CW00797197

THE BUILDINGS OF ENGLAND
FOUNDING EDITOR: NIKOLAUS PEVSNER

LANCASHIRE:
MANCHESTER AND
THE SOUTH-EAST

CLARE HARTWELL, MATTHEW HYDE
AND NIKOLAUS PEVSNER

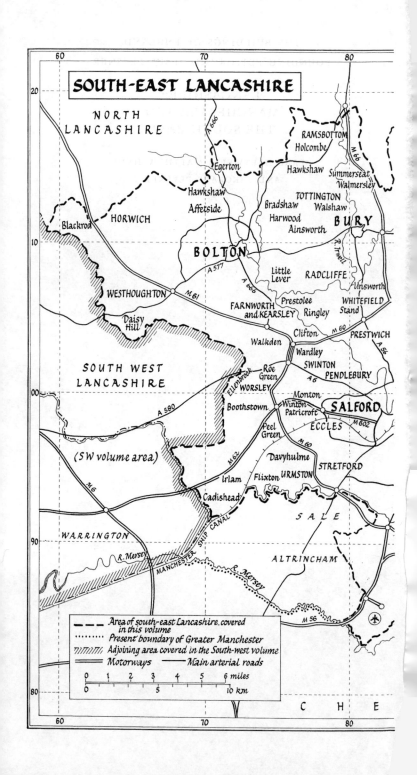

SOUTH-EAST LANCASHIRE

NORTH LANCASHIRE

RAMSBOTTOM
Holcombe

Egerton
Hawkshaw
Summerseat
Walmersley

Hawkshaw
Affetside

TOTTINGTON
Bradshaw Walshaw
Harwood
Ainsworth

BURY

Blackrod
HORWICH

BOLTON

Little
Lever
RADCLIFFE

Unsworth
WHITEFIELD
Stand

WESTHOUGHTON
M 61

FARNWORTH
and KEARSLEY

Prestolee
Ringley

Clifton

PRESTWICH

Daisy
Hill

Walkden

Wardley
SWINTON
PENDLEBURY

M 60

SOUTH WEST
LANCASHIRE

Roe
Green

Ellenbrook
WORSLEY

Monton
Winton
Patricroft

SALFORD

ECCLES
M 602

Boothstown

Peel
Green

M 60

(SW volume area)

Davyhulme

STRETFORD

M 52

Irlam
Flixton
URMSTON

M 6

Cadishead

SALE

WARRINGTON

R. Mersey
MANCHESTER SHIP CANAL
R. Mersey

ALTRINCHAM

M 56

C H E

Area of south-east Lancashire, covered
in this volume
Present boundary of Greater Manchester
Adjoining area covered in the South-west volume
Motorways   Main arterial roads

0 1 2 3 4 5 6 miles
0   5   10 km

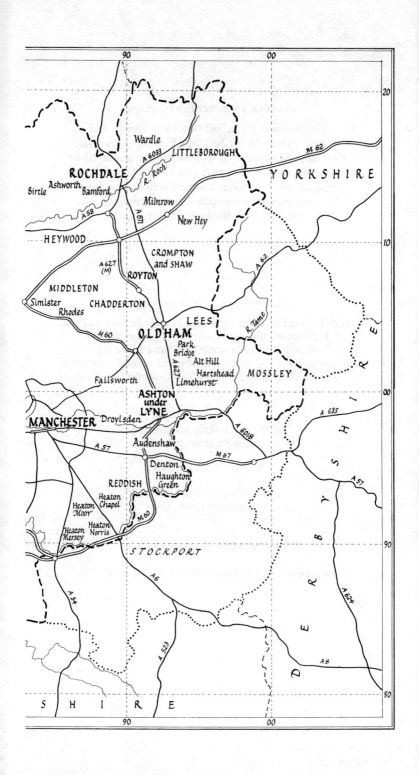

PEVSNER ARCHITECTURAL GUIDES

The Buildings of England series was created and
largely written by Sir Nikolaus Pevsner (1901–83).
First editions of the county volumes were published by
Penguin Books between 1951 and 1974. The continuing
programme of revisions and new volumes has been
supported by research financed through
the Buildings Books Trust since 1994

THE BUILDINGS BOOKS TRUST

was established in 1994, registered charity number 1042101.
It promotes the appreciation and understanding
of architecture by supporting and financing
the research needed to sustain new and revised volumes of
The Buildings of England, Ireland, Scotland and *Wales*

The Trust gratefully acknowledges
a major grant from

ENGLISH HERITAGE

towards the cost of research,
writing and illustrations

and an additional grant from

TRAFFORD METROPOLITAN BOROUGH COUNCIL

Lancashire: Manchester and the South-East

BY

CLARE HARTWELL

MATTHEW HYDE

AND

NIKOLAUS PEVSNER

THE BUILDINGS OF ENGLAND

YALE UNIVERSITY PRESS

NEW HAVEN AND LONDON

YALE UNIVERSITY PRESS
NEW HAVEN AND LONDON
302 Temple Street, New Haven CT 06511
47 Bedford Square, London WC1 3DP
www.pevsner.co.uk
www.lookingatbuildings.org
www.yalebooks.co.uk
www.yalebooks.com
for
THE BUILDINGS BOOKS TRUST

Published by Yale University Press 2004
2 4 6 8 10 9 7 5 3 1

ISBN 0 300 10583 5

Printed in China
through World Print
Set in Monotype Plantin

CONTENTS

LIST OF TEXT FIGURES AND MAPS

Every effort has been made to contact or trace all copyright holders. The publishers will be glad to make good any errors or omissions brought to our attention in future editions.

PHOTOGRAPHIC ACKNOWLEDGEMENTS

We are grateful to English Heritage photographer Keith Buck for taking most of the photographs for this volume (© English Heritage Photo Library) and also to the sources of the remaining photographs as shown below. We are grateful for permission to reproduce them as appropriate. Where older images have been used, every effort has been made to contact or trace copyright holders. The publishers will be glad to make good any errors or omissions brought to our attention in future editions.

Austin-Smith:Lord: 126
Bolton School: 103
Chetham's Library: 18, 26
Co-operative Insurance Company (CIS): 118
Len Grant: 70
Clare Hartwell: 46
Elain Harwood: 119
Matthew Hyde: 2, 3, 4, 10, 37, 39, 40, 50, 55, 63, 65, 72, 105, 109, 123
Nick Harrison: 5, 38, 73, 93, 108, 124
English Heritage: 7, 27, 48, 49, 52, 57, 58, 59 (Tony Perry), 60 (Tony Perry), 71, 74, 75, 88, 89, 90, 92, 99, 100, 101, 102, 120
Manchester Art Gallery: 22, 30, 33
Manchester City Council: 64
Richard Pollard: 43
Mark Watson: 23, 24, 34, 56, 61

The photographs are included in the indexes, and references to them are given by numbers in the margin of the text.

MAP REFERENCES

The numbers printed in italic type in the margin against the place names in the gazetteer of the book indicate the position of the place in question on the index map (pp. 2–3), which is divided into sections by the 10-kilometre reference lines of the National Grid. The reference given here omits two initial letters (formerly numbers) which in a full grid reference refer to the 100-kilometre squares into which the county is divided. The first two numbers indicate the *western* boundary, and the last two the *southern* boundary, of the 10-kilometre square in which the place in question is situated. For example, Eccles (reference 7090) will be found in the 10-kilometre square bounded by grid lines 70 (on the *west*) and 80, and 90 (on the *south*) and 00; Oldham (reference 9000) in the square bounded by the grid lines 90 (on the *west*) and 00, and 00 (on the *south*) and 10.

The map contains all those places, whether towns, villages, or isolated buildings, which are the subject of separate entries in the text.

EDITOR'S FOREWORD

This book is the first part of a planned three-volume survey of the buildings of Lancashire, completely revised and thoroughly expanded from Nikolaus Pevsner's two volumes of 1969. The author admitted disarmingly that his South Lancashire *covered 'the most difficult area I have had to describe'. Since that time, waves of de-industrialization, demolition and new building have changed the face of South Lancashire drastically. To allow full coverage it was clear also that the southern part of the county would have to be split in two. This has allowed the south-eastern area to expand northwards, to correspond to the old Greater Manchester MBC boundary.* Lancashire: Liverpool and the South-West *and* Lancashire: North *are in progress. They will be followed by a revised* Cheshire *volume, which will include the southern part of the former Greater Manchester area.*

Pevsner was grateful to have found local experts to guide him through the barely charted riches of Lancashire's buildings. The authors of this revised edition are both North-Westerners by birth or adoption, with a profound knowledge and understanding of the area they describe. They have collaborated throughout, visiting the major sites, reading each other's descriptions, and writing the Introduction together. The gazetteer entries are not separately credited, but the split goes roughly thus. Clare Hartwell has covered much of Manchester, and also Oldham, Salford, Stretford, Ashton-under-Lyne and the rest of Tameside. Matthew Hyde's territory comprises Bolton, Bury, Rochdale, and several areas of outer Manchester: Blackley and Heaton Park in the N, and in the S Didsbury, Withington, Chorlton-cum-Hardy, Whalley Range and Burnage, plus Manchester's annexe S of the Mersey: Wythenshawe, Northenden, and the airport. In addition, certain major buildings in Manchester have been described by outside contributors (identified on p. xviii), and other specialists have supplied introductory chapters on geology and archaeology.

The larger format and revised boundaries have allowed subjects to be covered in greater depth. Industrial and vernacular architecture, medieval buildings, Victorian churches and church furnishings all come high up this list. There are short histories and evocative descriptions of places that were passed over last time. Architectural patronage has also been treated more fully, and is searchable by means of a new Index of Patrons and Residents. So the book presents what is in every way a more densely populated architectural landscape – which, for South-East Lancashire, is exactly as it should be.

ACKNOWLEDGEMENTS

Nikolaus Pevsner toured Lancashire in 1967. The starting point for this book was his account of Manchester and the south-eastern part of the county as it appeared in *South Lancashire*, to which are added a few places on the southern fringe of *North Lancashire* which are now within the Metropolitan Boroughs. Pevsner's account, charged with his characteristic insights and informed by his knowledge and experience, also formed the start-ing point for Clare Hartwell's *Manchester* paperback of 2001 (edited by Bridget Cherry), upon which the account of the city centre in this book has been based.

Pevsner was helped by Edward Hubbard and Dr Tom Wesley, who, as he recorded, 'worked every night until late, planning and mapping and making my life generally easier.' Donald Buttress provided much information on churches, and the help of many others was acknowledged, including John H. G. Archer, Jeffrey Howarth, A. W. Sewter, Denis Evinson, Ivan Hall and others. Some of these, including Tom Wesley and John Archer, helped with the new volume too. The opportunity to visit every signifi-cant building within a relatively short time has made possible a reassessment of the area's generally undervalued architecture, and the coverage has been greatly expanded in the light of our observations and information made available by recent research. The many and deep-seated changes which have taken place in the area over the last thirty years are recounted, and corrections and new information sent in by readers have proved useful.

We are indebted to the English Heritage Regional Office in Manchester, especially to the director Malcolm Cooper who offered us every assistance, and to Henry Owen-John, Marion Barter, Andrew Martindale and Clare Reading. The book could not have been published without a major grant from English Heritage to support the research, and the work of Gavin Watson, Secretary of the Buildings Books Trust, in administering it. We are further indebted to English Heritage for its generosity in pro-viding most of the photographs through Bob Skingle and his col-leagues, including many that were taken specially by Keith Buck. Trafford Metropolitan Borough Council gave generous support to the project, and thanks also go to the former Trafford Con-servation Officer Alexandra Fairclough. The University of Man-chester and its Field Archaeology Centre, through the Director Dr Michael Nevell, provided office facilities and access to research files, for which we are extremely grateful. Dr Peter

Arrowsmith of the Centre ably assisted with aspects of the research. The Assistant County Archaeologist Norman Redhead not only contributed the essay on the area's archaeology, but supported our research throughout the project.

John H. G. Archer is owed a major debt as the author of the entries on Manchester Town Hall, the John Rylands Library, Deansgate, and the Free Trade Hall; we are very grateful indeed for this valuable contribution. We are also grateful to Julian Holder who contributed the entry on the Central Library and Town Hall extension and advice on the city's post-war architecture. Fred Broadhurst wrote the cogent and informative essay on the geology of the area. Special thanks go to Dr Rory O'Donnell who gave valuable advice on all of the principal C19 Roman Catholic churches covered in the volume. Teresa Sladen (TS) kindly allowed us to use information she compiled on Anglican churches in Manchester. The accounts of ancient glass which appear in the gazetteer rely upon information from Penny Hebgin-Barnes, who generously gave us access to her research and expertise. Terry Wyke of Manchester Metropolitan University has helped in many ways, and we are particularly grateful for his assistance on the public sculptures and monuments in the area. We are also grateful to W. J. Smith, especially for his advice on Middleton buildings.

Officers of the various local authorities within the area are owed thanks for their help, especially David Hilton, Manchester City Council Plankeeper, who gave us the benefit of his extensive knowledge of Manchester's Victorian architecture. Mick Nightingale in Bury MBC was wonderfully helpful in arranging transport and access to many buildings. Many other conservation officers and council staff were generous with assistance and support, including Philip Sweet and Peter Shaw of Oldham MBC, Rebecca Waddington of Rochdale MBC, Paul Hartley of Stockport MBC, Gerry Shaw of Trafford MBC, Kate Borland of Tameside MBC and Joe Martin of Salford City Council. Nick Harrison of Salford City Council was responsible for several of the photographs, and we are very grateful to him and to Salford City Council for their permission to use them. We also wish to record very special thanks to Mark Watson for his help with the photography, and thanks also to Colin Cunningham and Leslie Holmes for help with illustrations.

Many other authorities have given us the benefit of their expertise: Mike Williams of English Heritage on cotton mills, Dr Sharman Kadish and Basil Jeuda on the area's Jewish heritage, Evelyn Vigeon on Eccles and Salford, David George on industrial archaeology, Steve Little on Ancoats and other subjects, and John Aldred on Worsley. David O'Connor and Andrea Sarginson helped with Victorian stained glass, Alan Petford and Mike Buckley with research on George Shaw, Jacqueline Roberts with council housing, and Michael Shippobottom gave us much useful information on Bolton buildings. Jeremy Milln advised on Wythenshawe and Smithills Halls, Ian Pringle offered invaluable help on Prestwich buildings, and Peter Ingram was a very helpful

guide to Rochdale and Heywood. Jonathan Clarke very kindly
made available findings of his research on steel-framed buildings,
as did Jeremy Lake and Paul Francis on aviation history.

The English Heritage buildings team in York were helpful,
especially Simon Taylor and Ian Goodall. Also generous with
information and advice have been E. Alan Rose, Christa
Grössinger, Anthony Blacklay, Meriel Boyd and Michael Hall.
Useful information has been offered by the committee of the
Portico Library and Gallery, Dr Paul Crossley, Joseph Sharples,
Chris Wakeling, Claire Gapper, Richard Pollard, Elain Harwood,
Helen M. Thomas, Anthony Torkington, Simon Inglis, Kathryn
Sather, William Longshaw, Frank Kelsall, and Neil Darlington.
We are grateful also to Tessa Watt, Paul Murray, Martin West-
horpe, Ivor Smith, Marcus Tillotson and Norah and John Brown
for help in Bolton. Our thanks go to Geoffrey Wellens who gave
us so much assistance in Middleton, and to Christopher Burton,
the late Derrick Catterall, John Powell, Martin Lessons, Norman
Wolstonecroft and Val Roberts. Jason Stead, Gordon Smith, Lois
and Roy Stonehouse and Sharon and David Snook all helped in
Rochdale. Thanks also go to Gareth Hughes, Ian Barnett, Geoff
Sword, the late Peter Ferriday, Harvey Bertfield, J. Holt and Tom
Cowle. Karen Evans is owed special thanks for her thorough and
prompt assistance on various research topics.

The backbone to the research for the volume is the collections
held in libraries, record offices and repositories, and we wish to
extend particular thanks to the staff of these institutions, including the local studies and archive centres in each of the main towns
in the area. Special mention must be made of Dr Michael Powell
and the staff of Chetham's Library, and of the staff of the local
history and archive sections of Manchester Central Reference
Library. We are also indebted to Val Gildea of the Kantorowich
Library at Manchester University, Canon Marmion and Fr
Peter Phillips at Shrewsbury Diocesan Record Office, and to
Manchester Metropolitan University library.

Several architects and artists kindly gave time to discuss projects with us, including Ken Moth, John Sheard, Eamon O'Neil
of Cruickshank & Seward, Harry M. Fairhurst, Peter Barrett,
Antony Grimshaw, Linda Walton, the late Antony Hollaway, and
David Clarke of Bradshaw Gass & Hope. It would be impossible to mention individually all the owners, custodians, clergy and
staff who gave up their time to open buildings, offer information
about them and to show us around; we are very grateful to all of
them. Special mention must be made of the Rev. Greg Forster
of St Wilfrid, Northenden, Fr Nigel Hawley of St Elisabeth,
Reddish, Fr David O'Malley of Thornleigh Salesian College, the
Rev. Ray Coward of St Cross, Daisy Hill, Fr Dennis Clinch of
St Mary, Manchester, the Rev. David Wiseman of Bamford
Chapel, Geoffrey Robinson of Manchester Cathedral, Mr Reg
Fisher, verger of St Michael, Ashton-under-Lyne, the Sisters of
the Presentation Convents in Manchester and Clonmel, and the
Rev. Martin Ashworth of St Margaret, Prestwich. Dr J. Patrick
Greene, former Director of the Museum of Science and Industry

in Manchester, and his staff must also be thanked. We are also grateful to Liz Mitchell, Anthea Jarvis and Ruth Shrigley of Manchester City Art Galleries, Philip White of the Co-operative Insurance Company, John Farrer and Paul Isherwood of Manchester Airport, Sue Good of Didsbury C. of E. School, Janet Cole of Bolton School and the High Master of Manchester Grammar School.

Many people at Yale University Press, including the staff of the Pevsner Architectural Guides, helped in the preparation of the volume. Simon Bradley has edited the book with a characteristic mixture of kindness and cruelty; kindness in the generous encouragement given at all times, cruelty over the punctuation, and in never allowing a sloppy sentence to get by. Special thanks go to Sally Salvesen, Emily Rawlinson, Emily Lees, Emily Winter, and (at Penguin Books, where work on the project began) to Sue Machin. The production of the book involved many people: Alan Fagan drew the maps and plans in the text, Reg and Marjorie Piggott the area map on pp. ii–iii, Kate Gallimore for copy editing, Patricia Taylor-Chalmers for proof-reading, and Judith Wardman for preparing the complicated indexes. As ever, the authors and publishers will be very grateful for information on errors or omissions.

The final acknowledgement the authors would like to make is to each other. It has been good to work together and we hope that the book benefits from our different perceptions, often separate, but sometimes, when the occasion demanded, focused together.

Clare Hartwell
Matthew Hyde
May 2004

INTRODUCTION

Climb any tall building in the centre of Manchester or Salford – and there are more and more of them – and the half-circle of the Pennines that encloses the conurbation to the N and E comes into view. They appear very close in frosty or snowy weather. In the towns, Bolton, Bury, Rochdale and Ashton-under-Lyne, it is not necessary to climb a building, for the hills are all around; and Oldham is itself on a hilltop. The Pennines curve round from NW of Bolton, through Holcombe Moor above Ramsbottom to Blackstone Edge at Littleborough and then S all the way through Shaw, Lees and Mossley. The high fringes, places such as Affetside, or Hey House at Holcombe, or Prickshaw at Rochdale, command the whole compass of this book: Oldham with its high-rise civic office block, Rochdale with its seven towers, Heaton Park with its telecom mast and temple, the towers of central Manchester dominated by the CIS building and, if you are lucky, the town hall, and the flatlands stretching away S and W over Chat Moss and the Mersey valley towards the sea.

The arc of towns NW to NE with their high moorland hinterlands had agricultural traditions based on upland farming and wool, and stone as the predominant building material. As the land falls, larger settlements are concentrated in the river valleys, brick becomes the predominant building material, and vernacular buildings are timber-framed. The sprawl of Manchester, Salford and their suburbs occupies a low bowl formed by the Irwell and Mersey valleys. Ashton-under-Lyne lies E on the River Tame and Stretford to the S.

This is one of the most densely populated regions of Europe, but there are some areas of attractive open country, such as the high heathery hills around Mossley, the lanes around Lees and the Pennine landscapes of outer parts of Ramsbottom, Littleborough, Crompton and Shaw. There are also frequent pockets of what Nikolaus Pevsner called the non-countryside, particularly in the N and W. A few fields, a scruffy farm or two, a river, maybe a canal, often a view. Prestolee provides a good example, Rhodes and Clifton others. Failsworth and Reddish are instances to the E. They are always welcome, sometimes surprising, providing just a sufficient buffer between towns to be able to say where one ends and the next begins. Very often, especially in the northern areas, the farms prove to be more than a single dwelling, rather a cluster of dwellings and associated buildings, which is called a fold. Prestolee again provides a good example: Seddon's Fold. Brandlesholme at Tottington and Ogden at New

View of Manchester from Salford, engraving, 1802

Hey are others, but they can also be identified within areas long since built up. This is the characteristic pattern of settlement, with the church at a spot convenient for the surrounding folds and not at the centre of a village. Ashworth is still exactly like this, but it is also clear at Milnrow and Littleborough, Radcliffe, and even Didsbury (Manchester). Further down into the plain recognizable villages could be found, such as Blackley (which was wiped out in the 1970s), or Withington (both Manchester). Flixton, far to the SW, is a more obvious example, and best of all is Worsley – and that was an estate village of the Egertons. There are only two or three examples of the classic church and manor nucleus: Manchester itself, Bury, Ashton-under-Lyne and Radcliffe, where the churches survive, though the actual manor sites have been lost, or survive as sub-surface archaeology.

Farming and textile production and marketing, including cotton goods from the C17, formed the economic base. The Industrial Revolution had origins in many different places, but the explosion of industrial activity in SE Lancashire at the end of the C18 was, without precedent, the beginning of a sensational era which created the modern world. Manchester was at the centre of global commercial trade, its streets bustling with foreign merchants, and Manchester wares were a brand known the world over. Oldham and Bolton were world centres for cotton-spinning, Bury and Rochdale too became major industrial towns. Industrial pre-eminence lasted until the first few decades of the C20. The result is that most of the area covered by this book is urban in character, and dominated by architecture and buildings of the

Victorian and Edwardian periods which reflect civic pride as well as economic and industrial success.

The Manchester that the industrial revolution created has been well recorded, and is still with us to some extent. Less familiar, except in the paintings of L. S. Lowry, is the environment created in the industrial hinterland. In 1879 a photographer, Mr Knott, turned his camera on his home town of Oldham, taking a 360 degree panorama from a high point near the centre of town. Today in Gallery Oldham we can walk along his picture, astonishing in its clarity (it must have been a holiday week, allowing the smoke to clear) and detail, noting the forest of chimneys, the miles of railway sidings, the mine headgear right in the middle of town, terraces and mills under hasty construction, an almost complete lack of vegetation, the *ad hoc* nature of the whole place. For a literary confirmation of such an environment we can turn to Fletcher Moss, on a pilgrimage (his word) from Didsbury (Manchester) through part of the Lancashire coalfield to Wardley Hall, near Worsley, in 1906: 'A badly worn paved road led through a blackened land dotted with coal-pits, or mills, overhung with a dull pall of smoke, through which the shrieking engines and the clanging trams rushed on their hideous way.'

The scene was changing when Nikolaus Pevsner and his driver, Tom Wesley, came here in 1967. The resulting book, *The Buildings of England: South Lancashire* (1969), of which this volume revises and updates one part, captured the early phases of the transition. The Lancashire cotton industry was on its way out. Buildings were beginning to be cleaned, and there was large-scale redevelopment in many places, but the remains of heavy industry were still everywhere and the land was tired and filthy. Tom Wesley recalls that the air left a constant sulphurous taste. An old boy of Oldham Bluecoat School in the 1960s, revisiting in 2003, was amazed to discover that it commanded a panorama of the hills – never seen in his day.

Thirty-five years have wrought an almost total transformation. Visually, and in deeper ways, SE Lancashire is a different place from the one Pevsner surveyed. The sulphur in the air has gone, soot no longer descends on washing lines, tender leaves and polychromatic architecture. More miraculous still are the rivers:

> I is for IRWELL
> for IRK
> and for INK
> But none of these liquids
> Is wholesome to drink.

So runs an old rhyme, but it is no longer true. Perhaps the most astonishing thing we have to record is the building in 2002 of a salmon ladder at Northenden weir, on the Mersey.

The history of SE Lancashire has determined that, by comparison with other Buildings of England volumes, we have to deal with a great shortage of buildings before the second half of the C18, i.e. the beginnings of the Industrial Revolution, and a great

View from a window of the Royal Technical College, Salford.
By L.S. Lowry, 1924

wealth of buildings of the C19 and C20. Nevertheless the surviving halls and churches of the late medieval period, the multiplying settlements of the C17, and the really remarkably few
buildings and landscapes of the C18, still have a coherent story
to tell – more so than industrial Lancashire has generally been
given credit for.

Finally, a note on boundaries and content. This book covers
the SE part of the historic county of Lancashire. The boundaries
W to NE correspond almost exactly with those of the Metropolitan

Boroughs of Salford, Bolton, Bury and Rochdale. Then comes Oldham, but Saddleworth, which is part of Oldham administratively but historically in the county of Yorkshire, has not been included, and nor have those parts of Tameside Metropolitan Borough Council which were in Cheshire until 1974. The remaining s boundary is defined by the Mersey, so that settlements now in Stockport Metropolitan Borough Council (Reddish and the Heatons) and Trafford Metropolitan Council (Stretford, Flixton, Urmston and Davyhulme), which lie N of the Mersey and the historic boundary with Cheshire, are included. So is Manchester International Airport and Manchester's satellite suburb of Wythenshawe, in the historic county of Cheshire but part of the City of Manchester administratively since the 1930s. The contents of the Pevsner City Guide, *Manchester* (2001), have been condensed and updated, forming the basis for the part of this volume covering the centre of Manchester and its immediate environs.

GEOLOGY AND BUILDING STONES

BY FRED BROADHURST

The materials found directly beneath the soils over most of SE Lancashire consist mainly of unconsolidated clays, sands and peat, collectively known as Superficial Deposits. They are also frequently referred to as Drift, because the material was once thought to be the debris from a great flood. The SUPERFICIAL DEPOSITS include material of glacial origin, formed mostly during the course of the last (Devensian) of the Pleistocene glaciations (2 million–10,000 years ago), and post-glacial material formed since, consisting of gravels in river terraces, wind-blown sands, peat, etc. The Superficial Deposits are of variable thickness up to about 260 ft (80 metres), but in some places are missing, either due to non-deposition or erosion, and here the underlying bedrock is exposed at the surface.

The BEDROCK (also known as 'Solid' rocks) consists mostly of stratified ancient sediments, some of which (the older) belong to the Carboniferous Period of geological time (360–290 million years ago), and the rest (younger) to the Permian and Triassic Periods (290–210 million years ago). The Carboniferous rocks include many tough sandstones and so form the higher ground of the region, for instance in the Ramsbottom area. In contrast the Permian-Triassic rocks are generally much less resistant to erosion and form the lowlands of the Lancashire–Cheshire plain.

The outcrop of the CARBONIFEROUS ROCKS in SE Lancashire includes the area of the Lancashire Coalfield, around Bolton in the W, Oldham in the E, and adjacent areas of outcrop of the Millstone Grit, notably in the higher ground around Ramsbottom (N Lancashire), N of the coalfield. These Carboniferous rocks contain ancient sediments with evidence of deposition from

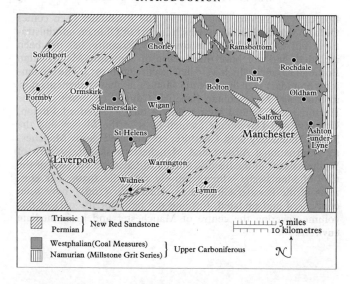

Sketch geological map of South Lancashire and surrounding area,
based on maps of the British Geological Survey

a vast river system carrying sediment from the N into an enormous deltaic complex across northern England and adjacent
areas. The delta, far larger in extent than any modern delta anywhere in the world, was associated with a region of major subsidence. Evidence from the rocks indicates a continuity of shallow
water conditions showing that deposition kept up with subsidence. On numerous occasions sediment was built up to water
level and plant growth led to the formation of peat, which, on
burial by later sediment, was transformed into coal. The total
thickness of Carboniferous sediment accumulated in this way in
SE Lancashire was probably about three miles. The evidence of
magnetism in the rocks (palaeomagnetism) indicates formation
at or close to the Equator, so the coal seams are interpreted as
tropical swamp deposits. This, and other evidence, indicates that
Britain and adjacent areas have drifted from the Equator to their
present latitudes over a period of about 300 million years, a con-
clusion consistent with the geological concept of Plate Tectonics,
involving drifting continents and ocean floors.

The Carboniferous in SE Lancashire contains a number of
sandstones, many of them formed in braided river systems which
led to the development of individual sandstone strata over large
areas. Other sandstones were developed only locally as channel
deposits. The rocks of the Lancashire Coalfield (the Coal Measures or Westphalian), rich in coal, and the underlying sequence
(Namurian), rich in sandstones and formerly known as the Millstone Grit, both contain tough beds suitable for building stone.

They also contain clayrocks (or 'shales') from which bricks and tiles can be made. Many of the sandstones are tough, erosion-resistant rocks due to the presence of a silica cement which occupies a substantial part of the pore space within the rock. This silicification appears to be related to the depth to which these sandstones have been buried. When fresh these rocks are white or light grey but on weathering they develop an attractive, brownish colour due to oxidation and hydration of the small amount of iron minerals present.

These sandstones have been used as building stones over a long period, first for local use, but later over a wide area as the construction of canals and railways allowed transportation over significant distances at an acceptable cost. The stone was used for buildings, walling, dam construction and, in the form of thin slabs (flagstones) as material for roofing ('grey slates') and for paving. Many of the mills and workers' houses associated with the Industrial Revolution were constructed with these materials. In the case of flagstones a number of quarries were converted to mines as overburden cover became excessive. The Haslingden Flags in the Rossendale valley were particularly important as a source of flagstones. Manchester Cathedral and the Town Halls of Manchester and Rochdale are good examples of the use of 63, 61 Carboniferous sandstones.

A Carboniferous (Westphalian) sandstone exposed at Collyhurst, 1½ m. NE of the city centre in Manchester, provided building stone during the late C17 and early C18 prior to the construction of canals or railways. This stone, to be seen in some of the earliest structures of Manchester, including Chetham's 18, School and Library (1421) and St Ann's Church (1709), has an 27 attractive purplish colour but contains numerous clay and silt fragments which weather readily. Replacement of damaged blocks by better quality materials has produced some interesting patterns in these early buildings, notably St Ann's Church. The name Collyhurst Sandstone has subsequently been adopted for another sandstone, also from Collyhurst, but of Permian age. Recently, the Permian rock has proved of great commercial interest in NW England in terms of oil and gas exploration, so the term Collyhurst Sandstone, as a Permian sandstone, is now accepted and well entrenched in the literature. A new name is required for the original, Carboniferous, rock from Collyhurst and the name Binney Sandstone, to commemorate the pioneer work of E. W. Binney in the area, has been proposed.*

The close of the Carboniferous Period is associated with a major change in the tectonic setting of northern England. The subsidence, which had allowed the accumulation of the thick stack of Carboniferous sediment, was replaced by uplift, in a process described as inversion. The change in late Carboniferous tectonics is associated with collisions between continents elsewhere in the world. These collisions completed a process of

* By F. M. Broadhurst and I. M. Simpson, *Proceedings of the Geologists' Association*, III, 2000.

continental aggregation to form a single supercontinent, to which
the name of Pangaea has been given.

Inversion brought the Carboniferous deposits back up towards
the surface, where they were subjected to weathering and erosion
under the desert conditions of the Permian-Triassic. The weathering involved oxidation which produced reddish and purplish
colours in the Carboniferous rocks. The Binney Sandstone is a
probable example. The erosion supplied sediment for accumulation as the (Permian-Triassic) New Red Sandstone.

In SE Lancashire the Carboniferous strata are generally
inclined downwards towards Cheshire and eventually disappear
beneath the cover of the Permian-Triassic red rocks, the NEW
RED SANDSTONES (which occur *above* the Carboniferous, as
distinct from the Old Red Sandstones which occur *below* the Carboniferous). Some of these rocks indicate deposition in the form
of sand dunes, others in stream channels, revealing that the
region was a land area. The lower (older) strata are rich in sandstone (some suitable as building stone), the higher (younger) rich
in clays and silts and containing substantial deposits of salt. The
highest and youngest strata of the Triassic have been removed by
erosion in SE Lancashire. Magnetic evidence indicates deposition within 10 degrees of the Equator during the Permian but by
the time of the Triassic the region had moved further away to 30
degrees. This is further evidence of the northward migration of
SE Lancashire (and adjacent areas) from the Equator during the
Carboniferous. By the Permian and Triassic the region had
reached the latitudes characteristic of today's Sahara Desert. The
fossil sand-dunes even provide evidence of a prevailing north-
easterly wind, the equivalent of today's Trade Winds in the northern hemisphere. The New Red Sandstone channel sediments
have features characteristic of flood deposits, which can be recognized in modern deserts and which result from flash floods.
The higher and younger strata in the New Red Sandstone
sequence contain deposits of rocks rich in clay, silt and, notably,
rock salt and gypsum. Such evaporite deposits are forming today
in the playa lakes of modern deserts.

Deposition of the Permian-Triassic (New Red Sandstones) in
Britain took place in detached basins, each related to a fault
system involving crustal extension and rifting. Deposition of
sediment took place as the faulting developed. The Cheshire
Basin is an excellent example of such a rift-basin, and contains
sediment more than $1\frac{1}{2}$ m. in thickness. The crustal extension is
related to the break-up of the supercontinent Pangaea, the fragments of which were gradually separated by the formation of new
ocean floor, ultimately producing the geography of the world in
which we live today.

In terms of building stones in the Permian-Triassic, the sandstones are of great interest. In general, they are much less
resistant to erosion than the Carboniferous rocks. They have not
been subjected to deep burial and lack the quantities of silica
cement so characteristic of the Carboniferous sandstones.
However, before the development of canals and railways these

red rocks were the only building materials that were available locally at reasonable cost. Nevertheless the red Penrith Sandstone (Permian) of Cumbria has been locally toughened by extra cementation and has been used in the construction of John Rylands Library on Deansgate, Manchester. The red Sherwood 90 Sandstone (Triassic) exposed in the area around Castlefield appears to have been similarly toughened and was almost certainly used for the construction of the Roman Fort and, later, the medieval Hanging Bridge, just S of the Cathedral. The younger (but still Triassic) Helsby Sandstone is tougher than most of its Triassic associates and at outcrop is resistant enough to form low escarpments in Cheshire, such as Helsby Hill and Alderley Edge. The stone was worked extensively on the Wirral and at Runcorn and Lymm. An interesting example of the use of the Helsby Sandstone is the former Parr's Bank (1902) at the junction of York Street and Spring Gardens in Manchester. The red sandstones on the exterior of the Bridgewater Hall in Barbirolli 120 Square come from the ancient sand-dune deposits of the New Red Sandstones in S Scotland.

To the S of SE Lancashire, around Wem and Whitchurch, close to the Cheshire/Shropshire border, there is a small area underlain by JURASSIC rocks. These rocks contain marine fossils so were deposited on a sea floor. Detail of the rock sequence can be matched with that of the main Jurassic outcrop in the Midlands and beyond. It is clear that the Cheshire Jurassic was once continuous with that of SE England but has been isolated by erosion. Research on detrital grains of apatite (a calcium phosphate mineral) in the Permian-Triassic of NW England has established the maximum temperatures to which the apatite grains have been exposed. These temperatures, in turn, provide evidence of the depth to which the apatite has been buried (in this case by a cover of Jurassic and younger sediments). It appears that in the S Lancashire region a cover of post-Triassic sediments up to about 1¼ m. is likely. The uplift required to bring about this erosion probably occurred at the end of the Cretaceous (about 70 million years ago) – at a time when the North Atlantic Ocean was opening, the ongoing process of the break-up of Pangaea. The evidence from the apatite grains indicates that the end-Cretaceous uplift was centred on the middle of the Irish Sea area and maximum erosion occurred here. This uplift (probably associated with the ascent, underground, of molten rock, a potential volcano) was apparently responsible for the general southeasterly tilt seen in the rock strata from the Jurassic up to the early Tertiary in S and E England. Later, the elevated region of the Irish Sea area collapsed to form the marine basin seen today. Further volcanicity to the north developed in response to tension to form the volcanic centres of Antrim and the Western Isles of Scotland. However, this volcanic activity failed to develop into an extension of the North Atlantic and it was replaced by successful fracture west of Ireland. The final opening of the North Atlantic has been linked to a general tilting of the British Isles, up in the north and west, down to the south and east. Erosion in the uplifted

north and west of Britain has exposed ancient tough rocks in contrast to the young and easily eroded rocks of the south and east.
The great variety of landscape in the British Isles owes its existence to this tilting process, a process which still continues,
though its effects are masked by the changes in sea and land levels
caused by the melting of ice sheets at the close of the Devensian
ice sheets 'only' some 10,000 years ago.

The post-Triassic rocks of the s of England have provided
some of the C20 building stones to be seen in SE Lancashire.
In particular, reference must be made to the Portland Stone
of Dorset, a late Jurassic (about 150 million years old) white
limestone, oolitic in nature and containing many fossils.
An excellent example of its use is the Central Library in
Manchester.

A world-wide cooling of the climate during the Tertiary Period,
combined with continuing northwards migration, eventually
brought Britain within range of ice sheets from the Arctic. The
earliest glaciation is linked to the commencement of the Pleistocene Epoch (and the Quaternary Sub-Era) about 2 million
years ago. Subsequent warmer intervals and further glaciations
followed climatic changes which are linked to astronomical controls on the amount of radiation reaching Earth from the Sun.
Such climatic cycles are known as Milankovitch Cycles (after the
work of Milutin Milankovitch in the 1920s–30s). The last glaciation (Devensian, named after the Roman town of Deva, the
modern Chester) ended about 10,000 years ago and at present
we are enjoying the warmer interval that followed. Future glaciations are certain.

The PLEISTOCENE DEPOSITS of SE Lancashire include layers
of clay with boulders, the so-called boulder clay, or till, deposited
directly from ice sheets. This material (together with the clayrocks of the Carboniferous) is a source of clay for brick
manufacture. Sands generated from melt-waters associated with
shrinking ice are common and include the Chelford Sands of
Cheshire, used for the manufacture of glass. Postglacial deposits
include river terrace materials, important for the production of
gravel and also peat, which until recently was an important ingre-
dient in compost and products used to improve soils.

Up to the time of the Industrial Revolution the construction
of permanent buildings relied on stone for support and decoration. However during the Industrial Revolution the frequency of
fires in the mills seriously raised the cost of fire insurance and
resort was made to the incorporation of CAST-IRON FRAMES in
buildings to reduce the scale of damage in the event of fire. By
the start of the C20 the price of STEEL had fallen to such a level
that it could be used in preference to cast iron. At this stage stone
(or brick) was no longer needed for the main structural support
in buildings. Buildings with a steel frame could now be clad with
thin panels of natural stone, the purpose of which was limited to
decoration and waterproofing. As the cost of this stone was now
a smaller proportion of the total building cost, it was possible to
utilize attractive materials from all parts of the world. This has

produced a situation where the oldest buildings in any given town or village reflect the local geology, later buildings reflect the improvements in transport that have taken place and the youngest buildings, based on steel frames, are covered with cladding stone from all corners of the world. Architects are now selecting stone from the same high quality worldwide sources, so the new buildings have a cosmopolitan aspect. Most towns in SE Lancashire contain examples of buildings clad with natural stone. In Manchester the Marks & Spencer/Selfridges store between Cross Street and New Cathedral Street is clad with Jura Grey, a limestone from Germany, rich in fossils such as ammonites. The same type of stone forms the floor of the concourse in the Bridgewater Hall. The use of natural stone in buildings has been extended into shopping malls where attractive, hard-wearing stone is proving an advantage in the floors as well as shop fronts. A good example is the Trafford Centre (Stretford), 5 m. W of Manchester city centre. In recent years the production of block stone for building has been replaced to some extent by production of aggregate for use in the preparation of concrete blocks, curbstones, etc, and referred to as reconstituted stone. Nevertheless natural stone is being used extensively for paving (replacement or new) in the streets of Manchester and elsewhere.

A good introduction to the geology of SE Lancashire is included in Aitkenhead et al., 2002 (see Further Reading). Especially useful are geological maps at the scale of 1:50,000 published by the British Geological Survey. Individual areas are covered by 'Drift', or 'Solid', or 'Solid and Drift' editions. The 'Solid' editions show the distribution of the bedrock formations as they would be seen if the Superficial Deposits were removed.

THE ARCHAEOLOGY OF
SOUTH-EAST LANCASHIRE

BY NORMAN REDHEAD

The Prehistoric Period

Archaeological evidence for the prehistoric period in SE Lancashire is relatively sparse, contributory factors being the acid, poor soil for arable farming, a wet and boggy landscape, a small and scattered population, and intensive development from the industrial period onwards. Despite this, considerable advances in knowledge have been made in recent decades.

The earliest evidence for occupation comes from the MESOLITHIC period of *c.* 10,000 to 5,500 years ago. Pollen analysis of peat cores on the central Pennine moors has shown that the upland environment during this period consisted of scrubby woodland and heath where clearings would have attracted grazing animals. In some parts the blanket peat is still 10–13 ft (3–4 metres) deep, but elsewhere it has eroded due to industrial pollution and drainage, revealing thousands of flint tools and waste flakes associated with temporary camp-sites. The acid gritstone soils have destroyed organic remains such as bone, leather and wood, which formed a large component of these nomadic peoples' material culture, leaving only hearths, stake-holes and patterns of stones as relics of their tents and shelters.

Archaeologists have catalogued many thousands of flints from these erosion patches. A broad pattern of technology has emerged, with the earlier Mesolithic comprising larger and more dispersed camp sites using broad-blade tools whilst the later Mesolithic is characterized by more numerous sites using much smaller tools called microliths. Except for some local cherts, the raw material appears to have been traded from as far away as the Lincolnshire and Yorkshire Wolds. The dense concentration of Mesolithic sites in the central Pennines may be due to this being such a narrow crossing point of the uplands, encouraging trade between tribal groups to the E and W.

The peat has been completely burnt away at Windy Hill, E from Milnrow, revealing many flint sites. An excavation in 1982 examined a late Mesolithic camp-site on a S facing spur overlooking Piethorne Brook. The people of this time were hunter-gatherers and such sites would have been warm and provided excellent look out points for spotting deer. Hilltop sites N of Bolton and Rochdale have also yielded flint finds suggestive of camp-sites, and these include Knowl Moor, Crook Hill, Great Hill, Brown Wardle Hill, and Rivington Moor.

The lowlands of SE Lancashire have revealed only occasional Mesolithic flint finds, reflecting perhaps the high level of urban and industrial development rather than a lack of prehistoric activity. Only two sites are well documented: a possible lakeside settlement at Radcliffe E'es dug in the 1950s and a small temporary camp-site on a sandy knoll at Astley Moss, excavated in 1996.

Whilst the NEOLITHIC period (3500 to 2000 B.C.) heralded the first farmers and a settled, as opposed to itinerant, lifestyle in much of Britain, there is little evidence for this in SE Lancashire. The archaeological record for this period is mainly in the form of chance finds of polished stone axes and adzes and flint tools and weapons. In the uplands continuation of the hunting tradition is represented in the form of leaf-shaped and transverse flint arrowheads. Whilst the farmland was marginal across much of the area, the lighter, better drained soils of the river terraces could have supported the first farmers in the late Neolithic and early Bronze Age. In the Irwell valley Neolithic flints have been found at Prestwich, Kersal Moor and Radcliffe E'es. The importance of the upper Irwell valley in this period is emphasized by two rare monument types. Near Radcliffe Cemetery is the site of a hengiform monument partially excavated in 1951, comprising a large bank encircling a ditch 8 ft (2.4 metres) wide; this could have been the focal point of seasonal ritual and communal activity. Just beyond the upper reaches of the Irwell (and slightly outside the area covered by this book) is a group of monuments at Cheetham Close N of Bolton, which includes a stone circle, two ring-bank cairns and at least two small cairns; this clearly was another centre of ritual/community activity.

The EARLY BRONZE AGE (*c.* 2000–1500 B.C.) appears to have been a time of favourable climate and rising population. There is an increase in finds, including the first metal objects and first widespread use of pottery in the area, and a number of funerary monuments date from this period, indicating the existence of settled farming communities.

In SE Lancashire there are thirty-six known or suspected BURIAL SITES including seven ring cairns and nineteen barrows. Whilst many were destroyed by C19 development or antiquarian investigations, a few of the better surviving sites such as Harper's Mound, Horwich, have been protected through scheduling. Important well-excavated sites include two cairns at Shuttle-worth and Whitelow, E of Ramsbottom, which have produced cremated remains in pottery urns, associated with grave goods including pottery food vessels, flint implements, and a faience bead. Whitelow Cairn, which has radiocarbon dates of around 1600 B.C., consisted of a bank of stones 6.5 ft wide and 1.6 ft high (2 metres wide and 0.5 metres high) forming a ring of 80.4 ft (24.5 metres) diameter. Within this was a central stone mound defined by an inner bank and a small terraced stone platform on the N side and with two standing stones to the SW. Whitelow was originally created as a single burial cairn, but subsequently as many as twelve more cremations were deposited in circular pits cut into the structure. Another well-recorded cairn site with many structural similarities to Whitelow is Wind Hill near Heywood. Cremation urns were sometimes placed in central pits or cists, such as the barrows at Lowhouse, Milnrow and Snoddle Hill, Littleborough.

The most important evidence for early Bronze Age settlement in the area has come from Manchester Airport's second runway, where archaeologists in 1999 recorded evidence for a long-lived occupation site on a sand and gravel terrace overlooking a ford across the Bollin. Remains include a series of circular and rectangular buildings beside a sunken trackway which was associated with a midden deposit. Finds such as domestic pottery, stone implements including flint tools and quern stones, and the presence of cereal grains, indicate a farming community.

Further N, beyond the Mersey, there are currently no known settlement sites in SE Lancashire for the Bronze Age, although chance finds and other archaeological evidence suggest the confluence of the rivers Irwell and Roch was a focus of activity. In the uplands many finely worked flint tools and weapons, such as thumb scrapers, barbed and tanged arrowheads and knives, have been found, and several recent archaeological excavations in the area have encountered such finds beneath later deposits. Other stone implements including axes and hammer stones are widely distributed.

There is evidence for climatic deterioration in the MIDDLE BRONZE AGE, from around 1300 B.C. to the mid-Iron Age of *c.* 400 B.C. This corresponds with a marked decrease in the number of find spots and funerary sites. Pollen core analysis shows expanding peat bog during this period and it is likely that in SE Lancashire marginal farmland became unworkable and the population declined.

Until recent years archaeologists had very little understanding of the nature and location of late prehistoric settlement in this area at the time of the Roman invasion. Evidence has been difficult to find for several reasons: sparse population, disturbance from extensive industrialization and urban growth, and a materially poor economy that was animal-product based. Pottery has been found in only small quantities, some of it so coarse that it is hard to recognize during archaeological excavations. Similarly, there has been a lack of metal artefact finds and visible earthwork monuments. However, over the last two decades several research excavations have begun to establish settlement types for the region.

One of the main forms was the DITCHED ENCLOSURE containing a farmstead with round huts. In SE Lancashire there are two excavated examples; one at Great Woolden Hall on a promontory overlooking the River Glazebrook N of Cadishead, the other at Castlesteads N of Bury. Both settlements began in the mid to late Iron Age and continued well into the Roman period (around A.D. 200). The open area excavation at Great Woolden revealed a nearly complete plan of a double-ring house, radiocarbon dated to 65–15 B.C. It consisted of an outer circular post-trench nearly 42.7 ft (13 metres) in diameter, with an entrance indicated by a gap of 5.9 ft (1.8 metres) width and two large post pits which once held entrance posts of 2 ft (0.6 metres) diameter. A line of small, circular post-holes c. 0.6–0.8 ft (0.2–0.25 metres) diameter formed the inner ring. A large rotary quern fragment and sherds of Very Coarse Pottery (used as salt containers) provided evidence for material culture. A third site, a hill-top enclosure at Rainsough near Prestwich, was largely destroyed by sand quarrying in the 1930s, however excavations around its periphery in the early 1980s revealed late prehistoric pottery sherds as well as an abundance of C1 and C2 A.D. Roman wares. There are likely to be many more such settlements awaiting discovery and aerial photograph analysis has revealed several potential promontory sites in the Irwell and Roch valleys and hill-top enclosures in the uplands.

IRON AGE finds are few in number and only two decorated metal objects are known: a torc with bronze beading from Littleborough and a bronze ox-head ornament from Manchester. Other indicators of settlement in the Iron Age are carved stone heads which have 'Celtic' features such as incised hair, lentoid eyes, a wedge-shaped nose, up-turned moustache, and a slit mouth with incense hole. These heads are difficult to date and many have been moved from their original locations to adorn house walls or gardens, but originally they may have been placed next to springs or pools. Their distribution is skewed towards the Pennine foothills and uplands. A good example can be seen at Touchstones Museum in Rochdale, this one being set on a cylindrical stone shaft which was inserted into the ground. Real human heads from the prehistoric period have been found in peat bogs in SE Lancashire. Particularly noteworthy are three skulls which retain skin and hair: those from Ashton Moss, Ashton-under-Lyne, and Red Moss, Horwich, date to the Bronze Age, and another from Worsley Moss, Salford, is of Roman origin. The largest surviving peat bog is Chat Moss, E of Salford, always a major feature in the landscape, and a barrier to transport until Stephenson floated his Liverpool-to-Manchester railway line across it in 1828–30.

South-East Lancashire in Roman Times

When the Roman army arrived in Lancashire during the 70s A.D. it would have come across a largely open and cultivated land-scape, probably dotted with farmsteads along the river valleys and with some defended hilltop enclosures in the uplands. The native population was part of a loose confederation of tribes called the Brigantes.

The Romans created a ROAD SYSTEM across SE Lancashire linking a network of forts, with Manchester being the hub. From Manchester roads could be taken SW to Chester legionary fortress, W to the military site at Wigan and NW to Ribchester fort, NNE to the fort at Ilkley, NE to York legionary fortress, E to Melandra fort and SE to the Roman site at Buxton. A number of more minor roads have been postulated; several have been confirmed through field observation, map work and excavation, but many more require sound archaeological investigation. Excavations on the main Roman roads have shown varying levels of survival and methods of construction, suggesting that engineers used local materials; for instance the main trans-Pennine highway between York and Chester has been found to consist of bands of gravel W of Manchester, whereas to the E in the Pennine uplands it is much better preserved and of thicker foundation, being made of gritstone cobbles on top of gritstone blocks set on a clay bed. The road from Manchester to Ribchester survives as a substan-tial earthwork above Tottington; at Affetside it can be seen as a straight road, still used today and named Watling Street.* The well-studied road from Manchester to the fort at Castleshaw, E of Oldham, is commemorated with a series of information plaques along its length. Roman coin hoards ranging from the C2 to C4 A.D. have been found across SE Lancashire and their distribution coincides with the known Roman road alignments. At Boothstown, E of Salford, two substantial hoards have been found close to the course of the Manchester to Wigan Roman road: one contained 550 bronze coins in two pottery vessels, the

---

* A well-preserved length of paved road at Blackstone Edge above Littleborough was long thought to be Roman in origin but in recent times research has suggested it may be an early C18 turnpike road, although the site of the Manchester to Ilkley Roman road is likely to be nearby.

other 1070 bronze coins from a straw-lined pit, both being deposited in the second half of the C3 A.D.

As a hub of the regional transport network, Manchester grew to be an important centre in the Roman period. The FORT was erected *c.* A.D. 78 in a strong defensive position, on raised ground overlooking the confluence of the Medlock and Irwell. In its original form it was square in plan, covering *c.* 3 acres (1.2 hectares) and built with a turf rampart with timber gates, stockade and corner towers. There is evidence for the fort being destroyed and abandoned in the mid-C2 A.D. but by *c.* A.D. 160 it was rebuilt, again in turf and timber, but on a larger scale covering 5 acres (2 hectares) to accommodate extra granaries. The final phase of construction came *c.* A.D. 200 when the rampart was faced with a stone wall and the gatehouses also rebuilt in stone. This phase is represented in the reconstructions of the N gate and sections of the N and W rampart and ditch system, which can be visited off Liverpool Road in Castlefield.

Alongside the Roman fort grew a CIVILIAN SETTLEMENT, the *vicus.* This appears to have been a linear development alongside the road from the fort's N gate, although recent excavations have shown it extended at least 328 ft (100 metres) W of the road. The cemetery and religious complex were on the E and SE side. Excavations through the 1970s found extensive evidence for successive building phases beginning in the late C1 and continuing

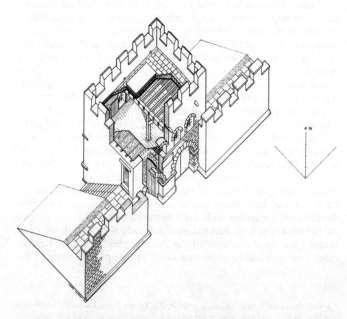

4 m

The reconstructed north gate of the early C3
Roman Fort at Castlefield, Manchester

into the early C3 A.D. The evidence consisted mainly of post-holes and beam slots indicating timber construction, but in a few cases dwarf stone walls were found, and these supported timber-framing. The buildings were typically rectangular, some having recognizable internal divisions, others being a single room. Variations included the addition of a veranda, a type comprising a shed open along one side, and a U-shaped complex around a central yard. The reconstructed stone footings of three of these buildings, including a hostelry fronting the Roman road, can be seen opposite the White Lion pub on Liverpool Road. Through the C2 A.D. the Roman fort and *vicus* had periods of large-scale industrial production, mainly related to iron working. A large number of hearths have been found, either within buildings or in the opening to the rear, and many of these were used to forge weapons, tools or other equipment. It is thought that these intensive periods of activity were to support military campaigns further N into Scotland.

Whilst the coin finds and evidence for re-cutting of the fort ditches shows that the fort continued in use throughout the C3 and C4, the *vicus* declined considerably during this period. In the C3 industrial activity gave way to domestic buildings and by the C4 the *vicus* was all but abandoned. Romanization of SE Lancashire appears to have been a transient affair and its impact on the native structure and economy was slight. There were no villas which might indicate large, managed estates and indeed settlement appears to have continued in the pre-Roman form of dispersed farmsteads dependent on a pastoral economy, with crops on the lower valley slopes or river terraces.

Medieval South-East Lancashire: the Pre-Conquest Period

There is remarkably little archaeological evidence for the post Roman and pre-Norman Conquest period. The only excavated features representing SETTLEMENT from this time were found just outside the N gate of the Roman fort in Manchester. These were a line of four rectangular or sub-rectangular pits, delimited by closely spaced stake-holes, interpreted as remains of early C5 sunken floored huts or *grubenhauser* cut into the Roman exit road and in-filled defensive ditches, and sheltering under the lee of the ruined fort wall. Whilst Saxon coin and jewellery finds in the vicinity of the former *vicus* suggest some settlement in this area, we cannot be certain that Manchester saw continuous occupation and in fact by the late medieval period the former fort and *vicus* area were unoccupied, being within a park named Aldport. However, we do know that in the year 919 King Edward ordered his army to 'repair and man' the *burh* at Manchester, which lay on the border of Mercia and Northumbria and which had presumably been damaged during conflict with the Danes. But the location of the *burh* is still not known, although there are two strong candidates: one at the former Roman fort site, the other at the opposite end of Deansgate on land overlooking the confluence of the Irk and Irwell and defended by Hanging Ditch.

Nico Ditch, s of Manchester, is interpreted as a late Saxon ditch defining a territorial boundary. It runs between Ashton Moss (Ashton-under-Lyne) in the E to Hough Moss near Chorlton-cum-Hardy in the w. An Audenshaw deed of c. 1200 refers to 'Mickle' (meaning large) Ditch, from which its name derives. Along much of its length its course has been preserved in the street pattern or as administrative boundaries. Two sections, at Platt Fields Park, Manchester, and Debdale Golf Course, Denton, have well-preserved earthworks. Archaeologists have excavated several sections across Nico Ditch but have yet to find evidence for an *in situ* rampart base, which suggests that the feature was a territorial boundary in a featureless landscape rather than a defensive earthwork.

Other archaeological finds indicative of pre-Conquest settlement include a C6 urn from Red Bank, NW of Manchester Cathedral, and an ash-filled pit excavated near to Whitelow Cairn, E of Ramsbottom, that was radiocarbon-dated to the late Saxon period. The bracken ash was probably used for fulling and represents early evidence of textile manufacture in the region.

PLACE NAMES play an important role in identifying settlements of potential pre-Conquest origin. An example is those names ending in 'ton' meaning farmstead. The Roman road from Manchester to Ribchester remained in use as the primary routeway, with isolated settlements lying nearby such as Pilkington and Tottington. Other Saxon settlements along this route were located at Radcliffe ('red cliff') and Prestwich ('priest's farm'). A fragment of wheel-head cross with interlace decoration, of C10 or C11 date, has come from near Prestwich parish church. Other decorated crosses of late Saxon date, indicating probable pre-Conquest church sites, have come from Bolton and Eccles. Manchester Cathedral also has an example of early stone sculpture, but the 'Angel Stone' incorporated into the cathedral wall may be of Norman rather than late Saxon origin. There is a suggestion that some of the early churches began as Celtic churches in the C6 or C7, these being characterized by a circular plan form with a series of cells ranged along the inside of a curvilinear court. Based on the circular shape of their original graveyards, Prestwich, Bolton, Eccles, Manchester, Rochdale and Middleton may qualify as such early sites.

The Domesday Survey of 1086 has few entries for SE Lancashire, which lay in the Hundred of Salford; this is due to incompleteness in the assessment rather than lack of settlement. Only Rochdale, Salford, Radcliffe, Northenden and Ashton-under-Lyne are mentioned. Gamel the Thane held Rochdale, which at that time was named 'Recedham' ('village of the people of Rheged') and may once have formed part of the C6 kingdom of Rheged which covered Lancashire and Cumbria. Close to Rochdale Parish Church is an early flag wall believed by some to be late Saxon.

Later Medieval South-East Lancashire

This period, from the Norman Conquest to the end of the C15, saw the system of parishes and manors established that survived to the C19. It was a time in which the economy of SE Lancashire was still based on agriculture but in which the manufacture of textiles was becoming increasingly important. Whilst the economy of Lancashire was poor by national standards, there was considerable population growth, and the scattered farmsteads, halls, hamlets and villages were augmented by the development of market towns. Castles and religious houses were few in number and had little impact on the economy, landscape or society.

MARKET CHARTERS were granted to Salford (1228), Rochdale (1241), Bolton (1251), Manchester (1282), Ashton-under-Lyne (1413), Farnworth (1426) and Bury (1440). In addition, Borough Charters were granted to Salford (*c.* 1230), Bolton (1253) and Manchester (1301), creating urban communities whose citizens or burgesses received plots of land in return for yearly rents to the lord of the manor. The plots of land, or burgages, were generally 20–33 ft (6–10 metres) wide and could extend up to 295 ft (90 metres) in length. Based on rentals, it is estimated that by 1473 Manchester had *c.* 155 burgage plots, with another sixty-five added by 1599. Sadly, no buildings survive on burgage plots from this period, but a deed of 1487 describes one as being occupied by a three- or four-storeyed courtyard building which contained a hall, parlour and chamber, with a garden and stables within the courtyard. A few TIMBER-FRAMED BUILDINGS do remain from the early post-medieval period, giving a flavour of the types of structures that once clustered around the medieval market places: the Old Wellington Inn (Exchange Square, Manchester), Man and Scythe (Churchgate, Bolton), the Two Tubs (The Wiend, Bury) and Halls Building (off Church Street, Eccles) are good examples. Excavations at Cathedral Yard, Manchester, where the Wellington Inn now stands, showed that this part of the town was used for leather working, with over 200 pieces of leather off-cuts being found. An inquest of 1288 refers to sixty-nine burgages in Bolton. The medieval settlement here grew up around the church, which overlooked the gorge of the River Croal and the rectangular-shaped market place stretching along Churchgate. Archaeological excavations in 1998 uncovered a number of medieval walls representing three burgage plots, with a corridor between the walls that provided access from the market place to back yards. Around a hundred sherds of medieval pottery were found, ranging from basic cooking pots to finer green-glaze flagons. The burgages had a narrow frontage onto the market place but extended a long way back. Originally the back yards were open and used for gardens, stock and small-scale industry, but by the end of the C18 they were infilled with buildings, some being used for textile manufacture and storage, reflecting the growth of the textile industry in the area. This pattern of infilling was aided by subdivision into separate tenancies so that in Manchester, for example, burgage plots at Long Millgate became packed with housing in the C17 and C18, leading to overcrowding.

Several short-lived CASTLES are known from SE Lancashire. The one at Manchester was held by the Grelleys and is first referred to in 1184. This was probably an earth and timber castle of ring-work form, the site of which is now occupied by Chetham's School and Library N of the Cathedral. In the C13 it was replaced by a manor house. Excavations have uncovered evidence for a medieval ditch running across Chetham's yard that may be the inner defensive ditch for the castle. The line of another defensive ditch, which reused a palaeo-channel, is preserved in the name Hanging Ditch. This enclosed a promontory overlooking the confluence of the rivers Irk and Irwell, encompassing both the castle and church that formed the historic core of Manchester's medieval settlement. Access across the ditch from the Chester road was by means of Hanging Bridge, which still survives and is now exposed in the basement of the Cathedral Visitors Centre. Another earthwork castle can be found at Castleton, S of Rochdale. Fishwick's plan of 1823 shows the earthworks of a Norman motte-and-bailey. It is still possible to see the truncated remains of the motte or mound, surmounted by the C18 Castle House, although the bailey has been defaced by modern housing. Ullerswood, SW of Manchester Airport, is recorded in 1173 as being one of the castles held by Hamo de Mascy against King Henry II. The motte survives, set in a commanding position high above a crossing over the Bollin.

Radcliffe Tower and Bury Castle are examples of late FORTIFIED manors rather than castles. Both were medieval manor houses that were fortified through a royal 'licence to crenellate', Radcliffe in 1403 and Bury in 1469. Radcliffe Tower, SW of Radcliffe Parish Church, survives as the consolidated ruin of a pele tower built in the local red sandstone. This form of medieval fortification was peculiar to northern England and evolved in response to frequent raids from Scotland. Radcliffe Tower is a long way S and may have been as much a status symbol as a defensive structure. Excavations and documentary evidence show that the stone tower had a fine timber-framed great hall attached, linked on its W side to an L-shaped timber-framed wing, all enclosed by a stone wall fronted with a broad ditch. When Thomas Pilkington erected Bury Castle it must have been one of the most impressive buildings in Lancashire, for archaeologists have found evidence for a massive tower house measuring 82 by 62 ft (25 by 19 metres) and with walls 7.5 ft (2.3 metres) thick. This building would have held both the great hall and private accommodation. It was protected by a broad moat that was revetted by a sandstone wall strengthened with buttresses. Excavations of the moat silts revealed many domestic and military artefacts, and also architectural fragments such as window tracery and corbels. The S arm of the moat and its buttressed wall are permanently displayed at Castle Street, Bury. Excavations at

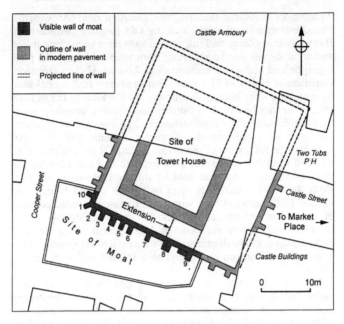

Plan of Bury Castle, Bury

Blackrod suggest the site of another late medieval fortified manor at Castle Croft.

Medieval hall sites were sometimes enclosed by MOATS, which have a broad date range of the late C13 to late C14. Excavation of moats provided drainage and upcast earth for a raised, dry platform on which a house could be erected, at the same time giving a level of defence and creating a fishpond; they also sent out a message of high social status. The size and shape of the moat could vary considerably; the few examples left in SE Lancashire are the circular moated platforms at Wardley Hall (Wardley) and Arley Hall (W of Blackrod), and the more common square plan form at Peel Hall Moat (Etchells, Wythenshawe), Clayton Hall (E Manchester) and Peel Moat (Heaton Moor). Many moats have been infilled and some important examples, such as Withington and Barton-upon-Irwell, had housing estates built over them in the C20. Excavations have found sandstone revetting of the inner moat edge at Peel Hall, Little Hulton, and Bradford Old Hall, E Manchester, both now built over.

HALL SITES are known for most of the medieval manors in SE Lancashire. Timber-framing from late medieval great halls survives at Baguley, Wythenshawe (both S of Manchester), 15 Chetham's School and Library (Manchester city centre), Hopwood (Middleton), Clayton (Manchester), Smithills (N of Bolton), 19 Ordsall (Salford), Wardley, Stubley Old Hall (Littleborough), 17

Taunton (N of Ashton-under-Lyne), Dearden Fold (Ainsworth), Brandlesholme (N of Bury) and the Old Rectory (Middleton). But sadly many large and impressive halls have been demolished and their details are known only from map evidence, old photographs and historic documentation. Lostock Hall in Horwich, Gristlehurst Hall N of Heywood, and Bradshaw Hall N of Bolton have all long since been pulled down, but the Hearth Tax of 1666 states that they had twenty, thirteen and thirteen hearths respectively, indicating their high status. Archaeological investigations have also shed light on the character of some hall sites. For instance, the full extent of sandstone footings at the De Traffords' C12 hall in Old Trafford has been exposed and recorded, as has that at Denton which was held by the De Duttons in the C15. Both these sites started as open halls with central hearths. At Ordsall Hall the site of the E wing was excavated to reveal remains of a C14 kitchen range. Perhaps the most remarkable site is Baguley Hall, where archaeological excavation and a detailed building survey have demonstrated structural development in the C13 and C14 from an aisled hall to a framed hall with service block.

Many of the medieval CHURCHES established in SE Lancashire retain medieval fabric, although this is often fragmentary due to later rebuilding. Large medieval parish churches with surviving late medieval fabric include: St Chad (Rochdale), St Mary (Radcliffe), St Mary (Eccles), St Mary (Prestwich), St Michael (Flixton), St Michael (Ashton), St Mary (Manchester), and St Wilfrid (Northenden). The last three are mentioned in Domesday Book and are therefore the oldest documented churches in SE Lancashire. Bolton and Bury, both of which have been entirely rebuilt, Eccles, Middleton, Prestwich, Radcliffe and Rochdale are mentioned in the C12 and C13. Prestwich church had a huge parish extending 13 m. E to W; this led to two chapels of ease being erected at Crompton and Oldham. St Leonard (Middleton), has some of the earliest and most interesting medieval fabric, with decorated Norman columns and reused chevron moulding in the chancel arch. The larger halls had private chapels and a good example can be seen at Smithills Hall, although most have been rebuilt or, as is the case with Clayton, demolished. SE Lancashire has no monasteries, but Kersal Cell NE of Salford takes its name from the monastic cell established in the C12 by the Cluniac priory of Lenton in Nottinghamshire. A cruck-built hall of the early C15 survives, and archaeologists have found in the garden carved stones of Norman and later medieval date that probably came from the site of the chapel and priory depicted on an estate plan of 1755.

In the late medieval period the LANDSCAPE was dotted with isolated halls and farmsteads set against a background of open field systems, pasture meadows and large tracts of woodland. Some of the wealthier lords had deer parks. Philips Park N of Prestwich retains a long stretch of bank and ditch forming the remnants of the medieval deer park boundary (park pale) built for the Pilkingtons of Stand Hall. Most manorial halls had water-powered corn mills which were an important source of revenue: under the custom of mill soke, tenants of the manor were required to grind their corn at the mill for a fixed proportion of their grain. In later centuries corn mills were often converted into textile mills, although a fulling mill on the River Irk near Manchester, referred to in the late C13, shows that harnessing of water power for textile manufacture began at a very early date. The remains of Hopwood Corn Mill, Middleton, have been exposed by excavation and, although C18 in date, give a good feel for the size and composition of a medieval corn mill. The classic openfield system of the medieval period is little in evidence in SE Lancashire, and broad reverse S-shaped ridge-and-furrow with headlands for the plough team to turn is very rare due to changing agricultural practices and C19–C20 development. However, land was improved on a large scale to provide common upland pasture for cattle and sheep. This can be seen around Affetside, NW of Bury, where the now enclosed fields were linked by packhorse-ways and drovers' roads which survive as sunken lanes (hollow-ways). Elsewhere, lowland mosses were gradually shrinking as they were reclaimed for pasture by drainage or slowly removed by 'turbary', (the right to extract peat for fuel). Iron working was an important part of the local medieval economy, and many valleys, where there was wood for charcoal and iron ore, would have been exploited by iron smelters. Meadowcroft Fold, Pilsworth, is one of the few examples of a deserted medieval village; as well as remains of medieval structures associated with the settlement, archaeologists have found evidence for iron smelting.

By the end of the C15 sheep rearing predominated across the area and the woollen industry was well established. A network of packhorse trails developed in the early post-medieval period, linking the farmsteads and hamlets involved in domestic woollen cloth production with local markets. Water-powered mills were used for heavy duty processing such as fulling and scribbling (carding). Reservoir catchment areas on the Pennine fringes across SE Lancashire contain remains of mills, farms, packhorse tracks and sheep pasture field systems, dating from the late medieval period to the C19 when these valleys were abandoned for reservoir construction.

CHURCH ARCHITECTURE TO THE C17

Earlier Medieval Churches

EARLY CHRISTIAN, ANGLO-SAXON and NORMAN remains in SE Lancashire are extraordinarily slight. There is no structure, and nothing incontrovertibly *in situ* of pre-Conquest or Conquest origin.* There is a rebuilt Norman arch and part of another one at Middleton, and an *ex situ* C11–C12 carved angel at

* For Anglo-Saxon fragments *see* Archaeology.

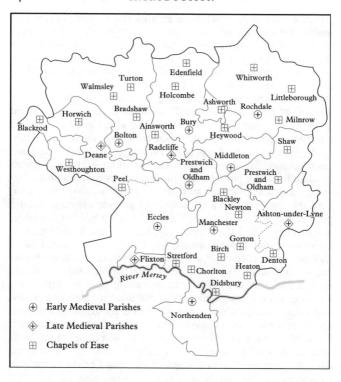

Area of the Diocese of Manchester covered in *Lancashire: Manchester and the South-East.* (The chapels of Whitworth, Edenfield and Turton fall into North Lancashire)

Manchester Cathedral. Apart from that there is nothing but a few loose Norman stones at Bolton and some reset fragments at Flixton. The ancient parishes were only seven, reflecting the sparseness of the population. Manchester and Rochdale were the biggest, Eccles and Prestwich, judging by their ecclesiastical and priestly names, the most important. Middleton lay between Prestwich, and its detached, and unruly, chapelry of Oldham. The others were Bury and Bolton. To these was added by incorporation in 1933 the ancient Cheshire parish of Northenden. The later medieval parishes of Ashton-under-Lyne, Radcliffe, Flixton and Deane, and the early chapels of ease such as Oldham and Ashworth, bring the number of places where we might hope to find a pre-Reformation church up to a dozen or so – still astonishingly few for an area so large and now so populous.

Nothing illustrates the poverty of early ecclesiastical architecture more than the absence of any abbey or indeed proper priory. There was only Kersal, in Salford, a Cluniac cell for two monks, and the granges at Marland (Rochdale), of the Cistercian abbey at Whalley (N Lancashire), and at Westhoughton, belonging to

Cockersand Abbey (N Lancashire). Excavations at Kersal produced minor carved stonework of the C12–C15, but no sign of the actual building site, while nothing at all survives elsewhere. So far as early churches are concerned, the arcade piers at Rochdale parish church are C13 EARLY ENGLISH, with stiff-leaf, upright leaves, little heads, and waterholding bases; but very modest in scale. That completes the tally. DECORATED work is not much more plentiful. The arch to the Lady Chapel at Manchester and a reset arch of the St Catherine Chapel at Eccles are both probably C14. A couple of (restored) windows with flowing tracery survive at Radcliffe, which has a Dec-era plan, and a possibly C14 arcade. The unusual arcades at Prestwich Church, tall and without capitals, and its outer walls may also be late Dec. That is all that can be mustered up to the C15.

Churches from the Late Fifteenth to the Mid-Sixteenth Century

A change in the fortunes of Lancashire can be dated from the Battle of Bosworth, 1485, when the Tudor dynasty established itself. The decisive role in the battle of the Stanleys, the dominant family of the North West, was well rewarded. The greatest patron of the age, both of pious building and of the New Learning, was Lady Margaret Beaufort, mother of Henry VII and wife of Thomas Stanley, 1st Earl of Derby. The names Stanley and Derby and the emblems of the Eagle and Child and the three Stags or Stags' Heads caboshed now become familiar. In SE Lancashire, with its lack of extensive monastic lands, this marks a greater watershed, architecturally speaking, than the Reformation, for church building and improvements continued into the mid C16.

The architecture of C15 England was of course of PERPENDICULAR character. At Manchester a collegiate church* was founded in 1421 by Thomas de la Warre (for the priests' house *see* below). The pre-existing building was rebuilt by the various wardens, and it reached its present large size at the turn of the C15 and C16. It is one of the finest and largest Perp parish churches in Britain, despite thoroughgoing restoration. The precise building history remains obscure, but the choir is almost certainly the work of Warden James Stanley II (incumbent 1485–1506) using a team of masons associated with the East Anglian workshop of *John Wastell*. This may also be the date of the nave clerestory and the chapter house. There is a striking resemblance between Manchester's arcades and Wastell's arcades with their decorative spandrels at Lavenham in Suffolk – also spoils of Bosworth, given by John de Vere, Earl of Oxford. The nave is traditionally said to be the work of an earlier warden, but it has a degree of uniformity with the choir (reproduced in C19 rebuilding), and the spreading aisles, which incorporate the areas once occupied by chantry chapels, the great size, and magnificent furnishings and timber roofs create a grand effect.

7

---

* Made a cathedral in 1847.

Radcliffe, St Mary, *c.* 1850, from a drawing by Selim Rothwell

Manchester stands in a class of its own and all the other surviving MEDIEVAL CHURCHES are smaller and less decorative. They have varied histories, and the only generalizations which can be made, are that most reached their present size in the late C15 or early C16, and by that time the general appearance was long, low and blunt with a squat embattled tower, a roof of low pitch over nave and aisles, and embattled sides. The relative sizes are instructive. Manchester is *c.* 155 ft (47 metres) from the inner tower arch to the chancel E end.* Eccles measures *c.* 110 ft (34 metres), and like Manchester, has large chancel piers containing rood stairs (at Eccles only in the N pier) and rising above the roof as pinnacles. The two churches have the same type of clerestory, with broad arched openings with uncusped lights with pointed heads, probably added or remodelled in the late C15 or early C16. The two have some similarities in their building histories as well, for in both cases the N arcade was moved outwards, leaving the tower offset, perhaps in the 1480s. The same thing seems to have happened in Richard Assheton's rebuild of 1524 at Middleton (*c.* 102 ft, 31 metres). Cardinal Langley had carried out an earlier rebuild in 1412; his tower survives but it is not certain how much else. Radcliffe too (only *c.* 70 ft, 21 metres) may have been widened, although the evidence of the masonry is not clear. All these have or had timber roofs of near-identical design, constructed in compartments with shallow arch-braced trusses each with figures in albs bearing shields against the kingposts and an identical series of repeating bosses. It seems certain that the same craftsmen must have been involved, and at about the same time,

* All of the following measurements are from the inner tower arch to the chancel E end.

perhaps during the 1480s.* St Michael, Ashton-under-Lyne (*c.* 110 ft, 34 metres), was rebuilt on grand lines, traditionally from 1413. The arcades of seven bays, timber ceiling, and a few fragments of the medieval outer walls survive, but the arcades were scraped and given new plaster detailing in the 1840s. C18 drawings show that it had the same sort of clerestory as those of Manchester and Eccles. At Prestwich, *c.* 105 ft (32 metres), the arcades and outer walls are probably C15. Here there is an unusually tall, slender tower of the late C15. Deane, Prestwich and Middleton   6, 8 have domestic-looking clerestories, probably early C16, with long rows of flat-headed mullions. Eccles has an arcade without local   9 parallels. The caps and mouldings are crude, but some of the shafts are set with niches in pinnacled surrounds; work which could be late C15 or C16, i.e. of a date with the clerestory. Other Perp arcades are also relatively crude, especially in comparison to Manchester: plain octagonal columns are the rule, although Radcliffe has nicely executed four-half-rounds-and-four-hollows, and twice-chamfered arches.

Of the other medieval churches, only the C15 base of the tower was left after rebuilding at Blackrod, while at Flixton the C15 E chancel wall and a respond inside survived the C18 and C19 remodelling. Those at Oldham, Bolton and Bury were all demolished. There is but one TIMBER-FRAMED CHURCH in the area, the only one to survive in the whole of Lancashire, although timber-framed chapels are recorded at e.g. Blackley, Gorton, Ainsworth and Bradshaw. St Lawrence at Denton is a low sturdy   10 building in the typical Lancashire black and white style, built in the 1530s, without aisles or tower, with decorative framing confined to close-studding and herringbone, and with a cove under the eaves. A few miles away in Cheshire, Chadkirk and Siddington churches offer parallels, both also simple long rectangles, with close-studding and herringbone and a cove.

For Perp CHURCH FURNISHINGS Manchester Cathedral has pride of place. The CHOIR STALLS, co-sponsored by Warden   7 James Stanley II *c.* 1500, are exceptionally intricate, and amongst the best in NW England. They can be linked with the workshop of *William Bromflet* and the stalls at Ripon (1489–94), Beverley (1520–4) and Bridlington (1518–19, dispersed), all in Yorkshire. They abound in Stanley emblems and have a full set of MISERICORDS. There are a number of C15 SCREENS too, including a magnificent pulpitum, or rood screen, and one in the Lady Chapel with figures of St George and female martyrs. Middleton has stalls as well, and a fine screen nothing like Manchester's, with boldly carved shields, probably early C16. At Northenden a chapel screen with lively carved tumblers dates from *c.* 1527. There are BENCHES at Deane, some of which look late C16, and a few bench ends, crude C16 work, incorporated into the stalls at St Lawrence, Denton. Preserved as museum pieces at Bolton parish church are a few stalls with simple misericords.

* There is a similar roof at St Wilfrid, Mobberley, Cheshire.

This brings us to STAINED GLASS. St Michael, Ashton-under-
12 Lyne is outstanding amongst English churches for the St Helen
glass, the most ambitious such cycle in English medieval art. It
was given by Sir Thomas Ashton c. 1516. Twenty panels chronicle the early life of St Helen, her journey to the Holy Land and
discovery of the cross upon which Christ was crucified. There are
also scenes from the life of her son, the Emperor Constantine,
including the Council of Nicaea. There is other good glass as
well, including three large reset mid–late C15 figures of canonized kings. At St Lawrence, Denton, there are reset fragments
and a number of well-preserved figures from the early C16. Apart
from this the only other ecclesiastical glass of importance is
11 the famous Flodden window at Middleton. Sixteen archers, all
named, are kneeling with their chaplain. The precise date is
arguable, so it seems best to accept the tradition that here we
have a unique thanksgiving for victory at Flodden Field in 1513.
The C16 Entry to Jerusalem window in Eccles parish church originated in Rouen and was brought to Manchester in the C18 for
the demolished St John. (Another importation can be mentioned
here, the three small late C15 PAINTINGS, probably Catalan,
bought in 1952 for Christchurch, Walmsley, at Egerton.) There
is hardly any other old glass. The windows which survived icon-
oclasm in the collegiate church at Manchester were dispersed in
the C19 or destroyed during the Second World War. There is no
indigenous glass at Eccles, and only fragments at Deane and
Radcliffe.

There are few medieval funerary MONUMENTS. So far as
BRASSES are concerned the best ensemble, indeed the best group
in Lancashire, is at Middleton. There are five, ranging from Sir
Ralph Assheton †1485, and Edmund Assheton, Rector, †1522, to
Ralph Assheton, †1650. In Manchester Cathedral the brass of the
first warden John Huntingdon (†1458) is over-restored. A few
other very abraded C15 and C16 brasses survive; the only other
one in good condition is that of Warden James Stanley II (†1515).
To this all that can be added are fragmentary C14 slabs at Eccles
and Radcliffe and part of a medieval sarcophagus of unknown
date in the crypt of Oldham parish church.

Seventeenth-Century Churches and Fittings

No complete C17 CHURCH exists. The tower at Didsbury is dated
1620 with an inscription to the founders Sir Edward Mosley and
Anne Mosley. The nave was rebuilt at the same time, but it is so
overlaid that it is difficult to say much about it, except that the
piers aspire towards the Doric. The tower at Radcliffe is inscribed
1665, with the names and arms of Radcliffe, Beswick and
Assheton. Like Didsbury it is Perp in form. Could they simply
be rebuildings reusing original material? The same goes for the
little tower at Bradshaw of c. 1640. It had a wooden belfry stage
on top, like that at Middleton (added in the 1660s). The w tower
at Sacred Trinity, Salford, of 1634–5, by contrast, is a strange
mixture of Gothic and classical motifs, with a triglyph frieze

below the crenellated parapet and crocketed corner pinnacles. The rest of the church was rebuilt 1752–3. At Blackrod the C15 tower was partially rebuilt in 1628 and a stair-tower added in 1647. We can be sure of the date of the tower at Ringley: 'Nathan Walworth builded mee 1625'. It is thin and unbuttressed, with three-light mullioned windows just like a house of the period, but tall obelisk pinnacles. The nearest example the area can give of a church of characteristic Lancashire C17 type is the Old (Parochial) Chapel at Milnrow, an early C18 rebuild of predecessors of 1496 and 1537, since turned into cottages. It was strongly Puritanical in character, with nothing churchy about it except for the bellcote which was on its w gable. The form seems to have been much like the grammar school at Middleton, with a full-height space galleried at both ends, as at the late C17 Presbyterian (now Unitarian) chapels in N Cheshire at Knutsford, Dean Row, and Macclesfield. The C17 history of SE Lancashire churches is full of breakaway Presbyterian congregations, either taking over the established building, or sometimes building a new one.

C17 CHURCH FURNISHINGS are no more plentiful. At Eccles 13 a stone TOMB-CHEST commemorating the Brereton family was commissioned in 1600: recumbent figures and a child in swaddling bands, in the late medieval tradition, though with angle balusters to the tomb-chest. Little more than fifteen years later the MONUMENT to Sir Nicholas Mosley †1615 at Didsbury is 14 the outstanding fully classical example in the area, with kneeling figures in aedicules with columns. It is fairly competently done so far as the architectural frame is concerned, but the figures are unsophisticated. At St Lawrence, Denton, that to Edward Holland †1655 is ambitious in scale and design but very crudely executed, with columns framing an oval inscription tablet and an achievement with mantling, helms, heraldic beasts, etc. There are minor BRASSES of the Mosley family in the Cathedral, and one in Flixton: Richard Radclyff †1602. The brass to Ralph Assheton †1650 with his family at Middleton is particularly valuable for his Commonwealth armour and boots. Deane has a late C17 PULPIT, and the new church at Ringley has retained some of the C17 furnishings and armorial STAINED GLASS. Not really belonging here are the C17 Continental furnishings collected by Robert Lomax in the 1840s for his little church at Harwood and the Flemish panels in Scott's church at Worsley. Similar pieces were incorporated in early C19 house decorations for their rich effect, e.g. at Smithills, Bolton and Hopwood.

DOMESTIC, COLLEGIATE AND SCHOOL ARCHITECTURE TO *c.* 1700

Medieval Domestic Building to c. *1500*

Early domestic buildings are sparse. There are no CASTLES except for the traces of one (more of a fortified manor) at Bury,

Radcliffe Tower, engraving, 1829

where a few footings are exposed. The only other fortified building is Radcliffe Tower, a pele or solar tower unusually far S, dating
from 1403. Here there is what seems to be a kitchen, with a
heated chamber over. Some MANOR HOUSES survive from the
C14 and are of more than local interest. The most important is
15 Baguley Hall, in Wythenshawe, Manchester, with its mightily
timbered great hall and a splendid spere truss – the latter a
North-Western speciality, in which fixed partitions flanked the
screen (and in some cases framed the dais, too). It employs an
interesting form of timber-framing in which the main timbers are
plank-like, flattened members. The hall associated with Radcliffe
Tower is said to have had similar timbers. The truncated E wing
of Ordsall Hall, dated 1360, has survived, comprising a parlour
and chamber with a crown-post roof. The nucleus of Smithills
near Bolton – the hall with its spere truss and service rooms,
detached kitchen, and solar wing – were probably built by
William Radcliffe in the mid-C14. There is a crown-post roof
here, too, showing that this building tradition was not confined
to the S of the country.* Other candidates for C14 or C15 dates,
with evidence for open great halls, are Brandlesholme at
Tottington (discussed in more detail below), Dearden Fold at
Ainsworth, and Stubley Hall, Littleborough.

MOATS are much less numerous than in neighbouring
Cheshire, and are dealt with in more detail in the Archaeology
section. The earliest is probably Peel Moat at Heaton Moor, with
a square platform which may be of C13 origin. Still with bridges,
though they are probably C17, are those at Peel Hall (the hall has

---

*There is also a crown-post roof at Chetham's School and Library (the college of
priests, for which *see* below), and another is reported at Clayton Hall.

gone), Wythenshawe, and Clayton Hall, both in Manchester. The
best-preserved ensemble of hall and moat is Arley, in the far w
at Westhoughton. Wardley Hall's moat is impressively wide, with
a very large platform.

Domestic Building from *c. 1500 to c. 1700*

The early and mid c16 saw the building or rebuilding of a
number of large TIMBER-FRAMED HOUSES. This was probably
prompted by the increasing prosperity in the decades of political
stability after Bosworth and consolidation of the supremacy
of the Stanleys, Earls of Derby. The easy land market after
Dissolution could also have contributed. The Radcliffe house at

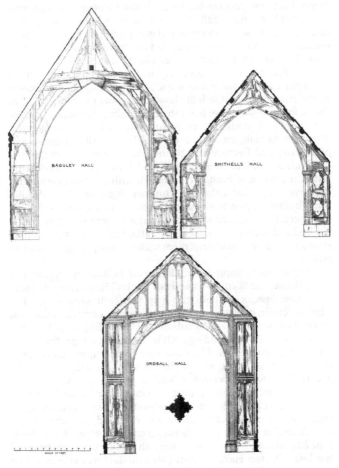

Spere trusses, drawn by Henry Taylor, 1884

17 Ordsall (Salford) was partially rebuilt with a huge open hall in
   1513, of lofty dimensions and with much decorative timber.
        There are speres with posts rising from unusual moulded stone
   bases, and a fragmentary spere truss at the high end, framing the
   dais position. This feature is also seen at Brandlesholme Old Hall,
   Tottington, built for the bailiff of Tottington Forest. Here the date
   is less certain – could it be C15? It is an important and little-
   known house, where a floor was incontrovertibly inserted into
   the open hall (Clayton Hall may be another example). This was
   then furnished with a big inglenook and smoke hood, which survives with a later masonry chimney inside it. There are wings at
   each end, the S one (upper end) rebuilt. The lesser Cinderland
   Hall, Droylsden, a cruck-framed house, possibly early C16, also
   had an open hall, now with an inserted floor.
        Other houses of similar date illustrate the building from the
   first of an upper chamber above the hall, with retention of a traditional screens passage below. Nicholas Cooper has suggested
   that chambers above halls at this time may be associated with
   houses of the lesser gentry who did not need open halls for manorial courts or other ceremonials, and this would fit to some extent
   with the story in SE Lancashire. The best example is Wardley
   Hall, which was rebuilt probably in the early–mid C16 with a
   cross-passage with three doorways. The mouldings of the timbers
   in the chamber over the hall show that it was primary, and that
   the ceiling too was there from the first, hiding the upper parts of
   the trusses. A similar story is suggested by what remains at
   Worsley Old Hall, probably early C16. Hyde Hall in Denton and
   Middleton Old Rectory also seem to have been built in the mid
20 C16 with a chamber over the hall, and Tonge Hall at Middleton
   (late C16) was also built two-storeyed, with a cross-passage this
   time running behind the hall chimney. Agecroft Hall, Pendlebury, built c. 1530 was a courtyard house, dismantled and taken
   to America in 1926. Studies made prior to removal state that it
   too had a chamber over the hall from the beginning, and the plan
   shows the traditional arrangement with a cross-passage at the low
   end.
        Adaptations to improve circulation are evident in a number of
   older houses. At Wythenshawe Hall the building history is likely
   to remain opaque without the help of dendrochronology, but
   what is certain is that an upper chamber was created in the C16,
   when there was probably a substantial rebuilding of at least the
   upper part of the building, while a cross-passage form was
   retained at lower level. Here the stair to the upper chamber is
   preserved. It is in a tower at the back of the hall, reached by
   a corridor running behind it, and it was topped with a little
   structure which may have been a banqueting house. The stair
   arrangements at Wardley were superseded when corridors and a
   stair-tower were added to the inner courtyard, probably in the
   C17. A similar development is suggested at Barlow Hall (Chorlton, Manchester) too, though here the hall range has been all
   but lost. Clayton Hall, Clayton (Manchester) was also modified
   (probably in the C17), with the introduction of a corridor on two

levels running alongside the hall, and a newel stair. At Agecroft
Hall the corridors on the inner faces around the E and S sides of
the courtyard were additions, said to have been originally in the
form of upper galleries supported on posts. At Smithills, Bolton, 19
a C16 timber-framed stair and two-level corridor runs along one
side of the courtyard. On the other was an upper gallery on posts
(as at Agecroft), which has been unconvincingly reconstructed.
These houses thus illustrate the use of chambers over the hall,
often retaining a screens passage, and later development of circulation in which corridors were added, typically on the inner
sides of courtyards. An important parallel in SW Lancashire is
Speke Hall, which has a similar building history.

TIMBER FRAMING is only rarely exposed in damp SE Lancashire. The best example, and the most decorative one, is Hall
i' th' Wood at Bolton of c. 1559–77, which is very jolly with its 16
varied geometric motifs. It can be compared with a fragment at
Worthington Hall in SW Lancashire, and with the Elizabethan
wing of Chorley Old Hall in Cheshire. All-over quatrefoil patterns are seen at Ordsall (1513), Tonge, Smithills, and possibly 17, 20,
once at Hopwood. Ordsall has been credited with starting a 19
fashion for this type of decoration, also seen at Samlesbury in N
Lancashire and Speke in SW Lancashire. Close-studding and herringbone predominates in buildings such as the C16 Middleton
Old Rectory, the transported Agecroft Hall (c. 1530), and Kenyon
Peel, Little Hulton, near Walkden which was as late as the 1630s
(tragically destroyed in the 1950s). The C17 corridor and stair-
tower ranges at Wardley are done in herringbone too. Square
framing is seen in later C16 and C17 examples such as Hough
Hall, Moston, Kempnough Hall, Roe Green, and the little
Scotson Fold at Radcliffe.

CRUCK CONSTRUCTION remained popular in SE Lancashire
through to the C16, as recent dendrochronological analysis has
shown, and not just for humble buildings. The crucks in minor
gentry houses such as Kersal Cell, Salford, date from the early
C16, and at Taunton Hall, Ashton-under-Lyne, the dates
suggested are in the 1490s. An early C16 date is possible for
Cinderland Hall at Droylsden Seddon's Fold at Prestolee, Brandlesholme at Tottington, and Haulgh Hall, Bolton, all substantial buildings, have impressive crucks, though dates have not been
obtained.

Tonge Hall at Middleton is a frightening example of the decay 20
of exterior timbering. It rots first on the S side where it is exposed
to extremes of temperature. The common solution was to build
the outer walls away in brick or stone, up to the eaves, leaving
some of the internal structure – wall-plates, posts and trusses –
in place. This was often done piecemeal, as at Tonge which has
lost its S side, with other sides following later. Hopwood Hall,
Middleton, was completely cased in brick in the C17 and C18,
leaving only the spere truss with its quatrefoils. Windy Bank at 23
Littleborough looks like a stone house of the C17 but the walls
enfold a four-bay timber-framed house of a century earlier. At
Dearden Fold, Ainsworth, brick and stone hide a timber-framed

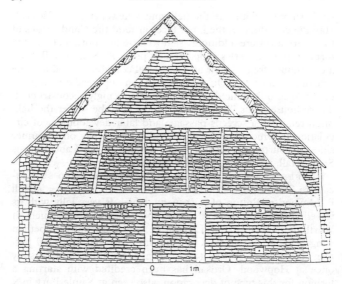

Cruck truss, Seddon's Fold, Prestolee
(University of Manchester Archaeological Unit)

great hall. Large parts of Smithills are cased in stone, though it appears that the outer walls of the great hall were always stone-built. The alternative was to cover the timber with plaster, planking or slate-hanging, often painting it to resemble the framing underneath. In many cases this has been removed again, necessitating replacement of the decayed timber underneath – as at Ordsall Hall, Smithills Hall, Wythenshawe Hall and Denton church.

Timber-framed TOWN BUILDINGS are very rare. Almost all of them are now pubs. The Boar's Head at Middleton, the Two Tubs at Bury (which has a cruck frame) and The Man and Scythe, at Bolton (rebuilt in 1636), are the main examples. To them can be added the minor Halls Buildings at Eccles, which once fronted the market place, and the C17 Old Wellington Inn at Manchester, which has been moved and completely reconstructed.

Collegiate and School Architecture

The most important and complete domestic complex, not only of SE Lancashire but of the whole North West region, is that of the COLLEGE OF PRIESTS near the centre of Manchester (now Chetham's School and Library), the best example of a secular college of priests of its date anywhere in the country. Erected in the 1420s, the building is of stone, with an open hall complete with screen, dais and canopy, and well-appointed lodgings for the warden at one end, buttery and pantry at the other, and a long kitchen and service range running at right angles terminating with a gatehouse. The priests lodged in sets in a stone cloister on 18 two levels, around a little courtyard w of the hall. The great kitchen, open through two storeys, is almost as impressive as the hall and would have met with Pugin's approval. All is preserved to a degree unparalleled elsewhere. The building was erected in closely spaced campaigns, and is of a remarkable degree of uniformity, especially the impressive crown-post roof.

Many SCHOOLS in SE Lancashire were founded in the C15 and C16: Middleton in 1412 by Cardinal Langley; Manchester in 1515 by Hugh Oldham; Rochdale in 1565; Oldham's was a little later, 1606. The earliest extant building, belonging to the Elizabethan age, is Middleton Grammar School, built by Alexander Nowell in 1586. It is a vernacular stone building, containing a double-height room in the middle lit by large mullioned-and-transomed windows, with two-storey ends. Robert Lever's similar building of 1665 at Bolton stood until 1880.

DOMESTIC FURNISHINGS rarely survive. The PANELLING at Smithills Hall, Bolton, of *c.* 1535 is the best of its date, and advanced, for linenfold panels alternate with medallions and small heads in profile, and with geometric puzzles in inlay, typical Early Renaissance motifs. Haulgh Hall at Bolton has similar inlaid panels, but no faces. The screen of Middleton Old Rectory has particularly fine linenfold panelling, with some of the folds inclining one way and then the other. Some of the DOORS and their surrounds at the Manchester college of priests are preserved, and uniquely in SE Lancashire, the hall retains its SCREEN and CANOPY. GLASS, mainly armorial and heraldic, survives at Ordsall Hall, Salford, Barlow Hall, Chorlton-cum-Hardy (Manchester) and at Smithills Hall (Bolton), though in every case the ensembles were gathered together from different sources and reset. The most complete and homogenous domestic collection is the armorial glass now in Middleton church, which originated in the old rectory there. The C16 glass at Smithills Hall is perhaps the most interesting, with a shield of Archbishop Cranmer from the period 1539–53, early C16 Royal Arms, and a spirited shield and crest of the Stanleys. PLASTERWORK 21 survives at Slade Hall, Levenshulme (Manchester) – crude C16 stuff and mainly heraldic, though with an entertaining hunting scene. C17 work can be found at Kersal Cell, Salford, where in addition to a heraldic scheme there is a charming frieze with lion masks and water creatures. The plasterwork in Hall i' th' Wood was imported or imitated in the early C20 Lever restoration, except for the coat of arms of the Starkie family, probably of 1654, in Crompton's room. There is an early C17 plaster ceiling at Ordsall Hall, Salford, with geometrical designs. Lower Fold Farmhouse in Alt Hill has the only identified example in SE Lancashire of (probably C17) PARGETTING, protected by the addition of a later wing. Fragments of C16 WALL PAINTING survive at Kersal Cell (Salford), but pride of place must go to Wythenshawe Hall where the chamber above the hall is painted to

22 resemble panelling and there is a frieze of 'Antique' work of *c.*
1580. In the same room is a very accomplished Renaissance-style
INTERNAL PORCH, perhaps imported, of much the same date.

The best C17 INTERIORS are undoubtedly at Chetham's
School and Library in Manchester, where a library and Bluecoat
School founded through the bequest of the merchant Humphrey
Chetham reused the C15 college of priests' building. The C17 fittings and decorative schemes, including plasterwork in trail
designs, panelling, doors and door furniture, a stair with splat
26 balusters, library shelves and much original furniture, represent
a unique ensemble in the Manchester area. The carved tympanum (possibly early C18) commemorating Chetham is highly
unusual and without local parallels.

*New Directions in Domestic Building from the Late
Sixteenth Century*

Late C16 and C17 GREAT HOUSES illustrate developments typical
of that time in style, symmetry and materials. In 1596 Sir
Nicholas Mosley built Hough End Hall, Chorlton-cum-Hardy,
Manchester, all in BRICK (the earliest large scale use in this area)
and symmetrical, with a central entrance, although the hall was
still set to one side. It was a decisive break; only twenty years
earlier his neighbour, Alexander Barlow, had rebuilt Barlow Hall
in timber, round a courtyard. The first building to express the
CLASSICAL ORDERS is Lostock Hall Gatehouse, Horwich, of
1591, with columns of Doric, Ionic and Corinthian orders superimposed on either side of the entrance arch. Another step is rep-
3 resented by Clegg Hall in the hills near Milnrow, built by the
Asshetons *c.* 1640 to a full double-pile plan and symmetrical on
all four sides. Clegg Hall can be related by the gauche classical
columns of its porch to Bradshaw Hall, Bradshaw, of which only
the porch remains. It was a tall compact house similar to
Gawthorpe of 1600–5 in N Lancashire. Bradshaw can in turn be
related to the 1648 wing and porch of Hall i' th' Wood, Bolton,
which has the same pointed obelisk pinnacles. So here at least,
in spite of the paucity of the remaining buildings, we can see a
coherent group. All of these houses retain the mullioned-and-
transomed windows so beloved of the cold northern counties.*

The W wing at Ordsall Hall is of brick, dated 1639, with mullioned windows and a three-storey entrance block, but it is
notable for its large size and the fact that it was designed to incorporate non-communicating apartments, perhaps for junior family
members or for staff. Barlow Hall acquired a brick wing at much
the same time. Also of brick, of 1625, is the gatehouse at Wardley
Hall. It is much-altered, but has basket-arched mouldings over
the windows like those at Ordsall. The family wing at Baguley

---

* For a house with windows shaped for casements we must turn to Newall Green
Farm in Wythenshawe, dated probably 1694 – but that is a Cheshire house in type
if no longer in fact.

was rebuilt in brick in the C17, cutting off the high end of the hall.

THE EIGHTEENTH CENTURY

Churches and Chapels

St Ann in Manchester (1709–12) is the queen of C18 ecclesiasti-   27
cal buildings. The patron was Lady Ann Bland, née Mosley. The grand pedimented porch with Corinthian columns, and super-posed pilasters of the nave lend the design sophistication.★ This and the lofty proportions set it apart from the dumpy brick or stone boxes more characteristic of the county. The only other of comparable scale is St George, Little Bolton, of 1794–6 by *Samuel Hope*, with its tall tower and pedimented side elevations, but it is much later, and is executed quite plainly in brick. These two are all of a piece, excepting the rebuilding of the upper part of the tower at St Ann and the E extension of St George, and that cannot be said of many of the others. St Thomas, Ardwick, came in 1741, but it was widened and lengthened in two campaigns and a tower was added in 1836. The church of St John the Baptist at Lees, far to the E on the outskirts of Oldham, was built in 1742 with an architecturally ambitious cupola, but it was repeatedly altered thereafter. At Ellenbrook the modest brick church of 1725 was extended and altered in the C19, and a little chapel built in Heaton Chapel in 1756 was much altered in the late C19. Sacred Trinity Salford was rebuilt (apart from the tower) in 1752–3; it is solidly done in stone, with competent detailing to the openings. The C15 church at Flixton got a new tower in 1731 with a very handsome pedimented doorway, and a new nave in 1756 with a charmingly amateurish Tuscan/Doric arcade. St James, Ashworth, 1789, and St Anne, Tottington, 1799, are both plain two-storey boxes with a bellcote but no tower. There were many more, e.g. St Mary the Baum at Rochdale of 1740, which was inventively rebuilt by *Ninian Comper* in 1909–11. Apart from this it should be recorded that the demolished St John, Manchester (1769) was   79
of special interest because it was Gothic.

That leaves the NONCONFORMISTS. The chapels at Ainsworth (1715) and at Dimple, Egerton (1713), were Presby-   39
terian (now Unitarian). Both probably were originally single-storeyed with the door in a long side, but were raised to take galleries later in the C18, and turned to face E in the C19. New Chapel, Bottom o' th' Moor, Horwich (Presbyterian, now Con-gregational) has a similar story: founded early C18, enlarged 1805. The Dissenting chapel at Platt (1699, rebuilt 1790) seems to have been more sophisticated, with a T-shaped plan and windows set in blind arcading, but it was substantially rebuilt in the C19. All

---

★ The design is based on that of All Saints, Oxford, by Henry Aldrich (1706–20) which Barker would have known through an engraving circulated to raise building funds.

other C18 Dissenting chapels are gone, e.g. those at Stand, Bury, Bolton, or were rebuilt in the C19, e.g. Dob Cross, Newton Heath, Manchester. The Moravian Church at Droylsden, is a special case, *see* p. 205.

St Ann in Manchester is the only place to retain a meaningful scheme of C18 church FURNISHINGS, albeit altered in the C19. The font, pulpit and altered box pews all survive. Some of the lovely ironwork, perhaps by the *Davies* brothers of Wrexham, is preserved. The Gothic style ironwork (1750–1) of Manchester Cathedral choir is as good. There is a fine late C18 pedimented reredos at St Thomas Ardwick (Manchester), and the organ from there, of 1787 by *Samuel Green*, is now in St Paul, Pendleton (Salford). Not one MONUMENT calls for special comment, but the following are better than the average for the area: at Rochdale, James Holt of Castleton †1712 by *William Coleburne*, London and in Manchester Cathedral, Thomas Ogden †1766, by *Christopher Moon*. There is no *in situ* STAINED GLASS. The windows by *William Peckitt* in St Ann, Manchester, came from the demolished St John, Byrom Street, Manchester, and this was the source too of a late C18 window now in St Chad, New Moston (Manchester).

Domestic Architecture

The engravings of EARLY C18 TOWN HOUSES with which Casson & Berry embellished their 1741 map of Manchester illustrates the ambitions of the town's merchants, e.g. that of Mr Marsden, with full-height fluted pilasters and a parapet with

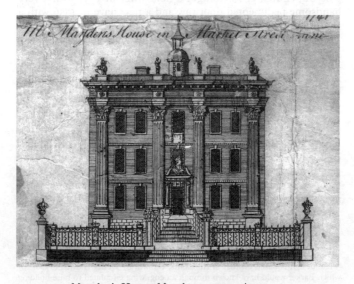

Marsden's House, Manchester, engraving, 1741

urns. Nothing as grand as this survives in the towns, except a
surprisingly sophisticated early C18 house in Yorkshire Street,
Rochdale, dated 1708. It has a curved front to allow for a street
corner, and is brick with superimposed stone pilasters, Ionic and
Composite. Rochdale Old Vicarage *c.* 1724 is also of brick, with
stone quoins, sash windows and a pretty doorcase with a small
shell carved inside the hood. The most accomplished early C18
GENTRY HOUSE, in the country but looking as if it belongs in
town, is Foxdenton Hall in Chadderton (*c.* 1720), built for a   29
branch of the Radcliffe family. It is unique in the area, for it is
all of brick, symmetrical, with tall sash windows, opposed pedimented entrances, and a compact plan with a basement kitchen,
looking urbane and sophisticated in its little park. Slightly less
grand was Sharston Hall (Wythenshawe, Manchester) of *c.* 1701.
It has been demolished, but its façade is reproduced on a new
building: three-storey, five-bay, with quoins and an open swan-
necked pediment over the door. This is very like Charles Roe
House in Macclesfield, Cheshire of *c.* 1700, and the early C18
Heaton Hall which was to be incorporated in Wyatt's rebuilding
(*see* below).

PALLADIANISM arrived on a grand scale with the building in
1735–7 of Alkrington Hall, Middleton, for Darcy Lever. It was   28
designed by a pioneer Palladian, *James (Giacomo) Leoni*, an architect of national status who knew at first hand the buildings of
Palladio and of Inigo Jones. It is very restrained, but impresses
with its fully developed *piano nobile* and giant order. Alkrington
was the plainest of a cluster of great houses by Leoni in the North
West, the others being Bold and Lathom Halls in Lancashire
(both demolished), and the magnificent Lyme Hall in Cheshire.
Alkrington is additionally interesting for having been modified in
the 1770s to incorporate Ashton Lever's prototype museum. Platt   30
Hall, Manchester, is more modest, and the work of practitioners
of regional rather than national renown. It is prettily done, of
brick, with side pavilions and its own small park. It was erected
in 1763–4 to the designs of *Timothy Lightoler*, but a great deal is
owed to *John Carr* who had prepared detailed proposals in 1761.
Lightoler put in a more generous stair, and designed artful
Rococo plasterwork for the interior. Healey Hall, Rochdale, of
1774, is a country cousin, of two storeys rather than three, and
of stone rather than brick, but otherwise very like Platt, relying
on exact proportion for its effect.

Heaton Hall is the most magnificent house in the area, unsur-   31
passed before or since. It represents the NEOCLASSICAL phase,
and was designed by *James Wyatt*, again a national figure. It was
done for Sir Thomas Egerton, later the 1st Earl of Wilton,
1772–8. Both were young men, and the house is a nice balance
of exuberance and considered poise, with its 'movement', as
Adam called it, in the garden façade, and its exquisite interiors,
with painted rooms by *Biagio Rebecca*. It is one of the first great   33
houses whose state rooms sit on the ground, abandoning the
Palladian *piano nobile*. *Samuel Wyatt* carried out some later
interiors, and built the fine stables, and *Lewis Wyatt* made

modifications including spectacular chimney clusters in the early C19.

Moving down the social scale, Parrs Wood at Didsbury of 1795 relates to Heaton in its sequence of spaces, and *James Wyatt* is known to have provided a design for a chimneypiece. It was the home of Richard Farington, East India Merchant and brother of the Royal Academician Joseph Farington, whose diaries record social visits both to Platt and to the town houses of Ardwick Green.

Heaton Park was the only principal seat of a great family in SE Lancashire, except Trafford Park, the seat of the de Traffords (and they had another at Croston in N Lancashire). The other major landowners lived far away, the Earls of Derby at Knowsley, SW Lancashire and the Egertons at Tatton in Cheshire. The absence of patronage helps to explain the fact that the ROCOCO style, for example, is represented only by the interior at Platt Hall, while Baroque and Adam styles are absent.

The same applies to DESIGNED LANDSCAPES. The few known formal landscapes were generally minor (as at Barlow Hall, Chorlton-cum-Hardy, Manchester, where there was a canal and pleached hedges, and at Hough Hall, Manchester, a formal avenue), or they were swept away by later developments, as were the avenues and parterres at Heaton Park. Those which remain – and they are remarkably few – are late C18 and later, so informality is the general rule. Trafford Park, in Stretford, was sold in 1897 and the park become the world's first industrial estate. The house, by then with railway lines up to the front door, was demolished after bomb damage in the Second World War. Only the lake and a reconstructed mid-C19 entrance with lodges are left. At Heaton the late C18 landscape, albeit overlaid and altered, survives within its great perimeter wall, the only significant remaining example in SE Lancashire. Making the most of its high, rolling site, it was designed by Sir Thomas Egerton and *William Emes* in the late C18-early C19, with lodges, a temple and a dower house. Large-scale works started in 2003 to return it to its C18 purity. *William Emes* also designed a landscape at Platt Hall in Manchester, but this has gone. Hulton Park, Westhoughton, is the only other substantial park to survive, though without its great house, and now agricultural in character. Alkrington Hall, Middleton, retains parkland and framing woods to its NW front, but on the SE the garden and park, right up to the house, have been incorporated into Alkrington Garden Village. At Wythenshawe Hall there is early C19 landscaping with judiciously positioned clumps in the park. Smaller-scale designed landscapes are at Healey Hall, Rochdale, with a ha-ha and walk, and Crimble Hall, Bamford. There was also a ha-ha at Parrs Wood, with parkland down to the Mersey; walled garden and stables survive. Smithills at Bolton has an unkempt park reaching up to the moors, with derelict walled gardens and, close to the house, a riverside rustic walk with dramatic rockwork and a formal terrace. There are fragments of the designed landscape at Hopwood Hall, Middleton, with a surviving *cottage orné* in the grounds. Jumping ahead for a moment, the mid-C19 scheme by *Nesfield* at Worsley New Hall, although abandoned, has not completely disappeared. The huge terraces and lake survive, as well as an intriguing grotto, which may have been part of his design.

Yeoman Houses and Farm Buildings

In the hills about Littleborough and Milnrow and Mossley, in fact all around the N and W fringe of the area, are many late C17 and early C18 YEOMAN HOUSES, a group which demands separate consideration. They are of strong character, low-set, with stone walls and roofs, long ranges of mullioned windows, and stony paths, yards and boundary walls. They are commonly neither isolated, nor gathered in villages, but clustered in the evocatively named 'folds' – tight groups of two or three houses and associated outbuildings. Underlying the late urbanization of the C19 are innumerable such settlements, all individually named (which have led to considerable difficulty in organizing the gazetteer). Firwood Fold in Bolton, and Prickshaw above Rochdale are two relatively unchanged examples, one swallowed up by the town, the other still isolated. Within the fold, the larger houses were often themselves in multiple occupation, as indeed were many of the great houses with their independent wings. Each family had its own front door, with date and initials carved on the lintel, and its own 'house' or house-place with its hearth and small fireside window. This is where the textile industry started and grew, for the poor Pennine land could never support such a population by upland farming alone. Windy Bank at 23 Littleborough, Birchinley Manor and Hall at Milnrow, Lee Gate Farm at Bradshaw, and High Crompton at Walshaw are all substantial houses showing evidence of multiple occupation. On a somewhat grander scale, Hall i' th' Wood at Bolton follows the 16 same pattern. The cluster of Castle Farm, Ogden, near New Hey is dated as late as 1715; the principal house is still asymmetrical, and still with mullioned windows. There are similar groups in Mossley, and on the outskirts of Ashton-under-Lyne. Cross-passage plan-forms predominate in earlier examples, with baffle-entry plans (where the entrance opens into a lobby in front of the chimney leading to rooms on either side), which better lend themselves to external symmetry, becoming increasingly common later.

Lowland houses of the same class are generally of brick, for example Brick House Farm at Unsworth of 1681, with raised decoration and mullions all in brick. Diamond Hall Farm in Failsworth is probably late C17 or C18, with raised brickwork decoration, windows without mullions, a symmetrical front and baffle-entry plan. Buckley Hill farmhouse in Droylsden is another example of similar type, and Yew Tree Farmhouse in Davyhulme, also symmetrical, with casements, is dated 1713. Newall Green Farm, Wythenshawe, probably latest C16, is more sophisticated: without mullions, symmetrical, and self-sufficient. Symmetry, though still with mullioned windows, is illustrated by

Oakdene Farmhouse in Mossley, 1755, while Audenshaw Lodge, 1774, is symmetrical with sash windows. Elsewhere asymmetrical houses with mullioned windows continued to be built through the late C18, such as Higher Alt Hill Farmhouse, Alt Hill, 1764, and Gorsey Farm Cottage, outer Ashton-under-Lyne, 1766.

There are relatively few working FARMS in SE Lancashire, and fewer still with pre-C20 ancillary farm buildings and coherent plan forms. The exceptions are some of the folds, such as Birchinley, Milnrow, where the houses and farm buildings are C17 and clustered around a common yard. Cruck barns exist at Seddon's Fold, Prestolee, and at Brandlesholme, Tottington, the latter with narrow aisles on one side. Apart from this there are few timber-framed farm buildings. One at Hyde Hall, Denton, is incorporated into a range of brick. This is one of the best examples of a courtyard plan farm, but the elements were added incrementally in the early and mid C19. A common Pennine type, represented by several upland examples, is the LAITHE HOUSE, where domestic accommodation, barn and shippon were integrated into one building. A good late C18 instance is Burn Farm, high in the hills above Shaw, where the farmhouse, with rows of mullioned windows, is at one end of a longhouse with an arched entrance to the shippon and barn. Others can be seen around Littleborough, and up on the moors at Affetside. A complex of decaying C18 brick barns survives at Cinderland Hall, Droylsden, including a threshing barn with integrated stables, and a good example of a shippon with a hayloft over. Others worthy of note survive at Diamond Hall, Failsworth, and Buckley Hill, Droylsden. A (probably) C18 brick barn at Audenshaw Lodge, Audenshaw, has raised brick decoration with heart motifs. An early C19 classical coach house and barn survive at Park Farm, Shaw, and there is an early C19 brick barn attached to Flixton House, Flixton with a classical cupola. Crimble Hall, Bamford has an C18 model farm, of brick with symmetrically planned buildings and walled gardens between. One of the most unusual agricultural buildings,

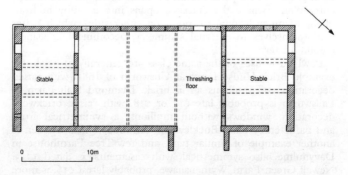

0   10m

Barn and stables, Cinderland Hall, Droylsden, plan
(University of Manchester Archaeological Unit)

and one of only a handful of examples nationally, is the c18 Winter Bee House at Littleborough, which incorporates a pigsty. 25

Late Georgian Town Houses

Intensive c19 expansion and rebuilding in the towns means that, unlike e.g. Liverpool, where extensive areas of Late Georgian residential streets can be found, Late Georgian town houses are thin on the ground in SE Lancashire. Cobden House in Manchester (*c.* 1770) has probably the best interior of any of its compeers. The builder or architect relied on pattern books for some details. There is a graceful stair, where fragments of Rococo plasterwork survive, and detailing identical to that used by Lightoler at Platt Hall is employed in the Venetian stair window. Other town houses in the area are more modest, but there are good groups of the late c18 and early c19 on St John Street and on Byrom Street, Manchester, where one row has Gothick doorcases. The Crescent and Encombe Place in Salford have splendid rows of early c19 town houses with stone doorcases, and there are one or two elegant houses in the main streets of Ashton-under-Lyne, put up as part of the planned expansion of the settlement.

Here must be mentioned the Moravian settlement at Fairfield, 32 Droylsden, which comes into a category of its own. It is exceptional, the most ambitious such settlement in the country. It was designed by *Benjamin Latrobe* in 1785. The plan is a square within a square, with modest terraced houses. The church is classical and brick, with a pediment and cupola. It is at the centre of the s side of the square, flanked by the communal quarters for unmarried men on one side (rebuilt) and women on the other, formerly a symmetrical group. The houses are all of brick, in similar but not identical sober style. The cobbled and flagged thoroughfares and the wooded burial ground are also preserved.

SOUTH-EAST LANCASHIRE IN THE INDUSTRIAL REVOLUTION

SE Lancashire became the first industrial economy and society in the world, in a process which accelerated almost uncontrollably from the late c18. A number of interrelated developments made this possible. Coal-mining techniques had been improved, and a canal system developed to take it where it was needed. The application of steam power to industry created factory towns, and Manchester became the centre of a global market in textiles. The lack of aristocratic control played a part, along with the absence of restrictive practices associated with a corporation and craft guilds. It has been suggested that the humidity of the climate, which made cotton easier to manipulate, could also have been significant. Perhaps the most important factor was the regional specialization in producing cotton-using cloths and the high level of expertise acquired in the purchasing, marketing and handling of the material, which had made the area the national centre for the production of cotton and mixed cotton cloth well before the end of the C18. Manchester's pre-eminence is reflected in the fact that an Act passed in 1736, which aimed to protect the wool industry from competition by taxing cotton goods, was known as the Manchester Act; Richard Arkwright was instrumental in getting it repealed in 1774. John Aikin in 1795 described 'the rapid and prodigious increase' of the trade as 'absolutely unparalleled in the annals of trading nations'. According to Daniel Paterson's Road Directory of 1821 'Manchester has long been celebrated for various branches of the Linen, Silk and Cotton manufactures. There are sixty Mills on the Irwell, within a space of three miles.' In earlier centuries the raw material originated in the Levant, but by this time cotton was being imported from America, reaching Manchester from the port of Liverpool.

Transport and Fuel

The roads from Manchester to Stockport, Oldham and Ashton-under-Lyne were all TURNPIKES by the early 1730s and road communications continued to improve through the C18. Links between Manchester and Liverpool were improved when the Irwell and Mersey Navigation was completed in 1736. The CANAL system was well developed by the opening of the C19. For the railways, which followed, see p. 49. The pioneering Bridge-water Canal (1759–65) was built by Francis Egerton, 3rd Duke of Bridgewater, to transport coal from his mines in Worsley to fuel-hungry Manchester. *John Gilbert* seems to have been initially responsible for planning the project. *James Brindley* became involved in 1759. The route was planned to follow a contour, avoiding the need for locks, and did not depend on improving an existing natural watercourse. Important early canal structures at Worsley include a late C18 dry dock. In 1761 the famous Barton Aqueduct opened, taking the canal across the River Irwell. The terminal basin at Castlefield, in Manchester, is the site of several early WAREHOUSES, though the survivors all date from the early C19. They illustrate the development of loading systems using internal wet docks. In 1776 the canal was extended to link with the West Coast and international trade routes. The Manchester, Bolton and Bury Canal Act was obtained in 1791. The canal was completed to Bolton and Bury by 1796 but the locks down to the Irwell in Manchester were only opened in 1808. The canal is 15 miles long and is beautifully built, with a stone-edged towpath, broad locks including a staircase at Prestolee, and several fine aqueducts. It fell into disuse in 1942, but restoration is planned.

The Manchester, Ashton and Oldham Canal Act was passed in 1792, and the canal was constructed for narrow boats of 7 ft (2 metres) beam. The engineer was *Benjamin Outram*, whose skewed aqueduct (1794–9) over Store Street in Manchester is one of the most notable structures. One of the best groups of CANAL BUILDINGS survives in the Fairfield area of Droylsden, including a late C18 agent's house and lock keeper's cottage, and an early C19 tollhouse, bridge and packet boathouse. Ashton-under-Lyne is the terminus of two other canals, also constructed in the 1790s with *Outram* as engineer. The Peak Forest Canal was built 1794–1805, connecting with the limestone quarries near Dove-holes, Derbyshire. The Huddersfield Narrow Canal, 1794–1811, runs from the E end of the Ashton Canal. The three meet at the Portland Basin, SW of the centre of Ashton, built in 1834.

The Rochdale Canal route was surveyed in 1790–1 by *John Rennie* and *William Crosley Sen*. After consultation with *William Jessop* an Act was obtained in 1794. In 33 miles (53 km.) and ninety-two broad locks, but without a tunnel, the canal crosses the Pennines between Todmorden and Rochdale. It was opened in 1804, completing a system linking ports on the E and W sides of the country. The terminal basin in Manchester has an unusual stone-built warehouse of 1806, still with the subterranean water-wheel which powered it. Disused from the mid C20, the canal was restored in the early C21.

The Lancashire COALFIELD was exploited from early times, and the industry developed in earnest from the late C18 to fuel the gathering pace of the Industrial Revolution and the steam-powered factories springing up everywhere. The timber-framed Scotson Fold at Radcliffe illustrates the antiquity of the indus-try, for it is C16 or C17 and was used as the mine manager's house from at least the C18. Transporting coal to the industrial centres gave a powerful impetus to the development of the canal system. Mines at Worsley were first exploited on an industrial scale by the 3rd Duke of Bridgewater, whose engineers *James Brindley* and *John Gilbert* built an extraordinary underground system of feeder canals to extract coal from the waterlogged mines. The Wet Earth Colliery at Clifton, some distance N beside the River Irwell, employed a sophisticated drainage system also devised by *Brindley*, which was later modified to form the Fletcher Canal for loading coal directly from the pithead. There was also an impor-tant coal industry in Oldham, where mines were built right in the centre of town, and in outlying parts of Ashton-under-Lyne, where the late C19 pump house of Rocher New Pit stands at Park Bridge. Signs of the pits in the Manchester suburbs of Bradford and Moston have completely disappeared. There is not one working pit left now. Two sites still give an inkling of the mess it created, both retaining minor buildings: Ladyshore at Little Lever, the source additionally of clay for the terracotta pioneered by *Edmund Sharpe* in the 1840s, and Outwood at Radcliffe.

The Early Textile Industry: Hand and Water Power

The name Manchester is still synonymous in many parts of the world with the TEXTILE INDUSTRY and cotton goods. The valleys with their rushing rivers were the sites of watermills, and were also where bleaching and dyeing took place. Manchester was the market. The inventions that made the spinning mill pos-sible, driven by the need to keep pace with the weavers, were all the result of painstaking experiment in the second half of the C18: James Hargreaves's Spinning Jenny in 1764, Richard Arkwright's water frame in 1771, Samuel Crompton's spinning mule in 1779. (They are all depicted in the wall paintings of the former council chamber at Rochdale Town Hall.)

Early mills were water powered and dispersed along the rivers at points where a head of water could be obtained. Few WATER-POWERED MILLS survive, and none is complete. Crimble Mill at Bamford was a woollen mill of 1761, rebuilt c. 1829 for spinning cotton, and again largely rebuilt in 1886. This is typical of the older, continuously evolving sites, such as Burrs at Bury, from the 1780s, and St Helena Mill at Bolton (see below). Handloom weaving continued into the C19 as a cottage industry, long after the invention of the powerloom in 1785. WEAVERS' HOUSES with long ranges of mullioned windows can be seen in many out-
34 lying upland areas such as Milnrow, Littleborough, Rochdale, Mossley and Lees. The survivors are almost all late C18 and early C19,* and range from isolated farm buildings to terraces in villages and small towns. The houses are typically of stone and of three storeys, in which lower floors formed domestic accommodation with the upper floor used for weaving. In some cases, such as Anthony Street in Mossley and Dale Street in Milnrow, upper taking-in doors survive at each end of short terraces. In others, the weaving floors were approached externally from stairs, as at Stormer Hill, Tottington, and Midge Hill near Mossley. Mount Pleasant near Walmersley, in the hills N of Bury, was a collection point for pieces hand-woven in the folds and farms of the area. It grew into a factory village in the early C19. Weaving took place in basement rooms in Horwich and in ground-floor rooms in Failsworth. The urban equivalent in central Manchester takes the form of three-storey brick houses, with ranges of attic windows lighting workshops used for textile finishing processes such as fustian cutting as well as weaving. Good examples can be seen on Liverpool Road, Castlefield. A related domestic industry was HATTING, but only one early C19 workshop has been identified. This is in Denton, which later became a national centre of the trade, though there is only one complete C19 works left to show for it.

Handlooms were sometimes gathered into mill-like WORK-SHOPS. Several were recorded in C18 Manchester, all of them gone, but one can be seen at Dob Wheel Mill at Smallbridge, Rochdale, a complex with a late C18 watermill. The handloom-weavers' shop dates from c. 1800 and is two-storeyed with windows in pairs. Not far away at Wardle is the three-storeyed Whittaker Mill of 1815, also for handloom weaving.

Textile finishing is represented by BLEACHWORKS for making woven cotton white before dyeing. Associated with it is paper-making, using cotton waste as its raw material. Both need copious supplies of pure water, so the works were situated in the steep,

---

* The late C19 examples in the centre of Milnrow reflect a local specialization in woollens.

confined, and often beautiful Pennine valleys, especially along the Irwell. These are some of the earliest industrial sites in the area, and curiously have sometimes survived long after the mills for cotton-spinning and weaving have been and gone. The best preserved bleachworks is probably Wallsuches, at Horwich, founded on this site in 1775 from an earlier site in Bolton. Wallsuches is being converted to residential use, and was inaccessible during the preparation of this book. Crompton's papermill at Farnworth was founded as early as 1686, and Creams at Little Lever, which is still going, was in production before 1773. Both industries engender strings of long, low, fairly nondescript buildings. The larger Holcombe Mill, now Mondi paper, is still in production at Ramsbottom. As competition for water became fierce it was rigorously controlled and hoarded. The holding pools were called LODGES, in distinction from reservoirs which are for canals or drinking water. The lodges often survive long after the industry has gone, and are still very common, making a distinctive landscape good for modern recreation. Groups of lodges can be enjoyed at Rhodes, Farnworth Country Park, and Healey Dell, Rochdale.

Specialized industry supplying the textile trade has left few traces. The best of the earlier works is Hazelhurst Engineering 35 Works at Ramsbottom, a striking semi-domestic range with houses underneath and a workshop with continuous mullioned windowing on top, built *c.* 1840 for making textile-printing rollers, and still in use by the original firm. Park Bridge, between Oldham and Ashton-under-Lyne, originated as an ironworks in the late C18 which quickly specialized in producing textile machinery parts, but only mid- and late C19 buildings survive.

Another related industry was the manufacture of CHEMICALS, especially bleaches and dyes. There was a concentration around Farnworth, in the Irwell valley, where there were half a dozen firms. Nothing significant is left of the buildings, and of the noxious riverside tips only one remains, clearly visible from the railway. In its early days the industry was extremely injurious to health and to the environment. It lived on with ICI's research 117 and development plant at Blackley, Manchester, a major employer into the late C20.

Textile Production in the Age of Steam

After the industry became based on steam power each of the towns developed in its own way, and different areas specialized in different branches of the trade. Manchester and Bolton produced fine yarn, while Oldham was a centre for coarse yarns. Bolton and Oldham dominated the spinning trade and became the main centres for cotton-spinning from the mid C19. Of the two, Oldham was pre-eminent, the leading cotton-spinning town in the world in the late C19. The processing of cotton waste to produce low-grade cloths was an important branch of the industry from the 1830s, and St Helena Mill in Bolton (1780, rebuilt for steam power, 1829) is an early example of a mill adapted for this purpose. Manchester was at the centre of the early boom in steam-powered mills. Internationally important groups of early steam-powered cotton-spinning mills survive close to the centre. Salford's industry was based on weaving and finishing, especially bleaching, using the pure water of the Irwell. There were important early mills as well, of which only Islington Mill (1823 by the builder *David Bellhouse*) has survived. Bury and Rochdale both had woollen manufacturing bases. Family firms in these areas were instrumental in changing over to cotton. In Bury it was the calico-printing Peel family firm, later the Peel Spinning and Manufacturing Co. Ltd (established in 1773), which created the cotton industry in the town. Rochdale had an important flannel industry as well as cotton. It was the former which saw it through the Cotton Famine when woollen goods could compete with cotton in price.

Early STEAM-POWERED MILLS are concentrated mainly in the Ancoats area of Manchester and beside the Medlock on the s side of town. Mills were grouped close to one another, in contrast to water-powered works where access to a head of water was essential. This had economic advantages in terms of shared infrastructure and access to a centralized pool of labour. Steam power was initially used to raise water for a waterwheel, as at the Arkwright mill of *c.* 1782 in Miller Street, but there are no surviving examples of this type, or of mills built for hand-powered machinery. The application of steam power to spinning mules was the real breakthrough, and the first mill in Manchester to use this system, powered by a *Boulton & Watt* rotary beam engine, was probably Peter Drinkwater's demolished Piccadilly Mill of 1789–90.

Early mills were typically long and narrow, often with wings used for warehousing and ancillary processes. They could be up to eight storeys high, and generally lacked anything but the most basic architectural ornament. Windows were relatively large, with segmental heads. Stairs were provided in full-height external towers, or internally, and there are also examples with staircases winding around the chimney (Brownsfield Mill, Ancoats, *c.* 1825).
92 Full-height external privy towers are usual. Mills of the McConnel & Kennedy complex, Murrays Mills (both in Ancoats), and Chorlton New Mills in Chorlton-on-Medlock include buildings conforming to this type. Internal construction falls into three main floor types, all with cast-iron columns providing support: timber floors, heavy timber floors without joists, and fireproof floors with cast-iron beams and brick jack arches. The warehouse part of Beehive Mill, Ancoats (1824) and the boiler house at St Helena Mill in Bolton illustrate an alternative form of fire-resistant construction employing a grid of beams supporting large stone flags, a system also found in Yorkshire and in some early C19 buildings of the Royal Naval Dockyards.

The earliest surviving mill in Manchester is Old Mill of 1798, part of the Murrays Mills complex in Ancoats. Eight storeys high, with external engine and boiler houses, it probably originally had timber floors and cruciform cast-iron columns which are still to be seen in another mill of the complex of 1804. Other examples in the immediate area illustrate the development of plan and fire-resistant construction, but the buildings are not completely representative since the survivors are more likely to employ fire-resistant construction and to be associated with large successful firms. 'Room and power' mills were common, used by smaller firms who paid for floor space and power in buildings which accommodated several different enterprises, and a few early examples remain such as Beehive Mill, Ancoats, of the 1820s.

By the 1820s many mills were lit by gas produced on site, and some of them piped gas around the buildings through the hollow structural cast-iron columns. The period 1825–60 saw continued improvements to textile machinery, power systems and building methods. *Eaton Hodgkinson*, working with *William Fairbairn*, made a breakthrough in the design of cast-iron beams through the analysis of tensile stresses. A lighter, more efficient beam was designed, which was cheaper than its predecessors. Their findings formed the basis for all future C19 structural cast-iron design. The new beam became standard in iron-framed buildings; the first known application was in *George Stephenson*'s Liverpool & Manchester Railway Water Street bridge of 1829–30 (demolished). Another significant development was the adoption of the powerloom for weaving. Loomshops were added to existing mills and integrated spinning and weaving mills were introduced. From the 1850s specialized weaving mills were built.

This is a convenient place to break off to consider other subjects. The story is resumed on p. 74 when Victorian and later developments are considered.

Early Railways

George Stephenson's Liverpool & Manchester Railway led the world when it opened in 1830, creating a new travelling public and generating whole new categories of structures, although it took a while for their forms to achieve anything approaching standardization. Liverpool Road Station and Warehouse of 1830 in Manchester are a case in point, borrowing their forms from commercial and canal architecture. Both have survived, to become the nucleus of the Museum of Science and Industry at Castlefield. Liverpool Road station was superseded by Victoria Station at Hunts Bank Approach, developed in stages 1844–1909. *Robert Stephenson* was the designer of the original building here. The Manchester South Junction & Altrincham Railway (MSJ&AR) was an early suburban commuter railway, built 1845–9. A brick viaduct of 224 arches carries the line from Piccadilly to Liverpool Road, an important landmark on the S side of the city centre, with several impressive cast-iron bridges. Engineering works – viaducts, bridges and tunnels – are everywhere. The most spectacular early work was the building of Summit Tunnel at Littleborough, 1841, by *George Stephenson*. The mighty tunnel mouth with its radiating voussoirs in the rocky landscape is nothing short of sublime. The most impressive brick viaduct, of 1840, crosses the Mersey valley from Heaton Norris to Stockport, with twenty-six brick arches rising more than 100ft (33 metres) above the river. Healey Dell viaduct N of Rochdale, 1867, is perhaps the most elegant; of stone, even taller, curved, and only single-track. By the middle of the century the network had spread to all the significant centres, and later developments will be returned to.

Early Nineteenth-Century Urbanization, Housing and Domestic Architecture

This was a period of mass immigration, not just from the surrounding areas, but from other parts of Britain, especially Ireland. The absence of planning in the explosive expansion of SE Lancashire's towns is what shocked people at the time, and it is apparent still in the mean placing of some of the greatest buildings. In our area, the rapid urbanization of Manchester produced – perhaps for the first time – a pattern of zoning (described by Engels in 1844), in which the commercial core was surrounded by a belt of factories and working-class housing, ringed by middle-class suburbs. The only example of a genuinely PLANNED TOWN is Ashton-under-Lyne. The Earls of Stamford expanded the settlement with a new axial layout in two main phases, 1787–1803 and during the 1820s, and despite much rebuilding and expansion, the layout and a few of the buildings, mainly the modest brick houses, and a few grander ones already mentioned, survive. The principal axial route has a circus, and views are terminated by the Church of St Peter (by *Francis Goodwin, see* Early C19 Ecclesiastical Architecture, below). In Manchester the grid of streets inherited from the late C18 and early C19 in parts of

Ashton-under-Lyne, Stamford Street.
Engraving by J. Harwood, 1832

the centre was the result of piecemeal development of parcels of land rather than any overall plan, though some developments, e.g. Stevenson Square N of the centre and Grosvenor Square in Chorlton-on-Medlock, included a central square. Ancoats was a special case, as the absence of restrictive covenants on land sales makes it seem that the land was consciously intended for industry and housing for the workers. At Worsley, which still has the character of a village rather than a town, housing for estate workers of the Dukes of Bridgewater survives from the 1760s onwards, when the workforce expanded as the canal got underway. They are mainly modest brick houses, erected to no particular plan, with terraces added to the outskirts or slotted into the existing settlement.

Industry often made the towns, not vice versa. Ramsbottom is a good example, entirely a C19 creation. Horwich is another, with some INDUSTRIAL HOUSING, although there was a pre-existing hamlet on the Chorley Road. Here a building society was formed in 1801 for the Ridgways' bleachworkers, followed by the building of rows of stone houses with basement loomshops. Barrow 36 Bridge, Bolton, was a model village built by Robert Gardner and Robert Bazley from 1831, with allotment gardens, a reading room and institute, and a Co-op, but no pub or church. Not far away, at Halliwell, Bolton, is more model housing of 1847 for John Hor- 37 rocks Ainsworth, grouped as a set-piece with St Paul's church (by *James Greenhalgh*), and schools. At Bradshaw, close to Bolton, the Scowcroft and Hardcastle families built terraces of stone cottages *c.* 1840 for their workforces. Eagley, at Egerton, was another example, laid out for the Ashworths from the 1820s. Arthur Greg of the well-known Styal (Cheshire) family was the mill manager. These places have long been held up as examples – Prince Albert and Disraeli both visited and were impressed by Barrow Bridge – and are now again very desirable as places to live, with the mills, if they have survived, converted to residential use too. This is what has happened at Summerseat, and again at Eagley.

Those who could afford it moved out of the polluted town centres, often into the gentler hills upwind of the factories. Migration gathered pace from the early C19 as the centres became more polluted. Manchester's MIDDLE-CLASS HOUSES or VILLAS were built first in the s suburbs, especially at Ardwick, Whalley Range and Victoria Park, then further out in Didsbury, and finally out into Cheshire at Alderley Edge and Bowdon. Others are on the heights to the NW, at Broughton (Salford), Prestwich and Pendlebury. Bolton and Rochdale had their villa suburbs, typically to the SW, and on higher ground. Chorley New Road is Bolton's villa district, Manchester Road is Rochdale's. The early and mid C19 saw the rise of the villa, and the style in SE Lancashire was predominantly Gothic, especially Tudor Gothic. Victoria Park in Manchester (layout and early houses by *Richard Lane*) was one of the earliest and most ambitious developments. It opened in 1837, with wide curving thoroughfares and judicious planting as a setting for houses in their own grounds. Lane's houses are mainly Tudor, though one or two are Greek.

By the 1850s Italianate styles had become popular. Samuel Brooks's villa suburb at Whalley Range (Manchester) was started in 1832, although it was only built up slowly. At Broughton Park (Salford), laid out for John Clowes in the 1840s, hardly any early houses survive, but nearby in Higher Broughton a number of interesting Early Victorian villas illustrate more variations of classical or Gothic. Summerhill, in Pendleton (Salford), a house by an unknown architect, is firmly in the Regency Gothic camp, while *Charles Barry* designed Buile Hill nearby, an interesting house of Greek inspiration. *Richard Tattersall*'s Chaseley here has been demolished, but his very similar Ashburne House in Rusholme, Manchester, ranks as one of the best Greek villas in the area, with a grand Corinthian vestibule and a spacious entrance and staircase hall. A more substantial house in the Greek style is Mauldeth Hall, in Heaton Moor, of the 1830s or 1840s, but the interior has been lost. An interesting strand is the early revival of domestic C17 black-and-white style at Worsley, where *James Evans* designed a hunting and fishing lodge (the Aviary) and a Court House from the late 1840s, and he or others followed the style for houses and cottages in the area.

Early Nineteenth-Century Public Buildings

The Greek Revival style was adopted for early C19 PUBLIC BUILDINGS and clubs all over the area. The earliest surviving example is *Thomas Harrison*'s Portico Newsroom and Library in the centre of Manchester, 1802–6, with its advanced interior and Soanic dome. Harrison also built the Exchange (1806–9, replacing that of 1729) and the Theatre Royal (1807) there, but they are long gone. Manchester's first town hall, by *Francis Goodwin* (1819–34) was a grand Ionic structure, using the ornate order of the Erechtheum in Athens. It is also demolished, but part of the colonnade was re-erected in Heaton Park. The Salford Market Hall (later the town hall), which is Doric, was designed 1825–7 by the chief local practitioner of the Greek Revival style, *Richard Lane*, who also did the Bolton Exchange and Newsroom in 1824–5, and the Chorlton-on-Medlock Town Hall and Dispensary (1830–1). The Botanic Gardens screen, Stretford (1828) is
45 very spare Ionic. The architect is unknown. *Charles Barry*'s Royal Manchester Institution (1824–35, now the City Art Gallery) is also Greek, but in a different class. That is to say that it was cross-fertilized by contemporary French (Dubout) and Prussian (Schinkel) examples with a good measure of personal inventiveness, creating a minor masterpiece. Greek was still the choice in 1841 for the Oldham Town Hall (by *Joseph Butterworth*), while only a year before Ashton-under-Lyne had settled on a grand Neoclassical design by *Young & Lee* for its new town hall overlooking the market square. 1842 is the date of the refacing in Greek style of the Wesleyan Theological Institute in Didsbury (Manchester) – probably by *Lane*, who built the Manchester & Salford Savings Bank on King Street, Manchester 'after the example of the Thrasyllic monument' in the same year. In Bolton,

Salford Market Hall, engraving by J. Harwood, 1832

Greek was the choice of *James Greenhalgh* for the former Assembly Hall and Public Baths on Lower Bridgeman Street, 1845. The style had almost died out in England by that time except for the Grecian mannerism of *Charles Cockerell*, whose cerebral Branch Bank of England was put up in Manchester in 1845. A similar style was used by *Irwin & Chester* for the Theatre Royal, which was going up nearby in the same year. A late classical manifestation was *Sydney Smirke*'s row of public buildings of 1850 or so in Bury, for the 13th Earl of Derby, of which the former Assembly Room and Courthouse are left. 48

The other dominant Regency style, Tudor Gothic, was used regularly for houses, as we have seen, but less often otherwise. The exceptions are mainly SCHOOLS by *Richard Lane*, of which only the Oldham Bluecoat School (1829–34) survives, replete with crenellations and octagonal turrets.* The Wesleyan Chapel at Didsbury College is as late as 1842, but in the same idiom and undoubtedly by *Lane*. Tudor Gothic too, but much more accomplished, is the Lancashire Independent College at Whalley Range, Manchester, of 1840–3 by *Irwin & Chester*, with its long collegiate front, covered cloister walks (more symbolic than useful) and tall gatehouse tower, spiky like Goodwin's St George, Hulme (*see* below). The Gothic carving of the oriel and the string courses is particularly good for its date. 47

Early Nineteenth-Century Ecclesiastical Architecture

A few NEW CHURCHES of the early C19 were replacements of earlier churches or chapels of ease. There are only two from

---

* His similar Blind Asylum & Deaf and Dumb school in Stretford has gone. The other example is in Wakefield, Yorkshire, now the Queen Elizabeth Grammar School.

before 1820, built before Commissioners' grants were available. All Saints Newton Heath, 1814–15 by *William Atkinson* (who did Abbotsford for Walter Scott, 1814–24), is low and stocky with two tiers of windows, which looks odd when done in Gothic. Holy Trinity, Littleborough, 1818, was built by *Thomas Taylor* of Leeds; a good building despite the opprobrium of later generations, with an extraordinary display of vernacular gargoyles.

The vast majority, however, were built with the aid of grants from the CHURCH BUILDING COMMISSION. An Act of 1818 voted a million pounds for church building, increased to a million and a half in 1825. Lancashire, an area of large and continuing population growth with burgeoning towns, was an obvious candidate for aid. It built more Commissioners' churches than any other county. We count thirty-three in the SE. The architects, especially in the first flush, were mainly London men: *Goodwin, Smirke, Barry, Philip Hardwick* and *Vulliamy*. Only *Lane, Shellard, Hayley* and *Shaw* were local, and they moreover tended to get the less expensive jobs. Many of the churches are in the Perp style, with thin W towers, thin buttresses, fat pinnacles, and interiors with three galleries and plaster vaults. The style has remained unpopular to this day, perhaps because it was vilified by the subsequent generation with its obsession for medieval precedent and archaeological detailing. In fact many of the churches are enjoyable, and some remarkably good by any standard.

Between 1820 and 1830 there are three by *Francis Goodwin*, a most prolific builder of Commissioners' churches. St Peter, Ashton-under-Lyne, 1821–4, is a fine church, with its unexpectedly transparent W tower. St George Hulme, 1826–8, is extraordinary, positively bristling with pinnacles, with a thin W tower. St James in Greenacres Moor, Oldham (1827–8), on the other hand, is poor, perhaps because money was tight. *Barry* did two in
41   1822–5: All Saints, Stand, in Whitefield and, to the same design but with a spire, St Matthew, Campfield, Manchester (demolished). Stand really is splendid. It was his first job, and he was recommended by Soane. With its crazily high and steep tripartite porch and an ingenious counterpoint of arcade and tierceron vaults it is quite a *tour de force*. Of the whole early group this is the best and the one best described as Gothick – there is a real Regency, theatrical feeling to it. His unexecuted design for St Mary, Oldham of 1824 (not a Commissioners' church) is if anything more inventive, with Dec window tracery, and a W tower rising from an extraordinary octagonal frontispiece, somewhat à la Fonthill, but perhaps inspired by Nash's classical All Souls, Langham Place, London, which has an arcade around a central tower and spire. *Richard Lane*, the local man, got the job at St
43   Mary, Oldham, 1827–30, in preference to Barry. This is a large and ambitious replacement of the medieval church. It is the interior which is memorable – full of lavish detail: generous cantilevered stairs, tall, slender clustered shafts, large galleries with elegantly curved undersides, plaster vaulting and bosses, etc. He did the similar but less ornate St Thomas, Pendleton, Salford (1829–31), with *Goodwin*. Of *Philip Hardwick*'s two churches,

Holy Trinity, Bolton, 1823–5, is large and confidently Perp, and St John Evangelist, Farnworth and Kearsley, probably designed by his father *Thomas Hardwick* and built 1824–6, is at least a splendid landmark. The classical style is seen only in *Robert Smirke*'s St Philip, Salford (1825), which is Greek and to a design 42 he had used before at St Mary, Wyndham Place in London. The long-demolished (non-Commissioners') St Saviour on Plymouth Grove, Manchester, of 1836 by *William Hayley*, had a front with giant Ionic columns.

By the 1830s there is greater variation within the basic Perp tradition. *T. W. Atkinson*'s St Luke, Cheetham is one of the most memorable instances, much more solid than most of the churches of the 1820s, with well-observed Perp windows, though only the tower and flanking walls remain today. Holy Trinity, Horwich, of 1830–1 by *Francis Bedford*, is in the usual Commissioners' style but good and solid. During the 1840s Commissioners' grants declined as a proportion of total costs, and their influence upon design waned. *E. H. Shellard* of Manchester is an interesting example of an architect who built in different styles at this time. Many of his churches are traditional Commissioners' 54 fare in typically thin lancet-and-buttress style, E. E. or Dec, but he experimented with Lancashire Perp for two, St John, Werneth (Oldham) and St Thomas, Lees. They have aisles and nave under one low roof, crenellated sides, stocky towers and, at St Thomas, pinnacles marking the transition between nave and chancel. *William Hayley*'s church at Heaton Norris (1846) has authentic-looking details to the surviving w tower, but had an auditory plan.

Of churches in the Norman or Italian Romanesque fashion which swept England in the 1840s the following may be mentioned. *William Hayley* did the highly surprising Italianate campanile tower to St Thomas, Ardwick in 1836, though the design is credited to a *Mr Frayer*. His All Souls, Ancoats in Manchester (1839–40) is lumpy Romanesque with an Italian feel. St Paul, Withington is more basic. The most elaborate is *Starkey & Cuffley*'s Holy Trinity in outer Oldham (1844), which combines Romanesque with Elizabethan motifs. St John, Irlams o'th'Height (Pendlebury) of 1842 is another example, by an unknown architect. One of *John Harper*'s three churches in Bury, All Saints, Elton (1841–3), is powerfully Norman with a square tower over the chancel where it can act as an eye-catcher from the town.

Many NONCONFORMIST CHAPELS were built, but relatively few survived rebuilding in the later C19. There have been losses as well. The Friends' Meeting House in Manchester is the largest and most elaborate Quaker house (there are not many), a grand and restrained Greek composition by *Lane*. Could he also have done the fine classical Independent chapel (*c.* 1840) in Cheetham Hill (Manchester)? The Methodists in Ashton-under-Lyne built a chapel with a solid-looking Doric portico in 1832. Hope Street Chapel, Rochdale (Particular Baptist), founded in 1810 and enlarged 1848, has a beautifully faded classical interior. Of

much the same date is Bamford Chapel, founded by two distinguished local families, the Kays and the Fentons. It is Gothic, in
style similar to that of the early Commissioners' churches, but
with all the architecture concentrated on the front, and of course
no tower. Perhaps the most interesting, at any rate in the story
of Gothic, is *Barry*'s Unitarian Chapel in Chorlton-on-Medlock
(1836–9), E.E. but combining archaeological considerations with
a personal approach, as was Barry's wont. A curious story is provided by St Andrew at Ramsbottom, now Church of England but
built Presbyterian in 1832–4; listed as being by *Welch* but no
doubt owing a good deal to the patrons, *Charles* and *William
Grant*. Its successor Presbyterian church of 1871, a showy building by *James & Robert Garnet*, is no more, but its materials were
bought by the Catholics and reused at Whalley Range, and possibly Chorlton too, in Manchester.

Which brings us to the ROMAN CATHOLICS. St Marie, Bury,
1841–2, is another of *John Harper*'s original churches, with an
openwork octagonal lantern of York inspiration teetering on its
giant arch of a front. At St Wilfrid, Hulme (Manchester) *A. W.
N. Pugin*, in 1840–2, put his new Gothic principles into practice,
albeit on a limited budget. St Mary, Manchester (1848), on the
other hand, infuriated Pugin who accused *Weightman & Hadfield*
of 'whoring after strange styles' – i.e. Rhenish Romanesque.
There is only one religious house of the early C19, and that is
the PRESENTATION CONVENT in Miles Platting, Manchester,
1834–6. The house of an enclosed teaching order, it ministered
to the children of Irish immigrant workers. It is a charming building, quite plain and classical with a pretty glass cupola and other
features of Late Georgian type.

Hardly any of the early C19 churches retain their FURNISH-
INGS to any significant degree, though there are still plenty with
galleries. An important exception (though in a medieval church),
is St Michael, Ashton-under-Lyne, where *Richard Tattersall*
remodelled the interior in the early 1840s with Perp-style plasterwork, using some convincing motifs, and rebuilt and
rearranged the late C18 furnishings, including the galleries, in
busy fashion. The pulpit, placed against the second bay of the N
side of the nave, and the box pews facing it, and away from the
chancel, escaped Ecclesiological correction. Here *Tattersall*'s fine
ORGAN CASE also survives, and there is another good example
by *Lane* in Oldham parish church. The only STAINED GLASS of
note is by *David Evans* at St Mary, Oldham, All Saints, Stand
and St Peter, Ashton-under-Lyne, all of the 1830s. His large
figures have very well drawn grey faces, and brilliant colours for
robes, especially a virulent purple.

Of MONUMENTS of the first half of the C19 the following may
be mentioned. *J. Bacon Jun.* did Charles Lawson †1810 in Manchester Cathedral with a good carved group, and a finely carved
tablet with an urn at Eccles to Thomas Butterworth Bailey †1802.
The monument to John Postlethwaite †1818 at St Michael,
Ashton-under-Lyne (by *T. McDermott*) has a display of Masonic
symbolism. St Andrew, Ramsbottom, has a fine collection of

Grant memorials. William †1842, the founder of the church, has a portrait bust by *Cardwell & Son* done from life, in a setting by *Knowles*. The free-standing monument to Joseph Ridgway †1842 at Horwich, by *Richard Westmacott Jun.* is worthy of note, with a young woman in prayer, in white marble. All Saints, Stand has some interesting memorials, for instance Tom Ramsbottom †1818 (Greek, portrait medallion, maritime trophy), James Clegg †1836 (portrait bust), by *Dunbar*, and James Ramsbotham †1835 (portrait bust and a long eulogy), by *Chantrey*; but the best is by *Sievier* to Frances Ramsbotham †1826, with all the poignancy of young death. There are other notable *Sievier* monuments at Prest- ₈₀ wich and Rochdale. Monuments by *Patteson* of Manchester are quite common. There are two good ones at Harwood, †1827 and †1814. At Bury is a curious monument by *T. Kirk*, 1824, to Lieutenants Robert and George Hood, explorers, with a walrus on an iceberg and an elephant.

The subject of mid-C19 and later C19 churches and their furnishings is returned to on p. 64.

VICTORIAN AND EDWARDIAN DEVELOPMENTS

Victorian Commercial, Public and Civic Architecture

SE Lancashire, especially Manchester, has some of the best Victorian civic and commercial architecture to be found anywhere. Manchester was the hub of international trade in cotton textiles, centred on the Exchange. The building of 1806–9 was enlarged in the 1840s and rebuilt in 1869–74 (for its early C20 replacement, *see* below). Proximity to the Exchange conferred advantages, and the streets round about became built up with commercial WAREHOUSES from the 1840s. They were designed to impress clients, with offices and well-lit showrooms. Italianate styles, based on C14–C16 palazzi, very quickly became predominant, for which *Edward Walters* was the leading architect during the 1840s and 1850s. His early warehouses on Charlotte Street are urbane, confident and innovative – five storeys high, of brick with pale stone dressings and exhibiting variety and boldness in the treatment of openings, with rooflines enlivened by chimneys. The new style was taken up wholesale and it evolved quickly. Watt's Warehouse (*Travis & Mangnall*, 1855–8) is a curiosity, brashly throwing disparate motifs together – though to great ₅₈ effect. By the 1860s Continental Gothic motifs were incorporated into the Italianate framework. The firm of *Clegg & Knowles* were premier warehouse builders from the 1860s until the early C20 (as *Charles Clegg & Son*). Warehouses by them and others line ₅₇ Princess Street in long unbroken stretches, exhibiting high standards of design and materials, and creating one of the most memorable commercial streetscapes in the country. As the century progressed there was experimentation with Elizabethan (No. 16

Nicholas Street, 1872–5 by *Alfred Waterhouse*), and even Scottish
Baronial styles (No. 74 Princess Street, 1880 by *Corson & Aitken*),
for the most part contained within five-storey buildings of multiple bays incorporating front-of-house offices, etc., with open
floors supported by cast-iron columns for the storage of cloth.

The palazzo style lent itself to other building types, such as (in
the centre of Manchester) *J. E. Gregan*'s Heywood's Bank (1845)
and *Walters*' Royal Bank of Scotland (1862). Italian High Renais-
49 sance was the choice for the Free Trade Hall (1853–6), *Walters*'
chef d'œuvre, monumental, refined and urbane. Oldham's most
dignified public building is the Lyceum by *N. G. Pennington*,
Italianate, of 1855–6. In Salford the County Court of *c*.1860–5
has gravitas. It was probably designed by *Charles Reeves* and his
pupil *Thomas Charles Sorby*. The County Court in Mawdsley
Street, Bolton, another palazzo, is by *Sorby* as well. In Bury the
former Bury Banking Co. premises by *Blackwell, Son & Booth*,
1868, with sculpture by *Joseph Bonehill*, is a lavish stone palazzo
with rounded corners, and a nicely differentiated manager's
house attached.

Ruskinian Gothic was introduced by *Alfred Waterhouse* with his
seminal Assize Courts in Manchester (1859–64), demolished
following damage during the Second World War. Talented
local architects developed the style in their own ways. Notable
buildings in Manchester of the 1860s–70s include *Thomas
Worthington*'s Memorial Hall and Police Courts, and *Edward
Salomons*' romantic Reform Club. The style was not taken up to
any great degree outside Manchester, though Salford's Gas
Board office of 1880 is a close copy of Worthington's style. *George*

Heywood's Bank, Manchester, from *The Builder*, 1849

Woodhouse had a go in Bolton with his Constitutional Club in Mawdsley Street, 1869–70. Another Bolton architect to enjoy Ruskinian polychromy was *Thomas Haselden*, who used it to good effect in his Twist Mill at Eagley, Egerton in 1887, and in Sharples Hall nearby. Another example is Ashton-under-Lyne's pretty Parish Offices (by *John Eaton*, 1869).

During the 1860s Manchester and the other important centres acquired new TOWN HALLS. 'Modern Gothic' was the epithet applied to *Waterhouse*'s Ruskinian town hall in Manchester, a   63
work of gravitas, subtly asymmetrical and displaying consummate planning and control of interior spaces. The configuration of greater and lesser staircases and the transition from the ground to double-height first floor have almost magical qualities. The   64
original interior schemes, including *Madox Brown*'s murals in the Great Hall, combine to make the building a seminal work of the Victorian age. In Rochdale *W. H. Crossland* (of Royal Holloway College fame) built a Gothic town hall in 1864 of rare pic-   61
turesque beauty, boasting splendid interior schemes and glass by   65, 66
Heaton, Butler & Bayne. *Waterhouse* was called in to replace the tower after a fire in 1883, and a good job he made of it. The citizens of Bolton chose Baroque with *William Hill*'s splendid town   62
hall, obviously derived from that at Leeds. It makes an unforgettable civic statement, with its generous approach flanked by mighty lions, though the interior is no match for the others.

With Owen's College, later the Victoria University of Manchester (started 1870), *Waterhouse* followed from the town hall, using the same practical modern Gothic to create a memorable ensemble s of the centre. He also designed the only large Victorian PRISON of the area, a spectacular polychrome giant at Strangeways, Cheetham (Manchester) of 1866–8.

Bolton has by far the best Victorian MARKET HALL. It was built   59
in 1851–6 by *G. T. Robinson* of Leamington Spa, with a beautifully airy interior of iron and glass. In Manchester there are two much smaller examples on Liverpool Road, Castlefield, done by *Mangnall & Littlewood* in the 1870s. The fragmentary wholesale fish market (*Speakman, Son & Hickson*, 1873) has splendid sculptural scenes by *Joseph Bonehill*. In Ashton-under-Lyne there is an attractive polychrome brick market by *John Eaton & Son*, 1867 with later additions.* Many of the towns had their markets, but most were torn down (or, as at Bury and Oldham, burnt down) at various times. The most notable retail building of iron and glass is the lovely Barton Arcade in Manchester (*Corbett, Raby & *   60
Sawyer, 1871), one of the best of its type in the country.

Social Reform and Cultural Improvement

Manchester and Salford were the first major industrial towns to create MUNICIPAL PUBLIC PARKS, largely through the efforts of the Manchester M.P. Mark Philips who served on the 1833 Parliamentary Select Committee on Public Walks. Three sites

* Recently badly damaged by fire.

were bought in 1845, two in E Manchester, Queen's Park, Harpurhey and Philips Park in Bradford, and the other in Salford, Peel Park. *Joshua Major & Son* won the design competition. Philips Park, named after Mark Philips, was the only one in which Major had a completely free hand in the design, but all three laid emphasis on the provision of public sports facilities. Many later municipal parks were designed to accommodate large promenading crowds. One of the finest is Alexandra Park, Oldham, laid out by *William Henderson* (who also did Birkenhead Park), with buildings by *Woodhouse & Potts* of Oldham (1863–5). Also laid out by *Henderson* was Farnworth Park, given in 1864 by Thomas Barnes M. P., whose gardener *Robert Galloway* assisted, and Queens Park, Bolton of 1866, but this has lost its buildings. In Moss Side (Manchester), Alexandra Park was designed by *Alexander Gordon Hennell* with a lodge and clock tower by *Alfred Darbyshire*. Broadfield Park, Rochdale, also opened in 1870, was made out of the steep banks surrounding the Town Hall, providing it with an effective green backdrop.

Legislation of the 1850s empowered local authorities to create CEMETERIES and so alleviate one of the great sanitary scandals of early Victorian towns. Before that time a few had been set up privately, one of the earliest being Rusholme Lane Cemetery in Manchester (1821, built over). The earliest survivor is the Manchester General Cemetery, Harpurhey, Manchester (1836), an evocative place despite the loss of its buildings. Of the municipal cemeteries hardly one has its full complement of buildings. The Oldham authorities acted quickly, establishing cemeteries in 1857 at Greenacres and Chadderton. Both have good entrance buildings (and a single chapel at Chadderton) designed by *N. G. Pennington*. Rochdale was quick off the mark too, opening its municipal cemetery with a fanfare in 1855. The loss of its chapels, by *Moffat Smith* and *Fowles*, is greatly to be regretted. However Heywood (1856) retains its twin chapels by *T. D. Barry* on its windy hilltop. Weaste, in Salford, opened in 1857, has lost its buildings but retains one of the best assemblages of Victorian 81 MONUMENTS of which the Brotherton memorial by *T. Holmes & W. Walker* of Manchester, with carving by *T. R. Williams* of Manchester, is outstanding.

Manchester was a relative latecomer to the municipal cemeteries movement. Philips Park Cemetery was the first, opened in 1866 with a layout designed by *William Gay* and notable buildings (now derelict) by *Paull & Ayliffe*. Of the later generation the following deserve mention: Crompton Cemetery, opened 1891, layout and buildings by *Wild, Collins & Wild*, and Hollinwood Cemetery (Oldham), with buildings of 1887–8, by *Potts, Pickup & Dixon*. Southern Cemetery, Manchester (1879), with buildings by *H. J. Paull*, was the site chosen for the city's first crematorium (1890), by *Edward Salomons*. CREMATORIA were a relatively new building type, and Salomons chose Byzantine and bright yellow terracotta to distance it from the established, or indeed any other, church. St Joseph's Cemetery, Moston (opened in 1875) was the first Roman Catholic cemetery in Manchester. There is an early

Jewish cemetery at Prestwich, 1841. Manchester Great Synagogue Burial Ground in Crumpsall, opened 1884, with a small
brick Ohel (chapel), by *George Oswald Smith*, while the Jewish
cemetery at Urmston probably opened in 1878. There is a good
array of monuments, and two very low-key brick Ohels, one by
William Sharp Ogden, 1894. Another Ohel, again low-key, is in
the corner of Southern Cemetery.

Sanitary reform was accompanied by provision of PUBLIC
BATHS AND WASHHOUSES. Bolton and Bury both provided
baths in their early municipal buildings, Bolton in its Assembly
Hall on lower Bridgeman Street, by *James Greenhalgh*, 1845, Bury
in the basement of its Athenaeum (by *Sydney Smirke*, 1850,
demolished). Oldham's first public baths (demolished), funded
partly through subscription, were opened in 1854. In Manchester and Salford a private company set up in the 1850s provided
facilities. *Thomas Worthington* designed three complexes for the
company, of which the only survivor (now derelict) is a grand
Italianate job on Collier Street, Salford of 1856. Salford's earliest
surviving municipal baths are on Blackfriars Street, designed
by the Borough Engineers *Brockbank & Wormall* 1879–80. In
Ashton-under-Lyne the extraordinary baths are amongst the
most imposing of the public buildings there, designed in 1870 by
Paull & Robinson in monumental Italianate. More widespread
provision came later, and we shall return to the subject.

We have to jump back in time to trace the origins of HOSPI-
TALS. The earliest survivor has already been mentioned, the Town
Hall and Dispensary at Chorlton-on-Medlock by *Richard Lane*
(1830–1, now part of the Manchester Metropolitan University),
which provided premises for a dispensary founded in
1825. Ancoats Hospital, Manchester (by *Lewis & Crawcroft*,
1872–4), the Royal Salford Hospital, and the Royal Manchester
Children's Hospital in Swinton by *Pennington & Bridgen*, 1872–3
(Italianate, on the pavilion plan), all grew from dispensaries
also founded in the 1820s. Other hospitals evolved from WORK-
HOUSES. At Withington (Manchester) is the Chorlton Union
Workhouse by *Hayley, Son & Hall*, 1854–5, with *Thomas
Worthington*'s Infirmary of 1864–6 behind. Worthington corre-
sponded with Florence Nightingale to find the ideal system
to minimize cross-infection. Draughty pavilions connected by
immensely long corridors, with high-ceilinged wards, open balconies, and no concession to visual satisfaction are the result. In
Ashton-under-Lyne a forbidding stone classical workhouse by
Mr Nicholson of Manchester, 1849, was the starting point for the
infirmary. In Crumpsall (Manchester), the Manchester Workhouse by *Mills & Murgatroyd* opened *c.* 1855, and Crumpsall
Hospital was built as its infirmary in 1876 by the same architects.
The Prestwich Union Workhouse was built by *Thomas Worthington*, 1866–70, Italianate, again with advice from Florence
Nightingale. The three institutions came together in 1919 when
the Manchester and Prestwich Poor Law Unions were amalgamated. Hope Hospital in Eccles also started as a Poor Law infirmary, built on the pavilion plan by *Lawrence Booth*, 1880–2.

Fishpool Workhouse at Farnworth, of 1858 by *George Woodhouse*, is now Bolton Royal Hospital, its show front Italianate, with a tower, like Withington. Birch Hill Hospital, at Dearnley, Littleborough, by *George Woodhouse & Edward Potts*, was one of the last of the big workhouses, built for the Rochdale Union 1873–7. Associated with the workhouses are the POOR LAW OFFICES in towns, which are often surprisingly florid buildings. The one at All Saints, Chorlton-on-Medlock (Manchester), and Bury Union Offices of 1865, are both Italianate and, if anything, over-decorated.

Schools and other educational institutions, for which survival rates are much higher from the later C19, are described on p. 79.

Salford was one of the first authorities to adopt the Museums Act of 1845 and the Public Libraries Act of 1850 to create the first free local authority LIBRARY in the country. Its MUSEUM was one of the earliest of its type to be free, and an ART GALLERY was incorporated. The Renaissance-style buildings were added incrementally from 1853 to the pre-existing Lark Hill Mansion, which was eventually demolished. It was years before Salford's achievement was matched elsewhere in SE Lancashire. Manchester built libraries in the 1850s, but it was not until 1882 that the City Art Gallery was created, when the Royal Manchester Institution donated its building and extensive collections to the corporation. The Oldham Art Gallery and Library (1883, by the local architect *T. Mitchell*) is Gothic, and quite extensive. Rochdale gallery and museum (now called Touchstones), by *Jesse Horsfall*, opened in the same year, but Bury had to wait until 1901 for its museum and library. It is an excellent building in Renaissance style by *Woodhouse & Willoughby*, with sculptural friezes by *J. J. Millson* (who also supplied the sculpture at Rochdale).

Even when cultural institutions were founded by local authorities, they were very often supported by PRIVATE PATRONS. In Salford, the art dealer Thomas Agnew gave generously to the new gallery, while at Bury the collection was based on that of the industrialist Thomas Wrigley. Oldham's collection includes many gifts from local industrialists, such as Charles Lees, who wanted to promote 'a cultivated as well as a commercial society'. Similar stories are common elsewhere in the area. To say that Lancashire merchants and industrialists never forgot their origins is a cliché, but there is some truth in it. Tales of rags-to-riches could come true, as never before or since, in C19 Manchester. James Jardine can be taken as an example. Born in 1818 of a poor family in the Irwell valley, he started as a clerk with Christy & Son, Fairfield, and rose to be manager. He was a junior partner with Hugh Shaw & Co., fine spinners of Ancoats, and rose to head the business, thence known as Shaw, Jardine & Co., the largest fine spinners and doublers in Manchester. He built himself a villa in Alderley Edge, Cheshire, but remained engaged in Manchester concerns. The children's wing at Ancoats hospital was built and endowed by him in 1888. Chairman of the Royal Exchange, Vice President of the Salford Savings Bank, on the board of Owens College, he also gave the S porch of Manchester Cathedral (where his likeness appears as one of the gargoyles), the E window at St Ann, and a window at Walmersley. Private patrons in the C19 provided facilities ranging from lads' clubs, technical schools, and hospitals to some of the most magnificent churches, mentioned in the appropriate places elsewhere. Jumping ahead to the end of the century, two of the most splendid additions to Manchester were provided by private individuals. The Whitworth Art Gallery and the John Rylands Library are major educational institutions financed by the bequests of Nonconformist industrialists. They could hardly be more different in style. The Whitworth Art Gallery by *J. W. Beaumont & Sons*, 1894–1908, is executed in solid Jacobean. The John Rylands Library (1890–9), by *Basil Champneys*, is Art-for-Art's-sake Gothic used freely as a medium for individual expression.

Major Victorian Houses

Some of the area's merchants and industrialists built fabulous MANSIONS for themselves but, having risen fast, they tended to fall hard – and so did their houses. Sam Mendel's palatial Manley Hall was built at Whalley Range (Manchester) in 1861, Italianate, with a winter garden, ornamental lodges and artificial grounds; but he went bust when the Suez Canal opened, and, after a period of public ownership, the house was destroyed in 1912. Ford Bank at Didsbury, by *Edward Walters*, 1854, built for Thomas Gair Ashton, was soberly Italianate and packed with art, but it too has gone. Italianate was also the choice for surviving houses such as the Lees family house at Werneth of *c.* 1849; for George Mayall's grand mansion in Mossley (1861–4) and of Sir Joseph Whitworth for his house of 1851 by *Edward Walters* in Rusholme (Manchester). In contrast Jonathan Wood chose Lancashire black-and-white for Drywood Hall, in Worsley (1855), picking up on a stylistic tradition established there by the 1st Earl of Ellesmere and his architect *James Evans*.

Ruskinian Gothic superseded Italianate as a popular choice from the 1860s. The brewer Sir Edward Holt, a noted philanthropist, lived quietly at Prestwich in Woodthorpe, a relatively modest Gothic villa of 1861 and 1889. In contrast the grandest surviving villa is The Towers at Didsbury, by *Thomas Worthington*, 1868–72 for John Edward Taylor, owner of the *Manchester Guardian*. It is Germanic Gothic, with a tower of the sort that Waterhouse favoured, built of superb materials and with lavish stone- and wood-carving and stained glass. Worthington also did the polychromatic Charlton House at Prestwich, 1866, and the demolished Timberhurst of 1853 at Bury for Thomas Wrigley, paper-maker and art collector. *Waterhouse* built a major Gothic villa, The Firs in Victoria Park, for T. R. Hetherington, 1874–5 (now the Xavieran College), and there are more luxurious houses (by others) of similar date nearby. In Audenshaw the millowner Abel Buckley had a Tudor house built *c.* 1860, with a glorious Gothic interior. Sedgley Park at Prestwich, *c.* 1854 for William Pearson, calico merchant, is large and Gothic, but its

86 magnificent interiors are chiefly the result of refurbishment in the
    1870s by *James Lamb* for Themistocles Petrocokino. Gothic too
    are a series of big houses on Chorley New Road, Bolton, by
    George Woodhouse. Woodside of 1877 is the best survivor, rather
    hard-looking with an almost over-inventive line in oriels. *J. S.
    Crowther* was in all things a true Goth. At Sunny Brow in Mid-
    dleton, 1865, his Gothic is more than skin-deep. Another almost
    certain Crowther house of much the same date is Gartness at
    Victoria Park, Manchester. Thomas Thwaites, bleacher, chose
84, 85 something different for Watermillock at Bolton, by *Bradshaw &
    Gass* of 1880–6. It is in an opulent Renaissance style, after Hall
    i' th' Wood close by, but overblown. In a similar vein is Thorn-
    leigh, Astley Green, Bolton, by *Henry Stead*, 1868 and *c.* 1890 for
    Arthur Lemuel Briggs, cotton-spinner.

    Few indeed are the substantial villas which are still family
    homes. Westcombe, at Heaton, Bolton, a plain comfortable villa
    perfectly preserved, including the *Thomas Mawson* garden, is the
    only one encountered in researching this book. Built *c.* 1881 for
    Thomas Winder, it was later the home of W. H. Lever for a while
    – he adored moving house and never lived anywhere for long,
    then of the Tillotsons who live there still.

    The newly rich (and not so new) sometimes took over historic
    houses, often carrying out major RESTORATION and extensions
    to make them look older still. The Ainsworths at Smithills,
    employing *George Devey* and others, extended the C14 and C15
    house and made it, bizarrely, more antique. At Wardley *John
    Douglas* restored the C16 house for the Earls of Ellesmere, though
    he was comparatively restrained. *Henry Taylor* was probably
    responsible for re-olding rather than renewing Wythenshawe Hall
    for T. W. Tatton and his wife in the 1860s and 1870s. Hopwood
    Hall, Middleton, received similar treatment in the 1850s, for Mrs
    Susan Hopwood, under *George Shaw*. Worsley Old Hall is another
    example, repeatedly extended and altered in black-and-white
    style, at first in the 1850s, probably by *Blore*.

    ## Victorian Ecclesiastical Architecture

    Victorian churches and their furnishings are an enormous subject
    in SE Lancashire, and will be divided into phases. We pick up the
    story where we left off in the 1840s, and start with early ECCLE-
51 SIOLOGY and with *G. G. Scott*. His estate church at Worsley
    (1845–6), an important early work, puts him plainly in the Pugin
    camp, but as Pevsner observed in 1969, it is 'on a scale and with
    a plenitude of means nearly always unavailable to Pugin.' Apart
    from the Ecclesiological plan – i.e. clearly expressed parts, espe-
    cially a deep and separate chancel, and the use of Middle Pointed
    (later C13 Dec) – the important attributes are the proportions
    and the solidity. There is a fine tower and spire enlivened by
    crockets and gargoyles; the timber roof is sturdy, far from the
    flimsiness of so many of the time. The arcade is solid, dignified
    and well detailed, the chancel and chapel convincing. The 1840s
    saw the alteration of existing churches to satisfy the new liturgical

preferences. One of the most interesting examples is *Lane*'s St John, Broughton (Salford) of 1836–9, where a chancel was added by *Gregan* in 1846, a project in which *A. W. N. Pugin* had a hand. With its Puginian sedilia, patron's tomb like an Easter sepulchre and *Hardman* glass designed by Pugin himself, it is a perfect example of the aims of the Ecclesiologists, meat that was too strong for the Bishop. Churches with clearly expressed parts, open timber roofs and (usually) Middle-Pointed detailing were proliferating by the end of the 1840s, for example *W. Young*'s excellent St Paul, Walkden and *J. Harrison*'s St Margaret, Whalley Range (Manchester), both of 1848–9. *Joseph Clarke*'s St James, Crompton (1847) is a good example of a church grasping at the new Ecclesiological orthodoxy, with a fully developed chancel, and Clarke reached full confidence with St Luke at Heywood, of 1860–2. *J. E. Gregan*'s St John, Longsight (1845–6) and *J. M. Derick*'s St James, Rusholme, of the same date, are relatively early SE Lancashire examples of offset (SW) towers. The churches of *Joseph Stretch Crowther* (1820–93) also belong here. With *Henry Bowman* he published *Churches of the Middle Ages* (1845 and 1853) with examples culled mostly from Lincolnshire Dec; one of the great source-books of the favoured style. *Bowman & Crowther* started with Unitarian churches, of which the best in the area was at Bury (1852, demolished). When Crowther set up on his own it was with Gothic Revival churches in the Gilbert Scott manner: St Mary, Hulme (1853–8), with a nice attendant group 56 of parsonage and schools, St Alban, Cheetwood (1857–64, demolished), and St Mary, Bury (1876), still Gothic Revival (Lincolnshire Dec) outside but more free inside. Later he was to switch to a cerebral Perp, for his additions to the churches at Rochdale and Littleborough, for example, which were based on his final great work, incomplete at his death: the restoration and partial rebuilding of Manchester Cathedral. *Weightman & Hadfield* did the enormously impressive Roman Catholic Cathedral in Salford (1855), also based on medieval precedent but avoiding a mechanical look, with the interior spaces impressively handled. Hadfield had worked with Crowther on *Churches of the Middle Ages* and the cathedral is based on the same sources as Crowther's St Mary, Hulme – indeed the two spires, both based on Newark, would have been visible one from the other as they rose.

1844 and 1845 are the dates of two of the most remarkable churches of the early Victorian period: St Stephen, Lever Bridge, 53 Bolton and Holy Trinity, Platt (Rusholme, Manchester), both by *Edmund Sharpe* (1809–77). Born in Knutsford, Cheshire, Sharpe was related both to Elizabeth Gaskell and the Bolton Whittakers. He took a degree at Trinity College, Cambridge, was recommended by the Master, William Whewell for a travelling scholarship (1833–5), spent a few days in the office of Thomas Rickman, then set himself up as architect at Lancaster. His first churches were for his cousin William Whittaker, Vicar of Blackburn. Sharpe's two famous 'pot' churches – so called because they are constructed as far as possible out of terracotta – came about through another relation, John Fletcher, owner of a coal and fire-clay mine in Little Lever. St Stephen only cost £2,600 despite much trial and error in the firing. Having published *Architectural Parallels* in 1848, another major source-book of the Gothic Revival, Sharpe quit architecture in 1851 to take up a career as a railway promoter, contractor and engineer, handing over the business to his brother-in-law and partner *Edward Paley*, who in due course took on *Hubert Austin*, for whom *see* below.

In the second phase we see a breaking away from Pugin, from Middle Pointed, and from copyism. Continental, particularly French and Italian precedents were sometimes adopted, and partly as a result brick and polychromatic effects became more popular. *Butterfield*'s Holy Cross in Clayton, Manchester (1863–6) with its brick polychromy is not his best work, but was influential locally. *E. W. Pugin*'s St Francis, Gorton, follows (*see* pp. 68–9), then *Crowther*'s St Benedict, Ardwick (1877–80), the most creative of his churches, with big windows set high, an Italianate tower, and a clergy house attached. *Waterhouse*'s St Elisabeth, Reddish, 1882–3, can be placed here: again of brick in a tough suburb and drawing on historical precedent in a frankly Victorian manner. Waterhouse built few churches, but here we have one of his very best buildings. *Street* is represented in Lancashire by one major work, St Peter, Swinton of 1869. It is full of variety, but looking, as Pevsner put it, 'strong and trustworthy with its bold, flat tracery'. Also by Street and contemporary are the frankly dull St James, Milnrow (1868–9), and the smaller but more entertaining All Saints, Little Bolton. *Scott*'s St Luke, Weaste (1865) is small and, by comparison with Worsley, minor, but here too is solidity in the great shafts at the W end supporting the tower.

Pevsner (following Goodhart-Rendel) characterized certain architects as ROGUES, and the name has stuck. *J. Medland & Henry Taylor* fit the bill perfectly, though the two brothers were very different. Henry was the antiquarian, author of *Old Halls of Lancashire and Cheshire*, 1884. Medland was the arch-rogue of SE Lancashire, said to have been associated with one of the greatest rogues of all, S. S. Teulon, before he set up his own Manchester practice in 1860, though no-one seems to know what form the association took. It is not that the firm's work resembles Teulon's, but there is quirky inventiveness, a love of oddity and an element of risk-taking and willingness to experiment. Favourite motifs include odd subsidiary towers or turrets like the one over the baptistery at St Mary, Haughton Green (1874–6), and peculiar tracery such as the circular windows with mullions at St Clement, Urmston (1868) and St Anne, Denton (1880–2). The latter rises up from a great basement, with forceful upward thrust. It is perhaps the most beautiful and contemplative inside (the rectory, almost equally rewarding, also survives). The internal polychromy, also seen at Holy Trinity, Ashton-under-Lyne and elsewhere, comes with a debt to Butterfield. A similar plan, based on transepts and chancel of equal dimensions is seen at the extraordinary Masonic church of St Edmund, Rochdale. At Haughton

Green, Japonaiserie meets Lancashire c16 timber-framing with a dose of pargetting for good measure. These are perhaps the partnership's most remarkable works, but there are many others, nearly always original. Two more can be found in Rochdale: the very good group of church, school and parsonage at St Mary, Balderstone, 1865–72, and nearby the retina-irritant polychromy of St Peter, Newbold, 1869. St Agnes, Levenshulme, Manchester (1884–5), charms with asymmetry and wonderful roof timbers.

George Shaw (1810–76) of Saddleworth is our other rogue, though in a different way. He was entirely self-taught, having worked and travelled as an agent for his textile manufacturing family until he suddenly blossomed as an architect in 1850, when he was forty. Architect and contractor that is: he was the original design-and-build man, able to supply from his works at Saddleworth everything requisite – stone, carved wood in profusion, stained glass. He did a fine line in ancestral chapels in the 1840s, redolent of antiquity with their dark and intricate woodwork, richly coloured glass, and worn brasses and tombs. The best was at St Chad, Rochdale. There were others at Calderbrook, Littleborough, at Healey, Rochdale, and at Hurst in Ashton-under-Lyne, but only the last is still complete. His buildings are peculiarly clumsy and coarse textured, his tracery sometimes laughably bad; but they are vigorous and unselfconscious, his irregular grouping is often good, and his distinctively tight and untrammelled spires can be excellent. Christchurch Healey, Rochdale (built 1850–77 in stages) is his best SE Lancashire church. Holy Trinity, Prestolee (1859–62), is also very good in the landscape, as is St James, Calderbrook at Littleborough 55 (1860–4). At St Thomas, Werneth, Oldham, 1853–5 (with *Trimen*) Shaw can be compared side-by-side with *J. S. Crowther*, who added a vestry and organ chamber. Crowther's work is infinitely more refined, but Shaw has more vim.

Then we come to *Bodley* and a return to a stricter historical Gothic, i.e. early Perp. His St Augustine, Pendlebury (1871–4) 73 was described by Pevsner as 'one of the English churches of all time'. The sheer brick exterior, with its high windows, is lifted a little by restrained pale stone banding and dressings, the whole body of the building is treated as one long vessel, with an insistent rhythm of buttresses. The interior is breathtaking in its majesty, with its great height and the march of the tall wall piers. Moreover it is all of a piece, with a decorative scheme almost exactly as Bodley envisaged, with glass and paintings by *Burlison & Grylls* designed under his supervision.

This brings us to the one local man of genius, for with *Hubert Austin* the firm of *Austin & Paley* achieved greatness, distinguished for their thoughtfully creative designs with masterful handling of space, line and plane. There is often much bare wall, and pared down simplicity; interiors can be subtly asymmetrical. The style often, but by no means always, Perp, the detailing sometimes exhibits subtle polychromy, with careful handling of masonry, and often incorporates restrained ARTS AND CRAFTS features, such as judiciously placed carved texts, inside and out.

There is more by the practice in N and SW Lancashire, but we have a splendid example of work on a tight budget, with a wonderful reredos at St James, Daisy Hill, Westhoughton (1879–81). St John Evangelist in Cheetham (Manchester), Romanesque – E. E., is larger and more monumental – serious, forceful and uplifting. St Thomas, Halliwell, Bolton (1875) is in its brick simplicity a powerful presence, and so is All Souls, Astley Bridge, (1878–81) not far away, built (with the demolished church of The Saviour, Deane Road) by the fervently Evangelical Thomas Greenhalgh. St Margaret, Halliwell, Bolton, is a gentler building, in stone, with Arts and Crafts detailing.

As the C19 century progressed, craftsmanship, materials, and money for churches were still plentiful (but unfinished churches get more common, especially unfinished towers). The influence of the Arts and Crafts movement, already noted in the work of *Austin & Paley*, can be seen in the approach to materials and fittings. The effect of the Aesthetic Movement and the Japanese fashion has already been noted in the work of the Taylors, while Free Style approaches can be seen in some of the later works. If the following reads like a list it is because there is an embarrassment of riches, and lack of space demands brevity. *Temple Moore* at Royton created a church of rare character and subtlety (1908–10), in which the layered spaces, with a sunken nave, wall- and window-passages, an island sanctuary and Lady Chapel, are extraordinary and effective. Another *Temple Moore* church, equally subtle, is St Aidan, Sudden, Rochdale (1913–15). *George Truefitt* did a curious church at Davyhulme (1889–90), with a great octagonal tower and odd detailing. *Ninian Comper*'s unorthodox and effective rebuild and extension of St Mary the Baum, Rochdale dates from 1909–11. Christchurch, or the Jesse Haworth Memorial church, at Walshaw near Bury (1889–92) is *Lawrence Booth*'s *chef d'œuvre*, with lavish carving and furnishings and a complete programme of stained glass. *R. B. Preston*'s churches at Rochdale (w) St Ann, and at Blackrod, Simister, and Littleborough all show his love of stone, though his cheap, brick churches are unmemorable. *R. Knill Freeman* of Bolton produced work not unlike that of R. B. Preston, with similarly effective but reserved Arts and Crafts detailing. *Frank P. Oakley*'s father was the Dean of Manchester, and Oakley worked with Crowther, and on his own after Crowther's death, on the restoration of the Cathedral. His All Souls at Heywood (1898–9 and 1908) is very Crowther-like, but St Andrew, Littleborough (1893–5), St John, Hopwood, Heywood (1903–5), and St Hilda, Prestwich (1904) are more personal.

Among ROMAN CATHOLIC churches not already mentioned (for the Cathedral in Salford, by *Weightman & Hadfield*, see p. 616) *J. A. Hansom*'s Holy Name of Jesus in Chorlton-on-Medlock (1869–71) is magnificent, his most impressive church, with a wonderful lightness in the interior spaces, thanks partly to the internal use of terracotta, and clever layering of space. The influences are early French Gothic. Where A. W. N. Pugin was usually forced to work to stringent budgets his son *Edward Welby Pugin* had as patrons the de Traffords, Sir Humphrey and Lady Annette (he had previously worked for her relatives, the Earls of Shrewsbury). For them he produced his masterwork, All Saints, Barton-upon-Irwell (Stretford). From the casket-like family chapel (with references to the Sainte Chapelle in Paris, 1243–8) to the soaring height of the apse, he created a place where there is both intimacy and nobility, all enhanced by the magnificent furnishings. St Francis, Gorton (1866–72), a friary church for the Franciscans, is his other important work, with a fantastic cliff-like w front, and a monumental exterior, though the interior, stripped and vandalized, awaits rehabilitation. His other church, also for the de Traffords, is St Ann, Stretford. The churches in this group lack transepts and have prominent rose windows, inspired by early French Gothic examples, but where the Stretford examples are executed in stone, St Francis Gorton is polychrome with much brick. St Joseph in Longsight (Manchester), by *Lowther & Rigby*, 1914–15, is minor, but it has an interesting Free Style tower and Art Nouveau detailing.

Few grand NONCONFORMIST CHAPELS have survived, and it is hard to think of an intact example of classic chapel architecture. Rich industrialists often shook off Nonconformist origins to embrace – and, often, endow – the Established Church in the later C19: the Heywoods, patrons of St Augustine, Pendlebury, and St Peter, Swinton (p. 661) are one example, the Whittakers of Ashton-under-Lyne another. The Claremont Chapel in Little Bolton, 1868–9 by *George Woodhouse*, and the near-contemporary Union Baptist chapel (former) in Stretford, both with grand Corinthian porticoes, are easily the most impressive works for the Baptists. Among other surviving chapels are Bridge Chapel (Methodist) in Radcliffe, 1881–3 by *Alfred W. Smith*, with its too-tall portico, and Providence Chapel (Congregational) at Middleton, of 1859–60 by *James Simpson*, without an expressed order. It is derelict, and so is his fine classical Methodist chapel in Shaw of 1863.

Some Nonconformist churches turned away from their characteristic classical vernacular traditions, aping the Church of England by taking on the full panoply of Pugin's examples and Ecclesiology. The Unitarians led the way. *Thomas Worthington* built for them two superb churches at Gorton (Manchester) and Monton. Worthington had worked with *Bowman & Crowther* on Gee Cross Unitarian church just outside our area at Hyde (1846–8), one of the first Dissenting churches in the country to look like a medieval parish church. The Congregationalists at Broughton, and Tottington Greenmount (1865–7, by *George Woodhouse*) went the same way. An unusually lavish example is the so-called Iron Church at Astley Bridge, Bolton (1895–8) which was built for W. H. Lever by *Jonathan Simpson*. Full-blooded Gothic among the Methodists is rarer, but St Paul Methodist Church at Didsbury, Manchester, is proudly Gothic with a spire and a rich interior, by *H. H. Vale* and *T. D. Barry &*

Sons, 1875–7. Very different is the domed Methodist Church at Halliwell, Bolton, of 1902 by *J. C. Topping*. It has domes over the stair-towers too.

Of other late C19 Nonconformist churches Albion in Ashton-under-Lyne (Congregational) is one of the largest and most ambitious (by *John Brooke*, 1890–5), with a high clerestory, transepts and a few roguish features in the spacious and beautiful interior. *Edgar Wood* makes his appearance with Temple Street Baptist Chapel, Middleton, 1889, and Silver Street Chapel (Wesleyan) at Rochdale, 1893. These are small fry, but the demolished Middleton Unitarian Chapel of 1892 was more ambitious. His

76 Long Street Methodist Church (1899–1901) with its attendant buildings, also at Middleton, makes a very refined and rewarding group, especially to be cherished now that it is under some threat. The list ends with a church which could have been a new

78 beginning, the First Church of Christ Scientist, in Rusholme, Manchester, also by *Edgar Wood* (1903–4, additions 1905–7): startlingly original, perhaps the most original of all his buildings. Pevsner called it 'the only religious building in Lancashire that would be indispensable in a survey of the development of C20 church design' which 'stands entirely on its own in England.' Wood was strongly influenced by Arts and Crafts ideas, some of his buildings have Art Nouveau characteristics and details, and some motifs recall Rennie Mackintosh. To this must be added novel planning, especially in the First Church, with its extraordinary splayed wings; the use of unexpected motifs such as the Arabic organ screen there, and a sort of proto-Expressionist sculptural boldness and plasticity, which looks forward to early-to-mid C20 trends.

The long-established Jewish community in Manchester built SYNAGOGUES mainly in the Cheetham area, but there have been

74 many losses. The best survivor is the former Sephardic Synagogue (now a Jewish museum) on Cheetham Hill Road by *Edward Salomons*, 1874. It is in Moorish style, inside and out, retaining its galleries and furnishings. Much later is the synagogue in Fallowfield (1912–13) which was the first major work of *Joseph Sunlight*. He named his inspiration as St Sophia of Constantinople. England's first purpose-built Armenian Church in Chorlton-on-Medlock, Manchester, is minor (by *Royle & Bennett*, 1869–70), but serves as another illustration of the diversity of Manchester's merchant community, while the grandly classical Greek Orthodox Church in Broughton (Salford) is a major work of *Clegg & Knowles* (1860–1).

Of CHURCH FURNISHINGS, St Augustine, Pendlebury retains a sequence paralleled in few other places. They are all designed by *Bodley*, or by him in collaboration with *Burlison & Grylls*, who did the extraordinary glass and the imposing reredos and other paintings. To this list of outstanding ensembles must be added the wall paintings, altars, reredoses and other furnishings in All Saints, Barton-upon-Irwell, assembled no doubt under the guidance of its architect *E. W. Pugin*, and the furnishings at *Hansom*'s Holy Name in Chorlton-on-Medlock. Of individual items the following deserve mention. Scott's St Mark, Worsley, has beautiful iron screens, probably by *J. B. Skidmore*. A reredos at St Thomas, Werneth, has an atmospheric painting by *Reginald Hallward*, 1905. Here there is perhaps the most unusual font (*c.* 1906), incorporating a bronze Christ cradling an ivory baby. In the years 1899–1920, through the influence of Edward Holt, brewer and philanthropist, the otherwise unremarkable St Margaret, Prestwich, was provided with wonderful Arts and Crafts furnishings carved by *Arthur W. Simpson* to the designs of *Dan Gibson*, both of Windermere.*

CHURCH MONUMENTS commemorate some of the area's most important local figures, even though public sculpture (*see* below) overtook memorial sculpture in the C19 as the chief form of patronage. In Manchester Cathedral *E. H. Baily*'s Thomas Fleming (1851) and *W. Theed*'s seated statue of Humphrey Chetham (1853) are the best of the Victorian monuments. At Worsley parish church the memorial to Francis Egerton, 1st Earl of Ellesmere †1857, is a tomb-chest with recumbent effigy designed by *Scott* with decorative carving by *J. Birnie Philip* and an effigy by *Matthew Noble*. Memorials designed by local architects include a table tomb to John Robinson Kay †1872, by *Crowther*, at Rowland Methodist Church, Summerseat (formerly in its own octagonal mausoleum), and the Peacock mausoleum at Brookfield Unitarian Church, Gorton, an impressively large and elaborate piece by *Worthington*.

The churches in SE Lancashire have rich collections of STAINED GLASS. Apart from *Burlison & Grylls*' outstanding work at St Augustine, Pendlebury, already mentioned, there are a few notable complete schemes. *A. W. N. Pugin* designed the chancel glass at St John, Broughton (Salford), in the 1840s, though some windows are badly damaged. The glass at St Anne, Denton, and St Mary, Haughton Green, is of the 1870s, by *Heaton, Butler & Bayne*. They also provided an interesting ensemble at Monton Unitarian Church, and most of the windows at St Ann, Manchester, including those in the apse designed by *Frederick Shields*. Their best ensemble is in a secular building: Rochdale Town Hall. The scheme by *Morris & Co.* of 1895–6 at Albion Congregational Church in Ashton-under-Lyne is not their best, but it creates a wonderful effect. A complete Masonic scheme by *Lavers, Barraud & Westlake* at St Edmund, Rochdale 1870s, is a curiosity. There is a good set by *James Ballantine* of Edinburgh at Prestolee, of the 1860s. Several churches in the Oldham area (e.g. St Thomas, Werneth) have assemblages of glass by *Capronnier* of Brussels, put together incrementally through the later C19. There is a complete ensemble by *H. Hughes* or *Ward & Hughes* of 1863–1902 at St James, Rochdale, and a near-complete scheme by the same firm at St Benedict, Ardwick. An evangelical programme at Christchurch Walshaw, each with its biblical reference, is by *Arthur Dix, Cakebread, Robey & Co.*, and *W. Pape*.

---

* Simpson also worked at Holt's celebrated holiday house, Blackwell at Windermere.

William Warrington can be represented by his big E window at Deane near Bolton of 1845, with many figures and hard colours, especially greens and yellows. Windows by *Wailes* of Newcastle, often with an overall blue cast, can be seen for example at Didsbury, 1855. The glass at Worsley, probably of the 1840s–50s, is by an unknown hand – but the bold, bright swathes of colour, relieved by jewel-like patterns in the tracery, is effective. There is an early scheme by *Kempe* at St Luke, Weaste, and his later work includes the scheme at St John Evangelist, Cheetham, Manchester. At St Ann, Stretford, the E windows were designed in 1863 by *Hardman & Co.* under the supervision of *E. W. Pugin*. A good collection at Bury parish church includes late C19 work by *Hardman* and *Clayton & Bell*. A window by *Shrigley & Hunt* at Deane, in memory of John Kynaston Cross M.P., †1887, is duskily Pre-Raphaelite, with some beautifully rich colours. The artists were *Almquist* and *Jewitt* – a notable early work of theirs. Fine windows by the same firm can be found at Prestwich parish church and St Andrew, Eccles. *Morris & Co.* did the superb E window of 1898 at Daisy Hill, Westhoughton, with plenty of fat twining foliage, as also in their window at Emmanuel, Didsbury. At St Chad, Rochdale we have Faith, Hope and Charity to cartoons by the firm that were used elsewhere, but with their antitypes beneath to fill the frame. At Christchurch, Walmsley, Egerton, windows of 1889 have large figures floating against floral quarries. More of their work can be found at St Peter, Swinton, where there are two good early C20 windows by *Whall & Whall*. *Christopher Whall* also did two windows in his distinctive style at St Leonard, Middleton, of 1911 and 1923. Also there, is a fine Boer War memorial window by *G. F. Bodley* and *Burlison & Grylls*. The list could go on. The interested visitor, after feasting on St Augustine, Pendlebury, could go on to nearby St Peter, Swinton, and St Mark, Worsley. If St Leonard, Middleton, and Bury and Deane parish churches were added, a good introduction would have been made, and apart from St Augustine, all are often open at the time of writing.

Victorian Public Art

The most important example of Victorian public art is *Ford Madox Brown*'s Manchester town hall murals of 1878–93, one of the city's treasures and an example of enlightened civic patronage. Rochdale town hall should have had a comparable prize in the giant mural of Magna Carta, by *Henry Holiday*, but it has not really come off (and is in any case very dirty now). The real treasure there is the wall decoration and stained glass by *Heaton, Butler & Bayne*, an inexhaustible source of delight. SCULPTURE at Manchester Town Hall includes statues mainly by *Theed*, incorporated into key architectural positions, while the Sculpture Hall houses a large collection of marble busts. The entrance vestibule has two of the city's finest examples of Victorian sculpture in *Chantrey*'s Dalton (1837) and *Alfred Gilbert*'s Joule (1893).

Also in Manchester, Piccadilly was laid out by *Joseph Paxton* in 1854 with an esplanade where national figures are commemorated. Most are still there, though in a different disposition. Peel (*William Calder Marshall*, 1853) and Wellington (*Matthew Noble*, 1856), were joined by *E. Onslow Ford*'s seated figure of Queen Victoria, 1901. In Albert Square the Albert Memorial, designed in 1862 by *Thomas Worthington* came first, with a statue of

Albert Memorial, Manchester, from *The Builder*, 1862

the prince by *Matthew Noble*. Later work mainly commemorates local dignitaries such as Bishop Fraser, by *Thomas Woolner*, 1887. Oldham has good Victorian statuary, concentrated in Alexandra Park, including John Platt M.P., by *D. W. Stevenson*, 1878 and Robert Ascroft M.P., by *F. W. Pomeroy*, 1903. The most unusual, because the subject is a working man, is that of Joseph Howarth by *Henry Burnett* (1868). Statues in front of the Art Gallery and Museum in Salford of Queen Victoria, 1857 and Prince Albert, 1864 are by *Matthew Noble*. In Ashton-under-Lyne the industrialist Hugh Mason is commemorated in a bronze statue by *J. W. Swynnerton*, 1887, repositioned near his mills on the edge of town. *Hamo Thornycroft*'s inspiring bronze, 'Education' (1905) has been ousted from the library to a churchyard corner in Crompton. Samuel Crompton at Bolton (by *Calder Marshall*, 1862), John Bright at Rochdale (by *Hamo Thornycroft*, 1891), Sir Robert Peel at Bury (by *E. H. Baily*, 1852), are each highly significant to their respective town, and the unveiling of each one was attended by scenes of fervent rejoicing. Bury's South Africa War Memorial of 1905, *George Frampton*'s cheering and waving Fusilier, was put up in the Market Place (moved since to the Whitehead Gardens). *Hamo Thornycroft* did Manchester's Boer War memorial (1907), which stands in St Ann's Square.

Mid-Nineteenth to Early Twentieth-Century Transport and Industry

By the mid C19 almost all the towns of any size had a RAILWAY STATION, several more than one. In Manchester at Piccadilly new iron and glass train sheds were built in the 1880s, by which time huge warehouses had been erected in the goods yard, of which the one surviving example is impressively stark. Central Station, built by the ambitious Midland Railway in 1880, closed in 1969 and is now the G-Mex Exhibition Centre. It has a single-span train shed 210 ft (64 metres) wide, with a spectacular substructure. Associated with it is the monstrous Midland Hotel, by *Charles Trubshaw* (1903). Between Central and Deansgate is the Great Northern Warehouse (1898), the last great railway work in Manchester, a giant of a building which combined an upper-floor goods station with canal and road interchange. Victoria, the city's other principal station, was partially rebuilt in the early C20, with a new street front. Parts of the train shed, and a delicious early C20 glass-domed café and bar, also survive. Outside central Manchester decent surviving stations are pitifully few. Old Trafford station (Stretford), *c.* 1856 and mildly classical, is one of the best. Urmston Station (1872) is attractive railway Gothic, but derelict. Bolton station, rebuilt in 1904, is preserved at platform level with long ranges of glazed-brick-faced buildings but not at street level. VIADUCTS and BRIDGES generally make more impressive survivals. There is a good display in Salford just s of Chapel Street where the parallel viaducts of 1844, 1865 and 1894 are supported on Egyptian or Greek columns, their parapets decorated with fluted pilasters or pilasters and swags. Threading through Castlefield in Manchester is another series of viaducts, including two high ones of iron, originally serving Central Station, which are castle-themed in deference to the place.

The MANCHESTER SHIP CANAL was one of the most ambitious engineering projects of the age, and a municipal endeavour without parallel in Britain. It made the city an international port by creating docks linked to the E coast by a huge cut, dug to the depth of the Suez Canal, which allowed seagoing vessels to reach the city. It was on a scale previously unknown in England. The swing road bridge and aqueduct in Stretford by *Sir Leader* 93 *Williams*, which carried the road and Bridgewater Canal over the Ship Canal, is a notable example of advanced technology associated with the project. The same period saw another ambitious municipal project, for Manchester completed a system for piping water from Thirlmere in the Lake District in 1894, a prodigious engineering feat, but one which has left little visible sign, apart from the AQUEDUCT at Agecroft, Pendlebury.

Now we must return to INDUSTRIAL DEVELOPMENTS. The mid C19 saw the rise of specialist COTTON-MILL builders, of whom *David Bellhouse* of Manchester was an important figure, while *William Fairbairn* was responsible for the improved design of structural ironwork. Fireproof construction became more widespread, but the relatively high costs meant that timber floors continued to be extensively used. Floors of reinforced concrete supported by rolled-steel beams were introduced from the late C19, but this method did not completely supersede the use of brick arches even in the early C20. Cavendish Mill, Ashton-under-Lyne, 1884–5 by *Potts, Pickup & Dixon*, was probably the earliest mill in the country to use concrete floors in fireproof construction, an innovation developed by *Edward Potts*. Roofs during this period were usually multiple ridges with light timber trusses, but by the early C20 flat roofs had become common. Of concrete with a bitumen layer, they could be flooded for feeding sprinkler systems. An early example was Abbey Mill, Oldham of 1876 by *A. H. Stott & Son* (demolished), and there was almost universal adoption of the feature for large mills from the early C20. The *Stott* dynasty of Oldham also designed some of the most striking late C19 and early C20 mills. Arrow Mill, Castleton, Rochdale (by *Sydney Stott*, 1908) is a particularly handsome and complete one. Other specialist mill architects included *George Woodhouse* and *Bradshaw & Gass*, important Bolton firms, and *F. W. Dixon* of Oldham.

A late C19 variation on the standard spinning mill came with the introduction of double mills. Two mills built end to end were powered from a central engine house, in some cases with a lapse between building the first and second mill. One of the best early examples is Houldsworth Mill in Reddish by *A. H. Stott* of 96 Oldham, 1865. Double mills continued to be erected into the C20, such as Swan Lane Nos. 1 and 2 mills at Daubhill, Bolton, 95 of 1901 and 1904. No. 3 Mill at Swan Lane, 1914, was *Stott & Sons'* last one. Another variation in design was a result of the introduction of ring spinning. The system was invented in America in the early C19 but brought to Lancashire in the late

C19, though it did not enjoy wholesale adoption. The machinery was smaller and heavier, the mills therefore had fewer storeys. A good example is Nile Mill, Chadderton, reputedly the largest ring-spinning mill in world in 1898. Electric lighting had been introduced to many mills in the late C19: Atlas No. 3 Mill, Bolton, had a steam driven electric light generator as early as 1877. By the early C20 the use of electricity as a source of motive power too was widespread; Kearsley Mill, Prestolee, of 1906, is a good example of a mill that generated electricity from its own steam turbines. Mains power was used when it became available, good early examples being Royal and Paragon Mills in Ancoats, Manchester (1911–13). Sir John Holden's Mill (1925–6 by *Bradshaw, Gass & Hope*), at Astley Bridge, Bolton is a later example, indeed the last cotton mill to be built in Bolton. Most new mills of the C20 had rope-drive systems, instead of shaft drives, and older mills were often adapted to the new system.

It is relatively unusual to encounter a mill of mid C19 or later date of wholly utilitarian appearance. Some kind of architectural display was almost always incorporated. Italianate was the style most widely adopted in the mid and late C19, for example at Gilnow Mill, Bolton, 1858, and for Miles Platting double mill (1869 and 1873, by *George Woodhouse*). At the turn of the C19 and C20 century Baroque, eclectic and even Byzantine styles were 94 employed, most spectacularly by the *Stott*s, whose mills in Chadderton and Reddish, for example, concentrate extravagant poly-chromatic ornament on the water towers. Almost all late C19 and early C20 mills sported at least some embellishment and many displayed the name of the mill on the chimney or water tower.

Decline began after the First World War and few firms survived into the 1960s, when the cotton industry finally came to an end in England. The mills which survive lie derelict or have been adapted as apartments, warehouses etc., or for light industrial uses. A very few are still used for spinning, such as those in Oldham and Ashton-under-Lyne taken over by Oxley Threads to produce sewing thread. Even so, there is hardly a town of any size in SE Lancashire which does not have at least one cotton mill left, and in many areas, like Ancoats in Manchester, the Beal valley in Shaw, the Tame valley in Ashton-under-Lyne and Mossley, Chadderton, Hollinwood in Oldham and the outskirts of Bolton, cotton mills continue to dominate the landscape.

The remains of SE Lancashire's HEAVY INDUSTRY are much more fragmentary. The area was a world centre of engineering, but hardly any physical evidence remains. Platt Bros in Oldham were the largest textile machinery manufacturer in the world in the late C19, but only the offices (1883 by *P. B. Alley*) and a few scattered remains are left, in the Werneth area. At Park Bridge, near Ashton-under-Lyne, only the late C19 housing and a works stable of 1870, a rare survival in SE Lancashire, are intact. The firms of Crossley (cars and buses), Whitworth (components and armaments) and Beyer Peacock (locomotive engineering) in E Manchester are all gone. Trafford Park boasted industrial giants such as the Ford Motor Co. and Metropolitan Vickers, but hardly a trace remains. The Lancashire & Yorkshire Railway's Horwich Locomotive Works of 1886–92 was a late establishment. Its buildings survive out of railway use. Railway engineering continues on a small scale at the preserved Buckley Wells works at Bury, of 1856, by *J. S. Perring*.

Before we leave this subject, brief mention can be made of the brewing industry. SE Lancashire is the home of a number of small independent BREWERIES, which have withstood amalgamations and take-overs in the late C20. The earliest buildings to survive, now converted to housing, are Bardsley Brewery in Limehurst, of 1832 with low stone buildings around a courtyard, and Walmersley Brewery, of 1842. The late C19 former Chester's Brewery in Salford (now offices) retains many of the buildings and an impressive tower. The best examples, all of the late C19, are Hydes Brewery in Moss Side, complete with ornamental gates and offices, the quieter Holt's Brewery in Cheetham (both Manchester) and the J. W. Lees Brewery at Middleton Junction, all still in use. Boddington's Brewery in Strangeways (Manchester) retains some C19 fragments, including a tall chimney, which is a prominent local landmark. Breweries' pubs, often executed in distinctive house style, are still important features of townscapes all over the area.

Buildings of Co-operation and Philanthropy

SE Lancashire, and specifically Rochdale, was the birthplace of Co-operation. At Rochdale the pioneer shop of 1844 is preserved as a museum, but no later buildings of any significance can be pointed out until we get to the late C19. CO-OPERATIVE SHOPS in particular (though they seldom function as co-ops any more) are still an important part of local townscapes. The larger ones sometimes incorporated libraries, reading rooms or public halls. There is a good line-up of premises in Bolton Street, Ramsbottom (*c.* 1862) and a good individual shop at Walshaw (dated 1891), advertising its grocer, clogger, news room and butcher. Shops can be seen everywhere in Oldham, including the vast former premises on Huddersfield Road, by *Thomas Taylor*, 1900, which combined extensive retail departments with a library and large public hall. *A. H. Walsingham* produced instantly recognizable eclectic designs with much colourful terracotta in the early C20, of which examples survive in Charlestown and Broughton, Salford, and in Cheetham Hill and Longsight, Manchester. Walsingham also had a hand in the impressive group of early C20 offices and factories off Broad Street, Pendleton (Salford), though these are all derelict. Other factories survive, for example in Denton, where they sport the local Co-operative Society's badge of a beehive.

One of the consequences of industrialization and rapid urbanization coupled with cyclical trade depressions was a new class of urban poor. Provision of facilities such as parks, public baths, hospitals and so on earlier in the C19 were followed later in the century by buildings of more specialist function, in the heart of

the afflicted areas. In many cases they replaced pre-existing facilities in reused buildings. Such PHILANTHROPIC BUILDINGS can be found in various locations. The best group survives in central Manchester and its industrial suburb of Ancoats. Here night shelters for men and women were opened by the Methodists; the women's shelter of 1899 by *W. R Sharp* included a home for domestic servants who would otherwise have to stay in common lodging houses. The Charter Street Ragged School and Working Girls' Home (1898) offered similar accommodation as well as a school for street children and a mission. Elsewhere in Manchester there are two early C20 children's refuges. Further afield, lads' clubs aimed to help and educate
88 working-class boys. Good examples include the Salford Lads' Club on Coronation Street, Ordsall, in Salford (by *Henry Lord*, 1904), the Crossley Club in Openshaw (*J. W. Broadbent*, 1912) and the Cannon Street Institute, Oldham (*Taylor & Simister*, 1910). An early C20 Jewish soup kitchen stands in the Cheetham area of Manchester. Late C19 and early C20 municipal model lodging houses can be found in central Salford (Bloom Street) and Manchester (Corporation Street). There are also almshouses of late foundation: Moss Side, Manchester (dated 1876, by *John Lowe*), Reddish (by *James Hunt*, dated 1882), the excellent group at Heaton Norris (*Peirce & Son*, 1907), Clifton (1925) and jumping far ahead in time, those in Didsbury (by *H. M. Fairhurst*) of 1960.

Late Nineteenth and Early Twentieth-Century Municipal and Public Building

Confidence and civic ambition which followed the opening of the Ship Canal to Manchester were expressed in high-profile projects, often executed with lavish use of terracotta and faience, so that the splendid new additions stood out like beacons amongst their smoke-blackened neighbours. London Road Fire Station must be one of the largest and most elaborate establishments of its type (by *Woodhouse, Willoughby & Langham*, 1901–6); Baroque, and embellished with an extensive sculptural scheme by *J. J. Millson* in *Burmantoft* terracotta. Many other places got similar facilities at about this time, of which the library, fire station and public baths complex in Reddish (1907–8 by *Dixon & Potter*) is a good example of public provision for a small town. In Salford the Education Offices on Chapel Street (1895, by *Woodhouse & Willoughby*), of pale yellow terracotta, are impressive. In Manchester the most memorable municipal baths are those designed by the City Architect *Henry Price* in the early C20. Of these Vic-
91 toria Baths in Chorlton-on-Medlock is probably the most opulent Edwardian municipal baths in the country, with highly decorative stained glass, mosaic and tiles, and suites of Turkish and
4 Russian baths. Meanwhile Bolton was refashioning its town centre with a programme of street-widening and straightening. The new buildings are ambitious in scale, in florid Renaissance or Baroque styles, and faced again in shiny terracotta in a variety of colours.

The architects were *Jonathan Simpson, W. H. Smith*, and *Bradshaw, Gass & Hope*. Though unattractive now, grubby and with their ground floors spoilt, their day may come again, as it has for the terracotta-faced buildings in the centre of Manchester.

Many of the smaller authorities built TOWN HALLS in the early C20. They are often associated with municipal LIBRARIES resulting from the generosity of Andrew Carnegie, who used part of his fortune to endow libraries in Britain, the United States and elsewhere. They form important and familiar points in many townscapes. The predominant style is the mannerist Baroque that came to be associated with officialdom, the materials hard red brick with much stone, usually the newly fashionable Portland stone, or terracotta. Libraries frequently have an emblematic dome or rotunda. Notable examples include Farnworth town hall and library, 1908, by *W. J. Lomax*; Radcliffe town hall, of 1911 by *W. M. Gillow & R. Holt*, and the library (on a different site) by *W. J. Lomax*; Westhoughton town hall and library, 1902–4, by *Bradshaw & Gass* and Chadderton town hall, 1912–13 by *Taylor & Simister*. Meanwhile Manchester was building libraries in the suburbs. Three were put up in S Manchester around 1915 (Didsbury, Withington and Chorlton), and one in N Manchester (Cheetham, 1909–11), by *Henry Price*, the Manchester City Architect. Three in the Bolton suburbs, at Halliwell, Astley Bridge and Great Lever, were all opened by Carnegie himself in 1910. The library at Eccles is large and grandly Baroque, by *Edward Potts*, 1907. Milnrow's was by *S. Butterworth & W. H. Duncan*, 1907–8; Heywood's of 1905–6 by *S. V. North & C. Collas Robin*. Both are very good buildings. Good examples also exist in Chadderton, which is Elizabethan, and Shaw, quietly Renaissance.

Lancashire has a special place in the history of state education. The Lancashire (later National) Public Schools Association was formed in 1847 to promote a locally controlled non-sectarian education system. The campaign finally bore fruit with the 1870 Education Act. BOARD SCHOOLS were the result, and those in Manchester and Salford were usually spare and Gothic. Dover Street School, Chorlton-on-Medlock by *Mills & Murgatroyd* (1881–6), on the other hand, is quite grand and Ruskinian. The greatest number to survive are of the next generation, late C19 and early C20, in blocky Queen Anne style. Looser Renaissance styles followed. Good examples include those in Chorlton-on-Medlock, Moston (Manchester), and at Pendleton, Salford (1906 by *John Woodhouse*). The records do not shed much light on their individual architects, but other sources indicate that these included *J. W. Beaumont, Woodhouse & Willoughby, Edward Potts*, and *Henry Lord*. In Oldham local architectural practices produced some memorable designs, such as Werneth Junior School, by *Thomas Taylor*, with a tall campanile clock tower (1891–3) and the splendid Higginshaw Board School, by *Winder & Taylor* (1894). Bolton again tended to employ local talent. The three big ones round the centre are each by a different architect but clearly out of the same pot: Clarence Street, Little Bolton by *Jonathan Simpson*;

1886; Great Moor Street of 1896–7 by *R. Knill Freeman*; and Hilden Street, Haulgh, of 1901–3 by *Bradshaw & Gass*. In a different league are Middleton's first two municipal schools, Elm Street and Durnford Street, designed in 1908 by *Edgar Wood & Henry Sellers*. Their classically derived symmetry and their pioneering use of reinforced concrete for roofs and floors to open up the plan are due to Sellers, for they were progressive in their spatial organization as well as striking in their architecture. Durnford Street School was demolished during the preparation of this book.

Most late C19 CHURCH SCHOOLS are quietly Gothic, for example the pretty stone St Thomas's School at Werneth (Oldham). More muted brick examples abound. Albion Congregational School in Ashton-under-Lyne (1861–2 by *Paull & Ayliffe*), on the other hand, is brightly, almost stridently polychromatic and Italianate. Those designed by *J. Medland* and *Henry Taylor* often have individual character, as might be expected. Good examples are Holy Trinity school in Ashton-under-Lyne (1885) with a large tower and apsidal hall, and the low and prettily polychromatic St Agnes School in Levenshulme, Manchester (1885). Later in date are *J. & J. Swarbrick*'s school of 1910 in Didsbury, Manchester, charmingly Baroque on a child-like scale, and St George's Street Sunday School (Congregational), Little Bolton, 1914 by *Ormrod, Pomeroy & Foy*, 1914, inventive with good detailing.

Technical education was needed to train a literate mechanically minded workforce for industry, and promoted through MECHANICS' INSTITUTES, often founded by industrialists. Many started in the early and mid C19, but most of the surviving buildings are later. An exception is the Lyceum and School of Science and Art in Oldham, which has been credited with making the town the greatest centre of cotton-spinning in the world. It was founded in the early C19 and got a splendid new Italianate building in 1855. Another relatively early example is the dignified palazzo by *J. E. Gregan*, 1854–5, for the Mechanics' Institute in Manchester. It was the precursor of the Municipal School of Technology, for which a large building was designed by *Spalding & Cross* incorporating an impressive Renaissance terracotta scheme by *Burmantofts* (1895–1902). The Technical and Art School in Ashton-under-Lyne (now a library and art gallery) was executed in Waterhouseish style in 1891. Bury has destroyed its handsome Athenaeum of 1850 by *Sydney Smirke*, but its Technical School, by *Joshua Cartwright*, Borough Engineer, 1893–4, now the Arts and Crafts Centre, is well-preserved. Heywood's Municipal Technical School is by *Woodhouse & Willoughby*, 1894, of red brick and terracotta with ornamental panels and a north-lit studio. The Royal Salford Technical Institute (by *Henry Lord*) opened in 1896. Of hot red brick and terracotta, Renaissance style, with a notable sculptural scheme by *Earp, Son & Hobbs*, it stands proudly beside Salford's Library and Art Gallery.

Now we must return to HOSPITALS. The hospital quarter in

Manchester is in Chorlton-on-Medlock, the site chosen as the replacement of Manchester Royal Infirmary, which was founded in 1752, moved to Piccadilly in 1754-5 and was demolished in 1909.* The land was donated by Owens College (subsequently Manchester University) to improve teaching opportunities for its Medical School. The new building by *E. T. Hall* with *John Brooke* is Greenwich Baroque. The Eye Hospital had already been established near the site in 1886, designed by *Pennington & Bridgen*, and St Mary's Hospital (for women and children), Edwardian Baroque by *John Ely*, followed in 1909. Other SPECIALIST HOSPITALS include the nearby Dental Hospital by *Charles Heathcote & Sons*, 1908, in their typical Baroque, and much too jolly for its purpose (now part of Manchester Museum). *Percy Scott Worthington*'s Skin Hospital of 1903-5 on Quay Street, Manchester, was sadly demolished in 1999. A big and spectacular Memorial Home for Crippled Children was founded at Ashworth by Walter Scott of Rochdale in 1913, designed by *G. F. Armitage* of Altrincham. The Blair Hospital for convalescents at Egerton, of 1884-9 by *J. Medland Taylor* and as odd as any of his churches, was founded according to the will of Stephen Blair †1870. Blair was a manufacturer of chemicals for bleaching and dyeing, a noxious business, so the money to build the hospital came from the same source as the sick to fill it. There were numerous TB hospitals too, such as Baguley at Wythenshawe (1911, developed from a fever hospital of 1902), which has become Wythenshawe Hospital.

Late Nineteenth and Early Twentieth-Century Housing

The inexorable increase in population was accompanied by new HOUSING as all the urban areas expanded. Manchester had closed numerous cellar dwellings after they were prohibited by a local Act of 1853. The Manchester Improvement Act of 1867 granted powers for closing houses unfit for habitation, the first in Britain to do so, and it included specifications for room sizes and minimum sizes for rear yards. IMPROVED HOUSING spread everywhere, with places like HULME (Manchester) becoming a working class suburb. EMPLOYERS sometimes built accommodation for the workforce. The largest and most complete example is the Oxford Community in Ashton-under-Lyne, built by Hugh Mason for workers at his cotton mills. Some of the houses were designed by *Paull & Robinson* in the 1860s and 1870s, with dwellings of different sizes and elaboration grouped in terraces, reflecting orders of seniority in the workforce. Workers' housing on a much smaller scale was built at Park Bridge from the 1860s by the Lees family at their ironworks and engineering factories (where the workers' institute survives) and by William Houldsworth at Reddish. The Lancashire & Yorkshire Railway housed its workforce by its new locomotive works at Horwich,

* One of the little classical lodges, by *Richard Lane*, was re-erected in Knutsford, Cheshire.

from 1884–7, in what was essentially a new railway town along the Chorley New Road. The streets have evocative names: Iron Street, Brunel Street, Gooch Street. A completely different story is seen at Worsley: the works yard was moved from the centre in the early C20 and new estate housing of the Port Sunlight sort was put up, in black-and-white style with an Arts and Crafts look.

Early MUNICIPAL HOUSING schemes were promoted by Manchester Corporation in Ancoats where Victoria Square (flats) and the adjacent terraces and shops were built in the 1890s by *Spalding & Cross*. The flats were, for SE Lancashire, an innovation: five storeys around a courtyard with communal facilities (laundries etc.) in the corner towers. The other housing there looked like traditional two-up two-down terraces but was mostly flats as well. Even more ambitious was the New Barrack Estate, at Ordsall in Salford, by *Henry Lord*; as at Manchester the style is vaguely Queen Anne, but the accommodation was mainly flats in two- and three-storey terraces. A privately sponsored lads' club and church formed part of this scheme, but the planned public hall remained unexecuted. Blackley Cottages, erected in 1903–4, were an early experiment by Manchester Corporation in relocation and rehousing from the slums. There are three terrace designs, attractive in themselves, but there was no ambition in the layout.

In the early C20 GARDEN VILLAGES began to take off, at first through private initiatives. The little Burnage Garden Village of 1911 was built and owned, as it still is, by a Tenants' Co-operative. The plan, by *J. Horner Hargreaves* in consultation with *C. G. Agate*, *Frank Dunkerley* and *Raymond Unwin*, was simple enough – just a loop of road with a communal sports club in the middle – and so are the houses, unfussy, roughcast, set low, with catslide roofs. Chorltonville at Chorlton-cum-Hardy, also of 1911–13, was a little bigger and more overtly pretty, and so was Alkrington, near Middleton, begun in 1909, planned by *Thomas Adams* of Letchworth, then *Peplar & Allen*, which included houses by *Thomas Arthur Fitton* and by *Edgar Wood*. The Oldham Garden Suburb, Hollins Green, was promoted by the 'Beautiful Oldham' movement, and the opening ceremony in 1907 was attended by Ebenezer Howard (author of *Garden Cities of Tomorrow*, 1902). Fairfield Garden Village, by *Edgar Wood & Henry Sellers* (1906–13) has the most interesting houses: Neo-Georgian but with Free Style touches typical of the practice. In Shaw the tiny Provident Park Estate was built by the local Co-op in 1911. These early experiments had an influence out of all proportion to their size in the great municipal schemes which came later.

Late Nineteenth and Early Twentieth-Century Commercial Architecture

The turn of the C19 and C20 saw a new generation of WARE-HOUSES in central Manchester, partly in response to renewed confidence after the success of the Ship Canal. Many are by *Harry S. Fairhurst*. His huge steel-framed and terracotta-clad buildings, such as Bridgewater House on Whitworth Street, incorporated sophisticated loading and transit systems. At about the same time there was a great rebuilding of FINANCIAL INSTI- TUTIONS. Huge banks and insurance company premises sprang up, one of the largest being *Alfred Waterhouse*'s Refuge Assurance (1891–5), expanded in two campaigns in 1910 and 1932. He also did the Prudential Offices in Manchester and Oldham. The Man- chester architect *Charles Heathcote* designed banks and insurance offices in a distinctively robust Edwardian Baroque, such as Parr's Bank and the Eagle Star Insurance. Heathcote was instrumen- tal, with the engineers *E. Wood & Co.*, in the introduction of fully framed steel construction in Manchester (as research by Jonathan Clarke has shown), which witnessed perhaps the earliest and most intensive adoption of the technique in Edwardian England.

In the Manchester suburbs BANKS could be more domestic in scale; two at Withington come to mind: the former Manchester and County Bank, by *Mills & Murgatroyd*, 1890, playfully Gothic, and the former District Bank by *Barker Ellis & Sons*, 1914, with charming Arts and Crafts half-timbering. Bury has a bank as grand as anything in Manchester, the former Bury Bank in Silver Street by *Blackwell, Son & Booth*, 1868. It is a richly bedizened palazzo (sculpture by *Joseph Bonehill*), with its attendant manager's house providing a nice contrast. Oldham's wealth is reflected in the extraordinary District Bank by *Mills & Murga- troyd* (1902–3), also as big and lavish as any in Manchester. Here the local architect *Thomas Taylor* designed a fine Midland Bank (1892) and another in Shaw. Oldham is favoured by one of the most innovative and unusual commercial buildings in the region, Dronsfield's Offices by *Henry Sellers*, 1906–7, with a Hawksmoor- ish top that manages to be more proto-Modernist than Baroque. Here too *Edgar Wood* built engaging small offices on Greaves Street, with an Art Nouveau flavour; one of his two banks in Mid- dleton survives as the Royal Bank of Scotland. In Ashton-under- Lyne the scale of commercial buildings is smaller, and the local firm *Messrs George & Son* did the crisp, dignified Post Office, the Savings Bank and probably some of the other good commercial buildings there. In Rochdale, the Royal Bank of Scotland repli- cates a vanished C18 house, but in urbane Portland stone; by *Cecil Jackson*, 1913. More interesting is the former Union Bank of Manchester by *Moulds & Porritt* of much the same date, Man- nerist in style with a tower and dome, and sculpture.

104

Leisure and Recreation in the Early Twentieth Century

The early C20 was a time of greater leisure for many. CINEMAS proliferated, and by 1914 Manchester had 111 licensed cinemas and Salford seventeen (not all purpose-built), a combined figure higher than for any other city outside London. Early examples, both Baroque, are the Picture House (1911) in Manchester and the Salford Cinema (1915). The Empress in Miles Platting, Man- chester, 1911–12 for W. H. Broadhead & Son, is unprepossessing outside but retains a wonderful original scheme within. An almost identical Broadhead cinema exists in Ashton-under-Lyne. THEATRES in Manchester include The Palace (1891 by *Alfred Darbyshire*, altered 1913 by *Bertie Crewe*) with its splendid interior, and the Opera House, a serious classical work of *Richardson & Gill* with *Farquarson* (1912). Further afield are the Victoria Theatre in Broughton (Salford), by *Bertie Crewe*, 1899, and the Crown Theatre in Eccles (*Campbell & Horsley*, 1899). The Hulme Hippodrome and Playhouse Theatres (1901 and 1902 by *J. J. Alley*, closed) still have elaborate interiors. Of Bolton's magnificent Theatre Royal (drama) of 1888, and Grand (circus and variety) of 1894, both by *Frank Matcham*, and its hideous Hippodrome of 1908, not a thing is left. Entertainment of a different type is illustrated in Eccles, which is one of the best places in England to see a concentration of little-altered Edwardian PUBS of the type resplendent with tiles, mahogany and etched glass. Once common, few of the interiors are left elsewhere. Pulling in the opposite direction, but almost equally showy externally, are early C20 TEMPERANCE BILLIARD HALLS, many by *Norman Evans*. These survive here and there, but only the ones in Chorlton-cum-Hardy, Manchester (now a pub) and Bury (a snooker club) are in good condition.

Provision of PUBLIC PARKS, another distraction from the alehouse, continued with acquisition by corporations of large country houses and some lesser mansions and their grounds in the early C20. Mossley got off the mark before the end of the C19, acquiring the Mayall mansion and its grounds in 1891. Manchester acquired Heaton Park in 1902 and Platt Hall in 1907. The trend continued after the First World War; Wythenshawe Hall and park was the gift of the Simon family in 1926 and in Oldham the Lees family house and park at Werneth were given to the corporation in 1935. The Smithills estate was bought by Bolton in 1938, Philips Park at Prestwich by Bury in 1946. Purists may with justice deplore some of the alterations to houses and grounds which followed, but without municipal patronage they may have been lost completely.

THE INTERWAR YEARS

Civic and Public Buildings

Civic building after the First World War included a handful of new TOWN HALLS, of which the Adamish Stretford Town Hall, 1931–3 by *Bradshaw Gass & Hope*, makes a grand statement. Their extension to the Victorian town hall at Bolton matches the C19 work, and their classical Le Mans Crescent gives it a grand setting, providing additional council offices and a library, art gallery and museum. Swinton's new civic buildings by *Percy Thomas & Ernest Prestwich* (1937) are disappointing, and at Bury the stripped classical town hall by *Reginald Edmonds* of *Jackson & Edmonds* of Birmingham (1939–54, interrupted by the Second

World War), is not much better. In Manchester *Vincent Harris*'s library and town hall extension was one of the most impressive 100 schemes of the 1930s; where the extension cleverly bridges the spatial and stylistic gap between Waterhouse's Gothic town hall and the classical bombast of the new library.

In Manchester, and everywhere, polite Neo-Georgian was the norm for other PUBLIC BUILDINGS, such as swimming baths, libraries and schools. An interesting example, though of the private sector, is the cleverly planned Manchester Grammar School, 1929–31 by *Percy Scott Worthington & Francis Jones*, which manages to combine uncompromising severity of form with generosity of space. *Percy Scott Worthington* was also responsible for engaging and humane halls of residence for Manchester University, started before the war and completed afterwards. Ashburne Hall and Hulme Hall, both in Rusholme, Manchester, have Neo-Georgian and Tudor motifs, with an Arts and Crafts flavour. Collegiate Tudor on the grandest scale is Bolton School, one of 103 William Lever's many benefactions, designed by *C. T. Adshead* following a competition in 1917 and built slowly over the next forty years. *Percy Scott Worthington* also did various HOSPITAL BUILDINGS at this time, including nurses' homes and other ancillary accommodation at Ancoats Hospital and the Manchester Royal Infirmary, but much of this has been, or will be demolished. The mildly Moderne Dental Hospital at Manchester (1939–40) is by his half-brother, *Hubert Worthington*. In the leafy Manchester suburbs the Christie Hospital and Holt Radium Institute at Withington, for cancer treatment, were built by *Harry S. Fairhurst & Son* in 1931–2, still on the pavilion plan.

AVIATION was an innovation that created a new class of building. Manchester Corporation built Barton Aerodrome, W of Salford and Eccles, from 1928, where the City Architect *G. Noel Hill* designed one of the first civilian control towers in 1933. 108 Barton was also the first airport to have designated runways. It remains an important early example of a municipal promotion, with surviving hangars and other early aviation buildings. It was too small for the Corporation's ambitions, however and a new site at Ringway (Wythenshawe) was bought in 1935. This is today's Manchester International Airport, opened in 1938. The original buildings, which were very like those at Barton, have all gone. The earliest accessible buildings here are the former Officer's Mess of 1941, and, by the end of runway 1, the Airport Hotel of c. 1938.

Manchester's COUNCIL HOUSING reached its peak of quality with the Homes for Heroes of the Higher Blackley Estate, started in 1919. In their pristine state (not today) they were as good as the best municipal housing of the day. More modest, less varied houses were built by the thousand in the 1920s at places such as Burnage and Withington. Wythenshawe was a huge garden suburb laid out from 1931 by *Barry Parker*, on land in Cheshire, far to the S of the centre, bought by the council for the purpose. It was an enormously ambitious scheme, but ultimately failed to create a satellite town, for although Parker planned a centre, it

was not started until after the Second World War and not completed until decades after that. The site was laid out with twelve
houses per acre, set in verdant surroundings, with wide, curving
105 roads. A new set of house designs was made by the *City Housing
Department*. Safe and solid, of brick and tile or slate; pleasing if
unexciting when new, but distressingly dishevelled today. Most
of the towns were building council housing at this time, Bolton
and Rochdale, for example, on a large scale, but the subject is
too large to analyse properly here. Suffice it to say that most are
brick houses and terraces, with some flats, e.g. those in Gorton,
though those on the most ambitious scale, Kennet House in
Cheetham (Manchester), have been knocked down. PRIVATE
HOUSING includes the attractive group of flats at Appleby
Lodge, Rusholme (Manchester) by *Gunton & Gunton* with *Peter
Cummings*, 1936–9, and there are one or two dashing Moderne
houses in Crumpsall (Manchester) and Broughton (Salford).

Public Art

FIRST WORLD WAR MEMORIALS can be the only beautiful
public artefacts in drab towns; for instance *W. H. Doxey*'s simple
but moving relief sculpture at Little Lever. Curiously, Manchester has little of note, apart from the Cenotaph in St Peter's
Square by *Lutyens* (1924) on the model of his Whitehall one, and
– one of the best anywhere in the area – *C. S. Jagger*'s sentry, a
privately commissioned memorial for employees of Watts & Co.
in their former warehouse on Princess Street (now the Britannia
Hotel). *Lutyens* also did Rochdale's cenotaph, like the Manchester one but in granite which dictates a bolder form, and the
more personal Lancashire Fusiliers' memorial in Bury (both of
97 1922). Best of all is *R. R. Goulden*'s heroic group in Shaw, a naked
man defending children from snarling beasts. The idiosyncratic
98 works by the brothers *Sydney* and *Vernon March* in Radcliffe and
Stand are almost too sensual for their purpose. *Albert Toft*'s group
of soldiers emerging from the trenches is one of Oldham's finest
ornaments, placed in a dramatic setting in front of the church.
Of others we may mention statues by *John Cassidy* at Heaton
Moor and Eccles, and *George Frampton* in Salford. At Dunscar,
Egerton, the memorial by *Gaffin & Co.* shows a young soldier
accoutred for war, but not warlike. The locomotive works memorial at Horwich, by *Paul Fairclough*, is of the same concept.

Churches and Synagogues

It is in the field of CHURCH ARCHITECTURE that Lancashire
most showed itself aware of progressive Continental architecture.
The fact that money was very tight in comparison with the pre-
war period may have contributed. The use of costly stone, especially carved stone, load-bearing arches, and wood was less
suitable than brick, steel and reinforced concrete, and post-and-
111 beam construction. St Nicholas, Burnage, Manchester (1930–2,
by *Cachemaille-Day & Lander*) was one of the first of a new

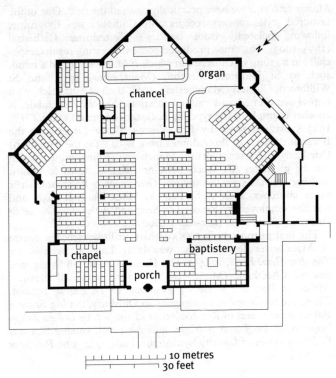

chancel

organ

chapel

baptistery

porch

10 metres
30 feet

St Michael and All Angels, Wythenshawe, Manchester, plan

generation, looking like a brick super-Odeon, with its internal spaces cleverly adapted to its position on an arterial road. The new suburb of Wythenshawe, deliberately conventional in its domestic architecture, was a laboratory for church design. St Michael and All Angels, Lawton Moor (1936–7, by *Cachemaille-Day* again), is a revolutionary church, on a centralizing if not fully centralized star plan. St John (R. C.), Benchill, by *Frank Reynolds* of *E. Bower Norris & F.M. Reynolds*, 1935, is less exciting, but follows all the Deco fads in its silhouette and brickwork. Rather similar are *Taylor & Young*'s St Luke, Wythenshawe and St Gabriel, Prestwich, but their St Paul, Blackley and St Matthew, New Earth, Oldham are Neo-Georgian.* Back in Manchester, St Christopher, Withington (*Bernard Miller*, 1935), was sadly demolished in 1994.

The ROMAN CATHOLICS built a great many churches in the 1930s. The boom was the work of very few architects and even fewer practices. When we have mentioned *E. Bower Norris, F.M. Reynolds, Greenhalgh & Williams* of Bolton, and *J. V. Mather* of

110

---

* Isaac Taylor was the son of J. Medland Taylor.

Mather & Nutter we have practically covered the field. One of the favoured styles, always recognizably Catholic, was Byzantine, following belatedly from Bentley's Westminster Cathedral (1895–1903). The craze produced some interesting results, especially in a group of churches in which *F. M. Reynolds* had a hand, such as St Dunstan, Moston, (Manchester) 1937, and St Willibrord, Clayton (Manchester), 1938, both of buff brick, with impressive domed and vaulted interiors. St John, Rochdale, is another example of the type, by *E. Bower Norris* and *Oswald Hill*, 1923–5, with mosaics by *Eric Newton*. *Walter Tapper* took the Byzantine theme of three domes from W to E for the (Anglican) Our Lady of Mercy, Gorton, Manchester. Romanesque, which can be given an Art Deco twist or stripped down to almost nothing, was the style favoured by *Greenhalgh & Williams* in their many churches, such as St Patrick, Miles Platting, 1936, and was also employed by *Reynolds & Scott* and *Arthur Farebrother & Partners* well into the post-war period.

The first purpose-built SYNAGOGUE in Prestwich, the centre of Manchester Jewry today, was Holy Law Synagogue, by *Theodore Herzl Birks*, 1934–5. The Higher Crumpsall Synagogue nearby, Cheetham (Manchester), is a monumental classical edifice in Portland stone by *Pendleton & Dickinson*, 1928–9. There are two sizeable synagogues in Didsbury, the big Shaarei Rahamim or Gates of Righteousness of 1925–7, by *Delissa Joseph* 'supervised' by *Joseph Sunlight*, and the much smaller Sha'arei Sedek or Gates of Charity Synagogue, built 1924–5 by *Pendleton & Dickinson*.

Commercial Architecture

Manchester has the finest COMMERCIAL BUILDINGS of the
101   interwar years. *Lutyens*'s Midland Bank (built 1933–5) must be mentioned first, classical in Portland stone with many of the Lutyens hallmarks, while on the Modern Movement side *Sir*
102   *Owen Williams*'s Daily Express of 1939, which has a front of black and transparent glass with rounded corners, can hold its own in competition with anything of that date. Lee House by *H. S. Fairhurst & Son* with *Henry Sellers* is the base to an unrealized American-influenced skyscraper, with Art Deco detailing. Minor buildings to note include the Dutch brick modernist Co-op buildings by *W. A. Johnson* with *J. W. Cropper* (1936) and the Art Deco Halifax Building Society in Oldham of 1934 by *Taylor & Simister*. Many CINEMAS were built at this time. In Bury the splendidly named Art Picture House of 1921–2 is by *Albert Win-stanley*, faced in white faience and with its auditorium, though overlaid, intact. The Forum at Northenden (1935, by *Charles Hartley*) was the unofficial entertainment centre of Wythenshawe until the Civic Centre was built. It is now an assembly hall of the Jehovah's Witnesses, but has preserved much of its interior. The most striking of all must be the Art Deco Essoldo Cinema in Stretford by *Henry Elder* of *Roberts, Wood & Elder* (1936), with a frontage shaped like a cash register.

SOUTH-EAST LANCASHIRE FROM
1945 TO *c.* 1990

Post-war Planning and Housing

Second World War bombing affected many areas, chiefly in Manchester and Salford, and attacks were directed at Trafford Park and its industry. In Manchester, the Cathedral and the Free Trade Hall suffered serious damage, and they were repaired, but *Waterhouse*'s Assize Courts were lost. Ambitious REDEVELOPMENT PLANS were prepared by many town and city councils immediately after the war, but the proposed new civic centres, roads and public amenities were not realized for decades, if at all. The most pressing problem in most places was HOUSING. Work on slum clearance had started before the war, but all the major centres inherited dreadful slums composed of C19 buildings. Temporary housing was an answer in some places. Of this a few PREFABS survive, for example a small group in Mossley, 1940s and another at Foxholes, Rochdale. The quite extensive Tin Town at Newall Green, Wythenshawe was built from 1946; these, not strictly prefabs, are two-storeyed and clad in light sheet metal. From the 1960s the answer was the tower block and high-rise deck-access schemes. In the 1969 edition of *South Lancashire* this was a big story both architecturally and socially. Pevsner was impressed by some of the schemes but he also had prescient misgivings. The story is now well known. Many high-rise and deck-access schemes foundered through a combination of poor building techniques and social problems, exacerbated by the unemployment which had come with the demise of industry. The redevelopment of Hulme, Manchester (by *Wilson & Womersley*, 1969–71) was a disaster, and the huge crescents were demolished in the early 1990s. The same fate attended many blocks in other Manchester suburbs, such as those known as Fort Ardwick and Fort Beswick. Many schemes combined high- and low-rise elements, for example in Oldham, where the ambitious housing of that time (by the *Ministry of Housing Development Group*) has gone, except for the low-rise elements. Salford's policy of rehousing on the spot as opposed to transplanting whole communities led to large concentrations of towers and smaller blocks, as at Pendleton, and individual tower blocks right in the very centre off Chapel Street. Other surviving examples are often scattered or in small clusters, e.g. in Eccles, Stretford, Haughton Green, the outskirts of Ashton-under-Lyne and Rochdale. Many were designed by local authority departments, some were system-built by contractors, and others were by private practices. In places like Pendleton there was a mixture. Bolton and Bury built no high-rise housing at all. *Wilson & Womersley*'s dense but low-rise St Thomas estate at Radcliffe of 1968 (project architect *John Sheard*), has proved more successful than the Hulme Crescents, but it is a tiny scheme in comparison. From the late 1970s onwards, especially in Manchester, more low-rise schemes were built, including two- or three-storey flats and individual houses with gardens; examples of this date can be seen in Miles Platting and Chorlton-on-Medlock (Manchester). More details of individual towns' policies can be found in the individual introductions.

Educational Buildings

The Neo-Georgian styles used for schools before the Second World War persisted into the 1950s, for example for the Chadderton Grammar School of 1959. A little later the 1960s–70s CLASP system of modular design for STATE SCHOOLS meant that they showed one of the sharpest breaks with pre-war traditions. It may have made economic sense but it did not foster innovation, and many of them have now reached the end of their useful lives, such as the very large Parrs Wood School at Didsbury, Manchester, of 1967, demolished in 2001. The most interesting schools of the 1960s–70s did not use the system (e.g. Urmston Grammar School by *Lyons, Israel & Ellis*, 1962–6, and Brentnal School in Broughton (Salford) by *Lee Monks* of *Cruickshank & Seward*) but these have either been radically altered or destroyed.

A few technical school and college buildings were put up during the 1950s, such as those in Stretford and Oldham but they were (predictably) cheap jobs. The boom in academic building came later. There was a burst of COLLEGE and UNIVERSITY BUILDING in Manchester during the early–mid 1960s. At the University of Manchester Institute of Science and Technology (UMIST) *W.A. Gibbon* of *Cruickshank & Seward* built great confident concrete Brutalist edifices which continue to impress, as does *H. M. Fairhurst*'s Chemical Engineering Pilot Plant. They deserve to survive the merger now taking place with Manchester University. *Fairhurst* also contributed much to that university in the 1960s, though perhaps the best building of that time is the Mathematics Tower by *Scherrer & Hicks*.[*] Other buildings of note are the Royal Northern College of Music by *Bickerdike, Allen, Rich & Partners*, 1968–73, and further afield (in Fallowfield, s Manchester), *L. C. Howitt*'s Hollings College (1957–60), known as the Toast Rack, Pop architecture as engaging now as it was then.

Public Buildings

There was little CIVIC BUILDING immediately after the Second World War, and when it started Modernist styles were generally adopted. Oldham started building a new civic centre in 1962, by *R. Seifert & Partners*, but it was left unfinished for a decade or so. More extensive projects were associated with local government reorganization in 1974. The Greater Manchester County came into being at this time, but the tier of local government administration created was dissolved in 1986, with powers devolving to the constituent boroughs. The headquarters was a

[*] Which could be lost as a result of the merger.

very unremarkable office block (now private offices) in central Manchester. The authority is mainly remembered in architectural terms for its commitment to conservation – it was instrumental in setting up the Museum of Science and Industry – and in the acquisition of Central Station in Manchester for an exhibition centre (*see* below). The newly created metropolitan towns absorbed their surrounding settlements, large and small, and they needed new facilities, and new expressions of status. In Oldham a new civic centre, which had been started in the 1960s (*see* above), was finished with the Queen Elizabeth Hall and Civic Centre by *Cecil Howitt & Partners* (1974–8), with a tower standing proudly on top of a hill in the centre of town. The 1980s council offices at Ashton-under-Lyne should have been more sensitively integrated into the existing civic buildings. Rochdale's response was the Black Box – Council Offices by *Essex, Goodman & Suggitt*. It is not a bad building, but it is unpopular. Reorganization had the interesting effect of prompting some of the authorities which were about to lose independence to spend money on municipal projects. Both Radcliffe and Middleton (both now part of Bury Metropolitan Borough Council) went down this route. Radcliffe Civic Centre stands out, 1974 by *John Sheard* of *Cruickshank & Seward*, with a free-form plan. Heywood Civic Hall, and Middleton (former) Town Hall, both by *Lyons, Israel & Ellis*, are also good.

Manchester built itself a new Crown Court, long and low, by the City Architect *L. C. Howitt* (1957–62). More innovative was his Blackley Crematorium (1959), with its weird stepped canopies. One of the best municipal projects of the time architecturally was the public baths at Broughton, Salford, by *Scott, Brownrigg & Turner* (1967), with a huge black cornice of a roof topped by glass pyramids. *William Gower*'s baths at Radcliffe (1968) is a faintly Moorish-looking white cube, with glass skylights. Also of note is the little Aqueduct Terminal Building at Heaton Park of 1955, by the Manchester City Engineers under *Alan Atkinson* and City Architects under *L. C. Howitt*, with a relief on slate by *Mitzi Cunliffe*.

ARTS BUILDINGS included a crop of theatres. Easily the most impressive, and daring in concept, was the Royal Exchange Theatre in Manchester by *Richard Negri* with *Levitt Bernstein Associates*, 1976. They designed a high-tech polygonal module and suspended it between the interior columns of the Edwardian exchange building. Wholly new structures include the Octagon Theatre at Bolton, by the Borough Architect *Geoffrey H. Brooks* (1967), which is good in a Brutalist way. In contrast, The Forum at Wythenshawe (Manchester), 1969–71 by the City Architect *S. G. Besant Roberts* is nothing special, but symbolic of the aspirations for the community. The Grange Arts Centre in Oldham by *Paterson & Associates* of Edinburgh (opened 1975) is cruciform and lends itself to different configurations of space.

The universities are the best places to see PUBLIC ART of the early–mid 1960s. At UMIST, *Antony Hollaway*'s highly unusual sculptural wall defines the E edge of the campus. *Victor Pasmore* did a mural in the Renold Building, and there are large mosaics by *Hans Tisdall* on the Chemistry Building. At Manchester University work of the period includes reliefs by *Lynn Chadwick* and *Hans Tisdall*, and sculpture by *Michael Piper* and *Michael Yeomans*. Large totemic concrete sculptures at Salford Technical College (now part of Salford University), too aggressive to be likeable, are by *William Mitchell*. *Mitzi Cunliffe*'s relief at Heaton Park Pumping Centre, 1955, has been mentioned. This and *Barbara Hepworth*'s Two Forms (Divided Circle), 1969, outside the Bolton Law courts, are probably the only good examples of art commissioned by a local authority during these years.

Religious Architecture

Some of the post-war CHURCHES, especially those in Wythenshawe, were searchingly experimental. St Francis, Newall Green, 114 by *Basil Spence*, 1959–61, is severely cubic. William Temple Church, by *G. G. Pace*, 1963–5, frankly steel-framed inside, is a big shed, arranged liturgically on a diagonal. Elsewhere, at St Mark, Chadderton, 1962–3, Pace deployed great laminated timber beams and timber lattice purlins, lending an industrial look, though the plan is conventional except for the exaggerated NE angle for the choir. Both churches have his typical limed oak and chunky black metal furnishings. *Maguire & Murray* built The Ascension in Hulme, Manchester (1968–70) with a centralizing liturgical movement plan and a ziggurat-like roof, designed to be overlooked by surrounding tower blocks, while All Saints, Stretford (*Leach, Rhodes & Walker*) should be mentioned for the bold W screen with glass by *Geoffrey Clarke, c.* 1958.

There was also a proliferation of ROMAN CATHOLIC churches in the 1960s to serve expanding suburbs and housing estates. The traditionally planned Immaculate Conception (1960–4) in Failsworth, by *Greenhalgh & Williams*, has a huge porte cochère with a suspended statue of the Virgin, and a detached baptistery. The swansong of the recognizably Romanesque longitudinal churches is St Anthony, Wythenshawe, by *Adrian Gilbert Scott*, 1959–60. In absolute terms it must be the finest building in Wythenshawe, but it was immediately an anachronism, as *Frederick Gibberd*'s stunning college chapel of 1963 at Hopwood, Middleton, makes clear. Like his Liverpool R. C. cathedral, of which this is a smaller and purer version, it is fully centralized with a central altar; the turning point for this was the second Vatican Council (1962–5), the great C20 watershed in the form and setting of the Catholic mass. Another Catholic wigwam is St Hilda (1968 by *Lanner Ltd*) at Northenden. *Desmond Williams & Associates* at St Augustine, Chorlton-on-Medlock, Manchester (1967–8), with the programme of ceramic reliefs by *Robert Brumby*, and especially their St Patrick, Rochdale (1965–7) also reflect the new era. The latter is cubic, with eight pierced buttresses supporting the concrete ring beam of a low dome.

A few other religious buildings call for notice. Hulme Hall

chapel (ecumenical), in Fallowfield (Manchester), 1966–8 by *Cruickshank & Seward*, is quietly effective, with an unusual whorled plan, while the spare Martin Luther German Church at Stretford (1963, by *T. D. Howcroft* of *Young & Purves*) is the antithesis of the showy expressionism so popular at that time. This trend is represented by St Mary, Denton (R. C.) by *Walter Stirrup & Son*, 1962, with its a great big swooping roof.

Developments in recent decades have mainly been aimed at creating SOCIAL CENTRES within the envelope. It is becoming rare to find a church in the area which has not had its interior subdivided. It can be done well, e.g. at St Nicholas, Burnage and St Martin, Castleton (Rochdale), both by *Anthony Grimshaw* of Wigan, 2000–3, or at St Katharine, Blackrod, 2001 by *Graham Holland*, and St Chad, Moston of *c.* 2000 by *Buttress Fuller Alsop Williams*. It can be done badly, as at Holy Innocents Fallowfield, which has been turned into a bleak barn, or at St Peter, Newbold, Rochdale (1984). A common feature of the bad conversions is the creation of a vast inaccessible void above the new subspace. Recently built churches are rare. A new and successful St Bartholomew, Westhoughton, was built after a fire by *Dane Ashworth Cottam*, 1994–5. There was major rebuilding by *Gordon Thorne* after arson in 1985 at St Margaret, Prestwich. A new Russian Orthodox church in Longsight (Manchester) by *Archimax*, 2003, is good, tall and spare with a copper onion dome. New SYNAGOGUES and MOSQUES, by contrast, are rarely noteworthy. Mosques are being built in increasing numbers, often reusing existing buildings. New ones usually follow formulaic designs in brick with plastic domes, such as the very prominent examples in Oldham, Rochdale and Bolton. An exception is the one in Rusholme by *N. Gedal*, 1999, with an unusual stepped

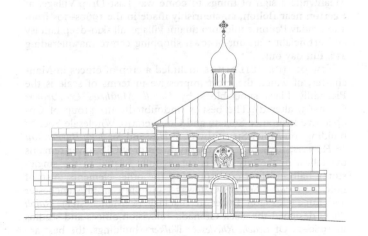

Russian Orthodox Church, Manchester, elevation

tower. There is a scattering of HINDU, JAIN and SIKH TEMPLES, but little of architectural note.

Of CHURCH FURNISHINGS, some of the best are STAINED GLASS schemes, of which the W windows in Manchester Cathedral by *Antony Hollaway* (1971–95) is the most important and complete ensemble. *Linda Walton* of *Design Lights* did good windows in St Katharine, Blackrod (1980, 1992, 1999) and more at the refurbished St Martin, Castleton, Rochdale, 2003. More old-fashioned, but very charming, is *Francis Skeat*'s biographical window of 1965 at St Ann, Belfield, Rochdale. *Stephen Dykes Bower* in the 1970s created memorable painted schemes and lighting fixtures at Oldham Parish Church and at St Paul, Pendleton. We must also note *Graeme Willson*'s 1990s Stations of the Cross at St Elisabeth, Reddish, and paintings at St Margaret, Prestwich and elsewhere.

Commercial Buildings

One important post-war development was the SHOPPING CENTRE, which in SE Lancashire were mainly built in the mid and later 1960s. They were largely enclosed centres, sometimes on more than one level, in the middle of traditional shopping areas. Many of these have gone, e.g. *Richard Seifert*'s centre in Oldham. Awful decaying centres survive at Eccles, in Walkden, and elsewhere. One or two, such as the small one at Urmston by *Leach, Rhodes & Walker*, *c.* 1968, and their centre at Swinton are at least thriving, if unlovely. The most monstrous was Manchester's Arndale Centre, an inward-looking scheme by *Wilson & Womersley* (1972–80), and that is being radically altered. The less said about Wythenshawe's shopping and cultural centre the better. Its site was only decided in 1945 and it was the mid 1960s before it took hesitant shape, thirty years after the first houses. Meanwhile a sign of things to come was Last Drop Village, at Egerton near Bolton, amateurishly made in the 1960s–70s from a workaday Pennine fold into quaint village, all skin-deep fantasy and artificiality; an out-of-town shopping centre masquerading as a fun day out.

New OFFICE BUILDINGS included a crop of offices in Manchester, of which the most impressive in terms of scale is the Piccadilly Plaza super-block by *Covell, Matthews & Partners* (1959–65, altered). The best is undoubtedly the group of Co-operative Insurance Society and Co-operative Wholesale Society buildings on Miller Street (by *G. S. Hay* and *Sir John Burnet, Tait & Partners*, 1959–61). The twenty-five storey CIS tower remains the tallest in the city and is successfully related to the single-storey hall and fourteen storeys of the other elements. Also of note are *Richard Seifert*'s Gateway House in central Manchester and huge Hexagon Tower in Blackley (N Manchester). *Ralph Tubbs* designed the sleek Granada Television offices and studios in 1960–2. Of *Leach, Rhodes & Walker*'s buildings, the best are the former Manchester Liners offices at the Salford Docks and Aldine House, central Salford. *Taylor, Young & Partners* designed an interesting FACTORY in Denton (1960), with a series of low, large-span tied concrete arches with upper glazing.

Transport and Communications

Interesting examples of 1960s technology are provided in some of the RAILWAY BUILDINGS. Oxford Road Station, Manchester 119 (1958–60 by *Max Clendinning* with *Hugh Tottenham*) is an example of conoid shell roofing in timber, deploying the type of laminated timber supports favoured by George Pace for some of his churches of that period (*see* for example St Mark, Chadderton). A striking bridge of the modern age is at Besses o' th' Barn, Whitefield *c.* 1968; a single enormous balanced concrete I-beam, by *W. F. Beatty*, civil engineer. By this time ROAD BUILDING was considered more important, and necessary to deal with the vast increase in traffic. Schemes to separate pedestrians from the roadside by vertical segregation, with upper walkways, were attempted but abandoned in Manchester. Something had to be done to relieve congested centres, but in places such as Ashton-under-Lyne and Middleton the effect of the relief roads was disastrous, cutting parts of the centres off from one another, destroying coherence and condemning some areas to decline through isolation. Parts of Stretford have been alienated from one another, and things were hardly better in Oldham, though frequent pedestrian bridges help to maintain links between the areas. The motorway system around Manchester has come close to completion in the early C21. The M60 ring has linked up pre-existing sections and routes N and S, creating new relationships between some of the towns. It is now the dominating feature on the map.

Conservation and Regeneration

From the 1970s there was increasing awareness all over the country of the threat to historic buildings and architecture from redevelopment schemes. Conservation groups successfully defended some of Manchester's best Victorian architecture, including the Albert Memorial. At the same time an appreciation of the importance of SE Lancashire's pioneering industrial past was fostered. Early successful schemes for the REUSE OF HISTORIC BUILDINGS included the conversion of Central Station in Manchester as the G-Mex exhibition centre in the 1980s. The restoration and presentation of the historic railway buildings at Liverpool Road, Castlefield by the Museum of Science and Industry from the early 1980s has been a triumph. In Ashton-under-Lyne the Portland Canal Basin was restored and the warehouse there turned into a heritage centre, with some of the nearby mills converted to flats. The Rochdale Canal, which had been abandoned and filled in during the mid C20 was reopened in 2002, after a £23,000,000 restoration including major bridgeworks. Commerce has come to the aid of *Waterhouse*'s Manchester Refuge Assurance building, now a hotel, while the striking reuse of the Royal Exchange for a theatre has already been mentioned. The other side of the coin is seen in the damaging and radical extension and reconstruction of the noble Free Trade Hall in 2003–4, and of *Cockerell*'s Branch Bank of England in 1995.

Changes in religious observance and population structure have continued to affect churches. The Churches Conservation Trust (formerly the Redundant Churches Fund) looks after a few, such as All Souls, Astley Bridge, Bolton (*Paley & Austin* 1878–81), closed in 1986. Its near twin, the Saviour on Deane Road, Bolton, 1882–5, was demolished in 1975; a great loss. Buildings by distinguished architects such as J.S. Crowther, Walter Tapper, and A.W.N. Pugin face an uncertain future. There is good news as well, with the repair and refurbishment of St Nicholas, Burnage, St John Evangelist, Cheetham, and strides towards the rehabilitation of St Francis, Gorton. It should also be recorded that following widespread church closures in the 1950s–70s the efforts of Donald Buttress and others resulted in a number of towers and spires being saved to stand as important landmarks, from *William Hayley*'s Christ Church, Heaton Norris (1844–6), far to the SE on the Stockport boundary, to *E. H. Shellard*'s St George (1858), to the W in outer Salford.

One solution is the CONVERSION OF CHURCHES for secular use. St Paul's Methodist church, Didsbury, was successfully converted to offices by *Downs & Variava*, 1990. Emmanuel, Daubhill, Bolton of 1837 was turned into flats *c.* 1990 with the eaves raised for continuous windowing above the parapet, a very striking motif. St George, Hulme was another flat conversion by *Provan & Makin* 2001–2, retaining the exterior character. Other residential conversions include the Congregational church at Broughton, a Methodist chapel at Tottington, and three Nonconformist chapels in a row at Ramsbottom. The rebirth of the Sephardic Synagogue at Cheetham as a museum is exceptional, and has proved a great success.

RECENT DEVELOPMENTS FROM *c.* 1990

SE Lancashire, and especially Manchester, has witnessed a renaissance over recent decades. Initiatives such as the creation of Development Corporations of the 1980s, and the City Challenge and European Community funding schemes, seemed to start the ball rolling, and changes started to accelerate in the late 1980s. There has since been an economic upturn, with the coming-of-age of new businesses and industries, and new confidence in the academic and housing sectors. The transformation has not been even, nor is it complete, but Manchester in the first years of the C21 can claim to be at the forefront of change in England's cities.

The 1980s and 1990s saw regeneration of the Trafford and Salford DOCKS, alongside the Manchester Ship Canal. The two sides developed in different ways. Trafford chose to create business and light industry parks to replace the heavy industry, which finally died in the 1970s, later augmented by the Trafford Centre for out-of-town shopping (*see* below) and related leisure developments. Salford, in contrast, promoted ambitious residential and office developments from the 1980s, accompanied by the cleaning and reopening of canal arms and presentation of some of the historic fabric. It is this area which has the greatest concentration of POSTMODERN architecture, none of it outstanding, though Quay West, a glittering office block on the Trafford Park side (by *The Ratcliff Partnership*, 1990), is redolent of the era. The Siemens building at Withington, by *MBLC*, 1989–90, has a Postmodern sense of irony, lacking in *Holford Associates'* extension to the Branch Bank of England in Manchester where a broken pediment motif was used as late as 1995. The style never really took in Manchester. It was a reaction against the Modern Movement of previous decades, with which the failures of social housing had become associated, and one development worth passing mention was the decision taken by authorities such as Manchester, Salford and Stockport (in Heaton Norris) to reclad some of the council tower blocks to introduce colour and even pediment motifs (e.g. those off Stockport Road and the Mancunian Way in Chorlton-on-Medlock). Postmodernism has been superseded by an expressive Modernist style, used from the early 1990s in Manchester by a clutch of locally based firms including *Stephenson Bell*, *Hodder Associates*, *Ian Simpson Architects* and *OMI*.

A harbinger of change was the LIGHT RAPID TRANSPORT SYSTEM ('METROLINK'), constructed by a consortium of *GEC*, *John Mowlem & Co.* and *AMEC* (depot facilities). The existing Bury and Altrincham suburban railway lines were adapted and connected with the centre of Manchester and a cross-town tram route, opened in 1992. The tram system was extended to Eccles via Salford Quays in 1999 and further extension to Rochdale, Wythenshawe, the airport and other destinations is proposed. It has been a great success as a transport system, and has prompted a return to trams in other major cities such as Sheffield. Its visual impact on Manchester city centre is less welcome, with ugly stanchions to support the cables and raised stations at key points such as St Peter's Square. There is a stylish new interchange at Eccles, on the other hand, and hopes for improvement to the present dispiriting transport interchange at Bury. In the same years the centre of Manchester was linked by rail to the AIRPORT, and the Airport Station of 1993 by *Austin-Smith:Lord* is the best new building there, with a take-off trajectory shape. Piccadilly Station was given new frontages and concourses by *BDP* at the beginning of the C21, and other improvements around the centre were undertaken in connection with the 2002 Commonwealth Games.

In other respects too, the transformation of the centre of Manchester has been more radical than in any other town or city in the region, and perhaps the country. New residential developments in Castlefield and off Whitworth Street West in the late 1980s heralded a revival in inner-city living. Buildings of the early

120   1990s include the Bridgewater Hall, 1993–6 by *RHWL Partner-ship*, built as a new home for the Hallé Orchestra, with an impressive auditorium and a landscaped setting.* The graceful and dynamic Trinity Bridge by *Santiago Calatrava*, 1993–5, was a Salford initiative, spanning the Irwell from Chapel Wharf to the centre of Manchester. A little later and outside the centre in Chorlton-on-Medlock, is the Contact Theatre by *Short & Associates* (1997–9) with its odd H-shaped ventilators and bright interiors, while the Hulme Arch, a bridge by *Wilkinson Eyre*, 1997, is the gateway to an area which has been rebuilt after demolition of the 1970s flats.

Devastation of the city centre by a terrorist bomb in 1996 was followed by further reconstruction. Some buildings had to be demolished, and the entire area around the s end of Corporation Street, where the bomb went off, was rebuilt. This seems to have provided the impetus for a phase of activity far beyond the immediate area affected. New streets, squares and shops have been accompanied by pedestrianization schemes and new building. Piccadilly Gardens were remodelled, though this involved the sacrifice of open space to commercial development. *Stephenson Bell* (with *Sheppard Robson*) were responsible for the commendable International Convention Centre on Windmill Street (1999–2001), and several other locally based practices have developed a similar neo-Modernist style for buildings in the area. The centre is still being rebuilt, with radical reworking of the Arndale Centre by *Chapman Taylor Partners*, a swathe of new development off Deansgate, where an early C21 architectural fashion for bulging shapes can be seen, and conversion of every sort of building into flats, hotels, etc.

APARTMENT BLOCKS are the most common new building type. The ambition of *Ian Simpson Architects'* great glass wedge, No. 1 Deansgate (2001–3), *Glenn Howells'* Timber Wharf and Boxworks, Hulme and *Stephenson Bell*'s Castlefield scheme have set the standard. *Terry Farrell*'s 'Green Building' in Chorlton-on-Medlock promises to be fresh, but many others are just boxes with corner towers trendily clad in glass, terracotta panels or brick. The boom in city centre living has caught on elsewhere, and conversions for flats and new building have started to reach inner Salford, Salford Docks and Stretford.

RETAIL ARCHITECTURE is an important part of the story, and another sign of the change in the economy. *BDP*'s sleek Marks & Spencer store in central Manchester replaced a predecessor destroyed by the bomb, and more retail outlets continue to be built. Some of the towns have built shopping centres in recent decades, in some cases, e.g. Oldham, replacing unpopular 1960s schemes. Many are accompanied by welcome pedestrianization. *Chapman Taylor Partners'* Market Centre scheme in Bolton started in 1988. Two examples gave the centre of Rochdale an almost complete indoor geography: Exchange Centre of 1978 by *BDP* (but transformed since), which incorporates the markets,

* Can it ever stand for Manchester in the way that the Free Trade Hall did?

and is connected to the seven tower blocks of College Hill, and the Wheatsheaf Centre by *Chapman Taylor Partners*, 1990, which incorporates the library, and is directly connected to the bus station and to the council offices. This brings us to the one retail development that is nationally notable, the TRAFFORD CENTRE, 1996–8 by *Chapman Taylor Partners*, which must also be the largest single building in SE Lancashire. An out-of-town shopping centre entirely dependent on road transport, it is a bizarre melting pot of architectural pastiche, creating a self-contained world of safety, comfort and make-believe.

The UNIVERSITIES have produced some of the best new architecture, the first sustained new building by academia in the area for several decades. *Stephen Hodder Associates* have produced a notable addition to Salford University with the Centenary Building on the Adelphi Campus (1994–5) and the crisp Career Services Unit (1995) on the Manchester University campus. *MBLC*'s Aytoun Library (1993) for Manchester Metropolitan University (MMU) employs the firm's trademark white cladding with suave curves. The best recent addition is All Saints West, MMU's new law department building, by *John McAslan & Partners*, 2002–3.

The turn of the C20 and the C21 saw new buildings spring up all over the country financed by money from the Heritage Lottery Fund and meant as special Millennium projects, typically ARTS CENTRES and MUSEUMS. The momentum created also saw new schemes built with money from other sources. The results include some of the largest and most striking new buildings of the region, some designed by practices of international stature. Trafford MBC was instrumental in the creation of the most impressive, the Imperial War Museum North on the banks of the Ship Canal. It is an extraordinary achievement, in which *Daniel Libeskind*'s sculptural architecture creates a powerful and disorientating inner world. Salford gave its dock redevelopment scheme a boost with the Lowry, by *Michael Wilford & Partners* 1997–2000: two theatres are enveloped by galleries and an exterior with a nautical feel, contrasting with the livid colours of the interior. Gallery Oldham by *Pringle Richards Sharratt*, 1999–2001, is fresh, engaging with Oldham's topography and neighbouring buildings. *Ian Simpson Architects* created a great glacial prow pointing into Manchester city centre for Urbis (2000–2), with exhibits on the modern city, and Manchester City Art Gallery was extended by *Michael Hopkins* in 2000–3. In Rochdale the Zen Internet Office by *Burr Design Associates* is good, while the museum and gallery was given an impressive makeover to create the Touchstones Arts and Heritage Centre.

Recent PUBLIC ART includes work funded by local authorities, the Heritage Lottery Fund and business sponsorship. In E Manchester The Runner by *Colin Spofforth*, 2002, and B of the Bang by *Thomas Heatherwick*, 2004, are outstanding. One of the most ambitious projects, the Irwell Sculpture Trail, runs beside the river through several local authority areas. The artworks are mostly disappointing, and have been vandalised. Probably the best is the enigmatic untitled chunks of granite by *Ulrich Ruckriem* (1998), at Outwood, Radcliffe. In Barbirolli Square, Manchester, Touchstone by *Kan Yasuda* (1996) is a big, curvy pebble, a good example of a work which pleases, but is resistant to vandalism. The best environmental sculpture and landscaping in Manchester is outside Urbis, with stone benches and artwork by *Stephen Broadbent* and *Melanie Jackson*, 2001. Apart from that, the bright glass by *Brian Clarke* (1993) in Oldham's central shopping centre deserves mention.

Outside the centre one of the most important new developments so far as Manchester is concerned has been the Manchester City Stadium built by *Arup Associates* for the 2002 Commonwealth Games and converted for football use, 2002–3. There is a cluster of other sports facilities here, including the sculptural velodrome by *FaulknerBrowns*, opened in 1994 as Britain's national cycling centre. Regeneration of the area with housing and retail schemes has started, and it is to be linked to the Metrolink system. Bolton's hopes lie in the spectacular Reebok Stadium at Horwich (1998, by *Lobb Sports Architecture*), the home of Bolton Wanderers FC, and its attendant Arena tennis centre (2001 by *Bradshaw Gass & Hope*).

When Nikolaus Pevsner was writing in 1969 the challenges and promises of new council housing were a major theme. They are still a preoccupation. COMMUNITY ARCHITECTURE in Hulme has produced a range of innovative schemes, including the Homes For Change complex, by *MBLC* (1999–2000). There is also new low-rise housing on traditional lines. This is the route that is being taken in a number of areas, though efforts to change the reputation and condition of surviving 1960s and 1970s tower blocks have been given a fillip by the taste for high-rise living in the private sector. In Ancoats construction of a new Millennium village is due to start in 2004 (lead developer *Urban Splash*, with *Alsop Architects*). The plan is to replace a depressed 1970s housing estate with medium-rise blocks, integrating shops, dwellings and small businesses around a system of new canal arms. Elsewhere, attempts have been made to restructure rundown estates by selective demolition, with introduction of more private space and gates to back alleys. Wide-ranging schemes of this type are being put into place for depressed areas from Salford through N and E Manchester.

At the opening of the C21 there is a feeling of optimism in many places, and civic and commercial pride is being expressed through architecture in a way hardly seen for a century. Manchester has reinvented itself and discarded its gritty image. It is a name to be proud of again. The other towns are following, but slowly. There is still a great contrast between the buzz and constant building activity of the Manchester centre, or the breezy optimism felt in the Trafford and Salford docks, and the underuse of, say, central Bolton or Oldham – but here the peripheries are often thriving, with many new residential developments enjoying the newly clean environment, and benefiting from motorway links. Extension of the Metrolink system could have an important part to play as well. The crucial thing will be to retain distinctive character, avoiding cloned buildings that could be anywhere, and stopping short of purging old buildings of all personality when they are restored. There is already proof that it can be done.

FURTHER READING

Coverage of SE Lancashire is patchy, with some areas well served and others relatively neglected. The most useful GENERAL and COUNTY HISTORIES are W. Farrer and J. Brownbill, *Victoria County History of Lancashire*, Vols 4 and 5, 1911; Edward Baines, *History of the County Palatine and Duchy of Lancaster*, 1836, and J. Aikin, *A History of the Country from thirty to forty Miles round Manchester*, 1795 (facsimile ed. 1968). For the diocese, *see* Arthur J. Dobb, *Like a Mighty Tortoise: a history of the Manchester diocese*, 1978. For GEOLOGY *see* N. Aitkenhead *et al.*, *British Regional Geology: the Pennines and adjacent areas* (British Geological Survey), 4th edn, 2002. For ARCHAEOLOGY *see* B. Barnes, *Man and the Changing Landscape*, 1982; M. Nevell (ed.), *Living on the Edge of Empire, Models, Methodology, and Marginality: Late Prehistoric and Romano-British settlement in North-West England*, *Archaeology North West* 3, 1999, and D. Hall, C. E. Wells and E. Huckerby, *The Wetlands of Greater Manchester*, *North West Regional Survey* 2, 1995.

There is no overview of ARCHITECTURE of the area, but an introduction to the medieval churches is given by S. R. Glynne, *Notes on the Churches of Lancashire* (Chethams Society), 1893. One of the best sources for the mid to late C20 is the journal *Architecture North West*, which was published between 1963 and 1970. Sources for individual towns are mentioned below. Studies of individual ARCHITECTS include J. H. G. Archer, 'Edgar Wood: a notable Manchester Architect' in *Transactions of the Lancashire and Cheshire Antiquarian Society* (TLCAS) 73–74, 1963–4; Anthony J. Pass, *Thomas Worthington: Victorian architecture and social purpose*, 1988; and C. Cunningham and P. Waterhouse, *Alfred Waterhouse, 1830–1905: biography of a practice*, 1992. A short article on Edward Salomons by Rhona Beenstock appears in *Manchester Region History Review* 10, 1996. The *Transactions of the Lancashire and Cheshire Antiquarian Society* 92–93, 1997, was devoted to subjects relating to the Manchester diocese and includes a study of N. F. Cachemaille-Day by Michael Bullen. Roger N. Holden, *Stott and Sons*, 1998 is a valuable study of a practice specializing in cotton mills.

For INDUSTRIAL ARCHAEOLOGY see R. McNeil and M. Nevell, *A Guide to the Industrial Archaeology of Greater Manchester*, 2000. A particularly useful study is M. Nevell (ed.), *From Farmer to Factory Owner, Models, Methodology and Industrialisation: the archaeology of the Industrial Revolution in North-West England*, 2003. Also useful are M. Nevell and J. Walker, *The Park Bridge Ironworks and the Archaeology of the Wrought Iron Industry in North*

West England, 1600 to 1900, 2003. For COTTON MILLS the best source is Mike Williams with D. A. Farnie, *Cotton Mills in Greater Manchester*, 1992. Also useful is R. McNeil and M. Stevenson (eds), *Heritage Atlas 2: Textile Legacy*, 1996. There are also a number of books on the cotton mills of individual towns, mentioned below. For CANALS and RAILWAYS *see* David Owen, *Canals to Manchester*, 1977; C. Hadfield and G. Biddle, *The Canals of North West England*, 2 vols, 1970; H. Malet, *Bridgewater: the Canal Duke, 1736–1803*, 1977; and M. Nevell and J. Walker, *Portland Basin and the Archaeology of the Canal Warehouse*, 2001. There is a large body of work on the Manchester Ship Canal including D. Owen, *The Manchester Ship Canal*, 1982, and P. M. Hodson (ed.), *The Manchester Ship Canal: a guide to historical sources*, 1985. For railways, *see* Geoffrey O. Holt, *Regional History of the Railways of Great Britain: the North West*, 1978.

For SCULPTURE, STATUARY, MONUMENTS and the DECORATIVE ARTS *see* Terry Wyke, *The Public Sculpture of Greater Manchester* (Public Monuments and Sculpture Association, forthcoming); B. Read & P. Ward-Jackson (eds), *Courtauld Institute Illustrations Archives 4, Late 18th and 19th Century Sculpture in the British Isles: Part 6, Greater Manchester*, 1978; James L. Thornely, *Monumental Brasses of Lancashire and Cheshire*, 1893, and P. Hebgin-Barnes, *The Medieval Glass of Cheshire and Lancashire* (*Corpus Vitrearum Medii Aevi Great Britain*, Summary Catalogue), forthcoming, and R. Bailey, *Corpus of Anglo-Saxon Stone Sculpture, Lancashire and Cheshire*, also forthcoming.

TOWN and TOWNSHIP HISTORY and ARCHITECTURE includes an extensive literature on MANCHESTER. The best recent history is by Alan Kidd, *Manchester*, 1993. L. D. Bradshaw, *Visitors to Manchester: a selection of British and foreign visitors' descriptions of Manchester from c.1538 to 1865*, 1987, is a very useful compendium. For early history *see* S. Bryant *et al.*, *The Archaeological History of Greater Manchester, Vol. 3: Roman Manchester, a frontier settlement*, 1987, and M. Morris, *The Archaeological History of Greater Manchester Vol. 1: Medieval Manchester*, 1983. C. F. Carter (ed.), *Manchester and its Region*, 1962, is especially useful for medieval and early modern Manchester; *see* also T. S. Willan, *Elizabethan Manchester*, 1980. The C17 and C18 remains a neglected subject. A. P. Wadsworth and J. de Lacy Mann, *The Cotton Trade and Industrial Lancashire 1600–1780*, 1931, and J. Walton, 'Proto-Industrialisation and the first Industrial Revolution: the case of Lancashire' in P. Hudson (ed.), *Regions and Industries: a perspective on the Industrial Revolution in Britain*, 1989 provide background to economy and industry, while the section on Manchester in C. W. Chalklin, *The Provincial Towns of Georgian England*, 1974, is a useful exposition of late C18 development of the town. W. H. Chaloner, 'Manchester in the latter half of the eighteenth century', in *The Bulletin of the John Rylands Library* 42, 1959–60, provides an introduction to the town on the cusp of the Industrial Revolution.

Books on MANCHESTER ARCHITECTURE include C. Hartwell, *Manchester* (Pevsner Architectural Guides), 2001, an

account of Manchester city centre and the immediate environs
which is included in condensed form in this volume. Other
sources include C. H. Reilly's short but informative *Some Manchester Streets and their Buildings*, 1924, and Cecil Stewart's *The
Stones of Manchester*, 1956. Short guides to the central area
include P. Atkins, *Guide Across Manchester*, revised edition 1987,
and E. Canniffe and Tom Jefferies, *Manchester Architecture Guide*,
1998. The best overview of Victorian architecture is the introduction to J. H. G. Archer (ed.), *Art and Architecture in Victorian
Manchester*, 1985, which also contains valuable essays including
studies of the John Rylands Library on Deansgate by John
Madden, the Whitworth Art Gallery by Francis Hawcroft, the
Royal Manchester Institution by Stuart Macdonald, Thomas
Worthington by Anthony J. Pass, and a reprint of M. Whiffen,
The Architecture of Sir Charles Barry in Manchester, first published
in 1950. For commercial warehouses *see* Simon Taylor *et al.*, *Man-
chester, the Warehouse Legacy: an introduction and guide* (English
Heritage), 2002, and A. V. Cooper, 'The Manchester Commercial
Textile Warehouse 1780–1914: a study of its typology and practi-
cal development', unpublished Ph.D. thesis, University of Man-
chester, 1991. For an overview of the building type *see* H. R.
Hitchcock, 'Victorian Monuments of Commerce', *Architectural
Review* 105, 1949. Studies of Manchester industrial buildings and
structures include R. S. Fitzgerald, *Liverpool Road Station Manchester: an historical and architectural survey*, 1980. The Chorlton-
on-Medlock mills are the subject of an article by S. Clark in
Industrial Archaeology Review 2, 1978. *Industrial Archaeology
Review* 10, 1988 and *Industrial Archaeology Review* 15, 1993 were
devoted to textile mills including Manchester examples. For post-
war architecture *see* D. Hands and S. Parker, *Manchester: a guide
to recent architecture*, 2000 and J. Parkinson-Bailey (ed.), *Sites of
the City: essays on recent buildings by their architects*, 1996. *Manchester, an Architectural History*, 2000, by the same author, covers
all periods and is especially useful for post-war architecture and
planning. D. Sharp, *Manchester*, 1969 is useful for buildings of
the 1960s.

There is a literature on individual MANCHESTER TOWN-
SHIPS, including a number of studies and memoirs of particular
areas published by Neil Richardson. Also useful are E. France
and T. F. Woodall, *A New History of Didsbury*, 1976, Fletcher
Moss, *Fifty Years Public Work in Didsbury*, 1915, and John M.
Lloyd, *The Township of Chorlton-cum-Hardy*, 1972. Wythenshawe,
because it is s of the Mersey and in Cheshire until the 1930s, has
its own bibliography; J. P. Earwaker, *East Cheshire* Vol. 1, 1877;
Peter de Figuiredo and Julian Treuherz, *Cheshire Country Houses*,
1988; W. H. Shercliff, *Wythenshawe (to 1926)*, 1974, and Derick
Deakin, *Wythenshawe: the story of a Garden City*, 1989.

ASHTON-UNDER-LYNE and the nearby townships in Tameside MBC, including Mossley, Denton, Droylsden, Failsworth
and Audenshaw, are well served by a series of books on the
history, archaeology and buildings of the area by Mike Nevell,
John Walker and others, published by Tameside MBC between

1991 and 1998. Also useful are J. Butterworth, *History and Description of the Town and Parish of Ashton-Under-Lyne, Mottram, Longendale and Glossop*, 1823; E. Butterworth, *An Historical Account of the Town and Parish of Ashton-under-Lyne in the County of Lancaster*, 1842, and W. M. Bowman, *England in Ashton-under-Lyne*, 1960. *See* also Ian Haynes, *Cotton in Ashton*, 1987; Ian Haynes, *Mossley Textile Mills*, 1996; and S. Taylor, *Failsworth Places and People*, 2001.

The best recent history of OLDHAM is Brian R. Law, *Oldham Brave Oldham: an illustrated history of Oldham*, 1999. *See* also Hartley Bateson, *A History of Oldham*, 1974; James Middleton, *Oldham Past and Present*, 1903; and K. McPhillips, *Oldham: the formative years*, 1981. John Beever, *History of Oldham Churches* is very useful, as is D. Gurr and J. Hunt, *The Cotton Mills of Oldham*, 1998. For SALFORD *see* Tom Bergin, Dorothy N. Pearce and Stanley Shaw (eds), *Salford: a city and its past* (1989); R. L. Greenall, *The Making of Victorian Salford*, 2000; Salford City Council, *A Civic History of Salford*, 2000. Useful guides to the BOLTON area include J. Scholes and W. Pimblett, *A History of Bolton*, 1892 (abridged edn 1994); G. Readyhough, *Bolton Town Centre: a modern history*, 1982; J. H. Longworth, *The Cotton Mills of Bolton*, 1987, and A. Wolstenholme, *The Industrial History of Farnworth and District (Greater Manchester)*, 2000. *See* also Thomas Mawson, *Bolton As It Was and As It Might Be*, 1916, a transcription of lectures commissioned by Sir William Lever. For BURY *see* F. Howarth, *Bury: a bygone era*, 2000, and M. Gray, *The History of Bury, Lancashire, from 1660 to 1876*, 1970, and *Bury: archaeology of a Pennine valley* (Greater Manchester Archaeology Unit), 1999. For ROCHDALE and neighbouring towns, Henry Fishwick, *The History of the Parish of Rochdale*, 1889, and John Street, *The Story of Littleborough*, 1999, are useful. For STRETFORD and adjoining towns *see* S. Massey, *History of Stretford*, 1976; K. Cliff and V. Masterson, *Urmston, Flixton and Davyhulme*, 2000, and J. C. Bailey, *Old Stretford*, 1985.

The most useful BIBLIOGRAPHIES are by Terry Wyke. His 'Nineteenth Century Manchester, a Preliminary Bibliography' is arranged under subject headings including architecture, art, housing, canals, railway, roads etc., and appears in a book which may be recommended in its own right, A. J. Kidd and K. W. Roberts (eds), *City, Class and Culture: studies of social policy and cultural production in Victorian Manchester*, 1985. His 'The Diocese of Manchester: an introductory bibliography' appears in *Transactions of the Lancashire and Cheshire Antiquarian Society* 92–93, 1997. Also useful is T. Wyke and N. Rudyard (eds), *'Cotton: a select bibliography on cotton in North West England'*, North Western Regional Library System, 1997. A Manchester region bibliography is published annually in the *Manchester Region History Review*, which started in 1987. For archaeology *see* M. Nevell, 'A Bibliography of North West Archaeology 1991–2000', *Archaeology North West* 5, 2000.

Those interested in carrying out more detailed research can consult The Department of the Environment and DCMS *List of*

Buildings of Historic and Architectural Interest for the relevant area. The local history and archive sections of the Manchester Central Reference Library have extensive collections covering the whole of the area, including local journals of relevance. Local collections may also be found at the local studies and archive centres for the individual towns, at the Greater Manchester County Record Office, the John Rylands Library on Deansgate, and Chetham's Library. The Sites and Monuments Record can be consulted at Manchester University Field Archaeology Department, where there is a collection of English Heritage reports on individual buildings (also available at the National Monuments Record, Swindon) and reports produced by the University of Manchester Archaeological Unit, as well as the archive on Greater Manchester cotton mills. Local architecture and architects are the subject of several theses and dissertations of the University of Manchester, including studies of classical architecture of the area, vernacular architecture, Victorian stained glass, St Augustine Pendlebury, and on Richard Lane, William Fairbairn, N. F. Cachemaille-Day and the churches of E. W. Pugin in the Manchester area.

Buildings of national importance in SE Lancashire are covered by GENERAL ARCHITECTURAL HISTORIES. Good starting points are John Summerson's *Architecture in Britain 1530–1830* (Pelican History of Art), last revised 1991 (and now counterbalanced by Giles Worsley, *Classical Architecture in Britain: the heroic age*, 1995); *Victorian Architecture* by R. Dixon and S. Muthesius, 1978; and *Edwardian Architecture* by A. Service, 1977. Elain Harwood, *England: a guide to post-war listed buildings*, 2000, includes incisive accounts of several examples from the area. Standard works on other building types and themes include J. Booker, *Temples of Mammon: the architecture of banking*, 1990, M. Girouard, *Victorian Pubs*, 1975, J. Earl and M. Sell, *Guide to British Theatres, 1750–1950* (Theatres Trust), 2000, Kathryn Morrison, *English Shops and Shopping*, 2003, and Harriet Richardson (ed.), *English Hospitals 1660–1848*, 1998.

INDIVIDUAL ARCHITECTS can be followed in H. M. Colvin, *Biographical Dictionary of English Architects 1600–1840*, 1995 (3rd edn), the *Directory of British Architects 1834–1900* (British Architectural Library), 1993 (expanded edn 2001, up to 1914), and A. S. Gray, *Edwardian Architecture: a biographical dictionary*, 1985. For sculpture, the standard works are Margaret Whinney, *Sculpture in Britain 1530–1830* (Pelican History of Art), revised by John Physick, 1988, R. Gunnis, *Dictionary of British Sculptors 1660–1851*, revised 1968 (3rd edn forthcoming), B. Read, *Victorian Sculpture*, 1982, and Susan Beattie, *The New Sculpture*, 1983. INDIVIDUAL BUILDINGS can often be investigated in contemporary periodicals, *The Builder* and *Building News* (later *Architect and Building News*) for the C19, the *Architectural Review*, *Architect's Journal* and *RIBA Journal* for the C20–C21. *Country Life* also covers selected country houses. A database of periodical articles is available at the British Architectural Library (RIBA), and on-line at *www.architecture.com*.

A full bibliography of GENERAL WORKS, including much on individual architects and artists, can be found at the Reference section of the Pevsner Architectural Guides' website, *www.lookingatbuildings.org.uk*.

GAZETTEER

AFFETSIDE

A ridge-top settlement stretched along Watling Street, the Roman Road from Manchester N to Ribchester. Sure enough, from the summit the road exactly frames the CIS building ten miles away in central Manchester. C18 marker CROSS at the highest point, a stubby cylinder mounted on three circular steps. CONGREGATIONAL CHAPEL (formerly Ebenezer), 1840, small, single-storey, with round-topped windows. BRADSHAW HEAD at the N end of the village is a laithe house, with house and shippon in line under one roof.

AGECROFT see PENDLEBURY

AINSWORTH

A small settlement in open country W of Bury.

CHRISTCHURCH, Church Street. 'A wooden chapel set round with trees' recorded Camden in 1586. Cockey Chapel, small and rustic but no longer wooden, lying diagonally across its churchyard, is still set about with trees. The oldest stonework appears on the S side, where timber decays first. This suggests progressive rebuilding of the timber-framed church, although the alignment of the many old ledger stones, at odds with that of the church, seems to contradict this. From the major rebuild by *Richard Kay* of 1831–2 must date the big bald lancets, the little chancel, and perhaps the tower. The N transept is dated 1842. The interior is plastered except for the organ transept which is boarded, so it reveals nothing of its construction. W gallery on slender octagonal posts with entasis and hybrid foliage capitals. Queenpost roof. ALTAR TABLE, TURNING LECTERN, PULPIT and VICAR'S STALL are all unmistakably by *George Shaw*. Of *c.* 1850, they were brought in from Bury parish church when it was rebuilt in 1876. The FONT in the outer porch was probably brought in too. It is of biscuit-coloured terracotta, small, octagonal and elegantly Dec with foliage diapering on the base. Perhaps from St Stephen, Lever Bridge (*see* Bolton, p. 157), in which case it is by *Edmund Sharpe*. – STAINED GLASS. In the upper half of the E lancets: outer lights signed *Alan Courtney*, †1953 and 1957.

The square CHURCHYARD is said to have been moated.

COCKEY NEW CHAPEL (Presbyterian, now Unitarian), 39 Knowsley Road. The puritans were only finally ejected from the parish church in the early C18. 'Erected 1715, enlarged 1773, altered and repaired 1845' says the inscription on the pediment over the W door, which must itself be of 1845. The

chapel stands in a delightful enclave, a square walled churchyard full of old trees and ledger stones. Four bays and two
storeys, two broad bays wide, with three-light mullioned
windows. The s wall is full of irregularities; the entrance may
have been on this side, and perhaps the chapel only had one
storey to begin with. A rustic double belfry perches on the w
gable. It has Ionic pilasters with little faces in the capitals. The
two-deck PULPIT stands against the long N wall, surrounded
on three sides by galleries on wooden posts. – BOX PEWS.

Next to the E front is the three-storey REST HOUSE and
STABLE, also of stone with mullioned windows in threes and
fours; a mounting block outside.

AINSWORTH NATIONAL SCHOOL, Bury Old Road. 1838. Long,
with Y-tracery and a heavy cornice.

DEARDEN FOLD, Bury Old Road. H-shaped house, half brick
and half stone, with a central entrance. The entrance leads to
a cross-passage behind an inglenook fireplace on the E side.
But, upstairs, there is the splendid central truss of an open
great hall. Cambered tie-beam with a carved boss at the apex
supporting a kingpost, and big braces with multiple pegging.
Part of the wall-post remains. So we have a timber-framed hall
house probably of pre-Reformation date, like Brandlesholme
Hall at Tottington, with the stack inserted in the middle of the
hall. The BARN shows evidence of a dwelling at the s end, with
a lintel inscribed DRP 1691.

ALKRINGTON HALL see MIDDLETON

ALT HILL

Alt Hill is an area of scattered farms and houses N of Ashton-
under-Lyne (of which it is now administratively a part), on the
Oldham boundary. Places of interest are on ALT HILL LANE
and tracks leading from it.

HIGHER ALT HILL FARMHOUSE, near the N end, is dated 1764
and yet still has mullioned windows and an even greater
number of lights to mark the housebody (main living space),
i.e. no Georgian symmetry yet. Central door with the datestone and initials WAH over, three bays and two storeys. It was
the home of the Heginbottom family who became prominent
industrialists in the C19. Further s, FAIRBOTTOM FARM-
HOUSE is partially timber-framed, with early and mid-C17
alterations, rebuilding and extensions. Front elevation of
narrow rubble courses with a central door, now a window, with
a doorcase with Doric columns and a pediment: presumably
early C19, which is probably also the date of the windows.
Rear wing with mutilated mullioned windows. Beside it a
moderately sized but very modestly detailed brick WESLEYAN
METHODIST CHURCH of 1837, low and domestic in charac-

ter. It was built as a Sunday school and is being adapted for
domestic purposes.
(LOWER FOLD FARMHOUSE On a track leading s from the
road. Dr Nevell reports a timber-framed house, probably mid
C17 and encased in brick in the C18 and C19. The older part
is three-unit with services, cross passage, housebody and
parlour. A cross-wing dated 1710 has the initials TIA above
the door. Continuous outshut to rear with dairy. The formerly
external w gable retains pargetted decoration, very rare in the
county.)

ASHTON-UNDER-LYNE
9090

INTRODUCTION

Ashton was granted a market in 1284 when it was in the barony
of Manchester, but independence was effectively achieved in
the early C15 when Sir John de Assheton negotiated a token
rent, and acquired the advowson of the church. Around this
time the town received its charter and the church was rebuilt.
The lordship passed to the Booths of Dunham Massey in 1516
and to the Earls of Stamford in the early C18. The 5th and 6th
Earls expanded the town with a new axial layout in two main
phases, 1787–1803 and during the 1820s. The population grew
from 2,500 in the 1770s to almost 15,000 in 1831, rising to
more than 35,000 by 1851. Town Commissioners were established in 1827, and the town became a municipal county
borough in 1847. Expansion came with the advent of cotton-
spinning and the construction of the canal system in the late
C18. Ashton-under-Lyne became an important industrial
centre and the terminus of three canal systems linking Manchester, Huddersfield, and the mines and quarries of the Peak
District. Cotton mills were erected at first in the centre and
then mainly alongside the canals. Industrialists provided public
and educational facilities in the later C19, by which time
increasing commercial success was reflected in the proliferation of civic and commercial buildings of the centre.
    The C20 has not been kind to the town, with busy roads
cutting parts of the centre off, the Council Offices and

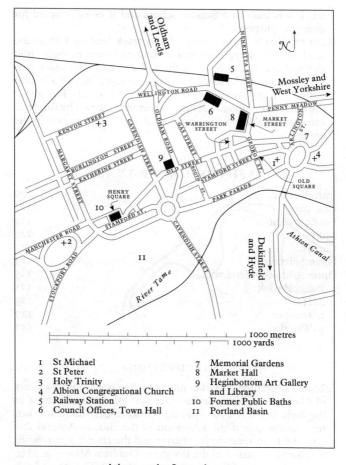

Ashton-under-Lyne, the centre

1	St Michael	7	Memorial Gardens
2	St Peter	8	Market Hall
3	Holy Trinity	9	Heginbottom Art Gallery
4	Albion Congregational Church		and Library
5	Railway Station	10	Former Public Baths
6	Council Offices, Town Hall	11	Portland Basin

shopping precincts spoiling the look of the market square and, unforgivably, the erection of huge buildings which obscure the relationship between two of the finest buildings of the centre, the Albion Church and the parish church. Mammon has even made a car park of the parish churchyard.

The centre is described first, with churches, public buildings, mills and canals followed by a perambulation. Outlying parts follow, listed alphabetically.★

★ Dr Michael Nevell of the University of Manchester Archaeological Unit kindly put the results of his unpublished work at our disposal. For his books on the area *see* Further Reading.

CHURCHES

ST MICHAEL, Stamford Street. The church is large and has an
impressively tall and sturdy w tower. But the churchyard to the
s is if anything bleaker than it was when Nikolaus Pevsner saw
it in 1968, thanks to the car park in it.

St Michael may be one of the two churches in the barony of
Manchester mentioned in Domesday, and there was certainly
a church by 1262 when Lords of the Manor of Manchester
held the advowson. There is some uncertainty about the dedication as it is sometimes referred to as St Helen's, though it
is not clear whether the prominence of the St Helen stained
glass (*see* below) was the cause of confusion. Rebuilding was
begun in the C15 (traditionally in 1413) by Sir John Assheton
who had acquired the advowson. He had negotiated the rights
to the manor in return for a token rent, so the rebuilding must
represent a celebration of independence from the Manchester
manor. His great-grandson Sir Thomas (†1516) left money for
the tower and gave much of the surviving glass. The interior
was pewed and the ceiling plastered over in 1792, following
storm damage. The screen and rood were removed at this time.
The N side was partially rebuilt in 1821 (which the tracery
heads show), but the lower part of the C15 wall is visible in
places inside. A fire at this time is said to have destroyed the
organ and much interior timberwork. The s wall was rebuilt in
1841 (though part of the original fabric can be seen in the SE
corner of the interior), the 'interior piers &c' restored in 1843
at a cost of £3,500, and the 'carved oak pews and galleries
wholly restored' in 1843–5. The work was done by *Richard Tattersall*, whose plan of the new Stamford pew is dated 1841.*
There are parallels with the plasterwork and detailing of the
nearby Dukinfield Unitarian Chapel (Cheshire), 1839–45. The
tower was rebuilt most recently in the late C19 by *J. S. Crowther*.
Of the grand C15 church, then, apart from the ceiling, only the
base of the N wall, the arcades and chancel arch survive, but
these have been scraped and given false plaster detailing.

EXTERIOR. Crowther's W tower of 1886–8 is nothing like its
predecessor (of which the top stages dated from 1818–19) but
is based on that of Manchester Cathedral, cf. the high paired
bell-openings, clusters of corner pinnacles, an open traceried
parapet and a large W window. Nave and aisles are embattled.
Outer walls, as we have seen, were wholly or partially rebuilt
in the C19. S aisle with four-light windows with Perp tracery.
A porch in the second bay has a stepped parapet and ogee
moulding over the door, a fairly close restoration of that shown
in a view of 1765. The two easternmost aisle bays are lower and
mark the position of the family chapel of the Earls of Stamford, previously an Assheton chantry chapel. The E wall and
seven-light Perp window are late C19. Nowadays the church is

---

* The historian E. Butterworth recorded in 1842 'an intention to renovate the whole
interior, in the Perpendicular Gothic style, from designs of Mr Tattersall'.

entered from the N porch, a First World War memorial by
R. B. Preston & R. Martin, 1921. The N aisle wall of 1821 is
perhaps by the same team of masons who worked on St Peter
(1821–4, below), with similar characterful headstops. The N
vestry is a former chantry chapel of the Lees/Leech family, with
a partially collapsed vault, refaced in the C19.

44   INTERIOR. The total effect is singular, and not easily for-
gotten, combining busy 1840s carving, panelling, frieze and
cresting to the arcade, and ornate plasterwork, with dark oak
contrasting with white-painted plaster. Furnishings represent
a sequence of rare completeness of the 1840s. Leeds Parish
Church has the most similar interior. Five bays, then the
chancel arch, then two more bays. The arcades have clustered
shafts, a high base with polygonal caps, and polygonal caps also
at the top. The detail is wholly of plaster, but to what extent
does it follow the medieval work beneath? The rich panelling,
frieze and cresting above is also plasterwork of the 1840s
restoration, and once again it is impossible to tell how much
is pure invention. Certainly the motifs in the chancel arch
spandrels look authentic, albeit crisp. The medieval ceiling is
masked by Georgian plasterwork, which follows the form if not
the detail of the original; heavy moulded beams with large
bosses. The vestry is in a much restored former chantry chapel,
N side, with what seems to be a squint towards the high altar,
now blocked. The former Assheton Chapel, s side, was remodelled at an unknown date, with new windows and probably the
loss of internal screens or dividing walls. The chancel was refitted by *Crowther,* 1881–9, with a good mosaic pavement and
painted decoration.

FURNISHINGS. The 1840s furnishings represent a late auditory arrangement in which the box pews all face a three-decker
pulpit placed against the N nave arcade, one bay before the
chancel. Some pews therefore have their backs to the chancel.
There are churchwardens' and parish constables' pews beneath
the w gallery. Parts of the older work were incorporated into
substantial refurbishment of what was probably the existing
arrangement. The three galleries are supported by plain cast-
iron columns and the basic structure could be C18. Cantilevered stone stairs leading to them at the w end with Gothick
cast-iron railings. Detailed description starts with the PULPIT.
Bits and pieces of earlier carving. The carved angel at the foot
of the stairs is probably C18 work, and also the two pelicans in
their piety on the rector's stall. Repositioned stairs with a mis-
matching rail, top deck possibly also partially C18. – BOX
PEWS. Some benches, others compartments with seats on four
sides. Some seem to be Georgian pews cut down, with C18
brass plates, all furnished with ornate poppyheads in the 1840s.
– GALLERY FRONTS. Very busy, with an intersecting upper
blind arcade and complex arcade with pendants below. In the
detail of the upper arcade, s side, little faces, initials TW and
GW (presumably the carvers), and the date 1843. Other motifs
appear elsewhere in the same position. – FAMILY PEW, SE. For

the Earls of Stamford, in the position of the Assheton chapel. *Richard Tattersall*'s plan is of 1841. The lower part is distinguished by the plasterwork of the underside of the gallery and simple dividing arcade, perhaps made of cast iron. Stairs with Gothic detailing lead up to the upper part. The earl's pew door has a little painted coronet and there is an elaborate plasterwork ceiling. – FONTS. There are three: a C18 baluster and bowl, broken, and two unremarkable Victorian pieces. Next to the one at the w end a STOUP. Late medieval, with four large well-preserved heads, recovered from the vicarage garden. – ORGAN CASE. Of a piece with the other work, i.e. of *c.* 1844 and very ornate. The instrument is by *Hill* of London, 1845, enlarged in 1889. – CHARITY BOARDS dated 1844, beneath the w gallery. Other boards and tablets here record restoration work of 1792, 1844 and 1903.

STAINED GLASS. The ancient glass includes the best- 12 preserved and most important medieval stained glass in NW England, outstanding nationally for a parish church and the most ambitious surviving St Helen cycle in English medieval art. It was given *c.* 1497–1512 by Sir Thomas Assheton (†1516). Twenty windows depict the life of the saint, and Assheton family donors to the building of the church are also shown. Each scene (except No. 20) is accompanied by a Latin inscription. White glass decorated with yellow stain predominates, blue and ruby is used for most of the garments and there is sparing use of murrey (a mulberry tint) and green. The painting is of some quality, and many figures are richly dressed with royalty shown wearing ermine-trimmed robes and crowns. The style of painting is typical of the late C15, and the design of armour relates to the 1470s, though this is merely an indication that the artists copied actual examples or scenes current twenty years before. The existence of a North-West regional school is hinted at through stylistic similarities between this and glass in Grappenhall in Cheshire, Abergele in North Wales and Morley in Derbyshire,* but the small number of examples means it is difficult to generalize. About three-fifths of the glass survives, the remainder restored during cleaning and conservation in 1913 and 1974. The scheme was moved from the E window to the S aisle in 1872.

The sequence starts at the E end, and the top windows, 1–13, read in order, E–W. Out-of-sequence windows beneath, starting with 18 beneath 1, then 17, 19, 14, 15 and 16, followed by six donor family windows and 20 beneath 13. The story starts with depictions of the saint's birth and girlhood (1–3) including a charming scene of the young girl in red being presented to a nun, with a timber-framed building in the background. Her marriage to Constantius and birth of their son Constantine are shown next (4–6). Scenes from Constantine's life follow, including a depiction of the Council of Nicaea and a stirring representation of the battle against Maxentius with

* According to Penny Hebgin-Barnes

well-drawn soldiers in armour (7–9). Next Helena's journey to the Holy Land and discovery of the cross on which Christ was crucified, with a scene of the resurrection of a shrouded corpse over whom the cross has been laid (10–16); the legend of Zambres the sorcerer and the bull follows, in which the bull is magically killed by the sorcerer and revived by Pope Silvester (17–19). 20 shows Helen at prayer. The donor windows on either side of the s porch show Sir John Assheton (†1428) and his children, dated 1499; Sir Thomas Assheton (†1516) with his wives; Sir John Assheton (†1494) also with wives, and Sir Thomas Assheton (†1457).

In the N aisle the window immediately E of the porch has figures of canonized kings, identified as St Edmund, Edward the Confessor and Henry VI; but the window is no later than 1466, so the third king cannot be Henry and the lettering attached to it must originate in a lost window. The next window eastwards is made up of medieval fragments with figures of saints, donors, St Anne, a Virgin and Child, etc. Next the Nativity, by *Mary Forsyth*, 1964, a memorial to Mr Wilson, a borough surveyor of Ashton. The last window on this side has some early C19 heraldic glass including the bogus arms of John Ross Coulthart. Fine E window 1872 by *James Ballantine & Sons* of Edinburgh.

MONUMENTS. Immediately W of the N door, John Postleth-waite †1818 'who obtained all the highest orders of Masonry without becoming PROUD'. By *T. McDermott* and a relatively early example of overt Masonic symbolism in a memorial. The text is framed by the columns Jachin and Boaz, and other Masonic motifs abound. – s aisle, E, Edward Brown †1857 by *Matthew Noble*. Or at least the bust is by him.

The fate of the CHURCHYARD has been noted. The earliest identified gravestone is of Katherine Fairfax †1623, near the vestry door. Beside the N gateway, a slab commemorating John Leech †1689, proudly celebrating 181 descendants living when he died aged ninety-two.

ST PETER, Manchester Road. The focal point of the w end of Stamford Street, but now on an island surrounded by daunt-ingly busy roads. 1821–4 by *Francis Goodwin*. The first of Goodwin's three Commissioners' churches in the Manchester area. Large and ambitious, Perp in the Commissioners' way, ashlar, with pleasantly fanciful motifs. It cost over £14,000, and the 6th Earl of Stamford gave the land, thereby providing for a landmark in the vistas of his father's planned town. The imposing w tower is what is seen in long E views, made mem-orable by the silhouette with two large, high, completely open paired arches of the bell stage. W door in florid surround, corner pinnacles, and an open traceried parapet. The high nave windows, like all the rest, have stone mullions and cast-iron tracery. Seven bays divided by buttresses with thin piers and finials. Stops to moulds are furnished with a lively collection of carved faces, similar to those in the N wall of St Michael (above). The E end has a low canted chancel-like vestry flanked by tall octagonal piers. Big circular rose window.

INTERIOR. Three galleries with arcaded fronts supported by quatrefoil cast-iron columns, the W gallery divided off below in the late C20. Organ loft above with what looks like an original ORGAN CASE, matching the gallery fronts. The roof is of low pitch and ceiled and connected with the walls with broad ribbed coving. The ribs rise from ornate foliated corbels. The barest of recesses at the E end, with bold Gothic plaster panelling above. The ornate canopied carving below is obviously by *George Shaw* of Saddleworth, with his trademark swirling forms, probably of the 1860s. Pretty Gothick niches with canopies on the E walls at gallery level. All the lower box pews and many of the furnishings have been removed. – STAINED GLASS. E rose window, 1830s by *David Evans* of Shrewsbury, richly coloured with the Twelve Apostles. N side, at the W end a window by *W. Pointer*, 1923; three windows by *T. F. Curtis, Ward & Hughes*, 1890s and 1901. Various late C19 work on the S side including allegories of charity by *Lavers & Westlake*. – CLOCK. Installed 1840. The face is at the E end and the mechanism at the W end connected by a drive shaft running the entire length of the church.

The churchyard has largely been cleared. MONUMENTS to note are the huge boulder, to Thomas Boulton † 1880, E, and the Gothic Heginbottom monument, of the C19 industrialist and philanthropist family (*see* Holy Trinity and the Heginbottom Library, below), SE.

HOLY TRINITY, Dean Street. By *J. Medland & Henry Taylor*, 1876–8, for the local industrialist George Heginbottom. Typical of the firm for the roguish details, strong texture and individuality. Brick, nave and aisles, N transept, chancel with wide apse. The windows are mostly plain lancets, with more decorative treatment reserved for the apse, where the openings are foiled. Taylor's oddities appear in the low lean-to W baptistery and the two big flying buttresses rising on either side, continuing between lancets with channelled brick surrounds, to support nothing more than a bellcote. This has a tier of three openings and much decoration in blue diaper brickwork and shaped brick. The NE end has beside the vestry a circular stair-tower, and the vestry roof is pierced by a flying buttress rising to a tall brick chimney.

INTERIOR. The 1990s subdivision of the W end and reordering by *Graham Holland* has not wholly robbed the interior of its force, richness and individuality. Arcade of fat, round, polished granite piers with simply moulded tops, chancel arch with clustered piers of red granite and foliate enrichment to the caps. The chancel needs piers; for it has a narrow ambulatory at a lower level. In the nave the W bay of the arcades is shorter and lower to link up with the three-bay screen of columns between nave and baptistery. Arch-braced kingpost roof with curved diagonal braces extending over nave and chancel. Clerestory of simple paired windows with detached brick shafts, the same motif to the W window. Walls of exposed brick, and reminiscent of Butterfield, patterned with bands of buff and red brick in the nave upper parts, and with crosses and chequers in the chancel. The ALTAR has been brought forward with an arcaded SCREEN and REREDOS surmounted by a North European Gothic style tabernacle. – STAINED GLASS. S side, St Augustine and St Chad; N side St George and St Alban; these and glass in the apse probably all by *Heaton, Butler & Bayne*.

The churchyard has a wall incorporating a drinking fountain, W side, and very elaborate stepped GATEWAYS with arched openings, SW and NW. The whole makes a group with a school, NE, and vicarage, SE, also by the *Taylors* and both, unusually, still in use for their original purpose. The brick SCHOOL, opened in 1885, was funded from the will of George Heginbottom. Apsidal hall and big battlemented tower. (The interior is said to retain the original plan, glazed screens, and arch-braced roof trusses). The VICARAGE of 1881 is large and gabled with bargeboards. Some decorative blue brickwork towards the church.

CHRIST CHURCH, Oldham Road. 1847–8 by *Dickson & Breakspear*. Brick, English bond. A large church but with a bellcote only. Transepts, chancel, and transept E chapel. The windows are mostly lancets. Five-bay arcades of octagonal piers; open arch-braced timber roof with pendants, and in the chancel, cusped windbraces.

ST ANN (R.C.), Burlington Street. 1859. Coursed sandstone rubble, gabled, with a plate-traceried circular window, five cusped lancets below and the stump of a SW tower.

ALBION CONGREGATIONAL CHURCH (now United Reformed Church), Stamford Street East, cut off from the centre by roads. One of the largest Congregational churches in the country, 1890–5, by *John Brooke* of Manchester, who was recommended by J. S. Crowther. Professor Binfield describes it 'in every respect rich man's Dissent overtaking the Anglican Joneses, a fifteenth-century minster upstaging the real parish church'.* The Congregationalists were clear about what they wanted. It was to be called a church, not a chapel. It was to be 'Gothic in design, with nave, transept and chancel, without galleries, except a shallow one over the entrance . . . rendered prominent by a lofty tower and spire . . . the entire structure should be of stone, the inside, however, to be of red sandstone.' There was a clear intention to adhere to Ruskinian principles regarding materials and decoration. The total cost came to *c.* £50,000, much of it defrayed by the textile manufacturer Abel Buckley. Transitional Dec-Perp. It cannot fail to impress, with NW tower and spire (liturgical orientation, as with all following compass points), complicated flèche, low aisles and flying buttresses. It seems mean-spirited to say that it does not quite

* *See* his excellent study of the church, *TLCAS*, vol. 85, 1988.

cohere architecturally; the many-windowed tower is slightly ungainly and the spire not large enough for it, the flying buttresses not wholly convincing and the transepts awkwardly handled internally. No matter. Its presence, scale and ambition create a powerful impression. NE hall, 1916.

INTERIOR. The narthex gives on either side to generous stairs to the W gallery. Then the drama begins. The first impression is of great spaciousness. There is much bare wall relieved by concentrated passages of decoration. Wide nave and very narrow aisles, scarcely more than passages. Octagonal piers with foliated caps, low transepts, each with a W porch, sheltered by a great expanse of unbroken aisle wall. Elevated chancel, sanctuary. Elaborate hammerbeam roof with angels, continued in the transepts. Richly carved furnishings, of which the ORGAN CASE is especially good. – ORGAN by *T. C. Lewis*. – PULPIT with tester. – REREDOS. A most striking painted tile First World War memorial by *Gordon Forsyth* of *Pilkingtons*. Pre-Raphaelite in tone, with a great sense of movement, clever asymmetry and interplay between matt and glazed surfaces. Christ with a wounded serviceman, St George and angels. – STAINED GLASS, by *Morris & Co.*, 1895–6. The composition and colours work to great effect, though it is not their best. E window, saints and allegories with a starry sky above and minstrel angels. In the transepts Old Testament figures N, New Testament S, including high clerestory windows. – MONUMENTS. Hugh Mason †1886, N transept. A fine white marble bas-relief, with an angel opening a door and portrait medallion. – Betsy Mason †1861. White marble, bas-relief recumbent figure and angel.

METHODIST CHAPEL, Stamford Street. 1832, austerely classical with an entrance colonnade of fluted Greek Doric columns. The rest is brick with simple arched windows and arched windows also in the pediment. Flat-headed ground-floor windows. On the outer W wall a stone from the parent chapel, formerly off Cricket's Lane, with the inscription: 'Can any good thing come from Nazareth? Come and see, John 1st–46th 1781'. Beside it a MONUMENT to James Dean †1819, a tinplate worker.

INDEPENDENT METHODIST CHURCH, Wellington Road. Dated 1877. Symmetrical, projecting gabled entrance block, classical in form but mildly Gothic in detail.

CHURCH OF THE NAZARENE, Stamford Street. *See* Perambulation, below.

PUBLIC BUILDINGS

The main public buildings face the market place, which is as spacious as any North Yorkshire example, and was given in 1829 by the 6th Earl of Stamford.

On the N side is the TOWN HALL, 1840 by *Young & Lee*, perhaps *Thomas Lee* of Manchester who had been Lewis

Wyatt's clerk of works, presumably at Heaton Hall (*see* p. 398).
Grand, of stone, seven bays with a five-bay centre. Two storeys
on a raised basement, rusticated below. The central entrance
has giant attached Corinthian columns and the outer bays have
end pilasters. Balustraded parapet. An extension to the l. by
John Eaton & Son continues in much the same vein, though
with giant pilasters. Very simple and restrained, although it is
as late as 1878. Grand entrance hall with screens of two pairs
of Ionic columns and an imperial staircase with cast-iron
balustrade, top-lit with a coved ceiling and fancy plasterwork.
Upstairs is the large and rather plain civic hall, with a curved,
coffered plaster ceiling.

The former WATER BOARD OFFICES at the NW corner of
the square carry on the theme of solid classical ashlar work.
Mid–late C19 and very austere, but topped with an endearingly
crude carved lion. This part now is only a façade, and between
it and the town hall extension, and rising up as a backdrop to
the whole of the N side, the COUNCIL OFFICES are atrociously ugly in yellowish brick, four and six storeys with an
eight-storey octagonal part. By *Cruickshank & Seward*,
1979–81. On the E side is the brick MARKET HALL, by *John
Eaton & Son*. Prominent central tower of polychromatic brick
with clock faces and keyed oculi, dated 1867. The hall is also
of brick, nineteen bays with arcades with semicircular lights,
consisting of the original core and extensions in similar style
of 1881 and 1930. Of 1881, splayed entrances on the S side with
lions on the parapet and stained glass over the doors.* Late
C20 shopping precincts fail to do justice to the other sides of
the square.

HEGINBOTTOM LIBRARY AND ART GALLERY, Old Street and
Oldham Road. 1891–3 by the Ashton-under-Lyne architects
John Eaton & Sons. The gift of a local industrialist, George
Heginbottom. In the High Victorian style of Alfred Waterhouse
of twenty years before. Stone, asymmetrical, with a tower
with a pyramidal roof dominating the composition. Projecting
arcaded entrance, windows integrated into the base of a
balcony above. To the r. a tall octagonal stair-tower, to the l. a
big gabled bay with an oriel. On the Oldham Road side, carved
roundels depict allegories of the Arts and Crafts. The interior
is delightful, with mosaic floors, glazed tiles, plasterwork and
a little kiosk in the hall. The library has cast-iron galleries with
openwork fronts on all four sides supported by decorative
columns. Grand stairs lead up to the art gallery, originally an
art and technical school, lit by a window with painted roundels
reprising those of the exterior.

DRILL HALL, Old Street, built for the Seventh Lancashire Rifle
Volunteers, now used by the Territorial Army. By *John Eaton
& Sons*, 1886. Part of a group with the library, but of brick.
The elements of the frontage are all stepped slightly back from

* Badly damaged by fire, 2004.

one another. First the gabled hall, then a square tower with circular stair-tower to one side. The main entrance follows, with a deeply recessed upper window, and finally a lower block with an oriel.

POST OFFICE, Warrington Street. Dated 1891, by *Thomas George & Son* of Ashton. An assured composition. Renaissance in red brick with stone dressings. Two storeys, with a prominent stone cornice, balustraded balcony, arched upper windows to Warrington Street with pilasters, some with scallop tympani. Other openings generally in rusticated stone surrounds, entrance with big brackets and a balustrade and urn finials over.

ALBION SCHOOLS (former), Penny Meadow Street. 1861–2 by *Paull & Ayliffe*. Said to have been the largest denominational schools of their day in England. Large, Italianate and rather startling in bright, densely patterned red and white brick. Symmetrical street elevation with central projecting three-bay pedimented range flanked by bays with elaborate stone entrances. On the l. side an Italianate tower. Upper hall with a queenpost roof and paired cast-iron columns with florid tops.

PUBLIC BATHS, Henry Square. 1870–1 by *Paull & Robinson*. An amazing performance. Brick, Italianate – or is it Transitional between Norman and E.E.? Anyway, it has a tower à la Siena Town Hall, with machicolations but adapted as a chimney, a landmark in views E down Stamford Street. Much of the effect is obtained by the great expanses of bare wall and repeating motifs of circular openings and small windows with round heads. Offices and entrance to the E with a smaller version of the chimney at the entrance. Inside the pool retains its galleries and hammerbeam roof. It has been empty and derelict for years. Saving it would help to atone for sins committed against other Ashton-under-Lyne buildings.

TAMESIDE GENERAL HOSPITAL, Fountain Street. The earliest part originated as a workhouse for 500 inmates, built on a hill overlooking the town. The competition of 1849 was won by a *Mr Nicholson*, probably *William Nicholson* of Manchester. A big forbidding E-shaped block, symmetrical with a later six-bay range attached to the r., all in roughly coursed smoke-blackened gritstone. Two storeys, classical, with some odd untutored details such as the quasi-Venetian windows. Projecting central pedimented entrance block, arched entrance. On the SE side of the site, on Darnton Road, is the former DISTRICT INFIRMARY dated 1880, but looking later. Red brick and dressings of pale stone and terracotta. Three projecting bays and a loggia with balconies on each side of the central entrance. Rising behind, a tall octagonal tower with oculi and blind arches, all topped with a little copper dome. Other buildings on the site include brick pavilion and administration blocks on Mellor Road of *c.* 1900 by *John Eaton, Sons & Cantrell*, and various C20 additions, none of special interest.

SIXTH-FORM COLLEGE, Darnton Road, formerly Ashton-under-Lyne Grammar School. Large, early C20, brick with

Ashton-under-Lyne baths (former), interior, from *The Builder*, 1870

English Renaissance detailing and Arts and Crafts touches,
such as the low spreading dormers.

TRAM DEPOT (former), Mossley Road. 1904 for the Ashton-
under-Lyne Municipal Tramcar Co. A series of red brick sheds
with shaped gables, offices to the r., tram sheds to the l.

MEMORIAL GARDENS. Only a short distance from the E end of
Stamford Street but cut off from the centre by busy roads.

Main entrance with tall stone piers with urn finials and grand balustraded stone steps. In the centre of the gardens a FIRST WORLD WAR MEMORIAL by *Percy Howard*, sculpture by *J. Ashton Floyd*, unveiled 1922. Two handsome bronze lions on stone bases guard a very tall Portland stone plinth with a bronze female winged figure representing peace supporting a soldier.

RAILWAY VIADUCT, Park Parade. 1845 for the Ashton-under-Lyne and Manchester Railway. An impressive stone structure running across the valley and the river.

MILLS

Of the early watermills on the River Tame Dr Arrowsmith reports the sandstone footings of the medieval manorial corn mill on the N bank of the river near Cavendish Mill (below), though these could relate to later rebuilding. Cotton-spinning and weaving was the main industry from the late C18, preceded by linen and fustian production. The first cotton mill opened in the 1770s and the use of steam power is first recorded in 1800. Mill building peaked during 1823–5 and 1832–7. Mills were mainly built in the centre in the early years, and thereafter largely alongside the Ashton Canal. Only the most prominent and significant are included. Further details of these and of mills not included can be found in Ian Haynes, *Cotton in Ashton*, 1987.

GOOD HOPE MILL, Bentinck Street. Cotton-spinning mill, three-storey part with offices to Bentinck Street, extended 1930, four-storey part at right angles with a chimney rising from a high base at the w end. This is the earliest part (now converted to flats), of 1824, extended before 1840. Timber floors with cast-iron columns.

CAVENDISH MILL, Cavendish Street, on the N side of the Ashton Canal. 1884–5 by *Potts, Pickup & Dixon* of Oldham. Five and six storeys. Visually the most distinctive feature is the octagonal stair-tower wrapped around the chimney on the SE side. It has paired arched windows in the upper stage. Almost certainly the earliest mill in the country to use concrete floors, rather than brick jack-arches, in the system of fireproof construction, an innovation developed by *Edward Potts*. Converted to flats 1994.

JUNCTION MILL, on the N side of the Ashton Canal W of Portland basin, originated as Samuel Heginbottom's works in 1831. Only the mid–late C19 chimney survives, a landmark in views along the canal. 210 ft (64 metres) high, octagonal, with decorative brick relief work at the base and top.

OXFORD MILLS, Oxford Street, Guide Bridge, on the N bank of the Ashton Canal. Started by Thomas Mason in 1845 with a six-storey NE block. A second, almost identical, SW block was added parallel to the first six years later. Stone plaques record the dates. Fireproof construction with cast-iron columns and brick jack-arches. Warehouses and office lie between the two, put up before 1863. The builder was *Edward Sigley* of Ashton. Cotton-spinning continued on the site until 1955. HOUSING was provided from the first, with 150 houses built over some fifty years. Hugh Mason, left in sole charge from 1860, provided most of it (also the demolished Institute with educational and recreational facilities on Ann Street, by *Paull & Robinson*, 1866–8). Much of the housing has also been demolished, including two-up two-down terraces of 1866 opposite the mill by *D. Lindley* of Ashton, who was probably responsible for much of the rest. More extensive two- and three-storey accommodation for senior members of the workforce was provided with JOHN BRIGHT TERRACE, Oxford Street, dated 1869 and the demolished Gibson Terrace of 1871, both by *Paull & Robinson* and named after prominent liberal politicians. Housing on TRAFALGAR SQUARE, also early 1870s, is the most elaborate, for managers. Similar but larger and more decorative than John Bright Terrace, and therefore probably also by *Paull & Robinson*. A terrace of twelve houses treated as one composition and nicknamed the Twelve Apostles. Three storeys with deep bracketed cornices, first-floor window arcade and gabled end bays. Standing across the road, opposite, a repositioned bronze STATUE of Hugh Mason by *J. W. Swynnerton*, 1887.

WELLINGTON MILL, Whitelands Road. 1857 with late C19 extensions. Large, brick, with a corner water tower. The best surviving example of a purpose-built spinning and weaving mill in Ashton.

OXLEY THREADS occupies the former GUIDE MILL, Stockport Road, Guide Bridge. Built for Ralph and James Kershaw, 1841–2, extended before 1863. The upper floors have been removed, but the offices, with a range of arched windows, survive. Still used for spinning thread in 2004.

CANALS

Ashton is the terminus of three canals constructed in the 1790s. They were part of one enterprise, with the same shareholders, and the engineer was *Benjamin Outram*. Part of the impetus was the drive to deliver locally produced coal to Manchester, for which the ASHTON CANAL to Manchester was constructed 1792–7 (*see* also Droylsden, Ancoats in Manchester and Manchester centre). The PEAK FOREST CANAL was built 1794–1805, connecting with the limestone quarries near Dove-holes, Derbyshire. The HUDDERSFIELD NARROW CANAL, 1794–1811, runs from the E end of the Ashton Canal. The three meet at the PORTLAND BASIN, SW of the centre of Ashton, built in 1834. The reconstructed ASHTON NEW WHARF WAREHOUSE here was built by *David Bellhouse & Co.* of Manchester, 1832–4. Badly damaged by fire in 1972, partially rebuilt in 1985 and fully restored as a museum, 1999. Brick, three storeys with timber floors and cast-iron columns (the upper two completely rebuilt), nine bays. Towards the basin a range of stone arched openings. The three central ones were shipping holes leading to internal wet docks. An external cast-iron breast-shot waterwheel was installed on the E side in 1839–41, restored 1988.

The Peak Forest Canal joins the basin from the S, where it is crossed by a narrow stone BRIDGE dated 1835, with stone slab sides and a cobbled deck. Immediately S an AQUEDUCT carries the canal over the River Tame. 1794–1801 by *Benjamin Outram* and *Thomas Brown*. Stone, with three brick arches divided by cutwaters from which buttresses rise.

PERAMBULATION

The original medieval street (Old Street) runs roughly E–W, and the 5th Earl of Stamford's new grid of streets was laid out to the SW. Its principal axial route was Stamford Street with its polygonal circus, which runs approximately parallel to Old Street and centres on a view of St Peter's Church (*see* above). Surviving late C18 and early C19 buildings are mostly altered, though the two- and three-storey brick houses establish the scale and character of those parts of the centre not wholly rebuilt.

We start near the E end of Stamford Street beside St Michael's Church (*see* above). The former PARISH OFFICES overlook St Michael's Court, a little square on the S side of the street. 1869, by the Ashton-under-Lyne architect *John Eaton*, Continental Gothic style with polychromatic brickwork, two storeys and an attic. Asymmetrical elevation to the square with an eventful roofline of gables and chimneys. On the other, W side of the square, No. 121 is one of the largest and best-preserved late C18 houses, with a pedimented doorcase and radial fanlight. Addition to the l. with a doorway with a Gibbs surround. Continuing W, N side, STAMFORD ARCADE, a pedestrian way through to Old Street, is paved with truly enormous slabs of stone, hence its old name, Flag Alley.

Continuing W brings us to OLD SQUARE, a polygonal circus. Only one and a half sides have the original plain brick C18 buildings, but their replacements are splayed at the corners to follow the original design. W of the circus, N side, MARKET AVENUE is another narrow pedestrian way, created in 1847–9, with decorative cast-iron arches between the buildings. For the Methodist Chapel *see* p. 117. Still on Stamford Street, N side, BARCLAYS BANK makes a show, early C20, Portland stone with giant fluted Ionic columns. Opposite CLARENCE ARCADE, 1894, inoffensively Renaissance, top-lit shopping arcade with a gallery and upper glazed tiles. Beside it the late C19 NAT WEST BANK (formerly the District Bank) is a bold Renaissance composition similar to the Post Office on Warrington Street (*see* above) and so possibly by the same local

firm, *Thomas George & Son*. Still on the S side, the former
ODDFELLOWS HALL is in two parts, that on the corner of
Booth Street dated 1855, with rusticated quoins and a sym-
metrical frontage of two storeys with an upper Venetian niche.
Stone extension r., 1898 by *W. Waddington & Son* in the typical
Renaissance style of the firm. A little further on, N side, the
CHURCH OF THE NAZARENE is a house of 1810–12 by *W.
Cowley* for Samuel Heginbottom. Brick, two storeys, symmet-
rical with later wings, pedimented entrance bay and projecting
portico with Ionic columns, now infilled on the sides.

Continuing and turning N along Oldham Road brings us to
OLD STREET, the original medieval route and hence not on
the grid. For the Library and Art Gallery *see* Public Buildings,
above. The general scale is again defined by the late C18 and
early C19 brick buildings. The STAR INN on the corner of
Oldham Road is one of the few still in recognizable form. Symmetrical, two storeys with wide tripartite upper windows and
a central entrance with a fanlight. Also on the N side the former
PICTURE PAVILION cinema, now a furniture warehouse.
Built *c.* 1912 for W. H. Broadhead & Son and almost identical
to their Empress Cinema in Miles Platting (p. 384). Symmetrical, red brick with white brick dressings, strong verticals.
Proscenium arch with scrolly plasterwork on each side,
pilastered walls with a fancy plasterwork frieze, and an elaborate plaster balcony front. Beside it the SALVATION ARMY
CITADEL, by *Oswald Archer* of London, dated 1908. Red brick,
stone dressings, a stepped gable giving the appropriately military tone. A short detour N up GAS STREET brings us to a
refreshing recent building, a night club (called Atomic at the
time of writing) by *Arca*, 2001, converted from a garage. Futur-
istic steel pylons with strange nozzle tops (a reference to petrol
pump feeders?) on each side of clear glazed walls. Returning
to Old Street and continuing E brings us to the large MECCA
CINEMA, formerly the Majestic, 1918–20. By *Arnold England*
of Lytham St Anne's. Splayed to the street corner, in pristine
white faience and terracotta. Edwardian Baroque with all the
usual motifs; keyed oculi, pilasters, etc. The corner of Warrington Street provides the next architectural incident, with the
former ASHTON-UNDER-LYNE SAVINGS BANK, 1911 by
Messrs George & Son. Splayed corner entrance with a splendid
lion's head grasping a large (replacement) key in its jaws over
the door. This was conceived as a revival of the practice of
placing signs on buildings to denote their purpose. Stone
ground floor with Doric colonnades, brick upper floor with
stone dressings, gable with big Baroque scrolls and the Ashton-
under-Lyne arms. Inside is a domed and vaulted ceiling constructed in reinforced concrete using the *Hennebique* system.
Returning N and E along Bow Street leads to the Market Place,
see Public Buildings, above. Turning S down WARRINGTON
STREET brings us to the Post Office (*see* above) and S of Stamford Street on the corner of Fleet Street, earlier SAVINGS

BANK premises, a partial rebuilding of 1881 by *T. D. Lindley* of
an early C19 building. Corner entrance, stone surrounds to the
windows.

OUTER ASHTON-UNDER-LYNE

1. Cockbrook

The settlement merges with the E side of the centre and
Stalybridge.

CURRIER LANE. A row of rendered cottages, of which No. 15a
is the truncation of a larger house, perhaps early C16, containing a cruck truss.

2. Hurst

Including Hurst, Higher Hurst, Hurst Brook, and Hurst Nook;
the area merges with the N side of the centre of Ashton.

ST JOHN THE EVANGELIST, King's Road, Hurst. 1847–9 by
Shellard. Transepts, tower and S chapel added by *George Shaw*,
1862, all in yellow sandstone rubble. The tower and chapel are
similar to Shaw's St James Calderbrook, near Rochdale (*see*
Littleborough). The tower with boldly done octagonal top
parts and spire is set W of the S aisle and visually independent
of it. Transepts have lancets to match Shellard's nave and N
and S windows with flowing Dec tracery, typical of Shaw. The
S chapel has an unusual frieze with his favourite swirling
designs. The additions were built by the munificence of
Oldham Whittaker, a member of the great mill-owning family
of Hurst. INTERIOR. Nave arcade of six narrow bays with clustered piers and open timber roof. Two-bay chancel with circular piers, S side. Shaw's transepts have very complicated
timber roofs with arch braces and kingposts. The WHITTAKER
CHAPEL must be one of Shaw's most ambitious and complete
surviving schemes, with a forest of Dec-style dark oak furnishings. Richly carved PARCLOSE SCREENS. – STALLS complete with arm rests and canopies with many-crocketed
pinnacles, carved CEILING with quatrefoils and pendants (now
painted). Both the STAINED GLASS windows are evidently his
work, figures in canopies with typical Shaw motifs. – LECTERN,
a fierce eagle, typical of Shaw's workshop. The chancel must
have been refurbished by Shaw at the same time, and has
similar canopied STALLS. – ALTAR RAIL with swirling openwork design, richly carved REREDOS, etc.
   CHURCHYARD. Two Whittaker MONUMENTS lie SE of the
church. An elaborate canopy with crocketed corner pinnacles
sheltering a chest tomb is obviously by *Shaw* and so probably
of the 1860s. Amongst others it commemorates Oldham Whittaker †1871 who was cremated, unusually for that date. The

other, late C19, is an octagonal pier with a pyramidal top with traceried panels. The church SCHOOL beside the churchyard is dated 1880. Large, gabled, yellow sandstone with tall windows with intersecting tracery.

ST JAMES, Cowhill Lane, Hurst Brook. 1863–5 by *George Shaw*, with his typical curvilinear tracery but having the unusual motif of two toy-like detached W octagonal turrets with tall stone spires. SE chapel, NE vestry. Aisleless with a low chancel. The Hurst mill-owner Oldham Whittaker gave most of the money for it. E of the church ST JAMES' SCHOOL, St James Street, is also of the mid-1860s and almost certainly also by *Shaw*. Large, stone and quite simple.

CEMETERY, King's Road, Higher Hurst. Opened 1892. CHAPEL by *T. D. Lindley*. Dec with a W cupola and chancel under a lower roof. Big, formerly open arches at the base of the square tower, which has corner pinnacles and an upper octagonal stage with a spire.

HURST CROSS, Hurst, at the junction of Queen's Road and King's Road. By *John Eaton*. Squat stone cross on a plinth, with the initials HC and Masonic symbols. Erected by public subscription to commemorate the Reform Act of 1868, reputedly on the site of an earlier cross.

LADYSMITH BARRACKS, Higher Hurst. 1841–3. All that survives now is a section of the forbidding stone wall alongside Mossley Road and the entrance with a heavily classical gateway flanked by pedestrian entrances. The barracks behind have been replaced by late C20 housing.

ODD WHIM, Mossley Road. A public house in a rendered brick building of 1825, very greatly altered. Historically interesting because it originated as a gatehouse built at the behest of the millenarian visionary John Wroe who was the founder of the Christian Israelites and a successor to Joanna Southcott. Wroe prophesied an apocalypse in which Ashton-under-Lyne would become the new Jerusalem. Four gatehouses or watch houses were built, of which this is the only survivor. A 'grand sanctuary', supposedly based on the design of Solomon's temple, was erected in the town centre (demolished). The cult, which observed Jewish dietary laws and customs, attracted a substantial following, but Wroe was forced to leave the town in 1830 after various scandals. He later founded communities in America, Australia and his native Yorkshire.

HOUSES. There are a few C18 stone HOUSES here and there, with a concentration in Higher Hurst near the junction of Mossley Road, Gorsey Lane and Old Road. Mostly greatly altered, e.g. the JUNCTION INN, Mossley Road, a mid-C19 rebuilding of an earlier house with a crude flat-cut Venetian window in the side wall. On GORSEY LANE near the junction with Ashbourne Drive, GORSEY FARM COTTAGE is dated 1766. Two storeys, central door, but asymmetrical with mullioned windows. More C18 or earlier buildings on Links Place, just off Gorsey Lane, of which No. 437a is probably timber-framed beneath all the render and alterations, while its three-storey neighbour is of stone with mullioned windows.

3. Taunton

NE of the centre of Ashton-under-Lyne, on the border with Droylsden and Failsworth.

TAUNTON HALL, Newmarket Road. A late medieval cruck-framed hall of the de Cleyden family who were associated with the site from the C15, now split into two dwellings. Three bays, two storeys with a slightly projecting wing to the l. C18 brick in English garden wall bond, l. side, rendered brick walls on the r. and awful new windows, porch, etc. Three cruck trusses survive, two in the former hall, now ceiled over and with an inglenook, the other in the cross-wing. Tree-ring analysis suggests that the southern cruck truss was made from one tree felled in 1495–6, while the other two trusses have repositioned purlins of similar date, suggesting the actual trusses might be of earlier origin. The GATEPIERS are probably C17, tall, stone, with ball finials.

4. Waterloo

The area merges with the NW side of the centre of Ashton.

METHODIST CHURCH, Oldham Road. By *J. C. Prestwich & Sons* of Leigh, opened 1968. Low, wedge-shaped forms, two full-height angled piers at the entrance.

WILSHAW DALE COTTAGE and FARMHOUSE, Wilshaw Lane, near the junction with Oldham Road. A strange little building, stone, the l. farmhouse part with Gothick ogee window and doorheads with pretty intersecting glazing bars, the other part conventional with heavy stone lintels, dated 1812 over the door.

ASHWORTH

In the high, still rural area NW of Bamford between the Bury and Rochdale Road and the Edenfield Road.

ST JAMES, Chapel Lane. All by itself – excepting only the Egerton Arms pub – on a hilltop. The rare survival of a pre-Victorian chapel of ease (to Middleton), a thing once common in the area (e.g. Heywood, Milnrow, St Mary the Baum in Rochdale). Plain box of 1789, the successor to a chapel of 1514. The C16 chancel remained until 1837. Of stone, with twin entrances and two tiers of round-arched windows with inserted wooden Y-tracery. Plain well-lit interior with just a little stained glass. The gallery was removed in 1961. – MONUMENT. Tablet to the Rev. Joseph Selkirk, vicar 1821–32, with miniatures of himself and his wife.

ASHWORTH HALL and FOLD. An attractive group. Gatehouse
range with a cottage on either side of the arch and a long barn
attached, all probably C18, stone with stone roofs. The Hall
behind is a long brick house with a long unarticulated roof of
stone. The brick apparently faces a stone building which in
turn encases C16 timber-framing. Farm, more cottages, and a
pair of listed PIGSTIES on the road across from the gatehouse.

SCOTT HOUSE, Furbarn Lane, was the Memorial Home for
Crippled Children, built by Walter Scott of Rochdale in
memory of his wife Ellen, 1913, by *G. F. Armitage* of Altrincham. Big and spectacular. Stone for the ground floor and the
entrance tower, black-and-white timbering for the upper
floors, originally with open balconies; but all rather crude
close to.

   The footpath between Ashworth and Scott House dives into
an astonishingly pretty dell with the romantic ruins of
ASHWORTH MILL (woollen) on Naden Brook; four-storey,
stone, fragmentary.

AUDENSHAW

Audenshaw lies S and W of Ashton-under-Lyne, with which it
merges. The first tiny village, in existence by the C17, was
swallowed up by reservoirs built 1875–84. The area became built
up in the C19.

ST STEPHEN, Audenshaw Road. 1845–6 by *E. H. Shellard*. Sandstone ashlar but with small masonry blocks. Essentially this is
still of the Commissioners' type, i.e. paired lancets and buttresses along the sides, but the W tower with broach spire and
two tiers of lucarnes already recognizes the new principle of
archaeological accuracy. The cost was in fact partly met by the
Commissioners (£500). Chancel built 1900, in matching style.
(Interior with quatrefoil piers with fat shaft rings, three
galleries with Gothic parapets.)

CEMETERY, Cemetery Road. Opened 1905. Spare stone Tudor
lodges on each side of the entrance. WAR MEMORIAL facing
the entrance, unveiled 1920. Pedestal with a bronze statue of
a soldier in battledress by *P. G. Bentham*.

RYECROFT HALL, Manchester Road. There are three or four
large houses of the 1860s–80s on this stretch of Manchester
Road, of which this is the largest and best preserved. Built for
mill-owner Abel Buckley, *c.* 1860. The gardens are now a
municipal park and the house council offices. It is a good set-
piece with a stone entrance lodge and a large asymmetrical
Tudor Gothic carriage house behind the main building. Sober
externally, but gloriously unrestrained within. Entrance front
with unequal projecting gabled bays with a bay window and
oriel respectively, single-storey porch, transomed windows with
hoodmoulds. E side similarly treated. Vestibule with plasterwork Gothic panels on the walls and an arched entrance to the

hall with shafts and foliated caps. The splendid hall has the same traceried plasterwork walls and ceilings and a central octagonal gallery with a lantern over. Doors with traceried panelling and surrounds with arched heads also with shafts with foliated caps.

FAIRFIELD ARMS, Manchester Road. The best of the rest of a group of large detached houses. *c.* 1870. Polychrome brick and stone, Gothic. Stable block in matching style.

AUDENSHAW LODGE, Cornhill Lane. A brick house dated 1774, two storeys, central entrance, with an eaves cornice and flat rubbed brick window heads with stone keys. A world away stylistically from houses of similar or even later date in outer Ashton-under-Lyne and Mossley, with their asymmetrical elevations and mullioned windows. Another datestone of 1629 suggests a date for a predecessor building. Beside it a brick BARN, probably earlier. Opposed cart doors and raised brick lozenge and heart motifs in the gable.

BAGULEY HALL *see* MANCHESTER, WYTHENSHAWE, p. 503

BAMFORD   8010

Separated from Heywood, s, by the valley of the Roch. Visually continuous with Rochdale, it was nevertheless in the old Heywood Borough until 1974. Bamford does not really have a centre, and most places of interest cluster around the Bury and Rochdale Old Road, which runs sw to Bury, or routes leading from it.

ST MICHAEL, Bury and Rochdale Old Road. 1884–5 by *H. C. Charlewood*. A church of extreme simplicity, barely Gothic, but not small. Of stone, with a bell-turret over the chancel arch. Long nave and chancel and short aisles, like transepts. Spacious interior without colour or focus. It cost £4,000. Opposite, in the acute junction with Coal Pit Lane, is the Gothic SCHOOL of 1874 in blackened stone, by Mr *Spencer* of Heywood.

BAMFORD CHAPEL (United Reformed), Norden Road. Founded in 1801 by the Kays of Bury, a distinguished Non-conformist family, and the Fentons of Crimble Hall, land- and mill-owners and bankers. A pleasing northern ensemble with a school and manse in blackened stone set behind large trees. The chapel is in the middle. Its thin and very tight lancet front, with three steep gables, looks more 1840 than 1801. Chancel-like extension, in brick, *c.* 1850. Simple interior with a gallery on slender iron columns, again mid C19 in character rather than 1801. – Group of wall MONUMENTS to the founding families. SCHOOL on the l. dated 1861; MANSE, rebuilt 1939, on the r.

BAMFORD HALL, reached from a drive running N from Bury and Rochdale Old Road just SW of the built-up area. A Neoclassical mansion of 1841 with a giant Ionic portico has gone, but the parkland and LODGES remain.

BEAUMONDS, formerly Meadowcroft, Bury and Rochdale Old Road, by the junction with Meadowcroft Lane. An additive house originally of 1688 belonging to the Kays, but it is now mostly 1860 and c. 1900.

No. 15 Broadhalgh Avenue, formerly WHIRRIESTONE, 1907–9, is by *Parker & Unwin* for Mrs Ashworth. A distinguished house – Parker wrote that it 'exemplifies, more than any other I can call to mind in my own practice, the application of those principles of architecture and furnishing for which I have been contending' – with an unfortunate progeny: the house would be described today as a dormer bungalow. Those principles were informal open planning within a fairly formal envelope, and furnishing '– down to the very handle of the coal box –' according to the owner's wishes, and largely built-in.

Four buildings, each hip-roofed in heavy stone slabs, are grouped around a paved courtyard. In the front wall, originally an open pergola, a substantial lychgate. Behind that the house with, linked on either side by a low veranda to make a U, the billiard room and motor house. They are all roughcast white, with stone dressings and battered corner buttresses. Front door set to one side; on the other side, tiny windows and a tall chimney indicate the inglenook. The house was partly open-plan both horizontally and vertically; on the ground floor only a large living room, a kitchen and a study which could be opened up to the rest. Upstairs in the roof, bedrooms linked by a gallery overlook the open centre (apparently now floored across), lit by the long ranges of dormers. The flanking billiard room and motor house were added in 1910–11 when Mrs Ashworth remarried. The group, low, airy, contained, with separate structures linked by a veranda, is strongly suggestive of British colonial houses.

Immediately W the suburbs peter out into a tract of open country, criss-crossed by paths, with a good flagstone wall with diamond link-rivets, and Broadhalgh Fold, a typical fold with old cottages and farm buildings.

CRIMBLE HALL and FARM, Crimble Lane, in open country near the River Roch. Formerly the home of the Fenton family. The hall is a plain, early C19 dolls' house, with an ashlar front and rubble sides, in a fine position overlooking Heywood to the S. There is a ha-ha and some good planting, the farm of brick with symmetrical estate buildings. Walled gardens between the two.

CRIMBLE MILL, Crimble Lane, in the unbuilt-up valley of the Roch, between Bamford (N) and Heywood (S). An industrial site with a long history, owned by the Kenyon family for two centuries. A woollen water mill of 1761 was rebuilt c. 1829 for spinning cotton, then rebuilt in brick in 1886 (datestone). Five

storeys. In the mid C19 it was returned to wool-spinning and
a tall engine house for a beam engine and a circular chimney
of blue brick added at the s end.

HOOLEY BRIDGE MILL, Bamford Road. w of Bamford on the
Roch. A cotton-spinning mill belonging to the Fentons, Built
in the 1830s. A long even brick building on a tight site by the
river. Integral engine house, indicated by a tall arched window.

BARLOW HALL see MANCHESTER,
CHORLTON-CUM-HARDY, p. 413

BARTON-UPON-IRWELL see STRETFORD

BESSES O' TH' BARN see WHITEFIELD

BIRTLE or BIRCLE   *8010*

A dead-end settlement. A lane winds up through rough but not
unattractive country, eventually turning into a packhorse track
over the moors. It serves numerous stone cottages and small
farms, quarries, and a mill with its lodges. The simultaneous
growth of many such communities is what produced the ten-
tacular urbanization of the area.

ST JOHN BAPTIST, up Castle Hill, a dirt track linking Birtle with
Bury. By *George Shaw* 1845–6; his first church, and a competent if uncomplicated exercise in revived Gothic. The cost was
just £1,350, to which the Commissioners contributed £200.
Nave with bellcote, chancel, N vestry transept with typical
Shaw chimney like a miniature spire. Cusped lancets throughout. Built of watershot stonework, which means tilting each
stone outwards slightly to throw off water, a vernacular technique unusual in a church. Hammerbeam roof with well-
modelled angels. Neatly reordered with an inserted two-storey
narthex in 1999 by *John Ashley*. – FONT. Perhaps the only
remaining *Shaw* fitting, simple Gothic. – STAINED GLASS.
Triple E lancet by *T. Willement* 1846, geometric grisaille with a
single figure. His 1845 design for the window had seven figures.
  Attractive CHURCHYARD. The rocks and rough moorland
vegetation of the old quarry in which it was built set the
crowded monuments and the little church off to perfection.

BLACKROD   *6010*

A hilltop village straggling along the old A6. Long associated with
coalmining, it had at least seven pits.

ST KATHARINE. A chapel of ease of Bolton is recorded here in
1338. It finally became a parish in 1858. Blunt w tower of asymmetric silhouette set at an angle to the rest. In its lowest part
it is Perp with diagonal buttresses, then of 1628 (datestone)

with odd Perp-survival tracery in the w window. Above that c18 with quoins, and finally of 1837 (the clock stage above the bells). A square stair-tower was added on the NE corner, dated (on the step) 1647, which was heightened with the other phases. The rest is simpler. Double nave, or nave and s aisle, and a long chancel, by *R. B. Preston*, with Dec windows alternately of two and three lights. The chancel and the two E bays came first in 1905, then in 1911 the old church in between was rebuilt to match. Preston's feeling for stone shows in the fine masonry of the nave and aisle. Low double-chamfered tower arch. A five-bay arcade with octagonal piers separates the two naves. In 2001 a two-storey parish centre by *Graham Holland* was inserted in the w bays of the aisle only; a successful solution to a common brief. – STAINED GLASS. An enjoyable modern collection. E window signed *M. Lowndes*, 1914. s aisle E, where there was a Lady Chapel altar, the Annunciation; 1943. Nave s side, Jesus in the carpenter's shop, by *Wippell*, 1991, and a roundel on the same subject. Three windows by *Linda Walton* of *Design Lights* whose studio is in the village. Nave NW, God and children from many lands, 1992. Chancel s, St Cecilia, 1999. Angel Voices, sw, partly obscured by the upper room, signed S.W. 1980.

WESLEYAN CHAPEL. 1899, of red brick and terracotta with some stone.

LIBRARY, opposite the church. Of 1975, i.e. immediately after Blackrod was taken into Bolton Metropolitan Borough. Square, with a tall pyramidal skylight, but this has been blocked off inside.

CHORLEY ROAD. No. 1 is the former Co-op, and entirely typical with its white terracotta front. It is now Design Lights stained glass studio.

RAMADA JARVIS HOTEL, on the A6 towards Westhoughton. It incorporates HILTON HOUSE, Georgian, brick, five bays and three storeys with two-bay links and two-bay pavilions. Interior not preserved.

ARLEY HALL, 2m. w. Now Wigan Golf Club, but in a salient of Bolton Metropolitan Borough. A delightful picture, with its moat and its odd and various Gothicisms. The s front with shaped gables and straight-topped windows must be c19, but the w wing has little quatrefoils and mullioned windows with concave-sided triangular heads and must be still c18. Pretty porch on this side in the Strawberry Hill mode. More delicate Gothicisms inside in the way of fireplaces, doors and doorcases, but a chunky cantilever stair between the wings belongs to the c19 phase. All this must be an overlay on an older house, traces of which may be seen in the former kitchen with its triple-arched fireplace with passageway behind – a classical motif but a vernacular plan-type.

The MOAT is circular and wide, enclosing a tiny platform. Handsome STABLE by the bridge, brick and stone, symmetrical, with oval hay holes. The Leeds & Liverpool Canal passes immediately to the E. Over the canal bridge ABBEY FARM,

c18, has a big Gothic window shape as decoration on its gable
end. The WATCH TOWER is a little eye-catcher at the W end of
the former garden.

BOLTON

INTRODUCTION

Bolton, or as it was once called, Bolton-le-Moors; a market town
in rough country. The market charter was granted in 1256. But
already in the C16 Leland had remarked that the market 'ston-
deth most by cottons and course yarne'. In 1807 *The Beauties of
England and Wales* called it a large thriving manufacturing town,
adding 'it is traditionally asserted that the cotton manufacturing
machinery originated here'. This refers to the C18 inventions of
Arkwright and especially Samuel Crompton (see Hall i' th' Wood
and Firwood Fold). Bolton's business was fine spinning in quantity, whereas Oldham's was coarse spinning in vast quantity. In
1920 there were around 160 spinning mills. Many still stand, a
few complete, but not one is still spinning.* Related to the cotton
industry was engineering, notably the firm of Hick Hargreaves,
who only quitted their premises of 1833 in 2002, and the fabrication of structural steelwork – still a Bolton speciality. In the
surrounding valleys, where water was plentiful, were the bleach-
and dye-works that finished the cotton: see for instance Barrow
Bridge, Bolton; Bradshaw; and Wallsuches at Horwich.† Now
that their polluting processes are at an end the rivers have slowly

---

*For a detailed account see James H. Longworth, *The Cotton Mills of Bolton
1780–1985*, 1987.
†Belmont dyeworks, just N of the borough on the A675, is still working, filling its
valley with steam and turning the stream every colour.

become clean and the land green. This must be one of the most striking changes between any first and second edition of *The Buildings of England*. The pity is that the land, newly revealed in beauty, is so often immediately covered with bijou houses.

The Metropolitan Borough of Bolton was created in 1974, combining the Borough of Bolton with those of Blackrod, Farnworth, Horwich, Kearsley, Little Lever, part of Turton, and Westhoughton. The population of the Borough in 2001 was 261,035, and growing. Bolton itself, although one of the largest towns in Lancashire, has a declining population, from 168,000 in 1901 to 160,000 in 1969.

One architectural distinction of Bolton and its dependencies is an absence: no high-rises. This is very evident in the panorama from Scout Road, above Smithills. The tallest structures were the mill chimneys. Now they are gone, allowing the Victorian town hall to be the dominating landmark; a rare privilege. The town, oddly, appears to have shrunk into itself.

Bolton has managed to preserve two historic halls, Smithills and Hall i' th' Wood, both of them with early connections with the textile industry, but Great Lever Hall and Darcy Lever Hall have been allowed to disappear. A good place to appreciate the early settlement pattern is N of the town, between Hall i' th' Wood and Firwood Fold, where the old lane winds its way (though heartlessly cut up by the ring road) from one little industrial settlement to another between Bradshaw Brook and the River Tonge.

There are several Bolton architects to watch. *James Greenhalgh* was Bolton's principal, certainly most interesting, architect of the early C19, able to build Greek (Lower Bridgeman Street Assembly Hall and Baths, *see* Streets, below), Gothic (St Paul, Halliwell), Tudor (cottages and schools by St Paul's) and Dutch (St George's School, Little Bolton). *J. W. Whittaker* (*see* St Peter, Halliwell), also working in the early C19, has caused confusion with his namesake and contemporary, the clergyman architect J. W. Whittaker of Blackburn. *George Woodhouse* (*c.* 1829–83) dominates mid-Victorian Bolton. He was, said *The Builder* in 1873, a 'local architect of more than average ability'. His buildings in Mawdsley Street bear that out. He was a prolific chapel builder in a variety of styles, collaborating with *William Hill* in the building of the town hall, and with other architects in the workhouses at Fishpool (Farnworth) and Dearnley (Littleborough). *Richard Knill Freeman* (1838/9–1904) was able to produce nice work, *see* the Old Grammar School by the parish church, St Augustine, Tonge Moor, and St Catherine at Horwich. The Miners' Federation Hall of 1913–14 on Bridgeman Place (*see* Streets, below), tough-looking, excellently built of hard-wearing materials in an Edwardian Baroque style, can introduce the pre-eminent firm in the C20, *Bradshaw Gass & Hope* of Silverwell Street. Still extant, and interesting because they reflect the character of Bolton so well, the firm was founded in 1862 by *Jonas James Bradshaw*, who took his nephew *John Bradshaw Gass* on in 1871, moving into Silverwell Street at about the same time. Gass became a partner in

1881, and in 1900 they were joined by *Arthur John Hope*. When Bradshaw died in 1912 they simply took the comma out. During the first half of the c20 the firm had a high reputation, building cotton mills, grand houses, Nonconformist churches, and public buildings across the country. The climax was the Manchester Royal Exchange in 1921. The firm was expert in flat roofs and structural steel. Today, led by *David Clarke*, they are busy with educational and hospital commissions. Bolton is also the home of the prolific c20 Catholic architects, *Greenhalgh & Williams*.

It is worth looking out for the c20 STAINED GLASS of *Edith Norris* of Tonge Moor Road, whose work appears in many of the suburban churches. She has a worthy successor in *Linda Walton* of *Design Lights* at Blackrod.

Finally, no account of Bolton would be complete without reference to Lord Leverhulme. William Hesketh Lever was born in Wood Street in 1851 (*see* Streets, below), went to the dame school across the road, where he made friends with his future architectural right-hand man, *Jonathan Simpson** and met his future wife. He learned his trade at his father's grocery warehouse in Manor Street, the continuation of Bank Street in Little Bolton. He went on to build an enormous fortune by revolutionizing the manufacture and the marketing of soap. He was created baron in 1917 and viscount in 1922. A man of intense loyalties, he never forgot a friend, and nor did he forget the place of his birth. Architecture was a passion, allied to social engineering. The rescue and refurbishment of Hall i' th' Wood is a typical combination of philanthropy, sentiment and the desire to educate. Immediately north of the borough, at Rivington (N Lancashire) he built himself a palatial bungalow and an astonishing garden, and gave Boltonians a mountain playground. Westcombe in Heaton was one of his many houses. The Congregational churches in Little Bolton and Astley Bridge reflect his religious views and devotion to his parents. In 1916, for Lever, *T. H. Mawson* gave and published a series of lectures called 'Bolton as it is and as it might be', proposing Beaux-Arts boulevards, a new museum in Queens Park of American appearance, an important precursor of the Lady Lever Gallery at Port Sunlight, Cheshire, and a peripheral parkway system. Bolton had already undertaken its own programme of street improvements, at Bradshawgate for example, and little came of the scheme, but its influence can be seen in Leverhulme Park and Deane Clough, in Bolton School, in Le Mans Crescent, and in the modern ring roads.

THE CENTRE

The centre is circumscribed by the rectangle of St Peter's Way on the E, Topp Way N, Marsden Road W, and Moor Lane and Trinity Street S.

---

* Jonathan Simpson (1850–1937) was articled to *James Lomax*, married his daughter, and named his son *James Lomax Simpson*, later James Lomax-Simpson.

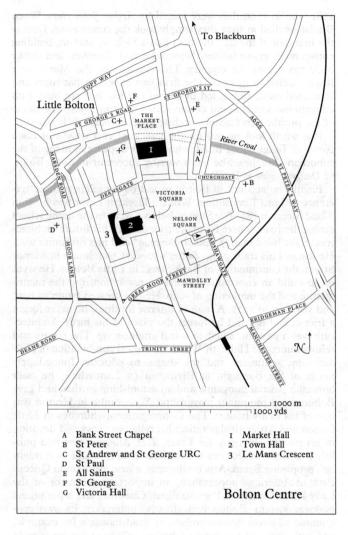

To Blackburn

Little Bolton

THE MARKET PLACE

River Croal

VICTORIA SQUARE

NELSON SQUARE

MAWDSLEY STREET

BRIDGEMAN PLACE

DEANE ROAD

TRINITY STREET

1000 m
1000 yds

A	Bank Street Chapel	1	Market Hall
B	St Peter	2	Town Hall
C	St Andrew and St George URC	3	Le Mans Crescent
D	St Paul		
E	All Saints		
F	St George		
G	Victoria Hall		

Bolton Centre

The centre is divided into Bolton proper, which follows, and Little Bolton across the River Croal on p. 147.

PLACES OF WORSHIP

Lancashire was and is a strongly Catholic county. Not so Bolton, which was called The Geneva of the North for its Protestant stance. Even now the Anglican churches of the area are nearly all distinctly low-church in their furnishings. The mother-church of the Catholic emancipation, St Peter and St Paul, is hidden out of town towards Daubhill.

St Peter, Churchgate. The medieval parish church, an oft-altered example of Lancashire Perp, was cleared away in 1866. Its late C18 GATES and GATEPIERS remain.

The formidable new church is by *E. G. Paley*, 1867–71. It has none of the prettiness of Paley's earlier partner, Sharpe, nor the inventiveness that Austin was to bring to the practice. The whole was paid for by Peter Ormrod, cotton-spinner, to the tune of £45,000, and he got nothing but the best: the most scholarly Dec from the acknowledged expert, the tallest tower in Lancashire, the finest ashlar inside and out, a vaulted chancel. At 180 ft (55 metres) the NW tower is actually too tall for comfort, giving the illusion of leaning towards the church. It is awkwardly jointed into four equal storeys, with too many set-offs to the buttresses. Nave and aisles, transepts, chancel and aisles are all pulled into a near-rectangular footprint. The outline is rectangular too, the chancel very nearly as high as the nave. The traceries of the principal windows are from published sources, e.g. the S transept from Temple Balsall in Warwickshire.

The interior is cold and tall, the nave with a high cradle roof, the short transepts with single-framing. Slender clustered piers for the five-bay arcade, which hardly alters its rhythm for the transepts. Paired clerestory windows of clear glass flood the church with cold light; triplets of blank windows for the transepts. The chancel is a fully cathedral-like ensemble, with its tierceron rib-vault and bosses, triforium, naturalistic capitals, and huge window. – The REREDOS is by *Paley & Austin*, 1878. – Fine decorative FLOORS at the E and W ends with mosaic, marbles and tiles. The rest relaid in the 1980s with the sort of white compo used for airport and station concourses.

An Anglo-Saxon CROSS was found when the old church was demolished, and is displayed just inside the NW door. Similar to the chief Whalley cross (N Lancashire) but with the interlace in compartments. The head is partly preserved. A few furnishings from the old church have been collected museum-style in the SW corner, including three MISERICORDS and the Perp STALL of Andrew Barton of Smithills, and some Norman fragments. – FONT and COVER, 1938, by *Cachemaille-Day*.

STAINED GLASS. In the N transept is the E window of the old church *c.* 1850, the traceries rearranged somewhat. Hot colours; said to be by *Wailes*. The present E window in memory of Peter Ormrod is by *Hardman*. – MONUMENTS from the old church are gathered in the NW and SW corners and under the tower. John Taylor †1824 by *Chantrey*; profile on a draped base. – Ralph Fletcher †1832; mourning woman by an urn. – Benjamin Hick, engineer †1842; a kneeling youth and a standing woman unveiling the portrait of the deceased. – By the S door, Mary Isabel Winder †1915 and her infant daughter, a

Anglo-Saxon cross, Bolton
(University of Manchester Archaeological Unit)

beautiful white low relief on blue slate. Outside in the churchyard, Samuel Crompton †1827; plain grey granite chest.

SE of the chancel is the OLD GRAMMAR SCHOOL by
R. Knill Freeman, 1883, now the parish centre. An enterprising
little building. Replacing a C17 building like the one remaining at Middleton (q.v.), it served only until 1897 when the
school moved to Chorley New Road. The Church Institute and
the Sunday School have gone, and the churchyard is bleakly
landscaped, with a large car park.

ST PAUL, Spa Road, facing the end of Deansgate, on a spot
which has a history of contentious Nonconformist building.
1862–5, by *J. Murray* of Coventry. The corner site is very tight
but prominent from the E and N. The architect has responded
with a picturesque composition, placing the spire at the NE
corner and multiplying the gables on both sides. Round
clerestory windows in a continuous row. The bare interior has
been crudely subdivided. Short polished granite piers with
clumsy foliage capitals. High roof supported by what look like

arched girders but are a form of scissor-bracing. – STAINED
GLASS. E, by *Heaton, Butler & Bayne*. The church was due to
be sold in 2003.

Former SCHOOL, immediately S, 1867–70.

HOLY TRINITY, Trinity Street. By *Thomas Hardwick*, 1823–6. A
Commissioners' church and an expensive one. The cost was
nearly £14,000. The church is of the Commissioners' type too,
but handled with uncommon earnestness, with convincing
Perp tracery and a substantial W tower. (The piers of the seven-
bay arcades have no capitals. The nave ceiling has depressed-
pointed transverse arches of wood, the aisles are given
octopartite plaster rib-vaults.) Declared redundant in 1993.
SCHOOL, S, in Crook Street. 1866, large, of stone and Gothic.

ST EDMUND (R.C.), St Edmund's Street. 1860. Nave and
chancel only, rising above an undercroft as the ground falls.

ST PATRICK (R.C.), Great Moor Street. 1861 by *Charles Holt*.
SW turret and rose window with spherical triangles in horizontal rows, not radiating. Gothic Presbytery. Short interior
with a single crooked aisle.

BANK STREET CHAPEL (Unitarian). By *George Woodhouse*, 1856,
replacing a T-shaped chapel of 1696. E.E. front of ashlar facing
Bank Street. The rest, hard to see, is of coursed rubble with
very tall lancets. The interior is tightly cruciform, tall and
fragile-looking like the Unitarians' Dukinfield Chapel in
Cheshire, dominated by the organ and pulpit. Steeply raked
galleries on slender iron columns. – STAINED GLASS by
Capronnier, E and W. Three late ones by *Morris & Co.*, 1920,
1928–9 and 1934. By *Walter J. Pearce*, at the sides, 1904–15. The
latter are bisected by the gallery, so that the lower figures have
their heads chopped off. This had been taken into account
by *Heaton, Butler & Bayne* with their portrait medallion of
Longfellow, S side, 1878. On the back wall three PEW DOORS
from the old chapel are preserved.

VICTORIA HALL, Knowsley Street. A Wesleyan Mission, by
Bradshaw & Gass, 1898–1900. The Forward movement at the
end of the C19 sought to reach the disaffected with 'Central
Halls' like this, unchurchy, open all the time, with a social as
well as a religious message. This, one of the first, was largely
paid for by Thomas Walker, a tanner. The entrance tower, all
bright red terracotta and brick, breaks through the then
recently completed block of Victoria Buildings, upsetting its
symmetry but hardly interfering with its fenestration. Behind
is the theatre-like auditorium. Raked seating, U-shaped gallery
also raked on iron pillars with Composite capitals, coved
ceiling with a canopy over the dais. Glass with Renaissance
strapwork in yellows. Dais and seating were updated in the
1970s. The extension on the S side, of 1932, is on the site of
the Ridgeway Gates chapel of 1776.

FRIENDS' MEETING HOUSE, Silverwell Street. 1970–1 by *W. T.
Gunson & Son*. Two-storey social building and caretaker's
house, low link, meeting room set diagonally, its tilted roof
floating on the fully glazed upper walls.

PUBLIC BUILDINGS

62 TOWN HALL, Victoria Square. Built 1866–73. Still the dominant
accent of low-rise Bolton, its 200 ft (60 metre) high tower
unchallenged now that the chimneys have gone. It is exactly
contemporary with Rochdale's town hall, and a year or so
ahead of Manchester's – but they are both Gothic. Bolton
wanted its town hall classical. A competition was held and
adjudicated by Professor Donaldson, which was won by Leeds
man, *William Hill*. He was assisted by the Bolton architect
George Woodhouse.

   The result is very like Leeds: a simple square clothed all
round by a giant Corinthian order, a tall domed tower over the
entrance and a prominent square ventilator stack on each side.
But it is perkier than Leeds, less heavily weighed down by its
cornice, slimmer in its tower and dome, and fronted by a fully
developed six-column portico with a pediment. SCULPTURE
in the pediment by *William Calder Marshall* represents Bolton
with Manufacture, Agriculture, Cotton, Commerce and Trade.
Bradshaw Gass & Hope put forward a grand redevelopment
plan in 1927 for the town hall and its surroundings, most of
which was implemented in the 1930s and completed in 1939
(*see* also Le Mans Crescent, below). The town hall was doubled
in size, repeating Hill's side elevations. New entrances were
built at ground level with the regrettable result that the great
portico with its lions and cascade of steps is now scarcely used.

   The original plan is simple: stairs at the corners, offices and
ceremonial rooms along the sides, a square of corridors, the
hall in the middle. The extension makes another square but
with an internal courtyard faced with glazed brick in place of
the great hall. *The Builder*, generally lukewarm about the building, criticized the lack of an internal grand stair. This has been
partially remedied with a new flight from the NE entrance. The
Great Hall was never satisfactory because of its excessive
height. It was burnt out in 1981 and has been rebuilt in two
storeys, the ALBERT HALLS, by the *Borough Architect's Department*. The upper hall, now with raked seating, preserves the
basic shape of the room with its (blocked) clerestory of lunette
windows with plaster figure groups at the corners of the four
seasons by *Mr Paul*; 'not high art, but well intentioned' said
The Builder. The Council Chamber was on the N side; now the
DINING ROOM, with little to distinguish it except for some fine
civic furniture. At the SE corner is the RECEPTION ROOM,
with paired-column screens at the ends and a magnificent
buffet and mirror sporting the municipal elephants. The 'over-
use of gilded vegetation, the figures in the ceiling representing
planets, months and elements, and the silhouettes of edible
animals round the walls' reported by *The Builder* have all disappeared. Mayor's parlour, Mayoress's parlour and ante-room
belong to the 1930s phase, with flush wood veneers.

   LE MANS CRESCENT. Also by *Bradshaw Gass & Hope* and
carried out at the same time as the extension to the town hall,

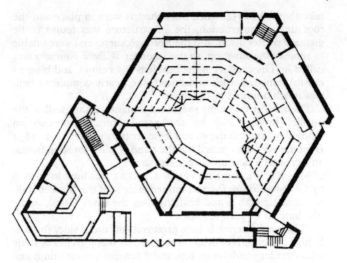

Bolton, Octagon Theatre, plan

1932–9. It gives the town hall, whose mean setting had aroused much criticism, a worthy backdrop. It is a long narrow building concave on the town hall side to form a quadrant, and flat on the other. Ionic columns frame the entrances at the ends. Museum, gallery and library are housed at the s end, council offices at the N. Three arches pierce the centre, like Admiralty Arch in London – but they lead nowhere. But there is, surprisingly, no tiredness. The panache is kept up.

OCTAGON THEATRE, Howell Croft South. 1967 by the Borough Architect *Geoffrey H. Brooks*. A welcome dose of honest Brutalism among the clad buildings of Bolton. A light glass and steel façade wraps round the concrete-framed foyers and café. Behind is the hexagonal auditorium block of brown brick with occasional slit windows cantilevered inwards. The auditorium itself is octagonal with flexible seating.

OCTAGON MULTI-STOREY CAR PARK, next door. 1987, by *Balfour Beatty Ltd*, project architect *R. Boyle*.

MARKET HALL, Knowsley Street. 1851–6, by *G. T. Robinson*, who was selected in a competition assessed by George Godwin. The brainchild of Councillor T. L. Rushton, who was mayor 1848–50, this was a huge undertaking. The market's previous home had been in what is now Victoria Square, whence it had been moved from the ancient Market Place – *see* Streets.

The site fell steeply away to the river, and was covered with a maze of cul-de-sacs and slum dwellings. The ground had to be built up to a level by means of a great vaulted undercroft. New streets had to be made – Market Street, Corporation Street and Knowsley Street – and a new river bridge at high level made for Knowsley Street. Only then could the hall itself take shape. In 1854, when the columns were in place and the roof under construction, the substructure was found to be giving way. Robinson, and the Borough surveyors, were unable to remedy the situation, so the engineer *William Fairbairn* was called in. His analysis of the problem (*see* below), and his successful remedial work underneath the nearly completed hall, was much admired at the time.

The market originally presented a blank curtain wall to the ouside, broken only by the grand entrance portico on Knowsley Street to the w, and lesser entrances s and e. In 1894 *Bradshaw & Gass* opened out the s and w walls for shop fronts, and created a new se corner entrance.

The MARKET PLACE SHOPPING CENTRE was built in 1980–8 by *Chapman Taylor Partners* immediately N of the Market Hall, interlocking with it and bridging over the River Croal; so the two have to be seen together.

Robinson's exterior is best preserved on the e side, towards Bridge Street. It is of brick, articulated by blank arches of stone with circular windows on top, and a generous stone plinth and cornice. In the centre is the Doric entrance with its sliding doors of wood and iron, and Bolton arms. The N side, now inside the Market Place Centre, is also largely complete. On the s and w are *Bradshaw & Gass*'s well-preserved shop façades of 1894, each with a mezzanine, and a run of cast-iron windows along the upper floor. There is a nice shallow oriel in cast iron on the se quarter. Robinson's s entrance is unaltered, and so is his grand six-columned Corinthian portico to Knowsley Street. On the roof are brick corner ventilator towers – but the sw one is lost.

Chapman Taylor Partners' MARKET PLACE CENTRE is in that most ephemeral of styles, a jokey Postmodernism. Many are the references that can be picked up in this indigestible concoction, the most obvious being the bell-shaped dome of the adjacent Victoria Hall which has pupped, not only on the aedicules which give the exterior its exciting skyline, but inside too in the many light shades. Shops are arranged about a two-level mall with top-lit interpenetrations at intervals which are decked out with marbled bogus architecture, imitation Tiffany chandeliers and mosaic and tile floors in loud colours. A flying stair hangs alarmingly from a pod-like landing high above the 'outdoor' café. The mall interlocks cleverly with the market hall by means of a big circular balcony piercing the c19 wall above a pair of escalators.

59   The interior of the 1855 MARKET HALL is like a lemon sorbet after all this: lucid structure simply revealed. It is covered by an elegant iron and glass roof with a cruciform clerestory within the rectangle. The crossing is marked by diagonals rising by means of iron hammerbeams to make an interrupted X, which originally carried a tall ventilator tower. Round all four sides runs a balcony, its decorative iron balustrade preserved on the e and N sides, together with, flanking the e entrance, one of the original flights of steps.

The UNDERCROFT, used for storage, is highly impressive in spite of subdivision and festoons of service ducting. A wider roadway runs around the periphery. This is what caused Robinson's substructure to fail, because the uneven vaulting spans loaded his square columns (clearly visible along the E and W roadways) unequally. Fairbairn's inserted brick arches run N–S. The undercroft opens by three arches piercing the massively rusticated basement storey facing the river, but this is now hidden by the substructure of the Market Place Centre.

Worth searching out on the Bridge Street steps are SCULPTURES from Sunnyside Mill at Daubhill (see p. 143), of *c.* 1880 by *J. Bonehill & Co.* They are wide pilaster capitals incorporating scenes of cotton growing, picking and processing.

COVERED MARKET, Ashburner Street. Of 1932, on the site of the Bolton Iron & Steel Co.'s foundry. The Borough Engineer is recorded, *W. Russell Brown,* but not an architect. It is less ambitious than the 1855 Market Hall, but nevertheless attractive and retaining more of the market atmosphere. Outer face of two-storey brick, Neo-Georgian, enclosing parallel rows of partially glazed steel roofs. The WEIGHTS AND MEASURES BUILDING on the N side is small in scale, but a full Palladian composition with a five-bay centre, low links and flanking pavilions.

LAW COURTS, Queen Street. 1982 by the *Property Services Agency.* Arbitrarily positioned in an open space and fortress-like, it looks more like a relic from the distant past than a recent addition to the town. Clad in sandstone slabs hung vertically, it is an irregular polygon with random projections and small windows. It stands in a defensive-looking dry moat, which doubles as a car-park, reinforcing the castle image. On the grass outside SCULPTURE by *Barbara Hepworth,* Two Forms (Divided Circle) 1969.

LADS' & GIRLS' CLUB, Spa Road. By *Michael Hyde Partners,* 2002. Large multipurpose building faced with yellow brick and glass with a trendy wave roof. The club was founded on Bark Street in 1889.

RAILWAY STATION, Trinity Street. By *William Hunt,* 1899–1904, for the Lancashire & Yorkshire Railway. Not much left at street level, just the little clock tower, of red terracotta and grey granite, rebuilt (lower) next to the new booking office. At platform level the long canopies are preserved, and the buildings faced with glazed brick in butterscotch and toffee colours, but severely underused.

STREETS

The two principal streets are Bradshawgate, running S–N into Bank Street and over the River Croal to Little Bolton (see below), and Deansgate, running W–E, past the parish church at Churchgate and over the river again towards Bury. The market cross, an Edwardian replacement, stands where they meet. Bolton's centre

is genuinely metropolitan, but it has none of the glitz that has
overtaken Manchester. It is regular and grid-like, surprisingly
grand in scale, but even and prosaic. The drama of Bolton was
all in its heavy industry, which has gone. 1901–14 were the years
of street widening and straightening, with a further phase in the
1930s. The rebuilt fronts are of terracotta or faience before the
war, Portland stone after it. Three or four storeys high, richly if
meretriciously decorated, they are too often now neglected, their
ground floors stripped out and the upper parts grubby.

The following is arranged in walkable order, although a grid of
streets is never easy to perambulate meaningfully.

VICTORIA SQUARE. New Market Place was opened out in 1832.
The Town Hall occupies much of it; what is left runs N and S
into Oxford Street and Newport Street North, all pedestrian-
ized in 1969 (an early scheme), creating an ill-defined space
with no sense of enclosure. This has perhaps been felt for a
long time, for the following are all placed in symmetrical relation to the town hall steps. STATUES of Dr Samuel Chadwick,
1873, by *C. B. Birch*, and of Lieut-Col. Sir B. A. Dobson, 1900,
by *John Cassidy*. WAR MEMORIAL, 1928, by *A. J. Hope*, a symbolic arch or gateway. Bronze sculpture by *Walter Marsden*
added in 1933 – 'Struggle' on the N side, 'Sacrifice' on the S.
Tacky FOUNTAINS, 1964. SCULPTURE: a pair of elephants and
castles, the municipal emblem, from Bolton Bleachworks in
Chorley Street, *c.* 1850; now on the pillars of a shelter. STEAM
ENGINE of 1886 made by Hick Hargreaves, preserved on
Oxford Street in a glass box. The only decent building, unbalanced since the demolition of the Commercial Hotel,
is the former EXCHANGE of 1824–5 by *Richard Lane*. Free-
standing, but looking as though designed to fit in a row. Of
finest ashlar, Grecian, of five bays, with two unfluted Ionic
columns *in antis* and panels with the caduceus sign of Hermes
and of Commerce, and wreaths. The former CO-OP on the
corner of Oxford Street is by *Bradshaw Gass & Hope*, 1931.
The frontage of the former ARNDALE CENTRE, 1971, throws
away the best site in town, facing the town hall. It is low and
mean, with a flat roof and token stone-cladding. It was given
a face-lift and rebranded as CROMPTON PLACE in 1989 by
Bradshaw, Rose & Harker. An uninviting entry in front of the
exchange leads throught to Mawdsley Street.

MAWDSLEY STREET. Thomas Mawson in 1917 lamented the
fact that some of Bolton's best buildings lined this short and
narrow street, whereas there was little to impress on Victoria
Square. It is still true. Interspersed with a number of Late
Georgian houses are, starting from the N end: the GALLERIA
Shopping Centre and ST ANDREW'S COURT of 1987 by
J. Holland of *GWBD Partnership*, neatly contrived on a tight
site, and BRIDGEMAN BUILDINGS of *c.* 1865, followed by the
former COUNTY COURT of 1869–70 by the County Surveyor
Thomas Charles Sorby: a palazzo, all sober ashlar, but now a

pub. Then comes a disastrous gap, showing the court's shorn-off end. Nos. 25 and 27, originally the Constitutional Club and an office annexe, are by *George Woodhouse*, 1869–70. Inventive Venetian Gothic, exhibiting constructional polychromy. Their backs are good too. Opposite another palazzo, this time with a central archway to a rear yard, and the former POOR LAW OFFICES of 1865. On the corner of Bold Street is the MECHANICS' INSTITUTE of 1868–70, which was handed over to the authority and reopened as the Technical School in 1891, and is now a gym. Brick and much stone, tall and Italianate, it makes the most of its tight site with machicolations and a big cornice at the top, but appears to have lost a corner tower.

From here a continuation may be made to Great Moor Street and Bridgeman Street, or a short cut through E to Nelson Square (*see* below).

In GREAT MOOR STREET is a big red SCHOOL of 1896–7 by *R. Knill Freeman*, for 1,080 children, later a technical college and now flats. Completely symmetrical except for the entrance, which dodges to one side in an upsetting way to avoid the central oriel. The classrooms were on the front and back. The whole of the centre was a transverse open hall, with dining room below and laboratories above. Opposite, the former TURKISH BATHS of 1890–1 by *Stones & Chadwell*: a sweet Italianate building in brick and buff matt terracotta. From here a foray can be made to BRIDGEMAN PLACE for the MINERS' FEDERATION HALL of 1913–14 by *Bradshaw, Gass & Hope* in Ruabon brick and Darley Dale stone, and typically Wrennish. Opposite on LOWER BRIDGEMAN STREET, the former ASSEMBLY HALL and PUBLIC BATHS by *James Greenhalgh*, 1845; classical, with monolithic Doric piers for the portico and doorcases. On ASH STREET between the two is the neat little GLOBE HOSIERY WORKS of 1884, altered 1929, with its chimney made a feature on a central pedestal.

NELSON SQUARE was completed in 1823. STATUE of Samuel Crompton by *Calder Marshall*, unveiled to great crowds in 1862. Reliefs on the pedestal of the young Crompton with his fiddle and mule, and of Hall i' th' Wood. Bolton Artillery CENOTAPH, a Portland stone stele by *Ormrod, Pomeroy & Foy*, 1920, stark and unadorned.

Nelson Square debouches onto BRADSHAWGATE, a drearily wide and under-occupied street like Great Moor Street. On the S corner of Nelson Square is a typically red and shiny former PRUDENTIAL of 1889, surprisingly not by Waterhouse (though he was consulted), but by *Ralph B. Maccoll* of Bolton. At the N end of Bradshawgate a fine run of early C20 faience [4] façades in mushy pea, ginger nut, liver, tripe and blood orange shades runs into Deansgate. The most pleasing of the plateful is the floridly Renaissance YATES'S WINE BAR of 1906, by *W. H. Smith*; symmetrical, with circular windows and a shallow oriel on the top floor. The PACK HORSE HOTEL of 1904 is by *Jonathan Simpson* for Magee Marshall, with *Robert W. Edis* of London, and was lavishly fitted out with mirrors, marbles

and mosaic. The corner building, now Subway Snacks, is by
W.H. Smith again.

Off the E side of Bradshawgate is SILVERWELL STREET,
built in 1810. Here are the offices of *Bradshaw Gass & Hope*,
established here in 1860 in a pleasant Late Georgian terrace
with carriageway arches through to the yard. No. 13, dated
1903, taller and faced in terracotta, was the Estate Office of
the Earl of Bradford. The archway opposite No. 13 leads to No.
1 SILVERWELL LANE, formerly Silverwell House, of 1790,
for many years attached to the now-demolished Drill Hall
which hid it completely. Now freed, its white painted façade
with three-storey canted bays makes a good addition to the
streetscape. Interesting recent small-scale HOUSING, by
Pozzoni Design Group, in front of No. 1 (in place of the drill
hall). Around CLIVE STREET, red yellow and blue brick terraces of 2002 for the Portico Housing Association. THE
ARCHES, *Urban Splash* apartments in tomato-red cladding,
yellow brick and silver metal, 2003. LANCASTER CLOSE,
1976, is negligible architecturally but of interest as Britain's
first RAF sheltered housing.

WOOD STREET is a dead end (blocked by a garden fenced with
Rochdale flags) of plain three-storey Georgian houses, including at No. 16 the birthplace of William Hesketh Lever, and a
single stone palazzo, the BOLTON SAVINGS BANK (now Pizza
Express), of shortly before 1849 by *J. E. Gregan*.

CHURCHGATE, the original market place, was the natural gathering place before the steep descent to the river crossing,
although the A666 fills the valley now. Once densely populated,
this short street sported until the 1960s two *Frank Matcham*
theatres, a cinema, seven pubs and two Temperance bars.
MARKET CROSS 1909 of Dartmoor granite, by *Bradshaw, Gass
& Hope*, with a potted history of Bolton inscribed upon its
sides.* Here in 1651 James, 7th Earl of Derby, was executed,
declaring on the scaffold, 'The Lord send us our King again,
and the Lord send us our old religion again.' MAN & SCYTHE,
rebuilt in 1636; small-scale, with vestiges of timber framing.
SWAN HOTEL rebuilt 1845, altered 1930 and 1981. Lumpish
office buildings frame the church gates, TRAVEL HOUSE,
NEWSPAPER HOUSE of 1998, and CHURCHGATE HOUSE of
1974.

DEANSGATE continues w from Churchgate. Like Bradshawgate
it starts off quite grand at the Churchgate end, but fizzles out
at the w. PRESTON'S jewellers on the corner of Bank Street is
a greeny-yellow terracotta palace by *Thomas Smith & Sons*,
1908 and 1913. It had a Time Ball on the corner turret, which
dropped at midday. In Mealhouse Lane is the former
EMPRESS BALLROOM of blood-red terracotta, 1900, lavishly
Baroque but maltreated. Next to it the former Tillotson's
Bolton Evening News building, of c. 1900 by *Bradshaw & Gass*,

* The old one, what is left of it, is at Bolton School; see p. 164.

is much more accomplished; of brick and stone, with its ground floor opened out but not totally lost. Back on Deansgate is the NATWEST BANK of 1852 by *George Woodhouse*, extended 1907, formerly the Bank of Bolton, a splendid palazzo faced with beautiful ashlar. MARKS & SPENCER, 1965–7. ROYAL BANK OF SCOTLAND, 1875, by *Cunliffe & Freeman*; Renaissance, with a tower, and pillared top-lit banking hall within. WHITTAKER'S department store occupies three diverse buildings between Howell Croft and Old Hall Street: a pastiche timber-framed block with a pepperpot turret of 1907 by *George Crowther*, the terracotta Aspinall's Buildings of 1912, symmetrical, with corner pepperpots, and on the town hall side the clunky concrete-clad PADERBORN HOUSE of 1968–9 by *Sutton* of Birmingham, with municipal offices above. Back on Deansgate is the POST OFFICE, 1913–16, composed like the new public front of Buckingham Palace minus its centrepiece and pediments – but who was the architect? Opposite is the Y.M.C.A., a rickety building of brick and terracotta, creatively asymmetrical, with shops on the ground floor. It was built as the Imperial Temperance Hall (dancing, billiards) in 1909, and reopened as the Y.M.C.A. by Sir William Lever in 1919.

From the w end of Deansgate ST EDMUND STREET descends to a small car park on the site of Booth's factory, where Samuel Crompton operated his mules. On the other side of the little river bridge is ST HELENA MILL of 1780 and credibly Bolton's first spinning mill, but largely rebuilt in 1820 for steam power. Stone, four storeys, with a later square chimney at the back. BACK KNOWSLEY STREET, w of Knowsley Street (off the N side of Deansgate via Ridgway Gates) preserves a rare fragment of Bolton's lost intricacy, diving beneath Victoria Hall to the river for an atmospheric view of the two hidden arches of Knowsley Street bridge, a mill and footbridges, and in steep foreshortening the N wall of Victoria Hall with many donor plaques.

LITTLE BOLTON

Immediately N of Bolton centre, but separated from it by the valley of the little River Croal, which is bedded with stone setts for its entire progress through town. Essentially one long street, St George's Street at the e end which changes at Bridge Street into St George's Road at the w.

ALL SAINTS, All Saints Street. A private chapel of 1726 was rebuilt by *G. E. Street* 1869–71. Closed in 1966, it is now the Ukrainian Catholic church. Not large, and without a tower, but with bold plate tracery at the ends and in the clerestory. Four-bay arcades with stiff-leaf. Diaphragm arches over the aisles; the aisle windows are internally grouped under blank arches too. Closely timbered roofs, that in the chancel renewed after arson in 2000. The introduced ICONOSTASIS does not fully hide the E end, as it would in an Orthodox church. Large square altar in the sanctuary on which is the big TABERNACLE like a complete Byzantine church. – STAINED GLASS. E by *Clayton & Bell*. S aisle E, and probably W too, by *Shrigley & Hunt*, 1926 and 1912. The SE chapel has double tracery.

ST GEORGE, St George's Road. Now a Craft Centre. 1794–6 by *S. Hope*, which probably means *Samuel Hope* of Manchester rather than Samuel Hope of Liverpool. A big Georgian town church of brick, with a tall W tower. The tower doorway is broad and without a pediment. The W window alone has an ogee arch. The sides are surprisingly domestic-looking, of seven bays and two storeys with a three-bay pediment. This feature also appeared on an elegant C18 design, its signature unfortunately lost, preserved in Bolton library, which shows single-storey fenestration in super-arches like Platt Chapel Manchester.

The 1796 church had a flat E end. It was given a full Ecclesiological chancel and S chapel as late as 1908–10 by *James Lomax-Simpson*, and very good they are too. The interior is highly deceptive. Old photographs show a tremendous auditory church with an oval gallery on slender iron columns, and a flat clearspan ceiling. Simpson rebuilt the galleries straight, in a more Wrennish form, strengthened their supports, and introduced Ionic columns above to support the roof. The tie beams were cut and the centre of the ceiling raised into a cove.

The last service was in 1975. Reopened as a crafts centre and café in 1994, architect *June Partington*, with remarkably little disturbance to the fabric or the space.

The fittings are deceptive too. – REREDOS, 1921. – ALTAR RAIL, CHOIR STALLS. – PULPIT, perched on a very tall baluster, the stair curved and vertiginous with three fluted balusters to a tread; astonishingly, all 1911. – FONT. Charming shallow marble basin with four cherubs' heads, on a baluster. – MONUMENTS. Hard to see behind the introduced craft stalls. Alice Ainsworth †1802. Small pensive male figure by a pillar. – William Wright †1814. By *S. & T. Franceys* of Liverpool. Kneeling woman by an urn with military trophies. – Richard Ainsworth, 1834. Sarcophagus and palm frond. – Rev. William Thistlethwaite †1838. Draped urn. – Rewarding C20 STAINED GLASS. The designers were careful to leave plenty of clear glass. E, a First World War memorial by *Heaton, Butler & Bayne*, Christ surrounded by contemporary figures. Lunette on the S side of the chancel, high up and easy to miss, but very rich. SE chapel, two by *E. Pickett & Co.* of Leeds, 1960 and 1962, and one by *Shrigley & Hunt*, 1956.

ST GEORGE'S SCHOOL (former), looking down Bath Street. 1847–8 by *James Greenhalgh*, an architect of some talent. Jacobean, with a big shaped gable, obelisk pinnacles and a central oriel.

ST ANDREW AND ST GEORGE (Congregational, now United Reformed), St George's Road. 1862–3 by *Oliver & Lamb* of Newcastle. Gothic, but 'too flat' said *The Builder*. It lost its spire in 1969. Elegant auditorium on the upper floor, with the slenderest iron columns of quatrefoil section supporting galleries. It was reordered and furnished in 1936 by *Ormrod, Pomeroy & Foy*. – STAINED GLASS. Two given by the second Lord Leverhulme in 1936 in memory of his parents, who were married here, and one of 1938 commemorating the Tillotson family. A second Tillotson window of 1969 in a bold Modernist style is by *Edith Norris*.

SUNDAY SCHOOL, attached to the w end. By *Ormrod, Pomeroy & Foy*, 1914. A good building with inventive detailing.

CLAREMONT CHAPEL (Independent, formerly Baptist), St George's Road. Of 1868–9, by *George Woodhouse*. Very grand, of red brick with stone dressings and a Corinthian portico on the show front. Extended at the back 1895 and 1909. The interior entirely reconstructed 1980 by *Andrew Lowe*, structural engineer. The auditorium is now at balcony level and a sports hall occupies the former chapel floor.

GILEAD HOUSE (Salvation Army), St George's Road. 1984, by *David Blackwell*, executive architects *Leach, Rhodes & Walker*. L-shaped block with a group of octagonal units sheltering cosily in the angle.

Former TOWN HALL, St George's Street. Of 1826, possibly by *Benjamin Hick*, who designed the lost Dispensary in Nelson Square in 1825. Disused and falling into decay. Ashlar, Greek, with rusticated door surround, pilaster strips with sunk panels, and a one-bay pediment. Tom Wesley points out that the cart entrance of the industrial building opposite (a brewery and then an oil works), has exactly the same rusticated surround.

BOARD SCHOOL, Clarence Street. By *Jonathan Simpson*, 1886. Big and red, as schools of this period are.

From the old town hall a walk can be made returning E–W.

STANLEY CASINO on the corner of Bridge Street is a former Methodist chapel of 1803–4 by *Peter Rothwell*, and very handsome it is. It closed in 1969. Brick, five by five bays, with arched windows. Three w doorways, the middle one with a pediment. The whole front is pedimented too, with a quatrefoil (a Gothic motif) and a modest garland below. The CARPET WAREHOUSE on Higher Bridge Street is the former New Jerusalem Chapel by *James Greenhalgh*, 1844. Three bays, brick, modest, with arched windows and a pediment across. Opposite the casino the big red terracotta corner building was the CO-OP DRAPERY DEPARTMENT of 1896 and 1902, by *Bradshaw & Gass*. It has lost its ground floor as is all too common in Bolton, and its corner spire too. The MOAT HOUSE HOTEL, 1990 by *Planning and Building Associates*, like the adjacent Market Place Centre, has a strong base of alternately rusticated stone but goes into distressing detail higher up, in this case a paraphrase of Palladian alternate triangular and curved pediments. The hotel incorporates the former ST MARY (R.C.) of 1845 etc. on Palace Street. The church was radically altered in the late C19 and the most salient feature now is a rose window with

flowing tracery. ST GEORGE'S ROAD is lined with early C19
two-storey brick terraces. SPINNERS' HALL was built in 1880
by *J. J. Bradshaw* as the Junior Reform Club, and enlarged in
1911 by *Potts & Hemmings* for the Cotton Spinners' Association in Edwardian Baroque style. At the W end, by the junction of St George's Road, with Topp Way and Marsden
Road, are two striking housing developments. ST GEORGE'S
COURT, the last gasp of *Bolton MBC Architects* under *Patrick
Taylor* in the early 1980s, is Germanic, with steep roofs incorporating several levels of dormers. KENSINGTON HOUSE,
c. 2001 for the Portico Housing Association, is in bright Lego
colours and shapes, yellow brick, blue glass bricks, and silver
roofs forming parallel curves, like horizontal sails.

OUTER BOLTON

Bolton's suburbs are extensive, and dividing them up into bite-
sized chunks is not easy. Starting at the N they are arranged clock-
wise: Astley Bridge; Tonge Moor; Breightmet and Tonge Fold;
Darcy Lever and The Haulgh; Great Lever; Daubhill; Deane;
Heaton; Halliwell; Smithills and Barrow Bridge. Bradshaw,
Harwood and Little Lever have their own gazetteer entries.

1. Astley Bridge

ALL SOULS, Astley Street. One of two remarkable churches by
Paley & Austin for the Evangelical Thomas Greenhalgh, mill-
owner.* Built 1878–81. It closed in 1986 and is vested in the
Churches Conservation Trust. Mothballing has if anything
added to its power. The majestic red brick W tower dominates,
but the buttressed body of the church with its polygonal apse
rises above the terraces too. There is a stair-turret against the
N side, and some flushwork in the tower and the small N porch.
The nave is, as Mr Greenhalgh instructed, a single undivided
space, with an astonishing clear span of 52 ft (15.85 metres).
The windows are set high. The roof has wooden vaulting at the
edges and a raised barrel in the middle, with varying fretted
decoration in the spandrels. A tiny GALLERY at the W end, set
right up at tie-beam level, commands a sensational view of the
great unobstructed space below with its long rows of pews. The
E end on the other hand is tripartite in plan, a shallow chancel
and polygonal apse and two side chapels, and they are separated by two-bay arcades of high and noble piers, giving a hall
effect. The church is furnished with Evangelical simplicity. –
CHOIR STALLS, PEWS, ORGAN CASE, and PULPIT are all by
the architects. – REREDOS and FONT are by *John Roddis* of
Birmingham. The font COVER, a perfect match, was added in
1930. – STAINED GLASS in the apse by *Clayton & Bell*, 1881.
SCHOOL. 1878–9, by *J. J. Bradshaw*.

* The other was The Saviour, Deane Road, 1882–5, demolished in 1975.

ST PAUL, Holland Street. 1848. In the Norman style, by *J. W. Whittaker* of Bolton. In 1868 *J. Medland Taylor* breached the walls and tacked narrowish Gothic aisles onto the broad nave, and a short chancel. The strong E.E. spire which is so effectively framed from Blackburn Road by the stone terraces of Birley Street looks like Taylor too. The 1848 nave is tremendously wide, spanned by tie-beam trusses only saved from being 'chapel' by their notchy decoration. The inserted arcades are short-stepping, with cylindrical piers. W GALLERY. The short upper windows now serving as a clerestory suggest that the church had N and S galleries too. – Dwarf SCREEN and REREDOS, 1906, in marbles and mosaic, by *A. J. Hope* of *Bradshaw, Gass & Hope*. – PULPIT. Also 1906. – STAINED GLASS. E and one S with unusually animated figures and colours dominated by orange. Four by *Edith Norris*, 1950s, and two by another local maker, *W. E. Lynch*, 1944 and 1949.

METHODIST THEATRE CHURCH, formerly Seymour Road Methodist Church, Seymour Road. 1866–8 by *George Woodhouse*. Red brick and yellow-painted stone, Italianate. Strong side elevations, with continuous banding.

CONGREGATIONAL CHURCH (Iron Church): *see* Halliwell, p. 166.

LIBRARY, Moss Bank Way. By *Bradshaw & Gass*. In the brick-and-much-stone-trim style of Edwardian libraries all over the country. Andrew Carnegie gave £15,000 for three libraries in 1908, building started in 1909, and the three – Astley Bridge, Halliwell, and Great Lever (q.v.) – were opened by Carnegie himself in 1910.

THORNLEIGH SALESIAN COLLEGE, Sharples Park. Thornleigh was a cotton-spinner's mansion of 1868 by *Henry Stead*, for Arthur Lemuel Briggs, extended *c.* 1890. Olde English hospitality personified. Big welcoming hallway with plenty of carved wood, panelling, decorative friezes and an inglenook fireplace with copper hood. More inglenooks, each bigger than the last, in the dining and billiard rooms. The main stair has been moved and simplified, as the Salesians have done in several of their NW properties. Service quarters well-preserved, but a conservatory has been removed.

CHAPEL. Connected to the house by a concrete loggia clearly of the 1960s. The chapel itself, large, of buff brick and Portland stone with a Wrennish cupola looks 1930s, but no: it is of 1966 and an interesting example of ambitious Catholic church-building immediately before the Second Vatican Council. The chapel is visually T-shaped but a lower section, now divided from the main chapel, makes it cruciform. This is the section connected to the house, and was for the community. Each priest was required to celebrate mass daily, so there are ten side chapels each with altar and mini-sacristy round a central clerestoried space. Subtly graded glass in purple hues. The main chapel is very light, with pale yellow tints in the windows, focusing on a very wide and simple baldacchino of concrete, its solemnity upset by decoration reminiscent of a Punch-and-Judy stand on top. – STATIONS OF THE CROSS.

A continuous frieze. A small apse at the w end filled with coloured glass acts as the War Memorial.

The Salesians also own THE LEES, close by to the N, an enjoyably incorrect villa of 1836 incorporating an older house. White stucco with black windows and decoration. The s front has triplets of windows presumably meant to be Gothic but with triangular heads, Anglo-Saxon style. In the centre, a semi-circular bay, the windows far too tall and moreover running together vertically. A balustrade on top upsets the balance well and truly.

SIR JOHN HOLDEN'S MILL, Blackburn Road, Sharples. The last cotton mill built in Bolton, 1925–6, by *Bradshaw Gass & Hope*. It was electrically powered from the mains, so it has no chimney, engine house or boiler house, but it still has the prominent corner water tower with a copper dome. All red pressed brick, with its architectural decoration done with 'specials' and a little terracotta. Six storeys articulated into a notional base, order and entablature, like an office building of the period. As so often there was provision for it to be doubled in size, at the N end.

85 WATERMILLOCK, on Crompton Way (the ring road). An opulent mansion by *Bradshaw & Gass* of 1880–6 for Thomas Thwaites, bleacher, and then his son Herbert. Now a posh pub. All of stone and beautifully executed, in a Jacobean style paying tribute to the stone part of Hall i' th' Wood across the valley to the E. Asymmetrical in all its parts. The principal rooms in the main block face s and E; a billiard room is nearly detached at the SW corner and services in a wing NW. Rich interiors by *Goodall & Co.* of Manchester are well preserved downstairs, but the upper floor has been opened out to make a fantasy suite of purple and silver. The E PORCH opens into a wide HALLWAY panelled in dark oak, from which rises the Imperial STAIR, framed by a triple marble arcade and lit by a glazed lantern. In the DRAWING ROOM a big inglenook fireplace with curved side windows, in the DINING ROOM *de Morgan* tiles. By the w entrance is the smaller MORNING ROOM, pan-elled and ceiled in pitch pine, originally with a painted frieze of coffee plants. Next to the billiard room, and so virtually detached from the main house, is the SMOKING ROOM, orig-inally with Japanese wallpaper and a painted frieze of branches
84 and birds. The spectacular BILLIARD ROOM is top-lit, with a great chimneypiece at one end and a triple arcade at the other which was intended to contain an organ.

The LODGE, architecturally as good as the house, is now sundered from it by the ring road.

2. Tonge Moor

NW of the town, in the V between Bradshaw Brook and the River Tonge.

ST AUGUSTINE, Thicketford Road. By *R. Knill Freeman*, 1883–6. A church of considerable dignity, although towerless, thanks to a basement floor which gives it extra height. Low aisles, tall clerestory. Red and yellow stone, free Dec. On the N side are two odd projections, either of which, visually, could have grown into a tower: a NW transept with lean-to porch, and a NE organ chamber which has a bell hung off its stair-turret. In fact Freeman's drawing shows that it was the organ chamber that was intended to sprout a low tower and gabled spire.

Tall, spatially resourceful interior, brick lined with plenty of stone dressings, and well-lit by the clear glass of the clerestory. The narrow passage aisles with cross-arches are darker, lit only by small paired windows. Tiny chapel at the E end of the S aisle and formerly N as well. Lady Chapel under the W gallery. The W transept is the baptistery. – REREDOS. 1953, by *D. S. Purnell*, blocking part of the E window. – Forward ALTAR. Both are classical, not Gothic. – FONT. Big stone bowl with a carving of Christ and children. – CRUCIFIX. Life-sized; now in the baptistery. It used to hang over the screen, which has gone. – STAINED GLASS. E, 1920, by *Henry Holiday*, a WAR MEMORIAL in gorgeous Pre-Raphaelite colours, representing Revelations Chapter 12. The little aisle windows are by *Shrigley & Hunt*, up to 1928. By *Edith Norris*, 1950s, Lady Chapel and SE chapel. The tall baptismal window, semi-abstract, is by *Andy Seddon*, late C20. So too are the abstract piece over the NW door, and some etched glass.

(ST COLUMBA (R.C.), Ripley Street. 1954–6, by *Geoffrey G. Williams* of *Greenhalgh & Williams*.)

HALL I' TH' WOOD, off Crompton Way. An uninviting approach through poor housing, a bleak playing field, a sudden vision of decorative C16 timber framing and C17 stone mullions and pinnacles, and an unsuspected river valley, steep and wooded. One of the most rewarding C16 and C17 houses in SE Lancashire, it owes its survival to W. H. Lever, later Lord Leverhulme, who in 1899 bought it and presented it to the Corporation. The way it is presented is largely due his careful restoration, by *Jonathan Simpson* and *Edward Ould* of *Grayson & Ould*. Its particular distinction is that here in 1779 Samuel Crompton, whose family rented a part of it, perfected his Spinning mule. For Hall i' th' Wood is not a gentry house. It was associated with industry from the C16, and grew to allow for multiple occupation, like the C17 houses around Rochdale (*see* Windy Bank at Littleborough, q.v.), rather than for polite entertainment. Indeed the house has four, and until the early C20 five, identifiable sections, each with its own entrance, staircase and chimneystack.

The Brownlow family was involved with the bleaching, fulling and finishing of cloth. The House at ye Wood appears first in 1550 in the will of Lawrence Brownlow II, consisting of hall, buttery kitchen, larder house and chamber and a barn together with a fulling mill and a malt kiln. It was perhaps built in about 1499 at the time of his father's marriage. This early part must be the NE wing, which is partly stone-built and is certainly the most puzzling in its internal structure. The SE or

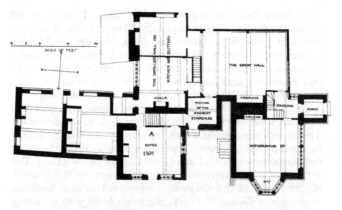

Hall i' th' Wood, plan showing demolished east wing.
Victoria County History of Lancashire, vol. 5, 1911

hall wing, one of the prettiest bits of half-timbering in the north
west, dates from *c.* 1559–77 and was built by Lawrence's son
Roger Brownlow II. It is two-storeyed with a continuous cove
and is decorated all over with quatrefoils, cusped Xs making
four half-quatrefoils, straight and wavy chevrons, and small
squares. The SE corner of the earlier wing has timber framing
to match, but the join is not well managed. On the W side a
timber stair rises within a stone tower (cf. Wythenshawe Hall,
q.v.).

The tall and plain NW wing of stone came next. It is signed
and dated 1591 L.B.B. – Lawrence Brownlow III (the datestone was recovered and placed here in the restoration). In
1614 the property was mortgaged to Humphrey Chetham, and
as a consequence passed to Christopher Norris, although the
Brownlows remained as tenants. Alexander Norris, his son,
made a two-storey S porch and a SW wing in 1648, in stone
and decidedly monumental, with baluster pinnacles ending in
steep cones, large mullioned-and-transomed windows, a
round-arched entrance and a two-storey canted bay. Finally a
two-room wing was built to the N. Its date is uncertain, but it
must be before 1780, when Samuel and Mary Crompton
moved into it on their marriage. The wing was demolished in
the early C20 when the lane had to be realigned to stop it falling
into the river.

Entrance is now by the E door, not quite in the angle of the
L. It leads straight into the HALL, single-storey but taller than
the rest. A former screens passage arrangement is suggested by
the matching W door, two service doors, and a morticed joist
overhead, although this last is unconvincingly framed in to the
rest of the building. The puzzling feature is the presence of
what looks like another screens passage running alongside it
immediately N, from the angle between hall and wing. The

stone fireplace is round-arched like the s porch of 1648 and
must belong to that phase. The rooms in the N wing were the
kitchen and buttery. The STAIRCASE spiralling round a mast
at the back is a C20 renewal but its top portion is genuine. The
lower room of the 1591 wing, originally unheated, was the
DAIRY. Its upper parts can be explored next. Over the dairy is
a pleasant panelled CHAMBER. No original panelling survives
– the importations are conscientiously recorded by small brass
plates; this panelling is from Hacken Hall, Darcy Lever. The
cross CORRIDOR is a full eight steps higher up and is not above
the screens passage but above the odd parallel passage noted
below. Over the hall is not a great chamber, as there is at
Wardley and Wythenshawe, but three modest rooms. Two fireplaces, belonging to the stack probably inserted in 1648, heat
two of the rooms, suggesting that the space has been subdivided since at least that time. The chimneypiece in CROMP-
TON'S ROOM has a plaster coat of arms of the Starkie family;
Alice Norris married John Starkie in 1654.

This is the time to explore the 1648 wing. It consists of two
fine apartments, a PARLOUR below and CHAMBER above, both
with imported panelling and copied plasterwork. (Chamber
panelling, overmantel and frieze from a house in Ashford,
Kent; Parlour panelling and overmantel from a house in
Buntingford, Hertfordshire). The tiny PORCH ROOM is windowed on three sides. The newel STAIR is crammed into the
space between door and chimneystack, i.e. in the baffle position. It has closely spaced stout balusters, lozenge and wave
mouldings, and a dragon in relief.

The ATTICS were fully accessible and lit. Here at last the
building phases become, if not clear, a good deal clearer. The
hall range and the N cross-wing are revealed as two independent structures with a full yard-wide gap between them (cf.
Wythenshawe and Baguley Halls, q.v.). It is this gap that is
filled by the corridor below and the extra screens passage on
the ground floor. The attic of the NW wing poses a further
puzzle, though: there is a corridor right up here above the
kitchen corridor, with its own beautiful wooden screens with
a pair of two-centre headed doorways. Can there have been
another dwelling, right up here?

Hall i' th' Wood never had a park or an estate. The GARDEN
was made in 1906–8 as part of the Lever restoration, with terraces, balustrades and alternately blocked gatepiers evoking an
imagined gentlemanly past. Heavily vandalized, it was greatly
simplified in the 1960s. The steeply curving setted lane clip-
ping the NW corner of the house tells a different story, of varied
country long exploited – but not irredeemably despoiled – by
industry.

CROMPTON'S BIRTHPLACE. FIRWOOD FOLD is a little rural
   enclave, but not a pre-industrial one, for the pool behind the
   cottages fed a bleachworks, now a timber yard. In No. 10
   Samuel Crompton was born. Probably C17, it is thatched, with
   mullioned windows, and turns its gable to the street. There is

only one spot, worn smooth by photographers, from which a giant pylon does not appear immediately behind it. Nos. 8 and 15 exhibit fragments of cruck trusses. Being built parallel to the street, they are probably later not earlier.

3. Breightmet and Tonge Fold

E of the town, along Bury Road.

ST CHAD, Longworth Street, Tonge Fold. 1937, by *Richard Nickson*. Of pale red brick on a blue brick base. NW campanile, gallery stair-towers, and a long nave with a low clerestory with square windows, like that of Deane. The sanctuary is raised, with its own four-gabled roof. The S chapel has one too. The interior is lined with grey brick with the horizontal joints channelled. Plain square piers and concrete beams, but arches for the sanctuary and the chapel sanctuary. The painted beams of the roof provide a welcome bit of subdued colour.

ST JAMES, Roscow Avenue, Breightmet. By *J. E. Gregan* and *W. R. Corson*, 1855–6. Ecclesiologically correct Dec with a broach spire, nave and aisles, S porch and a long chancel. The interior is very long and low, the arcades low with alternating round and octagonal piers, the paired clerestory windows low over the arcades. – Low-set fat PULPIT, 1927. – STAINED GLASS, all small scale and by no means a complete set, including several by local makers. E 1850s by *Wailes*. Chancel S 1876. S, at the W end, a three-lighter by *Heaton, Butler & Bayne*, 1901. Chancel N by *Reuben Bennett*, 1904. S aisle E by *Walter Pearce*. Two by *Wippell*, both pleasing; Christ welcoming children, the children in 1838 dress, and a Second World War memorial, St George and the Dragon, complete with Spitfires and a Churchill quote. NW corner by *Edith Norris*, 1957.

ST OSMUND (R.C.), Long Lane. 1960, probably by *Greenhalgh & Williams* of Bolton. Buff brick, green concrete roof tiles, an oblong tower. In the simplified Romanesque typical of C20 Catholic churches; simplified so far that the window- and door-heads are two concrete flags leaning together. (There are Bolton precedents for this, *see* e.g. The Lees at Astley Bridge). Interior built round a pair of concrete trusses E and W in Gothic-arch shapes, and elbowed intermediate trusses. Low baptistery with a red marble FONT on the N side. – STAINED GLASS. Chancel and baptistery with abstract fractured backgrounds, the rest fully pictorial – Christ's life and Passion on the S, miracles on the N; all by *Lightfoots*. The first church, of 1925, is now the PARISH HALL.

4. Darcy Lever and the Haulgh

An interesting, steeply cut little area immediately SE of the centre, where the Tonge and the Bradshaw Brook join the emerging River Croal.

ST STEPHEN, Lever Bridge. Famous as the first of *Edmund Sharpe*'s three 'pot churches', built 1842–4.* Part experiment, part advertisement, everything visible is terracotta, made from the fireclays of Ladyshore Colliery in Little Lever (q.v.) which was owned by Sharpe's brother-in-law, John Fletcher. Nave, wide transepts, short chancel. The blackletter inscription around the w door demonstrates how crisp terracotta can be, and the ballflower, wavy parapet and pinnacles that adorn the wall tops so lavishly make the most of its potential for mass production. It is a great shame that it has lost its w steeple: the delightful Germanic openwork spire in 1939, the rest 1966. The spire, 'of solid terracotta from top to bottom, dowelled together with terracotta', was like that of Freiburg Minster, recalling Sharpe's continental tour of 1833–5 which, apart from a few days with Thomas Rickman, constituted almost his sole architectural training.

Despite faulty firing that resulted in considerable wastage the church cost only £2,600. The *Illustrated London News* liked 'This truly elegant structure ... believed to be the only attempt that has yet been made in this kingdom to build an entire church of Terra-Cotta'; but 'Pretense and affected decoration' thundered *The Ecclesiologist*; 'one large window, one small window, one pinnacle, one yard of parapet, one set-off, one yard of string course – behold all that is necessary for the exterior of an elaborately enriched cast-clay church!' Terracotta soon became an essential of urban architecture particularly in the smoky north, but after Holy Trinity in Manchester, 1845–6 (q.v.), it was hardly used for churches and certainly not on the outside, except by the unrepentant Sharpe at his own church in Lancaster in 1874.

The interior is exceptionally pretty, owing its prettiness to the crispness of the terracotta and its light biscuit colour. The porch which is all that is left of the tower has a terracotta vault with bell hole. The wide unaisled nave has an open timber hammerbeam roof, more decorative than businesslike. A terracotta cornice frieze with two bands of foliage frames a blackletter text ('Wis of Sol chap iii'). More running foliage for the dado, all miraculously 'undercut'. The pew ends with three or four designs of poppyheads, and their open arcaded backs, are all terracotta. The church has a proper crossing with X-framed roof, and substantial transepts. The organ in the s transept has a pretty case decorated with terracotta canopies like the stalls at Lancaster Priory. The chancel (really the sanctuary, for the chancel step runs across the transept) is short, but very rich. Two tiers of arcading, all-over diapering, canopied niches framing the raised lettering of the Ten Commandments, Creed and Lord's Prayer: all terracotta. Altar, font and pulpit were originally largely terracotta too.

*The others are Holy Trinity, Platt, s Manchester, q.v., and St Paul, Scotforth, N Lancashire.

At this point in the Gothic Revival it is fascinating to see how, while Pugin sought to bring everyone to their knees, Sharpe with his matchless knowledge of medieval Gothic was content to delight the eye. Pugin wanted a return to the Middle Ages; Sharpe simply to be able to reproduce its forms by practical means. If Sharpe had had Pugin's powers of persuasion, how different the revival might have been! – STAINED GLASS. By *Willement* the E window and all the tracery heads, which set forth a programme of martyrs including Charles I; but some have yet to be done. Transept S, the stoning of St Stephen, by *Wailes*. One on the N by *Henry Holiday*, 1884.

The church has an attractive but messy setting, a steeply wooded river valley with its works, crossed by a high latticed railway VIADUCT of 1848. The terracotta of the missing tower appears to be buried in the bank on the N side of the churchyard. (The Fletchers lived at a house called The Hollins, which had been altered by *John Douglas,* at the top of the bank.)*

CEMETERY. Bordered by the River Tonge. By *George Woodhouse* and *Charles Holt*, 1857. Fine GATES and LODGES to Cemetery Road, axial roadway lined with stone pine trees; but one of the pair of CHAPELS has gone, upsetting the plan. The remaining chapel is typically exaggerated Gothic. Outsized door under its own gable. Two thin colonnettes standing uncomfortably on the gable lend notional support to the corbel table of an absurdly miniaturized turret.

HAULGH HALL, Hilden Street. Right by the A666. C16 or C17, timber-framed, with a splendid cruck at the E end and a two-storey jettied bay S. Hall below, great chamber above, with a stone stack across the W end and a cross-passage beyond that. In the bay built-in seating with panelling inlaid with geometric designs.

Overshadowing Haugh Hall to the S is HILDEN STREET SCHOOL, the former PUPIL TEACHERS' CENTRE, of 1901–3 by *Bradshaw & Gass*. Brick and terracotta, symmetrical, with an openwork parapet in the middle.

LEVERHULME PARK. Given to the town by William Lever in celebration of his election as mayor in 1918. It was laid out by *Thomas Mawson* and was the first of a proposed chain of parks intended to ring the town. Here was Darcy Lever New Hall, formerly called Bradshaw Hall. Darcy Lever Old Hall, a picturesque timber-framed house, was demolished in 1951.

At the junction of Radcliffe Road and Castle Steet is TWO CATS HOUSE, the Earl of Bradford's Lodge of 1854, by *Charles Holt*. The home of Fred Dibnah, celebrity steeplejack, responsible for demolishing many of Bolton's unwanted chimneys and steeples including that of St Stephen. Twin gables with an ornamental parapet not shown on old photographs, so perhaps from St Stephen. Massive four-way stack in the valley, trefoil-headed windows, coat of arms with the two cats that give the

---

*Thanks to Michael Shippobottom for this and much other information.

cottage its nickname. A miniature industrial complex has been created on the wooded slope below with machinery, chimneys, and sheds.

Michael Shippobottom points out two housing schemes in The Haulgh: THE AVENUE, *c.* 1900, laid out by the surveyor *David Frederick Green,* brother-in-law to Charles Holden and displaying some of his mannerisms such as a window sandwiched between two chimneystacks; and MODEL HOUSING on Halstead Street and Castle Street for the Dr Chadwick Charity, 1883 and 1890, by *Jonathan Simpson.* The POLICE STATION and COURTROOM on Castle Street is by *Henry Littler,* 1876.

5. Great Lever

ST MICHAEL, Manchester Road. 1851, by *Dickson & Breakspear.* Made difficult of access by the railway and the by-pass, but when you do get there it is almost rural, with a steep clough on the S side. The church is small and fussy, of rough pale gold stone, E.E. in style with lancets in ones and twos and a triplet for the E end. It has a belfry on the W gable and a toy turret for the vestry chimney.

ST SIMON AND ST JUDE, Rishton Lane. Church and former school by *R. Knill Freeman,* 1899–1901. Red brick and red Ruabon terracotta, the terracotta used to fine effect. Perp, with a SW tower nicely crisp but a little undersized.

LIBRARY, now a community centre, Bradford Road. 1909–10, by *Bradshaw, Gass & Hope.* Brick and dark red stone. Symmetrical, with a cupola, mildly Baroque.

BEEHIVE MILLS, Crescent Road. No. 1 Mill of 1895, and No. 2 of 1902, both long and level with stripes of yellow and blue brick, are linked by a common entrance. The stump of one chimney, and one engine house, survive at the back by the railway line. The office is at the Bolton end, and is much more decorative than the rest.

GREAT LEVER HALL, rebuilt by Bishop Bridgman, with a chapel, in 1631–4, is another of Bolton's lost timber-framed houses. After serving as a Conservative club and a rectory it was demolished in the mid C20. Its site is buried under the A666.

THE BROOKLYN, Green Lane. Now a pub. A great Gothic house of 1859 by *George Woodhouse* for Thomas Walmsley, a wrought-iron manufacturer. Date and initials are on the little tower. Set sideways to the road, and retaining its LODGE and GARDEN. Of brick with much stone, with crisp carving. The stair remains inside, but not much else.

THE SOUTHFIELDS, formerly the Walker Institute, almost opposite on Green Lane, is another large Gothic house also converted into a pub. Of stone; the original house L-shaped and thoroughly Gothic, a W extension dated 1877 less so, with sash windows. The interior is opened up but retains some moulded ceilings.

6. Daubhill

EMMANUEL, Cannon Street. 1837–8, by *Edward Welch*, the short
chancel 1848 by *Gregan*. Engagingly gauche, with a thin w
tower, stepped triple lancets, and comical faces as hoodmould
stops. The spire has been removed. Closed in 1990 and converted into flats, with the eaves raised for continuous windowing above the parapet; a successful motif. The PRESENT
CHURCH is the former parish room, extended in 1989 with a
dual-purpose space framed with laminated cruck-like timbers,
and a shuttered-off sanctuary. – Four COLOURED GLASS
windows of 2000, by *Classical Glass* of Breightmet.

ST GEORGE THE MARTYR, Roseberry Street. 1878–80, by
J. Medland & Henry Taylor. Of ordinary brick with an odd
oblong spirelet on the w gable. Wide transepts, and chapels set
diagonally, to make a five-part E end, each with its own gables
at two levels. The windows, round-arched lancets, are all
grouped in fours. (The interior shows Taylor at his trickiest.
The transepts are two bays (of the arcade) deep, and then the
walls cant in towards the chancel. The woodwork takes care to
stress this irregularity.)

95 ST PHILIP, Bridgeman Street. By *E. H. Lingen Barker*, 1909–11.
Immediately E of Swan Lane Mills and dwarfed by them. Built
of the same hard red brick as No. 3 Mill (see below) and the
relentless grid of terraced houses that characterizes the district.
The church has independently roofed aisles, a lean-to w
narthex, and a bellcote.

ST PETER AND ST PAUL (R.C.), Pilkington Street, in an area
now industrial, not residential. 1897, by *Sinnott, Sinnott &
Powell*, replacing Bolton's first Catholic church – well out of
town – of 1798–1800. Of red brick, with lancets, and very
austere, without even buttresses to articulate the sheer walls.
Only the NW tower makes a display, with its tall paired belfry
windows under their raised eyebrows and pyramid roof. Six-
bay arcades of granite piers, each made out of two stones
jointed by a shaft ring, with gross foliage caps. Short wide
chancel, transept chapels. Massive architectural REREDOS,
crucifixion in a Gothic frame flanked by Peter and Paul in
niches under tall pinnacles. Dado of coloured TILES. The
LADY CHAPEL was fitted up as a First World War memorial
with mosaic walls and floor. It is top-lit with a skylight and
hidden lighting for the statue niche.

SHREE KUTCH SATSANG SWAMINARAYAN TEMPLE (Hindu),
Adelaide Street. 1993. Of red and blue brick, nearly square,
with a shallow-stepped gable to the street. In front of this a
two-storey forebuilding surmounted by the Sikhara, a convex-
sided square pyramid, in pink stone. Canopied porches in the
same stone to the street and to the car park on the s side.
Inside, upstairs, a single great room, the wide flat ceiling raised
in the middle. Unfurnished except for the the shrine at the far
end, made in India and all in orange wood. This has three sections, each with a Sikhara roof, and a lower one at the r.

MOSQUE, Derby Street and Peace Street. Nearing completion 2003.

SWAN LANE MILLS, Bridgeman Street. No. 1 and No. 2 mills of 1901 and 1904, built end-to-end as was often projected but seldom acheived, were claimed as together the largest in the world. No. 3, taller and more shiny, with distinctive rounded 95 corners (corbelled out over the road at the SE), was added in 1914. All are by *Stott & Sons* and No. 3 was to be their last mill. Double engine house for No. 1 and No. 2 mills; No. 3 has a taller one. All three cluster round the single chimney, which carries the Swan motif in glazed brick but has unfortunately lost its decorative top. The office building at the Swan Lane end is relatively quiet, but No. 3 Mill has a spectacular corner entrance in the yard, with the Swan again, all in white glazed brick.

SUNNYSIDE MILLS, off Adelaide Street. Belonging to Tootal Broadhurst Lee; but mostly demolished in 1980. There remains SUNNYSIDE HOUSE, and the CLOCK TOWER which can be seen from Derby Street, of stone with a Germanic spire and the dates 1862 and 1872. The architect was *George Woodhouse*. Parts of a narrative stone frieze rescued from the engine house of No. 4 Shed (the mill was mostly single-storey) have been built into the basement of the Market Place Centre in town (q.v.).

7. *Deane*

ST MARY. Saynte Mariden (Saint Mary Deane), in its wooded 8 dean, was mentioned in 1227 as a chapel of ease in the parish of Eccles, not Bolton. In 1541, with ten townships, it was made a parish. Most of the building belongs to that date, i.e. latest Perp. Only the undersized W tower, unbuttressed except at the bottom, is older, and the reset C13 N door. The church is long and low, with continuous battlements, a continuous clerestory, and mullioned windows in threes and fours. They are arched but not cusped, and the church is without tracery except at the E end. In 1833 the aisles were raised to accommodate galleries and made two-storey, i.e. with an upper row of windows. The short porch dates from this time. With the galleries gone the second storey of aisle windows adds light and space to the interior, which is otherwise very plain. The octagonal piers are irregularly spaced, suggesting eastward extension in stages, with twice-chamfered arches. The capitals at the W end have a little elementary motif of decoration, including shields (cf. Eccles). The continuous low clerestory ignores the arcade rhythm. The flat roof is a reproduction of 1884. There is no chancel arch. The short chancel, with its big window on the S, was lengthened by ten feet in 1884.

FITTINGS. ALTAR. Intended to be seen, not covered with a frontal. It is carved with a representation of the martyrdom of the Protestant George Marsh (*see* Smithills, p. 171n.) in 1555. – REREDOS. 1886, with canopied niches. – PULPIT. Late C17.

Cut down, but still very fine despite the treacly varnish. The tester and small canopy mounted behind was the clerk's desk front. – PEWS. A notable feature of the church; of various dates, but all simple oak benches with scalloped ends. – CHANDELIER, commissioned in 1737 from *George Tarlington* for the brass, *J. Pearson* for the iron. The NE chapel under the organ was made by *G.G. Pace* in 1969–76, with characteristic stone altar, limed oak fittings, ceiling and coloured glass. – Hulton HATCHMENTS in the SE chapel. – MONUMENTS. The only notable one hangs on a spandrel of the N arcade, to Roger Holland †1828, his wife †1823 and son also †1828, with portrait medallions of all three; signed *S. Manning*. – STAINED GLASS. The E window, probably originally uncusped like the others, is by *William Warrington*, 1845. Rows of small saints, much canopy work, bright colours. In the SE chapel two armorial roundels with fine mantling, probably commemorating a Hulton marriage of 1663. On the S side one by *Kempe & Co.*, 1907, with the tower symbol of *W.E. Tower*. NE chapel E by *G. G. Pace*, 1976. The four-lighter N by the chapel, and the aisle clerestory window above it, are by *Shrigley & Hunt* in memory of John Kynaston Cross M.P., †1887. Duskily Pre-Raphaelite, with some beautifully rich colours. In the second light, an angel with a chalice; in the third, Jesus at Gethsemane. The artists were *Almquist* and *Jewitt* – a notable early work of theirs. Still on the N side, the George Marsh window of 1897. And at W end, an unusual window of 1959 by *H. R. Keedy*, depicting the two Wesley brothers and their mother with, below, scenes of their lives.

In the spacious CHURCHYARD: CROSS of 1893 commemorating George Marsh, set in an ancient cross socket. Freestanding PULPIT, 1880s. LYCHGATE, 1903, a proper little building, with doors.

CROAL MILL, Blackshaw Lane. By *Bradshaw, Gass & Hope*, 1908. A fine sight, the Baroque tower with two tiers of scrolls to achieve the octagonal top, the engine house with its big arched windows, and the more domestic office, all in red and grey brick and grouping well with the fall of the lane. The body of the mill is unadorned, with horizontal windows; the chimney has gone.

DOVE MILL, now Dovedale Mill, Deane Church Lane. By *Stott & Sons*, 1904. For super-fine mule spinning. Reinforced concrete structure. Five storeys of endlessly repeating segment-arched windows. The engine house, unusually with segment-headed arches too, survives at the r. end but the detached chimney has gone.

8. Heaton

W of the centre and N of the Croal valley, along Chorley New Road.

CHRISTCHURCH, Chorley New Road and Markland Hill. 1895–6 by *R. Knill Freeman*. A nice, relaxed composition, with a turret with wooden top attached to the two-storey organ chamber/vestry. Yellow and red stone. Aisles but no clerestory. Opaque interior, the effect of textured greenish glass and dark stone and wood. The tall six-bay arcades take no notice of the two bays of the transepts. Boarded barrel roofs except in the aisles. – FONT. A real giant clam shell, nacreous within, encrusted with sea creatures without, on a Corinthian column of alabaster. The other half of the shell is said to be in St Thomas and St John (see below). – STAINED GLASS. Confined to the aisles, and all by *Wippell* and mid C20. Some are signed, e.g. *A. F. Erridge*, *Cooper Abbs*, the latter characterized by Dan Dare lantern jaws even for the infant Christ.

PARISH HALL, NW. 1987, by a parishioner, *John Brindley*. Excellent group in orange brick with pyramid roofs; two linked blocks, the higher one containing the hall, which is square and well-lit, with a coved ceiling and French windows.

ST MARGARET, Lonsdale Road. The parish was founded in 1902 with the building of VANNEN HALL, named after the first vicar. The church was built by the second vicar in 1912–13 and is by *Austin & Paley*. It is of stone with a long level roofline and shouldered gables, the chancel arch indicated by a buttress. The aisles look as though they could be later. S porch, and a SE porch too. Was a tower intended? There is not enough land to extend W, but the blank walling at the W end, W buttresses and turning stair suggest that one could be built within the mass.

The interior was subdivided in 1982, with no attempt made to light the resulting W end rooms or use the void above. The shortening of the nave emphasizes its cave-like quality, the gold mosaic of the reredos glinting against the dark stone of the walls. Nave piers alternately round and octagonal, a very high chancel arch with sunk panelling, then a quicker rhythm in the chancel with two tall narrow arches N and three lower ones S. The SE chapel has a canted E end. Window designs are varied, as the firm liked them. – REREDOS, 1954, mosaic and *opus sectile* probably by *Whitefriars*. – FONT and PULPIT bases are like Perp pier bases. – STAINED GLASS. E by *Powell & Sons*, 1937. On the N side, St Margaret, with a budgie, of 1966 and signed E.N. – *Edith Norris*. The double window S is signed *Humphries Jackson & Ambler*, Manchester, 1921, and is good, with strong colours and modelling and no filling-in. They probably also did the window in the chapel, also 1921.

ST THOMAS AND ST JOHN, Tempest Road, Lostock. By *Jonathan Simpson*, 1914. Wooden and weatherboarded, with a little cupola. It has unequal transepts and a short chancel. Large Parish Centre *c.* 2000, of brick, connected by an octagonal link. The group is nicely placed on the hillside under a copse.

SOMERSET ROAD CHAPEL (United Reformed). Two early C20 linked buildings of hammered blackened stone with pale Bath stone dressings. Broad uncluttered chapel interior with shallow transepts. Hammerbeam roof with longitudinal braces. Organ in the shallow polygonal apse.

103 BOLTON SCHOOL, Chorley New Road. The great Runcorn sandstone length of the school with its collegiate gatehouse ranged behind expansive green lawns is one of the sights of Bolton. It is one of William Lever's major benefactions. In 1898 he was made a governor of the Grammar School, then still by the parish church. Within a year, by buying up houses, he had moved the school up onto Chorley New Road. In 1913 he brought it together with the Girls' High School in a new and re-endowed foundation. His brief for a new building was a U-shaped building with the base of the U on Chorley New Road, of red Runcorn stone, Elizabethan or Tudor. A competition, held in 1917 and judged by Bradshaw, Gass & Hope, was won by *C. T. Adshead* of Manchester. Lord Leverhulme, as he had become, died in 1925 leaving the school half-built. As at Liverpool Cathedral, built from the same quarries, work dragged on until after the Second World War at inflated cost and reduced ambition. The twin halls were finished in 1953 and the two quads, one on each side of the U, completed only in the 1960s, by *Bradshaw Gass & Hope*, with brick facing to the courtyards, which would have been unthinkable to Lever. On the boys' staircase a WAR MEMORIAL with STAINED GLASS by *Shrigley & Hunt*.

Lever wanted the new school to be co-educational on the American pattern, but 'one wing will be distinct for boys and one for girls'. Like the Fairfield Moravian Settlement (*see* Droylsden), boys' and girls' departments are mirror images, each with its great hall and quad. They meet only at the gatehouse, which contains the library. The intended central court with its huge chapel was scuppered by the need to allow access to a villa Lever had failed to buy. So the gatehouse arch leads only to a disparate group of ancillary buildings.

SWIMMING POOL of 1906, by *James Lomax-Simpson*, supervised by his father *Jonathan Simpson*, in brick and stone with a hammer- and collar-beam roof. It was converted and extended in 1993 by *Cassidy & Ashton* of Preston to make the ARTS AND SPORTS CENTRE. Its foyer has a cruck frame of laminated timber. BEECH HOUSE is now the Junior School; a mildly classical mid-Victorian villa with a Doric portico. The OLD MARKET CROSS on the lawn behind the boys' hall came from Churchgate in Bolton (q.v.). It looks C17.

CHORLEY NEW ROAD. Along the ridge and the s-facing slope rich C19 Boltonians built their villas. It is still the preserve of the well-to-do, but their requirements are different. Redevelopment proceeds apace, and many of the Victorian houses are represented today only by their names and gateposts. Among the best of the survivors are:

WOODSIDE, on Chorley New Road opposite Christchurch, now Clevelands School. One of several Gothic mansions by

George Woodhouse.* Built in 1877 for J. Mellor, but soon sold to his cousin J. P. Thomasson. Of darkened stone, with two Germanic stair-towers. Angled and corner oriels supported on single buttresses are a favourite motif. Good carving here and there, but there are still lumps waiting to be carved. WEST-COMBE, Beaumont Road. Built *c.* 1881 for Thomas Winder and said to be by *Frank Winder*. It was bought by W. H. Lever for a few years, and then by the Tillotsons. Plain solid house of uncoursed rubble, with some decorative half-timbering and tall deeply ribbed chimneys of brick. The classical porch was added in 1912–13 by *Jonathan Simpson*, who also made the Adam-style ceiling in the dining room. The house is excellently preserved, and so is the *Thomas Mawson* GARDEN with its rockwork, rose garden, beech hedges, vegetable plot and a greenhouse by *Halliday*'s of Middleton. Lever adored moving house, and after the birth of his only son in 1889 the family moved to Hillside on Chorley New Road, which has gone.

Michael Shippobottom also identifies ELDERCOT, by *Ormrod & Pomeroy*, 1905–6, on Chorley New Road and Greenmount Lane; SIDCOT by *Hermon Crook* for J.H. Smethurst, 1925, whitewashed in Arts and Crafts manner; MARSHCOTES on Oakwood Drive also by *Crook*, for himself; GREY GABLES on Chorley New Road by *Jonathan Simpson* for himself.

9. Halliwell

NW of the centre, along Chorley Old Road and Halliwell Road. For St Margaret, *see* Heaton.

ST PAUL, Halliwell Road. Church, schools and houses all of 1847 for John Horrocks Ainsworth, 'after seeing a similar layout in the south of England'. The architect was *James Greenhalgh*. They make an eye-catching set piece, the terraces and schools grouped around the little church on its raised green like the wings and offices about a Palladian house.

The church is relatively quiet, although it has an excessively steep roof, with a bellcote balanced on the w gable. It has Y-tracery but with the tympana filled with blocks of stone, and tall triple lancets E. No aisles. The steep roof is supported inside by delicately arcaded trusses. – Gothic BOX PEWS in four rows, i.e. with side aisles as well. – STAINED GLASS. E, SECOND WORLD WAR MEMORIAL with the *Wippell* monogram and the artist's signature and device, *A. F. Erridge*. – Arms of the Ainsworths, reset. – BRASSES to John Horrocks Ainsworth †1865, and to Col. Richard Ainsworth †1926. The flanking TERRACES were clearly back-to-backs, named Victoria and Albert Terraces on the two outer sides, and St Paul's Terrace on both of the sides facing the church. At the far end of the s terrace is the original VICARAGE, with bay windows. All have bold Tudor detail, the serried drip-moulds so pronounced as

* Others were Fernclough (for J. K. Cross), Ravenswood, and Westbourne.

to be the major motif of the group. The girls' school on the N side has similar detail, although it was added in 1856.

ST PETER, Church Road. 1838–40 for John Horrocks Ainsworth, by *J. W. Whittaker* who is buried here. Transepts and a short chancel were added in 1844 when the tower had to be rebuilt. The clumsy pinnacles, the long lancet windows with buttresses between, and the masonry itself, rock-faced but mechanically coursed, are all characteristic of the period. No aisles. The tie beams have summary tracery over, leaning to r. and l. They form an X at the crossing. – STAINED GLASS. Ainsworth arms, s transept. – MONUMENT. J.H. Ainsworth of Moss Bank †1865, of alabaster.

Detached but linked PARISH ROOM on the N side, of 1984, by *John B. Potts*, when the church was re-ordered and largely stripped of furnishings. Big churchyard with some fine trees.

SCHOOL. 1810. Of two storeys, and plain; now the Parish Office.

ST THOMAS, Eskrick Street. By *Paley & Austin*, 1875, and in its brick simplicity sensational for the date. It is for ever a pity that the N tower was not completed. The brick walls are unadorned, the aisles have just eight deeply set lancets, the clerestory fourteen. The arched vault of the N porch is brick. Only the W and E walls have more elaborate fenestration, that on the E entirely original, with its one long middle lancet and the flanking smaller lancets, and incidentally one of the few places where stone appears. Access, even by appointment, was not permitted. (The arcade arches are of brick, and brick is exposed above them. The arcades are of five bays with round piers and very simplified E.E. leaf-and-crocket capitals. The source of Paley & Austin's inspiration was probably the Bodley of Pendlebury. SEDILIA and PISCINA, in all this insistence on lancets, have round arches.) SCHOOL, w, 1877, by *R. Knill Freeman*, who trained in Austin & Paley's office.

CONGREGATIONAL CHURCH and MANSE, now IRON CHURCH ANTIQUES CENTRE, Blackburn Road and Draycott Street, i.e. at the Bolton end of Blackburn Road. Built 1895–8 for William Lever and his brother James in honour of their parents, by Lever's childhood friend *Jonathan Simpson*. The Iron Church nickname, a hang-over from its temporary predecessor of 1877, is still oddly apt. Of Lever's favourite rust-red Runcorn sandstone, now greenish with algae outside and white with efflorescence inside. Wiry SW steeple with an emphatic parapet at the base of the spire, three-sided apse linked to the manse. The absence of corner buttresses gives it a tight look. Spacious interior on the same system as Albion Congregational church in Ashton-under-Lyne, i.e. with half-height transepts, their arches taller than the aisle arcades but not as tall as the chancel arch. So there is not a proper crossing and the centre is relatively dark. Lavish carving; the piers inlaid with panels of foliage, the principal arches with paterae. – Lovely STAINED GLASS. Three E in memory of Eliza

Lever †1893 by *Henry Holiday*. s transept, Christ the Teacher, by *Walter J. Pearce*, 1928.

Across the road are the former SUNDAY SCHOOL of 1900, also by *Simpson*, and COOPER MEMORIAL INSTITUTE added in 1909; now The Islamic Society. Large, red, the School with red terracotta, the Institute with contrasting yellow stone.

HALLIWELL METHODIST CHURCH, Harvey Street. c18 or early c19 five-bay stone façade with arched windows in two storeys, but two have been raised into dormers, and an entrance introduced at one end.

METHODIST CHURCH, Chorley Old Road. 1902–3 by *J. C. Topping*. With its three domes this is something quite exceptional in Methodist architecture. Pink brick, yellow stone. Symmetrical façade with columns in two orders and shallow domes over the stair-towers. At the back a larger dome on a cubic crossing. It has lost its lantern, and is in any case set too low, so that the roofs cut into it. For sale in 2003, the Methodists having retreated to the adjacent SCHOOL of 1892, also presumably by *Topping* and quite showy.

UNITARIAN CHURCH, Chorley Old Road. By *Bradshaw Gass & Hope*, 1931. Tiny in comparison with the great bulk of St Thomas's behind, but it has the full complement of an oblong w tower with a saddleback roof, nave and aisles, and chancel, all of brick with brick tracery.

VEDA MANDIR and Community Centre, Thomas Holden Street. It was ST BARNABAS by *F. R. Freeman*, 1913. Built entirely of Accrington brick except for the chancel steps. A tower and full-length nave were intended (as shown in the STAINED GLASS).

QUEENS PARK. Laid out in 1864–6 to provide work during the Cotton Famine, by *William Henderson* of Birkenhead. Named Queens Park in 1897. Its 43 acres (17 hectares) on the s-facing slopes above the river buffered the villas of Chorley New Road from the smoky town. Its layout, boundaries and buildings have all been simplified. PARK ROAD LODGE is the only remaining building. STATUES of Disraeli by *T. Rawcliffe*, 1887; of J. T. Fielding by *J. Bowden*, 1896; and of James Dorrian by *John Cassidy*, 1898. WAR MEMORIAL 1928 by *Bradshaw Gass & Hope*.

LIBRARY, Hadfield Street. 1909–10, by *Brown & Henderson*, in the Bradshaw, Gass & Hope idiom.

MERE HALL, Brownlow Way. Now the Registry Office. The GATES to the park state that it was given to the town in 1890 by J. P. Thomasson, and carry his portrait medallion by *John Cassidy*. The park is tiny, but so elevated as to be quite an event. The house was built in 1837 for Benjamin Dobson. It is four-square, three bays each way, brick. Porch with paired fluted Doric columns on the s, and a semicircular bay, E.

(VICTORY HOTEL, Chorley Old Road. By *Jonathan Simpson* for Magee Marshall, 1888. Grand, Queen Anne, with three gables.)

ATLAS MILLS, Chorley Old Road. The seven mills of John Musgrave & Sons were a major concentration of spinning capacity, employing 2,000 at their peak. Now MORRISON'S SUPERMARKET, of 1989 by *John Brunton Parnership* of Leeds, occupies most of the site. In its café are displayed photographs of the demolition of the great chimney by Fred Dibnah in 1992. The Northern Mill Engine Society is housed in the windowless WAREHOUSE, built *c.* 1890 to store raw cotton bales. Also surviving are the derelict workshops and canteen of No. 4 mill.

FALCON MILL, Handel Street. By *George Temperley & Son*, 1907. Six-storey mule-spinning mill of red brick, unadorned except for stripes of blue bricks and yellow. Corner tower with Frenchified roof and the name in white brick on green. It has terracotta capitals but the pilasters have been removed. It was electrically driven by its own steam turbine and generator, and has concrete filler joist floors.

EGYPTIAN MILL, Slater Street. Five-and-a-half storeys with the top and bottom emphasized, i.e. a notional giant order. Engine house at the back but no chimney. Corner tower with a telescopic top. SKAGEN COURT, 1970s, immediately w of Egyptian Mill. A system-built, deck-access housing development of the sort that went out of fashion almost as soon as it was built. The *Jesperson* system developed in Copenhagen was used. Laing's were the British licencees, and the factory was in Heywood. Extruded like some industrial moulding around a large communal space, it is of five storeys throughout, in grey concrete with flat roofs and strong horizontal emphasis. Flying bridges connect the decks across the open corners.

10. Barrow Bridge and Smithills

Moving up into moorland country, N of the ring road.

DEAN MILLS. In 1844 a mill-owner could declare, in Disraeli's *Coningsby* 'Why, in the way of machinery, you know, Manchester is a dead letter. If you want to see life, go to Stalybridge or Bolton. There's high pressure'. Disraeli visited Dean Mills in 1840, and so in 1851 did Prince Albert, after seeing the company's exhibits at the Great Exhibition. It was also a notable example of industrial philanthropy. Robert Gardner and Robert Bazley founded the enterprise in 1831, building a pair of six-storey mills linked by an engine house by the river. The mills have gone (they stood where the bus turnaround is today), but they also built a MODEL VILLAGE called Barrow Bridge, and this survives. It consists of five rows of stone houses, many with pretty single-stone canopies over the door, with the first in each row turned so that its entrance is at the end, and a further row of taller ones. Three blocks of gardens interrupt the rows, so there was plenty of room. The rows with gardens on both sides seem to have been back-to-backs. The houses were provided with water and gas. On the other side of

Bazley Street is the very large INSTITUTE of 1846, now called Barrowdene House, of 2 + 7 + 2 bays with a hall on the upper floor. On the road below, near the site of the mills, was the shop and, further up the valley, the managers' houses, singly or in pairs, pretty three-bay houses with hipped roofs. Unlike Millbank's mill in *Coningsby*, the partners refused to have either a pub or a church, maintaining that both were potential sources of disturbance.

HALLIWELL BLEACH WORKS was immediately downstream. The largest in Bolton, it was established by Peter Ainsworth of Moss Bank in 1739. His grandson Richard, who had pioneered the use of chemical bleaching, bought the Smithills estate in 1801. All that remains is the giant CHIMNEY built by John Horrocks Ainsworth in 1863, rising sheer from the earth. It is octagonal, 30 ft (9 metres) across at the base, and was originally 306 ft tall.*

SMITHILLS HALL. A large country house on the moorland edge, of a picturesqueness more accidental than designed, and an architectural history more beset with entanglements than most. It consists of three ranges E, N and W of an open court.

William Radcliffe obtained the manor in 1335 and the nucleus of the present house appears to date from the middle of that century: hall with its screens passage at the W end, buttery and pantry in line, and a kitchen originally detached slightly further W. The solar was over the buttery and pantry. A new family cross-wing was added at the E end some time later, perhaps in the early C15. In 1485 the estate passed by marriage to Andrew Barton. He or his son was responsible for the nearly separate E range with its large square bay. An external timber stair was tucked in at the angle, and from this sprang corridors along the courtyard side on both floors of the S range, as at Speke (in SW Lancashire). The chapel at the S end of the range was built c. 1580–90, although its W end was rebuilt after a fire in 1856. In the early C16 a W range was built in line with the kitchen. This had two-storey corridors matching those of the E wing, but they were open, like those of an inn. Early C19 sketches show a gate arch at the S end of the W wing, but it is not certain whether the court was ever closed by a S range. In 1801 the estate was sold to the Ainsworths (*see* p. •• above), who were probably initially concerned as much to protect their water rights as they were with the old house. By 1850 they had made the W wing into a fashionable residence, but beyond the Hall the E range was falling into decay. Colonel Richard Ainsworth inherited in 1870 and engaged *George Devey* in 1874–8 and again in 1882–4 to remodel the W end. It is this, with its gaily unconvincing black-and-white work, that makes the strongest initial impact. Nigel Ainsworth sold the hall and the estate, which stretches NW right up to Winter Hill, to the County Borough of Bolton in 1938.

*The Ainsworths also showed notable philanthropic concern for their workforce; *see* St Paul, Halliwell.

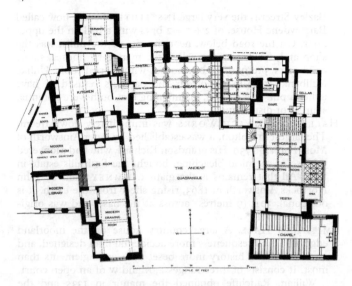

Smithills Hall, plan by Henry Taylor, 1884

The outer walls are predominantly of stone, with timber-framing only showing in parts of the w end, where it seems to be almost totally renewed, and in the court, where the two-storey corridor with its continuous windowing, quatrefoils and cove is particularly pretty. The massive hall door with its tiny courtesy door has survived under its steeply pointed stone arch, and two wooden-framed windows. The walls of the hall range have been heightened, perhaps to counteract its diminutive appearance in the greatly expanded house. The early C19 parts, which are substantial, are in plain watershot stone with mullioned windows. *Devey*'s stonework is of superior craftsmanship but harsh texture. His timbering, while often reproducing old forms, is dotted with large black sunk quatrefoils of no known provenance.

The massively timbered C14 HALL is a room as impressive as the halls at Baguley (Manchester) and Ordsall (Salford), although here the effect is lessened by the building up of the floor levels so that the plinths are buried and the doors dwarfed. The roof with its three tiers of quatrefoil braces sits on the original eaves and retains its steep pitch, with a later shallower-pitched roof on top to allow for the heightening of the walls. The w wall has bold elongated quatrefoils, and so does the spere truss. There are the usual three service doors to kitchen, buttery and pantry, their heads cut into the huge mid-rail, plus a fourth which probably led, like that at Chorley Old Hall in Cheshire, up to the solar. It seems that the side walls were always of stone, for there is no evidence of missing timbers. The E wall is as impressive as the W, with a middle tier of uncusped braces, but it belongs structurally to the E CROSS-WING. The big braces run all round the upper floor of this wing, interrupted only by the rebuilding of the N wall in stone, and by the stone stack on its E side. Steeply cambered tie-beams in the upper chamber support kingposts. The intermediate floor has been replaced with a C16 one, finely moulded and square framed, probably at the same time as the fireplaces were inserted. The C16 E RANGE is a separate building, connected awkwardly to the rest by the porch-cum-stair-tower.* Plain rectangular framing is exposed in the corridor, but has been replaced elsewhere. Bay, stair-tower and corridors are all structurally independent but appear to have been added in close sequence. The ground-floor WITHDRAWING ROOM, with its finely moulded ceiling joists, is fully panelled; it is complicated linenfold stuff, with in addition pairs of male and female heads in profile, geometric fancies, and Andrew Barton's rebus. It is odd that the panelling blocks three smaller windows; but see the Oak Dining Room, below. The clumsy rebuilding of the outer walls suggests that a stack has been lost. The CHAPEL is a stone building at the S end of the E wing. It suffered a fire in 1856 and was restored by Peter Ainsworth, when the vestry with its fireplace, now blocked, was made into a transept with a family pew above. The E window, mullioned-and-transomed with uncusped arched lights, has a remarkable display of mid-C16 heraldic STAINED GLASS. Top centre is the royal arms, flanked l. by a splendidly spirited Eagle and Child 21 with the shield of Ferdinand Stanley, who succeeded as 5th Earl of Derby in 1593, and r. by the shield of the See of Canterbury impaling Archbishop Thomas Cranmer †1556. At either end and in the middle row are the shields of Lancashire families. The bottom row is mostly Victorian, with Ainsworth shields. Two good Ainsworth MONUMENTS, 1833 and 1870.

Returning now to the hall we can explore the W end. Its many changes of level and orientation make it easy to get lost; nor is navigation made easier by the visually discordant diagonal corridor running across the NW angle. The C14 detached KITCHEN exists only as a ghost, but it has imprinted itself on the structures that have grown up around it and its crooked orientation has affected the whole of the W range. The N wall has gone, as has part of the W wall. The S wall has an internal corner, with stone mullioned windows incorporating a supposed dole window, opening onto a tiny hidden courtyard. The space is like a shapeless corridor. In the wing overlooking the quad are the GREEN HALL and the WHITE DRAWING ROOM. The structure is C16 and the decor *Devey*, but the narrow pointed arched doorways with their reeded reveals are Gothick, i.e. perhaps early C19. The fireplace in the drawing room is Devey's but it is in a C16 stack and three of the

---

* Here is shown the footprint of the Protestant martyr George Marsh, condemned at Smithills in 1555.

moulded stones of the surround are C16. The fireplace in the room above is the same, so perhaps they have both simply been widened. Tucked in by the stack is a sweet staircase with a corner of mullioned windows on the landing. It looks like Devey outside but is clearly C17 and C18. The LIBRARY comes next. It is a splendid C19 pastiche, dark and rich with pieced-together panelling and carving. Next door is the teashop, a large bare L-shaped room. It was the OAK DINING ROOM, considered in 1855 to be the leading feature of the house, erected by Peter Ainsworth 'in admirable keeping with the rest of the edifice'. It was made the same size and shape as Andrew Barton's Withdrawing Room in order to purloin its panelling, which remained here until Bolton took over the house. An ornate chimneypiece carrying the initials AB together with the arms of the Bartons and the Ainsworths, and a damaged pendant ceiling remain. The MAIN STAIR is appropriately wide and oaken. Halfway up is a fireplace in the Chinese taste, beneath a large window; an extravagance and a talking point no doubt. Little can be seen at present of the BILLIARD ROOM at the extreme W end, but it is fully panelled with a damaged pendant ceiling and a giant inglenook. It remains to mention, because it is easily missed, the EDUCATION ROOM, which occupies part of the internal court, was a fore-runner of Devey's billiard room, and has a glass dome. A good deal of the warren-like upper floor is disused.

The KNOT GARDEN (probably a C19 recreation of a Tudor one) in the S quad has been recovered from under turf. Long S terrace with a mount, bastions and a ha-ha. The STABLES across the valley, picturesquely unattractive in stone and timber-framing, are by *George Devey*, 1874–8.

MOSS BANK PARK. The house was built by Peter Ainsworth II in 1786–90. Enlarged several times, it was deserted by the family in 1870 and demolished in 1951. The environs became a public park in 1928. (AVIARY and OBSERVATORY TOWER remain.)

MONTSERRAT is a large Council estate of good quality housing with some Neo-Georgian detail. Outside ST JAMES (R.C.), a dual-purpose building of 1954, is a stone CROSS of Dark Ages character, though undateable. It was used as a footbridge over Doffcocker Brook and one side is worn smooth. Simple, powerful.

BOOTHSTOWN

W of Worsley, and bordering the Wigan boundary. Booths was part of the manor of Worsley and the estate was created in the C14 for a younger son of Henry de Worsley. For St John Mosley Common *see Lancashire: Liverpool and the South-West*.

BOOTH'S HALL. Booth's Hall Road. There was evidently a house of some sort from early times, but little is known of it and the present building dates from the early or mid c18. A rainwater head dated 1782 with the initials SC presumably records alterations made by Samuel Clowes who owned it from the later c18. Rather unprepossessing, painted brick, symmetrical, three bays and three storeys. c20 rear extensions and replacement windows.

BRADSHAW

7010

Bradshaw lies NE of Bolton and runs into it, but it retains a strong sense of an early industrial community clustered round Bradshaw bridge.

ST MAXENTIUS. A very unusual dedication. The tiny tower of the old chapel of ease, now free-standing, is dated by the Victoria County History to 1640 though it may be older. Diagonal buttresses, simplest arched bell-openings. It had a wooden top stage, like Middleton (q.v.). Photographs of the old chapel show the s side of c17 stone, the N of 1775 brick; but the piers were wooden, suggesting that it was a timber-framed building progressively rebuilt. The new church, which lies a little s and w of the tower, is by *E. G. Paley*. It took a long time to build, 1863–72. Dec with Geometric tracery. It has a bellcote, transepts, and a vestry with a cross-gable. Austere interior. Long nave with a hammerbeam roof; the chancel has close-coupled rafters. – FONT dated 1550, octagonal. – MOSAIC above the N transept partition, 1960s, depicting the fancied life of St Maxentius; crude. – STAINED GLASS. Two by *Shrigley & Hunt* in startling contrast. E, conventional, probably by *Almquist*, 1896. s transept 1950s, boldly abstract, representing the sacraments; perhaps by *R. Hayes*.

BRADSHAW HALL, ½ m. N. It was a tall early c17 house of the Gawthorpe (N Lancashire) type, but had already been considerably reduced before final demolition in 1949. Now all that is left is the porch, and many of its stones are replacements. Round-arched entrance, Roman Doric columns, and baluster pinnacles as at Hall i' th' Wood. The sill of a five-light mullioned window to one side is almost buried. Remains of a pleasure garden in front. BARNS and extensive early c19 farm buildings to one side.

BLEACHWORKS buildings behind have been converted and proliferated *c.* 2000 into a residential enclave, by *Longden NW*.

The church stands at an important junction of the roads to Ramsbottom and Harwood, and the proto-industrial settlement is very attractive today. Raw cotton was laid to bleach in the meadows, and the necessary copious supply of water came from the brook, broadened out into a reservoir behind the church. The Scowcroft and Hardcastle families built terraces of stone COTTAGES *c.* 1840 for their workforce, some three-storeyed, many of them facing away from the road. The CROFTER'S ARMS however is of brick which must then have

stood out. Named after the bleaching crofters, it was built by
William Scowcroft in 1790. LEE GATE FARM, just beyond the
cottages on Lee Gate Road, belongs to the late C17. The farmhouse is quite distinguished in its architectural motifs but they
are artlessly disposed. The door, set to one side of the shallow
projecting wing, has a huge lintel stone incised to make
a scallop shape. Above it is one of the characteristic but
uncommon Lancashire bottle-shaped windows, a triplet under
an ogee hoodmould. String courses step up and down as
required. In the re-entrant angle are two tiny round windows,
like gunloops. In the wing a fire window, lighting the fireside.
The l. wing was a separate dwelling. The adjacent BARN carries
the date 1729 and a pious inscription. POLICE HOUSE, opposite the church, 1900, unmistakable with its pressed red brick
and generous stone dressings, Tudor style with a shaped gable,
and Lancashire arms.

8010   BURY

INTRODUCTION

The smallest of the Metropolitan Boroughs of Greater Manchester. Bury M.B.C., which was created along with the others
in 1974, is long and thin, with Ramsbottom at the N end and
Prestwich at the S. Bury proper is also the smallest of the major
towns that ring the metropolis (population 60,000 in 2001,
reduced from 90,000 in 1876, out of a borough population of
180,000). For this reason, perhaps, it retains more of the feeling
of a Lancashire market town than any other. Fields and moors
are the background to every view, even from the market place.
    Bury was owned by the Earls of Derby, who ousted the Pilk-
ingtons as Lords of the Manor after Bosworth in 1485. It has
tended to be High Church, in opposition to its neighbour Bolton.
Following the Napier report of 1840 it became a military town,
the headquarters of the XXth Lancashire Fusiliers, with a substantial barracks on Bolton Road built in 1842–5. Like the other
SE Lancashire towns its prosperity was built upon its industries.
'The cotton manufactures of this town and its vicinity are carried
on to an almost incredible extent' reported the *Beauties of
England and Wales* as early as 1807. Chief among them was the
'very capital manufacturing works of Sir Robert Peel, Bart and

Co. on the banks of the Irwell' (*see* also Summerseat and Rams-bottom). His son, also Sir Robert, was the Prime Minister. Peel Mills, immediately N of the town centre, represent the develop-ment of the family firm. In 1981 the business transformed itself into the mighty Peel Holdings, owners and developers of, among other things, the Trafford Centre (Stretford, q.v.), the Manchester Ship Canal (Manchester, p. 302) and Chat Moss. Papermak-ing was another industry making use of the waters of the Irwell, which continues today. There was also widespread coal mining. The remains of industry are not so visible today as in Bolton or Oldham, except for the revived East Lancashire Railway – *see* p. 182 below – with its frequent steam and antique diesel sounds and smells.

The town centre, which was never large, was in the 1970s tightly ringed by major roads. Bury, like Birmingham, may live to regret this. Roads have cut off even the town hall from the centre, although this and other buildings immediately outside the ring have been included here.

Bury has its quota of home-grown or nurtured architects. *John Harper* (1809–42), born near Blackburn, trained under Benjamin and Philip Wyatt. Although he practised at York, Bury is the best place to see his work. In the last five years of his short life he built three churches, each in a different style: St Marie (R.C.), 1841–2, Perp; All Saints, Elton 1841–3, Norman, with its tower on the chancel, and St Paul 1838–42 in lancet style. He also did two schools, at Elton and Tottington. *James Maxwell* of Bury, arti-cled to Thomas Holmes (*see* also Holcombe) went into partner-ship with *William Charles Tuke* of Bradford 1865 to form *Maxwell & Tuke*. Their work varies, perhaps reflecting the personalities of the partners; some relatively conventional like the Congrega-tional Church of 1885, some having a distinctively precise skin-tight look, with minimal projections: Christchurch, Walmersley, 1883 and St Mary, Hawkshaw, 1890–2. *Lawrence Booth* is the other local man to note. He did Christchurch, or the Jesse Haworth Memorial Church at Walshaw 1889–92, a showy design with exceptionally lavish carving. His St Thomas, Rochdale Road (1866) is more fussy than lavish. Also by him is Barclay's Bank, formerly Bury Banking Co. on Silver Street, 1868, a rich stone palazzo with polychromy and sculpture.

CHURCHES

ST MARY. Church and steeple have never been happy with each other. The earliest pictorial record shows a Georgian classical building (by *Thomas Towneley*, 1777–80) with a diminutive late medieval tower and spire. The tower was rebuilt in 1842–4 by *A. H. Cates* of York with a broach spire, too tall for the C18 nave and uncomfortably at odds with it in style. At the insti-gation of Canon Hornby the Georgian church was pulled down and a new one built in 1872–6 by *J. S. Crowther*. So today

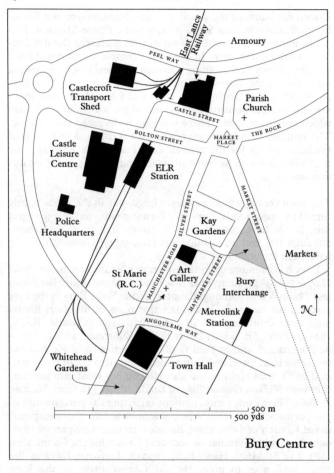

Bury Centre

we see Crowther's church and Cates's steeple, still at odds with one another – a classic case of alternating redevelopment. Steeple and church, although both Victorian Dec, are comically different in scale. Crowther's church, in golden Darley Dale coursed rubble, looms over Cates's little ashlar gritstone steeple, its ridge higher than the start of the spire. It is richly Geometrical and very tall, with prominent stair-turrets flanking the chancel arch and a three-sided apsidal E end. There was no thought of returning to the Lancashire Perp which must have stood here once. Instead we have Lincolnshire Dec, with the polygonal E end modelled perhaps on Lichfield and the twin turrets, which Crowther used so often, recalling those of Manchester Cathedral. He left a gap between

his W wall and the little tower, bridging it with a low transversely roofed narthex. At its S end is the porch, at the N a
polygonal baptistery, so it reads as a miniature version of the
church itself. The grand S porch leads into a low space with
the polygonal baptistery ahead under a wooden rib vault and
an open arcade on the right. Turning through the arcade
reveals a breathtakingly high version of the same thing, the
arcaded space and the polygonal apse under a wooden rib
vault. Surprisingly the interior is brick-lined, and the arcades
are pushed outwards, making the aisles relatively insignificant.
Arcades and aisles are unsynchronized, with just four arcade
bays to the six of the aisle windows. The high clerestory has an
internal walkway with a quatrefoiled parapet, like that in the
nave of Chester Cathedral. The nave roof is a very steep double
hammerbeam with alternate high-level ties. A double transversely roofed chapel opens off the S side of the chancel –
another Victorian, not medieval, feature. The sheer, fully glazed
W wall is only faintly shadowed by the W steeple; a rare achievement. Dozens of PORTRAIT HEADS, carved by *Earp & Hobbs*,
terminate the drip moulds. The architect, with sideburns and
a worried expression, is on the W arcade SW corner. The Earl
and Countess of Derby are on the chancel arch, Bishop Lee
on the S chapel arches, but Bishop Fraser, who considered this
'the gem of the diocese', is hidden behind the reredos. Children in the baptistery.

REREDOS, a memorial to Captain Bridge †1919, by *J. Harold
Gibbons*. Brightly coloured and gilded figures under a hood. –
CHOIR STALLS. 1893, by *Austin & Paley*. – SCREEN. Iron,
1899. – PULPIT. Delicately carved, of many different stones,
by *Earp & Hobbs*. – FONT, 1850, from the old church, with a
tall three-tier filigree cover; by *George Shaw*.* – S CHAPEL
REREDOS, also brightly coloured; a memorial to the Rector's
son †1916, by *F. E. Howard*. – CHAPEL SCREENS. Iron. To the
chancel, probably by *Crowther*; to the nave, by *Giles Gilbert Scott
c.* 1910. – PAINTINGS. On gilded copper, in the wall arcading
of the apse, given by Sarah Openshaw 1880s. – The FLOORS
are a tour-de-force. The narthex, centre alley of the nave, and
the chancel are laid with brilliantly coloured geometric mosaic
in large sweeping circles; by *Minton & Co.*

STAINED GLASS. An unusually consistent scheme. Chancel,
chapel, W wall and baptistery are all by *Hardman*; figures in
cartouches against a geometrical background. The exception
is a single NE lancet in the baptistery, undated, by *Kempe*.
Nave, with canopy work, all by *Clayton & Bell*. – MONU-
MENTS. Many tablets recalling that this is a garrison church.
The best is in the tower, signed *T. Kirk* 1824; Lieutenants
Robert and George Hood, while engaged in the overland
Arctic expedition, the former assassinated by an Iroqois. A

---

* Other *Shaw* fittings were transferred to Christchurch, Ainsworth (q.v.).

walrus on an iceberg represents the Arctic; an elephant, Africa.
– Brass to Geoffrey Hornby, Rector, †1850, chancel floor.

WAR MEMORIAL in the churchyard wall, SW, by *Sir Reginald Blomfield*, 1924. Grey granite cross and curving wings. Bronze reliefs by *J. H. Cawthra*; soldiers, sailors, nurses and wounded in informal procession l., workers on the home front r.

The RECTORY, like the church, has been repeatedly rebuilt, but its big walled garden is a remarkable survival in the middle of town. In THE WYLDE, N of the church, is the BISHOP ASHTON ROOM, formerly Bury Grammar School. Of 1784, by Mr Robinson, presumably *Lawrence Robinson* of Middleton, clerk of works to James Wyatt at Heaton Hall (*see* p. 398). Handsome single-storey range of ashlar with the windows and door under linked superarches. The interior was a single room, with a curved apse at each end. At right angles is a contrasting Gothic wing of 1862 by Mr Whittaker, perhaps *J. W. Whittaker* of Bolton, again a single room, with a hammerbeam roof.

ST MARIE (R.C.), Silver Street. 1841–2, by *John Harper*, of York (but born near Blackburn). An openwork octagonal lantern balancing on a giant arch forms the eye-catching W front. Arch and lantern are filled with Perp tracery. St Helen's in York is the model. The rest bears little relationship to its frontispiece. Open interior without aisles or side galleries. Few windows either; the church is principally lit by the six-light Perp E window in its short chancel. Dado of glossy brown and green moulded tiles, like a pub. – STAINED GLASS. E by *William Wailes*. In the few side windows, glass by *A. Ferdinand Ltd* of Didsbury.

HOLY TRINITY, Spring Street. 1863–5 by *E. G. Paley*. Sombre double-naved church, towerless, with the chancel attached to the S nave. Heavy plate tracery E and W. All the details which were to be carved have been left in the block. (Airy interior, with few fixtures. Five-bay arcade, with round piers on high bases and naturalistically carved capitals. The N aisle ends at the E in a three-bay arcade. Beyond is the small Lady Chapel, with a brightly painted REREDOS by *J. Harold Gibbons*, a First World War memorial, introduced in 1987.) Large stone RECTORY immediately W, simpler and rather better than the church.

UNITARIAN CHAPEL, Silver Street. A dark brick cube with rounded corners, by *Terence Ratcliffe*, 1974. Nothing, inside or out, is preserved of its three predecessors, which were of 1719, like the one at Ainsworth (q.v.); 1837, classical; 1852, Gothic, by *Bowman & Crowther*. Nor does it reveal anything of its interior disposition, or its purpose. The walls are in discontinuous sections, interrupted by dark slit windows. The chapel turns out to be in the NE corner; all white, full-height, with a light scoop on the roof. SCULPTURE by *Elizabeth Mulchinek*, of five children.

CONGREGATIONAL CHURCH, Rochdale Road. 1885 by *Maxwell & Tuke*. Red brick and yellow stone. Gothic dress, with a pair of large four-light windows over a single entrance in between the usual staircase shoulders.

PUBLIC BUILDINGS

THE CASTLE, Castle Street. The names Bury or Burgh, and The Rock, which is the name of the street S of the church, are suggestive. The Pilkingtons were given licence to fortify their manor house in 1465, but forfeited it to the Stanleys twenty years later, following the battle of Bosworth. It was already ruinous in Leland's time, half a century later still. Part of the buttressed moat wall is exposed.

CASTLE ARMOURY, Castle Street. By *Henry Styan* of Manchester with the Borough Surveyor *James Farrer*. Toy fort architecture, very old-fashioned for its date of 1868. In 1906–7 it was extended, unbelievably in identical style, by *Alfred Hopkinson* of Bury. It is a mock-military pastiche in the Norman mode with arrowslits, crenellations, turrets of various sizes, and gargoyles. Everything to the r. of the thinnest and tallest tower belongs to the extension, including the splendid military trophies carved in relief over the entry arch. As architecture it is none the worse for its anachronism. The long asymmetrical front composes very well along the narrow street, especially when the parpoint stonework (in which the stone is dressed to a rock face in a mechanical way) glitters in raking sun. Behind, the plain brick DRILL HALL.

ART GALLERY AND LIBRARY, Moss Street and Silver Street. Thomas Wrigley, paper-maker, of Timberhurst,* left his collection to the town on condition that a suitable building was provided to display it. A competition was held in 1897, assessed by R. Knill Freeman, and the present building by *Woodhouse & Willoughby* opened in 1901. The style was said by the architects to be English Renaissance of the C18, freely treated. It is faced with the finest ashlar and punctuated by three gable-fronts with an applied gatehouse motif of superimposed orders of three storeys, one on Moss Street and two on Silver Street. The galleries are on the first floor, as the blank upper walls make clear, with an off-centre entrance on Moss Street by a four-column portico on the gable-front. The ground floor is given over to the Library, entered through a loggia between the Silver Street gable-fronts. Processions of sculpted allegorical figures, by *J. J. Millson*, wrap around the projecting gable-fronts behind the middle order: above the Gallery entrance, Architecture and Sculpture; on the library front, Literature and the Applied Arts. STAINED GLASS is by *Walter J. Pearce*.

TECHNICAL SCHOOL, Broad Street (now the Arts and Crafts Centre). By *Joshua Cartwright*, Borough Engineer, 1893–4. A similar composition to the Gallery. Ashlar, with a three-storey frontispiece on a two-storey building, the upper storey blank

---

* A house nearby by *Thomas Worthington*, 1853, demolished.

but top-lit. Relief figure SCULPTURE in panels of the Arts, Crafts and Applied Sciences by *J. J. Millson* and *J. R. Whittick*. LAMPS by *Janet Lubinska*, 1995. The building reaches back to Moss Street where there is another façade. All the flues are gathered into a single prominent chimney, square and ribbed. The long corridor is enlivened by Lancashire roses in coloured glass set into the doors, and radiators with atlantes. Cantilever stair with flowing iron balustrading.

TOWN HALL, Knowsley Street. On the edge of the town centre, outside the ring road. By *Reginald Edmonds* of *Jackson & Edmonds* of Birmingham, 1939–40, then 1947–54. Sir Hubert Worthington was the assessor of the competition. Large and dull, unfeelingly clad in fine ashlar stone and visually flat roofed. The front faces away from town over a sunken railway line. Semicircular portico entrance with clumsy oblong columns. Three giant recesses, the centre containing the borough arms, the outer ones the Lancashire rose, fatly carved and brightly coloured with horrid garlands. The massing of the building and the giant recesses owe something to Egyptian temples; the windows, where they are not simply punched through, are Greek, with paterae.

The RAILWAY BRIDGE carrying Knowsley Street, presumably of 1846, is very fine, with radiating voussoirs.

WHITEHEAD MEMORIAL GARDEN AND CLOCK TOWER, across the railway cutting in front of the town hall. Given in 1914 by Henry Whitehead in memory of his brother Walter, a surgeon. The clock tower is by *Maxwell & Tuke*. Of Portland stone with an ogee cupola and fussy, evenly distributed Arts and Crafts Gothic detailing. Bronze plaques by *Thornton & Co.* flanking the door under its ogee arch, and a dancing figure of Time by *Moreau* above. – Also in the park the SOUTH AFRICA WAR MEMORIAL, 1904, of the Lancashire Fusiliers. On a stone plinth a surprisingly jubilant soldier in bronze, by *George Frampton*, waves his shako at the oncoming traffic. Plaques on each side carry the names in artistic lettering under a stylized Art Nouveau oak wood. – COASTAL FORCES MEMORIAL. A tribute to Robert Whitehead, the inventor of the torpedo, an example of which is mounted on a rock. – FOUNTAIN, long dry, by *T. R. Kitsell* of Plymouth, 1897, in debased Renaissance forms. Grey granite base, red granite columns, worn Portland stone canopy topped by a Scottish flying crown supporting an iron weathervane.

DIVISIONAL POLICE HEADQUARTERS, Irwell Street. *c.* 1968. A pair of point blocks of six and five storeys with a low linking section. Post and beam structure of Brutalist concrete, with the posts set well back, allowing the exciting recessions which make these buildings so assertive on the skyline.

BURY MARKET is locally famous, but the buildings are not up to much. MARKET HALL, Market Parade, by *Harry S. Fairhurst*, 1971. Butterfly-winged but not graceful. The spine beam is uncomfortably heavy and low, its support uncomfortably invisible. The adjacent FISH AND MEAT MARKET by

Leslie Jones, 1999, is more fun. Jelly-bean plan with a circular
bulge near the middle. Stalls facing outwards as well as
inwards. A clerestory with a silver brise-soleil lights the
interior.

MILLGATE SHOPPING CENTRE, off Market Parade, 1980s.
Unambitious but successful, perhaps for that reason. Simply a
series of covered streets. The glazing supports are white and
tubular, the floors cheerfully tiled.

BURY GRAMMAR SCHOOL. Bridge Road, in the angle between
the Manchester and Bolton roads, and now cut off by the ring
road. A series of Accrington brick buildings by *William Venn
Gough* of Bristol. The boys' school, 1900–3; girls', 1904–6;
central hall, 1906–7.

BURY COLLEGE, on the continuation of Market Street beyond
the ring road. Woodley Centre building of 1937, large and symmetrical with an implied giant order and twin Egyptianizing
entrances. Hall tacked on the S end. Millennium Building,
2001 by *Bond Bryan* of Sheffield. Steel frame clad in two tones
of grey with flush windows. Orange brick reserved for the stairways and the circular entrance. Entry is by a bridge to the
second floor.

PERAMBULATION

In the irregular MARKET SQUARE, in front (S) of the parish
church, is the PEEL MONUMENT, over life-sized, by *E. H. Baily*,
1852. The inscription with its corn wreath refers to his repeal of
the corn laws. The TWO TUBS public house, W, is probably late
C17 and originally timber-framed.

Four principal streets radiate from here. We take them in turn.

SILVER STREET, S, the town's grandest, leads to the town hall
and on to Manchester, although it is cut by the ring road.
BARCLAY'S BANK, formerly Bury Banking Co. By *Blackwell,
Son & Booth*, 1868–9, with sculpture by *Joseph Bonehill*. A
lavish stone palazzo with rounded corners. String course of
grey granite and a pair of polished red granite pilasters above
the entrance. The manager's house, striped in stone and brick,
is at the rear. Former CONSERVATIVE CLUB and UNION
BANK, 1904. Atlantes carry the corner entrance hood, reclin-
ing figures prop up the intermediate semicircular pediments.
Between the library and St Marie's (*see* above), the TEXTILE
HALL, 1893–4 by *David Hardman*, with SCULPTURE by
Whittick & Royle. Around St Marie's are terraces of brick two-
storey houses, purely Georgian though dated 1845 etc.

The short length of MARKET STREET, SE, is dominated by
DERBY HALL (now THE MET) by *Sydney Smirke*, 1850, for
the 13th Earl of Derby. Corinthian temple façade on a rusticated basement, with circular niches above the three windows.
To the l. a lower seven-bay section with a semicircular pediment. Inside was the assembly room, a lofty courthouse, the

police station, and in the basement public baths. To the r. of the temple, distressingly, is nothing worth talking about. Smirke's handsome Athenaeum, and his Derby Hotel on the corner of the market place, were foolishly knocked down in the 1960s. Opposite is the former Manchester & District Bank, now YATES'S WINE BAR, a palazzo of 1860. Market Street leads s to KAY GARDENS, created in 1901 on the site of the Derby Market. In the middle of the triangular garden is the KAY MONUMENT by *W. Venn Gough* of Bristol, a belated recognition by the town of the importance of John Kay (born here in 1704) and his flying shuttle. A kind of solid pavilion of granite and Portland stone, with a stone dome. Bronze Fame on top, small bronze figures of workers on the four pediments. Bronze portrait medallion and reliefs of handloom and power loom, signed, faintly, *John Cassidy* 1907. Facing the gardens is the ART PICTURE HOUSE by *Albert Winstanley*, 1921–2, faced in white faience and symmetrical. The auditorium, though obscured, is intact: paired curvy boxes and a semicircular gallery, fronted with dancing cherubs. Stage with semicircular proscenium arch. Former CO-OP building, 1930s. The Portland stone towers are recognizable, but the rest has been hidden by black glass. Beyond the Ring Road but still in Market Street is the BURY TIMES GROUP BUILDING, an engaging little building on a triangular site by *Thomas Barnes* of Bury, 2001. Yellow brick, pinkish render and silver cladding differentiate the working parts, stairs, and lift respectively, with a continuously glazed top storey demonstrating the structural system and blunt aerofoil section roofs over all.

Not much in BOLTON STREET, W. SNOOKER CLUB. One of *Norman Evans*'s Temperance billiard halls of *c.* 1910, of which a complete example survives at Chorlton-cum-Hardy, Manchester (q.v.), but this is a double-span version. Tiling and mosaic survive on the façade, but the dormers have gone and nothing of the original interior is visible. BOLTON STREET STATION, the revived East Lancashire Railway headquarters. Built in 1846 but now mainly of 1952, plus a new pastiche buffet building on the platform. At the back of the small car park opposite the station a footpath named Castlecroft drops down to CASTLECROFT TRANSHIPMENT SHED, 1846. Strong stone building with three gables and three parallel roofs, and three arched entrances on all four sides. That is all, except for a suggestion of pilasters at the corners and the undifferentiated surrounds – no keystones, no springers – to the openings. The roofs are carried on iron columns and have only very shallow longitudinal bracing.

THE ROCK, E. By the chancel of the parish church is the UNION CLUB and BANK of 1874. It could almost be by Crowther with a different hat on. Tall, of header-bond brickwork with stripes of blue and red stretchers and some tile insets. Fancy stone side entrance with plate tracery above. The top storey is timber-framed. Steep roofs with round chimneys at the corners. The MARSDEN BUILDING SOCIETY next door has a carved crocodile and a lioness on the bay. Then comes the former Yorkshire Bank, a toy fort but of painted ashlar. A parpoint stone building follows, and then a typical former Burton's in Egyptianizing Deco. A little further on, and set back to widen the street, is HORNBY BUILDINGS of 1933 by the *Borough Architects*. Cream faience, with half-hearted Greek detailing. Round the corner in Rochdale Road is the former ODEON, 1936. Streamlined façade, asymmetrical to allow for the angle of the street, of cream faience applied without bonding, with thin green or blue stripes at the top. In TITHE-BARN STREET is the former BURY UNION OFFICES building of 1865. Brick and fine ashlar façade, with the emphasis on the ashlar. Big cartouche on the roof. Asymmetrical, Italianate, overdesigned.

OUTER BURY

Bury's suburbs are relatively diffuse, bisected N–S by the River Irwell with no road bridging points except in the centre, and additionally dissected by lesser streams coming down from the w.

North and West: Elton, Woodhill and Woolfold

ALL SAINTS, Walshaw Road, Elton. 1841–3 by *John Harper*. The big square flat-topped tower is on the chancel, where it makes a fine landmark from the town. Wide aisleless nave with shallow-pitched roof, w porch, transepts. All done in a crude Norman style, but it is a forceful building. Church and churchyard are derelict, but under restoration 2004. SCHOOL, N. Long, low, Romanesque, with a corbel table in between flat buttresses. Similar to Greenmount School, Tottington (q.v.); perhaps both were by *Harper*.

ST JAMES, Walshaw Road, Woolfold. 1930–1 by *R. Martin*. Low, of squared stone randomly coursed, with a squat crossing tower. Four-light windows of late Gothic character. The new PARISH CENTRE parallel to the church copies its half-hipped Westmorland slate roof.

ST STEPHEN, Bolton Road, Elton. 1882 by *G. T. Redmayne*. Unusually quirky, and unfinished at the w end. Polygonal E end, two-storey N transept, with a thin turret in the angle. No clerestory; instead there is a pair of outsized gabled dormers N and S, each sprouting a flying buttress. W narthex added. (Inside, the walls are of exposed brick).

MEMORIAL to the XXth Lancashire Fusiliers, Bolton Road. 1922, by *Sir Edwin Lutyens*. He declined a fee, being the son of Captain Charles Lutyens of the Regiment. Slim obelisk of Portland stone on an altar or sarcophagus plinth standing on a couple of shallow circular steps. The Union and Regimental flags are carved in stone but fully coloured, as at Rochdale, but this is more moving in its modesty than Lutyens's municipal monuments. Behind was the martial square of Wellington Barracks of 1842–5, unnecessarily demolished in 1969. The only remaining building is the chapel-like Quartermaster's Store, 1845, now the REGIMENTAL MUSEUM. Slender iron columns support great baulks of Baltic pine for the upper floor. POWELL STREET and POWELL SQUARE, nearly opposite, provide a late C19 echo of the barracks. Trim and orderly, in two grades of brick and roughcast with joggled terracotta lintels.

PEEL MILLS, Woodhill Road, Woodhill. Immediately N of the centre, but difficult of access. Originally three large mills in a row, but No. 1 of 1885–7 has gone. Standing are No. 2 of 1892, and No. 3 of 1913–15, which was electrically driven from the start. N of the site a former railway BRIDGE of stone with five skew arches gives pedestrian access to the country park (below).

BURRS COUNTRY PARK, Woodhill Road, Woodhill. Here are the ruins of two of Bury's earliest mills, built in 1790 and demolished in 1980, and the stub of a great octagonal chimney. A navigable feeder for the Manchester, Bolton & Bury Canal crosses the river by a three arch AQUEDUCT of blue brick. The Irwell has cut itself a rocky gorge – it is a pretty spot. – SCULPTURES. By *David Kempe*, 1996: Waterwheel, and Picnic Area – a stainless-steel mousetrap (tourist trap). Stone Cycle by *Julie Edwards*, 1997: concentric circles of large stone blocks which have been cut in half diagonally, like sandwiches. The little CALROWS FARM on the approach road carries the engaging inscription STANDLEY – DERBY, the Stanley Eagle and Child crest, and the date 1770 PLM. Untouched by fashion, it has three- and four-light mullioned windows.

South and East: Buckley Wells, Fishpool, Fernhill,
Freetown and Chesham

ST PAUL, Church Street. By *John Harper,* 1838–42. Distinguished from afar by the clumsy gables, like apologetic eyebrows, which break through the tower parapet over its attenuated belfry lancets. Of ashlar, with paired narrow lancets and gallery entrances embracing the tower. Islanded in a big square churchyard which has been too thoroughly cleared, and now closed. Declared redundant in 1995. Burnt, 2004.

Former PARSONAGE, now Shelley House, E of the church. By *T. Holmes,* 1851. Gothic, irregularly massed, with windows as richly traceried and drip moulded as those of the church are bald. Circular chimneys each with a carved garland draped round the top.

ST THOMAS, Rochdale Road. 1866, by *Lawrence Booth* of *Blackwell, Son & Booth.* NW tower and broach spire. Steeply pointed windows with plate tracery, or grouped in twos and threes with intermediate shafts.

ST PETER, off Manchester Road. 1871–2 by *Maycock & Bell*: nave, chancel and apse carried through without a chancel arch,

aisles, and the lower part of a NW tower; the clerestory disproportionately tall, with pairs of large two light windows with
flat plate tracery. 'If only the apparent lightness of the structure carries with it durability, one of the great aims of good
architecture will be achieved', commented the *Bury Times*. A
percipient remark, because weaknesses soon manifested themselves and in 1899–1901 *J. Medland Taylor* took down and
rebuilt considerable parts of it. His are the buttresses of the
apse and the W narthex. He removed the tower base, proposing instead to build a steeple attached at forty-five degrees to
the N aisle – hence the canted stub wall with a single bell hung
under the jutting roof.

CEMETERY, St Peter's Road. 1866–9. GATEPIERS, LODGE, and
CHAPEL by *Henry Styan* and the Borough Surveyor, *J. Farrar*,
with sculpture by *Joseph Bonehill*. It is curious how some Victorian architects, when faced with the job of designing for a
cemetery, lost all restraint. The CHAPEL follows a common
formula with overlarge transepts, a dwarfish NW tower growing
into a spire very low down, a SW porch and a small polygonal
apse. No fewer than four tiers of gargoyles mark the transition
from tower to spire: hugely overscale angels, grotesque faces,
bats, and, wriggling down from the lucarnes, crouching beasts.

PILOT MILL, now Antler Luggage, Alfred Street. Cotton-
spinning and doubling mill, 1905. Bury is not dominated by
mills, but this is a big one. Five storeys, the top and bottom
differentiated to make a notional classical order. Brick and buff
terracotta. Corner tower, engine house at the back, but no
chimney. Iron columns, concrete floors.

RAILWAY WORKSHOPS, Baron Street, Buckley Wells. Built as
carriage sheds for the first East Lancashire Railway in 1856, by
J. S. Perring. Of brick, with parallel roofs supported on iron
stanchions. Truncated at the S end but even so immensely long.
Nowadays it is used for the repair of preserved locomotives.

EARL OF DERBY'S ESTATE WORKSHOPS, Manchester Road.
1866, by *James Green* of Todmorden. Now SWINTEX, manufacturing road cones, but originally supplying building materials of every description, and manufacturing and repairing
wagons and carts, for the extensive Derby Estates in the area.
Prominent Italianate gatehouse and clock tower, asymmetrical, of best orange brick and much stone, the ground floor
rusticated. It is a pity that the Eagle and Child weathervane
has gone. Low workaday brick sheds behind.

In front, a former MOTOR SHOWROOM by *Northern Design
Group*, 1963. Exciting at the time with its virginal glass and
steel but, its virtue compromised by crude advertising, hardly
worth a glance today.

STARKIES, Manchester Road. A tight huddle of brick buildings,
some with stone basements. They are odd because of their
many oval openings, repeated over three storeys in places. The
group is incomplete-looking, making it hard to determine its
function. On a pair of adjacent doors is inscribed JHE (John
and Elizabeth Hammond) 1717.

A few large HOUSES remain along Manchester Road, e.g.
HEATON GROVE, an Italianate villa in finest ashlar with a
Doric porch. Rebuilt in the remains of the garden, three bays
of terracotta arcading.

BRIDGE HALL, off Rochdale Road E of the M66, i.e. really
in Heap Bridge (*see* Heywood) but on the Bury side of the
River Roch. A significant early settlement overtaken by industry, then the motorway, and now housing. The favourable position of the C17 house above the river can still be recognized,
as can the very large mullioned-and-transomed window lighting the hall, with the entrance at one end and fireplace at the
other. Victorian bays at both ends.

CADISHEAD

7090

A small settlement which grew up along the route between
Manchester and Liverpool.

ST MARY THE VIRGIN, Penry Avenue. 1929 by *R. Martin.*
Unremarkable except for the irregular cyclopean stonework
favoured by Martin.

A few older HOUSES are clustered around the junction of
Liverpool Road and Hayes Road. The earliest is No. 155a
Liverpool Road, set back at an angle to the road. Probably
late C17, thatched, rendered, with casement windows and
gable chimneys. Also on Liverpool Road the attractive Late
Georgian PLOUGH INN, symmetrical, with big windows in
lugged architraves. Arched entrance with reeded pilasters,
fanlight, etc. Just around the corner on Hayes Road are some
C18 cottages of which the least spoiled are Nos. 34–36, rendered brick, stone slate roofs.

CHADDERTON

9000

Chadderton originated as scattered farms and settlement along
the roads between Middleton and Oldham. Expansion came with
industry, starting with silk weaving in the C18. The first impression, approaching from the S along Broadway, is still of a mill
town: huge mills and a fair sprinkling of chimneys reflecting early
C20 growth. On the E side the settlement merges with Oldham,
of which the area became administratively a part in 1974. To the
W there are still open fields.

CHRIST CHURCH. 1870 by *H. Ainley*, who was head draughts-
man at the huge engineering firm of Platt Bros & Co. (*see*
Oldham, Introduction). SE tower with a tall parapet and stair-
tower with a tall pyramidal top. Dec window tracery.
Clerestory with circular lights and trefoil lights, which look like
portholes inside. Five-bay arcade of slender clustered piers.
The nave ceiling was replaced in 1963.– CHANCEL FURNISH-
INGS probably by the workshop of *George Shaw*, with canopied

stalls, etc. – MONUMENT. Emily Clegg Lees †1889. Large, white marble, with an angel holding a wreath.

EMMANUEL, Chestnut Street. By *A. J. Howcroft*, 1911. Very red brick. Mechanical Perp details. No tower, but the dullness is relieved by a little octagonal NW bell tower.

ST LUKE, Queen's Road. 1882 by *Stott & Sons*. A big ambitious church, but the projected NW tower was never built. Tall nave and chancel under one roof. Low aisles, clasped on each side by a pair of flying buttresses springing from piers topped with octagonal spires. The division between nave and chancel is marked by a buttress breaking through the roof line. Geometrical tracery. The flying buttresses do not support a vault, but a kingpost roof of uncommon span (34 ft, 10 metres).

VICARAGE, Queen's Road, S of the church. Dated 1896. Red brick with tall chimneys. Eventful roof-line including a dormer with an extravagant terracotta finial.

ST MARK, Ogden Street. By *G. G. Pace*, 1962–3. Pevsner in 1969 commented: 'One must leave it to Mr Pace – he is always fresh and never afraid of experiment, and he does not follow all the latest fashions.' Thirty years on, the freshness has not been lost. Elements of the design, in particular the saddleback tower and steep gables, are related to Pace's St Leonard and St Jude in Doncaster (1957–63), while the cruck-like beams were used there and in several other designs, including the chapel at Keele University (1959–65). Otherwise the materials are blue engineering brick, perhaps as a nod to the industrial character of the area, and graduated slate roofs. The gables have small windows with five tiers with unmoulded mullions and broad flush transoms in random places. Long W range housing the day chapel with the tower at the S end, vestries etc. in a narrow range at right angles and behind; low top-lit narthex. The main body of the church is longitudinal and orientated, but canted out on the NE side to give room for the choir; the roof dips low at the angle and swoops up again on either side. The W

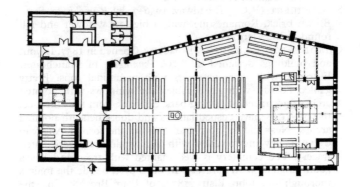

St Mark, Chadderton, plan

gable rises up above the narthex. It leaked, and secondary glazing has been installed. Light airy interior, with white-painted brickwork, exposed concrete beams and cream stone paving. The roof supports are great primitive Y-shapes, with contrastingly industrial-looking timber lattice-work purlins. Two shallow steps up to the sanctuary, NE organ chamber with a timber screen. – The FURNISHINGS are mainly by *Pace*. Fixed stone SEDILIA. – ALTAR, long and blocky, of limed oak, placed forward from the E end. – ALTAR RAIL. Limed oak rail, thick black metal supports. – PULPIT. Originally fixed with a brick base at the extreme S side of the sanctuary, reconstructed using original timbers and placed closer to the altar. – CRUCIFIX. Typical Pace ironwork, with a gilded figure, said to be C17 German work, provided by the architect. Additional CHOIR FURNISHINGS, limed oak CHAIRS, etc., by *Alan Hurst*, *c*. 1990 following the Pace style. – FONT, placed at the W end axially to the altar. Stone cylinder with beside it a slimmer cylinder rising above, with a spout. This contains a tap so that running water can be used for baptism. – FONT LID. Cast aluminium in swirling shapes rising up to form a crown of flame-like finials. – BENCH SEATING. Late C19, from another church, painted matt black. – STAINED GLASS. In the E window only, randomly incorporating fragments of C19 glass said to originate from demolished churches in the area. – ORGAN by *G. Sixsmith* of Mossley, 1983. The day chapel has a scissor-braced timber roof and furnishings including a black metal CRUCIFIX by Pace and a TABERNACLE by *Donald Buttress*.

ST MATTHEW, Chadderton Hall Road. By *E. H. Shellard*, 1848–57. SW tower and spire by *Stott & Sons*, 1877. It is this addition which gives the building character, with triple lancets and octagonal pinnacles at the corners. Otherwise very simple, with Dec window details.

ST SAVIOUR, Denton Lane. 1960–2 by *Taylor, Roberts & Bowman*. Square, of brick, with in the W wall a low round arch as the portal, asymmetrically placed, and at the E end a higher brick semi-cylinder, glazed in the front, i.e. to focus light on the altar. Disused and boarded up.

ST HERBERT (R.C.), Broadway. 1956–7, by *Reynolds & Scott*. Brown brick, Romanesque, with a big low W tower and tall round-headed lancets.

CHADDERTON CEMETERY, Broadway. Opened in 1857. Layout and buildings designed by *N. G. Pennington* of Manchester. Entrance with large gatepiers with pyramidal tops. Pretty gabled LODGE with steep gables and windows with pointed arches and traceried glazing bars. Set back from the entrance, the OFFICES have cusped lancets and doors beneath pointed arches. Near the SE corner of the site the former Anglican CHAPEL, low and towerless with an E window with reticulated tracery. The cemetery is well planted with trees and has a good range of MONUMENTS. In the S part, beside the main S thoroughfare, John Platt †1872, of Platt Bros & Co., the engineering firm (*see* Oldham, introduction). Canopy with the piers and underside carved with fantastic flowing Celtic-style designs. Like Greenacres Cemetery, Oldham, also by Pennington and opened at the same time (*see* Outer Oldham E), it was designed for public recreation at a time when the Oldham area lacked public parks.

TOWN HALL, Middleton Road. 1912–13 by *Taylor & Simister*. Red brick and much stone. The centre is a semicircular columned porch and a stone dome at the top with a lantern. Three bays l., three bays r. Entrance hall with a double staircase and Doric columns. Council chamber with barrel roof, proscenium at one end and gallery at the other, with liberal plasterwork.

CARNEGIE LIBRARY, Middleton Road. By *J. Lindsey Grant* of Manchester. Dated 1905. Elizabethan accents, with transomed windows, gables and an oriel. Entrance tower to the r. which has lost its dome. The stone canopy over the door incorporates a figure of a reading child. Entrance hall with Ionic columns.

POLICE STATION, Victoria Street. Dated 1901, part of a group with the library (above). Dutch gables and transomed windows in red brick with stone dressings.

SWIMMING BATHS, Middleton Road. Art Deco style, opened 1937. Symmetrical, brick with stone dressings and some black glazed brick. Recessed entrance block with vertical window strips and lower flanking blocks with horizontal window bands. Entrance with green terracotta-clad piers and original glass panels prettily engraved with designs of a seagull, fish and a figure amongst waves.

NORTH CHADDERTON COMPREHENSIVE SCHOOL, Broadway. Long and low, probably late C19. Symmetrical, with separate boys' and girls' entrances at either end, each with a perky little slated turret.

RADCLYFFE LOWER SCHOOL, Broadway. Formerly the Chadderton Grammar School. Opened 1959, but in Neo-Georgian style which could as well be of 1939. Symmetrical, brown brick, with a grand central stone entrance bay with cupola and pedimented door.

BURNLEY BROW COMMUNITY SCHOOL, Victoria Street. 2001 by *Oldham Metropolitan Borough Council Architects' Department*. Fresh and bright with a blue metal roof with oversailing eaves and a gull's wing canopy high over the entrance. The low, friendly late C19 school it replaced stands quietly decaying in Eustace Street, nearby.

WAR MEMORIAL, Middleton Road. In front of the Town Hall (above). By *Taylor & Simister*, statue by *Albert Toft*, unveiled 1921. Granite obelisk with a projection near the base on which stands a bronze soldier holding a rifle.

HOUSES. Nos. 422–426 Middleton Road. Mid-C19 brick terrace. Entrances with Doric columns and very shallow arched overlights.

FOXDENTON HALL, Foxdenton Lane. Set in an attractive 29 municipal park, in a little area of open fields on the western edge of Chadderton. Built by Alexander Radclyffe, traditionally between 1710 and 1730. It incorporates stonework from a house of 1620, put up by his distant relative and forbear William Radcliffe. It was leased from the Radclyffes by Chadderton Council in 1922 and was finally acquired by them in 1960, in poor condition. Major restoration followed.

The hall is a beautiful early C18 brick house with stone quoins, the entrance front of seven bays with a recessed three-bay centre and a big hipped roof with deep bracketed eaves. The opposite (s) side is flush except for a very slight projection of the eaves over the entrance. Central entrances on each side have pediments, and there are sash windows throughout, except for the basement. There are no parallels stylistically in SE Lancashire, though nearby Chadderton Hall, now demolished, was of similar date and style. The house sits on a red sandstone basement lit by two-light mullioned windows. A door lintel beneath the main entrance on the N side has the initials WR and the date 1620.* This has led to speculation that the C18 house was built directly on to the basement or ground floor of the predecessor building. However all the openings line up, with mullioned windows directly beneath the sashes, and the plan can hardly be 1620.

The plan is symmetrical with ground-floor rooms of equal dimensions flanking the slightly larger ENTRANCE HALL. This is a lovely light space with a large C18 fireplace with a bolection-moulded surround. Exposed reused C17 timbers in the ceiling look very incongruous, and their configuration makes little sense. Could they have been put in as part of a misguided repair using timbers from the basement level? The panelling, apart from that around the fireplace, is also C17. It may have originated in the predecessor house, but it is of two different types and does not fit the room properly, in stark contrast with the stylish space, and the early C18 mahogany doors and bolection-moulded panelling in the rooms on the W side. More C17 panelling appears in the room to the E. The western rooms were thrown together during refurbishment, and only one chimneypiece survives, probably mid-C18. A sturdy STAIR with big newel posts, a closed string and turned balusters lies on the E side. It is difficult to imagine that the same craftsmen could have been responsible for the comparatively advanced panelling and chimneypieces. The UPPER FLOOR has been altered and the rooms subdivided, except for that on the E side, which has bolection-moulded panelling like the rooms below, and a mid-C18 chimneypiece with Rococo scrolling. The room above the entrance hall, now subdivided, has C17 panelling and another mid-C18 chimneypiece. It is odd that some rooms have elegant C18 interiors and others make do with rough C17 work. Perhaps the intended schemes were never carried out and the

---

* Presumably C17 stonework was reused, but inside the 1620 doorway retains the iron fittings for the door. Why place a basement door immediately below the front door? Could there have been external access to the basement here?

reused panelling became a permanent fixture, or perhaps the
building was subject to a misconceived antiquarian refurbishment, possibly in the C19. In the BASEMENT the ceiling has
largely been replaced as part of the 1960s restoration, and there
are other alterations, but the walls are thick and solidly built,
there is a large fireplace below the entrance-hall fireplace, and
the mullions of the windows are well-preserved with deep
hollow mouldings. There is a possibility that this was the
kitchen and services, which would have been an advanced
arrangement for this part of the world.

FOXDENTON FARM, Foxdenton Lane. Immediately W of
Foxdenton Hall, and perhaps originally its home farm. A very
thoroughly modernized cruck house, encased mainly in rendered and painted brick, with a C17 stone W wing and a brick
E wing, thought to be a C18 recasing of earlier work in stone.
Cross-passage plan, with two surviving cruck trusses, and an
inglenook fireplace. In Lancashire cruck construction continued into the C16, which could be the date of this example.

MILLS AND WORKS

Chadderton has a number of very impressive cotton mills, of
which only a selection has been included.* One of the best
groups is on the NW side of Broadway, where early C20 mills have
in common the use of Accrington brick with stone, terracotta or
contrasting brick dressings, flat roofs and display concentrated
on corner water towers. The splendid GORSE MILL, Gorse
Street, 1908 by *P.S. Stott*, has a great tower with a pyramid roof. 94
RUGBY MILL just beyond, also on Gorse Street, by *F. W. Dixon
& Son*, 1908, has lost its chimney but retains the ornate corner
tower. Nearby, RAM MILL by *Stott & Sons*, 1907, has the most 94
elaborate tower of all. Six storeys with full-height pilasters terminating with finials, then a tall octagon with traceried terracotta
banding and pilasters, topped by a recessed dome. On Broadway
itself are ACE MILL and OLDHAM AIRCRAFT FACTORY
(former). Ace Mill was built in 1914 by *P.S. Stott* in his instantly
recognizable style, though it is mutilated. The site was adapted
and expanded as a factory for the assembly of Handley Page
0/400 heavy bombers in 1918. Maintenance sheds, stores, assembly sheds, offices, etc. survive on the site, unprepossessing red
brick buildings. (Some of the sheds, as English Heritage reports,
have Belfast truss roofs, others lightweight iron roofs.)

MANOR MILL, Victoria Street. By *G. Stott*, 1906. A very complete ensemble, with engine house, tall circular detached
chimney, offices, lodge, boundary walls, etc. Typical early C20
design, red brick and stone dressings, with a flat roof to
the mill. An imposing corner water tower has at the top an

---

* For more information and the other mills, *see* D. Gurr and J. Hunt, *Cotton Mills
of Oldham*, 1998.

octagonal lantern crowned by a copper dome with brattishing and a flagpole.

NILE MILL, Fields New Road. 1898 by *P. S. Stott*, and the largest ring spinning mill in the world of its day. A large flat-roofed double mill with central engine house with the typical arched windows, and a water tower over. Ring spinning was invented in America in 1829 but brought to Lancashire in the late C19. Ring frames spun yarn as a continuous operation and did not require highly trained operatives for running. The frames were smaller and heavier, and the mills consequently had fewer storeys than the standard type. Here there were originally three storeys, with another added in 1905.

CLEGG HALL *see* MILNROW

7000
CLIFTON

NW of Pendlebury, and merging with it, on land which drops to the N and the River Irwell. Clifton was an important coal mining area from the mid C18. Pilkingtons Royal Lancastrian Pottery was established in the valley bottom in 1891.

ST ANNE, Manchester Road. 1872–4 by *E. M. Barry*. The cost was £16,000, met by local colliery owners. Their legacy is also to be seen in the internal and external tie-rod bracing, put in to combat subsidence caused by mine workings. Not a run-of-the-mill design, though in the Middle Pointed of the High Victorians and with geometrical tracery and paired cusped lancets. Everything about it is purposeful, the elements of the structure accentuated by the use of angle buttresses. The W rose is uncommonly prominent, and so are the transept fronts, also with rose windows. Cruciform plan, apsidal E end with an arcade of lancets, prominent S porch. No tower, only a bellcote on the nave E gable. Stone with red tile roofs. (Three-bay arcade, cylindrical columns, large chancel arch with colonnettes rising from stiff-leaf corbels. Raised chancel with encaustic tiles, wrought-iron GATES and choir furnishings, early C20 stencilled walls. – STAINED GLASS. S aisle, a fine window by *Gordon Forsyth* of the Royal Lancastrian Pottery, Hugh Brocklehurst Pilkington †1915.)

FIRST WORLD WAR MEMORIAL, Bolton Road, near the junction with the M60 motorway. *c.* 1920 by *Gordon Forsyth* of the Royal Lancastrian Pottery. Stone, a splendid roaring lion on a tall plinth.

MEMORIAL COTTAGES, Bolton Road, beside the war memorial (above). 1925, for Edward Pilkington. A low rendered U-shaped range with stone slate roofs, arched doorways, and an open-arched chimney in the centre of the rear range, which has the Pilkington arms over the central door.

CLIFTON PARK HOTEL, Manchester Road. A small symmetrical Late Georgian house set well back from the road, approached via a disproportionately grand entrance and drive. Ionic doorcase, fanlight, etc.

FLETCHER CANAL and WET EARTH COLLIERY. Off Clifton House Road. The Clifton Colliery, also known as the Wet Earth Colliery, started in 1740 when a deep shaft was sunk close to the River Irwell. In 1750 Matthew Fletcher took over the mine and *James Brindley* was called in to solve the problems of flooding. Brindley installed a waterwheel to draw water up from the mine. A feeder stream (to power the waterwheel) was created by tunnelling beneath the river and siphoning water up some 30 ft (10 metres) above river level. Water was returned to the river via a tailrace. In 1790 Fletcher built a loading basin at the pithead and enlarged the feeder stream to form a canal, which was linked to the nearby Manchester, Bury and Bolton Canal and so to major centres. After various changes in ownership the mine closed in 1928, with the essentials of Brindley's system still working. Ornate chimney, *c.* 1840, nearby.

CROMPTON and SHAW   9000

There is no clear distinction between Crompton and Shaw, both originally part of Crompton Urban District, which was absorbed into Oldham Metropolitan Borough Council in 1974. The settlement is concentrated in the valley of the River Beal, where the railway runs, with moorland rising up on the E and W sides. Before the advent of large-scale industry the little settlement in the valley was surrounded by scattered farms. There was a chapel of ease of Prestwich Church from the C16 or before. The Victoria County History records a Mormon meeting place in 1850. There is not one now.

HOLY TRINITY, Church Road. Existing in 1515. Rebuilt in 1739, again in 1800, and lastly in 1870–1 by *J. Drew*. A sizeable and ambitious building, with a great crossing tower with broad paired bell-openings, octagonal stair-turret and a pyramid roof instead of the intended spire. Windows with Dec tracery, including large three-light clerestory windows. Chancel lower than the nave, and attachments to the chancel yet lower. Externally this attachment of transept, vestry etc., partly one-, partly two-storeyed, is picturesque.

ST JAMES, St James Street. *c.* 1847 by *Joseph Clarke*. Built with a small contribution from the Commissioners. SW broach spire, with a carved frieze at the base. Lancets and plate tracery. Small paired clerestory windows, carefully expressed parts in the Ecclesiological spirit. Five-bay arcade of alternating round and octagonal piers with caps with attractive foliage carving, each one different. Fully developed chancel and chancel arch.

  SCULPTURE. Hidden in a clump of bushes E of the church. A good bronze by *Hamo Thornycroft*. A woman with book in lap and one arm around a young boy, the other outstretched.

On the base, the word 'Education'. It is a copy of one of the four supporting groups made for the London Gladstone Memorial in 1905, purchased by the local industrialist James Cockroft and presented to the people of Shaw and Crompton in 1919. It was placed in the library (*see* below), but removed in 1975 to make more space.

St Mary, Thornham Lane. 1878 by *Wild & Collins*. Set back from the street and at an angle to it. Dec with an undersized SE octagonal turret and SW porch.

Wesleyan Chapel (former), Rochdale Road. By *James Simpson*, 1863, and imposing indeed. Ashlar, Italianate, with a big pediment all across containing an oculus, arched upper windows, and a projecting porch with corner antae and Doric columns. It is set back from the street with railings around, and an overthrow over the entrance. Attached at the rear on Chapel Street, a large Sunday School (former) by *John Wild*, 1871, with a pediment over the central three bays and two entrances with round heads.

Methodist Chapel (former), Buckstones Road. High up in a fold of the bare hillside. Built in 1823, at a time when Sunday in the area, according to a Methodist commentator, 'was the devil's own day for drinking, gambling, cockfighting, wrestling and pigeon flying'. Stone, with arched windows and central doorway in the gabled front elevation. Other windows and internal alterations relate to a domestic conversion of 1996.

Crompton Cemetery, Fraser Street. Opened in 1891, the layout and buildings by *Wild, Collins & Wild*. Imposing entrance with tall gatepiers and an unusually large two-storey Tudor-style stone Lodge. The large Chapel is set on a hill. Like a little church, with Dec window tracery, SW broach spire with lucarnes, a pair of gabled S chapels and an expressed chancel. The cemetery has a strange, sad look. Oldham Council fears the monuments are unsafe and many of them have been felled, lying everywhere like trees after a hurricane.

Crompton House Church of England School, Rochdale Road. A large mid- to late-C19 Tudor-style stone mansion with projecting wing, battlemented porch in the angle and traceried windows beneath flat heads. Set back from the road behind tall gatepiers with fearsome cone-like finials. Miss Crompton and Mrs Ormerod gave it for use as a school in 1926. The 1920s additions are low and of brick.

Swimming Baths, Farrow Street East. Red brick with minimal Baroque detailing and the date 1899.

Carnegie Library (former), Beal Lane. 1906–7 by *Jesse Horsfall*. Baroque, one- and two-storeyed. Canopy over the entrance with Art Nouveau style lettering and carving supported by an exaggerated keystone, integrated with the sill of an upper Venetian window. Money for purchase of the land was raised through public subscription and around 3,000 books were donated by the Crompton Co-operative Provident Society. Today it is empty and boarded up and the fine sculpture bought for it is placed unceremoniously in a churchyard (*see* St James, above).

MIDLAND BANK (former), Rochdale Road. 1897, by *Thomas Taylor* of Oldham. Baroque, low and powerful in stone, with much bare wall. Entrance offset to the l. with beside it a little row of five windows framed within a pilastrade. Attached at the rear is a manager's house of brick.

BLUE BELL INN, Market Street. A large three-storey stone house with mullioned windows. Dated 1763, but the stone is a reproduction probably dating from substantial late C19 or early C20 alterations, which included insertion and alteration of ground-floor openings and remodelling of the interior. The twenty-light window at the top for handloom workshops has been removed.

WAR MEMORIAL, High Street. Unveiled in 1923. One of the best 97 in SE Lancashire. Tall stepped granite plinth with a bronze group by *Richard R. Goulden*. A man, naked save for a cloak, fends off two snarling panthers with a sword, protecting with his other arm a group of children who huddle against him and beneath the cloak. The writhing beasts recall depictions of Satan, and the sword-wielding figure St Michael. A bronze mother and child, also by *Goulden*, was displayed at the British Empire Exhibition in 1924 before being brought to Shaw to honour the war work of the women of the area. Most shamefully it was stolen in 1968.*

PROVIDENT PARK ESTATE, N of the centre, Park Parade, Dingle Avenue, and Shore Avenue. Brick semi-detached houses of 1914 of entirely predictable design by *J. Whittaker & Son*, interesting because they were built by the Crompton Co-operative Provident Society and are placed on wide curving streets in garden suburb style.

MILLS

A group of big early C20 mills lies in the valley along the railway line on the E side of town. Amongst the largest are LILY, DAWN and LILAC mills, sounding like a group of Edwardian sisters. The last two are by *P. S. Stott*, 1901 and 1904 respectively, with his typical powerful corner towers bearing the names. Lily Mill, by *G. Stott*, was put up in 1904.†

OUTLYING FARMS AND HOUSES

BURN FARM, Buckstones Road. A laithe house, that is a farmhouse with attached shippon and barn with a large cart

---

* As Terry Wyke records.
† For full details of these and others in the area *see* D. Gurr and J. Hunt, *The Cotton Mills of Oldham*, 1998.

entrance, all of one build. Probably mid- or late-C18. The house has four- and five-light mullioned windows.

HIGHER PARK, off Milnrow Road. Six late C18 or early C19 cottages, built piecemeal in typical Pennine style, of stone with mullioned windows.

MOORFIELD HAMLET, Rochdale Road, near the junction with Thornham Road. A little group of stone two-storey late C18 houses with mullioned windows.

PARK FARM, Milnrow Road. The early C19 farmhouse is elegant and forward-looking for this area, where traditional forms with mullioned windows persisted well into the C19. Symmetrical, with an ashlar front, sash windows and a pedimented doorcase with Doric columns. Arched lights to the attic in the end gables, and a rear wing with a central arched window lighting the stair. Also at the rear, stone outbuildings including a COACH HOUSE and BARN of the same date, with bulls eye windows, the former converted, the latter dilapidated.

STOCKFIELD FARM, Rochdale Road. A stone C18 house, two storeys, with rows of mullioned windows, five-light below, three-light above.

(TOP GREEN HILL FARMHOUSE and BARN. The DCMS list records a mid- or late-C17 stone house with mullioned windows and an attached barn.)

DAISY HILL *see* WESTHOUGHTON

DEANE *see* BOLTON p. 161

7090

DAVYHULME

Davyhulme lies immediately E of the Manchester Ship Canal. It is indistinguishable from Flixton, SW, and Urmston, S. To the N are the M60 motorway and Trafford Park.

ST MARY, Davyhulme Road. Of 1889–90 by *George Truefitt*, who won the competition in 1887. A building of considerable character. Short aisles, nave, shallow transepts and a huge octagonal crossing tower with paired lancet windows, angle pinnacles and a pyramid roof. Other windows have plate tracery. All of yellow sandstone with red sandstone dressings and timber framing in the topmost parts of the gables. The chancel E end has a high reredos, and consequently the five E windows are arranged so the outer two are placed much lower than the stepped inner three. (The capitals of the crossing have deliberately simplified E.E. caps. The string course all around has no other purpose than to hide a pipe. Goodhart-Rendel called it 'a filthy sham').

CHRIST CHURCH, Lostock Road. 1968–9. A dull brick effort enlivened by four large STAINED GLASS windows, S nave, by

Kenneth Gordon Bunton. Curving abstract designs in bright colours.

YEW TREE FARMHOUSE, Davyhulme Road. Dated 1713. Symmetrical with a narrow full-height gabled porch and casement windows. Rendered brick.

(GOLF CLUBHOUSE, Gleneagles Road. By *McCutcheon & Potter*, 1937, according to Simon Inglis. A striking moderne design.)

URN, Davyhulme Road (off). An unadorned stone urn, *c.* 10 ft. high, amid trees. Probably early or mid-C19 and said to commemorate racehorses belonging to the Norreys family.

DENTON   9090

The area was little more than scattered farms until the late C18, when coal extraction started in earnest. There were five collieries by the mid C19. Denton was a national centre of hatting in the C19, but the physical evidence for this is being effaced. Today the settlement is fragmented by busy roads, and the M57 motorway rudely cuts it in half. Its chief ornaments are two outstanding churches: the C16 timber-framed St Lawrence, and the late C19 St Anne.

NICO DITCH. A linear earthwork stretching between Ashton Moss (Ashton-under-Lyne) and the former Hough Moss in Moss Side, Manchester. (Other sections are visible in Levenshulme and Rusholme, Manchester. *See* also Carr Ditch, Urmston). Its line, clearly visible on mid-C19 maps, is preserved in the street pattern and in many administrative boundaries. The earliest documentary evidence for it is *c.* 1200, and the name is probably a derivation of 'mickle' meaning large. It has been interpreted variously as a Roman or Saxon boundary or defensive ditch.[*] Archaeological investigation suggested an original width of *c.* 20 ft (3–4 metres), but failed to establish a date. One of the best-preserved stretches survives in Denton golf course, near Corn Hill Lane, where it reaches a depth of about 4 ft (1.5 metres) in places, and continues for almost 30 yds (300 metres). This section runs S in the line of Laburnum Road and Dane Bank (still the administrative boundary between Manchester and Tameside), and to the N in the line of Lumb Lane in Audenshaw and Droylsden. From this point it ran into Ashton Moss, where there seems to have been a related ditch along the NW side.

ST LAWRENCE, Town Lane, at the corner of Stockport Road. A chapel of ease of *c.* 1530, made parochial 1854.[†] It is the only 10 surviving timber-framed church in SE Lancashire; small,

---

[*] For a discussion of its origins and purpose *see* M. Nevell, *Tameside Before 1066*, 1992.
[†] The original dedication to St James was changed *c.* 1800, supposedly because of the discovery of medieval glass depicting St Lawrence, though this does not survive.

charming and notable for the sensitivity of the additions by *J. Medland & Henry Taylor* of 1872. Rendered exterior with painted timber framing, exposed framing, s wall. Central w door, jettied gable and timbered cupola. At the E end projecting gabled and jettied chancel and transepts of 1872. Part of the s nave wall was renovated in 2002–3, when original timbers were found beneath the plasterwork showing that the pattern of painted timbers follows the original, i.e. close studding below herringbone.

INTERIOR. Six bays of original timbers of *c.* 1530, arch-braced trusses with diagonal braces and cusped windbraces. Plaster ceiling at collar level. The interior was reordered and new pews installed, 1859. The sanctuary is busy with plaster lozenge and flower reliefs. w gallery with quatrefoil cast-iron columns and a strangely detailed C19 wooden gallery front with ogee openings, quatrefoils and incised floral designs. – ROOD SCREEN. Of 1927, highly detailed, arcaded, with open curvilinear tracery. – CHOIR STALLS probably by the *Taylors*, with unusual poppyheads, one with a Japanese-looking roundel. They incorporate some C16 bench ends, traceried or foliated, except for one with very crude carvings of a dog and an entertaining centaur wearing a hat. – CHURCHWARDENS' PEW with a brass plate dated 1726 and another recording a restoration of 1862. Of 1726, a section of dark panelling topped by an open segmental pediment and an urn. – STAINED GLASS. Two two-light chancel windows with late medieval glass. s side: Gabriel from an Annunciation and St John the Evangelist standing on a plinth. N side: a donor, probably William Hyde, kneeling at a *prie-dieu* with an open book, and a Hyde shield. Late C19 E window by *Lavers, Barraud & Westlake*. Elsewhere, three-light windows, several with medieval centrepieces. These include various arms and badges of the Spencer, Reddish and Hyde families, and figures including another donor (probably Katharine Hyde) at a *prie-dieu*, the Virgin, and St John the Evangelist. One panel with a leaping unicorn (N side) is probably Netherlandish domestic. – MONUMENTS. In the N transept a large wall monument, Edward Holland †1655. Oval inscription plate between two lumpy columns with acanthus capitals. Top achievement with double scrolls on each side of the mantling and arms, capped by helmets and crude heraldic beasts. A small marble tablet beside it is also C17, to Eleanor Arden, but the inscription is effaced. s transept, Dame Mary Asheton †1721. A shaped marble wall tablet with urns.

67 ST ANNE, St Anne's Road, N of the motorway. Of 1880–2 and part of a group with lychgate and rectory by *J. Medland & Henry Taylor*. The patron was the local industrialist Joseph Sidebotham and the dedication was inspired by the names of his mother and his wife. The marguerite, or daisy, a symbol of St Anne, abounds in the decorative scheme. Free Arts and Crafts Gothic. Everything is odd about the church. Red brick, tiled roofs, assertive crossing tower with a massive square base.

The powerful grouping, seeming to force the tower upwards, is said to have been influenced by medieval Norwegian stave churches. No aisles, but transepts and a straight-ended chancel. Emphatic tall chimneys contribute to a domestic feel. The tower has a truncated pyramid roof, an inset timber stage then a swept pyramid roof. The stair-turret in the angle between nave and S transept is separate, octagonal with a conical tiled roof and angled entrance. At the W end is a tall baptistery projecting triangularly. The S transept rose window has tracery with mullions as if it were not a rose, like one of the aisle windows of the Taylors' St Clement, Urmston (q.v.). Arched N transept window, transomed nave windows. The building is set over a generous undercroft giving it height and solidity.

INTERIOR. The impression is of great generosity of space, given by the wide crossing with transepts and chancel of the same dimensions, brick crossing arches, and an octopartite timber vault. But the weirdest thing is the E angles of the crossing. They are short fat granite columns, and behind them the angle is chamfered off so as to form a kind of squint. Similar columns support the crossing tower of the Taylors' St Edmund, Rochdale (q.v.). Hefty arch-braced roof with principals rising from stone corbels carved with motifs and texts and, in the chancel, two large angels on the beams to mark the sanctuary. The richness of the decoration intensifies towards the sanctuary, with restrained use of gold mosaic (by *Salviati & Co.* of Venice) to heighten the effect. Walls are exposed brick, buff and red with some cream glazed-brick banding, the chancel patterned in lozenges and crosses (cf. the Taylors' Holy Trinity in Ashton-under-Lyne). – REREDOS with gold mosaic. Low chancel wall with red terracotta arcading topped by beautiful IRONWORK by *Freeman & Co.* of Manchester, with large springing daisies. – Inset PULPIT with similar ironwork top. – Ironwork SCREEN to the organ chamber in the chancel N side. – Floor tiles in the nave give way in the chancel to marble, terrazzo and MOSAIC with texts and daisies, the terrazzo by *Messrs Patteson* of Manchester, the mosaic by *M. Ludwig Oppenheimer*. Blind arcade on each side of the reredos with gold mosaic. Mosaic text beneath the windows of the baptistery, which has a mosaic floor with daisies. More mosaic over the S door. – Original bench PEWS. – FONT. Marble bowl with a gold mosaic frieze. – STAINED GLASS. All by *Heaton, Butler & Bayne*. E window, Adoration of the Shepherds, transept windows with foliage reminiscent of Morris & Co. designs, baptistery windows with the baptism of Christ, etc. Nave windows have floral motifs, with the names of the flowers, on a plain ground. – MONUMENT. Large brass on the N transept wall, Captain James Nasmyth Wedgewood Sidebotham † 1916. Figure in battledress framed by a canopy mounted on green marble.

LYCHGATE. Sturdy timber structure with kingpost trusses and a tiled roof.

68   The RECTORY of 1882 is exactly as strange as the church.
Large and quite ornate, of the same red brick and tiled
roof. Gabled cross-wings, a porch in the angle, an upper
transomed six-light window of stone in the central part.
Octagonal tower in the other angle, topped by a conical roof.
The l. wing has a funny little gabled oriel. Tall elaborate chimneys. (The interior is said to retain many original furnishings
and to feature imaginative use of internal spaces.)

CHRIST CHURCH, Manchester Road. By *G. G. Scott*, 1848–53.
A plain, honest piece, of stone. Not exciting, but there is
quality in the massing and the use of much bare wall between
the lancets. Nave, chancel and aisles under separate roofs, large
and solid NW tower with broach spire with lucarnes, E and W
windows with C14 tracery. (Nave arcades with alternating circular and octagonal piers, arch-braced roof trusses springing
from carved corbels. Wagon roof to chancel. Alabaster FONT
and PULPIT, both 1901. – STAINED GLASS. E and W windows
by *Wailes*, c. 1866. TS)

ST MARY (R.C.), Duke Street, 1962 by *Walter Stirrup & Son*.
Wildly Neo-Expressionist roofs, swooping up at the corners,
with deep eaves, and set at an angle.

COUNCIL OFFICES, off Market Street. 1888–9. Rather dull,
of brick, with two tall storeys over a basement, sparing
Renaissance motifs such as shaped gables, etc. The building
started as a free library, designed by *J. Lindley*, altered for use
as a town hall by *J. Clayton* in 1899.

LIBRARY, formerly also a technical school, Peel Street. The
library part is Queen Anne style, by *J. W. Beaumont*, 1894. Red
brick with channelled chimneys, gables, transomed windows
and all the usual motifs. The attached half-timbered building
is earlier, though not by much: described as a gymnasium on
Beaumont's plan and now used as function rooms.

COUNTY POLICE STATION and POLICE COURT, Stockport
Road. Dated 1896. Red brick and stone dressings, cleanly and
nicely detailed, Renaissance style with shaped gables with
scallop designs. Could it be by *Thomas George & Son*, who did
the similar post office in Ashton-under-Lyne? Separate doors
with carved stone heads labelled Constables, l., Magistrates,
centre, and Sergeants, r.

BAND STAND, Victoria Park. Late 1890s. Swept octagonal roof
supported by fluted columns.

There are a few early C19 houses here and there on STOCKPORT
ROAD. They are generally of brick, some with doorcases, e.g.
Nos. 51–55, of three storeys, with flared brick headers to give
a chequered effect.

HATTING FACTORIES

Denton, and Stockport in Cheshire, were the main centres of C19
hat production in the North, dominating the industry nationally
from the 1860s. Denton's factories have largely disappeared.

Origins as a cottage industry are recalled at DANE BANK HOUSE, on Windmill Lane, an early C19 farmhouse with scribed stucco and quoins which has an attached workshop, now altered and used as a garage. The Woolfendens' factory which developed here has disappeared, but three large late C19 houses opposite were built for family members. Of surviving factories the largest and most complete is J. MOORE & SON on Heaton Street, started in 1872 but rebuilt in 1892. Of this date the main brick block with the tall circular chimney. Workshops on each side of a courtyard were added as the business expanded. To Heaton Street, two- and three-storey ranges with a parapet rising behind bearing the firm's name. The ruinous remains of JOSEPH HOWE & SONS' WORKS, on Annan Street near the centre, are notable because of the domestic appearance of the frontage buildings (now reduced to one storey), attributable to the fact they were designed in 1869 to be converted into housing if the business failed.

FACTORY, Windmill Lane. By *Taylor, Young & Partners*, 1960. Designed to produce concrete components, now used for light industry. What is noticeable is the series of low concrete arches, post-tensioned to form large-span tied arches, with upper glazing.

DROYLSDEN

9090

This was an area formerly of scattered farms lying SW of Ashton-under-Lyne, which had developed a domestic linen bleaching and weaving industry by the mid C18. The open rural situation and availability of land was presumably what attracted Moravian settlers who built their community in 1785, and this survives as an other-worldly enclave S of the centre. Things began to change with the opening of the Ashton Canal towards the close of the C18; industry followed swiftly, and has now largely departed.

ST MARY, Church Street. 1846–7 by *E. H. Shellard*. Yellow sandstone, no tower, only a bellcote. Aisles and chancel. Mostly lancets, but the clerestory windows spherical triangles. After the spare exterior the interior is surprisingly ornate. Six-bay arcades with quatrefoil piers, thin shafts in the diagonals, and stiff-leaf capitals. W gallery with arcaded front and organ loft. High chancel arch, long chancel. Narrow nave with high hammerbeam roof, simpler arch-braced chancel roof. The roof principals rise from short E.E. shafts resting on headstops which were carved from the unfinished blocks *c.* 1880. – FURNISHINGS. Pitch-pine PEWS with shaped poppyhead ends. – CHANCEL FURNISHINGS of the early and mid C20, with linenfold panelling.

ST ANDREW, Edge Lane. By *Percy Walker*, 1914–17. Accrington brick with decoration mainly reserved for the W end facing the road. Here there is a low polygonal baptistery, offset bellcote and tall lights set into heavy buttresses. Aisles and transepts, windows with cusped tracery of red terracotta. (The interior is Romanesque in character with arcades of round arches and narrow aisles).

St Stephen (R.C.), Sunnyside Road. By *Greenhalgh & Williams*, 1960. Brick. Gabled w end with a slim offset w tower and a window strip beside it extending from the gable down to the entrance screen. Glazing all in honeycomb and lozenge shapes, including a deep window strip to the nave.

Moravian Church. *See* Perambulation, below.

Council Offices, Manchester Road. *c.* 1970 by *J. Poulson*. Large, white, with a curving pattern in relief framing the windows. The service towers are clumsily treated, and the whole thing completely out of scale with its surroundings.

cemetery, Greenside Lane. Large late C19–early C20 stone Dec chapel with a tower with an open arcaded base and a tall spire. Possibly by *T. D. Lindley* who did the cemetery chapel at Hurst in Ashton-under-Lyne (q.v.). The cemetery has an axial layout and original attractive railings on the street sides.

library, Manchester Road. Dated 1937. Neo-Georgian, low and of fawn brick, with a stone plaque over the entrance showing a child reading.

police station, Manchester Road. Mid- to late C19, with the words 'County Constabulary Station' over the door. Symmetrical, two storeys with a central door treated as a Venetian opening, all exactly as at the one in Mossley (q.v.), but in brick instead of stone.

war memorial, Cemetery Road. Slender stylized three-sided stone shaft with understated crosses at the top. Unveiled 1921.

New Inn, Greenside Lane. A 1930s Moderne pub and attached shops, an unusual style in the Manchester area and completely unexpected here. Rendered with a flat roof, the elevations stepping out with curving forms and a semicircular end. On the Scott Road side an entrance with a balcony over has original ironwork and glazing. Fake Victorian makeover inside, masking the original clean lines.

Buckley Hill Farm, Cross Lane. An interesting C17 brick house of two storeys and an attic, with three gables, windows under hoodmoulds and very flat summarily shaped relieving arches, and plenty of raised brick lozenges, singly and in groups. Most windows have been replaced but mullions survive in the attic and r. return elevation. The l. gabled bay is a rebuilding, perhaps early C19, which follows the original form closely. (The listing description reports an interior with an inglenook, cyma-moulded beams with ogee stops, and a dogleg stair with splat balusters.) A barn beside the house is also of brick, with opposed cart entrances and decorative ventilation holes. Probably C18.

Cinderland Hall Farm, Lumb Lane. Perhaps built by the Byron family in the C15 or by the Hultons who acquired the estate in the early C16. Timber-framed, partially rebuilt in brick, partly rendered. Three-unit, with gabled porch to the main part, gabled cross-wing, and rebuilt single-storey service

wing. (Dr Nevell reports a cruck-framed hall, now ceiled over
but with a full-height cross-passage with the original three
doorways.) Around the yard, altered and partially rebuilt brick
BARNS, probably C18 and early C19, including a shippon and
one with a cart entrance and threshing floor flanked by stables.
CO-OPERATIVE SUNDRIES MANUFACTORY (former), Greenside Lane. One of the only big works left in the area, and
prominent in the centre. Early C20. The two-storey office
block has a bold ground-floor arcade with an entrance in a
Diocletian opening and windows in the same form, and a stone
frieze at eaves level with lettering and the local Society's
beehive badge. The four-storey, five- by ten-bay main block is
plain apart from polychrome brick at the top, where pilasters
break above the parapet.

PERAMBULATION

Fairfield, s of the centre, has the most interesting buildings in
Droylsden, which include one group of national interest, the
Moravian Settlement. Start at the junction of Fairfield Road
and Market Street. Here the ASHTON CANAL can be reached
from the road bridge. Striking w along the towpath past the
remains of C19 mills quickly leads to a basin where the
(disused) Fairbottom canal branch diverged, and on to a good
group on the N side. First a former TOLLHOUSE, probably
early C19, brick, a single room with a door with semicircular
head to the r. and a corner chimneystack. The LOCK is of the
usual type with stone steps, turned into a double lock in the
1820s. Graceful BRIDGE, like the one in the Portland Basin in
Ashton-under-Lyne (q.v.), of stone with a cobbled deck, dated
1838 and known locally as the camel's hump. Set back from
the canal is the late C18 former CANAL AGENT'S HOUSE,
symmetrical, two storeys, with stone lintels and sills. Just to the
w and more modest, a LOCK KEEPER'S COTTAGE. Late C18,
windows with very heavy stone lintels, doors with arched
heads. Continuing w of the bridge gives views of the stone
PACKET BOATHOUSE dated 1833. Long and low with an
arched opening to the canal in the gable end. The group is
given added cohesion by the coped stone walls alongside the
canal and cottage path. The former VICTORIA MILL which
forms the backdrop to the buildings here was built in 1845.
Remains of the original works, and a polygonal chimney.

Return to Fairfield Road and turn sw for the MORAVIAN
SETTLEMENT, entered from the s side of the road. This is the
largest and most ambitious Moravian settlement in England,
the last of three established during the C18, and still occupied
by a Moravian community.* The Moravians originated in the
mid C15 as followers of Jan Hus, the Bohemian Reformer. The

* The others are at Fulneck, Yorkshire (West Riding), of the mid 1740s and Ock-
brook, Derbyshire, started in 1750.

group was persecuted and eventually re-established itself in Saxony in the early c18, from where several parties came to England in 1730 with the intention of travelling on to America. They became associated with John Wesley and some decided to form settlements in England, drawing in local people disillusioned with the Established Church. The North-Western group settled in Dukinfield, Cheshire, but decided to move because they could not acquire land on suitable terms there. Principal buildings were put up 1784–5; the main movers were John Lees, a local mine-owner, and Benjamin Latrobe. Latrobe's twenty-year-old son *Benjamin Henry Latrobe*, who became famous as an architect after emigrating to America in 1796, was responsible for drawing up the plan and designing the buildings. The plan was determined partly by the tradition of segregation of men and women, common to other c18 Moravian settlements. The unmarried lived communally in single-sex houses. The division of the sexes is expressed further in this community through an E–W subdivision of space, with the girls' school and quarters for unmarried women on the E side of the site, with matching arrangements for men on the other side. Women originally worshipped on the E side of the church, and were buried on the E side of the burial ground. In addition the community considered several plans, including placing the church at the centre of the site, but the s end away from the road was chosen because of the relative seclusion offered. The plans were sent for approval to the Unity Elders' Conference in Barby, Germany.* The community aimed to be self-sufficient and a number of different activities were undertaken as well as farming, including handloom weaving, hatting, commercial baking and so on.

The settlement has an air of seclusion and calm. Buildings are similar in scale and materials, but not uniform in design, so there is no feeling of regimentation. The entrance is on the N side, the plan a square within a square, the streets cobbled with flagged walkways, the brick houses of two and three storeys. Earlier houses are in header bond. Those (chiefly on the NW side) which have been refronted, added, or rebuilt, date variously from the mid c19 to late c20, but they are in keeping. The houses are mainly terraces, but some are detached and some semi-detached. Three-storey houses opposite the entrance are said to have been used as a weaving factory; if so, they have been altered, or light must have been brought in from the roof. Cotton-spinning using spinning jennies was also undertaken, and some houses on the N side are said to have been converted from a cotton warehouse established in 1786. The grandest house is on the NE side of the outer square. It has five bays flanked by recessed single bays, and a central pedimented doorcase. It is said to have been a doctor's house which operated as a cottage hospital. The house on the w side

32

* *See* Margaret Geddes, 'The Coming of Moravians to Cheshire and Lancashire', *Moravian History Magazine*, Autumn 1998.

Droylsden, Moravian Settlement, engraving by J. Swirtner, 1795

of the entrance was used as an inn until the Temperance Movement caught up with the community in 1848.

Taking either Brethren's Street or Sisters' Street s leads to the showpiece buildings, which would have been visible from the main Ashton-under-Lyne road, s, as shown in a late C18 engraving. The CHURCH is placed centrally. The four slightly projecting central bays are pedimented, with a cupola over, similar in appearance to the Moravian school in Fulneck, where the Latrobe family had earlier been based. Central entrance. Only the small windows of the outer bays are original. The tall narrow windows are early C20 enlargements inserted when the interior was re-oriented. Originally the congregation faced N, and there was a s gallery. Now everything faces E, and the fittings and decoration date from the early C20 changes. w gallery with fancy cast-iron columns, raised E end with an upper loft and an organ with an elaborate case, on each side minimal plaster decoration of paired pilasters and cartouches. – PULPIT placed centrally at the E end, simple CHOIR FURNISHINGS on each side, and central COMMUNION TABLE.

Attached on each side of the church, lower two-storey two-bay wings which served as the manse (w) and steward's house (E). Detached three-storey blocks on either side were originally provided for single men and women, the SISTERS' HOUSE, E, and the BRETHREN HOUSE, w. The buildings were used as boarding schools from the later C19, and the Brethren House, still a school, was rebuilt in 1871, though the general shape and proportions echo the original. The Sisters' House, now a community centre, has late C19 fenestration. The interior is greatly altered.

The BURIAL GROUND, s of the settlement, is wooded, with
an overgrown avenue aligned with the chapel. It is a lovely
evocative place, with simple stones laid flat in rows, all of them
numbered and lettered with bare details of names and dates.
Latrobe's son, brother of the more famous architect, lies here,
on the men's side. When burial of spouses in shared plots was
instituted, larger stones were used to give room for both
names. A stone baluster SUNDIAL base at the intersection of
paths is of 1785, but the dial and gnomon have disappeared.

A path running s on the w side of the burial ground leads
to Fairfield Avenue and the housing of FAIRFIELD TENANTS
LTD, 1913–22 by *Edgar Wood & Henry Sellers*. The company
was formed in 1912 and twenty-two acres of land were
obtained on a 999-year lease from the Moravian Church. A
number of Moravians who wished to remain near their home
settlement were members. The Manchester Tenants' scheme at
Burnage, s Manchester (q.v.) was visited while it was under
construction and T. C. Horsfall and E. D. (later Lord) Simon
became involved in the scheme. Thirty-three of the thirty-nine
houses were built 1913–14, the others after 1920. The street is
called Broadway, that frank English name recalling the Worces-
tershire village and reflecting the generosity of the street width
and verges, which are planted with trees. Garden walls are of
sandstone rubble, and paths are flagged (many replaced by
tarmac). The site slopes slightly upwards w to e and n, and
there is a green in the centre. According to J. H. G. Archer
'the imaginative exploitation of levels and texture suggest
that Wood was responsible for the layout, but the chaste Neo-
Georgian character of the houses undoubtedly reflects the taste
of Sellers.'

The homes seem at first to be the standard Neo-Georgian
semi-detacheds coming into fashion just before the First World
War, but then one notices such features as the severely cubic
shape of the projecting part of each house. In fact they vary in
detail and in form, with detached, semi-detached and terraced
housing, doubtless a nod to the houses of the Moravian settlement. Frontages are varied, some set well back behind open
lawns, others with gardens hugging the street. Everything is
subtle and restrained. The houses are of red brick, with sparing
dark brick dressings and patterning, and they reward careful
study. The deeply inset entrances are generally arched, with
fanlights, many with pediments raised some distance above,
some flat, others with open triangular stone pediments, and
one with fluted columns pushing above the entablature in a
thoroughly Mannerist way. Sash windows with slightly cambered heads, a few bold polygonal bows; upper windows are
generally casements. Arrangements of entrances to the gardens
include groups of arches formed by a door, a niche and then
another arch to the garden. Where the street turns to the N,
and becomes Broadway North, the corner is taken by a
sudden, deep, concave expanse of brickwork with chimneys on
each side and pairs of inwardly curved windows – the only big

architectural statement. The walk back is rewarding for all the details of composition and grouping seen for a second time at a slightly different angle.

ECCLES

Eccles is an ancient settlement, with a church with C12 or earlier origins. It became a small town, and was Incorporated in 1892. The boom years were the two decades before 1891 by which time there were 36,000 inhabitants. The figure for 1871 was only 19,000. The staple industry was textiles (cotton and silk). Industry has almost gone, and the area is now linked to surrounding settlements by suburbs. The centre is around Church Street, and the little group of civic buildings, pubs and shops, with the church on a slight eminence to the N, have some sense of coherence, marred by a depressing and now partially abandoned 1960s shopping centre (by *Leach, Rhodes & Walker*). The Metrolink tram with a transport interchange which came in 1999–2001, and anonymous retail and business parks to the S of the centre, are the most recent arrivals.

St Mary the Virgin, Church Street. The first mention is in 1180, but parts of an Anglo-Saxon cross discovered nearby in 1889 (*see* below) are a possible indication of earlier origins. The advowson was acquired by Whalley Abbey in 1230. The refounding of the St Catherine chantry in the S transeptal chapel in 1450, the granting of a papal indulgence for those giving alms for repairs in 1467 and a bequest for building work in 1525 by Robert Langley of Agecroft, suggest a date range for the main pre-C19 works seen today. The building is of red sandstone. Short W tower with straight-headed three-light bell-openings. The S porch was C15, as the door shows, but it was rebuilt at various times, most recently as a First World War memorial in 1923. Nave and aisles are all embattled. N and S chancel chapels, and a transeptal S chapel. The aisle and clerestory windows have panel tracery, but it is entirely uncusped. Before early C20 restorations it was possible to detect a differing treatment of the window mouldings which suggested that the S aisle was somewhat earlier than the N, and there was evidence, in the form of a plinth, for an earlier S aisle as well, which may have related to the period of rebuilding of the S transeptal chapel *c.* 1450. At the W end of the N aisle is a half-uncovered C15 three-light window close to the nave. The chancel (but not the flanking chapels) was rebuilt by *Isaac Holden* in 1862–3. Most of the rest was refaced 1907–8.

INTERIOR. The high tower arch was filled in by a porch in 1862–3 and the upper part converted into a sham window. The tower is earlier than the arcades. When they and the aisles were built they were made wider, so the tower is not now on axis. The sequence of alterations seems to be as follows. First the S aisle was rebuilt and the S transeptal St Catherine Chapel

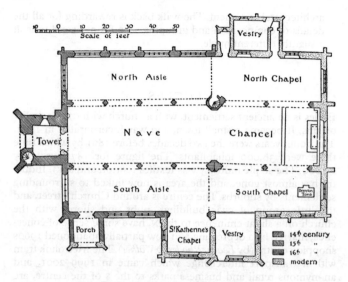

Eccles, St Mary the Virgin, plan.
Victoria County History of Lancashire, vol. 4, 1911

reconstructed retaining the original C14 N arch, *c.* 1450. Later
the nave was widened on the N side and the N aisle reconstructed, for which F. R. Johnston suggests a date of *c.* 1480.
The nave roof must date from the same campaign. The four-
bay nave arcades, like the clerestory and aisle windows, look
late C15 or early C16. Perhaps they were rebuilt when the
clerestory was inserted or enlarged, preserving the earlier roof.
The chancel piers also look early C16 but may be later (*see*
below). The nave arcades have chamfered projections and thin
hollows in the diagonals. Capitals are elementary, some with
two designs of blank shields. Statue niches face W in two of the
N piers; pedestals with a shield, canopy with crocketed pinnacles, all crudely done. Two more niches on the S arcade face S;
the one on the SE respond towards the St Catherine Chapel
has carvings of her wheel as well as tongs and a hammer.

The NAVE ROOF is the chief treasure of the church. Shallow
pitch with arch-braced principals rising from corbels, blind
tracery in the spandrels and cresting over. The bosses, figures
and many of the beams look original but most of the arch-
braces have been replaced, probably during restoration in
1846, which is commemorated by an inscription in the spandrels of the easternmost truss. The roof is almost identical to
the nave roof of Manchester Cathedral (q.v.), though of course
on a smaller scale. The date of the Manchester roof is not
known, though it is traditionally associated with Warden Ralph
Langley, incumbent 1465–81, and the sun-in-splendour motifs
of both examples have been associated with the York family

badge and a pre-1485 date. It may be that the widening of the
nave and construction of the roof at Manchester were closely
followed by a similar programme of work at Eccles by the same
craftsmen. The patron could have been Laurence Booth, who
held various positions, including the Archbishopric of York,
under Edward IV. There are large central bosses with sunbursts
beneath the kingposts, which all have a figure wearing an alb
and holding a shield, almost identical to those in Manchester.
Each bay is divided into thirty-two panels, with bosses, chiefly
foliated but with a repeated motif of a sunburst with four
praying figures above, also seen at Manchester.

Large piers mark the chancel, that to the N with a rood stair.
The inserted arch is due to *Holden*. The axis of the chancel is
skewed some 18 in. (45 cm.) to the S, according to one theory
because it was set out at a different time of year from the nave.
Its dating is problematic. There are two-bay arcades, similar to
those of the nave. Tradition has it that work was abandoned in
1537 when the Abbot of Whalley was hanged, or two years
later when the Abbey was dissolved. A Letter Patent of 1566
describes the chancel as 'quite fallen downe to the grounde
and nothing left thereof but onely a smale quantity of stones
which is utterly defaced'. The document ordered that £133 6s.
8d. should be paid for its repair, so perhaps the piers and a
makeshift roof visible in early C19 views date from this period.
The piers were retained by Holden in his rebuilding, when triangular clerestory lights were inserted. His roof borrows motifs
from Manchester Cathedral.

The arch of the S transeptal chapel must be C14, perhaps of
1368 when the chantry of St Catherine was founded by
Thomas Booth of Barton Hall. The chantry was refounded by
Laurence Booth in 1450.* Apart from the arch everything was
rebuilt during the C19 and the chapel has now been designated
a 'heritage area' with various items brought from elsewhere in
the building. The N chapel is associated with a chantry founded
in 1460 by William Booth, Archbishop of York (†1464) and his
half-brother Laurence (who later held the same post), who
founded a college of six priests in 1462 (for the site of their
house *see* College Croft Flats, below). C19 accounts describe
the E window as having reticulated tracery, of which the
present window is said to be a copy. The S chancel chapel
almost certainly relates to a chantry founded by Sir Geoffrey
de Massey of Worsley in 1453. It was turned into a meeting
room and café, late C20.

FURNISHINGS. REREDOS. Very elaborate, alabaster and
mosaic, installed 1883. – PULPIT. 1862, with charming carvings
around the base of animals and foliage. – FONT. Stone, *c.* 1862.
The N chancel chapel was refurbished 1952–4 by *W. Cecil
Young* who was responsible for the peculiar, ugly Renaissance-
style SCREEN. – STAINED GLASS. E window S aisle, early C16

* St Catherine with her wheel is the crest of Booth of Barton.

glass depicting the Entry into Jerusalem, from a convent in Rouen. Installed in St John, Lower Byrom Street, Manchester, during the late C18, and moved here in 1929 when that church was demolished. It was split between three lights and distorted and elongated, giving rise to its local nickname 'The Long Donkey Window'. N aisle, W end, Mayo memorial, with saints including St Luke, rather good, by *Francis H. Spear*, 1929. Also in the N aisle a war memorial showing an airman on a plain ground by *W. Pointer* of Manchester, 1948. E window, 1862 by *Hardman*, damaged during the Manchester Blitz of 1940. The missing pieces were later replaced with plain glass as a reminder of the event.

MONUMENTS. Nave arcade, Christopher Dauntsey †1718, tablet surmounted by a jaunty putto. – Dauntsey family brass, W wall, 1648; N aisle. George Leigh †1679, painted arms. – S chapel, Dorothy Brereton †1639, erected in 1600 for herself, her husband Richard †1598, and their infant son. The family were heirs in title of the Masseys of Worsley and Tatton. Well-preserved recumbent figures with the child in swaddling bands beside his mother. She has an elaborate head dress and ruff, her husband wears armour. The tomb-chest has square angle balusters and otherwise only shields. Moved from the S chancel chapel in the late C20. Affixed to the wall of the S chapel are three COFFIN LIDS, liberally decorated with copper studs, and their COFFIN-PLATES recovered in the late C20 from a vault in the S chancel chapel. John Gilbert, †1795 and his wife Lydia †1797. Gilbert was one of the chief engineers of the Duke of Bridgewater's canal and became his steward. The other is that of John Egerton †1700, the infant son of John Egerton of Worsley. – W porch, S side, Thomas Butterworth Bailey †1802, by *J. Bacon Jun.* finely carved tablet with an urn draped in flowers. Moved from the chancel. – TOMB SLABS. Two damaged slabs were recovered during repairs to the church floor in 1856. They have carved and incised cross designs and are probably C14.* – SCULPTURE. At the E end of the N nave arcade (but likely to be moved to the S transeptal chapel) part of an Anglo-Saxon cross shaft with knotwork, found nearby during the construction of the Ship Canal, and part of a C15 lantern cross with the Trinity, found in the wall of Barton Old Hall (demolished).

ST ANDREW, Chadwick Road. 1879 by *Herbert Tijou*. Big, stone, with a good S tower, polygonal apse with tall windows, and powerful grouping of the various elements. Geometrical tracery, with aisle and clerestory windows varying only slightly in detail. The tower, by *J. S. Crowther*, 1889, is based on Tijou's design but with subtle differences. It is less decorative in the lower stages, particularly in the detailing of the angle buttresses, yet the pinnacles at the top are hexagonal in place of Tijou's square ones, and they are more emphatic, too. Nave and chancel under one tall arch-braced timber roof. Seven-bay

* Miss Evelyn Vigeon provided information on these and other items in the church.

arcades of circular piers with capitals with knobbly leaves in the C14 fashion. This and much of the other detail was carved during the early 1880s. Highly ornate Dec style CHANCEL and CHOIR FURNISHINGS added c. 1900; canopied REREDOS installed 1898. – STAINED GLASS. E windows by *Kempe* showing the Life of Christ. Good glass by *Shrigley & Hunt*: W windows, Christian warriors, 1916; N chapel E window Daniel and Elisha, the latter shown as a bald man blessing a child with luxuriantly flowing locks. Other windows by them in the S aisle. Several other aisle windows by *A. O. Hemming*, 1902–3. He also painted extensive MURALS during the same period, showing figures such as Queen Victoria, soldiers, nurses and mill girls as well as Biblical scenes. Painted over, 1960s.

ST JAMES, Eccles Old Road. 1860–1 by *W. Scott* of Liverpool. Yellow sandstone, late C13 style with a NW broach spire facing the road, low aisles with double lancets, clerestory with triple lancets.

ST MARY (R.C.), Church Street. 1897–8 by *W. H. Rowle*, on land given by the de Trafford family of Trafford Park, on the other side of the Ship Canal (*see* Stretford). Stock brick and red brick, the planned NW tower unexecuted. Romanesque elements with very tall narrow lancets to the low aisles. E window with plate tracery. Arcades of octagonal piers, elaborate stone REREDOS with pinnacles and an arcade containing statues, said to be a gift of the de Trafford family.

SALVATION ARMY, Church Street. Dated 1907 and quite plain, with the usual crowstep detail to the gable, red brick, buff terracotta and relief lettering.

TOWN HALL (former), Church Street. 1880–1 by *John Lowe*, extended 1899. Originally built for the local Board of Health, it became a town hall after Incorporation in 1892. It is a lacklustre affair, said to have been described by L. S. Lowry as the second ugliest building in Lancashire. Symmetrical, arched main windows, but pavilion roofs on either side of a tall stone clock tower with a domed top.

LIBRARY, Church Street. A Carnegie library by *Edward Potts*, 1907, doing justice to the little square it fronts. Eclectic Renaissance-cum-Baroque style, brick with much stone, including copious carving. The main windows are Venetian under a super-arch with sculpture in the spandrels: allegories of learning and the arts. Baroque portal. Vestibule with an arcade of Ionic demi-columns and a coffered tunnel-vaulted ceiling. The reading room is generously lit by windows to the gallery and a high clerestory. Tunnel-vaulted ceiling, arcaded gallery with ironwork balcony fronts and cartouches in the spandrels, portrait medallions of writers from Homer to Tennyson on the walls. In the clerestory, pretty Art Nouveau glass with names of more writers.

WAR MEMORIAL, Church Street. By *John Cassidy*, c. 1920. Tall plinth with an angel of Victory holding a palm, and a bronze panel with a soldier in battledress with the word 'Pax' over.

PUBLIC BATHS, Cromwell Street. 1913, altered 1926. Long and

low, Baroque, of red brick with a great deal of yellow terra-cotta. The main entrance, now altered, was symmetrical with entrances for men and women. The striking channelled brick chimney, given vertical emphasis by bright red brick detailing, is a local landmark. Converted to a therapeutic centre in 1988.

HOPE HOSPITAL, Eccles Old Road. Originally a Poor Law infir-mary built on the pavilion plan by *Lawrence Booth*, 1880–2, almost completely engulfed by extensions and later buildings. Red brick, vaguely Renaissance, with four long narrow ranges terminating with full-height angled pavilions linked by sturdy two-tier iron bridges. E of the early buildings, a very large former NURSES' HOME dated 1923, pale speckled brick and red brick with shaped gables and three storey canted bays. Apart from this the usual conglomeration of later building including tall 1960s blocks and low, brightly coloured brick late C20 additions on the S side of the site.

TRANSPORT INTERCHANGE SHELTER, Church Street. A glass wedge with branching steel columns exposed within, by *EGS Design*, 2001.

CROWN THEATRE (former), Church Street. By the Eccles architects *Campbell & Horsley*. Opened in 1899 as the Lyceum theatre and turned into a cinema in 1931. Large, red brick and terracotta, Renaissance style, with a truncated corner tower. (Interior with three balconies supported by four tiers of columns.)

REGENT CINEMA (former), Church Street. By *N. Hartley Hacking*, 1920. Red brick and buff terracotta, Baroque and rather nicely done, i.e. Hacking has not tried to cram too much in to the narrow frontage. Central entrance bay with big arch enclosing an oriel, entrance with columns, balustraded parapet.

MIDLAND BANK, Church Street. By *Drury & Gomershall*, 1936. Dignified, in fine red brick, stone cornice, central entrance with Ionic pilasters and a segmental pediment.

MANCHESTER AND COUNTY BANK (former), Church Street. 1871. One of the best buildings of the centre. Large, Eliza-bethan, stone, with gables, mullioned-and-transomed windows and foliated shafts at the entrances.

MONKS' HALL, Wellington Road. The front is roughcast, Tudor, of *c.* 1840. Symmetrical two-storey range with a porch, single-storey range added in the late C19 in matching style. This neat front masks C17 origins, for there is a timber-framed range behind the frontage, and parallel to it. This has some visible framing in square panels, but alteration and additions obscure the details.

COLLEGE CROFT FLATS, College Croft. Immediately S of the churchyard on an area named for the house of the college of six priests founded by Laurence Booth in 1462 (*see* St Mary, above). Three fifteen-storey blocks put up in 1963 and another sixteen-storey block of 1967, all by *Wimpey*.

HALLS BUILDINGS, off Church Street. A C17 timber-framed house, now derelict. Stone plinth, brick and wattle-and-daub infill. (The interior has back-to-back fireplaces, a timber-framed cross-wall and tie-beam roof trusses.)

PUBS. Eccles is the best place in SE Lancashire to see early C20 gin palaces. Some of those built for Joseph Holt's brewery retain little-altered interiors, now a great rarity.

LAMB HOTEL, Regent Street. By *Mr Newton* of *Hartley Hacking & Co.*, for Joseph Holt's brewery. Red brick with buff terracotta dressings, Baroque and asymmetrical. Central entrance bay with a gable bearing the date 1906 and a narrow oriel beneath. The interior is almost completely intact. Mahogany entrance screen, elaborate bar, Art Nouveau tiles, Jacobean staircase, rooms with original doors in Jacobean surrounds, lobby screens. Original fixed seating, including raised seating in the billiard room, which has its original (billiard) table.

ROYAL OAK, Barton Road. By *Mr Newton* of *Hartley Hacking & Co.*, for Holt's brewery, dated 1904. Edwardian Baroque in red brick and buff terracotta with a full-height canted bay with a big central chimney to the street corner. Stables and yard, with an entrance with terracotta finials to the entrance piers. Like the Lamb (above) it has a little-altered plan and fittings.

GRAPES HOTEL, Liverpool Road. The earliest of the pubs in the area by *Mr Newton* of *Hartley Hacking & Co.* Dated 1903, Jacobean style in red brick and red terracotta, less ambitious than the other two, but almost as good inside. Art Nouveau tiles, Jacobean stair, elaborate bar, separate rooms with original doors and surrounds, lobby screens and original fixed seating.

TOWN HALL INN, Church Street. 1909, Baroque, of stone. Narrow central entrance bay crowned by a little dome. A smaller entrance to the r. with demi-columns, presumably to the former outdoor department. On the whole better than the Town Hall itself (*see* above), which is nearly opposite.

DUKE OF YORK, Church Street, beside the Town Hall. A big three-storeyed early C20 Jacobethan affair with a range of timbered gables and stone transomed windows.

EGERTON

7010

Together with Bradshaw (q.v.), and including Eagley, Dunscar and Bromley Cross, Egerton was part of Turton township in N Lancashire, but all are now in Bolton MBC.

CHRISTCHURCH, Walmsley. 1839–40, by *Edmund Sharpe*. Well sited on a knoll. A sizeable church built of horizontally channelled stone, but with lancets so narrow and closely grouped as to give it a cross-eyed look. Meagrely buttressed W tower with big pinnacles. Double transepts were added in 1867, still in channelled stone but with Geometric tracery and carved faces to the hoodmoulds. The tall interior must initially have been excessively plain and narrow. Slender monolithic piers of four-shafts-and-four-hollows section, arches with two sunk hollows – i.e. archaeologically accurate motifs. The transepts opening out behind the arcades have added some breadth and richness. – REREDOS. 1872, a low stone arcade with mosaic panels. Side panels were added in 1901 with much more lively mosaic scenes. – ALTAR, REREDOS and CANOPY in the s chapel, made to accommodate a late C15 painted predella bought by the vicar in 1952. It is in three sections, Christ before Pilate, Man of Sorrows, and Lamentation, divided by gilded tracery. Christa Grössinger compares it to the work of the Catalan artist Jaime Huguet. – WAR MEMORIAL. Alabaster plaque with angel and wreath, *c.* 1920. – STAINED GLASS. Painted coat of arms, now in a late C20 w lavatory. The rest of the early glass is geometric with small scenes. E window, 1872, very blue, by *Wailes*. S transept 1896 by *Ballantine & Gardiner*. Facing each other in the nave two by *Morris & Co.*, 1889, designed by *Burne-Jones*. Pairs of large figures with small associated scenes below floating against floral quarries.

NATIONAL SCHOOL, by the church gate. Dated 1839. In the same channelled stonework as the church so perhaps also by *Sharpe*. Vernacular in style with round-headed mullioned windows and hoodmoulds. SCHOOL, alongside, of 1882. Plainer, with plate tracery at the ends; adapted as a theatre.

ST JOHN THE EVANGELIST (R.C.), The Crescent, Toppings. By *J. V. Mather* of *Mather & Nutter*, 1966–7. An oblong tile-hung spire rises apparently out of some back gardens of the Toppings estate, where building started in 1939 and continued up until the 1950s. Peering closer, it can be seen to stand in the centre of a low flat-roofed brick building with concrete and slab glass windows. Effective cave-like interior, cruciform but wider than long, lit only by the lights at the base of the spire and four corner windows. The four inclined legs of the spire define the sanctuary; its lantern and a shallow inner dome create a ciborium over the altar. SLAB GLASS by *Dom Louis Charles Norris* of Buckfast Abbey; in the lantern 1985, the rest, not completely abstract, brought here in 1994 from St Aldhelm, Turton. – SCULPTURE by *Ray Schofield*: Stations of the Cross, in metallic fibreglass; figures of St John, Our Lady of Mount Carmel and the risen Christ. He also made the ETCHED GLASS WINDOW depicting St Anselm and St John in a local setting, 1994.

UNITARIAN CHAPEL, Blackburn Road, Dimple. Just inside the MBC boundary. Datestone 1713. A vernacular building of three bays and two storeys with mullioned windows in threes, those of the upper storey stepping down as the ground falls. Fussy narthex and bellcote added in 1874. (– BOX PEWS. – PULPIT in the middle of the side facing the entrance.) Beautiful GRAVEYARD running down to a stream. By the door is the massive grave slab of *John Bradshaw Gass* †1912, done by the firm no doubt.

SCHOOL, in the grounds of the chapel. 1851, Tudor.

BIRTENSHAW METHODIST CHURCH. Arts and Crafts Gothic, 1925, of local squared rubble with Runcorn stone dressings. SCHOOLS, 1888.

EGERTON UNITED REFORMED CHURCH (Congregational). 1873–4, by *George Cunliffe*. With plate tracery.

BLAIR HOSPITAL (former), Hospital Road. Now AL JAMIAH ISLAMIYYA DARUL ULOOM, an institute of higher education. The hospital, for convalescents, resulted from the bequest of Stephen Blair †1870, chemical manufacturer (*see* Farnworth). It was built in 1884–9 by *J. Medland Taylor* in an unusual mix of stone and brick in equal quantities, either striped or chequered. The brick is harshly red, the stone channelled horizontally and blackened, the effect grim.

LAST DROP VILLAGE, Hospital Road, Bromley Cross. Not a village. Orrell Fold, a typical sub-Pennine cluster of dwellings and farm buildings, was transformed by Mr Carton Walker in the 1960s–70s into a retail, hotel and leisure complex disguised as a quaint village street. The model was perhaps Firwood Fold (*see* Bolton, Tonge Moor). The challenge is to work out which are the original buildings. The restaurant of 1964 for example was a shippon, and retains its stone-flag cattle stalls, and the cocktail bar was a covered midden. The transformation was insensitively done, with the liberal application of cement mortar and taverna-style plaster and the incorporation of much reclaimed material. The latter includes, over the cocktail bar door, a Romanesque arch and cushion capitals in biscuit-coloured terracotta, like that of St Stephen Lever Bridge, Bolton (q.v.).

WAR MEMORIAL, Dunscar, at the junction of Blackburn Road and Darwen Road. By *Gaffin & Co.*, 1921. A bronze soldier – so young – in battledress with pack and helmet on his back, bayonet sheathed and rifle reversed, stands on a Portland stone and granite pedestal.

EAGLEY MILLS, in the wooded valley between the Darwen and Blackburn roads. An early industrial complex of great interest, converted in the late 1990s to residential use by the *J. D. K. Partnership* of Newcastle and the *P. J. Livesey Group*. James and Robert Chadwick developed the business (smallwear weaving, sewing-cotton manufacture, twist bleaching and dyeing) and the associated community from the 1820s. By the river is an early three-storey MILL with five-light sash windows and a hipped roof. No. 3 TWIST MILL with its clock tower, by *Thomas Haselden* 1887, dominates the site. Five stories, distinctively striped in red brick and rock-faced stone. Behind it is No. 2 MILL, 1881, of four storeys and strongly buttressed, with a corner bell-cupola. Both mills are now residential. Some of the windows have been recessed to create balconies for the flats. Two large mills (one by *Bradshaw & Gass*, 1892) and extensive north-light sheds have been demolished. By the bridge on Hough Lane is the former CO-OP STORE and HALL of 1873, now EAGLEY HALL, by *Maxwell & Tuke*, once a handsome building. Separate tailoring building by *Bradshaw & Gass* in 1895. SCHOOL, School Street, 1851–2, by *W. W. Whittaker & George Woodhouse*, done up to the nines for residential use in 2003. COTTAGES in Paper Mill Street and School Street. By Mill No. 2, more residential streets. A superior group known as Bash Row, properly Vale View, is where the gaffers lived. Nos. 115 and 117 Hough Street have ashlar fronts with Grecian doorcases. Clustered at BANKTOP immediately s is the main company village; Playfair Street, Park Row and Park View of the 1830s and 1840s, simple stone cottages attractively grouped around gardens, with a few larger houses at the edges. MORADA, brick with timber-framed gables, was for the mill manager. EAGLEY BANK retains some of its wooded grounds; ashlar front with Georgian doorcase and fanlight, but the curved SW corner is surely Victorian, suggesting that the date at the back, 1854, goes for the whole. Italianate STABLE with a clock tower.

SHARPLES HALL, immediately E, was *Thomas Haselden*'s own house. An Italianate villa of golden stone in his favourite stripes, rock-faced alternating with fine ashlar. It has lost its grounds to residential development.

7000   ELLENBROOK

The settlement, probably originally centred on the medieval chapel of ease, now merges with Walkden, N.

ST MARY THE VIRGIN, Bridgewater Road. Possibly on the site of a chapel of the de Worsleys for which a licence was granted in the C13. There was certainly a building here by the late C16. The present brick church dates from 1725, and was extended to the E in the late C18. Low and humble, with the expected round-arched windows. The chancel, with lancets, polygonal W baptistery and S aisle were added in 1842, also in brick with some polychrome detailing. (Round-arched nave arcade, roof with kingpost trusses. – STAINED GLASS. E window given by Sir Francis Egerton, and similar to the E end glass of St Mark, Worsley (q.v.). Probably mid-C19 and of Continental origin. TS)

BROADWAY. A little C18 group marooned in suburbia. Parrs Fold Farmhouse is C18, rebuilt, according to the datestone, in 1850 and rather plain. Two groups of cottages beside it are C18, but partially rebuilt in the mid or later C19 with picturesque chimney clusters, bargeboarding and half-timbering.

MINES RESCUE STATION (former), Ellenbrook Road. 1933 by *Bradshaw Gass & Hope*. The only visible legacy of the many pits in this area, built as a regional training and rescue centre by Lancashire and Cheshire Coal Owners. Chequered brick with hipped projecting bays with flat parapets and urns, flanking a brick entrance loggia. Around it houses for the staff, brick and modestly Arts and Crafts in style. Large superintendent's house, s side, and semi-detached houses on the N side facing Ellenbrook Road and along the N side of Orchard Avenue.

FAILSWORTH

The typical settlement in this part of the county, neither town nor village, the direct unnoticeable continuation of the Oldham Road, NE from Manchester, through Newton Heath, yet with one area, Daisy Nook, still rural in character.

HOLY TRINITY, Oldham Road and Broadway. 1909 by F. R. *Freeman*. Yellow sandstone with red sandstone dressings. Perp style. Incomplete at the E end.

ST JOHN, Oldham Road. 1845–6 by *E. H. Shellard*, W tower added in 1879 – by whom? It is the one memorable part, with a tall graceful broach spire, clasping buttresses, large bell-openings and elaborate clock surrounds with canopies and crocketed pinnacles. The rest is typical Shellard, with paired lancets and spherical triangles for clerestory windows. – MONUMENT. N of the church. John Taylor †1883. An elaborate Gothic affair with upper canopies and a crocketed spire.

IMMACULATE CONCEPTION (R.C.), Lord Lane. By *Greenhalgh & Williams*, 1960–4. Large, brick, the dominant feature the W front where the tall arch of a full-height porte cochère has suspended within it a large statue of the Virgin. Rising above, a bizarre concrete spire looking like a semi-furled umbrella. Narrow aisles with stone friezes with scenes from the Life of Christ in relief. Circular clerestory windows. Top-lit sanctuary with large MOSAIC of the Assumption. Circular NW baptistery attached to the main building by a short corridor.

COUNCIL OFFICES and LIBRARY (former), Oldham Road. 1880 by *J. N. Firth*, the library of 1909 by *E. Ogden & P. Cartwright* who encased the whole façade at the same time. Brick with Portland stone dressings and patterns. A very pretty composition, with well-judged projection and recession of window and entrance bays, enlivened with chequering and attractive carving over the library door.

FAILSWORTH POLE, Pole Lane. Failsworth is famous for its pole. The site is at the heart of the old settlement, traditionally occupied by a maypole. In 1793 a pole was put up as a 'Loyal Standard' in a ceremony attended by the hanging and burning of an effigy of Tom Paine. Successive poles followed in 1850, when a ship's mainmast was erected, in 1889, in 1924 and finally in 1958. A metal pole stands atop a tame brown brick pylon incorporating clock faces, by the district surveyor *E. D. Turner*. Plaques record previous poles.

SCULPTURE, beside the pole, Outside Inn by *Timothy Shutter*, 1993. A stone rendition of a pub interior with a seat, fireplace, lamp, beer mugs, etc. Put up to commemorate the bicentenary of the erection of the first official pole.

PACK HORSE INN, Wrigley Head. A two-storey stone C18 house flanked on each side by brick early C19 extensions. Symmetrical, with openings with stone architraves, the windows perhaps early C19 replacements of mullioned windows.

THE FIRS, Oldham Road. Now a care home, but built for the local mill-owner Henry Walmsley, *c.* 1850. Red brick and stone dressings. Two storeys. Three widely spaced bays. One-bay pediment, projecting stone porch; still in the classical tradition.

FAILSWORTH LODGE, Broadway. A simple red brick house of five bays, dated 1770, with three tall storeys, a central doorway with a broken pediment, and two-bay lower wings. Now a club, set incongruously in a sea of tarmac.

OLDHAM ROAD. Nos. 407–411, beside the Rochdale Canal. Combined shops and warehouse of 1804. Of brick, with two storeys to the street and four storeys to the canal. The block is curved to the canal side, where there is a wharf. Loading doors on this side have been glazed and other alterations made in a late C20 conversion to a pub.

FERRANTI OFFICES (former), Tweedale Way. By *J. R. G. Seward* of *Cruickshank & Seward*, 1965. Slick white-tiled offices of three storeys around an internal courtyard, set off by the grubby brick factories that they front.

REGENT MILL, Princess Street. By *G. Stott*, 1906. The largest and most complete surviving mill in Failsworth. Typical of the early C20 mills of the Oldham area. Red brick with stone dressings. A great long flat-roofed four-storey range, and a prominent water tower with a pyramidal roof.*

ASHTON ROAD WEST. Nos. 28–32, a little late C18 brick terrace with large ground-floor windows lighting former weaving workshops.

DIAMOND HALL FARM, Medlock Road. Probably early C18. A brick house with central gabled porch and central chimney, hence a baffle-entry plan. Raised brick patterns: cross on the l. and lozenge on the r. Original windows with shallow brick arches over. Large brick BARN opposite with lozenge-shaped blue brick ventilation holes, arched cart entry and integral stables with pointed-arch heads to doors and windows.

MEDLOCK HALL, Daisy Nook. A much-restored timber-framed C17 house with stone cross-wing with mullioned windows. Cross-passage plan. (A single cruck truss survives inside.)

(WOODHOUSE GREEN FARMHOUSE, Cutler Hill Road. The list of listed buildings records a C17 timber-framed house and stable.)

FAIRFIELD *see* DROYLSDEN

FARNWORTH and KEARSLEY

7000

The parish church straddles the boundary between the two places, which is nowhere clear, but Kearsley Mount remains distinct and is taken as outer Farnworth – *see* below. Prestolee, N of Kearsley and E of Farnworth, has its own entry.

Papermaking from rags developed in the late C17 and C18 in the Croal and Irwell valley, using the plentiful clean water.

* For more information on this and other mills in the area, *see* D. Gurr and J. Hunt, *The Cotton Mills of Oldham*, 1998.

Cotton-bleaching followed, and then the most injurious of all C19 industries, chemical manufacture of soda and bleach, producing hydrochloric acid gas, sulphuric acid in the water, and dumps of evil-smelling calcium sulphide. The demise of these industries (though papermaking continues nearby in Little Lever and Radcliffe, q.v.) has left little architectural legacy (but *see* St Stephen, Kearsley Mount, below, and Blair Hospital at Egerton). Cotton-spinning on the other hand has left a series of great mills of varying distinction, a few of which are identified below. The recovery of the river valleys in the last decades of the C20 is astonishing (*see* Moses Gate Country Park, below).

St John Evangelist, Church Street. The parish church of Farnworth and Kearsley, built for the Commissioners in 1824–6 by *Thomas Hardwick*.* It is a typical ashlar box, the w tower with polygonal buttresses, the tall pinnacles removed in 1912. Two-light windows N and S, not too narrow. The unusual tracery, with a second instalment under a lower semicircular sub-arch, belongs to alterations of 1873, when the three-bay chancel was added. Here again there is some confusion because the church asked for plans from both *Freeman & Cunliffe* and *Paley & Austin*. Interior galleried on slender iron columns, the cutaway of their undersides matching the sub-arches we saw outside. Flat ceiling, with plaster bosses. – REREDOS and PEWS of 1874. – STAINED GLASS. E, Baptism of Christ and Crucifixion. Under the galleries, by *Heaton, Butler & Bayne*, 1908, *G. Wragge*, 1923, *Shrigley & Hunt*, 1939, and *W. Pointer*, 1958.

The SCHOOL opposite, s, is rather good. Of brick, with three equal gables. The centre section is almost all window. By *R. Knill Freeman, c.* 1880.

St James, St James Street, New Bury, 1 m. wsw of St John. 1862–5 by *Isaac Holden & Son*. Of rock-faced stone. Undivided nave with a bellcote, narrow chancel with vestries. Paired trefoil-headed lancets. Wide scissor-braced roof. – FONT. Small Neo-Norman tub with archaic figures in dogtoothed arcading. – STAINED GLASS. War memorial of *c.* 1920 in the tall w lancets, Pre-Raphaelite colours. s side E, Christ in the Temple, *c.* 1910 signed *Jones & Willis*. Expressionist figures, 1965, w on both sides.

St Thomas, Dixon Green, Farnworth. By *J. S. Rawson*, 1879. Closed and falling into dereliction, which is a pity because it is a fine building. No tower, but a sheer semicircular apse and tall nave and aisles. Evenly spaced lancets in the clerestory, plate tracery elsewhere, with a big five-lighter for the w end.

(All Saints, Moses Gate. By *R. Knill Freeman*, 1897.)

St Gregory (R.C.), Church Street (disused). Of 1873–5 by *Edmund Kirby*, yet all lancets, as if it were 1825. Large, with a

---

* A church history of 1999 claims that *Charles Barry* prepared the design and states that *Philip Hardwick* was present at the laying of the foundation stone.

N transept. Abandoned in favour of the parish hall (by *Green-halgh & Williams*, 1960). Large red brick PRESBYTERY, 1896.

OUR LADY OF LOURDES (R.C.), Plodder Lane. 1957. The plan is exactly that of a coffin, with a tower linked to the feet end. The lid is a pitched roof, so its eaves slope down to a point on each side. Five tall windows in the longer side elevation, hexagonal glazing filling the shorter.

TRINITY CHURCH (Congregational and Methodist), Manchester Road, Farnworth. 1974. Octagonal with a monopitch roof. Connected by low ancillary buildings to the much more ambitious BICENTENARY HALL of 1862, an elongated Gothic octagon with a high pyramid roof and its own tower entrance. The cornices are richly decorated with carved paterae, and there are two splendid gargoyles, crouching figures with crossed feet.

CONGREGATIONAL CHAPEL (United Reformed), Albert Road. 1862. Big, red brick, and classical, but very plain.

In MARKET STREET, Farnworth, a group of three buildings faces the park, managing to convey for a moment a sense of civic dignity. All three are of hard pinkish brick with ample stonework. The TOWN HALL is of 1908 by *W. J. Lomax*. It is symmetrical, of nine bays and two storeys, with a steep, i.e., C17-type pediment, a more-than-semicircular porch with Ionic columns, and a cupola. Subsidiary semicircular pediments r. and l. The CARNEGIE LIBRARY, also by *Lomax*, was built in 1910. It has columns, an oversized semicircular (i.e. also C17-type) pediment, and a dome. Under the pediment is an enormous dropped keystone incongruously swagged with lusciously carved fruit. Carved portraits of Carnegie and of Mr Richardson, chairman. The third building is unfortunately derelict: the EVANGELICAL BAPTIST CHURCH of 1906 by *Bradshaw, Gass & Hope*. The semicircular pediments appeared here first, and so did the characteristic palette, although here it is terracotta not stone that provides the contrast.

Across the road is FARNWORTH PARK. Opened in 1864 by William Gladstone. It was designed by *William Henderson* of Birkenhead and *Robert Galloway*, head gardener to Thomas Barnes M.P., the donor of the park. His generosity is recorded in a pitifully vandalized MONUMENT by *Bradshaw & Gass* put up in 1895 at the top of the park, with a bronze portrait relief by *W.C. May*. WAR MEMORIAL by *J. & H. Patteson* of Manchester, 1924. Gritstone column and undersized bronze Fame, blowing a trumpet.

POLICE STATION, Church Street. 1879. Lancashire's police stations are usually Tudor with a central emphasis but paired entrances. This is a big one, with seven gables all fussily shouldered and pinnacled. It was presumably designed by the County Architect, *Henry Littler*.

(THE SHAKESPEARE, Glynne Street. Large intact 1920s corner pub.)

BOLTON ROYAL HOSPITAL, Plodder Lane. The nucleus is the Fishpool Workhouse of 1858 by *George Woodhouse*. Italianate, with a central tower and six lesser towers. It faces the town rather than the lane. Many additions, of 1866, 1894, 1925 etc., infilled as usual with modern temporary-looking structures. The main entrance and accident and emergency block is by the *Gilling Dod Partnership* of Chorley, 1996, who also completed a large accommodation and treatment block in 1985. In the foyer, main corridor and around the chapel, temple and mosque are the fruits of an arts project of 1997 including STAINED GLASS by *Classical Glass* of Bolton, artists *Richard Kay* and *Andrew Seddon*; MOSAICS by *Rachel Cooke*, CERAMICS by *Gerald Buchanon*.

HORROCKSES MILL, 1915, Lorne Street. The best of a group of three mills which step down the hillside towards the railway. Strongly modelled, with corner towers grooved at the sides and corbelled out at the top, one carrying a pyramid roof. At the back is the stone-lined cooling reservoir, called in Lancashire a lodge; an unusual survival. Immediately W a single-storey north-light weaving shed, making little impact on the street apart from its tall engine house, but impressive inside for its receding vistas of iron columns and skylighting.

CENTURY MILL, George Street, near St James. Built 1902–3 for ring-spinning. Only three stories high but very long and wide. Of brick, unadorned except for the stone blockings on the tower, with concrete floors on iron columns. The scar of the demolished engine house can be seen at the back, with glazed brick, but the fine octagonal chimney stands, of dark brick with a corbelled-out top. Part of its foundation cone of rough brickwork can be seen.

The Manchester & Bolton Railway, which opened in 1837, is marked by a series of elegant BRIDGES between Farnworth and Kearsley, stations elliptical-arched, with radiating voussoirs, and often rising steeply to the middle. The great *Jesse Hartley* was the engineer.

MOSES GATE COUNTRY PARK, Croal and Irwell valley. Progressively industrialized and polluted from the founding of John Crompton's paper mill in 1670 (*see* pp. 218–9, above) until the mid C20, but in the C21, with the return of clean water and air, verdant and increasingly beautiful again. Nothing obvious is left of the industrial buildings, but three large LODGES (reservoirs) remain, and so does ROCK HALL of *c.* 1807, occupied originally by the manager of Crompton's works and now the visitor centre. A standard five-bay, two-storey house of brick, with a pediment, but with engagingly over-large windows and fanlight and correspondingly little wall. The mills were immediately below and to the N. The setted lane by the side of Rock Hall leads up to Farnworth CEMETERY, for a magnificent panorama.

KEARSLEY MOUNT is 1m. SE, beyond the bypass. Three churches are grouped together on the summit:

ST STEPHEN, Manchester Road. By *J. Medland Taylor*, 1870–1, for Stephen Blair, proprietor, with his brother, of Kearsley

Chemical Works. Taylor's roguish side comes out in the bell-openings of the tower and the three-light windows at the E end of the nave, looking like two two-lighters overlapping. The N aisle is as wide as the nave but there is no S aisle. Stumpy quatrefoil-section arcade columns, two with naturalistic capitals currently painted in naturalistic colours. – PULPIT, FONT and FONT COVER have received the same treatment. – FIRST WORLD WAR MEMORIAL by the font, done in painted tiles. – STAINED GLASS above it, with in the lower lights an army padre giving Communion, and a field hospital. Also Blair memorial window by *Alfred O. Hemming*, 1901, and *Shrigley & Hunt* windows of 1954 and 1963.

The parsonage, also by *Taylor*, had plenty of roguish touches, but unfortunately it has been demolished.

METHODIST CHURCH, opposite, on Manchester Road. 1914. Hard brick and stone front in Renaissance style, with twin doors. An older SCHOOL adjoins.

ST JOHN FISHER (R.C.) and SCHOENSTATT SHRINE. A narrow track off Manchester Road turns a corner to deliver a genuine *coup d'œil*. The church and presbytery of 1967–8 by *Desmond Williams & Associates*, in brown brick with monopitch roofs, provide in their crudeness the perfect foil and frame for the gem-like shrine and an unexpectedly splendid panorama over the Irwell valley to the distant Pennines. The shrine is a tiny German chapel, white, thick-walled, with a little belfry and a polygonal apse. Built in 2000, it is a copy of the C12 mortuary chapel near Koblenz where the Schoenstatt renewal movement began in 1914. It is the first in England; there are 160 world-wide. The Baroque ALTARPIECE with its twirly columns, and the SCULPTURE of St Michael were carved in Germany.

FLIXTON

7090

Flixton lies immediately E of the Manchester Ship Canal and N of the Mersey, overlooking Carrington Moss. It merges with Davyhulme, NE, and Urmston, N.

ST MICHAEL, Church Road. An enjoyable church, with the rare distinction in this part of Lancashire of having a free view to the S over green fields. A church was recorded here in the C12. Abraded stones with what could be chevron ornament are reset in the chancel E gable, and have been cited as evidence for the Norman predecessor. The chancel E wall is C15, with diagonal buttresses; the restorers (in 1853) of the Perp E window may have followed the original tracery pattern. Of 1851 the chancel N vestry and organ chamber; the rest of the building is C18 and C19. The W tower with rusticated quoins, urn finials and a window with Y-tracery is an 1888 rebuilding of a tower put up in 1731. Some C18 stonework was reused, but the bell-openings were Victorianized. A plaque records the C18 tower, and some of the round-arched windows and the splendid S

Flixton, St Michael. *Victoria County History of Lancashire*, vol. 5, 1911

door with pilasters and a pediment look original. The nave and aisles were rebuilt in 1756, with round-arched windows on pilasters. Neo-Georgian s porch, 1919.

INTERIOR. Arcades of columns on high bases, misaligned with one another, and awkwardly related to the chancel arcade. Typical country classicism, probably meant to be Doric. *Mr Birch* was paid two guineas for the work, and parish documents record two meetings 'about the pillers', when ninety pints of ale were consumed. The two-bay chancel has octagonal piers, probably made during rebuilding in 1815. The C15 SE octagonal respond suggests the early C19 work may have followed the original. Simple kingpost roof. A carved PANEL in the tower arch, four shields with initials and crude emblazonry, is said to show badges of the masons involved in the C18 rebuilding. – FURNISHINGS. Mainly of 1877, including an elaborate stone REREDOS with canopied niches, stone PULPIT and an octagonal stone FONT. Large, circular, spiky ironwork CHANDELIER, 1968. – STAINED GLASS. E window by *William Wailes*, c. 1860; s aisle E and SE, brightly coloured glass by *R. B. Edmundson*, 1858; two others, late C19 by *Heaton, Butler & Bayne*. Two N aisle windows by *Mayer & Co.* W window, St George, St Aidan and St Oswald, probably early C20. – MONUMENTS. S aisle. BRASS to Richard Radclyff †1602 and family, kneeling figures, one group facing the other. He is in armour and the inscription records his loyal role in the siege of Leith (1560) and the Northern Rising (1569). – Ralph Wright †1831, tablet with an urn on sarcophagus. – Wright Lee Wright †1847, tablet with drapes and a draped urn. N aisle, Robert Norreys †1784, marble tablet. – PARISH CHEST. Simple, with three locks, acquired 1602.

CHURCHYARD. Baluster SUNDIAL s of the tower, on which the date 1772 was formerly visible. MONUMENTS. John Jones †1751, tomb-chest with inset balusters at the angles. There was a fashion here in the mid–late C19 for enormous ledger stones, some as big as 5 by 6 ft (1.5 by 1.8 metres).

ST JOHN, Irlam Road. 1968–9. By *R.B. Wood-Jones* in association with *Marsden & Arschavir*. Square, with glazed gables on each side and a channelled copper roof. Bright interior with C19 furnishings, said to come from Manchester Cathedral, and a good range of late C19 STAINED GLASS from various sources. The building is attached by a covered walkway to the original humble brick MISSION CHURCH of 1925.

PUBLIC LIBRARY (former), Bowfell Road. 1930s, brick, classical, and slightly strange. The main body is almost like a church, with a tall entrance arch and a rounded apsidal end with plain brick columns supporting the oversailing roof. Lower transept-like wings with similar rounded ends and brick columns. Gabled entrance bay, the entrance framed by tall columns.

RECTORY (former), No. 52 Carrington Road. A plain brick two-storey house of 1825 with a central arched doorway with inset Doric columns.

FLIXTON HOUSE, Flixton Road. Probably built by Ralph Wright, who acquired property in the centre of Flixton *c.* 1801–6. A large two-storey house, of chequered brick, with four bays and a handsome offset doorway with a broken pediment and Doric columns. Victorian additions to the rear and side, and an ugly conservatory at the front added when the local authority acquired house and grounds in the 1930s. Immediately behind and attached to the house by a wall, a brick BARN with circular pitching eyes in stone surrounds and a dear little octagonal cupola. Kingpost roof.

THE VILLAGE is a thoroughfare off Church Road w of the church. It is no longer villagey. Nos. 18–20 is a timber-framed house dated 1672 with square panels and an iron-studded door on the r. side. The eaves were raised and additions made on each side in brick, probably in the late C18. The neighbouring No. 16 is also probably late C18, brick and render, much altered.

No. 351 CHURCH ROAD, almost opposite the church. A pretty polychromatic brick house, probably 1870s.

FOXDENTON HALL *see* CHADDERTON

HARTSHEAD

A tiny isolated settlement in the moors N of Ashton-under-Lyne on the slopes of Hartshead Pike, a prominent hill.

HARTSHEAD PIKE TOWER on the top of the hill is by *John Eaton*, started in 1863 by public subscription to mark the marriage of the Prince of Wales and completed several years later. Stone, circular with a conical top, cusped lancets and dormers with stepped gables. An earlier structure is recorded in the mid C18, rebuilt in the late C18. LILY LANES, a narrow winding road up towards the pike, has alongside it a number of C17 and C18 houses, cottages and farmhouses, most of them drastically altered and restored, with a concentration at HARTSHEAD GREEN. Surprisingly for such a small remote place there is a former mission church, ST AUGUSTINE, standing on the hillside. Mid-C19, small, with coupled lancets and a quatrefoil W window. Nave, apse and porch. Stone with a stone slate roof. Converted to a house. Houses to note, both on the N side of the lane, are HARTSHEAD GREEN FARM, of late C17 origin with later additions, the older parts of very narrow courses of stone, and JEREMY'S COTTAGE, dated 1642, rebuilt retaining the inglenook inside. (The outlying FOUR WINDS is a late C18 house with a classical front and a pedimented doorway with Gibbs surround, recorded by Dr Nevell.)

HARWOOD

NE of Bolton and merging with it.

CHRIST'S CHURCH, Stitch Mi Lane. Of 1840–1, for Robert Lomax, cotton manufacturer and collector of antique woodwork. W tower thin, telescopic in two stages, with a short spire rebuilt in 1918 and decidedly wonky. Boxy nave without aisles or structural chancel. S transept 1847. It is all built in an intractable stone without any smooth bits even for the jambs or mullions. The style is a rustic artisan Romanesque and the result engagingly chunky.
   Cosy small-scale interior, still in its pre-Ecclesiological state. W gallery on paired iron piers with little Norman capitals. Tie-beam roof, arcaded, with huge bosses. Tiny chancel, little more than an alcove, framed by a tall narrow arch with zigzag but no capitals. Stubby blank arcading, and a second upper tier opening into notional galleries. They are just the upper parts of the two vestries, whose doors r. and l. of the chancel arch are big enough to suggest a basilican three-part E end. – ALTAR RAIL. A Romanesque arcade. – BOX PEWS at the sides, open ones in the middle; no central aisle. The rich furnishing of the S transept, which was the LOMAX CHAPEL, has unfortunately been lost. – ALTAR. A vestment cupboard from Nuremberg incorporating carved scenes and dated 1561. – PULPIT dated 1660, from the Chapel Royal in St James's Palace which was refitted in 1836–7. It has been cut down and is without a tester. – STALLS, a pair with misericords, cut down out of a row; Flemish, mid C17. – LECTERN, oak, an unusually animated eagle on an orb; probably Flemish of *c.* 1700. –

ORGAN, free-standing, said to be from Edgware, i.e. the Chandos–Handel neighbourhood. The case however is standard Victorian minimum-Gothic. – MONUMENTS. The best are to John Lomax †1827, yet an asymmetrical Rococo cartouche, and Robert Lomax †1814 and Mary his wife †1822, a conventional Gothic canopy; both by *Patteson* in white marble. – STAINED GLASS. E, 1921; Psalm 21.

LYCHGATE, dated 1840. It was the old vicarage porch, re-erected here in 1913. A fragment of the house still stands in the churchyard.

SCHOOL and schoolhouse 1848, SW of the church, on the corner of Newby Road.

WESLEYAN CHAPEL, Hardy Mill Road. 1862. Of stone, and still severely classical.

WALSH'S EDUCATIONAL INSTITUTE, Hardy Mill Road. 1872. Like a chapel of the period but the staircase set to one side only, so an asymmetrical front.

HAUGHTON GREEN

9090

The settlement lies S of the centre of Denton and merges with it. Apart from the enclave formed by the church and churchyard, Haughton Green is not a pleasure to look at, and the three high 1960s tower blocks immediately N of the church do not help. Rows of early–mid-C19 terraces survive on Meadow Lane and Haughton Green Road. Apart from the odd one with side-sliding sashes they have all been thoroughly modernized. An early C17 glassworks on the banks of the River Tame near Hyde Hall (*see* below) associated with the French glassmaking Du Houx and Pillmey families, does not seem to have survived the Civil War. Some of the kilns were excavated in the 1970s.

ST MARY THE VIRGIN, Haughton Green Road. 1874–6 By *J. Medland & Henry Taylor*. A typically roguish composition, this time timber-framed, with Aesthetic Movement accents. Nave with a steep roof, dormers, and coved eaves. N porch with, in the angle, a funny octagonal brick tower with a pyramidal tiled roof with gables in alternate faces, with the baptistery below. Long chancel with quatrefoil banding and bargeboards with Japanese-style roundels and similar pargetted roundels on the side walls. Timber buttresses on each side and at the angles of the chancel, perhaps derived from French examples. The gabled S side looks almost domestic. Windows are generally mullioned, that at the W end transomed and tiered after Pennine vernacular examples. Chancel windows have traceried openings with carved flowers in the spandrels. The interior is highly idiosyncratic and playful, delighting in experimentation with the timber construction, and with many unusual decorative features. There is a strong sense of influence of Japanese design. Some of the detailing is intricate, some quite crude, making one think of Sarah Losh's church at Wreay, Cumberland, of 1842. The nave is very wide, the s aisle cross-gabled, and the weirdest fretwork openings are set between the nave roof and the aisle bay roofs. The arcade has timber posts with filigree openwork carving in the spandrels of the aisle, pierced mouchettes below, and pierced roses in the spandrels to the nave. Nave roof with embattled tie-beams, pendants, raking queenposts and scissor-bracing. The purlins are oddly supported against the chancel wall by arch-braces. The chancel arch is cusped and the organ chamber has an elaborate open-work SCREEN of very unusual design, with arcading containing a grid of pierced quatrefoils, pierced mouchettes below, and to the nave, tall branching floral designs. Pargetted fleurons to the sanctuary, similar to those of the sanctuary of St Lawrence, Denton (q.v.). Pargetted panels also appear over the entrance to the baptistery. – REREDOS. Quite crudely carved oak arcading, with beautiful paintings of foliage and flowers in the style of William Morris. Original timber furnishings designed by the architects, including an openwork timber PULPIT. – FONT. Marble bowl with carved floral designs. – Very unusual READING DESK with a complex design of buds in brass. – Complete set of STAINED GLASS by *Heaton, Butler & Bayne* (some badly faded), incorporating designs derived from William Morris's Willow wallpaper. The nave and aisle windows have floral and sacred symbols on a plain ground.

A low link on the s side joins the church to a late C20 breeze-block CHURCH HALL of almost unbelievable ugliness.

RECTORY (former), Meadow Lane. Presumably of the 1870s and by *J. Medland & Henry Taylor* too. Altered for use as a restaurant, but with some surviving odd touches such as the strangely detailed door with a peculiar fanlight and the full-height gabled bay, with cusped lights to the windows and miniature quatre-foiled ground-floor windows.

METHODIST CHURCH, Two Trees Lane. 1810. Very plain, brick, of three bays with a pediment and arched windows. Spoiled by a horrid mid-C20 porch.

DENTON CEMETERY, Cemetery Road, Haughton Green. Opened 1894. Large stone two-storey domestic Tudor LODGE. Stone CHAPEL, dated 1896. The design is a more elaborate version of *T. D. Lindley*'s cemetery chapel at Hurst (*see* p. 126), and so is probably also by him. Dec, with a central tower of which the base is treated as a porte cochère. Square tower above with buttresses and crocketed pinnacles becoming octagonal in the third stage, with an octagonal stone spire. The cemetery layout is axial with a circus sw of the chapel.

HYDE HALL, Town Lane. An interesting timber-framed house probably of the mid C16. It is in poor condition, and the interior could not be inspected, so the following is based on a Royal Commission report. Two storeys, with a hall and chamber over, and cross-wings. It seems that it was built from the first with a chamber over the hall. The sequence of building is approximately as follows. The mid-C16 house had a N parlour and s services. Later in that century a two-storey oriel was added to the N end of the E side of the hall, and soon after the s wing was encased in brick. A projecting two-storey porch with the Hyde arms, dated 1625, was then added to the w end of the cross-passage. It did not match the old first-floor level of the house, and a staircase was inserted. The N wing was rebuilt *c.* 1700, and various extensions and alterations were made thereafter. Render obscures much of the timber framing. C18 additions to the r.

FARM BUILDINGS. Stables, barns and ancillary buildings on three sides of the courtyard N of the house, a pattern more commonly seen in Cheshire. The earliest part on the w side is timber-framed with brick infill, the rest all brick and built, according to the keystone dates, in 1839, 1850 and 1859. The two-storey entrance bay, dated 1839, has a wide arched entrance and ogee windows, with a dovecote in the inner gable. Flanking barns have blind round-arched openings pierced by ventilation holes. (Interior construction is of brick with brick vaults.)

MANOR FARMHOUSE, Haughton Green Road. A greatly restored two-storey double-depth stone house, dated 1735. The window details are all altered, but what is certain is that, although the façade is symmetrical, they were low and of two lights, i.e. pre-classical.

HAUGHTON DALE HOUSE, Meadow Lane. Probably early C19, stone, two storeys, pyramidal roof with a central stack. Mullioned windows with hoodmoulds.

7010   HAWKSHAW

On high ground between Ramsbottom and Bolton. Properly Hawkshaw Lane Ends; Hawkshaw itself is a still-isolated farm settlement 1 m. or so N.

ST MARY. 1890–2 by *Maxwell & Tuke*. A precision job, of finely laid and coursed stone. Nave, chancel, N transept, SE vestry, unfinished tower porch. The side windows are stretched right across from buttress to buttress, eliminating the upper wall altogether. The spandrels of the four-light windows are smooth diaphragms of stone, each under a huge single lintel. Otherwise only two buttresses, at the w. Wide, light, unaisled interior covered with a businesslike hammerbeam roof without chamfers or stops. The plaster walls were originally stencilled and gilded. The voids between the buttresses are bridged independently of the outer skin by equally unadorned paired inner lights.

BISHOP'S LODGE, the former vicarage immediately w, is the residence of the Bishop of Bolton.

METHODIST CHURCH, Bolton Road. 1891, the parallel SCHOOL, 1910.

Hawkshaw was an industrious little community. Of the coal mines there is little evidence apart from place names. Still to be seen on the main road are BLEAKLOW MILL, established in 1834 by Riggs's and working now as BLACK SHEEP TEXTILES; and CROWN MILL, also of the 1830s, now residential, stone, three-storeyed, with the engine house at the E end. A row of associated cottages to the E. The late C18 TWO BROOKS BLEACHWORKS was ¼ m S. Largely demolished, but evidence for extensive water engineering can readily be seen. The square stone CHIMNEY stands alone some distance away. Fred Whowell, whose father took on Two Brooks in 1850, rebuilt CROICH HEY on the main road in 1904, as a family residence in glaring red brick and tile-hanging.

THE HEATONS
8090

Heaton Norris is the old name for the township N of the Mersey from Stockport, now split into several areas which merge with one another. They lie between the boundary with the City of Manchester and Reddish, N, and with Stockport, S, of which they have been administratively a part since 1913. In the early C19 only Heaton Norris existed as a real settlement, with scattered buildings amongst the fields elsewhere. The other, largely residential areas, grew up later in the C19. Now that the Mersey has largely been culverted the visual S boundary is the M60 motorway, which generally follows the N side of the river in the valley bottom.

HEATON CHAPEL
8090

ST THOMAS, Wellington Road. Originally a chapel of ease standing alone in the fields, with the Chapel House pub for company from the early C19 (rebuilt in the late C19). An odd sight. A humble nave, rendered white, with a flèche, and a tall, square, brick chancel with vertical window slits rising above the nave added by *Bernard Miller* in 1937. Low W late C20 porch. The core is of *c.*1765 and has arched windows. The church was altered in the 1870s by *J. Medland Taylor*, who may have inserted plate tracery to the round-arched windows and put in the Gothic W windows. (Several TABLETS, classical and Gothic; STAINED GLASS by *John Scott* of Manchester).

ST THOMAS'S SCHOOL, Wellington Road, beside the church and making a group with it. Low and gabled, red brick with a big flèche. Dated 1891.

MCVITIE & PRICE BISCUIT FACTORY, Wellington Road, on the border with Levenshulme. A large works in red brick with red terracotta dressings dated 1917. The main two-storey range has big windows in giant arches. Utilitarian, but with Baroque details such as the pediment over the main entrance and the firm's badge and name in a cartouche on the N gable. Subsidiary buildings in similar style, mid- and late C20 additions.

ERRWOOD PARK WORKS, off Crossley Road, behind McVitie
& Price. Now largely late C20, but some much-altered older
buildings on the N side of the complex were part of the works
of Crossley Bros of Openshaw, purpose-built for car production in 1917.

MARBURY ROAD, near the junction with Nelstrop Lane. A little
group of early buildings, survivors of a larger complex shown
on early C19 maps. SHORES FOLD COTTAGES is a low single-
depth range of two dwellings of at least two builds, greatly
altered, but probably C16–C17 in origin, judging by surviving
roof and ceiling timbers. White-painted brick, possibly replacing timber framing. SHORES FOLD FARMHOUSE almost
opposite is probably late C17 or early C18, painted brick with
a pedimented brick door case within a C19 porch. Two storeys;
large, slightly off-centre chimney. (Inside, chamfered ceiling
beams and a dog-leg stair with splat balusters).

HEATON MERSEY

ST JOHN BAPTIST, St John's Road. 1846–50 by P. Walker. Thin
W tower (which lost its landmark spire in 1995), aisleless nave,
all in stone. The architect went in for excessively steep lancets
for his side windows, still with buttresses between, Commissioners' fashion, and also for his porch entrance. The chancel
and chancel chapel are by Preston & Vaughan of 1891, and well
in keeping. (Hammerbeam roof, arcaded W gallery with royal
arms, 1850s glass.) Attractive stone lychgate by Taylor & Young,
1927. A stone archway with a tiled roof and foliated banding
around the openings. The stone chosen for the interior inscriptions was so poor that they have been almost completely
effaced.

RECTORY (former). Opposite the W end of the church.
Large, c. 1850, brick with blue brick dressings, and a big gable
with fancy bargeboards facing the road.

STELLA MARIS SCHOOL (formerly St John's School), NE of
the church. Mid-late C19, single-storeyed with steep gables,
quite ornate with varied churchy windows, including cusped
lancets and a little rose window in a dormer. Truncated turret,
r. side. The former SCHOOL HOUSE stands beside it, of two
storeys with tall chimneys and windows with trefoil heads.

CONGREGATIONAL CHURCH, Mersey Road. Formerly the
Sunday School to the demolished church. Early C20, with a
commemorative date 1825 over the porch. Warmly attractive,
with a row of gables to the street and much banding and brick
diaper work in orange, white, blue and pale grey. Large
windows in the gables lighting the upper hall, smaller ones
below. On the l. side a gabled porch with a timbered upper
storey. The main upper room has a timber roof. Furnishings
include an oak PULPIT and SCREENS from the demolished
church. BRASS with good lettering by Shrigley & Hunt. To

James Watts of Abney Hall, nearby in Cheshire, †1892, patron
of the church and one of the most successful of Manchester's
C19 merchants (*see* Watts Warehouse, now the Britannia Hotel,
Portland Street, Manchester centre).

DIDSBURY ROAD PRIMARY SCHOOL, Didsbury Road. 1950s.
Pale brown brick; well-grouped blocks with flat roofs and a low
tower with a clock face.

CROWN INN, Didsbury Road. Probably late C18. L-shaped,
brick, with sash windows and part of a group with the C17
house on Vale Close (below).

HOUSES

This is an area of large Victorian and Edwardian villas, of which
some of the best can be seen on DIDSBURY ROAD. No. 279, by
Alfred Darbyshire, is one of the biggest. Tudorish details, with timbered gables and a blocky octagonal tower with a pyramid roof.
Not far from it Nos. 241–243 are large early C20 semi-detached
brick houses in quiet refined Arts and Crafts style, with garages
treated as pavilions and linking ranges with archways to the
garden. Steep tiled roofs with swept eaves, dormers with hipped
roofs, etc. No. 245, set back from the road, is in similar style.

Nos. 1–3 HIGHFIELD PARK, a pair of early C19 Tudor
Gothic houses with details typical of *Richard Lane*. Scribed
stucco, windows with paired arched heads and margin lights,
label moulds, bays and doors with parapets.

Nos. 2–4 VALE CLOSE is probably C17, one and a half
storeys, timber-framed in square panels with brick nogging
replacing wattle-and-daub. Brick C18 addition, S end. The
gable to the street, N side, has a cambered tie-beam, kingpost
and diagonal struts. It originated as a three-bay building with
typical cross passage plan. The remainder of the street to the
S, and nearby PARK ROW, have attractive early–mid-Victorian
terraces.

HEATON MOOR

8090

ST PAUL, Heaton Moor Road. 1876–7 by *Bird & Whittenbury*.
F. P. Oakley extended the nave by two bays in 1896 and added
the SE tower in 1900. This, with its unusual octagonal top
stage, is what gives character. Large paired bell-openings and
pinnacles, the upper stage with a busy arcaded parapet. All in
stone, with lancets and Geometrical tracery. (Arcade with circular piers, reredos and piscina by *R. B. Preston*, 1910. Good E
and W windows by *Albert Moore* of London, 1897 and 1901.
TS)

THE VIRGIN ST MARY AND ST MINA Coptic Church (formerly Congregational), Heaton Moor Road. 1896 by *Darbyshire & Smith*. Slender SW steeple with gables containing

prominent clock faces. Geometrical tracery. Set back on the NW side a SUNDAY SCHOOL, slightly more simply treated and nicely grouped with the church.

PEEL MOAT, Heaton Moor Golf Course. Reached via a footpath from North Area College, Buckingham Road. A well-preserved moat and platform which is *c.* 32 yd (29 metres) square, possibly identifiable with a 'chief messuage' recorded in this area in 1282.* If so this would be the earliest known moat in the SE part of the county.

FIRST WORLD WAR MEMORIAL, Heaton Moor Road, in front of St Paul's church. By *John Cassidy*, and up to his usual high standard. Unveiled 1921. Bronze life-size soldier in battledress on a Portland stone plinth. Cassidy agreed not to use the same design within a thirty-mile radius. The layout of the space, a simple arc of stone wall set into the churchyard perimeter with the monument standing in the centre, was designed by *Henry Sellers*.

TOWN HALL AND OFFICES (former), Thornfield Road, Heaton Mersey. By *Woodhouse & Willoughby*, dated 1901. Symmetrical, yellow sandstone with red sandstone dressings. Central entrance block with a scalloped gable, domed cupola and big transomed windows flanked by lower ranges with similar end gables and details. The arched entrance has columns supporting consoles with a canopy with fancy ironwork railings.

TITHE BARN SCHOOL, Mauldeth Road. Probably late 1960s. Low single-storey blocks clustered together with variety in the flat and angled roofs, dark grey brick.

ELECTRICITY STATION, Heaton Moor Road. Early C20. Large and rather impressive, red brick, red terracotta and red sandstone banding. Baroque, with blocked and blind windows. Central segmental pediment to the street with the Manchester Corporation arms, showing it was put up before incorporation of this area into Stockport in 1913.

SAVOY CINEMA, Heaton Moor Road. Opened in 1923. Baroque, red brick with white terracotta dressings, and the name in red terracotta over an altered ground floor.

REFORM CLUB, Heaton Moor Road. 1886–7, by *Alfred Darbyshire*, who won the competition. Extended 1906. Odd and asymmetrical with a triple entrance arcade, offset square oriel rising above eaves level, r., and a funny octagonal turret with a conical roof, l. Brick with stone dressings.

MAULDETH HALL, off Mauldeth Road in the midst of Heaton Moor golf course, which has taken over its little park and most of the gardens. A large Greek Revival villa put up between 1832 and 1840 for Joseph Chessborough Dyer, an inventor who came to Manchester in 1812. Ashlar, bold rather than refined. Entrance front with central projecting bay and a big Doric portico. E side of five bays articulated by oversized attached Ionic columns. W side with a full-height three-bay semicircular

---

* According to Dr Arrowsmith's research.

bow. A very early example of recently developed fire-resistant building techniques for a dwelling, using Hodgkinson cast-iron beams. These had been developed in Manchester during the 1820s and were first used probably in 1829–30. An E wing was added during the 1840s and was substantially rebuilt in matching style in 1880–2 by *Charles Heathcote*, who converted the building to a hospital for incurables. The building became derelict in the late C20 and has been converted to offices.

A classical LODGE on Mauldeth Road, disfigured by a late C20 mansard, is probably also *Heathcote*'s work.

HEATON NORRIS

8090

CHRIST CHURCH, Wellington Road North. By *W. Hayley*, 1844–6, built with a Commissioners' contribution on land donated by Wilbraham Egerton of Tatton Park. It is Hayley's most ambitious surviving work, although only the W tower survives, with the flanking walls to the aisles. It has an odd appearance these days: a coating of soot clings to the ashlar dressings and spire, while the rock-faced stone of the remainder remains clean, making very stark what was before a contrast of pale colours. Ornate, with large corner and smaller intermediate pinnacles, slender shapely spire. The interesting thing is the E.E. portal, W window with plate tracery and paired bell-openings in an E.E. arcade. The church was otherwise decidedly pre-Pugin and pre-Scott in character. The tower is a striking landmark on the very crest of the hill on the main road between Manchester and Stockport, appearing in the centre of views along the main road between the two. The Churches Conservation Trust must be congratulated for preserving it.

ALL SAINTS, Manchester Road. 1886–8 by *Preston & Vaughan*. Pale brick with terracotta dressings, and motifs of *c.* 1300. N aisle and S chapel so the E end presents three gables to the road. No tower, but a bellcote between nave and chancel. Timber-framed SW porch with brick nogging. Beside it, S side, the large RECTORY employs the same materials and palette.

ST MARTIN, Didsbury Road. 1901 by *R.B. Preston*, in his trademark pale brick with red brick and red terracotta dressings. Dec window tracery. No tower, only a flèche. A great windowless W wall facing the road was probably meant to be completed with a tower. Bold gabled chapels, S side.

ST MARY (R.C.), Roman Road. By *Pugin & Pugin*, 1897. Perched high above the motorway overlooking the Mersey Valley. Not large, without aisles, and with a canted apse and Dec window tracery. W bellcote and large rose window, reminiscent of E. W. Pugin's All Saints, Barton-upon-Irwell of thirty years before (*see* Stretford), but simpler and smaller. Timber roof with principals rising from corbels which act as canopies for statuary. Chancel arch, W organ gallery. – REREDOS. Alabaster, with canopies for statues and the monstrance. –

ALTAR RAIL. Also alabaster. – STAINED GLASS. In the nave, scenes from the Life of the Virgin, 1929.

BETHESDA PRIMITIVE METHODIST CHAPEL (former), Manchester Road, almost opposite All Saints (above). Dated 1890, vaguely Italianate. Pedimented door, sides with rows of round-headed windows. The interior has been subdivided, keeping the curved gallery on cast-iron columns.

WYCLIFFE CONGREGATIONAL CHURCH, Wellington Road North. By *Edward Walters*, 1849. Symmetrical front to the road, complete with railings, gatepiers and iron standards for gas lamps. Central gable with a large Dec window flanked by inset gabled bays for the N and S galleries, each with an entrance and steps up. The gallery arrangement is slightly unusual, the roof pitch necessitating upper as well as lower cast-iron columns, all with moulded floral designs to the shafts. Timber roof with wrought-iron stays, dormers framed in cusped panels. E organ gallery. – Original PULPIT and ground-floor box PEWS. – STAINED GLASS. W window by *R.B. Edmundson & Son* of Manchester, with Faith, Hope and Charity in the upper lights.

CHRISTADELPHIAN CHURCH, Lancashire Hill. Formerly a school; late C19. It stands atop a great cliff of sandstone above the motorway, and is notable therefore as a landmark. Yellow sandstone, gable with a circular window to the motorway, steep paired gables to Roman Road.

PENDLEBURY HALL, Lancashire Hill. By *J. W. Beaumont*, 1880–2, built as an orphanage, now a care home. Imposing, as it was meant to be, but rather graceless, with a great tower with domed corner turrets and a two-stage domed top rising from the centre. Ranges with an array of chimneys, gables, oriels and transomed windows.

AINSWORTH ALMSHOUSES, Green Lane. Named for the bene-factor who was a local businessman. By *Peirce & Son*, who won the competition in 1907. An unusual group, six pairs of houses arranged in a gentle curve. Grey brick with red brick and red terracotta dressings, transomed windows, big central stacks. Pairs of dormers with segmental gables, which have sheets of lead with floral motifs. The end houses have corner turrets with lead domes. Communal gardens at the front and rear, sur-rounded by a wall with a central arched gateway. It has a shaped parapet and segmental gable with the name and the date 1907.

NURSERY INN, Green Lane. 1939, A typical example of an 'improved' pub. Symmetrical, brick and render, with a tiled hipped roof. What makes it special is the unspoilt interior, now a great rarity. Oak panelling, original bar with painted glass overlights, coloured glass windows on a gardening theme; plants, watering cans, etc. At the rear a bowling green, part of the original design.

STOCKPORT RAILWAY VIADUCT, by *G. W. Buck* for the Manchester & Birmingham Railway. Completed in 1840 and widened to four tracks 1888–9. A giant span of twenty-six brick arches. Magnificent, and magnificently tall over the lowest part of the Mersey valley, where it rises *c.* 108 ft (33 metres) above the level of the river. It took twenty-one months to build.

HEATON NORRIS GOODS WAREHOUSE (former), Wellington Road North, where the land starts to fall down to the Mersey. Of 1877, for the LNWR. A massive block, the side to the road 360 ft (110 metres) long with thirty-one windows. Four storeys over a high basement. Polychrome red and blue brick with an emphatic grey brick cornice. It was fully integrated into the railway with internal tracks, platforms and turntables. Detached engine and accumulator house for the hydraulic system, N, detached three-storey offices, S.

ALBION FLOUR MILL. A landmark on the crest of Lancashire Hill, beside the infilled canal, *see* below. 1893, replacing an earlier building. Brick with sparing polychromy and terracotta banding, of four storeys with corner turrets. At the rear a tall water tower and a range of large late C20 grain silos.

WELLINGTON BRIDGE, Wellington Road North. Many-arched stone road bridge over the Mersey. Built *c.* 1826, the parapet renewed 2000.

ASHTON-UNDER-LYNE CANAL, STOCKPORT BRANCH TERMINUS, Wharf Street. The Act was passed in 1793 and the canal opened in 1797. A small, much-altered early-mid–C19 house at the entrance to the works now on the terminus site may have been originally associated with the canal. Otherwise there is nothing to see apart from some stretches of brick walling and foundations.

THE PYRAMID offices, 1989–1992 by *Michael Hyde & Associates*. Between the motorway and the river, so technically in old Lancashire. A great glass pyramid and a prominent landmark, giving rise to the local name for the area, 'the Valley of the Kings'.

SHOP, No. 52 Wellington Road North. Dated 1889. Notable for profuse Jacobean-style red terracotta decoration, busy friezes with putti, etc. It was probably designed as a showroom for the timber merchants listed in the directories at this address.

HOUSING

TOWER BLOCKS, Hanover Towers and Bentley Towers, Lancashire Hill. 1967–9 by *Stockport County Borough Architects' Department* under *J. S. Rank*, in association with *Laing Sectra*. A system-built project. 'Uncommonly good and splendidly slender,' was Pevsner's comment. Twenty-two-storey slabs and lower blocks, well grouped. The deck access was later modified and infilled to create maisonettes. Strident late C20 green and cream recladding with Postmodern motifs has spoiled the effect.

WELLINGTON ROAD NORTH. The main road between Manchester and Stockport. On the W side a few brick early C19 terraces, some with handsome door cases and fanlights, can be seen between the big Victorian villas. The best groups are Nos. 183–187, and further s, the more modest Nos. 99–105 (Heathfield Terrace).

HEATON PARK *see* MANCHESTER p. 398

8010

HEYWOOD

'It looks like a great funeral on its way from Bury to Rochdale, consisting of little more than a mile of brick-built cottages and shops. The very dwelling houses look as though they too worked in factories,' wrote Edwin Waugh in his *Lancashire Sketches*, 1881. 'The heights and depths cultivated in Heywood appear to be those of factory chimneys and coalpits', concluded Waugh, but 'Heywood may yet emerge from its apprenticeship to blind toil, and, wiping the dust from its eyes, look forward to things quite as essential as this fight for bread for the day.' Yet here, as in many SE Lancashire towns, there seems to be a good deal of nostalgia for the age of blind toil, and one of the things the town looks forward to is the re-opening of the railway to Bury, with steam engines.

ST LUKE. The little C17 Episcopal chapel (to Bury), domestic in its architecture and 'highly offensive' to C19 taste, was taken down after the Christmas services in 1859. The aspiring new parish church, a major statement, is by *Joseph Clarke*, 1860–2. It is markedly similar to Crowther's newly completed St Mary Hulme in Manchester (*see* p. 451), even down to the traceries. Lincolnshire Dec in golden stone with a broach spire, tall and generously windowed, the chancel very nearly as high as the nave. It has chancel aisles as well as nave aisles so the building is rectangular in plan as well as even in height, broken only by the tower which is outside the N aisle (an improvement over St Mary), by the porches, and by the Fenton Chapel, NE. The interior is very tall and light, dominated by the high chancel arch and enormous E window. The chancel as one would expect is richer, with detached colonnettes on the piers instead of plain quatrefoils and a panelled barrel ceiling instead of an open hammerbeam roof. SEDILIA and PISCINA decorated with hop and grape crockets under an organ GALLERY with seven angel musicians. There is an EASTER SEPULCHRE too. The interior carving, of Bath stone, is by *Joseph Bonehill* of Manchester.

REREDOS, PULPIT and FONT are all of alabaster, 1880s, designed by *Joseph Clarke & F. Lennox Canning* and executed by *N. Hitch* of Vauxhall. – WAR MEMORIAL, 1921, a wooden screen with a canopied shrine and lamp, by *Taylor & Young*. – STAINED GLASS. Huge W and E windows by *Hardman*, 1875–6, Old and New Testament respectively. Aisle windows mostly by *Clayton & Bell*. Aisle W windows by *Wailes*, 1860s, with char-

acteristic purples and turquoises. In the Fenton Chapel three
by *Capronnier*. Most interesting, though no great shakes artis-
tically, is the N aisle E, a Masonic window commemorating
the laying of the cube stone in 1862. It is by *George Shaw* of
Saddleworth. Pugin-like design in primary colours with
elaborate canopy work. The faces have faded badly.

St James, Tower Street. 1837–8, built at the expense of the
Kershaws and other mill-owning families. Long, with an
undersized W tower. Y-tracery of wood, replaced with stone
where stained glass has been inserted. The short chancel with
its Geometric E window was added in 1861. The interior is
dominated by the single-span roof, unnecessarily massive, with
cusping, petal shapes, a Maltese cross and pie-like bosses. GAL-
LERIES on slender iron columns. Eccentric heavily carved
PEWS and CHOIR STALLS, although these date from 1875.
PULPIT and REREDOS of alabaster, 1920s. – STAINED GLASS.
E, by *Hardman*, a Fenton memorial †1857.

The adjacent SCHOOL of 1835–6, also with Y-tracery, has
had its top storey removed and a wide-eaved roof put on (by
G. B. Howcroft, mid-C20). An improvement, making it look like
an overgrown *cottage orné*.

St Joseph (R. C.), Taylor Street. 1915, signed and dated *W. T.
Gunson & Son*, as was their laudable habit, on what is left of
the school. Unimpressive outside – brick, Romanesque – but
a fine interior. Nave of just two square bays defined by giant
arches in the side walls and overhead. Another for the crossing, then a hemicycle and semidome for the apse. The
transepts are disappointingly not full squares. Are they an
addition? They have two altars in apses apiece, with hidden
top-lighting. MOSAICS in semidome and side entrance. –
PRESBYTERY immediately S.

All Souls, Rochdale Road. A grand church by *Frank P. Oakley*,
1898–9, the nave tall with plate tracery, the chancel and polygonal apse with Geometric bar tracery. The tower porch outside
the N aisle was added by *F. P. Oakley & G. Sanville* in 1908.
Brick-lined interior but with plenty of stone. The capitals are
rough octagonal lumps still awaiting the carver. The E end is
rib-vaulted, a lavish refinement paid for by the first vicar,
Rathbone Hartley. W end partitioned off in 1994, an expensive
job but leaving unresolved the dead space above it. The tower,
its porch base also rib-vaulted, was given by Rathbone Hartley
too. Although good, it is a little underscale and so detracts from
the nobility of the church. This is made plain by the pre-1908
BANNER juxtaposed with a large modern MODEL in the
church.

St George, Heap Bridge. Close to Bury, but in Rochdale
MBC. By *J. Lowe*, 1891. Perched on a hillside surrounded by
last-gasp industry (car breakers and the like) and only accessible by a dirt track. The chancel was consecrated only in 1912.
Nave and chancel all in one. NW turret, low baptistery, S
aisle. (The circular stone PULPIT looks High rather than Late
Victorian.)

St John, Manchester Road, Hopwood. By *Frank P. Oakley*, 1903–5, replacing an iron church of 1881. With its wide, intricately tripartite w window, marked asymmetry, and sw turret it could be taken for one of Austin & Paley's. The wide five-bay nave is flanked on the n by a fully developed aisle, but on the s just a narrow passage. There are tall hall-church-type arcades on both sides however, open on the n, but acting as wall piers on the s. The stonework makes it clear that this was always the intention. The chancel was not built. Instead we have a short temporary-looking structure of brick. On either side of the chancel arch are square rib-vaulted compartments set diagonally. Are they a spatial conceit, or the beginnings of a crossing tower? There is plenty of land for a grand e end.

There is not much in the way of a centre. On Church Street is the Civic Hall, by *Lyons, Israel & Ellis*. Supposedly, like that at Royton, built by Heywood Borough Council to spend its reserves before being swallowed up by Rochdale, which was in 1974. Blue brick cube with smaller and lower cubes at the corners.

Carnegie Library, Church Street. An excellent building of 1905–6 by *S. V. North & C. Collas Robin*. Creamy ashlar front with two large mullioned-and-transomed bays framing an Ionic doorcase with a hood. Allegorical figures recline, bookend fashion, each side of the hood. The brick and stone side elevations undulate due to subsidence. Octagonal lobby with stairs to one side. Tripartite interior, clumsily top-lit, the floor and the concrete post and beam structure again rocking disconcertingly.

War Memorial, in the gardens by the library. By *Walter Marsden*, 1925. Granite pylon and an over-life-sized bronze mourner. The names were not carved until 1986.

On the corner of Hind Hill Street is the small but powerful Barclay's Bank, Edwardian Baroque with alternately blocked columns. Close by is the Police Station and Magistrates' Court, 1935. Good civic architecture on a modest scale. Nearby is the Municipal Technical School by *Woodhouse & Willoughby*, 1894, of red brick and terracotta with ornamental panels and a n-lit studio. The extension of 1912 employs the same architectural elements but without the ornament.

Mutual Mills, Aspinall Street. A huge complex, now very empty, dominating n and w views of Heywood. No. 1 Mill (1884), No. 2 Mill (1893), and No. 3 Mill (1914–23) are all in the same style, of common brick with stripes of hard red and blue brick and continuous sills of stone, the stair-towers with baluster parapets and ball finials. The offices and engine houses remain but no chimneys.

Queen's Park Road leads toward Bamford. Queen's Park, once the grounds of Heywood Hall, was given in 1879. Three-tier fountain, ornamental lodge and café, concrete stage with a rainbow-stepped canopy; all somewhat battered, but a £963,000 National Lottery grant was awarded for restoration in 2003. On Queen's Park Road are the former HIGH SCHOOL of 1892, just a single room but an eye-catcher in polychromatic brick and stone with four dormer gables, and the OLD SCHOOL HOUSE in soft-looking header-bond brickwork and yellow stone dressings, with mullioned-and-transomed windows and a quatrefoil over the front door; *c.* 1860 and entirely typical of *J. S. Crowther.*

CEMETERY, Rochdale Road. 1856. On a windy hilltop, offering a panorama of the town with its mills and steeples. Twin chapels – and yet not quite twins – at either end of the summit terrace; by *T. D. Barry* of Liverpool.

EDGECROFT, Manchester Road, at the s edge of town. A house by *Edgar Wood*, 1921, his last known building before he retired to Italy. Of common brick and still with its stone roof, with unmoulded mullions and transoms in the bay. The street wall is cut away in semicircular scoops allowing a peep into the front garden with its two old medlar trees.

HOLCOMBE   7010

A hillside settlement on the SE flank of Holcombe Hill with its monument. Ramsbottom, a relative upstart, is in the valley below and runs up to it from the E.

EMMANUEL. By *Thomas Holmes* of Bury, 1852–3, replacing a C16 chapel of ease. The best thing is its romantic position, embosomed in trees on a spur of the hill high above Ramsbottom. An earnest but gauche attempt at full-blooded Dec. Tall nave and aisles, clerestory with spherical-triangle windows, large N transept, narrow chancel, all executed in coarse rock-faced masonry. The w tower and broach spire however, with its three tiers of alternating lucarnes and not too attenuated, could not be bettered, especially when seen from higher up. The interior is nicely proportioned and not too big. Circular and octagonal piers alternate. The tower arch is still blocked by the temporary entrance needed at the consecration because the tower had not been finished. – CHANCEL FURNISHINGS all 1931, except the PULPIT which is built into the side of the chancel arch. Spirited ROYAL ARMS. – STAINED GLASS. E, greenery-yallery, by *Heaton, Butler & Bayne* †1907. The windows are mostly clear, giving views of trees and airy height ouside.

Large and interesting CHURCHYARD with many old ledgers and some surviving iron enclosures. A group of grandiose tombs by the chancel SE is built up on the lip of the hill like the beginnings of a necropolis.

DARUL ULOOM, Holcombe Old Road. A large Early Victorian house belonging to the Aitkin family, extended in 1864, which later became a TB sanatorium with the addition of the usual open-fronted wards. It closed in 1970 and was converted into a Muslim theological college, with house and wards transformed by Islamic windows and golden domes.

Hey House, on the slopes of Holcombe Moor, above and to the w of Holcombe Old Road. It carries a datestone R.B. 1616 at the back, towards the Moorbottom Road. Hey House was a hunting lodge associated with the de Traffords, which evolved as the headquarters of the Holcombe Hunt and home of the master of hounds. Long H-shaped house extended at both ends, with the door in the w cross-wing. Ground-floor windows mullioned-and-transomed, upper floor with mullions only, and both with drip moulds. Ball and obelisk finials, kneelers, and castellated parapets. The chimneys are corbelled out into miniature castles at the top. The interior is a mish-mash of historical features but the plan-form is clear – a cross-passage runs behind the great inglenook fireplace of the central house-place, with its heck, or stub wall, on the N side. The Holcombe Hunt was reorganized in 1708, and the Gothick fireplaces, doors and door-heads probably date from then. The carved overmantels assembled out of antique pieces, painted glass shields in the windows, along with the castellations, are probably associated with Thomas Gorton, Master of Hounds 1840–59, whose initials appear in one of the windows. The KENNELS were enclosed by the high retaining wall at the w end of the house. Behind in the yard are the STABLES.

Peel Monument. 1851–2, in memory of Sir Robert Peel, by *Grant, Ashton, Knowles & Gorton*. Not quite on the summit of Holcombe Hill, it is an inelegant chimney-like tower, 120 ft (37 metres) high, with the single word PEEL above the entrance. The flat top and the top of the base structure are corbelled out and castellated, as Mr Grant liked it.

HOPWOOD *see* MIDDLETON

HORWICH

Three phases can be identified. There is the mining and textile-finishing Horwich along the winding Chorley Old Road, much of it stone, of small shops, terraced cottages, and big chapels with the factories by the water courses. The late C19 railway Horwich, of Accrington brick, stretches along the dead straight Chorley New Road which runs along the lower ground to the SW. Now at the turn of the C21 there is the new Metropolitan Borough Horwich brought by the M61, a white and silver retail district centred on the Reebok Stadium and Arena along De Havilland Way.

Holy Trinity, Chorley Old Road. Horwich was a parochial chapelry within Deane parish in the C16. The chapel was first rebuilt in 1780. The present church, large and dignified, broad and black, with a tall, slender w tower, was built in 1830–1 by *Francis Bedford* for the Commissioners and the Ridgways of Wallsuches (*see* below) for £5,999. The w view is impressive, with seven graded blank lancets and the unexpected motif, high up, of the Ridgways' kneeling loaded camel. A short unbuttressed chancel was added in 1903 by *R. Knill Freeman*. Broad interior with galleries. It is a hall church with a ribbed plaster vault supported on widely spaced and slender square piers set diagonally. – The FITTINGS are all very plain, except the ALTAR TABLE, a fine piece with panelled front designed to be seen, not hidden by a frontal, in the Bolton fashion. – MONUMENT to Joseph Ridgway of Ridgmont †1842 by *Richard Westmacott Jun.* of London. Free-standing, white marble, a kneeling young woman in prayer. – STAINED GLASS. The E window appears to incorporate an early Ridgway arms in the tracery.

SCHOOLS immediately E and W. One is of 1793, with Venetian windows downstairs, and a Diocletian window above which has been repeated in the large dormers, which are clearly later. The other, minimally Gothic, is the NATIONAL INFANT AND SUNDAY SCHOOL of 1832. Still a school.

ST CATHERINE, Richmond Street. It originated as a mission to the railway immigrants in the 1880s. The nave is by *R. Knill Freeman*, 1897, in red brick with broad red terracotta windows under blank arches. The temporary chancel was not replaced until 1932, by *Frank R. Freeman*. His E section, with a large N chapel, has simplified stone tracery. No tower. The interior is broad and spacious with an Arts and Crafts feel. Exposed brick with stone stripes in the arcades; just the clerestory plastered. The nave has been halved by a wood and glass partition. – ALTAR TABLE, 1902, designed to be seen, with carved fruit. Unusual STALLS, COMMUNION RAIL and PULPIT by *Charles Cressey*, 1902, openwork made up of square section wood, interlocking and visibly pegged. – LECTERN, a pelican with hungry babies, by *Earp, Hobbs & Miller*. – FONT also by Cressey, square, supported on eight and then four stone legs. – War memorial SCREEN at the back incorporating two large ceramic plaques to Catherine Ainsworth †1916. Probably made by *Pilkington* of Clifton. One portrays an English garden idyll, the other wartime devastation. – STAINED GLASS. E window signed *Pointer* of Manchester, 1955. In the chapel re-used pieces probably mounted by Pointer, 1950s. At the back a small unsigned piece of much the same date, probably by *Edith Norris*.

ST MARY (R.C.), Chorley New Road. The architects were *Randolph & Holt*. The PRESBYTERY, of stone and prominently dated 1905, masks the chancel. The church, also of 1905, is behind, hard against a back road. It is cruciform with a bell-cote on the transept gable, E.E. in style of creamy ashlar with reddish dressings of Alderley Edge stone from Cheshire, an unlikely choice. Tall interior: a three-bay nave with non-projecting transepts behind pairs of narrow arches, a short chancel with chancel chapels. – REREDOS with three-dimensional scenes of the Annunciation and the Nativity. – ALTAR with the Last Supper, and Lady Chapel ALTAR, are all of a piece, with fat dwarf colonnettes.

To the r. is what is left of the brick SCHOOL, partly demolished in 2002, carrying a damaged datestone, probably 1886.

Opposite the church the TRAMCAR SHED of 1900, which
was the terminus of the Bolton system, effectively marks the
northern limit of the Manchester conurbation.

LEE LANE CHURCH (Anglican and United Reformed), was
built in 1856 as a Congregational chapel by *George Woodhouse*.
Stone, Gothic.

(INDEPENDENT METHODIST CHURCH, Lee Lane. 1906.)

NEW CHAPEL (Congregational), Bottom o' th' Moor. 1 m. E,
on high ground with a sweet graveyard. Founded in the early
C18 as a stormy Presbyterian offshoot of the parish church. As
enlarged in 1805 by Thomas Ridgway of Ridgmont it is a plain
square building of three bays each way. A chancel-like extension was opened by William Lever, who worshipped here when
he was at Rivington, in 1905. Cosy interior with a gallery on
three sides and elegantly curved pews.

Over the road is the former SCHOOL of 1877, extended in
1935.

PUBLIC HALL, Chorley Old Road. Of 1878, given by Mrs
Martin in memory of her husband. Nearby in Jones Street are
the LIBRARY of 1936 and similar CLINIC.

WALLSUCHES, 1 m. E. An early, extensive and well-preserved
BLEACHWORKS was undergoing residential conversion in
2003 (and hence inaccessible). The Ridgway brothers moved
their operations here from Bolton in 1775, making use of the
plentiful pure water and the coal. By 1798 a five-storey
Gingham House had been built (now reduced to two) and a
Boulton & Watt steam engine introduced. The bleaching buildings are arranged in parallel rows on the E part of the site. The
W part, more haphazard, was given over to warehousing. The
stream is culverted across the site but the reservoirs and their
leats can be seen. Thomas Ridgway lived amongst the works
at WALLSUCHES HOUSE, ashlar, of five bays, with a shallow
bow with tripartite window and a pillared porch. Joseph
Ridgway's house was RIDGMONT, high up on the S side of
Chorley Old Road overlooking the works. Now the Masonic
Hall. A long house of *c.* 1800, stuccoed, with a three-bay
pediment not quite in the middle, and a semicircular pillared
porch. A cantilever stair rising in a semicircular recess survives.

The Ridgways formed a building society in 1801. The CLUB
HOUSES, opposite Holy Trinity – three hollow squares of
terraced two-and-a-half-storey houses – are the result. Two
datestones 1806. They were seen as superior to the Ashworth
houses at Barrow Bridge, Bolton, which were rented. Attractive now in their watershot stone, they must have been pretty
cramped when built. Steps up to the front doors, some with
original railings. Steps down too, to weaving shops in the
basements with six-light mullioned windows. At the backs
more steps up and down suggest that they were back-to-backs.
On the main road Nos. 54–70 incorporate bowed shop
windows of 1806, a rare survival.

Locomotive Works now Horwich Loco Industrial
Estate, off Chorley New Road. A series of long brick sheds
built by the Lancashire & Yorkshire Railway in 1884–7.
Horwich was an odd choice. The town had been by-passed by
the primary railways, was served only by a late branch line, and
was in decline. For that very reason however land was cheap.
The first new loco (which has been preserved), left the works
in 1889. The works, employing over 3000 men, tripled the
population and created a distinct railway town. The works
closed in stages in the second half of the C20, and there is now
no physical link with the railway.

Housing. Many short streets named after C19 engineers spur
off the main road. The Railway Mechanics' Institution of 1888
has gone, but company-financed schools, a cottage hospital,
and recreation ground remain. The locomotive works' own
war memorial faces the main road. A youthful soldier on a
plinth, by *Paul Fairclough*, 1921. Unfortunately being of marble
he is slowly dissolving.

Round De Havilland Way, which connects the SE end of
Horwich with the M61, are the industrial park and retail and
leisure areas which, it is hoped, will breathe new life into
Horwich. The centrepiece is the Reebok Stadium opened
in 1998, by *Lobb Sports Architecture*. The home of Bolton Wanderers FC is an emblematic gateway to Greater Manchester
from the NW and a symbol of Metropolitan Bolton. Four white
tubular masts, topped by the floodlights, incline inwards
steeply, braced apart by tapering girders. From the oblong thus
formed, echoing the shape of the pitch, are hung the four petals
of the roofs, beneath which, but hardly touching, is the oval of
the stadium with its steeply raked seating. The whole is
enclosed by a sleek curtain wall. There is plenty of room under
the seating for a hotel at the S end and an exhibition centre, E.

A smaller companion to the Reebok, linked to it by a footbridge suspended from an off-centre wishbone of tubular
steel, is the Arena, opened 2001, an indoor tennis centre by
the venerable Bolton firm of *Bradshaw Gass & Hope*. Oval,
white, with an umbrella roof. Entrance atrium reaching up
three floors. Beyond that a huge whispering space for eight
tennis courts, the floor rubbery and blue, the roof gently
arched with holey girders. Round about is Middlebrook
Retail Park; the usual low rise sheds covering much ground,
tricked out with a few architectural suggestions and set in
sterile acres of car park with bits of boring grass in between.

Lostock Hall Gatehouse, Mill Lane, at the E fringe of the
Lostock Industrial Estate. Of 1591. A striking survival in the
wide valley, still facing open country to the E. Its ambitious
architecture, if not strictly correct, proves that the area was
not a wilderness before the Industrial and Post-industrial
Revolutions. Large, of three storeys and three bays, with boldly
moulded cornices, entablatures and parapets, and the three
classical orders conventionally superimposed. Big mullioned-
and-transomed windows over the archway. The parapet is

crenellated with semicircles once topped with obelisk pinnacles. Large barns adjacent. The hall, which was timber-framed, stood immediately w, near the present farmhouse.

HYDE HALL see HAUGHTON GREEN

IRLAM

The settlement originated as ribbon development along the Manchester to Liverpool Road.

St John Baptist, Liverpool Road. 1865–6 by *J. Medland Taylor*. Small and compact, with a crossing tower with a low slated broach spire, very short transepts, and an apse. The roughly coursed uneven rubble – red sandstone with yellow sandstone dressings and banding – gives it a slightly rugged look. The w wall has the most unorthodox rose window. Odd rose windows to the transepts, too. N clerestory only, slated with small cusped lights. (Internally the Taylor touch is the crossing arches with voussoirs of alternating thickness – just as in certain Georgian door surrounds. And whereas this motif is used simply and straightforwardly in the arches of the s windows, in the crossing arches it is done in two orders. The roof timbers start very low, and the church is made lighter by the dormers in the roof.)

St Teresa (R.C.), Liverpool and Astley Roads. A straight-forward job of 1903 by *Oswald Hill*. Grey brick with red brick dressings, lancets, towerless with a canted apse.

Methodist Church of St Paul, Liverpool Road. Early c20, conventional except for the bold full-height octagonal tower, offset to the r. This has flat-headed windows below, arched above, an embattled parapet and low pyramidal roof.

IRLAMS O' TH' HEIGHT see p. 561

KEARSLEY see FARNWORTH

KEARSLEY MILL see PRESTOLEE

LEES

Lees started as scattered farms and settlements, mainly along roads between Oldham to the w, Ashton-under-Lyne to the s, and routes E to Yorkshire. It was part of Ashton-under-Lyne parish until the mid C19 when it was taken in to the parish of Oldham. It lies on rising ground and is visually part of Oldham, but with a Pennine feel, as red brick gives way to stone as a building material. The settlement falls into two areas on either side of High Street, centred on St Thomas, s, and St John, N.

St John, St John's Street. Built in 1742. Of stone with windows in two tiers. The two E bays were added in 1772, and the two w bays look like additions as well, judging by quoins in the stonework. The most striking element is the pretty W cupola, octagonal with a domed roof and finial, Doric columns, balustrading, and urns at the angles. It is an ambitious piece of work for a far-flung country parish. Unfortunately the rest was made respectable in 1865 by *H. Cockburn*. He introduced new windows with flowing tracery, renewed the galleries, and made a chancel by inserting two-bay piers so as to create a 'hall-church' type space – but a fire in 1986 destroyed the balconies and other fittings. – STAINED GLASS. *Capronnier* was busy here. The dates are 1884–96 (signed in 1896 by *Comère & Capronnier*).

VICARAGE (former), Sun Hill, N of the church off Stamford Road. Built partly by public subscription, completed 1770. A large double-pile house, symmetrical, five bays, with a central pedimented door. Windows in stone architraves.

St Thomas, St Thomas Street. Of 1844–8 by *Shellard* and remarkable in that it is based on Lancashire Perp. The solid W tower, embattled aisles, low-pitched roof and s porch of two storeys are archaeologically perfectly convincing, and the Perp tracery is correct. It is the proportions, more than anything else, which give it authenticity. The chancel is marked externally by pinnacled turrets, one of several details suggesting that Shellard may have looked at, for example, Manchester Cathedral (*see* p. 267) for inspiration. It is a more elaborate version of St John, Werneth (1844–5, *see* p. 545), also Lancashire Perp in style. The tower was added in 1855, presumably to Shellard's design, as it is consistent with the rest. Large springing gargoyles at the angles. Chancel chapel added in matching style, 1887. Inside, the detailing is less convincing, but the progressiveness is felt everywhere. Hammerbeam roof, though with a thin, plank-like look. The trusses rise from stone corbels with large heads. Traceried openwork in the spandrels. No clerestory, but pairs of dormers on each side. Could these be later insertions to improve the lighting? They have reverse-S tracery typical of *George Shaw*. Arcades of octagonal piers; steps up to a proper chancel; W gallery with blind arcading. – Carved stone REREDOS of 1852. – Canopied DECALOGUE BOARDS on each side of the E window, by *George Shaw*, like many of the furnishings. – Elaborate canopied STALLS incorporating painted arms of local families, typical of Shaw's workshop and similar to those at St Thomas, Werneth (*see* p. 546). – PULPIT. Octagonal with canopied sides. – BOX PEWS. In three blocks, those in the centre with poppyheads. – STAINED GLASS. Quite a number of windows by *Capronnier*, dating from 1874–98. The Good Samaritan of 1888 is the popular favourite. Badly faded windows, N aisle E and s aisle w, looking typical of *Shaw*. – MONUMENTS. In the chancel, Rev. W. Jungbluth †1897, brass panel with Arts and Crafts-style repoussée work, by the *Keswick School of Industrial Art*. N aisle, Thomas

Taylor †1887, canopied Gothic wall memorial by *Hilton* of
Manchester.

ST AGNES, Knowls Lane. Combined with ST AGNES SCHOOL.
Low and humble, stone, with a w bellcote. Started in 1869,
when it was used as a school. Chancel added and church dedicated, 1880, when school buildings were added on the N side.

WAR MEMORIAL, Lees Cemetery, St Thomas Street. Bronze
soldier in battledress on a Portland stone plinth. By *Maile &
Sons*, unveiled 1921.

GRAPES INN, St John's Street, s of the church. Dated 1741.
Stone, with mullioned windows and a large BARN attached to
the r. with a big arched opening.

THE DEVONSHIRE, St John's Street, beside Acorn Mill (*see*
below). A big stone block of a building, probably early C19.
Symmetrical front with rusticated entrance and sash windows.
Mullioned windows (renewed) in the sides.

WELLFIELD HOUSE, Hartshead Street. Built for a local mill-
owner *c.* 1840. Restrained and symmetrical, of stone. Five bays,
with a door with fanlight and elaborate iron trellis porch. Small
gabled LODGE and Italianate COACH HOUSE on High Fold,
the latter converted to a house and the large arched entrance
blocked.

ACORN MILL, St John's Street.* Built for James Dyson in 1800
as a cotton-spinning mill, and successively extended. Four
storeys, of stone. Of the 1800 mill only a short section of wall
survives. It was damaged by fire in 1825 and rebuilt shortly
afterwards, then extensively remodelled in the 1840s using
fireproof construction of cast-iron columns and brick arches.
In the late C19 another storey was added. The different phases
can be unpicked in the long SE elevation to St John Street. The
s block, known as New Mill, was built in 1825 and is fairly
intact. Eleven bays with Venetian windows in the gable ends,
timber floors and cast-iron columns. NW of the main buildings
are long stone-built weaving sheds, eight ranges in all, probably mid-C19.

LEESBROOK MILL, High Street. 1884 by *J. Stott*. Four storeys,
with a typical projecting water tower bearing the name, and a
tall circular chimney, also with the name, in white brick. The
detailing is Italianate, in brick with stone dressings.

OUTLYING BUILDINGS

Houses, farms and cottages of the C17 and C18 lie in the open
country w of the centre. Almost without exception, they are of
stone with mullioned windows and greatly altered. Those to note
are: the houses and attached cottage of MANOR FARM on
Knowls Lane, a complex with late C17 and C18 elements. FLASH
COTTAGES on Thornley Lane, including C18 extensions to an

---

*Mr Ivan Hradil kindly made the results of his research into this building
available.

earlier laithe house, i.e. a house with attached barn and shippon
all of one build. The arched barn entrance is infilled, and the
cottages attached on each side. Nos. 125–131 Lane Head Road,
a terrace of three-storey late C18 weavers' cottages sharing a long
eleven-light attic workshop window. Nearby, Nos. 133–147, more
small late C18 houses.

LIMEHURST   *9000*

Limehurst lies NW of Ashton-under-Lyne on the River Medlock
and boundary with Oldham.

BARDSLEY VALE MILL, off Oldham Road beside the River
    Medlock. Originally a cotton mill of 1857, with an earlier
    adjoining mill, badly damaged by fire in 1891. The remains
    were incorporated into a large pharmaceutical works, started
    c. 1896. The dominant feature is a tall water tower in red brick
    with yellow brick dressings and the words 'Thomas Kerfoot
    Manufacturing Chemist'. Low brick buildings all around, and
    a tall octagonal chimney with iron strapping, perhaps part of
    the earlier mill. Kerfoot's started as a Manchester firm, and
    pioneered tablet-making machines.
BARDSLEY BREWERY (former), off Oldham Road. Founded in
    1832 by Robert Bentley. Of stone, with two-storey ranges
    around a courtyard. A wide cambered arch with the date 1832
    leads into the yard from the W. An opposed arch in the E range
    is blocked, and the whole has been greatly altered in connec-
    tion with its present use as flats. Ancillary buildings have gone.
LIMEHURST FARMHOUSE. Reached from a track leading NW
    from Oldham Road. Of *c.* 1600. Timber-framed, the W part
    with brick infill and a kingpost truss, the E part rendered. Large

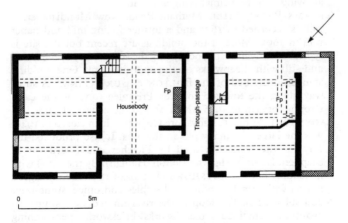

Limehurst Farmhouse, plan.
(University of Manchester Archaeological Unit)

projecting gabled parlour and service bays at either end. Late
C20 windows. (Dr Nevell records the expected three-unit plan
with a cross-passage, and an inglenook in the housebody.)

7000   LITTLE LEVER

SE of Bolton.

ST MATTHEW. By *E. Paley*, 1865, replacing a church of 1791
which was on the other side of Market Street; a few headstones
mark the spot. Paley had a bit of fun giving the church a Transitional archaeology, suggesting that the transepts with their
round-arched windows are older than the plate-traceried
nave. Big flat rose above the W porch. The decoration has
all been left uncarved. The SE tower was completed above
eaves level in 1924 as a war memorial. Aisleless nave of wide
span, the transepts slightly narrower so that the upper collar
beam roofs do not make a proper crossing. – Modest stone
REREDOS. – FONT and PULPIT are both heavy stone tubs. The
former VICARAGE, E, of 1875 is now the Police Station; red
brick in garden bond, with blue banding.
JESUS KING'S CENTRE, formerly Congregational chapel, 1850.
A steep-roofed Gothic box of stone, with lancet windows, in a
packed graveyard.
CHRISTCHURCH (Methodist and United Reformed), Mytham
Road, *c.* 1995, the fifth chapel on the site. Warm brick with a
little stone. Big roof. Old graveyard at the back.
LIBRARY. A standard Lancashire small library design of the
1930s, mildly Deco and tile-clad. It was modified to take the
WAR MEMORIAL on the front wall, which was was not
finished until 1940. Low relief sculpture by *W.H. Doxey* of a
warrior under a blanket as though asleep, with only his face
showing and the helmet lying above it.
CREAMS PAPER MILL, Mytham Road. Now Mondi paper. A
mill is recorded in 1677 and a former fulling mill and paper
mill in 1699. Most of the buildings are recent but the site is
typical of early industry, occupying the steep valley of the Irwell
and still with sheepwalks on the opposite bank. One building
stands on the bed of the BOLTON & BURY CANAL. A short
way along the towpath towards Prestolee (q.v.) is the cata-
strophic breach of 1936 which caused the canal's closure.
LADYSHORE, ½ m. SE. Ladyshore Colliery, which closed in 1949,
was the largest of many pits in the area. It also produced the
clay for the terracotta used by Fletcher and Sharpe at St
Stephen, Lever Bridge (*see* Bolton, Haulgh). By the canal with
its loading bay is LADYSHORE HOUSE of 1833, the manager's
house, with attached office and stables and office, stone-built
and substantial. The loop of the river immediately S, now so
beautiful, contained a bleachworks, brickworks, pea-canning
factory and a pottery tip.

LITTLEBOROUGH

Originally an area of scattered hamlets or folds in the hills, centred on the C15 chapel of Littleborough or Little Brucke. When the town did coalesce, which was not until the C19, it took its name from the chapel.

HOLY TRINITY. By *Thomas Taylor* of Leeds, 1818–20, replacing the old chapel of ease, recorded in 1471. Robust gritstone box with a W steeple but no chancel, with a row of the local vernacular flat-faced gargoyles on each side. Awkward gablets were added at the spire base in 1866 to take a clock. The finely carved dedication stone above the W door, with rose and thistle, is signed *Nield sculpt.* To this was added in 1889 a long cathedrally chancel by *J. S. Crowther*. This is taller and altogether more solemn, of cheesy yellow ashlar, with large and deeply cut foliage carvings in the string course, and large Perp windows characterized, like those of Manchester Cathedral (which Crowther was restoring at the time), 'by the use of the two-centred arch, equilateral, or nearly so, in principle'. An exposed part-arch on the N side and the start of one of Crowther's favoured rood turrets on the S show that he intended to build a new nave too; indeed William Law of Honresfield (*see* p. 252) had offered to pay for it.

The INTERIOR is even more like two buildings, reflecting in architectural terms the warring High and Low Church factions that have characterized the congregation until very recently. Taylor's airy nave has a delicately Gothick clear span roof and lightly supported galleries. It has two LECTERNS. The first, donated in 1866, was pinched and hidden in 1867, ploughed up and returned 1942; the second, 1890. Heraldic STAINED GLASS with grisaille on the S side is from the old E window of 1842. Crowther's chancel belongs to a different sort of church, epitomizing the words of the Victorian hymn 'Angel Voices'*:

> Craftsman's art and music's measure
> For thy pleasure
> All combine.

It is lined with dark red stone, under a double hammerbeam roof full of angel musicians. – Triple SEDILIA, and AUMBRY. – Long CHOIR STALLS with Gothic fretting, different in each panel, and brass reading lamps with shades like upturned glass bells. – Mosaic FLOOR designed by Crowther and made by *Minton*, with seven steps up to the altar. – Dark STAINED GLASS, the E by *Hardman*, the rest *Clayton & Bell*.

Outside, a Masonic mausoleum signed *Lawrence Booth* architect, *T. & E. Williams sculpt.*, to Laurence Newall, Grand Master, †1871.

---

*Published in 1889. It was written for St John Westhoughton in 1861.

5 ST JAMES, Calderbrook. A blackened stone church on a green
hillside, built for James Dearden in 1860–4. Its pyramidal
steeple, irregular massing and eccentric traceries proclaim the
hand of *George Shaw*. On the S are the tower and spire and a
founder's chapel, with an external approach to its burial vault
– but James Griffiths Dearden, who had laid the foundation
stone on his twenty-first birthday, is the only occupant. The
chapel, with its frieze of S and O shapes, and the steeple, distinctively pinched in halfway up the belfry windows where the
octagon starts, are essentially the same as those at Shaw's St
John, Hurst near Ashton-under-Lyne. 'The roofs will be open
to the timbers and every roof will be different in style from the
others' states the opening brochure. The interior is low, the
windows set very low, as at Shaw's Christchurch Healey. Alternating octagonal and circular piers with a band of foliage in
the capitals in the N arcade and the two-bay chapel arcade. –
Oak ALTAR and REREDOS of 1948, beautifully executed, in
memory of Pilot Officer A. T. Dearden †1941. They hide an
earlier scheme in richly coloured tiles and alabaster whose centrepiece, dated 1872, has been moved to the N side of the
chancel. – ALTAR RAIL of cast iron, grained. – STALLS by *Shaw*
with poppyheads, displaced from the chancel and the Dearden
Chapel. – STAINED GLASS. Complete 1860s scheme of
Dearden memorials in the chancel by *Clayton & Bell*. Nave S
side, a memorial to the founder by *Shaw* himself, 1862, with
curiously photogravure-like faces which have weathered badly.
In the chapel more Dearden windows, of 1948 by *George
Cooper Abbs* for *Wippell*. They presumably did the ceiling painting too. N aisle by *K. G. Bunton* †1963, and a Second World War
memorial by *Shrigley & Hunt*.

In the churchyard, N of the chancel, a stout granite Celtic
cross marks the grave of Enid Stacy †1903, Socialist campaigner and suffragette.

ST ANDREW, Dearnley. Nave and aisles 1893–5, by *F. P. Oakley*,
brother of the first vicar. Chancel and chapel 1914, in a new
style, by *F. P. Oakley & G. Sanville*. Stone outside, brick inside.
Big rose in the W gable. Clerestory windows single and evenly
spaced outside, but grouped in threes inside. The chancel has
pared-down Geometric tracery.

    VICARAGE immediately NE, signed and dated *Oakley,
Sanville & Blayney*, 1967. Of stone rubble cast into blocks.

ST BARNABAS, Shore. 1901 and 1906 by *R. B. Preston*. Of stone.
Big tower in the angle of the S transept with ancillary rooms
grouped at its foot. The interior is brick-lined to dado level,
plastered above. Nave divided off at W end *c.* 1996. Glazed
throughout with opaque greeny glass, but STAINED GLASS was
introduced in 2003 with a new E window, Christ in modern
Littleborough, by the local artist *Walter Kershaw*, made by
Jaycee of Bacup. Sparing use of glass-painting and of swirled
glass, the rest done with plain colours and textures.

METHODIST CHURCH, Dearnley. Two buildings of 1868 and
1899 side by side with a turret in the valley between the two.

Of stone. The 1868 chapel has exaggerated architectural features; window and door surrounds protrude and there is ballflower over the door.

BIRCH HILL HOSPITAL, Rochdale Road. It was built as the huge Rochdale Union Workhouse in 1873–7, by *George Woodhouse & Edward Potts*. Landmark clock tower, sheer, of red brick, with a pyramid roof and corner ears. It was one of the last Union Workhouses to be built and had an attendant SCHOOL, a long two-storey block, by the same architects.

HARE HILL PARK. Purchased by the town in 1901 from the Newall family. Plain Georgian house, adapted with heavy-handed additions for Council offices and a Carnegie LIBRARY. Much rockwork in the grounds, and the grave of Mephisto the monkey (1891–3).

WHEATSHEAF HOTEL, Littleborough Square. 1868. A showy three-storey building with Gothic detailing, built semicircular to command both road and railway approaches.

BACK-TO-BACKS. The forty-eight houses in the little grid of streets off Barehill Street: Leah, Pioneer, Jerrold, Smith and Nelson streets, were built by the Littleborough Co-operative Society in 1868.

The MANCHESTER & LEEDS RAILWAY, opened in 1841 and engineered by *George Stephenson*, follows the river immediately SE of the church. The stone VIADUCT crosses the Halifax Road by the parish church on a skew arch flanked by two pedestrian arches, also skewed. Beyond the arches, where Blackstone Edge Road and Halifax Road diverge, is a concentration of worthwhile C17 and C18 YEOMAN HOUSES and associated barns and stables.

WINDY BANK, at the W end of Blackstone Edge Old Road, is an excellent house of tough character, L-shaped, of blackened gritstone with kneelers and finials to the gables and four fear-some gargoyles. The three-gabled W front is inscribed over the door IB (for John Butterworth) 1635. It leads to a cross-passage behind the fireplace, as is indicated outside by the stack and the two-light fireside window. The short E wing has its own entrance dated RL (for Robert Lightowlers) 1611, its own cross-passage and its own fireside window. A lower and rougher extension at the N end has been a third dwelling. Inside it is clear that the W wing is the stone casing of a four-bay timber-framed house, its roof trusses fully preserved and its wall posts at least indicated by the shoulders and mor-tices. The three W gables correspond to the bays of the timber-framed house, not the present room division. The N bay, indicated by the northernmost gable, was taken up by the cross-passage and a smoke hood with the fireside window within it. The roof timbers of the 1611 wing are altogether rougher, suggesting that it was a new build. The join between the wings is confusing.

Close by, below Halifax road, are 'both Bent Houses', a typical appellation for a cluster of dwellings and outbuildings. The very pretty OLD BENT HOUSE is inscribed IMS (for John and Mary Stott) 1691 on the porch. Still asymmetrical, but more horizontal than Windy Bank, without gables. There is a second porch on the s elevation, which looks as though it was a short wing which constituted a second dwelling exactly as at Windy Bank. But here the angle has been filled in to make the house a double pile. The infill is sash-windowed, and is probably C19.

25 Immediately E on Lightowlers Lane, amongst a converted group of C18 and C19 farm buildings called Pike Barns, is a rare treasure, the WINTER BEE HOUSE. A diminutive square building of high quality stonework, C17 in style. The low base storey was for pigs and fowl, providing a certain amount of warmth for the bees. The upper room, its door reached by external steps, has two rows of eight recesses for the bee skeps. The bees would have been taken up to the heather in summer.

Close to this group on Halifax Road is HONRESFIELD, a big plain house of 1873. By *Benjamin Ferrey*, and built, surprisingly, by Dove Bros of Islington. It cost William Law, mill-owner, £5068.

The old PACKHORSE ROAD over Blackstone Edge is rightly famous. It may be C17 rather than Roman as is often claimed, but it is impressively direct, scorning the gradient-easing S-bends of later roads. It is paved with large stones with a central groove for braking.

TOWN HOUSE. Actually on the N fringe of town, at the end of Town House Road. A fold rather than a single dwelling. Plain five-bay Georgian house of 1798 with a pediment and nice doorcase. Stone inscribed L1685N at the back, probably *ex situ*. Woollen WAREHOUSE bearing the Newell arms and the inscription NLS (Lawrence and Sarah Newell) 1732, three storeys and three bays, with arched double doors on each floor. Now residential. Attached three-storey COTTAGES. Unconverted BARN at the back.

SHORE HALL, 1 m. WNW. IB (for James Bamford) 1605 is roughly carved on a lintel. L-shaped, and scraped clean. It has the horizontal look of the later halls, without extraneous gables. The house place is indicated by transomed windows. The door position indicates a cross-passage behind its fireplace.

On the main road W into Rochdale is STUBLEY OLD HALL. Low-set H-shaped house of brick and stone with some external indications of timber framing. (The late C15 open hall survives, and at least one cruck of the three in the s wing. Armorial STAINED GLASS.)

A little further on is DEARNLEY HALL, an engagingly crooked, long, whitewashed C17 house. Double entrance under a single drip mould, so it was two dwellings. (Timber-framed screens partition with three doors). Behind, on its estate, was built the Workhouse (*see* above).

HOLLINGWORTH LAKE is a local beauty spot, popular for water sports and once immensely so. It even has a Promenade along the N shore, and seasidish bungalows on Hollingworth Road, also N. It was built as a reservoir for the Rochdale Canal of

1804. The M62 RAKEWOOD VIADUCT of 1968, a brutal post-and-tensioned-beam structure, cuts across the valley high up.
SUMMIT, 1 m. N, is named for the Rochdale Canal which crosses the watershed here without a tunnel. This last section was completed in 1804. The turnpike road followed in 1824, and finally the Manchester & Leeds Railway (*see* above). The railway tunnel was the longest in the country at 1 mile 1,125 yds, and cost £300,000. The TUNNEL ENTRANCE is a powerful expression of the undertaking, heroic in scale with radiating voussoirs and two enormous horizontal roll-mouldings. The Company's arms and the date 1839 are carved on the road

Littleborough, Summit tunnel, engraving by A. F. Tait, 1845

overbridge immediately s. The infant River Roch crosses the
railway in an elegant S-bend AQUEDUCT of iron and stone.

ROCK NOOK MILL is nearby, mainly of 1886 and 1896; of black
rock-faced stone, four storeys, with unequal towers at the ends.

Further yeoman houses are N and W. On Calderbrook road by
St James is HANDLE HALL, an attractive house with two
doors, so originally two dwellings, and a barn all in line as is
the local pattern. The barn, with the usual central round-
arched door and tiny circular openings, has a showy end elevation with round windows and the date 1673. Its front
windows have curly drip ends, like crude Ionic volutes. The
house has ogees incised in the door lintels. A plaque records
that the house of 1610 was restored by James Dearden in 1829;
a defaced inscription recorded the rebuilding of the barn in
1842. The involvement of Dearden's antiquarian friend *George
Shaw* is likely.

MANCHESTER

WITH CONTRIBUTIONS BY JOHN H. G. ARCHER AND JULIAN HOLDER

INTRODUCTION

Manchester is one of Britain's great cities, the largest conurbation in SE Lancashire, with a population of around 422,000. Liverpool, with a similar population, is the only rival in the region. The centre of the city is concentrated on the E bank of the River Irwell, which forms the boundary with the City of Salford. Immediately surrounding townships on the N, S and E sides were absorbed following incorporation in 1838, and the boundaries expanded successively thereafter, culminating in the

256 MANCHESTER

1930s with the creation of Wythenshawe and Manchester Airport
to the S, in an area formerly part of Cheshire. The city as a result
is a funny shape – over ten miles long and only about two miles
wide. It was for a while administratively part of the Metropolitan County of Greater Manchester, formed as a result of local
government reorganization in 1974, but dissolved in 1986 when
its functions were devolved to the constituent metropolitan
borough councils. Manchester's early pre-eminence is reflected
in the size and elaboration of the C15 collegiate church. Its
seminal role in the Industrial Revolution is well known, and its
manufacturing, distribution and financial base is reflected in
impressive Victorian and Edwardian industrial, commercial and
civic buildings. Post-war decline was reversed, most noticeably in
the past decade, and traditional industry replaced by commercial, financial, public sector and information technology businesses, though the northern and eastern suburbs have yet to reap
the benefits. With two universities and a number of colleges, the
city is also credited with having one of the largest student pop-
ulations in Europe. The appearance of the centre has altered radically in recent years, with new buildings and landscaping
schemes; one of the biggest changes is the fashion for living in
the city centre, which now has a resident population of between
11,000 and 13,000.

The story of Manchester starts with its Roman fort, established
A.D. 79 at Castlefield, S of the city centre. A Saxon *burh* may have
been extant in the C10, but there does not seem to have been
substantial settlement until after the Conquest. The Grelley
family had established a manor house by the C13 at the confluence of the rivers Irwell and Irk, and the medieval town grew up
7 around it. The parish church (made a cathedral in 1847) is probably one of the two churches mentioned in Domesday. It was
almost completely rebuilt following collegiation in 1421, becoming one of the largest and most lavish Perp parish churches in
England, with notable furnishings. The priest's college (now
18 Chetham's School and Library) was built on the site of the
Grelley manor house. It is the best and most intact example of
its type in the country, with a great hall, kitchen, and priests'
lodgings in a cloister. If we add the C15 Hanging Bridge near the
church, we have named all that survives architecturally of
Leland's 'fairest, best builded, quikkest and most populus tounne
of al Lancastreshire.'

The MANCHESTER PARISH encompassed the whole of the
present city N of the Mersey, but the villages within this area had
their CHAPELS OF EASE. Those at Birch (Rusholme), Blackley,
Chorlton, Didsbury, Gorton, and Newton Heath, small and often
timber-framed, have been replaced except for some C17 fragments at Didsbury. Northenden (in Cheshire until the 1930s) is
the only other medieval parish in the city. Its church retains its
tower and some furnishings. There are a number of impressive
timber-framed HALLS beyond the centre, however, of which the
15 C14 Baguley Hall in Wythenshawe is one of the earliest and most
interesting. Wythenshawe Hall was rebuilt in the late C15 or C16.

Barlow Hall, Chorlton-cum-Hardy, and Clayton Hall, Clayton (probably C15), are less complete. Good examples of smaller houses are the C16 Slade Hall, Levenshulme, and Hough Hall, Moston (probably C16 with C17 additions). In the centre the Old Wellington Inn is probably C17, but it has been radically restored and re-erected away from its original site.

The town had become a regional centre by the late medieval period, thanks to its pre-eminence in textile production and marketing. The manor was bought in 1595 by Sir Nicholas Mosley, a cloth merchant and former Lord Mayor of London. He built the up-to-date brick Hough End Hall at Chorlton-cum-Hardy. 26 Not much can be said of the C17 otherwise, but there are interiors without parallels in the region in the C15 building of the college of priests, where a Bluecoat School and free library was created 1654–8 through the bequest of Humphrey Chetham.

St Ann's church is the most sophisticated C18 CHURCH in SE 27 Lancashire. It was built in 1709–12 and St Ann's Square was laid out in 1720, s of the old centre, the first major planned development outside the town. By the second half of the C18 Manchester had an exchange, an infirmary and a crop of eight more churches in addition. Not one of them remains. Dissenters and Roman Catholics had meeting houses or chapels too, though none are left, and Jewish traders probably met in Synagogue Alley, recorded in the 1740s. Further afield, St Thomas at Ardwick was built in 1741, and a little chapel at Heaton Chapel (*see* p. 229) *c*. 1756. There were DISSENTING CHAPELS at Gorton, Dob Cross (Newton Heath), and in Rusholme, where the only pre-C19 example survives at Platt. This was rebuilt in brick in the C18, and much altered in the C19, retaining the T-shaped plan.

Development gathered pace from the late C18, when large areas of the centre were parcelled up and laid out for residential development. Associated TERRACES survive here and there, the best examples on Byrom Street and St John Street. Cobden House, nearby, boasts the best interior. Houses with attic workshops for handloom weaving and textile finishing can be seen in various locations, while Ancoats was developed for industry and workers' housing – a story we shall return to. The major GEORGIAN MANSIONS were right out in the country in their own grounds, the first being Platt Hall in Fallowfield of 1764 by *Timothy Lightoler*, 30 based on designs by *John Carr*, and – far on the N side – *James Wyatt*'s Heaton Hall of 1772–8 with late C18 additions by *Samuel* 31 *Wyatt* and more of the early C19 by *Lewis Wyatt*. Aping the Wyatt style is Parrs Wood of *c*. 1795–8 in Didsbury.

Grecian was the style chosen for most of the PUBLIC BUILD-INGS AND INSTITUTIONS of the early C19 town. The Portico Newsroom and Library (1802–6) on Mosley Street, by *Thomas Harrison* of Chester, is an advanced building with a sophisticated Soane-inspired interior. *Francis Goodwin* designed the first town hall (1819–34, demolished), while *Charles Barry*'s Royal Man- 45 chester Institution of 1824–35 (now the City Art Gallery), Mosley Street, is a major early work of that architect. The chief local practitioner of the Greek style was *Richard Lane*. His Chorlton-on-

Medlock Town Hall and Dispensary of 1830–1 is typical. The
Wesleyan Theological Institution in Didsbury of 1842 was still
Grecian (and probably also by *Lane*), but the accomplished Lan-
47 cashire Independent College, Whalley Range (1840–3, by *Irwin*
& Chester), is Gothic.

EARLY C19 CHURCH BUILDING started with All Saints,
Newton Heath, by *William Atkinson* (1814–15), Georgian in
form but Gothic in style. Thereafter most were built with grants
from the Church Building Commission (established 1818).
The most splendid is *Francis Goodwin*'s Gothic St George
(1826–8) in Hulme. *Barry*'s Unitarian Chapel of 1836 in
Chorlton-on-Medlock is also Gothic, and interesting for his
command of the E.E. style, while of other early C19 Nonconformist chapels only *Richard Lane*'s Grecian Friends' Meeting
52 House (1828–31) in the centre and the classical Independent
Chapel of 1840 in Cheetham, survive. *A. W. N. Pugin*'s Gothic
church of St Wilfrid in Hulme (R.C., 1840–2), low and cheap,
nevertheless marked the beginning of a new phase of church
design.

TRANSPORT LINKS were well developed by the opening of the
C19. The pioneering Bridgewater Canal (1759–65) has its terminal basin at Castlefield, and by 1776 it was extended W to
link with international trade routes via the Mersey estuary. The
Manchester–Bury–Bolton, Manchester–Ashton–Oldham and
Manchester–Rochdale canals followed between 1790 and 1805.
The canal warehouses of the Bridgewater and Rochdale
basins exhibit development of loading and transit systems via
internal wet docks. The terminus of the world's first passenger
railway, the Liverpool & Manchester, with the original station
and warehouse of 1830, survive near the Bridgewater Canal Basin
in Castlefield. Long before this, in the early 1780s, the first Manchester cotton mill had been built for Richard Arkwright on
Miller Street, and a boom quickly followed. Important groups of
early steam-powered mills survive in Ancoats and in Chorlton-
on-Medlock. Further afield, a sole surviving monument to the
silk industry can be found in the early C19 mill in Newton
Heath.

INDUSTRIAL MANCHESTER became a prodigy, one that was
frightening and bewildering, as well as exciting. Schinkel, the
Prussian court architect, visited in 1826 and wrote in amazement:
'At Manchester since the war 400 large new factories for cotton
spinning have been built, several of them the size of the Royal
Palace in Berlin, and thousands of smoking obelisks of the steam
engines 80 to 180 ft high destroy all impression of church
steeples.' Carlyle in 1843 wrote that Manchester was 'every whit
as wonderful, as fearful, as unimaginable as the oldest Salem' and
Disraeli called Manchester 'the most wonderful city of modern
times.' The population trebled between 1801, when it was around
75,000, and 1841; by 1851 it was over 300,000. Industrialization
and mass immigration created an urban environment of a sort
never seen before. Engels in 1844 drew attention to what seemed
to be a new urban plan type: the commercial core was sur-

Manchester, mills alongside the Rochdale Canal.
Sketch by Karl Friedrich Schinkel, 1826

rounded by a belt of industry and workers' housing, with middle-class residential areas forming an outer circle. Slums of almost indescribable squalor mushroomed; those in Ancoats, Angel Meadow and lower Deansgate were notorious before the mid C19. The conditions of the poorest city-dwellers were highlighted by James Kay, whose *Moral and Physical Conditions of the Working Classes* appeared in 1832, and Edwin Chadwick, who published his *Report on the Sanitary Condition of the Labouring Population* in 1842. Elizabeth Gaskell's *Mary Barton* came in 1848, with an account of working-class life in Manchester which shocked readers.

Emigration to the SUBURBS had begun before 1800, and it accelerated in the following decades. Houses and terraces of the early and mid C19 can be picked out, especially in Chorlton-on-Medlock, Ardwick and along Wilmslow Road towards Didsbury. One of the best is on Plymouth Grove, Chorlton-on-Medlock, where the home of Elizabeth Gaskell of *c.* 1840 has Greek detailing. Nearby another house of similar date, also preserved for its associations (with the suffragist Pankhursts), has Gothic details, neatly illustrating predominant villa styles of the period. The planned villa development at Victoria Park in Rusholme, laid out in 1837 by *Richard Lane*, retains its cohesion and some of its early houses, while a few of the grand villas of Samuel Brooks' development from 1832 at Whalley Range survive.

By the mid C19 there was a multiplicity of industries, foundations that led to the city becoming a world centre of engineering, with the (demolished) factories of Beyer Peacock, Joseph Whitworth and Crossley concentrated in the eastern suburbs. In the centre itself COMMERCE and TRADE were more important. The Exchange, extended in 1836, had to be enlarged again in 1845. The archaic local government was replaced by a municipal corporation in 1838, when absorption of the surrounding townships began. The manorial rights were bought by the Corporation ten years later. Queen Victoria visited in 1851, and in 1853 Manchester became administratively a city. Railway stations had been established in the centre of town, Piccadilly in 1842 and Central Station in 1875–80. The Manchester South Junction & Altrincham Railway, a suburban commuter line, came in 1845–9.

The ARCHITECTURE OF THE VICTORIAN AGE is dominated
by Gothic and Italianate styles. *Charles Barry*'s palazzo-style
46 Athenaeum on Princess Street came in 1836–7, and the model
was immediately taken up, initially by *Edward Walters*, for the
city's archetypal Victorian building, the commercial warehouse.
Later, firms such as *Clegg & Knowles* specialized in warehouses,
developing a flexible vocabulary incorporating Continental
motifs from the 1860s, and creating unique streetscapes in the
centre. Manchester's role as the home of the Anti-Corn Law
49 League is commemorated by *Edward Walters*' Free Trade Hall
of 1853–6 (now the Radisson Edwardian Hotel), described by
Nikolaus Pevsner as 'perhaps the noblest monument in the
Cinquecento style in England.' Ruskinian Gothic was introduced
by *Alfred Waterhouse*, but his seminal Manchester Assize Courts
of 1859–64 has been demolished. The crowning achievement was
63 *Waterhouse*'s Town Hall (1868–77), one of the outstanding
achievements of Victorian architecture, which retains its interior
fittings and decorative schemes. *The Builder* in 1896 predicted
that 'it will probably be accounted one of the most excellent
works which the nineteenth century has bequeathed'.

VICTORIAN GOTHIC was adopted by local talents such as
Edward Salomons, *Thomas Worthington* and *J. S. Crowther*, one of
Manchester's most serious students of Gothic, who restored the
Cathedral during the 1870s and built high and noble churches in
the suburbs. *J. Medland & Henry Taylor*, *Edmund Sharpe*, *Worthington* (for the Unitarians), and *George Shaw* built others of
note. *Weightman & Hadfield* did the first R.C. church after
Hulme; also for the Catholics were *E. W. Pugin*'s extraordinary St
70, 75 Francis, Gorton, of 1866–72, and *J. A. Hansom*'s daring Holy
Name of Jesus (Chorlton-on-Medlock) in 1869–71. They are as
different as could be spatially and in terms of materials, but both
exhibit Early French Gothic influence. The former Sephardic
74 Synagogue in Cheetham Hill (*Edward Salomons*, 1874) is
Moorish in tone, the only Victorian synagogue to survive
unscathed.

EDUCATIONAL INITIATIVES included the Mechanics' Institute, whose premises from 1855 were *J. E. Gregan*'s noble palazzo
on Princess Street. The first free library was built in 1852. The
Victoria University of Manchester started as Owens College in
1851. Its buildings in Chorlton-on-Medlock are a product of
Alfred Waterhouse's maturity, erected between 1870 and 1902
(later parts by *Paul Waterhouse*) in the practical modern Gothic
of the Town Hall. An inclusive admissions policy encouraged the
proliferation of Nonconformist training colleges. The Wesleyans
at Didsbury of 1842 and the Independents at Whalley Range were
joined by the Primitive Methodists at Hartley Victoria College,
Whalley Range, by *Tate & Popplewell* 1878–9 and later. Thirty-
nine Board Schools were erected in Manchester after 1870, at
first in Gothic, later in Queen Anne and Renaissance styles. A
good late C19 example is the former Dover Street School in
Chorlton-on-Medlock, in Ruskinian Gothic style. Typical examples of early C20 schools include those on Plymouth Grove, in

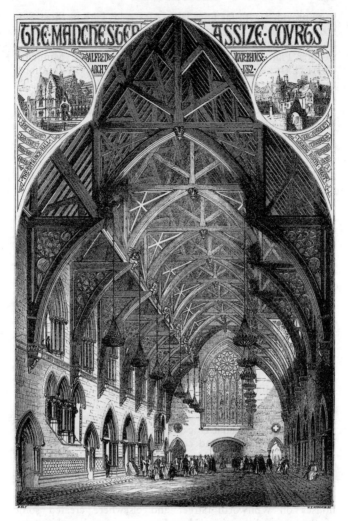

Manchester Assize Courts (demolished), from *The Builder*, 1859

Chorlton-on-Medlock, at Moston, next to Hough Hall, and Oswald Road School, 1908–9, at Chorlton-cum-Hardy. Church schools, like the early Board Schools, were usually modestly Gothic. One of the best is St Agnes in Levenshulme (1885), by *J. Medland & Henry Taylor*. Much later, with charming Art Nouveau detailing, is *J. Swarbrick*'s Church of England school in Didsbury, 1910.

Manchester created its pioneering PUBLIC PARKS in areas E of the centre. Queen's Park, Harpurhey and Philips Park, Bradford, were laid out on land bought in 1845. Other suburban areas were provided with facilities later; Alexandra Park in Moss Side (1870) is a good example. Later still, parks were created through the acquisition of country houses and their grounds: Heaton Park in 1902, Platt Hall, 1907, Wythenshawe Hall in 1926. Municipal CEMETERIES started with Philips Park Cemetery (*see* Bradford) in 1866, the layout by *William Gay,* the fine buildings by *Paull & Ayliffe.* Southern Cemetery, Chorlton-cum-Hardy (opened 1872) is the site of the city's first crematorium, designed in Byzantine style in 1890 by *Edward Salomons.*

Meanwhile little had been done to address the problem of housing. The first MUNICIPAL HOUSING was in Ancoats, where Victoria Square and the associated terraces were built 1894–9 by *Spalding & Cross.* They were far too expensive for most of the local inhabitants. The extent of the social problems at that time is illustrated by the Ragged Schools, lads' clubs, model lodging houses, and night shelters, including two for street children. Some were founded by the Methodist Church, which also built two large establishments combining chapels with other facilities; Central Hall on Oldham Street (1885–6) and the enormous Albert Memorial Hall, Peter Street (1910).

By the end of the C19 Manchester had piped water from the Lake District, a project only overshadowed in scale and techno-logical innovation by the construction of the MANCHESTER SHIP CANAL, which opened in 1894. It was one of the most remarkable engineering achievements of its day, making Man-chester a port of international stature, and diversifying the eco-nomic base of the region as industry became concentrated in the Trafford Park Industrial Estate (*see* Stretford). Renewed confi-dence was behind the burst of new commercial buildings in the centre, many of them fully framed in steel – following in part from the construction techniques used for warehouses and transit sheds of the Ship Canal Docks. It seems possible that they rep-resent the most rapid and concentrated early adoption of the technique in Britain. The Manchester engineering firm *E. G. Wood & Co.* and the local architect *Charles Heathcote,* both with expe-rience of building at the docks, played an important role.* *Harry S. Fairhurst* was another local man, whose innovatory ware-houses on Whitworth Street and elsewhere created some of the most distinctive Edwardian commercial architecture. Baroque and Renaissance styles predominated, and the use of terracotta and faience became common, employed to spectacular effect by, for example, *Waterhouse,* whose enormous, lavishly decorated Refuge Assurance Offices (begun 1891) are still a city-centre landmark.

Baroque and various Renaissance styles were also favoured for some of the most conspicuous MUNICIPAL BUILDINGS from the early C20, for example *Woodhouse, Willoughby & Langham*'s police and fire station on London Road (1901–6), and the mag-91 nificent Victoria Baths in Chorlton-on-Medlock (1903–6). The

*We are grateful to Jonathan Clarke of English Heritage for information on this subject.

crop of early C20 Carnegie libraries in the suburban centres by the City Architect *Henry Price* are smaller, but well-composed. Greenwich Baroque was chosen for the Royal Infirmary, rebuilt in 1905–8 in Chorlton-on-Medlock by *E. T. Hall* and *J. Brooke*. Other public facilities were provided through the wealth of local industrialists: *Basil Champneys* used free Perp for his dramatic John Rylands Library on Deansgate, while the Whitworth Art 90 Gallery in Chorlton-on-Medlock (*J. W. Beaumont & Sons*, 1894–1908), the gift of Joseph Whitworth was executed in respectable Jacobean. One of the most original buildings of its day, *Edgar Wood*'s extraordinary First Church of Christ Scientist 78 (1903–4), is tucked away in Victoria Park (Rusholme). A brilliant work of great individuality, it speaks for the spirit of an age searching for an alternative to historical precedent.

After the First World War COMMERCIAL BUILDING returned in force. The Midland Bank on King Street by *Sir Edwin Lutyens*, 101 designed in 1928, is easily the best example of interwar classicism in the city. The Kendal Milne department store is an imposing example of German-influenced post-classical style (*J. S. Beaumont*, 1939), and Lee House, by *Harry S. Fairhurst & Son* with *Henry Sellers* (1928–31), the base of an unrealized skyscraper, is notable for sophisticated interplay of materials, texture and form. The Modern Movement is represented by the Daily 102 Express building in Ancoats, by *Sir Owen Williams* (1936–9), as good as anything of its day in England, while Dutch brick Modernism was the style chosen by the Co-op, for offices on Dantzic Street, in 1936.

MANCHESTER UNIVERSITY did some building between the wars, including a library by *Percy Scott Worthington* (1935–7); more interesting work by him, started before the war, can be seen in Rusholme and Fallowfield, where Hulme Hall and Ashburne House (halls of residence) are excellent, low and friendly, with deft Arts and Crafts touches. *Worthington* also designed Manchester Grammar School, Rusholme, with *Francis Jones*. It is Neo-Georgian, like council schools of the time, but singular for the force of the design and clever planning. Major CIVIC PROJECTS included the Central Library and the Town Hall exten- 100 sion, both by *E. Vincent Harris* (1934–8), and a municipal airport, established near Eccles in 1928, and relocated at Ringway from 1935. This, with the creation of the suburb of Wythenshawe in 1931 (*see* below), established the final extent of the city, which stretches more than ten miles from Heaton Park in the N to Manchester Airport in the far S.

HOUSING CONDITIONS in the older inner suburbs were still appalling. A limited programme of slum clearance took place, but in 1945 it was estimated that 68,000 houses were unfit for habitation. One answer was expansion of the suburbs. More than 27,000 council houses were erected between 1924 and 1938, covering huge areas in Burnage, Withington and Blackley. The new garden suburb at Wythenshawe (laid out by *Barry Parker*) was 105 the most ambitious of these schemes. Private housing also proliferated, and CHURCHES were built to serve the expanding

110 suburbs. *N. F. Cachemaille-Day*'s St Michael in Wythenshawe
(1936–7), is notable for Continental influences and its star-
111 shaped plan, and his St Nicholas, Burnage, 1930–2, was
described by Pevsner as a milestone in the history of church
architecture in England. Churches of Byzantine influence with
domed interiors were built by the Catholics in Moston and
Clayton. *Walter Tapper*'s unfinished Our Lady with St Thomas of
Canterbury in Gorton (1927) took up the style for the Anglicans.

After the Second World War the cotton industry, which had
been failing since the 1930s, collapsed. The most dramatic period
of INDUSTRIAL DECLINE began in the late 1960s. Mills were
abandoned, their chimneys overtaken by new high-rise and deck-
access COUNCIL HOUSING erected after slum clearance. Some
of these were poorly built, and social problems were exacerbated
by widespread unemployment. Pevsner in 1969 considered
'industrial housing' at once visually indifferent and socially
dubious. 'Do we really want these towers of flats everywhere? Do
tenants want them? . . . Will they not be the slums of fifty years
hence?' In the event the problems started to manifest themselves
in less than a decade.

The most impressive CHURCHES of the 1960s are *Sir Basil*
114 *Spence*'s St Francis, 1959–61, and *G. G. Pace*'s William Temple,
1963–5 in Wythenshawe. Others were built in the new estates,
such as *Maguire & Murray*'s Church of the Ascension in Hulme,
1968–70, with a roof designed to be looked down upon from the
high-rise blocks. This and *Desmond Williams & Associates*' St
Augustine (R.C.) in Chorlton-on-Medlock (1967–8) reflect the
new liturgy of that decade, but *Adrian Gilbert Scott*'s St Anthony
(R.C.) 1959–60 at Wythenshawe is traditionally planned.

The best COMMERCIAL BUILDINGS of the 1960s are the
118 group of Co-operative Insurance Society and Co-operative
Wholesale Society buildings on Miller Street (by *G. S. Hay* and
Sir John Burnet, Tait & Partners, 1959–62). The three elements of
the Piccadilly Plaza (*Covell, Matthews & Partners*, 1959–65,
remodelled 2001–2) are undeniably impressive in size and ambition. Others deserving mention are *Casson, Conder & Partners*'
former District Bank (1966–9) and *Brett & Pollen*'s Pall Mall
Court (1969), both on King Street; *Ralph Tubbs*'s sleek Granada
offices (1960–2), Atherton Street; Albert Bridge House (*E. H.
Banks*, 1958–9), Bridge Street and *R. Seifert & Partners*' sinuous
Gateway House (1967–9), Piccadilly Station Approach, all in
117 Manchester. *Seifert* also did the Hexagon Tower (1971) in Black-
116 ley, where Blackley Crematorium is a notable work of the City
Architect *L. C. Howitt*. Another building of the public sector,
119 Oxford Road Station (1960 by the staff architects of British Railways, project architect *Max Clendinning* with engineer *Hugh Tottenham*), is the most ambitious example in the country of conoid
timber shell roofing.

The universities and colleges expanded from the early 1960s,
but the UMIST campus is the only one with real cohesion. Here
W. A. Gibbon of *Cruickshank & Seward* designed impressive Brutalist edifices of Corbusian influence. The buildings of the Uni-

versity of Manchester of these years are less impressive, with only a few exceptions, e.g. *Scherrer & Hicks*'s Mathematics tower, but they incorporate sculptures and reliefs by artists such as *Lynn Chadwick*, *Hans Tisdall* and *Michael Piper*. *Bickerdike, Allen, Rich & Partners*' Royal Northern College of Music (1968–73) is expressive, with upper-level walkways which were part of an unrealized plan to link academic buildings by high-level pedestrian routes. In Fallowfield, Hollings College (*L. C. Howitt*, 1957–60), known as the toast rack, is an engagingly light-hearted job, and a popular landmark in s Manchester.

BUILDINGS OF THE 1970s were generally less ambitious, though *Levitt Bernstein*'s wonderful high-tech Royal Exchange Theatre pod of 1976 is a memorable exception. The appearance of the centre was dramatically changed by the erection of the ugly, inward-looking Arndale Centre (*Wilson & Womersley*, 1972–80). In the decades which followed some undistinguished Postmodernist buildings sprouted up here and there, but some of the most successful schemes involved REUSE OF HISTORIC BUILDINGS, such as the conversion of Central Station, Windmill Street, as an exhibition centre, G-Mex, opened in 1986. Castlefield was designated an Urban Heritage Park in 1982, and the Liverpool & Manchester Railway buildings there were preserved as part of the Museum of Science and Industry in Manchester. The Jewish Museum was formed in the Sephardic Synagogue in Cheetham Hill, and the National Museum of Labour History relocated in a hydraulic pumping station off Bridge Street. There have been drawbacks and losses as well. The early C19 Havelock Mills, the last group of mills in the centre, were demolished in 1991, and it is quite shocking that buildings of the quality of *Percy Scott Worthington*'s Skin Hospital (1903–5) on Quay Street should have disappeared as recently as 1999. Another sad loss was *J. S. Crowther*'s St Alban, Cheetwood of 1857, demolished in 1998. Both the Free Trade Hall and *Cockerell*'s Branch Bank of England have lost their identity and integrity by being extended.

Manchester at the time of writing is a site of BUILDING ACTIVITY, part of a process which started in earnest in the mid 1990s. It is on a greater scale than the burst of building in the 1960s, and probably as intense and wide-ranging as the boom in the early C20. An early sign of change was the Light Rapid Transport System METROLINK, constructed by a consortium of *GEC*, *John Mowlem & Co.* and *AMEC* (depot facilities). A cross-town tram route, opened in 1992, connected with the adapted Bury and Altrincham suburban railway lines. It was extended to Eccles and Salford Quays in 1999, and further extension is planned. It has had a damaging visual impact on some parts of the centre, but is a great success as a transport system. In the same years a railway link was made with the airport, where the Airport Station of 1993 by *Austin-Smith:Lord* is the best new building there.

An upturn in the local economy, the process of renewal following devastation by a terrorist bomb in 1996, and the hosting of the 2002 Commonwealth Games have also been important factors. The renaissance started with projects such as the

120 Bridgewater Hall (by *RHWL Partnership*, 1993–6) and *Short & Associates*' unusual Contact Theatre near the University in Chorlton-on-Medlock. Many new buildings have adopted a Modernist style, such as the International Convention Centre on Windmill Street (*Stephenson Bell* with *Sheppard Robson*, 1999–2001), which is a demonstration of good new design fitting well with C19 neighbours – here the Central Station and the Great Northern Warehouse. Other projects have benefited from lottery and Millennium

122 funding – they of course are ART GALLERIES and MUSEUMS. Urbis, by *Ian Simpson Architects*, for housing an exploration of the modern city, has a high glass prow rising in views to the N from the centre. *Michael Hopkins* extended the City Art Gallery, 2001–3, using glass to connect Barry's original to an extension of the Athenaeum building.

There has been new ACADEMIC BUILDING as well, as Manchester consolidates itself as one of the student capitals of the country. A lot of it is undistinguished accommodation blocks, but Manchester Metropolitan University has led the way with the Aytoun Library (*MBLC*, 1993) and All Saints West (Chorlton-on-Medlock), a stylish new block by *John McAslan & Partners* (2002–3). *Hodder Associates*' Career Services Unit (1995) on the Manchester University campus (not actually part of the University), is excellent. Meanwhile Manchester University and UMIST began the process of merging in 2003, and *Terry Farrell*'s Masterplan for redevelopment of the campus is in preparation.

The 1996 bomb exploded near the S end of Corporation Street causing severe damage to surrounding buildings. This area and that to the N around the cathedral have since been transformed, with new pedestrian streets and squares, new buildings, refurbishment and repair of damaged buildings and a new park near the Cathedral. Other parts of the centre have also changed almost beyond recognition – with new gardens at Piccadilly, a surge of development in the Northern Quarter on the N side of the centre, and rebuilding of the area between Spinningfield, off Deansgate, and the Irwell. As well as conversions (hardly a warehouse in the centre has not been turned into flats), purpose-built apartment blocks seem to spring up on every corner, usually with plenty of glass, metallic or brick cladding, and an architectural statement of a corner tower. Many are formulaic, but there are well composed schemes by architects such as *Glenn Howells*, *Stephenson Bell* and *Ian Simpson Architects*. *Terry Farrell*'s Green Building in Chorlton-on-Medlock (under construction 2004) is part of wholesale mixed residential redevelopment of the Chorlton Mills complex. Smaller-scale developments of the same kind can be found in the S suburbs, e.g. No. 417 Barlow Moor Road, opposite Chorlton Park, by *Stephenson Bell*, 2000–1.

Manchester City Stadium was built for the 2002 Commonwealth Games some distance from the centre in E Manchester by *Arup Associates* (lead architect *Dipesh Patel*) and reconfigured afterwards for use by a football club (*see* p. 364). Regeneration of the surrounding area has started, but housing and decayed suburban centres remain one of Manchester's most pressing problems. The rebuilding of Hulme following demolition of the huge deck-access blocks has been a success, and *MBLC*'s Homes for Change (1999–2000) is one of the most interesting RESIDEN-TIAL SCHEMES, designed with the input of prospective tenants, the first such experiment in the city to produce an architecturally notable result. The experience of community architecture will doubtless be drawn upon during the planning of the Millennium Village, New Islington, in Ancoats, and in schemes for changing the fortunes of depressed areas, mainly on the E and N sides of the centre, which are being put into place. If they are successful, Manchester will truly have reinvented itself.

The centre of Manchester is described first, with religious, public and academic buildings followed by the streets of the inner area in alphabetical order. Perambulations then cover outer parts of the centre. The suburbs are divided into three areas, S, N and E, each with the townships arranged in alphabetical order, some grouped together for convenience.

CENTRAL MANCHESTER

MANCHESTER CATHEDRAL

Manchester has one of the most impressive examples in England of a late medieval collegiate church. It stands N of the modern town centre, probably on the site of one of the two Manchester churches mentioned in Domesday. The present building dates essentially from after the foundation of the college in 1421, although its predecessor was probably of similar length by the C14, and evidence for C13 and C14 work was found during restorations. The regular plan of aisled nave and aisled chancel, each of six bays, was expanded piecemeal by additional chapels to N and S to reach the present exceptional width in the early

C16, under Warden James Stanley II. He was also part-donor of the magnificent set of choir stalls, the cathedral's chief treasure. The elaborately decorated exterior with its lofty W tower and the general uniformity of the Perp style also impress, although much of the fabric has been renewed. The church was raised to cathedral status in 1847.

History

In 1421 Thomas de la Warre, Lord of the Manor, obtained a licence from Henry V for a collegiate foundation. It was a chantry college, where masses were to be said for Henry V, the Bishop of Coventry and Lichfield, Thomas de la Warre, and their progenitors. The church was dedicated to St Mary, St George and St Denys. The domestic premises survive; they were built on the site of the manor house, N of the church, and became Chetham's Hospital and Library in the C17 (*see* Public Buildings, below). The building history of the church has yet to be satisfactorily resolved. The will of the first warden John Huntingdon (incumbent 1422–58), dated 1454, and an inscription on his brass, suggest that he rebuilt the choir. The nave is traditionally attributed to the wardenship of Ralph Langley (1465–81). The fifth warden, James Stanley II (incumbent 1485–1506, subsequently Bishop of Ely, †1515) is known to have contributed a chantry chapel and choir furnishings. He started work on the Chapel of St John the Baptist (now the Regimental Chapel) N of the chancel. His badge appears on the S choir stalls; on the N stalls is the badge of the merchant Richard Beswick, who also founded the Jesus Chapel on the S side, given a licence for worship in 1506.

C19 restoration started in 1814 with disastrous alterations by *John Palmer*, who rebuilt the NW corner and covered the nave interior with Roman cement. The exterior was repaired and refaced during the 1850s–70s, and the nave arcades rebuilt by *J. S. Crowther*; the W tower was largely rebuilt by *J. P. Holden* in 1862–8. *Basil Champneys* added porches and vestries in 1898, and a large S annexe in 1902–3, and *Sir Hubert Worthington* after the Second World War restored and rebuilt what was necessary.

Exterior

The general impression is of a large, lavishly decorated Perp church, although late C19 refacing and the C20 rebuilding of much of the NE corner mean that little or no exterior stonework is medieval. The original work was largely followed in outline but not in detail. The rebuilt W tower is sheer below but richly appointed at the top. Early views suggest that the lower stage was originally Dec.

At the upper level are Perp two-light transomed bell-openings with panelling above. Openwork battlements (as on the rest of the church), grouped pinnacles at the corners, above set-back buttresses decorated with canopied tracery. *Holden* raised the

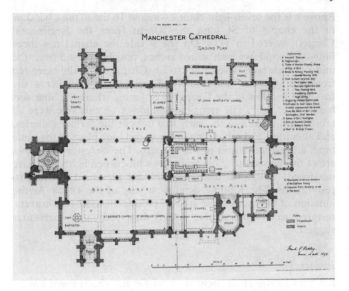

Manchester Cathedral, plan, engraving, 1893

tower by 20 ft (6 metres), increasing the proportions and basing
the design loosely upon the original. The elaborate w porch
added in 1898 is by *Champneys*. The nave outer walls are those
of the medieval chantry chapels added beyond the aisles, though
in some cases this was achieved by rebuilding aisle walls on a new
line.

The tour starts from the sw. Adjoining *Crowther*'s ornate s
porch of 1892, two four-light windows to the slightly projecting
St George's Chapel (*c.* 1503). Then two five-light windows to the
chapel of St Nicholas, dated variously 1470–86 (both C19 restorations). Further e the view is obscured by *Champneys*' vestries and
annexe (1902–3), excellent, as one would expect, subdued in contrast to his porches, yet charmingly varied in the grouping and
with felicitous decorative passages such as the bay windows to
the s. On *Percy Scott Worthington*'s extension of 1933–4, over the
Dean's entrance, is a beautiful relief of the Christ Child with St
Mary, St Denys, and St George, by *Eric Gill*, 1933. The Jesus
Chapel (1506), its windows with heavy supertransoms, is next in
the main sequence. The small octagonal Perp Chapter House is
attached (its exterior a rebuilding after the Second World War),
and the window to its e is of the same design as those to the Jesus
Chapel. Another example, reset, appears in the adjacent Fraser
Chapel of 1890.

The e view is impressive, thanks chiefly to *Hubert Worthington*'s
bare e wall, part of a rebuilding of the whole of the NE corner
including the outer walls of the Lady Chapel after the 1940
bomb. In a niche a gilded Mother and Child by *Charles Wheeler*.

Above it is the seven-light choir E window. To the N, the E window to the chapel of St John the Baptist (now the Regimental Chapel), started in 1513. On the N side the chapel has three four-light windows with stilted arches, possibly reused from the mid-C15 aisle wall. The early C16 Ely Chapel originally extended from this side; it was a casualty of war damage. Further W the five-light window lit the Chapel of St James, where the altar was hallowed *c.* 1507. The remaining windows on this side were all rebuilt and altered in the early C19 to light the former galleries, and alteration and rebuilding of the W end took place at the same time, all restored again in the late C19. The clerestory windows are of five lights, the choir originally with cusped lights, the nave uncusped, though the distinction was not preserved in later C19 restorations. The roofline detail is wholly of the 1870s. At the junction of nave and choir are two prominent rood-stair-turrets, restored to a more ornate design than early C19 engravings suggest.

Interior

7   Six bays to the choir arch; six bays for the choir; there are no transepts, but the semblance of outer aisles provided by the remains of the chantry chapels gives an impression of great width to both nave and choir. Detailed examination should start at the extreme E end with the small LADY CHAPEL. Only the inner W wall and entrance arch survived the 1940 bomb. Its round shafts rise from polygonal bases to polygonal banded caps. A narrow fillet on the fronts of the piers is carried through to the cap, the arch has broad hollows to the mouldings. The details suggest the C14, and C18 and early C19 engravings show Dec windows. Perhaps the chapel was retained for a special reason, such as the existence of a miracle-working statue or relic. The E wall of the choir and aisles appears to be of one phase: Perp shafts with polygonal bases and banded and battlemented polygonal capitals. The upper part shows signs of having been rebuilt, the arch above the Lady Chapel entrance has awkward stilted sections and the spandrel decorations above are similar to those of nave and choir. They must have been introduced to harmonize with the rest of the building.

The CHOIR has arcades divided from the five-light clerestory windows by a crested frieze. The date is problematic. The arcades are slimmer and more delicate than those elsewhere in the building. Circular shafts rise from polygonal bases to circular banded capitals; all the mouldings are deeply undercut. A slim shaft rising from its own polygonal base on the front continues over the capital to the top band of the frieze, re-emerging as the central member of a cluster of shafts which terminate in a pretty cap with lacy edges. This supports the wooden angels and eagles of the roof. The shaft thus draws together the whole composition, balancing the strong horizontals of frieze and cresting. A curious feature is the splayed plan of the arcades: the W end is 25 ft 4 in. (7.69 metres) wide, narrowing to 22 ft 1 in. (6.73 metres) at the

E end. The E responds have polygonal bases with a hollow moulding between the shafts, and polygonal banded capitals. They must
have been kept as a starting point for the new choir arcade, but
the junction is awkward, as is shown by the differing heights of
the string courses. This suggests that only the responds and part
of the E wall may remain from Huntingdon's C15 choir, and that
the arcades may be a late C15 or early C16 rebuilding by James
Stanley II.* The splay may have been deliberately contrived to
make the choir appear longer, cf. the tapering plans of late C15
churches such as Astbury, in Cheshire. The decorative detail supports a late C15 or early C16 date for both choir and nave. The
choir arcade spandrels have a pattern of cusping and foiled circles
containing shields, crowned by a foliage frieze. A similar scheme
appears in the nave, and the window spandrels of the clerestory
there. The parallel in the region is the nave of Mold parish church
in Flintshire, of c. 1500, a member of a group of Welsh churches
remodelled or embellished through the patronage of the Stanley
family, though Manchester lacks the abundant Stanley badges
seen at Mold. Farther afield the connection is with East Anglia,
where the churches of Great St Mary, Cambridge (1491),
Lavenham (1495), and Saffron Walden (1497) exhibit similar
treatment to the arcades, and are all the work of John Wastell.†
This suggests that the chancel arcades are unlikely to be as
early as the 1420s and it seems possible that Stanley was responsible, using masons from East Anglia, where he had strong
connections.

The CHOIR ROOF has cambered beams with open arch braces
and delicately traceried panels. There are eagles, a Stanley badge,
and angels bearing shields at wall plate level. Greatly restored by
Crowther, and again after serious damage in 1940. Huntingdon's
rebus – on one side a man goes hunting, on the other he draws
drink from a tun – appears on the spandrels at the W end of the
roof, though this could be reset or commemorative (the rehearsal
of these motifs in the entrance to the Lady Chapel is C19).

Stair-towers at the entrance to the choir gave access to the loft
and on up to the roof. Outwardly they are similar, but have different diameters; could the S tower be a recased survivor from
Huntingdon's time or even earlier? The choir arch must be
Stanley's work. It has parallels with Mold, if Crowther's restoration can be relied upon. Between spandrels and leaf frieze are big
animal carvings, and the shafts have foliated caps, both features
of the Mold nave arcade.

ST JOHN THE BAPTIST CHAPEL, now the Regimental
Chapel, on the N side of the choir, was probably started in 1513
by James Stanley II and finished after his death by Sir John
Stanley, who was reputed to be his illegitimate son or grandson.
E wall rebuilt after the 1940 bomb. Part of the N wall was perhaps
reused from Huntingdon's original choir aisle. The windows are

---

* Crowther believed that Huntingdon's arcades were re-erected and the timber
ceiling remodelled by Stanley.
† Professor Paul Crossley pointed out the East Anglian parallel.

flanked by wall brackets supported by a variety of grotesques and beasts. The arcade to the choir aisle is distinguished by a very deep hollow moulding to the arches and flared polygonal caps to the shafts. In bays one and two the hollow mould between the piers is enriched by a slim central pier, thereafter this is omitted. This change may indicate where John Stanley took over after James Stanley II's death.

The JESUS CHAPEL on the S side was licensed in 1506. Both arcade and outer wall seem to have escaped wholesale restoration; the latter is probably the original aisle wall reused. Traceried panels flank the windows; the W arcade has circular piers rising from high polygonal bases with rather crude banded and battlemented caps. A new sequence of arcades, beyond the chapel to the E, is similar in style but more crisply executed, relating to the CHAPTER HOUSE. Only the entrance is original, with cusped panelling over the paired doorways, and there is cusped panelling too in the reveal. For the Fraser Chapel of 1890 at the end of the S aisle *see* monuments, below.

The NAVE was almost completely rebuilt during C19 restorations, when the floor level was lowered and the arcades reconstructed by *Crowther*, who emphasized that he reproduced the original 'line for line and joint by joint'. The arcades are heavier than those of the choir (although they have the same slim central pier superimposed on the main shaft), but the details are different. The clerestory lights are late Perp, so perhaps the arcades were remodelled when these were introduced. The inner face of the tower with its high arch has gouged surfaces to receive Roman cement, though the remains of cusped panelling can be discerned. The full-height vertical channel on the r. side, not repeated opposite, is another mysterious feature; possibly the tower design was compromised by earlier work. The nave arcade is offset to the N on the N side, presumably to align with the splayed choir.

The NAVE ROOF is one of the glories of the building. It was replaced to the original design during the 1880s, reusing the bosses and minstrel angels. Crowther found evidence of alteration which he interpreted as an accommodation of the moved line of the N arcade. Like the choir it is a camber-beam roof, but the design differs in that each bay forms a complete compartment and the bosses, unlike those of the choir, were carved from the solid. The local parallel is the nave roof of Eccles parish church (q.v.),* where the figures on the kingposts and a repeating boss design with four praying figures over a sun motif are almost identical, suggesting that the same team of craftsmen were responsible. The beams are supported by braces with quatrefoils and shields similar to the arcade spandrels; beneath, a musical angel forms an ornamental supporter. The series of angel minstrels at Manchester is particularly good and complete. The seven angels on each side each play a different instrument, wind on the

---

* Eccles has a similar building history, the clerestory is similar, and the N arcade was also moved outwards.

N, strings on the S (the clavicymbal on the N side was accidentally transposed with the portative organ on the S side during restoration).

Furnishings, described clockwise from the east

LADY CHAPEL. SCREEN. Dated *c.* 1440 by Henry Hudson,* and if so the earliest screen in the church. Mutilated female statuettes, possibly virgin martyrs and confessors, flank the central St George and dragon beneath the tabernacles, with C19 replacements at each end. Entertaining grotesques on the strip below the canopies. – Oak REREDOS no doubt to Worthington's design, and most effective. – PISCINA. Medieval, relocated; likewise the gilded SCULPTURE of an angel. – TAPESTRIES designed by *Austin Wright* and made by *Theo Moorman* in 1957. – Engraved GLASS of similar date in the high N and S windows by *David Peace*.

CHOIR. SCREENS in the E part, wrought iron, with Gothic pinnacles, and a wrought-iron COMMUNION RAIL, all delightful. They date from 1750–1, and Dr Ivan Hall thinks they are probably by *Robert Bakewell*. Above these the upper part of Perp wooden SCREENS, thought by Hudson to be contemporary with the stalls. They were remodelled *c.* 1750 to form one large ogee arch per bay. – BISHOP'S THRONE, 1906 by *Sir Charles Nicholson*, Perp style. – STALLS. Without a doubt amongst the very finest in the North of England. Installed *c.* 1500–6. Badly damaged during the Second World War and restored by *James Brown*. James Stanley II, fifth warden, was mainly responsible, witnessed by the proliferation of Stanley arms and badges. The absence of episcopal emblems suggests the work was finished before he became Bishop of Ely in 1506. Richard Beswick, a contemporary of Stanley, paid for one side, and his arms appear on the desk standard of the NE stall.

The Manchester stalls can be linked with the workshop of *William Brownflet* or *Bromflet* who was responsible for the stalls at Bridlington Priory *c.* 1518–19 (demolished, but fragments survive in Yorkshire churches), which are closely related stylistically to those at Ripon Minster of *c.* 1489–94, and Beverley Minster of 1520–4. There are thirty stalls, twelve on each side and six returned. The exquisite canopies are intricately carved with great exuberance. The stalls of honour at the W end, the Dean's and Residentiary's, are distinguished from each other and from their fellows. The canopies have four-sided fronts instead of the usual three, and are more ornate, with the Dean's outstripping the Residentiary's for wealth of detail. Hudson called this 'probably . . . the most elaborate structure of its kind in existence'. Above is another tier of simpler canopies. Crowning everything is a tester with cresting and pendant arches. It was a most felicitous invention, apparently used here for the first time (though it was used at Beverley a

---

* His *The Mediaeval Woodwork of Manchester Cathedral*, 1924, is indispensable.

few years later), which has the effect of unifying the whole composition and placing it within a frame. The STALL DESKS are set on a stone plinth. The desk ends have projecting fronts in the form of a diagonal shaft, a feature typical of the Bromflet workshop, housed at the base in charming little tabernacles with crocketed gables and tiled roofs. The uppermost stage has open tracery and supports a bracket with animals or beasts.

A full set of MISERICORDS.* The designs and subjects can be related to the Ripon misericords, dated 1489–94, and those at Beverley of 1520–4, both linked with the workshop of *William Bromflet*. N side, from W to E: angel bust with a shield; the Pelican in her Piety; two dragons fighting; Joshua and Caleb carrying a giant bunch of grapes (mutilated); man breaking his wife's cooking pot; dragon biting its back; child issuing from a whelk shell fighting a dragon; two men playing backgammon; the fox as a hunter; deer hunt; hunter and stag; defaced; cock and cockatrice; unicorn; the rabbit's revenge. The last, showing a rabbit cooking a hunter and his dog, is taken from a late C15 engraving by Israhel Van Meckenem. The supporters on this side are all flowers, foliage or fruit.

S side, E to W: gryphon; antelope; sow playing bagpipes and piglets dancing with pig supporters; Wild Man and dragon fighting; lion and dragon fighting; lion couchant; bear-baiting; pedlar robbed by apes, with ape supporters; fox stealing goose with fox and fox-and-cub supporters; Wild Man on camel fighting another on a unicorn; elephant and castle; angel with shield bearing the arms of the Isle of Man; dragon, eagle with supporters; Eagle and Child. The latter seat (for the Dean, previously the warden's seat) is wider than the others.

CHANDELIERS. In the chancel. Of brass, given in 1690 and 1715. – Fraser Chapel SCREEN, partly medieval, brought from elsewhere in the building. – PAINTING over the entrance to the chapter house and the inner doorway by *Carel Weight*, 1963. – SCREEN to the Jesus Chapel, medieval with ogee arcading, restored. – ROOD SCREEN or pulpitum dividing choir from nave. The only screen in the church wholly based on arched forms. Four-light openings l. and r. of the doorway. Drastically altered and later restored by *Sir G. G. Scott* in the 1870s, when the replacement parapet was added. At some time doors were inserted into the side bays. – SCULPTURE, CII or CI2, reset in nave NE respond. Small relief of an angel bearing a scroll. – Regimental Chapel SCREEN only very partly original, incorporating the arms of Sir John Stanley. In the chapel an CI8 FONT, octagonal bowl on a baluster stem.

STAINED GLASS. The scheme of five windows at the W end is a major work of *Antony Hollaway*, commissioned in 1971 and prepared in consultation with the Cathedral Architect, *Harry M. Fairhurst*. Windows dedicated to the three patron saints of the cathedral are flanked by designs based on Genesis and the Creation, S, and Revelation, N, invoking the spiritual journey

* This description is based on an account by Dr Christa Grössinger.

from birth and baptism to the afterlife. At the E end of the Regimental Chapel the Fire Window by *Margaret Traherne*, 1966, in memory of the Manchester Regiment and of Sir Hubert Worthington. The E window by *Gerald Smith* was executed after 1945.

MONUMENTS. Clockwise from the E. – Fraser Chapel. Bishop Fraser †1885 by *J. Forsyth*. Recumbent effigy in a low niche in the S wall. – Chancel. BRASSES in the floor: Warden Huntingdon †1485. 3 ft 3 in. (1 metre) figure, heavily restored in 1907; nearby another to Dean Maclure, 1906. – S choir aisle. Wall MONUMENT: Thomas Ogden †1766, with an obelisk, by *Christopher Moon* of Manchester. – BRASS: Warden Richard Heyrick †1667. – MONUMENT: Hugh Birley, M.P., recumbent alabaster effigy, 1886; by whom? – two fragmentary *ex situ* C15 BRASSES on the outer Jesus Chapel arcade, to the Byrom family. – Jesus Chapel, S wall. BRASSES: William Hulme †1691; – two Mosley family brasses: Anthony †1607 and son Oswald †1630. – S nave aisle. Two wall tablets of *c.* 1997 by *John Shaw*, one a tribute to the work of the emergency services in the aftermath of the 1996 terrorist bomb, and the other commemorating Humphrey Booth †1635 whose charity helped to cover the cost of post-bomb repairs to the cathedral. – MONUMENTS: Elizabeth Trafford †1813, a figure weeping over an urn. – Several BRASSES commemorating cathedral chapter clerks and registrars. Those to Lewis Alfred Orford †1948 and Lewis Hadfield Orford †1972 have beautiful lettering by *Donald Jackson*. – STATUE of Thomas Fleming, by *E. Baily*, 1851. – SW nave aisle. MONUMENTS to Dauntsey Hulme †1828. Attributed to *Richard Westmacott*, but it does not look good enough. Could it be by *Westmacott Jun.*? – N aisle, W end. Free-standing seated figure of Humphrey Chetham, by *W. Theed*, 1853, a schoolboy at the foot of the base. – N aisle wall. Simple tablets with fine lettering to Raymond Bernard Wood-Jones, Cathedral Architect, †1982 and Hubert Worthington †1963. – Between these a square tablet, Rawstorne Lever, no date but C17 in appearance. – Tablet to Lever family children, six of them, † between 1635 and 1647, with an affecting verse. – Outer St John the Baptist (Regimental Chapel) arcade, two *ex situ* fragmentary and abraded medieval brasses, memorials to the Radcliffe family, one *c.* 1480, the other *c.* 1540. The female figure is a palimpsest, and the other side has the figure of a nun of *c.* 1450.

N chapel, NE side. BRASS to Warden James Stanley II in episcopal robes, 1515, fragmentary, and now 29 in. (74 cm.) long. – Against the W wall of the chapel MONUMENT to Charles Lawson, 1810, by *J. Bacon Jun.*

OTHER PLACES OF WORSHIP

ST ANN, St Ann's Square. 1709–12. Founded by Lady Ann Bland *née* Mosley, who built her church as a Whig and anti-Jacobite alternative to the High Church Tory faction centring on the collegiate church. *John Barker* was described as 'undertaker' of the project, and the cost was £5,300. Purple-red Collyhurst sandstone with much patching. The W tower looks blunt, but it had originally a three-stage cupola, removed 1777 and replaced by the present upper stage. Six-bay sides with two tiers of round-headed windows and coupled pilasters above and below, the lower ones fluted with Corinthian capitals. N and S entrances have pediments and coupled fluted Corinthian columns. A Baroque door was inserted into a window opening of the N wall, possibly by *Waterhouse*, who restored and remodelled the church 1887–91. Apse with giant Corinthian pilasters and carvings in the frieze. There was originally a balustraded parapet with urns. The design of All Saints, Oxford, by Henry Aldrich (1706–20), which was disseminated in the form of an engraving to raise building funds, was the model for St Ann. The motifs of coupled pilasters, pedimented doorways and balustraded parapets are almost identical, though St Ann is larger.

INTERIOR. *Waterhouse*'s interventions were remarkably restrained and sensitive. At the E end the apse was panelled, a platform inserted and altar and reredos added. Carved cherubs and swags in the panelling above the altar are copied from the Grinling Gibbons original in the choir of St Paul's Cathedral (the church was for many years attributed to Wren). Three galleries with replacement Tuscan columns, original slim upper columns. S chapel and N vestry. Waterhouse retained many furnishings including: COMMUNION RAIL. Partially original with beautiful scrolling wrought-ironwork. Dr Ivan Hall thinks it is probably by the *Davies* brothers of Wrexham. – PULPIT. Three-decker with angle columns and marquetry panels, given the right proportions by sinking it into a well in the floor. – PULPIT RAIL. Early or mid-C18 work, probably by the same hand as the altar rails. – FONT. Shaped marble polygonal bowl with baluster stem, dated 1711. – BOX PEWS, remodelled but with the original brass plaques. – S chapel: some reset woodwork including a PEW with carved foliated panels. – ALTAR TABLE with a dense array of columnar balusters on urn bases. – STAINED GLASS. In the apse a scheme by *Frederick Shields*, made by *Heaton, Butler & Bayne*. Figures in rich Germano-Swiss architectural surrounds, in pale tones. Other windows are mostly by *Heaton, Butler & Bayne* as well, of a variety of dates but with unity of style. N side, E, three painted figures, St John, St Peter and St Matthew, of 1760 by *William Peckitt* of York. From the demolished St John, Byrom Street (*see* p. 349). In the S chapel an unusual etched abstract Art Deco design, in memory of Hilda Collens †1920, founder of the Northern School of Music.

ST MARY (R.C.), Mulberry Street. 1848 by *W. G. Weightman & M. E. Hadfield*, the second being the Catholic church specialist in the firm. Built on the site of a chapel erected in 1794. The design is a modification of one by Hadfield published in *The Rambler*, which so infuriated Pugin that he wrote a pamphlet to denounce this and other churches. He said (among many other equally defamatory remarks) that it 'shows to what depth of error even good men fall, when they go whoring after strange styles'. The choice of Rhenish Romanesque was both anti-Puginian and novel, and probably reflects the imagination of Hadfield's young assistant George Goldie. It had few immediate Catholic progeny, though Goldie later developed the style in Ireland. The early use of structural polychromy is notable, though this applies only to the exterior: there was no hesitation in painting the columns inside to resemble marble. Red brick, with sparing use of pale sandstone. Richly carved portal and sw tower with Rhenish helm roof.* The window arches are banded in red and yellow sandstone, as is the surround to the wheel window. The INTERIOR is basilican, with six bays and tall round-arched clerestory windows. Exposed timber roof with a lantern, w gallery with an ORATORY with a glazed screen on the s side.

The interior is dominated by an array of marble and Caen stone mid-late C19 STATUARY (now partially painted), in architectural settings, a scheme attributed to *Mr Lane* of Preston. It replaced painted figures and shows how Catholic iconography moved away from the strict medieval precedent Pugin preferred. – STATIONS OF THE CROSS. By *Norman Adams*, paintings installed in 1995. – STAINED GLASS. The best is a brilliantly coloured late C19 window showing the Virgin. Attached to the r. side of the church the PRESBYTERY. Red brick and painted stone, with churchy window to the ground floor and an oriel over. The unspoilt interior has an impressive full-height top-lit staircase and a door leading to the oratory in the church.

FRIENDS' MEETING HOUSE, Mount Street. 1828–31 by *Richard Lane*. This has presence, partly by being given space and dignity by being well set back from the street with generous steps up to the entrance, and partly for the restraint and purity of the design. Five bays with a three-bay portico of attached unfluted Ionic columns after the example of the Ilissic temple from Stuart and Revett's *Antiquities of Athens* (1762–1816). The rest is mainly brick, the side elevations with projection and recession articulated by stone pilasters and sillbands. Doric interior removed, C20.

METHODIST CENTRAL HALL, Oldham Street. 1885–6 by *George Woodhouse*. Substantially rebuilt following war damage. It replaced Wesley's Methodist chapel nearby, of 1781. The exterior is undistinguished, in a weak and flat Renaissance mode, but the site is important historically as the centre of Manchester Methodism from which a large and well-organized social services mission spread during the C19 and earlier C20.

ALBERT MEMORIAL HALL, Peter Street. Built for the Manchester and Salford Wesleyan Mission. 1910, by *W.J.*

* The only surviving English medieval example is at Sompting, Sussex. The motif had earlier been revived by O. B. Carter, at St Peter, Southampton, 1845–6.

Morley of Bradford, who won the limited competition. The Methodist Forward Movement of the late C19 and early C20 created Central Halls to reach inhabitants of inner cities, and this was one of the largest in the country when built. It is just approximately churchy in some details, with a mixture of Gothic and Baroque elements. Octagonal turret with a domed top, all clad in yellow *Burmantofts* terracotta. The ground-floor rooms, now used as a pub, included lecture halls, classrooms, etc. Stairs lead up to the huge (disused) upper hall, which seated more than two thousand, with a horseshoe gallery and a rostrum with an ornate organ case.

REFORM SYNAGOGUE, Jackson's Row. 1953 by *Peter Cummings* with *Eric Levy*. Reddish brown brick. Set back from the street, with a central entrance flanked by thin piers. Projecting bays on each side have tall narrow window strips. Galleries, including a choir gallery behind the Ark; clerestory lighting. Oak furnishings: ARK where the Torah scrolls are kept, with a marble surround; in front of this a BIMA, from which the Torah is read. Ground-floor windows with unusual figurative STAINED GLASS by *C. Lightfoot* of Manchester, 1953 to designs by *John Bradshaw*.

FOURTH CHURCH OF CHRIST, SCIENTIST, Peter Street. A conversion of 1950s offices by *OMI Architects*, 1998. The interior has a remarkable double-height auditorium rising from the basement in which white walls form planes, cut away and recessed to create a complex but uncluttered light-filled interior.

For the CROSS STREET CHAPEL, *see* Cross Street, centre; for the CONGREGATIONAL CHURCH (former), Castlefield, *see* Perambulation 4.

PUBLIC BUILDINGS

1. Civic, Administrative, etc.

63 TOWN HALL, Albert Square.* Designed by *Alfred Waterhouse* and built from 1868 to 1877; credit for this masterly work is owed to informed civic patronage as well as the architect. The project was conceived in 1863 and the council resolved to proceed in 1864. It was to be 'equal if not superior, to any similar building in the country' and was to be funded accordingly. The patronage was sustained and an account of 1886 gives the building cost as £521,357 12s. 1d., and the total cost, including land, furnishing and fees, as c. £859,000.

The forethought devoted to the commissioning led to the introduction of the two-stage architectural competition, hailed by *The Builder* as 'for the age and country, an immense innovatory stride'. From 137 first-stage entries submitted in 1867, eight finalists were assessed by Professor T. L. Donald-

---

* John H. G. Archer contributed this entry.

son and G.E. Street, and on 1 April 1868 Waterhouse was
appointed.

From an initial plan of great simplicity and effectiveness,
without any loss of clarity Waterhouse produced a building of
great subtlety and refinement. Approximately a hollow triangle, the form fills the site, and the Great Hall is placed in the
void and perpendicular to the w side, which faces Albert
Square and contains at first-floor level the state apartments.
Separate entrances for different functions are strategically
placed, with the main entrance facing Albert Square. Public
access is at the main angles; there is a private entrance for the
lord mayor, and beneath the Great Hall was a police station,
entered from the s courtyard. The four floors of offices face
outwards along the sides, and concentric within the form is a

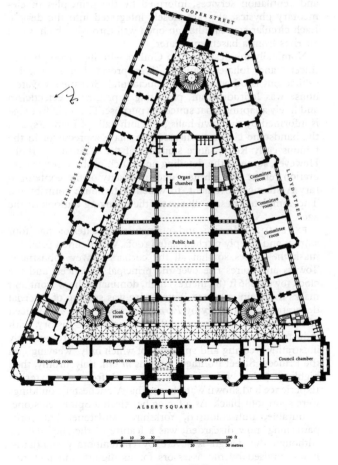

Manchester Town Hall, plan

corridor at each level which serves general circulation. The vertical circulation is equally direct: a pair of grand staircases, located close to the main entrance, lead to the first floor and serve ceremonial purposes. Other uses are served by circular staircases in each major angle and by additional stairs off the N and S corridors. A private stair links the mayor's apartments to Princess Street.

The plan and structure are very closely integrated and fireproof construction of segmental concrete vaults, the *Dennet* system, is exploited architecturally. Large spaces are spanned by wrought-iron beams which support the vaults. In the principal rooms the construction is masked by ceilings, but in offices the rhythm of beams and vaults forms an attractive feature. Rib- or groin-vaulting is used for the prime circulation areas, and by combining this with open arcading Waterhouse obtained dramatic views through and across spaces. Heating and ventilation services, informed by the principles of elementary physics, also are closely integrated into the design. Each circular staircase has an open well through which warm air rises from a basement heater.

Nominally the design is C13 Gothic, with its uncomplicated tracery and foliated capitals. This provided a serviceable vehicle but is otherwise almost incidental. Stylistically Waterhouse was latitudinarian, practising a pragmatic eclecticism and freely adapting what suited his purpose. The main frontage is informed by the town halls and cloth halls of Flanders, and the handsome circular staircases also have a precursor in the famous early Renaissance staircase of the Château de Blois. However, some of the detailing and much of the interior decoration reflect the lightness and originality of the contemporary Aesthetic Movement, to which Waterhouse contributed. The completed design illustrates the changing outlook of the age.

EXTERIOR. Massive and powerful, the exterior has four storeys and steeply pitched slated roofs. Well-defined pavilions mask the angles so that all the corners convey robustness. Towers and spires rise over the principal entrances, and the clock tower, 286 ft (87 metres) high, dominates the W front and marks the main entrance. Waterhouse was sparing of external decoration but statuary by *Farmer & Brindley* was introduced at focal points. The figures reflect Manchester's history, with industry represented by two admirable roundels respectively illustrating weaving and spinning, of which only 'Weaving', on the Princess Street frontage, remains *in situ*. Polychromy, then highly popular, was virtually eschewed from the exterior. Experience had shown Waterhouse that Manchester's buildings were soon soot-black. As a facing he selected Spinkwell stone, a durable, dun-coloured, Yorkshire sandstone, but tonal patterning, now discarded, was a feature of the roof slating. Although the design is severe by contemporary standards, it was praised by the assessors for its dignity and picturesqueness, but because the site is enclosed except for the W elevation, its varied skyline of towers and spires, impressive from many different viewpoints, is only observable from a distance. The site, plan, form and its towers closely interrelate, and with the differentiation of the parts and the expression of materials and techniques, owe much to Pugin's radicalism. The alternating depths of the masonry courses, for example, express their toothing into the brick backing: the narrow faces are the bonding courses.

The play on asymmetry is Ruskinian in inspiration and arises from the observation of nature, in which a dominant form often provides a strong focal point that is unaffected by variety in the related details. This concept pervades the design, beginning with the main frontage. The dominating clock tower is approximately central but its adjoining frontages are varied and the N and S pavilions are of markedly different design, yet the frontage remains architecturally authoritative and is often assumed to be symmetrical. The same applies to the other elevations although less dramatically.

The N pavilion presents the most public angle of the building and illustrates a confident freedom in combining symmetry and asymmetry. It is defined by its projecting form and resolves the awkward corner by cutting across the angle to create the leading face of the pavilion. It relates directly to the W frontage and carries its scale into Princess Street, where a staircase tower forms a terminal point for both the pavilion and the adjoining smaller-scaled four-storey offices. The three faces embracing the angle are consistent with the character of the main frontage, but each is symmetrical. The W face, with a single, central window flanked by pairs of canopied niches and their historical figures, effectively closes the front elevation. The central face gains spectacular prominence from a canted and corbelled oriel, also flanked by niches, supported metaphorically by a short but massive flying buttress that bisects the angle and spans to the boundary. The adjacent E face, although narrow, also has an oriel similar to its neighbour but unbuttressed. Beyond this the wall is inset and the grand scale is reduced by windows arranged asymmetrically although within the governing horizontals continued from the main frontage. Finally the staircase tower not only completes the ensemble but signifies the importance of dual doorways, respectively for the public and the mayor. As subtle as it is powerful, this pavilion virtually presents the building in microcosm.

Emphasis on massiveness and vigour of expression also reflects Ruskinian influence. The 'Lamp of Power' points to the sublime effect of an overhanging cliff and calls for buildings with 'a solemn frown of projection'. Waterhouse's design is heavy with such effects which occur internally but are most dramatic externally, as in the expressive modelling of the N pavilion. Almost equally forceful are effects on the S face of the S pavilion and in the drama of the E prospect down Lloyd Street.

INTERIOR. Spaciousness is one of the most memorable features of the town hall. Unexpected views occur either into individual spaces or across a whole sequence of them. Most remarkable of all are those from the S corner staircase, revealing the main foyer and its screens and staircases. These effects arise from the command of plan, space and structure that is Waterhouse's hallmark.* Also outstanding is the deftness of the planning and the manipulation of axes, although this is so accomplished that it passes largely unnoticed whereas, from first entering, the all-pervading sense of the richness of the decorative treatment is palpable. It is ordered according to functional status; ceremonial and social, administrative (with its own hierarchy) and variously utilitarian. The richest treatment includes rib-vaulting, with the webs striated in contrasting stones (blue-grey Forest of Dean and a buff Bath stone), walls lined above a tiled dado in terracotta, banded by patterning and colours similar to the vaulting. More modest treatment has groin vaults decorated with a variety of painted designs. Terracotta lining and tiled dados are used throughout both the lower floors, but the dados are not treated uniformly and are tiled to give individuality to the different areas. Similarly the mosaic flooring is panelled to define areas and patterned to express status. Decoratively the circulation areas are as important as any individual room.

Two themes appear in the decorative programme: Manchester and its history and the nature and extent of its commerce. The first is seen in the external sculpture and the murals by *Ford Madox Brown*, and the second in motifs incorporated in internal finishes and decoration. Where this is not thematic it is frequently innovative and characteristic of the Aesthetic Movement.

In character the interior and exterior are consistent. The polychromy is Ruskinian but the precise mechanistic detail of the carved geometrical patterning of joinery and masonry is contrary to his tenet that workmen should be entrusted with creative design. Waterhouse preferred to maintain consistency and introduced variety by other means.

Provision for ceremonial occasions and the reception of distinguished visitors was a major requirement that is answered by the generosity of the reception areas and the impressive route to the first-floor foyer and the major apartments. Ingenuity was needed because although the main entrance, set within the clock tower, is approximately centrally positioned, the site's configuration caused the Great Hall to be offset to the S. Waterhouse adroitly linked them by placing the entrance axis centrally in the most northerly of the four bays common

---

* Two major changes have detracted from the design spatially, both affecting the first floor. In the N angle an open well in the vaulting linked the mayoral apartments to the corridor. More serious and regrettable is the insertion of a kitchen across the N courtyard. It affects the adjacent corridor and is disastrous to the courtyard.

to the entrance hall, the foyer above it, and the Great Hall. The principal staircases flank this space and complete the ceremonial route.

The ENTRANCE VESTIBULE is the building's most sumptuous chamber. Small, rib-vaulted and glittering, it fills the base of the tower. In its floor it incorporates a bold design in coloured marbles and porphyry that is a section of a Roman pavement presented to the city by Waterhouse. Sculpture worthy of the location is the only major addition. Face-to-face across the chamber are the seated figures of two of Manchester's most eminent scientists, Dalton (1837), by *Sir Francis Chantrey*, and Joule (1893), by *Alfred Gilbert*. Behind Joule is an open arcade giving a glimpse of the WAITING HALL (now the SCULPTURE HALL), an extensive space, also four bays long, and well suited to its original purpose. It overlooks Albert Square, has a generous canted bay and, on the s wall, an impressive baronially scaled chimneypiece. Its height suggests an undercroft although it is richly finished, rib-vaulted and decoratively striated. A line of massive piers and an excellent floor design, with an emblematic pattern of red Lancashire roses, divide it from the cross-corridor. Busts and memorials now line the walls.

The ENTRANCE HALL, immediately across the corridor from the vestibule, also is fully vaulted, generously proportioned and continguous with the Sculpture Hall. It is enclosed N and s by the ceremonial staircases, each rising, dog-legged in two flights that are separated by a half-landing set in a vaulted semicircular apse. Ranges of tall windows light the landings and the upper flights. The principal stair rises directly from the entrance axis and is distinguished by a small, open-arcaded spiral stair on the axis of the half landing and projecting above it. This majestic, fully arcaded *tour de force* is best appreciated from the first-floor foyer which overlooks the staircases and offers longer views beyond. The foyer itself is contained by the arcading, its glazed wagon-roof ceiling and its panelled and symbolically patterned floor: the bees represent Manchester's industriousness, and the cabled border, ropes of spun cotton. From this point the staterooms are directly accessible.

The GREAT HALL, 100 ft long by 50 ft wide (30 by 15 metres), is of seven bays, divided by clustered shafts and lit by tall windows. Its ceiling suggests hammerbeam construction, but the allusion is dispelled by its cusped lightness; it supports only the panelled wagon-roof ceiling. The space is impressive; facing the entrance is a vaulted apse containing a finely cased organ, and the walls are lined with the famous murals by *Ford Madox Brown*. The ceiling is richly emblazoned to represent the nations and cities with which Manchester traded. The windows are set high, and beneath the sills and above an oak dado are the murals, six on each side, with subjects that relate, in some cases tenuously, to Manchester's history. In order, from the NW corner, the titles are: The Romans Building a Fort at Mancenion A.D. 80 (1879–80); The Baptism of Edwin

(1878–80); The Expulsion of the Danes from Manchester (1880–1); The Establishment of Flemish Weavers in Manchester A.D. 1363 (1881–2); The Trial of Wyclif (1885–6); The Proclamation Regarding Weights and Measures A.D. 1556 (1881–4); Crabtree Watching the Transit of Venus A.D. 1639 (1881–3); Chetham's Life Dream A.D. 1640 (1885–6); Bradshaw's Defence of Manchester A.D. 1642 (1892–3); John Kay, Inventor of the Fly Shuttle A.D. 1753 (1888–90); The Opening of the Bridgewater Canal A.D. 1761 (1890–2); Dalton Collecting Marsh Fire Gas (1886–7).

Brown commenced the commission in 1879 and completed it in 1892, six months before his death. Each mural is 10 ft 6 in. by 4 ft 9 in. (3.2 by 1.44 metres) and the first seven were painted *in situ* using the Gambier Parry method, which is akin to fresco. The remainder were painted in the studio on canvas in oils. Individually the murals are boldly composed and in scale and character are admirably suited to the architecture.

Sculpture has a minor role in the room. In one of the two niches flanking the apse is the figure of C. P. Villiers (1876) by *Theed*. Centrally at the w end is Gladstone (1879), also by *Theed,* and at higher level busts of Queen Victoria and Prince Albert, by *Noble,* are superimposed above those by *Marshall Wood* of the Prince and Princess of Wales.

The state rooms fill the entire w frontage and are entered from a corridor of matching richness to the reception area, but the greater height shows the vaulting to better advantage and the turning of the internal angles is particularly impressive. From the s the rooms are the former Council Chamber (now the Conference Room), which is separated by a vestibule from the Mayor's parlour and (former) General Committee Room. The principal vestibule is within the clock tower and divides the reception suite. To its N are a further reception room, and the Banqueting Room. All the rooms interconnect and each is made asymmetrical and spatially varied by at least one substantial bay. All have notable chimneypieces and, except for the Council Chamber, all have panelled oak dados decorated with strictly geometrical patterning.

Spatially the most complex is the COUNCIL CHAMBER, designed to seat forty-eight aldermen and councillors. The mayor and principal officers presided on a low dais, and the gallery above this accommodated the recording clerks. The gallery to the E was for the public, and the recess beneath it was for the press. Some original fittings remain. Above ashlar walls is a deep frieze, painted attractively with sweeping, intertwining tendrils of cotton plants laden with the bursting white bolls of the ripened crop. Interspersed are shields bearing the devices of neighbouring cotton towns. Geometrically panelled, the ceiling is in strong colours and complements the more delicate ones of the frieze. In its decorative importance this room is second only to the Great Hall.

The RECEPTION ROOMS are alike and the panels flanking their chimneypieces were intended to have murals by leading

artists, but the civic nerve finally failed and woven-patterned
fabrics, now renewed, replaced them. The ceilings are of great
interest: light in tone and effect, their colours and patterns
reflect Aestheticism and the advanced taste of the 1870s. This
occurs also in the design of the chimneypieces.

The BANQUETING ROOM, in addition to a bay, has the two
oriels of the N pavilion, two chimneypieces and a musicians'
gallery. Above the dado the trellised pattern of the painted decoration is original, and the ceiling is panelled in oak and decorated by gilt suns. Furnishings include curtains believed to
have been designed by HRH Princess Louise and made by the
Royal School of Art Needlework, South Kensington. They have
a place in the history of Victorian design.*

The UPPER CORRIDORS, simplified but not dull, incidentally provide stimulating views of the courtyards. Their other
great attractions (*see* especially the E corner) are the open-
trussed conical roofs that cap the circular stairwells and again
illustrate Waterhouse's mastery of space and structure.

The building's decoration is one of its important aspects and
reflects Waterhouse's active participation. Three firms were
responsible for the design and execution of the painted decoration. *Heaton, Butler & Bayne*, of London, decorated the
Great Hall; *Best & Lea*, of Manchester, the Council Chamber
and the Reception Room; and *Pollitt & Coleman*, of Manchester,
the Mayor's Parlour. Waterhouse designed the zigzag decoration of the corridor vaulting; also ceiling designs in the staterooms show a consistency which suggests his close attention.
Outstanding, with its brilliant Japonaiserie, prominent in
the contemporary vocabulary, is the S vestibule; the central
vestibule, now regrettably conventional, has a fine original
ceiling. Related to the decoration and also personal to
Waterhouse is the glazing. Most of the quarry glazing is white,
but the margins are in seemingly infinitely varied patterns and
tones of grey and wine colours from claret to rosé. At the turn
of the century C. R. Mackintosh used a similar palette.

Waterhouse's hand can be seen everywhere: he designed the
furniture for the public rooms, the alphabet for the etched lettering, the coat-hooks, the fire-irons and the dinner service. He
was consulted even about the inscriptions for the bells, for
which he suggested drawing upon contemporary literature.
Lines from Tennyson's *In Memoriam* were chosen, but the
legend above the clock tower, 'Teach us to number our days',
is biblical.

Manchester's sustained patronage was well rewarded. The
works of Waterhouse and Ford Madox Brown are now
regarded as classics. Their achievements share an extraordinary
dynamism, seen in the boldness of Brown's compositions and
the originality of his characterization; and in the vital inventiveness that informs the whole of Waterhouse's design. Independently of each other they created a joint work which

---

* These are at present in store.

continues to astonish and impress and is more truly representative of Gothic than any set of revived historic forms. Manchester Town Hall stands as one of the greatest and most
original architectural works of Victorian England.

100 TOWN HALL EXTENSION, St Peter's Square and Mount
Street.* Won in competition by *E. Vincent Harris* (1876–1971)
in 1927, built 1934–8. Pevsner viewed it as his 'best job' whilst
Charles Reilly found it 'dull' and 'drab'. Conceived of as an
understated link between the grandeur of the Gothic Revival
Town Hall and the classical bombast of the Central Library,
Harris's design manages to pay due deference to both whilst
proclaiming its own integrity. This is essentially done by an
eclectic mix of Gothic forms for the skyline, translated via
more domestic stone mullioned-and-transomed windows to
the main façades down to the more civic Neo-Georgian
character to the w where it faces the Central Library. Eight
storeys plus attic with the seventh and eighth storeys set back
behind a parapet. Faced with Darley Dale sandstone, the
whole enlivened by ornate carved tracery grilles to the staircase bays, in a late Gothic style, which incorporate heraldic
devices for England, Scotland, Ireland and Wales with the
Lancashire cotton flower. Each of the two stair-lights is surmounted by an allegorical statue carved by *J. H Cawthra* to
represent a Philosopher and a Counsellor. Beneath the
windows to the top storey are decorative panels of faience by
Shaw's Glazed Brick Company, Darwen.

The ground-floor arcades were conceived of not merely as
enjoyable urban spaces but as the setting for the showrooms
of the Manchester Corporation Gas and Electricity
Committees; the dying mouldings to their arches echo the
ecclesiastical late Gothic work of contemporaries such as
Temple Moore and Walter Tapper. The concave façade linking
the sets of showrooms, which formed an exciting new pedestrian route in the heart of the city, contained the Rates Hall.
To the Town Hall end the extension is linked by two bronze-
faced enclosed bridges at the level of the Council Chambers.
The original interior schemes have been swept away and the
clarity of the ground floor is only partially apparent in the
former Rates Hall. To the Council Chamber ante-room, and
Council Chamber itself are stained glass windows by *George
Kruger Gray* of ancient badges of the House of Lancaster, the
walls faced in Hopton Wood stone with bands of Ashburton
marble.

ALBERT BRIDGE HOUSE (tax offices). *See* p. 347

CROWN COURT, Crown Square. 1957–62 by *L. C. Howitt*, built
to replace Waterhouse's Assize Courts of 1859–64 which were
severely damaged in the Blitz. Symmetrical and feebly playful.
What a come-down after Waterhouse's brilliant early work. The
building has a façade 289 ft (88 metres) long and is clad in
Portland stone. Stripped classicism with steps up to a central

* Julian Holder contributed this entry.

entrance, used only on ceremonial occasions, with a wavy canopy with eagles on top. The other entrance is in the forbidding blocky grey extension to the r., completed in 1986, by the *Property Services Agency*. It houses additional courts and offices. Statuary salvaged from Waterhouse's building is on display inside, part of a full-blooded Ruskinian scheme by *Thomas Woolner*, which illustrated the history of Common Law. It is the largest collection of his work. The life-size figures in the foyer represent allegories, kings and lawgivers. More statues are housed in a basement gallery. Also preserved are the two capitals from the main entrance, mounted on piers. These are by the *O'Shea* brothers, in the vital style of their work at the Oxford Museum.

CITY POLICE AND SESSIONS COURTS (now part of the Crown Court). Minshull Street. 1867–73 by *Thomas Worthington*. The building is informed by Worthington's absorption of Ruskinian principles and his knowledge of European Gothic. The design has a vigorous urban quality imparted by the flat areas of brickwork, deeply recessed openings and bold outline. The site is awkward and the asymmetrical composition with corner tower and central campanile chimney turns this to advantage. Orderly rhythm is given by the ranks of tall closely set windows, and decoration becomes more concentrated at the top, in the stonework of the chimney with its spiky gargoyles and the corner tourelles and open arcading to the tower. The carving by *Earp & Hobbs* includes fierce beasts placed at eye level at the entrances, as Ruskin would have liked. The separation of different users was achieved by placing pairs of courtrooms on each side of an open courtyard, each separated from its neighbour by offices and flanked by corridors. The original courtrooms have panelled roofs and high windows framed by ornate pilasters. The pitch-pine furnishings effectively combine open, glazed and blind Gothic arcading.

The EXTENSION to the Aytoun Street side is by *James Stevenson* of the *Hurd Rolland Partnership*, 1993–6. Worthington's forms are simplified for the new work, which echoes the tall windows and gables. The courtyard was glazed over and four new courtrooms inserted into the ground floor, with two new courts in the extension. The atrium is the hub of the separate circulation routes with an open deck for the public and glazed walkways for jurors and judiciary. The STAINED GLASS of the jury walkway is by *Lavers, Barraud & Westlake*. It was moved from the former judges' rooms and copied where necessary to provide a complete scheme. The figures of Moses, St Michael and Solomon symbolize Law, Justice and Wisdom.

MAGISTRATES' COURT, Crown Square. A new building is being constructed by *Gensler Architects*, 2004. Plenty of red sandstone and matt silvery cladding. A large atrium with an angled roof contains upper-level walkways and palm trees.

POLICE AND FIRE STATION, CORONER'S COURT, London Road. The court is in use, the remainder is empty. By

Woodhouse, Willoughby & Langham, 1901–6, winners of a competition judged by Waterhouse. A magnificent municipal showpiece, now shamefully neglected, the detail blurred by a thick layer of dirt. A huge near-triangular block ranged around a courtyard used for drill. As well as all the usual facilities there was accommodation for firemen and their families. The style is Neo-Baroque in red Accrington brick, tawny terracotta and brown faience, with Hawksmoorish turrets as part of a picturesque skyline. The terracotta is by *Burmantofts* and the sculptural and architectural modelling by *J. J. Millson*. The generous, classically inspired figures have a hint of Art Nouveau attenuation and symbolize Courage, Vigilance, Justice, Truth, etc.

POLICE HEADQUARTERS, Southmill Street, w side. 1937 by *G. Noel Hill*, City Architect. The Portland stone front is in stripped classical style. Pale brick buildings behind around a courtyard.

POST OFFICE, Spring Gardens. By *Cruickshank & Seward*, opened 1969. Three-storey podium block and an eight-storey tower. Upper walls inside are lined with bold fibreglass relief panels.

2. Galleries, Libraries, and Concert Halls

45 CITY ART GALLERY, Mosley Street. By the young *Charles Barry*, 1824–35, for the Manchester Institution for the Promotion of Science, Literature and the Arts, founded 1823. The building is Grecian, his only public work in this style. His success lay in his ability to make the interior fit the glove of the Greek style, partly through the use of top-lighting with the consequent reduction in the number of windows, and partly through his clever adaptation of designs for villas by L.A. Dubut published in 1803. There is a debt also to Schinkel's Schauspielhaus in Berlin, of 1819–21. From these he developed the idea of a portico flanked by wings and topped by an attic. The portico has six unfluted Ionic columns with a pediment, then three recessed bays with two columns *in antis*, and then come three-bay solid pavilion-like ends.* SCULPTURE by *John Henning Jun.*, executed in 1837. Metope panels in the upper part of the pavilions depict allegorical figures with attributes and putti. Plain metope panels continue around the other sides.

The portico expresses the presence of a full-height entrance and staircase hall, which has a Greek Doric colonnade on three sides. The lofty space, with clerestory lighting all round, is mediated by a gallery, reached from a stair which rises between plinths and divides on either side of the (disused) entrance to the former lecture theatre. At ground level there is visual penetration beyond the colonnade on each side. In this way expres-

---

* Marcus Whiffen suggests that the bold modelling and strong contrasts may owe something to the ancient temples Barry had seen in Egypt.

sion is given to the spaces lying on each side and above. The Institution's building and extensive collections were donated to Manchester Corporation in 1881. The resulting alterations included the removal of a large lecture theatre which lay immediately behind the entrance hall. Upper top-lit galleries now lie on three sides around the entrance hall. Further alterations came with the erection of an extension, 1999–2002, *see* below. A vivid decorative scheme with bright stencilled friezes, instituted by Timothy Clifford and Julian Treuherz in the 1970s and 1980s, was largely removed, and the glazed lanterns have been obscured by new artificial lighting. The scheme did not deserve such summary treatment, and the entrance hall, divested of the sculpture and paintings previously displayed there, seems bare. The first thing the visitor sees is the box for voluntary donations.

The gallery from 1938 used as an annexe the former ATHENAEUM in Princess Street, behind, the premises of a   46 club promoting adult education. Also by *Barry*, 1836–7. As Manchester's first palazzo, it can claim to be the inspiration for a genre which Manchester was to make her own as the model for commercial warehouses. The design has much in common with Barry's Reform Club in London of 1838–41. Nine bays with pedimented *piano nobile* windows. The ground floor is raised high over a half basement so there are steps up to the entrance. Inscribed frieze, after the Palazzo Pandolfini, Florence. Historicism also in the big expanse of wall above the upper windows. The proportions are crushed by the heavy roof added after a fire in 1873, which destroyed part of the interior. The work was by *Clegg & Knowles*.

Land was acquired in the rear angle of the two buildings in 1898, with the intention of building and extension, but a century passed before *Sir Michael Hopkins* brought the plan to fruition, 1999–2002. The original Royal Manchester Institution building is linked to the extension via a first-floor bridge and through doors made by extending existing windows at ground level. In this way Barry's rear elevation retains its coherence. A glass box links the buildings and leads into a transparent central part with stairs and lifts. In contrast the N part of the extension is expressed as a block matching and balancing the dimensions and solidity of the Athenaeum, clad in stone, with much light brought in from the roof.

Treating the extension as two linked units has integrated the building into a composition of three parts, which in turn relates to the rhythms of the Institution building. The interior spaces work well, but any sense of the Athenaeum as a discrete building has been lost. The original entrance is no longer used, and the hall is not in the public domain. The attic lecture theatre added by *Clegg & Knowles* in 1873 is now a gallery devoted to decorative arts. Splendid, with the best plasterwork of its date in the city (now painted pale grey). Top-lit, with paired pilasters with lyre motifs, and a coved ceiling, with life-size figures in classical dress representing Music, Dance, Education, etc.

90 JOHN RYLANDS LIBRARY, Deansgate.* Commissioned by Enriqueta Rylands (1843–1908) as a memorial to her husband John (1801–80), a Nonconformist, pre-eminent in the textile business and a philanthropist. It was intended to house his theological collection and provide a free library, but after his death Mrs Rylands added two major private collections, creating a nationally important scholarly library. In 1890 she appointed *Basil Champneys*, the architect of notable collegiate work including Mansfield College, Oxford, which had Nonconformist and Mancunian associations and appealed to Mrs Rylands. Little expense was spared: the library cost £230,000 and took until 1899 to complete. Champneys wished to give it a religious character, which Mrs Rylands resisted. Its design draws on Gothic precedent, but underlying the historicist surface are contemporary aesthetic values expressed in the quiet play on asymmetry, the attenuation of vertical forms, the studied contrasts between plain surfaces and concentrated detail, and above all in the play of space and structure for aesthetic effect. Imagination and artistic licence rather than strict historicism or rationalism are the keys to the Rylands Library.

The site is a long, narrow parallelogram with a short frontage to Deansgate. Narrow streets, Wood Street and Spinningfield, were to its N and S. The building is distinctive through the composition of the frontage and also, because the plan is rectangular and aligned to Wood Street, it skews from Deansgate and catches the eye.

The frontage suggests a gatehouse of three bays. Built in red sandstone, it consists of a low, two-storey block with an imposing superstructure of towers, battlements and octagonal corner turrets that rise from the leading external angles. The slightly recessed central bay contains the richly decorated main entrance. The end bays have paired windows of different design at each level. Symmetry is avoided by counterchanging the pairs, which suits the internal needs. Rising above each end bay is an octagonal tower and behind each, stark and rectangular, is a taller tower. Deeply recessed from the street but in line with these is the end gable of the Reading Room, the heart of the scheme. This concentrated geometry establishes the identity and character of the building. The powerful massing is complemented by intricate patterning expressed in wall panelling, window tracery and delicate open-screen work. Solid battlements on the end blocks contrast with open work, and concentrated panels of detail with plain ashlar. The richest display is reserved for the reticulated tracery at the head of the Reading Room window, and above this is a crown of spiky openwork that combines the slanting lines of a conventional gable in a design that is silhouetted against the sky. This inge-

*John H. G. Archer contributed this entry.

nious finial replaced the proposed gable of an earlier design
after Mrs Rylands insisted that the roof should be incom-
bustible, and low-pitched concrete superseded conventional
trusses.

The remaining form is relatively simple. Like the nave of a
double-aisled church, the Reading Room provides the main
vessel, with a clerestory, a lower stage containing the reading
bays, and aisles housing corridors. The longitudinal emphasis
is halted by a tall tower, deceptively like a transept, which spans
the site. At the w end is a central semicircular apse, now
masked by extensions. The first of these, a NW addition of
1913–20 by *Champneys* and his son *Amian*, integrates smoothly
with the original.

The design of the nave-like centrepiece, the principal
element of the side elevations, is revealed from the s. It is the
full development of a concept that is incipient in the Mansfield College Library. Seen from Spinningfield, buttresses and
flying buttresses subdivide the main vessel and aisles, and in
each bay a two-storey oriel gives a vertical stress that is further
emphasized by the slender buttresses and the sculptural treatment of those to the aisles, which provide a springing point for
the flying buttresses. Architecturally this elevational treatment
is an admirably lucid statement that is completed on both the
N and s sides by the return walls of the entrance block. Each
is treated individually and asymmetrically.

INTERIOR. The ENTRANCE HALL and the PRINCIPAL
STAIRCASE on its s flank span the site's width. Spacious and
double-storeyed, both are rib-vaulted and form the most
expressive spaces in the building. They are designed to be seen
sequentially, with a short main axis from the entrance to the
cross-axis of a lateral aisle from which the main staircase rises.
At the focal point is a heavily didactic SCULPTURE by *John
Cassidy*, Theology Directing the Labours of Science and Art,
which closes the axis. The vaulting relates to the aisles and the
structure. Small vaults, narrow, steeply pitched and carried by
slender, deeply moulded piers, flank the main aisle, but the
lateral aisle is marked off by a row of double piers linked by
ogee fretwork; these carry the weight of the E gable. In the NE
corner the columns and vaults support an octagonal tower.
From the entrance the size of the aisle bays is progressively
increased to the tierceron vault that canopies the turning point
and the symbolic sculpture. The character of the space is of
lofty complexity, and between the piers the two flights of the
arcaded staircase can be seen rising within it. Their ascent
reveals further drama, first in the view over the hall, then, above
the half landing, an oculus penetrates the vaulting and opens
into the octagonal tower and, finally, seen from the upper
flight, from beneath cross-arcading it is gradually revealed that
the facing wall is the soaring rear wall of the s rectangular
tower: the drama of the design is undeniable.

Cathedral-like and tierceron-vaulted, the READING ROOM
is eight bays long, with gable walls filled by large, traceried

windows that provide a field for stained glass. At the entrance
stands an impressive statue of Enriqueta Rylands and at the w
end, in a vaulted apse, is an equivalent sculpture of John
Rylands. Both are by *John Cassidy* and are in Carrara marble.
The room is treated sculpturally and is not unlike J. L.
Pearson's church of St Augustine, Kilburn (1870–80). Double-
storey reading bays extend along each side and the laterally
deep central piers are penetrated at gallery level by a passage.
Each bay is arcaded at both levels. The lower bays are
divided by central piers, the upper arcades span the full bay,
and above them is the clerestory, which is the principal source
of natural light. The spatial character of the bays is enriched
by the double-storey oriel windows, the openwork gallery
fronts and the open, traceried screens that give the bays
seclusion.

The Reading Room is not over-richly decorated, but the
gallery fronts are assertive with Victorian Dec carving, and the
capitals of the mid-piers of the lower arcade provide pedestals
for sculptures of literary or religious figures, selected by Mrs
Rylands and carved by *Bridgeman's* of Lichfield. Each gable
window is panelled by two rows of figures in stained glass by
C. E. Kempe; with philosophers, writers and artists in the e
window and prophets and theologians in the w.

The wall finishes throughout are red sandstone or panelled
oak, and the unvaulted ceilings are of lightly modelled plaster
panels by *George Frampton*, a prominent Arts and Crafts
designer. The vaulting of the main library is striated in two
tones of sandstone, a Ruskinian detail.

Champneys and Mrs Rylands did not have an easy relationship. The design of the furniture was entrusted to *Stephen
Kemp*, the clerk-of-works, and Mrs Rylands chose the figure
sculpture, which Champneys considered to be 'tame and
inartistic', ordered the iconography of the stained glass, and
commissioned the green glazing and the fine bronze railings
and electrical fittings. The latter, by *Singer's* of Frome, is most
successful and is a notable Art Nouveau feature in its own
right. Nevertheless, when completed the library was recognized as Champneys' principal work. Technically it was notably
advanced, and stylistically, despite its medievalist overtones,
it illustrates remarkable aesthetic freedom, and the spatial
progression from the entrance to the Reading Room is a
masterpiece.

The library, now part of Manchester University, currently is
subject to major alterations. A pitched roof, as first intended
by Champneys, will create a gable to Deansgate and enclose
the clerestory, therefore affecting natural light in the Reading
Room; and an extension on Spinningfield will form the entry
for general use. Consequently the architectural progression
conceived by Champneys will no longer be accessible as the
normal means of entry from the street to the Reading Room.
The architects for these works respectively are *Lloyd Evans
Prichard* and *Austin-Smith:Lord*.

CENTRAL LIBRARY, St Peter's Square.* One of the great 100
monuments of Manchester. Built 1930–4 and one of *Vincent
Harris*'s most confident, assured, and bombastic essays in the
Roman Imperial manner he developed during the 1920s.
Harris won the commission in competition in 1927 (part of the
same two-stage competition for the Town Hall extension,
above) with a scheme for a steel-framed, Portland-stone-clad
building of four storeys plus attic with an extensive four-level
book storage area partially below ground. Harris's Pantheon-
influenced design may also reflect the needs of the circular
plenum heating plan for the high-voltage electrode heating
plant.

The five-bay portico of Corinthian columns, tetrastyle *in
antis*, with round-headed arches to the returns, provides a landmark entrance to the city centre from the s. It also provides a
classical foil to the Gothic Revival of Manchester Town Hall
to the N. The round arches of the portico sides are echoed in
the façade which is composed of a heavy two-storey rusticated
base surmounted by a continuous Tuscan colonnaded screen
to the upper storeys.

Despite the apparent weight of the exterior it is in fact more
of a façade which encloses a large, top-lit and domed circular
reading room in the manner of the former British Museum
Reading Room. It housed subsidiary functions such as catalogue rooms, study carrels, and special collections. The ingenuity of Harris's design is seen in the way he placed this grand
space, with its Tuscan colonnade of Sienna scagliola, on top of
the stacks (as in the American Library of Congress), in defi-
ance of the fashion for creating book towers on top of reading
rooms as seen at the Universities of London, Leeds, and Cambridge. The original FURNITURE was designed by Harris;
STAINED GLASS windows in the double-height entrance hall
by *George Kruger Gray* and *Robert Anning Bell*.

CHETHAM'S SCHOOL AND LIBRARY, Long Millgate. The
domestic premises of the collegiate church (now the Cathedral), where the priests lived together as a community were
built following collegiation in 1421. They are almost intact,
lying some distance N. They are the best-preserved buildings
of their type and date in the country. On the foundation of the
college, *see* Cathedral, p. 268 above. The establishment consisted
of a master or warden, eight fellows, four clerks, and six cho-
risters. It was dissolved in 1547 and the buildings acquired by
the Stanley family, Earls of Derby. The college was refounded
but the buildings remained in Stanley hands until their estates
were sequestered in the Civil War. They subsequently became
dilapidated before being acquired by the executors of the will
of the wealthy merchant Humphrey Chetham †1653.† The

* Julian Holder contributed this entry.
† For studies *see* S. Guscott, *Humphrey Chetham 1580–1653: fortune, politics and
mercantile culture in seventeenth-century Britain*, Chetham Society, 2003, and
C. Hartwell, *The History and Architecture of Chetham's School and Library*, 2004.

building was fitted up in accordance with his wishes as a free
library and Bluecoat School in 1654–8. The result was the
preservation of the medieval building and an exceptional early
town library complete with original furnishings. C17 documents show that a number of lost buildings, including two
barns and a second gatehouse, were standing at that time; they
probably formed part of the original college of priests complex.

After the initial adaptation few changes were made until the
C19, when the condition of the fabric and increased numbers
of pupils prompted restoration and alteration. The feoffees
astutely chose some of the most able and conscientious of C19
Manchester architects for the work. There were three major
phases, in the 1850s by *J. E. Gregan;* in 1876–8 by *Alfred Waterhouse,* and in 1883–95 by *J. Medland Taylor.* C20 expansion was
largely into neighbouring C19 buildings. The charity school
continued until after the Second World War, becoming a music
school in 1969. The library has remained open to the public
since inception.

The buildings are not unduly decorative, but there is some
architectural display, and the accommodation for nineteen
people, their servants and guests was ample and well
appointed. The buildings are of red sandstone with a stone flag
roof. There is a rectangle with hall and lodgings around a
cloister, then the kitchen and other rooms in a long E wing with
a short SE angled range, ending in the gatehouse. The build-

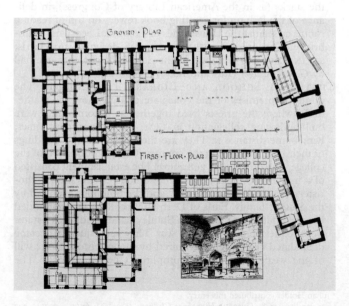

Manchester, Chetham's School and Library, plan.
From *British Architect and Northern Engineer,* 1876

ings appear to have been erected in two or more closely spaced campaigns. Later alterations probably included refenestration of the hall, and addition of the porch and hall chimney.

The gabled GATEHOUSE on Long Millgate has a heated upper chamber reached from an external stair. A large archway leads into the courtyard where the main block can be viewed. All the visible windows of the range have cinquefoil-headed lights under a four-centred arch, most with labels. Windows in other elevations (apart from the cloister, *see* below) are more simply treated. The HALL is lit by three transomed two-light windows and a low window at the dais end. To the l. the WARDEN'S LODGINGS have a two-storey projecting square bay with a niche in the gable. To the r. a two-storey PORCH, which *J. E. Gregan* rebuilt in the 1850s to match the bay of the warden's lodgings. It is awkwardly stepped back to accommodate the hall window, and blocked upper openings in the kitchen (*see* below) suggest that it must be secondary.

INTERIOR. Inside the porch, entrances to kitchen and cellar, and then the SCREENS PASSAGE with the expected paired entrances to the buttery and pantry, thrown into one room during the C19. The 7 ft (2 metre) high screen is of the spere type with two entrances. The central section was originally moveable, and it is all sturdy C15 work apart from the cresting. The stone-flagged HALL is marvellous, one of the best preserved of its date in Lancashire. Here the roof can be seen. It is of an unusual type for the N of England* with arch-braced tie-beams, common rafter trusses with collars and diagonal braces, and a collar purlin. However there is no real crown-post, only a stub between the curved braces which attach the collar purlin to the principals. The soffits of the arch braces and collar purlins are moulded and the feet of the principals extend below the wall-plate. All this is of one consistent design throughout the building. Paired trusses indicate the position of a louvre, made redundant when the fireplace (below) was inserted. Windows on both sides are misaligned with bay divisions of the roof, and the bases of the trusses have been cut to make room for the windows. While this can be explained on the w side by alterations to insert the chimney and C17 stair, on the other side it suggests that there was a complete refenestration, though the window design is consistent with a C15 or early C16 date. The huge fireplace with its external stack on the w side, probably inserted in the C16 or C17, was rebuilt in 1894 by *J. Medland Taylor*. The fine original battlemented canopy over the dais (s end) is another remarkable survival. There is an alcove with a bay window towards the cloister s of the fireplace. At the sw corner of the room there is a doorway, which leads to a LOBBY with access to the upper and lower chambers of the warden's lodgings and the cloister. The lower room, called the AUDIT ROOM, is fitted with C17 panelling

---

* But not unknown. A small family of crown-post roofs has been identified in the North West including an example at nearby Ordsall Hall in Salford.

and a plaster frieze of trails. The remarkable original oak ceiling has parallels with the ceiling of the choir in the Cathedral. Its moulded beams have carved bosses at the intersections, including a Mouth of Hell mask devouring a sinner, and the panels have diagonal ribs and central bosses. The bay is ornate too, with a design of stone quatrefoils in the vault.

The upper room, now the LIBRARY READING ROOM, is the most lavishly decorated of all. The bay is more elaborate than its counterpart below, with a Tudor arch with shafts rising from polygonal bases. The panelling is C17. Stanley badges applied to the wall plate and to the bay vault are later additions. Above the (renewed) fireplace is a splendid timber tympanum. It occupies the whole width of the N wall, framed by an arched band. The centrepiece is Chetham's arms with an eagle above grasping ropes of foliage and flowers. On either side wreathed obelisks rise from piles of books and support shell lamps. Flanking the obelisks, birds; on one side the Pelican in her Piety, on the other a remarkably vigorous cockerel (perhaps a restoration) grasping ears of corn. Paint and varnish were probably introduced in the C19. The Solomonic obelisks, lamps of learning and books speak for themselves, as does the pelican, a symbol of Christian sacrifice. The cockerel could be a symbol of Mercury and a reference to Chetham's successful career as a merchant. The piece is probably the work of a local firm which had absorbed the fashions and conventions disseminated by the workshop of Grinling Gibbons, and an early C18 date seems plausible.

A passageway leads off to the N to a narrow room lit by a range of nine mullioned windows with pointed heads. It also has quatrefoil openings giving views to the hall, but its original purpose is unclear.

18   The CLOISTER has a walk around a garth with three-light openings to only three sides, the fourth side being filled by the hall range. Along it lay the fellows' sets, much as in Oxford or Cambridge colleges, except that the cloister is two-storeyed, and sets do not have individual stairs, but were served by walkways on two levels.* Stepped buttresses divide the bays. Lower windows have cinquefoil heads, upper windows, in alternate bays only, trefoil heads. There is a camber-beam roof to the lower cloister (the upper cloister roof has been replaced). Access to the upper cloister was via a stair, now removed, at the NW corner where part of the structure can be seen in the ceiling. The S cloister range (at least) postdates the hall, witness the cloister buttress sitting on top of the hall plinth in the SE side of the garth. Cloister and hall plinths differ, as do internal floor levels.

FELLOWS' SETS have heated ground-floor rooms with two-centred arched entrances with continuous hollow mould-

---

* Some parallels are offered by the late C15 Prior's Lodgings at Wenlock Priory, Shropshire.

ings. Upper rooms were converted to form the library, with new windows to give more light. Partitions were removed but the bay divisions are visible in the pattern of roof trusses. The upper cloister walk and the entrances from it are preserved. The sets are of a similar size, *c.* 16 ft (5 metres) square, but they are not identical. There are problems of interpretation of the S side, where we have already seen evidence that the cloister is secondary. The room adjacent to the Audit Room is larger than the others, and distinguished by a mould around the arched entrance. There is no upper cloister entrance to it, only doors leading from the Warden's accommodation. It may have therefore been part of the senior lodgings, and there is a tradition that it was a chapel. The upper part of the library here is known as the Mary Chapel, though when it acquired this name is not known.

Now to the LIBRARY, an almost equally remarkable survival, 26 described by T. Kelly as 'By far the most important [public] library formed in this period – indeed the greatest of all the early town libraries'. The present entrance from the SW side of the outer courtyard was instituted by *Waterhouse*, as part of a campaign of alterations in 1876–8 which provided separate circulation for library and school. He inserted a stair into the SW set. At the same time he rebuilt and refenestrated all the ground-floor sets on the W side and made them interconnect. There were two C17 library entrances, one from the N where visitors climbed external stairs to an entrance at upper level, the other, which also gave access to the Librarian's and School Master's rooms, via the stone STAIR beside the hall, at the NE side of the cloister, which was built in 1656 reusing the medieval entrance to the cloister garth. Oak rail, newels with finials, and shaped and pierced splat balusters, probably the work of *Richard Martinscrofte*, who did the library furnishings.

The library is L-shaped, taking up the upper fellows' rooms on the S and W side of the cloister. The book cases are ranged at right angles to the outer walls. They were constructed during 1656–8 by the local joiner and surveyor, Richard Martinscrofte, and the books were chained. Originally 7 ft (2 metres) high, they were raised on two occasions. Chaining was continued until the mid C18. After the chains were removed gates with wavy finials were introduced to the bays. Although it is not the custom of this series to describe moveable furniture, the C17 library stools, similar to those found at St John's College Cambridge, deserve mention, as do the wonderful tables in the reading room, two with unusual legs shaped like consoles.

Now for the E range. The front was largely refenestrated in the 1850s as part of a substantial campaign of repair and restoration by *J. E. Gregan*. Both the original windows, and those probably inserted or renewed in the C17, were made uniform throughout and newly furnished with trefoil heads and labels on the ground floor. The polygonal bellcote with a lead roof is shown in an engraving of 1741. It was probably put in during the C17 conversion.

The splendid KITCHEN is a huge space open to the roof, with fireplaces beneath joggled lintels on two sides. One of the upper windows was blocked when the porch was rebuilt in the 1850s. The window rebate extends for the full width of the room; the W part was presumably blocked when the porch was erected. A narrow corridor leads to a room to the E and a passageway between the main courtyard and a small rear courtyard divides this from rooms further E, which were probably used for baking and brewing. The large angled upper room beyond to the E is reached from the external stair beside the gatehouse, and must have been quarters for servants and guests, used latterly as dormitories and now as a library.

THE C19 BUILDINGS. *Alfred Waterhouse* designed a new freestanding red sandstone schoolroom in 1871. It was finally erected in 1876–7 to the SW of the main building. It is modest and nicely detailed, looking a little like a chapel. Perp, but the motifs of the main building have not been slavishly adopted.

Further expansion took place in the late C20 when neighbouring buildings were acquired. The buildings of the Manchester Grammar School along Long Millgate were taken over in 1955 (for the present buildings and history, see p. 471). The N part, by *Barker & Ellis*, 1869–70, has a high gatehouse motif in the centre with a high chimney towards the schoolyard. An extension to the S is by *Mills & Murgatroyd*, 1877. On the W side of the site the former Palatine Hotel was built in 1842–3 by *I. & J. P. Holden*. It was acquired and converted in 1969. NE of the main building are two tall gabled accommodation blocks of the 1980s.

122 URBIS, Corporation Street. Designed to house exhibits on the theme of the modern city. By *Ian Simpson Architects*, 2000–2. Shaped like a rearing transparent prow with an exciting sculptural feel, but with slightly forbidding sheer opaque glass sides, which inhibit engagement with the surroundings. Sloping copper-clad roof. The entrance from the low N end leads to a progression of spaces through six storeys to a restaurant and viewing gallery in the tallest, S part. Visitors ascend in an inclined lift and progress down through the tiered floors.

120 BRIDGEWATER HALL, Barbirolli Square. By *RHWL Partnership*, 1993–6, the first free-standing auditorium of its size built in Britain since the Royal Festival Hall in 1951. Set at an angle to the square, it has a transparent prow pointing towards Albert Square and the town hall. Angled bays on the canal side house function rooms and foyers, etc. To Lower Mosley Street a glazed stair juts out from a stepped wall clad in silver-coloured aluminium panels. Finally there is a semicircular plant tower with tiers of glass planks. GERB vibration isolation bearings, developed to protect buildings in earthquake zones, were used for the first time in a concert hall to insulate the foundations

from the superstructure to shield the building from vibrations of traffic and trains. The undercroft is an impressive sight with silver service ducts snaking through the space. The (surprisingly small) GERB units, metal boxes with transparent panels revealing rows of springs, are sandwiched between huge white concrete piers.

INTERIOR. A tier of airy galleries with foyers and bars on four floors enjoys views between levels and out over the city and canal. The underside of the auditorium sails into the space through four floors, as at the Royal Festival Hall, a white inclined plane adorned with rippling enamelled and painted steel strips designed by *Deryck Healey*. The auditorium seats 2,400 and combines the traditional shoebox plan with the 'vineyard' format of terraced seating of Hans Scharoun's Philharmonie in Berlin (1963). The visual focus is the striking arrangement of the (functioning) silver-coloured pipes of the huge *Marcussen* organ behind the podium. In contrast to the whites and blues of the foyer, colours are muted, with oak floors and cherry-veneer acoustic boards. Tall piers support a heavy concrete roof structure but its density is counterbalanced by the height of the space and by the steel tensioning structure which doubles as a lighting rig.

3. Educational

MANCHESTER UNIVERSITY. *See* Chorlton-on-Medlock, Academic Institutions, p. 425.

UNIVERSITY OF MANCHESTER, INSTITUTE OF SCIENCE AND TECHNOLOGY. *See* Chorlton-on-Medlock, Academic Institutions, p. 431.

MANCHESTER METROPOLITAN UNIVERSITY AYTOUN CAMPUS, Whitworth Street, Aytoun Street and Chorlton Street. This was the site of the College of Commerce which joined with the College of Art and the John Dalton College of Technology to become Manchester Polytechnic in 1970 (for a fuller history and the University's other central Manchester buildings, *see* Chorlton-on-Medlock, Academic Institutions, p. 424). A twelve-storey tower and podium clad in grey precast concrete by *S. G. Besant Roberts*, the City Architect, 1966, was the college's first purpose-built premises. In front, and linked by a two-storey glass entrance block, the impressive contrast of AYTOUN LIBRARY AND COMPUTER CENTRE by *MBLC*, 1993. It has an irregular plan, made to fit the site. Five storeys, clad in shining white powder-coated aluminium panels. Inside a ramp sweeps up from the entrance foyer and turns back to the first floor.

SHEENA SIMON SCHOOL, Whitworth Street. By *Potts & Pickup*, opened in 1900 as Manchester Central School. Red brick and orange and buff terracotta with a tall corner turret. The building fronts a small park but the architects could not rise to the challenge; the Queen Anneish elevation is straggly and unimaginative.

4. Utilities, Transport and Bridges

ELECTRICITY STATION, Winser Street, beside the Rochdale Canal. Opened in 1901. Red brick, sandstone dressings, with giant round-headed arches with keystones. The large octagonal chimney is a local landmark. At the time the plant was one of the most compact in the country, reflecting the limitations on space in this crowded district. It was also one of the earliest combined heat and power stations in the country, providing steam heating for many nearby warehouses.

CENTRAL STATION, now the G-MEX CENTRE, Windmill Street. Manchester's fourth railway terminal, erected 1875–80. *Sacré, Johnson* and *Johnstone* were the chief engineers of the three companies that came together as the Cheshire Lines Committee to undertake the project. They were the Midland, the Great Northern and the Manchester, Sheffield & Lincolnshire railways. The huge wrought-iron and glass train shed is in the form of a segmental vault, spanning 210 ft (64 metres), only 30 ft (9 metres) less than St Pancras in London. There are eighteen main arch frames – the gable ends are double arches, giving fifteen bays – standing on a vast brick undercroft with intersecting tunnel vaults. Closure came in 1967 and the future of the building was not secured until the Greater Manchester Council acquired control in 1978. The building was converted to the Greater Manchester Exhibition and Events Centre, or G-Mex, by *Jack Bogle* of *Essex, Goodman & Suggitt* and opened in 1986. The shed ends were glazed and the scruffy frontage buildings replaced with low glazed foyers.

DEANSGATE STATION. See p. 350.

LIVERPOOL ROAD STATION. See p. 353.

119 OXFORD ROAD STATION, Oxford Road Station Approach. 1958–60. One of the most remarkable and unusual stations in the country for architectural form and technological interest. It is sited high on the 1849 MSJ&AR viaduct. An inverted timber prow rears up over the entrance, part of a roof formed by three prefabricated timber shells on huge laminated cruck-like timber beams. They are like the sort of structures George Pace was experimenting with for churches at this time, on a much larger scale. More beams support curved platform canopies with lines of porthole windows. The use of timber is continued with the booking office, café and seating. The design is by the British Railways London Midland Region architectural team (project architect *Max Clendinning*) with the engineer *Hugh Tottenham* of the Timber Development Association, who developed the use of laminated timber to create conoid shell roof forms. This was the Region's most architecturally dramatic experiment with timber shell technology, and it is an important example of its deployment to achieve large roof spans incorporating clerestory lighting. In this instance the fact that the lightness of the structure reduced foundation loads was a consideration. Substantially restored and repaired, 1996.

Prestolee. The River Irwell, crossed by the late C18 Packhorse Bridge, an aqueduct of 1797 carrying the Bolton & Bury Canal, and in between a C20 pipe bridge (p. 563)

2. Rochdale, College Bank flats, by R.D. Thornley succeeding W.H.G. Mercer, Borough Architects, 1966, from the Mayor's Parlour, Rochdale Town Hall (by W.H. Crossland, 1866–71, stained glass by Heaton, Butler & Bayne) (pp. 587, 596)
3. Milnrow, Rochdale Canal with warehouse, C19 weavers' houses, and Clegg Hall, early or mid-C17 (p. 522)
4. Bolton, early C20 commercial buildings, Bradshawgate (p. 145)
5. Salford looking W from Manchester

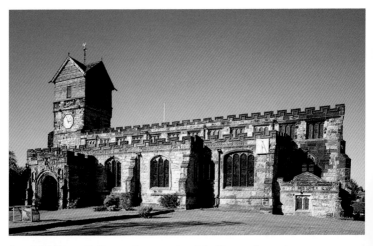

6. Middleton, St Leonard, C15 and C16, belfry C17 (p. 507)
7. Manchester Cathedral, C15 and C16, interior, stalls *c.* 1500–6 (p. 270)

8. Deane, St Mary, *c.* 1540s (p. 161)
9. Eccles, St Mary, interior nave roof, probably late C15, arcades and
    clerestory early C16 (p. 208)

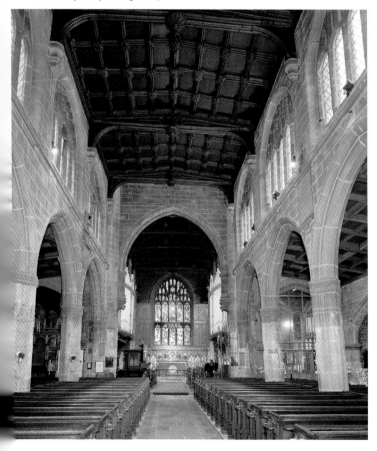

5. Manchester (Wythenshawe), Baguley Hall, hall, C14 (p. 504)
6. Bolton (Tonge Moor), Hall i' th' Wood, s side, C16 and C17 (p. 153)
7. Salford (Ordsall), Ordsall Hall, N side, early C16 (p. 636)

34. Milnrow, weavers' houses, Charles Lane, mid to late C19 (p. 522)
35. Ramsbottom, Hazelhurst Engineering Works, c. 1840 (p. 579)
36. Bolton (Barrow Bridge), millworkers' houses, early C19 (p. 168)
37. Bolton (Halliwell), bleachworkers' houses, 1847 (p. 165)

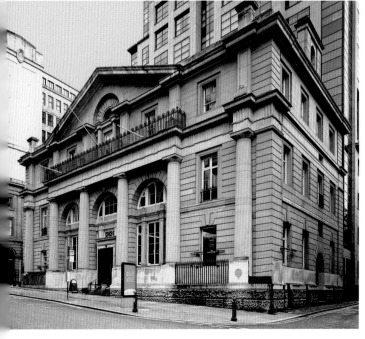

53. Bolton, St Stephen, Lever Bridge, by Edmund Sharpe, 1842–4, interior (p. 157)
54. Manchester (Blackley) St Peter, by E.H. Shellard, 1844, interior (p. 385)
55. Littleborough, St James, Calderbrook, by George Shaw, 1860–4 (p. 250)
56. Manchester (Hulme), St Mary, by J.S. Crowther, 1853–8 (p. 451)

57 | 59
58 | 60

61. Rochdale, Town Hall, by W.H. Crossland, 1866–71, tower by Alfred
    Waterhouse, 1885–7 (p. 594)
62. Bolton, Town Hall, by William Hill with George Woodhouse, 1866–73
    (p. 140)
63. Manchester, Town Hall, by Alfred Waterhouse, 1868–77 (p. 278)

64. Manchester Town Hall, by Alfred Waterhouse, 1868–77, entrance
    vestibule with statues of Joule by Alfred Gilbert, 1893, foreground, and
    Dalton by Sir Frances Chantrey, 1837, opposite (p. 283)
65. Rochdale, Town Hall, by W.H. Crossland, 1866–71, interior (p. 595)
66. Rochdale, Town Hall, Great Hall, stained glass by Heaton, Butler &
    Bayne, c. 1870 (p. 595)

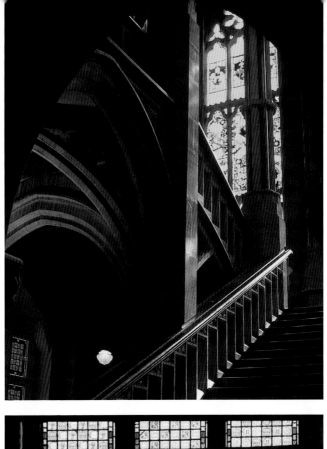

67. Denton, St Anne, by J. Medland & Henry Taylor, 1880–2 (p. 198)
68. Denton, St Anne's rectory, by J. Medland & Henry Taylor, 1882 (p. 200)
69. Rochdale, St Edmund, Falinge, by J. Medland Taylor, 1870–3, interior (p. 590)
70. Manchester (Gorton), St Francis, by E.W. Pugin, 1866–72 (p. 372)
71. Manchester (Ardwick), St Benedict, by J.S. Crowther, 1880 (p. 356)

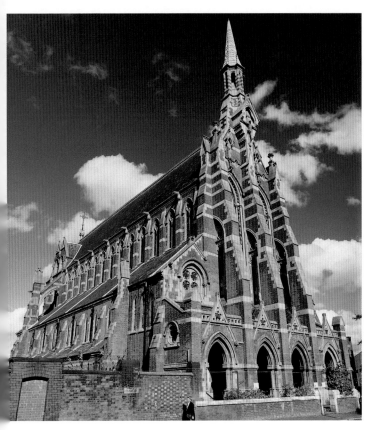

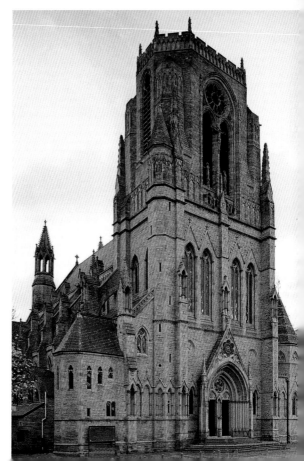

4. Manchester (Cheetham and Strangeways), Spanish and Portuguese Synagogue, now the Jewish Museum, by Edward Salomons, 1874 (p. 390)

5. Manchester (Chorlton-on-Medlock), Holy Name of Jesus, by J. A. Hansom and J.S. Hansom, 1869–71 (p. 419)

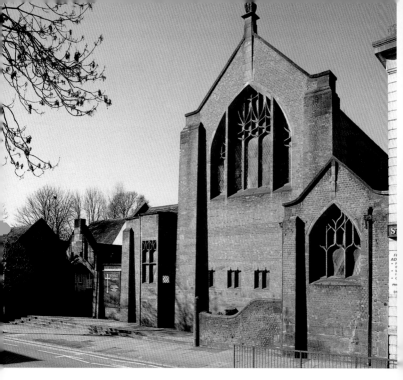

80. Prestwich, St Mary,
Monument to the Rev.
James Lyon, by R.W.
Sievier, *c.* 1833, detail
(p. 566)

81. Salford (Weaste and
Seedley), Weaste
Cemetery, Brotherton
Memorial, by T. Holmes
& W. Walker, carving by
T.R. Williams, after 1857
(p. 646)

82. Westhoughton, St James,
Daisy Hill, E window, by
Morris & Co., 1898
(p. 677)

83. Middleton, St Leonard,
design by G.F. Bodley,
made by Burlison &
Grylls, 1903, N aisle
window, detail (p. 508)

NAMES OF THE FALLEN

1939–45

7. Crompton and Shaw, First World War memorial, by Richard R. Goulden, 1923 (p. 195)

8. Radcliffe, First World War memorial, by Sydney March, 1922 (p. 574)

103. Bolton, Bolton School, by C.T. Adshead, designed 1917 (p. 164)
104. Oldham, King Street, Dronsfield Offices, by Henry Sellers, 1906–7 (p. 540)
105. Manchester (Wythenshawe), Leybrook Road, cottage flats, by Manchester City Council Housing Department, 1937 (p. 490)
106. Manchester (Blackley), Victoria Road, housing, by Manchester City Council Housing Department, 1903–4 (p. 387)
107. Middleton, Long Street, Fencegate and Redcroft, by Edgar Wood, 1895 (p. 516)

108. Peel Green, Barton Aerodrome, control tower, by G. Noel Hill, 1933 (p. 557)
109. Manchester (Heaton Park), aqueduct Terminal Building, by Alan Atkinson and Manchester City Engineers, and City Architects under L.C. Howitt, 1955, relief by Mitzi Cunliffe (p. 401)
110. Manchester (Wythenshawe), St Michael and All Angels, by N.G. Cachemaille-Day, 1936–7, interior (p. 493)
111. Manchester (Burnage), St Nicholas, by Cachemaille-Day & Lander, 1930–2 (p. 410)

121. Manchester
(Withington), Sir
William Siemens
House, by MBLC,
1989–90 (p. 487)
122. Manchester, Urbis,
by Ian Simpson
Architects, 2000–2
(p. 298)
123. Rochdale
(Castleton), Zen
Internet Office, by
Burr Design
Associates, 2001
(p. 606)
124. Stretford, Imperial
War Museum North
by Daniel Libeskind
1997–2002, interior
of air shard, looking
up (p. 653)

121	123
122	124

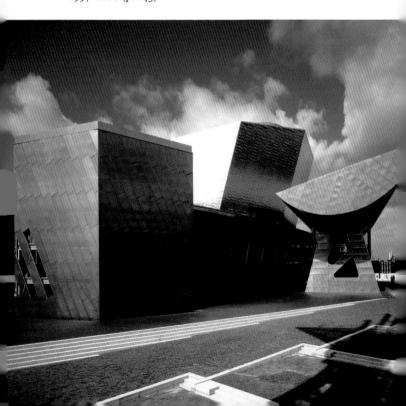

PICCADILLY STATION, Piccadilly Station Approach. The first station here opened in 1842, jointly operated by the Manchester & Birmingham Railway (later the London & North Western Railway, LNWR) and the Sheffield, Ashton-under-Lyne & Manchester Railway (later the Manchester, Sheffield & Lincolnshire Railway, MS&LR). Enlarged in 1866 and again in 1880–3 when the present roof was installed. The mutilated frontage on London Road includes the goods office entrance, Renaissance style with pilasters with fanciful ram's-head caps. The station frontage was rebuilt in 1959–66, and again in 2001–2 by *BDP*.

MS&LR LONDON WAREHOUSE, immediately N of Piccadilly Station. Of 1867, the survivor of a group of four. Massive, starkly grand seven-storeyed block of brick with stone dressings and small segmental-headed windows. The cast-iron columns, those on the ground floor with base diameters of over 2 ft (65 cm.), diminish in circumference on each floor and support a grid of riveted wrought-iron box girders with intermediate cast-iron beams carrying brick jack arches. There were originally eighteen internal hoists. The building was converted to apartments, 2000–1.

VICTORIA STATION, Victoria Station Approach. Opened in 1844 by the Liverpool & Manchester Railway and the Manchester & Leeds Railway. An L-shaped block on the corner of Hunts Bank Approach and Victoria Station Approach. *Robert Stephenson* was the designer of the original Hunts Bank Approach building. Stone, Italianate, with an added upper storey and wings. The station was extended in 1864–5, enlarged again in 1909 for the Lancashire & Yorkshire Railway, and adapted during the 1990s to accommodate the Metrolink. The long stone Baroque elevation to the street is unexciting, but there is attractive detail such as a glazed canopy to the street with the names of destinations and a painted map beside the northern entrance showing the railway network. Beneath it a bronze WAR MEMORIAL by *George Wragge*'s studio, unveiled 1922. Inside, the Edwardian booking hall survives, also a range consisting of a first-class restaurant, domed refreshment room, and bookstall, all with gold mosaic lettering on a turquoise ground. The refreshment room interior has marble-lined walls, mosaic and tiles, and the underside of the dome is richly decorated with festoons of fruit and flowers. Grafted on to the back of the station is the MANCHESTER EVENING NEWS ARENA by *Austin-Smith:Lord* with *Ellerbe Beckett*, 1995–6, a huge soulless sports and entertainment complex. The structural interest is in the use of reinforced concrete to improve sound insulation, and in the huge size of the roof which is spanned by a 345 ft (105 metre) steel truss.

MANCHESTER SOUTH JUNCTION & ALTRINCHAM RAILWAY VIADUCT (MSJ&AR). Built 1845–9 for an early suburban railway, started as a joint venture between the two original companies on the Piccadilly Station site. The 224 brick arches run between there and Liverpool Road, following approximately the route of the River Medlock and forming the visual boundary to the s side of the city centre. Constructed by the builder *David Bellhouse Jun.*; several of the cast-iron bridges were built by his son, the engineer and iron founder *Edward Taylor Bellhouse*.

LIGHT RAPID TRANSPORT SYSTEM 'METROLINK'. Constructed by a consortium of *GEC*, *John Mowlem & Co.* and *AMEC* (depot facilities). A Parliamentary Bill was deposited in 1984. Its first stage, opened 1992, linked the existing Bury and Altrincham suburban railway lines. The route is all overground, running from Piccadilly Station to Victoria Station and thence to Bury, with the Altrincham route branching off in Piccadilly Gardens. Ugly traction poles support most of the overhead wire system, and obtrusive ramps at the stops damage the setting of some important buildings in the city centre (*see* St Peter's Square). It has been a great success for commuters, and the system was extended to Eccles via Salford Quays in 1999, with further extension proposed.

MANCHESTER SHIP CANAL. The Canal is actually outside the City of Manchester, running on the line of the River Irwell between the boroughs of Salford and Trafford and on to the Mersey estuary. It was a Manchester Corporation scheme, however, and one of the greatest engineering projects of the Victorian age. The 1880s had seen manufacturing profitability in Manchester undermined by ruinously high transport costs, dock dues and handling charges, and the result had been factory closures and an economic downturn. The Canal transformed Manchester into an international port and diversified the industrial basis.

The Manchester Ship Canal Co. was instigated by the local industrialist Daniel Adamson in 1882, and the Manchester Ship Canal Act was passed in 1885. £5 million was raised by floating a share issue, and construction began in November 1887. Following the withdrawal of many backers, Manchester Corporation raised a further £5 million, and took over 51 per cent of the shares. The engineer *Sir Edward Leader Williams*, who was the general manager and engineer of the Bridgewater Navigation Company, became associated with the project in 1882. The project contractor was *Thomas Walker*, who had built the Severn Tunnel for the Great Western Railway, but he died before work was completed in 1894. The canal covers a distance of a little over thirty-five miles, linking Manchester to the Mersey estuary at Eastham, a few miles s of Liverpool. Docks were built in Salford and Trafford. The cut was made to the depth of the Suez Canal to ensure that large ocean-going ships could use it. It was a remarkable engineering feat, accompanied by technological innovations such as *Leader Williams*'s swing aqueduct at Barton-upon-Irwell (*see* Stretford).

Opened by Queen Victoria in 1894 in a ceremony attended by more than a million people, the Canal was dealing within two years with over one million tons of cargo annually, and

The opening of the Manchester Ship Canal, print, 1894

by 1914 it accounted for 5 per cent of national imports and 4.5 per cent of domestic exports. Manchester eventually became the country's third largest port. Economic upturn resulted, and the region was protected from some of the worst effects of interwar and post-war industrial depression. Decline set in from the 1960s. Regeneration of the docks in Trafford and Salford (*see* Stretford and Salford Quays, Salford) began in the 1980s.

ASHTON CANAL, Ducie Street. Built to transport coal from Ashton-under-Lyne and Oldham to fuel-hungry Manchester (*see* also Ashton-under-Lyne and Droylsden). The Act was passed in 1792. Narrower than most of the inland waterways in the North, it was for boats of 7 ft (2 metres) beam. *Benjamin Outram* was responsible for the part between Great Ancoats Street and the BASIN, which lay on the s side of Ducie Street beneath the railway goods yard, where it can be seen truncated just NE of the London Warehouse (*see* above). An AQUEDUCT, *c.* 1794–9, also by Outram, crosses Store Street, NE of the basin. Skewed construction, derived from William Chapman's pioneering designs for the Grand Canal at Naas in County Kildare, Ireland, of a decade before. It is the earliest surviving example of the improved 'English System' of building skewed bridges.

BRIDGEWATER CANAL. *See* Castlefield, p. 351.

MANCHESTER & SALFORD JUNCTION CANAL, 1836–9. This runs beneath Barbirolli Square, between the branch of the Rochdale Canal beside the Bridgewater Hall and the Irwell near the w end of Quay Street, a distance of ⅝ mile. The E part was closed and backfilled when Central Station was built. In 1899 the remaining w part received a boost when the Great

Northern Railway Goods Warehouse was constructed (*see* p. 334), incorporating an interchange with the canal which allowed goods to be transported to and from the railway via the Irwell and the Ship Canal.

ROCHDALE CANAL, Dale Street. The Rochdale was the first transpennine canal, linking the Bridgewater Canal in Manchester with the Calder & Hebble Canal in Sowerby Bridge, completing the route between Hull on the E coast and Liverpool on the W. *John Rennie,* assisted by *William Crosley,* undertook surveys during 1791, and Crosley went on to act as engineer, with advice from *William Jessop.* The Act was passed in 1794 and the canal was completed 1804–6.

The TERMINAL BASIN on Dale Street has an entrance with a castellated stone archway of 1822, with a tiny LODGE attached behind and the unassuming early C19 OFFICES of the Canal Company to the l. The basin is being redeveloped (2004) with new buildings and canal branches. Two canal buildings survive. The first, l. of the entrance, is a four-storey WAREHOUSE, dated 1806 and constructed from millstone grit blocks. The initials WC on the datestone suggest it may have been designed by William Crosley. The elevation to the street (W) has a slightly projecting central bay, and there is a Venetian window in the N gable end. Of considerable interest as the earliest surviving canal warehouse in the city which differs structurally from those of the Bridgewater Basin (*see* Castlefield, Perambulation 4), it is the only survivor of the period in Manchester to use cast-iron columns throughout. It has timber floors supported by unusual branched cast-iron columns with octagonal bases. They have two struts attached to fish-bellied plates supporting timber beams. On the upper floors columns have flanges to receive shuttering for flexible division of the floor space. There are arched shipping holes to the E towards the basin, so that goods could be unloaded from internal wet docks. (Conversion to offices is planned, 2004.)

A high breast-shot WATER WHEEL of cast iron and timber served this and a demolished warehouse to the E. Attributed to the engineer *T. C. Hewes,* and installed in 1824, it survives in a subterranean stone chamber to the S of the building. On the far, NE side of the basin a brick WAREHOUSE of 1836, with small windows with round heads and a range of shipping holes on the S side. It was a grain warehouse, with timber floors and cast-iron columns; converted to flats, 2003–4.

ALBERT BRIDGE. *See* p. 347.

BLACKFRIARS BRIDGE, Blackfriars Street. 1818–20. *Thomas Wright* of Salford won the competition in 1818. Three stately arches with coupled Ionic columns rising from cutwaters.

HANGING BRIDGE. *See* p. 342.

IRK BRIDGE, Hunt's Bank Approach. The River Irk was culverted between the Irwell and Victoria Station in five campaigns through the C19. This was a principal crossing-point into Manchester from the N, on the line of the Roman road to Ribchester. City Engineers' plans show three separate phases of stone bridges over the Irk beneath the road, perhaps including the remains of C18 and earlier bridges.

TRINITY BRIDGE. *See* Salford, p. 622.

VICTORIA BRIDGE, Victoria Street. 1837–9, replacing the C14 bridge over the Irwell which linked Manchester with Salford. Stone, with a heavy parapet and in the middle on each side the Queen's orb on a massive Grecian scroll.

STREETS: THE COMMERCIAL CORE

The central area of Manchester is bounded on the W side just short of Deansgate, on the N side by Market Street, Piccadilly Gardens and Piccadilly, on the E side by London Road, on the S side by Whitworth Street West, Granby Row, and the boundary with Chorlton-on-Medlock (see map p. 306–7). This is the area to the S and SE of the medieval town, which was developed in the C18 and then intensively rebuilt as the civic and commercial centre in the C19 and C20. Its streets are so rich architecturally that they need to be described individually. They are arranged alphabetically.

ALBERT SQUARE. Created when the Town Hall (*see* Public Buildings, p. 278) was built on the old town yard. Only the S side can make any claim to be a worthy foil for the town hall. On the corner with Mount Street, l., Nos. 20–21 is by *G. T. Redmayne* for the Scottish Widows Fund Life Assurance Society, dated 1872. Redmayne, a pupil of Alfred Waterhouse, uses motifs such as tourelles and tall traceried windows echoing his master's town hall. Beside it No. 17, CARLTON HOUSE, free Gothic with three-storey oriels crowned by gabled dormers, 1872 by *Clegg & Knowles*, and more ornate than their contemporary warehouses. Also by them No. 16, ALBERT CHAMBERS, 1873, Venetian Gothic with arched window heads springing from giant pilasters and a busy frieze at the top, crowned by spiky battlements. The MEMORIAL HALL, on the r. corner, 1863–6 by *Thomas Worthington*, was erected to commemorate the secession of Nonconformist clergy in 1662. An awkward site with its longer side to Southmill Street. Brick and stone and decidedly Venetian Gothic with ranges of traceried windows lighting the hall on the topmost floor. Worthington had returned from his second tour of Italy in 1858, and this reflects what he had absorbed. LLOYDS HOUSE pokes its nose into the SW corner of the square. By *Speakman & Charlesworth*, 1868. Gothic, a relatively early use for a warehouse. The focus is at the corner entrance with an open colonnade supporting an octagonal tower with a tall pyramidal roof. It was probably the city's first purpose-built packing warehouse, becoming a model for the building type.

The W side has little to offer apart from No. 1, in Portland stone, by *Percy Scott Worthington* c. 1919. Tall, with a narrow

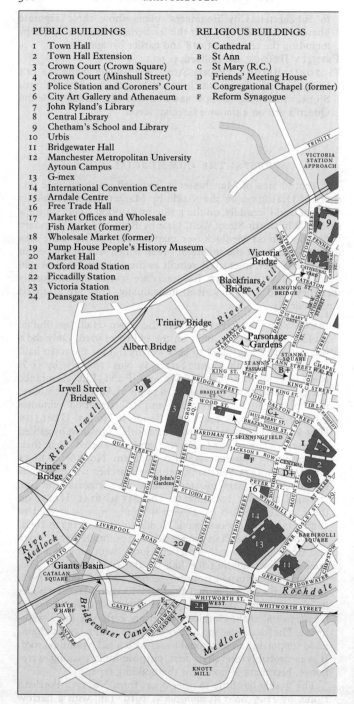

PUBLIC BUILDINGS

1 Town Hall
2 Town Hall Extension
3 Crown Court (Crown Square)
4 Crown Court (Minshull Street)
5 Police Station and Coroners' Court
6 City Art Gallery and Athenaeum
7 John Ryland's Library
8 Central Library
9 Chetham's School and Library
10 Urbis
11 Bridgewater Hall
12 Manchester Metropolitan University
      Aytoun Campus
13 G-mex
14 International Convention Centre
15 Arndale Centre
16 Free Trade Hall
17 Market Offices and Wholesale
      Fish Market (former)
18 Wholesale Market (former)
19 Pump House People's History Museum
20 Market Hall
21 Oxford Road Station
22 Piccadilly Station
23 Victoria Station
24 Deansgate Station

RELIGIOUS BUILDINGS

A Cathedral
B St Ann
C St Mary (R.C.)
D Friends' Meeting House
E Congregational Chapel (former)
F Reform Synagogue

Manchester, the centre

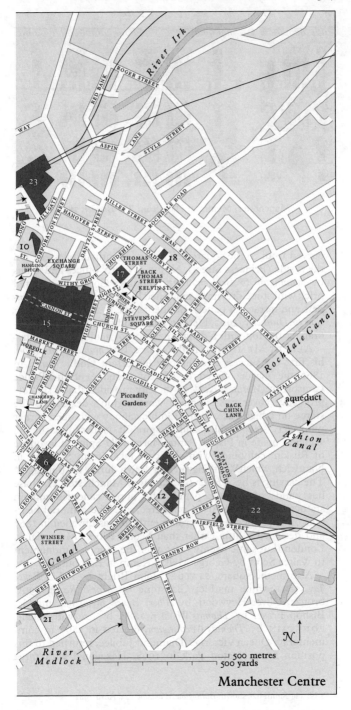

Manchester Centre

Manchester, Memorial Hall, from *The Builder*, 1865

curved front to the square and giant Corinthian pilasters. On the N side (Princess Street), Nos. 1–7, pretty offices and shops by *Pennington & Bridgen*, 1877. Tudorish Gothic, in soft red brick with stone dressings, enlivened by delicate traceried parapets and terracotta panels. Beside it Nos. 9–21 by *Waddington, Son & Dunkerly*, 1902, is stone-faced and much grander, elaborate at the top with a conglomeration of gables and turrets.

ALBERT MEMORIAL, in the square. By *Thomas Worthington*, his first big success and his first important Gothic work. In 1862 the mayor offered to present a statue of the Prince Consort by *Matthew Noble* to the city provided that a suitable protective cover was supplied. Worthington's design has the statue on a high base, with a Gothic canopy with open corner pinnacles, steep gables and a spire. It is based partly on sketches made in Pisa of Santa Maria della Spina, a favourite of Ruskin, combined with elements taken from St Mary in Nantwich, which Worthington had drawn during his pupilage.* The carving is by *T. R. & E. Williams* of Manchester. The base has bands of heraldic panels, the upper canopies contain statues representing Art, Commerce, etc. The armorial bearings of the Prince feature prominently. It was unveiled in 1867 and designed a little earlier than Scott's Albert Memorial in London (but some twenty years after the canopied monument to Walter Scott by George Meikle Kemp in Edinburgh).

Also in the square, STATUES: John Bright by *Albert Bruce Joy*, 1891, white marble; Gladstone by *Mario Raggi*, 1901, bronze; Oliver Heywood, by *Albert Bruce Joy*, 1894, marble; Bishop Fraser by *Thomas Woolner*, 1888, bronze with reliefs. FOUNTAIN by *Thomas Worthington*, erected in 1897 to commemorate Queen Victoria's Diamond Jubilee, returned to this position from Heaton Park in 1998. Hexagonal with three

* As Nicola Smith has shown, *Burlington Magazine* 123, April 1981.

basins, bronze dolphin on top and winged beasts below by *John Cassidy*.

ALBION STREET. On the E side the façade of a canalside warehouse of 1869 by *Mangnall & Littlewood* with unusual cast-iron traceried windows, new offices behind.

AYTOUN STREET. THE GRAND, NE side, started as a warehouse of 1867–8 by *Mills & Murgatroyd* and was converted to a hotel by them in 1883. Stone, Italianate, rusticated ground floor, two upper floors linked by a giant arcade and two more floors above. Conversion to flats has ruined its proportions by giving it two extra storeys.

BARBIROLLI SQUARE. By *RHWL Partnership*, 1990s, as the setting for their Bridgewater Hall (*see* Public Buildings, p. 298). Nos. 100 and 101 loom over the N side, office buildings, also by *RHWL Partnership*, 1998–9. Pale grey granite and reflective glass. Built as part of the funding package for the Bridgewater Hall, which they upstage by their large size and showy finishes. SCULPTURE by *Kan Yasuda*, 1996, Touchstone, a big, smooth, sensuously curved pebble of marble.

BLOOM STREET. The interest is on the E side. From the N, No. 11, by *Pennington & Bridgen*, 1889, a severe stripped palazzo, not at all like their usual work. Further S a range of small offices and warehouses, the best No. 17, ALBERT HOUSE, of 1903 by *Mills & Murgatroyd*. Red sandstone, fine red brick and terracotta, with Art Nouveau detailing. Further S beyond Sackville Street there are some plain early C19 houses of two and three storeys.

BOOTH STREET. From NW end, at the junction with Pall Mall. No. 1, N side, was built 1846–7 for R. H. Greg & Co. by *R. E. Whittaker*. A large palazzo warehouse on an island site, the half-basement vermiculated, ground floor ashlar, the rest brick with stone dressings. Important as an example of fireproof construction applied to a warehouse, with cast-iron columns and beams and brick jack arches. Manchester warehouses seldom adopted this form, preferring to stick to the cheaper option of timber floors. Opposite, two attractive buildings by *Edward Salomons*. No. 6, MASSEY CHAMBERS, 1872, ornate Renaissance style, symmetrical, with a parapet with a central pedimented dormer supported by putti. The *piano nobile* features carved heads (one veiled). Its more robust neighbour, Nos. 8–10, is the former MANCHESTER & SALFORD TRUSTEE SAVINGS BANK, opened in 1874. Three storeys with a tall *piano nobile* featuring graceful windows and carved arched window heads.

BROWN STREET. The SCOTTISH PROVIDENT building, by *Cruickshank & Seward*, 1971, has an aggressive look given by the closely set slits on the ground floor. Opposite Nos. 46–48, the former Brook's Bank, by *George Truefitt*, dated 1868, with an intricate openwork iron crown atop a three-storey semicircular corner oriel. The beautifully crisp carving is by *Williams & Mooney*. Further S, on the E side, the sober mid-to-late C19 CHANCERY CHAMBERS. Its stone rusticated base, brick

upper floors and heavy top cornice are echoed in simplified
form in the attached office building around the corner in
Chancery Lane, by *Hamilton Associates*, 1994.

CENTRAL STREET. N side. A big four-storey palazzo warehouse
of *c*. 1865, so similar in style to No. 109 Princess Street by *Clegg
& Knowles* that it must also be by them.

CHAPEL WALKS. On the N side OLD HALF MOON
CHAMBERS, by *Speakman & Charlesworth*, 1870. The first two
storeys are ornate, with entertaining animal carvings and
grouped arched windows.

  Further E, TUDOR HOUSE by *Barker & Ellis*, 1889, brick
below and elaborate half-timbering above. On the corner with
Pall Mall a palazzo-style warehouse of *c*. 1868 looks like a
typical *Clegg & Knowles* effort.

CHARLOTTE STREET. The S side has one of the very best and
most complete ranges of mid-C19 commercial warehouses.
Built between *c*. 1850 and *c*. 1865, all are by *Edward Walters*, in
his personal and highly influential interpretation of the palazzo
style. With one exception each occupies a block with access to
the loading bays from the side streets. All are of fine brick
dressed with stone, of five storeys over a basement. What
matters in all is the conscientious and discriminating decoration, the amount of which depended on the purse of the client.
From the E: No. 36, *c*. 1855–60, has a rusticated stone plinth
and ground-floor windows with segmental heads. Above,
grouped windows with round heads, the storeys divided by
dentilled sill bands. Heavy cornice surmounted by a parapet
and big corniced chimneys at the corners. Next No. 34, *c*. 1855,
the simplest, with round-arched openings to the ground, segmental above, stone sill bands, and quoins. The ground-floor
window keystones are linked to the sill band above. Now a
block is skipped and Nos. 14–16, *c*. 1856–8 is richer. The
ground floor and basement, in stone, are linked in a continuous
arcade with central paired doors. Second-floor windows have
alternating segmental and triangular pediments. Along the
eaves a staccato rhythm of chimneys.* The corner is splayed
and rusticated, the cornices nicked and the corner chimney
angled to the splay. Finally, No. 10, the most ornate and probably the latest, *c*. 1865. Combined sills and pediments and crisp
detailing create a sophisticated interplay between vertical and
horizontal.

CHATHAM STREET. S side, on the corner of Raby Street, a Free
Style composition with Arts and Crafts touches, with an attrac-
tive understated entrance front and a rooftop playground. By
F. B. Dunkerley, dated 1910, built for the Manchester and
Salford Boys' and Girls' Refuges and Homes Society.

CHEPSTOW STREET. Facing the junction with Great
Bridgewater Street, CANADA HOUSE, a ten-bay, six-storey
warehouse fronted in pale orange terracotta. 1909, by *W. &
G. Higginbottom*. The rear is a glazed screen with full-height

---

* Some of the chimneys were probably ventilators.

octagonal piers. CHEPSTOW HOUSE, to the sw, is a former packing warehouse (now flats), built in 1874 for Samuel Mendel by *Speakman, Son & Hickson*. The usual corner turret, and a long façade with the openings grouped and treated differently to give variety.

CHORLTON STREET. Near the e end, n side, two former warehouses. First No. 47, MINSHULL HOUSE, probably mid-C19, with later additions to the rear and l. It has a huge rusticated arched entrance (now infilled) in the centre. To the rear on the former Grocers' Company Coal Wharf (now a car park), there is a jetty at first floor level. Inside the upper floors have an impressive system of iron tie-rods and struts for the overhanging upper floor. Next, No. 45, a mid- or later C19 warehouse. Beside it a lock house, rebuilt in the early C20, straddles the canal. Near the junction with Portland Street a seven-storey office building, ARTHUR HOUSE by *Cruickshank & Seward*, 1962, conspicuous for the use of white concrete favoured by the firm at that time.

COOPER STREET continues Fountain Street to the sw. No. 9 WALDORF HOUSE, was designed by *W. Mangnall* for the Freemasons in 1863. Masonic emblems proliferate and there are richly carved Venetian Gothic motifs, rows of pilasters and niches with statues, but the elevation is crowded and the details fail to cohere.

CROSS STREET, linking Albert Square to Market Street, is lined with large C19 and C20 commercial buildings, several by *Charles Heathcote*. For the Royal Exchange *see* Exchange Street, for Nos. 1–7 Princess Street, *see* Albert Square. At the s end, w side, early C20 insurance offices in *Heathcote*'s blocky and vigorous Baroque, of red sandstone with grey granite. A good example of this architect's skill at handling corner sites. BOW CHAMBERS opposite, offices and shops of 1869 by *Speakman & Charlesworth*, has showy polished granite columns to the ground-floor shops. No. 62–68, w side, EAGLE STAR HOUSE, on an island site, is by *Charles Heathcote & Sons*, 1911, not large, with a powerful cornice, rounded corners, huge Norman Shaw-style chimneys and nice Edwardian Baroque motifs convincingly and firmly controlled. One of the best of his city-centre buildings. Opposite (e side) on the corner with King Street is No. 37, 1895, also by *Charles Heathcote* for the Northern Rock Building Society. On the other corner LLOYDS BANK, completed 1915. *Heathcote* again, an overpowering confection, richly Baroque, in Portland stone. The carvings and statuary are by *Earp, Hobbs & Miller*. The banking hall is resplendent in coloured marble with a big glazed barrel vault.

MR THOMAS'S CHOP HOUSE, w side, dated 1901. A sudden, almost comical change of scale. One narrow bay only, three storeys with an attic. Red brick and buff terracotta with Art Nouveau motifs. The corner entrance, two-storeyed oriel and elaborate crowning gable combine with lively effect. This part, originally a shop and offices, was designed by *Mills & Murgatroyd*; the chop house behind, facing St Ann's

Churchyard, and also dated 1901, is by *Woodhouse & Willoughby*, in similar style. Next, HANOVER HOUSE, w side, built as a Conservative club in 1875–6, by *Robert Walker* with *Horton & Bridgford*. Italianate with richly carved window tympana contrasting effectively with smooth ashlar walls. On the NW corner of St Ann's Street ALLIANCE HOUSE by *Heathcote & Rawle, c.* 1890. All in stone in eclectic style.

The OBSERVATORY on the E side, an office block by *Holford Associates*, 1995–7, is notable only for its size and the fact that it incorporates the CROSS STREET CHAPEL (Unitarian), on the ground floor. Founded in 1698, the chapel was destroyed during the Second World War and replaced during the 1950s. The new chapel was designed by *Edwina Wilson* of Holford Associates in consultation with the congregation. To the r. a hall with separate street access, to the l. the entrance to the chapel, in a splay at the corner. The meeting room is a double-storey drum with a circular colonnade of cylindrical piers with foyer and corridor curving around it.

COMMERCIAL BUILDINGS further N, more offices and shops of *c.* 1868 by *Walters, Barker & Ellis*. Walters had retired by this time and so had nothing to do with this rather lacklustre composition. The interest is in the use of stone facing instead of brick and the introduction of Continental Gothic motifs, with ranks of grouped windows and variation in the form taken by the window heads.

EXCHANGE STREET is physically and visually part of St Ann's Square. It now links with New Cathedral Street, a pedestrian route running N to the Cathedral (*see* p. 267). Exchange Street was laid out in 1777 to link the square with the market place. It is dominated by the ROYAL EXCHANGE. This has a grand classical Edwardian exterior of 1914–21 by *Bradshaw Gass & Hope*; within is a radically modern theatre by *Levitt, Bernstein Associates*, completed 1976.

The Lord of the Manor Sir Oswald Mosley built the first exchange in 1729, N of the present building. It was replaced by a Neoclassical building by *Thomas Harrison* in 1806–9, enlarged by *Alex Mills* in 1847–9, then replaced by *Mills & Murgatroyd* in 1869–74 before the present building came. Business was initially transacted between mill and warehouse owners, importers, finishers, etc. but before long trading was left to their representatives – managers, agents and salesmen. Decline came through slumps in trade, the advent of new communications and rationalization of many little businesses into large conglomerates, though trading continued until 1968.

In 1973 the empty building was used to house a temporary theatre. The theatre-in-the-round plan followed a line of succession from Elizabethan circular playhouses to Sir Tyrone Guthrie's improvised theatre instituted in 1946 in Edinburgh, and subsequent buildings at Stratford, Chichester and Sheffield. The idea of creating a permanent structure followed and the theatre group collaborated with *Richard Negri*, who was subsequently appointed as the designer. *Levitt, Bernstein*

Associates were chosen as architects with *Max Fordham & Partners* and *Ove Arup* as engineers. *Levitt, Bernstein Associates* came back to carry out necessary repairs and introduce improvements after severe damage caused by the 1996 bomb.

The present building had to cater for eleven thousand members and boasted of being the largest place of assembly for trades in the world. It takes up the E side of the street and part of St Ann's Square. All in stone, with giant columns and pilasters and a round angle tower at the corner. In rebuilding after war damage the hall was truncated. Entering the building is a theatrical experience in itself. A glass lift (part of the 1990s improvements) brings one to the entrance of the enormous hall, with giant columns and three glass domes. Beneath the largest, central, dome and suspended from the four central columns is a tubular steel theatre-in-the-round, a high-tech 'Lunar Module' (as it was soon christened). The design is ingenious. The four piers support welded tubular steel trusses spanning 98 ft (30 metres). Secondary trusses then span between the two main ones so that a square is formed. Within the square the theatre is seven-sided, so that the tiers of seats are not directly opposite one another. The 1990s refurbishment introduced new lighting and colour schemes. The domes were reglazed and swathes of colour splashed on the upper glazing and glass entrance doors, to designs by *Amber Hiscott*.

FAIRFIELD STREET. Outlying, E of the London Road junction, the STAR AND GARTER pub, dated 1877, Queen Anne style, including panels with sunflower designs. W of the junction, S side, a former Temperance coffee house by *Charles Heathcote*, 1902. Plain, of red brick, with big gables.

FAULKNER STREET. The CHINESE IMPERIAL ARCH, a traditional design built by Chinese craft workers in 1987, straddling the street close to the junction of Nicholas Street, proclaims that we are in Manchester's Chinatown. The E side is lined with former commercial warehouses. Nos. 41–43, by *Thomas Fish Taylor*, 1846, is Grecian, with an absurdly high stone base and attached Doric columns supporting a pediment – hopelessly incorrect, but done with such panache that it is difficult not to like it. Warehouses of more conventional design follow until the corner with Nicholas Street is reached. Here is No. 55, a big brick job by *Clegg & Knowles*, 1870, a departure from their usual style, with verticality emphasized by giant pilasters. On the same side Nos. 59–61 was a mid-C19 milliner's shop. Door and windows in stone surrounds, attic workshop with a continuous range of windows.

FOUNTAIN STREET is a continuation of Cooper Street. Nos. 66–68 on the corner of Booth Street is a colourful Venetian Gothic affair by *Clegg & Knowles*, dated 1868, in warm red brick with sandstone dressings. No. 60, by *Ratcliffe Groves Partnership*, 1992, clad in pale stone, has a very prominent gracefully curving eaves cornice. Beside it a deferential extension to Alfred Waterhouse's No. 60 Spring Gardens, by *Cullearn & Philips*, 1988–9. The best building is No. 46, W side, by *Thomas*

Worthington. Built for Overseers' and Churchwardens' offices in 1852, with the two top floors added in 1858. Each floor is treated differently, with a range of œil-de-bœuf windows in stone frames in the attic. Towards the N end of the street the SHAKESPEARE pub, rebuilt 1923 by *W. Johnson & Sons*, incorporating parts of a demolished building from Chester. Some of the carving and bargeboards, as well as the crude caryatids of the tympanum over the entrance, are probably authentic C17 work, the rest mock timber-framing.

GEORGE STREET. At the N end, W side, the former telephone exchange, RUTHERFORD HOUSE, built by the *Ministry of Public Buildings and Works* in 1967. A disciplined elevation of six storeys. Slim vertical ribs front a white grid with the horizontals stressed by dark strips. To the S, E side, a mid-C19 stone warehouse on the corner of Charlotte Street, sometimes attributed to *Walters*. Texture is carefully controlled: rusticated basement, channelled ground floor, four storeys above, with ranks of windows between superimposed pilasters. Further S on the corner of Nicholas Street No. 33, a warehouse by *I. & J. P. Holden*, 1845. Further S still, Nos. 39–41, by *Walters*, c. 1845, all fronted in stone, rusticated ashlar below and (unusually) coursed rubble above. On the other side of Princess Street, No. 63 is a palazzo warehouse of c. 1857. The quality of the design has led some to attribute the building to *Walters*.*

GRANBY ROW. An area of imposing Edwardian warehouses, now the centre of Granby Village, designed by *Halliday Meecham*, 1989. New blocks of flats were added in imitation Edwardian warehouse style, and existing buildings converted into flats. ORIENT HOUSE by *G. H. Goldsmith*, c. 1914, is one of the most extravagant, six storeys with attics, of white faience with a giant Ionic colonnade. The back and part of the side is exposed, showing the steel frame with glass curtain-walling. Beside it GRANBY HOUSE (Nos. 61–63), also by *Goldsmith* but of 1908 and completely different in spirit and style. Red brick with Portland stone dressings and Art Nouveau motifs. The gabled corner bays are framed by polygonal piers giving a faintly Elizabethan accent.

GREAT BRIDGEWATER STREET. Attached to the Tootal Broadhurst, Lee & Co. building (*see* Oxford Street), LEE HOUSE, S side, is the eight-storey base of a proposed seventeen-storey tower. It is by *Harry S. Fairhurst & Son* with *Henry Sellers*, 1928–31, and one of the very best interwar buildings in the centre. The steel frame is clad in fine, small brownish bricks in delicately ribbed panels between canted window bays. Doors and loading bays in Portland stone surrounds with understated Art Deco mouldings; similar mouldings to attach the rail at the top. The bronzed multi-paned glazing was removed in late C20 refurbishment, so some of the subtle interplay has been lost. It was designed so that additional storeys could be added, and a plan of 2003 proposes to do just that, to the original design.

* Dr A. V. Cooper attributes it to *J. Pickard*.

Further w on an island site the jaunty early C19 PEVERIL OF THE PEAK pub holds its own thanks to a refurbishment of *c.* 1900, when the street elevations were cased in coloured tiles. The interior is good too, with small rooms and coloured glass screens. Further w, s side, the early C19 BRITONS PROTECTION pub is early C19 revamped in the 1930s, with much interior decoration of that date.

JOHN DALTON STREET. On the s side No. 16, a five-storey polychromatic Italianate office building of 1865 by *Edward Salomons*, incorporated into TRINITY COURT, offices and shops by *Roger Stephenson* of *Stephenson Architecture*, 1991–2. A superior façade job, in the quality of the new spaces and in the treatment of old work too. New shops are set back to the l. with the entrance to the offices to the r. The office accommodation is in two blocks divided by an impressive and generous atrium pouring light into the heart of the building, with a stair which starts as stone and changes to steel. Finishes are in limestone and marble.

KENNEDY STREET runs parallel to Booth Street. The interest is on the NE side, where the most notable building is the delightful MANCHESTER LAW LIBRARY by *Thomas Hartas*, 1884–5, home of one of the oldest provincial law libraries, founded in 1820. Venetian Gothic, only three bays, each divided into three again with richly traceried and strongly moulded frames to the openings. An oriel marks the first-floor reading room; steps lead up to the entrance, r., recessed behind a traceried screen. Three floors with two main staircases. Entrance foyer with the entrance to the library itself to the l. and a top-lit staircase leading up to the reading room and to second-floor rooms which could be let separately. The ground floor housed a circulating library (now with C20 furnishings). Stairs lead directly from it to the reading room with most of the (slightly rearranged) attractive original fittings, e.g. tall bookcases with cresting and slender detached shafts, and stained glass by *S. Evans* with roundels showing judges in wigs.

A gap where good C19 buildings were allowed to collapse in 2003 is to be redeveloped. No. 36, by *Nicholson & Mottram*, 1878, stone, Gothic, with strongly moulded elements, is in parlous condition. At the N end of the street, three late C18 houses which are now pubs.

KING STREET. Described by an American visitor in 1777 as the best built of Manchester streets: 'long and sufficiently wide; most of its houses noble'. The s part has kept its Georgian proportions but only two buildings of that date survive. The rest date mainly from the later C19, mostly shops. They are not large, generally of three or four storeys only, with varied narrow frontages, some with delicate cast-iron window arcades. It is on the N part that there is real excitement.

The start is at the W end near the junction with Deansgate. On the s side, Nos. 8–14, offices and shops by *Clegg & Knowles*, 1875. The office entrances have fine carved detail. Opposite,

Nos. 15–17 by *Maxwell & Tuke*, 1902, high and elaborate, all in half-timbering. For Old Exchange Buildings on the N side, *see* St Ann's Square. Nos. 35–37, N side, is a five-bay brick house, originally with wings, built in 1736 for Dr Peter Waring, which became a bank in the late C18. Its interior has gone and the wings were replaced by 1990s glass-shop fronts. No. 56, opposite, has early C18 origins, though you would hardly know it to look at the façade with its C20 shutters and balconies.* Further along, S side, No. 62 is by *Pennington & Bridgen*, 1874, Gothic, but lacking the delicacy of much of their other work.

King Street continues E of Cross Street. (For Lloyds Bank and the former Northern Rock Building Society premises *see* Cross Street.) The wider top part leads into the otherwise crowded banking and financial quarter. *Waterhouse*'s minor but unmistakable PRUDENTIAL ASSURANCE building of 1888–96, S side, red brick and terracotta, has the top part shorn off and the ground floor now opened out for shops.

No. 82, S side, is the former BRANCH BANK OF ENGLAND by *Charles Cockerell*, 1845–6. The bank was given the right to establish branches in 1826 as compensation for its loss of monopoly of joint-stock banking. Cockerell succeeded John Soane as the Bank's architect in 1833. He was asked to design branch buildings in Manchester, Liverpool and Bristol in 1844. The Manchester design is the earliest and most expansive, though the spirit is the same. Only five bays with giant attached columns and a crowning motif of an aedicule window in an arch which pushes up the pediment. The pediment is three bays wide, and in this part the lower windows are large and arched with a recessed tripartite arrangement with lunette over. They correspond to the banking hall. Cockerell uses one of the simplest of Greek orders, from the Temple of Apollo at Delos, which he had employed at Oakley Park, Shropshire. Inside, a tunnel vault leads to a saucer dome, continuing as another tunnel vault. The dome stands on four cast-iron Tuscan columns with pierced capitals. The King Street entrance is an early C20 insertion and the original arched opening on the W side of Pall Mall was reinstated in 1995, when the building was reduced to the status of an entrance foyer to the office block behind, by *Holford Associates*. This is too large and high, of fifteen storeys, with a tired broken pediment motif on top.

Still on the S side, on the E corner of Pall Mall, Nos. 84–86 was built in 1841–2 by *Richard Lane* 'after the example of the Monument of Thrasyllus' as he put it, for the Manchester & Salford Savings Bank. The ground floor arcade with polished granite trim is a rebuilding of 1904 by a deferential *Charles Heathcote* for the Sun Insurance Co. The upper part, of sandstone ashlar, is indeed closely based on Stuart & Revett's illus-

---

* The interior retains C18 panelling and early C18 plasterwork, according to the list description.

tration. Giant pilasters and laurel wreaths in the frieze, surmounted by a pedestal.

Next SHIP CANAL HOUSE (s side), 1924–7 by *Harry S. Fairhurst*. Portland stone and classical, eight storeys stepped back at sixth- and seventh-storey levels. Statue of Neptune by *Earp, Hobbs & Miller*. ATLAS HOUSE, 1929, by *Michael Waterhouse*, is squashed up next to it on the corner of Brown Street. Opposite (N side), two of the city's most interesting commercial buildings of the 1960s. The first is the former DISTRICT BANK by *Casson, Conder & Partners*, 1966–9. It is only six storeys high, entirely faced with granite, vertically ribbed, and that is a relief after all the raw concrete and tinny curtain-walling of many of its contemporaries. The general shape is a slab set back from the streets and at its two ends irregular octagons elongated at right angles to the slab. On the ground floor the area between the slab and streets is filled in, and there are here also canted projections, just as the roof is canted too. The impressive banking hall is no more, lost during a conversion to shops, 2000. Next to it No. 55 PALL MALL COURT, by *Brett & Pollen*, 1969 for London Assurance Ltd. Strongly modelled and striking with tall angled service towers, that to the street with a single window slit. The lower part is tiered, with ranks of boxed-out windows. Cladding throughout is bronze patinated aluminium, and blue-bronze Staffordshire brick or mosaic.

The MIDLAND BANK, s side, occupies an island site at the top (E end) of the street. It is the King of King Street, the major work in Manchester of *Sir Edwin Lutyens* in collaboration with *Whinney, Son & Austen Hall*, who took care of the practical side. Carving was by *J. Ashton Floyd* of Manchester. Designed 1928, erected 1933–5. It is a nearly square block and treated as such, with the upper motifs identical on all four sides. The two angle porches are in King Street, and the entrances all have pilasters which die away and disappear, as at Lutyens's Midland Bank on Poultry in London. The elevation steps back and contracts and the tops of the centre motifs have French pavilion roofs. Sheer walls with simple openings contrast with the texture of the lower entrances and the upper stages. The proportions are ingeniously calculated, as Lutyens in his later years adored to do. The top stage is two-thirds of the stage from the obelisks to the next set-back, and that middle stage is two-thirds of the bottom stage. Also the walls above the first floor sill have a very slight batter: 1 in. in every 11 ft (2.5 cm in every 3.35 metres).* The banking hall could not be skylit, so Lutyens gave it arcading on all four sides and wooden galleries much as in Wren churches. The galleries have large arched windows to let enough light in. The Delhi order, with bells, which Lutyens devised for the Viceroy's House in New Delhi (1913–29), is used.

*Eitan Karol suggests that the rising set-backs show the influence of Charles Holden, e.g. his Law Society in Chancery Lane, London.

Opposite, the REFORM CLUB by *Edward Salomons*, 1870–1, in his romantic interpretation of Venetian Gothic. One of the largest surviving provincial clubhouses in the country. The street elevation is symmetrical, but it is the verticality of the corner oriels surmounted by graceful turrets and the external expression of the internal spaces which one notices. The two-storey hall on the *piano nobile* has a range of large windows, matched in the soaring oriels, that at the centre with a balcony. Beneath is a fanciful portal, richly adorned with carving. Plaques with allegories of the Arts on the E turret and Sciences on the W turret were designed by *Robert Pollitt* and carved by *T. R. & E. Williams*. The ground floor of the interior is of two periods, one contemporary with the exterior, the other of 1910 by *Maxwell & Tuke* who converted some of the rented ground-floor offices for use by the club. To the first period belong a fine full-height staircase from a spacious entrance hall, the grand main dining room two storeys high on the *piano nobile* and an enormous billiard room, running the whole length of the building, in the roof – this part now offices. Of the second phase the best surviving rooms are the magnificent ground-floor lavatories with marble basins and marble panels in the ceiling.

LINCOLN SQUARE. STATUE of Abraham Lincoln by *George Grey Barnard*, 1919. Presented to the City of Manchester by Mr and Mrs Charles Phelps Taft of Cincinnati, Ohio. It had been destined for Parliament Square in London but the American Commission of Fine Arts considered it insufficiently reverent and ruled in favour of a copy of the figure by Augustus Saint-Gaudens at Lincoln Gardens, Chicago.

LONDON ROAD. Outlying S of the railway viaduct, is the BT BUILDING, by *J. W. Hammond*, 1972. Angled to the curve of the road, with tapered piloti hugging lower glazed parts on either side of Travis Street, which runs between. Above, frankly expressed concrete decks.

MARKET STREET. Originally a lane leading from the medieval market place out into open country. It was widened in 1821–2, and established as a principal shopping street by the mid C19.

At the E end on the N side Nos. 109–127, RYLANDS BUILD-ING (Debenhams), completed 1932, by *Harry S. Fairhurst & P. G. Fairhurst*. The largest wholesale textile warehouse of its day in the city. The frontage is over 230 ft (70 metres) long. Stripped classicism in Portland stone with huge corner turrets turned from the frontage at an angle of forty-five degrees, all enlivened by ornamental metalwork and zigzag patterns. The remainder of this side is dominated by the ARNDALE CENTRE (1972–80, *Wilson & Womersley*) which occupies a 15 acre (6 hectare) site. The unlovely tile-clad Arndale tower is a landmark, and the whole was designed as an inward-looking block with long blank frontages except on Market Street. New shop frontages are being inserted, 2004, and the whole of the N part is being rebuilt by *Chapman Taylor Partners*. There is more variety on the S side, though the only really notable building is No. 70, of c. 1825. All that survives is the upper part of the façade with giant unfluted Ionic columns. It was designed – by whom?* For the short-lived Thomas Crewdson & Co. Bank. New shops behind this and the neighbouring early C19 façade were designed by *Stephenson Bell*, 2000. STEPHENS BUILD- INGS on the corner with Brown Street, a Waterhouseish effort, c. 1896 by *Booth & Chadwick*. Very fine red brick, red terra- cotta and red sandstone. Perky corner turret and richly deco- rated shaped gables.

MOSLEY STREET. Named for the Lords of the Manor who laid out this and neighbouring streets in the early 1780s. It quickly became one of the most elegant streets in town, but after c. 1840 it was a premier site for warehousing. Much of this was swept away for the present banks, offices and commercial buildings. Starting at the Piccadilly Gardens end, on the W side, Nos. 14–16 COBDEN HOUSE, 1839, an early work of *Edward Walters* and his first Manchester commission, can claim to be the first palazzo-inspired warehouse in the city. Brick with stone dressings with emphasis reserved for the second-floor windows. The ground floor is a restoration. On the N corner with York Street Nos. 24–30, 1898 for the Mercantile Bank of Lancashire by *J. Gibbons Sankey*. Portland stone, upper Ionic colonnades and corner turrets set back in stages above the entrances. The modelling and detail start to go Free Style towards the top. Next the ROYAL BANK OF SCOTLAND, between York Street and Spring Gardens. The first block is by *Walters*, his last great work, for the Manchester and Salford Bank in 1862. Walters' assurance shines through. Two-storeyed rusticated giant pilasters below, so that the pedimented *piano nobile* windows are on the second floor. Here giant angled pilasters point to the pinched-in corners of the very emphatic cornice, which is topped by a balustrade punctuated by big stone urns and corner chimneys. The top part draws the whole composition together, balancing the strength of the ground- floor rustication. To the l. of the lower entrance block a match- ing 1880s extension by Walters' successors, *Barker & Ellis*. The latest extension, 1975, *Harry S. Fairhurst & Son*, has simply treated openings palely following the C19 rhythms. The same firm also did the expensive-looking No. 45 on the other (E) side, now Royal Bank of Scotland offices, in 1963–5. A tower on a podium, all clad in dark green marble and light green granite.

At the corner with Charlotte Street is the noble and unas- suming PORTICO LIBRARY, 1802–6, the only surviving work in the city of *Thomas Harrison*, and the immediate successor to his Lyceum (1800–4) in Liverpool. It is an early example of urban Greek Revival, incorporating an advanced Soane- inspired interior. To Mosley Street a pedimented central loggia has four unfluted Ionic columns, probably based on Stuart &

---

* Richard Lane would be the obvious candidate, but the detailing does not seem like his work.

Revett's drawings of the Little Temple on the Ilissus. On the side to Charlotte Street a rank of attached columns and ground-floor windows with alternating flat and pedimented heads, all done in finely finished Runcorn stone. The steps up to the Ionic portico and the recessed entrance emphasize the exclusive nature of the club, but they now lead to the disappointing pub conversion. The ground floor was the newsroom, which had an open well with a galleried first floor. This had been closed in and furnished with a dome by 1900, and is floored over. The library upstairs is preserved, reached from a side entrance. Here the space is dominated by a Soanic dome and segmental tunnel vaults to E and W. Harrison presumably knew Soane's Bank of England interiors, and may have had contact with Soane through his membership of the Architects' Club. The library and its fittings are intact, and the library continues in use.

MOUNT STREET. Nos. 2–4, former Inland Revenue offices by *Pennington & Bridgen*, 1874–6. Crocketed gable with tourelles and a statue of Queen Victoria beneath a canopy. The corner entrance (to Central Street) has an elaborate two-storey oriel, encrusted with carving.

NICHOLAS STREET. No. 16, by *Alfred Waterhouse*, 1872–5. Elizabethan details with gables and chimneys, creating an eventful roofline in contrast to all the Italianate cornices hereabouts. Brick with stone dressings, six storeys with the upper three slightly recessed between the gabled end bays.

NORFOLK STREET. At the junction with Brown Street No. 10, the former PALATINE BANK by *Briggs, Wolstenholme & Thornely*, 1908–10. Great circular corner towers with conical roofs, upper arcade on the Norfolk Street side, giant colonnade to Brown Street. Details such as crowstepped gables and dog-tooth ornament, looking rather odd in Portland stone. Further W, S side, Nos. 2–6 was the NORTHERN STOCK EXCHANGE by *Bradshaw & Gass*, 1907. Edwardian Baroque, with a low orderly three-storey façade of Portland stone. Converted to a restaurant in 2000. The magnificent hall has a dome supported at the corners by pilasters clad in sensuous green and cream marble. On the S side to the street, the arcading incorporates lunettes. Bulky plasterwork festoons and wreaths in the spandrels.

OXFORD STREET has some of Manchester's more spectacular offices and warehouses. We start at S end with the PALACE HOTEL at the corner of Oxford Street and Whitworth Street, former offices for the Refuge Assurance Company. Built in three phases: No. 1 Building by *Alfred Waterhouse*, 1891–5, at the corner of Whitworth Street; No. 2 Building by *Paul Waterhouse*, 1910–12, doubling the Oxford Street façade and linked to No. 1 Building by a 217 ft (66 metre) clock tower over the new entrance; No. 3 Building, 1932 by *Stanley Birkett*, doubling the Whitworth Street façade. Clad with imperishable pressed brick and dark red terracotta (by *Doulton*), only relieved by the grey granite of the tower base and orange terracotta at its top.

The decoration is of the Northern Italian C16 type. A power-ful effect is achieved by the richly textured side blocks set against the sheer mass of the tower when seen in foreshort-ened perspective. The sheer back elevations faced with white glazed brick are almost devoid of ornament – in their way almost as spectacular. The INTERIORS show equally imper-ishable and highly wrought materials. *Burmantofts* faience and glazed brick in butterscotch shades are used for No. 1 Build-ing, with characteristically muted stained glass and excellent ironwork. The richest display is reserved for the corner entrance, now blocked. Apart from the entrance and stair the whole ground floor, including the glassed-over light well, was one vast open business hall. No. 2 Building employs a wider palette, including greens and copper shades, and more bulgy forms. It incorporates a sumptuous full-height marble and bronze staircase. No. 3 Building is similar to No. 2 but red tiles are substituted for faience. Converted to an hotel by *Richard Newman*, opened 1996.

The PALACE THEATRE on the corner with Whitworth Street, E side, by *Alfred Darbyshire*, 1891, altered by *Bertie Crewe* 1913. Clad in ugly beige tiles in 1956, but the splendid domed auditorium was retained. On each side of the proscenium arch two tiers of boxes with atlantes and caryatids and a pedimented Ionic colonnade. Two tiers of curved balconies. The elaborate plasterwork is an exuberant mixture of classical and Egyptian motifs. Beside it on the same side ST JAMES'S BUILDINGS by *Clegg, Fryer & Penman*, 1912–13 for the Calico Printers' Association. High and broad and all Portland stone: Baroque. A tower, rising from a broken pediment, crowns the central entrance block. The entrance hall is the most opulent in the surviving Manchester warehouses, with an elaborate plaster ceiling and everything else clad in marble: grey and white walls, green columns and a sumptuous stair. Opposite, No. 56, the almost equally impressive offices of the textile manufacturers TOOTAL BROADHURST, LEE & CO., 1896–8, by *J. Gibbons Sankey*. Large too, in red brick striped with orange terracotta, but comparatively classical. Polygonal corner towers frame an arcade with giant Corinthian columns. The INTERIOR has been refitted, keeping on the stairs a war memorial by *Henry Sellers*: a frame of layered coloured marbles with a niche (from which the figure was stolen) above a cream marble inscription panel.

PICTURE HOUSE of 1911 by *Naylor & Sale*, further N and on the W side. The earliest purpose-built cinema in the city centre, retaining something of its original form, though the ground floor has been horribly ruined and the tower over the entrance removed. Orange terracotta and red brick with seg-mental gablets punching through the balustraded parapet. On the other (N) Chepstow Street corner, a 1980s toy Georgian office development is fronted by PRINCES BUILDINGS (Nos. 18–28 Oxford Street), built as offices, shops and warehousing by *I. R. E. Birkett* in 1903. Only the terracotta-clad façade is left, but this has verve, with a row of tall chimneys linked by a sweeping curved parapet. The detail is Art Nouveau. Opposite is the interwar ODEON by *F. T. Verity & S. Beverly*, with flattened pilasters and stylized capitals above garish tiles.

PETER STREET. The name is for St Peter's Field, and the site of the Peterloo massacre of 1819 (*see* Radisson Edwardian Hotel, below). Starting from the St Peter's Square end, S side, ST GEORGE'S HOUSE, the former YMCA designed in 1907, completed 1911, by *Woodhouse, Corbett & Dean*. A great solid block of a building, built of reinforced concrete construction using the *Kahn* system. The cladding is brown and buff *Burmantofts* terracotta with very shallow projections. The front is not symmetrical; central entrance in a big semicircular arch, with undulating, slightly projecting bays on each side of a recessed lunette, r. side, simpler treatment to the l., the whole drawn together by a big bracketed cornice. Restrained and judicious use of ornament, including a copy of Donatello's St George in a niche. The incorporation of swimming baths, gymnasia and other sports facilities can be traced to New York prototypes, in particular the Brooklyn YMCA, 1885, and West Side Branch YMCA, 1897. Like these the Manchester building had a gymnasium with an oval running track around it and a swimming pool, in this case on the top floor, but everything was unfortunately removed when the building was converted to offices in the 1990s.

On the same side, W, the THEATRE ROYAL (now the Royale night club) dated 1845, by *Irwin & Chester*, altered inside by *Edward Salomons* in 1875. A splendid classical composition in stone, one of the best examples of theatre architecture surviving anywhere in England from the first half of the C19. Projecting entrance bay with giant recessed portico with Corinthian columns and pilasters. A central semicircular arch breaks through into the gable above. Steps up to the (altered) entrances, the central one surmounted by a pedimented niche with a statue of Shakespeare after the Westminster Abbey example by Peter Scheemakers. Flanking bays have tall pedimented first-floor windows with balconies. A debt is surely owed to Cockerell, whose Branch Bank of England was being erected at the same time (*see* King Street), though as Dr Ivan Hall points out, there is also a parallel with the E end of Hawksmoor's St Alphege, Greenwich.

49   Next on this side, the RADISSON EDWARDIAN HOTEL (site of the former Free Trade Hall).* The hotel occupies a site of great historic note. In 1819 it was the scene of the infamous Peterloo Massacre when the Manchester Yeomanry intemperately attacked and dispersed a large and orderly meeting gathered to promote political reform. Later it was used for two succeeding public halls serving the national campaign to repeal laws imposing a tariff on imported corn. It succeeded in 1846 largely through Manchester's endeavours. From 1855 until

* This description is by John H. G. Archer.

1999 it accommodated the third Free Trade Hall, created by public subscription to house a wide variety of political, social and cultural purposes that brought lustre to the city. Designed by *Edward Walters*, a master of the palazzo style, it was nationally outstanding and his masterpiece. Substantially rebuilt by the City Architect *L. C. Howitt* after extensive war damage, its exterior was a model of careful conservation, and in 1969 Nikolaus Pevsner described it as 'perhaps the noblest monument in the Cinquecento style in England'. In 1996, the hall, then in the ownership of the city, closed and subsequently was sold for conversion to hotel use, and in 1999 a scheme by *Stephenson Bell* of Manchester was approved. It was completed in 2004 and it incorporates the original palazzo frontage and three bays of the adjacent South Street elevation.

The site is approximately trapezoidal, with the main frontage facing north and falling E–W. South Street, on the E side, rises to Windmill Street, facing S, which has the longest frontage. The W side abuts an existing building, and adjacent buildings on Peter Street and those facing the hotel are similar in height to the original building. The hotel, however, has a fourteen-storey accommodation block extending along Windmill Street and a lower section, for reception and entertainment, scaled to and adopting the original frontage.

The façade is classically orthodox in design and is in fine, ashlar Yorkshire sandstone. It is of nine bays and consists of superimposed semicircular-arched arcading. The slope of Peter Street is absorbed by a ground-floor arcade, boldly Roman in scale, character and detail, which forms a base for the immensely rich, similarly arcaded superstructure. Massive corner piers define it and a bold cornice caps it. Pevsner aptly summed it up as 'monumental and yet amazingly refined'. At first-floor level a moulded, modillioned string course forms a tabling for the arcading of the *piano nobile* and its paired Roman Ionic columns. Within each bay is a framed and triangular-pedimented window beneath a tympanum filled with allegorical figures representing international commerce and the arts and industries. Central is the open-handed figure of Free Trade, flanked by sheaves of corn and backed by sails, masts and rigging: no message could be clearer. The artist for the architectural sculpture was *John Thomas*, the former superintendent of stone-carving at the Palace of Westminster. The elevation is completed by a garlanded frieze, the cornice and its balustraded parapet. At the NE corner the design is maintained almost intact for three bays along South Street to the junction with the new structure.

Throughout the design the carved detail is of high quality and is often symbolic. The spandrels are filled with well-composed and finely cut foliage, but at different levels dif-ferent features are skilfully integrated into their design. In the upper arcades these are wreathed disks of red granite, possibly a Ruskinian influence, and beneath each a well-designed group of musical instruments echoes one of the hall's uses. The spandrels of the lower arcade introduce the coats of arms of towns related to Manchester through the cotton trade and the repeal campaign. A final symbol occurs in the frieze of the entablature of each pier of the lower arcade, where carved miniature corn sheaves may remind all who enter or leave that the Free Trade Hall commemorated a campaign for daily bread.

For the site of the Free Trade Hall four successive hotel schemes, all by different architects, were proposed. All were controversial because they flouted the principle of finding a compatible alternative use for an outstanding historic building. After a public inquiry in 1998, *Stephenson Bell*'s later proposal was approved by the city council and English Heritage. It cannot be commended as a conservation scheme for a major historic building; the frontage is a dutiful token, but the accommodation tower, which presents an elegantly designed face to Windmill Street, has an overpowering effect on the context and, seen from Peter Street, intrudes on the outline of Walters's classic design, which is now surmounted by the irregular form of the tower and its two projecting spurs.

The underlying fault lies with a proposal which was misconceived from the outset, and it is extraordinary that a civic authority with such a wide range of needs chose to sacrifice a building of such exceptional distinction architecturally and historically. City councillors and members of official bodies, or the architectural profession, or relevant committees should learn from this that works of such quality merit greater respect than to be reduced to the equivalent of stage scenery.

Opposite, on the N side a pair of warehouses, both *c.* 1868, on the corners of Southmill Street. No. 47, E side, is by *Walters, Barker & Ellis*. A typical palazzo of the date. On the other corner HARVESTER HOUSE by *Clegg & Knowles*, stone-faced, five storeys, with the usual tall ground-floor arcade. For the Albert Memorial Hall, w, *see* p. 277.

The sw part of Peter Street was opened out as part of the scheme by *Leslie Jones Architects* for the conversion of the Great Northern Warehouse (*see* Watson Street). A square with gardens and water features was laid out in 1999 on the site of the goods yard which served the warehouse. On the Deansgate corner the yard walls have been furnished with a tower which seems to serve no purpose beyond punctuating the corner.

PICCADILLY forms the approach to the town centre from Piccadilly Station (see Public Buildings). We start at the foot of Piccadilly Station Approach, E. GATEWAY HOUSE runs alongside the ramp, offices by *Richard Seifert & Partners*, 1967–9. A very impressive, long, sweeping, undulating façade, the horizontals stressed throughout. One of the best 1960s office blocks in Manchester. Opposite, on the other side of Ducie Street, III PICCADILLY (formerly the Rodwell Tower), 1963–6 by *Douglas Stephen & Partners*, of concrete with an eighteen-storey tower and a lower part. Visually it reflects the influence of Louis Kahn's Medical Research Building, Philadelphia, with its boldly articulated uprights. Spanning the

canal on the other side is the MALMAISON HOTEL, incorporating the Joshua Hoyle Warehouse by *Charles Heathcote*. 1904,
clad in brick, terracotta and faience. The splayed corner bay
containing the main entrance is crowned by a turret and
flanked by gabled and turreted bays. The new hotel entrance
on Piccadilly is marked by a spiky raked and angled canopy
linking the original building with the new. This part and the
conversion are by *Darby Associates*, 1998, extended 2001–2.

No. 107 PICCADILLY, E side, is offices and warehousing
(converted to a hotel 2002–3) by *Charles Heathcote*, dated 1899.
Typical Neo-Baroque with gable and round angle turret, and
with alternatingly blocked columns, but distinguished by
subtle asymmetry in the elevations and robust muscularity.
Simpler linked warehouse behind. Dwarfed by its neighbour,
No. 97 is a late C18 inn, the only survivor on Piccadilly of the
buildings shown on Green's 1794 map. Stuccoed, with doorways with Doric columns and pediments. The side elevation
to Paton Street incorporates two late C18 former houses with
crude pedimented doorcases. On the other side No. 12,
BARCLAYS BANK, an individual and powerful classical essay
by *Percy Scott Worthington* for the Union Bank, dated 1911,
strongly modelled in Portland stone. On the other, E side, Nos.
77–83, dated 1877, conventional eclecticism up to the eaves,
but then the architects (*Clegg & Knowles*) suddenly go in a
completely different direction – unless we are looking at later
additions. Wide band of richly moulded fruit and foliage
motifs, then a variety of oversized sculptures and gargoyles,
topped by a timbered gable and the obligatory corner turret.
Beside it Nos. 69–75 is Venetian Gothic, probably 1870s, with
the entrance bays at each end given emphasis and the doorways with ornately carved consoles.

PICCADILLY GARDENS. A wide square with gardens in the
centre. This was the site of the Manchester Infirmary, erected
in 1775 on the edge of the C18 town and demolished in 1909.
New gardens by *EDAW* and an elongated concrete pavilion by
Tadao Ando were opened 2002. The pavilion presents a long
brutal expanse of concrete to Parker Street on the SW side of
the square. On the other side it is glazed on each side of an
opening linking the gardens with the street. The gardens have
fountains and axial walks, but the SE side has been taken up
by a new retail development by *Allies & Morrison*, 2002–3,
despite protests at the loss of open space and blocked views.
An expressed grid clad in red brick, much glass, and a walkway
linking Portland Street with the gardens. STATUES are ranged
along the NE side. Wellington by *M. Noble*, 1856, then the
Queen Victoria Memorial by *Onslow Ford*, 1901, with a stately
and dignified seated bronze figure against a Baroque architectural background. Watt by *Theed*, 1857, a copy of Chantrey's
statue made for Westminster Abbey. Sir Robert Peel by *Marshall*, 1853, bronze with two bronze allegories below. Adrift, a
symbolic group by *John Cassidy*, 1907, is due for re-erection in
the square, 2004.

On the s side of the square, PICCADILLY PLAZA by *Covell, Matthews & Partners*, 1959–65, remodelled by *Leslie Jones Architects*, 2001–2. A huge commercial super block consisting of three buildings linked by a podium. The HOTEL is a high slab parallel to Piccadilly, cantilevered out on a sloping underside, creating a very powerful effect when viewed from the side. The low restaurant projects towards Piccadilly and has three funny little roofs. The slab is stressed horizontally. The high office slab, twenty-four storeys high, SUNLEY HOUSE, has not got that horizontal emphasis. Also it stands at right angles to Piccadilly, and has towards it a wall decorated with relief designs derived from circuit boards, with just one long window slot. The third element, BERNARD HOUSE, was replaced with a building which palely echoes the swooping roofline of the original. The group, instead of reading together, has always looked desperately disparate. It completely fails to take account of its surroundings, but the sheer confidence and scale impress.

On the w side of the square No. 10 MOSLEY STREET, 1836–8, is attributed to *Richard Tattersall* for the Manchester and Salford Bank: stone, with giant Corinthian columns on a high base bizarrely decorated with triglyphs, which does not seem like Tattersall (cf. his accomplished Ashburne Hall, p. 475). Then the former LEWIS'S department store, here from the 1880s. The original building was replaced by a huge untidy Baroque pile of 1915 by *J. W. Beaumont & Sons*, then the biggest store in the provinces, rivalling the attractions of London shops. Extensions of 1924–7 and 1927–9. On the N side, from the w: No. 1 PICCADILLY, by *J. Lynde*, 1879, a jolly incident on the corner of Tib Street, with corner turret and upper bays articulated by short iron columns framing canted windows. No. 11, r., by *P. Hothersall*, 1922, was a cinema. Portland stone, with giant pilasters and a balustraded parapet. Further along, the NATWEST BANK of *c.* 1930 is by *J. Hembrow* of *Mills & Murgatroyd*. A nicely austere frontage of Portland stone with stylized Ionic pilasters and a row of solemn lions. No. 47 is a stuccoed late C18 survivor, diminutive beside its neighbours. No. 49, the former J. P. & E. Westhead & Co. warehouse, probably built 1846–7, is a severe palazzo; red brick and stone dressings; two great stone arched loading entrances at the rear on Back Piccadilly. Nos. 51–53, dated 1904 and Nos. 59–61, dated 1907, two versions of the same design by *W. & G. Higginbottom* separated by a rather dull 1870s effort. ST MARGARETS CHAMBERS on the corner of Newton Street, 1889 by *Heathcote & Rawle*, has tall, ornate shaped gables and a wide carved stone frieze. Note the carving in the gable facing the square.

PORTLAND STREET runs along the E side of Piccadilly Gardens and continues sw to Oxford Street. It is a street of great C19 warehouses, still impressive, despite intrusions caused by demolitions and war damage. The most distinguished buildings are three former warehouses all designed by *Edward Walters* between 1851 and 1858 in his accomplished palazzo style. He was designing the warehouses on Charlotte Street (q.v.) at about the same time, but here there was room – and the funds – for larger, more impressive buildings, all in stone. They make an imposing group, each one with fine, deeply cut carved detail. Nos. 3–5 and 7 are now the PORTLAND THISTLE HOTEL, and No. 9 offices. The façades only survive, beginning with No. 9 on the corner of Aytoun Street, 1851–2. Four storeys, rusticated ground-floor arcading and a central entrance. Second-floor windows with segmental pediments; balustraded parapet. No. 7, to the l., 1852, has five storeys with attic and basement and a ground-floor arcade. The two upper storeys are linked by giant pilasters. The proportions have been damaged by the additions above the cornice. The best of the group is Nos. 3–5, 1858, a refined version of No. 7, with more assurance and élan than its neighbours. Walters was occupied at the time with the Free Trade Hall (*see* Peter Street), cf. the ground floor arcade with spandrel carving. The horizontal stress of the second-floor pediments is balanced by the verticality of giant pilasters linking to the floor above. This and the integration of sill with lintel, the whole united by the controlling forces of cornice and quoins, marks it as a product of Walters' maturity.

Continuing SW brings us to the BRITANNIA HOTEL, formerly Watts Warehouse, king of the home trade warehouses, a vast and ambitious affair of 1855–8 by *Travis & Mangnall*. S. & J. Watts was the largest wholesale drapery business in Manchester and the owner James Watts typical of the city's new mercantile princes, a self-made man who espoused the free-trade cause. His warehouse aptly encapsulates the spirit of self-confidence mixed with a touch of brashness. The length is twenty-three bays or *c.* 300 ft (90 metres), the height nearly 100 ft (30 metres). There are four roof towers but the ranges of gables between and on top have been lost. The general outline resembles the Fondaco dei Turchi in Venice. Each of the six floors is given a different treatment ranging from Italian Renaissance to Elizabethan, culminating with wheel windows in the roof towers. This fantastic mixture is held together by an orderly rhythm and the confidence of the composition, so it is more than just a curiosity. Inside, the original sumptuous staircase has generous landings with ornate cast-iron columns. In the entrance foyer a FIRST WORLD WAR MEMORIAL, 1921. The Sentry, by *C. S. Jagger*, a strongly expressive bronze soldier with a rifle, aptly suggesting both vigilance and contemplation.

The pattern breaks at this point, a result partly of wartime bomb damage. BANK CHAMBERS, 1971 by *Fitzroy Robinson & Partners*, stands on the NW side, and there are two early 1960s towers, SE side. No. 73, W side, is a former warehouse at the corner of Nicholas Street by *Pennington & Bridgen*, 1873. The style is becoming eclectic and Italian Gothic motifs are employed. Greatest emphasis is still reserved for the *piano nobile* where the window surrounds are elaborate. Beside it a

58

row of modest buildings gives an indication of late C18 scale. The long attic windows show that some were designed or converted for workshops. The tall intruder in the middle of the block with its large windows is by *J. M. Porter*, 1883. Two little pubs have partly original C19 interiors. The CIRCUS (No. 86) has a bar in the entrance hall, grained matchboard partitions, and bench seating: an almost miraculous survival considering the tiny scale of it all.

On the corner of Princess Street is No. 101, the former PICKLES BUILDING (now the Princess Hotel). By *Clegg &*

Manchester, No. 101 Portland Street, from *The Builder*, 1870

Knowles, *c.* 1870, stone with a corner entrance, and Continental Gothic motifs; in the eclectic style adopted by the firm at this time. The composition has been damaged by the loss of the tall eaves chimneys. Grouped windows of diminishing size create an orderly rhythm, but with no indication of a *piano nobile*. For Portland House on the other corner, *see* Princess Street. The whole of the remaining SE side has more big late C19 warehouses, all of red brick with stone dressings, all exhibiting more or less elaborate treatment of the openings. Together they create a powerful effect. The ground floor and basement of Nos. 113–115 were converted by *Hodder Associates*, 1998, for CUBE (Centre for Understanding the Built Environment), exhibition galleries with a bookshop and lecture theatre. Everything was stripped back to bare brick, timber beams and cast-iron columns, used as a backdrop for white screens and panels of opaque glass which admit diffused light. The BEHRENS building is the last in the sequence on this side. A long four-storey warehouse built for multiple occupation with a rounded corner to Oxford Street, by *P. Nunn* for Louis Behrens & Sons, *c.* 1860. The giant arcade creates a relentless rhythm, linking first and second floors and extending unbroken for twenty-three bays. The late C19 buildings opposite on the corner of Oxford Street have been demolished. They made an important contribution to the street scene and should not have been allowed to go. Others on this side were demolished behind their façades. A new hotel and health club by *Leslie Jones Architects*, 2000–1, fills the space.

PRINCESS STREET. The most impressive Victorian street of the city. Like Portland Street it is lined with warehouses, but here more survive and there are long unbroken sequences. Few are without interest and almost all keep within a single scale, having four or five storeys over a half-basement. In general they occupy a block each and most date from the 1860s onwards. A high proportion are by *Clegg & Knowles*, or by *Charles Clegg* alone, the leading warehouse firm of the late 1860s to the 1880s. The buildings are so tall and close to the edge of the street that it is only possible to see them from the opposite side, so several blocks will be described sequentially to avoid crossing and recrossing this busy thoroughfare.

We start at the junction with Mosley Street (for Princess Street NW from here see St Peter's Square and Albert Square). The earliest in the sequence is No. 83, on the corner of George Street. By *Travis & Mangnall*, *c.* 1847, with round-headed windows and an arcaded ground floor and basement, looking heavy-handed compared with its near contemporaries on Charlotte Street. Then as far as Portland Street this side is mainly over-restored C18 or early C19 houses. On the W side Nos. 14–16, *c.* 1875, take the corner with Mosley Street gracefully; brick with stone dressings and a balustraded parapet. Next Nos. 18–24, Dugdale's warehouse, *c.* 1877–8, sandstone, in a free European Gothic style with a striking open arcaded parapet and tall chimneys. It has all the hallmarks of *Clegg &*

Knowles. Next Nos. 26–30 by *C. Clegg*, 1883, with corner oriels and two sets of paired entrances. No. 34, by the same architect, is also of 1883, but has a Tudor flavour. On the corner of Portland Street, occupying an island site, No. 36 is by *Clegg & Knowles*, 1880. Stone, in a variation of their usual eclectic style of the time. Note the elevation to Faulkner Street with the openings grouped more closely, to suit the relative narrowness of the street.

SE of Portland Street, first the E side. After the Pickles Building on the corner (*see* Portland Street), No. 101 by *Clegg & Knowles* again, 1869, in the earlier version of their palazzo style. Brick with stone dressings, a high stone rusticated half-basement and first-floor windows emphasized with alternate flat and pedimented heads, all crowned with the usual emphatic cornice. On an island site, No. 103 is the former MECHANICS' INSTITUTE (founded in 1824), of 1854-5 by *J. E. Gregan*. This refined palazzo was Gregan's last work. It set a standard for the scale of the commercial warehouses which were to follow, but the nobility and purity of the design sets it apart. The proportions, with three tall storeys with a basement and blind attic storey, also contrast with the five-storey warehouse norm. Brick with stone dressings, central entrance and first-floor windows with segmental pediments. The site is awkwardly shaped and the parallelogram plan is stepped at the sides to make maximum use of space and light. The arcaded first-floor windows on the Major Street elevation mark the lecture hall. The interior has been altered, but the elegant entrance hall remains, and a full-height cantilevered stone staircase with an ironwork balustrade at the rear. It now houses the archives of the National Museum of Labour History. Nos. 105–107 is by *Clegg & Knowles*, 1871, a variation on their usual formula, this time in buff brick. No. 109, also by them, 1863-4, resembles No. 101.

57   Now for the W side. PORTLAND HOUSE, on the corner with Portland Street, is a huge eclectic effort by *Pennington & Bridgen*, 1887, red brick, with pale stone bands and hipped gables with finials. Squashed up beside it No. 46a LANGLEY BUILDINGS, *c.* 1895 by *W. Waddington & Son*, with a corner entrance with a ship's prow over it. The remaining buildings on this side as far as the canal are all late C19 variations of similar materials and scale.

The BRIDGE over the Rochdale Canal has a late C19 cast-iron parapet and a separate footbridge to one side. Just beyond, W side, a departure from the Italianate norm with No. 74 (now part of the Dominion Hotel), 1880, by *Corson & Aitken*. Scottish Baronial style with angle tourelles and dormers with paired chimneys. A solid design accentuated by stone dressings and header-bond brick. Corson was a Scot who trained in Dumfries, but his foray into Scottish style was not emulated by anyone else in Manchester. At the corner of Whitworth Street, the former Dominion House, now part of an hotel, by *I. R. E. Birkett*, 1893.

Across Whitworth Street, on the E side, the premises of Morreau & Spiegelberg, by *C. Clegg & Son*, 1912. Arcaded below and topped with a range of big shaped gables. On the other side two quite splendid early C20 packing and shipping warehouses, No. 82 (ASIA HOUSE) and No. 86 (MANCHESTER HOUSE), by *I. R. E. Birkett*, 1906–9, six storeys with attics and basements, essays in Edwardian Baroque stylishly executed in brownish red sandstone and pink bricks. No. 82 has an exceptionally rich entrance hall and stairwell lined with veined marble and green and cream faience, with designs of trees and Art Nouveau stained glass. It is a good example of the warehouse type, designed for multiple occupation and furnished with offices with secure self-contained warerooms behind, arranged in two blocks on either side of loading bays. The company running the warehouses provided portering, making-up, packing and despatch services, carried out by their own staff in the basement and sub-basement.

SACKVILLE STREET runs SE from Portland Street across the Rochdale Canal. Warehouses, all probably 1870s, of which Nos. 42–44 by *Pennington & Bridgen* is particularly well detailed. In the park, opposite, BEACON OF HOPE by *Warren Chapman* and *Jess Boyn-Daniel*, 2000. Steel column dedicated to those affected by HIV/AIDS. A seated STATUE of Alan Turing by *Glyn Hughes*, 2001, honours Turing as a mathematical genius and victim of homophobia. The setting is appropriate as this area and the nearby Canal Street have become known as the Gay Village for the concentration of bars, cafés and clubs popular with the gay community.

ST ANN'S SQUARE was named for the church (*see* Other Places of Worship, p. 275). It was laid out in 1720 on Acresfield, the site of an annual fair from the C13 until 1823. The square represented the first major development away from the medieval centre around the Cathedral. It was originally a select residential area, shown on a 1741 engraving with formal rows of trees. On the W side some late C18 or early C19 houses, generally quite plain, though Nos. 6 and 20 have nice stuccoed decoration. WINTER'S BUILDINGS E of the church is a big colourful mixture of brick, stone and terracotta, by *J. W. Beaumont*, 1901. To the S, a mid-1990s shop by *Buttress, Fuller & Alsop* with a nautical-looking turret and the rear of Mr Thomas's Chop House (*see* Cross Street) form interesting points on the little enclave around the church. OLD EXCHANGE BUILDINGS, a red sandstone block dated 1897 by *Royle & Bennett*, S of the church, incorporates ST ANN'S PASSAGE, leading through to King Street, with ornate pilasters to the passageway. On the SE side of the square the St Ann Street corner is graced by the urbane No. 25, now the Royal Bank of Scotland, built in 1848 for Benjamin Heywood's bank by *J. E. Gregan*. One of the finest palazzo-inspired buildings in the city, three storeys, of pale sandstone, beautifully finished. Care was taken to place the stone on its natural bed to avoid premature decay.

The rusticated ground floor has arcades of windows; pedimented windows on the upper floor have balconies. The corner is taken with a generous splay. The lower, brick-built manager's house on St Ann's Street is a more simply treated palazzo, with a splay to Cross Street drawing the composition together. It is attached to the single-storey entrance, an arrangement recalling the Palazzo Pandolfini in Florence, successfully relating its smaller scale to the noble proportions of the bank.

Beside it to the l. Nos. 17–23, later C19, has ornate plasterwork decoration which has been extensively replaced by fibreglass. Next, on the corner of Old Bank Street, OLD BANK CHAMBERS (Barclays Bank) is of Portland stone with a very narrow corner splay with relief sculpture. By *Harry S. Fairhurst* for Manchester Liners, c. 1925. For the Royal Exchange, *see* Exchange Street.

STATUES in the Square: Richard Cobden, by *Marshall Wood*, 1867, bronze; Boer War memorial by *Hamo Thornycroft*, 1908, a rifleman protecting his wounded comrade. Also a FOUNTAIN with a fanciful bud of red granite on a dark stone drum. By *Peter Randall-Page*, 1995.

ST PETER'S SQUARE. St Peter's Church was built on the edge of the town in 1788–94 by *James Wyatt* and demolished in 1907. On the site a memorial garden designed by *L. C. Howitt* and dedicated in 1949, which incorporated a Portland stone cross by *Temple Moore*, 1908, commemorating the church, and the Portland stone CENOTAPH by *Lutyens*, 1924, similar to the one in Whitehall. As a public space the square does not work and the lack of coherence is exacerbated by the visual mess and physical barrier created by the Metrolink stop and the graceless stanchions for overhead wires. STATUES: at the N end, opposite the rear of the town hall, Messenger of Peace by *Barbara Pearson*, 1986, bronze, whimsical stylized female figure with doves. Opposite the Town Hall Extension, Struggle for Peace and Freedom by *Philip Jackson*, 1988, bronze, a group of linked figures.

The MIDLAND HOTEL, 1898–1903 by *Charles Trubshaw* for the Midland Railway, stands on the S side – a vast and varied affair, red brick and brown terracotta, with the French touches of e.g. the Russell Hotel in London. Louche and undisciplined, but so confident as to be an essential part of the Manchester streetscape. The exterior is clad in polished granite and generous quantities of *Burmantofts* faience in which the company's wyvern emblem features prominently. The Midland was probably Manchester's first fully steel-framed building, and one of the contractors was the Canadian engineer *James Christian Stewart*, who had been working on buildings at Trafford Park (*see* Stretford) for the British Westinghouse Co.* The huge mass is hollowed out by two light-wells, like the Town Hall but there is none of the Town Hall's logic of design or circulation. The interior has lost a good deal of its opulent detail, but it is

* According to research by Jonathan Clarke.

still possible to identify the Winter Garden and Octagon which, with the saucer-domed corridor linking the hotel with the (former) route to Central Station (*see* Public Buildings, p. 300), make up the chief reception area. Upstairs the Lancaster Suite has bold Jacobean plasterwork and panelling and a canted and angled oriel overlooking one of the light-wells. The Adamesque Derby Suite has some very handsome and probably genuine C18 doors and doorcases, wainscotting and chimneypiece. The magnificent Concert Hall is lost, its presence commemorated today by just a stained glass window by *George Wragge* in a lower corridor, and the four tympana on the Lower Mosley Street façade depicting the Arts by *F. C. Spruce*.

On the N side of the square a row of Late Georgian houses with doorcases all looking greatly restored. Nos. 73–75, Gothic, polychromatic and strongly – almost crudely – textured, is by *Ernest Bates* of 1868.

SOUTH KING STREET, parallel to the S part of King Street, is a backwater preserving some attractive late C19 cast-iron shop-fronts along the N side. No. 41 and No. 19 are the best and most complete.

SPRING GARDENS. From the junction with Mosley Street there is an intriguing glimpse of Lutyens's Midland Bank (*see* King Street). At the junction with Fountain Street on the l. corner, s side, an office building by *Edward Walters*, 1851, with a splayed corner to Spring Gardens. Four storeys and added attic storeys. Rusticated stone below, red brick above, with pedimented second-floor windows which have sills integrated with the lintels below. On the r. corner, N side, No. 49, a former warehouse by *Clegg & Knowles*, 1879. A disciplined and satisfying composition in stone with curved corners to Fountain Street and Concert Lane. On the l. corner, N side, Nos. 60–62 is a former warehouse of 1881–3 by *Alfred Waterhouse*. Pale stone laid in his favoured alternating narrow and wide courses. Splayed corner with an octagonal turret, the ground floor rusticated with a continuous arcade of openings. For the extension *see* Fountain Street.

The street curves around to the r. (for the Chancery *see* Brown Street). Here a group of imposing bank and insurance buildings close the view E along King Street. No. 47 was built in 1881 for the Commercial Union Assurance Society by *Heathcote & Rawle*. Renaissance with richly decorated dormers and corner turret. The exploitation of this awkward site shows that Heathcote's considerable skill was already well developed. The adjacent Nos. 43–45, of 1888–90, was the premises of the Lancashire and Yorkshire Bank. By *Charles Heathcote & Sons*. Free Renaissance, not yet the fully blown Baroque he is best known for. Stone, with a tall turret giving emphasis to the principal entrance bay, l. The huge and splendid banking hall, with twin saucer domes, polished granite columns and marble-lined walls retained some original furnishings, such as the customer writing cubicles on the l. side, when converted to a pub. Adjoining it is No. 41, curving around the corner of York Street.

Stone, built for the National Provincial Bank by *Alfred Water-house*, 1888–90 and not at all Gothic. The style might be called free German Renaissance, with its variety of gables. The stone front is in high relief, thanks chiefly to very prominent brackets for balconies and pediments.

On the corner of York Street, opposite, is *Charles Heathcote*'s superb former PARR'S BANK of 1902. His usual bold Edwardian Baroque, with Art Nouveau motifs in the ironwork. All of red sandstone with an angle dome and corner entrance. Arched windows with paired Doric columns between, supporting nothing more than big scrolled brackets. The interior (now a pub/restaurant) is amongst the most opulent of the date surviving in Manchester, or for that matter, in London. First a foyer in mahogany with Ionic columns framing the doors, then the sumptuous banking hall, with green marble walls and Ionic columns. The ceilings are encrusted with richly moulded plasterwork, and some of the original stained glass survives in the windows.

TIB LANE is a little street between Cross Street and Booth Street with a couple of c18 former houses, of which No. 10 is the least altered. Beside it, and almost as narrow, but of four storeys over a tall basement, a jewel-like warehouse of 1876, by *Smith & Heathcote* in Italian Gothic style.

WATSON STREET. The gargantuan GREAT NORTHERN WAREHOUSE was opened in 1898. It was planned by *A. Ross* of the Great Northern Railway, consulting engineer *W. T. Foxlee*. It is a hugely impressive block, with five tall storeys, of blue brick below, red brick with blue brick dressings above, and lettering in white brick at the top. Steel stanchions each capable of bearing a load of 650 tons, with wrought-iron girders, support arched brick fireproof floors. It acted as a railway, road and canal interchange (the Manchester and Salford Junction Canal (*see* Public Buildings, p. 303), *c.* 40 ft (12 metres) beneath ground level, was reached by shafts). The future of the building was uncertain for many years. Eventually the carriage ramp and viaducts serving the upper-level goods station were removed as part of a conversion of 2000–2, which incorporates the building into an extensive leisure complex by *Leslie Jones Architects* (*see* also Peter Street). The new buildings to the s stretch the full length of Watson Street to Great Bridgewater Street. The link between old and new is marked by an abrupt change in plane and materials, and fiddly detail.

WHITWORTH STREET. One of the great Manchester streets, the w part as impressive as Princess Street but of the next generation. We start at the w end at the junction with Oxford Street, where LLOYDS PACKING WAREHOUSES dominate. The company was formed in 1896 and within thirty years it was packing and despatching one third of the foreign cotton trade of Lancashire. The warehouses here were built in response to the boom in trade and confidence following the opening of the Manchester Ship Canal in 1894, when easy access and efficient loading facilities were essential. The huge buildings are steel-framed and built to high-quality fireproof specifications. Terracotta and faience fronts contrast with the rear elevations where the steel frame is exposed and glazed. The architect, who was the leading expert in the design of these advanced warehouses, was *Harry S. Fairhurst*. They have all been converted to flats or offices.

First, backing on to the Rochdale Canal, BRIDGEWATER HOUSE, 1912, ambitious business architecture of its time, granite below, white faience above, with a ripple of canted bays. Eight storeys with attics and basements. Probably the most advanced building of its type when erected. Fairhurst's design revolutionized the business of loading and unloading of goods, and here twenty-six lorries could be dealt with simultaneously using a drive-through system. Opposite, INDIA HOUSE, 1906, Edwardian Baroque, clad in orange terracotta. Next the entrance to the rear yard between the buildings, with a lovely arching ironwork gate. Lastly LANCASTER HOUSE, built in two phases between 1905 and 1910. Edwardian Baroque, of red brick and orange terracotta. It is the scale which impresses rather than the detail. The corner to Princess Street is emphasized with an ornate four-storey corner turret.

Further NE, apart from a gap alongside the canal, there are ranges of big warehouses, all more or less of a height, all of the late C19 or early C20, all of red brick. Individually they are not outstanding, but the visual coherence and massing is a vital part of the street scene. For the University of Manchester Institute of Science and Technology, s side, *see* Chorlton-on-Medlock; for the Manchester Metropolitan University buildings, *see* Public Buildings, p. 299.

WHITWORTH STREET WEST continues w of Oxford Road. The CORNER HOUSE (s side) is a complex of cinemas and exhibition space converted in 1985 by *The Millard Partnership* and *Fletcher Priest Architects* from an early C20 store. The cinema opposite with the curved corner is part of the complex. By *P. Cummings*, 1934–5, refitted in 1998, by *David Chipperfield* who clad the upper part with green glass strips. A huge apartment block, opposite (by *MBLC*, 2001–2), has an interesting corner tower, circular at the top, with green copper cladding. From this point the MSJ&AR viaduct follows the s side of the street. The GREEN ROOM THEATRE further w, inaugurated in 1987, is accommodated within two of its arches, with entrance and front of house remodelled in phases between 1992 and 1996 by *Ian Simpson Architects*. A little farther w, the RITZ, a dance hall built in 1927–8 with a white faience front sporting trophies with musical instruments. It was one of *Cruickshank & Seward*'s early commissions. Not far beyond, on the same side, another white-faience-clad block is a warehouse of 1914, by *Harry S. Fairhurst* again. The arches of the viaduct open out as the junction of Albion Street is approached, giving views of a former gasworks site and of GRAND ISLAND by *P. Shuttleworth* of *Building Design Partnership*, 1991. A great square office block clad in purple-grey panels with a central atrium, heavy-looking because of the client's requirement to reduce solar gain. Opposite, the HAÇIENDA is a humdrum apartment block, 2002–3, on the site of the famous club of the same name, which opened in 1982.

WINDMILL STREET. INTERNATIONAL CONVENTION CENTRE by *Stephenson Bell* and *Sheppard Robson*, 1999–2000. A coolly sophisticated building, with a glass foyer on two levels fronting Windmill Street. An 800-seat stone-clad auditorium, shaped like a scallop shell in plan, rises above the entrance with an angle jutting out to the street. A multipurpose hall at the rear (S) is separated from the auditorium by a taller service stack.

YORK STREET. S side. No. 26, *Leonard Stokes's* former Telephone Exchange, was built *c.* 1909. Free Style, an original and subtle design with gently canted bays of fine red brick, in places laid in herringbone pattern, with blue brick banding and sparing white faience decoration.

PERAMBULATIONS

1. Dale Street to High Street

This is a fairly long walk covering the area NE of the central part of town, known as the Northern Quarter, bounded by the centre to the SW, Ancoats (*see* p. 376) to the NE, and Shude Hill to the NW.

The area N of Piccadilly was largely open land until after *c.* 1770, when Sir Ashton Lever of Alkrington began selling it in large blocks to developers. Some buildings of that period survive, of which most are modest brick houses, some with attic workshops. Late C19 and early C20 textile warehouses, offices and other commercial buildings now crowd the streets nearest the town centre, which largely retain the scale of C19 Manchester. The part W of Oldham Street includes areas where narrow streets and a network of alleys give a flavour of how the place must have been before later C19 rebuilding. Much of this area had already been built up by the mid C18 as the town expanded E from the medieval core around the Cathedral, and some late C18 and early C19 houses and warehouses survive here. Regeneration, initially centred on Oldham Street, started in the late 1990s with new bars, cafés and shops as well as residential conversions.

We start at the SE end of DALE STREET, at the junction of Ducie Street. For the Rochdale Canal Basin *see* Public Buildings, p. 304.*

---

*LAYSTALL STREET, NE of the basin, has one interesting building, a former warehouse of 1880 by *M. Seanor* with an extravagant front of richly moulded terracotta. It was built for a manufacturer of firebricks and of terracotta, for which the frontage was probably designed as an advertisement. We are grateful to Steve Little for supplying these details.

Dale Street runs NW, and it is lined with late C19 and early C20 commercial warehouses, hugely impressive, but lacking the homogeneity of e.g. Princess Street, for here there is more eclecticism and variation in scale. The Baroque No. 57, E side, 1913, has a streamlined interwar rear extension. Nos. 53–55 next to it, LANGLEY BUILDINGS of 1909 by *R. Argile*, is a treat, making the most of its narrow frontage with a lively terracotta façade sporting a curved oriel and giant composite pilasters and a segmental pediment. Note Back China Lane, SE side, a private street for loading, with original gates. No. 56, W side, *c.* 1875, is a warehouse with a Venetian Gothic front, stone below and polychrome brick above. More warehouses follow; one of the largest, E side, is No. 35, of 1903 by *J. W. Beaumont*. Six storeys in pink terracotta and a splayed corner with upper octagonal piers and turrets. BRADLEY HOUSE of *c.* 1850 sits on a triangular site between Newton Street and Port Street, a late classical warehouse (five storeys, brick on a stone ground floor). The narrow elevation to Dale Street has a tripartite window with pilasters.

The junction of Dale Street, Newton Street and Port Street is a good vantage point. On the NE side of Dale Street, Nos. 29–31 by *W. & G. Higginbottom*, 1909, is a big early C20 warehouse in bright red brick with white stone dressings. Opposite there is a little row of late C18 houses with doorcases. On the NW side of NEWTON STREET two 1880s warehouses by *Clegg, Son & Knowles*: the first on the corner of Back Piccadilly, red brick and stone dressings, with rounded corners and prominent chimneys; its neighbour, on the corner of Dale Street, similar though more elaborate.

HILTON STREET is reached by cutting NE along Port Street beside Bradley House. A group of late C18 houses survives on the N corner. Nos. 45–47 have crude pedimented doorcases and steps from the street down to cellars. More houses extend along each side of Port Street where one or two have long attic workshop windows. Hilton Street continues NW. On the S corner of NEWTON STREET, No. 50 is a very attractive warehouse by *C. Clegg & Son*, 1907. Baroque, strikingly designed to maximize light with giant three-storey glazed arcades on the three exposed sides. A short detour N to the corner of Faraday Street brings us to the POLICE MUSEUM in a police station of 1879, low and unpretentious in red brick. The range along the Newton Street front was rebuilt as a Weights and Measures Office later in the C19, but the station, entered from Faraday Street, retains the original Charge Office and windowless cells. Returning to the corner of Hilton Street brings us to STEVENSON SQUARE and the site of St Clement, of 1793, demolished in the 1870s. This was the centre of a development by William Stevenson, who bought the land from Sir Ashton Lever in 1780. No. 9, N side, was an early C19 thread-winding mill, but almost all the other buildings are late C19 or early C20. The former premises of I.J. & G. Cooper on the S side were designed in 1906 by *John Bowden*. The huge warehouse occupies an island site stretching through to Dale Street. The style is eclectic with tall shaped gables, all done in pressed red brick with matching terracotta and a red sandstone ground floor. On Dale Street, sw side, is an extravagant arched stone entrance with carved Renaissance and Art Nouveau motifs, while on Spear Street, NW side, the loading bay is lined with white glazed bricks.*

LEVER STREET leads NE from the square. Late C18 Manchester housing is graphically illustrated by Nos. 69–77, NW side, a row of five brick houses with pedimented doorcases, backed on BRADLEY STREET by the city centre's only surviving examples of one-up one-down houses. The contrast between the smart houses on the street frontage and the tiny dwellings behind is striking. The latter were probably originally occupied by artisans, and had many advantages compared with cellars, back-to-backs, and common lodging houses which were the lot of less skilled workers. The whole range was rebuilt in 1996 so it all looks regular and new. Retracing our steps SW brings us to the junction with Dale Street where there are more warehouses. The Italianate No. 22 on the NE side, by *Smith, Woodhouse & Willoughby*, 1875, has arched entrances rising through two storeys with carved keystones and ironwork screens. No. 20 on the other, SE side, by *J. W. Beaumont*, 1895, has an arcaded corner entrance and a pair of large arched windows. Looking back across to the N side of Dale Street from the street corner gives a view of the frontage of the Coopers' warehouse (*see* Stevenson Square, above) and beside it on the other corner of Spear Street, No. 3, a former millinery warehouse of *c.* 1905, red brick and yellow terracotta with Baroque touches. Further s down Lever Street, E side, is a group of late C18 or early C19 town houses (now offices) fronted by elegant stone doorcases and semicircular stone steps: Nos. 12–14, scribed stucco, Nos. 8–10 exposed brick.

On the opposite (w) side of the street the narrow BACK PICCADILLY runs NW and brings us out on OLDHAM STREET. This was one of Manchester's premier late C19 and early C20 shopping streets. After years of decline regeneration has come with residential conversions and a smattering of stylish new shops and bars. We begin at the s end with a mixture of shabbily grand early C20 shops, e.g. Nos. 6–12, E side, with an upper Doric colonnade, completely outdone by Nos. 21–33, opposite, by *J. W. Beaumont*, 1914, with its grand upper Ionic colonnade. For the Methodist Central Hall, *see* p. 277.

The SMITHFIELD BUILDING, w side, is actually several separate buildings around a central courtyard, converted to flats by *Stephenson Bell* for the developers Urban Splash in 1997–8. Shops below with flats recessed behind balconies

---

*The building was considered sufficiently advanced to merit a full-page description in the *Building News* in 1906. It was lit throughout by electricity, and solid steel columns diminishing in size on each successive floor were used for their superior fireproof qualities. A staff canteen catered for 400.

above, held together with a tight urban vocabulary of grids. Upper floors generally retain the late C19 façades. To the N more late C19 and early C20 shops and offices follow, then we reach two interesting pubs. THE CASTLE, E side, built in 1789, used as a pub from at least 1816, was refitted c. 1897. Arts and Crafts lettering outside and late C19 plan and fittings inside. THE CITY, W side, also late C18, has a good late C19 timber front with carved pilasters and fanlights with radiating bars. Above, a (probably early C19) panel depicts the arrival of William and Mary in England attended by Britannia, an angel and a rejoicing clergyman (the pub was called the Prince of Orange from c. 1800).

There are one or two interesting buildings on SWAN STREET which runs NW at the top of Oldham Street, for those who feel equal to a detour. Nos. 2–4, N side, a former MIDLAND BANK, by J. B. Whinney, was completed in 1922. Classical, in Portland stone, with a curved end to Oldham Road. Further NW, on the same side, there is a terrace of early C19 houses and the late C19 entrance to SWAN BUILDINGS, with a nicely carved red stone plaque with a swan. Further along, S side, the BAND ON THE WALL, formerly the George and Dragon, was an Edwardian music-hall-cum-pub which retains a bold ground-floor arcade outside and splendid plasterwork ceilings with pendants inside. Its neighbour, No. 11, is Ruskinian Gothic in red brick. Rejoin the perambulation by returning along Swan Street and turning r. down Tib Street.

The narrow TIB STREET runs SW, parallel to Oldham Street. It originated as a footpath alongside the River Tib, which was culverted in 1783. A few C18 houses survive, most of them greatly altered. Nos. 47–53, W side, had originally basement cellar dwellings and attic workshops. The (restored) workshop windows and N gable taking-in door survive. On the N side low-rise brick local authority housing of the late 1970s, the first public-sector housing in the centre after slum clearance and exodus in the 1960s.

THOMAS STREET runs NW, but there is not much to see until Nos. 48–50, SW side, is reached. It has long ranges of upper workshop windows and a warehouse extension with its loading bay at the rear on KELVIN STREET. This area was built up by the mid C18 and the maze of tiny streets reflects the essentials of the layout shown on Green's 1794 map. There are several interesting late C18 houses, some with attic workshops, and some early-to-mid-C19 warehouses here and on TURNER STREET and BACK TURNER STREET. Back on Thomas Street near the NW end Nos. 30–35, NE side, is a row of houses with late C18 or early C19 doorcases, placing them a cut above the humbler Kelvin Street dwellings, though the attics have workshop windows.

Thomas Street continues NW to the top of HIGH STREET. Opposite, Nos. 75–77 is a showy Venetian Gothic warehouse, c. 1875, sandstone and red brick, with elaborate corner entrances with big carved heads.

At the NE end of High Street a number of the buildings of the former SMITHFIELD MARKET can be found. The market grew up in the late C18. In 1846 the Corporation bought land on the SE side of Shudehill, and the site expanded throughout the C19. By 1900 it was the largest covered market in Britain. The former MARKET OFFICES, on the NE corner of Thomas Street, are by *Travis & Mangnall*, 1877. Three storeys, red brick with stone dressings, with round-headed first-floor windows. On top a conglomeration of tall chimneys and pedimented gables crowned with urns. Attached to the r. is the eccentric WHOLESALE FISH MARKET by *Speakman, Son & Hickson*, 1873. Only the gabled brick façades and some cast-iron columns survive, and a new building of 2003 has been slotted between them as part of the ICIAN redevelopment (*see* below). The style is Italian Romanesque with stepped gables and prominent Lombard friezes. Vigorous sculpture in the tympana by *Joseph Bonehill* of Manchester shows scenes of fishing at sea, landing the catch and selling it on, etc. Some of the attractive ironwork gates survive also, by *Hodkinson, Poynton & Lester*.

To the NE, on GOADSBY STREET, the WHOLESALE MARKET HALL, by *I. & J. P. Holden*, dated 1857, altered 1867. Classical, in a style described by *The Builder* in 1859 as 'Roman composite'. Stone, pedimented, with pilasters incorporating bulls' heads and arched openings. The old market place is to be the site of a mixed retail, commercial and residential scheme by the developers ICIAN, with conversion of existing buildings and new buildings, in progress 2004. The CRAFT VILLAGE reuses the Retail Fish Market building of *c.* 1895, which lies near the SE corner of the site. Glazed roof, arcaded brick sides – nothing special, but suited to the new use, craft studios and shops inserted in the 1980s.

Returning to High Street, continue s for No. 66, E side, a pub of 1882 by *Watson & Justice*. Eclectic Gothic detailing with Tudor moulds over the doors. Further along, CHURCH STREET runs E. On the s side a large former warehouse of 1928 by *Jones, Francis & Dalrymple* has a grand stone front with fluted Doric columns. Almost opposite, UNION STREET runs N. No. 2, E side, is a derelict late C18 brick house. The grandest in the area, with three bays and three storeys.

Returning to High Street and continuing s leads to the centre and Market Street. Perambulation 2 can be joined by proceeding w along Market Street and turning r. into Corporation Street.

2. *The Medieval Core and Corporation Street*

This walk covers the NW side of the city centre, from the Irwell and the boundary with Salford on the w side, to Miller Street and Dantzic Street to the N and Shude Hill to the E.

The medieval core of the city lay near the river, between the Cathedral (*see* p. 267) and Victoria Station (*see* Public Buildings, p. 301). It had become a squalid slum by the early–mid C19, partially rebuilt with warehousing thereafter, but remaining a backwater until the end of the C20. A terrorist bomb in 1996 exploded near the s end of Corporation Street causing severe damage to the immediate area, which has been extensively rebuilt. The urban design competition launched in response covered not only the damaged area but also the neglected hinterland to the N. The winners were a team consisting of *EDAW*, *Ian Simpson Architects*, *Alan Baxter Associates*, *Benoy* and *Johnson Urban Development Associates*, whose proposals included linking the cathedral area with the centre by a new pedestrian route (New Cathedral Street, below) and new public open spaces (Exchange Square and City Park, the latter to a design by *BDP*), as a focus for regeneration and development.

CORPORATION STREET is a continuation of Cross Street (*see* central area, p. 311). The N part was cut through a muddle of tiny alleys and courtyards in 1848, the year in which the Corporation purchased the manorial rights of the town from Sir Oswald Mosley. We start at the s end where the 1996 explosion occurred. Here the whole area has been rebuilt keeping most of the basic street pattern. The MARKS & SPENCER and SELFRIDGES store, w side, by *BDP*, opened in 1999. An enormous free-standing block with a central lightwell and big glass screens. Despite its size it does not dominate, thanks to the careful detailing of the elevations and respect for the cornice line of neighbouring buildings. The store was split when Selfridges took over the N half in 2002. Interior spaces were redesigned, with a basement food hall by *Future Systems*. A high-level footbridge between the two halves crosses Corporation Street. By *Hodder Associates*, engineers *Ove Arup & Partners*, it is a hyperbolic paraboloid in the form of a translucent hourglass, with triangular glass panels. It links with the w side of the Arndale Centre (*see* also Market Street), but cannot bridge the stylistic gap between the classy refinement of the M & S store and the unexciting Arndale Centre frontage, with formulaic towers, by the *Ratcliffe Partnership*, completed 2000.

To the N is a new public space, EXCHANGE SQUARE, by *Martha Schwarz*, 1999–2000. The shape was determined by the lines of Hanging Ditch, on the N side (*see* below), New Cathedral Steet, w, and Corporation Street, E. The fall of the land is taken by angled terraces from the platform upon which Marks & Spencer sits, but it is not possible to traverse it in desired directions, as walls on the edge of the terraces divert walkers away from the principal destinations around the square. The scheme has also been let down by gimmickry, e.g. the strange pop SCULPTURES by *John Hyatt*, 1999, like giant children's windmills set at different angles. The lighting scheme is imaginative, however, and at the base of the terraces there is a curving linear water feature with blocks of stone rising above the water so that it can be crossed at any point. On the E side of the square the whole of the N part of the Arndale

Centre (*see* also Market Street) is being rebuilt by *Chapman Taylor Partners*, 2004.

The CORN EXCHANGE, dated 1897 and 1903, takes up the N side of the square. The site is triangular and the straggly four-storey Renaissance style building took thirteen years to build. *Ball & Elce* did the brick part to Fennel Street and *Potts, Son & Pickup* the rest. Post-bomb repair and refurbishment resulted in loss of most of the comfortable Edwardian interior, replaced by new retail outlets, with the general idea of galleries lit by the central dome retained. The building fronts HANGING DITCH, a street named from a watercourse running in an arc between the rivers Irwell and Irk which enclosed the heart of the medieval settlement.

CATEATON STREET runs W as a continuation of Hanging Ditch. The OLD WELLINGTON INN and SINCLAIR'S OYSTER BAR, N side, are known collectively as the Shambles of which they were originally a part. They were modified in 1925, jacked up from the medieval street level to Shambles Square (now beneath New Cathedral Street, below) in the 1970s, and moved here in 1998–9 as part of the post-bomb redevelopment. The WELLINGTON INN, probably C17, has close-studded framing with angle braces and mullioned windows, the jettied gables decorated with lattice framing. The framing of the upper floor is a later addition. Of 1998–9 the odd rear extension which reproduces timber framing in stone cladding, and the stone linking block to the OYSTER BAR. This was of brick, the internal timbers reused, so its origins are obscure though a C16 date has been suggested for it. Mid–late C19 bar fittings have been preserved inside. More important Manchester buildings have disappeared without a trace in the last decade, so perhaps the main point of this exercise will be to illustrate an enduring C20 love affair with timber framing. The buildings form the visual termination of NEW CATHEDRAL STREET, a welcome new pedestrian route, running from St Ann's Square along the W side of Marks & Spencer. The W side is taken up by a large formulaic retail development, 2001–3. For No. 1 Deansgate, *see* Perambulation 3.

The CATHEDRAL VISITOR CENTRE, by *Hurd Rolland Partnership*, 2001–2, reuses Hanging Bridge Chambers of 1880–1, a narrow office building with ranges of boxy oriels. Inside it is possible to see HANGING BRIDGE, which spans Hanging Ditch between Cateaton Street (s) and Cathedral Yard (N). The bridge formed a principal approach from the town to the parish church (now the Cathedral) during the medieval period. The earliest reference occurs in 1343, but the present structure is probably a later rebuilding or remodelling; a likely date is *c.* 1421–*c.* 1500, the period when the church was rebuilt. Coursed and dressed sandstone, two Tudor arches with a central pier. The arches are of unequal width and slightly differently treated, that to the s with ribs on the underside. They appear to be of one build, however, and Dr Arrowsmith surmises that the differing treatment may reflect different donors.

The footings of the s arch and a (buried) buttress on the NW side could relate to an earlier structure. Stone footings placed at an angle from the E side of the central pier may be an indication that the water was diverted at some time through the S arch, leaving the N side dry. Last on Cateaton Street, MYNSHULL'S HOUSE further w on Cateaton Street, N side, is an engaging little building with an openwork parapet and Jacobean detailing. It was built for the trustees of a charity founded through the will of Thomas Mynshull in 1698, replacing an earlier building on the site. The idea was that the rental would provide funds for apprenticing poor Manchester boys to a trade. By *Ball & Elce* with carving by *J. J. Millson*, dated 1890.

Retracing our steps to Exchange Square, continue N alongside the Triangle building to Fennel Street. For Urbis, *see* Public Buildings, p. 298. The CITY PARK beside it was designed by *BDP*, 2001–2. Undulating greensward, with stone benches and a watercourse incorporating artworks on the theme of the seasons designed by *Stephen Broadbent* and *Melanie Jackson*, 2001.

The remaining E side of Corporation Street N of Urbis is dominated by the buildings of the CO-OPERATIVE WHOLESALE SOCIETY and CO-OPERATIVE INSURANCE SOCIETY. First the CO-OPERATIVE BANK, 1977 by *CWS Architects*, red brick with a deep mansard, built on a horseshoe plan. Beside it a copy of a STATUE of Robert Owen by *Gilbert Bayes*, 1953, erected 1994. Next the CWS offices, Baroque, by *F. E. L. Harris*, 1905–9, with coupled giant Corinthian columns and arcading at the top. The unbalanced look is due to the loss of the corner domes. Then more offices, originally a bank, this time of 1928, by the CWS chief architect *W. A. Johnson*. Uninspiring and severe with giant upper pilasters. PARKERS HOTEL, by *Bradshaw, Gass & Hope*, 1906, on the N part of Corporation Street beyond Miller Street, started as the CIS head office. Edwardian Baroque, red brick and Portland stone, with a curved frontage to the street corner and a copper dome. Simpler stone addition, l. Continuing N brings us into an area known as Angel Meadow and to ASHTON HOUSE, E side, former model lodgings for women built by the Corporation 1908–10 by the City Architect *Henry Price*. On an island site, with a very narrow rounded NE end to the junction with Crown Lane. Free Style, red brick and cream terracotta. It catered for 222 women, who occupied dormitories with individual cubicles and cooked for themselves in communal kitchens. Further along on DANTZIC STREET, the CHARTER STREET RAGGED SCHOOL AND WORKING GIRLS HOME is a relatively rare survivor of this type, with a largely intact plan. The range to Little Nelson Street dated 1891 is by *Maxwell & Tuke* who added the block to Dantzic Street in 1898. The earlier part has tall channelled chimneys and top-floor oriels, the rather plain later building one or two Baroque touches. As well as educating street children, accommodation was provided for vulnerable servant girls who would otherwise have had to use common lodging houses. Return along Corporation Street to MILLER STREET, named for Arkwright's mill of *c.* 1782, probably the first Manchester mill to use steam to raise water to the wheel.

On the s side more offices of the CWS and CIS. The complex consists of a twenty-five-storey tower, a five-storey lower part, and the fourteen-storey NEW CENTURY HOUSE to Corporation Street, a curtain-walled slab. The CIS TOWER is the best of the Manchester 1960s office blocks, done with discipline and consistency and inspired by the achievements of Skidmore, Owings & Merrill, in particular the Inland Steel Building in Chicago, which was amongst the buildings inspected by the design team on a trip to America. The team were *G. S. Hay* of the CWS and *Gordon Tait* of *Sir John Burnet, Tait & Partners*, the building date 1959–62. When the building was being planned the CIS General Manager set out three aims: to add to the prestige of the Society and the Co-operative Movement, to improve the appearance of the city and to provide first-class accommodation for staff. The aims were fulfilled, and continue to be forty years on.

118   First the CIS TOWER. Steel-framed with a windowless service tower of reinforced concrete clad with mosaic and rising to 400 ft (122 metres). Glass, aluminium and black enamelled steel were chosen for the exterior instead of concrete or stone, which become dirty so quickly in Manchester's atmosphere, and this decision has paid off. It remains the tallest building in Manchester and one of the most distinguished. The details around the entrance from Miller Street are the only weakness. The entrance hall is excellent, the cool spaciousness only slightly marred by a new controlled entry system. The mural by *William Mitchell*, of bronzed fibreglass, fits perfectly with the optimistic 1960s ambience. *Professor Misha Black* and the *Design Research Unit* designed the interiors, including the executive dining rooms in cherry veneer and the executive suite with teak veneer and vertical green glass strips.

NEW CENTURY HOUSE is approached from an entrance forecourt from Corporation Street, with an abstract relief by *John McCarthy* on a screen wall at r. angles. Between the two buildings a conference hall for 1,000. *Jonathan Green Associates* and a CWS in-house team designed the interior, *Stephen Sykes* the figurative sculptured panels inside.

DANTZIC STREET runs s between the CIS and CWS buildings. Here and in surrounding streets are other Co-op buildings, including REDFERN HOUSE, CWS offices designed in 1936 by *W. A. Johnson* with *J. W. Cropper*. The inspiration is Dutch brick Modernism, a style already used for a much larger CWS building in Prescot Street, East London. Seven storeys with a flat roof, pale brown brick with a blue brick base. Tall service tower to the l. and receding curved blocks with continuous window bands with Portland stone frames and metal casements. Adjoining, HOLYOAKE HOUSE, by F. E. L. Harris for the Co-operative Union, dated 1911. Three storeys and a basement. Baroque in blue-green and cream faience with an extension in similar style on HANOVER STREET, N. Another 1930s building on the opposite side of Dantzic Street seems to be a missing part of Redfern House and must have been designed by the same team.

VICTORIA BUILDINGS lie further s on Dantzic Street. A triangular block of offices, warehouses and workshops by E. J. Sherwood & R. Thomas, 1874. Grouped windows and doorways, linked by round-headed arcades. The street continues s to Withy Grove, from which SHUDE HILL runs NE. Older buildings to note are, on the NW side, No. 29, a stuccoed mid-C19 warehouse with a full-width first-floor window fronted by four graceful twisted cast-iron columns, and on the NE side, No. 46, the HARE AND HOUNDS pub, late C18 in origin with a remarkably complete interwar interior. The N side of the tramway is to be the site of a large new transport interchange. Beyond, at the corner of Hanover Street, the SMITHFIELD pub, built for the Lancashire and Yorkshire Bank in 1904 by Jesse Horsfall. Conventional apart from an attractive Free Style corner tower. Attached, N side, the early C20 STOVELL BUILDINGS, formerly an umbrella works.

OUTLYING BUILDINGS

SHARP STREET. The SHARP STREET RAGGED SCHOOL was founded in 1853, this austere brick building erected in 1869. An early and remarkably intact example of a purpose-built Ragged School. (It is said to have a little-altered interior with a ground floor partition which divided the reception class of wild street children from those who had been subdued).

Returning s and continuing w along Withy Grove brings us back to Corporation Street. Perambulation 3 starts just to the w, at the bottom of Cateaton Street on Deansgate.

3. Deansgate to the Banks of the River Irwell

This walk explores the area on the w side of the centre to the boundary with Salford. Deansgate, on the line of the Roman road to Ribchester, linked the medieval centre with the site of the Roman Fort. The N part was partly built up by the mid C17 and expansion continued in the C18. By the mid C19 the s part was little more than a slum. Deansgate was then widened, starting from the N in 1869, with new offices, shops and commercial buildings. Some C18 houses, including Manchester's best-preserved Georgian terraces, survive near the s end.

DEANSGATE. Starting at the N end, w side, the uninspiring RAMADA RENAISSANCE HOTEL, 1972, former offices by *Cruickshank & Seward*. A fifteen-storey tower, all in grubby white concrete, rises above a lower part. Opposite, No. 1 DEANSGATE, a landmark fourteen-storey apartment block by

Ian Simpson Architects, 2000–2. First a podium, then a huge exposed steel cradle supporting a high glass wedge. Nos. 62–66, HAYWARD'S BUILDING, shops of *c.* 1877, w side. Free Renaissance with three large twin-arched first-floor windows but six smaller ones above; four storeys. By *Corbett, Son & Brooke*, the carving by *Williams & Millson*. Opposite are BARTON'S BUILDINGS of 1871 by *Corbett, Raby & Sawyer*. A long and thoroughly ignorant façade – the ground-floor pilasters must be seen to be believed. On the first floor a cast-iron window arcade and an intricate balcony, a hint of what is to come: for behind the façade is the BARTON ARCADE, a gorgeous glass and iron shopping arcade with two octagonal domes rising from glass pendentives, probably the best example of this type of cast-iron and glass-roofed arcade anywhere in the country. There are two entrances from Deansgate and another reached from St Ann's Square, in a wonderful cast-iron and glass curtain wall. Inside everything is light and airy, with three tiers of balconies with ornamental balustrades curving around the U-shaped arcade, which is quite narrow but very high, rising to 53 ft (16 metres). Shops below, and, unusually in a British arcade, offices above. The ironwork came from *Macfarlane*'s in Glasgow. The obvious influence was the Galleria Vittorio Emanuele in Milan, illustrated in *The Builder* in 1868. Everything was repaired and restored in 1982.

KENDAL MILNE'S department store, on an island site, w side, by *J. S. Beaumont*, 1939. Unlike his usual work, or anything else in Manchester.* A sublimely monumental block with splayed corners, clad in Portland stone. In the German style of store architecture created by Messel early in the century, but stripped down. Windows are vertical strips of greenish glass blocks, with a barely perceptible camber introducing subtle curves and enlivening the stark elevations with reflecting light. Opposite Nos. 83–93, the earlier Kendal's store, by *E. J. Thompson*, 1872–3. Stone, with tripartite first- and second-floor pedimented windows framed by Doric and Ionic columns, and a curved corner to King Street.

ST MARY'S STREET runs w beside Kendal's with the five-storey ARKWRIGHT HOUSE at the end, 1928 by *Harry S. Fairhurst*. Portland stone, with giant Corinthian columns above the entrance.

PARSONAGE GARDENS was the site of St Mary's Church, built 1753, closed 1890, demolished 1928. On the w side the terracotta-clad NATIONAL HOUSE, 1905–9 by *Harry S. Fairhurst* again, converted to flats 2000. Further N, BLACK-FRIARS HOUSE, s side, is also by *Harry S. Fairhurst* for the Bleachers' Association, 1925. Portland stone, in the crisp classical idiom favoured by the firm between the wars. Back in the square, ST MARY'S PARSONAGE runs s. At an angle to the

* Mr Ferriday thinks it could be the work of a German émigré working in Beaumont's office.

street, E side, a Venetian Gothic warehouse by *Clegg & Knowles*, 1868. Warm red brick with stone dressings and attractive details. For Trinity Bridge *see* Salford p. 622. Continue to the junction with BRIDGE STREET, dominated by ALBERT BRIDGE HOUSE, tax offices by *E. H. Banks* (Ministry of Works), 1958–9, one of the first and best big post-war buildings in the city. Eighteen storeys high with Portland stone cladding, and low blocks coming forward to make a group. To the W, on the riverside in front of Albert Bridge House is a STATUE of the Salford M.P. and philanthropist Joseph Brotherton, by *Matthew Noble*, 1858, moved from Peel Park in Salford in 1986. ALBERT BRIDGE, by *Jesse Hartley*, 1844, replaced a bridge of 1785. A single low segmental arch of stone with pilaster terminals and curved abutments.

WATER STREET leads S, and beside the river THE PUMP HOUSE PEOPLE'S HISTORY MUSEUM is housed in a hydraulic power station by the City Architect *Henry Price*, 1907–9. The conversion was by *OMI Architects*, 1993–4, to accommodate part of the collection of the National Museum of Labour History. It is best seen from the Salford side of Albert Bridge: two huge water tanks on each side of the central engine house, accumulator tower to the l. Along the waterfront S of the museum large apartment blocks and offices are under construction, 2004.

Back on Bridge Street we continue E back towards Deansgate. The MASONIC HALL is by *Percy Scott Worthington*, dated 1929. A monumental block in Portland stone with shallow wings, rusticated at ground-floor level. There is an obvious debt to Lutyens, whose Midland Bank was going up in King Street at the same time. Inside, a splendid hall, Ionic columns and a coffered top-lit barrel-vault ceiling. Further E, s side, the former premises of the MANCHESTER AND SALFORD STREET CHILDREN MISSION. By *W. & G. Higginbottom*, dated 1896. Green and cream faience with lettering, and above, charming panels with smiling children's heads. Attached to the rear (on Wood Street, reached either from Deansgate or via Bradleys Court, a tiny alley to the r.), are the Mission offices and (former) WORKING MEN'S CHURCH, dated 1905. The organization, founded in 1869, came to this site in 1873. Back on Bridge Street No. 64 RATIONAL HOUSE, s side, by *Samuel Davidson*, 1897, and KENWORTHY BUILDINGS, N side, 1902 by *Brameld & Smith*, are examples of the pleasant modestly scaled late C19 and early C20 commercial buildings along the remaining stretch of the street towards Deansgate.

On the s corner of Bridge Street the mid-C19 SAWYERS ARMS adds a splash of colour with its extravagant early C20 red- and yellow-tile-clad ground floor. Opposite, at the N corner of John Dalton Street, an office building, 1876 by *Pennington & Bridgen*: Gothic, but no longer High Victorian Gothic. The portal may still be that, but on the façade there is too much bare wall, and the rhythm is already turning Late Victorian. We turn r. onto Deansgate. The former GAS

COMMITTEE SHOWROOMS AND OFFICES by *Edward Salomons*, 1890, W side, very badly weathered red sandstone. Narrow three-bay frontage, three storeys with a Dutch gable. LINCOLN HOUSE, E side, by *B. Johnson* of *Holford Associates*, 1986, has pink granite piers and reflective glass, the earliest example of brash 1980s glitter in the centre.

SPINNINGFIELD is a small square opposite, W side, retaining its C18 field name. The area from here down to the riverside is being redeveloped, 2002–4. Large commercial buildings are being erected on the S and W sides of the square, including a new building for the Royal Bank of Scotland by *Sheppard Robson*, end-on to Deansgate. Exposed steel cradles the base, and it bulges out on the S side, following a recent fashion in architecture for fluid shapes. For the Magistrates' Court and Crown Court *see* Public Buildings, pp. 286–7.

ELLIOT HOUSE, Deansgate E side, 1878, is former School Board offices by *Royle & Bennett*. Queen Anne style, red brick, red terracotta and red sandstone. In the corner splays, at eye level, oval windows in surrounds of beautifully carved red sandstone. Still on the E side, 201 DEANSGATE by *Holford Associates*, 1995–6, pompous offices with brick and glass towers framing a cornice and single giant column. Beside them the irrepressibly cheerful Nos. 205–209, ONWARD BUILDINGS, 1903–4 by *Charles Heathcote*, built for a federation of Temperance societies, with bold stripes of red brick, pale yellow sandstone and yellow Terracotta. Opposite, ROYAL LONDON HOUSE, a big Baroque stone block by *Charles Heathcote* of 1904.

GREAT NORTHERN RAILWAY OFFICES. On the S corner with Peter Street the entrance to the former goods yard of the Great Northern Warehouse (*see* Watson Street, centre), then a long, remorseless, uniform range of shops and offices of *c.* 1899, stretching along the whole E side as far as Great Bridgewater Street. Only one room deep, they form a screen wall to the former goods station behind. On the W side CONGREGATIONAL CHURCH HOUSE, Baroque, Portland stone, 1909–11 by *Bradshaw & Gass*. Church-like in an English Renaissance mode, with a domed tower at one end, a rusticated basement and double-height windows seeming to imply a gallery. We return to QUAY STREET which leads W, laid out in 1735 from Deansgate to a new quay on the Irwell.

OVERSEAS HOUSE, on the corner, is a typical *Leach, Rhodes & Walker* office block of 1974. Beside it a striped Edwardian Baroque job, then No. 15 Quay Street by *Stephenson Architecture*, 1991–2, a design of some subtlety with high quality detailing and materials. The stone-clad attic and stair-tower to the r. frame the projecting brick front. Opposite, N side, SUNLIGHT HOUSE is a towering Portland stone office block designed by *Joseph Sunlight* in 1932. When put up it was the tallest building in Manchester. The immense bulk, more evident from distant views, is articulated by soaring corner towers with vertical window slits and winged angel heads designed by *J. Lenigan*. Ten storeys, with four attic storeys set back in tiers. Inside is a basement swimming pool (now used by a health club), part of the original design. Next on this side the OPERA HOUSE, formerly the New Theatre, 1912 by *Richardson & Gill* with *Farquarson*. Classical Mannerism in an appropriately theatrical style with an obvious debt to Cockerell, and also, perhaps, with a nod to the nearby Cockerell-inspired Theatre Royal (*see* Peter Street). The main elevations are in imitation stone. Symmetrical, pedimented, and strongly textured with horizontal emphasis throughout given by channelled rustication. At the centre, over the entrance, three pairs of giant fluted Ionic columns, the outer pairs breaking forward to frame an arch in the tympanum which contains a fine bas-relief 'The Dawn of the Heroic Age', modelled and executed by *John Tanner & Son*.

Opposite, COBDEN HOUSE, on the SW corner of Byrom Street, is a large 1770s town house. Despite an unprepossessing exterior, the result of the loss of the original entrance steps and doorcase, it is the best preserved house of its date in the centre. Brick, symmetrical, with a slightly projecting entrance bay and a late C19 doorcase. To the rear a full-height polygonal bay has to the r. a very nicely detailed stone Venetian window, a smaller version of a window at Platt Hall, by Timothy Lightoler (*see* p. 473). An impressive entrance and staircase hall has a cantilevered stair with a wrought-iron balustrade similar to Adam's work at Osterley, Harewood and Kenwood. The well is lit by the Venetian window modelled on details published by Lightoler in the *Modern Builder's Assistant*, 1757. The surviving scrap of Rococo plasterwork in the stair-well ceiling (according to Dr Ivan Hall) is taken from Matthias Darley's *The Compleat Body of Architecture*, 1773. All main rooms have elaborate doorcases with broken pediments, of which one or two are original. Built by the Byrom family, it was occupied by Richard Cobden in 1836–50, then by Owens College, the precursor to Manchester University, 1851–73: it later became the County Court. The new building to the r. is by *Stephenson Bell*, 1999.

BYROM STREET runs S. The Byroms had laid out a grid of streets for building by 1788, but take-up was slow. Colin Stansfield's research shows that *Charles McNiven* probably built some of the earlier houses. A park at the S end was the site of St John's Church, 1768–9 (demolished 1931), the first major Manchester example of Gothic Revival. Opposite, r. side, a row of late C18 houses with charming Gothick doorcases, most of them extant by 1794. No. 31 has attached at the rear a tiny late C19 chapel, built for the Convent of St Mary who moved in during the mid 1870s. Running E off Byrom Street, ST JOHN STREET has the city's most complete Georgian terraces. Of three storeys and generally of one or two bays, but not a unified scheme. The plots were taken up piecemeal during the late C18 and early C19. Some have pedimented Doric doorcases and some recessed doorcases and slim Ionic columns. No. 24,

N side, is probably 1840s, five bays with a central segmental-headed doorway.

ATHERTON STREET is reached by returning to Byrom Street and striking W across St John's Park. GRANADA HOUSE, W side, is by *Ralph Tubbs*, 1960–2 for the Granada Television Centre. A simple unpretentious design of eight storeys, curtain-walled and topped with signage and, to one side, a spiral stair. The low studios behind, also by *Tubbs*, were an early purpose-designed television complex, built in 1956. Two storeys, of pre-cast concrete units. Also part of this complex, S of the main building, the STAGE ONE building (studios) uses polychromatic brick to match a restored C19 accumulator tower which was incorporated into the building. By *Building Design Partnership*, 1985. To the W Coronation Street's 1960s outdoor set, a scaled-down copy of a C19 terrace, was replaced in similar style in 1981 by *Ken Moth* of *Building Design Partnership* with set designer *Denis Parkin*. The former County Municipal School opposite the main Granada block is dated 1912. Minimal Renaissance detailing and a rooftop playground with piers between the railings giving it a fortress-like look. Atherton Street brings us back to Quay Street. The greatly restored block of C18 houses on the N side was built on part of the Byrom family estate (*see* above).

WATER STREET at the W end of Quay Street runs alongside the Irwell. Beside the river the VICTORIA AND ALBERT HOTEL, warehouses of *c.* 1840, converted in 1991–2 by *Trafalgar House*, project architect *A. Hallworth*, retaining part of the interior structure of timber beams and cast-iron columns but not much of the character. On the r. an (altered) mid-C19 covered quay, close to the site of a large quay and warehouses built by 1740 on the Irwell Navigation.

4. Castlefield

Castlefield was named for Manchester's Roman fort, which was located at the confluence of the Medlock and Irwell. The area's greatest importance historically and internationally is in the substantial remains of early canal and railway structures. The pioneering Bridgewater Canal reached Castlefield in 1765, and interchange with sea-going vessels on the Mersey came in 1776. When the Rochdale Canal joined the Bridgewater Basin in 1804–6, it completed a canal route linking the W and E coasts. The railway buildings include the world's first passenger railway station and the oldest surviving railway warehouse. The area, designated an Urban Heritage Park in 1982, retains some of the most dramatic industrial scenery in the city. Since that time there has been regeneration with new buildings as well as refurbishment of the old, and the visual excitement of the area owes something to both. The perambulation starts near the S end of Deansgate at its junction with Whitworth Street West.

DEANSGATE STATION, E side, opened in 1849 on the MSJ&AR line. Rebuilt 1896. Curved to the street corner, paired corner entrances with mock portcullises and battlemented parapet. Just to the s, e side, is DEANSGATE QUAY, a superior eight-storey apartment block by *Stephenson Bell*, 1999–2000. On the w side, right up against the s side of the railway viaduct, the former CONGREGATIONAL CHAPEL, 1858, is by *Edward Walters*. Brick with stone dressings, a design of interpenetrating temple fronts, the central part with an upper arcade of round-headed windows and a wheel window in the pediment. A tall slender Veneto-Byzantine campanile attached to the s has blind arcading to the first stage, with a stone arcaded belfry stage and a steep concave roof.

Returning N beneath the railway viaduct brings us to CASTLE STREET, which runs w from Deansgate. Here there are impressive views of the viaducts and skewed bridges of the 1849 railway as they cross first the street and then the Rochdale Canal, on the N side of the street. On the other side the BRIDGEWATER CANAL BASIN can be seen, the terminus of one of the first canals in Britain to run cross-country between watersheds without relying on the courses of streams or rivers. It was built for Francis Egerton, 3rd Duke of Bridgewater, to transport coal from his mines in Worsley (*see* Worsley). *James Brindley* acted as consulting engineer, and *John Gilbert* was resident engineer.

Castle Street overlooks the CASTLE QUAY, the original terminus and coal wharf of the basin. The sandstone cliff was cut back so that coal could be heaped alongside the canal. The GROCERS'WAREHOUSE on the wharf was rebuilt in 1987 after demolition in 1960. The original was built in two phases, the first completed in the early 1770s, over an existing canal arm of *c.* 1765. This was part of Brindley's system for hauling coal up the sheer sandstone face to Castle Street. Boats were taken into a tunnel driven directly into the cliff from which 8 cwt (406 kg) coal buckets were raised up a shaft more than 20 ft (6 metres) to street level using a water-powered crane. The l. archway leads to Brindley's tunnel, with side shafts housing a replica waterwheel and hoist. The other archway is for a second wet dock, added before 1807.

On the s side of the wharf, up against the Bridgewater Viaduct, the QUAY BAR by *Stephenson Bell*, opened in 1998. Double-height bar, slightly angled full-height fins to the canal, recessed glass walls between. The layout was derived from the geometry of spiral shells. A path runs w along the quay, where Castle Street can be rejoined near the Merchants' Warehouse. Alternatively, returning up the steps to Castle Street gives a closer view of EASTGATE (N side), a well-detailed office conversion of an 1870s warehouse by *Stephenson Architecture*, 1992. Continuing w alongside the quay brings the magnificent MIDDLE WAREHOUSE into view across the basin to the s. The enormous five-storey brick structure was built 1828–31. A giant blind segmental arch houses two arched shipping holes, and paired round-headed windows alternate with loading slots on

each side. Converted to flats and offices in 1988. The street
continues to follow the line of the basin and curves to the N.
Here on the W side is the brick MERCHANTS' WAREHOUSE,
dated 1825, the oldest surviving warehouse of the basin. The
repair and refurbishment in 1995–7 was by *Ian Simpson Architects*. Brick, three storeys to the street, four to the canal. To
Castle Street loading slots alternate with two-window bays, the
windows small with round heads. To the canal, paired central
shipping holes with supplementary loading slots on each side.
Inside it has transverse walls dividing it into six bays. The renovation was achieved by placing services in slim glass blocks
on each gable end.

A narrow C18 bridge carries Castle Street over the Rochdale
Canal just as it flows into the Bridgewater Canal Basin. Beside
it is a late C19 lock house. To the E the canal is crossed by
the elegant understated ARCHITECT'S FOOTBRIDGE by *Ian
Simpson Architects*, 1996, a slender span with a steel frame clad
in stone. To the W the slightly silly BARCA café bar by *Harrison Ince*, 1996, is built into the 1849 viaduct arches facing on
to CATALAN SQUARE. The MERCHANTS' BRIDGE, 1996 by
Whitby & Bird, crosses the canal in a curving sweep here, stabilized by a cantilevered sickle arch. It was inspired by Calatrava's Ripoll Bridge in Gerona. To the W on the other side of
the basin SLATE WHARF, 1990s apartment blocks, designed
to match the materials and scale of the older buildings.

Castle Street continues N beneath an impressive array of railway
viaducts, which are best appreciated from the N side of the
basin and will be described from that viewpoint, *see* below. We
are now following a canal arm which was reopened in the early
1990s as part of a scheme by *DEGW*, who designed the
stepped spectator stand sheltered by canvas tents which overlooks the canal arm from the E, and the VISITORS' CENTRE
of 1993 above the basin to the N on Liverpool Road. Along the
other (W) side of the canal is the YMCA, called the Y hotel, by
David Lyons Associates, *c.* 1990. Pitched roofs, polychromatic
brick, bright red trimmings, an attempt to fit in with the character of the area which does not really come off. A walk S along
the edge of the basin beside the YMCA brings us to the Youth
Hostel Association's CASTLEFIELD HOSTEL by *Halliday
Meecham*, 1995, two simple brick boxes with barrel roofs set at
an angle to each other, with an entrance in the angle. Understated and suited to the environment, unlike its neighbour,
offices with an upcurved roof with a glazed spine and folksy
collection of green funnels, 1996–9. This is reached from
POTATO WHARF by crossing the GIANTS BASIN, designed by
Brindley to take outflow from the canal into the River
Medlock, which emerges from a tunnel on the other side of
the road. It was originally a huge clover-leaf weir, modified in
the late C18 or early C19.

The RAILWAY VIADUCTS span the canal basin to the S and this
vantage point affords the most memorable view. In the foreground the two which served Central Station (*see* p. 300) of

c. 1898 and *c.* 1877. They march across the basin supported by huge castellated steel columns. They frame a view of the MSJ&AR viaduct with an elegantly arched bridge with Gothic pierced spandrels and castellated brick piers (the other branch of this line runs immediately behind the YHA). Lowest and latest, the Merchants' Bridge arcs across the water.

Potato Wharf runs N to join LIVERPOOL ROAD. The N side of the street is taken up by the buildings of the MUSEUM OF SCIENCE AND INDUSTRY IN MANCHESTER. The museum was opened in 1983 following the purchase in 1978 of the site of the Liverpool & Manchester Railway terminus by the Greater Manchester Council. The process of restoring and converting the buildings has been a great success. The main entrance is further E on Lower Byrom Street, but starting at this end allows us to follow the historic sequence of building.

The site settled on by the railway company, after many setbacks, was close to the concentration of warehousing around the canals and the Irwell with easy access to Water Street and Deansgate. *George Stephenson* was the engineer, and after initial setbacks he inherited a route proposed by *C. B. Vignoles* under *George and John Rennie*. The complex consists of the viaduct and bridges over the Irwell and Water Street, the passenger station, the station agent's house, and ancillary buildings along Liverpool Road. A railway warehouse of the first phase lies to the N, beyond it to the E a warehouse of 1880 and goods transfer shed of 1855. The volume of traffic both in terms of passengers and goods had never been tackled on such a scale before.

WATER STREET at the W end of Liverpool Road is our starting point. Opposite the road junction a car park alongside the Irwell is the vantage point for *Stephenson*'s stone BRIDGE over the river of 1830, two stone segmental arches on a slightly skewed plan. Converging with them to run parallel across the river is the South Junction part of the 1849 MSJ&AR viaduct. Stephenson's viaduct continues in brick from this point and has alongside Water Street an animal ramp. The viaduct to the N serves the Byrom Street and Grape Street Warehouses (*see* below).

Recrossing Water Street and returning E along Liverpool Road brings us to the PASSENGER STATION completed in 1830. It has first- and second-class entrances with separate booking offices on the ground floor, reached from Liverpool Road, and waiting rooms above which led out to the platform. The front is classical and faced in stone and stucco. The brick house beside it on the corner of Water Street is earlier, of *c.* 1810, and became the station agent's house. (The platform side of the station and the following sequence of buildings can only be seen from inside the museum, and this involves a detour E to the entrance on Lower Byrom Street, returning inside the museum precinct to the W end of the site).

The RAILWAY WAREHOUSE, N of the passenger station, was the first building of the complex to be completed in 1830. It was built in just five months, and it was almost certainly designed by the Liverpool architect *Thomas Haigh.** Three storeys alongside the railway, curving with the line of the viaduct, with rail loading at first-floor level, street level loading at the rear. Railway wagons ran from the viaduct into the building via turntables where they were unloaded and reloaded. The internal structure is of timber, but with cast-iron columns in the basement. The design can be compared to river and canal warehouses, particularly in structural features such as the use of timber floors and timber posts, and transverse cross-walls facilitating the movement of goods between viaduct and road. Bringing wagons directly into the building for loading has parallels with the use of internal wet docks in canal warehouses. The restoration and refitting is by *Building Design Partnership*, project architect *Ken Moth*, in three phases over the period 1992–6.

The POWER HALL is next in sequence. It was a goods transfer depot of 1855, a long two-bay shed running alongside Liverpool Road, the roof hipped at each end. The wagons entered the W side and were unloaded to road vehicles on the S side. The building was opened for museum use in 1983, the alterations largely confined to introducing top-lighting and glazing openings.

The LOWER BYROM STREET WAREHOUSE, 1880, is a goods warehouse served by a viaduct supported by squat cast-iron columns on stone bases. Fireproof construction with brick jack arches and primary and secondary iron beams on large square-section columns. A full-height interior ramp was inserted and a glass-fronted lift slotted into a loading bay in 1987 by *Building Design Partnership*. In 2000 *Austin-Smith:Lord* created a new main entrance, suitably industrial in appearance, and inserted a top-floor restaurant and rear stair-tower.

Beyond to the N, now part of the Granada Television site (*see* Perambulation 3), the GRAPE STREET WAREHOUSE of 1869 is part of the group, visually and functionally. It was served by a separate viaduct across Water Street with the wagons going straight into arched openings. Red brick with blue brick dressings.

Another part of the museum, the AIR AND SPACE HALL, lies opposite the entrance. This is housed in a market hall, called Lower Campfield Market, by *Mangnall & Littlewood*, 1876. Large, rectangular, cast-iron and glass, with ornate detailing. This and the nearby Higher Campfield Market (*see* below) is one of relatively few Victorian markets to use a utilitarian glass and iron frame for the exterior. It was adapted for the display of aeroplanes in 1983 by acting City Architect *E. Clark* for the City Council and taken over by the museum in 1985.

---

*Dr Greene and Keith Falconer identified unexecuted designs for warehouses at Gloucester Dock which are strikingly similar in design.

Lower Byrom Street runs s back to Liverpool Road. Opposite the junction is St Matthew's Sunday School, dated 1827, converted to offices in the 1980s. Brick, two storeys, with an apsidal s end and windows with pointed arches and simple Y-tracery. Turning l. takes us to the site of Manchester's Roman Fort, set back from the s side of Liverpool Road. Established *c*. A.D. 79 in a strategic position at the meeting point of an E–W route linking the bases at York and Chester and the route N to Ribchester and Carlisle. At this time it was of timber and turf, square in plan and designed for an infantry unit of 480. After a period of abandonment a larger timber fort was built *c*. A.D. 160 and this was rebuilt in stone *c*. A.D. 200. A civilian settlement had grown up outside the fort but it is not known how long it persisted after the end of Roman rule.

A path runs s between low walled enclosures, based on excavated plans of buildings of the *vicus* or civilian settlement. Sections of the defensive ditches have been excavated and grassed. They protected the North Gate, and the reconstruction of 1986 was based on the excavated foundations of the twin-portalled early C3 gateway in this position. The design was taken from Continental and British examples and the masonry detail from parts of the wall found during excavation. To the SW the foundations of a granary and another part of the perimeter wall have been consolidated and reconstructed.

Back on Liverpool Road, on the s side there is a row of late C18 and early C19 houses with ranges of windows lighting former attic workshops, probably the best preserved such group in Manchester. Opposite there is another Market Hall of 1878 by *Mangnall & Littlewood*, known as Higher Campfield Market, and similar to their market now used as the Air and Space Hall. It is linked by a glazed roof to a (former) Free Library, by *George Meek*, 1882, fronting Deansgate. Red brick, stone dressings, two storeys. Central entrance with a big segmental pediment with strongly modelled carving. The upper floor is lit by a range of stepped triple windows and at the top a pierced stone parapet and central stone pediment with the city's coat of arms. Diagonally opposite, the corner of Deansgate and Great Bridgewater Street is to be the site of Beetham Tower, a huge forty-seven-storey hotel and apartment block by *Ian Simpson Architects*. Drawings published in 2003 show a sleek glazed tower cantilevered out at the twenty-third floor, where the apartments are set over the hotel, terminating with a slim, transparent, tapering crest rising above the penthouse apartments. It will stand over 560 ft (170 metres) high, taller than anything else in town, in fact taller than anything else in Britain, outside London.

OUTLYING BUILDINGS

The area s of Deansgate Station in a loop of the Medlock is known as Knott Mill, with small-scale mid- and later C19 light industrial works and warehouses and new apartment blocks. Some of the buildings have been imaginatively converted by e.g., *Ian Simpson Architects*, *Harrison Ince* and *Stephenson Bell*, for their own use and as offices, studios, etc. The former ST PETER'S SCHOOL, St Peter's Street, is dated 1876. Large, brick, stripped Gothic.

EAST MANCHESTER

ARDWICK and BESWICK

Ardwick was largely open land when part of the area was acquired by the Birch family in 1636. By the late C18 houses and villas were being built, of which a few, mainly early C19, survive. The estate was eventually bought by Thomas Marsland Bennett in the C19. Beswick was joined with Ardwick to form a ward when Manchester was incorporated in 1838, and was almost completely undeveloped until the mid C19. The city spread its industry and cheap housing over the whole area by the end of the C19, and slum clearance followed from the 1930s and after the war. Only the w part around Ardwick Green now has any cohesion and character. The boundaries are the River Medlock and Ashton New Road, N side; Grey Mare Lane, E side; Ashton Old Road, Gorton Road, Vaughan Street, Bennett Street, Hyde Road, Exeter Close, Langport Avenue, Stockport Road and Ardwick Green South, s side; and Downing Street, w side.

Churches

The depopulation of the area is reflected in the fact that of the eight churches described by Pevsner in *South Lancashire*, only three survive, and of these only St Jerome is currently in use as a church.

ST BENEDICT, Bennett Street, Ardwick. 1880 by *J. S. Crowther*.
71   A remarkably large church, done with panache, and quite unlike any of Crowther's other churches. Some of the unusual

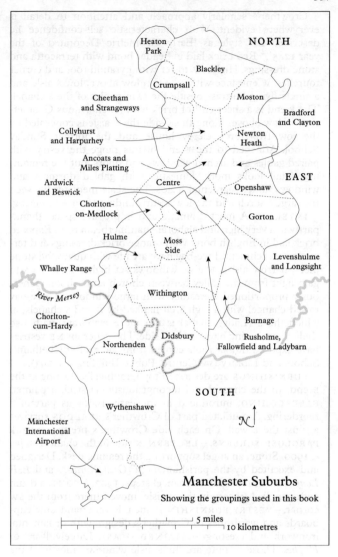

NORTH

Heaton Park

Blackley

Crumpsall

Cheetham and Strangeways

Moston

Bradford and Clayton

Collyhurst and Harpurhey

Newton Heath

Ancoats and Miles Platting

Ardwick and Beswick

Centre

EAST

Openshaw

Chorlton-on-Medlock

Gorton

Hulme

Moss Side

Whalley Range

Levenshulme and Longsight

River Mersey

Withington

Chorlton-cum-Hardy

Burnage

Northenden

Didsbury

Rusholme, Fallowfield and Ladybarn

SOUTH

Wythenshawe

N

Manchester International Airport

Manchester Suburbs

Showing the groupings used in this book

5 miles

10 kilometres

features, such as the attached school and clergy house, can perhaps be attributed to the input of the Anglo-Catholic Bennett family. John Marsland Bennett, who built and equipped the church at his own expense, was a prosperous merchant who settled in Ardwick in the 1850s. According to his son he wanted a church which would be 'plain but massive . . . it should possess a shell which would be standing years after many cheap, "dressy" churches had crumbled to ruins.'

Crowther's scholarly approach and attention to detail is everywhere evident. With characteristic self-confidence he described the style as 'Early Geometric Decorated of the year 1245'.* Red brick laid in header bond with terracotta and stone dressings. High NW tower with pyramid roof and corner tourelles. W entrance with rose window above, low S aisle and a single flying buttress beside the twin gables of the S chapel. The E end is a sheer cliff of brick with an enormous Geometric window above. Along the N side the N aisle is concealed by the low two-storey clergy house and the former Sunday School. Attached to the E end of this range the vestry with paired gables and arched windows and doors, but the remaining detail looks more domestic, with gabled dormers and windows under segmental heads. The scale mediates between the large church and the lower surrounding terraced housing.

INTERIOR. A most dramatic and impressive space, thanks partly to a very high and elaborate hammerbeam roof. Exposed brick laid in English bond with orange brick dressings and terracotta enrichment. Five-bay nave arcade with quatrefoil stone piers; narrow aisles, N aisle windows set higher than the S to gain light from the valley between church and school. Generously proportioned clerestory with large windows. Three-bay raised chancel with a high arch flanked by N and S chapels, of which the S (Lady) chapel is the more elaborate, with two shallow projecting bays on the S side. The generous NE vestries have exposed timber roofs copied from the roof at Chetham's School and Library (see Centre, Public Buildings, p. 293).

FURNISHINGS are described topographically starting at the E end. In the chancel and incongruously classical, a painted BALDACCHINO, introduced in the early 1960s as part of a reordering. A mutilated part of Crowther's REREDOS survives against the E wall. On each side Crowther's pretty ironwork PARCLOSE SCREENS. – LECTERN, N side of the chancel steps, c. 1900. Stone, an angel supporting the reading desk. Designed and executed by the parishioners W. Cecil Hardisty and E. F. Long. – PULPIT, S side of chancel steps, 1907. – FONT, a drum with panelled tracery in the N aisle, moved there from the SW corner. – VESTRY FURNISHINGS include very handsome cupboards and wardrobes to Crowther's design, with ornamental ironwork and cresting. – STAINED GLASS. Largely Ward & Hughes. Those to note are the S aisle windows, mostly of the 1890s. Saints, mostly those associated with the Benedictine order, in architectural surrounds. The odd ones out are a good window of 1924 showing St George, and a brightly coloured window of 1935 by M. E. Aldrich Rope. W end N side, the archangels, 1889 by Ward & Hughes. N side, three good 1890s windows showing Benedictine nuns and abbesses.

---

*Crowther must have had Westminster Abbey, actually begun 1246, in mind and this is the source of some of the motifs such as the clerestory and rose window. It is clear that he had also made a study of Butterfield's St Cross in Clayton, 1863–6 (q.v.).

CLERGY HOUSE. The interior has typical *Crowther* joinery details. Entrance and reception rooms at the w end; staircase up to a long series of rooms over the school rooms. The route from the upper floor down to the vestry and the transition between secular and sacred space is marked by a change from square to arched openings, with each successive doorway becoming more ecclesiastical in appearance.

ST JEROME, Baden Street, Beswick. 1913 by *E. Lingen Barker*. Small, brick, with a w bellcote. Steeply pitched roofs. Low w baptistery beneath a sloping roof.

ST THOMAS, Ardwick Green North. Set back from the street frontage in a yard paved with gravestones. The columnar gateposts look c18. Built in 1741 on a small scale, widened in 1777, lengthened by two bays to the E in 1831, and provided with its w tower in 1836 by *William Hayley* to the designs of a Mr *Frayer*. This is the one really remarkable feature, an Italian Romanesque campanile, a type not generally favoured before the 1840s. Three stages above the cornice, the first with three tall blind arches pierced by slits, then a similar blind arcade. The top stage has an open arcade of the same design, capped by a shallow pyramidal roof with a projecting cornice. The main body of the church is brick laid in Flemish bond, with sandstone dressings including a cornice which continues around the tower. The side to the green is absolutely plain and flat. Two tiers of arched windows with Y-tracery. Following redundancy in 1978 it was converted to offices preserving part of the nave as a large meeting room. The galleries are supported by cast-iron columns, original fluted columns below, unfluted replacements above. Flat, deeply coffered ceiling divided into square panels by moulded ribs. The c18 REREDOS, probably dating from 1777, divides the E wall into three bays with fluted Corinthian pilasters supporting an entablature and central pediment.

ST BRIGID (R.C.), Grey Mare Lane, Beswick. The church of 1878–9 on Mill Street has gone. The present building, dedicated in 1996, originated as the church hall of *c.* 1975 by *Burles, Newton & Partners*. Brownish brick with a copper mansard and slits of high-set windows to the entrance part, clerestory lighting to the hall.

Perambulation

Almost everything of interest can be seen in the course of a walk starting at the w end of ARDWICK GREEN, a shadow of its former self. In 1794 it had a serpentine canal and a few houses along the N side. A guide of 1839 described it as a 'pleasing suburb . . . ornamented by a fine miniature lake, surrounded by handsome dwellings'. It certainly is not that now. The canal has gone and the green is a standard municipal park with, near the SW corner, a FIRST WORLD WAR MEMORIAL of the Eighth (Ardwick) Battalion by *George Hall*. Portland stone. A domed cenotaph with Ionic columns at each corner

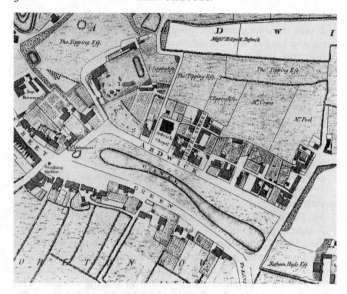

Ardwick, shown on William Green's map, 1794

supporting a cornice. The battalion's original home was the
TERRITORIAL ARMY DRILL HALL AND OFFICES, 1886 by
Lawrence Booth, overlooking the w side of the green. The function is expressed in the use of both military and domestic
motifs. Booth was clearly influenced by the Castle Armoury in
Bury (*see* p. 179) of 1868 by Henry Styan and Alfred Hopkinson, both for the general outline and the use of Romanesque
motifs. Three storeys with a battlemented roofline, rubble with
ashlar dressings. Central entrance bay, corner tower with a
tall octagonal turret. Continuing NW brings us to MANOR
STREET, running N from the green. Here a terrace named
Ardwick Grove was laid out *c.* 1830. Brick houses, two and
three storeyed with doorcases. Similar houses are on the corner
of adjoining ARDWICK GREEN NORTH. A little further E on
Ardwick Green North, No. 31 is probably the earliest, symmetrical with two storeys over a raised basement and a central
pedimented doorway (now a window) with a shouldered
architrave. This is probably the remains of a house shown on
Green's 1794 map.

The E end of the Green offers views of the APOLLO
THEATRE by *Peter Cummings* with *Alex M. Irvine*, on the
corner of Hyde Road and Stockport Road. Opened 1938 as a
cinema, now used as a concert hall. White terracotta front with
discreet Art Deco ornament, good auditorium with a sweeping horseshoe gallery and Art Deco trimmings. A detour can
be made here for the APSLEY COTTAGE pub, immediately
beside the E end of the Apollo off Stockport Road. Two storeys,

only one room deep, with a central pediment. It seems to have originated as a range of early C19 stables or service buildings for large villas (demolished) facing Hyde Road.

Back at the E end of the Green, HIGHER ARDWICK runs in a curve to the N and E. One or two buildings of note, e.g. E side, No. 4, FENTON HOUSE, *c.* 1840 with a delicate ironwork entrance canopy. Further N on the same side, the No. 32 CLUB, a former Primitive Methodist Sunday School. *William Dawes* won the competition for the buildings in 1874; the neighbouring church has been demolished. A picturesque assemblage of elements in sandstone rubble; Gothic detailing. Two-storey polygonal hall with gabled dormers, entrance block and an octagonal tower with a tall pointed roof. Following the street N around the corner brings us to the former CONSERVATIVE CLUB, on the S side. Designed by *Slater & Kendal* and dated 1878. Red brick with stone and terracotta dressings, two tall storeys with arcades of windows flanking a narrow entrance bay crowned by a segmental pediment. From here PALFREY PLACE runs S. Nos. 2–4, W side, a pair of stately three-storey town houses, early–mid-C19. Stucco, rusticated at the ground floor, porches with Doric columns. Their elegance is incongruous in the present surroundings, characterized by large decaying late C19 and early C20 works. At the end of the street turn E along Harkness Street, then S down Dalberg Street to Hyde Road. A short walk E brings us to the former NICHOLLS HOSPITAL, now part of Manchester College of Arts and Technology. 1879–80 by *Thomas Worthington*. Established as a Bluecoat School by Benjamin Nicholls, as a memorial to his son who died prematurely in 1859 after working with the poor in Manchester. Worthington was commissioned to prepare designs in 1867 for a building to be constructed after Nicholls's death, which came ten years later. It was Worthington's last major work in the city. The design is related to his Police Courts (*see* p. 287) and his entry for the Town Hall competition, all being worked on at about the same time. European Gothic style, of red brick with stone dressings. The architectural embellishment gradually intensifies from basement to top, so apart from the entrance, reached from a flight of stone steps, the treatment is simple at lower levels. First-floor windows have delicately moulded label stops, then a range of befinialed gabled dormers strikes upwards. Stone tourelles at the corners. The central tower is without buttresses. A machicolated stone parapet with octagonal corner tourelles supports a saddleback roof; tall gabled dormers with traceried windows. The interior is simply planned: the entrance leads to a foyer and then an impressive hall, from which rises a top-lit stair with a cast-iron balustrade with wheel motifs. Classrooms are ranged on each side. Original forecourt walls, gate piers and gates to Hyde Road. Late C19 and 1960s rear extensions, to the W an addition of 1996 by *R. King*, City Architect. Two four-storey classroom blocks, with angled roofs and projecting eaves; off-centre projecting brick stair-tower.

Outliers

PIN MILL, Pin Mill Brow, Ardwick. A fairly complete mid-C19 cotton mill complex. Near the centre is an engine house with distinctive arched windows and a tall brick octagonal chimney. Weaving sheds on each side have ranges of saw-tooth north-light windows and there is a curving office range to the street.

BESWICK *see* ARDWICK, above

BRADFORD and CLAYTON

The areas merge with one another and seem remote from the centre, with most of the industry gone and much council housing mixed with late C19 terraces. New sports buildings came to Bradford for the 2002 Commonwealth Games, accompanied by a regeneration scheme, which has started with large retail outlets and housing improvements. The boundaries are (not including) Ashton New Road, S; the borders with Tameside and Oldham, E; The railway line and River Medlock, N; and Hulme Hall Lane and Alan Turing Way, W.

ST CROSS, Ashton New Road, Clayton. 1863–6 by *Butterfield*, and unmistakable inside. Outside it is a very high red brick building with blue brick and pale stone banding. There is a high sw tower, the top part with chequered brick and stone and a pyramid roof. High clerestory, S chapel with paired gables, very high E window. The features are Middle Pointed i.e. *c.* 1300.*

INTERIOR. Five-bay arcades, the westernmost narrower than the others, with alternating quatrefoil and round piers. Above all is red brick with diapers, the aisles with blue brick bands instead. Arch-braced timber roof. The chancel arch is high and behind it there are Butterfield's favourite two-light openings into chapels under one big blank arch. The chancel has stone paving and encaustic tiles, a carved stiff-leaf frieze, and blank trefoil-headed arcading in the sanctuary. The patterns of coloured stone and tiles in the walls here have been incorporated into late C20 stencilling which does not follow the original design. Two-bay S chapel, with twin roofs with exposed timbers and between them a single timber pier rising from an extraordinary spiky stone base. The W end was partitioned off in the late C20 for meeting rooms etc., but it has been done with care, and the glazed openings have engraved minstrel angels. Above the rooms, an organ loft.

FITTINGS. Most of the choir furnishings have been removed. PULPIT in the NW chancel arch. Timber with open-work designs. – FONT, a bowl supported by detached piers with a lid with elaborate ironwork. – STAINED GLASS. In the chapels late C19 figures reset in brightly coloured late C20 surrounds.

---

* It is clear that J. S. Crowther made a study of the building for his St Benedict Ardwick, of 1880 (*see* Ardwick and Beswick, above).

The windows to note are all late C19: the four patron saints of
England, Scotland, Wales and Ireland, N chapel and N aisle,
and four windows in the N aisle with unusual Old Testament
scenes stretching across the paired lights.

ST WILLIBRORD (R.C.), North Road, Clayton. 1938, by
Reynolds & Scott. Brick, Byzantine, with similarities to St
Dunstan, Moston, by Norris & Reynolds (*see* N Manchester
suburbs). Massive, with a low square central tower with
splayed corners and a band of small rectangular windows at
the top. The aisles are expressed as three tall gabled projections with tall round-headed lancets in blank arches. Central
entrance and gabled S porch with a statue in a niche, low N
chapels. The tower is not expressed internally, and neither are
the aisle gables, but the interior is impressive. There are three
sail-domes with transverse arches, on wall-piers pierced for
aisle passages with semicircular arches at the tops. The domes
are continued to the N and S by short tunnel vaults. Lower
chancel and apse, the latter windowless with a MOSAIC
showing the Holy Spirit as a dove on a blue ground. This and
other mosaics in the side chapels are by *L. Oppenheimer*,
installed at various times after the Second World War. It is an
interesting plan, inspired very probably by Tapper's Our Lady
with St Thomas, Mount Road, Gorton (*see* p. 371).

PHILIPS PARK CEMETERY, Alan Turing Way, Bradford.
Opened in 1866. The layout was designed by *William Gay* and
the office, entrance lodges and chapels by *Paull & Ayliffe*, who
won the competition in 1863. Of these only the offices
and entrance lodge on the corner of Briscoe Road and the
Anglican Chapel E of the main entrance survive. Flanking the
entrance, the stone LODGE, r., with a stair-turret, and
OFFICES, l., with a clock tower, in eclectic Gothic style. They
make a striking group, but both are partially unroofed and in
appalling condition. The Anglican cemetery CHAPEL is of
stone, Dec, with a SE tower and spire, nave and apse and S
aisle, early French details. This too is badly decayed.

Axial layout, with a wide spine road running E–W through
the site. Each denominational area had its own entrance;
Anglican, W; Roman Catholic, E, and Nonconformists in the
centre. The River Medlock divides the site from Philips Park
(*see* below).

PHILIPS PARK. Alan Turing Way, Bradford. Manchester was the
first major industrial town of the C19 to create municipal
public parks. The scheme was promoted by the Manchester
M.P. Mark Philips who served on the 1833 Parliamentary
Select Committee on Public Walks. A grant was obtained from
the Government and three sites were bought in 1845, one in
Salford (*see* p. 624). The competition was won by *Joshua Major
& Son*. Philips Park, named after Mark Philips, was the only
one in which Major had a completely free hand in the design.
He incorporated areas for a variety of sports within a land-
scape planted with shrubs and trees. At the entrance on Stuart
Street there is a red brick LODGE, by *Alfred Darbyshire* of 1868,

replacing an earlier building by *J. E. Gregan*, and just beyond
a DRINKING FOUNTAIN erected in 1896 to mark the half-
centenary of the opening. Serpentine paths, and in particular
the winding circuit drive, were a main element in Major's
design, and the layout remains largely intact. The River
Medlock to the N divides the park from Philips Park Cemetery
(*see* above).

MANCHESTER CITY FOOTBALL CLUB STADIUM, Rowsley
Street, Bradford. By *Arup Associates*, lead architect *Dipesh Patel*,
1999–2002, designed for the 2002 Commonwealth Games. It
can be seen from all sorts of surprising places around the city,
a low spiky presence on the horizon. Concrete bowl frame suspended from twelve huge masts. Eight of them rise from spiral
ramp towers, which look like coiled concrete springs, impart-
ing energy and dynamism to the design. Patel used a similar
feature for his Johannesburg Athletics Stadium of 1995. Undulating roof clad in silvery metal panels. After the games were
finished an athletics track was removed and 32 ft (10 metres)
of earth excavated to create another rank of seats in the conversion to a football stadium. The N side, which had temporary stands for the duration of the games, was then infilled.
Landscape GARDENS by *Gillespies*.

The stadium setting is enhanced by SCULPTURE, off Alan
Turing Way. B of the Bang by *Thomas Heatherwick*, 2004, is an
exhilarating spiny metal starburst, 184 ft (56 metres) high.
Nearby, The Runner by *Colin Spofforth*, 2002, is also good, a
springing athlete on a globe.

SPORTCITY SCREEN WALL, Ashton New Road. A supermarket is screened by a low wall illuminated by sweeps of
coloured lights. By *Trevor Horne Architects* with the lighting
engineers *Speirs & Major Associates*, 2003.

NATIONAL CYCLING CENTRE or VELODROME, Stuart Street,
Bradford. By *FaulknerBrowns*, from a concept by *HOK Sports
Facilities Group*. Opened in 1994 as Britain's national cycling
centre. In long views the huge curving shape, with its alu-
minium-clad roof, is impressive. The sculptural form was
generated by the elliptical shape of the racetrack, and the backbone of the arching shape is formed by a 400 ft (122 metre)
clear span steel arch springing from concrete thrust blocks. The
main area has a curving steel roof and clerestory lighting giving
the impression of lightness and strength. It seats 3,500 with
provision for an additional 1,000. Within the main stadium a
SCULPTURE, life size bronze of the champion Manchester
cyclist Reg Harris, by *James Butler*, 1994. SPORTS FACILITIES,
tennis courts, etc., N of the football stadium, are housed in
metal pods.

GASWORKS, Alan Turing Way, Bradford. Established by the Corporation in the 1870s. The present holders are mid-C20 and a
landmark in the area.

ABATTOIR, Riverbank Road, Bradford. By *S. Besant Roberts*, City
Architect, 1966. Ingeniously planned, a vast complex of which
the most striking element is a huge meat market, a near-

circular polygon with a continuous window strip of vertical planks.

CLAYTON HALL, Clayton. An attractive green island in this rather bleak area. There is a moat (dry at the time of writing) crossed by a stone BRIDGE, probably C17, with two segmental arches. The HALL consists of two distinct parts, a truncated hall house probably of the C15 or C16 and an attached C17 or early C18 house.

The moat suggests that the site has origins in the C14, and it may be a good deal older, as the site was owned by the Byron family from the C12. They sold the house to the Chethams in 1621, and it was occupied for a while by Humphrey Chetham, founder of Chetham's School and Library (*see* Centre, Public Buildings, p. 293). After various changes of ownership the hall was bought by Manchester Corporation in 1896. Restored in the early C20 and again in the mid C20. An C18 drawing shows the hall with a timber-framed wing on the SW side and it seems likely that the present house on the N side (not visible in the C18 view) replaced another range or wing.

The two-bay hall is timber-framed and has a massive external chimney, probably C17, at the S end, and a corridor extension running the length of the W side, also probably C17. A timber-framed stair-tower with a bellcote serves the corridor. There has been much restoration, but the bellcote is shown on early C19 views, and it may well be of a date with the stair. Inside there are two large arch-braced trusses which may have originated as an open hall. The central truss has been infilled to divide the space, and it looks as if ceiling has been inserted. The doors in the dividing wall have Tudor-arched heads, suggesting a C16–C17 date for this, and the corridor and stair were presumably added at the same time to serve the newly created

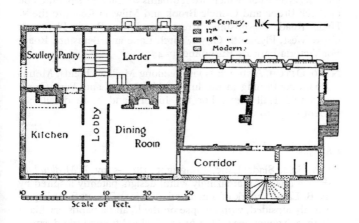

Clayton Hall, plan, *Victoria County History of Lancashire*, vol. 4, 1911

upper floor. The roof is reported to be a crown-post and collar-purlin roof, which would be further evidence for a local tradition of a type of construction more commonly seen in the s of England. The building would reward further study, as it is one of very few examples in se Lancashire where a floor seems to be an insertion into an open hall, while the corridor additions fit with locally typical c17 improvements to circulation.

The attached house to the N is of brick and quite grand with stone quoins and a slightly off-centre door also with stone quoins. Double-pile plan with a central staircase. Rooms at the front have remains of inglenook fireplaces, that on the l. with a blocked fire window. The crudity of some of the exposed beams, which are very roughly chamfered and stopped, contrasts with the elegance of the reeded door surrounds and suggests that the building may incorporate parts of an earlier structure.

CLAYTON *see* BRADFORD, above

GORTON *see* OPENSHAW, below

LEVENSHULME and LONGSIGHT

This area was nothing more than scattered houses and farms in the early c19, with ribbon development along the main Manchester–Stockport road and a smattering of industry. By the late c19 the area was predominantly residential, which it remains. Longsight is notable for the fact that both the Ukrainian and Russian Orthodox churches, which more often reuse other buildings, have purpose-built churches there. The area merges with Levenshulme to the s, and the boundary with Stockport.

The E boundary is Mount Road, and the lines of Nico Ditch and Nelstrop Road which are footpaths or tracks; s side, the line of Black Brook and Cringle Brook and Milwain Road; to the N, Hyde Road, Devonshire Street, Stockport Road, Plymouth Grove West, Plymouth Grove, Birch Lane and Beresford Road. For Victoria Park *see* Rusholme, p. 477.

NICO DITCH. A stretch is visible along Melland Fields, Mount Road, continuing in the line of Matthews Lane, Park Grove and Old Hall Lane. For the history and more details *see* Denton, p. 197.

Churches

ST AGNES, Slade Lane, Longsight. 1884–5 by *J. Medland & Henry Taylor*. An amazingly wilful design, patently inspired by E. B. Lamb's work of a generation before. The W front is perversely lopsided, with an apse on the l., and a baptistery like a high polygonal apse. One of the Taylors' funny little dormers appears high on the s side, and there is a quirky little bell-turret. The chancel ends in an apse, and inside there is more wondrous detail than one can describe. The church was aisle-less (a N aisle, added in 1895, has been partitioned off) and is dominated by the tricky timbers of the roof and arch-springers. To the r. of the chancel is a two-bay chapel, one bay W, one E of the chancel arch. The arcade from chancel to chapel has two brick-built E.E. columns with shafts set two deep. It is all without doubt deliberately confusing, but the atmosphere is friendly. – STAINED GLASS. N aisle, three-light First World War memorial window by *W. Pointer* of Manchester.

ST ANDREW, Stockport Road, Levenshulme. 1907–8 by *R. B. Preston*. Pale brick laid in header bond with red brick and red terracotta dressings, Perp style, thin S entrance tower. Typical of Preston's cheap early C20 churches. Disused.

ST JOHN, St John's Street, Longsight. 1845–6 by *J. E. Gregan*. A design of archaeological ambition, only a few years after Pugin's St Wilfrid, Hulme (see p. 453). *The Ecclesiologist* described the style as 'First Pointed'. It stood alone in the fields when it was built. Yellow sandstone, large, with a SW broach spire, a fairly early example of a tower and spire set to one side of the main part of the church, aisles, and large transepts added in 1853 which were designed to be galleried. The INTERIOR was subdivided and reordered in the 1970s. Five-bay arcade with circular piers, arch-braced timber roof. – STAINED GLASS by *Willement*, probably the good 1840s glass in the N transept N, in which case it must have been moved when the transept was added. N transept internal window to nave and N aisle, good glass perhaps by *Lavers & Barraud*.

ST MARK, Barlow Road, Levenshulme. 1908 by *C. T. Taylor* of Oldham. Red brick and much stone with much patterning of the two. Obviously inspired by Leonard Stokes. Lively W group of a short tower and the polygonally projecting baptistery. Memorable interior, of exposed brick and terracotta, low and wide, with a spreading chancel arch starting on strange convex, not concave, curves before turning depressed-pointed. Wide aisles. Pretty, freely Flamboyant SEDILIA. – STAINED GLASS. Modestly Arts and Crafts.

ST PETER, Stockport Road, Levenshulme. By *Alfred G. Fisher*, 1860, enlarged in 1872 by *Maycock & Bell* and again in 1896. E.E. and terribly dull in yellow sandstone with SW broach spire. The *Building News* in 1870 cruelly described it as 'an amorphous, hog-backed abortion'.

ST JOSEPH (R.C.), Plymouth Grove, Longsight. By *Lowther & Rigby*, 1914–15. Red brick with a striking NW tower, which has splayed angle buttresses with stone terminations punching up through the pyramid roof. Free Style and Art Nouveau touches. The very tall clerestory has tall narrow paired windows with traceried heads in alternating patterns. Fancy tracery and Art Nouveau mouldings round the doors. The arcade piers are elongated, chamfered lozenges, and the depressed pointed arches die into them. The aisles have full roof trusses, and the nave has exposed trusses also. The chancel arch springs from a high point, adding to the airy atmosphere.

St Mary of the Angels and St Clare (R.C.), Elbow Street, Levenshulme. 1975, by *Greenhalgh & Williams*. Brick, a central octagon with stained glass after Gibberd's Liverpool R.C. Cathedral.

St Robert (R.C.), Hamilton Road, Longsight. 1969–70 by *Mather & Nutter*. A slightly aggressive design in concrete, brown brick and metal cladding. Stabbing funnel over E end flanked by smaller ones.

Russian Orthodox Church, Clarence Street. By *Archimax (Peter Barrett & Natalia Maximova)*, 2002–3. Two tall storeys with a rounded apse facing the street; meeting rooms etc. upstairs. Purplish-grey brick with red brick dressings, hipped copper-clad roof, central copper dome with a cross. The dome was the gift of the Patriarch of the Orthodox Church and was made in the workshops of the monastery of St Sergius Lavra, Sergiev-Posad, near Moscow.

Ukrainian Orthodox Church, off Plymouth Grove West. By *F. Holowko*, 1971. Red brick and very plain except for the turrets flanking the gabled front with metal onion domes.

United Methodist Church (former), Dickenson Road, Longsight. Dated 1907. This and St John's Church (*see* above) stand out amongst the otherwise uninspiring buildings of central Longsight. Red brick and red terracotta with fanciful terracotta tracery. A forceful central entrance has battered sides flanked by turrets.

Bethshan International Church, Crowcroft Road, Levenshulme. Formerly the Bethshan Tabernacle. 1957 by *J. C. Prestwich Brown*. A local landmark. Brown brick with a fan-shaped plan and a bold curving front with a tall square tower to the l.

United Reformed Church, Stockport Road, Levenshulme. By *John Lowe*, 1888. Yellow sandstone, Dec, assertive spire with spiky gargoyles bringing a bit of life to this part of Stockport Road. Attached early C20 Sunday School.

Public Buildings

Town Hall (former), Stockport Road, Levenshulme. 1898–9 by *James Jepson*. Red brick, Renaissance, seven bays with arched upper windows and a cupola. Portal with big brackets. Subtle asymmetry in the treatment of the openings on either side of the entrance. Spacious entrance hall, and an impressive stone stair leading up in one flight and returning in two to the former council chamber. Converted to antiques shops, late C20. The attached stone police station is executed in businesslike Tudor Gothic.

swimming baths, Cromwell Grove, Levenshulme. 1931 by *G. Noel Hill*, City Architect. Neo-Georgian, symmetrical, of brick with Portland stone dressings. The composition is neatly tailored to the street corner.

CARNEGIE LIBRARY, Cromwell Grove, Levenshulme. 1903, by James Jepson, more modest than those in southern suburban centres. Symmetrical with big shaped gables and terracotta panels with Jacobean motifs. Exposed timber roofs.

ST AGNES SCHOOL, Hamilton Road, Longsight. By *Henry & Medland Taylor*, opened in 1885. A charming little building, with typical Taylor details. Gothic, low and gabled, of poly-chrome brick with an octagonal bay with lancets to the street.

BELLE VUE, Hyde Road. The famous pleasure and zoological gardens, which grew to be one of Manchester's premier C19 attractions, originated as a pub, *c.* 1820. By 1865 it was esti-mated that 50–60,000 people visited on holidays. The site retained its popularity until the mid C20. The gardens closed in 1981, but greyhound racing and speedway continue, both in the GREYHOUND STADIUM, which was the first in Europe when it opened in 1926. The former entrance on the corner of Hyde Road and Kirkmanshulme Lane sports a dashing 1960s upturned concrete canopy. Otherwise the stadium is conventional.

SLADE HALL stands end-on to Slade Lane. Converted to flats, 2002. Edward Siddall, whose initials appear over the door beside the date 1585, bought the estate in 1584. Two-storey timber-framed house with jettied upper floor, hall-and-cross-wing plan, with a porch in the angle. Porch and cross-wing have jettied gables. Most of the timber framing is herringbone, but the smaller porch gable has lozenges painted to appear quatrefoiled. A late C19 timbered wing attached to the r. (E) of the cross-wing is said to be a rebuilding of a C17 wing. To the rear (S) is a brick early C19 extension with a timber parapet and brick corner pilasters. The interior has a hall with a chamber above, but everything has been greatly altered with loss of original features. The main surviving point of interest is the naïve PLASTERWORK of the chamber. On the S wall a frieze of heraldic shields with crude female figures between them. The arms of Queen Elizabeth are flanked by the Stanley arms on one side and Siddall arms on the other. On the oppo-site wall is a hunting scene with huntsmen, stags and dogs on either side of the Stanley crest of the Eagle and Child in a tree.

Streets

CHAPEL STREET, Levenshulme. On the S side a mid-C19 former COTTON MILL. A fairly complete ensemble with fireproof engine house and stair and attached yard with weaving sheds.

PLYMOUTH GROVE, Longsight. RICHMOND HOUSE is a large brick early C19 house with a slightly projecting central bay and a doorcase with Doric columns.

NORTHMOOR ROAD, Longsight. CO-OPERATIVE HALL (former), 1913 by *A. H. Walsingham*. Typical of his Co-op buildings, and the one lively incident on the street. Cheerful

Edwardian Baroque in brick with liberal green and buff terracotta, and a turret at the N gable end. Shops below, hall above
with space for more than 500, this part converted to flats, 2001.

SLADE LANE. LONGSIGHT NEIGHBOURHOOD CENTRE. A
villa of *c.* 1850 in its own grounds beside the railway. Symmetrical, sash windows with margin lights, steep gables with
fancy bargeboards.

STOCKPORT ROAD, Levenshulme. LEVENSHULME HEALTH
CENTRE. An early C20 house radically altered by *Hodder Associates* in 1998. White planar walls, and a new entrance between
the street and rear car park. The rear extension, of rendered
cross-wall construction, is infilled with glazed and cedar-clad
rainscreen panels. Further S, E side, the former LEVENSHULME
GRAND THEATRE, an early cinema for the Grand Picture
Theatre Co. by *Frederick Fenn*, 1913. Quite grand and classical
with a pilastered ground floor and upper Ionic balcony
colonnade.

LONGSIGHT *see* LEVENSHULME, above

NEWTON HEATH *see* BRADFORD, p. 407–8

OPENSHAW and GORTON

Openshaw and Gorton were isolated settlements until the advent
of industry, when they became famous for their engineering
works. One of the largest was the Beyer Peacock & Co. locomotive manufacturing company. Joseph Whitworth opened his
factory nearby in 1880, and went on to manufacture heavy armaments. Another important firm was Crossley Engineering and
Crossley Motors. By the mid C20 most of the factories had closed
or relocated. Only a scattering of undistinguished sheds etc. off
Gorton Lane and Pottery Lane survive. The centre of Gorton
has largely been rebuilt, late C20.

The boundaries are the Stockport and Tameside boundaries
and Nico Ditch alongside Melland playing field to the E; Mount
Road, Hyde Road and (not including) Bennett Street, and
Pottery Lane, W; Ashton Old Road, N.

For Nico Ditch *see* Denton, p. 197.

Churches

ST CLEMENT, Ashton Old Road, Openshaw. By *Entiknap &
Booth*, 1879–81. Sober, stone, unexecuted tower. Polygonal
apse, plate tracery windows, clerestory with stepped round-
headed arched windows. The neighbouring VICARAGE, also of
stone, is early C20.

ST JAMES, Cambert Street, Gorton. 1871 by *G. & R. Shaw*.
Replacing a chapel of ease of 1755 which in turn replaced a
chapel of 1422. The church was rebuilt at the expense of
Charles Beyer of the Gorton Foundry at the same time as

the building of Brookfield Unitarian Church (*see* below) for
Beyer's partner Richard Peacock, to provide for both Anglican
and Dissenting members of their workforces. One of *George
Shaw*'s best churches and one of the few important buildings
to survive C20 clearances in Gorton. Yellow sandstone. Dec
with a fine NW broach spire, with everything carefully and separately expressed. The eyecatching details are the clerestory
with alternating triple and sub-triangular lights and the tower
with a NW circular stair-tower with a crenellated top. Window
traceries are all variations of Shaw's individual interpretation
of curvilinear style. INTERIOR. Single-chamfered arcade supported by alternating circular and octagonal piers, perhaps
based on the C13 arcade at St Chad, Rochdale (q.v.) where
Shaw worked in the 1840s. Roof of unusual design with arch-
braced timbers and pendants. Most of the elaborate FUR-
NISHINGS were designed by the architect, an important
ensemble produced in his workshop in Saddleworth. Carved
REREDOS flanked by canopied DECALOGUE and CREED
BOARDS. – ALTAR with ogee tracery. – ALTAR RAIL with open
curvilinear roundels. – READING DESK with an elaborate
canopied front. – PULPIT with canopied sides and openwork
roundels in the stair rail. – LECTERN, a fierce eagle, in memory
of Shaw †1876, perhaps also the product of his workshop. –
FONT, an elaborate Dec piece with a conical cover of 1905. –
W SCREENS with open arcading. – STAINED GLASS. Two early
C20 windows are of local note; s aisle by *R. Bennett* of Manchester, N aisle by *George Wragge* of Manchester.

ST PHILIP, Brookhurst Road, Gorton. 1908–9 by *W. Cecil
Hardisty*. Brick, stripped Romanesque. Big semicircular apse,
N transept, very narrow low aisles with wide windows with
semicircular heads, other windows narrow with round heads.
The interior, with its simple forms in exposed brick, has lost
its power through subdivision and insertion of a false ceiling.
It could hardly be more different from Hardisty's Christchurch, Moss Side (*see* p. 460). – FONT. A big square marble
affair with mosaics. – STAINED GLASS. s aisle, St Gregory and
the Angels by *E. H. Attwell* of Manchester, 1928; three E
windows of similar date possibly by the same.

OUR LADY WITH ST THOMAS OF CANTERBURY, Mount
Road, Gorton. 1927 by *Walter Tapper*, narthex added in 1983
by *Buttress Fuller Architects*. Now disused and boarded up.
Funded by a bequest made by Angelina Clarke who made the
dedication a condition and stipulated that it should be in
Renaissance style with three domes. Only a stump of the
intended building. Two bays. The sheer brick walls and simple
forms are strikingly expressive. W side with a pedimental gable
and without openings – just a niche with a bell. Lean-to
narthex below, with a steep tiled roof. On each side, two
projections with giant blind arches, each with a high round
window; a round window also in the low linking block. Then
the chancel with a cambered window and a semicircular apse.
The intention was to have three bays and to cover them with

saucer domes connected by short tunnel vaults extended towards the outer walls by short tunnel vaults as well. The aisles would be low and run through the piers between these latter transverse tunnels and continue below them.

(Plastered interior. Domed nave and chancel, semi-domed apse, all linked by tunnel vaults. Domed NE chapel. The division between nave and chancel is marked by a large rood loft at gallery level which is sited beneath the W arch of the main dome of the chancel. Lady Chapel, N with wrought-iron screen and window of 1965 brought from St Philip Blackburn.)

St Agnes, Reddish Lane, Gorton. By *L. K. & C. T. Mayor*. 1908. Pale brick, red brick, red terracotta. The main entrance, N, faces a side street. Arts and Crafts tower over the entrance and other slightly roguish features, windows with red terracotta tracery. INTERIOR. Exposed brick with a four-bay arcade with octagonal red sandstone piers, aisles, two-bay S chapel. Sanctuary with stoup and sedilia. Arch-braced timber roof. – Modestly Arts and Crafts CHOIR FURNISHINGS and PULPIT. – STAINED GLASS. Mainly mid-C20, much by *W. H. Cotton*. S aisle by *E. H. Attwell*, 1929. Good glass in the chapel, the Virgin and St Anne, *c.* 1900.

70 St Francis (R.C.), Gorton Lane, Gorton. By *E. W. Pugin*, Started 1866, consecrated 1872, the E end completed after his death by *Pugin, Ashlin & Pugin* in 1878, but evidently to the one design. Built for the Recollect branch of the Franciscan Order who came to Manchester from Belgium in 1861 at the invitation of Bishop Vaughan of Salford. Their intention was to run a major church and parish. They finally withdrew in the 1980s. Much of the work was done by direct labour, with a brother acting as clerk of works. It was the last of three large Catholic churches built by the younger Pugin in the area. The others were St Ann (1862–7) and All Saints (1863–8) (for both *see* Stretford), both built through the munificence of the de Trafford family. All three show C13 French influences, but St Francis has the most ornate exterior, strikingly polychromatic, unlike the others, and where they sport over-ornate rose windows at the W end, here the front is dominated instead by big stepped buttresses. Like All Saints it has no tower but a W bellcote.

It was meant to be a demonstration, and it has remained a showpiece despite the best efforts of vandals. No-one could deny that it is over-detailed. It is of red brick with generous stone dressing. The façade is four bays wide and has four portals into a narthex. Behind, the sloping roof lines of the aisles appear, and their fronts have rose windows. The centre rises high, with two tall two-light windows and three buttresses oddly connected with the wall behind the tracery. They are hugely overscaled for the job they have to do. Out of the middle buttress grows a stepping-out panel with the Crucifixus, and on the top of the gable over this is a high bell-turret, a lowered replacement of the original. The E end is a very high polygonal apse, lit by enormous gable-windows and from dormers at the roof line, all focused on the altar. The interior with a thirteen-bay nave and two-bay chancel treated as one vessel, is impressively tall, 100 ft (30 metres) to the ridge of the roof. There are narrow aisles, with confessionals generously laid out on the monastery side. Typical E.W. Pugin capitals and other details; most of the furnishings have been stripped out apart from the badly damaged REREDOS by *Peter Paul Pugin*. Tall, stepped and gorgeously bepinnacled, but smashed by vandals. Life-size statues of the Twelve Apostles from the arcade await refixing. – STAINED GLASS. E end by *R. B. Edmundson* of Manchester.

MONASTIC BUILDINGS are attached to the r. and form a cloister around a courtyard. Red brick, three storeys, very simply treated. They were begun in 1863, also to *Pugin*'s design.

After a major campaign to save the buildings they are closed pending redevelopment as a community, exhibition and visitor centre and wedding chapel.

ST ANNE (R.C.), Ashton Old Road, Openshaw. 1884–8 by *Simpson*. Red brick and painted stone. High bellcote with a Crucifixus below, exaggerated buttresses and low entrance porches, showing the influence of St Francis, Gorton (*see* above). Otherwise quite plain apart from some Dec windows at the E end.

SACRED HEART (R.C.), Levenshulme Road, Gorton. By *Reynolds & Scott*, 1962. It looks *c*. 1930. Brownish brick with pale grey stone dressings and a recessed entrance with a screen and a red sandstone Crucifixus.

BROOKFIELD UNITARIAN CHURCH, Hyde Road, Gorton. By *Thomas Worthington*, 1869–71. In the C17 Gorton was notorious as a centre of dissent, described by one commentator as 'a nest of vipers'. A chapel was built in 1703 for a congregation which had been meeting in houses nearby. There were ties with the Cross Street Chapel in Manchester (p. 312). The little C18 chapel was replaced by a very large and strikingly prosperous-looking church. It has a setting exceptional for Manchester. To its S and W there is a landscaped dip and the Sunnybrow Park. Moreover, Far Lane, skirting it (*see* below), is clearly a village lane and still has some cottages. It was built at the expense of Richard Peacock of the Gorton Foundry at the same time as the rebuilding of the parish church of St James by Peacock's partner in his engineering and locomotive works, Charles Beyer (*see* above). The idea was to provide for both Anglican and Dissenting members of their workforce. Stone, E.E. style, with a NW steeple attached to the aisle. The church has a bold, simple, and perfect Ecclesiological interior. Six-bay arcades of dark sandstone on pink granite columns which contrast well with the plastered walls. Chancel arch with detached columns. Panelled roof. – REREDOS of stone with the carvings of the Evangelists. – PULPIT, stone, on a cluster of marble columns. – FONT, a stone bowl supported by cluster of columns, 1891. – WALL PAINTING. Twelve painted medallions in the nave arcade depict teachers, spiritual leaders and dissenters, including Erasmus, Socinus and Calvin. Said to be contemporary with the church and to be by *Mr Allen* of London. Over the chancel arch, early C20 angel chorus, all wings, ribbons, and clouds. – STAINED GLASS. E window with a palm tree, rose tree, lily and vine. – MONUMENT. The best one is in the chancel, s side. George Wells †1888, tablet with an unusual castellated surround. – TABLET commemorating the bicentenary of the Gorton Chapel, nicely done in Arts and Crafts style.

w of the church is the MAUSOLEUM of Richard Peacock †1875, by *Worthington*. A large three-bay shrine of white stone, each bay with an arch with two lights and a roundel over. Steep roof and statues at the corners beneath canopies – an engineer, blacksmith, draughtsman and architect, supposedly a portrayal of Worthington himself.

LODGE and attached gates, l. of the church, presumably also by *Worthington*. Single storey, gabled, with an arched mullioned window to the road and a pair of cylindrical chimneys.

BROOKFIELD UNITARIAN SUNDAY SCHOOL (former), Hyde Road, Gorton. Dated 1899, by *Thomas Worthington & Son*. A long range facing the road is crowned by a flèche and lit by arched traceried windows and square-headed transomed windows. Lower wing attached to the r. Converted to flats, 1997, with no attempt to make the new doorway and replacement windows harmonize. To make matters worse a new apartment building to the l. spoils the grouping with the church.

MORAVIAN CHURCH, Wheler Street, Openshaw. By *Taylor & Simister* of Oldham, 1928–9. Chequered brick, slightly canted E end. Italian Romanesque motifs. Two large circular windows are opposed at the E and w ends. w gallery. Brick pilasters support the beams of an arched concrete roof. E dais with oak CHOIR FURNISHINGS, and COMMUNION TABLE. – PULPIT, s side. – STAINED GLASS. Roundels with Moravian motifs, chalice N side, lamb and flag s side. E window with striking coloured glass with much blue in Art Deco style. Attached to the r. a low 1960s block, then a SUNDAY SCHOOL, 1911–12 by *John Eagle*. Brick with an unusual cross-shaped window at the front. The ensemble is only a mile or so from the Moravian Settlement in Fairfield (*see* Droylsden).

GORTON CEMETERY, Alvaston Road, Gorton. Opened in 1908, laid out as a grid. The centrepiece is the CHAPEL range, looking late C19 rather than early C20. Dec, yellow sandstone, three chapels, the central one with a cupola, linked by tall open arches.

Public Buildings and Parks

CROSSLEY HOUSE, Ashton Old Road, Openshaw. Dated 1912 and built as a lads' and men's club; still used as a young people's centre. By *J. W. Broadbent* for the widow of Sir William Crossley of Crossley's Engineering, who was the club's patron,

EAST MANCHESTER: OPENSHAW AND GORTON   375

commemorated in a large copper plaque above the stone fireplace of the hall. A plain three-storey building with Baroque
touches and slightly projecting bays flanking an entrance with
paired arches. The interior retains a lecture theatre on the top
floor with a stage and gallery. It is part of a group, attached to
the r. with the disused WHITWORTH INSTITUTE AND BATHS
by *J. W. Beaumont*, 1908. Built for the engineering magnate
Joseph Whitworth who had his factory nearby. The red brick
and red terracotta institute, which housed a library, is in Beaumont's typical unexciting Jacobean. Between this and the lads'
club the derelict baths and washhouses are obscured by 1980s
extensions at the front.

DEBDALE PARK AND WATER PARK, Hyde Road. The parks
incorporate reservoirs created from 1826 by the Manchester
and Salford Waterworks Company. The park was extended
after the Second World War when the late C18 GORTON
HOUSE and its estate was bought. The house (now offices) is
set well back, approached by a long drive from Hyde Road.
Large, red brick, symmetrical. Central door with an Ionic
doorcase flanked by full-height polygonal bays with pyramidal
roofs. The interior has a top-lit stair with wreathed handrail,
open string and closely set balusters. Altered outbuildings
to the r. include what was probably a STABLE with round
windows and blind arcading. The entrance on Hyde Road is
flanked by a pair of single-storey square brick LODGES with
hipped roofs and central chimneys.

Streets and Twentieth-Century Housing

BROOKHURST ROAD, Gorton. On the corner of Old Hall Lane,
GORTON HALL LODGE, *c.* 1865. Red brick, gabled, with a
polygonal bay and a cartouche above with Richard Peacock's
monogram. The hall is first mentioned in 1681. It was damaged
by fire in 1847 and taken over and presumably wholly or partially rebuilt in 1865 by Peacock. Demolished 1906.

FAR LANE, Gorton. On the N side a row of three brick cottages
dated 1782, all now with replacement doors and windows.

HYDE ROAD, Gorton. PLOUGH INN, corner of Wellington
Road. Late C19, retaining original plan and fittings. A little
further E, set back, the LORD NELSON pub occupies late C18
or early C19 cottages.

TAN YARD BROW, Gorton. A row of three plain late C18 brick
cottages faces on to the road. A little further up the hill on the
W side, SPRINGBANK FARM is probably also C18. A low L-
shaped range: rendered with replacement windows to the r.,
attached brick former barn or stable to the l. with two side-
sliding sashes. (Attached barn to the rear with a kingpost roof).

Gorton has several large COUNCIL ESTATES, mainly interwar,
with some later schemes. The most interesting are the 1930s
flats. Those on MILLWALL CLOSE and SWINDON CLOSE,

opposite St James's church, have three storeys with upswept eaves, recessed balconies, and windows with horizontal glazing bars.

NORTH MANCHESTER

ANCOATS and MILES PLATTING

Ancoats was largely open land until the late 1780s. Within a few decades it became one of the most intensely developed industrial centres in the world, with large steam-powered cotton mills and a variety of other factories and works as well as homes for thousands of people attracted by the work. The population, swelled by immigrants from Ireland as well as surrounding areas, rose from 11,039 in 1801 to 53,737 in 1861. The grid of streets represents late c18 speculative development.* After decades of decay and clearances regeneration has begun with conversions, refurbishments and residential and retail developments. Miles Platting merges imperceptibly to the N and NE. The boundaries of the two areas are Great Ancoats Street and Swan Street, SW; Bromley Street, Oldham Road and Hulme Hall Lane, N; New Viaduct Street, Palmerston Street and Councillor Street, E.

Churches and Religious Buildings

No fewer than nine churches have disappeared since the first edition of *South Lancashire* (1969). Romanesque was the favoured style in the area, perhaps because the primitive forms were thought suited to the industrial environment or the temperament of the residents.

*For the Ancoats estates *see* J. Roberts in *Manchester Regional History Review* 7 (1993).

ALL SOULS, Every Street, Ancoats. A Commissioners' church. By *William Hayley*, 1839–40, and pre-archaeological, though looking unlike any other Commissioners' church in the locality or probably the country. Redundant in 1981, now workshops. Brick, idiosyncratic Romanesque, a plain rectangle with solidly square uncouth pinnacles with pyramidal caps. Projecting central W entrance bay with a round-headed portal, frieze of intersecting arches over and a wheel window above. The shallowest possible recess at the E end, with a blind Norman arcade and three stepped lancets. Three galleries supported by slender clustered cast-iron columns. Timber roof with shallow trusses and open round-headed arcading.

ST PETER, Blossom Street, Ancoats. 1859 by *Isaac Holden & Son*. Romanesque, with round-headed openings throughout. It was built for a newly created parish made necessary by the population explosion. After years of dereliction the exterior was restored in 1998–9. Red brick with brick and stone dressings. Nave and apsidal chancel under one concave-sided roof. Big NW campanile in three stages with paired belfry windows and blind arcading above, topped by a (restored) upper part with a concave-sided roof. The big blunt forms and curving apse and roof make an impressive picture. The INTERIOR has five lofty bays with slender octagonal cast-iron columns with foliated caps with volutes, and semicircular brick arches. The roof divided into bays by four elegant trusses of cast iron with enriched spandrels. Part of a W gallery survives.

ST ANNE (R.C.), Carruthers Street. 1976 by *Gordon Parry & Partners*. Brown brick with a high apsidal E end rising like a funnel. Roof sloping down over a low narthex. Impressive sheer brickwork apse.

CORPUS CHRISTI (R.C.), Varley Street, Miles Platting. 1905–6 by *Ernest Gunson*, instead of the scheme prepared by *Leonard Stokes* in 1891 for which money could not be found. Large, of red brick with pale sandstone dressings, in the Italian Romanesque style. Broad façade with incomplete SW tower and an apsidal baptistery projecting from it. The W portal tympanum and large lunette window have tracery of no known prototypes, of course not Italian Romanesque, but not Northern either. Interior with columns with block capitals ornamented with vine and wheat motifs. The arches slightly horseshoe. Timber ceiling of the type of S. Zeno at Verona. Tunnel-vaulted S aisle with a series of chapels in low arches. Vaulted chancel and apse (added in the 1930s) lit by an arcade of eleven windows. – BALDACCHINO. Green marble with gilding.

ST MICHAEL (R.C.), George Leigh Street, Ancoats. Founded in 1858, palely Gothic and now only a truncated stone façade with a late C20 building behind. The original building may be by *Corbett, Son & Brooke* who did the neighbouring Gothic SCHOOL in 1879. *O. C. Hill* extended the school and added a CLERGY HOUSE in 1887.

ST PATRICK (R.C.), Livesey Street, Miles Platting. 1936 by *Greenhalgh & Williams*, replacing a church of 1832. Stripped Romanesque with an Art Deco flavour. A big monumental design, very similar to his St Anne (R.C.), Greenacres, Oldham (*see* p. 551) of 1937. Red brick with white stone dressings. Windowless apsidal sanctuary. Eight-bay arcades with marble shafts. At the w end a two-storey module of *c.* 1990 with meeting rooms. Sanctuary with Byzantine-style MOSAIC, 1951 by *L. Oppenheimer*, who also did the mosaics in the N and S chapels of 1961. – Handsome red marble BALDACCHINO. – First World War memorial, a marble Pietà repositioned in the upper part of the new module. RECTORY on the l. side. A large very plain brick house, dated 1895.

PRESENTATION CONVENT, 1834–6 with an attached (later) school, r. of St Patrick's church on Livesey Street, Miles Platting. Erected for an educational order founded in 1778 in Ireland and established in England in 1836. The annals of the convent state that the building is based on the plans of the Presentation Convent in Clonmel, Co. Tipperary, which were drawn up by the Mother Assistant, *Mother Magdalen Sargent* in 1828. Because the order was closed the plan had to permit sisters to see visitors and enter the school without leaving the building. The main part looks like an elongated Late Georgian town house, apart from the tall, elegant glazed bellcote over the central entrance bay. Two storeys, red brick with stone dressings. Entrance with Doric columns and pilasters, four-bay ranges on each side. Attached to the l. a later C19 chapel and refectory of red brick with red terracotta dressings. Ground-floor refectory windows transomed, upper chapel windows Dec with terracotta tracery. Attached to the r. the mid–late C19 SCHOOL with additions of 1927.

INTERIOR. Beyond the (replaced) enclosure door is a stair with a wreathed handrail, lit by a tall stair window. The corridor to the r. ends with doors leading in to the school, that to the l. has an original enclosure door with radial fanlight at the end leading to the REFECTORY of *c.* 1870 and upper CHAPEL. Arch-braced kingpost roof with iron ties, C20 glass. To the rear a garden with the nuns' BURIAL GROUND in the NE corner. The sisters' graves are marked by identical headstones.

TRINITY METHODIST CHURCH, Butler Street, Ancoats. By *J. C. Prestwich & Sons* of Leigh. Consecrated in 1964. Brick. Single-storey community rooms and offices to Butler Street. Taller meeting room rising behind, decorated with Mondrianesque panelling and lit by full-height windows arranged in closely set vertical strips. On the site of Victoria Hall, opened in 1897 by the Methodist Mission.

PARTICULAR BAPTIST CHAPEL, Rochdale Road. By *J. Wills & Son*, dated 1907, on the site of predecessors of 1789 and 1823. Brick with pale faience dressings, Free Style. Central gabled entrance bay flanked by full-height octagonal piers with little domed caps, and lower battlemented wings. (The interior has an immersion tank and furnishings salvaged from the earlier building.)

Public Buildings

G.P.O. SORTING OFFICE, Oldham Road, Ancoats. *c.* 1995. A vast shed fronted by a brick office range. On the NE side a FIRST WORLD WAR MEMORIAL to men of the Manchester Post Office by *J. Ashton Floyd.* Unveiled 1929, rededicated 1997. Bronze angel bearing a torch with child supporters. Originally sited in the old post office in Spring Gardens.

FIRE STATION (former), Boond Street, Ancoats. 1865, the city's first purpose-built fire station.* The firemen's accommodation has gone except for the elevations with blocked openings forming the yard N side. An L-shaped range around the SE corner has fire-engine sheds and offices. To Boond Street the front of the offices, brick with stone dressings, with a (blocked) Venetian window and a cornice topped by a parapet.

POLICE AND FIRE STATION (former), Goulden Street, Ancoats. By the Borough Surveyor *J. G. Lynde* for A Division. A forceful, even monumental, design of *c.* 1870. A high windowless façade has a giant blind arcade topped by a pediment, all in stone. The rest is brick. Within the courtyard a tall channelled chimney. Badly damaged by fire, 2002.

ANCOATS HOSPITAL (former), Old Mill Street, Ancoats. By *Lewis & Crawcroft,* 1872–4. It originated as the Ardwick and Ancoats Dispensary, started in 1828 in an area with many patients but few subscribers, to use the words of a recent study.† The first physician was James Phillips Kay, whose experiences were used as a basis for his famous *Moral and Physical Condition of the Working Classes* of 1832. The present building acquired its first hospital beds for in-patients in 1879. Gothic, symmetrical, with a tower with elaborate tourelles in brick with polychrome bands and stone dressings. The saddleback roof has gone. Due for conversion as part of the neighbouring New Islington Millennium Village (*see* p. 384).

Canals

The E side of Ancoats is crossed by two canals, the ROCHDALE CANAL completed in 1804–6 and the earlier ASHTON CANAL, completed as far as Great Ancoats Street in 1796.

ROCHDALE CANAL. For the history, see p. 304. A well-preserved section can be seen from Redhill Street, starting at the junction with Great Ancoats Street with Lock No. 82, and following the canal NE. A late C19 cast-iron FOOTBRIDGE links the towpath to Redhill Street. In the next stretch the blocked entrance to the TUNNEL to the former Murrays Mills canal

---

* Information from Tom Burke.
† By R. Cooter and J. Pickstone, in *Manchester Regional History Review* 7 (1993).

basin can be seen (for the mills, *see* below). The wall has a parapet of huge slabs of millstone grit. At the N end of the street UNION BRIDGE, rebuilt in 1903. Road bridge flanked by a separate footbridge, both with cast-iron panelled parapets, and a spiral horse ramp on the S side.

ASHTON CANAL. For the history *see* p. 303. A good group of canal structures survives off VESTA STREET: LOCK with stone stairs flanking the lower entry; brick lock-keeper's COTTAGE of *c.* 1800 (altered) with three storeys to the canal. Just to the E a towpath bridge of *c.* 1800 has a curved parapet and cobbled deck. Similar locks and a few bridges can be seen as the canal is followed NE. Far to the NE a late C18 AQUEDUCT carries the canal over the River Medlock beneath New Viaduct Street, part of a wondrous complex of road, rail and canal bridges spanning the steep river valley here.

Cotton Mills

Ancoats contains an internationally important group of cotton-spinning mills sited mainly in the E part of the township. They illustrate the development of plan, power system, cast-iron technology and fireproof construction over a period of more than a century and include the best and most complete surviving examples of early large-scale steam-powered factories concentrated in one area.*

The sight of the huge mills lit up at night by gas, the tall chimneys darkening the skies with their smoke, was without parallel in the first few decades of the C19, when the area was almost invariably included in the itineraries of visitors to Manchester. Some evidently approached the visits in the spirit of Picturesque tourism, dwelling on the sublime, awe-inspiring qualities of the scene. The Gothic sensationalism of French writer Leon Faucher described how 'you hear nothing but the breathing of vast machines, sending forth fire and smoke through their tall chimneys, and offering up to the heavens, as it were in token of homage, the sighs of that Labour which God has imposed upon man' (1844). This contrasts with the drier observations of Schinkel who noted in 1826 that the buildings 'as big as the Royal Palace in Berlin' were erected without the benefit of an architect.

The largest of the survivors are the McConnel & Kennedy works and neighbouring Murrays Mills (Redhill Street). These are not typical. Mills of the period were generally smaller and many were designed for multiple occupancy (room and power mills), rather than being purpose-built for one firm. It was partly the large size of the companies which allowed these two examples to weather the economic storms into the C20.

*For more details of these and other mills here and elsewhere in Greater Manchester, the survey undertaken by the RCHME during the period 1985–90 can be consulted at the National Buildings Record at Swindon and the Sites and Monuments Register at Manchester University Department of Field Archaeology.

McConnel & Kennedy's Mills, Redhill Street, Ancoats, 92
alongside the Rochdale Canal. James McConnel and John
Kennedy came to Manchester from Kircudbrightshire and set
up the firm in 1791, initially to produce textile machinery. They
built their first cotton-spinning factory in Ancoats in 1798 on
the site now occupied by Royal Mill (*see* below). The firm
became the largest in Manchester. It was responsible for the
first successful application of steam power to mule spinning,
and probably established the standard Lancashire cotton-
spinning mill arrangement of having the spinning mules
located transversely on the upper floors, one per bay, with
preparation of the cotton taking place on the lower floors. The
mills were lit by gas using a system installed by *Boulton & Watt*
in 1809. The four main buildings on the site illustrate development from 1818 to 1913.

    Sedgwick Mill, Redhill Street. Eight storeys, fireproof
construction. Begun 1818, probably designed by *William Fairbairn* with the owner John Kennedy. Seventeen-bay canal-side
range, eight-bay wings projecting NW at each end; the courtyard was closed on the NW side by a block of *c.* 1820. The
three-storey internal engine house is located at the W end of
the main block. In 1865 Fairbairn replaced the columns on all
but the ground and first floors so that self-acting mules could
be installed.

    Sedgwick New Mill, to the NW, is attached to the W
wing of Sedgwick Mill. Built 1868. Five storeys, fifteen bays,
used for doubling the yarn produced in the other mills on the
site. Last in the sequence Royal Mill and Paragon Mill,
1911–13. The drawings are signed by *Mr Porter* of the Fine
Cotton Spinners' Engineering Division. Red brick with terracotta and stone dressings and Baroque detailing. Six-storey
nine-bay steel and concrete buildings designed to house electrically powered mules, with electric motors housed in towers.
These mills are in the first generation of those purpose-built
for electricity, which was supplied by the Corporation.

Murrays Mills, Redhill Street, Ancoats, alongside the
Rochdale Canal. The careers of the brothers Adam and George
Murray followed a similar path to that of their neighbours and
main rivals, McConnel & Kennedy. Between 1798 and 1806
they developed the area between Murray Street and Bengal
Street into the largest mill complex in the town. The buildings
are ranged around a courtyard containing a canal basin, now
filled in, connected to the Rochdale Canal by tunnel. Offices
and entrance on the Murray Street, W side, with a central stone
arched entrance flanked by arched doorways. The remaining E
and W sides, 1806, had narrow blocks used for warehousing
and ancillary processes, but the E range was demolished in the
1990s. Overlooking the canal, S side, Old Mill, 1798, and
the attached Decker Mill, 1801–2, to the r. Each has eleven
bays and seven storeys, served by a fireproof stair-tower on
the N side. On the opposite, N, side of the courtyard, New
Mill, 1804; six storeys, with a prominent circular stair-tower

attached to the courtyard side. The remains of a detached engine house and octagonal chimney in the courtyard, s side, relate to improvements of *c.* 1870–80.

The complex was enlarged by building E of the main complex on the other side of Bengal Street. On the corner with Jersey Street LITTLE MILL, 1908, replaced a building of 1820. To the l. DOUBLING MILL and FIREPROOF MILL, added *c.* 1842 and powered by a single internal beam engine; these two converted to offices by the developers *Urban Splash* in 2002. All three were connected with the main complex by tunnels beneath the road.

BEEHIVE MILL, Jersey Street, Ancoats. Converted in 1996 by *Provan & Makin* to offices, studios, etc. Two blocks of the 1820s with later extensions. The earliest part is an L-shaped block of five storeys and thirteen original bays to Radium Street with three bays to Jersey Street, s. The attached WARE-HOUSE wing on Jersey Street is dated 1824. It was built using a sophisticated and rarely surviving form of fireproof con-struction in which interlocking cast-iron beams supported by cast-iron columns form a grid which receives huge stone flags. The roof structure is of advanced design and similarly devoid of timber: cast-iron trusses are held under tension by wrought-iron ties.*

BROWNSFIELD MILL, Binns Place, Great Ancoats Street. Of *c.* 1825, L-shaped with blocks of six and seven storeys. Circu-lar external stair-tower in the angle of the blocks, wrapped around a chimney. Conventional design for the date, with an internal engine house, but unusually complete and well-preserved.

BRUNSWICK MILL, Bradford Street, Ancoats, on the Ashton Canal. Of *c.* 1840. One of the largest and best preserved of a distinctive type of mid-C19 fireproof mill associated with the designs of *William Fairbairn*. Quadrangular plan with a central courtyard. Seven-storey block to the canal for spinning, wings on each side for a combination of spinning and ancillary processes. A four-storey warehouse and office block along the street frontage links the wings. External engine house for a double beam engine in the courtyard.

SPECTATOR SILK MILL, Spectator Street, Ancoats. Part of a complex of industrial buildings on the SE side of the Ashton canal. Early–mid-C19, brick and render, six storeys with a stair-turret at the SE corner and a full-height latrine tower pierced by diamond-pattern ventilation holes.

VICTORIA DOUBLE MILL, Lower Vickers Street, Miles Plat-ting. Built in two phases, 1869 and 1873, to the designs of *George Woodhouse* for William Holland. A building of great pres-ence and a landmark in the area. Two large six-storey cotton-spinning mills stand on each side of a tall round chimney,

---

* Edward Holl was using a similar form of construction by 1813 for buildings of the Royal Dockyards in Chatham and Devonport.

which has a stair-tower wrapped around the lower part. Italianate, red brick with yellow brick dressings, the corners of the
mill blocks treated as pilasters with bracketed cornices. The
conversion to offices and community facilities which saved it
came in the 1990s.

Streets

ANITA STREET *see* Oldham Road, Ancoats.
GREAT ANCOATS STREET, Ancoats. The largest and most strik-   102
ing building not only on the street frontage but also of its type
in the city is the DAILY EXPRESS BUILDING. By *Sir Owen
Williams*, 1939, following the example of his Daily Express in
London (1931). His one other Express Building, of 1936, was
built in Glasgow. An all-glass front, absolutely flush, with
rounded corners and translucent glass and black glass. The top
floors are set back in tiers. A little turret at the l. corner. The
printing presses were in the triple-height press hall, a most
impressive sight from the street, particularly when lit up at
night. The building has been extended four times since 1960,
most recently in 1993–5 when *Michael Hyde & Associates* converted it to offices. Their extension to Great Ancoats Street, l.
side, is seamless. Behind, a silvery block of offices and apartments by *O'Connell East Architects* (2003) echoes the rounded
corners of the 1939 building.
    METHODIST WOMEN'S NIGHT SHELTER, E corner of
George Leigh Street. By *W.R. Sharp*, opened in 1899. Four
storeys on a narrow site, with an oversailing timbered attic and
an oriel to Great Ancoats Street. There was a coffee tavern on
the ground floor, and the rest was divided between a night
shelter, a home for women needing 'further care and discipline'
and a home for domestic servants, who were offered an alternative to the moral perils of the lodging house.
HOOD STREET, Ancoats. METHODIST MEN'S HOSTEL by
J. Gibbons Sankey, dated 1903. Its sheer size gives some idea of
the demand for decent lodgings and the strength of Methodist
commitment to social service. It is not wholly utilitarian either,
with buff and brown terracotta banding and a central pedimented entrance bay flanked by turrets.
GEORGE LEIGH STREET, Ancoats. GEORGE LEIGH SCHOOL,
1912. Red brick with tall corniced chimneys and slightly projecting entrance bays. Note the rooftop playground. For the
municipal housing, *see* Oldham Road.
OLDHAM ROAD, Ancoats. VICTORIA SQUARE. A vast slum
replacement of 1897. The Corporation sponsored a competition won by *Spalding & Cross*. The result is a five-storeyed
block with an inner courtyard or square round which balconies
run on four levels. The iron railings show at once that the architects wanted to do more than was strictly necessary without
at all going elaborate. The eighteen-bay front to Oldham
Road has indeed good brickwork, a middle gable with some

terracotta and Dutch side-gables. The sides of the block are
stock brick with large segmental-headed windows in pairs
alternating with small round windows in pairs. It originally
comprised 235 two-roomed and forty-eight single-roomed
flats, paired on each side of a communal lobby with a sink and
water closet. The turrets contained communal laundries and
drying rooms. This initiative did not do the slum dwellers any
good since they could not afford the rents and had to move to
squalid conditions elsewhere, but it was the first municipal
housing in Manchester and it is still occupied and in public
ownership.

The adjacent block to the s was built at the same time, with
shops and dwellings above, while behind there is more municipal housing of the same period on ANITA (formerly Sanitary)
STREET and GEORGE LEIGH STREET, modest brick terraces.

OLDHAM ROAD, Miles Platting. EMPRESS CINEMA, originally
the Empress Electric Theatre. 1911–12 for W. H. Broadhead &
Son, and very similar to their Picture Pavilion cinema in
Ashton-under-Lyne (*see* p. 124). Red brick with white brick
dressings, symmetrical with a central crenellated parapet and
a large cartouche with the word 'Empress'. (The interior has
a double-height auditorium with balcony and lavish timber and
plasterwork decoration including Baroque-style organ cases
framing the proscenium arch.)

OLD MILL STREET, Ancoats. NEW ISLINGTON MILLEN-
NIUM VILLAGE. Ancoats Hospital (*see* above) and the area to
the w bounded by Weybridge Road, Woodward Place and
Darlington Street, N, the Rochdale Canal, w and Cardroom
Road, s, have been approved as the site of a Millennium
Village, lead developer *Urban Splash*, with *Alsop Architects*. The
new scheme proposes demolition of a depressed 1970s estate
and everything else except the original hospital building, with
development around newly created canal arms, integrating
shops, dwellings and small businesses.

PALMERSTON STREET, Ancoats. ARDWICK LADS' CLUB and
ARDWICK MEN'S CLUB (former). By *W. & G. Higginbottom*,
opened in 1898. Red brick with a little ornamental faience.
Two-storey gabled blocks flanking a lower entrance part.

POLLARD STREET, Ancoats. A range of large warehouses
and works lines the SE side of the street. First a Co-operative
Society warehouse of *c.* 1900, brick, three storeys and thirty-
two bays, then immediately to the NE the Vulcan Works of
1888–9, a four- and five-storey former ironworks with a tall
chimney on the w side.

ROCHDALE ROAD, Ancoats. The MARBLE ARCH by *Darbyshire
& Smith*, dated 1888, is the only one of the scattered pubs in
the area of architectural pretension. The interior has an
unusual jack-arch ceiling with exposed cast-iron beams
supported by tile-clad brackets.*Walls and ceiling of the main

* Darbyshire had considerable experience of designing fireproof cotton mills and
pioneered fireproof safety theatre designs with Henry Irving.

bar are lined with glazed bricks and tiles and a lettered frieze advertises types of drink.

BLACKLEY

The Rochdale boundary is on the N, Heaton Park to the W, the River Irk to the S and then Factory Lane and Boggart Hole Clough. On the E side the boundary is taken as the North Manchester High School for Boys.

There were three village centres, Blackley itself (pronounced as once spelt, Blakely), which was a substantial settlement down by the River Irk; Higher Blackley or Crab Village; and Charlestown. Of the three, Blackley was destroyed by the City Council in the 1970s, leaving Old Market Street as a mockery of emptiness. The 'quaint village' of Charlestown has gone too, so only Crab Village on its breezy height is left. The churches and buildings of interest are grouped according to these three clusters.

The landmark of Blackley, completely out of scale as well as out of place in its sophistication, is HEXAGON TOWER. It was built 117 in 1971 for ICI as a research building, and is by *Richard Seifert & Partners*. It fills the little valley where Blackley village was, towering eleven storeys on a spreading two-storey base and dominating the landscape with its massively Cubist prismatic forms. Two further blocks were planned. The cladding modules are arrow-shaped, linking together to leave hexagonal windows in deep reveals. Each module is moreover slightly folded, so that the points where the modules touch sticks out. The building is powerful from every angle, but particularly so in steep foreshortening, when the points line up and make black shadows, and the great V-shaped end window unzips to reveal the endless stair within.

The building takes its name from nearby HEXAGON HOUSE, a lumpish brick building of the 1950s by *H. S. Fairhurst & Son*. The name was chosen for the hexagonal benzene ring, the foundation of all synthetic dyes.

ST PETER, Old Market Street. There was a private chapel here 54 in 1548 which was sold to the inhabitants in 1611. In 1736 this was rebuilt in stone. The present building, set further back from the road and offered up on a grass mound, like a villa of the period, was built in 1844 by *E. H. Shellard*. It is a Commissioners' church (total cost £3,162), and very complete. Boxy nave decked out with buttresses and clumsy pinnacles, blunt W tower half-embraced by the gallery stairs with their own side-entrances. Paired narrow lancets. A narrow chancel with a big Geometric E window was added in 1880. The interior is aisled, with slender quatrefoil piers supporting three galleries. – Gothic BOX PEWS, complete. – Several MEMORIAL TABLETS saved from the previous church. – ROYAL ARMS. –

STAINED GLASS. On the S side, eight panels of brightly coloured armorial glass from the 1844 E window.

The CHURCHYARD has been insensitively levelled, apart from the upper part, which is abandoned to wilderness.

Nothing is left to tell of the village except a couple of pubs and a small mill on the corner of Domett Street. Even the SCHOOL, a typical big red brick and terracotta Queen Anne building by the *City Architects*, 1907, has closed.

ST ANDREW, Upper Blackley, off Crab Lane. 1864–5, by *J. Medland Taylor*. Stone; nave, chancel with a bell-turret on the chancel arch, S aisle. No clerestory, just one gabled dormer at the E end of the nave. The Rectory, to which it is connected by a cloister-like corridor, is dated 1871 on inset tiles: fanciful, with tricky brickwork. – STAINED GLASS. E, dated 1881 but unsigned, as is the cartoon preserved at the church. Four S windows by *S. Evans*.

On Crab Lane are old cottages, by-law cottages and new cottages determinedly cottagey, the garden boundaries often of thin flagstones set on end.

ST PAUL, Victoria Avenue. By *Taylor & Young*, 1930–1, in a Georgian classical style. Incomplete at the W end, with a temporary wall. It should have had a nave of five bays instead of the existing two, plus a narthex and a bell-turret. Even so the interior is pleasing in pink and apricot, brightly daylit and carefully proportioned and furnished. Apsed sanctuary, curved on the inside though three-sided outside, strong crossing with corner spaces almost as though a dome was contemplated, truncated nave, and a Lady Chapel on the S side linking to the RECTORY of 1931. FITTINGS, such as the paired oak pens for reading desk and pulpit are simple but of high quality. The Lady Chapel was only fitted out in 1954. The adjacent PARISH HALL of 1952 which replaced the tin Mission Church of 1914 is an early work by *Leach, Rhodes & Walker*, then of Middleton.

OUR LADY OF MOUNT CARMEL (R.C.), Old Road. 1907–8, of red brick, Perp, with a very tall clerestory and a NW turret. Thin hammerbeam roof. The PRESBYTERY is large with deeply ribbed chimneys, dated 1904.

ST CLARE (R.C.), Victoria Avenue. The Franciscans came here in 1929 and built a small church and a school, both extant. The Friary was built in 1951 to the designs of *Weightman & Bullen* of Liverpool, and finally the present church by the same architects in 1956–8. It is an aggressive design, the frame showing externally and overhanging slightly – an alarming motif. Wide undivided interior with a spectacular roof, the ribs scissoring like the chapel vault of Borromini's Propaganda Fide in Rome. – Three STAINED GLASS panels of Franciscan exemplars.

ST JOHN BOSCO (R.C.), Charlestown Road. 1958–60, by *Geoffrey G. Williams* of *Greenhalgh & Williams*. Uncomfortably overwindowed, as can be achieved in reinforced concrete, but the windows arched as though structural. The steeply cambered concrete roof beams are visually uncomfortable as well, being untied, and balanced on very little. Otherwise a conventional Catholic design, residually Romanesque with a tall campanile. (STAINED GLASS and iron SCREEN in the baptistery, by the architect.)

CEMETERY, Victoria Avenue. A beautiful rolling landscape is set out informally except for the short avenue linking the two principal buildings, both of 1959 by *L. C. Howitt*, City Architect. They pay tribute to the bow of Heaton Hall and the rotunda of its temple, so clearly visible on the opposite hilltop. – CREMATORIUM. Long symmetrical façade, with a big bow 116 in the centre with closely set mullions and two transoms high up. At each end is a flying two-stage porte cochère of thinnest concrete. Inside are three chapels; they are not denominational but allow concurrent funerals. The central chapel has concrete beams arranged fanwise, and is effectively lit by the huge window with its gentle coloured glass. Facing is the sixteen-sided CHAPEL OF REMEMBRANCE, with its concrete framing exposed and bending gallows-wise on top of the roof. It is lit by round glass bricks in a little central dome. Under it a lens-shaped table of white marble, like an altar. Small courtyard behind.

BOOTH HALL CHILDREN'S HOSPITAL, Charlestown Road. By *T. Worthington & Son*. The Infirmary of the Prestwich Poor Law Union was built in 1907–8 on the familiar system of a central administration block with pavilions to l. and r. connected by a long corridor. The style of the central block is Early Georgian but its materials hard brick and red terracotta. The pavilions have paired corner towers like so many dovecotes. The corridor is gently curved and slopes up and down the hill. A Children's Hospital was created in 1915 and now occupies the whole complex. The Nurses' Home was built in 1925, and the two angled s-facing wards at the w end of the site with continuous balconies in 1927.

BLACKLEY COTTAGES of 1903–4, between Victoria Avenue and 106 Alworth Road, are an early experiment by the City Council in rehousing from the slums. There are 149 houses built at twenty to the acre, in short terraces of three different designs. The HIGHER BLACKLEY ESTATE was put up from 1919 around Erskine Road; 1,104 were planned, 546 done by 1921. They were built to a superior standard, probably the best the city ever did, and are nicely varied in design. The whole progress of Manchester Council housing can be followed in Blackley as the specifications gradually declined. Simpler but still pleasant housing of the 1920s can be seen around Symond Road; Thurlby Avenue is typical, but made remarkable by the tall brick TOWER which rears up behind it. This was associated with an early attempt at district heating and hot water supply. Wythenshawe-type housing (q.v.) was built in the 1930s including occasional special designs: e.g. in Evesham Road, WHITE MOSS GARDENS and CLOUGH HOUSE, identical respectively to Mitchell Gardens and Chamberlain House in

Wythenshawe but here facing each other across a green. The 1950s Wythenshawe designs were extensively used here as well.*

CHEETHAM and STRANGEWAYS

Immediately N of Manchester centre. Manchester's Jewry were concentrated here in the C19 and signs of their presence remain. One of Manchester's most notable High Victorian buildings, *Alfred Waterhouse*'s Manchester Assize Courts (1859–64), stood on Bury New Road in front of his Strangeways Prison until it was demolished following war damage (for the surviving statuary, *see* Crown Court, p. 286). The southern part of the township is a near-desert of retail warehouses and light industrial works bisected by the busy road. Residential and shopping areas lie to the N. The boundary is on the N and E sides (including) Crescent Road, Greenhill Road, Woodlands Road, Smedley Road, and the River Irk; on the S side New Bridge Street; W side, the boundary with Salford, which is only present visually alongside the River Irwell.

Religious Buildings

ST JOHN THE EVANGELIST, Waterloo Road. 1869–71 by *Paley & Austin*. Built at the expense of Lewis Loyd. A serious, thoughtful design and a strikingly forceful and blunt treatment of transitional Romanesque/E.E. Stone, with a massive four-stage SW tower with a big pyramid roof and pinnacles also with pyramid roofs. S entrance with four orders of arched moulding and pipe corbels. The windows are mainly lancets, which leaves much sheer wall, giving a slightly forbidding look. The W windows are placed unusually high up. W porch 1894, in matching style. INTERIOR. Brick walls with stone dressings. Three-bay nave, two-bay chancel, no structural division between. Round apse with two tiers of blank arcading and arcaded side walls with octagonal N piers and circular S piers. Nave arcade with quatrefoil N piers and octagonal S piers. Timber arch-and-scissor-braced roof. N organ chamber a continuation of the N aisle, S chapel, a continuation of the S aisle. FURNISHINGS. REREDOS. Traceried panels, *c.* 1916. – CHOIR STALLS. Pine with arcaded fronts and ends with sunflowers and other Japanese-inspired roundels. – PULPIT with similar motifs. – SCREEN, openwork with cresting. – FONT. Very plain. Oak COVER with finialed gables and a tall spire. – STAINED GLASS. All good, including windows by *C. E. Kempe*, saints, church leaders and unusually, Sir Philip Sidney.
ST LUKE, Cheetham Hill Road. 1836–9 by *T. W. Atkinson*, on land given by Edward Smith Stanley, 13th Earl of Derby. Sited prominently at the top of the hill, it is one of the few uplifting

---

* We owe much information on Manchester council housing to Jacqueline Roberts.

sights in the area. A remarkable design of which only the w tower and the w end of the aisles and vestry survive.* It is still pre-archaeological, but more credible than most Gothic churches of the 1830s. Perp, three-stage slim stone tower with a tall four-light window with blind tracery over, pierced parapet and crocketed pinnacles. It originally had a fine crocketed spire, perhaps based on the example of Wakefield Cathedral. The crowded CHURCHYARD retains its perimeter walls with delicate traceried iron railings and stone gatepiers with cusped panels.

ST CHAD (R.C.), Cheetham Hill Road. 1846–7 by *Weightman & Hadfield*. Stone, Perp, and on the way to archaeological accuracy, though window proportions and tracery detail have been varied and mixed up, not grouped to suggest different building campaigns. It could hardly be more different from their St Mary Mulberry Street of only a year later (*see* Centre, p. 276). All the parts are separately expressed and there are enjoyable asymmetries in the design. SW tower with a higher stair-turret, aisles punctuated by big gargoyles, nave, and lower chancel. Attached on the E side a large PRESBYTERY, of stone like the church, with steep gables and gabled dormers.

Six-bay nave with octagonal piers and a hammerbeam roof, two-bay chancel, aisles, two-bay N chapel, two-bay S chapel with one bay beside the chancel and the other beside the aisle, creating the effect of a transept and allowing the chancel to be lit by two high windows on this side. Good FURNISHINGS. PULPIT with much Gothic panelling and a tall pinnacled canopy. – S chapel. Very elaborate coved wooden REREDOS with angels; ALTAR with painted carving; richly carved ALTAR RAILS. – STAINED GLASS. E window, *c.* 1847–8, by *Barnett & Son* of York. N chapel E window by *Edith Norris*, 1956. – MONUMENT. Seated statue of Monsignor W.J. Canon Sheehan, rector of the church, erected by the parishioners 1906.

INDEPENDENT CHAPEL (former), Cheetham Hill Road, at the corner of Park Street. *c.* 1840. An excellent classical design. Ashlar, with a three-bay front with slender arched windows, a big portal, and a one-bay pediment. The side has giant pilasters. Five bays long with windows in two tiers. The end bays are blank, with banded rustication. Inside there is only a simply treated S stair to the former gallery, now with an inserted floor.

TRINITY UNITED CHURCH, Cheetham Hill Road. 1899–1900. The architect is recorded as *Henry Price*. Could this be *Henry R. Price* of the firm Price & Linklater rather than the Henry Price who became Manchester City Architect in 1902? It certainly does not measure up to the usual standard of the latter. Red brick, red terracotta, thin battlemented tower with slate-clad spirelet, Geometric windows.

---

*The C18 Flemish pulpit was moved to Manchester City Art Gallery after demolition.

74 SPANISH AND PORTUGUESE SYNAGOGUE (former), Cheetham
    Hill Road. By *Edward Salomons*, 1874, for the Sephardic Jews
    in what Salomons described as 'Saracenic' and 'Moresque'
    style, appropriately recalling the ancient architecture of
    Moorish Spain, and avoiding either Gothic or classical with
    their respective Christian and pagan associations. The use of
    the style for the exterior as well as the interior is quite unusual,
    though T. H. & F. Healey did something similar in the Bowland
    Street synagogue in Bradford in 1880–1.* Rescued after
    closure in 1981, the building reopened as the Manchester
    Jewish Museum in 1984. Not large, set back from the line of
    the street, in warm red brick with stone dressings. Projecting
    entrance bay and central door framed by a Moorish arch, with
    an arcade of five windows with horseshoe heads above. On
    each side are two-storey bays, windows with ogee heads below
    and horseshoe heads above. The INTERIOR has been kept
    much as it was when closed apart from the removal of seats in
    the ladies' gallery upstairs, where there are exhibitions. Open
    timber roof, galleries on three sides, with an intricate ironwork
    parapet and cast-iron columns with fancy capitals. At the E end
    is a recess framed by a Moorish arch with a classical ARON,
    where the Torah scrolls are kept, with paired columns and a
    segmental arch. – TEVAH, or BIMA, from which the Torah
    is read, at the W end with openwork sides in Arabic designs,
    probably inspired by the *mushrabiyya* fretwork screens found
    in Egyptian mosques. At the rear there is a converted SUCCAH,
    used during the festival of tabernacles, which had originally a
    removable roof. – STAINED GLASS. An extensive early C20
    scheme. Big circular E window with a menorah, 1913. The rest
    downstairs show Biblical landscapes. Upstairs, E end: on one
    side the pillar of fire, on the other the pillar of cloud.

    SYNAGOGUE (former), Cheetham Hill Road. By *W. Sharp
    Ogden*, 1889. Red brick, stone dressings, central pedimented
    entrance with a circular window with a Star of David design,
    set back from the street with gate piers and stone steps up.
    Horribly altered, and stripped-out inside.

    CENTRAL SYNAGOGUE (former), Heywood Street. 1927–8 by
    J. Knight. Derelict. Small. Brick and white stone, Grecian
    detail. The structure is reinforced concrete by *Lambourne &
    Co. Ltd.*

    HIGHER CRUMPSALL SYNAGOGUE, Bury Old Road (at the
    point where Crumpsall, Cheetham and Salford border each
    other). 1928–9 by *Pendleton & Dickinson*. Large, Portland stone
    on the exposed faces, pale brick on the others. Classical, with
    the Ark end facing the street. A central projecting domed
    apsidal bay is flanked by tall windows with consoles and
    pediments, smaller domed bays on each side. Lion masks in
    the cornice of the apse are a very unusual feature, possibly (as
    Dr Sharman Kadish reports) unique in Britain. Sculpted
    animals very rarely feature in Jewish art. (Interior with good

    * Dr Sharman Kadish pointed this out to me.

STAINED GLASS, including a Vision of Jerusalem window with an Art Deco sunburst.)

NORTH MANCHESTER JAMIAH MOSQUE, Woodlands Road. 1982. An early British example of a large purpose-built mosque. Large, brick, with a big gold-coloured metal dome and finials.

Public Buildings

TOWN HALL (former), Cheetham Hill Road. 1853–5 by *T. Bird*. A sober classical composition of red brick with prominent stone quoins and a heavy bracketed eaves cornice. Two tall storeys, seven bays with a projecting three-bay centre and lower wings. Austerity is offset by the delicate iron porte cochère in front of the central entrance. The upper hall has a semicircular end wall.

POOR LAW UNION OFFICE (former), Cheetham Hill Road. 1861–2. Three bays and two storeys flanked by single-storey wings. Decidedly more florid than the town hall, to which it was subsequently used as an annexe. Central entrance with a porch with fluted Ionic columns, the volutes linked by bulging festoons, flanking bays with Venetian windows.

FREE LIBRARY (former), Cheetham Hill Road. By *Barker & Ellis*. Yellow brick and stone dressings, dated 1876 in the frieze. Above the portal a handsome five-bay window arcade. Side bays with upper pedimented windows only; the walls below are sheer and contribute to a monumental look. Above the cornice segmental gables on each side of a balustraded parapet. There is nothing left inside.

PUBLIC LIBRARY (former), Cheetham Hill Road. 1909–11 by the City Architect *Henry Price*. Stone, Edwardian Baroque with two symmetrical gables and a semi-domed porch. Boarded up.

STRANGEWAYS PRISON, Southall Street. 1866–8 by *Alfred Waterhouse*. The high minaret-chimney, actually part of the ventilation system, is a landmark. Of the rest one does not see much, except the 1990s additions and alterations (*see* below). The architectural motifs are Romanesque, with an octagonal raised centre like a North Italian cathedral or a British workhouse, in dark red brick with pale stone dressings and banding. Waterhouse took as his model Joshua Jebb's radial plan of Pentonville, in London, of the 1840s, and consulted Jebb, who was Surveyor General of Prisons, on the plans. Six wings radiate from the centre, a short entrance wing then five four-storey cell blocks. The gatehouse, now superseded by a new entrance, has octagonal turrets with tall pyramidal roofs flanking the big entrance arch. Extensive damage during a prolonged riot in 1990 prompted refurbishment in 1991–3. The *J. R. Harris Partnership* did the work and prepared a masterplan. Later accretions were demolished, but the only part to disappear completely was the Magistrates' Court on the SW side. The main cell wings were divided into sections to improve staff/inmate access and circulation. Before the refit the long views along the wings from the controlling hub contrasted with the claustrophobic cells and contributed to an oppressive atmosphere. The cells were refitted and the windows enlarged. The new entrance complex, by *Austin-Smith:Lord*, is at the angle of two new blocks, set back from Southall Street.

Jews' School (former), Derby Road. By *Edward Salomons*, 1868–9. Three storeys, brick, gabled end bays with a little sparing decoration in the form of oriels with blue diaper brickwork and stone dressings. Converted to warehousing and much altered. The school was established in 1842 and this building remained in use until 1942.

Talmud Torah School (former), Bent Street and Torah Street. By *Ogden & Charlesworth*, 1894. Modest, brick with stone dressings, and panels of brick with Star of David motifs. Single-storey with two-storey gabled wings, one dated 1931. Central arched entrance beneath a gable.

BUS DEPOT (former), Queens Road. By *J. Gibbons*, Manchester's first electric tram shed, opened in 1901. Office range with an array of gables and dormers along Queens Road, splayed corner to Boyle Street with a big exaggerated segmental arch and a bulging carved keystone over a large window. The Boyle Street elevation to the tram sheds has a long brick screen wall. Attached to the N end, two buildings erected for a bus depot in 1928 and 1935, housing a TRANSPORT MUSEUM, opened in 1979.

Other Buildings

There is no perambulation. Most buildings of interest can be seen on or from Cheetham Hill Road, but this is too long and inhospitable for a comfortable walk and there are long stretches with nothing of interest.

BURY NEW ROAD. Nothing to report except the BODDINGTON'S BREWERY, E side, of which a very tall octagonal chimney is a landmark and the only notable late C19 survival.

CHEETHAM HILL ROAD was laid out in 1820, when it was called York Street. Its buildings, some recalling former prosperity, are mostly altered or mutilated. Near the S end, W side, the DERBY BREWERY ARMS pub originated as a hotel in the early 1860s. Red brick with stone dressings. The five-bay pub part has a central arched doorway with Ionic pilasters and rich foliate carving in the spandrels and tall windows with inset shafts. Offices and shops to the r. complete the group.

Civic buildings and some synagogues can be seen to the N (*see* above), but then there is little of interest until the Waterloo Road junction is approached, more than a mile to the N. Just S of the junction the scene is enlivened by a row of jolly SHOPS, E side, at the corner of Esmond Street. By *A. H. Walsingham*, 1913, for the Co-operative Wholesale Society. Red brick and yellow terracotta naughtily combining Venetian window motifs with timbered gables. Further N in the same row, a

TEMPERANCE BILLIARD HALL (former), 1906, by *Norman Evans*. Roughcast and quite ornate with a big segmental arch containing a (blocked) Venetian window flanked by square turrets with pyramidal roofs and pilasters with attractive moulded Art Nouveau decoration.

DERBY STREET. The E end is dominated by big late C19 and early C20 warehouses and works, historically notable because many were built for big Manchester Jewish firms, e.g. No. 46, N side, a purpose-built Marks & Spencer warehouse of 1900–1. For the former Jews' School, *see* Public Buildings, above. The MANCHESTER ICE PALACE, N side, by *E. W. Leeson*, 1910–11, was a skating rink, closed in 1967. Baroque, red brick with yellow terracotta dressings. Above the central entrance a pediment breaks through the bracketed eaves cornice. Ground-floor windows form an arcade of segmental arches. The sides are plain brick with an arcade of lunette windows above the eaves. A little further W, N side, the CHEETWOOD HOTEL is a cheerful little pub, of red brick with terracotta and faience dressings and a corner turret with a pyramidal roof. By *N. Hartley Hacking*, dated 1907. Further W a number of large works of the 1920s–30s, many by *Joseph Sunlight*, of which the best preserved and most ambitious is VICTORIA BUILD-INGS, S side, of 1922. Two giant Baroque Ionic columns frame the entrance, the pediment above has Egyptian motifs.

CHEETHAM PARK, Elizabeth Street. Near the centre, a hexagonal cast- and wrought-iron BANDSTAND of *c*. 1890 with Art Nouveau detailing.

EMPIRE STREET. HOLT'S BREWERY, dated 1860 and remod-elled in 1890. Brick, neat and utilitarian. The office with its pedimented stone doorcase originated as Joseph Holt's house, built for himself alongside. Holt's son Edward lived at Woodthorpe, Prestwich (*see* p. 570) and his holiday home was Blackwell, in Windermere.

NORTH STREET. No. 86, BEDMAKER. Textile manufacturing warehouse by *P. Bintliff & N. Evans* of *Studio BAAD*, 1993. A breath of fresh air after the acres of cheap shabby brick sheds on this side of Cheetham Hill Road. A conventional shed is fronted by a tube of silver corrugated steel, housing the offices. An offset glazed panel marks the entrance, and three angled funnels rise from the roof to light the double-height reception area.

SMEDLEY LANE. A row of C19 houses face St Luke's church (*see* above). The grandest is Temple Bank, a classical villa of *c*. 1840 with deep bracketed eaves and a central slightly projecting gabled entrance bay. Stone porch with Doric pilasters and a pierced parapet. Beside it to the E, two pairs of more modest houses of similar date with stone doorcases and canted bays.

SOUTHALL STREET. Near the N end, the PHILANTHROPIC HALL, dated 1906, by *T. Bushell* for a Jewish charity which ran a soup kitchen from it. Red brick with some half-hearted Queen Anne detailing.

COLLYHURST and HARPURHEY

Collyhurst stands high above Manchester and the River Irk, where the hill is crowned with 1960s–70s tower blocks. Quarries here provided Manchester with building stone until the C19. There is nothing else to report other than to say that the three churches described in the first edition (1969) have been demolished. Harpurhey lies N of Collyhurst, and here there is some sense of a centre, with C19 buildings, churches and shops. The boundaries are Moston Lane and Factory Lane, N; the River Irk, W; Oldham Road, Collyhurst Street, Rochdale Road and Dalton Street, S; and on the E side Ashley Lane, Church Lane and Thorp Road. Busy Rochdale Road cuts N through the townships.

CHRIST CHURCH, Church Lane, Harpurhey. By *Edward Welch*, 1837–8. At that time it stood alone in the fields. Built by subscription and with a grant from the Manchester and Eccles Church Building Society. Stone, with a W tower of very unusual appearance; steep gables, big pinnacles, and a clock by *Joyce* installed in 1851. The bell-openings are a stepped triplet of lancets, so are the side windows of the church, between close-set buttresses. Shallow polygonal apse with tall arched three-light windows. Porches on each side of the tower and the S vestry were added in 1888, with other alterations. INTERIOR. Galleries on three sides with octagonal cast-iron columns and blind arcaded fronts. Roof trusses with open arcading from the 1888 restoration, as also most of the FURNISHINGS. Choir furnishings and the original pulpit have been removed and some of the fabric incorporated into late C20 furnishings, including an ALTAR TABLE and FONT. The original FONT survives at the SW end. Stone, an octagonal bowl with roundels. – ORGAN by *Jardine*, 1913, the case with flowing carving and angels. – STAINED GLASS. The E windows of 1855 are probably by *Wailes*. 1860s heraldic glass in the nave by *R. B. Edmundson* of Manchester.

MANCHESTER GENERAL CEMETERY, Rochdale Road, Harpurhey. *Mr Moffat* won the competition for the buildings in 1836–7, but they were demolished in the 1960s. It is an atmospheric place nonetheless. Starting on level ground near the road, the land falls to the edge of the Irk valley with dramatic views to the W. Divided from neighbouring Queen's Park (below) by a low wall.

HARPURHEY BATHS, Rochdale Road, Harpurhey (just N of the boundary). By the City Architect *Henry Price*, dated 1909. In the jolly Baroque Price used for such establishments. Red brick and orange and buff terracotta, symmetrical, with two entrance bays with pilasters rising from arched doorways to semicircular pediments. Central and flanking bays have arched windows below and tripartite windows above. The usual arrangement for the time: first- and second-class men's baths and a smaller women's bath (in this case reached from an entrance at the rear). The interior has green and cream tiles, probably by *Pilkington*, and original cubicles etc. Near the centre of the complex there is a tall chimney, and beside it the former laundry. The baths have been closed for years, and a scheme of 2004 envisages demolition of the laundry and women's bath and the construction of a sixth-form college on the site. The main entrance and men's baths would be converted to exhibition halls etc. for use by the school and community.

QUEEN'S PARK, Rochdale Road, Harpurhey. One of three parks laid out in Manchester by *Joshua Major & Son*. Opened in 1846. For the history of this and the other early Manchester public parks *see* Philips Park, p. 569. The land originally formed the grounds of Hendleham Hall. Red brick LODGE probably of the 1870s on Rochdale Road. The land falls from a plateau on the E side down to the W, providing varied prospects. Major's design provided a circular main path with side paths leading off to the pleasure gardens on the fringes. Areas were set aside for various sporting facilities. The centrepiece of the park is a MUSEUM AND ART GALLERY (now used for storage and administration) by *J. Allison*, 1883–4, on the site of Hendleham Hall. Red brick, with a gabled porch and otherwise just an even set of ground-floor windows and no upper windows except in the entrance bay, as the upper rooms are top-lit. In gardens facing the museum was a STATUE by *John Cassidy* of Benjamin Brierly, a prominent literary figure in the city and dialect poet, erected in 1898, but only the plinth is left.

MOSS BROOK ROAD, Harpurhey. Crofters House. A small early-C19 rendered villa overlooking the culverted Moston Brook with a symmetrical front with round-arched bays and heavy Doric pilasters. Now part of a dogs' home.

ROCHDALE ROAD, Harpurhey. Nos. 691–695, just N of Queens Park (*see* above). Three early C19 brick houses treated as one composition, the central one with a pediment, the sides with prominent semicircular bays with pilasters.

COLLYHURST ROAD, Collyhurst. At the entrance to the GHM paint factory. SCULPTURE. Nothing to Worry About by *Jonathan Woolfenden*, 1994. Steel plate sculpture of a large ship (loosely based on a Dreadnought) nearly 23 ft (7 metres) high sinking into the ground. The work was commissioned by the owner of GHM Paints.

CRUMPSALL

Crumpsall lies on land rising to the W from the Irk valley. The huge North Manchester Hospital complex dominates the NW side of the settlement. Otherwise it is largely residential. The boundaries are the River Irk to the E and N, the Salford boundary, W, and Woodlands Road and Smedley Lane, S.

ST THOMAS AND ST MARK, Hazelbottom Lane. By *George Shaw*, 1863. Low, of coursed sandstone rubble, no tower or aisles. N and S porches, S chapel, low chancel. Dec windows with details

typical of Shaw. The long N vestry extension is dated 1903.
(STAINED GLASS. A number of windows by *Shrigley & Hunt*.)

ST MATTHEW, Delauneys Road, Crumpsall. 1908–10 by *Isaac
Taylor*. Stone, conventional late Perp but with some early C20
touches, e.g. piers without normal capitals and arches with one
broad hollow chamfer. The chancel has short diagonal side
walls with one-light windows. Large NW tower, S chapel, wide
aisles, wide three- and four-light clerestory windows. (An arch
at the E end of chancel leads into the sanctuary, with windows
in the canted corners, and side windows to the sanctuary too.
Rich Renaissance style STAINED GLASS, and almost complete
interior fittings. TS)

ST ANNE (R.C.), Crescent Road, Crumpsall. 1957 by *Greenhalgh
& Williams*. Of brick. Detached saddleback tower with concrete
openwork top linked to the church by a wavy canopy. Gabled
nave with a central vertical window strip. A Neo-Georgian
presbytery to the r. is attached by a low link.

For the Higher Crumpsall Synagogue, *see* Cheetham and
Strangeways.

MANCHESTER GREAT SYNAGOGUE BURIAL GROUND, off
Crescent Road. Opened in 1884, high on a hill overlooking the
Irk valley. Axial plan with an array of C19 obelisks and other
monuments. Small brick OHEL (chapel), by *George Oswald
Smith*, 1888, simply treated with windows with triangular
heads.

NORTH MANCHESTER HOSPITAL, Delaunays Road, Crumpsall. A huge complex on high ground overlooking the valley of
the River Irk. It consists of several different institutions which
have been drawn together. The Manchester Workhouse by *Mills
& Murgatroyd* (later called Springfield Hospital) was opened
c. 1855, and Crumpsall Hospital was built as its infirmary in
1876 by the same architects. The Prestwich Union Workhouse
was built by *Thomas Worthington* in 1866–70. The three
institutions came together in 1919 when the Manchester and
Prestwich Poor Law Unions were amalgamated. Various
additions were made at this time. In 1975 the North Manchester General Hospital was formed from the institutions, and
incorporating a number of other hospitals in the area. A major
programme of expansion started in 1994, swallowing up
Springfield Hospital. The other two C19 elements remain
distinct.

CRUMPSALL HOSPITAL was intended in 1876 to cater for
1,400 inmates. Seven four-storey ward blocks in red brick
banded with stone terminate with full-height polygonal bays.
Between them an administrative block fronting a courtyard,
where most of the show is concentrated. Three-storey block
with a central entrance bay crowned by a pediment with the
words 'Poor and Needy the Lord careth for me'. A recessed
bay on each side has full-height polygonal bays, flanked in turn
by three-storey pavilions with gabled roofs.

The PRESTWICH UNION WORKHOUSE of 1866–70 followed from *Thomas Worthington*'s successful Chorlton Union

Crumpsall, Prestwich Union Workhouse, from *The Builder*, 1872

Workhouse (*see* p. 486), which had attracted praise from Florence Nightingale. Worthington sent the North Manchester plans to her, and the design was modified to accommodate her suggestions regarding sanitary accommodation and ventilation; windows were enlarged and large hearths inserted into the gable ends of the pavilions. The buildings lie on the highest part of the site. They were designed to house all classes of inmate, numbering in total 312, with male and female wings and hospital accommodation. Worthington wrote of them: 'all attempt at architectural effect has been carefully avoided, but the work is substantial and good.' The entrance buildings to the courtyard have been lost, but the main range still has presence, brick, two and three storeys with staircase and latrine towers, modestly Italianate and symmetrical.

MIDDLETON ROAD. Nothing to report except a few houses on the N side. Nos. 21–25, a row of altered early C19 brick cottages with door heads with pointed arches. A few grand late C19 and early C20 detached houses remain. Amongst the least altered are No. 89, the BELMONT HOTEL, a red brick mansion with half-timbered gables and an entrance bay with a tall turret, and No. 121, ARNCLIFFE, hard red brick with an angled corner turret and an elaborate stone porch. In a different vein is No. 195, a Moderne house by *Roberts, Wood & Elder*, 1935. Large buff bricks, and details such as narrow projecting quoins making it seem over-textured. Parapet, and a rounded stair projection with angled window bands with Art Deco glass.

CRESCENT ROAD. Set back from the road and reached from a long entrance drive, WOODLANDS is a handsome five-bay brick house of *c.* 1810. Two storeys and a basement. The shallow porch with Adamish columns and the window above it are set in a blank giant arch. Three-bay pediment.

(Groin-vaulted hall and an open-well staircase of stone with cast-iron balusters beneath a domed skylight).

HARPURHEY *see* COLLYHURST, above

HEATON PARK

31 The salient points were made by Aikin in 1795. 'Heaton-house, the seat of Lord Grey de Wilton, about four miles from Manchester, is beautifully situated on an eminence in a rich park. This truly elegant seat was built from a design of Wyat'.

Sir Thomas Egerton, later the 1st Earl of Wilton, inherited Heaton while still a minor in 1756. In 1772 he commissioned *James Wyatt* to prepare a design to remodel the house, which was exhibited at the Royal Academy. Egerton was twenty-three; Wyatt, triumphant from the success of his Pantheon in London, twenty-six. Pevsner considered the result the finest house of its period in Lancashire, and one of the finest in the country, Summerson thought it the most important of Wyatt's classical houses. It was his first country house commission, and one of the first country houses to abandon the Palladian *piano nobile* for state rooms on the ground floor. The initial design is lost, but it may appear in the large PAINTING of Sir Thomas as an archer in the entrance hall; notably the links have statues in niches, instead of the executed windows.

Building proceeded slowly. The Dining Room was complete by 1775, the Billiard Room by 1776, when 'the men from Leeds' were paid for the iron for the staircase, the Saloon by 1778. The Music Room behind the colonnade of the E link was only completed in 1789, by *Samuel Wyatt*. Was it a change of intention? The 2nd Earl and *Lewis Wyatt* completed the library in the E pavilion in 1823. At this time ranges of bedrooms were added along the N front, and the chimneys grouped into Vanbrughian temples. The 2nd Earl was a racing man, and needed extra accommodation offered by the additional bedrooms for the Heaton Park races, established in 1827 (but transferred to Aintree in 1839). The W wing was probably finished before the E, but has been much altered.

Attempts were made to sell Heaton as early as 1866. The City of Manchester, wishing to make a reservoir and needing more public open space, bought it in 1902 for £230,000. The W wing of the house, containing kitchen and services, burnt out in 1983 and is still, shockingly, derelict.

Sir Thomas had inherited a plain mid-C18 house of brick, of three storeys and seven bays, as can be seen on the N side. *Wyatt* made the three storeys into two, added the pediment, rendered it, and fronted it with a portico of four columns with Adamish capitals and a straight entablature. Stretching l. and r. are *Lewis Wyatt*'s bedroom wings, with unifying giant pilasters, evenly spaced. James Wyatt built an entirely new range attached to the

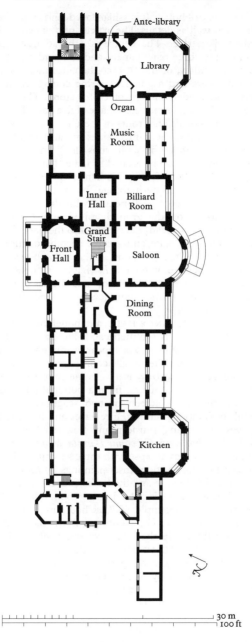

Heaton Hall, plan

s side of the c18 house. It is ashlar-faced, and exquisite in composition as well as details. The articulation of centre, links and
pavilions is perfect. The centre is a broad bow with demi-
columns and three relief panels, and to l. and r. just one large
Venetian window, of the type contained under a blank arch.
Giant pilasters and a guilloche string course; capitals, string
course and medallions are of *Coade* stone. Then follow the
straight links, each with a colonnade of five bays. The end pavilions are octagonal. The fronts of these have again a contained
Venetian window, the canted sides garland panels. A fluted
frieze with garlanded ox skulls runs along links and pavilions.
The composition can be related to James Paine's garden-front
design at Kedleston for Sir Nathaniel Curzon (to whom Sir
Thomas was related by marriage) but with two novel differences. Firstly Wyatt has dispensed with the *piano nobile*. The
state rooms sit on the ground, raised only by a couple of
shallow steps, with ready access out into the park. Secondly he
has extended the state and service accommodation into the
links as well as the pavilions, making the house unusually
compact. Appended on the r. is *Lewis Wyatt*'s CONSERVATORY,
originally with glass pavilion roofs and a glass dome over the
octagonal centre. Portico entrances at the ends lead out onto
a square parterre.

INTERIOR. The ENTRANCE HALL, a remodelling of the c18 hall,
is austere and strictly symmetrical. It has apsed ends, and the
three arrows of the Egertons appear prominently in frieze and
fireplace. Traversing the equally cool staircase hall in the centre
of the house, the SALOON is a welcome contrast in its warmth
and richness. We see it first from a notional passage, tunnel-
vaulted, through a screen of two scagliola columns with
capitals of Wyatt's invention. Fireplaces and frieze with lyres –
this was the original music room. Low-relief plasterwork by
Joseph Rose Jun. and *Giovanni Battista Maini*. The DINING
ROOM to the r. has an apse with three serving tables designed
by Wyatt for this position. Inset paintings by *Biagio Rebecca* of
bacchantes in the apse and the Seasons in the centre. The corresponding room to l. is not a drawing room but the BILLIARD
ROOM, an early example. *Gillows* had supplied Sir Thomas
with a table in 1771. The paintings after subjects from Ovid,
in built-in frames in the fabric-covered wall, are by *Michael
Novosielski*. The MUSIC ROOM follows, in the link. It was
inaugurated in 1789 with a performance of Handel's *Acis and
Galatea*. The organ by *Samuel Green* terminates the enfilade
from the dining room. It cost £350, and *Biagio Rebecca* was
paid £40 for painting its case in grisaille on a greyish-green
ground, with putti and winged genii holding a portrait of
Handel. The exquisite chimneypiece is by *John Bacon Sen.*,
after a design of *Piranesi*. Through a jib door by the organ is
the LIBRARY, fitted out by *Lewis Wyatt* in 1823, although the
shell of the pavilion must have been there. It is less pretty, more
strictly Neoclassical than the rest. Apsed ante-library, screen

of two Ionic columns, octagonal and domed library proper. Some of the mahogany *Gillows* bookcases remain; the rest are in Manchester's Central Library. The ante-library leads to the E CORRIDOR, then out to a loggia and the CONSERVATORY; all by *Lewis Wyatt*. The corridor and INNER HALL receive little natural light.

Back in the staircase hall is the GRAND STAIR, airily cantilevered under a coved ceiling with umbrella fans and an oval skylight, rising Imperial-fashion in one flight and returning in two. Elegant balustrading of iron, lead and brass. Tripod lamp standards, after one discovered in Herculaneum. The airy effect is obtained by dispensing with supporting columns for the stair head and using instead an iron girder. The decorative iron, and probably structural iron, of which there is more under the floors of the E wing, was supplied by *Tobin* of Leeds. The landings are screened by scagliola columns, disguising their different widths, a relic of reuse of the C18 house? The grandeur of the ascent is justified by placing the choicest room, the CUPOLA ROOM, over the Saloon. It was the Dowager 33 Lady Egerton's dressing room and boudoir, en suite with her Palm Tree Bedroom (which has lost its decoration), and perhaps also functioning as a withdrawing room, and is circular with a shallow dome. James Lomax suggests that the delicate 'Pompeian' decorative scheme, by *Biagio Rebecca*, is derived from the Mannerist C16 Villa Giulia near Rome. The ceiling paintings of the Elements, Virtues and of gods and goddesses are also by *Rebecca*. Eight tall mirrors focus on the centre of the room, and from here can be seen not only the park in three-fold panorama but, through the open door, the spoked circle of light from the dome and a miniature circular world in the convex mirror across the staircase hall: a rich spatial experience.

A few things can be seen in the burnt-out W wing. The BACK STAIR, also of cantilevered stone, is back-to-back with the grand stair. From it the long brick-vaulted SERVICE CORRIDOR reaches out to the KITCHEN, counterpart to the library in the opposite pavilion. It does not occupy the full height but is nevertheless, by dropping a couple of steps, impressively tall, with enormous fireplaces on the flanking walls.

On the S side of the house a characterful lead lion and lioness lie in front of the bow, from the yard of *John Cheere* after Van Nost, their backs polished smooth by the bottoms of generations of Manchester children.

The Park

An estate map of *c.* 1750 shows a road climbing from the SW to pass by the W end of the house, then branching NW and NE. Parterres are indicated on the E side, presumably somewhat lower than the house. Echoes of both features could until 2002 be seen, in the junction of paths between house and stables, and in the flat car park at the top of the Smithy Lodge drive. The road was diverted in 1777. Sir Thomas Egerton and *William Emes* were already reshaping the park landscape in 1770–3 on fashionable Brownian lines. The works continued under *John Webb* in 1807–14, while Lewis Wyatt was working on the hall, including the building of the perimeter wall. Little change was then made from the 1820s until the early C20, when Manchester Parks Department terraced the E front of the house with formal gardens, below which were bowling greens, and built a huge tea room on the w end; converted the stables into a pets' corner; dug the boating lake on the race-course site; made a municipal golf course; laid tarmac roads, put up iron railings, and planted pink cherries, poplar and plane trees, and rhododendrons.

The red brick STABLES, w of the house, very like those at Tatton in Cheshire, are by *Samuel Wyatt* and dated 1777. Like the house they have a central block, low straight links, and pavil-ions. Carriages were kept in the pavilions, horses were led in through the centre arch to be stabled around the courtyard. On an eminence NE of the house, and commanding a terrific prospect, is the TEMPLE, probably also by *Samuel Wyatt*. It was mentioned by Aikin in 1795. Cylindrical cella with a Doric colonnade and ribbed dome. On top of the dome is a minia-ture version of the whole temple.

The remainder of the park buildings are taken topographically, working clockwise. To the N of the house is the C18 DOWER HOUSE, a Doric temple portico with a small house built behind it. Near it and unmissable is the TELECOMMUNICA-TIONS TOWER with its fat concrete shaft and shovel-like con-traptions all around the top. It dates from *c.* 1964 and is indeed like sculpture of the 1960s. By the St Margaret's gate is the BOWLS PAVILION, by *Stephen Williams* of *McBains Cooper* for the Commonwealth Games in 2001. An entertaining little building of warm brick and pure white render. It is hard to describe, indeed hard to tell exactly what is going on. This is because the plan is not governed by a grid, nor are the eleva-tions, and the walls do not necessarily stop within the enve-lope. The salient feature is the fan-shape of the clubhouse, with its big curved wall of glass overlooking the greens on the s and its oversailing roof. Within, the kitchen and office are inde-pendent white-painted shacks. Clustering outside, shower block, toilet block, and groundsman's store are likewise inde-pendent buildings, utilitarian in themselves but adding to the complexity of the whole. It sounds messy, but it works.

The RESERVOIR takes a big bite out of the park. It was planned in 1904, started in 1907, but not completed until 1926. Perched on its N rim is the pylon-like TERMINAL BUILDING of 1955, by the City Engineers under *Alan Atkinson* and the City Architects under *L. C. Howitt*, which controls the influx of water from Haweswater, 82 miles (130 km) away. As the visible sign of a largely invisible but mighty undertaking, it has been given a monumental character. Stone, windowless on the land side, flat-roofed, with unnecessarily grand steps and ramps to the upper level. The blank wall is covered by an incised RELIEF by *Mitzi Cunliffe* of Lake District slate. The aqueduct emerges from Haweswater, top l., three men pour lead to seal a joint in the centre, pure water pours forth cornucopia-like, bottom r. Beneath it five more slate panels give the history of the undertaking. Inside, a hushed temple of 1950s technology. Terrazzo floor, cream and green marble-clad walls, blue-painted valve gear, silver railings, black indicator cabinets, built-in electric fires. On the blank wall a huge sectional diagram of the aqueduct showing in exaggerated relief the tunnel, cut-and-cover and siphon sections. Models of the Lake District reservoirs in display cabinets.

Below the house to the s is the BOATING LAKE, made by the City Council in 1912. At its w end was re-erected in 1912 the PORTICO from Manchester's Town Hall in King Street. Superseded by Waterhouse's Town Hall (q.v.), it was by *Francis Goodwin*, 1819–34. It is startlingly overscaled for a park building. Just four giant Ionic columns, strangely enough without entasis, and at each end a closed bay with a niche. Heavy entablature, crisp honeysuckle frieze after the order of the Erechtheum in Athens. Edgar Wood was among those pleading for it to be saved.

The GRAND LODGE at the sw corner of the park was 'now building', together with the park wall, in 1807, so is probably by *Lewis Wyatt*. A Doric triumphal archway with paired columns and no pediment. Little lodge houses are contrived in each side, their upper storeys lit by side lunettes. The octagonal SMITHY LODGE, at the Middleton Road entrance on a green knoll, antedates the park wall, and is probably by *James Wyatt*. A powerful essay in primitive classicism, it is constructed of just sixteen great stones for the plinth, eight for the columns upended without bases upon it, and eight for the lintels. On top is a pyramid roof and a chimney, inside the ring is a little house. The GOLF CENTRE of *c.* 1995 by the *City Architects*, with a nod to nearby Smithy Lodge, is circular, of yellow brick with a continuous window strip below the eaves, with a conical roof and central skylight. A slice of the outer ring has been omitted to allow side lighting into the centre, which is the bar.

In 2002 the park, tired, overused, and with many of its features overgrown or decayed, entered a new, lottery-funded phase under *Lloyd Evans Pritchard*. The aim is to return the C18 sweep of turf up to the house by smoothing out the City's terracing, recreating the ha-ha, removing car parks, bowling greens and tennis courts, and, by thinning the trees, re-revealing the principal landscape features such as the Dower House.

MILES PLATTING *see* ANCOATS, above

MOSTON

Moston is a straggling township with the older centre to the w
and New Moston to the e. The former has the character of a
community and the appearance of a centre, near the junction of
Moston Lane and Kenyon Lane, where there is a tiny green. Coal
was extracted in the area from the early c17 or before, and
coalmines were established in the early c19 on the e side of St
Mary's Road. The last one closed in 1960 and no visible trace of
it survives. The boundaries are: to the e, the boundary with
Oldham; on the s, the railway and Church Lane; to the w (including) Ashley Lane, Moston Lane, Bute Street, Boggart Hole
Clough, Belthorne Avenue, Charlestown Road, Moston Lane
and Greengate; to the n, the Rochdale boundary.

St Luke, Kenyon Lane, Moston. 1909–10 by *E. Lingen Barker*.
Red brick, stone dressings. Low transepts, nw entrance, polygonal vestry to road. Narthex with a screen of open arches and
piers of polished granite. Four-bay nave arcade of round piers,
barrel roof. ne two-bay chapel. – stained glass. w, St
Bartholomew, by *Abbott & Co.* of Lancaster, 1931. Chapel
n by *Shrigley & Hunt*, 1931.

St John, Ashley Lane, Moston. By *R. B. Preston*, 1908. Of grey
brick with red brick banding and dressings. A bellcote at the
nw corner faces n and the w end has paired windows separated by a buttress. Five-bay nave arcade of polygonal piers.
A reordering of *c.* 1991 by *Nicholas Rank Associates* placed the
altar at the w end and divided off the e end for offices, meeting
rooms etc. – stained glass. w windows by *Graeme Willson*,
1991. – paintings also by him. – The large vicarage beside
the church on Railton Terrace is also by *Preston*.

St Mary, Nuthurst Road, Moston. By *Horton & Bridgford*,
1869. Small, and cheap-looking in polychromatic blue and red
brick with stone dressings. Symmetrical gabled façade to the
road with three lancets and a bellcote. Otherwise there are thin
lancets and a low apse.

St Chad, Hazeldene Road, New Moston. 1931 by *R. Martin*.
Red brick with stone dressings, very plain and low. A
reordering of *c.* 2000 by *Buttress Fuller Alsop Williams* placed a
partition and organ loft across the e end and the altar at the
centre of the s side. – Painted reredos, the liturgical seasons
by *Irene Halliday*, 2001. – font. A big pink marble vessel with
cherubs. – stained glass. The 1930s e window was given by
the freemasons. Large figures on a plain ground, Solomon and
Hiram of Tyre. The late c18 w window came from St John,
Byrom Street (demolished). It shows Christ teaching. Above
the repositioned altar, a window by *Irene Halliday*, 1999. Pleasant 1930s figurative glass in the chapel and baptistery.

St Dunstan (R.C.), Moston Lane, opposite Kenyon Lane. By
E. B. Norris & F. M. Reynolds, 1937 and similar in some ways
to St Willibrord, Clayton (*see* e Manchester), by Reynolds &

Scott. Romanesque, large, of fine brown brick with sparing stone banding and red brick dressings. Gabled s (liturgical w) front, with a tall round-headed lancet in a blind arch with a stone carving of St Dunstan below and a central entrance. Monumental square SE tower, the sheer walls broken only by pairs of tiny windows, a band of small paired windows at the very top, and high paired bell-openings rising from corbelled pedestals. Three-bay nave with round-headed lancets, low flat-roofed aisles, very shallow gabled transepts and a low octagonal Italian crossing tower with round windows in alternate faces. The tunnel-vaulted aisles have three-bay arcades of low semicircular arches, tunnel-vaulted nave, windowless semicircular apse with MOSAIC similar to the one at St Willibrord and so probably also by *L. Oppenheimer*.

ST JOSEPH'S CEMETERY (R.C.), Moston Lane. Opened in 1875, the first Roman Catholic cemetery in the city. It was home to a community of Alexian Brothers whose residence was demolished *c.* 1969 (for their present premises, *see* below). The red brick chapel and offices are of 1875, extended and altered in 1981. A clergy vault was established in 1876 and the remains of notable Roman Catholic ecclesiastics re-interred there. The layout is axial. The Campo Santo, erected in 1904 on the s side of the site, was modelled loosely on the C14 Campo Santo in Pisa. Red brick, three sides of a rectangle. The ends of the wings are gabled and have sloping buttresses to the l. and r. Big pointed arched openings. In the re-entrant angles pavilions are placed diagonally, also with big arched openings. Centre with three such openings and pinnacles. In between is blind arcading, some of the arches containing memorial stones. The cemetery has a good range of Victorian and Edwardian memorials, including three brick mausolea, mainly concentrated near the main entrance on Moston Lane. A large pauper burial area in the SE part of the cemetery has rows of simple shaped headstones with lists of the names of the dead by month and year. A memorial to the 'Manchester Martyrs' by *J. Geraghty* of Bootle, 1898, lies SW of the entrance. The three men were hanged in 1867 for their part in an armed confrontation in Manchester when Fenian organizers being taken to prison were freed and a policeman killed. The evidence for their guilt was slight and they were celebrated as martyrs to the cause of Irish independence. Large Celtic cross on a stepped pedestal with many Irish symbols such as wolfhounds, a figure representing Erin and an Irish Harp. Stones at the base represent the counties of Ireland and were each quarried from the respective counties. Portrait medallions of the three men appear on the sides.

ALEXIAN BROTHERS' NURSING HOME, St Mary's Road. The brothers have been in Moston since 1875 (*see* St Joseph's Cemetery, above). A complex of late C20 brick ranges around a forecourt dominated by an octagonal CHAPEL by *David Mansfield & Associates*. Pale brown brick, built 1991–2. (REREDOS and ALTAR from an Alexian nursing home in

London. – STAINED GLASS by *Irish Stained Glass* of Dublin
with subjects relating to the life of St Alexis and the mission
of the brothers).

SIMPSON MEMORIAL HALL, Moston Lane. An early work of
J. Gibbons Sankey, dated 1886. Red brick and very spare, with
a gabled front to the road and the upper hall approached by
an external staircase with a central door and round window
above. On each side big transomed oriels with flat heads
(probably replacing gables). Extensions of 1900. The building
houses a public hall, library and community accommodation.

MANCHESTER COLLEGE OF ARTS AND TECHNOLOGY,
Moston Campus, Ashley Lane. The building, probably of the
mid 1960s, was a Manchester City Council technical college.
The main block, of five storeys, is a bold Y-shape, with a bowed
front. It was probably designed by the City Architect's team,
led at that time by either *L. C. Howitt* or *S. Besant Roberts*.

HOUGH HALL, Hough Hall Road. The only physical reminder
of Moston's pre-industrial past, an interesting and well preserved house with some unusual features. Two storeys, timber-
framed, late C16 or early C17 with various later C17 additions
and some C19 interference. Three-bay range with irregular
framing and taller two-bay E cross-wing, all on a stone plinth.
A large stone external stack projects from the SE side of the
cross-wing, and beside it is a very narrow full-height projecting
entrance bay with a gable, also timber-framed. The original S
entrance with projecting porch is at the angle with the wing
and surmounted by a miniature oriel. The framing l. of this has
been interfered with to introduce larger windows to the
ground-floor chamber, and to light a later stair. On the N side
there is an inserted entrance in the wing. Infill between the

Moston, Hough Hall. *Victoria County History of Lancashire*, vol. 4, 1911

wing and the main range on this side is in the form of two unequal gabled bays. They are both timber-framed and may be late C17, perhaps dating from when the hall was bought by the Lightbowne family in 1685.

INTERIOR. Chamfered and stopped primary and secondary ceiling beams, tie-beam roof with angle-struts and windbraces. There are some peculiarities of plan. The s entrance gives on to a large room with a notional cross-passage and a range of three doors to the r., the middle one (which corresponds to the traditional kitchen passage position) leading to a narrow passage and the E entrance. A staircase was inserted into the entrance hall, perhaps *c.* 1880, when the hall was bought by the Ward family. The stair is late C17 or early C18 in style, as is the panelling, but the work is crude by Victorian standards. There seems to have been a passageway N of the entrance hall, but later alteration has obscured the arrangements; this may have been the original stair position reached from a fourth door in the cross-passage, as at Chorley Old Hall, Alderley Edge, Cheshire. The chamber follows, W, all panelled in the same style as the entrance hall, with a renewed fireplace. Parlour beyond (w). The upper cross-wing rooms have stone fireplaces.

NEWTON HEATH

Newton Heath had a chapel of ease from the late C16 or before, but it was essentially rural until the C19. The boundaries are (including) Oldham Road, N; the boundary with Oldham, E and the railway, S and W.

ALL SAINTS, Old Church Street. Built in 1814–15, by *William Atkinson*, enlarged in 1844, the chancel added 1880. The church replaces one existing in 1573. Of 1814–15 the ashlar-faced exterior, except the two E bays of 1880. Short W tower with polygonal buttresses with embattled tops; embattled parapet. Two-storey stair-turrets on each side. The oddity is the two tiers of side windows, smaller and with four-centred arches below, larger and pointed above; just what one would expect in a classical Georgian church, but looking strange in Gothic. The side walls are buttressed and the tops embattled. The chancel is lower, and has a Perp E window. (Galleries on three sides on cast-iron columns. Fine C15 FONT from St Bartholomew, Covenham, Lincs. Two windows by *William Wailes*, 1860s.) The CHURCHYARD has traceried railings and gates probably of 1815.

ST WILFRID, Oldham Road. By *Austin & Paley*, 1909. Typical of the later work of the practice, Perp with Arts and Crafts accents, of hard red brick and stone dressings to suit the urban and industrial context. The S (liturgical W) side is to the road, and display is concentrated here. Canted end with a chequered stone parapet to the road, with two- and three-light windows. Beneath the sill, at eye level, a carved text, a favourite motif

of the architects. On the l. a forceful bell-turret rises as a slab
with its narrow end to the road, with blind tracery and an open
bell arch. Porches flank the nave, each treated slightly differently. That on the l. projects slightly and there is a niche above
the door, formerly with a statue of St Wilfrid. Nave and
chancel under one roof. Octagonal arcade piers without capitals, open timber roof, wide chancel arch. Disused and due
for conversion, 2004.

   VICARAGE on the E side of the church, also by *Austin &*
Paley, probably of the same date.
EVANGELICAL CHURCH, Old Church Street. A tin tabernacle
clad in corrugated iron with arched windows with simple
Y-tracery, probably early C20 and notable only as an example
of an increasingly rare type.
DOB LANE UNITARIAN CHAPEL, Oldham Road. On the
border with Failsworth. Founded in 1698, an important centre
of Dissent at the time. The present building is a replacement
of 1878 by *Adams & Son* of King's Lynn. Red brick with
timbered gables, late C20 porch and windows.
SILK MILL. Holyoak Street. Said to have been built in 1826 and
enlarged in 1832, which is the date on a stone plaque on the
front. Five storeys over a high basement, brick with stone
dressings, large lunette in the gable, stair-tower on the w side.
Fireproof construction with cast-iron columns and brick
jack arches. It was one of the largest silk mills in the country
in its heyday, and is one of the few surviving silk mills in
Manchester. Converted to offices, late C20.

                STRANGEWAYS *see* CHEETHAM, above

                    SOUTH MANCHESTER

BURNAGE

A long narrow township, bounded on the N by the Cringle Brook near Burnage Hall Lane and Millwain Road, on the E by the Stockport boundary, S by Parrswood Lane and E by Parrswood Road and the railway.

ST MARGARET, Burnage Lane. By *Paley & Austin*. Red sandstone, with no tower or clerestory. The church was not built in one go. The three-bay nave, chancel and S aisle are 1874–5, the N aisle 1911 and the W bay, baptistery and S porch 1925–6. The apse of the baptistery is framed by heavy stub walls, as though in preparation for a W tower, as had been proposed in 1911. Well-proportioned interior with a single-framed roof. – REREDOS, 1885. – First and Second World War memorials, made to match, with the lettering on little tiles separated by strips of gold mosaic, probably by *Walter J. Pearce*. – STAINED GLASS. Faith, Hope and Charity in the S aisle, 1894. Chancel S, *c.* 1920, signed *Walter J. Pearce*, figurative and traditional. S aisle E by *T. F. Willford* of Marple, *c.* 1950. Baptistery, 1950; Scout, Guide, Cub and Brownie in the uniforms of the time.

III St Nicholas, Kingsway, by Mauldeth Road Station. 1930–2, by *Cachemaille-Day & Lander*. A milestone in the history of church architecture in England. Of buff brick, high, sheer and sculptural, with a German-inspired passion for brick grooves and ribbing both vertical and horizontal. Sheer apse to Kingsway, as high as the rest of the church, with the windows set very high up. The main entrance is on the S side of the apse, with jazzy finned brickwork. Slender, long windows in the chancel aisles, tight between buttresses. To the S, transept-wise, a squat tower and another sheer apse. The W bay of 1964, lower and tired-looking compared with the rest, is also by *Cachemaille-Day*. He liked to say that St Nicholas was both his first job and his last.

Noise from Kingsway was already a problem, so the apse from the first was filled by vestries and offices below the sanctuary. The low and narrow S aisle with its finned brick piers acts as a processional way to the W end of the nave, and a fine explosion of light and colour. Dean Hewlett Johnson, Dean of Manchester, wanted 'great cool spaces . . . enlivened here and there with a splash of colour, a figure, an incident.' Cachemaille-Day kept the furnishings low, the walls bare, the windows clear, but the ceiling is coffered in blue, red and gold. Tall narrow openings give a glimpse of blue transepts. The high apse is not wasted after all. Staircases rise up on either side of the altar, which is very wide, into the apse at high level, and it is here, behind a tall iron screen, that the Lady Chapel is placed. The screen is braced to the great boss of roof (which is illuminated) forming a cross. – A PAINTING after Murillo acts as reredos for both altars. Up here on the S is the original choir gallery. Returning to ground level, PULPIT and LECTERN are low brick pens, ALTAR RAIL black and gold with chunky balusters. – The FONT with its vertiginous telescopic cover is dramatically framed by the S transept. Inside the cover a little figure of a child. – The HYMN INDICATOR rises as well, on pulleys, and is triangular.

St Nicholas was reordered in 2001–3 by *Anthony Grimshaw* of Wigan. The church's spatial complexity is not spoiled but rather added to, by hanging the required social room above head height, just as the Lady Chapel is raised, and making it sheer and circular, echoing the curve of the apse. Its walls are sand-blasted glass, with just one slit left clear to peep down into the nave. In steep pens in front of it, like coconuts at a shy, sit the choir and organist. Underneath is the moveable partition separating the W end and, tucked into the NW, toilets and kitchen.

St Bernard (R.C.), Burnage Lane. By *Reynolds & Scott*, 1958. Brick Byzantine with transepts, and a W transept too. Barrel ceiling with the clerestory lights cut into it. – Three STAINED GLASS windows at the W end in the style of Harry Clarke. The parish hall and presbytery is a Victorian villa.

Burnage is overwhelmingly City Council housing of 1923–7. The spacious layout with its circles and octagons looks nice on the map, and the double avenue of Errwood Road is fine on the ground. The houses themselves are almost all semis, generously proportioned with hipped roofs and simple but effective contrasts in brick colour.

The municipal estates had a notable precursor in BURNAGE GARDEN VILLAGE of 1911, a little enclave immediately s of Grangethorpe Drive. 136 houses were built on an 11-acre (4 hectare) site by Co-partnership Tenants Ltd who manage the estate to this day. The plan was by *J. Horner Hargreaves* in consultation with *C. G. Agate*, *F. B. Dunkerley* and *Raymond Unwin*. The houses are of a type made familiar by imitation – simple, roughcast, low-ceilinged with ample roofs. The estate includes a communal tennis and bowling club.

On Slade Lane, YORK HOUSE is a large early C19 house with a doorcase with Ionic columns, while an earlier, rural Burnage is represented by a few late C18 cottages such as HYDE FOLD and BROOK COTTAGE on Burnage Lane by St Margaret's church, and the increasing influence of Manchester by Victorian villas such as the wonderfully monstrous SANTAIDD of 1887, or the more modest pair of 1847 that are now the SUN IN SEPTEMBER pub, both on Burnage Lane.

CHORLTON-CUM-HARDY

Chorlton is bounded on the s and w by the winding River Mersey with its water meadows, and defined by the long line of Barlow Moor Road which runs parallel to it on drier ground. The C16 village centre, now a backwater, is between the two by Chorlton Brook. The change from village to suburb was brokered as usual by developing transport links. A railway station opened in Stretford in 1849, initiating villa development in High Lane and Edge Lane. Chorlton did not get its own station until 1880, but before that the building of Wilbraham Road in 1869 created a new centre where it crossed Barlow Moor Road. Wilbraham was a first name favoured by the Egertons of Tatton; the Egertons had been Lords of the Manor since the C18. Chorlton today is a busy suburb but it retains much open land by the Mersey, both its old halls, and a recognizable pre-suburban village.

Places of Worship

ST CLEMENT, High Lane. By *Pennington & Bridgen*. Started in 1860, roofed in 1866, not consecrated until 1896. N (1883) and s (1896) transepts by *W. Higginbottom* block some of the clerestory lights. Higginbottom also did the Lady Chapel of 1895. Of stone, spreading in shape, Dec in style, with an octagonal sw turret like that of the old church (*see* Perambulations) and a timber porch. In an early and contentious reordering of *c.* 1976 the nave and aisles were partitioned off and a floor inserted at the level of the capitals. The problems of lighting the resultant spaces have not been solved. – STAINED GLASS. E, *c.* 1870, is a big five-lighter, intensely coloured. The heavens above, fires of hell below, but not done with medieval relish. s transept E, by *Lavers, Barraud & Westlake,* 1870. N transept W, by *George Wragge* of Manchester, 1917.

ST WERBURGH, Wilbraham Road. 1899–1902, by *R.B. Preston.* Grey brick headers and red terracotta dressings, the W view with three parallel gables. Flèche now with conspicuous loudspeakers. Wide and low interior, quatrefoil piers in terracotta. – SCREEN. 1922 and 1925, a war memorial, by *R.B. Preston* and *R. Martin.* – STAINED GLASS. An interesting assemblage. s transept, by *Humphries, Jackson & Ambler* of Manchester; the risen Christ, 1931. E, 1950, by *Barton, Kinder & Alderson;* Christ appears twice, rather disconcertingly. Nave NE by the same firm 1953; the boy Jesus with a model boat. Nave NW, 1960, and SE, 2000, both by *Wippell.* A handsome RECTORY adjoins; 1934, Neo-Georgian with ashlar base and doorcase. A good Art Deco stair window remains at the side.

OUR LADY AND ST JOHN (R.C.), High Lane. Immediately opposite St Clement (above) and orientated the other way round, so the E ends face one another. Opened in 1927. Red brick and buff terracotta, Dec and Perp tracery. No tower. The interior is wide and aisleless, with a double hammerbeam roof (which may incorporate parts from St Andrew's Presbyterian church at Ramsbottom (q.v.) and *see* also Whalley Range, p. 481), but with three parallel E chapels, all with fine ALTARPIECES. – GLASS is leaded with contrasting textures but hardly any colour, an attractive effect. – MOSAIC covers the whole of the E wall of the nave, and the chancel; apocalyptic. Probably by *Oppenheimer.* The PRESBYTERY is a sizable Victorian villa of notchy red brick.

ST AMBROSE (R.C.), Princess Road. 1958, by *Reynolds & Scott.* Grey brick in stretcher bond, with a modest SW (liturgical NE) tower. The interior displays a common C20 formula for Catholic churches. Plain piers support a nave with a barrel ceiling with the largest arches; middle-sized arches for the arcades and, a variation, groins rather than arches for the narrow aisles.

METHODIST CHURCH, Manchester Road. 1873 by *H.J. Paull* and a little grim, like his Southern Cemetery chapels (*see* below). Stone, with a thin SE steeple and Geometrical tracery. Red brick SCHOOL behind, 1883.

GITA BHAVAN HINDU TEMPLE, Wilbraham Road. Plain 1990s shed with a cheerful frontispiece carrying five graded Sikharas, or convex pyramids, in white, gold and yellow. They are square in section and triple in their applied decoration. At the back is a former Congregational chapel of *c.* 1900.

SOUTHERN CEMETERY, Barlow Moor Road. Opened in 1879. At 187 acres (76 hectares) the largest cemetery in Manchester, with a comprehensive collection of Late Victorian and Edwardian memorials. The competition of 1873 was won by *H.J. Paull*, who went in for cemeteries (*see* Philips Park, p. 569). The adjudicators were Mills & Murgatroyd. It is laid out unromantically on its flat site, the plan geometric and symmetrical. The buildings, all of pitch-faced (roughly finished) stone from Elland Edge with green slate roofs, are on the other hand highly asymmetrical and Romantic in inspiration, though not pretty.

The OFFICE and LODGES, set in a long run of walling with ornamental ironwork, are both spired. The three CHAPELS are on the cardinal points of the central elliptical roadway. Axial with the main gate is the Anglican chapel, a complicated little building with a slated spire. The R.C. one, SE, is simpler, with a stone spire, the Dissenters', NW, with an apse and a stone spire with big lucarnes. Near the latter is what must have been the showiest monument, for John Rylands †1888. It is by *Charles Heathcote*, a Baroque affair shaped like a Renaissance shield on a hexagonal base, of granites and, despite the injunction against softer stones, white marble. It has lost its canopy and gilded angel trumpeters as well as its railings. Very low-key Jewish OHEL (chapel) in the W corner, towerless, with raised gables on each side. It is not shown on early maps; the oldest Jewish stone is 1892. CREMATORIUM near the NW corner, by *E. Salomons*, 1890, relatively early for a crematorium. Romanesque in bright yellow terracotta. The campanile disguises the chimney. The aisles open outwards instead of inwards to form loggias which act as columbaria. The capitals of their arcades are a good advertisement for the non-weathering properties of terracotta. Further loggias and hollow walls have been and continue to be added for ashes.

Major Houses and Public Buildings

BARLOW HALL, Barlow Hall Road. A house and mill existed here in the C13, but everything today dates from the 1570s or later. Today it is the clubhouse of Chorlton Golf Club, founded 1902. Three sides of a quadrangle (the gatehouse range was knocked down in 1962) with what is left of the great hall in the middle range, and wings extending E; a N wing which probably had the family rooms, and a S wing with C17 or C18 additions. Of brick of many periods and very irregular, but the hall bay in the NW corner and a square gabled room above it still timber-framed. The house was built by Alexander Barlow, grandfather of the Catholic martyr Ambrose Barlow, in about 1574, the date on the sundial and in the glass of the bay. The sundial carries the pointed motto 'Lumen me regit, vos umbra' – the light rules me, the shade you. The hall range and N and S wings probably date from this time. The house was updated, perhaps in the C17, by the addition of corridors round all four sides, making a small courtyard smaller still. The corridor cuts through the hall bay, which was seven sided, as at Ordsall (q.v.). Its plaster ceiling, divided into seven sections like a pie, remains. Whether the hall was always two-storeyed or was divided horizontally subsequently is not possible to say because it was burnt out in 1879. The stair-tower is against the N wing with a modern entrance. In the C17 or early C18 a second complete dwelling was built at the SE corner. Again Ordsall is a parallel case. The large semicircular bay on the SW corner is early C19. The splendid finials should not be missed; one on the hall bay, the other on the SE gable of the S wing, called the lady's wing probably for the female figure in a niche.

The interior is much altered. After the fire the hall was rebuilt with lush new fittings and decoration for Sir William Cunliffe-Brooks, possibly by *George Truefitt* whom he employed elsewhere. C16 STAINED GLASS survives in the hall bay. It was probably commissioned in 1574 but not necessarily done all at once: shields of Holland, Reddish, Kendall, Barlow, and Edward Stanley, Earl of Derby. The sixth is the C19 shield of Sir William Cunliffe-Brooks himself. Scratched on one quarry is 'Spero Me hora qu w Smythers 1580'. Was he the glazier?

Barlow Hall commands a fine prospect of water meadows, now the golf course. Below the semicircular bay a line of horn-beams, once shaped, marks the position of a rectangular canal with rounded ends, infilled in 1966, running NW–SE at a diagonal to the hall. The flat terrace SE of it seems to have been a formal garden and orchard.

HOUGH END HALL, The only substantial Elizabethan mansion in SE Lancashire, but it was nearly lost, as Pevsner recorded in 1969.* It was built in *c.* 1596 by Sir Nicholas Mosley, cloth merchant, who had just purchased the lordship of Manchester. He was knighted as Lord Mayor of London in 1599 and is splendidly commemorated in Didsbury church (q.v.). Broad in effect, it is a very up-to-date house for this part of the world – compare Barlow Hall (above), built only twenty years earlier. It is solidly constructed of brick, laid in a Flemish bond and showing a diaper pattern in good light. Three storeys high, with an array of five gables, flat-fronted except for the bringing-forward of the wings, and symmetrical, with the door in the middle. Its mullioned and transomed windows are not quite symmetrical however; the r. centre has an extra pair of lights, indicating the hall, and there are extra upper lights on the l. too, for the winter parlour. Massive chimneystacks prop up both ends and there is another, hidden now, at the back. There is no decoration. The house relies for its effect purely on symmetry and mass. Comparisons can be made with Hacking Hall

*Hough End Hall has been a conservation issue since 1924 when concern for its future led the architect John Swarbrick to found the Ancient Monuments Society.

Garderobe
over

Dining
Parlour

Withdrawing
Room

Ante Space

Staircase
Annexe

Hall

Gatehouse

Porch

Stair

Pantry

Corridor

Larder

Kitchen
and
Bakehouse

Winter Parlour

Garderobe
over

□ Later additions

10 m

30 ft

Hough End Hall, plan

of 1607 in N Lancashire, also three-storeyed, five-gabled and
symmetrical but retaining an asymmetrical entrance, and with
Stayley Hall (Cheshire) which has a more concentrated
echelon of gables.

The interior is all but lost; an open plan office on two floors
has been created inside the shell. Just enough is left to show
that the hall was set asymmetrically to the r., as the extra
window lights suggested, with a huge fireplace in the rear wall.
The stair was the other side of the screens passage, on the l.,
leading to the great chamber above. A second stair, quite
grand, was made behind the hall fire-place, suggesting division
into two dwellings; it has been removed to Tatton (Cheshire).
The plan shows that the little outshut at the SE end, which has
its own gable and round windows, was a garderobe. Another
is indicated at the N corner and shown on a plan prepared in
the C19.

The setting and scale of the hall is spoilt by the 1960s office
blocks that so disgracefully encroach upon it, but the car park
in front represents a small enclosed garden shown on early
maps, and over the road in Chorlton Park is a memory of the
axial avenue to Barlow Moor Road.

LIBRARY, Barlow Moor Road and Longford Road. 1914, the first
of a trio by *Henry Price*, City Architect, following a gift of
£15,000 from Andrew Carnegie. The others are Didsbury and
Withington (below). Each was built in a different style but
to the same general plan of a wedge or fan shape. This one
is Baroque. Brick with generous Portland stone dressings.
Octagonal dome over the issue desk, which, since a ceiling was
inserted, it no longer serves to illuminate.

OSWALD ROAD SCHOOL, behind the library on Longford Road.
1908–9, big, red, robust and florid in the city's usual Queen
Anne style.

CHORLTON BATHS, Barlow Moor Road, of 1928–9, sober and
classical, (cf. Withington Library, p. 485). By now the City Architect was *G. Noel Hill* and the preferred style Neo-Georgian.

Perambulation

From the New Village Centre, Starting at the library, to the Old
Village, and on to Chorltonville.

We start on Barlow Moor Road. Immediately S of the library
and composing well with it is the SEDGE LYNN, built as a
Temperance billiard hall in 1907 by *Norman Evans*. Now a
pub, but well-preserved. Long barrel roof, with dormers, supported on composite wooden trusses. Bold hexagonal porch
with a little dome, set to one side. Semicircular bay with a long
window of Venetian composition above it. Art Nouveau glass.
Bizarrely cheek-by-jowl is the CO-OP FUNERAL PARLOUR,
and very grim it is, a cube of dark brick laid sawtooth fashion.
It is a 1970s refronting (by *Harry S. Fairhurst & Son*) of a
late 1920s cinema whose side elevations, surprisingly carefully
designed, are unimpaired.

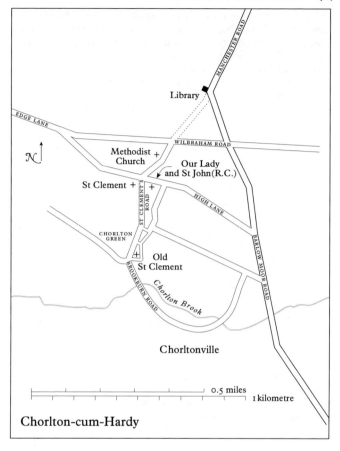

Chorlton-cum-Hardy

MANCHESTER ROAD diverges behind GRAEME HOUSE, a
1970s slab block, and the little CHORLTON PLACE shopping
precinct at its foot, both by *Cruickshank & Seward*. Nos. 11
and 13 Manchester Road are an idiosyncratic pair in red and
grey brick by *Henry Goldsmith*, illustrated by him in his *Eco-
nomical Houses* of 1895. They have a squashed dormer each and
share a tall timber-framed one in the middle. Long cove for
the eaves, basket arch for the porch. There appear to be
inglenooks at the ends on all three floors. The houses cost £500
each. LLOYD PLATT HOTEL (now Hardy's), 1870, is a landmark where the new Wilbraham Road intersects Manchester
Road. Mr Platt was the developer, Mr Lloyd the landowner
E. J. Thompson, the architect. Orange brick and fine sandstone
dressings with Masonic insignia. Galleries have been added to
overlook the bowling green. On the opposite corner is the
CONSERVATIVE CLUB of 1891 of brick and terracotta with

blue timber framing and a corner clock turret. Diverting W onto Edge Lane, No. 12 is a FREEMASONS' HALL, presenting a showy tripartite front to the street. It was created out of a pair of semi-detached houses of *c.* 1860 by the addition of an upper hall in the middle. The style is Italian Gothic, the material is brick, the decoration polychrome. Nine close-set lancets light the central lodge (the added upper hall) which has a shallow square domed ceiling and Masonic stained glass. The 1931 extension for the Chapter at the W end weakens the façade. Back on Manchester Road and close together are the Methodist church, St Clement, and St John (*see* above). St Clement's Road leads to CHORLTON GREEN, a diminutive triangle of grass and trees with the long low HORSE & JOCKEY with half-timbering ranged along its N side and, facing its apex, the little bellcote-cum-gateway of the old churchyard. OLD ST CLEMENT, a small timber-framed chapel of *c.* 1512, stood here, then a plain brick church of 1779, which was given aisles in 1837. It was demolished in 1949. Its footprint is outlined on the ground and rusty indentations in the base stones recall an iron arcade. The diminutive timber-framed bellcote-cum-gatehouse was the gift of William Cunliffe Brooks in 1888. Faint but definite traces linger of the pre-railway village; a few late C18 or early C19 cottages and farmhouses remain, such as No. 62 Beech Road, and where Brookburn Road crosses Chorlton Brook gives the area some geography – a dip in the road, a stream, a bridge – a brief illusion of a country lane. By the bridge is the BOWLING GREEN pub, rebuilt in 1907. The associated bowling green is said to have existed in the C15.

S of the bridge a row of Edwardian semis, tall, narrow and fussy, provides the ideal prelude to CHORLTONVILLE. The company was set up in 1911 'to provide beautiful, healthy, conveniently-planned homes, with plenty of light and an abundance of fresh air, at reasonable rents' and the estate of around 40 acres (16 hectares) was declared open in 1913. 'The houses are grouped with special regard to architectural beauty and effect. The roads are wide and well laid out with grass verges, seven feet wide on either side, and are planted with trees of various kinds.' The 'wise forethought' thus trumpeted in the company's brochure has abundantly paid off, for Chorltonville is as pretty and as desirable as ever. The houses are almost all semi-detached and amply spreading (no architect is given but the builder was *Thos. Whiteley*). Pebbledashing is everywhere rather than exposed brick, and all the devices that say 'home' – bays, porches, catslide roofs.

CHORLTON-ON-MEDLOCK

Chorlton-on-Medlock lies to the S of the centre, S of the River Medlock, which forms the N boundary. The E boundary is Ardwick Green South, Stockport Road and Plymouth Grove

West; s, Hathersage Road and Moss Lane East; w, Lloyd Street, Denmark Street, Boundary Road and City Road. The area around the present Grosvenor Square, formerly known as Chorlton Row, was sold in the 1790s to create a residential suburb. By 1821 there were more than 8,000 inhabitants. Rapid development of Manchester led to middle-class emigration after the mid C19, and the area filled up with cheap housing. In 1869 Owens College (which later became the University of Manchester) moved here, followed from the 1880s by hospitals along Oxford Road to the s. Municipal slum clearance started in the mid C20. The area has become, as a result, dominated by academic institutions in the N part and a large hospital complex to the s, with a more mixed area, including 1970s housing estates, along the E flank.

Churches are described first, then public buildings, with separate sections for the hospitals and academic institutions. Individual houses follow, then two short perambulations.

Churches

HOLY NAME OF JESUS (R.C.), Oxford Road. 1869–71 by 75 *Joseph Aloysius Hansom*, with his son *Joseph Stanislaus Hansom*. Contemporary with their Arundel Cathedral, Sussex, and one of their finest buildings. The elder Hansom was doubtless responsible for the daring structural design and the younger for the detail and many of the furnishings. The design had a steeple 240ft (73 metres) high (based on those of Amiens Cathedral) which remained unexecuted; the octagonal top of the tower is by *Adrian Gilbert Scott*, completed 1928. It could not be better suited for its task. Hansom's tower is much broader than it is deep. The façade is deliberately not identical to its l. and r., and on the r. side is also a baptistery with a conical roof. The sides and apse have flying buttresses, and along the s side low outer chapels are expressed by small gables and small windows. The E end consists of transepts, a short chancel, and a high polygonal apse with a narrow ambulatory and cross-gables. Two E turrets rise where the chancel sets in.

The INTERIOR was designed for the preaching of the Jesuits, who left in 1994. It is overwhelmingly airy, because of the extremely slim piers. The whole church is rib-vaulted using lightweight polygonal terracotta blocks (by *Gibbs & Canning*) instead of stone. Terracotta is also used as a facing material, in some places with ornamentation. The disastrous decision in 1972 to sandblast the interior removed the original surface and lightened the colour. Vaulted narthex and W organ gallery screened by a very high three-bay arcade. Four-bay nave, transepts entered by a high arch continuing the nave arcade. The chancel is very high too; its width equals that of the nave only by adding to it the ambulatory entrances, as at Gerona Cathedral in Spain. Nave and chancel are linked by very tall diagonal arches to soften the transition. The chancel is flanked by pairs of chapels with low vaulted ceilings incorporating oculi, divided by open two-bay arcades.

Of individual motifs it may be said that the chancel and apse piers are of the French type of Chartres, Rheims and Amiens, and that Hansom favoured rose windows and windows of the so-called spherical-triangle shape. Inner traceried openings are given to the clerestory and transept windows, adding to the richness. The S chapels were made into one long space to become the CHAPEL OF THE MADONNA DELLE STRADE (Madonna of the Wayside), a masterpiece of *J.F. Bentley*, 1891–4. Walls and piers were panelled in painted and stencilled wood. Wooden frontal, reredos and triptych with painting by *N.H.J. Westlake*. Unfortunately structural instability resulted and the dividing walls had to be reinstated, re-creating the three original chapels, in 1997. The exquisite octagonal BAPTISTERY, at the SW corner, was completed in the 1890s by the younger Hansom.

FURNISHINGS. The church has an unusually complete set of late C19 furnishings. HIGH ALTAR, by *Joseph Stanislaus Hansom*, 1890, a marvellously detailed architectural piece of the Benediction Altar type, carved by *R.L. Boulton* of Cheltenham. E chapels: N side N, ST JOSEPH CHAPEL with an ornate gilded wooden triptych altar. Beside it OUR LADY OF VICTORIES CHAPEL. On the S side the chapels were completed in 1885. First the SACRED HEART CHAPEL with an altarpiece by *Charles Alban Buckler*, sculptor *R.L. Boulton*. Beside it the CHAPEL OF THE HOLY SOULS, the altarpiece almost certainly by them also. – PULPIT by the younger Hansom, *c.* 1886. Also by him is the alabaster FONT, *c.* 1890, and the fine cast- and wrought-iron baptistery SCREENS. – Many marble STATUES of saints disposed around the interior, most of *c.* 1900 by *J. Alberti*. – STAINED GLASS. Mostly by *Hardman & Co.* of the late 1890s. S transept: two tall lights by *Paul Woodroffe*, a First World War memorial with Morris-like interleaving foliage.

The 1960s CHAPLAINCY in Oxford Road by *Mather & Nutter* is a rather mannered design with a saw-tooth roof rising from detached piers. Behind, to the E on Portsmouth Street is the Jesuits' PRESBYTERY by *Henry Clutton*, 1874–5. An attractive design in brick with stone dressings. Domestic Tudor motifs successfully convey the relationship with the church. Stone early C20 extension to the S. Attached to the N is the (former) CHURCH HALL, a crisp brick job by *Edmund Kirby*, dated 1892 in raised bricks. Converted to a pub.

ST AUGUSTINE (R.C.), W side of Grosvenor Square (Lower Ormond Street). By *Desmond Williams & Associates*. Of 1967–8, and so in the first generation of R.C. churches designed for the new liturgy. Dark brick gives it an austere appearance. Load-bearing brick piers support steel trusses which are positioned to provide north-light clerestories. Recessed central entrance with a service projection, to the l., and four full-height brick piers, r. A bell tower rises behind from the link to low meeting rooms, chaplaincy etc. INTERIOR. Pairs of slim brick piers each with a slit of coloured glass chips by the *Whitefriars Studio*. At the E end a narrow glass ceiling strip casts natural light over a large ceramic MURAL in muted tones, Christ in Majesty by *Robert Brumby*. Ceramic PLAQUES and wall-mounted light fittings also by Brumby.

UNITARIAN CHAPEL (former), Upper Brook Street. 1836–9 by *Charles Barry*. The mother house was the Cross Street Chapel (*see* p. 312) and this building was erected at a time when the middle classes were moving into the suburbs growing up in this area. The various Unitarian chapels in the inner Manchester area had evolved, like Cross Street, from C17 Dissenting congregations but this was the first purpose-built specifically for Unitarian worship.

The relatively early use of archaeologically ambitious Gothic by Nonconformists perhaps reflects the progressive views of Manchester Unitarian circles, or it may have been the personal choice of the architect, who would have been known to leading Unitarians through his involvement with the Athenaeum (*see* p. 288–9). The design postdates Barry's churches at Stand, Whitefield of 1822–6 (q.v.) by more than a decade. The style is correspondingly more mature in that the detail is subsumed to the whole, contrasting with the accretion of motifs and filigree detail seen in the earlier work. Lancets separated by gabled buttresses along the sides in the accepted Commissioners' fashion, but with none of the etiolation. Stone corner turrets with blind lancets and pyramid tops. E rose window. Only the W side is more personal, with a giant niche integrating window and door with much shafting, perhaps based on Peterborough Cathedral. The deeply set window has a quatrefoil and two cusped lancets with the W door integrated below. (The interior has a pointed plaster ceiling divided into six compartments by bold ribs. The arrangement with three moulded arches opening into the westernmost bay, similarly vaulted, is elegant. Three galleries; the lancet windows begin at gallery level.) The building has been abandoned for a decade or more. It deserves better.

On the N side and attached at the rear is the SUNDAY SCHOOL – by whom? It looks like a later addition, but all the records seem to have been lost. It has more incident and is less monumental than the chapel, with ranks of gables, windows with stepped lancets and an apsidal W projection forming a foil to the big bones of the chapel.

ARMENIAN CHURCH, Upper Brook Street. By *Royle & Bennett*, 1869–70. The first to be purpose-built for the Armenians in England. Windows with pointed heads and simple intersecting tracery, gabled W porch, circular window in the W gable with tracery in the form of the Armenian Cross. Rounded apse. The INTERIOR is whitewashed and simple, in keeping with Armenian tradition. At the E end an arch with polished granite columns, and on a high platform in the top-lit apse an elaborate ALTAR with gilded columns. According to the Armenian rite the choir is separated from the nave only by a low arcaded SCREEN, in pitch-pine like the PEWS and other furnishings. – FONT in a recess in the N wall at the E end. The mildly Gothic PRIEST'S HOUSE is set back and attached to the r.

For St Joseph (R.C.) *see* Longsight, p. 367.

Public Buildings

1. General

For the former Town Hall and Dispensary *see* Academic Institutions, p. 436.

PLYMOUTH GROVE PRIMARY SCHOOL, Plymouth Grove West. Early C20. Robust Queen Anne style, red brick and red terracotta, big blocky forms. The type can be seen everywhere in Manchester; this is a good unspoiled example.

91 VICTORIA BATHS, Hathersage Road. 1903–6 by the City Architect *Henry Price*, based on designs of 1901–2 by the City Surveyor *T. de Courcy Meade* and his assistant *Arthur Davies*. The most opulent Edwardian municipal baths to survive anywhere in England. Exuberant in striped red Ruabon brick and pale yellow terracotta, making it look like a large friendly humbug. The architectural detailing of the terracotta was designed by Price's team and supplied by *J. C. Edwards* of Ruabon. Symmetrical in massing and outline, with steep gables and a clock cupola. Separate entrances for first- and second-class men, and for women, and another for a flat provided for Manchester's Superintendent of Baths and Wash Houses. INTERIOR. The first-class entrance foyer is the most lavish, with tiles by *F. C. Howells* of *Pilkingtons*, a generous tiled stair and a mosaic floor with attractive fish designs (by *Patteson*). A large copper plaque by *George Wragge* commemorates the opening. Second-class men enjoyed less decoration, and women less still. Two main pools, with individual changing cabins, and a third converted to sports hall, all with galleries and glazed roofs. Marvellous suites of Turkish and Russian baths. STAINED GLASS with, *inter alia*, scenes of people playing various sports, probably by *W. Pointer*. The whole thing is a wonderful set piece, due to be brought back into partial use following a decade of campaigning by a local group.

CONTACT THEATRE, Devas Street. By *Short & Associates*, 1997–9. The first impression is created by two ranks of fantastic chimney ventilators, part of a natural ventilation system, drawing on research by *Max Fordham & Partners* (cf. the architects' Queens Building, De Montfort University, Leicester). The first tier of stacks is in buff brick, a second tier, set back, clad in zinc. The serious ecological considerations are combined with motifs expressing a punning language of theatrical forms. The round brick tower, for example, has something of Elizabeth Scott's Shakespeare Memorial Theatre, Stratford-upon-Avon. Struts bracing the stacks are in the form of theatrical spears and the entrance is a layered, curtain-like silver screen. The auditorium and stage were retained from the 1960s predecessor by *Building Design Partnership*, but everything else is new, with a curving foyer leading to a double-height space and stairs to the upper level.

WHITWORTH ART GALLERY, Whitworth Park. Named for Sir Joseph Whitworth, whose bequest provided the funding. A 20-acre (8 hectare) parcel of land was acquired in 1887 and laid out as a park. The competition for the new gallery building, replacing an adapted older house called Grove House, was won by *J. W. Beaumont* in 1891. Waterhouse was the assessor, and that explains the building nearly completely. It was built in phases from 1894. N, central and S galleries came first, as extensions to Grove House. Outer galleries have arcades with terracotta panels to Denmark Road (N) and the park (S). The entrance front which replaced Grove House was not ready until 1908. Red brick and red terracotta, Jacobean and symmetrical; two low towers and polygonal buttresses on the angle parts. A central semicircular porch has paired grey granite columns. INTERIOR. Only the vestibule retains its original appearance, top-lit and lined with columns. New galleries by *John Bickerdike* were completed in two phases, 1963–4 and 1966–8, after the gallery was handed to the University of Manchester in 1958. Alterations included a mezzanine inserted over the N and central galleries and the introduction of large windows in the S gallery giving views over Whitworth Park. A SCULPTURE GALLERY by *Ahrends, Burton & Koralek*, 1995, was inserted between the entrance block and the lower gallery behind, retaining the original rear exterior wall. A new angled roof appears to float above the space.

WHITWORTH PARK. Now largely featureless apart from a STATUE on the S side. Edward VII by *John Cassidy*, unveiled in 1913. Bronze. For the circumstances surrounding the creation of the park *see* Whitworth Art Gallery, above.

2. Hospitals

A new site on the E side of Oxford Road was chosen for the Manchester Royal Infirmary in Piccadilly which was founded in 1775 and demolished in 1909. The land was donated by Owens College (subsequently Manchester University) who wished to improve teaching opportunities for their Medical School. The Eye Hospital had already been established near the site, and St Mary's Hospital followed. The hospitals have spread over 42 acres (17.5 hectares), replacing mid-C19 terraces, and are being extended with a variety of new facilities, 2004.

ROYAL INFIRMARY, Oxford Road. 1905–8, the great work of *E. T. Hall* who won the competition with the Manchester architect *John Brooke*. The assessor was J. J. Burnet. Vast, and in the Greenwich Baroque style, brick and much Portland stone, on the traditional pavilion plan. Of the main administration block to Oxford Road the l. side was destroyed in the war. A central domed tower has an open pediment high over the entrance with a relief showing the Good Samaritan. The surviving linking block to the r. is in the form of a bridge with an open walkway with a Tuscan colonnade. Another block with a corner tower follows. The CHAPEL, behind to the N, has at the W end a stone gable with an open pediment and niche. The E Venetian window has STAINED GLASS by *William Sales Arnold* of *Dudley Forsyth*, London, 1908. At the rear a MONUMENT, Richard Baron Howard, physician, by *W. Theed*, dated 1853.

ADDITIONS include an assertive brick private patients' block, dated 1936, by *Percy Scott Worthington*. Major extensions along Upper Brook Street are by *BDP*, completed 1992. To the E a large new ward block is by *Abbey Hanson Rowe*, 2000–1, and a Clinical Research Facility on Grafton Street by the *Taylor Young Partnership*, 2000–2. New building continues on the site, 2004.

ROYAL EYE HOSPITAL, Oxford Road. 1886, by *Pennington & Bridgen*. Symmetrical, in the style popularized by Norman Shaw a decade or so before, all in red brick, red terracotta and red tiled roofs. Terracotta panels attributed to *Mr Holding* show Christ healing the blind. OUT-PATIENT DEPARTMENT and NURSES' HOME, Nelson Street. Neo-Georgian by *Percy Scott Worthington*, 1937.

ST MARY'S HOSPITAL, Oxford Road. 1909 by *John Ely*. Red brick and terracotta, mildly Edwardian. Big domed towers at each end of a range with projecting gabled bays. The upper-floor CHAPEL has an ornate hammerbeam roof and original furnishings. On the main stair, STAINED GLASS; St Luke, St Mary and healing miracles, by *Heaton, Butler & Bayne*. An E extension by *Watkins Gray & Partners*, 1966–70, was reclad in white panels *c*. 1990.

3. Academic Institutions

Manchester has the largest urban higher education precinct in Europe and Chorlton-on-Medlock is the site of the majority of the academic institutions: the University of Manchester (a merger of the Victoria University of Manchester and the Institute of Science and Technology (UMIST), which is in process, 2004), Manchester Metropolitan University (MMU), and the Royal Northern College of Music (RNCM). Each has developed in its own way and there are few places where one feels that one's movements are directed by a plan. *The City of Manchester Plan* of 1945 envisaged expanding the educational centre from the site of Manchester University on Oxford Road and integrating it into a new road system in a scheme drawn up in collaboration with *Sir Hubert Worthington*. Little came of this though some of the underlying ideas were incorporated into the subsequent development of the site.

In 1963 the City Council, Manchester University, UMIST and Manchester United Hospitals appointed *Sir Hugh Wilson* and

Louis Womersley to prepare a development plan for the whole of the education precinct (the hospitals occupy a site immediately s of the University, *see* above), which was published in 1967. They produced a grand design to create one campus, more or less on the scale of Berkeley, California, and rather like the Smithsons' 1953 competition plan for Sheffield University. Vertical segregation of pedestrians and traffic would have been achieved by high-level walkways linking the University campus with the College of Art and Design (now part of MMU), the RNCM and UMIST. Several buildings put up in the wake of the plan were designed to link in with the upper walkways, but the spending squeeze which followed in the 1970s ensured that the more ambitious elements of the scheme never came to fruition, and there was little new building until the late 1990s.

Plans to merge the Victoria University of Manchester and UMIST were confirmed by the councils of the two universities in July 2003. *Terry Farrell & Partners* were appointed as the lead consultants for the masterplan and estate strategy, and the process of consultation started in mid 2003. The combined universities will have a student body in excess of 30,000, with over 6,700 staff. In the following account the UMIST campus is described separately, for convenience and because it is still physically distinct from that of Manchester University.

3a. The University of Manchester

Introduction

The University of Manchester started as Owens College in 1851 under the will of John Owens, for students who could not subscribe to the Anglican creed. Reorganized in 1870, it incorporated the Royal Manchester School of Medicine in 1872, and moved to the present site in 1873. It became the first college of the new Victoria University in 1880, with Liverpool joining in 1884 and Leeds in 1887. In 1904 it achieved independence and autonomy. Expansion up until the First World War was followed by a gap, then by the burst of building in the 1960s–70s which financial restraint soon reduced to a trickle. Architectural development since the Second World War is a sad record. If the University of Liverpool asked too many architects to design its buildings and the result was lack of unity, the University of Manchester showed too little initiative, too easy a sense of satisfaction, and the result was lack of architectural interest. The most innovative buildings are by outsiders, *Scherrer & Hicks* and *Building Design Partnership*. Most others are by local firms, such as *Cruickshank & Seward* and *Harry S. Fairhurst & Son*. The most significant new buildings, the School of Management by *ORMS* and *Hodder Associates*' Career Service Unit, are not really University buildings at all, though they are part of the Precinct Centre group.

The University of Manchester area extends from Booth Street East and Booth Street West, N side, to Cambridge Street on the w, Upper Brook Street on the E and Denmark Road to the s. Since the 1980s there has been overspill on to the w side of Cambridge Street. Roughly speaking, to the w are Arts, to the E the Sciences. The former UMIST Campus is located in the SE, and described separately. The description gives a perambulation covering the Waterhouse quad and its environs, mainly buildings in the first generation, and another covering the more interesting later buildings.

Perambulations

i. The Waterhouse Quad and its Environs

Owens College appointed *Alfred Waterhouse* in 1869 and building began in 1870. The buildings are arranged around a quadrangle on the w side of Oxford Road with a subsidiary courtyard behind, to the w. A plan, different from today's in many ways, was exhibited at the Royal Academy in 1872. Work was not completed until 1902 (*Paul Waterhouse* finished things off), but the buildings of the quad form a convincing whole in style, form and massing. They are of stone, in alternating narrow and wide masonry courses as at the Town Hall (*see* p. 436), with steep tiled roofs. The idiom was aptly described at the time as modern Gothic. There is economy and practicality of plan and construction, which is largely on the *Dennett & Co.* fireproof system. It is not possible to devise a straightforward walk, because if the order of building is disregarded the development of the site cannot easily be conveyed. In consequence there is some chopping and changing between the main quadrangle and Oxford Road.

We start in the main quadrangle. The w range (1) was built first, along with the Chemical Laboratories and Medical School behind (*see* below), all completed by 1874. It is quite low and intimate in scale. The outline with projections and recessions and the skyline are nicely varied. Polygonal entrance bays flank a central pavilion, and there is variation in the wings and in the detail, e.g. the differently stepped lancets of the entrance bays expressing the presence and direction of the staircases within.

The next phase was the N part of the range along Oxford Road and the N side of the quad, including the Museum and Beyer Laboratories, 1883–7. This was a building for a new university, so everything had to be grand. Waterhouse was equal to the

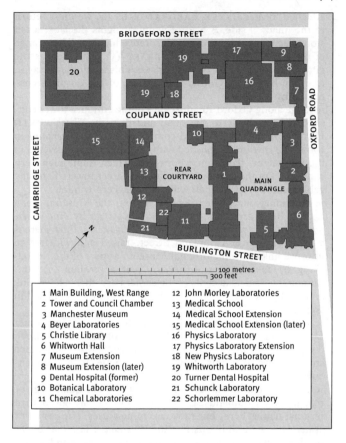

University of Manchester, the Waterhouse quad and environs

challenge. From Oxford Road the high tower, fronting the block containing the council chamber (2) is crowned with one of his steep pyramid roofs. A bay window to its r., with Geometrical tracery, houses the main staircase. On entering you find yourself in vaulted spaces of E.E. character. Display is concentrated on the grand staircase approach, which also serves the Whitworth Hall to the s and the Museum to the n. The staircase is intriguing and visually rewarding, from the detail of the floor surfaces to the glimpses into subsidiary upper caged-in staircases, one of them treated as an oriel.

The MANCHESTER MUSEUM (3) is firmly utilitarian, with tripartite windows, of no period character whatever. Full-height buttresses set up a rhythm and extend above the eaves, ending in pyramidal caps. The interior has a double-height ground floor and an excellent upper floor with wide galleries on two levels. *Ian Simpson Architects* did a successful interior remodelling and a new entrance (*see* below), 2000–3. For the attached former BEYER LABORATORIES (4) we must return to the quad, N side. A grid of windows lights the labs, a tall stone flèche provides the only decorative incident. The S range of the quad, the CHRISTIE LIBRARY (5), 1895–8, was the gift of Prof. Richard Copley Christie. This is another essay in free non-historicist Gothic with ranges of big dormers connected by arches.

The range along Oxford Road to the S of the entrance tower consists of an archway to the quad and then the WHITWORTH HALL (6), started 1898 and completed by *Paul Waterhouse* in 1902. The rhythm established with the Museum is answered in the full-height, flat-topped buttresses which frame high Perp windows. On the corner of Burlington Street towers flank the gabled end bay of the hall with its great Perp window.

The remaining parts which extend N from the Museum along Oxford Road are the MUSEUM EXTENSIONS by *Paul Waterhouse* of 1911–27, finished by *Michael Waterhouse*. First there is a bridge link over Coupland Street, raised and widened to improve links with the original Museum as part of the remodelling by *Ian Simpson Architects*. Next a pavilion (7) continuing the vertical accents of the earlier part, then a lower link and finally the latest part (8), a five-storey block completed in 1927.

The Museum extension is attached to the pre-existing former DENTAL HOSPITAL (9), on the corner of Bridgeford Street, designed by *Charles Heathcote & Sons* in 1908. Brick with much stone, of five bays only, Edwardian Baroque, with a semicircular half-domed porch.

The rear courtyard, immediately W of the main quad, can be reached via Coupland Street. The buildings are given their original names here, but most are in new uses. The rest is by *Waterhouse* with additions by *Paul Waterhouse*. The rear of the original 1873 building takes up the E side, simply and crisply treated. Attached on the N side is the BOTANICAL LABORATORY (10), 1911 by Paul Waterhouse, also crisp, but more ornate. The remaining buildings are stripped Gothic of 1871–1909, all of buff brick with stone dressings, with chimneys, pinnacles, turrets and flèches creating a picturesque roofscape. On the S side the understated CHEMICAL LABORATORIES (11), 1871–3 (for the Burlington Street side *see* below). Attached to the r. on the W side is the relatively ornate JOHN MORLEY LABORATORIES (12), by *Paul Waterhouse*, opened in 1909, with a pretty stair-tower. Beside it the MEDICAL SCHOOL (13), opened in 1874, and to the r. an extension of 1882–3 (14). Finally another extension (15) was added to the W in 1891–4 along Coupland Street.

Coupland Street, N side, E end. First is the new museum entrance, part of the remodelling by *Ian Simpson Architects*, cleanly done. Then the PHYSICS LABORATORY (16) by *J. W. Beaumont*, 1900–1, with transomed windows and an elaborate entrance. Rear extension (17) of 1912, also by *Beaumont*. The self-effacing NEW PHYSICS LABORATORY (18) of 1930–1 follows, by *Percy Scott Worthington* attached by a later link to the much larger WHITWORTH LABORATORY (19) of 1909, by *J. W. Beaumont*, with two orders of pilasters. Another part of this building faces Bridgeford Street, an arrangement made necessary by older buildings. The TURNER DENTAL SCHOOL, now the Dental Hospital (20), by *Hubert Worthington* 1939–40, is quite plain, free-standing with curved corners and horizontal emphasis given by white stone bands. It was completed by a fourth, s range in 1951–2; 1990s additions in matching style.

Walking s around the Medical School extension (15) brings us out on the w end of Burlington Street. First on the N side is an oddity, the SCHUNK LABORATORY (21), dated 1871. This was the personal laboratory of the distinguished chemist Dr H. E. Schunk, brought from Kersal in Salford in 1904 and re-erected by *Paul Waterhouse* as a mirror image of the original. The neighbouring polygonal laboratory of 1904 has attached at the rear the SCHORLEMMER LABORATORY (22), by *Alfred Waterhouse*, opened 1895. Finally the s side of the Chemical Laboratories (11) has buttresses echoing the s side of the original building of the main quad, the tumbled-in brickwork aptly acknowledging the change from stone to brick.

ii. Later Buildings of the University of Manchester

The later University buildings were erected mainly from the 1920s to the 1970s. There are a few recent additions, mostly of the 1990s. Those of particular architectural note are described, others only mentioned in passing.

We start at the PRECINCT CENTRE on Oxford Road. By *Wilson & Womersley* in association with *H. Thomas*, University Planning Officer, 1970–2. It was conceived as the key building of the 1967 plan. Red brick and red tiles spanning Oxford Road. Upper level shops and offices are ranged around two interconnected squares with glazed tent-like roofs. An upperlevel walkway to the RNCM (*see* p. 436), w side, crosses Booth Street West to the N. Only the E side works, with coordination and connection with other buildings. Here ST PETER'S HOUSE, by *Cruickshank & Seward* in matching red brick and tile, was part of the original scheme. In 1994 the University and UMIST decided to merge certain departments to form the FEDERAL SCHOOL OF BUSINESS AND MANAGEMENT, based partly in the Precinct Centre. The merger produced some new buildings of quality. The SCHOOL OF MANAGEMENT by *ORMS*, 1997–8, can be seen from the upper deck of the Precinct Centre, NE side, and is connected to it by a footbridge across Booth Street East. A stone-clad base contrasts with glazed upper floors. Still on the E side, but to the s of Booth Street East, is an attached white drum containing the 400-seat LECTURE THEATRE of the School of Accounting and Finance, based on a concept of 1996 by

Hodder Associates (but carried out through a design and build arrangement). Take the steps down to the ground level here for the CAREER SERVICES UNIT, to the SE. *Hodder Associates* won the competition in 1995. The L-shaped building is carefully related to its surroundings. Three storeys, rendered white, with strong forms and patterns of projection and recession, solid and void. Return to Oxford Road where a group of buildings is attached to the E side of the Precinct Centre. The best is *Scherrer & Hicks'* MATHEMATICS BUILDING,* 1967–8. The tallest of the University buildings, a sixteen-storey tower standing on one corner of a three-storey podium with cantilevered lecture theatres, clearly influenced by James Stirling's Engineering building at Leicester University of 1963. Concrete-framed, with brick facing. The tower is assertively composed of free cubic shapes stepping vertically and horizontally in the expressionist Brutalist style of the moment. In the podium courtyard a SCULPTURE by *Michael Yeomans* looks like an organic growth attacking the walls.

It is necessary to cross the road and turn l. along Bridgeford Street for the ARCHITECTURE AND PLANNING building. By the building's then inhabitants, Professors *N. L. Hanson*, and *R. H. Kantorowich*, with *M. C. Schonegevel* and *G. Skacel*, 1970. Set amid spacious lawns, it is uninspiring in grey concrete, but inside there is a large attractive courtyard with pools. Returning to Oxford Road and continuing S leads to Brunswick Street, E side, where a group of buildings, 1957–67, was designed around the monumental W–E axis of the street which had been proposed by Worthington. With two exceptions they are by *Harry S. Fairhurst & Son* (i.e. *H. M. Fairhurst*), of brick with copper-clad ribs and roofs. They incorporate external art works by *Lynn Chadwick* (Williamson Building), *Michael Piper* (Schuster Building) and *Hans Tisdall* (Chemistry Building). The odd one out of this group is the ROSCOE BUILDING, N side, by *Cruickshank & Seward*, 1964. White concrete, with a six-floor glass façade. Back on Oxford Road, continue S past the Waterhouse quad and turn r. into DOVER STREET. The former HIGH SCHOOL FOR GIRLS, S side, by *Mills & Murgatroyd*, 1881–6, is now used by the University. Red brick heightened by a few touches of stone and red terracotta, in the sort of Northern Gothic established by Waterhouse and Thomas Worthington as a civic style a decade before. Next to it is the SOCIAL SCIENCE AND ECONOMICS BUILDING by *Cruickshank & Seward*, 1966–7, white concrete, with a core clad in dark grey brick, the windows boxed out in canted surrounds.

Return to Oxford Street and cross to the W side into a courtyard, almost opposite. On the N side a dull 1960s block faces the stately FACULTY OF ARTS by *Percy Scott Worthington* 1911–19. Of red brick and Portland stone, symmetrical with a classical stone portico. The entrance leads to a noble hall, top-lit, with

---

*A possible casualty of the University merger.

Ionic columns and a coffered barrel roof. The white concrete and Portland stone extensions at the rear (s) and running E from the w wing are additions of *c.* 1970 by *Cruickshank & Seward*, with Corbusian external stairs and a curving rooftop pavilion.

Across the courtyard w of the Arts Faculty is the JOHN RYLANDS UNIVERSITY LIBRARY, 1935–7, by *Percy Scott Worthington*. Portland stone below and red brick and stone dressings above, with an L-shaped rear (w) extension by *Sir Hubert Worthington* of the mid 1950s (attached to the N is a large red brick four-storey extension with a new main entrance by *Dane, Scherrer & Hicks*, 1982). s of the library is the Mansfield Cooper Building (*Cruickshank & Seward*, 1975–7) then an attractive linking block clad in timber planks with variously horizontal, slanting and zigzag window strips, by *Short Ford Associates*, 1999. This connects with the AQA (Assessment and Qualifications Alliance) building, formerly the Joint Examination Board, strictly not put up by the University. First is an extension by the *Playne Vallance Partnership* of *c.* 1975, then the main building by *Playne & Lacey*, 1962. Octagonal, with a pointed roof ending in a nice lantern. Altogether it is an intimate building, as befits its function.

Immediately E, behind the Arts Faculty, is the HUMANITIES BUILDING, 1961–7 by *G. G. Baines* of *Building Design Partnership*. A building of some power. It is of brown concrete, bush-hammered, with the verticals of the frame projecting. Low l. addition with abstract concrete reliefs designed by *William Mitchell* of the sort which were so overdone at that time. Turn r. and return to Oxford Road and continue s past the huge church of the Holy Name (*see* Churches, above), where on the corner of Grafton Street the STOPFORD BUILDING is a huge medical school by *H. S. Fairhurst & Son*, 1969–72. The attached BIOTECH building to the rear is by *Fairhurst Design Group*, completed 1999, being extended by the same firm 2004. WHITWORTH PARK STUDENT ACCOMMODATION lies a little to the s, off Oxford Road w side. By *Building Design Partnership*, 1973–4. Low blocks in traditional materials create a pleasant domestic atmosphere, in reaction to the big accommodation units of the previous decade.

iii. Outlying Buildings

MCDOUGALL SPORTS CENTRE, Burlington Street. 1885 by *J. Hillkirk*. Originally the drill hall of the Third Manchester Rifle Volunteers, converted to a physical education centre for the University in 1939 by *J. S. Beaumont*.

3b. University of Manchester Institute of Science and Technology (UMIST)

UMIST remained an autonomous body dealing direct with the University Grants Committee until it merged with the Victoria

University of Manchester in 2004 (*see* Academic Institutions, introduction, p. 424). It started as a successor to the Mechanics Institute which became a municipal college. New buildings were erected s of the C19 buildings from 1962 and the area was incorporated into the *Wilson & Womersley* 1963 Educational Precinct Plan (*see* p. 424), following *Sir Hubert Worthington*'s original proposals. The MSJ&AR viaduct of 1849 cuts across the precinct, with older buildings on its N side and most of the newer to the s, on low ground in a loop of the (culverted) Medlock.

We start with the earliest part, to the N, with the front to Sackville Street, built for the Municipal School of Technology by *Spalding & Cross*, 1895–1912. A splendid expression of municipal pride and confidence. It is a grand composition in the Loire style, five storeys, with a gabled gatehouse-type entrance bay. Brick with red sandstone, lavishly decorated with tawny-red terracotta panels with Renaissance motifs by *Burmantofts*. The deep plan consists of rooms in four blocks along the street frontages, with superimposed halls at the centre flanked by light-wells faced in white glazed brick. The foyer is lit by an entrance screen with stained glass, part of an extensive and attractive scheme by *Walter J. Pearce*. The lower hall is an impressive space with large square piers clad in terracotta while the upper hall has a vaulted ceiling encrusted with plasterwork. The enormous extension, separated by a courtyard behind, was designed in 1927 by *Bradshaw Gass & Hope*, but only completed in 1957, a gross anachronism by then. Red brick and much yellow terracotta, Norman Shaw gables, and a high set-back top at right angles.

  CHANDOS HALL by *Cruickshank & Seward* (in charge *W.A. Gibbon*), 1962–4 overlooks the gardens from the E. Fifteen storeys, with ribbed white concrete walls and a roomy glass staircase tower on one side. On the s side of the viaduct is a pleasant elevated walkway beside the arches, many of which are open, creating a visual link between the old and new areas.

The OTHER POST-WAR BUILDINGS, s of the railway, have a sense of purpose lacking in most of their contemporaries at the University. This is largely owing to the confidence of those designed by *W.A. Gibbon* of *Cruickshank & Seward*. Corbusier and Niemeyer influences are evident. We start at the heart of the complex where a turfed precinct forms a little square reached from the viaduct walkway by a handsome flying staircase descending in two arms. To the w the RENOLD BUILDING by *W.A. Gibbon*, 1962, a six-storey tower on a two-storey base. It housed lecture theatres which would otherwise have been dispersed departmentally, a new initiative in British academic planning at that time. Generous transparent stair-tower on the NW side. The E face is a folded white concrete wall with angled window strips. Impressive entrance hall on two levels with a MURAL: Metamorphosis by *Victor Pasmore*, 1968, in the lower part.

To the E the STUDENTS' UNION (Barnes Wallis Building) with the WRIGHT ROBINSON HALL, a podium with a fifteen-storey tower of residence behind, 1963–6 by *W.A. Gibbon*. All in white concrete with shuttering marks. Vertically stabbing roof erections like funnels give light to the stairs.

STAFF HOUSE, on the S side of the square, by *Thomas Worthington*, 1960, extended 1968, slots in behind the mill building (*see* below). An uncompromising frame of big squares and four storeys. E of the Union and Renold Buildings a blocky sculptural boundary wall by *Antony Hollaway*, c. 1965, marks the site perimeter. Prefabricated textured concrete panels slotted into concrete columns. It extends S as far as the CHEMICAL ENGINEERING PILOT PLANT by *H.M. Fairhurst* of *H.S. Fairhurst & Son*, 1966. Engineering brick S, glass N, boldly dividing the building into two halves. The glass part is open through four storeys and crowned by a contrastingly solid-looking cooling plant hovering above the roof.

To the w JACKSON STREET MILL (Chemical Engineering), a large brick mid-C19 cotton-spinning mill by *Stott & Sons*, utilitarian apart from an unusually ornate Italianate entrance bay. Converted to laboratories by *H.S. Fairhurst & Son*, in 1959. S of this MATHEMATICS AND SOCIAL SCIENCES, by *W.A. Gibbon* of *Cruickshank & Seward*, 1966–8, a fifteen-storey tower block, and a landmark. A subtle composition with careful grouping of the blocks, which have huge brutal expanses of precast shuttering. Attached to the E, a two-storey lecture theatre block continues the brutal vocabulary of bare concrete. Attached on the SW side of the main building the low FERRANTI BUILDING (Electrical Engineering), by the same architects. In the grassed courtyard an entertaining SCULPTURE, Insulator Family, three high-voltage ceramic insulators supplied by *Allied Insulators* of Stoke-on-Trent, installed 1987. To the NW the PARISIER BUILDING (Civil, Structural and Mechanical Engineering); *H.M. Fairhurst*, 1963, brick with copper cladding. Opposite, the FARADAY BUILDING (Chemistry), also by *H.M. Fairhurst*, 1967, concrete and quite extensive with abstract patterning by *Antony Hollaway*. There is a high slab, a bridge across Sackville Street, and a four-storeyed part. The entrance opposite the Parisier building incorporates MOSAICS, The Alchemist's Elements, by *Hans Tisdall*, 1967.

To the w, also by *Fairhursts* is the GEORGE BEGG BUILDING, 1974 (Mechanical Engineering). Fronting the w side of Sackville Street, just to the N, WESTON HALL (14), 1991 by *Downs & Variava* with extensions completed in 2000 by *Halliday Meecham*. Conference centre, student residences, etc. Inside, the foyer with a working Foucault pendulum is engaging, otherwise the big, dull brick blocks with pitched roofs have no memorable features whatever. What a comedown after all the 1960s bravado.

For the Federal School of Business and Management *see* p. 429.

3c. Manchester Metropolitan University

The John Dalton College of Technology, the College of Commerce and the Regional College of Art were merged as Manchester Polytechnic in 1970. University status came in 1990. Spread over seven different sites, it is one of the largest universities in the UK. The main buildings in central Manchester occupy the area N of the University between Oxford Road (E), Cambridge Street (W), Rosamund Street West (S) and Chester Street (N). For the Aytoun Buildings, originally the College of Commerce site, *see* Centre, p. 299. The centre of the site is Grosvenor Square.

Grosvenor Square was designated a cultural centre in the *City of Manchester Plan* of 1945 and confirmed as the main campus for the city's colleges in the 1967 *Wilson & Womersley* plan for the educational precinct (*see* Academic Institutions, Introduction, p. 424–5). Buildings of the John Dalton College of Technology and the School of Art were already established in the area (*see* below) and the City Council had acquired land there, partly through the construction of the Mancunian Way (*see* p. 438) which divides Grosvenor Square from the College of Technology buildings to the N. *Sheppard Robson* were appointed architects for the new polytechnic in 1971, with *Gordon Taylor* in charge of the project. Their Development Plan of 1972 was never fully realized and more of the pre-existing buildings around the square were retained and converted than originally intended. The effect is pleasing in variety.

N of the Mancunian Way on the W side of Oxford Road, the FACULTY OF TECHNOLOGY, a descendant of the Mechanics' Institute and Municipal College of Technology. The first building of 1966 by the *City Architect's Department* is a conventional tower. Extension of 1974 by *W. Heppell, City Architect's Department*. Five storeys, all but the ground floor with continuous windows with slanting glazing bars angled upwards from the concrete frame, somewhat in the manner of the GLC's Pimlico School of 1966–70. Beside the main entrance on Chester Street a bronze STATUE of John Dalton by *William Theed* after *Chantrey*, 1855, moved from Piccadilly in 1966.

GROSVENOR SQUARE lies immediately S of the Mancunian Way, W of Oxford Road. It is known as All Saints, after an early C19 church which stood in the centre, until demolition following war damage. A park has been created on the site. The ALL SAINTS BUILDING by *Gordon Taylor* of *Sheppard Robson*, 1978, takes up most of the N side, housing the Arts Library, offices and administration. Brownish-red brick, with parts of three, four and five storeys. The entrance to Oxford Road was remodelled by *MBLC* in 1999–2000. Attached, W, ALL SAINTS WEST, the Law Department, was put up in 2002–3. By *John McAslan & Partners*, with cool greenish glazed surfaces and dull metallic cladding, contrasting with the red brick neighbours. Inside there is an atrium into which the curved wall of lecture theatres bulges out on two levels. Next the

LOXFORD BUILDING by *City Architects*, 1974, the first of a series of multi-purpose buildings on the site, combining teaching suites with accommodation. Brick with eleven-storey towers rippling out above a three-storey lower part.

On the w side of the square is the BELLHOUSE BUILDING (Lower Ormond Street, w side), the façade of a house of 1831. Three storeys with a central entrance and a pedimented window above. Converted to offices 1987. The ORMOND BUILDING, s, is on the corner of Cavendish Street. By *Mangnall & Littlewood*, 1881, as offices of the Poor Law Guardians and a Registry Office. Taken over by the Polytechnic in 1970. Ornate in red brick with stone dressings. The building gathers itself up towards the Cavendish Street corner where there is an octagonal upper-floor oriel surmounted by a turret with an elongated dome and cupola. Ranged along Chatham Street to the w and straddling Cavendish Street, the CAVENDISH BUILDING, *Sheppard Robson*, 1978, similar in style to their other buildings here, for teaching and accommodation. The RIGHTON BUILDING occupies the s corner of Cavendish Street and Lower Ormond Street. Built as a draper's shop, named and dated 1905 in a raised parapet over the entrance, and taken over in 1970. Two storeys, white glazed brick and buff terracotta. It has probably the best-preserved Edwardian SHOP INTERIOR in the city. Two light wells, with a common gallery reached by the original Jacobean-style stair. Balustrades around the wells have Art Nouveau style ironwork.

The GROSVENOR BUILDING (Faculty of Art and Design) on the s side of the square is actually two buildings: the original Manchester School of Art building to the w, the Chorlton-on-Medlock Town Hall and Dispensary to the E. First the remarkable School of Art building, 1880–1, designed by *G. T. Redmayne*. Gothic and symmetrical, with a central entrance, but take the period details away and you have Mackintosh's Glasgow School of Art of 1898, i.e. an ornate treatment of the centre but otherwise all frank large studio windows. The entrance has a moulded arched head, richly carved spandrels, and a little three-light oriel above with, on each side, circular tourelles with conical caps. This is flanked by three arcaded bays and one continuous strip of north-light studio glazing across the roof. At each end gabled wings have large simply treated upper windows with pointed heads. The Manchester School of Art began in 1838. By 1880 women formed part of both student and teaching bodies, and a segregated studio and stair for them was part of the original design. At the back is an excellent extension of red brick and orange terracotta, dated 1897. It is by *J. Gibbons Sankey* and has three plain gables and one tier of terracotta E. E. two-light windows with angels in the tympana, designed by *W. J. Neatby*, the head of the Architectural Department at *Doulton*'s. The interior has three linked top-lit studio/exhibition halls at upper level, separated by corridors with round-headed terracotta arcades with more beautiful Art Nouveau motifs in the

capitals and spandrels, by *Neatby* again. Various early C20
extensions.

Next the former Chorlton-on-Medlock Town Hall and Dispensary, dignified by being set back from the line of the street.
By *Richard Lane*, 1830–1, nine bays wide, with a Greek Doric
pedimented portico. Severity is relieved by lion masks and
wreaths in the frieze. Only the façade survives. Adjoining, E,
on the corner of Oxford Road, the MABEL TYLECOTE
BUILDING (Drama Department) by the *City Architect's
Department*, 1973, a purpose-built college of adult education
designed to link in with the high level walkways of the Wilson
& Womersley plan (*see* p. 424). Oversailing upper floor of
exposed concrete, brick lower part with concrete ribs. Taken
over by the University in 1991.

The GEOFFREY MANTON BUILDING (Humanities), 1996–9
by *Sheppard Robson*, fronts Oxford Road to the S. A ground-
floor glass screen gives views of the atrium. The principal
entrance is from a courtyard on the W side. At the corner is a
full-height triangular tower, from which a glass-sided first-
floor bridge connects with the Grosvenor Building. Inside a
large airy atrium with a tubular steel roof. To the W is another
bridge, with unexpected geometrical shapes, and hexagonal
roofs to each section, part of the nine-storey CHATHAM
BUILDING (Faculty of Art and Design), connecting it to
the Grosvenor Building. By the *City Architect's Department*
(*S. G. Besant Roberts*), 1966.

For the buildings of the Aytoun Campus *see* Manchester centre,
see p. 299.

ROYAL NORTHERN COLLEGE OF MUSIC, Oxford Road and
Booth Street West. By *Bickerdike, Allen, Rich & Partners*,
1968–73. The Royal Manchester College of Music was founded
in 1893 and had as its first principal Charles Hallé. In 1972 it
merged with the Northern School of Music, which began as
a private music school in 1920 and became a public institution
in 1943.

A concrete rectangle only two storeys high, the top solid
except for window slots; double-height spaces below, slightly
recessed behind tall stilts. On the S side glazed bays to the r.
light the original foyer and the stair. It was designed to accommodate high-level walkways linking with surrounding buildings, but only the one to the Precinct Centre, S (*see* p. 429),
spanning Booth Street West, was built. The others are truncated at the ends of the deck on the E side of the building,
pointing to unrealized projects. The impressive interior has
expansive double-height spaces and auditoria, served by a very
generous stair rising majestically on the S side of the building.
An extension was added on the W side by *MBLC*, 1997–8,
blocks faced in granite and grey brick in similar tones to the
original building, to which it is linked by an airy double-height
glazed entrance block.

Houses

Some notable examples of the surviving houses and terraces built for the middle classes in the early or mid c19 are listed below. Almost all have been converted for use as offices, flats, etc.

NELSON STREET. Nos. 60–62, a pair of villas of *c.* 1840 of which No. 62, l., was the home of Emmeline Pankhurst when she founded the Women's Social and Political Union in 1903. Slightly projecting entrance bays. The l. house has a full-height polygonal bay attached to the l. with arched windows with intersecting glazing bars.

OXFORD ROAD. Nos. 176–188, W side. A terrace of *c.* 1830 called Waterloo Place, between Tuer Street and Bridgeford Street: seven three-bay two-storey houses with wide arched entrances with inset Doric columns. Most have delicate fanlight glazing. Nos. 176–182 have attractive early C20 attic additions.

Nos. 323–333, E side, at the junction with Dover Street: a row of four quite grand three-storey stuccoed town houses. No. 323 is the largest, with ground-floor channelled rustication and first-floor windows with cornices. The next two have respectively a wooden porch with square pillars and a stone porch with Tuscan columns. The last, No. 333, has a recessed entrance with Doric columns.

Nos. 316–324, W side, near the junction with Dilworth Street: a large detached house set back from the street, originally composed of three separate dwellings. Expansive five-bay frontage with a central arched entrance.

PLYMOUTH GROVE. No. 84, *c.* 1838–40, is of note as one of the largest and most elaborate early C19 houses in inner Manchester. It was the home of the novelist Elizabeth Gaskell after 1850. Stuccoed with full-height pilasters and a portico with columns and pilasters, all with unusual capitals derived from the Tower of the Winds in Athens. The same order was used, probably by *Richard Lane*, for the Wesleyan Theological Institute (*see* Didsbury College, p. 445), also of the early 1840s. Lane was no stranger to speculative building (*see* nearby Victoria Park, Rusholme, p. 477) and may have dabbled in building here as well. Almost equally impressive symmetrical elevation to Swinton Grove, and a large oval bay to the rear. The interior has original doorcases, plaster friezes and a top-lit stair with brass balusters.

SWINTON GROVE. Nos. 2–4, N side. Pair of brick houses of *c.* 1840 at r. angles to the street, with full-height semicircular bays.

Perambulations

1. Oxford Road, from Charles Street to Booth Street East

The starting point is the junction of Oxford Road with Charles Street (E) and Hulme Street (W).

OXFORD ROAD on the W side has the DANCEHOUSE THEATRE, formerly a cinema, by *Pendleton & Dickinson*, 1929–30. A long classical façade clad in pale cream faience with orange faience detailing. Elaborate Art Deco plasterwork, of a richness rarely found in England, in the one surviving double-height auditorium. Converted for theatre use 1992. Opposite, E side, is the dull Manchester headquarters of the BBC by its chief architect *R.A. Sparks*, opened in 1975. Beside it to the S, and in sparkling contrast, is the NATIONAL COMPUTING CENTRE by *Cruickshank & Seward*, 1964. White concrete and white tiles. Three storeys, the top cantilevered out and crowned with angled roof projections lighting the stairs, like those on their Barnes Wallis building at UMIST (*see* above). The street frontage was unfortunately altered to incorporate shops and offices 2000–2. The arid gloomy undercroft which follows lies beneath the MANCUNIAN WAY inner-city motorway, which crosses the S side of the centre largely as a viaduct. The part from Chester Road (in Hulme) to Upper Brook Street (Chorlton-on-Medlock) was built 1964–7 by Manchester City Council's *City Engineers* and *G. Maunsell & Partners*. The extension to Pin Mill Brow (Ardwick), by *City Engineers*, was opened in 1992.

S of the motorway Oxford Road forms the E side of GROSVENOR SQUARE, which was almost completely rebuilt for the main Manchester Metropolitan University buildings (*see* p. 434).

GROSVENOR STREET runs E from the S end of the square. The former GROSVENOR PICTURE PALACE is on the E corner with Oxford Road. Designed in 1913 by *Percy Hothersall* and opened in 1915, when it was described grandiosely as 'Roman-Corinthian of the later Renaissance influence'. Faience and terracotta in dark green and cream shades, with a domed entrance bay at the corner. Inside, the balcony and an amount of florid plasterwork survive. Further E, S side, the (former) ADULT DEAF & DUMB INSTITUTE by *John Lowe*, 1878. Stone, Gothic, symmetrical with a central arched entrance. Above this a pedestal and statue of Christ healing a deaf man and a lettered frieze. The building was designed to offer social, religious and educational services to adults. Back now to Oxford Road. The MANCHESTER AQUATIC CENTRE S of Grosvenor Street, by *FaulknerBrowns*, 1999–2000, was designed for use in the Commonwealth Games held in Manchester in 2002. To Oxford Road it presents a profile with a curving roof recalling in outline the attitude of a diver. Inside one notes the asymmetrical roof shape, the shallower slope with a suspended ceiling with big rippled panels.

2. Chorlton Mills and Macintosh Works

The group of mills and works on the NW edge of the township include important examples of early C19 fireproof construction and part of one of the earliest purpose-built rubberized cloth manufactories in England.* Most of the complex has been converted, mainly to flats, in a process starting in the 1990s with mills on the E side of Cambridge Street. New building has started in this area, and the conversions continue, 2004.

We start on Chester Street with CHATHAM MILL, Chester Street, a cotton-spinning mill built in 1820 with an extension of 1823 along Lower Ormond Street. A truncated chimney is attached to the rear. Continuing W brings us to the N end of CAMBRIDGE STREET. The group of early and mid-C19 mills and works here has an intertwined history which started with the factories of the Marsland and Birley families. There was a fleeting input from Robert Owen. Many were eventually taken over by the Birleys, and in turn by the company they set up to produce waterproof cloth by Charles Macintosh's method, patented in 1823.

The building between Chester Street and Hulme Street, E side, is the remains of two mills; that on Chester Street corner, MARSLAND'S MILL, originating in 1795, was rebuilt in 1813. The adjoining CHORLTON OLD MILL was built for Robert Owen in 1795 before he moved to New Lanark. In 1803 this building was extended along Hulme Street. The buildings were eventually taken over by the Macintosh works (see below) and partially rebuilt.

CHORLTON NEW MILLS, N of Hulme Street, E side, three multi-storey blocks built in phases for the Birley family. The first, of 1813–15, is set back from the road. Six storeys and two basement storeys; an early example of fireproof construction. Next came the twelve-bay fireproof wing added to the S on Hulme Street in 1818. Finally in 1845 a linking block at the corner of Hulme Street was added. The big chimney dates from 1853.

MACINTOSH WORKS, Cambridge Street, W side. The Birleys built a factory to produce Macintosh's patented waterproof fabric in 1825–6. The original building was demolished but a second building, completed by 1838, stands on the Hulme Street corner. Attached to the W, a block of 1849 housed a vulcanization boiler. The tapering octagonal chimney here is of c. 1851, built for Chorlton New Mill to which it is connected by an underground flue. Interwar and post-war building reflects Dunlop's expansion in the C20.

Lastly on Cambridge Street, W side MEDLOCK MILL, c. 1811 on the N bank of the Medlock. A range of C19 offices front and follow the curve of the road, and the converted mill (Hotspur Press) rises behind.

Opposite the Macintosh works alongside the Medlock the GREEN BUILDING by *Terry Farrell & Partners* is under construction, 2004. As the name suggests, the aim is to create an energy-efficient building in which the design, materials and special features will reduce energy consumption and take

---

* For a full account of the mills and their owners see Sylvia Clark in *Industrial Archaeology Review* 2 No. 3, Summer 1978.

advantage of renewable sources of power. A ten-storey
tapering cylinder with apartments will sit on a podium housing
a nursery, doctors' surgery and other facilities. Electricity will
be generated by a roof-mounted wind turbine and solar panels
will be used to provide hot water. A central atrium with
retractable windows will provide natural light and ventilation,
and the flats will be equipped with energy-efficient appliances.

Outliers

CHARLES STREET. The Lass O' Gowrie pub has a cheerful
glazed terracotta exterior of *c.* 1900. On the corner of Brook
Street beside the Medlock a stylish 1990s conversion of C19
buildings for Factory Records, now a club.
PLYMOUTH GROVE HOTEL, Plymouth Grove. Ornate pub of
1873 with a prominent clock tower.
CITY ROAD. No. 1 City Road, office block by *Architects Group
Practice*, 1990. A row of faceted reflective glass clad towers
with domed tops – flashy pop architecture.

DIDSBURY

The early settlement was by St James's church, extant in the C13
or C14. What is now called Didsbury Village grew up half a mile
N after the coming of the Midland railway in 1880. The Styal line
followed in 1909, the new road Kingsway with its trams in 1920,
and the area is now, apart from the Mersey flood plain, solidly
built up. It is by no means uniform however. The villas of the
wealthy lie S of the village along the Wilmslow Road and, of
slightly later date, at Fielden Park. Solid bourgeois housing is at
Albert Park around Palatine Road and, again a little later, immediately N of the village on both sides of the Wilmslow Road.
Dense terrace housing lies on either side of the present village
street. 1930s semis occupy the Ford Bank estate and the further
reaches of Didsbury Park, and there is now a great deal of infilling and subdivision.

The boundary on the S is the River Mersey with its wide
flood plain, on the E Parrs Wood Road and Parrs Wood Lane,
including Parrs Wood itself, on the N Fog Lane and Lapwing
Lane, and on the W Burton Road and then Barlow Moor Road
to Princess Parkway.

Places of Worship

ST JAMES, Stenner Lane. The ancient chapel is thought to have
originated as a private oratory in the C13. It was made parochial
in 1352, one of a string of medieval churches along either side
of the Mersey. It became the parish church of Didsbury in
1850. The dumpy W tower is dated 1620 and an inscription
refers to Sir Edward and Anne Mosley as founders, although

it looks medieval apart from its crown. The pinnacles and loops were put there in 1801.* The church is all of pinkish ashlar with old stone showing in the N and W walls. Nave and aisles under one roof, chancel, and an oversized S extension dated 1895 running parallel to it. The windows are very assorted, but include several large square-headed ones with transoms.

The interior is odd. There is early C17 fabric, but later additions and alterations have changed its character. There are two chancel arches, one four bays from the W, the other six. The nave arcade, up to the first chancel arch, is vaguely Doric with semicircular arches, but the columns are too tall for their width and strangely crude and lumpy. Beyond the first chancel arch, which carries an engagingly gloomy pair of carved and painted angels as corbels, is a pair of octagonal columns. Then comes a straightforward Victorian chancel arch and chancel, extended on the S, as we saw outside, to make vestries, an organ chamber and a transept.

The nave columns were probably heightened for galleries in the C18 galleries. Fletcher Moss (for whom see p. 447) says they were 'chiselled smaller' to improve the view in the late C18 or early C19. In 1771 the chancel was made the same width as the nave, and probably lengthened, so that dates the octagonal columns. A plan made of 1843 shows a rectangular building with its E end where the Victorian chancel arch is now, and galleries round all four sides except under the E window. 1855–6 saw considerable alterations, including a new E window and the W door in the tower; the window above it was presumably altered at the same time. The second chancel arch was broken through the previous E wall in 1871 when the present chancel was added, by *Horton & Bridgford*, for Miss Mabel Louisa Barnes, and the galleries removed. Joseph Farington R.A., the diarist (see Parrs Wood, below), had died after a fall down the gallery steps 'encumbered with Hat, Umbrella & prayer-book' in 1821. In 1875 the W windows of the aisles were made, and the N door of the tower inserted; *Horton & Bridgford* again.

Low SCREEN, PULPIT and ALTAR RAIL, of white marble and sticky-looking onyx; 1911. – LECTERN. Brass angel of 1905, probably by *Jones & Willis*. – STAINED GLASS. A full C19 set by assorted makers darkens the interior. By *Wailes* of Newcastle the chancel window, 1855, reset in the 1871 E end. Around it are four by *Lavers, Barraud & Westlake*, the two on the S side displaced when the vestry and baptistery were built. The best are two adjacent shipwreck scenes at the NW and another by the same maker near the pulpit. The nearby memorial window to the contumacious Rev. Kidd †1880. – MONUMENTS. Sir Nicholas Mosley †1612, the builder of Hough End Hall (see Chorlton-cum-Hardy, p. 414). He kneels in a

14

---

* According to Diana Leach the C17 topknot of miniature battlements, obelisks and faces, was transferred at the same time from the tower to the curious little square vestry in S porch position.

Corinthian aedicule, dressed in the robes of the Lord Mayor
of London (1599). Below, in three Ionic aedicules, kneel his
two wives and two of his sons. The monument is crowned with
coats of arm and blunt obelisks, and is made of alabaster and
Derbyshire marbles. – Close by, Sir John Bland †1715, big
tablet of dark Derbyshire marbles. – Chancel arch N, Ann,
Lady Bland †1734, daughter and heiress of Sir Edward Mosley
and long-suffering wife of Sir John. She was the founder of St
Ann's church in Manchester. – Other C18 tablets on the N wall,
Thomas Briarly †1776, William Broom †1764, James Bayley
†1778.

CHRISTCHURCH, Darley Avenue, West Didsbury. By *Henry
Littler*, 1881–2. Its big square tower is a landmark on the entry
to Manchester from the SW. The church was the gift of William
James Roberts of this parish and of Darley Dale in Derbyshire,
the source of much Manchester stone. Large, in the style of
*c.*1300, but the squared-off massing and flat continuous roof
show that Mr Littler, unusually, took some account of the
local late Perp. Transepts of aisle height, not interrupting the
arcades whose piers are circular with four flat ridges. Road
widening in 1980 brought the great artery of Princess Parkway
right up to the W door. The church was then reordered by
Gordon Thorne with a new SE entrance on Darley Avenue and
a spectacular organ slung over the tower arch. – Alabaster and
marble PULPIT, 1910. – Low alabaster SCREEN and REREDOS,
1921, erected as a war memorial, displacing an iron and brass
one to the N transept. – STAINED GLASS. A nearly complete
set in the nave and transepts by *Lavers & Westlake*. That in the
N transept commemorates the donor: the Nativity. Mr Roberts
as one of the Magi presents Christchurch West Didsbury to
the Christ child. The exceptions are on the S side by *Jones &
Willis* 1924, and on the N side one by *Wippell* of Exeter 1943;
Martha and Mary are depicted in wartime style, Martha like
a staff nurse with a bunch of keys at her waist.

EMMANUEL, Barlow Moor Road. 1858, by *Starkey & Cuffley*.
Thin SW tower, the upper parts polygonal with a short spire
(rebuilt in 2001). Dec, with triple pointed roofs and no
clerestory. Long unaspiring interior of nave and aisles, a S
transept, and chancel. It was made a nonsense of in 1986 when
Nicholas Rank Associates removed all the fittings and partitioned off the chancel and transept, making the rest into a
completely flexible space, although it is normally arranged
with the altar on the N side. The principal entrance, of wood
and glass, is now in the SE corner. Emmanuel is permanently
equipped as a studio for radio broadcasting. – STAINED
GLASS. Pevsner thought that the *William Morris* glass of 1889
in the S transept, with its bold leaf scrolls filling the lower
lights, made the rest look despicable, though the ensemble
includes windows by *Hughes* of 1864 (E), *Capronnier* 1874 in
the former SE chapel and *O'Connor* in the S aisle.

ST LUKE, Burton Road. A simple brick mission church, of 1881
until 1890, then again 1934–84. The discontinuity was due to

the erection of a large and fancy 'tin tabernacle', St Mary, on
Palatine Road. Following its regrettable demolition the First
World WAR MEMORIAL was brought here. Fronting the
church are the SCHOOLS of 1890, converted to offices.

ST CATHERINE OF SIENA (R.C.), School Lane. First came the
dual-purpose HALL in 1929, then the adjoining HALL, 1936–7.
Lastly (this is a common pattern) the PRESBYTERY and the
CHURCH, by *Arthur Farebrother & Partners*, 1956–7, project
architect *Desmond Williams*. Simplified Romanesque, with
round arches and a campanile. The pillared porch was added
in 1961. Wide flat-ceilinged interior with low side aisles behind
segmental arches. – The ALTAR RAILS, removed in the centre,
are done with marble blocks cut to the same segmental shape
carried on blue mosaic columns, like a decorative viaduct, by
Alberti, Lupton & Co.

ST PAUL METHODIST CHURCH. The modest brick building of
1961, distinguished only by a canted entrance bay of glass, is
today's church. The former church to its N, a proud Gothic
stone building with a SW steeple, is a commercial office. Built
to serve the Wesleyan Theological Institute (*see* Didsbury
College, below), it was designed by *H.H.Vale* of Liverpool and
completed after his suicide by *T.D. Barry & Sons* of the same
city in 1875–7. It was a memorial to James Heald of Parrs
Wood, given by his sister Miss M. Heald and nephew William
N. Heald who bore the entire cost of £20,000. The style was
said to be transitional from E. E. to Geometrical but the motifs
are freely treated, e.g. the aisle windows of five arched lights
per bay. Dormers instead of a clerestory. Rich interior with fat
polished granite colonnettes and inhabited foliage corbels and
capitals.

The office conversion is an exemplary job, by *Downs &
Variava*, 1990. The crossing kept open to the roof, criss-
crossed by flying stairs and galleries all as light as possible. Two
intermediate floors are inserted in each of the four arms but
at slightly different levels, so that each level in the chancel overlooks two levels of the nave, and vice versa.

GROSVENOR ST AIDAN'S (United Reformed), Palatine Road.
So named because the congregation of Grosvenor Square
chapel in Manchester nominally merged with this one. By
Henry Lord, 1901. Of Accrington brick and red terracotta, with
a pair of flying buttresses on the front indicating, over-
dramatically, the narrow aisles within. – STAINED GLASS of
1901–13, all by *Walter J. Pearce*. The Evangelists, transepts; W
window SS Columba and Aidan, originally in the E end. In
that position now, a *Whitefriars* window of 1957, the Road to
Emmaus.

The SCHOOL on Parkfield Road, also by *Henry Lord*, opened in
1890,

CHRISTCHURCH (United Reformed), Parrswood Road, 1931. A
strong exterior, gambrel-roofed with two big dormers and a
split W window. Narthex in front with a little octagonal room
at each end and a porch in the middle with battered buttresses.

Surprisingly elegant interior considering its short wide proportions and its dual-purpose use, as a social hall as well as a
church. Five-sided chancel space with big Perp windows.
Wide nave with narrow passage-aisles, the nave articulated by
paired semicircular arches and a plaster vault cut away for the
dormers, the aisles given interest by a light-dark-light alterna-
tion of high arches and low lintels.

IVY COTTAGE EVANGELICAL CHURCH, Barlow Moor Road,
takes its name from Ivy Cottage (No. 18) across the road. It
was founded by Oliver Brockbank in 1893, because Emmanuel
was not serving the servants of Didsbury. Probably by *J. & J.
Swarbrick*. Of hard red brick with mullioned-and-transomed
windows and a flèche, dated 1899, extended 1904 and 1974.
Inside, a fine T-shaped auditorium with powerful hammerbeam trusses. Excellent joinery and coloured glass with ivy
leaves.

SYNAGOGUES. There are two on Old Lansdowne Road, which
was the centre of a sizeable Jewish population. The big one is
the SHAAREI RAHAMIM or Gates of Righteousness of
1925–7, by *Delissa Joseph* 'supervised' by *Joseph Sunlight*. Brick
with some Portland stone. Severely Neoclassical with unusual
articulation and details, a spread Venetian window being a
recurring motif. The front is powerfully sculptural, like a great
sphinx with the white stone porch held between its paws.
Equally powerful interior, basilican, with just two giant Ionic
columns on each side to support the galleries and the mon-
strously deep cornice of the clerestory. – BIMA, from which the
Torah is read, and ARK where the Torah scrolls are stored, of
marble and bronze. – Bronze CHANDELIERS.

A few minutes' walk S is the SHA'AREI SEDEK or Gates of
Charity Synagogue, built in 1924–5 by *Pendleton & Dickinson*
for a breakaway congregation of the Shaarei Rahamim (above).
Dr Sharman Kadish reports that it was for the 'oriental Jewish
community'. Set in a charming hidden garden, a modest brick
building with a triple entrance arcade. Slender iron columns
support the gallery.

ISLAMIC CENTRE, Barlow Moor Road. Formerly Albert Park
Wesleyan Chapel, 1883. Red brick with a corner spirelet.

Public Buildings

LIBRARY, Wilmslow Road and Barlow Moor Road. 1915, by the
City Architect *Henry Price*. The result of a gift of £5,000
solicited from Andrew Carnegie by Fletcher Moss of the
Old Parsonage (*see* p. 447). An inventive little building on a
wedge-shaped site, planned around a clerestoried octagon.
Perp, in Portland stone and brick, the Gothic doors and
ironwork well-preserved. Compare Chorlton-cum-Hardy and
Withington libraries (q.v.), each in a different style. Pleasing
GLASS, elaborately leaded including coats of arms, but without
colour.

DIDSBURY COLLEGE, Wilmslow Road. 1840–2. Originally the Wesleyan Theological Institute, now a campus of Manchester Metropolitan University. The Methodists bought the site in 1840 for the training of ministers. There was a handsome house of *c.* 1785. It still exists, encased in the centre of the present main building; its red brick carcase can be seen from the court-yard at the back. The style chosen by the Methodists was Grecian and the architect almost certainly *Richard Lane.* Long ashlar front of eleven bays with a three-storeyed five-bay centre which represents the house. The order, very crisply done with acanthus below and a lotus leaf above, is from the Tower of the Winds as illustrated by Stuart and Revett; it also appears on the Gaskells' house in Plymouth Grove (*see* p. 437). Inside, an elegant oval stair with delicate iron balustrade sweeps through two floors behind a screen of two columns. Lower ashlar-faced wings reach back to make a courtyard behind.

The STUDENTS' UNION immediately S is also of 1842 and very characteristic of *Lane.* It was the chapel until St Paul's was built. Red brick and Gothic with corner turrets like a starved King's College Chapel. On either side symmetrical tutors' residences make a Palladian composition. Wide plaster vault inside. The newer buildings belong to the post-war years as a teacher-training college, and are mostly by the *City Architect's Department,* e.g. the Simon Building of 1957, Hall and Drama Studio 1963–4, Birley Building 1968. Over the road is Broomhurst, a seven-storey hall of residence also by *S. G. Besant Roberts,* City Architect, 1963. It has worn well.

NAZARENE COLLEGE (Wesleyan), Dene Road. Established here in 1958 in two Arts and Crafts houses. The White House, originally whitewashed but no longer white, was built in 1914 by *F. B. Dunkerley.* Symmetrical front and back, of common brick with a stone roof. Pretty stable or garage range, l. Inside, oak wainscoting and barrel-shaped plaster ceilings with naïve-looking Elizabethan motifs. The big music room to the r., lowered so it is entered from above, is given a cross shape by the inglenook and a square bay facing each other midway. The excrescence at the far end was made for an organ. The other house, w, is dated 1927, again of common brick, but asym-metrical, with some half-timbering and a tiled roof. It has a built-in garage. The 1960s residential range on the site of the tennis court is an unusually tactful job for the time.

DIDSBURY SCHOOL (Church of England), Elm Road and Grange Lane. The plain 1880 range, in header bond, has lost its central spire. On the Grange Lane end is a school WAR MEMORIAL. The 1910 range along Elm Road, attractive and inventive Arts and Crafts work by *J. & J. Swarbrick,* is the reason for singling the school out. It has a pleasing miniature quality, e.g. the little Baroque cupola on the tower. On the rainwater hoppers chubby-cheeked children's faces. Tall windows on the street front indicate the hall, which has had a mezzanine inserted at one end. At the back a gently rippling row of mullioned-and-transomed windows lights the class-rooms. But these two parallel blocks are staggered to allow for the tower and the entrance: it is a complicated little building.

PARRS WOOD. The 50 acre (20 hectare) estate was bought by the City Council in 1920 in order to build Kingsway, which terminated here. PARRS WOOD HOUSE, now part of Parrs Wood School (below) is a white stucco mansion with semicircular bays E and S, a semicircular porch with bucranium frieze W and straggling service quarters to the N. Bought in 1795 by Richard Farington, brother of the famous diarist, the artist Joseph Farington, for £6,450. It was probably unfinished then as the sum included just £150 for fittings. Joseph Farington died here in 1821, see St James, above. From 1840 it was the home of James Heald who was prominent in political, Methodist and financial circles.

The house is planned like a poorer man's Heaton Hall (q.v.), and has a similar sequence of principal rooms: apsed entrance hall, a central Imperial stair under a dome, a drawing room with a semicircular bay, and upstairs an oval boudoir, the finest room, but now lost. As at Heaton there is concealed structural ironwork here and there. Joseph Farington recorded (27 May 1798): '[*James*] *Wyatt* I called on this morning he gave me a design for Dick's chimneypiece.' This is probably the caryatid fireplace in the withdrawing room. Handsome contemporary STABLES, burnt out, but reinstated in 2002. The original buildings all suffered theft and damage during the most recent development, which has turned Parrs Wood from a semi-rural educational enclave into a leisure complex – bowling, bingo, multi-screen cinema and health club – occupying enormous sheds along Kingsway. The site of the 1964–5 Parrs Wood School is a desert of car parking. The new PARRS WOOD HIGH SCHOOL, 2001, occupies spectacular £11,000,000 premises by the venerable firm of *Edmund Kirby & Sons* of Liverpool, under a Public Private Partnership between the City Council and Thornfield Developments. The school is red, with swoopy roofs, and concentrated on three floors unlike its spreading predecessor. It has a central top-lit axis aligned with Parrs Wood House, blocking its view over the river valley. Just one part of the older complex is incorporated, Frank Hatton Hostel of 1981.

FIELDEN PARK COLLEGE, Barlow Moor Road. 1969 by the *City Architect's Department*. How busy they were at that period! Classroom block of five storeys with exposed concrete beam-ends; narrow window bands between them at each ceiling level. Low workshop block of dark brick, and an assembly hall linking the two.

Perambulation

A choice of the villas can be seen from the library S along Wilmslow Road to Parrs Wood, returning via Didsbury Park. For the library *see* above. Immediately N are two pairs of Egyptian-style shops by *Mills & Murgatroyd*, 1930, with canted-in window tops and a lotus frieze on the cove. Between them is the tall and narrow RAILWAY INN *c*. 1880. Opposite is the diminutive Rhodes Memorial Clock Tower of 1909. Didsbury station was here.

The village street calls for little comment apart from its phenomenal recent conversion to a café society, with numerous café bars replacing shops. An intruder between the village cottages arrived in 2003, the MARKS & SPENCER FOOD-STORE, with three storeys of apartments above, by *JGSP Design*; dark blue brick, grey paint, brise-soleil. On the same side, the POLICE STATION is dated 1900, strictly symmetrical with a central bay and the arms of the Duchy of Lancaster, i.e. not yet Manchester. At the s end of the village on Dene Road is HOLT HOUSE of 1960 by *H. M. Fairhurst*, a five-story block of flats built for the Sir Edward Holt Trust: almshouses in fact, although not looking like them. Dark brick, punched square windows. Balconies on the ends and triangular bays running the full height of the building at the back. The extensive use of copper is characteristic of the architect.

BROOME HOUSE, opposite, is a modest Georgian house with a central semicircular bow in which the pretty doorway is set, and two more bows, this time angled, added at the ends. Opposite again is LAWNHURST, built for Henry Simon in 1894 by *Salomons & Steinthal*. Red brick and yellow terracotta, very asymmetrical. Terracotta loggias and balconies in Renaissance style. For Broomhurst Hall of Residence, the Methodist church and Didsbury College, *see* above.

THE ELMS is a plain roughcast house in minimal Greek style with corner pilasters and an Ionic portico, almost certainly by *Richard Lane*. Elegant entrance hall with an Ionic screen and a cantilevered stair, top-lit from an oval dome. Slender iron veranda at the back.

Two big pubs at the bend in the road, the Old Cock and the Didsbury, mark the position of the old village green. Behind them is St James (*see* above), a surprising vista of open land and greenery, and the OLD PARSONAGE, Stenner Lane. The gateway to the garden was the doorcase of the Spread Eagle Hotel of 1876 in Corporation Street, Manchester. It was re-erected in 1902 by Fletcher Moss, who lived here from 1865 until his death in 1919 and whose name has become transferred to the immediate area and gardens. No visitor to Didsbury can long escape the name of Fletcher Moss, an 'astonishingly attenuated alderman and absurdly antiquated author' (his words). His writings, with photographs by James Watts of Abney Hall (across the river in Cheshire), are a prime if idiosyncratic source of local information. The house is long, low, roughcast, C17 in origin, and presently almost lost in vegetation. There is faint evidence of a vernacular plan type in the cross-passage passing behind a hearth to long rear passages, and slight evidence for a timber-frame in the single visible purlin which is morticed for a windbrace. The higher rooms at the ends with pyramid roofs, and probably the delicate porch with its tent roof, were added in about 1830. Fletcher Moss added the olde beames, stained glass, panelling, and clumsy twisted balusters. THE CROFT in Fletcher Moss Gardens is an upside-down house with the front door and reception rooms on top; the fall of the land makes this practicable. The interior suggests an early C19 date although the façade is Late Victorian. The well-known gardens are evidence of the favourable microclimate of this S-facing bank of the Mersey.

Further E on Wilmslow Road (N side) THE GROVE, or Watts's Folly, by the S gate to Didsbury College. Of c. 1870, a tight little close of houses in header-bond brick, stone and timber framing with fanciful detailing in the way of buttresses, balconies, bays and colliding arches. It was built by James Watts of Abney Hall (Cheshire).

87 Further E, S side, is THE TOWERS. Set well back in the Business Park of the same name is the grandest of all Manchester Victorian mansions, only comparable with Abney Hall across the river in Cheadle, Cheshire. It was designed by *Thomas Worthington* in 1868–72 for John Edward Taylor, proprietor and editor of the *Manchester Guardian*. Asymmetrical, picturesque, showing the fruits of his travels to the Loire (the dormers) and even, possibly, Prague (the Germano-Gothic spired NW oriel). The kitchen at the l. end with its tall louvred roof perfectly balances the off-centre Germanic tower with the porch below. Of finest orange brick and generous amounts of buff Derbyshire ashlar, a typical Worthington palette. The lively stone carving, including gargoyles, long and thin in the Continental fashion, is by *Thomas Earp* of London. The interior is presently occupied by different offices. The long vestibule and outer and inner halls lead straight back, passing only the staircase in its stone cage on the r. and the long servants' wing on the l., until the family rooms ranged along the sunny garden side are reached. STAINED GLASS on the stair: portrait medallions, flowers, and mottoes extolling the delights of home and the virtues of honest work. An unusual feature, opening off the drawing room, is Mr Taylor's windowless and top-lit private art cabinet.

From 1919 to 1988 The Towers was the Shirley Institute for textile research, with new buildings on a curved axis in front of the house by *H. S. Fairhurst & Son*, 1952 and 1963. Since then many large office blocks have appeared. They are given some unity by their dark green coloration; the architects are *Leach, Rhodes & Walker*. The harbinger at the gate is Worthington's LODGE, with fat columns and a pyramid roof. The electricity substation next to it has taken up the challenge with its own pyramid roof. Immediately behind that is another lodge of the Fairhurst era, with rounded corners and a concrete slab roof. A pleasing little group.

Back on Wilmslow Road, PARK HOUSE at the corner of Didsbury Park is white, Gothic; it could be by *Lane* in his Gothic mode. THE CEDARS is white too, mid-C19, Italianate

and nearly symmetrical, but with an Osborne tower at one end
and an incongruous mansard roof at the other. It is said to be
by *Walters*. The mid–late C19 DIDSBURY LODGE, the last of
the series, is the finest house, built of best orange brick and
creamy ashlar like The Towers, with symmetrical semicircular
bays and an impressive stone porch. The small white LODGE
looks earlier, perhaps early or mid-C19.

From here it is convenient to continue E to Parrs Wood, or to
return via DIDSBURY PARK, where there are several good
early C19 houses on the l. and 1930s housing on the r. At the
N end is PARK END HOUSE, a striking five-bay house of Georgian proportions but with early Victorian trim. PINE HOUSE
is Gothic and white with fancy bargeboards, a companion to
Park House at the other end of the street. From here you can
walk through the recreation ground and along Grange Road
and William Street parallel to Wilmslow Road, regaining the
Library via Warburton Street, noting old and new terraced
cottages on the way. The new ones occupy the site of Heald's
Dairy.

Other Houses

The following housing areas may also be distinguished.

Around PARKFIELD ROAD SOUTH is a leafy region of post-
1880 houses, of a common design with variations. They are all
late C19 and characterized by tricky internal planning, notably
the so-called Cheshire Key. The houses are L-shaped and
interlocked, so that one has a double front and the other a
double back. Examples are Nos. 29–31 and Nos. 33–35 Pine
Road. Nos. 5, 7, 9, and 11 Elm Road are a particularly spectacular group, with much half timberng. *Henry Goldsmith* is a
likely candidate as their designer.

FIELDEN PARK is a compact area of large villas immediately S
of Barlow Moor Road, laid out after Palatine Road intersected
it in 1863. Of those that remain the following may be singled
out:

WOODSTOCK, Barlow Moor Road; now a pub. Built in 1877 for
E. Rogerson by *Asahel P. Bell & George Freeth Roper*. An excellent house of Norman Shaw derivation with tall chimneys, cut
brick decoration, inglenooks and floral stained glass. The front
door, unobtrusive under a heavily bracketed balcony and large
stair window, opens into a generous inner hall, now the bar,
originally with its own fireplace. The interior has been opened
up somewhat but the typical villa plan is clear. A panelled
dining room of masculine character, a lighter, more feminine
drawing room facing S, with a big bay and an inglenook, a
smaller morning room facing E, and the service wing to the N.

FAIR OAK, Spath Road, was given by the Needham family to
the University and used by it, and latterly the Metropolitan
University, as a hall of residence. Yellow brick mansion of
Waterhouse type but not listed in his oeuvre: the totem-pole

faces on the porte cochère suggest *Alfred Darbyshire*. Wide
central hallway lit by a big skylight and by the stair window;
built into the overmantel of its fireplace is a brass clock with
the signs of the zodiac. Good 'artistic' glass of flowers and
birds. CAIRNCROFT, also on Spath Road, was built in 1898–9
by *J. Swarbrick the younger* for John Brockbank; a large house
in Renaissance style of finest red brick.

Also in Fielden Park are GREYSTOKE and ROSEBANK, Palatine
Road. Two houses with a linked history. Greystoke was built
for the Silkenstadt family. It is of yellow brick, formally
Georgian in style, with a fine internal hall from which the stair
rises to a wide upper landing with four Ionic columns and an
oval dome. Rose Bank, much more florid with French
overtones, was intended as a wedding present to their only
daughter Marie Louise. It has an unusual oak-panelled
basement ballroom. Tragedy intervened: her fiancé was killed
in the Boer War and she herself died in 1899. The family then
set up the two houses as a school for domestic service. A
century later this had grown into Greystoke Hall of Residence,
with extra accommodation blocks of 1963 by the *City
Architects*. It closed in 2001. MARIE LOUISE GARDENS of
1904, her memorial, is on the other side of Palatine Road. It
has a small red brick pavilion with a heavy cove and fanciful
ironwork, and a pretty lodge, by *Joshua Cartwright* of Bury.

FALLOWFIELD *see* RUSHOLME, FALLOWFIELD AND
LADYBARN, below

HULME

Until the late C18 this area SE of the Bridgewater Canal was
largely open land. A few Georgian villas sprang up alongside the
main routes and spilled over from Chorlton-on-Medlock. The
boom came later, and by the mid C19 most of the area was
packed with terraces, mainly of by-law housing, laid out on a
gridiron plan. Clearance started in the mid C20 but the 1970s
deck-access flats which followed became a byword for the failures of post-war social housing. For these and their replacements
see below. The 1970s rebuilding imposed a new pattern on the
old grid plan, except on the fringes. Stretford Road, which ran
E–W through the centre, was truncated as part of a policy of separating pedestrians from traffic. This had the effect of isolating
the area, which lost its main shopping street and link with the
centre. The reinstatement of Stretford Road and the integration
of the new housing with the road system were seen as priorities
in the 1994 Masterplan (*see* below), which also provided for a
new park, designed by *Neil Swanson*, just N of Stretford Road.
This area seems destined to become a centre for the community.
The buildings of interest are scattered and the most significant
are churches.

The boundary is on the N side the Centre, on the E side (not including) Cambridge Street, Lower Cambridge Street, Higher Cambridge Street, Lloyd Street North, on the s side (not including) Moss Lane East and West, on the w side the border with Trafford.

Churches

ASCENSION, Stretford Road. By *Maguire & Murray*, 1968–70. Externally of brown concrete blocks and an aluminium roof, formed from a series of overlapping squares built up to provide central lighting. The idea was to provide a composition which looked attractive when viewed from the neighbouring high-rise flats, but these have all been demolished. Inside, the square space is subdivided by an L-shaped gallery for the organ and choir extending along the whole of the (liturgical) w wall and part of the N wall. Attached to the w, offices and a hall expressed as tiered boxes, and attached to the N a rectory.

ST GEORGE, Chester Road. By *Francis Goodwin*, 1826–8. A Commissioners' church in fact, not only in appearance. The original cost was as much as £15,000. Ornate, decidedly pre-archaeological w tower with diminishing pinnacles but big pinnacles on top, seemingly from the example of Hawksmoor's St Michael Cornhill. Porches set diagonally at the NW and SW angles, breaking up the box of the plan effectively, high three-light Perp windows separated by buttresses, two big E pinnacles, and a high polygonal apse. Only the latter is an unexpected motif, but the whole makes a lively and memorable picture. The twenty-year search for a use which would preserve the interior volumes proved fruitless, and the building was converted to flats by *Provan & Makin*, 2000–2. The interior can no longer be read as a whole. Six-bay arcade of slim, soaring clustered Perp piers and an unusually well-lit apse thanks to the tall windows. Plaster tierceron vault. The CHURCHYARD is walled and has entrances with octagonal stone piers decorated with traceried panels.

ST MARY, Upper Moss Lane. By *J. S. Crowther* 1853–8, his first 56 major job after the end of his partnership with Henry Bowman. It has stood through two complete cycles of urban decay, dereliction, destruction and renewal, standing alone amid utter desolation in the 1960s and again in the 1990s. It is a moving tale of survival, but St Mary has not survived as a church, having been declared redundant in 1981, and nor has the fabric come through unscathed.

St Mary's is as much Crowther's manifesto as St Wilfrid (*see* below) was Pugin's, but unlike Pugin he had the wherewithal to do a grand job, and the church is much more prominent. Of golden stone, it is Geometric Dec in style after Lincolnshire exemplars, with a steeple and E and W windows that can genuinely be called soaring. The slender 241 ft (73.5 metre) NW spire is one of s Manchester's major landmarks. Characteristic

Hulme, St George, engraving by J. Harwood, 1832

of Crowther are the stair-turrets with their spirelets flanking the chancel arch, here with an extra pair on the outer walls, the elaborate foliated crosses on every gable, the tracery mullions in two thicknesses, and the crisp carving. The chancel is as wide and as high as the nave, making the footprint a simple rectangle except for the N and S porches. The interior is very tall, with the chancel arch set as high as it would go. It has been horribly divided up. Octagonal piers in the nave, clustered shafts for the chancel. Steep open hammerbeam roof to the nave, with angel musicians clothing the hammerbeams. The chancel roof is single-framed.

No significant furnishings left. – PAINTINGS. Roundels on canvas in the spandrels of the arcades; saints in the chancel, more sophisticated narrative scenes in the nave. – The STAINED GLASS has survived reasonably well but is hard to see. Very fine Jesse tree in the 45 ft (14 metre) high W window, multiple scenes of 1862 in bright colours in the even taller E window. Boldly modelled and coloured figures in the chancel clerestory.

St Mary's gains greatly as townscape from the group of lesser buildings that cluster at its feet. At the E end a SCHOOL and SCHOOLHOUSE, and SE the PARSONAGE, all charming examples of Crowther's domestic Gothic in header-bond brickwork. Across Parsonage Street another SCHOOL, of 1873 with plate tracery, by *John Lowe*.

ST WILFRID (R.C.), Bedford Street. By *A.W.N. Pugin*, 1840–2, and the chief benefactor was Lord Shrewsbury, a faithful Pugin patron. A seminal building in the history of C19 church architecture, yet in striking contrast to the regeneration all around, it is in shockingly poor condition. E.E. style and memorable as a very early case of the archaeologically inspired church. The red brick exterior with lancet windows is low and massive. The parts are separately expressed, with low roofs clustering around the body of the church. The tower, never completed, is NW not W, and this end is impressively sheer, with small openings. The structure rises from a massive stone plinth, and Pugin delights in setting back the wall surfaces and expressing points of tension, such as the corners of the tower, with flat buttresses. It all had to be done cheaply – Pugin's bane. The financial restrictions forced him to concentrate on fundamentals, but he allowed himself the touch of archaeological fun laying his bricks in English bond, not Flemish like the hated Georgians. The S aisle has three separately gabled projections for confessionals (which Pugin so often omitted), added in the 1860s by *E.W. Pugin* who also extended the sacristies.

INTERIOR. A conversion to offices in the 1980s was achieved by inserting a free-standing two-storey unit in the nave so that in theory the volumes could be restored, but the W end has been crudely subdivided and altered and only the chancel is preserved as open space. Six bays of octagonal piers, double-chamfered arches and two-bay N chancel chapel with a round arcade pier. The S chapel has one bay, not two, to avoid over-symmetrical design. Complicated queenpost roof. The chancel arch springs from polygonal shafts. On one side the arcade with stiff-leaf E.E. capitals and original screens to the N Lady chapel, on the other SEDILIA and PISCINA. There is an arcade with cusped heads behind the altar, three lancets above, and finally a wheel window. – PULPIT, set into the S side of the chancel arch and reached by a stair in the thickness of the wall which continues up to the rood loft position, marked by a door. – STATUE, The Virgin, *c.* 1850s. Puginesque pedestal beneath a tall crocketed canopy against the N chancel arch. In the Lady Chapel a Puginesque wooden altar and reredos. – *Pugin's* polygonal FONT has large hinges on the lockable flat lid. – STAINED GLASS. E end. Rose window, *c.* 1880 and three lancets all with good interwar glass by *Harry Clarke & Co.* of Dublin.

For Zion Congregational Church (former), see below. For Christ Church, Lloyd Street North, and the R.C. Church of Divine Mercy, Moss Lane East, *see* Moss Side, below.

Public Buildings

LORETO COLLEGE, Chichester Street. The convent of a teaching order of nuns was established here in 1851 and a school founded at the same time. A co-educational sixth-form college since 1977. The present mixture of relatively undistinguished late C19 and C20 buildings includes a Neo-Georgian extension by *Hill, Sandy & Norris*, 1934. Only the CHAPEL of 1874–6 by *H. Tijou* is of special note. It projects into the courtyard N of the convent buildings. Polychromatic brick, five bays, canted E end, two tall storeys; chapel above with traceried windows, hall below with transomed windows. The chapel has a raised ALTAR and elaborate REREDOS in the form of an ornate carved canopy with niches containing statues. Interior surfaces are richly decorated with tiles and MOSAICS by *L. Oppenheimer*, of 1946 and *c.* 1958.

HULME ARCH, Stretford Road. By *Chris Wilkinson* (of *Wilkinson Eyre Architects*) and *Ove Arup & Partners*, 1997. A mighty angled parabolic arch with tension cables carries a road bridge over a dual carriageway in a cutting (Princess Parkway). In the late C20 fashion of bridges exploiting spectacular engineering techniques for effect. Here the simple form and solidity of the arch was needed for the large scale and hard urban setting. It is intended to act as a visual and physical link with the city centre, from which Hulme had been isolated in the 1970s by Princess Road and the truncation of Stretford Road.

ZION ARTS CENTRE, Stretford New Road. Huge former Congregational church of 1911 (paid for by a bequest of Enriqueta Rylands) on the site of its 1841 predecessor. Converted to an arts centre with a theatre in 1999 by *MBLC*. Red brick with stone dressings and Renaissance detailing, the entrance bay to one side with a wide arch, an elaborate Venetian window over and a gable with a turret. INTERIOR. Originally there was a hall seating eleven hundred. The entrance hall has typical Edwardian trappings – green and white tile-clad walls, original stairs to the r., but a new theatre part bulges into it in a surprising and dramatic manner and new corridors on each side, lit by glazed screens, lead to the theatre entrance. Manipulation of the space around the original features gives glimpses through to upper and lower levels, linking the spaces and knitting old and new together. In the foyer ceiling a circular opening, giving views of the upper section of the new part and cleverly giving expression to the double-height space of the theatre beyond.

HIPPODROME THEATRE (former), Chichester Street. Built 1901 as the Grand Junction Theatre Circus and Floral Hall by *J.J. Alley*, as part of a complex which includes the Playhouse, (*see* below). The Hippodrome specialized in melodrama, the Playhouse in music hall. The exterior has been altered in the mid C20 with cladding etc. leaving little visible evidence of the original, but the interior is said to be splendid, with galleries, boxes and elaborate Rococo plasterwork, balconies supported by ornate iron columns and a proscenium flanked by giant fluted Ionic columns.

PLAYHOUSE THEATRE (former), Warwick Street by *J. J. Alley*, 1902. Part of the Hippodrome complex, above, and similarly disfigured externally. The interior was altered in a conversion to a concert hall in 1990, but it is said to retain the auditorium, galleries and rich plasterwork.

Housing and Other Buildings

The 1969 edition of the *Buildings of England* found Hulme 'the largest redevelopment area of Manchester, many say of England, and some Europe. At the time of writing whole blocks lie waste, streets are blocked and new streets are made.' In the interval between then and now a complete housing scheme has come and gone. 3,284 deck-access homes and fifteen tower blocks were completed in 1971. The centrepiece was four quarter-mile-long six-storey deck-access 'Crescents', constructed to designs by *Wilson & Womersley*. They were named, in an act of hubris, after the architects Charles Barry, John Nash, William Kent and Robert Adam. Problems were apparent from the beginning, and in less than a decade this was one of the most notoriously defective and dysfunctional housing estates in Europe. Demolition began in 1991. All the deck-access housing went, but some nine- and thirteen-storey towers survive amongst the new housing.

In the wake of such spectacular failure the pressure to create successful social housing was intense, and rebuilding was made possible by a successful bid for City Challenge funds in 1991. Resident participation was seen as fundamental, and an extensive consultation programme was set up. *MBLC* drew up a masterplan in 1994. The resulting new housing includes projects by *ECD Architects*, *Ainsley Gommon Wood*, *OMI Architects*, *MBLC*, *PRP* and *Triangle*, and the North British Housing Association. Privately owned and rented accommodation is provided in a mixture of terraces, semi-detached houses and small blocks of flats around new and reinstated streets. They range in style from pastiche through quirky to frankly modern.

The showpiece of the new housing and the most striking individual element is HOMES FOR CHANGE, Chichester Road. By *MBLC*, 1999–2000. The tenants opted to recreate some of the features of the system-built housing the accommodation replaced: deck-access, maisonette type dwellings within a structure of heavy precast concrete. On the other hand, the mixture of different types of living space (fifty units in all), and integration of shops, cafés and studios into the scheme, as well as the more intimate scale, is in direct contrast to what went before. It is a four-sided, four- and six-storey block around a courtyard, looking slightly haphazard, as if it had come together in an *ad hoc*, organic way. There are curving roofs, and cutaway walls in cream brick and render. A tall angled metal-clad stair-tower at the NW corner draws the eye upwards and directs attention to the recessions and projections of the composition. A circular brick drum punctuates the SE corner.

BARRACK STREET. Terraces of brick houses, actually flats, built in the early C20 for NCOs attached to the neighbouring (demolished) barracks of 1817 (*see* Princess Street, below). Each unit has paired doors for access to the upper and lower flat, an unusual configuration in Manchester, though common on Tyneside.

CHESTER ROAD. A principal thoroughfare between Manchester city centre and neighbouring Stretford. A smattering of late C18 and early C19 housing survives. Nos. 2–4, thrown together as one building, red brick and a doorcase with Doric columns. Between Crown Street and Great Jackson Street, two five-bay houses with three-bay pedimented centres. Further W there is a terrace, Nos. 215–219, N side, red brick, two with doorcases with Doric columns.

PRINCESS STREET. No. 10, *c.* 1807, now divided into flats, is the survivor of a pair of houses probably built for the mill-owner John Pooley. To the l. a slightly projecting pedimented entrance bay with an added loggia. The building was later used as part of the Hulme Barracks of 1817, which occupied a neighbouring site to the E and N. Of this no other trace remains except for the houses on Barrack Street (*see* above).

WORSLEY STREET runs parallel to the Bridgewater Canal where new apartment blocks for the developers *Urban Splash* have been created, some from existing industrial buildings, some from scratch. The impetus was the proximity to successful new residential development around the Castlefield Basin to the E (*see* p. 349–51). TIMBER WHARF is a glittering glass-fronted eight-storey apartment block by *Glenn Howells*, 2000–2. On the adjacent site to the E the BOX WORKS apartments, 2000–2, retaining the cream faience front of a 1930s warehouse, with corner towers and continuous horizontal window strips. At the corner of Worsley Street and Egerton Road, W side, the Urban Splash SALES OFFICE looks like a giant insect, an elliptical metal-clad pod on stilts, erected in 1999. It is not certain if it will stay here, though it seems (by 2004) to have become a fixture.

The remaining buildings of interest are too scattered to fit into a walk, so are listed by street.

CHESTER ROAD. The TURVILLE pub, late C19, on a prominent triangular site. Red brick with oversailing eaves, prominent dormers and arcaded upper windows.

CITY ROAD. No. 204 is a doctor's surgery by *Hodder Associates*, 1996. Two-storeyed, brick, with a recessed central entrance and glass-block window strips, topped by a gull-wing roof which appears to hover above. Issues of security were paramount, but the design manages to look welcoming rather than defensive.

EGERTON STREET, E side, beside the Bridgewater Canal. Former flour mill by *William Waddington*, 1896. Italianate, red brick with a tower and campanile chimney. Integral canal basin with loading facilities. From the w side of the street a surviving part of HULME LOCKS can be seen, where a branch divides from the main canal and runs alongside the railway viaduct. The locks opened in 1838, creating a direct link between the canal and the River Irwell, which connected the canal system with the Port of Liverpool. For the railway viaduct, *see* Castlefield, p. 352.

ELLESMERE STREET runs parallel to Chester Road, N side. A number of late C19 and early C20 industrial buildings survive on the N side. One of the most prominent, ALBERT MILL at the w corner of Hulme Hall Road, is dated 1869. Red brick with stone dressings and ranks of segmental headed windows. Cast-iron column and timber floor construction, towers with fireproof staircases, privies and hoists.

LADYBARN *see* RUSHOLME, FALLOWFIELD AND LADYBARN, below

MANCHESTER INTERNATIONAL AIRPORT

In 1929–30 Britain's first municipal airfield operated briefly at Rackhouse Farm, Wythenshawe. In 1930 Barton (*see* p. 557) was selected for an aerodrome, but it proved fog-prone, so in 1935 the City bought a site out at Ringway for £80,000. The airport has grown continuously since then and is now the third largest in the country.

Ringway Airport, as it is still often called, opened in 1938. The original terminal, control tower and hangar, have all gone. They were by the City Architect *G. Noel Hill*, with *Norman Dawbarn*; the architect on the job was *Leslie Penman*. The airport was almost immediately overtaken by war, although it was never formally requisitioned. 1941 saw the first flight of the Lancaster bomber, the most famous of several Ringway prototypes. Wartime developments gave the airport a flying start in 1945, when the *City of Manchester Plan* predicted that it would be as important to the city as the Ship Canal had been.

In 1957–62 a new terminal and control tower were built along the old Ringway Road, whose wiggly line thus determines the geometry of the whole airport. This building, repeatedly extended and altered, is today's Terminal 1. It was extended in 1969–74 with a multi-storey car park on the landside, a new front on the airside, and the addition of Pier C. In 1984–6 the International Departures Lounge (IDLEX) was added, with an operations tower on top, and the Pier C satellite extension built. In 1989 the present Terminal 1 was extended again to make a domestic terminal. All the work thus far was by the *City Architects*, but henceforth it was contracted out. In 1988–93 Terminal 2 was built. Meanwhile Terminal 1 received another new airside front. Both the airside additions are jettied out on columns over the old Ringway Road, which still exists underneath, complete with kerbs and pavements. In 1998 the domestic terminal was extended further and is now called Terminal 3, and the space between IDLEX and Pier C was infilled, all by *Nicholas Grimshaw & Partners*.

The airport outgrew its site in 1982 when the main runway was extended out and over the Wilmslow–Altrincham Road. The building of a second runway in 1997–2001 lancing out SW into Cheshire towards Mobberley and Tatton Park, was highly controversial. Tatton is less than the length of the runway away.

And now a description.* BUILDING 217 (used to store archives and museum collections) by the roundabout at the end of Ringway Road, the former Officers' Mess of 1941, is the only accessible building left from the war years (there are also a couple of hangars). Of buff brick with pinky brick trim, concrete dressings, and steel windows, all surprisingly good in quality.

TERMINAL 1. Originally by the City Architects *L. C. Howitt* then *G. Besant Roberts*, with interiors by *James Cubitt*, 1957–62. It has been swallowed up by a multi-storey car park with ramps of 1989 on the land side and two successive new frontages on the airside. The lower part of the control tower, now set well back, is all that can readily be seen of the first exterior, but the full-height Departures Hall running N–S across the building is still the principal interior space. Two original fittings remain, both resited: a bronze SCULPTURE of a flying man, commemorating Alcock and Brown's transatlantic flight of 1919 by *Elisabeth Frink* now in the retail area of Departures, and a coloured glass screen by *Margaret Traherne* in memory of the wartime Parachute Training School symbolizing a parachute jump, is in the prayer room. At the land end of this hall a shallow ramp indicates the 1974 – or is it 1984? – join. At the airside end a double line of columns indicates the junction of the 1962 and 1974 fronts and then we are in a long white airy space with a wave roof overlooking the tarmac. This is the *Grimshaw* addition of 1998.

High level tubular WALKWAYS connect Terminal 1 to Terminal 2 via the railway station and the Radisson Hotel, giving good views around.

TERMINAL 2 is by *Scott, Brownrigg & Turner*, 1988–93, and very similar to their Terminal 4 at Heathrow of 1982–6. It is a great

---

* A large model of the airport, mounted vertically, is in the foyer of Olympic House (*see* p. 459). It is kept up to date and indicates future developments.

contrast to Terminal 1; a single coherent design, cool and grey with great uncluttered spaces. Even so it is only two-thirds built, incomplete at the NW end. What the building has gained over Terminal 1 in logic, with well-defined functional zones and its principal axes marked out by glass roofs, it has lost in excitement. It is designed for calm; a mood-controller.

TERMINAL 3, for domestic and British Airways flights, is tighter and more intimate in scale than the others. It evolved as an extension of Terminal 1 and is confusing in its geometry. The 1989 section with brown glass and stove enamel is by the *City Architects*. The 1998 section, all white within, all corrugated metal and green glass without, is by *Grimshaw*.

RAILWAY STATION, 1993 by *Austin-Smith:Lord*. Although modest in size, it belongs to an international breed of excitingly sculptural recent stations such as Lille and Lyon. Ironically it is the only structure at Manchester Airport that attempts to symbolize the romance of flight. From a point at the platform end the roof rises on a take-off trajectory, broadening out at the same time, to finish at a wide semicircle of glass under a sharp peak. It rises in three steps, over the platform, the booking hall and the high level approaches. The architects have made the most of the spatial possibilities of the descent from the high-level walkway entrances down to the foyer and the platforms. Extensions were under way in 2003; not an easy building to extend without spoiling it. [125]

SAS RADISSON HOTEL. 1996, by *Patrick Davies*. The building as executed is considerably different from his design. Cleverly built at an angle of the high-level walkway, which gave rise to the kink in the building. Silver-grey bedroom floors above this level, buff rock-faced offices below, a wide and complex atrium connecting these with the walkway entry. A high-level observatory lounge echoes the airport control tower.

COMMONWEALTH HOUSE. 1997, by *Austin-Smith:Lord*. Another cool silver-grey building with green glass and a brise-soleil, kinked in the middle like the Radisson hotel.

OLYMPIC HOUSE. Offices by *Leach, Rhodes & Walker*. A shallow S-shape, i.e. kinked twice, with pointed ends, forming a coherent group with the last two, in the model at any rate, or from the air. Elegant, cool and spare except for the superfluous stone-faced triumphal arch motif over the entrance.

Finally the AIRPORT HOTEL on Ringway Road is a link with the early days. Built *c.* 1938 for Bell & Co. who had an architect called *Mr Swan*. Big hipped roof with tapered chimneys. Wide white façade, understated except for an incongruous Gothic door surround. When the wind is right planes wheel round for take-off immediately outside the pub garden; a popular place to recapture the romance of flight without actually flying.

ULLERSWOOD. 1.2 m. SW of Manchester Airport. C12 earthwork castle with a sizeable motte, or mound, capped by a late C20 house and part-covered by trees.

MOSS SIDE

Moss Side became built up with by-law housing from the mid C19. The township is divided by the busy Princess Road, with a 1970s low-rise estate to the W and C19 terraced housing to the E. The boundaries are: on the N side (including) Moss Lane East and Moss Lane West, E (including) Lloyd Street South and Upper Lloyd Street, S, Demesne Road and W (excluding) Withington Road.

CHRISTCHURCH. On the corner of Monton Street and Lloyd Street North. By *W. Cecil Hardisty*, 1899–1904, on the site of an C18 proprietary chapel. The design was exhibited in 1897. His best job in Manchester. Arts and Crafts Perp style, red brick with red sandstone dressings and chequering. Tracery with over-much cusping. Display is concentrated on the W front, where a bellcote sits roguishly on one shank of the gable. Elaborate porch with traceried parapet and octagonal pinnacles; aisles. Four-bay nave arcades of octagonal columns

Moss Side, Christchurch, from *The Builder*, 1898

without capitals, barrel roof, w gallery. Most of the original furnishings have gone. – Large REREDOS by *G.F. Bodley*, brought here from his church of St Edward, Holbeck, Leeds, 1903–4, demolished in 1981. Gilded and painted wooden triptych with figures beneath Gothic canopies. N Chapel: ALTAR, also by *Bodley* and from St Edward; REREDOS by *J. Harold Gibbons* from St John, Werneth, Oldham (*see* p. 545). – FONT, polygonal, with marble shafts. By *Walter Tapper*, from St Erkenwald, Southend. – ORGAN CASE by *J. Oldrid Scott*, from St Peter, Northampton. – BENCHES in the nave by *E.W. Pugin* from St Francis, Gorton (q.v.).

ST CRISPIN, Claremont Road. By *Hubert Worthington*, 1927–30. Brick, Romanesque, unfinished and altered in the late C20. Plain Neo-Georgian VICARAGE to the S, also by *Worthington*, 1926.

R.C. CHURCH OF DIVINE MERCY (Polish), Moss Lane East and Lloyd Road. Former Methodist chapel, *c.* 1875. Yellow sandstone with red sandstone dressings, three-bay arcaded entrance front, NW tower, very shallow transepts. Horseshoe gallery with cast-iron columns. – Brightly coloured STAINED GLASS, late C20, put in by the Polish church.

CHURCH OF GOD (former Nonconformist chapel), Raby Street. *c.* 1880, yellow sandstone, Dec. SW tower and spire, small transepts, shallow apsidal chancel, school attached at the E end. – REREDOS with Decalogue and painted panels of 1908 showing mothers and miraculous babies from the Old and New Testaments. – STAINED GLASS. E windows by *E. Wright*, 1947.

MILLENNIUM POWERHOUSE CENTRE, Raby Street. Community and youth centre. By *MBLC*, completed 1999. One- and two-storey rendered ranges in bright colours housing offices, café, etc. around a dramatic hall with an elliptical roof clad in metal. The hall bulges out on the N side, supported by angled struts. It is designed to allow the space to be extended into the adjacent drama area, which can in turn be opened into an attractive courtyard.

TRAM DEPOT (former), Princess Road. 1909, probably by the *City Architect's Department*. Red brick with stone dressings, made memorable by the big monumental corner block with a square flat-topped clock tower and a huge blocked archway. Office range etc. r., otherwise brick sheds.

HYDES' ANVIL BREWERY, Moss Lane West. Founded 1861 for Greatorex brothers as Queen's Brewery, occupied by Hydes' Brewery since 1899. A remarkably complete and relatively unaltered ensemble, which remains in use. One- and two-storey brick buildings, grouped around a courtyard entered through ornate gate piers with a pedimented pedestrian entrance and office range to the l., all with painted stone dressings. Facing the entrance a range with a central gable with a clock and finial. Other ranges with rooftop louvres.

LAGER FACTORY, Princess Road. Mid–late C20, on the site of the C19 Albert Brewery. The huge silos dominate the surrounding area.

The following HOUSES merit attention. ALMSHOUSES, Raby Street. By *John Lowe*, dated 1876, a rather late date for a new foundation of this sort. Erected by John Robinson in memory of his sister. Attractive E-shaped block of six houses, Tudor style in red brick and terracotta dressings. The remains of early C19 stucco TERRACES survive on Moss Lane East: Nos. 466–468, with paired porches with pilasters and wreaths in the frieze; nearby Nos. 366–372, with porches with Doric columns *in antis*.

ALEXANDRA PARK, Princess Road. Land was acquired by Manchester Corporation in 1868 and the park was opened in 1870. The 56-acre (23-hectare) park was designed by *Alexander Gordon Hennell* of London to accommodate large promenading crowds. At the NE entrance a picturesque red brick LODGE with a clock tower, by *Alfred Darbyshire*, 1868. A little to the SW is a cast-iron DRINKING FOUNTAIN erected by the Band of Hope (a temperance organization) in 1876. A long raised terrace runs along the N side of the park, and a lime avenue runs along the W perimeter. There is a lake in the SW corner.

NORTHENDEN

Northenden was in Cheshire until 1931 when it was incorporated into the City of Manchester, which had acquired the area and open land to the S for the garden suburb of Wythenshawe (*see* below) in 1926. The village was round the church above the ford and mill. Narrow lanes, many pubs and distressingly few old houses testify to that. PALATINE ROAD was created in 1862, forming a direct link via Withington to Manchester, to the N. In its wake came Victorian terraces, often exhibiting fancy brickwork in indigestible colours. A further overlay came in 1926 when 142 council houses were built by Manchester on KENWORTHY LANE, the only ones allowed by Bucklow RDC after purchase of the land but before incorporation in 1931. Then came two parades of shops with maisonettes above on Palatine Road, and much typical housing in the further reaches. The shops, one block Neo-Georgian of the 1930s and the other of the 1950s, remain viable, whereas in the one-dimensional world of Wythenshawe they have mostly failed.

ST WILFRID, Ford Lane. In a large churchyard overlooked by the Georgian former rectory. It looks like a late medieval Cheshire church, but slightly too good to be true. The explanation is that *J. S. Crowther*, commissioned to repair the old church in 1872, found 'no foundations at all!! except the tower, the fabric having been built on the surface of the ground!' So he rebuilt it, except for the Perp tower, in 1873–6. The new church, of Alderley Edge stone, is a copy of the old but tidied

Northenden, St Wilfrid, detail of screen, drawn by J. P. Earwaker, 1877

up and improved according to Victorian precepts. The clerestory is made taller and more decorative, the chancel chapel windows more conventionally grouped and cusped, and the s porch much prettier. Crowther introduced two octagonal stair-turrets in the outer walls between aisles and chancel chapels, a favourite motif, and inhabited string courses. He prepared a new tower design too, based on the old but again prettier and taller, but in the end had to make do with renewing most of the detail on the medieval one. Its six bells, with jolly C18 inscriptions, are hung diagonally, perhaps indicating longstanding doubts about the foundations. The interior presents much the same picture of a late medieval church corrected according to Victorian principles. Typical of Crowther are the angel musicians of the chancel roof, after the admired angel consort of Manchester Cathedral, the deep yellow glass of the clerestory windows, and numerous details from the Gothic sink in the vestry to the snake-headed bolts of the doors.

Some of the medieval SCREENS have survived. – In the s chapel, which was endowed in 1527, a screen carries an inscription from Psalm 50 interrupted by a three-faced head.* Above the doorway are a pair of tumblers carrying a goad and a flail, and a monkey sitting on a drum. The tumblers can be read in two ways, so that they really do seem to tumble. The N chapel screen is C16 as well, but both show signs of rejigging. – STALLS in the chancel and s chapel by *Crowther*, with good poppyheads. – COMMUNION RAIL. – COMMUNION TABLE in the s chapel. Jacobean. – FONT. C18 with a baluster

---

*The rector points out a similar medieval head on the E face of the tower.

stem and minute bowl, set on a medieval base. – STAINED
GLASS. A full set, mostly given by the Tattons of Wythenshawe
Hall or the Watkins of Rose Hill. E by *Wailes c.* 1850, so presumably saved, with its tracery, from the old church. s chapel
E by *Hughes* of London; the two side windows early *Kempe*. At
the W end of the N aisle is a grungy window by *Percy Bacon*,
1896. In the vestry a charming Te Deum signed *Humphries,
Jackson & Ambler* of Manchester, 1924, with the appropriate
chant by Woodward in the key of D. – MONUMENTS. A
number of good wall tablets: s chapel, Thomas Worthington of
Sharston †1856 and his parents by *M. W. Johnson*; an angel
figure weeps over their three coffins. N chapel, Thomas and
Mary Tatton both †1827. Above it a tablet to Robert Tatton
†1689, with two uncouth putti; to William Egerton †1806, son
of William Tatton, with a woman lying on a sarcophagus, by
J. Bacon Jun. On the vestry wall Mary †1784, second wife of
William Egerton of Wythenshawe and Tatton; a fine urn draped
with flower garlands.

ST HILDA (R.C.), Kenworthy Lane. Designed and built in 1968
by *Lanner Ltd* of Wakefield. Two half-octagons with pyramid
roofs, one slightly bigger than the other, interlock in such a
way as to admit light at the join. The structure is of elbowed
laminated timbers. There are ten members, not eight; their
uneven spacing and unequal sizes are disconcerting and so is
the extraordinary shaped piece of steel required to hold them
together at the apex. The altar, as is implied by the direction-
ality of the lighting, is not central. – PAINTING. St Hilda offers
her church in Northenden, by *S. J. Proudfoot*, 1980. The first
church was built in 1904 as a private venture by Mrs Zeba
Ward of Cringlewood, Yew Tree Lane, and offered to the
Bishop of Chester. When he refused her nephew as incumbent
it went to the Catholic church instead.

WESLEYAN CHAPEL, Palatine Road. 1876–7, by *H. F. Slater*. T-
shaped, Gothic, brick. The front has generous stone dressings
and the brick is laid in a header bond. At the sides moulded
brick is substituted for stone and the bond is English garden
wall.

ASSEMBLY HALL OF JEHOVAH'S WITNESSES, Palatine Road.
It was the FORUM CINEMA of 1935 by *Charles Hartley*, the
major place of entertainment for Wythenshawe-dwellers.
Prominently sited, with a show front at one end and a fly tower
at the other. The windowless side walls are articulated by a
good deal of advance and retreat. Five double entrance doors
under a canopy with five windows above, the centre three with
canted heads. In the foyer are paired sweeping staircases and
a blue and gold terrazzo floor patterned like waves. The auditorium has a single deep balcony and a ridged segmental
ceiling. The side walls narrow in towards the stage, with multicoloured grilles representing the organ pipes behind. The
stage itself is framed by a triple wave of fat acanthus, but at
the audience end of the organ grilles are a pair of unfinished
squared-off Ionic pilasters suggesting a displaced proscenium

arch. A tank for baptism by immersion has been introduced in front of the stage.

AIRPORT HOTEL, Palatine Road, 1971. A landmark from Princess Parkway. No-nonsense design. Eight-storey bedroom block raised on piloti with the usual gubbins on the roof hidden by vertical concrete slatting. Reception and dining in a low horizontal block at right angles.

TATTON ARMS, Boat Lane. By *James Redford*, 1874. 'The banks of the river became a busy bustling Bacchanalium, where boating men and beanfeasters made boisterous revels'. So Fletcher Moss (*see* Didsbury) recalled in 1920. The revels continued well into the C20 but are, alas, no more. Redford's pub is determinedly jolly, with raised diapering and polychromy in the brickwork, timber framing and fancy bargeboards for the gables and stone for the Gothic door surround, but the lumpish extension to the l. and the bleak car park have dampened its frivolity. The STABLE at the back, although now painted white, exhibits even trickier brickwork – see the way the end buttresses with their tumblehomes run into the two oriel windows. It is fully equipped as a theatre.

The WEIR in the once infamously polluted River Mersey was rebuilt in 2002 with a salmon ladder.

ROSE HILL, Longley Lane. The home of Sir Edward Watkin (1819–1901), railway king and cross-channel visionary. The house, pointlessly re-named ASHLEY GRANGE, was being converted in 2003 to flats. By that time its park had been covered in little houses, its terraced gardens wrecked; even the Mersey which it overlooked has been diverted. Boldly rusticated perimeter WALL, its gatepiers moved further apart *c.* 1995 to take the modern roadway. The house bought by Absolom Watkin in 1832, with chequered Flemish bond brickwork, appears to be substantially preserved underneath his son's alterations. Grafted on the front is a single-storey loggia of the finest ashlar with Doric pilasters of exaggerated entasis framing a double doorway. More additions in similar style, with toy battlements, appear elsewhere. The interiors were especially fine. Absolom Watkin is commemorated by a massive stone carved with appropriate biblical texts, at the top of the scarp. Near the gates, on Watkin's Cheshire Lines railway, an extremely tall signal box of the 1870s peers over the Longley Lane overbridge.

BEECH HOUSE, Yew Tree Lane (w of the motorway; accessible by footbridge, or from Sale Road, Wythenshawe). Plain Victorian house with bays, disfigured by replacement windows and nondescript additions. It was the late C19 home of Thomas Lings, comptroller of the J. S. Crowther restoration of the Cathedral and rebuilding of St Wilfrid, Northenden. In the garden are many carved stones. The newer-looking ones match the bay of the Cathedral knocked out when the Fraser Chapel was built in 1890. Old photographs show a re-erected doorway, very like that of Langley's s porch at Middleton (q.v.). Was it from St Wilfrid's, or the Cathedral?

PLATT HALL *see* RUSHOLME, FALLOWFIELD
AND LADYBARN, below

RINGWAY *see* MANCHESTER INTERNATIONAL
AIRPORT, above

RUSHOLME, FALLOWFIELD AND LADYBARN

This area was almost completely rural until the early–mid C19 when it became fashionable for villa residences, away from noise and industry in town but within easy reach via the busy main road. Some were erected in groups as a speculation, the most ambitious scheme being Victoria Park, opened in 1837. Proximity to the University of Manchester (see p. 425) made the area popular for halls of residence, starting in the late C19, often reusing existing houses, and continuing with new student accommodation through to the C21. The boundary is on the N side (not including) Hathersage Road and Plymouth Grove, on the E side (not including) Birch Lane, Dickenson Road, Birchfields Road, Kingsway, on the S side (including) Mauldeth Road, on the W side (including) Yew Tree Road, Claremont Road, Parkfield Street, Moss Lane East.

Places of Worship

HOLY INNOCENTS AND ST JAMES. Wilbraham Road, Fallowfield. 1870–2 by *Price & Linklater*. In an indigestible colour combination of yellow sandstone with red sandstone dressings, with Geometrical window tracery. Aisles, S porch, S chapel. Square detached SE tower with paired bell-openings and corner pinnacles, octagonal spire with details that are personal and effective. Simply treated windows apart from those to the rounded apse, which have linked crocketed moulds. The INTERIOR was reordered 1983–4 by the *Ellis Williams Partnership*. W end altar, subdivided E end. Five-bay arcade of octagonal red sandstone piers, high chancel arch, three-bay chancel, arch-braced timber roof. Almost all the furnishings have been removed. – CRUCIFIX by *W. D. Caröe*, probably early C20, is mounted on the wall behind the altar (brought from St Mary's Home, Alton, Staffs). – STAINED GLASS. An extensive scheme mostly of the 1890s, mostly by *Lavers & Westlake*.

HOLY INNOCENTS SCHOOL (former), E of the church. Now a pub. By *F. H. Oldham*, 1882, using the same rather strident combination of red and yellow sandstone as the church, and the same details of the tracery. Symmetrical, with low gabled bays flanking a long range with very tall gabled dormers which have transomed windows with traceried heads.

HOLY TRINITY, Platt Lane, Rusholme. 1845–6 by *Edmund Sharpe*. A remarkable church with an interesting history. It was built for Thomas Carrill Worsley of Platt Hall (*see* below). The Worsley family chapel had been Platt Chapel (*see* below), which moved to a Unitarian position in the early C19. The idea for a new Anglican church was given impetus by the fact that in 1844 Mr Anson of Birch Hall decided to build St James (*see* below). Worsley, who hoped to complete first, stole a march on his rival by consecrating his church before it was finished. The dedication was a riposte to the Unitarian standpoint.

Considering his unrivalled connoisseurship of the Dec style, here Sharpe is curiously loose in his use of historical authority. The majority of the motifs are of *c.* 1300, but there are ogee details too, and the bell-openings of the SW steeple have Geometrical tracery. But the most interesting thing is that Sharpe used yellow terracotta as his facing material, throughout and inside as well as outside. Holy Trinity was the second of Sharpe's terracotta churches. On the circumstances of his foray into building 'pot churches' as they were disrespectfully called, *see* St Stephen, Lever Bridge, p. 157. Thomas Penson had already started using the material for interior arcading and rib-vaulting at Christ Church, Welshpool, 1839–44 and for exterior openings a year later at St Agatha, Llanymynech, Shropshire. The blocks at Holy Trinity are done in such a way as to simulate the mason's tooling, and Sharpe was proud of the fact that they were often mistaken for stone. *The Ecclesiologist* rejected terracotta as unworthy; criticism for using the material to imitate another would not come until later, with dissemination of the ideas of Ruskin and his followers. Sharpe learnt from mistakes made at Lever Bridge and reduced the size of the mouldings and ensured that the larger pieces were made hollow and then filled with concrete. John Fletcher supplied the terracotta, as at Lever Bridge, but there was a dispute about the costs. Another supplier was used for the spire, whose terracotta proved to be inferior and it had to be rebuilt in 1912. Long, low chancel and aisles, W porch and S porch in the tower, both, capitals and all, of terracotta. The top of the tower is handsomely if playfully made an octagon, and the octagon is held up by flying buttresses. The spire follows.

INTERIOR. Even the piers are terracotta. They are quatrefoils with foliated caps of four different designs, and the bays are wide so the two clerestory windows correspond to one bay. Arch-braced timber roofs of great complexity. Terracotta arcading in the chancel arch, two-bay chancel with a five-light E window. – PEWS have traceried details to the bench ends in terracotta, painted to look like pitch pine. – FONT. Stone, octagonal bowl with quatrefoils. – STAINED GLASS. In the chancel memorials to the Carrill Worsley family of *c.* 1849–50. N aisle, a window of 1871 by *Lavers, Barraud & Westlake.* – MONUMENT. In the N aisle, a pretty tile plaque in Burne-Jones style. Sophie Ellen Johnson †1924.

CHURCH HALL. Attached to the E end. 1966–7 by *Leach, Rhodes & Walker.* Brick, with angled windows to the churchyard. Although it is low it impedes the view of the church from Platt Hall and park (*see* below).

ST CHRYSOSTOM, Anson Road, Victoria Park. 1874–7 by *G. T. Redmayne.* A church had been planned here from the first, indicated on Lane's Victoria Park plan (*see* below). E.E., of yellow sandstone. Nave and chancel treated as one, aisles with lancets, conical tower at the (liturgical) E corner of the N aisle. W end with a nicely detailed entrance porch with a canopy over containing a statue of St John Chrysostom. Polygonal apse, five-bay arcade of round piers, extended to seven bays SE side to accommodate the two-bay Anson chapel. All the furnishings and the roof date from rebuilding by *John Ely* after a fire in 1904. – REREDOS. Good late C20 painting by *Graeme Willson*. – STAINED GLASS. A fine scheme by *Burlison & Grylls*, including the Doctors of the Church, English saints and many First World War memorials. Another memorial window in the chapel is by *Walter J. Pearce*.

ST CHAD, Mauldeth Road, Ladybarn. 1905–7 by *W. Cecil Hardisty*. His three Manchester churches (Christchurch, Moss Side, p. 460 and St Philip, Gorton, p. 371 are the others) are all different, and this is the least interesting externally. Low, red brick and stone dressings, windows with reticulated tracery, polygonal baptistery projection at the W end. The projected NW tower was never built. Well lit interior, thanks to the generous three-light clerestory. Five-bay nave arcades, octagonal brick piers with stone banding, the walls above of chequered brick and stone. High chancel arch, chancel roof with large carved angels. – Beautifully carved ROOD designed by *Hardisty* in 1919. – PULPIT. Oak with fine openwork carving and a stone base, probably also by Hardisty. Baptistery with a carved stone PANEL over. – RELIEF over the vestry door, St Chad, given by the architect. – STAINED GLASS. Several good aisle windows by *Burlison & Grylls*. S aisle, St Hilda and Caedmon by *Geoffrey Webb*, 1944, and a war memorial window by *Karl Parsons*, 1916.

ST JAMES, Danes Road, Rusholme. 1845–6 by *J.M. Derick* for Mr Anson of Birch Hall. Converted to an old people's home in the 1980s, now used as a social services centre. The S aisle lost its roof in the conversion. A building with archaeological ambition. The exterior is dignified, with much bare wall, even if it is not exciting. E.E., SW tower with broach spire, windows with plate tracery. The aisles have paired lancets and the clerestory an arcade of closely set lancets in triplets, flanked by blind arches. The Anson Chapel, S, was added in similar style in 1907 by *Isaac Taylor*. (The interior has been subdivided. Five-bay arcades with round piers, chancel arch and proper chancel. Rose window, and below three pointed lancets with detached inner shafting.) For the vicarage *see* Manchester Grammar School, below.

ST EDWARD (R.C.), Thurloe Street. 1860–1 by *E.W. Pugin*. Small, sober exterior of yellow sandstone rubble, nave with low aisles, apse, stump of an unexecuted SW tower. Details of *c.* 1300, circular foiled clerestory windows. (Inside, short, polished granite columns with summary capitals typical of E.W. Pugin.)

METHODIST CHAPEL (former), No. 188 Ladybarn Lane, Ladybarn. Gabled to the street with a stone plaque inscribed

MOUNT PLEASANT 1862. Red brick, three storeys and quite austere, with round-headed windows. This was probably the institution which aimed, according to a writer in 1888, to 'lighten the sodden mass of intemperance this place has become'.

PLATT CHAPEL (former), Wilmslow Road, Rusholme. Now used by a club. Rebuilt in 1790 and remodelled in 1874–6. A Dissenting chapel which had become Unitarian by the early C19. The first building was put up in 1699 on land donated by Ralph Worsley of nearby Platt Hall (*see* below). Brick with stone dressings. Three-bay arcade of windows, the entrance originally in the southernmost bay. Round-headed windows set in blind arches recall a motif used at Platt Hall, and the whole design superficially resembles John Carr's Farnley Chapel, Leeds of 1761. Centrally placed wing on the W side, giving a T-shaped plan. C19 alterations included replacement of the hipped roof with end gables, remodelling of the S end with a new entrance and bellcote, and the creation of an apse instead of a vestry at the N end. The INTERIOR has largely been stripped out. The exposed roof timbers and S (liturgical W) gallery are of 1874–6, when the interior was re-orientated on the N apse instead of facing a table opposite the wing. Scribed stucco walls; tall arch to the central wing, which is said to have accommodated the Worsley family pew.

The GRAVEYARD was truncated in the late C19 but two early C18 slabs with crude skulls and crossbones survive S of the chapel.

HULME HALL CHAPEL. *See* Victoria Park, p. 480.

FIRST CHURCH OF CHRIST, SCIENTIST (former), Daisy Bank 78
Road, Victoria Park. 1903–4 by *Edgar Wood* with additions mainly of 1905–7.* The first purpose-built church for the Christian Scientists in Britain and the second in Europe. The church was founded by Mary Baker Eddy in America in 1879, and established in Manchester through the efforts of Lady Victoria Alexandrina Murray. The basic requirement was a main space for worship, and another for a reading room. Services lacked ritual and symbolism, so the way was clear for something new and free from precedent. The result was one of the most original buildings of that time in England or indeed anywhere. 'One would be tempted to call the style Expressionist, if the date were 1923 and not 1903' was Pevsner's comment. Of brick, white rendering and some stone. The church has a steep gable with a stone chimneystack up the top and beyond it. Below the place where that stack starts is an extremely long round-headed window, extending l. and r. below the springing of the arch into two very small oblong two-light windows. It is reminiscent of a cross, and that must have been deliber-

---

* This account has benefited in many ways from John H. G. Archer's study, 'Edgar Wood and The First Church of Christ, Scientist, Manchester, a Record and Evaluation', 2003.

ate. The entrance is deeply recessed, beneath a semicircular arch of cut bricks which springs from splayed masonry reveals. Two wings project diagonally from that centre, a motif also used by E. S. Prior (cf. The Barn, Exmouth). One of them was the reading room, the other the hall. The reading room has to the forecourt a canted bay window, its gable broken round the angle of the canted sides. Between the hall range and the church front finally is a fat, short round tower with a conical roof, lower than the church gable. This part, in particular, recalls motifs used by Rennie Mackintosh. Along the w side of the church is a porte cochère with a little dome. The church is lit by gabled dormers, and the courtyard is entered via an arched gateway with a steep gable and oriel window. Pevsner in 1969 commented 'One can hardly drive originality and wilfulness farther, unless one is called Gaudi.'

The plan is a development of Wood's Wesleyan church and school on Long Street, Middleton (see p. 512), where the buildings occupy three sides of a courtyard with a screen closing the other side, but lack of space and a reduced budget led to modifications of the early designs and development of Wood's ideas. In 1905 vestries and a board room were added in a wing to the rear of the church. At the same time a rectangular apse and transepts were added.

The INTERIOR is as individual and non-historicist as the exterior. First a vestibule with access to the wings, and doors to the church. A bright, cool space with an open timber roof with paired trusses between high dormers. At first sight the absence of mouldings to the openings and consequent planar effect make the roof timbers appear out of place, as if they were an anachronism. There are aisles, and low round-arched arcades. The transepts and apse have vaults of reinforced concrete and are divided from the main space by semicircular arches. The two focal points are the rostrum in the apse with a marble REREDOS of different types of marble in green, buff, red and white with narrow borders of black and white marble. Tall panels flank a central panel with an oval of white marble with the Christian Science emblem, in bas-relief. The inset bronze lettering above and the inscriptions on the walls (from the Bible and the works of Mary Baker Eddy), have been removed. Opposite the main entrance has a double door flanked by marble panels. This end is dominated by the organ loft with a canted central bay and a painted panelled front with small designs, including Latin and Greek crosses. Above is a superb ORGAN SCREEN in the form of a *mushrabiyya*, an Arabic openwork screen. This screens the pipes and forms a highly decorative passage, introducing counterpoint to the recession of spaces provided by the balcony-like front to the loft and the inner space it partially encloses. Other FURNISHINGS have largely been lost.*

---

* Ceremonial chairs designed by Wood and some of the stained glass by *Benjamin Nelson* are preserved in the Whitworth Art Gallery.

The wing with the public reading room is tunnel-vaulted, with a fireplace in the N wall flanked by small windows. Above it is a damaged plaque, a copy of a panel by Ghiberti on the doors of the Baptistery at the Duomo at Florence. Private rooms and offices occupied the other wing, and the board room is in the N wing. It has a notable chimneypiece with a marble surround and green-glazed oblong tiles set end-on within the frame.

The building is Edgar Wood's *chef d'œuvre*, and a work unmatched for originality in the country. John Archer suggests Otto Wagner's St Leopold am Steinhof (1905–7) in Vienna, with its light interior, semicircular vaulted apse and *mushrabiyya*, as a source of some parallels, although Wood had already embarked on the final stage of his designs when this was opened.

SYNAGOGUE, Wilbraham Road, Fallowfield. 1912–13, the first major work of *Joseph Sunlight*, who won the competition. He named his inspiration as 'St Sophia of Constantinople' and Bentley's Westminster Cathedral in London. Central plan with a low concrete dome spanning 35 ft (10.7 metres). To the road the sequence starts on the r. with a low staircase block, then the main entrance in the square tower with a dome and four angle tabernacles. Next the main part with a wide gable, large tripartite segmental window above, a range of small flat-headed openings below. All faced in buff terracotta.

MOSQUE, Victory Road, Rusholme. By *N. Gedal*, 1999. More individual than the formulaic designs so often seen nowadays, thanks to the assertive stepped tower topped by a gilded crescent. Otherwise banded brick, green domes, and openings with pointed heads. This fronts the older part of the mosque which reused the brick McLaren Memorial People's Institute, dated 1910.

For St Agnes, Slade Lane, *see* Longsight, p. 366.

Public Buildings

MANCHESTER GRAMMAR SCHOOL, Old Hall Lane, Rusholme. Founded in 1515 by Hugh Oldham, a protégé of Margaret Beaufort, who bought two mills on the River Irk from the Lord of the Manor to provide it with an income. It incorporated a recent chantry bequest of Richard Beswick for two priests to train choirboys in Latin. The original buildings stood on Long Millgate, and were successively rebuilt and expanded (see Chetham's School and Library, p. 293). They were vacated in 1931 when the new building by *Percy Scott Worthington & Francis Jones* was opened. The design was exhibited in 1929.

The buildings, approached by a formal entrance drive from Old Hall Lane, face S across generous grounds and playing fields. Despite the strict budget Worthington and Jones created an efficient and attractive building, in beautifully detailed red brick, Neo-Georgian, and strictly axial. The motif of arched windows set in arches is evidently borrowed from

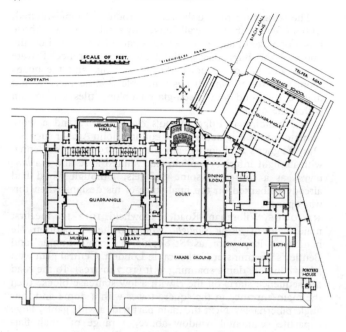

Rusholme, Manchester Grammar School, plan.
Architect and Building News, 1931

nearby Platt Hall (*see* below). A large quadrangle is entered by a tripartite archway under a cupola with a clock, S side. The hall is across the N end of the quadrangle with classrooms on two storeys in the W range, art rooms and the lushly panelled library in the S range, and more classrooms and the panelled High Master's rooms in the E range. A second quad to the E has a theatre on its N side, the dining hall on its E side, to the NE a yet smaller quad (now infilled) for science rooms, set diagonally. A large gymnasium and swimming pool lie SE of the dining hall. INTERIOR. The entrance in the centre of the N main quadrangle leads to a generous foyer followed by a tunnel-vaulted corridor then a domed anteroom. The large hall beyond has a high dais with carved panels and fluted pilasters in oak. WAR MEMORIAL over the inner entrance with a good bronze figure symbolizing Youth by *William McMillan*. Also by him the bronze STATUE of the founder, Bishop Oldham, outside the theatre, dated 1930.

Later additions include a low-key brick block of 1965 attached E of the main entrance. Other buildings to note lie W of the main complex. The former vicarage of St James's church (*see* above), is a pleasant Tudor house of red brick with stone dressings of *c.* 1850, altered and converted for school use.

Beside it a sports hall by *Hattrill & Partners*, 1997. The prefabricated timber frame is stayed externally and clad with
stained timber.

MANCHESTER HIGH SCHOOL FOR GIRLS, Grangethorpe
Road, Rusholme. By *J.S. Beaumont*. Opened in 1952 to
replace buildings destroyed in the Blitz. Weakly Neo-Georgian,
brick with flat roofs, various later additions. The entrance front
has a stone portico with a relief over: two women flanked by
abstract panels, by *Mitzi Cunliffe*, 1953.

PLATT HALL MUSEUM OF COSTUME HISTORY, Platt Lane,
Rusholme, a house by *Timothy Lightoler*, *c.* 1763–4. After
Heaton Park the best Georgian building in Manchester. The
Platt family estate was here from the C12 to the C13, until it
was sold to the Worsley family in 1625. The present hall was
built for John and Deborah Carrill Worsley. They had designs
for a new house prepared by *William Jupp* in 1760 and *John
Carr* of York in 1761, before settling on Lightoler. He modified Carr's severe Palladian design, changing the proportions
and making the main building slightly more ornamental and
lighter in character, in keeping with the Rococo interior. The
building was converted in 1947 to house the collection of one
of the first serious students of costume history, Dr C. Willett
Cunnington. Most of the rooms were altered, losing what
remained of their decorative schemes.

The house, which faces S, is of red brick, only seven bays
long, and with two and a half storeys. The two-bay links are
treated as arcades of large round-headed openings in blind
arches, topped with ball finials, as in Carr's design. The centre
has a three-bay pediment, and the mid-window a pediment
too.

Porch of two pairs of unfluted Ionic columns. The details of
the capitals, with nodding roses above the volutes, are followed
throughout inside. At the back of the centre is a decidedly

Rusholme, Platt Hall, south elevation:
design by John Carr, 1761; below as executed by Timothy Lightoler

awkwardly placed Venetian window lighting the stair. On the
W side there are two opposed GARDEN PAVILIONS for which
Lightoler's drawings survive. The rear was to have had two
courtyards with semicircular N walls, one relating to stabling
in the E pavilion, and service and kitchen activities in the other,
also broadly following Carr's proposals.

The PLAN is also a modification of Carr's design. It centres
on an entrance hall leading to a staircase hall, with principal
rooms planned centrally on the upper floor and links to service
accommodation in the pavilions. The entrance hall has two
screens of two columns with corridors leading off on each side
to service rooms. Ahead, the very handsome staircase, starting in one flight and curving back in two. Iron balustrades of
lyre shapes, which Dr Ivan Hall thinks are to designs by *Robert
Bakewell*, executed by Bakewell's pupil and successor, *Benjamin Yates*. Lovely plaster ceiling with vine motifs. Between the
staircase and front rooms on the upper floor runs a short corridor of one oblong bay flanked by two small groin-vaulted
ones. Venetian opening between the staircase and this corridor.
All this is more elaborate than Carr's proposal, which lacked
the double staircase. The dining room is in the centre on the
upper floor, the only room to retain the original decorative
scheme. It has a plain ceiling but beautiful Rococo stucco
panels on the walls, artfully incorporated into the frieze in the
manner of Lightoler's illustrations in *The Modern Builder's
Assistant* of 1757. The fire surround and the doorcase, which
has *trompe l'œil* fluting to the columns, use the Ionic of the
entrance portico. Lightoler's watercolours showing the interiors are preserved at the hall, which has allowed the original
blue and white colour scheme to be reinstated.

The PARK, since 1910 a municipal park called PLATT
FIELDS, lies to the S and W. Designs for the landscape were
drawn up by *William Emes c.* 1762, his earliest known commission. He widened the Birch Brook and planted clumps of
trees and perimeter belts S of the hall, of which nothing has
survived. Much of the Worsley estate was sold in the early C20,
and Manchester Corporation bought the house and the park
W of Wilmslow road. The most interesting feature is a stretch
of Nico Ditch (*see* Denton, p. 197 for details) which runs from
Wilmslow Road immediately S of Platt Chapel almost as far as
the boating lake.

Manchester University Fallowfield Campus

The Campus occupies the E side of Wilmslow Road from Thorne
Road, N, to Wilbraham Road, S.

We start with ALLEN HALL alongside Thorne Road, built for
Roman Catholic students, 1960–1 by *Reynolds & Scott*.
Further E on Whitworth Lane, RICHMOND PARK by *Downs
& Variava* is a rather frightening group of yellow brick accom-
modation blocks of the mid 1990s, with one of their favourite

motifs, stabbing terminations to the gables. HOLLINGS [113]
COLLEGE, now the faculty of Food, Clothing and Hospitality Management, follows at the corner of Old Hall Lane. By
the City Architect *L. C. Howitt*, 1957–60. Here is a piece of pop
architecture if ever there was one. The people have found it a
nickname: they call it the toast rack, for its visible construction by means of a large number of very closely set steep angled
concrete piers looping over at the top as parabolic arches. The
floors, owing to this, decrease in depth from bottom to top:
seven, six, five, four, three windows. The staircase windows
slant like the arches. Workshop extension with zigzag roof to
the rear. A circular block to the road (known as the fried egg)
originally had a central hall, replaced by a circular library by
MBLC in 1995–6, with an outer band of offices. It works
remarkably well as part of the group. Brown render cladding,
exposed internal steel roof structure designed to avoid internal columns.

ASHBURNE HALL, Old Hall Lane, s side. The complex includes
the house of the Behrens family, given to Owens College in
1906 and used as a women's hall of residence. The building
was extended in 1910 and further accommodation erected
1909–31 by *Percy Scott Worthington*. Entrance lodge in convincing Regency style dated 1926, by Worthington's half-
brother *Hubert Worthington*, then the drive leads to the original
house of *c.* 1830. It is a smaller version (which archive photographs show) of Chaseley, a demolished house in Pendleton, Salford (q.v.), by *Richard Tattersall*, so probably his design
too. Scribed stucco, three bays with a central high pedimented
portico of four monolithic unfluted Ionic columns. Entrance
with scale-pattern fanlight, then a vestibule with a coffered
ceiling and a glazed screen with Corinthian columns based on
those of the Temple of Apollo at Didyma. In the hall coupled
pilasters frame entrances to the main rooms. Ahead the staircase rises in one flight and returns in two. Cast-iron scrolled
balustrade and large newels of iron with brass tops for lights.
The well is lit by a glass dome.

The purpose-built accommodation is ranged around a
grassed quadrangle. Brick, in Arts and Crafts style with Neo-
Georgian and Tudor motifs. The composition is symmetrical but
the subtle variation in the size of the gables, entrances recessed
behind big arches and the treatment of the roofline mean that
it does not read formally. Motifs are borrowed from women's
colleges at other universities, with, for example, the covered
corridors lit by arched windows following Champneys at
Newnham College, Cambridge (1875–1910), and the massing
of the central block owing a debt to Maitland at Somerville,
Oxford (Edmund Fisher, 1910–11). The N range has full-height
polygonal bays with flat tops which rise above eaves level. The
main block has a large upper hall with a dais with fluted Doric
columns, a comfortable panelled library below, and spacious
corridors with round-headed niches. The s side has late C20
buildings of similar scale and materials, and to the road, w

side, expensive Neo-Georgian gates designed by *Hubert Worthington*.

CHANCELLORS, Whitworth Lane, W side. Another hall based around a large house given to the University, this time the home of Sir Joseph Whitworth, by *Edward Walters*, 1851. Italianate, scribed stucco, of two storeys with an attic storey to the E, and a service wing. This part has upper tripartite windows in which consoles act as mullions. Bays to the garden front. Staircase with ornamental balusters and a wreathed rail. It was converted to a conference and teaching centre 1995–7 by *Short & Associates*. The playful new buildings E of the villa delight in the variety of materials: polychrome brick, cedar shingles and metal roof cladding.

WOOLTON HALL, S, on the other (W) side of Whitworth Lane is by *Hubert Worthington*. It was opened in 1959 and looks 1929, and is as far as could be from the panache of Hollings College (above), which was going up at the same time. Pitched roofs, thin Neo-Georgian detailing. Back on Wilmslow Road, OWENS PARK is by *Building Design Partnership*, 1964–6. The complex is dominated by a square nineteen-storey tower which has at the base a fibreglass RELIEF, Cosmos I, by *Mitzi Cunliffe*. Last in this sequence and S of Owens Park, OAK HOUSE: more halls of residence, bland late C20 brick boxes.

For Hulme Hall, Langworthy Hall, St Gabriel's Hall and Dalton Hall *see* Victoria Park, below.

Streets

APPLEBY LODGE, Rusholme. Off Wilmslow Road, opposite Platt Fields. By *Gunton & Gunton* in association with *P. Cummings*, 1936–9. An attractive and unspoiled group of three blocks of three-storey flats with 100 apartments around a central garden. Moderne style, of brick with stone dressings and flat roofs. Recessed stair-towers, curving cantilevered balconies.

LADYBARN LANE, Ladybarn. A few small early and mid-C19 houses and cottages on the W side, amongst later housing. Those to note are ROSE COTTAGES near the N end, reached from a footpath. Terrace of five tiny early C19 brick cottages, with outdoor privies attached to the front. Nearby, Nos. 96–98, small early C19 brick cottages, No. 96 with Gothick intersecting glazing bars.

MOON GROVE, Rusholme. A charming little enclave off Dickenson Road with small Late Georgian houses, built as a speculation in the 1830s. Chequered brick, doors with fanlights.

PLATT LANE, Rusholme. Near the E end, NIGERIA HOUSE, large, stuccoed and symmetrical. Further W, opposite Holy Trinity Church (*see* above), Nos. 66 and 68, a pair of Late Georgian detached houses. Brick, doorcases with Ionic pilasters, pedimented windows in the gables.

WILMSLOW ROAD, Rusholme. On the corner of Brighton Grove, very large semi-detached 1830s houses treated as one

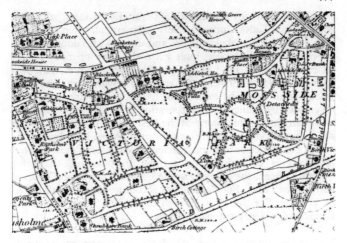

Rusholme etc., Victoria Park as shown on the 1848 OS map

composition. Neoclassical and stuccoed, with channelled rustication. Incongruous label moulds over the windows. End bays with orders of attached Doric and Ionic columns and pilasters superimposed, attic storey pilasters with lotus leaf detail. Further s, w side, OAKLEY, a large early C19 Gothic house in its own grounds, one of the only survivors of a number of large detached villas of this date in the area.

Victoria Park*

Victoria Park is an early example of a planned residential suburb all laid out in one go; the first gated suburban residential park in Manchester, and one of the first in the country. Earlier examples, such as Hakewill's Park Estate in Nottingham, of the mid 1820s were not nearly as ambitious. The plan is largely intact and many of the C19 buildings survive. The layout and some of the houses were designed by *Richard Lane*, a founding member of the development company formed in 1836. The scheme was prompted by the migration of professional classes from the centre, and the prospectus described the site as offering 'total freedom from manufacturers and their disagreeable effects'. Lane's plan shows 220 plots, and most of the work of planting and laying out the roads was complete when the park opened in 1837. The design encompasses Picturesque principles of sinuous curving thoroughfares and crescents planted with clumps of vegetation and trees. Lane designed most of the houses erected

*For the history and evolution of the park *see* M. Spiers, *Victoria Park Manchester*, Chetham's Society 1976.

before the company foundered in 1842. His favoured villa style was stripped Tudor Gothic, usually symmetrical, often stuccoed, with steep gables, label moulds, and doors with Tudor heads.

Nine houses had been built when the park opened, but of nineteen built by 1839 only eight were occupied. A trust was formed in 1845 to preserve the area as a private park, and large villas continued to be built up to *c.* 1880. The park was finally taken over by Manchester Corporation in 1954. Despite infilling and many losses this is one of the best places in Manchester to see Victorian villas in their own grounds. Most have been converted for offices or multiple residences, and some incorporated into various educational institutions. Purpose-built halls for Owens College, the ancestor of the University, were going up as early as the 1880s. Further student accommodation continues to be erected. For the First Church of Christ, Scientist and the Church of St Chrysostom *see* above.

The earliest houses, most of which are by *Lane* or can be attributed to him on stylistic grounds, were built *c.* 1837–40. Some of the first were erected on PARK CRESCENT, where the VICTORIA PARK HOTEL is three houses treated as one composition. Stuccoed and E-shaped with projecting gabled bays, a central entrance with a Tudor Gothic arch and windows with margin lights. Just around the corner on KENT ROAD WEST, another similar house. On CONYNGHAM ROAD, Nos. 6–8 are more versions of the same thing. At the N end of the same road LANE COURT is in contrast Greek, with an Ionic portico and full-height bowed bays to the garden with tripartite windows. Once Lane's Tudor style has been encountered it is easy to spot, and there are about half-a-dozen other examples scattered about.

Other houses to note are as follows: The former MILVERTON LODGE, No. 17 ANSON ROAD, is now a pub, a thing originally prohibited from the park. Mid–late C19, brick with stone dressings, Gothic with very steep gables and traceried windows. On DAISY BANK ROAD No. 65, SUMMERVILLE, is probably mid-1850s. Large, stuccoed, asymmetrical, with a portico with Ionic pilasters. No. 80, NEWBURY, N side, another large stuccoed house of the 1850s, this time Gothic. Set back on the same side is ADDISON TERRACE, *c.* 1848–50. A very pretty stuccoed Tudor Gothic terrace treated as six pairs of houses of two slightly different alternating designs. No. 102 was the home of Charles Hallé and subsequently of Ford Madox Brown while he was painting the murals in Manchester Town Hall.

LOWER PARK ROAD, E side. No. 1 GREYGARTH HALL, *c.* 1880–90. Brick, eclectic Italianate style, with a tall stair-tower with a pyramidal roof. Other large houses on this road were taken over by the XAVIERAN THEOLOGICAL COLLEGE, founded here in 1907. Their main building, W side, incorporates No. 8, THE FIRS, by *Alfred Waterhouse* for T. R. Hetherington, 1874–5. Red brick with blue bands and chequers. A picturesque show with a timbered main entrance and a tall tower with a splayed, gabled bay on one side, reminiscent of some of his University buildings. A gabled archway to the r. leads to an attached Neo-Georgian interwar range with upper-floor chapel. Interior planned around a magnificent full-height top-lit staircase with arcades on each side and corridors leading off. Much stained glass in the muted tones by *J. M. Allen, Heaton, Butler & Bayne* and *F. T. Odell*. Tiles to the designs of *J. M. Allen, Heaton, Butler & Bayne, D. Conway* and *W. Godwin* were used. The 1930s chapel addition has a semi-circular apse flanked by mosaic angels. Attached to the rear, large red brick buildings of the college, put up in 1911. Next on the same side MARYLAND (formerly Regent House), *c.* 1870, Gothic, grey and yellow brick with stone dressings. Tricky details with much variety in the texture and wall surfaces. Splendid entrance hall with a Gothic arcade and a gorgeous inglenook with Arts and Crafts detail, including stained glass, brass repoussé work, mosaic, and carved wooden panels and settles, part of a later refurbishment. No. 3, opposite, is a very grand villa of *c.* 1840–50, with the college motto 'Concordia res parvae crescunt' inscribed above the entrance. Stuccoed with quoins, high basement and a central pedimented entrance bay with a portico with paired Ionic columns.

GARTNESS, on UPPER PARK ROAD, can be attributed to *J. S. Crowther, c.* 1865. End-on to the road, Gothic, with a tower, and of brick laid with three rows of headers to every row of stretchers. Each part – family rooms, entrance and stair, service end – is expressed and roofed separately in a Puginian fashion. The tower room is reached by a tiny stair also poetically expressed. A tall Gothic window lights the stair and, via a screen of short fat columns and trefoiled arches, the inner hall. Upstairs a similar but simpler device to light the landing. All this is eminently typical of Crowther. From 1922 to 1983 the house served as the Manchester branch of Toc H, a Christian organization for servicemen started in the First World War. Various additions, including a low residential range of 1969, are due to them. At the other end of the road, LANGDALE HOUSE, 1846, is by *Henry Bowman*. Symmetrical front with steep gabled bays, ashlar but with small masonry blocks. The detailing is Tudor. Architectural rainwater heads with the initials H. B. The entrance sequence is well handled. First an open Gothic screen, then a lobby with Gothic screen and door, followed by the hall with doors with Gothic surrounds, and beyond the stair lit by a tall window with brightly coloured heraldic glass.

Halls of Residence and Other Educational Institutions

DALTON HALL, CONYNGHAM ROAD, is a Manchester University hall of residence originally for Quakers. By *G. T. Redmayne,* 1881–2. Stock brick and red brick with stone dressings, gabled. The street frontage is quite simply treated, but with subtlety. The main entrance arch has over it a beautiful terra-cotta panel with lettering and foliage.

HULME HALL (Manchester University hall of residence), OXFORD PLACE, s side. The interest is in the inner quad with a charming L-shaped block by *Percy Scott Worthington*, 1906. Brick with stone dressings in a quiet domestic Tudor and Arts and Crafts idiom. On the l. side a range with a lower arcade, like a cloister, then ranges of full-height polygonal bays. At the corner a tower with a crenellated stone parapet and a Gothic canopied niche. An archway in the l. range leads to another grassy enclave and a free-standing ecumenical CHAPEL of 1966–8, a satisfying composition of the heyday of *Cruickshank & Seward*, by *J. R. G. Seward*. Dark brown brick and white window strips, a whorled ovoid in plan with a low entrance block to the l., behind which a taller curving corridor wraps around the rear and leads into chapel, the highest part. Inside the ascending spaces and curving approach to the main space create a sense of progression.

ST GABRIEL'S HALL, OXFORD PLACE, N side. A hall of residence by *Oakley & Sanville*, dated 1939. Founded by the Bolton Sisters of the Cross and Passion as university accommodation for former pupils. The main part is arranged on three sides of a courtyard in the manner of almshouses. Neo-Georgian, brick, full-height polygonal bays alternate with paired and single doorways. Attached to the l. is a block by *Reynolds & Scott*, 1963.

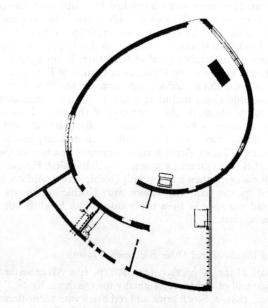

Rusholme, Hulme Hall, chapel, plan

MANCHESTER METROPOLITAN UNIVERSITY ELIZABETH
GASKELL CAMPUS, HATHERSAGE ROAD. The main building originated in 1912 as the School of Domestic Economy and
Cookery, which went on to become the city's first teacher
training college. Large, symmetrical, Queen Anne style, of red
brick and red terracotta. Unremarkable 1960s additions.

WHALLEY RANGE

In a desolate place called Jackson's Moss, only a couple of miles
s of the city, Samuel Brooks, banker, bought two farms in 1832.
He drained the land, laid out roads, and built gentleman's villas
with landscaped gardens. He named the place Whalley Range
after his boyhood home in Lancashire. Did he mean Whalley
Grange?

ST MARGARET, Whalley Road. The foundation stone was laid on
   11 February 1848 by Bishop Prince Lee on the afternoon of
   his enthronement, the first act by the first bishop of the
   new diocese of Manchester. He was to consecrate 123 new
   churches, including this one in 1849. It is by *James Harrison*
   of Chester and was paid for (£6,000) by Samuel Brooks. It
   looks like a village church overtaken by urban development,
   its orientation across its big green churchyard at odds with the
   alignment of the streets. Dec, with inventive traceries to the E
   windows. W tower with broach spire. Arcades with octagonal
   piers, two-light clerestory windows above the spandrels not the
   apexes of the arches – i.e. all is in the new attitude of archaeological correctness. The interior plaster has been stripped
   leaving the brickwork uncomfortably exposed but demonstrating that the SE chapel is an addition (*c.* 1920). – PEWS of
   an unusually organic design. – Oak LECTERN, a proud eagle
   signed by *G.A. Vitty* of Manchester. – STAINED GLASS. SE
   chapel S, a memorial to Alfred Neal Hyde (see Hydes'
   Brewery, Moss Side) †1918, with his portrait, twice. Dramatic
   E window, Crucifixion, *c.* 1932.

ST EDMUND, Alexandra Road South. 1881–2, by *Henry R. Price*,
   who is to be distinguished from the Manchester City Architect
   Henry Price. Geometrical tracery, polygonal apse, incomplete
   NE tower. Price's initial design of 1879 shows a spire, and a
   semicircular stair-tower to galleries under a cross-gabled roof.
   Cavernous seven-bay interior in poor condition. Disused since
   the early 1980s.

ENGLISH MARTYRS (R.C.), Alexandra Road South. Long
   nave, aisles, and the base of a NE tower all of 1895–6 by *F.H.
   Oldham*. Sanctuary and chapels 1908. The tower was completed in 1927 with a belfry stage and an eye-catching spire
   which has an openwork section with a ring of columns, inter-
   polated halfway up. Belfry and spire formerly adorned St
   Andrew's (Dundee) Presbyterian church in Ramsbottom (q.v.)
   of 1873 by *James & Robert Garnet*. The rebuilding here was

carried out by *E. B. Norris*. – STAINED GLASS. On the N side, English martyrs, by *Atkinson Bros* of Newcastle, and one by *Mayer* of Munich. At the E end, bold and strongly coloured glass of the 1920s by *Daniells & Fricker*, only fully preserved on the N side. Saints and martyrs on the S side, added after the war, following bomb damage.

Handsome PRESBYTERY of 1955.

Whalley Range is full of EDUCATIONAL ESTABLISHMENTS.

WHALLEY RANGE HIGH SCHOOL, Wilbraham Road. By the City Architects under *G. Noel Hill*, 1939; Neo-Georgian. Additions 1962, 1997.

WILLIAM HULME'S SCHOOL, Spring Bridge Road. 1886–7 by *A. H. Davies-Colley*. The hall 1920. Red brick and terracotta and a little yellow brick high up.

ST BEDE'S COLLEGE (R.C.), Alexandra Road South. 1877–80 by *Dunn & Hansom*, who also built on a large scale at Stonyhurst. An overgrown palazzo in orange brick and terracotta. Unfinished at the N end, but even so of eleven bays and four stories. Portrait heads crane out from the pediments of the ground-floor windows, and majolica reliefs by *Doulton* of Lambeth adorn the three-bay porch. What we see however is not a new building, but the refronting of the Manchester Aquarium, by *Joseph Sherwin* and *M. Seanor*, which opened in 1872 but failed in 1876. Its Italian Gothic arches in yellow brick with red stone dressings can be glimpsed to the r. of the main entrance where the refronting stops, complete with a chameleon finial. The academic hall and the low rooms on each side of it were all part of the aquarium, hence the marine creatures on the corbels of the hall.

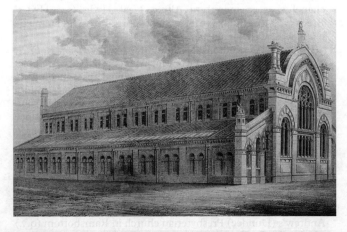

Whalley Range, Manchester Aquarium, from *The Builder*, 1874

The villa now attached at the s end of the school, with its little tower, is Hampton Grange of 1872. s again is St Gertrude's House, 1871, built as part of a convent and still with its garden and walls.

HARTLEY VICTORIA COLLEGE, Alexandra Road South. Now the Kassim Darwish (KD) GRAMMAR SCHOOL (Muslim) for boys. It was a training college for Primitive Methodist Ministers. William Hartley gave the land and supported three phases of building. The first buildings by *Tate & Popplewell* of 1878–9 are on the s, Gowan Road, end. To the r. of the original entrance is the three-storey principal's residence; to the l. the lecture room below, and the library above, marked by a run of closely-set windows. A long wing behind housed the study bedrooms. Both architects had worked in the Waterhouse office, and it shows in things like the decorative ironwork, the restrained coloured glass, and the varied open roofs. The college was doubled in size in 1896–8 by *J. Gibbons Sankey*, including the present main entrance, and a second residential wing. His CLOCK TOWER with its stone top ties together the long range and the different phases. In the third phase at the N end, of 1904–6, *F. W. Dixon* dropped all period allusions, although the structure is still freely Gothic. At the back is a complete residential quad and a large lecture theatre. Dixon's former CHAPEL is identifiable by its tracery and miniature flying buttresses. Its STAINED GLASS of 1914 was destroyed in 1940 by the same bomb that damaged English Martyrs (*see* above). In its place there remains a bold representation of the Heavenly City, 1951, a happy choice for its present use as a Muslim prayer room.

LANCASHIRE INDEPENDENT COLLEGE (Congregational), College Road. Now the headquarters of the GMB Union. Set in fine grounds. A long, very impressive, ashlar-faced Gothic front, impressive in particular if one considers the date: 1840–3. The architects were *Irwin & Chester* of London. Nine bays plus slightly projecting one-bay wings. In the middle a tall, fanciful tower, its top with openwork parapet and pinnacles octagonal and transparent. The recessed lengths of the façade have a ground-floor arcade of arches with four-centred heads, like a college cloister turned inside-out, and more emblematic than useful. Mullioned-and-transomed windows above, a two-storey Gothic oriel in the tower. The motifs of the tower are all a little tight, but the rest has much breadth and self-assurance. At the sides the facing switches to yellow brick, and then at the back to red. The entrance hall and assembly hall which were rearranged by *Waterhouse* in 1876–80 are disappointing after all this display, but the rooms along the *piano nobile* are very charming, their Gothic fireplaces, ceilings and doorcases nicely varied. The extensive collection of Trade Union banners is remarkable.

CARRIAGE & TRAMWAY CO. DEPOT (former), corner of Range Road and Withington Road. It looks more like a market hall.

Of brick with stone dressings, *c.* 1870. Four bays (once seven), each with a porch-like entry under a plate traceried window which rises into a gable. They are linked by a run of square windows which, outrageously, goes straight through the plate tracery – the original, odd arrangement. Behind can be glimpsed a taller building with four louvred cupolas.

The WHALLEY HOTEL, at the site of Brooks's Bar in the angle of Upper Chorlton Road and Withington Road, heralds the new suburb. Hulme, Moss Side and Whalley Range all come together here, with Trafford Borough on the other side of Upper Chorlton Road. The hotel was built *c.* 1875 and extended in 1901 by *Ernest Gunson*, so the earlier part may have been by his father, W. T. Gunson. Built of the finest orange brick and creamy stone, it has a semicircular bay with conical roof to the apex of the two roads.

VILLAS. The delectable villa suburb laid out by Mr Brooks is delectable no longer. Many of the villas have gone, including Brooks's own house on Wood Road and Sam Mendel's palatial Manley Hall immediately W of the Independent College. The earliest remaining houses are at the N end on WITHINGTON ROAD. Three pairs of houses stuccoed and colourwashed, the middle pair (Nos. 8 and 10) Gothic, and three short terraces, of which Hampton Terrace is almost Georgian. MADINA HALL. A pair of very large and plain stuccoed Tudor-Gothic semis of the 1840s. In Carlton Road is ABBOTSFORD, another pair of gaunt Tudor-Gothic semis. Italianate villas in their own grounds are represented on Carlton Road by ROWAN LODGE now the Carlton Club, and No. 18, HAREWOOD LODGE, now Dom Polski. Huge semis seem to have been a Whalley Range type. The best remaining pair is on Whalley Road, now called AFTON MANOR. *c.* 1870, Italianate in yellow brick with a few accents of blue brick and stone.

WITHINGTON

ST PAUL, Wilmslow Road. 1841, by *Hayley & Brown*. Blunt, of brick, very plain. W tower with square buttresses, octagonal pinnacles and a Neo-Norman portal, the sides with round-headed lancets. Barn-like interior with a W gallery and originally only the shallowest of chancels. Chancel, organ chamber and S chancel aisle were added by *J. Lowe* in 1863. In 1919–20 the aisle was made into a war memorial chapel with the addition of an apse. – STAINED GLASS in the E windows by *Ward & Hughes*. In the nave S, the Light of the World after Holman Hunt; opposite it Queen Victoria. Both are by *Walter J. Pearce* (who lived locally), and of 1901, but the Queen has been given a young face. – MONUMENTS. Several simple tablets e.g. Robert Tebbutt †1842 'to whose efforts the erection of this church is mainly due, and who is, alas!, the first tenant of its vaults'; by *Patteson & Co.*, Manchester, with an urn at the top.

ST CHRISTOPHER, off Princess Road, by *Bernard Miller*, 1935,

was demolished in 1994. It is a pity. RECTORY and CHURCH
HALL remain.

ST BERNADETTE (R.C.), Princess Road. By *Geoffrey G. Williams*
and *A. Walmsley* of *Greenhalgh & Williams*, 1959–63. Right next
to the road, which rises here to cross a railway. Built on a rectangular steel cruck-like system with the church above, at road
level, and the hall below. Campanile with open bell stage. The
church interior walls are decorated with a list of the saintly
virtues: Self-Control, Chastity, Fear of the Lord, Justice and
so on.

ST CUTHBERT (R.C.), Palatine Road. By *George Goldie*, 1880–1.
An ambitious church on a restricted site, not much bigger than
a house plot. The style is Neo-Romanesque. Four bays in a fine
orange brick with a mighty ritual s porch and small w apse,
presumably intended for a baptistery. The building was completed with transepts and three polygonal apses in 1902 by
W. T. Gunson. The newer work is in a darker brick. Fine austere
interior dominated by the powerful transept and the three
apses, which are semicircular inside, as is the w apse. Windows
set high and filled with simple geometric glass. Brick wall shafts
in the nave spring from architectural canopies to the statues.
The late C20 forward altar and its steps have been done
uncommonly well.

The adjoining PRESBYTERY, by *Gunson*, was built in 1911.

METHODIST CHURCH, Wilmslow Road. Dated 1865, of stone
with a little polychromy, Gothic, T-shaped, with paired
porches, one now enclosed in glass. It is surprising to find a
splendid plaster vault within, but only after venturing upstairs:
it was divided horizontally, by *Byrom Clark Roberts* in 1998,
with a foyer for coffee and the rest of the ground floor given
over to social and health organizations. The upper level is subdivided too, with one room left for worship. The tracery and
stained glass of the big transept windows were unfortunately
lost. The school at the back by *Herbert Turner* of Levenshulme,
1909, has been demolished but its attached entrance remains
to the r. of the church, and so does its decorative but institutional stone and iron staircase, used to reach the upper level
of the church.

For St Chad *see* Fallowfield, p. 468.

WITHINGTON TOWN HALL is well to the s of the village centre,
on Lapwing Lane. Yellow and red brick and red terracotta,
with sunflowers. Central clock turret. The date is 1881 and the
architect probably the older *J. Swarbrick*.

FIRE STATION, Wilmslow Road. Probably 1930s. The children's
faces on the hoppers is a signature of the younger *J. Swarbrick*.
Three-storey flats attached along Arnfield Road with cantilevered concrete balconies are part of the complex.

LIBRARY, Wilmslow Road. 1927, by the City Architect *Henry
Price*. On a splayed site like his Chorlton and Didsbury
Libraries (*see* pp. 416, 444) but this time sternly classical. Of
Portland stone and brick. Concave entrance, behind which
rises a hexagonal entrance hall with black and white marble

floor. Three clearly defined areas like every Carnegie Library
– reference, lending, children's – the central one with circular
skylights.

WITHINGTON BATHS, Burton Road. 1911–13 by the *City Architects*. Brick and terracotta. More modest than others of the
genre and, perhaps because of this, still in use.

ST PAUL'S PRIMARY SCHOOL, Wilmslow Road. Rebuilt in
1896 in a Flemish Renaissance style and attractively asymmetrical in header brickwork and stone.

CHRISTIE HOSPITAL and HOLT RADIUM INSTITUTE,
Wilmslow Road. One of the country's leading cancer hospitals. The original buildings by *Harry S. Fairhurst & Son* of
1931–2 are Neo-Georgian, in brick with a few Portland stone
accents. The Holt Institute is on the main road, a low symmetrical block, its twin entrances framed by Corinthian
porches. The hospital is behind, to the N, its pavilions and
central administration building fanning out from a circular
lawn to the N in the angle of Wilmslow Road and Palatine
Road. Continual expansion and modification have obscured
the plan and made the original buildings almost invisible. The
main entrance is now s onto Oak Road. The new buildings
are nearly all by the *Taylor Young Partnership*, except for the
Molecular Imaging Centre just starting in 2002, which,
appropriately enough, will be by *Fairhursts*.

WITHINGTON HOSPITAL, Nell Lane. The Chorlton Union
Workhouse was built by *Hayley, Son & Hall* in 1854–5. It
presents quite a show to the road, with florid gates and
railings and matching lodges framing the Italianate chapel,
whose visible front and tower are of fine ashlar. Behind this it
is institutional enough, just one very long brick range of three
stories and a hall at the back. Immediately to the N are the
seven pavilions linked by an immensely long corridor – still the
principal axis of the hospital – of *Thomas Worthington*'s Infirmary of 1864–6. The pavilions are made frankly hideous by
their centre-opening windows, excessive floor heights and end
balconies. Florence Nightingale wrote to Worthington 'No
ward is . . . a good ward in which the sick are not at all times
supplied with pure air, light and a due temperature. These are
the results to be obtained from hospital architecture, and not
external designs or appearance'. Worthington's hospital is
overlaid with a bewildering tangle of makeshift infillings and
linking corridors, some even flying over intermediate roofs.
The hospital closed in 2003 and the site is being redeveloped,
probably with loss of some of the above-mentioned buildings.

The village centre is s of the library along the Wilmslow Road.
A few low early C19 buildings with undulating roofs, e.g. The
Albert Pub and the cottages adjoining, contrast with High Vic-
torian ones, which are usually dated and often polychromatic,
e.g. Oak Bank Buildings, 1876. Three BANKS stand out. The
NATWEST, E side, formerly the Manchester and County

Bank, is next to the Methodist Church; by *Mills & Murga-troyd*, 1890. Ashlar, a single storey only, with shaped gables and a pierced parapet with a running leaf in the cornice. Entry is under an openwork screen under the central gable. In the banking hall on the l. a shallow octagonal dome has been contrived on eight little hammerbeams. BARCLAYS, also of fine ashlar, is not such a good building. The BANK of SCOTLAND is of Portland stone, inserted into the long terrace of Lansdowne Villas of 1868. Further S, CINE CITY, W side, was originally the Scala Electric Palace of 1912, so it is an early one. A curious mixture of Art Deco motifs with Lancashire black-and-white. Beside the junction of Palatine and Burton Roads, the WHITE LION HOTEL of 1880 by *William Mellor*, is quite a spectacular building, given texture by different types of moulded brick and made a landmark by its circular tower, from whose conical roof sprout four dormers and a clock turret.

From here Palatine Road heads SW. It was made in 1862 and is lined with villas. Slightly to the E, Wilmslow Road continues its winding way S, and this is our route. St Paul's School (*see* above), E side, forms a good group with William Friday's FORGE and Carriage Works of 1881, red brick with a central archway and a long range of low buildings at the back. On the W side is the RED LION, perhaps C17, long and very low. Opposite (W side) is the tiny WITHINGTON GREEN. Behind it is the long wall of Withington Hall (which has gone), and THE GRANGE, now MANCHESTER MUSLIM PREP SCHOOL, a villa with two towers of orange brick and stone, well-preserved and larger than most. It was built *c.* 1870 for Max Baerlin, the cotton-spinner and dyer. Square footprint, with entrance lobby and top-lit stair in the centre of the house linked by a broad corridor set slightly to one side. Three reception rooms command the favourable aspects. The unfavourable NE corner, containing the kitchen, is connected to a service wing. For the Christie Hospital and Holt Radium Institute opposite the Green, *see* above.

SIR WILLIAM SIEMENS HOUSE, Princess Road and Nell Lane. 121 By *MBLC*, 1989–90. Spectacular from afar, as was surely intended, but less appealing close up with its mechanically flush white powder-coated aluminium panels. Whiteness is its overriding characteristic. Drum shape to Princess Parkway and Nell Lane, with a courtyard behind aligned with the surrounding streets rather than forming a simple square. Two more courtyards are intended.

COUNCIL HOUSING of 1927 onwards fills a large area between Mauldeth Road and Whitchurch Road. It is planned around two octagonal roads with culs-de-sac inside and outside. In Eddisbury Avenue in the NW corner is the City's 10,000th council house, and sporting a fine plaque giving its date, 1928.

MERCANTILE BANK, Lapwing Lane. 1903, by the older *J.*

Swarbrick. L-shaped, single-storey, big basket-arched windows, with a Queen Anne flavour.

DISTRICT BANK (former), Lapwing Lane and Palatine Road junction. By *Barker Ellis & Sons*, 1914, charming, half-timbered in an Arts and Crafts manner.

WYTHENSHAWE

'Wythenshawe is a typical bit of Cheshire, fertile, historical, well wooded, well cultivated, with ancient manor houses and prosperous farms,' wrote Alderman Fletcher Moss (see Didsbury) in 1920, 'but the city ever encroaches and hungers for Wythenshawe, if only to build thereon houses innumerable.' Wythenshawe was intended to be Manchester's Garden City. Initiated under *Barry Parker* in 1931, it was the first example in Britain of a municipally owned satellite suburb. It is hard to get to grips with, having no natural centre, few landmarks, and no topography to speak of. Even residents get lost in the endless maddeningly curving residential roads. The target population was 100,000. Today it is 70,000, and ageing.

After the First World War Manchester was energetically rehousing people from its central slums, and it was clear that it would have to overstep its boundaries. The chief advocate for the Wythenshawe scheme was the socialist alderman William Jackson, powerfully backed by the Liberals Ernest and Shena, later Lord and Lady, Simon. Fletcher Moss's prophecy coincided with a favourable report on the site by *Patrick Abercrombie*, author of the Greater London Plan. The City Surveyor reported on alternatives. The north was bleak and smoky, difficult to build on, and unpopular with tenants. The eastern and western boundaries were already built up. So Wythenshawe it had to be.

First the land had to be bought. This became possible in 1926 with the death of T. E. Tatton of Wythenshawe Hall. Alderman Jackson's visit to Letchworth in 1927 resulted in an invitation to its co-designer *Barry Parker* to produce the development plan. Next control had to be wrested from Cheshire. Bucklow Rural District Council put up a fight, but at midnight on 31 March 1931 5,500 acres (2,230 hectares) of Cheshire were incorporated into the City of Manchester, and so became part of Lancashire.

The following account, instead of following the usual *Buildings of England* order, considers the houses first because they did come first; houses and yet more houses is the overwhelming impression of Wythenshawe. Only after that will the Centre be found – it was a very late arrival. Then come the churches, and then industrial areas and the hospital. Finally, the few pre-Garden City buildings suffered to remain will be considered.

Pre-war Housing

Building started at the NE corner, with Rackhouse, Kenworthy and Royle Green, Baguley and Royal Oak, Benchill, Crossacres

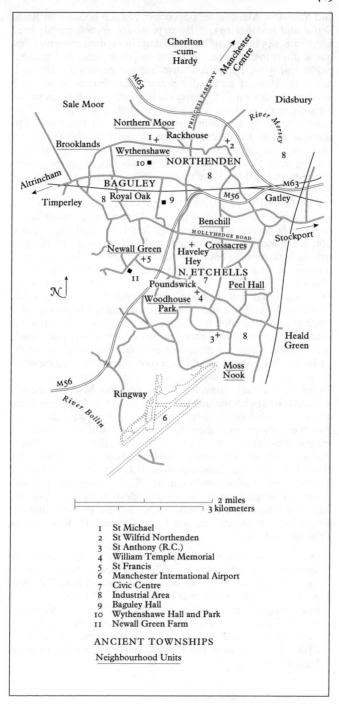

Chorlton
-cum-
Hardy

Manchester
Centre

PRINCESS PARKWAY

M63

Sale Moor

Didsbury

River Mersey

Northern Moor

Rackhouse

Brooklands

1 +

+ 2

Wythenshawe

10 ■

NORTHENDEN

8

Altrincham

BAGULEY

M63

Timperley

8 Royal Oak

■ 9

M56

Gatley

Benchill

HOLLYHEDGE ROAD

Stockport

Newall Green

+ 5

Crossacres

Haveley
Hey

N. ETCHELLS

N

II ■

7

Peel Hall

Poundswick

+

Woodhouse
Park

4

3 +

8

Heald
Green

Moss
Nook

M56

Ringway

River Bollin

6

2 miles
3 kilometers

1   St Michael
2   St Wilfrid Northenden
3   St Anthony (R.C.)
4   William Temple Memorial
5   St Francis
6   Manchester International Airport
7   Civic Centre
8   Industrial Area
9   Baguley Hall
10 Wythenshawe Hall and Park
11 Newall Green Farm

ANCIENT TOWNSHIPS

Neighbourhood Units

Wythenshawe Garden City and adjacent areas

and Sharston. Manchester's 20,000th council house is in Rack-house and is dated 1934.* By 1939 nearly 40,000 people lived here, in 8,145 houses of high standard in verdant surroundings, but with no town centre, with few shops or pubs, and tenuous public transport. Parker & Unwin had not provided such facilities in the Hampstead Garden Suburb, and Parker did not wish to make the same mistake here. He planned a centre; only unfortunately nothing of the sort was provided. So, although Manchester spoke of a satellite town, they did not build one. The showpiece was PRINCESS PARKWAY, the link with the parent city, resplendent with wide grass verges, meandering side paths and big trees. Now it is the M56 motorway. Lesser parkways such as the N end of Hall Lane or Hollyhedge Road give an idea of what it was like.

The first HOUSES are all cottage dwellings typical of council housing in other suburbs of the day. They were designed by the *Housing Department*, not the City Architect, and are conventional, Quakerishly undecorated, with a clean footprint. None of the old light-robbing back extensions or dismal cellars here; even porches and bays are uncommon. Roofs are usually hipped – the absence of gables was noted at the time – of slate or flat red tile, the latter often now needing replacement. Walls are of brick, occasionally rendered and colourwashed cream. Three courses of brick at first-floor sill level laid slightly proud provide a minimal string. In their simplicity they can be very attractive, particularly the B3 type, which is a three-bedroom semi with parlour, or the variant with a gambrel or fold-over roof, often with colourwashed walls. All the types can be seen in the area bounded by Hollyhedge Road, Brownley Road, and the M56. Occasional SPECIAL DESIGNS include COTTAGE FLATS at Leybrook Road of 1937, which look like pairs of oversized semis but incorporate two flats below, with their front doors at the sides, and two maisonettes reached by stairs off the central entry. On Hollyhedge Road are the almshouse-like MITCHELL GARDENS. Round the corner in Brownley Road is CHAMBERLAIN HOUSE of 1937 (named after Neville Chamberlain), twelve flats on three floors for single women, white and clean with balconies and corner windows and parabolic arches for the two entrances. A simplified version can be seen on Greenwood Road facing Princess Parkway.

BENCHILL SHOPS, with steeper hipped roofs than the norm, form a loose open square with Hollyhedge Road running through it. Two-storey flats above are reached from balconies at the back. The N side was built in 1932, the S side in 1934, indicating two phases of house-building. The Neo-Georgian SALE CIRCLE, really a polygon with a road running through the middle, is dated 1934, and so is the single row at Royal Oak. The shops have not thrived, nor have the few privately built pubs.

---

*The 10,000th is in Withington, q.v.

SCHOOLS were incorporated in all the housing areas. Benchill
was the first in 1934, then Rackhouse and Royal Oak (a well-
preserved example of the type), and St John's (R.C.): '350 children, six teachers and no books'. Haveley Hey followed in
1935. The first secondary schools were Yew Tree in 1934 and
Sharston and Brownley Green in 1937. They are often built on
the open-air principle with the classrooms off open loggias.

Post-war Housing

War brought all building to a standstill in 1939. It can still be
seen how building stopped dead in the fields at Nos. 256 and 343
Brownley Road. Barry Parker retired in 1941, and the City commissioned a new masterplan from the City Surveyor *R. Nicholas*,
which came out in 1945, the year Alderman William Jackson died
'whose vision and persuasive power was responsible for the purchase and development of Wythenshawe'. Parker's principles
were maintained with some dilution. Houses were now 13 rather
than 12 to the acre, which is hardly noticeable, but the architectural language changed. The standard roof pitch was retained
but the hips went, as did the string course. An unattractive
feature, endlessly repeated, is a cutaway at the end of a block or
a corner, where part of the block is inset, so that the eaves line
breaks upwards. Pre-war and post-war houses can be compared
side by side at Nos. 156 and 158 Lawton Moor Road, behind St
Aidan's church.

Baguley Hall was the first new district, built in 1945–50. Then
came Newall Green, Northern Moor, Crossacres, Woodhouse
Park, Moss Nook; and Brooklands, begun 1952. A distinctive
area of Newall Green, and the only part of Wythenshawe that
could be called cheerful, is that called TIN TOWN. There are
two similar systems here, both of 1946: 236 *Riley* houses w of
Greenbrow Road, and 250 BISF houses E of Greenbrow Road,
designed by *Frederick Gibberd*. Both are constructed on light steel
frames with channelled metal roofs (originally asbestos) and rendering on expanded metal or channelled metal sheet for the
walls. Once the frame was up they were built from the roof downwards. Bright colours for the roofs and upper walls sit well with
the prevailing greenery; the corrugations give good shadows in
raking sun.

Since the 1980s the City has relinquished total control, and
Wythenshawe has relapsed to normal planning regulations and
private development. The Parker standards are out, bourgeois
decoration is in. It is something of a relief.

The WYTHENSHAWE CENTRE was a late arrival. A Civic
Centre was planned from the beginning, roughly where St
Martin's church is now, but nothing came of it. In the 1945 plan
a new triangular site was allocated further SE with a spacious
administrative and shopping centre designed by *G. Noel Hill*, the
City Architect. What eventually materialized conclusively dispels
any notions of independent garden-city-dom for Wythenshawe.
Only the Fire Station of 1957 at the NE corner, and the

Methodist church at the SE corner bear any resemblance to the
generous Scandinavian style of Hill's scheme. The most prominent feature is a utilitarian multi-storey car park with a supermarket underneath. A couple of parades of shops on a pedestrian
street were built 1960–3 by *S. G. Besant Roberts*, the City Architect. It had flying bridges and glass loggias but these have gone.
The Market and Food Hall of 1974 are a bit more lively. The
FORUM CENTRE 1969–71, named after the cinema in Northenden (q.v.), is again by *S. G. Besant Roberts*. Theatre, library,
meeting halls and sports centre. Dumb from the outside, low and
horizontal, clad in white mosaic tile. Not a lot more eloquent
inside; black floors, wide spaces.

Churches

The CHURCHES followed after the housing in every case. They
often had to make do with less than prime sites, and rarely make
much impact on the townscape. The denominations on the other
hand made great efforts for the new community. The Church of
England in particular conducted some serious architectural and
liturgical experimentation, contrasting strongly with the strictly
traditional housing all around. The Anglican Diocese of Manchester expanded to include Wythenshawe and Northenden, but
the Catholic boundaries were unchanged, so that Wythenshawe
is still in the R.C. Diocese of Shrewsbury.*

A common pattern can be observed, still within living
memory. First, a congregation worshipping in a makeshift building, which is often still standing. Next, the appointment of a
priest or minister, then the building of a clergy house. A school
was often built next. The permanent church, with a peak of
enthusiasm and dedication, last.

ST FRANCIS, Greenbrow Road, Newall Green. By *Basil Spence*,
1959–61. One of the small suburban churches of which Sir
Basil Spence did some equally excellent ones at Coventry. 250
seats only. An austerely simple design, saved from bleakness
by a few deft touches. In front is a tall, free-standing concrete
cross supported by a tapering brick tower of triangular section.
Another, shorter cross is attached to the W front of the church,
which is a box of buff brick, flat-roofed and windowless except
for two tall slits at the E end. The W front is a subtly cubist
abstraction. A chunk of masonry has been notionally moved to
make a darkened void, leaving an upturned L of brick. This
appears to rest upon a smaller white box of (painted) Portland
stone which looks as though it has been rotated to make the
void. Balance is restored by a vertical grille on the other side,
with the concrete cross on top.

The darkened void turns out to be the entrance, although
this was not obvious because the glass is hidden behind a heavy
wooden grille. Behind the cross another heavily grilled window

*St John the Divine, Brooklands, will be dealt with in *Cheshire*, forthcoming.

lights a gallery. The white box is a small chapel at right angles to the main building, originally used for weekday services. The church itself is the simplest rectangle of bare brick with a planked ceiling, articulated only by hidden canted windows illuminating the E wall.

FURNISHINGS are as minimal as the rest. Simple pens for LECTERN and PULPIT. – Small FONT, the lettering of the cover by *Ralph Beyer*. – Cartoon-like line PAINTING of St Francis on the E wall by *Chattaway*, 1961.

ST LUKE THE PHYSICIAN, Brownhills Road, Benchill. 1938–9 by *W. Cecil Young* of *Taylor & Young*, who wrote 'No striving after sensational effect is aimed at' – a reference to St Michael (*see* below), perhaps. Long boxy church in yellow brick. Oblong W tower with a bell-cage on top (the bells were never installed). Prominent and crudely coloured mosaic clock on the W front, but the tower is subtly detailed, see the progressive setbacks to the corner chamfers, and the minimal gargoyles.

White-painted brick interior with a flat compartmented ceiling and a W gallery with organ. Narrow aisles lit by small star-shaped windows. The shuttered-concrete piers have cylindrical Art Deco lights near the top. The interior proportions were substantially altered in 1984, perhaps for the better, when the sanctuary was blocked off to make a community room, leaving a huge void above in which can be glimpsed a painted starry ceiling. The spectacular wooden REREDOS, Christ in Majesty with attendant angels, was brought forward onto the new dividing wall. Original FURNISHINGS in different woods, part ebonized, including ALTAR, LECTERN and READING DESK. Fine silver hanging LAMP from *Mowbray*'s, 1948. The font has been dismantled and the SW baptistery is disused. The Lady Chapel at the NE corner, left stranded by the reordering, has a 1930s version of a ceilure, with concealed light bulbs in the stars.

Grouped at the E end are the CHURCH HALL, two flats formerly a small hall, and a substantial RECTORY all set in a little square precinct; quite an ambitious set-up.

ST MARTIN, Blackcarr Road, Baguley. 1959–60, by *Harry S. Fairhurst*. Deeply conventional when compared with its neighbour William Temple Church (*see* below). Long and churchy with a NE tower. The big grid-like S windows lighting the chancel and the baptistery are distinctive. The rest are small and round-topped, with domestic metal frames. Zigzag-roofed porches N and W, thin tower with clock and bell. Spacious austere interior, a sea of pews. – A HANGING of Christ in Majesty fails to cover the slightly canted E wall, inviting comparison with Coventry but characteristically much more muted in its colours and imagery.

ST MICHAEL AND ALL ANGELS, Orton Road, Lawton Moor. 1936–7, by *Cachemaille-Day & Lander*. A sensational church for its country and its day. The plan is a star consisting of two interlocked squares. The material is brick, bare in four of the corners, with large brick windows in the other four, which are

110

the cardinal compass points. The intersecting arches of the windows, suggesting tracery, are the only period allusion. The roof was flat with a cross rising from the centre. The cost was less than £10,000.

The interior is raw but spatially subtle. Thin cross-shaped concrete piers support the flat ceiling with a diagrid pattern of ribs, anticipating Coventry Cathedral. The piers are not equally spaced but set up a clear orientation towards the altar in the point beneath the huge folded E window. The architects' drawings show that despite the centralizing shape a central altar was not contemplated; in fact an early drawing, marked 'in accordance with the Bishop's Instructions' shows a distinct nave, and indicates how the points of the star relate to a classic three-apse E end; so the age-old dialogue between centralized and longitudinal churches continued. – STAINED GLASS by *Christopher Webb*; heavenly hosts. Repetitive angels in blue and red filling the pointed E window. – FONT and PULPIT both massively octagonal, with simple incised and coloured line drawings of John the Baptist and the sower.

The adjoining RECTORY, also by *Cachemaille-Day*, was built just before the church. Flat-roofed with swooping corners by the front door and a health-giving open balcony adjoining the main bedroom. Pevsner commented 'the church makes it clear that the architect had studied Continental experiments. The parsonage points to Germany and Mendelsohn.'

ST RICHARD OF CHICHESTER, Peel Hall Road. 1969, by *Gordon Thorne*. A windowless box of blue brick, visibly expecting trouble. The entrance has been fitted with a steel shutter. A cross on the chamfered SE corner, matched by a chamfer for the entrance corner. Four skylights peek over the parapet. This is all that can be seen from the outside. Very simple interior, not white but grey, with low built-in pulpit and reading-desk arranged diagonally, as suggested by the chamfers, and lit of course entirely from above. The five STONES imported from great cathedrals seem a little pathetic in these surroundings.

WILLIAM TEMPLE MEMORIAL CHURCH, Simonsway, near Wythenshawe Centre. 1963–5, by *G. G. Pace*. William Temple (†1944) was successively Bishop of Manchester, Archbishop of York then of Canterbury.

The church called forth one of Pevsner's most personal responses: 'All praise to the clients who were willing to accept so daring a design. Much praise to the architect who had the daring to submit so uncompromisingly 1960s a design. And apologies from the author of this volume who cannot appreciate for worship so aggressive a building'. Today we can unhesitatingly endorse the first two sentences. As for the third, either the church has mellowed or we have.

The building is oblong, nearly square, of blue bricks under a big shallow copper roof, the gable walls filled with slit windows in a syncopated rhythm and the roof dotted with dormer windows and a concrete funnel of Corbusian (La

Tourette) derivation. It is not well sited, sitting in a damp dip and screened by trees and grassy banks from the Civic Centre. The interior is a revelation, a beautifully wide open space with the light and colour carefully controlled. Black steel beams and organ pipes, pale woodwork, common brick and concrete left bare, green from the trees outside. The internal axis runs diagonally from the N corner, through a semicircle of seating arranged Early Christian style behind the altar, the cross and the altar itself, and then through the font which stands in the middle of the church under a canopy of three black steel girders which also holds up the roof. Like the beams, these are standard rolled-steel section.* Seating is arranged in a fan shape around the axis. In the S corner of the church is a free-standing white chapel. Its serene little interior is lit only from the funnel above, apart from a square internal window by the altar which reveals that this too is on the diagonal axis of the church. The view from here through the girders of the baptistery to the main altar and cross is particularly satisfying.

FITTINGS are all by *Pace* except for the pews which were rescued from closed Manchester churches; bleached and limed, they look well. In his fittings Pace shows that he was as much an Arts and Crafts man as a Modernist.

The attached VICARAGE is by *Pace* as well. Of brick, with a tile roof, and staccato small windows on the side facing the church.

ST AIDAN (R.C.), Wythenshawe Road, Northern Moor. By *Reynolds & Scott*, 1953–5. Of buff brick. Quite a brave show, with its central and W towers and the presbytery in line and joined to the apse. Both towers are really just raised transepts, i.e. open on the inside. Because funds were short it was designed to be built in two halves; presumably the E half first because the presbytery was already finished, but in the event it was built in one go. Long flat-ceilinged interior with low aisles continuing round the apse as an ambulatory. The structure is based, as in so many C20 Catholic churches, on a Romanesque formula of three sizes of arches; the smallest for the aisles (here they are flattened), middle-sized for the arcades, and biggest across the nave. Piers are square and plain but in the apse explicitly Romanesque, with cushion capitals.

ST ANTHONY (R.C.), Cornishway, Woodhouse Park. By *Adrian Gilbert Scott*, 1959–60, and one of the few real landmarks of Wythenshawe. 'The Green Hut', a Nissen hut, was built in 1951. The SCHOOL followed in 1953 (by *Velarde*), the PRESBYTERY in 1954, so the permanent church, as usual, came last. It cost well over £100,000 and is the largest church in the Shrewsbury Diocese, rivalled only by St Peter and St Paul in New Brighton. Local legend has it that the copper on the green spire is from threepenny bits collected by the children.

*The off-the-peg character of the steelwork is partly a reflection of budgetary restraints.

The design was finalized in 1958. The plan is long and cruciform with a wider central space under the tower. St Anthony's is beautifully built in a distinguished narrow greyish brick and Portland stone. A giant parabolic arch at the ritual W end (actually E) announces the structural system, which proves to be the same as that of St Aidan, based on three sizes of arches, but rendered as parabolas. Photographs of the construction show that this involved some spectacular formwork. The windows have cusped tracery but set within round-arched openings, perhaps to avoid painful clashes of slope with the parabolas, in which case it is only partially successful.

The interior is richly fitted out, the dado in Hornton stone, the spacious sanctuary floored in marbles. – BALDACCHINO over the main altar and REREDOSES from Italy for the side altars. The Stations of the Cross are of carved limewood and the built-in PULPIT has carved symbols of the Evangelists.

ST ELIZABETH (R.C.), Peel Hall. Church hall plus a small chapel which can be opened out into it; 1973. Canon Marmion says by *Greenhalgh &Williams*. The Elizabethan Room, by *John Sheridon* of Wilmslow, 1982, is friendlier; it is built around three heavy roof trusses of Columbian pine.

ST JOHN FISHER and ST THOMAS MORE (R.C.), Woodhouse Lane, Benchill. Church and presbytery are by *Frank Reynolds* of *E. Bower Norris & F.M. Reynolds*, 1935. The first Catholic church in Wythenshawe, and the first in the country dedicated to the newly canonized saints. Powerful Deco W front 'in the modern German style', consisting of a wide tower with a triple

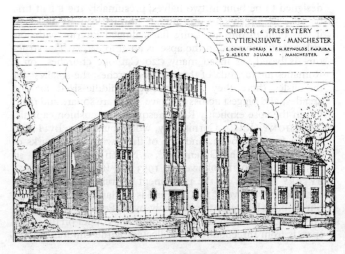

Wythenshawe, St John Fisher and St Thomas More,
drawing, 1935

doorway flanked by muscular shoulders, given verticality by fins in the brickwork. The contemporary PRESBYTERY is by contrast politely Neo-Georgian. The interior is a surprise because although the church is visibly articulated into nave and aisles it is without internal supports. The clerestory, strictly a blindstory, is supported only on huge longitudinal beams. The wide space reveals in its entirety a three-part E end, with a Lady Chapel l. and sacristy r. Pale wood wainscoting, marbles for the two altars. – STAINED GLASS by *Earleys* of Dublin, varied in style. E roundel, Mary and Child, its jewel-like quality reminiscent of Harry Clarke. Art Deco sunbursts for the triple rectangular lancets at the sides, with small roundels of the Evangelists and two titular saints. The latter also appear in the two rather anaemic windows to the narthex.

ST PETER (R.C.) Firbank Road, Newall Green. Ungainly church of 1953 by *Reynolds & Scott*. Three tall gabled windows on each side alternate with almost vertical roofing reaching down low, like a triple dormer bungalow. The interior suggests a more illustrious prototype. The arcades have giant arches alternating with little low entrances, the giant arches corresponding to big windows rising much higher than the roof. The low sections are like little rooms, but with a narrow aisle running through them. The principle recalls Alberti's St Andrea in Mantua.

The PRIMARY SCHOOL next door, by the same architects, preceded the permanent church in 1949–51.

SACRED HEART (R.C.), Floatshall Road, Baguley. By *Thomas E. Wilson* of Leicester, 1973. Hard to find, so apologetic is its architecture. Church, presbytery and parish centre all under one long low roof – two shallow monopitches meeting in the middle at the lowest point. Each is differentiated within the whole, e.g. the presbytery's upper floor appears above the overall roof. Bare brick and slit windows make for a dispiriting church interior. The reredos is pushed out to gain some sidelighting which continues as a minimal clerestory overhead.*

ST MARK (United Reformed), Portway Road and Oatlands Road, Woodhouse Park. Datestone 1958. Quite a good group, the church with its low tower or Westwerk, social centre, and (former) minister's house arranged round an open square. The church is a dual-purpose 'off-the-peg design'; the raised section, which can be curtained off, contains pulpit, altar table, and a little stained glass.

JESUS CHRIST AND THE LATTER DAY SAINTS (Mormons), Altrincham Road. By *T. P. Bennett & Son*, 1964. The front steps forward with windows in the folds, the roof angles upwards at the eaves. A sharp white obelisk stands free.

For St Hilda (R.C.) *see* Northenden.

---

*The contemporary HABITAT store across the road, a glass and steel box of the simplest elegance, is much the better building.

Other Twentieth-Century Buildings

Three INDUSTRIAL ESTATES, clean, modern, electric, were
planned from the beginning, for Wythenshawe was intended
to be self-sufficient.

SHARSTON INDUSTRIAL AREA straddles the Stockport–
Altrincham railway, which incidentally plays no part in
Wythenshawe, between the M56 and Northenden. There are
several 1930s Deco factories such as WYLEX, 1934 by *Cruickshank & Seward*, and RUFFLETTE on Sharston Road. Notable
is the former BUS GARAGE by *G. Noel Hill*, City Architect, of
1938–42. A huge clear span of 296 by 185 ft (90 by 56 metres)
covers space for 100 buses. Although the thin concrete shell of
the *Chisarc* system is the main engineering feat, the six vast
arches which support it are the visual treat. They are artfully
pierced through at the haunches for a little walkway at win-
dowsill height. Behind it and built on the same system are the
washing room and repair hall. On completion it was handed
over to Messrs A.V. Roe for building Lancaster bombers.

ROUNDTHORN INDUSTRIAL ESTATE on the E boundary
includes the large factory of the European Glass Group and
an office and a warehouse of 1963 by *Harry S. Fairhurst & Son*,
both on Southmoor Road.

MOSS NOOK INDUSTRIAL ESTATE at the SW corner of
Wythenshawe includes two complexes by *Cruickshank &
Seward*: FERRANTI LABORATORIES of 1950–4 and, across the
Styal Road, RENOLD HOUSE of 1954, now Manchester International Business Centre. Renold House, still crisp and fresh,
has a long three-storey range facing the road with solid
bookends of brick and an emphatic flat roof, but outside both
the solid ends a very light transparent stair-tower. Within this
frame each window is framed by the fin-like grid of concrete.
Recessed central entrance beneath a slender canopy and an
office cantilevered out on the top floor. Behind is a parallel
range of two storeys.

WYTHENSHAWE HOSPITAL, Floats Road, is immediately S.
The red brick and terracotta pavilions of Baguley Fever Hospital have been here as an outpost of Manchester since 1902.
In 1911 it was developed into a TB sanatorium, with two
narrow ward buildings angled to catch the sun. Councillor
Jackson's regular visits convinced him of the healthiness of
Wythenshawe and engendered his ardent advocacy for the
Garden City. The next phase is by *Powell & Moya*, humane
but businesslike in character. Their Maternity Unit, 1962,
replaces one of the open-fronted TB wards, upsetting the symmetrical plan. It is low and flat-roofed with a hammered concrete frame in front of the blue brick and generous windowing
of the curtain wall. S of Floats Road are a residential block and
midwives' hostel; but these have been abandoned. In 1973 a
wartime hut encampment was redeveloped into the main hospital, again by *Powell & Moya* and with the same palette. It is
planned round a series of courtyards, generally two-storey

except for a single taller block in white tile and glass brick. Several ranges are raised up above the ground so that the courtyards are continuous underneath. Large-scale developments along the N side late 1990s–2001, by various architects including *Halliday Meecham* (heart transplant unit and Accident and Emergency extension), provide an instructive contrast with Powell & Moya's work: no visible frame, bright polychrome brickwork, small square windows, pitched roofs. All three principal phases can be seen from the café courtyard inside the E entrance.

Pre-Garden City Buildings

WYTHENSHAWE HALL. The Tatton family continued here in unbroken succession from the late C13 until 1926, when the hall and park were purchased by Ernest and Sheena, Lord and Lady Simon, and given to the City of Manchester. The house, facing due E, stands in a flat 250 acre (101 hectare) park, the largest in Manchester after Heaton. Responsibility for the park and, crucially, for different parts of the house, is divided between different City Council departments.

The centre of the house is timber-framed, with herringbone and close studding. It is assigned to the time of Robert Tatton, about 1540, but the time of his son William, *c.* 1580, is just as likely, and it is possible that both had a hand in what is now here. Two low cross-wings, their gables standing well forward, frame the central hall range. This is also two-storeyed, with a shallow cove, but stands considerably taller. It has nearly symmetrical porch and dais bays, both two-storeyed.* Except for the carved bargeboards and bressumers of the two hall bays, the external timbering is unconvincingly renewed. The rest of the house straggles away in brick of various dates, some of it rendered, with some Victorian half-timbering at the N end.

The marriage of William Tatton of Wythenshawe to Hester Egerton of Tatton in 1747 transformed the family fortunes. They added a range of rooms to the N for family use, displacing the C16 kitchen and services. The rooms at the high end of the hall, to the S, became service rooms, with extensions to the S in brick. The W side was refronted in brick, the old hall stuccoed, and its windows made Georgian. A room in the new N range was altered again in the early part of the C19 for use as a LIBRARY, probably by *Lewis Wyatt* who was much employed on Egerton properties. A large canted bay and octagonal-paned windows were added. The *Gillows* bookcases there were ordered in 1813.

Edward Blore submitted a scheme in 1839, which was not implemented. It was left to T. W. Tatton and his wife Harriet in the 1860s and 1870s to carry out a phase of Victorian

---

*Goyt Hall in Bredbury, Cheshire, of *c.* 1570, has the same composition.

Wythenshawe Hall, plan

medievalizing. *J. Medland & Henry Taylor*, as well as their work in the C16 hall (*see* below), added a BILLIARD ROOM at the N end of the library *c.* 1862. The rooms E of the billiard room, in red brick with two timber-framed gables, incorporating a SMOKE ROOM, are by *A. William West* of London, 1880. The TENANTS' HALL at the extreme N end is by *James Redford*, 1879.

The City Architects under *L. C. Howitt* were responsible for ham-handed repairs and partial demolition in 1946–51. The stucco was removed from the E front and the present timber pattern created. A SE wing was demolished and so was the attached conservatory of 1885.

The porch does not lead ahead into the hall, as it once did. The door was blocked and an inner side-door leads into the ANTE-ROOM created in *c.* 1867 in the W part of the N cross-wing. The lower hall or DINING ROOM is a Victorian re-creation of a Tudor room, with shiny orange-tinted woodwork and smoothly chamfered canted beams above. 'This room was restored A.D. 1871–72: TWT & HST' is painted behind the bay joist. Thomas William and Harriet Susan Tatton are thought to have employed *John Shaw* and then *J. Medland & Henry Taylor* on it. Filled mortices in the northernmost joist indicate the position of a screens passage. The position of the peg holes shows just how far the beam, once no doubt heavily moulded, has been cut back. The fireplace is certainly Victorian, but the overmantel and dado panelling with their crude Ionic pilaster look at least partly Tudor, though it is not known if it is indigenous or imported from elsewhere.

Behind the scenes on the N side are the three service doors and kitchen passage, where the C18 additions retained some of the spatial relationships, if not much of the fabric – so there was a medieval plan. In the N cross-wing the top-lit N STAIR-CASE is S of the anteroom. It has alternate twirly and plain balusters, and is an early C19 creation, probably by *Lewis Wyatt*, though examination of balusters and strings show that it is a reconfiguration of earlier work, possibly of early C18 date. It rises up to a landing which, strangely, is slightly below the level of the upper rooms; they are all reached via steps up from it. The CHAPEL BEDROOM, above the N wing on the W side, has a barrel ceiling and an oak chimneypiece with the inscription ROBERT : TATTON : ESQUIER : ANNO : DOMINI : 1634, but it is an assembly, indeed only the inscription itself is of that date. Two crude pew ends are incorporated each side of the fire.

The WITHDRAWING ROOM or Great Chamber is the finest apartment, wider than the hall immediately below it by the width of the cove (and just possibly by a hidden cove at the back), and with a virtual wall of glass on the E containing six stained glass coats of arms, probably C19. The door from the landing, N side, has an INTERNAL PORCH, perhaps imported from elsewhere, with Corinthian pilasters with beautifully carved acanthus, and inlaid with black vine trails. The room has an inserted plaster ceiling, a crude imitation of C17 work. Could the remains of an original plaster ceiling survive above it? That there was one is indicated by the genuine-looking vine trails and pendants in the bays. The walls are richly panelled, the lower part similar to the dining room below. The upper part, said to have been inserted c. 1610, is arcaded with deeply recessed inlaid panels. Doric and Ionic pilasters and egg-and-dart are employed. In 1979 the panelling was removed at the N end to expose the timber frame of the wall behind it, herringbone patterned with bold carpenters' marks above a massive horizontal timber, close-studded in a different plane below it. WALL PAINTINGS cover frame and infill. Above a crude representation of panelling is an accomplished frieze of the sort known as Antique work – grotesque winged torsos, fat roses and foliage swirls derived from Italian Renaissance artists who in turn derived from the antique, executed in black and white, with colour reserved for the heraldry. David Park suggests c. 1570–80, which is about the time of Robert Tatton's death (though his widow Dorothy Bothe of Dunham lived until 1600), and William's inheritance.*

The Withdrawing Room has a door at the SW end, and this was probably the original main entrance to the room, for it gives on to a STAIR-TOWER. This is impressively wide, rising in four flights between brick walls and a square central cage of wood. Underneath its deal risers are treads of solid oak, morticed, quite crudely in places, into the outer walls of the hall range. It is undoubtedly a later addition. The stair could have been put in when the upper chamber was created, and when that might have been is considered in more detail below. An upper external corner, close-studded, of the great chamber can be seen. On it are more fragments of wall painting, some of it the black-and-white Antique work, some graffiti-like lettering and faces. Access to the stair on the ground floor is via a stone-flagged CORRIDOR which runs behind the hall. It continues straight through the Tudor stair from the early C19 stair

*Antique work, rare in the North-West, is also at Little Moreton Hall in Cheshire, and Lanercost Priory in Cumberland.

in the N wing, just as the corridor at Barlow Hall (Chorlton-cum-Hardy, p. 413) runs through the hall bay. On top of the stair-tower, reached by its own smaller stair, is the CROMWELL ROOM, perhaps a banqueting room, with a Tudor stone fireplace. C18 views of the hall show that it once had a little domed turret-like structure on top of it. Higher still, the roof space above the great chamber is mightily timbered with curved windbraces, but it seems too short and ill-lit to be the long gallery mentioned in inventories. The roof structure is sturdy and well made, but it is roughly finished and lacking decorative features, and so not made to be seen from either an open hall or the chamber – a point which will be returned to. From here the full complexity of the building, with its manifold interstices, can be seen. There are dead spaces, right down to the ground, between the hall range and the two cross-wings. This could indicate different building phases, but the construction of hall and wings separately in this way could simply reflect closely spaced sequences of building.

The exact sequence of building remains opaque. It seems clear that this is not an example of an open hall with a floor inserted into the existing structure. The roof structure was not designed to be seen, and there is no visual or obvious structural indication that the floor between hall and chamber is a later introduction. It could be that the hall was built two-storeyed from the first, though with a lower cross-passage, as at Wardley Hall, Wardley (q.v.) or Worsley Old Hall (q.v.), but there are indications that this may not have been the case. The exposed N wall of the great chamber gives food for thought. Its massive cross member looks like the tie-beam of a close-studded great hall. It fits with the eaves level of the adjacent cross-wing, and with the bits of close-studding noted elsewhere. The upper herringbone, on the other hand, with distinctive and prominent carpenters' marks, is found only in upper levels of the hall range. The upper chamber could have been created by inserting a floor at the level of the gallery over the screens and building up from it. In other words, the whole of the upper part of the hall range above the level of the tie-beam, including the roof-structure, could have been added to give the dimensions required for the upper chamber. It is difficult to explain the differences in the character of the timber framing above and below the tie beam otherwise, and the fact that the upper timbering is in a different plane (like a reversed jetty) is very puzzling. The stair-tower may have been introduced at the same time to provide a grand approach to the upper room.

Bordering the garden on the W are the pretty C18 STABLES. Walled garden with bothies and head gardener's house to the s. The pleasure gardens to the W and N were laid out in the 1850s by T. W. Tatton with *John Shaw* of Manchester. A modest PARK was set out E of the house between 1810 and 1830 with a ha-ha *c.* 650 ft (200 metres) E of the house. Some of the clumps were created from existing woodland and field boundary planting shown on a map of 1641. STATUE: bronze of Oliver

Cromwell on a high granite base, by *Matthew Noble*, 1875, faces the E front of the mansion. He has lost his sword. He was moved from the city centre in 1968. The bowls and tennis PAVILION to the W is an entertaining building of 1957–9 by the *City Architect's Department*; white and flat-roofed, it is raised up and supported by just the small brick entrance building at one end and a single fat circular pier at the other. On the N boundary is the Victorian LODGE of 1878, typically more showy in its timber framing than the house.

BAGULEY HALL, Hall Lane. A mighty anachronism in the wastes of Wythenshawe, built in the Cheshire of the C14, and nothing to do with latter-day Manchester. Manchester however acquired it with the rest of the Wythenshawe estate in the 1920s, and in due course knocked down the farm buildings, built a road at a nonchalant angle straight through the walled front garden, and surrounded it with a neighbourhood shopping centre and school. The hall itself was turned into a store for Direct Works. This was its condition in 1968. Today the shopping centre and the school are gone, and the hall is owned by English Heritage. Repairs and archaeology have been done, but its future is no more settled.

Baguley is a classic example of a medieval H-plan house, with each of its components of a different age. The nucleus is the magnificent C14 Great Hall, heavily timbered, with simple cusped X-bracing. The service wing at the N end is also

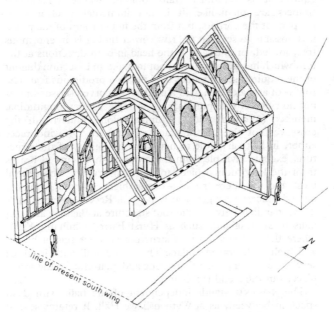

line of present south wing

N

Wythenshawe, Baguley Hall, construction drawing
(University of Manchester Archaeological Unit)

vestigially timber-framed, but on a different principle, and anyway largely built away in brick. The timber-framed PORCH is later still, and cuts across the low dole window of the hall in a clumsy way. The few remaining original timbers show the same carpenter's marks as the great chamber at Wythenshawe Hall, so suggesting a C16 date. The family wing at the S end is of C17 or early C18 brick and cuts the high end of the hall short. Finally the kitchen extension at the N end is a lean-to of indeterminate age. Archaeological investigation has shown that the present Great Hall was preceded by an aisled hall, and that a timber structure preceded the S wing. So almost every component of the house has been rebuilt at least once, but never at the same time.

15

The post-pits of the aisled hall were found about 5 ft (1.5 metres) in from the present hall walls, which seem to be in the same place as their predecessors. Its date is not known, but may have been C12 or C13. The present hall was built *c.* 1325–50 by Sir William de Baguley or one of his sons. It is very distinctive in its construction. The timbers are huge, often measuring two feet or more across; but they are planks, not posts or beams, a uniform seven inches or so thick. This is highly unusual in English timber-framing traditions, although it is known that Radcliffe Tower, Radcliffe (q.v.) and Tabley Old Hall (Cheshire) were similar. W. Startin and others have suggested that it may be part of a building tradition prevalent at this time in the area of the Dee estuary. The closest standing equivalent is Smithills Hall, Bolton, whose service-end timbers are plank-like. It is not immediately clear what happens at the corners, but from the upper room of the porch it is possible to see that the NW corner timber is an enormous tree, jowled, or enlarged at the head in both directions at the top, which has been hollowed out to make an L-section dugout of the required seven inches thickness – a prodigious feat. The roof is of archaic form with a phalanx of curved scissor-braces but no ridge or side purlins, only a single slender longitudinal member (a collar purlin) running along underneath the crossovers of the scissor-braces. There are no windbraces either, in fact very little to maintain the rigidity of the structure, except, invisible from the ground, short curved braces from the longitudinal piece to the main trusses. The central truss and the spere truss have very high collars and mighty curved braces, very generously pegged. Recent research* has drawn parallels between the roof structure at Baguley and C14 halls in SE England, such as Hurst Farm, Chilham, Kent, where the collar-purlin roof structure also has scissor-braces and high arch-braced collars. The N end wall with its three service doors, upper-level arcading and quatrefoils is the showpiece, but the S end is missing.

The N WING stands independent of the hall, with dead space in between, as at Wythenshawe Hall. It retains several

* By D. Stenning.

massive timber posts, with huge jowls on the top. They are not planks, so the structure is not related to the hall. A portion of the wall-plate preserved in the porch room shows that the wall was close-studded, but behind the screens passage, on both floors, are large straight upper braces. This is very similar to the cross-wing at Smithills, Bolton, and both probably date from the early C15. There is a very odd upper mezzanine room behind the N wall of the hall, partly open by means of a screen of balusters. What was it? There is some evidence that the service doors were blocked at some stage, allowing the N wing to function as an independent dwelling. Evidence for multiple occupation, probably by related families, is a recurring feature of both great and yeoman houses in this part of England.

The brick S WING chops off seven feet of the hall, i.e. about the width of the screens passage at the other end. It must have been a most difficult operation to carry out. The ends of the wall-plates are simply housed in holes in the brickwork. There is a small cellar with three little stone mullioned windows, and a very sparsely balustered stair. Little is known of the preceding structure.

Not much is left of the setting. The pretty enclosed garden at the front, with walls probably going with the N wing, has lost its front wall and ball-finialled gateposts. There are minor out-houses facing the yard at the back.

SHARSTON HALL, Altrincham Road. The house of *c.* 1701, in decay when Pevsner visited in 1967, has gone. A little further back is a parody of it, a large brick office building whose central portion replicates, in harsh materials, the *c.* 1701 part of the hall including the lovely doorway with open scrolly pediment.

ETROP GRANGE HOTEL, formerly Moss Hall, Thorley Lane. Five-bay, three-storey Georgian house, neat and chunky, with a pediment. Built *c.* 1780, but the end walls and staircase both look later. Next door KINGSLEY HALL on Bailey Lane incorporates, outrageously, another version of Sharston Hall. Again the Sharston façade has been treated simply as the centrepiece of a big office, this time with a pediment bunged over the whole thing and the bays reduced to three instead of five. The proportions, the unequal quoins and the scrolly open-pedimented doorcase are unmistakable.

PEEL HALL, Peel Hall Road. A moated manor house is recorded in the C14. The dower house there, which appears in Robert Tatton's will of 1578 as, 'not sufficiently builded for my wife to dwell in', and its successor farmhouse, have gone. The MOAT remains with its small but rather splendid three-arched stone BRIDGE with refuges. It is probably C17.

NEWALL GREEN FARM, Clay Lane. Dated 1594 on the recut lintel which would make it contemporary with Hough End Hall, Chorlton-cum-Hardy (q.v.). So 1694 is more likely. It is very similar to Shotwick Hall (Cheshire) of 1662. Pretty E-shaped symmetrical house of brick laid in garden wall bond, with a moulded brick string-course and stone quoins. Shaped gable to the two-storey porch. Windows shaped for casements, with no mullions. Circular windows in the gables with four little arrowpoints of moulded brick at the cardinal points.

Newall Green Farm stands on the very edge of Wythenshawe. The considerable density of older houses and the network of lanes in the green belt beyond makes it clear how much was obliterated by the garden city.

For Rose Hill and Beech House *see* Northenden, p. 465.

MICKLEHURST *see* MOSSLEY

MIDDLETON

INTRODUCTION

Middleton sits halfway between Manchester and Rochdale, only five miles from each of them, and even less than that from the centre of Oldham. There is no let-up in the urban fabric to the s or the E; only the motorway and the change in local authority to mark the boundaries. Nevertheless Middleton is a town of considerable individuality, historically important, and more distinguished than most in its architecture. Its medieval parish church is the most complete, and complex, of SE Lancashire, its remaining great houses are of exceptional interest, and it nurtured one of the most interesting architectural partnerships of the early C20, that of *Edgar Wood & Henry Sellers*.

As late as 1770 Middleton was little more than a village, but, as Aikin wrote in 1793, 'Buildings are increasing daily, and we here view with pleasure the outlines of what one day promises to be a great flourishing town.' Its trade was silk, then cotton, along with coal mining. The 1st Lord Suffield had obtained a market charter two years earlier and built a handsome market house (by *George Steuart*) near Middleton Hall. Nothing is left of either hall or market. The triangular market place itself was obliterated by a roundabout in the early 1970s. As a result the centre of gravity has moved s, away from the parish church on its hill. A second triangular space created between the Old and New Manchester Roads *c.* 1928, called Central Gardens, is the closest Middleton now has to a focus, facing the Arndale Shopping Centre of 1972,

and *Edgar Wood & Henry Sellers'* pretty trio of shops (1908) standing there like a single remaining tooth.

With the driving through of the road and the loss of its
autonomy to Rochdale in 1974, Middleton has lost heart. As a
result important buildings are neglected or standing derelict.
Hopwood Hall is derelict and at risk. In 2002 Durnford Street
School, a ground-breaking design by *Edgar Wood & Henry Sellers*
of 1908, was needlessly demolished. Even when the good
buildings are close together they never add up to anything; there
is too much tat in between. It makes a depressing picture, but
Middleton still gets the longest entry of any of the smaller towns;
there is plenty left.

CHURCHES

ST LEONARD, Long Street. One of the most rewarding medieval   6
churches of SE Lancashire. Built of a distinctive pale greeny
sandstone, now much weathered, it stands on a small but commanding hill. Typical of Lancashire are its long low proportions with clerestory and battlements from end to end. The
stumpy tower carries a comical weatherboarded belfry, almost
like a dovecote, as observed by Ralph Thoresby in 1682. New
bells were hung in 1667, which suggests its date. The S is the
show side, with a fine porch and with quatrefoils and inscriptions, indecipherable now, ornamenting the battlements. This
side narrows at the E end, by the SE door.

There are three phases of building. First a Norman church
of which we have the problematical tower arch and some displaced billet moulding. Then in 1412 Cardinal Thomas
Langley, Bishop of Durham and Chancellor of England but
born in Middleton, rebuilt the church. His is the tower but it
is not certain how much else of 1412 survives. In 1524, as was
recorded on the now-decayed S parapet, came a rebuilding by
Richard Assheton, brother of Edmund, the priest who is represented in brass in front of the altar. The little square SE vestry
with its pyramid roof was added in 1662. *George Shaw* rebuilt
parts of the E wall and the E window in 1869. The boiler house,
NE, with its decoratively incised Yorkshire lintel and distinctive
square chimney are probably by *Edgar Wood*, or *Henry Sellers*.
In 1957–60 a new N porch and vestries were added by *G. G.
Pace*: a carefully thought-out job but not a trouble-free one.

The interior is broad rather than tall or long, the nave and
S aisle notably so. The arcades, which go right through without
a chancel arch, are simple Perp with octagonal piers and caps,
like those at Deane. That on the N has been rebuilt further N,
as is very clear outside, throwing the tower arch off centre. It
is the tower arch, and an arch of the N arcade, which catch
the eye, for here is Norman work. The tower opening has three
orders of colonnettes, and a pointed arch inexpertly made of
sections of zigzag which have been carved for a tighter radius.

More bits of zigzag can be seen in the wall above, and there is a billet frieze incorporated into one of the arches of the N arcade. At the height of the arcade top is the scar of a cambered roof. Langley's church was celebrated for its beautiful roof, but an almost-flat one set so low and without a clerestory would have been a queer sight. At any rate it was replaced in the C18, and the C18 roof was in turn replaced in 1902 by *Edgar Wood* in restrained Perp style with enrichment at the E end.

Two questions remain. First, what do the Norman fragments represent? If the colonnettes are *in situ* then this is the W door, probably widened. If, as is more likely, it is all *ex situ* it could be the former chancel arch. The radii of the arch voussoirs point to a width of only about seven feet, which for a small two-cell Norman church is plausible. Second, is the church we see today all Assheton's, or is it Langley's church pushed around, widened and heightened? A deep base course encircles the whole building outside, only interrupted by porch and vestry. Apart from the rebuilding of the N arcade the only obvious discontinuity is where the N porch butts up to the wall. So, with these exceptions, it looks to be all of a piece. The style, especially the clerestory with its uncusped arched lights, and the recorded inscriptions on the parapets, point to Assheton as the author and 1524 the date, apart from the tower and perhaps the porch.

Middleton church is especially rich in FITTINGS. The chancel SCREEN is a very bold piece probably of the late C15. Its lower panels are square, with heraldry, the lights arched with late Gothic tracery. It is continued to the side walls, plainer but at least partly still C15. Its restoration and the addition of the cove and rood were done by *Bodley & Garner* in 1898. – STALLS with misericords with simple foliage against the E side of the screen. Choir stalls partly C16, partly modern. – REREDOS 1927. – HOPWOOD PEW in the S aisle, late C17; it has lost alternate balusters. – PULPIT, 1843. A recasting by *George Shaw*, to judge by the newels, of a C17 one. – Turning LECTERN also by *Shaw*, like those at Rochdale and Manchester Cathedral. – LIGHT FITTINGS by *G. G. Pace*.

Much good STAINED GLASS. In the chancel S window, by the altar, are the famous Middleton archers. The glass is not now in good shape. The date, no longer visible, has been recorded as 1505, but it has always been called the Flodden window, and as the battle of Flodden was in 1513, we can suggest 1515 or 1525 (to go with the Assheton rebuilding) as more likely. What is so special is that the sixteen kneeling archers are individually named, and so is their chaplain Henricus Tayler at the head of the procession. – In the clerestory (hard to see) C16 coats of arms, originally in the Old Rectory. – E window by *Lavers, Barraud & Westlake*, 1869, in hot colours and pretty good, especially in the tracery. – N aisle, Boer War window of 1903 by *G. F. Bodley* and *Burlison & Grylls*. Khaki tinted overall and as valuable for its depiction of soldiers and their gear as the Flodden window, which was orig-

Middleton, St Leonard, Ralph Assheton, brass, detail

inally here. – Langley chapel (NE) E, 1909 by *Archibald K. Nicholson* with plenty of clear glass. – Two gem-like windows by *Christopher Whall*. Grisaille, not clear glass, contrasted with intense colour; S side, Fides, Amor, Spes, 1911; Assheton Chapel (SE) E, 1923, a five-lighter: the Ascension plus John the Baptist and St Michael, with a wonderfully moody eternal city in streaky purple.

MONUMENTS. The most extensive set of BRASSES in Lancashire, all small in scale, is collected together in the chancel. Sir Ralph Assheton, wife and children, †1485; Edmund Assheton, priest, †1522, a 23 in. (58 cm.) figure*; Alice Laurence and her husbands †1531, 18 in. (45.7 cm.) figures; Richard Assheton, Mary his wife and children, 1618; and finally Ralph Assheton, Elizabeth his wife, and children,

* In 2004 this brass was found to be a palimpsest.

1650. His Parliamentary uniform and Cromwellian boots are particularly enjoyable, as is his relaxed pose. Other monuments include incised slab in wall niche on N side. In the chancel, Rev. James Archer †1832 by *W. Spence* with a not very grief-stricken mourner. Gathered in the tower, several more including Sir Ralph Assheton †1709 on the stair-turret.

RECTORY, Mellalieu Street, below the W end of the church. By *G. G. Pace*, 1957. It is in the garden of the OLD RECTORY, an unprepossessing house of 1894, a rebuild of an earlier C19 house, truncated at the ends. Hidden inside, a great treasure, is a substantial fragment of the C16 timber-framed rectory. Inside the Victorian front door is a very wide cross-passage. A doorway with an engagingly gauche Ionic doorcase leads through a wooden screen wall into the barbarically splendid OAK ROOM. Here it can be seen that the screen in fact has two doors, one blocked. It is a very splendid piece, with three tiers of scrolly linenfold panelling, very boldly carved. The folds of the upper panels lean this way and that. The rails are decorated with a tiny flower and tracery motif, and the top rail with a running oak trail. These are made of separately carved pieces inserted into a groove. Colonnettes frame the doorways, their top sections twisted. The rest of the panelling is said to have been brought from Middleton Hall. The chimneypiece is dated 1894; its overmantel is a Jacobean bedhead, and other bits of antique furniture are built in to the bookcase and cupboard. Armorial stained glass made for this room is now in the parish church. The ceiling/intermediate floor is massively framed with deeply moulded joists. It ignores the screen; the whole space, oak room plus cross-passage, measures 48 by 24 ft (14.6 by 7.3 metres).

Unfortunately there is little to relate to this magnificent room and tell us how it was used. The service cross-wing at the N end of the house, which contains the stair, appears to be C19, except for a bit of older flooring visible from the cellar. Nothing is left of a S cross-wing, although old photographs show that there was one. The upper floor is divided up and there is little to be seen except a portion of close studding, rather crudely executed, in the N end wall of the hall range. The roof is Victorian, but a couple of earlier trusses have been left, doubled by the C19 ones. They are of utilitarian kingpost type, not made to be seen.

In the 1960s the house was empty for a while and in poor condition. W. John Smith was able then to ascertain that the upper floor had been jettied, at least at the front, to observe brick nogging in between the studs, and to see evidence that the upper ceiling had been similar to the lower one.

It would seem therefore that Middleton Old Rectory was built two-storeyed, with a staircase perhaps located where the present one is, and a screens passage retained as a conservative feature. In the absence of any evidence from dendrochronology it can perhaps be assigned to the time of Edward Assheton, rector from 1585.

In the much-reduced garden are possible traces of a MOAT.
ST JOHN, Rochdale Road, Thornham or Slattocks. 1½ m. NW.
By *R.B. Preston*, 1906–7, given by the Smalley family. Quite
big, with a SW tower of similar silhouette to Preston's St Ann
Rochdale, and a W baptistery. Free Perp style with ogee details
in some of the tracery. (Spacious interior with low aisles. Walls
of coursed rubble, piers and dressings of smooth sandstone.)
HOLY TRINITY, Parkfield, Archer Park. By *George Shaw*, 1862.
The church is part of the park layout and looks moreover like
a big garden ornament for the Gothic former VICARAGE, no
doubt also by *Shaw*. Dec, of stone, aisleless, with a five-sided
apse and a bell-turret on the W gable. Double S transept added.
Simple interior with a lightly framed roof except for a great
post at the focus of the apse, braced out to all the angles. The
only Shaw fitting, apart from the unusual PEWS with individual armrests, is the massive LECTERN, a splendid oaken
eagle on a hollow octagonal stem braced out to the cross-
shaped base like his turning lecterns – STAINED GLASS. The
apse window nearest the organ of 1862 may be by *Shaw*. The
others in the apse are by *R.B. Edmundson* of Manchester,
1864; In the nave N and S by *Shrigley & Hunt*; and W, a *Kempe
& Co.* window of 1912 with the tower emblem of *W.E. Tower*.
In the transept (or is it a two-bay S aisle?) two large windows
by *Powells*, the W being a war memorial of 1920 associated with
the memorial BRASSES on the facets of the arcade pier.
ST MICHAEL, Townley Street. By *Austin & Paley*, at the expense
of the brewer J.W. Lees, replacing a church of 1839. E end
1901–2, nave *c*. 1910. The strong tower standing W of the S aisle
was not built until 1930. Large-scale austere interior, stone-
lined, with wide aisles and a W baptistery. The built-in stone
pulpit makes an interesting comparison with Wood's contemporary one at Long Street Chapel. – STAINED GLASS. A good
C20 collection mostly by *Shrigley & Hunt*, who worked so
often with Austin & Paley. Also a distinctive child-centred
series, after 1946, arranged asymmetrically with much clear
glass. The contemporary detail is pleasing: Christ blesses a boy
in 1950s shorts with soap-box and pram-wheeled cart.
ST PETER (R.C.), Taylor Street. 1910. Perp in red brick and
yellow terracotta.*
PROVIDENCE INDEPENDENT CHAPEL (Congregational),
Market Place. 1859–60 by *James Simpson*. Grand and confident, a big red brick and stone box backed by the green slope
of St Leonard's churchyard. Italianate, with twin entrances
and finely carved pediment decoration in stone. Brick polychromy at the eaves. Disused. Its interior is said to be good.
The adjoining school has been demolished.
BAPTIST CHAPEL, Temple Street. *Edgar Wood*'s first church, of
1889. He informed the press that the style was 'C13 English',
but it is C19 eclectic, German Romanesque if anything. Here

* Possibly by *Greenhalgh & Williams* of Bolton.

is the beginning of a line of experiment and evolution through Silver Street Chapel in Rochdale (p. 607) and Middleton Methodist church, to his famous First Church of Christ Scientist in Manchester (p. 469). Of red and yellow brick and red terracotta. In the gable front a chequer of red and yellow tiles, a rose window, an arcade of nine round-arched windows and a big round-arched door, framed by stripy corner buttresses. At the sides continuous windowing between buttresses.

Nearby are three terraces of COTTAGES also by *Edgar Wood*: Hilton Fold Lane, Norman Street and Amy Street, all 1899. Not at first worth a glance, but a second look shows the calculated asymmetry of each row and the characteristic canopy porches.

76 METHODIST CHURCH (Wesleyan Chapel and Schools), Long Street. *Edgar Wood* was appointed 1899; foundation stones 1900; dedication 1901. The tall Gothic gable of the chapel with its windows high up is set beside an inviting courtyard garden, opening to the street by an arched gateway, round which are grouped the Schools and Institute. The principal buildings are of soft red brick in header bond on a red stone base, the stone running up into the brick here and there in an organic way, the roofs all of heavy stone flags. The school buildings are roughcast. The disparate buildings are visually cross-referenced. Thus the church is linked to the street by one side porch and to the courtyard by the other. The domestic scale of this second porch is picked up by the dinky Small Hall at the SE corner, and its bay by the Parlour bay in the court. The axially placed Institute with its battered corner piers echoes the piers of the gateway.

INTERIORS. The SMALL HALL interior is as sweet as its exterior, heavily timbered in its open roof but miniature in quality. The PARLOUR has the same atmosphere, with a good fireplace and bay. The BIG HALL is robust but unmistakably Wood in its detailing, lit by lunettes above the side corridors.

The CHAPEL is a knockout, flooded with light from the big clear windows with their unconventional tracery and subtly coloured from the exposed powdery-looking brick, stone and wood. Everything is tightly controlled. There is no extraneous
77 colour, only the tiniest stained glass roses in the doors, no mouldings except for unstopped chamfers and the carved detail on the furnishings. It is aisled, with Gothic arcades without capitals, and there is a fully expressed and equipped raised chancel. The important FITTINGS are integral with the architecture and were executed by *Thomas Stirling Lee*, who was master of the Art Workers' Guild in 1898. – The PULPIT is a stone drum with colonnettes and a ring of carved roses at the top, the bookrest held up by an angel supposedly modelled on the local baker's daughter. – Matching FONT, a big bowl on a battered base with a bronze madonna and children set in front. – LECTERN, PEWS (originally painted green), and ALTAR furniture all by *Wood*, but not the present holy table.

CEMETERY and CREMATORIUM, Boarshaw Road. Late C19. Small stone chapel with streamlined forms – see the bellcote. Larger crematorium of concrete blocks attached. Near it is the gravestone of the artist F. W. Jackson †1918 by his friend *Edgar Wood*, with chevron tiling.

PUBLIC BUILDINGS

MUNICIPAL BUILDINGS. Middleton was a Municipal Borough until 1974. In Fountain Street is the BATHS building of 1938 by the Borough Architect, *John Pollard*, with its main space modelled on the Horticultural Hall in London of ten years earlier, and the CIVIC CENTRE of 1975. PARKFIELD HOUSE, Manchester Old Road was the TOWN HALL. It is by *Lyons, Israel & Ellis*, 1965–6, and replaces a villa of the same name which was given to the Council in 1925. Of four storeys, L-shaped, clad with heavy-looking white pre-cast concrete panels. It has had a pitched roof of corrugated metal put on. The relationship between Alkrington Hall on its sweep of illusory parkland, Parkfield House in the valley, and Sunny Brow (*see* below) on the opposite hilltop is very satisfying.

The adjacent walled GARDEN OF REMEMBRANCE of *c.* 1920 with its lodges and loggias determined the angle of the L.

OLD GRAMMAR SCHOOL, Boarshaw Road. The school was founded by Cardinal Langley in 1412. The present building was put up by Alexander Nowell in 1586 on low land by the river. A strong plain building of stone, long, low and symmetrical. The façade indicates the internal disposition. The string lifts over the large mullioned-and-transomed windows in the centre, which light the full-height schoolroom. Small domestic windows at the two-storey ends, which were served by spiral steps in the outshuts at the back.

LIBRARY, Long Street. By *Lawrence Booth*, 1889. Its three timber-framed gables take their cue from the Boar's Head opposite (*see* below). Asymmetrically placed tower and short spire. The PARK behind it was opened shortly afterwards.

ELM WOOD SCHOOL, Elm Street. 1908–10, by *Edgar Wood & Henry Sellers*. A brick building with Portland stone trim, very formally composed. A tall transparent hall rises at the back, with a memorable pylon-like tower at each end. Reaching out from the hall to the boys' and girls' entrances on the street are twin open arcaded and vaulted passages. The inviting garden thus enclosed, and glimpsed through the railings, is the centrepiece of the composition, as it is at Long Street Chapel. In front of the hall and connecting the two passageways is a low concave forebuilding. Classroom blocks at both ends, and enclosed playgrounds. Apart from that of the hall the roofs are of reinforced concrete.

DURNFORD STREET SCHOOL, by *Edgar Wood & Henry Sellers*, 1908–10. The demolition of this building in 2002 was one of the year's most serious architectural losses, and one that Middleton could ill afford. It was a larger building, but the elements were much the same. The centre, with another pair of pylon-like towers with Egyptian tops, was a grid of mullioned-and-transomed windows, the outer ones in full-height canted bays. The largest windows were reserved for the top floor, as in Bess of Hardwick's C16 houses. Roofs and floors were of reinforced concrete. The low infants' building which formed a T in front of the main building, also with a pylon, has been spared.

OTHER BUILDINGS

WARWICK MILL, by the centre on Oldham Road. 1907 by *George Stott* of *Joseph Stott & Sons*. A powerful presence, even after the loss of its boiler house and chimney. Mill and stair-tower, office with much terracotta, engine house with the usual tall arched windows remain.

20 TONGE HALL, William Street. A dilapidated but rewarding old house, timber-framed and stone-roofed, standing on a small hill that makes an island of rough country near the centre of town. It was built probably shortly after 1587 by Christopher Tonge. The Tonges were minor gentry who improved the house, especially in 1703 (rainwater-head date), but were never able to rebuild it. Two-storey hall range with a two-storey bay, and family wing. The service part, which was in line with the hall, collapsed in the C19 to be replaced by a low brick kitchen. A two-storey porch has gone too, although the great door is still there. It led into a cross-passage behind the hall fireplace, i.e. not a proper screens passage. The house must have been extremely showy. It is jettied and coved twice on the N and E sides, and decorated all over with quatrefoils in a square-panelled frame. The S side was the same but, as so often, it has had to be built away in brick.

The interior is muddlingly subdivided but essentially complete. The hall fireplace with its mighty bressumer has an ingle window at the back. W. J. Smith found that the smoke hood above it is of stone flags set on edge. Diagonal dragon beams for the jettied corners. A stone stack heats the family wing, with a wooden turning stair spiralling round a mast tucked in beside it. The *pièce de resistance* however is not Tudor but of 1703, when Richard and Alice Tonge put in a beautiful small parlour or dining room with characteristic panelling, door, and fireplace of the period, and reputedly an overmantel painting now covered up.

BOAR'S HEAD. Below the parish church in Long Street. Pretty timber-framed building with three unequal ornamental gables and two entrances side-by-side. W. J. Smith suggests that it was originally two dwellings, as is common in the outlying farms. The date 1632 is reported in the cellar.

Outside the MIDDLETON ARCHER, a J. W. Lees pub of 1974 on Kemp Street, is a SCULPTURE of the left-handed archer,

Edmund 'Crouchback' Plantagenet, Earl of Lancaster, victor in 1265 of the battle of Bowlee (Rhodes). By *Constantine Smith*, in bronze-coloured fibreglass, with grotesquely big hands and feet and a very broad bow.

ROYAL BANK OF SCOTLAND, formerly the Manchester and Salford Bank, Market Place. 1892, by *Edgar Wood*. Faced with matt pink terracotta, with a tiled roof. The upper floors show a threefold symmetry with bold dormers linked to the middle floor windows and four magnificent Art Nouveau hoppers. The ground floor is asymmetrical, the bank entrance and the manager's front door clearly differentiated.

SUNNY BROW, Archer Park. Now a nursery school. This is where Edgar Wood grew up. It was built by his father, T. B. Wood, in 1865. Gothic, of soft red brick laid in header bond (as Edgar Wood was to use at Long Street Chapel), and Bath stone. It is attributed on grounds of family connections to *Mills & Murgatroyd*, but style, materials and plan all point to *J. S. Crowther* who perhaps ghosted it. Plan and massing are identical in all but detail with two of Crowther's Cumbrian houses, Kendal Vicarage (demolished) and Wynlass Beck at Windermere. The door is in the double-gabled NE end, set to one side to allow direct light into a spine corridor. Three-storey cross-wing at the rear. The sunny S front is given to the family rooms, the shady back largely to circulation, and the rear wing to service plus a big dining room. The spectacular feature is a line of three Gothic arches along the spine corridor, one for the lobby and two for the stair – an updating of the medieval screens. The stair has Gothic detailing. The upper corridor has a coved ceiling reaching into part of the roof space, as do the principal bedrooms. Of the three houses Sunny Brow has the most generous allocation of decorative detail.

How fascinating it is that *Edgar Wood* grew up in a Crowther house with a George Shaw church and vicarage (Trinity, *see* above) at the other end of the street. Between the two, he built two substantial villas. Dunarden was demolished in the 1970s. WEST DENE of 1894 is a gawky house, too tall for comfort and not sure whether it faces downhill or sideways. Polygonal bay with stone mullions and transoms next to a curved Home Counties bay with tile hanging. The stair rises from a big entrance hall, its baluster type changing twice as it rises. The principal room has figurative plasterwork and carving, and coloured glass featuring angels and briar roses. A string of lower buildings has been lost from the W side of the house – conservatory, ballroom and gardener's cottage.

The following are also by *Edgar Wood* or *Edgar Wood & Henry Sellers*.

In Jubilee Park between Long Street and St Leonard, EXEDRA and fountain of 1906. Steps lead up to a stone semicircular seat. The fountain head and statue are lost and the effect of a grand approach to the church diminished by poor maintenance and the overgrowth of rhododendrons.

107 On Long Street and its continuation Rochdale Road are Fence-gate and Redcroft of 1895, semi-detached, but a very unequal pair. FENCEGATE is the smaller. Attractive frontage with a wooden lychgate and a polygonal bay with flush mullions and transoms in stone. Its plan is disappointingly standard, with the long kitchen outshut typical of the period. It was built for the manager of the family's mill, possibly a little later than its unequal twin. REDCROFT was Wood's own house until 1916 and is, as we might hope, highly individual and very much the home of the artist-architect. Entrance at the side by a spacious wooden porch. The hallway is a trapezoid space, with the stair tucked in beside the door as indicated outside. A removable section of floor allows furniture to be taken upstairs, and a speaking tube communicates with the attic studio. The principal room at the front of the house is darkly panelled with a large fireplace in an inglenook, one of whose windows looks out to the garden but the other is set sideways into the porch. Painted gesso figures of the Arts and secret drawers in the over-mantel. The first-floor landing is even more curious in shape than the hall below, with a curved wall as well as the canted doors. Wood's studio at the top of the house is light and spacious. Tiny stained-glass flowers are set into the plank doors.

Opposite at Nos. 34–48 ROCHDALE ROAD is a simple terrace of seven cottages and a shop, 1898. Simple, that is, until the asymmetric rhythm is noticed, and the flat canopy porches suspended by wrought-iron stays, each with a little fanlight above it. The shop had round-arched windows – that on Cheap Street still outlined. Nos. 51–53 ROCHDALE ROAD is a pair of 1900, of brick with a lot of stone including Yorkshire lintels, made asymmetrical by the bay treatment.

Immediately behind Rochdale Road are two later houses. No. 36 MELLALIEU STREET, 1906, is *Edgar Wood & Henry Sellers'* first house with a reinforced concrete flat roof, although this was by then a commonplace of mill construction. ARKHOLME, No. 1 Towncroft Street, was built a little earlier; an angular composition with very big windows and a flat section of roof.

SHOPS, Nos. 33–37 Manchester Road (facing Central Gardens). 1908. The façade is covered in white and green tiles boldly chevroned, the roof is flat. The façades must have been startling when new amongst the drab sooty brick of Middleton, but are now more attractive in Wood's drawing than in the flesh.

OUTLYING DISTRICTS

Alkrington

Immediately S of the centre along the Manchester Road.

28 ALKRINGTON HALL. One of the few surviving works of *Giacomo*, or as he usually signed himself, *James Leoni*, translator of

Palladio and Alberti. It was built for Darcy Lever in 1735–7. Leoni was the first architect of national status to build in SE Lancashire, and Alkrington the first full Palladian design, with a *piano nobile*. It is superb in scale but very plain. The central block of nine by three well-spaced bays is framed by low pavilion wings, all of brick with stone quoins. Two giant pilasters on a rusticated stone base frame the centrepiece which has a heavy entablature but no pediment.* The SE front is flat, and only articulated by the 3 + 3 + 3 rhythm of the windows, the pedimented doorcase, and slight emphasis of the centre windows. (Despite years of rough treatment the interiors are reasonably well-preserved, including a number of deep relief plaster ceilings. The two staircases, not greatly differentiated in scale or decoration, are lit by tall windows in the ends.)

At Alkrington was 'the elegant and magnificent museum of my friend, Ashton Lever, Esq.', as John Whitaker the historian called it. Sir Ashton initiated his famous collection of natural history and curiosities in about 1760, supposedly after he shot and preserved a white sparrow. By 1773 when he was elected to the Royal Society he was receiving as many as a thousand people in a day. A visitor in 1774 described it as occupying 'four large rooms ranging almost the whole front of the building, the wall formerly dividing the apartments being formed into arches to support the chambers above'. These were the three rooms along the N front and the W wing, which had been rebuilt by Sir Ashton for the purpose. The E wing was also rebuilt, probably for catering. Following the museum's move to Leicester House in London in 1774–5 the hall reverted to domestic use, though the arches were probably not filled in again until 1802. After municipal use the hall was restored as four dwellings by *Keith Harnden* in 1993–5.

By the N end of the house is a long BARN with shouldered doors, converted to five cottages with long mullioned windows, and a small STABLE, also converted, probably contemporary with the house.

The PARK, framed by woods, sweeps down from the N front to the River Irk. BRIDGE, in line with the house, dated 1636 on the upstream side, enlarged by Darcy Lever 1735 on the downstream side. On the W a series of ponds, and parallel to the SW front a formal canal, are mixed up with the houses of the Garden Village.

ALKRINGTON GARDEN VILLAGE. Begun 1909, a middle-class equivalent to Blackley Cottages just across the Manchester boundary (q.v.). Planned by *Thomas Adams* of Letchworth, then Messrs *Peplar & Allen* (also Burnage Garden Village, Manchester, q.v.). The speculation failed in the First World War and it is now mostly 1930s in aspect. Generous layout with some old trees. Early houses with characteristic long roof

---

*Leoni's vanished Bold Hall near St Helens was comparable in scale and restraint and had similar architectural elements but differently disposed.

slopes and roughcast in e.g. Rookway and Alkrington Green,
including in the latter several by *Thomas Arthur Fitton* and Nos.
22 and 24 Mount Road by *Edgar Wood* 1907: a symmetrical
pair for once of brick with some stone striping and stone flag
roofs (replaced on No. 22).

ALKRINGTON CONGREGATIONAL CHURCH (United
Reformed), Manchester New Road, by *Bradshaw Gass &
Hope*, 1928. Brick, laid in Flemish bond. Narthex, then the
low chapel with shoulders at both ends. Parish room behind,
at right angles. The larger windows have simple brick tracery.
A MEMORIAL, N, commemorates the union of Salem and
Alkrington chapels in 1929, and the war dead. Two columns
become one, bearing a cross.

Hopwood

A mile or so NE, Hopwood is split from Middleton by the M62
motorway. For St John, *see* Heywood. For St John, Thornham,
see p. 511.

HOPWOOD HALL is a rambling irregular house of brick with
stone roofs, built round a tiny courtyard. The hall range was
on the S side, the gatehouse range on the N. Of the medieval
building there is but one substantial relic, the upper part of
the spere truss. This is enough to prove that there was an open
great hall, to indicate that it was timber-framed and to suggest
that the framing had decorative quatrefoils, like Tonge or
Ordsall. Its position shows that the screens passage has been
incorporated into the large-bayed room to the E. In the C17 the
timber framing was built away in brick, an intermediate floor
inserted in the hall and a four-fireplace chimney stack plonked
in front of the dais, which became the snug. A corridor was
added along the courtyard side, and stairs inserted at the
family end. There were large scale additions in the C18 and C19
too, including the pele-tower-like block on the E side. In the
1850s Mrs Susan Hopwood, pioneer campaigner for smoke
abatement and an enthusiastic antiquary, reversed the clock,
Tudorizing the windows and filling the place with antique and
reproduction carved wood expertly blended by *George & John
Shaw* of Saddleworth. The whole of the upper storey has since
been stripped out, and the hall is currently empty and at risk.
    In the little valley below the hall are the foundations of the
C18 CORN MILL.

HOPWOOD HALL COLLEGE. The De la Salle Brothers established a teacher-training college in the hall in 1947, but left in
the 1990s. HALLS OF RESIDENCE, quite ambitious in their high
and gabled forms, 1952 and 1956 by *Reynolds & Scott*. Among
the other scattered buildings of 1961–3 etc. is the SPORTS
ARENA by *Cruickshank & Seward*, 2002. The stunning former
CHAPEL is by *Frederick Gibberd*, 1963–5. His Liverpool
R.C. Cathedral was built in 1960–7 so this is neither a try-out
nor a refinement of it; rather it represents the Liverpool

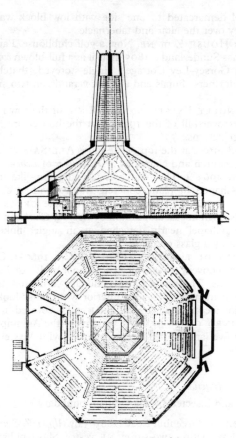

Hopwood Hall chapel, section and plan

concept in its pure form, without the flying buttresses or the ring of chapels, and with the lantern narrower and unadorned, so that the building is more like a funnel than a crown. It has eight instead of sixteen sides, so it is a definite polygon rather than the approximation of a drum. It floats on its green hillock, the sides recessed into shadow at ground level. Of very basic materials: exposed concrete, grey blocks, simplest coloured glass (by *D. Atkins*), and none the worse for that. Interior of Brutalist simplicity, with an impossibly live acoustic, and like Liverpool, bigger than you expect. It is lit only by the lantern and the circumferential slit window, but that is plenty. The structure which is invisible outside is clear inside: eight concrete members connected by two concrete ring beams and stiffened by X-braces in the roof. Central altar on an octagonal dais, with the organ behind, also as at Liverpool. Single chapel demarcated to one side with low block walls and a canopy over the altar and tabernacle.

DOWER HOUSE ½ m. NE. Now a golf clubhouse. Paintings by Thomas Sunderland *c.* 1805 show it as a full-blown *cottage orné*, called Gorsey-Ley Cottage,* single-storeyed, thatched, with large dormers, finials and a rustic veranda on two sides.

The LANGLEY ESTATE, on the hill NW of the town, is Manchester overspill of the 1950s, but the houses are not Manchester designs.

On Wood Street at the top of the hill is ALL SAINTS. Hall, vicarage, church and chapel by *A. H. Walker* of *Leach, Rhodes & Walker,* 1963–4. The church is jaggedly ship-like in outline, coffin-shaped in plan, concrete framed with a cladding of narrow bricks and copper roof. Tree-like CROSS 37 ft (11 metres) high in cast aluminium by *Geoffrey Clarke* on the E wall inside. Chapel nearly detached at an angle, linked to the church by a glass corridor.

OUR LADY OF THE ASSUMPTION (R.C.), 1960–1. Grey brick church, convent, presbytery and school by *W. & J. B. Ellis* of St Helens. The church conventionally Romanesque with a strong campanile. Spacious interior with flimsy-looking piers carrying a continuous beam. The E end is covered in MOSAIC. – STAINED GLASS in the W window of the Assumption, and in the five lancets of the transept, the Joyful Mysteries of the Rosary.

Middleton Junction

½ m. E, and bisected by the Oldham boundary.

ST GABRIEL, Greenhill Road. 1883–5 by *Alfred W. Smith.* Stone, towerless, with a two-storey NE vestry. Short polished stone arcade piers. (– STAINED GLASS. E, 1946, by *Humphries, Jackson & Ambler* of Manchester.)

GREENGATE BREWERY (J. W. Lees), Oldham Road. Good traditional complex of 1878 and 1883, all in brick with a little polychromy. Opposite the brewery one of its pubs, THE JUNCTION, formerly Green Lane Cottage – not a cottage but a villa of 1881, in harsh brick. STAINED GLASS by *Heaton, Butler & Bayne.* 'A man may have learning, he may have what is called genius, but he must have industry', among other appropriately Lancastrian sentiments. BRITISH VITA, Soudain Street, occupies Soudain Mills Nos. 1 and 2, early C20 by *George Stott.*

MILNROW

A linear settlement, linking with Rochdale at one end and New Hey at the other. It was only in the C19 that Milnrow and New

---

* Thanks to Andrew Martindale for this information.

Hey coalesced within Butterworth, one of the four townships of the vast Rochdale parish.

Rochdale was considered to be the centre of the genuine Lancashire dialect; John Collier (1708–86), known as Tim Bobbin, dialect poet and painter, was schoolteacher at Milnrow from 1729.

ST JAMES. Replacing a church of 1799, rebuilt in 1814, which stood in the SE corner of the churchyard. But an older chapel stands by the river (*see* below). What we see now is by *G.E. Street*, 1868–9. It was built at the expense of the Schofield family, flannel manufacturers, and at the instigation of the antiquarian vicar, Francis Raines. It was the Schofields, with connections at Swinton (q.v.), who insisted on Street as architect rather than Raines's friend George Shaw, who might have done something more interesting.

The church is a very sober exercise, solid and serious but hardly lively enough to excite enquiry into the name of the architect. W tower without pinnacles but a low recessed pyramid roof, wide nave and aisles, a shortish chancel and the small Schofield Chapel in the angle of the S aisle and chancel. The interior is wide rather than high. The octagonal piers have naturalistic foliage capitals carved by *T. Earp*. – FONT, PULPIT, STALLS, PEWS all by *Street*. His REREDOS was a cause of controversy on account of the red Maltese cross in the centre panel. The replacement Captain Schofield agreed to was a bleeding heart. Now there is a blazing sun – an odd progression. – STAINED GLASS. E and Schofield Chapel E by *Hardman*. S by *Clayton & Bell*, 1860s. W aisle windows perhaps by *Wailes*, 1874 and 1879. The N side windows are C20, showing how canopy work and edging steadily disappear; including one signed *Shrigley & Hunt*, 1911.

Large open rectangular CHURCHYARD surrounded by tough council housing. The little MEETING HOUSE by the N side of the chancel is not by Street but by *Henry Blackburn* of Rochdale. Canon Raines's MEMORIAL, 1879, is an obelisk of red and grey granites by the S porch.

Raines's Tudor Gothic VICARAGE of 1833, now St James House, is on Kiln Lane. He built a school too, in 1840, W of the church where the present school is.

In BRIDGE STREET by the river is a row of three cottages which was the OLD CHAPEL. Built 1496, enlarged 1537 and largely rebuilt 1725 after flooding, it was abandoned in 1799. The cottages have typical multiple-mullioned windows in the rebuilt S wall, but arch-headed lights in two storeys remain in the end walls. The naïve chapel doorway, probably of 1725, has been reset. It was originally on the upper floor, approached by steps. It has Ionic pilasters and in the pediment what looks like a Masonic triangular eye, developed into a shield instead.

MUNICIPAL BUILDINGS, New Hey Road. Progressively disused since Milnrow lost its municipal status in 1974 but under restoration in 2003. Fire Station of 1889, blunt unfinished-looking Clock Tower, Town Hall office of 1885, all minimally Gothic. Police Station, typically stern Tudor with a central bay and paired entrances either side of it; probably by the County Architect *Henry Littler*. The little CARNEGIE LIBRARY, by *S. Butterworth & W. H. Duncan* 1907–8, set back between them, is much suaver, its beautiful ashlar contrasting with the coursed rubble of the others. Arts and Crafts detailing, including roses and thistles, in the stonework; shades of Art Nouveau in the glass. The building spreads at the rear to accommodate borrowers' hall and lending library, reading room with a coved ceiling, and ladies' and boys' rooms, with dados of different colours in glazed brick.

DALE STREET is the principal thoroughfare. On its E side rows of late C19 WEAVERS' HOUSES. Milnrow was a centre for fell-mongering, i.e. stripping wool from hides. The workshops here specialized in the production of woollen cloth which combined stripped with shorn wool. This is the reason for the late date of the houses, which were rarely built after the early C19 elsewhere in SE Lancashire. Nos. 45 and 47 are three-storey, very deep, with original windows; No. 47 has been painted brick colour over the stone, an amusing conceit. Nos. 55–65 are three-storey as well, with taking-in doors on both upper floors of No. 65. Nos. 111–129 form a long two-storey row. All of these are built around a continuous grid of sills, lintels and mullions on the upper floors so that windows can be opened up or blocked as required. The openings are relatively wide and the stone members simply square and set flush with the wall, all signs of a late date. More of the same at Nos. 25–29 Charles Lane, leading SE off Dale Street. On the W side the houses have their backs to the road, showing how unplanned the urbanization was. No. 40 is moreover a gentlemanly C19 double-fronted house, with its arched stair window, and continuous weavers' windows, to the street. The adjacent houses are half-width, with blank walls to the street but weavers' windows overlooking the river.

CLEGG HALL, 1 m. NE. Still isolated, on a dirt road where it crosses the canal. Magnificent but long deserted and now a ruin, which is a pity because it is an ambitious house. The date is uncertain; possibly built 1617–18 by Theophilus Assheton of the Middleton family, but Nicholas Cooper suggests *c.* 1640. It is four-square – i.e. a double pile – with three gables on each side, two storeys and attics on a basement, with a ramp up to the front door. The continuous top string jumps up and down over the mullioned-and-transomed windows, and steps down at the sides to link the fenestration of the taller grand rooms at the front with the lower ones of the service quarters at the back. The two-storey porch, front and SW side are of ashlar, the rest coursed rubble. The porch has, or had, naïve fluted classical columns, paired and probably meant to be Doric below, single and Corinthian above. Prominent waterspouts at the valleys, but without the faces exhibited by later houses. The loss of the roof exposes the astonishing row of chimneys set diagonally along the spine wall. The few floor joists remaining

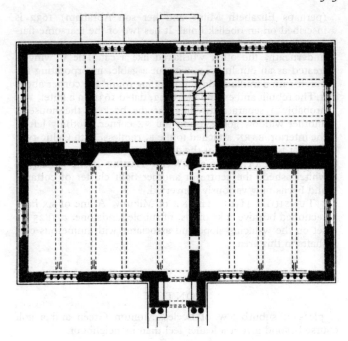

Milnrow, Clegg Hall, plan

are heavily moulded. In its squareness and symmetry, its precocious deep plan with all the stacks ranged on a spine wall, and its front-to-back split-level planning Clegg can be compared with Gainford Hall of 1604 in County Durham, which was the pioneer in the north of such innovations.

Surrounding the hall is a typical cluster of working buildings, including four WEAVERS' HOUSES, SW, solidly built with multi-light windows on the top floor only, a DYE-HOUSE and MILL, NE, and the site of a three-storey stone WAREHOUSE (burnt down, 2003) on the canalside. Mill and houses were built by Joseph Fenton of Bamford in 1811. At the NE corner of the site is the MILL MANAGER'S HOUSE. Water was supplied by the long narrow lodge, SE.

On Wildhouse Lane there are several C17 yeoman houses, clustered as was usual into folds. BIRCHINLEY MANOR and BIRCHINLEY HALL stand on either side of what was a common yard with numerous farm buildings. Both are U-shaped rather than H-shaped, i.e. with flat backs. The Hall's entrance is behind the hearth in the w wing. The date 1619 is carved on the porch, with five sets of initials indicating multiple ownership. (In 1556 an earlier house was recorded as being divided 'streight up to the top' between two sisters and their families.) The Manor is a charmer, but maltreated. EAM (perhaps Elizabeth Milne and her son Abraham) 1632 is inscribed on an obelisk finial. It has two of the fearsome flat-faced gargoyles characteristic of the area, one with little arms underneath, the other whiskered like a cat. The w wing is treated as an outshut, i.e. without a gable, incorporating the porch with a mullioned window going round the corner above it. The rebuilt and extended E wing, dated 1631 on a lintel, was probably a separate dwelling. At the back of the house is another window going round the NE corner. Nothing left of the interior. BARN attached to the E, roofless, with Celtic-type faces at the springing of the arch.

On the E side of the lane is WILD HOUSE itself, H-shaped, whitewashed, the centre of another tight cluster of cottages and barns now variously converted.

TUNSHILL HILL, 1 m. NE of Milnrow. A line of six half-sectioned beehive coke ovens, of rubble sandstone, *c.* 1825–30 set on the W-facing slope and associated with numerous coal shafts in this area.

MONTON

A pleasant suburb NW of Eccles. Monton Green and a golf course beyond give it a leafier feel than its neighbour.

ST PAUL, Egerton Road. 1911, by *R. B. Preston*. Stock brick and red brick with red terracotta dressings. Lancet windows, no tower.

UNITARIAN CHURCH, Monton Green. Of 1875, by *Thomas Worthington*, who won the competition in 1870. The dominating building of Monton. It stands in its own graveyard beside Monton Green, on or near the site of earlier chapels of 1698, 1715 and *c.* 1800. Well-composed and sited on a corner, so the S and W elevations are of equal importance. SW tower and spire, 150 ft (46 metres) high, low aisles, transepts and a polygonal apse. On the W side a progression from the N: stair-tower with a tall conical roof, nave with large Dec window, and the tower: elements connected with one another by low links, actually a narthex which runs the whole width of the building.

INTERIOR. The progression of space in the narthex is marked by differing treatments of the roofs, with scissor-bracing at the entrance on the S side, and panelled ceilings with bosses marking the other spaces. At the N end, an open stone arcade with steps up to the W gallery. Nave with a high hammerbeam roof with tie-rods and two tiers of windbraces. W gallery with panelled front, five-bay arcade of circular piers, generous transepts and steps up to the chancel. The chancel scheme is complete. – CHOIR STALLS with canopies. – Encaustic TILES by *Minton*. – PULPIT. Octagonal with a wrought-iron balustrade with designs of passion flowers. – Marvellous GASOLIERS (adapted for electricity), of similar intricate ironwork, at the entrance to the chancel and in the

transepts. – Original BENCH SEATING. – STAINED GLASS. In
the narthex, Faith, Hope and Charity by *Heaton, Butler &
Bayne*. They also did the unusual clerestory windows of *c.* 1899,
illustrating passages from the Benedicite and Te Deum with
artists, philosophers, writers and religious leaders as well as
saints and martyrs: Homer, Dante, Shakespeare, Milton,
Wesley, Bunyan, Erasmus, Michelangelo, Phidias, Socrates
and so on. In the S transept and probably also by the firm, the
Sermon on the Mount, with beautiful Morris-style foliage in
the upper lights. A set of brightly coloured mid-C19 windows
from the predecessor building by *H. Beiler* of Heidelberg, two
in each transept, show Luther, Huss, Zwingli and Wycliffe.
Good N transept window, Christ blessing children, by *T. R.
Spence, c.* 1880–90.

Gabled stone LYCHGATE of 1895 with elaborate iron gates.

MONTON MEMORIAL SCHOOLS (former), Stableford Avenue,
behind the Unitarian Church. By *Thomas Worthington & J. G.
Elgood*. Dated 1888. Large, asymmetrical, Gothic and of stone.
Entrance arcade with the door flanked by windows, gables
with triple and paired arched upper windows.

WESTWOOD LODGE, alongside the Bridgewater Canal, off
Parkin Lane. Mid-C19 lodge, picturesquely treated with tall
angled chimneys and bargeboards. Probably erected as part of
a series of rides and lodges in the area by the 1st Earl of
Ellesmere of Worsley Hall.

MOSSLEY   9000

A dramatic site with steep banks and views to the hills, separated
from Ashton-under-Lyne to the SW by open land. Mossley is
formed from three centres originally in three old counties;
Mossley, S, in Lancashire, Micklehurst, E, in Cheshire and
Roughtown, N, in Yorkshire. The areas were unified under a local
board in 1864 and became a borough in 1885. In 1974 they became
part of Tameside Metropolitan Borough Council. In character
Mossley is a Pennine hill town, with buildings largely of stone, and
an economy initially based on agriculture and wool-processing.
C18 and early C19 houses with upper attic workshops for handloom
weaving and related activities survive throughout the area. The
valley bottom between Mossley and Micklehurst is the course of
the River Tame, the Huddersfield Narrow Canal and the railway.
Industry was concentrated here. There were twenty wool mills in
the village by 1830; by this time cotton-spinning was also established, and was already becoming pre-eminent.

ST GEORGE, the parish church. First built 1755–7, rebuilt
1879–82 by *A. H. Davies-Colley & Brooke*. The NE porch tower
was added in 1887. Stone, Dec, and rather dull. N and S aisles,
triangular-headed clerestory windows, expressed chancel,
polygonal W baptistery. The tower has prominent bell-
openings and corner pinnacles. (Chamfered-arched nave

arcades with circular columns. – STAINED GLASS by *F. Comère* and *Capronnier*. – Good wall MONUMENT from the previous church, Catharine Kenworthy †1776. A shrouded figure lifting the coffin lid. TS.)

CHURCHYARD. E of the church is a stub of the wall of the 1755 church. On one side an inscription recording the fact, on the other a reset memorial to John Whitworth †1848, recording his career as a drummer, field bugler and finally drum major of the 7th Royal Fusiliers. Trophy with drums, bugles etc.

ALL SAINTS, Church Street, Micklehurst. 1891–3 by *Potts, Son & Pickup*. Stone, Dec, aisleless, with an odd NW tower incorporating a porch. Big pinnacles frame the octagonal top stage. Short spire with prominent lucarnes.

ST JOHN THE BAPTIST, Carrhill, Roughtown. 1878–9 by *Wild & Collins*. Austere, and of stone, but without conviction, though the very tall slim spire is impressive, and a prominent local landmark. Nave and chancel under one roof, S aisle, N porch, Geometrical window tracery. Detached SW broach spire with lancet bell-openings. (E window by *Reuben Bennett* of Manchester, 1901.)

ST JOSEPH (R.C.), Argyle Street. Opened in 1965. Brick with a gabled front with deep eaves, cupola with an upturned copper roof and spirelet.

TOWN HALL (former), Stamford Road. George Mayall, one of the most successful local industrialists, built a grand and rather stern Italianate house high on the hill in 1861–4, commanding views across the valley to the Pennines beyond. In 1891 it was bought and converted to the town hall. Stone, two storeys and asymmetrical. A projecting bay has a pedimental gable, and the elaborate porch has a rusticated base and heavy bracketed eaves cornices, with austerity relieved by carved allegories of plenty and upper balustrading with urns at the angles. Elaborate pedimented upper windows, with stone balconies linked to the lintels of the windows below by consoles. Single-storey stone entrance LODGE on Old Brow. The gardens have balustraded terraces. They are now a park and the site of a FIRST WORLD WAR MEMORIAL, of *c.* 1920 by *Kilpatrick* of Mossley. White marble female figure holding a book on a stone pedestal.

POLICE STATION, Argyle Street. Mid–late C19, two-storeyed with the central entrance treated as a Venetian opening, and the words 'County Constabulary Station' above the entrance. It is exactly like the one in Droylsden (q.v.) but in stone rather than brick.

STATION, Manchester Road. 1849 for the London & North Western Railway. Stone, quietly Gothic. The waiting rooms etc. alongside the platform have all been truncated and bricked up.

MILLS

Mossley had more than forty mills by the end of the C19, mainly along the Tame and Huddersfield Narrow Canal. Others were

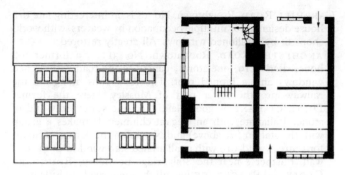

No. 18 Carrhill Road, elevation and plan

concentrated along Micklehurst Brook in Micklehurst and in Sandbed beside Lees Road, and in the centre of Mossley, where part of the 1860 Brookbottom mill survives. Almost all have been demolished.* The most imposing and only fairly complete example is WOODEND MILL, beside the river just off Manchester Road. It is a landmark in views into the valley from all around. Founded by Robert Hyde Buckley in 1848, it became a combined spinning and weaving factory in 1850, and was expanded in stages until 1913. Stone, with a tremendous four-storey frontage of forty-five windows to the Tame, all dominated by a tall circular chimney. Beside it the brick-built CARRHILL MILL. Started in 1801–2, but the surviving flat-roofed four-storey building is of 1897–9.

STREETS

ABNEY ROAD, Mossley. APSLEY HOUSE is a large stone Tudor Gothic house probably of the 1840s. Rather plain, with a symmetrical front with two projecting bays with very steep gables flanking the entrance, and a smaller gable.

ANTHONY STREET, Mossley, near St George's church. An early C19 terrace and a good example of three-storey houses in which the upper floors were designed as workshops and lit by mullioned windows. Nos. 7 and 17, at either end, have taking-in doors at workshop level.

AUDLEY STREET and BOTTOMS FOLD, Micklehurst. The oldest buildings of Micklehurst centre are concentrated in these adjoining streets. Various C18 stone houses, most of them greatly altered, but No. 28 Audley Street retains a relatively unspoilt elevation with two-, four- and five-light mullioned windows.

---

*For the history and remains of the ten or so for which some physical evidence survives, *see* Ian Haynes, *Mossley Textile Mills*, 1996.

CARRHILL ROAD, Roughtown. No. 18 is an interesting late C18 house designed for multiple occupation by weavers, with workshops lit by mullioned windows. All greatly restored.

MANCHESTER ROAD, Roughtown. No. 317 is a former toll house. Early C19, one storey, canted to the road with arched windows and a hipped roof. The road runs alongside the railway into the lower part of Mossley. Here the former DISTRICT BANK is good, late C19, one storey only and of stone, Italianate with an elegant chimney. It makes a group with the station (*see* above) and No. 62 on the corner of Stamford Street, mid-C19 with a tall arched stair window in the end wall. Further s near the Stalybridge boundary, BOUNDARY CLOSE and BLACKROCK just off the main road are little PREFAB settlements, rarely seen today, groups of 1940s houses of the *Tarran* type; vertical pebbledashed concrete slabs, some with corrugated iron roofs.

ROUGHTOWN ROAD, Roughtown. QUICKWOOD is the name of a terrace consisting of an early C18 house with C18 cottages attached. The house, called the Manor House, has a strangely configured front, surely the result of alteration. Three storeys and an attic, symmetrical with a central pedimented door, mullioned windows, and paired gables, each with a circular window placed to one side of the centre. Central pedimented window between. The attached terrace is of three builds, all of stone, seven houses in all, with mullioned windows.

The road continues on the s side of Carrhill Road and there are several C18 houses and cottages hereabouts on the steep slope overlooking the valley. One of the best-preserved lies near the junction with High Street, an early or mid-C18 house, two storeys, stone, with mullioned windows.

STALEY ROAD, Micklehurst. Nos. 71–77, a range of altered early C19 houses of which No. 77, dated 1802, was probably the first to be put up. Beside them No. 79, Oakdene, is dated 1755 with the initials RHE. Symmetrical, with a central door, but still with mullioned windows.

FARM BUILDINGS AND OUTLYING HOUSES

Farm buildings and cottages are scattered along the high and lonely lanes of the upland fringes. They would reward further study, and only a few indications are given here. Those of interest are almost all of the C18, some with C17 origins. They exhibit single- and double-depth plans, some (but by no means all) symmetrical, and illustrate the wholesale adoption of stone as a building material, the gradual and uneven abandonment of traditional plan forms, and the use of mullions through to the C19. In many of them wool preparation and handloom weaving were combined with farming as a source of income, and attic workshops were provided for the purpose.*

* A good introduction to houses of this type can be found in M. Nevell and J. Walker, *Tameside in Transition*, 1999.

BROADCARR LANE, S of the centre. No. 9 is mid–late C18, a double-depth house of three storeys with serried ranks of five-light mullioned windows. At the top of the lane the COLLIERS' ARMS is a low late C18 or early C19 farmhouse with a later and taller attached barn and shippon. The farmhouse is of two storeys, stone, with (probably replacement) sash windows and an entrance to the l. beside the barn. The front rooms were converted to a beerhouse, presumably serving miners at the former Broadcarr Colliery nearby, and early C20 fixtures remain in the tap room.

HOWARDS LANE runs from the Huddersfield Road E of Micklehurst up into the moors. First HOWARD'S FARMHOUSE, actually three three-storey double-depth houses of the early–mid C18. Further along, ALPHIN HOUSE is of similar date, double-depth, two and three storeys, while OVERGREEN is earlier, perhaps of the late C17, but much restored and altered. Last, PLEASANT VIEW, which aptly describes its situation, high on the heathery hill. House, cottage and barn all probably mid-C18.

LEES ROAD, N of the centre. HOLLYBANK FARM is dated 1744 with the letters MMS on the door lintel, perhaps relating to the partial rebuilding of an older house. L-shaped, single-depth, with an attached barn to the W.

LUZLEY ROAD, S of the centre, runs S across the moors to Ashton-under-Lyne and Stalybridge. Scattered buildings, some C18 and early C19, most altered. One of the largest is LUZLEY HALL, dated 1771, but probably with earlier origins. A large L-shaped house, greatly altered and restored, but with mullioned windows in the gable; two tall lights flanked by two shorter ones beneath a continuous label mould above, a long range of six lights with a mould extending on each side to the edge of the bay, below. On the other side of the courtyard altered barns and stables.

STRAWBERRY LANE, off Stockport Road, N of Roughtown. A number of early C19 houses, including a good terrace of four three-storey double-depth houses with four-light mullioned windows. QUICK FARM consists of an early C19 house with a rear C18 range with mullioned windows, a long low barn with a ball finial to the end gable, and an altered cottage, probably early C19, with slender mullions.

STOCKPORT ROAD, N of the centre. Just off the main road, MIDGE HILL is an interesting C18 complex of three houses with attic workshops, built into the hillside so that the workshop floor is reached from behind by a short flight of steps. Flat-cut Venetian window in the gable.

NEW HEY

Milnrow and New Hey are divided only – but it is a decisive divide – by the M62.

ST THOMAS. 1876–7. The site lies high above the town, so *H. Lloyd* was concerned to make a brave show – perhaps over-concerned. Of hard local sandstone dressed to the unattractive finish called pitch-faced, which has gone black. It is pointed in red. Doors and windows are edged nervously with Bath stone which has gone white. White Bath stone for the spire too, but the pinnacles are gritstone, now jet black. The roofs are banded with plain green and purple scalloped slates and crested in red. Continuous windowing in the clerestory collides with the transept roofs. A whole row of steep gables for the NE vestry. The arcade arches are steep too, with wide, square foliage capitals on short monoliths of brown fossiliferous stone. Wider and taller arches for the transepts, flanked by exceedingly narrow ones, like a Gothic triumphal arch. – FONT carved with Old and New Testament scenes, but painted. – STAINED GLASS. Two by *Heaton, Butler & Bayne*.

The SCHOOL at the foot of the hill, of stone with mullioned windows in threes and fours, preceded the church.

ELLENROAD ENGINE HOUSE, Bentgate Street. Although only a fragment, this is one of the best places to sense the power and life of the Lancashire cotton industry. The mill was by *Stott & Sons*, 1891–2. It burnt in 1916 and was rebuilt in 1921 by *John Russell*. This was demolished in 1985, so what remains are just the 1891 engine house, boiler house and chimney. The engine house, of brick and stone, was as usual given some architectural dignity. Tall arched windows at the sides give plenty of light. The end windows had to be big enough to bring in the engines. A huge arch at the mill end houses the giant flywheel. Wall columns on the inside, which is lined with glazed brick, carry an overhead crane. The circular chimney, 220 ft (70 metres) tall and free-standing, has the ring of pilasters near the top, a device which from 1886 was a signature of Stott & Sons. The mighty engines are steamed regularly.

At OGDEN, 1 m. E, the cluster of CASTLE FARM illustrates the architectural conservatism of the area. The main house is inscribed IT (James Taylor) 1715, but is little different from what would have been built a century before, just neater (i.e. not breaking forward at the ends), and more horizontal (i.e. without gables on the façade). Still asymmetrical, with long ranges of mullioned windows and a porch, formerly castellated. At the side of the porch, commanding the steps, are a gaping flat-faced gargoyle and a loop-hole.

OLDHAM

INTRODUCTION

Oldham stands high on a breezy hill, with views out to suburbs
on lesser hills, and the Pennines beyond. Before the Industrial
Revolution it was no more than a hamlet – by contrast with e.g.
Rochdale, which was a market town. The first landmark was a
chapel of ease of Prestwich parish, probably present by 1379

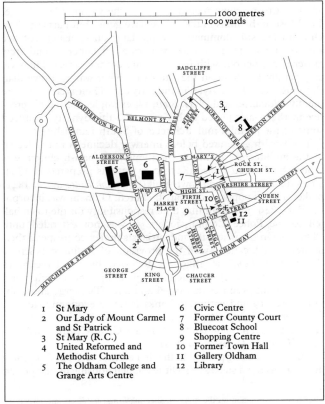

I	St Mary	6	Civic Centre
2	Our Lady of Mount Carmel	7	Former County Court
	and St Patrick	8	Bluecoat School
3	St Mary (R.C.)	9	Shopping Centre
4	United Reformed and	10	Former Town Hall
	Methodist Church	11	Gallery Oldham
5	The Oldham College and	12	Library
	Grange Arts Centre		

Oldham, the centre

when a baptism is recorded, and mentioned in 1406. Oldham was an important centre of handloom weaving by the early C19. The cotton-spinning industry, specializing in production of coarse yarn, was initially based around small firms which often shared mills. In the early C19 the settlement centred on the Market Place and the streets radiating from it, principally the main Manchester–Huddersfield route, Yorkshire Street. Mumps, at the E end of Yorkshire Street, had started to develop as a subsidiary centre, and Union Street, now the grandest city-centre thoroughfare, had been laid out but not built up. Within a few decades the church towers were outstripped in height and number by cotton-mill chimneys, for by the late C19 Oldham was the leading mill town in the world. The population was 12,024 in 1831, 52,820 in 1851, and 147,483 in 1911.

Professor Douglas Farnie points out that keys to this success were the excellent facilities for technical education and the willingness to adopt new technology on the part of the inhabitants. For instance, during the 'cotton famine', caused by the American Civil War, local engineering firms adapted machinery to spin Indian cotton. Farnie describes the town as 'the best place to study the mill in its perfected form'. It was also the home of the greatest C19 machine manufacturer in the world, Platt Bros & Co. Most of the mills in the centre have gone, but parts of outer Oldham are still dominated by the later ones, usually of five storeys, up to 150 ft (46 metres) wide, of concrete and steel girder construction, with flat roofs and corner towers. The style is generally Italianate in the late C19, giving way to Edwardian Baroque and eclectic styles in the early C20. Their architects were mainly Oldham-based. *A. H. Stott*, for example, started his practice in 1847, later joined by his sons, and this dynasty produced some of the premier mill architects of South Lancashire.*

The wealth generated before interwar decline is not reflected in the architecture of the town, though the parish church was rebuilt by *Richard Lane*, 1827–30 to designs prepared in 1824. The Greek Revival style Town Hall (by *Joseph Butterworth*, 1841) makes a show opposite the parish church. Oldham was incorporated in 1849, and until that time responsibility for the town hall fell to the Police Commissioners. It was not extended until 1879–80. On the whole the industrialists preferred to spend their money on education, with the provision of a Bluecoat School (by *Richard Lane*) in 1829–30, followed by the Lyceum (a mechanics' institute), founded in 1839 and provided with grand purpose-built premises in 1855–6 and later. The large and elaborate late C19 and early C20 banks indicate economic success, but there is little first-rate C19 or C20 ecclesiastical or public architecture. The new landmark is the Civic Centre tower (by *Cecil Howitt & Partners*, 1974–8).

The new housing praised in the first edition of *South Lancashire* in 1969 was not a success – so little council housing of that period

---

* For more information on the mills, engineering firms, architects and owners *see* D. Gurr and J. Hunt, *The Cotton Mills of Oldham*, 1998.

was. Some of the low-rise elements of the schemes off Horsedge Street and at Primrose Bank survive, but the favoured style today is traditional red brick housing. In 2004 the town centre is a scene of building, with a large supermarket under construction near the new art gallery (by *Pringle Richards Sharratt*, 1999–2001), and plans for a new library and performing arts centre.

The centre, including Mumps, is described first, with churches and public buildings followed by streets in alphabetical order. Then the outer areas follow. Outer Oldham N includes Besom Hill, Burnley Brow, Coldhurst, Derker, Heyside, Higginshaw, Moorside, Northmoor and Watersheddings. s and sw includes Bardsley, Hathershaw, Hollins Green, Hollinwood and Werneth. E and SE includes Alt, Glodwick, Greenacres, Greenacres Moor, Low Side, Pitses, New Earth and Waterhead. w includes Westwood.

CHURCHES

ST MARY, Church Street. By *Richard Lane*, 1827–30. The design dates from 1824, with amendments of 1825. It was exhibited at the Royal Academy in 1826. It is worthy of its hilltop setting, although the proposed scheme by *Charles Barry* would have been better.* The medieval church it replaced was also of great interest (partially rebuilt in 1476 by Ralph Langley), and by no means beyond repair – the tower base had to be removed by dynamite. Designs for a new church were drawn up by various architects, including *Francis Goodwin* and *Matthew Habershon* as well as Lane and Barry. The Bishop of Chester tried to impose Barry's scheme on the Oldhamers, who put up fierce resistance, and in the end Lane's prevailed. It was a financial disaster. At a time when an adequate Commissioners' church could be put up for £5,000 or less, more than £30,000 was spent, partly on a large crypt in the hope that costs could be offset by selling burial spaces.

Lane's church is large, and it is his best and most lavish church. It conforms in many ways to the Commissioners' type, i.e. it is etiolated Perp with a w tower and shallow apse. But the joyful, even florid detailing marks it out, though the loss of the exuberant finials to the tower has damaged its proportions. Display is mainly concentrated at the w end. Full-height octagonal buttresses at the angles of the tower are castellated at the top and flanked by similar turrets forming a sort of screen, with embattled porch bays on each side. w window with complicated tracery and knobbly ogee surround. There is much blind panelling and ornamented detail including a clock surround placed diagonally, and a bold frieze with anthemion-like motifs. Three-light bell-openings, stepped crenellated parapet. The sides are more conventional: windows with

---

*His proposal drawings are kept in the church.

intersecting tracery and pinnacled buttresses breaking through the parapet. The apse is emphasized by pinnacles at the angles.

43 INTERIOR. The first impression is created by the very tall five-bay arcades of slender clustered piers and the wonderful decorative scheme of 1975 by *Stephen Dykes Bower*. All the walls are painted in rich colours with Gothic designs, the piers and ceiling are done in reds and greens, and the details picked out with gilding. At the same time all the stained glass except that in the E window was removed and new lighting introduced. Soaring chancel arch, plaster-vaulted ceiling with pretty bosses. Three galleries with elegantly curved undersides, plaster ribs and traceried fronts. At the w end doors are on each side with flat heads and Tudor-style hoodmoulds, and there is a central recess with a Tudor arch and the churchwardens' pews. Generous cantilevered stone stairs to the galleries with wreathed rails and pretty Gothic traceried balusters. The huge CRYPT is tunnel- and groin-vaulted, with many large imposing cast-iron doors to the vaults. In the chancel late C19 or early C20 FURNISHINGS. – REREDOS. Painting of Christ in Majesty by *E. Stanley Watkins* of Ealing, 1908. – N chapel, another triptych PAINTING by him: the Nativity. – MONUMENTS. E end, s side, an elegant tablet with an urn, to Thomas Barker †1839, by *G. Lewis* of Cheltenham. – BRASS, Ralph Taylor †1769. – s side, an ambitious piece with a weeping figure, big volutes and putti, all rather crudely carved. – James Gee †1829, by *Scott & Bros* of Oldham. – Tablet with Gothic crocketed spirelets etc., John Duncroft †1852 by *John Knowles* of Manchester. In the crypt there is part of a medieval stone SARCOPHAGUS found during building work. – STAINED GLASS. The E window is good. Large figures of Prophets and Evangelists by *David Evans* of Shrewsbury, *c.* 1830. – PARISH CHEST. C15 or C16 with three locks. – ORGAN. By *Eliot & Hull*, 1830, with a superb traceried case decorated by *Dykes Bower*. – CHANDELIERS. By *Dykes Bower*, made by *Philip Tennant*.

OUR LADY OF MOUNT CARMEL AND ST PATRICK (R.C.), John Street. 1869–70 by *T. Mitchell* of Oldham, remodelled 1907. E.E. style. w front with three stepped lancets and a bellcote. Paired lancets, projecting gabled confessionals, N side. Four-bay arcades of alternating circular and octagonal piers, timber roof with pierced quatrefoils, canted apse with richly canopied niches with statues. – ALTAR with an aedicule with a tall spire by *George Goldie*. w of the church, a severe red brick PRESBYTERY of three storeys, dated 1898.

ST MARY (R.C.), Shaw Street. 1870. On the site of the town's first Catholic church, erected 1839. A very low-key design, stone, with lancets and a short tower with pyramidal slated roof.

INDEPENDENT METHODIST CHURCH (former), George Street. Built 1815. Brick with four very tall windows with stone sills and margin lights with coloured glass. Pedimented doorcase, r., which looks like a mid-C19 addition, and railings along the front. The land slopes away to the rear, where at

basement level a range of openings in stone surrounds originally gave access to eight two-room dwellings, let to generate
income. Above, another range of tall windows like those at the
front. (Little-altered interior with galleries on three sides, panelled box pews and a queenpost roof.)

UNITED REFORMED AND METHODIST CHURCH, Union
Street. Built as a Congregational chapel in 1855. The architect
was *R. Moffat Smith* of Manchester. w tower with a niche for
a portal with doors off on each side and a six-light window
over with Geometrical tracery. The upper stage of the tower
and the crocketed spire have been removed. Lancet windows.
Well-lit, thanks to the continuous row of clerestory lights with
cusped heads. Everything inside is dominated by the large
extravagant ORGAN CASE with crocketed spires and spirelets,
which stands on an E gallery and probably dates from a refitting of 1871. Gallery fronts with quatrefoils, supported by tall
slim circular piers, and an arched timber roof with principals
rising from carved stone corbels. Late C20 w end subdivision
slightly forward of the w gallery. – BOX PEWS.

FRIENDS' MEETING HOUSE (former), Greaves Street. By *P. B.
Alley*, opened 1869. Distinctly unchurchy. It could as well be
a public library, and was used as such for a while after the
Second World War. Symmetrical, with a projecting pedimented
entrance bay with paired arched windows above paired arched
entrances. Prominent dentilled eaves, and brickwork quoins.

PUBLIC BUILDINGS

TOWN HALL (former), Yorkshire Street. By *Joseph Butterworth*
of Manchester, 1841. Seven bays, two storeys, ashlar-faced.
Pedimented four-column portico of unfluted Ionic columns
after the Little Temple on the Ilissus in Athens. The flanking
bays have full-height pilasters, and the sides are brick. In
1879–80 additions were made and finished with a grand façade
to Greaves Street (E side) by *George Woodhouse* of Bolton and
Edward Potts of Oldham, with giant Corinthian pilasters
framing upper arched windows and lower windows with flat
heads. Extensions were made again in 1917, by *Taylor &
Simister* of Oldham, this time with giant Ionic columns rising
from high bases, the elevation to Firth Street (s side) treated
as a giant Venetian opening with paired Ionic columns resting
on a powerful rusticated base with a central entrance. The w
elevation, previously masked by other buildings, is utilitarian.
The building lies derelict, riddled with dry rot. The entrance
to the early part leads to a corridor with a pair of Ionic columns
at the entrance to a grand staircase hall, with a coved ceiling
and lantern. The stairs have iron balusters with anthemion
motifs. In the later extensions two courts (of 1879–80 and
1917) retain some of their original splendour, but none of the
fittings will survive the rot or plans to incorporate the
building into a shopping centre.

CIVIC CENTRE, Rochdale Road and West Street, on top of a hill on the w side of the centre, visible for miles around. To Rochdale Road the low parts are by *R. Seifert & Partners*, designed in 1962, three-storey ranges with window grids. The fourteen-storey tower and Queen Elizabeth Hall behind are by *Cecil Howitt & Partners*, 1974–8. The tower is a straightforward job, clad in Portland stone, well proportioned, with a service tower and two full-height vertical window strips. Double-height entrance hall with the piers clad in stone. Beneath the counters etc., silver-coloured metal panels with a roundel design.

To the N, across a big windy square, is the QUEEN ELIZ-ABETH HALL, a concert hall. Grey textured concrete and white concrete, with vertical window strips. The entrance is recessed behind a dominating and slightly aggressive sculptural frontispiece. Tiers of dark grey fibreglass oblongs looking like truncated organ pipes jostling together, all end on, with those behind rising higgledy-piggledy above the others. Inside, the palette is cream and dark grey, relieved by the same silvery panels seen in the Civic Centre.

COUNTY COURT (former), Church Lane. Not at all of the ashlar solidity and taciturn dignity of mid-C19 county courts. This is of 1894 by *Sir Henry Tanner* and decidedly gay. Red brick and yellow terracotta with plenty of Louis XII and Francis I motifs. Oriel supported by a great elongated bracket, round-arched entrance with tripartite windows with a pretty terracotta panel above. Converted to offices and a café, with alteration and loss of most fittings, though the courtrooms still have their exposed timber roofs. It occupies the site of a cotton mill established right next to the parish church in 1780.

POST OFFICE (former), Union Street. 1875–7 by *Robert Neill & Son*. Understated in brick with stone dressings, and given a touch of gravitas by urns and low pediments at the corners and over the centre. Ground-floor openings between pilasters.

LIBRARY AND ART GALLERY, Union Street. By *T. Mitchell* of Oldham, with sculpture by *J. J. Millson*. Opened 1883. Vaguely Gothic with a strictly symmetrical frontage. Bulging entrance bay with an oriel, three bays on either side, the middle one emphasized by tall windows with gables breaking above the roofline. A stone panel above the entrance has figures reading in relief, and a figure holding a book and a wreath tops the central gable. The art gallery extends to the rear, with roundels with portrait reliefs of artists, musicians, engineers and writers beneath a clerestory, with a glazed roof above. Rear extensions, including a lecture hall, by *Winder & Taylor*, 1893–4 in matching style, with more portrait roundels. There are plans for a new library and refurbishment of the building as a museum, and some of the upper galleries are closed pending reorganization and integration into the new art gallery (below).

GALLERY OLDHAM, Union Street. By *Pringle Richards Sharratt*, 1999–2001. Striking and suitably industrial-looking – there is nothing pretty about it. A long thin plan, gathering natural light from both sides. A tall lower part faced with red terracotta panels incorporates a central glazed entrance hall rising through two storeys, flanked by meeting rooms, café etc. The spaces are generous throughout, the entrance hall airy and inviting. Galleries stretch along the top, flanked by open walkways protected by curved steel ribs, forming a sort of cage cradling the inner spaces. Disappointingly there is no access to these walkways owing to fears for public safety. The end galleries can be top-lit or artificially lit, that in the centre is all glass. This offers superb views s over the town to the Pennines beyond, and creates a space ideal for the display of sculpture. The building is connected to the predecessor art gallery to the N (*see* above) by an understated upper-level bridge.

SCHOOL OF ART AND LYCEUM (former): *see* Union Street, below.

OLDHAM COLLEGE (formerly College of Technology), Middleton Road, immediately w of the Civic Centre. The crisp three- and six-storey blocks (Walton Building, Bevan Building, Brontë Building) with window grids are by *Sir Percy Thomas & Son*, 1965–7. The DAVID BELLIS BUILDING, *Ellis Group*, 2001, replaces the original building of 1950–4 by *Sir Percy Thomas* and *E. Prestwich*. Long and low, like its predecessor, but with a white rendered exterior and a box-like projection clad in cedar planks over the entrance.

The GRANGE ARTS CENTRE, Alderson Street, lies N of the main part of the campus. By *Paterson & Associates* of Edinburgh, opened 1975. Red brick with projections on three sides which express the presence of a cruciform theatre. At the front a somewhat intimidating screen of reflective black glass with recessed entrances below. The theatre has seating for 500 in the arms of the cross, and the facility for creating thrust and proscenium stages as well as theatre-in-the-round. Ancillary studios etc. in the corners.

BLUECOAT SCHOOL, Horsedge Street. Built 1829–34 as a charity school under the provisions of the will of the hatter Thomas Henshaw. On a hill yet higher than the one on which the church sits. In this way *Richard Lane* placed his two Oldham buildings in the most prominent positions available, at least until later developments obscured the school. It has a long ashlar front of seventeen bays, in the Tudor Gothic style Lane used for all his schools, based loosely on the front of Hampton Court Palace. The articulation is 3–4–3–4–3, the conception a three-storey entrance bay linked to three-storey end pavilions by two-storey ranges. Tall octagonal castellated turrets frame the entrance, and similar turrets appear at the external angles of this and the end bays. Originally they were topped by tall pinnacles capped by elaborate finials, giving a much spikier and more picturesque appearance. The details of the entrance bay echo the w front of Lane's church, though here the windows are domestic, transomed with label moulds.

Oldham Bluecoat School with the parish church in the background.
Engraving, 1843

Generous entrance hall with double stair and Tudor-arched doorways. A little Tudor-style LODGE stands at the entrance to the grounds.

SIXTH-FORM COLLEGE, John Street. By *Cruickshank & Seward*, 1991–2. Four interlocking blocks clad in polychromatic brick, each with a central courtyard. On the site of the Royal Oldham Infirmary, demolished in 1989 (for the new building *see* outer areas N), it incorporates the hospital's main doorway. Late C19, stone, with a Tudor-arched doorway and a balcony with blind traceried arcading.

CHAUCER STREET SPECIAL SCHOOL (former), Chaucer Street. Now a youth centre. By *Winder & Taylor* of Oldham, who won the competition judged by E. R. Robson. Opened in 1903 as a school for mentally and physically handicapped children. Queen Anne style, low and friendly, with a symmetrical gabled front and tall windows, decorated with terracotta cartouches and keystones. A range to the r. has bowed windows, with a gabled return to the street corner.

BUS STATION, Cheapside. By *Austin-Smith:Lord*, 2001. Sinuous and elongated with a lightweight aluminium canopy, glazed sides and branching steel piers within.

DRILL HALL (former), Rifle Street. Late C19. A long, low, frowning eminence of red brick, symmetrical with castellated central and end bays.

STREETS

There is no perambulation. Streets are described alphabetically and can be identified from the map on p. 531.

ALBION STREET. HALIFAX BUILDING SOCIETY, Albion Street. By *Abbey & Hanson, Rowe & Partners*, 1985. A stylish glass box with deeply recessed entrance, echoing the lines of the Yorkshire Bank, on High Street behind (below).

BOW STREET. Midway along is an attractive pub, HARK TO TOPPER, 1900 by *C. T. Taylor*. Brick and orange terracotta with paired stuccoed gables and nice detailing, e.g. the window heads, Renaissance-style terracotta panels, and door overlight with Art Nouveau glass.

CANNON STREET. The CANNON STREET INSTITUTE (former), a lads' club by *Taylor & Simister* of Oldham, opened in 1910. A big blocky Edwardian Baroque design, in red brick and yellow terracotta. Two-storey tower flanked by single-storey wings, housing offices and activity rooms. Large gymnasium behind, placed axially and lit by big lunettes.

CHURCH LANE. A narrow cobbled street running to the W side of the parish church. Nos. 7–9 are a pair of late C18 or early C19 three-storey brick houses. The windows are all in stone surrounds, with a second-storey string course and smaller openings to the attics. Entrances with rusticated stone surrounds. No. 11 also has three storeys, this time with a central pedimented doorcase. Opposite, No. 8, of the same period, but with only two storeys, and Nos. 10–14, 1880s versions of Georgian houses with pedimented doorcases but with cambered window heads.

CHURCH TERRACE. No. 11 is of brick, early or mid-C19, incorporating the base and side of an older stone building.

CLEGG STREET, w side. A few mid-C19 houses with Doric doorcases and stone cornices.

FAIRBOTTOM STREET. The COLISEUM THEATRE started as a circus, constructed of timber by *Thomas Whittaker* in 1885 in Henshaw Street for the Grand American Hippodrome Circus. Whittaker ended up owning the building, which he dismantled and moved to the present site in 1887 as the Colosseum Theatre. It changed hands in 1939 when the spelling of the name was altered and the auditorium partially rebuilt by *Armitage & Lees*. The basic timber structure remained until rebuilding in 1965, which retained the gallery and auditorium seating. A most unprepossessing exterior, with a blank rendered gable and understated entrance, but a cosy auditorium with a gallery front with festoons and flowery roundels.

GEORGE SQUARE. A pleasantly landscaped pedestrian area with SCULPTURES. 'Vertex' by *Shirley Diamond*, 1993. Three pairs of steel and copper blades looking like sharks' fins rising from the paving. 'Here' by *Andy Robarts*, 1993. Three bronze lumps disposed along a sloping walkway. They represent glacial boulders which have collected objects resonant of Oldham life, such as buttons, clog-irons, parts of mill machinery etc., as they moved along.

GREAVES STREET. No. 5 is an interesting small office building by *Edgar Wood*, built in 1901 for solicitors. It is not on a town-centre scale and has decidedly villagey features, though it fits with its low neighbours. Warm golden stone, stone-flag roof. Symmetrical front with large windows and three little dormers with weatherboarding in the gables. Above the door a large Art Nouveau panel, an extended lintel with a thrusting keystone and carved trees on each side. The double doors have large hinges and copper plates sweeping across the centre, cut through by very slim vertical windows with Art Nouveau glazing. The rear is asymmetrical, with a central full-height canted bay, and variation of dormers, windows and roof lines on each side.

Immediately s is a large former BILLIARD HALL, 1912 by *Winder & Taylor*. Long and low with a steady rhythm of square windows with exaggerated green terracotta keys between green terracotta pilasters. On the corner of Firth Street, a former WAREHOUSE of *c*. 1880, all of stone with heavy detailing, e.g. the big eaves brackets and the voussoirs of the giant arcade enclosing ground and first-floor openings. Taking-in doors on the Firth Street side.

HIGH STREET. One of the main shopping streets, a continuation of the w end of Yorkshire Street. The s side is taken up by the SPINDLES SHOPPING CENTRE (opened 1991, replacing *Richard Seifert*'s 1960s shopping centre), of no moment architecturally, but with bright, optimistic painted and stained glass by *Brian Clarke*, installed in 1993 in the octagon over the main hall and over upper-level walkways. Tight grids of chequers alternate with coloured panels, the whole overlaid by big splashed crosses.

Otherwise the interest is all on the N side. Starting at the E end on the corner of Church Street and Yorkshire Street, BARCLAYS BANK, a huge eclectic effort by *W. Waddington & Son*, started in 1896. Corner entrance with a dome over and a strongly horizontal rhythm of windows, the upper ones with round heads. Nearby, the HILTON ARCADE of 1893 by *Wild, Collins & Wild* has a tall narrow high-arched entrance with stepped round-headed windows over. The long narrow arcade is top-lit, with restored timber shopfronts.

The continuation of High Street to the w is MARKET PLACE. N side, the YORKSHIRE BANK, by *John Brunton & Partners*, 1970, a brutal concrete block cantilevered out over the street to form a covered walkway and entrance recess. On the same side, to the w, is a former BURTON'S shop. Typical interwar Burton's architecture, but with the entertaining motif of stylized elephants' heads as caps to the notional pilasters (a design used elsewhere, e.g. in Wolverhampton).

KING STREET. UNITY HALL (former). The premises of a Friendly Society, *c*. 1930. Symmetrical with ground-floor pilastrade with lotus capitals and a Greek-key frieze over, doors on each side in recessed openings with roundels, overlights with metalwork, and more roundels above with a lion holding a key. Continue s across the bypass for DRONS-FIELD'S offices, w side. By *Henry Sellers*, 1906–7. Historically much more remarkable than it is visually startling, for the originality and subtleties impinge gradually. Symmetrical, with three-bay blocks on either side of the entrance bay, of which the upper part is deeply recessed and rises above, with blocky piers and chimney shapes reminiscent of Hawksmoor. Pevsner in 1969 noted: 'the window and the door surrounds of stone cut into such anti-period angular shapes that the building must be accepted as valid pioneer work for a C20 style.' The materials are glazed green brick (now horribly painted), Cornish granite, and glass.

MUMPS is the continuation of the E end of Yorkshire Street. Once a premier shopping street, but everything has a decayed look today. The area is dominated by the astonishing DISTRICT BANK (former), by *Mills & Murgatroyd*, 1902–3. Enormous in scale, with a high Baroque corner tower with pedimented aedicules topped by a dome. Windows in two storeys separated by paired columns which start naughtily on brackets halfway up the ground-floor windows. Giant arches frame the end entrance bays. The banking hall has Ionic piers and is lined with veined marble. Attached on the r. side, a very grand range of early C20 shops, red brick with much white terracotta.

QUEEN STREET. A few early C19 three-storey brick houses on the E side (Nos. 11–15, Nos. 23–27) are followed by No. 29, early C20 offices with an oriel with Westmorland slates and a pair of entrances, gaily banded in brick and stone. The mid–late C19 offices at No. 31 are more serious in tone with a central pedimented entrance bay, and windows in stone surrounds, the upper ones arched.

UNION STREET, one of the main streets of Oldham, is wide and has some of the town's most prominent buildings. Starting at the E end, the VICTORY CINEMA, N side, started life as the Adelphi Theatre by *T. Crossley*, opened in 1875. It reopened as a cinema in 1920, when it was remodelled and cased in cream faience. Very spare, with unadorned pilasters and 'Victory Cinema De Luxe' in white tiles on a purple ground. Further along on the same side is a little group of brick early C19 houses, Nos. 115–117 and No. 121, of which the last is the grandest – three storeys with a projecting central entrance bay, stone parapet with a little central gable, and windows beneath flat gauged brick heads. Still on the same side, the MIDLAND BANK (now HSBC) is by *Thomas Taylor*, dated 1892. An assured design. Slightly projecting end bays with slated pavilion roofs with brattishing. Entrance in the l. bay by a porch with granite Ionic columns. Upper Ionic pilastrade with arched windows. For the neighbouring United Reformed Church, and public buildings opposite (Library and Art Gallery, former Post Office) *see* p. 535–6 above. The UNION CLUB, N side, now a Masonic Hall, is of 1869, by *Thomas Mitchell*. Two tall storeys, coursed and squared rubble with ashlar dressings. Very severe and rather unsettling; the small masonry blocks seem to intensify the bare expanses of wall (the upper windows in bays three to six have been blocked) and sit uncomfortably with the smooth ashlar porch. Bays two and six are advanced, with pediments; the first bay (l.) is a later addition in matching style. Entrance in bay two, a strict Greek Doric porch with fluted columns.

A little further w on the same side the SCHOOL OF ART AND LYCEUM, now home to the council's music services and other departments. The Lyceum was essentially a mechanics' institute, set up in 1839 and supported by leading local industrialists. Purpose-built premises by *N. G. Pennington* were erected in 1855–6, and a School of Science and Art added in 1865. It was these institutions which, according to Professor Farnie, 'raised Oldham to the front rank of British towns as a centre for technical education and trained students for posts as mill managers'. The 1865 building quickly proved to be inadequate and it was rebuilt in 1880–1 to match the Lyceum in style. A long dignified front, Italianate, with upper arched windows and urns along the parapet. The Lyceum, l., has a central entrance bay with a round-headed door, large arched window above with an iron balcony, and a gable breaking through the parapet with the word 'Lyceum'. Three-window ranges on either side, the upper ones with wreaths above. The School of Science and Art, r., repeats the design, with only minor differences. The Lyceum is entered via a vestibule with a barrel vault, all encased in very pretty green, cream and ivory glazed tiles, probably in the 1880s. Next is a grand entrance hall, with a handsome stair which goes up in one flight and returns in two. It is lit by a large window with painted glass

Oldham, The Lyceum, engraving, 1856

showing Socrates. Tall arched doorways with Corinthian pilasters to the principal rooms.

A little further along is an office of the PRUDENTIAL ASSURANCE (former). By *A. Waterhouse & Son*, 1898–1901, red brick of course, but not the intense red of some of the practice's other commercial buildings. Here there is a cooler look, with buff terracotta banding and green terracotta detailing to the entrances. Polygonal four-storey angle turrets with round-headed doorways beneath pediments supported by columns. Main three-storey range with a ground-floor arcade of three large windows, upper mullioned-and-transomed windows with a band of terracotta cartouches between the floors.

On the opposite side near the junction with Brunswick Street a three-bay Doric screen, created from salvaged material from the Union Street New Connexion Methodist Church of 1875, demolished 1984. Further along on this side the CASTLE PUB, 1930s, has an unspoiled exterior, brick and white faience, and windows with yellow Art Deco sunbursts. Last on the street, s side, the former GRAND THEATRE, designed by *Thomas Taylor* and 'a London architect', 1908. Reopened as a Gaumont cinema in 1937, it is now a club. Large and sprawling with sparing Edwardian Baroque features, given a strange appearance by the crude Art Deco corner entrance which came with the cinema.

YORKSHIRE STREET. Starting near the E end, at the junction with Fairbottom Street, N side, the ARTISAN'S REST (now Harry's Bar) is by *C. T. Taylor, Roberts & Bowman*, 1937. Canted corners and strong horizontals: stone strips at the top, windows with horizontal glazing detail. Carved panels over the entrance show craftsmen at work and at leisure. A little further along, another pub, the OLD MESS HOUSE. Probably early to mid C19, remodelled 1881 by *James Hilton*. Stone quoins, and a fancy projecting porch added in the 1890s. The former HALIFAX BUILDING SOCIETY, s side, has been converted to a café bar. 1934 by *Taylor & Simister*. Art Deco, handsomely done in stone with polished granite trimmings. Pylon-like entrance tower angled to the street corner. Upper windows are divided by cylindrical mullions treated as terms, one holding a house and key, the other with a trowel. WAR MEMORIAL, N side, in front of the church, unveiled 1923. High granite base supporting an ambitious bronze by *Albert Toft*, with a soldier standing aloft directing his fellows to join the attack from the trenches. They are shown all around moving forward to take position, so the sculpture can be viewed from all sides, as Toft intended. The site was laid out and a new retaining wall built to the churchyard to designs of *Thomas Taylor*. Opposite, beside the Town Hall (*see* above), and a worthy neighbour, is the NATWEST BANK. A stately classical composition. It was probably put up in the 1890s. Could *Barker, Ellis & Jones* of Manchester, who made various alterations in 1896, be responsible? Two tall storeys, rusticated with round-arched openings below, the upper windows with segmental and triangular pediments. The banking hall has a coffered ceiling and Ionic columns. The return on Greaves Street has attached to it a quietly dignified five-bay manager's house with a central pedimented doorcase and sash windows.

OUTER OLDHAM

1. North

Comprising Besom Hill, Burnley Brow, Coldhurst, Derker, Heyside, Higginshaw, Moorside, Northmoor and Watersheddings.

HOLY TRINITY, Godson Street, Coldhurst. By *E. H. Shellard*, 1847–8. Stone, lancets and just a bellcote.

ST MARK, Perth Street, Heyside. 1878 by *Wild & Collins*. Small and low with a w bellcote and lancet windows.

ST STEPHEN, St Stephen Street, Higginshaw. By *G. Mitchell* of Oldham, 1873. Tracery in the style of *c.* 1300. Short SW tower with a slated pyramid roof, SW stair-turret. S transept. Empty and derelict.

ST THOMAS, Northgate Road, Moorside. By *H. Cockburn*, 1872. The show is all in the W tower with its openwork parapet, truncated octagonal pinnacles and octagonal NE stair-turret rising to a spirelet. Cusped lancets. Triple clerestory lights, paired aisle lights. (Arcades with clustered shafts. – STAINED GLASS. N aisle, *Mayer & Co.*, 1902 and 1908, S aisle all by *Capronnier*, 1881–91.)

UKRAINIAN CATHOLIC CHURCH (formerly All Saints, Anglican), Chadderton Way, Northmoor. 1888–91 by *Winder & Taylor*. Very red brick, with a NW tower with pinnacles and pierced parapet in stone. Mostly lancets, paired in the aisles, triple in the clerestory. A type characteristic of the date. It was taken over by the Ukrainian church in 1988.

WESLEYAN METHODIST CHURCH (former), Library Street, Northmoor. 1909 by *J. Wills & Son* of Derby. Red Brick, Portland stone dressings, paired lancets, and a proper W tower, all of stone at the top with blind arcading and corner pinnacles.

ST AMBROSE SCHOOL AND CHURCH (former), St Ambrose Street, Watersheddings. By *Thomas Taylor*, dated 1908. The buildings are linked. Red brick decked out in yellow terracotta, banded tower with pyramidal roof.

ROYAL OLDHAM HOSPITAL, Rochdale Road, Burnley Brow. On the site of the Oldham Workhouse founded in 1840. The Board of Guardians built an infirmary here in 1870, called Boundary Park Hospital. Following the closure of the Royal Oldham Infirmary premises off John Street, in the centre,* the hospital re-established itself here in new buildings designed by

---

* Where the main doorway is incorporated into a Sixth-Form Centre.

Taylor & Young, 1981–9. Facing Rochdale Road, three-storey blocks with small gables and exterior walkways. Some older red brick buildings, mainly of the interwar period, survive on the w side, with, on the corner of Sheepfoot Lane and Rochdale Road, an attractive Venetian Gothic block probably of *c.* 1870.

HIGGINSHAW BOARD SCHOOL, Shaw Road, Higginshaw. By *Winder & Taylor*, plans approved 1894. The king of Oldham's surviving board schools. Large, resplendently decorated with terracotta, with upper octagonal pilasters and an eventful roofline with Dutch gables and cupolas. Twelve bays to Shaw Road, two tall storeys. Between the storeys, an attractive strapwork frieze of pale terracotta on a red ground.

ALBERT MOUNT, Bartlemore Street, Derker. A very jolly four-square block of sixteen houses around a courtyard, built in 1862 as a speculation for the industrialist William Rye. Red brick with red and white brick arches to doors and windows, a Greek-key design at the eaves, and yellow terracotta string courses.

JAMES STREET, Watersheddings. A little low stone C18 house amid brick C19 terraces. Asymmetrical, with an off-centre entrance aligned with the stack, hence a baffle entry plan. Mullioned windows.

RIPPONDEN ROAD, Besom Hill. High up on the edge of the moors, Nos. 848–864, a row of nine early C19 houses all with mullioned windows.

WERNETH MILLS, Henley Street, Burnley Brow. No. 1 and No. 2 mill stand beside one another, with two proud Italianate water towers to the street. Despite their similarities they are not by the same architect. No. 1 (l.) originated in 1875 and was rebuilt by *G. Stott*, 1899. No. 2, by *F. W. Dixon*, was built in 1891 and successively extended until 1937.

2. South and South-West

Comprising Bardsley, Hathershaw, Hollins Green, Hollinwood and Werneth.

Churches

HOLY TRINITY, Ashton Road, Bardsley. 1844 by *Starkey & Cuffley*. A very odd-looking church thanks to the large overhanging pinnacle pyramids and the overdone Romanesque motifs, all executed with gusto. The sides still have long lancets, with shafts and chevron mouldings. No aisles, but transepts with wheel windows in the gables. Chancel with stepped round-headed lancets. The w tower is the strangest part, weighed down by the pinnacles, with a peculiar open-work parapet and Romanesque beasts supporting the corbels.

ST JOHN, St John's Street, Werneth. 1844–5 by *E. H. Shellard*. The Commissioners contributed £1,000; other costs were met by Mr Kay Clegg. Perp, with a w tower to convince the antiquarian and an expressed chancel. There are transepts, possibly later additions. It seems that Shellard had looked at Lancashire churches for inspiration (cf. his St Thomas, Lees, built at about the same time). The low three-stage tower has a crenellated parapet, and the sides are crenellated as well, with aisle and nave under one roof. The five-bay arcades have octagonal piers with fleurons – again archaeologically informed. The church was closed in the 1970s and crudely subdivided for use as workshop units.

St MARGARET, Chapel Road, Hollinwood. By *R. Knill Freeman*, 1880, replacing a church of 1766–9. Rather charmless, of narrow coursed rubble with large Dec windows to the transepts and w end. Lancets to the aisles and large two-light clerestory windows. The best feature is the fine NW tower with triple bell-openings at the top, and that is of 1906.

St THOMAS, St Thomas's Circus, Werneth. 1853–5 by *A. Trimen* and *George Shaw*. A late Commissioners' church, though the grant was only £125. Other costs were defrayed by local industrialists. On the crown of a hill, and part of a planned development. It sits in a circus at the centre of a grid of streets with terraces for mill workers. Sturdy NW tower with a broach spire, E and W windows with flowing tracery, triple lancets to the aisles. *George Shaw* added the transepts in 1868. Their large windows have flowing tracery incorporating s shapes typical of Shaw. Choir vestry, organ chamber, etc. added by *J. S. Crowther* in the 1880s. Perp-style w porch, 1908. Arcade of circular piers, and a high arch-braced roof, that in the chancel with cusped wind-braces and angels at the corbels replacing the original roof: work carried out *c.* 1860 probably by *Shaw*, at the expense of John Platt of Platt Bros & Co. (see Hartford New Works, below).

FURNISHINGS. A memorable ensemble, with some outstanding pieces, the gifts of wealthy families who lived nearby. Chancel furnishings by *Shaw*, *c.* 1860. Elaborate canopied STALLS similar to those of St Thomas, Lees (q.v.), incorporating emblems of the Platt and Radcliffe families. – PULPIT. Also by *Shaw*. Highly ornate, with intricate canopied sides. – LECTERN. A great fierce eagle, typical of *Shaw*'s workshop. – REREDOS. Atmospheric painting of the Adoration of the Magi in an elaborate painted and carved frame, by *Reginald Hallward*, 1905. – BAPTISTERY, w end of s aisle, created and fitted up with marble-lined walls and a mosaic floor in 1908–9. The FONT is a highly unusual piece, previously exhibited *c.* 1906 at the church art section of the Church Congress in Manchester. A large square bowl with attractive reliefs on the sides showing angels instructing and protecting children, with a pedestal on one side supporting a bronze Christ cradling an ivory baby. – FIRST WORLD WAR MEMORIAL. Triptych by *H. A. Payne*. The names of the dead flank a moving painting showing Christ bringing light to a stricken landscape inhabited by ordinary people.

STAINED GLASS. E window by *Capronnier*, 1883. Chancel side windows of 1892 with armorial bearings, nicely done. S transept, Parable of the Talents, 1895, perhaps by *Ward & Hughes*. S aisle, Peace, Love and Hope, 1910 by *Heaton, Butler & Bayne*. Baptistery, Peace, Purity and Temperance by *Gustav Hiller*, 1911. Several other windows by Hiller's firm with dates up to 1930 appear in the baptistery and S aisle, evidently by another hand in the workshop and not as good. W window by *Mayer & Co.*, badly faded. N aisle: *A. G. Moore*, 1932, and *G. E. R. Smith*, 1958. N transept: David and Solomon, 1889; the Virgin by *A. G. Moore*, 1935.

ST PAUL, Ashton Road, Hathershaw. 1879–80 by *Wild & Collins*. The W end has tall cusped lancets. Clerestory with roundels incorporating alternating quatrefoil, S-shape and star motifs. Low aisles with paired lancets. Unexecuted SW tower.

HOLLINWOOD CEMETERY, Roman Road, Hollinwood. The buildings are of 1887–8, by *Potts, Pickup & Dixon*. Large Gothic OFFICES with an impressively tall clock tower and slated spire. Simpler gabled LODGE opposite. ENTRANCE SCREEN with a gabled arch flanked by pedestrian entrances.

Public Buildings, Parks and Houses

HATHERSHAW AND FITTON HILL COMMUNITY CENTRE, Ashton Road, Hathershaw. A new building by *Hodder Associates* is planned, 2004.

WERNETH GRANGE CONVENT, Grange Road, Werneth. A large asymmetrical stone Gothic house dated 1871, with pretty details: angle turrets, oriels, steep gables with bargeboards, an elaborate timber porch. It became a convent of the Sisters of Mercy in 1907, and due to them is the large chapel on the E side of the house. Simple and plain, in matching yellow sandstone rubble, with lancets.

ST THOMAS SCHOOL, St Thomas's Circle, Werneth. *c.* 1870. Stone, with motifs to match the church, opposite (above). Nicely picturesque, many-gabled and with a sprinkling of traceried windows.

WERNETH JUNIOR SCHOOL, Coppice Street, Werneth. By *Thomas Taylor*. A tall campanile clock tower on the r. side dominates the main range. Entrances with carved panels over bear the name of the school and the dates 1891 and 1893. The adjoining INFANTS' SCHOOL is early C20 with the barest Baroque detail and many alterations and additions.

HULME GRAMMAR SCHOOL, Chambers Road, Werneth. 1894–5 by *J. W. Firth*. Founded through the Hulme Trust, an educational charity. Both boys and girls were educated, in separate classrooms. Red brick, gabled, with Elizabethan accents. Central hall with a very tall handsome flèche and tall transomed windows. Symmetrical low blocks on each side of the hall. Behind, five low classrooms each with its own gable.

WERNETH PARK, Manchester Road and Frederick Street, Werneth. Given to the people of Oldham in 1936 by the Lees family (see Lees Memorial, below). Beside the Frederick Road entrance an unpretentious gabled LODGE, of *c.* 1870. Then come the house and related buildings (see below) on a broad terrace sloping down to the S. A wall divides this area from the rest of the park, which has perimeter planting and a C20 avenue.

LEES HOUSE. Built *c.* 1849 for the Lees family. Given to Oldham for use as a museum by Marjory Lees in 1935, when extensions to the rear (NE) were made by *J. H. Heywood* to house the collections. Now it is an adult education centre. Italianate and quite unpretentious, brick with stone dressings. Stone porch with a shell hood, stone quoins, bracketed eaves cornices and pedimental gables. Inside it is thoroughly institutionalized but with some ceilings, fireplaces etc. Stair with cast-iron balusters, ground-floor doorcases with pediments. A downstairs sitting room has a pretty Rococo-style painted ceiling with faces at corners, said to be portraits of Lees womenfolk.

MUSIC ROOM and CONSERVATORY, *c.* 1860, NW of the house. Single-storey range with Doric portico, tall windows and a bay and balustraded parapet with urn finials. The octagonal music room rises behind, with a pyramidal roof and cupola. Attached, l., is a symmetrical conservatory with a polygonal entrance flanked by large circular bays. Boarded up and derelict.

LEES MEMORIAL, SE of the house. By *W. Hargreaves Whitehead*, 1937. Art Deco stone pylon with imposed crosses and a circular base with bronze reliefs: a portrait medallion, figures representing the seasons, and signs of the zodiac, with typical Art Deco sunburst and zigzag motifs. This rises from a circular pool (now with an ugly cage over it) with drinking fountains on the edge at the cardinal points.

Dame Sarah Lees (†1935) was a remarkable woman: a suffragist, Oldham's first female councillor, and the first woman Mayor, 1910–11.

NE of the park, on the other side of Frederick Street, a GATEWAY of *c.* 1870 leads to a former coach yard of Lees House, now populated by late C20 houses. Archway with a pedimental gable with an urn finial and curved flanking walls.

WERNETH LODGE, Manchester Road, opposite the park. Said to have originated in the early C19 as a coach house and ballroom. A mid–late C19 refronting and late C20 alterations have effaced any outward sign, and the building is now a care home.

WERNETH HALL, at the corner of Frederick Street and Werneth Hall Road, Werneth. Now a care home. The earliest part is at the rear, facing Werneth Hall Road. Two-storey C17 wing of narrow coursed rubble, five-light windows with flat hood-moulds and renewed mullions and transoms. It would take too long to describe all the extensions and alterations. Enough to say that most are in matching style and that the most recent was done in the 1990s.

THORNEYCROFT, Newport Street, Werneth. A large and rather ugly house, probably built in the 1870s. One of a small number in this area to survive thoroughgoing alteration.

HATHERSHAW HALL, Hollins Road, opposite Howgill Crescent, Hathershaw. Perhaps early C17, much altered and subdivided. The oldest part is the recessed central range, of two storeys with mullioned windows and an entrance to the r. At the l. end a projecting bay, probably a cross-wing, but without the expected gable, perhaps as a result of alteration or truncation. Attached to the l. and slightly projecting, a startlingly over-windowed range, on which the date 1694 was formerly visible. There are six large mullioned-and-transomed windows on each floor. They could hardly be more closely spaced.

GARDEN SUBURB, Green Lane, Northgate and connecting streets, Hollins Green. The 'Beautiful Oldham' movement was launched in 1902 by Mary Higgs and Sarah Lees (*see* Werneth Park, above). They were instrumental in setting up a company to create a Garden Suburb in 1907, and Ebenezer Howard attended the opening ceremony in 1909. The plan and first phase of houses were by *Heywood & Ogden* of Oldham. By 1914 183 houses had been built and let on Green Lane and streets running from it in the SW corner of the site. Straight lines are avoided, and all the streets converge upon the centre at the highest point. The (mainly) semi-detached houses are rendered or exposed brick, Arts and Crafts in tone. Building continued after the First World War but the houses were smaller and cheaper.

(SELBOURNE STREET, Bardsley. BANK TOP FARM. An early C18 stone farmhouse.)

Mills and Works

Two impressive groups of mills are situated in the area, with others scattered about. Most are early C20 cotton-spinning mills, all in red brick with yellow sandstone or brick dressings, with flat roofs, prominent water towers and Baroque motifs. Many remained in production until the 1960s and have found new uses as warehouses, etc.

The first group is in streets off Hollins Road, Hollinwood. HERON MILL, Millgate Street is of 1905 by *P. S. Stott*. A great palace of a mill, five storeys, with a water tower rising up at one corner with inverted Diocletian windows (a favourite P. S. Stott motif) at the top and the name emblazoned upon it. The tall circular detached chimney has another Stott trademark, two bands near the top. It had 104,000 mule spindles and a 1400 horse-power engine. Similar mills nearby include DURBAN MILL, Millgate Street, opposite Heron Mill and somewhat smaller, also of 1905, also by *P. S. Stott*; DEVON MILL, Chapel Street, by *G. Stott*, 1908; and ROYD MILL, Chambers Road, 1907 by *A. J. Howcroft*, who worked in P. S. Stott's Oldham office before setting up on his own in 1898.

The second group stands in Hathershaw, overlooking the SE side of Oldham. MAPLE MILLS, No. 1 (1904) and No. 2 (1915), on Cardwell Street, and EARL MILL, Dowry Street, 1891 extended 1893, are all typical of *P. S. Stott*. BELGRAVE MILLS, Honeywell Lane, form a rather mutilated group. The earliest was built 1881 (by *Potts, Pickup & Dixon*); others of 1907, 1910, and 1914 are by *F. W. Dixon & Son*.

HARTFORD NEW WORKS, Suthers Street and Featherstall Road South, Werneth. This was the main works of Platt Bros & Co., from 1854 the largest textile machine manufacturer in the world. In the 1840s the company became the biggest employer in Oldham. According to Professor Farnie 'Platt's mules were the true basis of the industrial supremacy of Oldham, being unrivalled in length, in speed of operation and in productivity.' The vast works, parts of which were designed by *T. S. Sington*, occupied an area W of the road opposite Werneth Station. The office and entrance building on Featherstall Road South is by *P. B. Alley*, the date 1883. French Renaissance in a wooden sort of way. Two long storeys with arcades of round-headed windows, and projecting pavilions at each end with hipped roofs with brattishing. In the centre a hipped-roofed clock tower with a large clock and a good deal of fancy iron-work brattishing around the top. Various parts of the works survive within the industrial estate now on site including OXFORD MILL, Suthers Street, a mid-C19 cotton mill altered for the company in 1909 by *A. E. Wolstencroft*.

3. East and South-East

Comprising Alt, Glodwick, Greenacres, Greenacres Moor, Low Side, New Earth, Pitses, Salem and Waterhead.

ST JAMES, Barry Street, Greenacres Moor. 1827–8 by *Francis Goodwin*. A Commissioners' church costing £9,652. The octagonal top of the tower with its flying buttresses and thin pinnacles looks a little like that of Charles Barry's St Peter, Brighton (1824–8) which also uses a lantern-like motif. The basic design may even be *Barry*'s – for it was he who originally won the commission, and foundations were dug to his plans.[*] He greatly underestimated the costs, and when the tenders came in he was replaced. Goodwin's attempt is not a success, but this was because he was forced to scale down the tower owing to lack of funds. The lantern is far too low to have any real effect and the proportions are all wrong. The tower has clasping buttresses and a prominent clock surround. Otherwise embattled parapets and three-light Perp windows with cast-iron tracery. The canted apse is a seamless addition of 1883 by *John Lowe* of Manchester. Inside, Perp piers of four chamfered projections with foliated caps. Three galleries with plain fronts;

---

[*] The tower of Nash's St Mary, Haggerston, London (1825–7) also seems to be a related design.

ribbed plaster ceiling. The interior was refitted in 1920 as a First World War memorial. Of this date the very ornate Dec-style ROOD SCREEN with carved figures, flanking panels with statues of St Michael and St George, and the names of the fallen. The chancel furnishings, including arcaded PAN-ELLING and timber SEDILIA, are probably part of the same scheme. – STAINED GLASS. E windows late C19. In the SE chapel, two of *c.* 1918, St George and St Joan, probably by *Shrigley & Hunt*. – MONUMENTS. S aisle, Rev. Gooday †1878. Large and elaborate, with Gothic niches and figures. – N aisle, Sarah Sidebottom †1856, tablet with urn by *J. Knowles* of Manchester. – Rev. W. Walker †1857, similar tablet with elab-orately draped urn by *Patteson* of Manchester.

HOLY TRINITY, Church Street, Waterhead. 1846–7 by *E.H. Shellard*. E.E., the sides with the Commissioners'-type paired lancets, but the W tower with a broach spire and the chancel with three stepped lancets. Unadventurous in comparison with his nearby St Thomas, Lees (q.v.), of only a year later. (INTE-RIOR. Arcades of clustered shafts, kingpost roof, chancel refitted 1884. – STAINED GLASS. By *Capronnier*, 1892; *R.B. Edmundson*, 1880 and 1897; *Mayer & Co.* of Munich, 1906; *R. Bennett* of Manchester, late C19; *Heaton, Butler & Bayne*, 1906.)

ST MARK WITH CHRIST CHURCH, Glodwick Road, Glod-wick. At the top of the hill, and a local landmark. 1876 by *John Wild*. Yellow sandstone rubble. SE tower with broach spire. Mainly cusped lancets, including triple lancets to the clerestory; five-light Dec E window. Part of a group with the SUNDAY SCHOOL (former), on Waterloo Street, W, with plate tracery, and VICARAGE and PARISH ROOMS (former), on Glodwick Road, N, with some churchy details to the house.

ST ANNE (R.C.), Cook Street, Greenacres. By *Greenhalgh & Williams*, 1934–5. Large, red brick and Romanesque, but with an Art Deco feel to the pylon-like W tower. The architects used a very similar design for St Patrick, Miles Platting (*see* p. 378).

GREENACRES WESLEYAN METHODIST CHURCH (former), Greenacres Road, Greenacres. 1857–8 by *James Simpson*. Clas-sical, with a gable treated as a pediment and elaborate pedi-mented upper windows. Altered for use as a shop.

GREENACRES CONGREGATIONAL CHURCH, Callard Street, Greenacres. Put up in 1853–4 on the site of an Independent chapel established in 1662 by Robert Constantine. The archi-tect was *R. Moffat Smith*. The oddness is in the SE tower, which has pinnacles at the angles from which flying buttresses rise to support a short stone pinnacle. Could this have been inspired by the tower of Goodwin's St James (above)? Otherwise the building is square with big gables on three sides, that at the E end with paired entrances. The rear range with meeting rooms etc. and an octagonal stair-tower was rebuilt in the late C20, when the interior was radically reordered.

PARSONAGE (former), Orbelin Road, near the Congrega-tional church (above). A very plain stone house of 1880. Two great chimneys rising from the eaves on the side are the notable feature.

CONGREGATIONAL SUNDAY SCHOOL (former), Callard Street, Greenacres. Dated 1889. Large, stone, with gabled end bays with large circular upper windows beneath pointed arches.

ST MATTHEW, Roundthorn Road, New Earth. Now a Salvation Army Hall. 1932–3 by *Taylor & Young*, and remarkable as a faithful reproduction of a Georgian chapel. Round-arched windows, pale brown brick with darker brick to plinth and cornice. Small timber lantern with a domed top. Only the portal in the w end with its Portland stone surround, and the expressed chancel, betray the date.

SALEM MORAVIAN CHURCH, Lees Road, Salem. Founded in 1824, but rebuilt in very plain brick, 1938.

ST VOLODYMYR, Onchan Avenue, Glodwick. 1911 by *J. Thorpe*. A mission church, now a Ukrainian Orthodox Church. Low and quite small but with some force in the blunt detailing. The expected red brick and Portland stone.

NEW JAMIAH MOSQUE, Greengate Street, Glodwick. Under construction 2003. Very large, formulaic with a green plastic central dome. Red brick with arched windows.

GREENACRES CEMETERY, Greenacres Road, Greenacres. Opened in 1857 at the same time as Chadderton Cemetery (*see* Chadderton), both conceived as public parks or walks at a time when the Oldham area lacked these amenities. The layout and buildings were designed by *N. G. Pennington* of Manchester. A walled entrance drive terminates with a large stone entrance block with a central gabled archway linked to a LODGE, r., and OFFICES l. The entrance is flanked by tall pinnacles with finials. Windows to the street are mainly cusped lancets. A good range of Victorian MONUMENTS. Those to note are: s of the entrance, Edwin Butterworth, historian †1848, by *E. Hall*, architect of Oldham. Erected by public subscription in 1859 'as a memento of his great moral and historical worth'. Truncated obelisk with a cap and urn finial. – Further s, Mary Austerberry †1863, broken column, fluted and wreathed with flowers, by *J. Lunt*. – SE of the entrance, John Sutcliffe †1916. Statue of a soldier in battledress.

ALEXANDRA PARK, Park Road, Glodwick. Built as an unemployment relief project during the cotton famine and opened 1865. *William Henderson* won the competition, with *Woodhouse & Potts* of Oldham, who designed the lodges. It was described by the *Oldham Chronicle* as 'an oasis in the dreary desert'. The land included plots for houses on Queen's Road, N side, and Alexandra Road, E side, to help defray the costs (*see* below). The skyline to the sw is still dominated by huge cotton mills. LODGES at the NW and NE corners, stone, Italianate and fairly substantial. The layout is based around a formal terrace with a broad walkway, from which land falls away to the s and sw. An axial path runs sw from the terrace, with less formal areas around the perimeter. A large boating lake along the western edge was added in the early C20. STATUES. At the w end of the terrace John Platt M.P., bronze on a plinth with four female supporters (Engineering, Mathematics, Art and Science), by *D. W. Stevenson* of Edinburgh, 1878. Platt founded one of the largest textile machinery companies in the world (*see* p. 550). Relocated from the town centre in 1924. At the E end of the terrace Robert Ascroft M.P., by *F. W. Pomeroy*, 1903. Bronze statue on a large granite pedestal. A FOUNTAIN of 1865 lies at the termination of the axial path SW of the terrace. Two bowls and a figure of a boy holding a fish.

Other structures lie in the S part of the park. A gabled GARDENER'S COTTAGE, presumably of the 1860s, stands near a lovely CONSERVATORY supplied by *Messengers & Co.* in 1907. Central part with a hipped roof topped by a domed lantern with brattishing, flanking smaller pavilions also with hips and lanterns. Walks lead W to an extraordinary, dumpy, pagoda-like OBSERVATORY, put up in 1899 to mark the fiftieth anniversary of incorporation. Chinoiserie with incongruous Gothic details, in particular the angle piers with foliated caps. Two-tier swept roof with deep eaves and a small dome. Beside it another STATUE, Joseph Howarth by *Henry Burnett*, 1868. Blind from birth and of humble origin, Howarth was the town's bellman and a Methodist lay preacher. The figure, wearing an old heavy coat and carrying a bell, contrasts with the other statues of well-dressed worthies. Elsewhere in the park, a BOWLS PAVILION and BOATHOUSE, nothing special but part of a good ensemble.

QUEEN'S ROAD, N of the park. The houses are effectively within Alexandra Park (above) – its walls and railings continue in front of each end of the road, which has its own gatepiers. The houses were built on plots leased to help to defray the costs of the park. None is individually special, but there is a good variety of little-altered 1860s–80s housing, much of it Gothic, e.g. Nos. 1–19 Shakespeare Terrace, 1869 by *Samuel Drinkwater* of Werneth. Others, including Nos. 25–31, were designed by *T. Mitchell*, 1869. ALEXANDRA ROAD, E, enjoys the same relationship with the park, with houses generally later in date.

RAILWAY WAREHOUSE, Park Road. A goods shed of *c.* 1850. Hugely impressive, but derelict. Curved, of four-storeys and seventeen-bays, in polychromatic brick. Four loading bays, windows with segmental heads, and another loading bay in each of the gabled ends.

WAR MEMORIAL, Heywood Street, Waterhead. By *George Thomas*, unveiled 1920. Bronze soldier in battledress holding his helmet aloft.

OLDHAM EQUITABLE CO-OPERATIVE SOCIETY PREMISES (former), Huddersfield Road, Greenacres Moor. By *Thomas Taylor*, 1900. Vast premises which combined public halls and a library with shops, including drapery, footwear, butchery and grocery departments. Two tall storeys articulated by a great window arcade, third storey with a busy rhythm of small windows. Truncated corner tower, r., and a gabled l. bay flanked by octagonal piers, with a huge semicircular upper window with mullions. Nowadays the ground floor is a mish-mash of late C20 fascias, etc.

GREENACRES LODGE, Greenacres Road, Greenacres. A large mid-C19 stone house in its own grounds. Probably built for a branch of the mill-owning Lees family, resident in 1861. Restrained, symmetrical, with a hipped roof and a slightly projecting entrance bay. An emphatic porch with an openwork parapet has arcades of piers with foliated caps on each side.

HOLTS LANE, Pitses, near the junction with Abbey Hills Road. Nos. 9–15, a brick terrace dated 1837 with Gothick windows with Y-tracery.

MANOR ROAD, Low Side. MANOR COTTAGE. Stone, late C18, still with mullioned windows.

ROUNDTHORN ROAD, New Earth. Nos. 259–267, a little group of rendered brick late C18 or early C19 houses with mullioned windows. Another terrace opposite, probably of the same date, has been modernized. Near the s end of the road was MANOR HOUSE, an early C19 house extended and altered in 1901 by *Henry Sellers*. The GATEPIERS by *Sellers* survive: stone with scrolls on the inner faces and ball finials.

Mills

Waterhead, far to the E, is still dominated by early C20 mills, of which CAIRO MILL in Crimbles Street (1903, extended 1914) and ORB MILL in Holgate Street (1907) are both by *P. S. Stott*, and typical of him.

Outlying

Alt Lane, Alt. ALDERS FARMHOUSE. Dated 1734, but possibly earlier and rebuilt or remodelled. Low stone house with mullioned windows (some with the mullions removed), cross-wing, and opposed entrances suggesting the presence of a cross-passage. Attached two-storey DAIRY, perhaps originally stables or of domestic origin, with mullioned windows, and BARN, probably C17 and ruinous. Further s and at right angles to the road TEN HOUSES, an early C19 brick terrace with sash windows, front, and mullioned windows, rear. Rebuilt and altered, 1991.

4. West (Westwood)

MORAVIAN CHURCH, Middleton Road, Westwood. 1868–9. The show is all to the road, where pinnacled piers frame a gabled entrance bay with round-headed arches to the door and windows. On each side bays with stairs to the galleries, with cornices and pinnacles at the angles.

MORAVIAN SCHOOL, Main Road, Westwood. By *C. T. Taylor*, dated 1906. Red brick and buff terracotta, Edwardian Baroque, with attractive details such as the oval windows flanked by banded Ionic demi-columns. The low central entrance bay is flanked by short flat-topped towers. Hall with a big lunette.

MANCHESTER COUNTY BANK (former), corner of Middleton Road and Featherstall Road, Westwood. By *Mills & Murgatroyd*, 1901, very crisply done in ashlar, with banded rustication to the ground floor, upper windows with consoled canopies and segmental parapets, and a strong bracketed cornice.

ANCHOR MILL, Daisy Street, Westwood. By *J. Stott*, 1881. The tall circular free-standing chimney with the date and an anchor picked out in white brick is the first thing to be noticed. Five storeys, fireproof construction with cast-iron columns and brick jack arches and an internal engine house.

OLD TRAFFORD *see* STRETFORD

PARK BRIDGE   9000

NE of Ashton-under-Lyne in the valley of the Medlock bordering with Oldham, and still an isolated settlement. Coal was extracted here from the C17, and an ironworks was established by the Lees family in 1786. It became an important centre for the production of textile machine parts. The remaining buildings are mostly of the mid C19 and later. None are of special architectural interest, except the stable, a rare surviving example of a large works facility, but they make an interesting group. In the valley bottom on Bridge Road, the former BOTTOM FORGE started in 1840, but with little recognizable of that date following late C20 conversion to warehousing. Off Park Bridge Road beside the Medlock, a brick chimney of a former mid–late C19 cotton mill, and further N, the truncated brick chimney of the former ROLLER WORKS of 1886, which produced parts for textile machinery. The large brick STABLES opposite, 1870, set into the hillside around a courtyard, were fitted out by *Musgraves* of Belfast. Converted to a heritage centre, 1970s. Steep gables, stone mullioned-and-transomed windows, wide arched entrance to yard. Next DINGLE TERRACE, running N: brick workers' housing of 1865 looking just as if transported from an urban centre. Branching NE brings us to DEAN HOUSE of 1844, built for the Lees family. Stone, quietly Gothic and gabled, with a pretty slated flèche. Further along, the PARK BRIDGE INSTITUTE by *John Eaton & Son*, with reading room etc., opened in 1905. The church and school of 1866 beside it have been demolished. The lane continues as DEAN TERRACE, more red brick terraced workers' housing of the 1850s. Beyond, the greatly altered KEVERLOW FARM, a late C17 stone house with attached barn with ventilation holes. Lastly on this stretch, and strictly speaking in Oldham, THE VILLAS, four semi-detached houses of 1910 for section managers. (Other industrial remains and ruins can be found in the immediate area, including the late C19 colliery PUMP HOUSE of the Rocher New Pit, to the E on the other side of the river.)

PATRICROFT

Visually the W part of Eccles.

CHRIST CHURCH, Liverpool Road. 1868 by *John Lowe*. Low, yellow sandstone. Gabled W end to the road with an offset spirelet and a large plate-traceried wheel window with trefoil openings. Clerestory with small quatrefoil windows.

HOLY CROSS (R.C.), Liverpool Road. 1961. A large and rather striking brick church with a tall SE tower, stone frieze with carved motifs, abstract mosaics at the E end, and relief of the Last Supper, S side. Large S windows through which Stations of the Cross reliefs can be seen inside, high on the N wall. The N side has only small square clerestory lights.

COUNTY POLICE STATION, Green Lane. Dated 1892. Stone, Tudor Gothic. Long range to the street, three projecting gabled bays, windows with hoodmoulds, etc. Probably by the County Architect *Henry Littler*.

ECCLES SPINNING & MANUFACTURING CO. (former), Green Lane. A big early C20 cotton mill with a large polygonal domed tower and fat circular chimney.

QUEEN'S ARMS, beside the railway line off Green Lane. Built in 1828 to serve the Liverpool & Manchester Railway, and therefore with a claim to being the first purpose-built railway inn. (The interior is reported to retain early C20 fittings.)

(JAMES NASMYTH WAY. Near here was the site of James Nasmyth's works established in 1836, where he invented the steam hammer in 1839–40. A small steam hammer is displayed beside the road.)

LIVERPOOL ROAD. No. 262 is a large and outwardly well-preserved brick house, *c*. 1830. Symmetrical with a central entrance with a pedimented door surround. A large STABLE behind has had its arched entrance infilled. The house has strong associations with inventors and engineers: the birthplace in 1877 of the aeroplane inventor A. V. Roe, it was also the residence from 1836 to 1843 of James Nasmyth who invented the steam hammer (*see* above).

BARTON AQUEDUCT, Barton Lane. By *James Brindley*, 1761, demolished 1893. One of the arches has been reset on the side of the road at the W end of Barton Lane.

For the Barton Swing Bridge and Swing Aqueduct *see* Stretford.

PEEL GREEN

W of Eccles and Patricroft, on the Liverpool Road.

ST MICHAEL AND ALL THE ANGELS, Liverpool Road, just E of the M60 motorway. By *Bernard Miller*, dedicated 1957. Low, brick and many-windowed. Emphasis is on the SW tower, which is sturdy and forceful, with a flat top. Short slightly recessed chancel, star-shaped E window with STAINED GLASS by *Harcourt M. Doyle*, 1957.

PEEL GREEN CEMETERY, Liverpool Road. Opened 1879. Large and well populated with monuments. The buildings were designed by *A. H. Davies-Colley* and *J. W. Beaumont* who won the competition in 1877. Simple LODGE, large CHAPEL of yellow sandstone with red sandstone dressings, low polygonal apse, and an unusual tower with an octagonal upper stage and a pyramidal roof.

BARTON AERODROME, Liverpool Road. An important early civilian airport, and the earliest municipal airport in the country. It remains in use for civil aviation as home to the oldest flying club in England, the Lancashire Aero Club (formed 1922). In 1928 it was handed over to the Manchester Corporation Airport Committee, in 1929 the landing field was approved by the Air Ministry, and the airport opened the following year. It was the first airport to have designated RUNWAYS, of grass laid over a cinder base. Its municipal career was short-lived, and by 1935 work had started on a new airport at Ringway (*see* p. 457).

Farm buildings on the site were adapted for use, including an OFFICE l. of the entrance, the earliest municipal airport passenger terminal buildings in England, converted from (of all things) a brick cowshed of *c.* 1880 in 1929–30. It had a booking hall, offices and customs offices. One storey, L-shaped, with transomed windows. Refurbished for offices, late C20. To the r. of the entrance is the main HANGAR and attached workshops of 1930, reputedly the earliest surviving civil hangar in England. Brick with a steel frame, thirteen bays, with a pitched single-span steel truss roof. The S gable incorporates a stone plaque with the municipal coat of arms. Workshops extend along the whole of the NE side, including a former boiler house where 'dope' for making and repairing fabric plane coverings was heated. A little to the NW is the CONTROL TOWER by the City Architect *G. Noel Hill*. It is a very early example, designed in 1933, the second civil aeronautical control tower in England after that at Croydon. The design was the result of lengthy negotiations between the Air Ministry and the City Council concerning wireless and meteorological facilities.* Three-stage octagonal brick tower rising from a podium which has angled and splayed wings. The tower is glazed at the top and has a concrete balcony. 108

Some of the other buildings relate to military use when the airport was requisitioned by the Air Ministry at the beginning of the Second World War. They include HANGAR I, thought to be a relocated First World War hangar, of timber, clad in asbestos sheets with a timber Belfast roof. The entrance is

---

* According to research by Jeremy Lake and Paul Francis.

flanked by low flat-roofed brick OFFICES or GUARD HOUSES with curved fronts.

PENDLEBURY
Including Agecroft and Irlams o' th' Height

N of Swinton, with which it merges. It was once a great area of coal mining, and housing for the miners, but almost all trace of the industry has been effaced, including the huge power station at Agecroft.

ST AUGUSTINE, Bolton Road, Pendlebury. By *Bodley & Garner*, 1870–4, and one of the most moving of all Victorian churches. Built at the expense of Edward Stanley Heywood, Manchester banker of Heywood Brothers, son of Sir Benjamin Heywood and brother of the Rev. H.R. Heywood, for whom Street built Swinton church in 1869. St Augustine cost about £33,000. The group including the gatehouse and school was by *Bodley & Garner* too. The school has been converted to offices. The whole group is of brick (with stone dressings) to deny any sense of luxury. *The Builder* in 1877 noted: 'There are large mills near the church, and it was advisable, by every means at the architects' disposal, to give an appearance of size and mass'.★

The GATEHOUSE separates the precinct from the road. It has a pointed arch and a tiny LODGE, with stone banding to the road and two unequal gables to the churchyard. To the l. is the SCHOOL, with two-storeyed gabled ends and a hall between, mullioned-and-transomed windows and a tall cupola towards the W end. If only someone in building the mid-C20 school on the opposite side of the precinct had taken care to do something a little better than run-of-the-mill stuff.

The CHURCH was built on a raft of concrete to counteract subsidence prevalent in this mining area. It faces you with its E wall. It is a high wall, and the window is placed high up (above the reredos inside). It has flowing transitional Dec-Perp tracery, as has the whole. There is blank panelling around, and two flanking pinnacles terminate this part of the composition. The sides of the church appear yet higher. The roof runs through without any break from W to E, penetrated only by the tops of the buttresses, and the side windows are of four lights in the chancel, of three in the nave. The chancel E bay is canted. High up, above the top of each window, is a blank arch, so that the window arch is slightly recessed against the top part, a motif Bodley got from Albi and Toulouse. On the N side W of the chancel is a low two-storeyed vestry. On the S side is a porch and a stair-tower serving the rood and organ. Windows on each side of this are blind, that to the E cut across

---

★ The parsonage (demolished), some distance away, was built to *Bodley*'s designs in 1868.

by the stair-tower. This was where Bodley planned his tower, which was to have been connected to the main body by a bridge. The w front has a doorway with statues over and a five-light window, bricked in below the transom.

The INTERIOR, 159 ft (48 metres) long and 80 ft (24 metres) high, is of breathtaking majesty and purity. Internal buttresses (or what the Germans call wall-piers) pierced only right at the bottom by aisle-like passages, and arches high up from pier to pier with short transverse vaults to the window tops. The fronts of the buttresses are sheer, with only a simple chamfer on each side. This scheme goes through to the very end. Like Albi it is derived from a common model in C13 mendicant architecture, the Dominican church at Ghent, which shares with St Augustine not just the internal buttress plan but also the internal elevation of full-height niches, pierced to form passages.* The space is unbroken from w to E. Starting at the w end and the main entrance, first there is a canted timber entrance lobby and a very narrow gallery running right across. The windows reveal themselves between the piers as the nave is traversed, and the absence of windows in the bays preceding the chancel, where the tower would have been, creates an area of dimness which heightens the light and decoration of the chancel. Here, s side, the door to the rood stair has beautiful gilded hinges shaped like branches with leaves. The stair emerges at the top in a little stone lobby with its own roof and slit window. The rood is then traversed to the organ, N side. The canted apse windows come into view only immediately before the rood is reached, adding to the richness of the E scheme.

FURNISHINGS. Commanding REREDOS with tiers of figure painting in North European style but incorporating Italian Renaissance models, e.g. St John the Baptist is after Mantegna. It appears doubly commanding because the sanctuary is raised by eight steps. It was designed by *Bodley* and executed by *Burlison & Grylls*, with whom Bodley says, in correspondence with Heywood, he had been studying 'old paintings'. Each scene is framed by gilded canopy work, and some of the details are in relief. The central figure of St Augustine has inset stones to the mitre and vestments, while the instruments of the Passion held by the angels at the bottom are of metal. The largest scene, an Annunciation, is at the top, then St Augustine and his attendants, with a crucifixion below. – Other furnishings are also by Bodley. SEDILIA. Like all the timber furnishings, executed by *Franklin* of Deddington. On a stone base, free-standing, treated as a settle with a flat tester. – Traceried ROOD SCREEN. – ORGAN CASE. Pipes set off by gilded traceried detailing. – PULPIT. Simple, square with linenfold panelling, attached to a pier one bay before the chancel. – FONT. At the w end, on a high stepped plinth. Stone, octagonal, with traceried faces. – COVER, a great spire with crocketed pinnacles, but not

73

* We are indebted to Michael Hall, whose monograph on Bodley & Garner is in preparation, for this and other points.

over-intricate. Topped by an angel, beneath a high golden
crown appended to the hoist mechanism.

PAINTINGS. The painted figures in tabernacles high up in
the E wall occupy niches between the wall-piers and the E
window. Musician angels, painted on raised copper. Repre-
sentations of the Doctors of the Church and other figures
appear in traceried surrounds on the W faces of the piers in
the nave (except the two westernmost bays). These, also with
raised gilded detail, relieve the plainness of the piers and help
to draw the eye eastwards. Four of them seem to have been
done by *Burlison & Grylls*, but it is possible that *W. O. & C.
Powell*, who redecorated the interior in 1900, did the others.
WALL PAINTING and STENCILLING was an integral part of
the original scheme, with Bodley & Garner's typical diapers
and broad bands of painted decoration beneath the windows.
Now all that survives is the chancel scheme, restored by
Stephen Dykes Bower in the 1970s.

STAINED GLASS. Very individual especially at the E end. The
colours are generally pale, with much plain glass, and the unity
of the scheme is critical to the character of the interior. It is
all by *Burlison & Grylls*, designed and supervised by *Bodley*
himself. In a letter to E. S. Heywood he wrote: 'We kept them
[the windows] broad in colour, each window having a leading
colour . . . It is about the first time it has been tried in modern
times, most new windows having so many colours in them. I
think the less variety of colour is more artistic.' The Apostles
and Evangelists in the E window are based on medieval glass
at Fairford, Gloucestershire (though with more muted
colours), concerning which Burlison & Grylls had been party
to correspondence in *The Ecclesiologist*.* The subject matter
concentrates on English saints, particularly missionaries,
martyrs and Christian kings. They, and the dedication to
Augustine, encapsulate the idea of mission to a desolate industrial area. In the nave the windows each have three large figures
on a plain ground with sparing decoration. In the chancel there
are two tiers of figures, and apse windows have three tiers of
figures on a blue ground.

St Augustine is one of the greatest of all Victorian churches,
unusual because so little has been added and so little taken
away. The interior almost exactly matches the scene shown in
the watercolour Bodley exhibited at the Royal Academy in
1875. The glass, painting and furnishings relate to the architecture as intended, and the effect is unforgettable.

CHURCHYARD. Michael Hall has discovered that Heywood
took a personal interest in the design of the churchyard, and
that he arranged purchase of shrubs for it. The entrance from
the lodge on Bolton Road leads to a path aligned with the E
end of the church. MONUMENTS. Placed axially with the E
front, E.S. Heywood †1914, the patron, and the Rev. Alfred
Dewes †1911, the first vicar. The men were brothers-in-law. A

---

* As research by Meriel Boyd has shown.

very tall stepped plinth, then an octagon with shields in the faces, topped by a slender tapering octagonal pier terminating as a canopied cross. Immediately before the E end, the Pendlebury Miners' Memorial, commemorating men killed in a disaster at the nearby Clifton Hall colliery in 1885. Headstone with a cross and Christ and angels in relief.

CHRIST CHURCH, Pendlebury Road, Pendlebury (originally Anglican, now Independent). By *W. R. Corson* of *Corson & Aitken*, 1856–9. The steeple with saddleback roof was added in 1861 by *Bodley* with the aid of money from the Heywood family, for whom he later built St Augustine (above). Coursed rubble body with two-light plate tracery windows. NW tower of ashlar, with three-light lancet belfry openings which temper the starkness of the outline through having banded shafts and little spandrel openings. Deep arch-braced roof with principals rising from enormous carved corbels set low in the walls. – STAINED GLASS. Opposed N and S nave windows by *Jones & Willis*, early C20, that on the N side a First World War memorial with SS Michael and George, quite good.

  VICARAGE (former), S of the church, red brick and very plain. Also by *Corson & Aitken*, 1868.

ST JOHN EVANGELIST, Bolton Road, Irlams o' th' Height. 1842. Neo-Norman, with a big W tower and side-windows of the Commissioners' type, but all in coursed rubble. Who did it? The tower has a row of five round-arched bell-openings and a shallow, rather Italian pyramid roof, which makes one think of *William Hayley* (cf. the Norman-Italianate treatment of All Souls, Ancoats and St Thomas, Ardwick, pp. 377, 359). The chancel was added in 1859–60 and the W baptistery in 1882, both in closely matching style. The interior was remodelled in 1881 when mouldings, ribs and wall shafts were added to the nave roof. (Alternating king- and queenpost roof trusses: W gallery supported by barley-twist cast-iron columns with cushion capitals.)

ST LUKE (R.C.), Swinton Park Road, Irlams o' th' Height. 1964 by *Burles, Newton & Partners*. Brick with an asymmetrical profile and a great big roof swooping down to terminate with a row of gables over canted bays.

AGECROFT CEMETERY, Langley Road, Agecroft. Laid out by the Borough Surveyor *Joseph Corbett*, buildings by *Sharp & Foster*, dated 1903. All in free Tudor Gothic and Perp, of yellow sandstone with red sandstone dressings. GATEWAY, an arch with blind panelling and a carved lion and unicorn. Chunky central finial. The LODGE, l., has applied timber framing. Stone OFFICES on the other side, with carved enrichments and a transomed bay. The ANGLICAN CHAPEL, also by *Sharp & Foster*, is placed axially and framed by the entrance arch. It is of unusual design, large and ornate, but fenced off and so decayed and ivy-covered as to defy detailed description. Great W tower, which has penultimate stage with a clock face framed by little oriels, and then a gabled timbered top with filigree timber panels. Nave with windows with flowing tracery and embattled W gable, SW timbered porch. The interior is said to have a fine tie-beam roof, with carving and arcading, but how long can any of this survive?

The CREMATORIUM stands at the N end of the main axial route. Formerly the Nonconformist chapel of 1903 by *Sharp & Foster*, altered by *G. Alexander McWilliam*, the City Engineer and Surveyor, in 1957. The chapel part has minimal Gothic detailing; flat-roofed ranges are the later additions.

THIRLMERE AQUEDUCT BRIDGE, Agecroft Road. 1892 by *J. F. Bateman* and *G. Hill*, engineers. Piping water to Manchester from the Lake District was, along with the building of the Ship Canal, one of Manchester Corporation's most ambitious and successful C19 projects. The bridge looks like a road or railway bridge, with much decorative cast iron, but carrying on the bed two large water pipes.

(AGECROFT HALL. A timber-framed house, partly of *c.* 1530 and partly of *c.* 1600 and later, was transported in 1926 to New Richmond, Virginia. It is now a museum. The publicity states that it stands 'in a setting reminiscent of its original site on Lancashire's Irwell River' which hardly sounds likely.)

PLATT HALL *see* MANCHESTER, p. 466

7000

PRESTOLEE

Practically an island. It lies in a loop of the River Irwell where the Croal joins it, with the Bolton & Bury Canal cutting across the neck.

HOLY TRINITY. Built at the expense of W. J. Rideout in 1859–62, with *George Shaw* of Saddleworth acting as both architect and contractor. Typically irregular in its massing, with long transepts and a big tower in the angle between nave and S transept. A stone staircase, its parapet decorated with Shaw's reversed S-shapes, rises up the outside of the tower, pierces a buttress, and continues to a narrow upper door. The steep set-offs to the angle buttresses, giving the steeple a strongly pyramidal form, are just as personal, as is the broach spire without lucarnes. Coarse Dec tracery. A full-height partition of wood and glass introduced in 1995 subdivides the nave. FITTINGS by *Shaw* include the PULPIT, cantilevered out from the crossing wall and reached from the vicar's vestry, and the VICAR'S STALL, both with miniature arcading. – STALLS, ALTAR, PEWS all by Shaw, and so probably is the FONT. Pevsner called this bumptious Neo-Norman; Shaw had a carver who specialized in Norman zigzag and Celtic interlace, which appears here on the base. All this is but a prelude to the dramatic STAINED GLASS. The shape of the building focuses attention on the four cardinal windows, which are unusually large and low-set. E, W and N were filled in the 1860s with vivid

pictures in luminous colours by *James Ballantine* of Edinburgh.
There is a smaller one on the N side as well.

KEARSLEY MILL, 1906. Unmissable. Six storeys, of red and
yellow brick. Engine and generator house, relatively small, at
the N end. The mill generated its own electrical power from
the start. 200 ft (61 metre) chimney with the name in white
brick and a yellow brick collar at the top. Stair-tower with a
dome at the opposite corner, and the office building which is
not showy.

Round about the confluence of the Croal and the Irwell is one
of the surprising interludes of open hilly country that give SE
Lancashire its character. SEDDON'S FOLD, Seddon Lane,
largely derelict, is a typical cluster of dwellings and farm buildings. Outlying to the SW is a stone BARN, probably C16, with
three, originally four, massive cruck trusses. The N bay has
fallen down. In the main cluster a Greater Manchester Archaeological Unit survey of 1985 found a C17 stone FARMHOUSE
with a baffle-entry plan, large timber-framed inglenook, and
mullioned windows. A second, slightly later dwelling backs
onto its N side. Attached on the W – so that the group makes
an L – is a surprisingly monumental brick building, probably
early C19, with a shallow-pitched overhanging roof and large
windows on the S only. Planning and decoration suggest a
public building rather than a dwelling. Three-bay STABLE with
Gothick arched windows.

Immediately N an exciting industrial landscape unfolds. Three
bridges cross the Irwell side by side. PACKHORSE BRIDGE is
only 5 ft (1.5 metres) wide, of five arches with diamond cutwaters but no refuges. J.D.U.Ward gives a date of *c.* 1790–1800,
which goes with its surprisingly monumental style, see the
alternately blocked voussoirs. Next, the four-arch canal AQUE-
DUCT came in 1797. Between the two is a C20 concrete suspension PIPE BRIDGE. Beyond the aqueduct the canal turns
sharp r. and ascends steeply by two sets of three staircase locks.
The top of the staircase commands a magnificent prospect like
a Lowry painting. The canal branches N along the Croal valley
to Bolton, curving round the bleak 1840s Tudor WELLFIELD
HOUSE, and E to Bury. Cream's Paper Mill (*see* Little Lever)
fills its steep sheep-walked valley with steam, Kearsley Mill is
brightly lit against the wooded Irwell bank and Farnworth
church (q.v.) is a bold silhouette above. The canal itself was
progressively abandoned from 1939 because of landslips, but
in 2004 preliminaries are in hand towards its restoration.

PRESTWICH

Prestwich-cum-Oldham was one of the largest parishes in
England, and in the C19 one of the richest. It has one of the finest
medieval churches in the area, although at first glance it looks
Victorian. The ancient rectory was the timber-framed Deyne,
demolished in 1837. It stood E of the church, off Rectory Lane.

Prestwich, St Mary.
Victoria County History of Lancashire, vol. 5, 1911

Only three miles NW of Manchester, but an appreciable climb above it, well wooded, with steep cloughs going down to the River Irwell: Prestwich had all that was wanted for a villa suburb. The story is one of C18 houses in their own parks, C19 villas in one or two acres, and C20 semis.

ST MARY, Church Lane. A major church, the centre of a very large parish. Approaching from the E the tall chancel with uncusped tracery catches the eye first, with its two-storey vestry and NE turret; but this is all by *Austin & Paley* of 1888–9, added to the E end of the chancel of the medieval church, which, although much altered, is complete from end to end. Tall C15 W tower, unusually slim and sheer (proportions 1:4.5), with slight-looking buttresses, few openings, a relatively light base moulding and only one intermediate string. Tracery panels on the buttresses, top and bottom. Desultory but amusing decoration under the parapet: on the S a procession of swans is harried from the back by a fox; the way they escape from the frame is surprisingly modern-looking. Heavy stone roofs to nave and aisles, with eaves, not parapets. Continuous closely windowed clerestory of domestic character. The aisle walls are Dec – see the NW window and roofline – but were 'raised' in 1756 to take galleries, with an extra tier of windows, as the S porch inscription tells us. A further programme of repairs is indicated by C18 dates on the tower. The SE chapel, originally C16, was rebuilt in 1874 by *John Lowe*. It indicates the length of the medieval chancel, which was under the same roof as the nave. Also by Lowe, 1875, is the little Birch chapel, now the Lady Chapel, at the SE end. *Austin & Paley*'s chancel of 1888–9 (replacing one by *Travis & Mangnall*, 1861) stands E of the medieval one. They rebuilt the N chapel too. The polygonal N porch is of 1895.

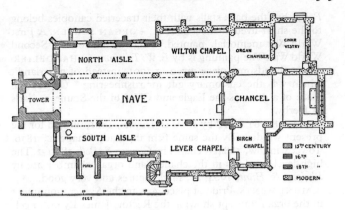

Prestwich, St Mary, plan.
Victoria County History of Lancashire, vol. 5, 1911

Things become clearer inside. Tall arcades without capitals; a Dec motif. The two sides are not in step with each other. The third pier from the W on the N side includes a piece of plain walling, indicating the position of the rood screen and stair. The easternmost pair also include a section of wall, which must be left over from an aisle-less chancel, i.e. before the chapels were added. This is confirmed by the outline of a S window in the spandrel. In the back of the NE pier is an aumbry belonging to that chapel. Splendid flat camberbeam roof, or strictly ceiling, for as we have seen there is a pitched stone roof above it. The construction and the bosses recall the chancel of Manchester Cathedral, suggesting a late C15 date and the patronage of the Stanleys, whose status in the parish was greatly increased after the battle of Bosworth at the expense of the Pilkingtons. Ceiling, roof and clerestory appear to be all of a piece, so perhaps the workaday clerestory, so different from that of Manchester or Eccles, is simply a reflection of the load it has to carry.* The E chapels, belonging to Heaton Hall on the N and Alkrington S, have largely lost their identity due to successive rebuildings and widenings. *Austin & Paley*'s E end is impressively sheer, if rather cold, with the windows set high above much blank walling.

It is possible then to propose a relatively simple chronology. First, arcades and outer walls, probably C14. Second, ceiling, roof, clerestory and tower, after 1485. Third, 1756 *et seq.*, S porch and raising of aisles. Last, the new C19 E end. The N and S chapels, C19 now, were originally added in the early C16.

FURNISHINGS. REREDOS, stone, in memory of Henry Arthur Drinkwater Birch †1863 aged eight, of scarlet fever. – ALTAR RAILS, STALLS, SCREEN and PULPIT by *Austin &*

---

*The E Cheshire churches with stone roofs, such as Prestbury, have clerestories of similar character.

Paley, but the back stalls with their traceried canopies belong to the short-lived chancel of 1861. – ORGAN SCREEN. A First World War memorial, painted. Wings added for the Second World War. The painting is by *E. W. Tristram.* – CHANDELIER. A very handsome piece given in 1701 'instead of a garland', which was the customary gift for rushbearing.* On top, in place of a dove, is the Eagle and Child of the Stanleys, Earls of Derby.

STAINED GLASS. E by *Ward & Hughes*, 1861, altered for the present window. By the same firm the Lady Chapel E, 1876. Tower window, 1884. N chapel by *Clayton & Bell*, 1890–2. The high-level windows in the chancel and organ chamber are by *Shrigley & Hunt*, 1904–27; single figures and very good.

MONUMENTS. Pride of place goes to the *Sievier* monument in the organ transept showing the Rector, James Lyon, in celebration of fifty years' incumbency in 1833, giving communion to four of his flock in what must be the medieval chancel. Bust of him as an old man above. – In the N chapel Sir Thomas Grey Egerton †1756, missing its top, and Sir Edward Egerton †1743. In the S chapel a series of brass coffin-plates including Sir Ashton Lever of Alkrington Hall (q.v.), †1788. In the chancel brass to Anna Allen †1634, with a two-sided hinged plate. Marble wall monument to William Ashton, rector, †1731.

The size of the original parish is reflected in the huge CHURCHYARD, enjoyably romantic with its varied monuments and inscribed poetry. They range from (W of the tower) the white Italian Renaissance mausoleum of John Brooks, †1849 and his wife †1851, with figures by *John Thomas* in niches; and the Slagg monument by *Waterhouse*, 1863, to the group of Heaton Park servants immediately SW of the tower. Others to note are: a slab with angel trumpeter signed *Sarah Patefield*, S; amateur botanists James Percival and John Horsefield nearby, and the poet Charles Swain †1874. On the lower terrace is James Lamb †1903, attributed to *Salomons*, and Sir E. Tootal Broadhurst †1922. By the E gate is the WAR MEMORIAL of 1921 by *Taylor & Young*, a Portland stone cross with a bronze sword.

RECTORY, by the E gate. By *Taylor & Young*, 1923. V-shaped with the front door in the angle – i.e. a half-butterfly plan. Wrennish details include the sash windows with their thick glazing bars, some segment-headed, and two tones of brick. Shades of Wood & Sellers too, in the round-arched doorway, the symmetrically placed obelisk chimneys and the partial flat roofs. Pleasing garden front, on a raised terrace recalling Croxteth Hall (SW Lancashire), symmetrical with four-pane-wide sashes conferring a sense of amplitude. The interior is planned about the diagonal axis of the hall. Glass domes in

---

* Rushbearing was an annual ceremony, which originated in renewing the rush floor coverings in churches, when it was traditional for local families to make gifts to the church.

the flat parts of the roof have been blocked, except above the Soanian servants' stair. SUNDIAL. C17, from the ancient rectory.

ST GABRIEL, Bishops Road, Sedgley Park. 1932–3, by *Taylor & Young*. The cost was no more than £5,000, except for the fittings, so the architects 'have been obliged to rely on dignity of proportion, good brickwork, carpentry and joinery, and beauty of material, on colour effects and one or two choice pieces of detail' said the *Manchester Guardian*. The result is an initially underwhelming church that grows on you. Long brick box with square windows set high and a low oblong tower. Bare white-painted brick within. Open tie-beam roof with kingposts and raking struts. The subtlety of the brickwork is in the gradual set-offs outside and the window splays inside; the choice detail is in a few bits of marquetry and the painted ROOD on the E wall, carved by *Sherwood Edwards*. REREDOS, STALLS, SCREEN, PULPIT and LECTERN all by the architects, in Renaissance style. – FONT. A big stone tub with a wave pattern, under the W gallery, which was partitioned off in 1984. LADY CHAPEL at right angles, NW corner, with STAINED GLASS of 1947.

VICARAGE, also probably by *Taylor & Young*, c. 1929.

ST HILDA, Whittaker Lane. 1904 by *F. P. Oakley*, with a vestry extension of 1922. Of red brick and terracotta, all under one roof, with a thin turret behind the NW porch. Baptistery at the W end under a six-light window. Brick-faced interior too, just the piers and a couple of stripes of red stone. Low stone wall for a screen, with the PULPIT, equally low, built in. Brightly painted and gilded REREDOS, with the Epiphany in a central niche. Very large free-standing AUMBRY, like a wardrobe, with relief and paintings by *Terry McGunigle* of Liverpool, 1990s. By the same artist STATIONS OF THE CROSS and Lady Chapel REREDOS. In the latter Heaton Park appears in the background, and St Hilda holds her church in Prestwich. The church also appears in the WAR MEMORIAL, a wooden relief, N aisle. SCHOOL. Immediately W, by *Maxwell & Tuke*, 1879. The same shape as the church – an overall roof extended at the sides and ends, but more cheerful in effect. Continuous glazing between buttresses at the upper level, tile-hanging at the ends.

ST MARGARET, Rooden Lane. 1849–52 by *Travis & Mangnall*, extended W in 1863 and 1899, and E in 1871. Long nave and aisles separately roofed, with a slim turret in the NE angle. Close-stepping arcades with octagonal piers. The aisle roofs are X-braced. The nave has a hammerbeam roof of light construction, the hammers inclined upwards and carved with small angels. In 1985 the church suffered a severe fire. Restoration, including a new N aisle roof, was carried out under *Gordon Thorne* (*E. G. Thorne*) of Prestwich.

The church's architecture is but a modest foil to the outstanding C20 and C21 FITTINGS. *Opus sectile* PANELS, E, by *Powell*, 1901. The foremost donor was Edward Holt, brewer, of Woodthorpe (*see* below). In 1894, when he was considering building a holiday home at Windermere,* he had visited the woodcarver *Arthur W. Simpson* at his Gill Head workshop. Over the next quarter century, mostly to the designs of *Dan Gibson*, Simpson furnished St Margaret's. Their work is entirely un-Gothic, horizontal in emphasis without pointy bits, decorated with Renaissance putti and beautifully carved roses, grapes, thistles, and oak leaves, and executed in light unstained oak. WAINSCOT †1904 and †1916, ALTAR RAIL 1903, STALLS 1899. The altar was lost in the fire. SCREEN, now at the W end, in memory of Holt's son Joseph †1915, installed in 1920 to a Gibson design of the 1890s. The figures of Joseph Holt and St Margaret were carved by *William Aumonier*. To avoid obscuring the W window the ROOD group itself, which surmounted the screen, has been placed over the NW vestry. In place of Simpson's screen now hangs a ROOD painted on glass by *Graeme Willson*. Christ is draped on the cross rather than nailed to it. By Willson also the forward ALTAR, with glass sides, and a PAINTING of 1994 acting as the Lady Chapel reredos. Mary is robed in swirling scarlet, the boy Christ is naked. Gordon Thorne's new ORGAN CASE incorporates an AUMBRY by Willson; the FONT COVER is by Willson too.

STAINED GLASS. W by *Ward & Hughes* in memory of the 2nd Earl of Wilton †1884. The family are still buried N of the church. *Shrigley & Hunt* windows of various dates on the N, plus one by *Francis Skeat*, 1963. Chancel s, *c.* 1978, to a former librarian of John Rylands Library in Manchester: two early woodcuts are reproduced, and among early printers' monograms is that of *Wippell*. By the organ, by *Meg Lawrence*, 1987, is Christ the carpenter and Mary, both modelled on modern people, and leaded in irregular hexagons.

CROSS, immediately w, by *R. B. Preston*, 1913. Tall, hexagonal.

OUR LADY OF GRACE (R.C.), Fairfax Road. Presbytery, 1894. Church/school, 1889. Church, anachronistically Gothic in Portland stone and red brick, 1931, by *Greenhalgh & Williams* of Bolton.

CONGREGATIONAL CHAPEL, Newtown Street. 1881. A good building in need of care. Colin Cunningham considers that it is by *G. T. Redmayne*, not by Waterhouse as was supposed. Of orange brick with a little terracotta, and yellow stone, with its many parts enclosed within a tight rectangle. Chapel upstairs, schoolrooms below, principal stair SW, lesser stair NW – all expressed by the fenestration and the rooflines.

HOLY LAW SYNAGOGUE, Bury New Road. The first purpose-built synagogue in the area. By *Theodore Herzl Birks*, 1934–5. He was the chief draughtsman in Joseph Sunlight's office, and Joseph's father Israel Sunlight was president of the synagogue.

---

* Blackwell, 1898–1900.

JEWISH CEMETERY. 1841, in the village centre. A long narrow plot behind the curved wall on Bury New Road. Original gates, interesting monuments.

ST MARGARET'S SUNDAY SCHOOL, Bury Old Road. 1851, by *Travis & Mangnall*, Gothic. It was a memorial to the Countess of Wilton.

WHITTAKER LANE SCHOOL is of 1879 by *Maxwell & Tuke*. More recent building attached.

LIBERAL CLUB, Bury New Road. 1879, by *Thomas Thorp*, with paired pilasters over a rusticated ground floor for its centre-piece. Allegorical figures representing industry and peace over the central window.

On Church Lane is the former CONSERVATIVE CLUB of 1879 by *W. Dawes*; Gothic.

Of the enormous PRESTWICH HOSPITAL of 1851 etc., by *Isaac Holden*, and its annexe of 1883–4 further SW in Clifton Road, little survives. In the valley below the remains of the annexe, now the Edenfield Centre, are CLIFTON AQUEDUCT and VIADUCT. The viaduct was built in 1846 for the Lancashire & Yorkshire Railway; thirteen elegant stone arches set on a curve, with a wider one for the river. The aqueduct, of 1796 for the Manchester, Bolton & Bury Canal, is heroic in its strength, though lower and of only three arches, with pointed cutwaters rooted onto the rocky riverbed.

The airy heights of Prestwich and Whitefield were favoured by the wealthy who built their villas here. None of the largest ones, in their own parks, survive.

PHILIPS PARK, the early C19 home of Robert Philips, one of Manchester's leading merchants, was bought for the public in 1946, but the mansion was demolished in 1950. Neglect and misguided intervention have robbed the park of much of its architectural and horticultural value, but not of its atmos-phere. The landscape is intricately folded and luxuriously verdant, and it retains more of the feeling of a private park than Heaton (q.v.). The mansion, possibly partly by *Barry*, stood on the car park site. ORANGERY and STABLES remain, and a small TEMPLE on top of a steep grass walk; the sculp-ture it housed is now in Bury Art Gallery. Outwood Lodge by *Johnson* of Lichfield, the mid-C19 home of Mark Philips M.P., was higher up in the park, by the surviving barn and farm-house. The N lodge represents its Tudor Gothic style. Skirting the northern edge and shocking in its sudden revelation is the eight-lane M60 motorway.

Of the remaining notable large houses Ian Pringle has identified the following.

On Hilton Lane, WRENWOOD and ROOKWOOD of 1881 by *Paul Ogden*, an entertainingly unequal pair with eclectic detailing. On Bury New Road at the corner of Butterstile Lane is OAK HILL, 1836 by *Mills & Butterworth*, plain brick, quietly clas-sical. CHARLTON HOUSE on Charlton Avenue, of 1866, is by *Thomas Worthington* according to the late owner. Tall, of header-bond brickwork, polychromatic and notchy, with a

Germanic tower. Renovated *c.* 2000 thanks to an enabling development of low linked houses. THE ROOST, Rectory Lane, is of 1895–6 by *J. L. Langham* for Mrs Barratt, in Home Counties style with tile-hanging and Norman Shaw bays. Tall vertically shadowed chimneys. Off Scholes Lane is BENT HILL, *c.* 1850 for Robert Neill, a Roman villa on a hill, used for a while as the town hall. Nearby is HIGH BANK, now NAZARETH HOUSE, a Georgian survival of *c.* 1792. Three-bay pediment, porch of two pairs of Ionic columns. Plastic windows of hospital type inserted. Stable block to one side. Continuing on to Bury Old Road, opposite the corner of Heaton Park is WOODTHORPE of 1861, with a billiard room extension of 1889. A Gothic house of unromantic texture and detail. The staircase and several chimneypieces survive. From 1889 to 1920 it was the home of Sir Edward Holt, brewer and patron of the arts (*see* St Margaret, above.) Now it is a Holt's pub itself.*

The choicest survivor is SEDGLEY HOUSE, now the nucleus of the Sedgley Park Centre, a police training college. Built *c.* 1854 for William Pearson, calico merchant, it is gauntly Gothic, with all its verticals emphasized, of red brick laid in Flemish bond and buff stone. The architect is not known. Standing on a knoll, it would have commanded a splendid view. In 1876 it was bought by Themistocles Petrocokino, stuff merchant and head of the Greek community in Manchester. He undertook a lavish redecoration under *James Lamb*. Shortly after 1900 the nuns of the Faithful Companions of Jesus took over. Since 1976 the police have been in charge; the site is densely developed, but the house is well-preserved.

Entry is through a porch and lobby into the broad HALL, floored with multicoloured tiles, which runs the full depth of the house. A fine fireplace with TP initials, i.e. after 1876, warmed visitors. The STAIR rises ahead, with a thin cast-iron balustrade and lit by a double-transomed window which surely was once coloured. The DINING ROOM retains its masculine feel in spite of pastel paint. Marble fireplace with bronze figures representing Music and Art, panelled ceiling. Egyptian gas fittings of bronze. The MUSIC ROOM opposite is decorated in Adam style. Delicately inlaid and gilded fireplace and two large pier glasses by *James Lamb*. Ceiling painting; musical trophy over the door. At the back of the house is the Garden or MORNING ROOM, smaller and more cheerful. The ceiling is painted with cornucopia, roses, olive leaves and swags, and dive-bombing blue tits, with TP initials. The frieze however, in a slightly heavier style, is signed by the Faithful Companions of Jesus. Fruit and swags again, but with starlings. Opening off the rear bay of the hall is the former BILLIARD ROOM. Dark wainscot and a terrific fireplace with built-in

---

*There are several good purpose-built Holt's pubs in the area, such as the FRIENDSHIP INN on Scholes Lane by *N. Hartley Hacking*, 1924, and the WELCOME INN of 1936 on Bury Old Road.

clock. Turned into a chapel by the sisters, who broke through the end and added a large apse with domed top-lighting and Romanesque arcading.

The sisters built a residential extension to the servants' wing of the house, by *Oswald Hill*, 1904; a larger free-standing chapel, and a hall of residence called Clitheroe Hall, by *W. R. Watson & C. W. Crush*.

THIRLMERE AQUEDUCT *see* Pendlebury.

HAWESWATER PUMPING STATION, Heywood Road *see* Heaton Park, p. 398.

RADCLIFFE

7000

Radcliffe bears the scars of heavy industry, and of its demise. There were for instance at least a dozen coalmines. Papermaking has been concentrated here and in Bury since as early as 1674. Radcliffe has also suffered, like many of the smaller towns of SE Lancashire, from losing its administrative identity to a larger neighbour, in this case Bury, and from being carved up by roads. In the closing years of its existence however Radcliffe Borough Council did some remarkably progressive building.

ST MARY, Church Green, i.e. about ¾ m. E of the present centre. Small and low-lying. A rare example of Lancashire Dec, although this manifests itself only in the originally cruciform plan and the flowing tracery of the transept end windows. The stumpy W tower (proportion 1:2.5), with its many set-offs, a fine piece of masoncraft, is dated 1665 on all three visible faces, with the names and arms of the donors – Radcliffe, Beswick and Assheton. Its W window could be genuine Dec reused. Nave of three bays, with four-light uncusped clerestory windows and a flat roof, which must be latest Perp. The chancel was unfeelingly rebuilt in 1817; the culprit was perhaps *Lewis Wyatt*, since it was paid for by the 2nd Earl of Wilton (*see* Heaton Hall p. 398). Restorations and extensions of 1870 and 1905, both by *J. Medland Taylor* and equally unfeeling, made the body of the church almost square in plan. His is the unpleasantly large and coarsely textured S aisle with its central gable, all that is left of the S transept. The central window repeats that of the N transept but with the extraordinary addition of two faces in the tracery. It is dated 1905 but perhaps reproduces what was there before restoration.

The interior is taller and more spacious than anticipated, and it is a surprise to find the nave of two bays only, not three as appeared outside. The arcades are finely moulded, the piers of four half-rounds and four diagonal hollows, the arch profile the same in more flattened form, as are the capitals and bases. On the E wall can be seen the outline of a steep roof springing from the arcade top. The chancel arch has been partly re-cut. As for the transepts, they appear rather to have been transeptal chapels. The S wall of the S transept is

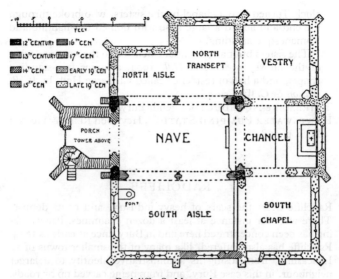

Radcliffe, St Mary, plan.
Victoria County History of Lancashire, vol. 5, 1911

well-preserved, unlike its outer face, with a PISCINA. N
transept and aisle are disconcertingly new looking; the internal walls were refaced by *J. Medland Taylor*. The nave roof of
1870 was said to be a re-creation of the late medieval one. If
so, it belonged to the same family as Eccles, with traceried
camberbeams, flat bosses, and angel figures standing as short
kingposts. The chancel is bleak, but the texture of the E
window reveals suggests reuse. The S aisle and SE chapel are
bleak too, but here again there may be reuse of at least one
square-headed Dec window. Portrait heads liven up the
chancel. Above the pulpit is the 5th Earl of Wilton, opposite
is Adam Crompton Bealey who paid for the 1905 restorations
– so that dates them. – REREDOS of dark wood, with five
panels in what looks like embossed leather but is painted gesso;
by *J. Medland Taylor*. – In the S chapel AUMBRY and REREDOS
PAINTING by *Graeme Willson*, 2002. – CHURCHWARDENS'
PEWS at the back, incorporating C17 woodwork. – STAINED
GLASS. In the SE chapel a tiny medieval fragment of a crowned
head; black and silver stain only. S transept by *Kempe* 1906.
E and Lady Chapel by *Shrigley & Hunt*. Several by *Wailes*.
Two in the N aisle by *Heaton, Butler & Bayne*. S aisle W by *T. F.
Willford* 1955. N aisle W by *Warrington*. – MONUMENT.
Alabaster slab under the altar, badly damaged, to James de
Radcliffe †1410.

The church lies in a wide bend of the River Irwell, where
the Roch joins it. On the W side of the churchyard is a moat-
like channel. What must have been a beautiful spot is slowly
recovering from despoliation by toxic tipping.

RADCLIFFE TOWER. Church and Tower should be seen together, although trees now obscure their relationship. The ruined pele tower is all that survives of the original seat of the Radcliffes, one of Lancashire's great families. It was sold in 1583 to the Asshetons of Middleton and thence descended to the Earls of Wilton. By the mid C19 the timber-framed buildings had disappeared, including the great hall which, it would seem, bore some resemblance to that at Baguley (Wythenshawe, q.v.), and the tower was ruinous.

What we see today is puzzling. In 1403 licence was granted to build two stone towers. The existing tower shows on its W side the scar of the great hall. The screens passage is known to have been at this end, so the tower is in place of the service wing. It was perhaps intended that the other tower should form the high end. Such an arrangement can be seen at Yanwath Hall in Cumbria. Was it a pele tower? It has walls four feet thick, mostly of large squared stones, with a double plinth and two tiny windows at low level on the E side. A tunnel vault at first-floor level collapsed soon after 1845. All this points to a defensive function, but how are we to explain the large semicircular arches at ground level on the N, E and S? The N retains a blocking of stone, but the others are now open. All three were on the evidence of their flues fireplaces, which can only signify a kitchen. The kitchen was usually detached beyond a buttery and pantry, but a fireproof building like this is exceptional (Yanwath again supplies a comparison). There is only a single doorway from the screens on the W side in place of the customary triplet, so the buttery and pantry must have been somewhere else. The doorway has deep slots for drawbars in its reveal, so the wing could be isolated from the rest. The kitchen, if such it is, was lit additionally by large N and S windows under the vault. The upper chamber, reached by a high-level doorway and an intra-mural stair, has a large fireplace above the W door, but its other walls do not survive. It was perhaps the solar. If, as seems likely, the fortified character of the building was more for show than serious defence, then the fireplace arches may also be a bit of public display, as perhaps were its four chimneys.

The only other standing building is a C17 stone TITHE BARN at the bend of the main road. Wide trusses without king- or queenposts, i.e. only a tie and a high collar. Purlins overlapping, not scarfed, and straight windbraces crossing over, not morticed in. The presence of wall-plates and mortices for wall braces suggests that it was fully timber-framed and that the stone is secondary.

ST THOMAS AND ST JOHN, Blackburn Street. A proud church of 1862–4 in the centre of present-day Radcliffe, by *William Walker* of Manchester, who is not known for any other work of architecture. It replaces a classical church built in 1819 for Countess Grosvenor, mother of the 1st Earl of Wilton, possibly by one of the Wyatts. The admirable tower was completed in 1871–2 by *Cunliffe & Freeman*. It is solidly built up to the clock stage, but the belfry is a light cage. The style is Perp, an unusual choice, but not the local Perp, for there is a separate chancel. Oddly old-fashioned are the gallery stairs with their own side entrances either side of the tower, indicated by the stepping-up windows. Only the w gallery remains, they were like those at Stand (*see* Whitefield, q.v.) of 1822. Symmetrical vestries either side of the chancel arch. The high roof, originally a hammerbeam, was renewed in the 1960s. – FONT and LECTERN from St John, Stand Lane (by *J. Medland Taylor*, 1866), demolished in 1976. The font was carved by the vicar there, *William Carter.*

ST ANDREW, Ainsworth Road. 1875–7, by *John Lowe.* An enterprising building. NW tower and spire. The tower starts to go octagonal low down, at clock level. A stair-turret wraps around the base, and, sheltering in the NE angle, a most unusual polygonal baptistery with its own pyramid roof. Narrow aisles, wide transepts, polygonal E end. Geometrical tracery.

Immediately N is the late C19 CONSTELLATION MILL, marked by a circular corner tower on the roadside. Five floors, the top one Italian Gothic with tricky brickwork and iron column-mullions.

ST MARY AND ST PHILIP NERI (R.C.). Church and presbytery, 1894, by *Jackson* of Manchester, in hard red brick with wooden windows.

BRIDGE METHODIST CHURCH, Milltown Street. 1881–3, by *Alfred W. Smith.* Of stone, Italianate, with a pedimented portico on attenuated columns. The capitals are lushly Composite.

CEMETERY, off Ainsworth Road. 1904. LODGE and CHAPEL are joined in the same building in a nice example of creative asymmetry. The domestic Gothic of the house, of two storeys with its chimneys and plain walling, is beautifully set off against the ecclesiastical Gothic of the church with its large windows and buttressing, with neither given undue weight.

Former TOWN HALL, Water Street and Spring Lane. Now residential. Edwardian Baroque of 1911 by *W. M. Gillow & R. Holt* in Portland stone and red brick, with angle turrets and segmental pediments.

98 FIRST WORLD WAR MEMORIAL, opposite the Town Hall, by *Sydney March*, 1922. Stone obelisk with three expressive bronze angels, of Victory (holding aloft a wreath), Sorrow (turning away, with a torch) and Hope (dove and roses). Much swirling drapery.

CIVIC SUITE, immediately W of St Thomas. 1974, by *Cruickshank & Seward.* A free-form plan, by *John Sheard.* Set low, almost sunken into the hillside, of unobtrusive brown brick, and almost windowless, with copper roofs providing the only accent. The building is all curves, with no corners outside or in. The inverted trusses of the foyer are striking. The auditorium can be divided by a coil wall partition. Brown brick, brown tile and brown wood is the colour scheme. It has worn well.

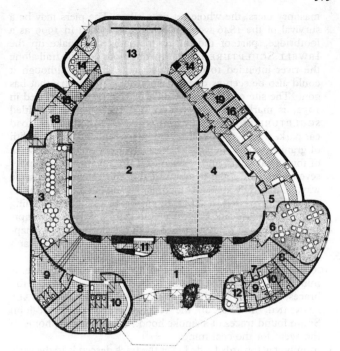

Radcliffe, Civic Suite, plan

LIBRARY, Stand Lane. Andrew Carnegie gave his usual £5,000
on condition that the town provided a site. A competition
was held in 1905 and the present building erected in 1906–7,
probably to the design of *William Lomax* who attended the
opening banquet. A strongly asymmetrical design with a
domed entrance tower and insistent use of Venetian windows,
each of which pushes the cornice up into a pediment; all in
red brick and yellow stone.

BATHS, Green Street. By *William Gower*, 1968. Prominent,
square, concrete-framed. The upper part of the frame is clad
in white mosaic, with an even range of pointed windows
lending an appropriately lively air. Below is a strong blue brick
base. Monopitch skylights protrude from the flat roof.

ST THOMAS ESTATE, immediately N of the church. By *Wilson
& Womersley*, 1968. The project architect was *John Sheard*.
New-towny, dense low-rise housing irregularly grouped
around and over pedestrian access paths. Of grey brick with
occasional red cladding with the seams following the roof lines.
The roofs are generally monopitches. More dense low-rise
housing, in dark brick, on Lord Street.

OUTWOOD VIADUCT. For the Lancashire & Yorkshire Railway,
1881. Five elegant iron arches, cross-braced, poised on pierced

masonry piers; the whole set on a curve. The piers may be a survival of the 1846 wooden bridge. Reopened in 1999 as a footbridge, part of the linked footpaths that make up the IRWELL SCULPTURE TRAIL, an ambitious 30-mile trail along the river intended to celebrate its regeneration, although it could also be seen as compensation for the industry that has gone. The site of Outwood Colliery, ½ m. s, which closed in 1932, is marked by grown over dirt rucks and an untitled SCULPTURE of 1998 by *Ulrich Ruckriem*. At the Ringley Road car park, where a few colliery buildings remain, is a monolith of granite, which the artist has caused to be split into a stack of four great cubes and reassembled. In a dell is a phalanx of seven more, of equal height and size and oriented the same way, so that they appear sometimes strung out and sometimes menacingly massed together. By the bridleway N and standing alone is the last and biggest of the stones. Serious attempts have been made to destroy two of the stones by fire, as happened at Avebury in the C18. Why should this be? 'You can't fix them to anything round here', said a passer-by.

SCOTSON FOLD is by the canal at the end of School Lane. A minor early C17 timber-framed house, box-framed with top braces, of two and a half units, unusually complete. (WALL PAINTING, flowers, on the cross-wall downstairs. W. John Smith found traces of a smoke hood.) It was later the home of the agent for the coal mines.

Continuing w towards Little Lever the track descends to the early C19 MOUNT SION PAPERMILL, an extensive works packed evocatively into its tight valley between river and canal. Brick sheds run parallel to the river, with at least a dozen roof vents, like little green cupolas each with its conical roof.

RAMSBOTTOM

7010

A calico-printing works was set up at the crossroads by Peel and Yates in 1783. The little town, stone built and happily situated in the wide Irwell valley, grew up around it. William and Daniel Grant of Strathspey bought the works in 1806, and in 1821–2 replaced it with a model calico-printing factory called the Square. This unfortunately has disappeared too. It was by the river at the s end of Square Street. The Grants dominated Ramsbottom for much of the C19, hence the occasional Scottish accent of the local architecture, for instance the tall and very plain ashlar frontages in the market place and Bridge Street, and the corbelled-out tower tops of St Andrew's, Hey House and the Peel Memorial at Holcombe, and Tower Farm at Tottington. The backbone of the town is two-storey terraced housing, solidly built of stone, nowhere mean, the rooflines often following the slope of the hillside.

ST PAUL, Bridge Street. 1847–50 by *I. & J. P. Holden*. The cost was £3,400 of which part came from the Commissioners, the rest by public subscription. The N or Palmerston aisle was

added in 1866 at the expense of William Grant. Thin tower and
spire, thin buttresses, narrow lancets done in a mechanical
near-ashlar. Steep roof. Iron N arcade with decorative spandrels. Thin arch-braced roof. The interior is darkened by
unmemorable STAINED GLASS of 1875–1916. – Alabaster
REREDOS, 1909. The rest of the chancel was panelled in
alabaster in 1940.

ST ANDREW, Bolton Street, set back between school and
vicarage. It has a curious history. It was built for a Presbyterian congregation in 1832–4 by *William Grant*, possibly to his
own design or that of his brother *Charles*, though the list says
by *Welsh* (surely *Welch?*) of Birmingham. In 1871 William's
nephew, also William, forcibly transferred it to the Church of
England. The Presbyterians' riposte was to build a more
impressive chapel, also St Andrew's, a few yards down the hill
on the corner of Kay Brow (by *James & Robert Garnet*). Only
its gatepiers and boundary wall remain.*

Sheer W tower with an oversailing top hamper. Its octagonal
buttresses are each topped with an overhanging sentry box
with its own pyramidal roof. Five-bay boxy nave, tall lancets
widely splayed, with wooden Y-tracery. Thin intermediate buttresses. The corner buttresses are octagonal, with fat pinnacles. Small polygonal apse E. Gallery entrances embracing the
tower, the S one carrying an iron coat of arms over its door.
The interior is broad, unobstructed and well lit, with a W
gallery on iron Gothic-panelled columns, but nine Grant
MONUMENTS lend it a mausoleum air. Clockwise from the
NW: Elizabeth †1848 signed *J. Burslem*; John †1855 signed *M.
Noble*, an urn, weeping ladies and portrait medallions; William
†1873, a Gothic aedicule signed *Burke & Co.*; John †1851, a
Gothic tablet signed *John Knowles*; William †1817 and Charles
†1825, by *Patteson*, 1864, each with a mourning angel and fanciful lettering; William †1842, the founder of this church, portrait bust by *Cardwell & Son* of 1839 depicting a bruiser in
plaid, the setting by *Knowles*; Robert †1864, elaborate fragile-
looking Gothic, unsigned; Daniel †1855, by *Patteson*, in the
style of the church; and Andrew Sherlock and Isabella *née*
Grant †1890.

The church was reordered in 1993–4 by *Paul Vipond* of
Byrom Clarke Roberts with the removal of one set of gallery
stairs and enclosure of the space under the W gallery. – CLOCK.
Fine brass face on the gallery front. The works, an architectural piece like a beam engine of the day, was made by
the engineer at the Grants' factory, *J. Buchanon*, in 1834. –
STAINED GLASS. E, from *Buckfast Abbey*, 1966–8. Only the
hands and face of St Andrew are painted.

SCHOOL and (former) VICARAGE on either side of the
church path. Both are excellent.† The school is Gothic with a

* Its complicated steeple was purchased in 1926 and re-erected at English Martyrs
(R.C.) at Whalley Range in Manchester (*see* p. 481).
† Perhaps by *James & Robert Garnet*.

Wells Vicar's Close chimney. The Vicarage, which post-dates the 1871 split, is less overtly Gothic but has a tall traceried window indicating the stair position.

ST JOSEPH (R.C.), Bolton Street. 1879–80, by *G. F. Whittenbury*. Nave and aisles with a tall clerestory but no tower or chancel. Proto-tracery in the W gable, paired lancets in the aisles, even procession of single lancets in the clerestory. Four-bay interior with circular piers. No chancel, although there is a chancel arch.

Attached PRESBYTERY. Plainest three-bay house dated 1862.

MARKET PLACE, at the crossroads, is a proper centre, irregular and steeply sloping. At the top the GRANTS ARMS *c.* 1807, of fine ashlar, five widely spaced bays and three storeys, unadorned except for the modest doorcase and slight emphasis on the centre windows above. Atrociously reconstructed interior. Stone- and brick-vaulted cellars at the back. It was originally Grant Lodge and the market place was its garden. In the middle of the market place, SCULPTURE, part of the Irwell Sculpture Trail (see Radcliffe, p. 576): Tilted Vase, bronze, by *Edward Allington*, 1998. On the E side the former METHODIST CHURCH by *James & Robert Garnet*, 1874. Symmetrical, Italianate, with paired entrances and end gables. A few paces up Carr Street is the LIBRARY of 1969 by *Lancashire County Architects*, of alien brick and concrete with long shallow roof pitches and central lighting. STAINED GLASS by *Bryan Farlow*, 2002, showing the towers which stood on each side of the valley: the Peel Monument (*see* Holcombe), and the Grant Tower which fell down in 1944.

BRIDGE STREET leads E down to the River Irwell past St Paul's. Nos. 50–60, 18–26 and 12–16, all in fine ashlar, have the Scottish look which may be remarked here and there. The STATION, save for the signal box of 1939, is a reconstruction; built 1846, demolished 1971, built anew 1989 by a private organization. Stone, single-storeyed with a wide, frilled, Swiss roof. By the swiftly-flowing river is the mid–late C19 HOLCOMBE MILL, now MONDI Paper. Fat iron-banded chimney with a cone in the top. In the small Riverside Park is an ARTWORK, The River, by *Kate Allerton* and *Hetty Chapman*; inscribed aluminium ribbon embedded in the ground.

BOLTON STREET climbs towards the Catholic Church and St Andrew. The former BAPTIST CHURCH of 1861–2 with its segmentally arched cornice under the pediment, the tall Co-op building with its top-floor windows linked vertically (there was an auditorium on the top floor), and the former Industrial and Provident Society Stores of 1862 make a fine group. Like many of Ramsbottom's buildings they are taller at the back because of the fall of the land. A further row, innocuous at the front, is built up at the back on great arches, with a terrace walk on top.

On Kay Brow is BARWOOD HOUSE and its STABLE, built *c.* 1780 for Henry Kay, calico printer; later owned by the Grant brothers, and used by them as St Andrew's manse, then as the works manager's house. L-shaped. Broad five-bay s front with a columned porch, five-bay E front also with central door.

SCHOOL HOUSE, originally Well House, No. 85 Dundee Lane. Built *c.* 1864, of second-hand materials from the demolished C17 courthouse at Holcombe on the hillside above, and supposedly also from Manchester Cathedral which was being rebuilt with Ramsbottom stone. Lintel inscribed 1664, on the door itself, a cross keys badge and faces can be recognized.

On Bolton Road West is the striking semi-domestic range of HAZELHURST ENGINEERING WORKS, built *c.* 1840 by John Spencer for making textile-printing rollers and occupied by the same firm today. Of stone, with a central entrance arch. Four houses (one door blocked) at the N end, two with bay windows. The third-floor workshop sails over the top, lit by continuous mullioned windowing, even round the gable ends. Square chimney behind at the s end, and a concrete-framed 1950s extension.

NUTTALL PARK, by the river. The Hall, the principal Grant residence, was where the car park and tennis court are today. From here the tower of St Andrew lines up precisely with the Peel Monument (*see* Holcombe). The STABLES dated 1817 remain, now Nuttall Cottages.

HIGHER FOLD, 1 m. NE at Shuttleworth. Datestone inscribed IKA 1732 over the porch, which is a charming piece made out of five thin flags, plus two more for the roof. Big quoins, multiple mullions for the windows, two tiny windows in the w gable. There is a second entrance into the cross-wing, which was therefore a second dwelling, and another house across the yard – a typical fold.

CHEESDEN LUMB MILL, 2 m. E of Ramsbottom. Erected in 1786 and operated by John Kay as a fulling mill. The s façade wall straddles Cheesden Brook and dominates the valley. Although now isolated in a relict industrial landscape, it is a powerful memorial to the ingenious harnessing of water power for textile manufacture. Following collapse in 1990 this wall was reconstructed by the Greater Manchester Archaeological Unit.

REDDISH

Reddish lies immediately w of the River Tame and Stockport, to which it has belonged administratively since 1901. The boundary with Manchester is formed by Nico Ditch, thought to be of Roman or Saxon origin (*see* Denton for more details). Industry was initially concentrated near the banks of the Tame, and then along the Stockport branch of the Ashton-under-Lyne canal, opened in 1797. The highlights architecturally and visually are almost all due to the late C19 industrialist Sir William Houldsworth who had his mills there and built the church of St Elisabeth, the club and school.

ST ELISABETH, Bedford Street. By *Alfred Waterhouse*, 1882–3, for W. H. Houldsworth. 'A superb job, big-boned, with nothing mean outside or in.' This was Pevsner's assessment, readily acceptable now but an eye-opener in 1969, indeed possibly instrumental in saving the church from destruction. Nave, aisles, chancel and apse, SE Lady Chapel with an apse too, SE tower with a short lead spire and pinnacles, and a big two-storey vestry and organ chamber on the N side. The tower, which stands outside the S aisle, is linked to the nave roof by a flying bridge and external steps: a typical Waterhouse conceit, both visually amusing and doubly practical – it gives access to the space above the ceiling and it contains heating and ventilation ducts. The church is built of narrow red bricks with stone dressings. The windows are round-arched, but Waterhouse never decides which style to commit himself to. In the tower is a Norman door with zigzag, the S doorway is Transitional, but the interior is Italian in many motifs and the chancel and the chapel are covered with Gothic rib-vaults. Yet Waterhouse is recognizable everywhere. The nave is amazingly high, with a wooden cradle roof. The brickwork is exposed, except for the marble facing of the apse. The arcade has short, fat columns of polished granite and very wide single-step pointed arches – so wide that the arcade consists only of four bays. Typical Waterhouse capitals. FITTINGS by *Waterhouse*. – SCREEN, of alabaster, Venetian, with the four Evangelists (by *Earp*) on top. The iron grilles were part of the Lady Chapel screen. – REREDOS, not as high as was intended; alabaster, with short fat columns and a tabernacle. – SEDILIA. – PULPIT, added in 1890, but suitably low and fat. – FONT, very fine. Of alabaster with a chunky base and Celtic knots. Conical cover, excellent iron bracket and crane. Waterhouse's decorative ironwork is always worth looking at, as are his TILES. The church was originally equipped with chairs; the PEWS date from *c.* 1910. – LECTERN, a brass angel by *Jones & Willis*; a First World War memorial. The LECTERN in the Lady Chapel was used in the upper room of the Institute across the road, and is therefore probably by *Stott*. – STATIONS OF THE CROSS. Startlingly modern, 1983, by *Graeme Willson*. They are based on wooden Xs and painted Os, the latter elongated and reminiscent of portholes in industrial buildings, but also picking up the shape of Waterhouse's windows. – STAINED GLASS. The church was fitted with Waterhouse's quietly coloured floral glass (by *F. T. Odell*), much of which remains. Panels designed by *Frederick Shields* and made by *Heaton, Butler & Bayne* in the clerestory and the odd triple group on the N side. They were originally ordered for Houldsworth's house at Coodham, Ayrshire. The apse glass is by *Kempe & Co.*, that in the Lady Chapel by *F. C. Eden*. – MONUMENTS. By the vestry door, beaten bronze panel by the *Keswick School of Industrial Art c.* 1901. Houldsworth Chapel, attached to the N side in 1919, though a further memorial to the founder hardly seems necessary. The architect is not known. Weak Gothic screen, groin vault, big lunette window. The tablet is by *Farmer & Brindley*.

ST MARY, Reddish Road, s of the centre. 1862–4 by *Shellard & Brown*. No tower, stone; late C20 porch extension, SW. The window details are remarkably incorrect, Dec, done as plate tracery, but with mullions treated as colonnettes with fancy caps. The heads of the lights look almost Moorish. *The Builder* described it as 'somewhat Continentalized in its details.' (First World War memorial glass with figures including King Alfred and Henry V; another window by *Walter J. Pearce*, 1930.)

ST JOSEPH (R.C.), Gorton Road. Squat brick NW tower, gable to the road. Consecrated in 1882, very substantially rebuilt during the 1960s.

For St Agnes, Gorton Road, *see* Gorton, Manchester, p. 372.

LIBRARY, FIRE STATION (former) and PUBLIC BATHS, Gorton Road. 1907–8 by *Dixon & Potter*. A slightly unlikely combination. Baroque. Cheerful red brick and yellow terracotta. The central three-storey fire station is used as a community centre and the big arched entrances are partially infilled. The single-storey library on the l. is side-on to the street, the baths on the other side end-on, with a lunette window in the gable.

NORTH REDDISH JUNIOR SCHOOL, Longford Road, early C20. A low, nicely grouped gabled complex, given distinction by the tall chimneys with flared tops of horizontal channelled brick, and a pretty flèche over the hall with a slender slated spire.

TAME VIADUCT, Reddish Vale. 1875 for the Sheffield and Midland Railways Committee. A great fourteen-arched giant striding across the wide, shallow valley of the Tame.

PERAMBULATION

The most interesting buildings can be seen in a short walk starting at HOULDSWORTH SQUARE, near the junction of Gorton Road and Broadstone Road. Here there is a MEMORIAL to Sir William Houldsworth by *J. & H. Patteson*, unveiled 1920. A clock supported by granite piers, originally with a drinking fountain and animal troughs below, and a bronze portrait medallion on the side. An inscription records the gratitude of local people for 'the bountiful gifts whereby he enriched and adorned their village'. Leamington Road leads N from the square to the HOULDSWORTH WORKING MEN'S CLUB. By *A. H. Stott*, opened 1874, and clearly meant to harmonize with the adjacent church of St Elisabeth (*see* above), though it is comparatively unrefined. Upper windows have round arches, transomed windows below, gabled porches. Towards St Elisabeth, on the corner, a great big, full-height, bulging semicircular bay.

Continue N along Leamington Street to ST ELISABETH'S WAY, where there is a real sense of space, with a pleasant green and a park beyond. On the E side the former RECTORY, like the church, is by *Waterhouse*, 1882–3. Red brick, tile roof to match

the church, unfussy and unremarkable. Projecting gabled end
bay, with a porch attached to the r., then a range with dormers
with tall pyramidal roofs. Just to the N *Waterhouse*'s quietly
done ST ELISABETH'S SCHOOL, 1876. Red brick with stone
dressings, E-plan with big gables at each end and tall lancet
windows. Across the green is the REDDISH SPINNING CO.
MILLS, on Houldsworth Street. Built in 1870. Less impressive than the other two mills here, the buildings grouped
around a tall water- and stair-tower which is a landmark in
views from the W.

Continue S along Houldsworth Street past HOULDSWORTH
PARK, another gift of Sir William Houldsworth, opened in
1907, to the magnificent HOULDSWORTH MILL. By *A. H.
Stott* of Oldham. A striking sight. On each side four-storey
ranges of sixteen windows, with a five-storey centre of nine
bays plus one-bay turrets with deep-eaved pyramid roofs, and
a middle clock feature rising above the parapet, with the date
1865. The windows above the arcade of ground floor openings
are set in giant blank arches. This is all centred on RUPERT
STREET from which impressive views are obtained, with the
splendid, very tall, detached, hexagonal chimney rising
behind. The central part was for offices and warehousing, the
rest for cotton preparation and spinning. This was one of the
largest double mills to be built in the region during the 1860s,
of fireproof construction, with brick vaulted ceilings and cast-
iron beams and columns. Now used as offices and flats. On the
E side of Houldsworth Street, opposite the mill, is a part of a
MODEL ESTATE, probably also by *A. H. Stott*. Only a few terraces survive, brick houses with bay windows and front
gardens on Houldsworth Street, more modest houses behind
on Liverpool Street.

Continue to the W end of Houldsworth Street and turn N
along BROADSTONE ROAD. This is a good vantage point for
seeing the mills ranged along the top of the valley which falls
away to the W. Almost opposite, set back from the SE side of
the road, is BROADSTONE MILL, 1903–7 by *Stott & Sons*. A
huge monumental block with ranks of large windows, in red
brick relieved by yellow brick banding. At the corner is an
extraordinary water- and stair-tower, with splayed corners and
vertical ribs rising up to finish as piers of yellow terracotta, the
top part looking like an elaborate crown, supporting a green
dome. The building has been truncated by half, losing a
matching tower at the other corner. Elaborate iron entrance
gates and railings survive along Broadstone Road. In front of
the mill, the GREY HORSE PUB uses similar red brick and
yellow terracotta and must have been built with thirsty mill
hands in mind. Edwardian Baroque, dated 1909, with entertaining cartouches showing a prancing horse and a horse's
head.

Just to the S BROADSTONE BRIDGE, by the Borough Engineer *John Atkinson*, 1909, replacing a late C18 canal bridge.
Here one can get an idea of the line of the Stockport branch

of the Ashton-under-Lyne CANAL, 1797, now infilled. It ran from a basin at the top of Lancashire Hill (*see* Wharf Street, Heaton Norris) to Clayton in Manchester. Below the bridge CANAL BANK FARM is probably early C19, brick with an attached barn. More houses of this date lie S of the bridge on the E side of the road. Returning N along Broadstone Road completes the circuit back to Houldsworth Square.

OUTLYING BUILDINGS

PRESCOTT'S ALMSHOUSES, Reddish Road. By *James Hunt*, dated 1882, a late almshouse foundation by Mr Prescott. Charmingly detailed, with a banded tile roof, big chimneys, speckled bricks with red sandstone dressings and gabled dormers with finials. Projecting central gabled bay with a shallow porch which has over the door a stone portrait relief of a melancholy Prescott, the name of the building and the date. Six houses altogether, the first five form a symmetrical composition, the one at the r. end is slightly set back from the others.

SPUR MILL, Broadstone Hall Road South. A cotton doubling mill of 1908. Unusual as it is of one storey only, with a central engine house with arched openings.

RHODES

8000

Along the Irk valley immediately SW of Middleton. All the SE Lancashire elements are here together. For once, even after the coming of the M60, no one has obliterated the others. Alkrington Hall (*see* p. 516) looks down from its aristocratic park on what is left of Schwabe's great calico printing works, on brick terraces and 1930s improved housing, and on the middle-class houses along the main road. The natural landscape, still open farmland immediately N, is ornamented not only by the parks of Alkrington, Rhodes House and Heaton but also by the industrial lodges or reservoirs along the Irk.

ALL SAINTS, Manchester Old Road. Of 1864, and supposedly by *E. G. Paley* (Terry Wyke) though that is hard to believe. Simple nave of stone and slate. Every window is different, so that it looks more like a demonstration of alternatives than a reasoned design. The chancel is an addition of 1924. There was a NE tower but this has been cut down to make a domestic-looking two-storey vestry. Detached graveyard and a good (former) vicarage off Boardman Lane.

ST THOMAS, Heywood Old Road, Bowlee. 1877. A sweet mission chapel up the hill, where farm labourers could attend in their working clothes. Side windows and brown brick porch, 1975.

The giant chimney of Salis Schwabe & Co.'s works has gone. It stood where Watt House is now, across the road from the boilers and the rest of the works, now Rhodes Business Park. The necessary LODGES, still fourteen acres in extent and supplied with copious pure water from springs and dams on what is now North Manchester Golf Course, are given over to fishing and dog walking. Schwabe's house, the plain RHODES HOUSE of 1811, is the Clubhouse.

Nos. 165–167 Old Manchester Road are by *Edgar Wood & Henry Sellers*, 1911. Highly disciplined, with a single window size and ruled by lintel and sill bands of Portland stone. In Broad Street and its continuation Schwabe Street opposite the works are several early works by *Edgar Wood*. RHODES SCHOOLS of 1884, now WOODS COURT, is out of the ordinary only in its simplicity and in its soft red brick. Symmetrical, with big windows above and an arcade below on the sunny and down-hill side, paired entrances reaching to the street and gable dormers on the other. Nos. 31–37 of 1899 is a nicely varied short terrace with shallow angled bays and leaded windows hung outside the wall plane. Flat porch roofs with fanlights on top, big stones for the garden gates. Nos. 2–4 Schwabe Street of 1895 are not immediately identifiable, because re-windowed, but they are very unequal, and have a stone flag roof. No. 2 has a pretty wooden porch like Wood's own house in Middleton.

WILTON ARMS HOTEL, Manchester Old Road, 1877. A monster pub in brick and stone with lavish naturalistic carved capitals. Converted stable range, w. Some interiors preserved.

RINGLEY

A pretty spot on the Irwell, now that the giant cooling towers of Kearsley power station have gone. BRIDGE, 1677; two arches with refuges over the cutwater. Concrete bridge next to it.

ST SAVIOUR, opposite the bridge. Inscriptions on the patheti-cally thin tower tell its history: 'Nathan Walworth builded mee 1625'; Repaired and raised 2 ft (0.6 metres) 1854. Referring to the church: 'Built 1626. All rebuilt 1826' (by *Charles Barry*). But all except the little tower was swept away for a new church of 1850–4, by *Sharpe & Paley* (probably Paley), set in the same churchyard much further back from the road. Three equal tall two-light w windows and a tight sw turret are its salient features. Dignified interior with circular piers and tall pointed arches, the clerestory of quatrefoil windows. The interest is in the FITTINGS, including several from the old church. Rococo CHANCEL RAILS, curved, with straight gates; ebonized frames with luscious gilded foliage infilling. – COM-MUNION TABLE in the N chapel, 1654. – C17 armorial STAINED GLASS in the three lancets on the N side of the chancel. – Later fittings include a lavish REREDOS and SEDILIA in alabaster, 1879, with mosaic and *opus sectile* pic-tures probably by *Whitefriars*; ROOD BEAM and figures, 1925; ALTAR and CANOPY at the NW end (a children's chapel), 1921. – MONUMENTS. At the NW corner, Matthew Fletcher

†1808, mine-owner and promoter of the canal which skirts the
N side of the church. A large standing figure with a sword leans
on a high pedestal with the portrait medallion. Also a pair of
scales in relief. – Ellis Fletcher †1834. A large female figure
weeps over a pedestal with portrait in profile.

ROCHDALE

8010

INTRODUCTION

Only 14 m. NE of Manchester, but a town of strongly Pennine
character, with high open moorland very close. Only 8 m. from
Yorkshire, yet a centre of the Lancashire dialect. Heavily populated, with one of the greatest town halls of England, but the
least urban of the big towns. The major medieval church of St
Chad was the centre of an enormous parish rather than of a substantial town. The very name Rochdale signifies a dale of the
River Roch, not a town. Its urban centre and those of its satellite towns are of relatively recent growth, beginning only in the
C17 and expanding mightily in the C19. The earlier pattern of settlement was an even spread of innumerable folds, little clusters
of agricultural and proto-industrial buildings, which are still
often identifiable within the later urbanization as well as out in
the country.

The town is built of gritty stone and harsh red brick, with
smooth sandstone making its appearance for the important
buildings (but not the Town Hall) in the C19, and incongruous
Portland stone in the early C20. Unusually for SE Lancashire,
there is no terracotta to speak of. Its hilly terrain is evident right
in the centre, with the town hall and the parish church linked by
a steep flight of steps, but the river makes little impact, having
been culverted in the early C20.

Rochdale is famous for its radical Liberalism – Cobden was
M.P. from 1859 to 1865, John Bright's brother the first mayor –
and with social progress. 'THE HOME OF COOPERATION' is its
boast. The co-operative movement was born in Rochdale in the
1840s, and its pioneer shop of 1844 is preserved as a museum of
the movement. It grew out of harsh necessity, the hardship

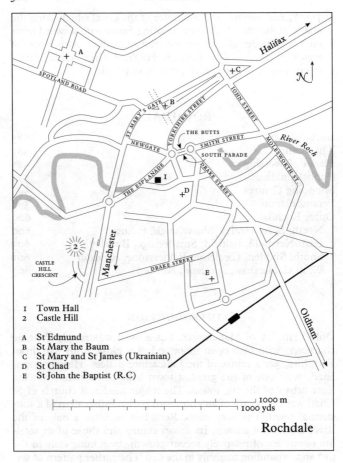

I   Town Hall
2   Castle Hill

A   St Edmund
B   St Mary the Baum
C   St Mary and St James (Ukrainian)
D   St Chad
E   St John the Baptist (R.C)

1000 m
1000 yds

Rochdale

created for most people by the Industrial Revolution, which in
turn grew out of the tough climate and stony soil – plenty of
water but a short growing season. Rochdale's business was wool,
hence the fleece emblem of the town which appears for instance
in the stained glass quarries of the town hall. Cotton arrived in
the 1790s, but only overtook wool in importance in the 1840s.
Part of Rochdale's industrial strength was the ability to switch
back to wool when the need arose. The wide Rochdale Canal,
completed in 1804, climbs up from Manchester and crosses into
Yorkshire by Littleborough. A generation later the Manchester
and Leeds Railway followed the same route, and in the late 1960s
the M62 motorway.

The huge Rochdale parish was divided into four quarters:
Spotland in the NW, Hundresfield NE, Butterworth SE, and
Castleton SW. It included Whitworth (N Lancashire), and Tod-
morden and Saddleworth (Yorkshire). These divisions were

superseded in the 1850s by the municipal boroughs. The Borough
of Rochdale was created in 1856, with a population at that time
of about 86,000. The boroughs were in turn superseded by the
Rochdale Metropolitan Borough, created in 1974. It is about the
same size as the ancient parish, but not quite the same shape; it
includes Middleton for example, but not Todmorden, Saddleworth or Whitworth. A look at the map will confirm that the
whole borough is an incomplete coming together of separate
parts, and that even today there is open country – just – between
all the main components. The population of the Borough in 2001
was about 208,000.

The most interesting architects to have worked in Rochdale
are mavericks, outsiders. *W. H. Crossland* (1803–1909) was the
creator of three prodigious buildings, all of the 1870s: Rochdale
Town Hall, and the Holloway Sanatorium and College in Surrey,
but he died in a boarding house leaving an estate of £29. The
prolific and original *J. Medland Taylor* of Manchester built four
churches here in the 1860s–70s, of which St Mary, Balderstone,
is remarkable for the completeness of the ensemble, and St
Edmund, Falinge, remarkable in any canon of C19 churches as
a shrine of Freemasonry. The self-taught architect and contractor *George Shaw* of Saddleworth was the most local. His work
can be seen in Rochdale parish church, at Healey and Norden
in the suburbs, and in outlying churches at Littleborough and
Wardle.

THE CENTRE

The seven tower blocks of COLLEGE BANK FLATS dominate ₂
the townscape. By *R. D. Thornley* succeeding *W. H. G. Mercer*,
Borough Architects, completed in 1966. The blocks are of
sixteen and twenty storeys, sometimes linked on a common
podium, built on the no-fines system with posts and beams
cast *in situ*. Luckily they are good of their kind, disciplined in
their sombre colouring and crisp detailing. They are irregularly
placed on the hillside but share the same orientation, so that
they group picturesquely as the advocates of tower blocks
hoped they would, appearing from some angles strung out
along the valley, from others powerfully massed. MITCHELL
STREET at their feet is an indication of what has gone – a
terrace of back-to-backs with front doors on both sides of the
row and chimneys rising not on the roof peak but halfway up
each slope.

PLACES OF WORSHIP

ST CHAD. The medieval church of a major parish. It stands on a
bluff, with the Roch valley falling away on the N, and the town
hall spire poking up startlingly from the valley below. It is distinctive in silhouette, with its W tower with paired three-light

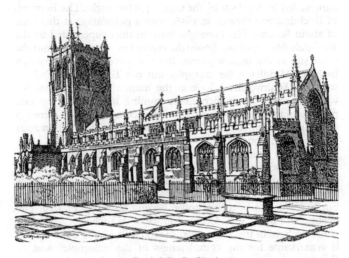

Rochdale, St Chad.
Victoria County History of Lancashire, vol. 5, 1911

belfry lights and detached pinnacles – not Lancashire motifs –
and its long chancel a little taller than the nave. It is battlemented and pinnacled from end to end, and the chancel has
its own aisles and clerestory. The impression is Victorian, but
the tower in its lower parts is C14, with altered buttresses and
openings. The Perp nave and its clerestory date from the 1550s,
but again there has been much renewing of windows and battlements. The N and S chancel chapels, of more regular stone,
existed in 1487 and appear to be all of a piece, though extended
E since; diagonal buttresses mark their original length.

The interior tells of an earlier building, for the six closely
spaced bays of the nave arcade are C13, although they are
damaged and have been heightened by a foot. Round and
octagonal columns alternate. The capitals of bays three and five
are decorated with stiff-leaf, upright leaves, and heads linked
by their hair. Waterholding bases, double-chamfered arches.
The FONT, a fat octagonal bowl dug up in the churchyard in
1893, is C13 or C14. Its prismatical base is said to be one of the
old clock surrounds from the tower.

The long chancel arcade, clearly Victorian, makes the church
a double sixer, i.e. with six-plus-six bays, like Manchester
Cathedral. In its double hammerbeam roof, East Anglian in
style, is a band of twenty-eight angel musicians, including a
saxophonist. The chancel arch is Victorian too.

The long series of C19 alterations started in 1815–16 with
repairs by *Thomas Taylor* of Leeds. Taylor had worked in the
Wyatt office; *Jeffrey Wyatt* inspected the work in 1816 and found
the repairs done in 'a workmanlike and superior manner'. Next
in 1854–5 came *Joseph Clarke*, who made a new nave roof and

rebuilt the N aisle. The porch and the top stage of the tower were done by *W.H. Crossland* in 1873 while he was building the town hall, with the same long French gargoyles carved by *T. Earp*. Finally the chancel was rebuilt and extended E by *J. S. Crowther* in 1884–5, with lavish carving again by *Earp*. The change from gritstone to creamy sandstone makes the new work obvious.

FITTINGS. St Chad is a rich repository of carved WOOD-WORK, with much to enjoy and much to puzzle. The puzzling part is the involvement of *George Shaw*, collector and recycler of old carved woodwork and manufacturer of high quality repro. The SE or Trinity chapel was richly furnished by Shaw (*see* below), and these furnishings are now scattered through the church. The chapel SCREENS are now arranged on either side of the chancel arch. Blackletter inscription along the rail, bold armorial panels below like those of Middleton, but unusually modelled on both sides. STALLS arranged college-wise the whole length of the chancel. The western stalls are early C19. There are some delightful figures on the bench ends; kneeling tonsured priests, armed knights, and slender battling beasts. Those at the E end, with gaping beasts, are from Canterbury, probably C15, acquired in 1865. The rest are by *Shaw*, heavily carved, with his trademark reversed cusped S in a circle. PRIESTS' SEATS by the altar, with some canopy work. Turning LECTERN, like those at Manchester Cathedral and Middleton.

The S or TRINITY CHAPEL was bought by James Dearden in 1823. In it a large standing MONUMENT by *Sievier* to Jacob Dearden †1825. On the wall, mounted in alabaster, five Dearden BRASSES, rivalling those at Middleton: †1545, 1586, 1598, 1609 and 1630. On the floor a worn stone slab with foliated cross, sword and shield, and an incised alabaster slab with a priestly figure with chalice. Recumbent effigies of a cross-legged knight and a bishop are lost, reputedly buried under the flags. Armorial STAINED GLASS by *Willement*, 1852, and by *George Shaw*, 1847. The church is rather shamefaced about these treasures, because, excepting the Sievier monument, they are all fakes. 'In the period 1847–9 the Dearden chapel was equipped with pseudo-medieval forgeries, to bolster the genealogical claims of the Lord of the Manor'. James Dearden and his antiquarian friend Shaw created a sumptuous manorial chapel, fenced with screens, fully stalled, and filled with ancestral monuments.* When the S chapel was rebuilt in 1883 the furnishings were dispersed in the rest of the church.

Other STAINED GLASS. Excellent *Morris & Co.* W, 1873, by *Burne-Jones*. Personifications of Hope, Charity and Faith, with their anti-types crouching beneath. The figures had to be repainted in 1882 because of a fault in the flux. N choir aisle:

---

* *See* also Hurst at Ashton-under-Lyne, Calderbrook at Littleborough (qq.v.), and Mottram-in-Longdendale, Cheshire. The Chadwicks of Healey Hall (outer Rochdale N) had been outbid by Dearden for the S chapel. Their chapel at Mavesyn Ridware in Staffordshire is also filled with bogus memorials.

action-packed window by *Burlison & Grylls*, 1887, Jesus and the traders. By *Powell/Whitefriars*: nave s, St Chad, artist *G.P. Hutchinson*, 1933; N nave 1939. – Other MONUMENTS. In the NW vestry, Jacob (or James) Holt of Castleton †1712. Fashionable standing monument with a fluted urn in an aedicule of pilasters and a pediment. Prominently signed *Wm Coleburne*, London. Many tablets, e.g. Thomas Smith †1806 with a woman by an urn, by *S. & T. Francis*, Liverpool; John Hopwood †1813 with a trophy; John Entwisle †1827 with a sarcophagus. Royds BRASS †1854 in the chancel floor.

The CHURCHYARD has mostly been grassed over, but round the tower is a fragment of the old stone field of ledgers. The NW boundary is composed of an archaic flag wall, with slotted stone posts instead of the usual iron cramps.

The OLD VICARAGE, W of the church, was built by the Rev. Dunster after 1724 and is supposedly modelled on his house in Marlborough Street, London. Brick with stone quoins, pretty doorcase with a small shell carved inside the hood, and an indecisive pediment. The interior has been institutionalized but retains its staircase with three balusters per tread, and some panelling.

ST EDMUND, Falinge, 1870–3. A masterwork of *J. Medland Taylor*, but the design input of the founder, *Albert Hudson Royds*, banker and Freemason, and of the first incumbent, *E.W. Gilbert*, artist and freemason, should not be discounted.

The foundation ceremonies of Rochdale's C19 churches were usually attended by the Freemasons in force, and many display Masonic symbolism, e.g. Christchurch Healey. St Edmund's is Rochdale's temple to Freemasonry, a total concept as exotic as Roslin Chapel in Scotland. It cost at least £28,000 at a time when a decent church could be built for £4,000. It stands on a diamond-shaped churchyard, the focus of four streets, at the highest point of the town. Approached from the s up the immensely wide Clement Royds Street, it seems to rise up out of the ground. First to appear is the five-pointed star of the weathervane, then a big square lantern tower, the four arms of the church, and finally the massive battered plinth on which the whole building sits. It is a Latin cross in plan, bullish in its proportions, without aisles but with a SE chapel, W and S porches and a W stair-turret. The windows are mostly square-headed, with crazy traceries incorporating stars and triangles. The blank panel in the W windows of the nave tell us that there is a gallery within, the rising windows in porches and turrets indicate internal stairs.

The disappointment of the INTERIOR is that the lantern tower has been ceiled off. It was done in 1887 on the advice of *J. Murgatroyd* in response to complaints about downdraughts. It is a pity because not only is the centre deprived of a flood of light, but its evocation of mystical proportions has been lost. The interior volume can be read as six cubes, one for each arm and two for the nave, plus that of the crossing. This is emphasized by the four fat granite columns that appear to carry the entire weight of the tower. The lantern was the seventh cube. The roofs are a tour-de-force of massive joinery. Exaggerated hammerbeams are exuberantly carved and notched over the chancel. Geometric figures fill the spandrels of the tie-beams elsewhere and cover the chancel ceiling. The Royds Chapel (SE), intruded upon by one of the massive buttresses which really carry the tower, is divided from the chancel by a screen of granite columns, their overscale capitals representing fig, passion flower and fern. A narrow stair descends to the private entrance.

FURNISHINGS. REREDOS by Bro. the Rev. *E. W. Gilbert*. Integral with the stone of the building and growing out over the architecture: the True Vine, deeply cut but not undercut, with the words I AM THE emerging. – DEDICATION BRASS very prominent over the N choir stalls; also by E. W. Gilbert, using as many fonts as possible like a circus poster of the period. – FONT. A fat bowl of white marble with symbols of the Four Evangelists, supported on short marble columns. – LECTERN. The symbolic climax of the whole scheme. On an imperfect block of dark stone stands a perfect white cube of ashlar. Upon that are three columns of brass; Doric, Ionic and Corinthian. Engraved upon their bases are the symbolic tools of masoncraft. On top is a horizontal brass tray, fretted with pomegranates, lilies and intertwined snakes, and finally, to carry the Volume of Sacred Law, a pyramid formed out of square and compasses.

STAINED GLASS. A complete scheme by *Lavers, Barraud & Westlake*, who were not quite up to the grandeur of the concept. On the S side the theme is Building, hence Noah's Ark and the Tower of Babel. On the N, Sacrifice, so Abraham and Isaac, and the Last Supper surprisingly shunted into a corner of the transept. The climax is in the Royds Chapel where are Nehemiah and Ezra, the masonic Tyler waving a sword, and the Building of the Temple in Jerusalem with A. H. Royds himself as master mason. In the N transept a Jesse Tree, bolder and greener than the rest, with Jesse stretched out over two lights. The S transept one is missing; it was a Te Deum, exhibited in Vienna in 1887.

ST JAMES (UKRAINIAN CATHOLIC CHURCH OF ST MARY). On a traffic island at the top NE end of Yorkshire Street, where it visually leaves the town centre. Rochdale's third Anglican church, built in 1821 of pebbly ashlar in the plainest Commissioners' Gothic. Blunt tower, buttressed side walls with transomed windows, short chancel. Interior without either aisles or side galleries, although the transoms suggest the latter. Plaster vault. The SCREEN is the obvious introduction for Ukrainian worship, although the removal of the organ may also be noted. Like an iconostasis it hides the sanctuary, and it is brightly and naïvely painted. It was made by members of the congregation *c.* 1950. ALTAR, large and square, made of redundant woodwork. Upon it stands the outsized Byzantine style TABERNACLE. – STAINED GLASS. E and the lower parts of the side windows, all by *H. Hughes* or *Ward & Hughes*, dating from 1863 (E) to 1902 (NW).

79 St Mary the Baum, Toad Lane. A plain two-storey church of 1740, Rochdale's second, was rebuilt in novel form by *Ninian Comper* in 1909–11, reusing some of the bits. The N aisle retains its C18 character, with arched windows and pilasters. Comper lengthened them, and the balustrade is his. He wanted that sense of flatness and cubic simplicity to set off his gables. Narrow red bricks outside, fine Alderley ashlar within. Entry is normally into the N aisle which is low, with a bulgy Tuscan arcade. The columns come from the old upper galleries. Beyond is a central aisle of medium height, lit by a minimally Gothic clerestory over the N arcade. On the S side is a sensationally high nave, lit by huge plain glass windows with tracery reminiscent of those in the C17 hall church of Warwick, and much bigger than could have been acheived in a conventionally aisled building. It has extremely tall piers, alternately round and concave-sided octagonal. The view from the N door of the three vessels stepping up in height, the unequal and unsynchronized arcades, and the wall of glass on the far side flooding all with light is uniquely effective. The S wall shows no separation of chancel from nave, but a beardless Christ in a mandorla, painted in beautifully faded colours, fills in the spandrel of the tie-beam above. The rest of the ceiling painting has faded beyond the beautiful.

Comper's SCREEN carrying his ROOD group and ORGAN stretches right across the church. It is transparent in the great S nave but makes a termination to the middle aisle – except for a low chapel under the organ. SCREEN round the N chapel too. – STAINED GLASS roundels in the N aisle. By *Wailes*, reset. The others, lightly coloured, are by *Comper*. In the great E window of 1911 an unbearded Christ appears twice in a mandorla. Middle aisle W 1923, E 1926.

Former VICARAGE by the W end, 1906, also by *Comper*. Brick, Jacobean with mullioned windows, battered chimney stack(s).

St John Baptist (R.C.), Dowling Street, by the railway station. Fr Henry Chipp wanted a Byzantine church with a dome and mosaics like Hagia Sofia. The design, Byzantine indeed, was made before the Great War by *E. Bower Norris* and *Oswald Hill*. The estimated cost was £12,800. When it was built in 1923–5, by *R. & T. Haworth*, the cost had risen to £21,000, even without the intended campanile. Luckily the drill tower of the adjacent fire station, also built by Haworth's (*see* Perambulation, below), does the job very well from a distance. The mosaics followed in the 1930s. The white dome and blue drum with its thirty-six small windows are quite a surprise. The body is a Greek cross, with short equal arms, of red brick and Portland stone. Pairs of angels prop the outer corners. The interior, in Byzantine fashion, is truly the inside of the outside, without hidden spaces. Dome, pendentives and barrel roofs are all of mass concrete – the shuttering is clearly seen. The dome was shuttered with straight timbers, so it is actually a shallow octagon. Its diameter is 65 ft (20 metres), the height of the crown, which is only five inches thick, 95 ft (29 metres). Niches with galleries fill the diagonals. MOSAIC covers the whole of the E end. It was designed by *Eric Newton* and installed in 1930–3. On the arch soffit trumpeting angels herald the Creation, represented as a big bang. The apse is filled by Christ the King. On either side are the judgments of the righteous, and of the wicked, with a spirited devil.

ST PATRICK (R.C.), Elliott Street. By *Desmond Williams & Associates*, 1965–7. Cubic building made up of staccato brick fins and slit windows supporting a low central drum. Successful interior, its sixties starkness softened by a moderate reordering of 1995. The brick fins form pierced buttresses, two per side, which support the concrete ring beam of a low dome, which exerts the usual calming influence. Curved concrete balcony front over the entrance. – ALTAR under the dome, but not central; a slab of polished black marble on rough grey granite legs. – Cubic FONT and LECTERN of the same rough granite. STATIONS OF THE CROSS painted by *Antonia White*, a parishioner, 2000. She also made the nine gallery front ICONS 1995, on Muscovite models, but the ninth is Alice Ingham, founder of the Catholic Rescue Society, who came from Yorkshire Street, close by. – Abstract STAINED GLASS in the Lady Chapel, which is behind the altar, by *Simon Harvey*.

HOPE STREET CHAPEL (Particular Baptist). Founded in 1810 by John Kershaw, and extended in 1848 to make the three-bay entrance elevation. No pediment. Its windows are tied together vertically by giant arches. The former MINISTER'S HOUSE l., now the caretaker's house, marks the original front line. Wonderfully harmonious interior, almost square. Slender iron columns with lotus capitals support the oval gallery and the central pulpit. Organ above, flanked by lyre music stands. Flat plaster ceiling. – BOX PEWS, elegantly curved in the gallery, lined with black baize with black cushions. – Mahogany RAILS with tulip balusters. – MONUMENTS. Tablets to John Stansfield †1868 and John Kershaw †1870 both signed *Stansfield*; Christopher and Mary Hodson †1860, with draped urn; Jabez Eddison †1914.

Former SCHOOL to the W of 1828, enlarged 1855; now called HOPE COURT.

KINGDOM HALL (Jehovah's Witnesses), Castlemere Street. *c*. 1900. Roughcast covers the whole building, even the windows, which is a pity because the design is worthy of Edgar Wood. As revealed by their shadows, the windows are of the Diocletian type, with a five-lighter on the front. Low welcoming arms reach forward at forty-five degrees, with sleeves stretching back. Shallow battered buttresses, and a steep roof; that is all we can see.

SILVER STREET CHAPEL *see* outer Rochdale, p. 607–8.

MARKAZI JAMIA MASJID (CENTRAL MOSQUE), Mere Street. Built on the former playground of Castlemere School of 1895 on Tweedale Street. By *Bullen Consultants* of Bradford, chief engineer *Atba Al-Samarrie*. A brick octagon with quoins, bands, and frames to the pairs of windows in reconstituted stone. Dull gold dome over the centre and a squat minaret. The interior is divided horizontally, with the lower level used for everyday prayer. Women and children in the upper gallery get the only good view of the dome.

PUBLIC BUILDINGS

61 TOWN HALL. One of the dozen most ambitious High Victorian town halls of England. The northern industrial towns in particular vied with one another in demonstrating new-found civic dignity in the magnificence of their town halls. Manchester and Rochdale were among the few who chose to build Gothic, but the two are very different.

Rochdale Corporation came into being in 1856, and a new town hall was under discussion almost immediately. A budget of £20,000 was set aside, and a competition was held in 1864, which was won by *W. H. Crossland* of Leeds. The site chosen was unpromising, on the edge of town and liable to flood. The foundation stone was laid by John Bright in 1866 and the building, enormously escalated in cost, was complete by 1871.

The building presents a splendidly craggy exterior of blackened stone, relieved by the four brightly gilded lions on the porte cochère and a touch of colour on the central flèche. The transverse great hall at the centre, the former courts on the r. and the mayor's apartments l. are all clearly expressed and independently roofed, as are spiral staircases at the ends and the principal stair at the back. The impression is of an overall E-shaped symmetry made up of separately expressed parts, offset by a strong tower

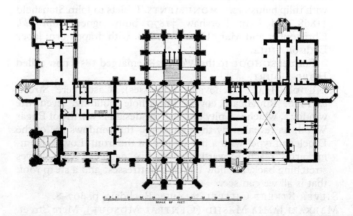

Rochdale Town Hall, design by W. H. Crossland, from *The Builder*, 1866

and spire at the NE end, but the symmetry is not absolute – and the present tower is by *Alfred Waterhouse* 1885–7, after Crossland's tower, taller and more colourful, was destroyed by fire in 1883. Crossland's tower was part of the main mass of the building, whereas Waterhouse, probably as much for aesthetic as technical reasons, made his tower step sideways, clear of the building but linked to it by an arch. At the back are the five arches of the former fire station whose proximity famously failed to save the first tower.

At night, and in the murky Pennine weather to which Rochdale is prone, the town hall glows with effulgent light from the brilliant stained glass which is its particular treasure.

The INTERIOR is beautiful, but the plan is awkward, making a logical tour difficult, because Crossland divided his building into three self-contained compartments: mayoral on the l. or NW, public in the middle, and judicial on the r. or SE.

We enter under the porte cochère into a three-naved vaulted hall, called the EXCHANGE but never used as such. The colourful heraldic tiles by *Minton* and the stone carving by *Earp* set the scene for what is to follow; *Heaton, Butler & Bayne* were in charge of the whole decorative scheme. The GRAND STAIR rises up 65 ahead in one and then two flights in a cage of stone and glass. The spaces beneath the landings should not be missed, with their openwork girder-like stone arches. Here and everywhere the architecture is inseparable from Heaton, Butler & Bayne's joyous STAINED GLASS, in this case delightful quarries. Facing us as we ascend is the most brilliant representation of the royal arms imaginable, filling the whole of a three-light, double-transomed window. In the other lights the arms of towns trading with Rochdale. A steamship and a locomotive in the tracery. The GREAT HALL above occupies the entire upper centre of the building. It is an apartment of great splendour and simplicity, a vast rectangle of polished floor under a great hammerbeam roof, from which the angels once dangled gasoliers. The stencilled wall decoration has been redone and looks overbright compared to the faded ceiling. The huge PAINTING of Magna Carta occupying much of the E wall is by *Henry Holiday*, 1870, assisted by *Carl Almquist* and *Henry Ellis Wooldridge*. It was meticulously researched, and took the best part of a year to complete, but is disappointingly stiff and undramatic, its colours dulled. To its l. balancing the door is a heraldic composition probably by *Clement Heaton*. The windows are filled with a pageant of kings and queens, by *R. T. Bayne*, from William the Conqueror to William IV. Monarchs are depicted full length, referring to known likenesses although sometimes erring on the side of flattery (*see* e.g. the slim George IV), together with their arms and attributes. The artistic problem of trousers has been avoided by dressing the kings in Garter regalia. Cromwell is given full prominence, indi- 66 cating Rochdale's politics as clearly as the subject of the mural.

Back on the ground floor is the RECEPTION ROOM, intended as the Council Chamber. The public were allowed to observe proceedings from behind the screen at the S end, which is now a corridor. Relatively low, it is dominated by openwork girders of stone – really flat arches – supporting the great hall above. The immediate source was perhaps Benjamin Bucknall's Woodchester Park, Gloucestershire, of 1858 etc., and the stone engineering theories of Viollet-le-Duc. The room is highly decorated, with a pair of fireplaces, stone and Gothic, and wall paintings of inventions and inventors of textile machinery, by *John Milner Allen*. Stained glass arms of C19 industrialists, together with combs and shuttles.

From here we enter, awkwardly, the Mayoral part of the building. In the MAYOR'S PARLOUR all-over decoration again, the walls delicately painted with birds and flowers, the ceiling with peacocks and sprigs, and a fine Gothic chimneypiece. The stained glass in the upper lights is a particularly charming series of the months, cleverly alternating busyness and calm; by *Allen*. The Mayor's Reception Room is rich and sombre with dark green walls painted like a formal forest. The carved corbels represent Crossland, with dividers and plan, Councillor Ashworth with the town hall itself, and on the other side shaking a fist at the pair of them Councillor Edward Taylor the Treasurer. As well he might, for by now it will come as no surprise to learn that the budget was out of control. The SMALL EXCHANGE is pointed out as the room where the money finally ran out; the wall painters seem to have left in mid-brush. In the ceiling panels, the trades of Rochdale. *Minton* floor tiles with arms and mottoes of England, Scotland and Ireland. Wales only makes its appearance in the stained glass. The TOWER ROOM was the base of Crossley's tower, and the striped vaulting remains. He intended it as the principal entrance to the mayoral apartments. The doorway is now filled with coloured glass by *Alfred Waterhouse* making an instructive contrast to the rest; cool, controlled and architectural. Finally the STAIRCASE, a stone cantilevered spiral, twin to the one at the other end, with delightful stained glass quarries.

There is less to see in the W end. The present COUNCIL CHAMBER was the courtroom and has been adapted considerably. Stone carving by *G. Law* of Rochdale, wood carving by *T. Earp*. Formidable judges and lawmakers, with a good deal of ruby red, in the stained glass above the bench.

Beyond is the MEMBERS' LOUNGE, once the magistrates' retiring room, with the most sumptuous fittings although the wall covering has been lost. Beneath and not shown to the public a warren of stores and offices fills the former POLICE PARADE ROOM. It was utilitarian, with iron columns to support the floor above. Around it on two sides are the untouched CELLS.

The final cost of Rochdale Town Hall was something like £150,000, at least five times the 1864 tenders. G.L. Ashworth said on opening day 'we cannot have beauty without paying for it'. Certainly Rochdale is greatly the richer for it.

Crossland gave his Town Hall dignity by terracing the riverbank in front to create THE ESPLANADE, thus inviting optimistic comparisons with the Houses of Parliament. The Roch was as filthy as the Thames, but being only a little river it was cul-

verted rather than cleaned up, in stages: 1904, 1910, 1923 and
1926. Now the river is clean, but when the bridging recently
needed replacement the opportunity to restore Crossland's
scheme was not taken. Sections of his balustrading remain at the
two ends of what Rochdale likes to call the widest bridge in the
world.

WAR MEMORIAL, Esplanade, facing the Town Hall. By *Lutyens*,
1922. Stele of grey Cornish granite, bolder and less subtly
modelled than his Portland stone memorial at Manchester. A
fallen soldier lies offered up on top, as at Manchester; a disturbing image. Furled flags carved in stone and fully coloured
on either side, as he wanted at Whitehall. Only the altar-like
WAR STONE in front exhibits Lutyens's famous system of
entasis. The sunken garden behind is the Second World War
memorial.

BROADFIELD PARK. Bought by the Corporation in 1865,
opened 1870. It occupies the slopes W and S of the Town Hall,
providing it with a verdant setting unusual for an industrial
town. The park makes the most of its steep site with steps,
rockwork and bridges. SCULPTURE. Statues of C. L. Ashworth,
of 1878 by *W. J. & T. Wills*, in marble and badly eroded; of
John Bright by *Hamo Thornycroft*, 1891, bronze. The Dialect
Writers' Memorial of 1900 by *Edward Sykes* is an obelisk with
(originally) four portrait medallions by *John Cassidy*.

TOUCHSTONES Art and Heritage Centre, Esplanade. Opened
2003. It is made up of three buildings: the former Library of
1883 by *Jesse Horsfall* of Todmorden, the Art Gallery and
Museum of 1903 also by Horsfall, and an angled extension of
1913 by the Borough Architect, *P. W. Hathaway*. The sculpted
panels of Art, Science and Literature were modelled by *C. J.
Allen* and carved by *J. J. Millson*. STAINED GLASS by *Walter J.
Pearce*. The River Roch reappears immediately behind it.

SCULPTURE. SPIRES, at the SW entrance to the Esplanade from
Manchester Road. 1997–8, by *Jeremy Waygood*. Twin lead-
coloured spires on cylindrical glass brick bases, echoing the
five flèches on the Touchstones buildings.

CASTLE. Just outside town SW towards Castleton, but visible
from the Spires. Fishwick gives a plan of the earthworks of a
motte and bailey castle here, commanding the Roch valley.
The plain Neoclassical CASTLE HOUSE stands on top, cubic,
of 3 x 3 bays in finest ashlar, with a Doric doorcase. Although
a fine landmark it is sadly encroached upon. It is on Castle
Hill Crescent, off the by-passed Manchester Road.

POST OFFICE, Esplanade. Planned in 1911 but not opened until
1927. By *C. P. Wilkinson*. Polite Wrennish Neo-Georgian in
Portland stone.

COUNCIL OFFICES, Smith Street. By *Essex, Goodman &
Suggitt* of Manchester, mid-1970s. Called by everyone The
Black Box, which is nearly but not quite sufficient for an architectural description. Machine-like box clad in black glass,
channelled to indicate the structure and with a service tower

clamped on to one side like a giant telephone handset. It stands on an aggressively organic base, clad in purple tiles laid vertically, bulging out here and retreating there in response to a vanished street pattern. Bus station and multi-storey car park attached.

SHOPPING CENTRES

Rochdale's centre has two alternative geographies, indoor and outdoor. Two adjacent shopping centres make an indoor world, with just a single street to cross in between.

ROCHDALE EXCHANGE SHOPPING CENTRE. A megastructure stretching from College Hill Flats SE down to Yorkshire Street, incorporating markets, car parking, offices and the Co-op department store. The architects were *BDP*, the project architect *Stuart Boott*. It was opened by Gracie Fields in 1978, but then it was clad in tiles of a sombre purple, and there was an excitingly jagged skyline and stairways without visible means of support. Today it is cheerful with red and yellow imitation stone, with all the sombreness and jaggedness ironed out. The transformation was completed in 1997. The original finish can still be seen here and there, e.g. above Woolworths.
On the other side of Yorkshire Street the WHEATSHEAF CENTRE by *Chapman Taylor Partners*, 1990, makes it possible to walk under cover all the way down to the Black Box and the bus station, but at street level the old and the new collide uncomfortably as the ground falls, and the outer walls of sheer brick are uninviting. It has a central atrium and a stained glass panel by *Jane Gray*. The PUBLIC LIBRARY is incorporated on top.

PERAMBULATION

The basic street pattern is simple. The road from Manchester, sticking to the high ground as Drake Street and picking up the Oldham Road, loops down from the S, crosses the river by Rochdale Bridge, and as Yorkshire Street curves up towards the NE and Halifax. At the crossing, on either side of the now-culverted river, are the short lengths of the Butts and South Parade. The Esplanade was built up on low-lying land in front of the Town Hall, forming a flatter connection from the bridge to the Manchester Road.

THE BUTTS is an irregular open space rather than a street. The ROYAL BANK OF SCOTLAND replicates the vanished C18 Butts House, but in urbane Portland stone; by *Cecil Jackson*, 1913. A Georgian fragment remains on its l. side; just a rich doorcase and a stair within. Next to that an engaging little early C19 Greek SAVINGS BANK. The REGAL MOON pub was the Regal Cinema of 1938. Its symmetry and massing are clearly classical in origin but some of the Deco detail defies analysis, such as the extraordinary balustrade, like an abacus. The interior is so heavily themed that it is difficult to tell how much is original. SOUTH PARADE answered The Butts on the other bank of the river. BAR 5, the former Union Bank of Manchester, is by *Moulds & Porritt*. Edwardian Mannerist with a tower and lead dome, much entertaining architectural dress and enterprising sculpture. The Butts in turn runs into SMITH STREET. Opposite the Black Box (*see* Council Offices, above), where the river disappears into its long culvert, is ELECTRIC HOUSE, 1930, built by the major Rochdale builders R. & T. Howarth. It does not live up to its name. Weak electrical symbols by the door and a weedy temple cupola above the corner entrance, too small to tell and in any case invisible from close at hand.

YORKSHIRE STREET curves up N and E from the old bridge towards St James and eventually to Halifax. Between the lowest part and The Butts is a tiny remnant of historic intricacy, with a couple of narrow alleys. Through an alley on the W side, on Newgate, is YATES'S WINE LODGE, 1911, built for the Rochdale Vintners' Company, with carved vines. Back on Yorkshire Street LLOYDS TSB occupies a sophisticated building of 1708 at the corner of a vanished street. It is a former inn but was probably originally a house. Of brick articulated by two tiers of pilasters, Ionic and Composite. Now it is shoved up against the entrance to the Exchange Shopping Centre. Immediately above the shopping centres an entry leads N to TOAD LANE, just a fragment of an old thoroughfare and a largely reconstructed one at that. Here is St Mary's and its former vicarage, a pub called The Baum (Balm), and the ROCHDALE PIONEERS MUSEUM, the modest building of *c.* 1800 opened as a co-operative shop in 1844. It is an engaging building with five-light sash windows, but not a lot is left of the original fabric. From here the College Bank Flats (*see* p. 587 above) make a menacing group.

Going the other way, DRAKE STREET runs S from the old Rochdale Bridge towards Oldham, but then curves back SW in a semicircle to meet the Manchester Road. The lower, southern part is scruffily urban, with the ponderous CHAMPNESS MEMORIAL HALL, the Rochdale Mission of 1925, built by R. & T. Howarth again. Behind it in Nelson Street the CHICAGO ROCK CAFÉ shows how far a building can be maltreated while yet retaining its essential structure. It was the Temperance billiard hall of 1909 by *Norman Evans*. Only the curve of the timber roof, showing at the ends, the dormers appearing above the bogus two-story elevations, and the bases of the composite timber trusses within, betray its identity. In the upper reaches of Drake Street, i.e. SW, are a number of good houses of Georgian character including No. 159, prettily Gothic with crocketed hoodmoulds. Immediately S towards the station FREEMASONS' HALL, Richard Street, of 1925 demonstrates the principles of Masoncraft but not those of architecture. House and hall are fronted with fine ashlar and the square and dividers are displayed in the pediment, but the sides are distressingly bald brick. The duality of the centrepiece gives it a cross-eyed look. The FIRE ENGINE STATION, Maclure Road, 1935, is of yellow stone and harsh red brick, with a strong tower. Appropriate low relief carving over the door. Pairs of houses for firemen are linked to it by arches.

OUTER ROCHDALE

Rochdale is an octopus rather than an amoeba. It has grown tentacularly, with open spaces between the tentacles. The spaces are the river valleys, still green although the earliest industry is to be found here, and high ground. The tentacles – to be incorrect zoologically – all have a major road as their spines, and they reach out to touch the next towns. The suburbs have been divided into N, E, S and W along the principal roads. To the N are Syke, Healey, Shawclough, Falinge; to the E, Newbold, Belfield, Smallbridge, Buckley; to the S Sudden, Castleton, Balderstone, Kirkholt; to the W, Caldershaw, Spotland, Norden.

FLAGSTONE WALLS are a distinctive feature. Ruskin in 1859 characterized the Rochdale countryside as 'A waste of grassless fields, fenced from each other, not by hedges, but by slabs of square stone, like gravestones, riveted together with iron'. They are too strongly rippled for paving or roofing, or for gravestones, but set on edge and cramped together they make serviceable and long-lasting boundaries. They were quarried and mined on Rooley Moor and around Whitworth (N Lancashire).

North

Along Whitworth Road and Shawclough Road. Comprising Syke, Healey, Shawclough, Falinge.

CHRISTCHURCH, Gandy Lane, Healey. By *George Shaw*. 1849–50. A spectacular church with its multiplicity of gables and gable-crosses and its slender spire, on a spectacular site. When consecrated in 1850 it consisted only of nave, S aisle and S tower porch, towards which the Commissioners had granted just £150. Chancel and S chapel followed in 1853, spire in 1861, and N aisle and vestry, completing the triple-gabled composition of the E end, only in 1877. Shaw's traceries are fussy and crude, but the build-up from E to W is excellent, and so is the sheer upward sweep of his spire, answered by the little spirelet over the vestry chimney.

The interior proportions are unusual; the arcades low and quick-moving, the aisles remarkably low, the clerestory windows small, but the nave roof high and far-reaching, allowing a very big W window. Sorely afflicted by dry rot, the E interior has been dismantled and walled off. It was very lavish. Still in place are the traceried stone arch over the former organ position, and the Royds Chapel screens with their Masonic symbols. The FURNISHINGS are scattered about, including several sets of STALLS, some with misericords, mostly by *Shaw* but some later. – STAINED GLASS. Excellent W window of 1900 and good side windows of the 1880s–90s all given by the Tweedale and Royds families and all by *Percy Bacon* of London. In the S chapel, Christ walking on the water, mid C20, by *Wippell*.

Immediately NW and grouping well with the church is the former VICARAGE, thoroughly Gothic, stone-roofed, L-shaped, with a stone oriel, some traceried windows and the rest mullioned. By *Albert Hudson Royds*, 1853, surely with guidance from Shaw.

HEALEY HALL. The old house of 1618 was a four-gabled affair with the door still set to one side. Its datestone is preserved at the back of the present house, which was built by Charles Chadwick of Healey and of Mavesyn Ridware, Staffordshire, in 1774. It is handsome and classical, of ashlar, with seven bays and a three-bay pediment. Chadwick evidently favoured inscriptions, including an immensely long Latin diatribe on the top and back of the single stone that comprises the pediment. Inside, a good cantilever stair, though it has lost its balustrade. Healey was the subject of an astonishing restoration by Jason Stead, 1998–2002, with new marble statuary chimneypieces from China and new moulded woodwork in MDF. The hall makes the most of its situation above Healey Dell with a HA-HA and long walk skirting the parkland. Below the house a rock-built TUNNEL.

HEALEY DELL is a famous beauty spot. Crossing high above it on a curve is a RAILWAY VIADUCT of 1867, 105 ft (32 metres) high, partly-skewed, and very slender.

FALINGE PARK, N of St Edmund (*see* centre, p. 590), was given to the town in 1902 by the mayor, Samuel Turner, and opened in 1905. All that is left of the late C18 mansion, home of Clement and Albert Hudson Royds, is the pathetic façade and the side pavilions. Of ashlar, five bays and two storeys, with a three-bay pediment. Ionic columned porch.

CRONKEYSHAW COMMON extends from Falinge Park W and then N as a long, narrow, cranked open space reaching open country at Syke. It is edged with several groups of stone weavers' houses and, right at the top, the METHODIST CHAPEL of 1868.

FALINGE FOLD is an unexpected C17 and C18 enclave overlooking the River Spodden. OLD FALINGE is dated 1721 and 1724, with mullioned-and-transomed windows and continuous drip-moulds.

East

Along the Halifax and Milnrow Roads. Comprising Newbold, Belfield, Smallbridge, Buckley.

ALL SAINTS, Foxholes Road, Hamer. 1863–6 by *J. Medland
Taylor*, who canvassed for the job as soon as it was announced.
SW tower and broach spire with some roguish detail about the
stair-turret, nave and aisles with quatrefoil and cinquefoil
windows for the clerestory, two-bay chancel. High interior
with scissor-braced roof, steep arches and dumpy arcade
columns with oversized capitals. Double-roofed transept on
the S side. STAINED GLASS. W (by *Wailes*) and E given respectively by the two principal donors of the church, W.W.
Schofield, and John S. Entwisle, who is also commemorated
by a fine BRASS on the chancel arch. Outside, N, are their two
grandiose columnar monuments.

Foxholes Hall of 1793 has gone. In Foxholes Close are single-
storey PRE-FABS, metal-clad, of *c.* 1945.

ST ANN, Milnrow Road, Belfield. 1912–13, by *R. B. Preston*. Of
rubble stones, some very big, with minimal dressings. S tower,
W baptistery, ogee-arched windows. Typically early C20 is the
way the buttresses are battered instead of having set-offs.
Equally typical the arcades with, instead of capitals, just
slightly projecting chunks. – STAINED GLASS. W by *Francis E.
Skeat*, 1965, in memory of the choirmaster Harry Aubrey
†1939. It is charmingly biographical, representing him as a
choirboy and as a child of the Chapel Royal, with portraits of
favourite English church composers, Sir John Goss, John
Stainer, and Sir Sydney Nicholson, brother of both the architect and the stained-glass artist. E by *Harcourt M. Doyle*, 1956;
St Ann.

ST JOHN, Halifax Road, Smallbridge. 1834, by *Lewis Vulliamy*
for the Commissioners. An oblong box of blackened stone,
projecting slightly at both ends, with closely set buttresses and
lancets along the sides. The church is symmetrical about both
axes, excepting only a comical turret on the W gable, low
gallery porches, W, and a vestry, E. (GALLERIES on cast-
iron columns; two tiers at the W end. – Good FURNISHINGS
including SCREEN, PULPIT, PEWS with poppyheads, STALLS,
and a hooded PRIEST'S CHAIR with misericord. – PAINTING.
Angel choir over the chancel arch. – STAINED GLASS. C18
roundel of St John, in the tower. E, by *Wailes*.)

ST PETER, St Peter's Street, Newbold. By *J. Medland & Henry
Taylor*, 1869. Startlingly polychromatic. Of red brick laid in
tricky fashion, and yellow stone laid crazy-paving-wise. The SW
porch was clearly the start of a tower, but in its truncated state
balances the NW baptistery. Spacious interior of four wide bays
and a three-sided apse, the nave subdivided crudely in 1984.
The baptistery is evidently a Medland Taylor foible; so are the
sculpted roundels in the spandrels of the arches, and the exhor-
tatory texts, here expressed in tile, at the altar rails, choir stalls,
and at the chancel step. – Damaged STAINED GLASS including a series by *Capronnier* and a fine one of 1914 by *Walmsley*.

SACRED HEART (R.C.), Kingsway. 1956–7, by *A. F. Farebrother
& Partners*. Constructed on a concrete A-frame system but
with side extensions to allow for aisles. The parish centre on

the (ritual) W end was added 1966–7, when the Farebrother campanile was taken down.

SMALLBRIDGE LIBRARY, Halifax Road, close to St John. 1971. Cute steel-framed rotunda with a folded glass curtain wall, but compromised by the weak attached office section, of brick and flat-roofed.

DYE HOUSE LANE, a potholed track leading S from Smallbridge to Clegg Hall (*see* Milnrow), served eight or nine mills and several coalpits in a few hundred yards. DOB WHEEL MILL is on a short spur E, by the River Roch, with several buildings of different ages. Two-storey stone woollen mill, originally water-powered. Advertised for sale in 1807, so probably late C18. Long brick handloom-weavers' shop of *c.* 1800, also two-storeyed with windows in pairs, some retaining small-pane glazing; a very interesting halfway-house between home and mill industry. The building is in poor condition. Larger flat-roofed brick mill, W, of 1854, when production switched to cotton. Tall engine house and three-arched boiler house at the W end.

South

Along the Manchester, Bolton, and Oldham Roads. Comprising Sudden, Castleton, Balderstone, Kirkholt.

CASTLE HOUSE, *see* centre, p. 597.

ST AIDAN, Manchester Road, Sudden. By *Temple Moore*, 1913–15. Well sited to be viewed from the N and E, its distinctive two-humped silhouette and E lancets appearing unexpectedly over the rooftops. Random-laid stone. E. E. in style with a broad W tower (completed 1931) and a small stair-tower on the S side with an external pulpit. The chancel, like that of St Chad, is taller than the nave. The interior, white and cream, plaster and stone, is full of originalities, and markedly stony in feel; the architect seems to have enjoyed the properties of stone and light. Three-bay nave, relatively low and almost square in plan, lit principally by three lancets in the W wall of the tower, which is part of the space. Square piers, broad unmoulded arches. The chancel is dramatically higher and brighter, its E wall filled with lancets in a 1:3:1 rhythm and the side walls hollowed out in three storeys, including a triforium. Chapels of three bays, S, and of two, N. – PISCINA, just a shallow fluted hollow on top of the sleeper wall by the altar. – STAINED GLASS. War memorial E, 1946, by *Harry Grylls*, with Celtic saints.

ST MARTIN, Castleton. The district, formerly Blue Pits, with Trub and Castleton Moor, only got its name with the opening of the railway station in 1877. The church of 1860–2 by *Ernest Bates* is a fine landmark on its hill. The NW steeple is particularly good, with its outsized aedicules and statues on the broaches of the spire, deep reveals to the bell-stage windows, and steeply raked buttresses. Late C13 style, veering between

Geometric and flowing in its traceries. Finely proportioned arcades, the piers alternately circular and octagonal and the latter resting on square bases with crisp miniature broaches. Two chamfers to the arches, the outer one concave.

The church was abandoned in 1991 and allowed to become derelict. Restoration and reordering 2002–3 is by *Anthony Grimshaw* of Wigan, with a new entrance through the NW organ chamber. The new altar is under the W window, i.e. orientation reversed. An intermediate floor fills the W end, with the stairs rising in front of the transept windows so their full heights can be seen. The new floor and the canopy roof above have been kept clear of the original architectural detail.

All the original FITTINGS have gone. Of the C19 STAINED GLASS there is only one survivor, the former E window by *William Wailes* of five lights. It has been remade by *Design Lights* of Blackrod for the W of four lights; the Ascension is the missing scene. New glass is by Design Lights, designed by the architect (the clerestory) or by *Linda Walton* using reclaimed fragments (from Wardle (q.v.) among others), and pale streaky glass with swirling leading.

ST MARY, Balderstone. An impressive group of church, school and parsonage, all paid for by the Radcliffe brothers, Joshua, Samuel, Josiah, James and John, owners of six mills and employers of 1,210 men and 1,890 women. *J. Medland Taylor* was the architect. All three buildings are of stone, the church with gaily coloured patterns in its slate roof.

Former PARSONAGE at the S end, inscribed AD 1865 JR. The *Rochdale Observer* described it as a 'stone built 12-roomed house with plenty of cupboards and pantries'.

The SCHOOL opened in 1866; a resourceful building with a complex spirelet on top and a curved enclosure at the back. Ornate double-arched porch on the better seen end inscribed 'Come ye children, hearken unto me' and 'I will teach you the fear of the Lord'.

The CHURCH, which cost something like £13,500, opened in 1872, completing the group on the NW with a splendid tower and spire with prominent lucarnes and corner tabernacles. Clerestory of large square-headed three-light windows; dwarf transepts each with a W door; 'Holiness becometh thine house O Lord for ever' carved under the E window. Under the W window the baptistery is expressed, as the Taylors liked to do, with a little lean-to extension. Its centre window is carved with lilies and pea-pods in place of open tracery. The interior was compromised by reordering in 1997, although the inserted structure stands free of the W wall and allows a spectacular view from its open upper deck. Arcade of short fat columns of polished granite alternately pink and grey, with lusciously carved capitals. Chancel richly fitted out with marbles, with openwork tracery screens on both sides. Carved roundels, New Testament in the arcade spandrels, and Old above the FONT. – STAINED GLASS. W by *Hardman*. Several by *Heaton, Butler & Bayne*, of which the chancel S of 1904 is best.

CASTLETON UNITED REFORMED CHURCH, Heywood Road. Mid-C19, with a grand Lombardic front with effective contrasts of ashlar and rubble plus a little carving and contrasted colour for the fat shafts framing the door.

The very large KIRKHOLT ESTATE was laid out by Rochdale Borough between the wars, but only built in the 1950s.

ST THOMAS, Kirkholt, of 1964 by *Moir & Bateman* of Rochdale, fails to dominate from its hilltop site. A tadpole-shaped building with a blunt nose, gills and a vestigial tail. The tail is the entrance, the gills are canted windows, the nose the E window. The roof ignores all this, running straight over the zigzag sides and coming to a point beyond the E window. It carries a flèche. Interior chopped in half with sliding partitions in the 1980s.

HOLY FAMILY (R.C.), Mornington Road, of 1954–5 with its presbytery has a dramatic site too. It has a campanile but is almost style-less.*

MORMON CHURCH, Manchester Road and Tweedale Street. By *T. P. Bennett & Son*, 1961–4. Big and prominent with 1960s motifs such as zigzag canopies, and a detached chimney-like tower and needle spire.

GEORGE AND DRAGON, Manchester Road, by the motorway bridge. By *Edgar Wood*, 1897, but so maltreated you would hardly know it. Two-storey section r., with a circular bay on the corner; three-storey cross-wing l. with an inglenook stack; porch in the middle. Sculpted inn sign on a beam: a lively St George with a broken lance, and a splendid crouching dragon.

Fake timber framing has been stuck over the façade, and on the end stack, roughcast applied to the stone base storey as well as the rest, and concrete tiles have replaced the stone-flag roof.

BARCROFT, Bolton Road, also by *Edgar Wood*, has lost its vital stone flag roof too, replaced with flat tiles. Curious stone porch, inscribed BC & JB 1894 under an eye. Roughcast, with projecting bricks forming a diaper pattern in the front gable and indicating the rise of the stairs. Roguish two-storey corner bay at forty-five degrees. Range of five mullioned windows in the SW gable, the middle light stepping up a little, as on the C18 houses at Prickshaw (*see* below). Extended to the l. after 1945, with a flush-mullioned oriel over the garden arch.

ARROW MILL, Queensway, Castleton. By *Sydney Stott*, 1908. A complete example of Lancashire cotton-spinning mill building at its zenith. Of brick, five storeys high and very deep, with stone dressings where it matters e.g. on the roadside office, on the engine house on the canal side (for cooling), and on the stair-tower with the mill entrance at its foot. The two-storey outshut along the road is a standard feature, housing the preparatory processes. The name, which had to be short, is proudly displayed on the tower and the chimney.

---

* The two churches can be compared to their equivalents on the Langley Estate in Middleton, q.v.

Queensway once ran as a canyon between mills. Opposite stands the lone engine house of the contemporary HARP MILL. Elsewhere MARLAND MILL, Nixon Street, Castleton, has lost its chimney but is otherwise complete. Stretching along Royle Barn Road is the immense length of Tweedale & Smalley's engineering works of 1901, now WOOLWORTHS' Depot.

On MANCHESTER ROAD in Castleton is a group of minor Edwardian buildings, typically red brick and yellow stone; the CARNEGIE LIBRARY of 1905, wedge-shaped on the corner of Queensway, the FAREWELL INN of 1909, CASTLETON BOARD SCHOOL, by *Edward Sykes* of Rochdale, 1901–4, and CASTLETON BATHS. This has a Baroque frontispiece with twin oculi, a dropped keystone over the central window, and grooved rustication, all done in artificial stone.

SANDBROOK PARK, Edinburgh Way. A small retail and office park built for the Co-op in the 1990s on the site of three mills. Stores, a fitness centre and a cinema are given some visual unity by the use of white tubular metal and multiple arched roofs. HOLIDAY HOUSE of 1995–6 by the *Taylor Young Partnership* represented a symbolic, but short-lived, move back to Rochdale for the headquarters of the Co-operative Retail Services. Arc-shaped, of stone and brick with a long pitched slate roof. Set in generous landscaping, by *Gillespies* of Altrincham, against the canal embankment.

BROAD LANE, Balderstone, winds its way SW to Shaw. Nos. 29–35 are stone WEAVERS' HOUSES, three-storied, with long ranges of mullioned windows. Nos. 33 and 35 are dated 17?7 on a joist. No. 33 has six-light windows, the mullions, which are rectangular, grouped 3 and 3 with a king mullion in the middle to support the joint in the lintel stones. No. 35 has eight-lighters, grouped 3-2-3. The houses are very deep, with two stacks in the end walls, but the top storey is without a spine wall. Did each consist of two houses back-to-back, with a loom shop on top? The attics intercommunicate, so it seems likely. Nos. 29 and 31 are taller and more regular so probably C19. More terraces along the lane, some with picturesque nicknames identifying peculiarities: Clog Iron Row, Blind Row, Oxo Row.

123 ZEN INTERNET, Moss Bridge Road. Excellent small office building of 2001 by *Burr Design Associates* of Rochdale. Built around a spine wall of polished blocks and a circular server tower, both of which show outside. The conference room is effectively outside too, circular, of glass; meetings are displayed as part of the show. The principal space is a two-storey open-plan office overlooking the canal.

MOSS MILL (mule spinning), nearby on Woodbine Street, is by *Stott & Sons*, 1888. It has lost its chimney, and the office block is derelict.

West

Along Rooley Moor Road, Edenfield Road and Bury Road. Comprising Caldershaw, Spotland, Norden.

St Clement, Wilbutts Lane, Spotland. By *Lewis Vulliamy*, 1832–5. More impressive than his St John Smallbridge (*see* p. 602). Lancets and buttresses in pairs, blocky corner buttresses, triple doors at the W end, but the turret and clock on the E gable where, it is said, they made a picturesque object from the drawing room window of Mr Clement Royds of Falinge Hall. (The interior has been re-ordered, with the W end partitioned off. Galleries.)

The Vicarage (SW) of 1840 could be by *Vulliamy* as well.

St George, Bury Road, Oakenrod. 1938–9 by *Robert Martin*. Light brick, with a long roof and no tower. Square attachments and straight-headed windows.

St Paul, Edenfield Road, Norden. By *George Shaw*, architect and contractor, 1859–61. Dec with flowing tracery, wide nave and wide N aisle, a short S transept, but no structural chancel, and a typical Shaw W tower with a slim broach spire without lucarnes. The S transept carries a bellcote, suggesting that the tower is an addition – but no, Shaw's drawing shows both. The transept is the vestry and the bellcote is its chimney made into an eye-catcher. The interior is wide and plain with arch-braced roofs. Shaw supplied the furnishings too. – Stained glass in the E window, angelic hosts, by *Walter J. Pearce*.

Villa Nostra, next to the church; a Grecian villa with inset panels of terracotta decoration. It has a large square industrial chimney in its front garden.

Until the second half of the C19 Norden, like so many of the districts of Rochdale, had no boundaries or even a name. The name Norden was chosen by James Dearden, Lord of the Manor, in a letter of 1859 when the new parish was created. The old settlements were Black Pits, Tenterhouse, Wolstenholme etc.

St Vincent de Paul (R.C.), Castleshaw Road. 1974–5. Designed for the Rev. Mortimer Stanley by *Bernard Ashton* of *Cassidy & Ashton Partnership*, Preston. A squashed hexagon in plan, much wider than it is long, with the presbytery attached behind the altar. Just two tapering cross-shaped piers to support the apex of the roof. Top-lighting for the altar, rooflights in the shortest sides. Strips of slab glass at the corners graded rainbow-style, designed by Eddie Blackwell and made at Buckfast Abbey by Brother Norris.

Methodist Free Church, Spotland. 1886. Brick and fine stone, a grand front in Renaissance style with relief carving and Corinthian pilasters. The sides as usual much plainer, with transepts to make a T-shape and the school at the back.

Silver Street Chapel (Wesleyan), Silver Street. 1893, by *Edgar Wood*. Small but striking. Powerful façade with the Tree of Life moulded in the gable apex above seven plain lancets

graded in an arc. The windowless base, framed by sloping
buttresses, is of striped brick and stone with a strong round-
arched door over which is carved another tree of life. Strong
elevation to Edmund Street too; continuous windowing
between the aisle buttresses and a gable and three lancets
arranged transept-wise at both ends. These are not repeated
on the other side, but it matters surprisingly little, because
slope of the ground makes symmetry unnecessary. The interior is now almost bare. A boarded ceiling follows the arc of
the end windows. Tie-beams between simple corbels. At the
dais end reinforced concrete piers and iron brackets replace
the wall buttresses and corbels. The walls here are lightly
partitioned so that the auditorium could be opened out into a
T-shape. A pleasing and practical building, showing how
Wood's thought was progressing towards his early masterwork,
Long Street Chapel in Middleton.

Close by is the former VICTORIA HOTEL, Spotland Road, also
by *Edgar Wood* and dated 1897 on a hopper. Stone for the
ground floor, smooth render above and fanciful half-timbering for the big gables. Queen-Anne-style shell hood over the
door, mullions and transoms on the ground floor, but wooden
oriels above. The roof is regrettably concrete-tiled, and the
chimneys have gone.

ROCHDALE CEMETERY. Dated 1855 on the gates. Three-arched
Gothic gateway with attendant lodges, by *R. Moffat Smith*. A
fine mature landscape with many good monuments. The Dissenting chapel (Ionic) and Episcopal chapel (Neo-Norman)
have gone, leaving only the minor R.C. chapel. The CREMA-
TORIUM of 1938 is some compensation, bearing as it does a
passing resemblance to the Saxon St Paul's Jarrow, with the
chimneys disguised in the oblong central tower.

(NORDEN LIBRARY. Early c20, Baroque, perhaps by
S. Butterworth & W. H. Duncan who did a similar library at
Milnrow (q.v.).)

Rooley Moor Road leads up NW to the hamlet of CATLEY LANE
HEAD, where it turns into a rough Pennine trackway. Here are
a number of stone-built vernacular cottages and farms, some
still derelict, including, by a mill lodge pool, SMALLSHAW
FARM dated ICM (James Crossley and his wife) 1632 on its
two-storey porch. The hall or house place is indicated by extra
mullioned lights, and a heightening by the simpler and taller
mullions upstairs. Rooley Moor Road continues to cross the
moors into Rossendale, connecting several large stone quarries that characterize this upland area. Well-preserved stone
sett surface with raised kerbs.

PRICKSHAW is still further NW. A fold of flag-roofed stone
houses up in the hills, right against the Rossendale boundary,
with extensive views and plenty of weather. The hamlet was
uninhabited from the 1950s and completely derelict by 1980
but has been restored and reoccupied. In the centre of the row
on Prickshaw Lane a pair of 1781 with mullioned windows. To

its r. the former Star Inn of 1823 with ground-floor sashes but mullions above, with the centre light raised a little. This same feature is on the row of four behind, also 1820s. The mono-pitched-roofed building, windowless to N and E, was the brewhouse. Croft Head is a laithe house, i.e. house and barn under one long roof. From here a network of narrow stone-setted lanes radiates between the fields, some of them, like the hamlet itself, astonishingly, originally gaslit.

ROE GREEN   7000

Just N of Worsley, beyond the motorway. In contrast to the surrounding suburbia it has the atmosphere of a village, with low houses around an ample green.

Everything of interest can be seen in a short perambulation. Starting just S of the green on Greenleach Lane, No. 175 is a low, late C18 or early C19 brick cottage with casements, with an added C19 timber-framed wing. Continuing W leads to the Green proper. Facing on to it from the E side is the INDE-PENDENT METHODIST CHAPEL, 1884, replacing a predecessor of 1855. Red brick with a flèche and a central entrance bay framed by piers terminating as pinnacles. Paired doorways beneath a round arch. In the grounds a PREACHING STONE is preserved. It was used as a platform for open-air meetings from 1808 by Independent Methodist preachers. A little way N on Greenleach Road is another, smaller green called Beesley Green. BEESLEY HALL here probably has C16 or C17 origins, though it seems to have been thoroughly rebuilt in the mid or later C19, and is now three dwellings. The steeply pitched roof may recall the original form but the tall gabled and timber-framed bays are C19 and the dormers C20.

Continuing W brings us to LITTLEWOOD on the corner with Lumber Lane, a brick C18 house with an early C19 brick extension (now a separate dwelling) along Lumber Lane with windows with slightly cambered stone lintels. This was the home of Richard Clarke, who used the lower part as a warehouse and fitted up part of the upper floor in 1824 as a preaching room for the Independent Methodists until their chapel was built on Roe Green. Opposite, and reached from a track running S from the road, KEMPNOUGH HALL stands on an ancient site, occupied by a branch of the Worsley family from the late C13 and the Starkie family in the C16. What can be seen now is C17, H-plan and boldly timber-framed in square panels in typical Lancashire style, with stone stacks. The larger cross-wing, r., has a jettied gable and a mullioned window with a sill panel carved with roses. The other wing is much smaller, and has been rendered. It was divided into three separate houses, probably in the C19.

ROUGHTOWN *see* MOSSLEY

9000

ROYTON

Royton originated as a tiny settlement on the main route between Oldham and Rochdale, described in 1780 as having 'only a few straggling and mean-built cottages'. Expansion came with the introduction of weaving and other branches of cotton manufacture. A local board was formed in 1863. The settlement lies NW of Oldham, merging with it.

St Anne, Broadway. By *Temple Moore*, 1908–10 (tower 1926–7), at the instigation of the Rev. J. T. Ormerod who visited a number of recently erected churches and was attracted by 'the beauty and originality' of the architect's designs. The result is one of Temple Moore's most interesting churches, and, while lacking some of the refinements of the others, more inventive and radical than most. In fact the only criticism one can make of the interior is that too many motifs are introduced. Externally there can hardly be criticism. The material is irregular roughly squared rubble, with amounts of bare wall, giving a rugged look. The ashlar dressings contrast strongly as they alone have been blackened by pollution. High, unbuttressed, i.e. sheer and square-topped, s tower with pierced stonework bell-openings and a primitive look. It stands out from the s wall of the church, balanced by a tall shallow N transept for the organ with a rose window high in the gable. The E end has

Royton, St Anne

a somewhat lower attachment housing the Lady Chapel, with low crenellated towers on each side. And whereas nave and chancel run on unbroken under one large steep roof, sweeping out gently over the aisles, the Lady Chapel is square at the top, with a flat roof. Also, whereas most of the windows have flowing tracery, there are here plain small Elizabethan or C17-type mullioned clerestory windows. The baptistery is yet lower and has a lean-to roof against the w wall.

The INTERIOR is hard to describe. It incorporates favourite Temple Moore motifs, such as passage-aisles and wall passages. The first impression is of spaciousness, light and dignity, belying the tight organization of a plan in which the nave is of only two bays. Chancel and w baptistery are raised up at either end of the nave. The interpenetration and progression of spaces, the rhythms of the arcading, and the grace of details such as the wide curved steps starting at the transepts and leading up on either side of the sanctuary, contribute to what Pevsner in 1969 described as 'an architectural polyphony which transforms precedent into something unprecedented'. The nave has a ceiled wagon roof on wall-piers, i.e. really buttresses placed inside (as well as outside), and connected on top internally by broad, plain pointed arches. They are pierced by low, round-arched aisle passages. The recessed windows, in groups of three, have arcading, the piers pierced by arched openings in each external face (i.e. front to back as well as laterally), carrying the heating pipes through the walls. Beneath the windows in each bay are two round-arched recesses. Similar details are taken up again for the chancel, after the interruption of transept and tower, but here the touch is lighter. There are three arched recesses beneath the windows and the piers between the lights are slimmer, pierced laterally only, reflecting the fact that they are three-light windows, rather than the groups of three separate single lights of the nave. The wagon roof runs through without any interruption. But the chancel is raised by four steps. The island sanctuary within is enclosed by low walls, with a chapel on the N side and wall seating on the other. Then, however, the Lady Chapel is separated from the chancel by a triple arcade of pointed arches. Two transverse arches spring eastwards from this arcade. Beyond and on each side are vestries etc., but the upper part of the E wall appears above with a central rose window above the chapel altar and arched windows on each side. At the w end is another triple arcade, between nave and baptistery (glazed in the late C20 to form a meeting room), but here the central arch is narrower, and the baptistery raised up by four steps.

Timber FURNISHINGS designed by *Temple Moore* include a fine PULPIT, two banks of CHOIR STALLS fronted by carved SCREENS, and an ORGAN CASE high in the transept. All have flowing traceried carving. – REREDOS. 1924, of copper, with a gilded gesso arcade framing paintings of Christ and the Apostles, by Moore's daughter *Mary Moore*, similar to her reredos at All Saints, Basingstoke, 1915–17. – FONT, repositioned opposite the pulpit at the W edge of the tower recess. A big polished stone bowl on a plain octagonal stem. – STAINED GLASS. At the W end, by *G. E. R. Smith* of St John's Wood. E end, by another hand, including Virgin and Child in the rose window in the Lady Chapel.

ST ANNE'S SCHOOLS, Broadway, N of the church. The E one is by *Temple Moore* himself, 1916, the other by *Leslie Moore*, his son-in-law, 1933–4. The group is hard to appreciate today, because the schools face a busy dual carriageway. They are a perfect prelude to the church, using similar stonework, varied in a very free Tudor way, kept low and hence not competing. The junior school (E) is near-symmetrical with gabled end bays and a hall side-on to the road with a strongly rhythmic range of windows between buttresses. The infants' school (W) is long and low with mullioned windows.

ST JAMES, Thornham Road, Summit, NW of the centre. By *R. Martin*, 1928, using the irregular masonry he sometimes favoured, long and low, with C16-style uncusped tracery. Money must have been too short for the tower or spire demanded by the hilltop site.

ST PAUL, Church Street. Built originally in 1754. The present building is of 1884–9, by *H. Cockburn*. NW tower and tall spire with an octagonal NW stair-tower. Paired clerestory lights. Inside, five-bay arcades of polished granite circular piers, thin scissor-braced nave roof, busier chancel roof. A succession of reorderings has given it a bitty look. Chancel with REREDOS and Comperish RIDDEL-POSTS with angels, 1919–22. SE chapel, 1926, an extraordinary Gothick-style confection in timber with florid ogee arches over recesses on either side of the reredos. – BENCHES by *E. Whittaker*, mid–late C20, with little gnomes at the feet of bench ends. – FONTS. Stone octagon on granite pier, W end. In the centre of the nave a little baluster font dated 1754. – MONUMENTS. N aisle, Katherine Pickford †1765. Tablet surmounted by a skull. Corbels at the base with the legend 'Life How Short!' on one side and 'Eternity How Long!' on the other. Nearby, Thomas Addison †1801, though the monument was probably made later. Signed *Bonehill*, perhaps *Joseph Bonehill* who was active in Manchester during the 1860s–70s. – STAINED GLASS. E window probably by *Hardman*.

TOWN HALL, Rochdale Road. By *W. H. Cooke*, opened 1880. Vaguely Renaissance, symmetrical with a tall clock tower capped by an elongated copper dome. Over the entrance a crowned head. Much plasterwork inside, especially in the Council Chamber, featuring lion masks, a motif repeated in the cast-iron balusters of the stair.

MARKET HALL, Rochdale Road. Opened in 1880. Part of the Town Hall development with some of the same features, and so probably by *W. H. Cooke*. Arched entrance with a head crowned with produce, frontage buildings with shops, rear market demolished *c.* 1955.

CARNEGIE LIBRARY, Rochdale Road, attached to the Town Hall (above). Dated 1906. Quietly Baroque, symmetrical, with windows with segmental pediments flanking an entrance with a triangular pediment. Tablets on the upper walls with names of writers.

DOWNEY HOUSE, Church Street. A large brick house of *c.* 1830. Tripartite ground floor windows and central doorway with Doric columns and a shallow arched head with a fanlight. On each side Neo-Georgian brick pavilions, probably 1930s.

THORP. A little settlement now engulfed in a late C20 housing estate. A track off Kirkdale Drive leads to a group of C17 and C18 buildings. Of these THORP FARM is a timber-framed house with a cross-wing. The outer walls were rebuilt in brick on a stone plinth with new windows, probably in the late C18 or early C19. The interior is said to have timber-framed walls and a tie-beam roof. A stone C18 BARN opposite with opposed cart entrances has been converted to stables. Other C18 buildings in the group have been very thoroughly rebuilt.

MILLS

A number of impressive late C19 and early C20 mills can be found in Royton, of which a selection has been made.*

LION MILL, Fitton Street, by *F. W. Dixon*, 1890. The notable feature architecturally is the balustraded corner tower.

MONARCH MILL, Jones Street. By *F. W. Dixon*, 1903. Typical of its date, with a central projecting water- and stair-tower, banded in yellow brick with the name in white brick.

PARK MILL and SANDY MILL, off Rochdale Road, with tall circular chimneys, both by *A. Turner*, erected 1912 and 1913 respectively.

SALFORD

7090

*For full details of these and others in the area *see* D. Gurr and J. Hunt, *The Cotton Mills of Oldham*, 1998.

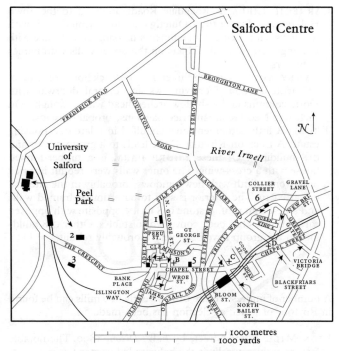

I	University of Salford Centenary Building	A	St Philip
2	Library, Museum and Art Gallery	B	Roman Catholic Cathedral
3	Former Fire Station	C	Independent Chapel
4	Former Royal Salford Hospital	D	Sacred Trinity
5	Magistrates' Court		
6	Former Greengate Baths		

INTRODUCTION

In the vast expanse of Manchester the River Irwell is hardly
noticeable. Yet it has ever since the Middle Ages formed the
boundary between the town of Manchester and the town of
Salford, and it still does between the two cities. Salford is as
proud of itself as Manchester, and it was a separate manor
already in the Domesday Book. In 1228 it received the grant of
a market and in 1230 its charter. The settlement then was concentrated around Greengate and the bottom end of Chapel Street
in a loop of the Irwell at the E end of the settlement, and the
streets as far W as Gravel Lane. The parish church, Sacred
Trinity, was founded only after the Reformation, but there was
a small Cluniac cell at Kersal from the mid C12. Ordsall Hall,
near the docks, was a large house in the country with no physical connection with Salford. It is one of the finest timber-framed
halls in the region, with an excellent C14–C16 interior. Kersal Cell

is a fairly substantial early C16 cruck house, with some contemporary and C17 interior decoration.

By the end of the C18 Salford's population was *c.* 18,000 (against Manchester's 70,000 in 1801). Industry proliferated during the early C19 with cotton-spinning, weaving and finishing. Islington Mill of 1823 is almost the sole surviving representative in the inner area. The 1820s–30s saw the erection of buildings of ambition and elegance along Chapel Street in the shape of the Market Hall by *Richard Lane,* and *Robert Smirke*'s church of St Philip, both in Greek style, both fronting little squares. By this time brick town houses were going up as well. Further N, alongside the Irwell, Broughton was becoming a fashionable area for villas, of which a few early and mid-C19 examples survive, and there are others in Pendleton. The development of church building follows predictable lines. The only C18 building is Sacred Trinity, Chapel Street, 1752–3, retaining the original tower of 1634–5. The Independent Chapel on Chapel Street was built in 1819. Commissioners' churches come in both Greek (St Philip) and Gothic (St Thomas, Pendleton, by *Goodwin* and *Lane*). The rate of growth accelerated from the 1830s: Pendleton, w of the centre, got a parish church 1829–31, Broughton (N) in 1836, Ordsall (SW) in 1842. The population stood at 70,000 in 1841, 102,500 in 1861 and 176,000 in 1881. Incorporation took place in 1844, the establishment of the Catholic see in 1850. The cathedral was begun in 1844 (in Chapel Street) and is ambitious indeed. Of the other Victorian churches none is of the first quality, though the chancel added to the Broughton Church by *J. E. Gregan* with *A. W. N. Pugin* in 1846 is of interest, lauded by the Ecclesiologists and hated by the bishop. St Clement, Ordsall, 1877–8 by *Austin & Paley* is good, but not their best, while the Greek Church of the Annunciation, Broughton is a fine classical building, one of the best works of *Clegg & Knowles.*

Salford was notorious for the slums of the C19, and it was the only authority (apart from Manchester) in SE Lancashire to build large-scale municipal housing at the turn of the C19 and C20. The New Barracks Estate in Ordsall by *Henry Lord,* though not fully realized, was more ambitious than Manchester's scheme, incorporating a lads' club and church (both privately financed) and an unexecuted public hall. The success of the Manchester Ship Canal had reverberations on the Salford side of the docks, but this was relatively short-lived. What prosperity there was during the C19 was not accompanied by development of financial and trading institutions – they were concentrated in Manchester, while wealthy bankers and industrialists favoured areas beyond, such as Pendlebury and Swinton (qq.v.), for the distribution of architectural largesse. The exception is the Art Gallery and Library, built in stages between 1845 and 1938, which was undertaken by the Corporation, and promoted by the art dealer and Mayor of Salford, Thomas Agnew, who gave generously to the collection. This progressive and early use of the Museums and Libraries Acts can be attributed to him and to Salford's first

M.P., Joseph Brotherton. The Royal Salford Technical Institute by *Henry Lord*, 1896, was the precursor to Salford University, formed in 1967. New buildings were put up from that time and recent developments include the Centenary Building by *Hodder Associates*, which won the 1996 Stirling Prize.

The squalor of the industrial age was replaced by poverty and deprivation in the post-industrial age. New housing was provided in tower blocks during the 1960s, often planted where the housing had been, so communities were kept together. Those at Pendleton are a striking sight, and efforts have been made recently to update them and to foster community spirit. At the end of the C20 the city was among the first to regenerate its docks with commercial, leisure and residential developments, starting in the 1980s and continuing with the promotion of the
126 spectacular Lowry arts centre (by *Michael Wilford* 1997–2000). Today the regeneration of the docks, now called Salford Quays, has proved a success, while the prosperity of Manchester has started to spill over the border of the central area as apartment blocks, cafés and bars begin to populate the area around Chapel Street.

Churches and public buildings are described first, then a perambulation covers the centre. Outlying areas follow, listed alphabetically. They are Broughton, Charlestown, Kersal, Ordsall, Pendleton, Salford Quays, and Weaste and Seedley.

CHURCHES

CATHEDRAL OF ST JOHN EVANGELIST (R.C.), Chapel Street. By *Matthew Hadfield* of *Weightman & Hadfield*, 1844–8, replacing an earlier chapel. A large and magnificent building by any standards, and one of the most ambitious R.C. churches of its day. A scale usually associated in these years with Pugin, who produced designs in 1842 but who later withdrew on 'a point of principle' (probably over the management of the contract). It became a cathedral in 1850. The design is based on three medieval churches, Newark, Nottinghamshire and Howden Minster and Selby Abbey, Yorkshire. There are reductions in scale, but many details are reproduced exactly, though it has been pointed out* that in some respects the building is closer to the illustrations in Edmund Sharpe's *Architectural Parallels*, where all three churches appear, than to the originals. Sharpe's book appeared only in 1848, but there may have been access to the engravings prior to that date. Contemporary criticism in *The Builder* suggested that it would have been better to cast the net wider for models. Despite the wholesale reproduction from a restricted range of sources, common in the 1840s, the design works well. Pale stone, cruciform, with a crossing steeple based on Newark but with the arcaded penultimate

---

*In the *Cathedrals of England* by Nikolaus Pevsner and Priscilla Metcalfe, 1985.

Salford, Cathedral of St John Evangelist (R.C.).
Engraving, 1872

stage of the tower missed out, and a spire of somewhat less noble proportions; otherwise all is copied exactly, including the triangular mouldings which link the windows. The W front to the street is symmetrical, the central entrance bay with a very tall Dec window flanked by pretty openwork spirelets, reprised at the corners of the aisles. This follows Howden, though with reduced proportions, so the window is without a lower transom.

INTERIOR. This has a bare look, owed partly to the 1983 reordering which needlessly removed much of the rich work in the chancel. The stonework is painted in magnolia and mush-room shades. Four-bay arcade of clustered shafts and high busy timber roof following Howden. The clerestory has deeply recessed windows between bare wall, implying but actually lacking the Howden wall passages. Stone vaulted chancel and chancel aisles, arcades with foliated caps, shorter and less rich than Selby is but with an exact reproduction of its E window, with lovely flowing tracery. Large STATUES beneath canopies above the piers.

A reordering by *Cassidy & Ashton* of Preston in 1972 made a new altar and sanctuary in the crossing, leaving the E end intact. In 1983 the pulpit, the high altar, side altars and other sanctuary furnishings, by *Weightman, Hadfield & Goldie*, 1853–5, were removed or altered. *George Goldie*'s gorgeous reredos was shorn off leaving only the base. Only the open-work stone SCREENS in the choir arcade survive. – The CHOIR FURNISHINGS carved by *Lane & Lewis* have been mutilated, though their bosses in the choir vault survive. – The Lee Chantry, NE, has an openwork stone SCREEN, a REREDOS with the Virgin, attendants and minstrel angels, and a canopied tomb, Daniel Lee †1877 with a BRASS by *Hardman*. The Leeming Chantry, SE, has a similar tomb, John Leeming †1858, also with a BRASS by *Hardman* and *Minton* tiles. – The Blessed Sacrament Chapel, S transept, is one of the only places where there is consistent richness in colour, materials and dec-oration. The fittings are by *P. P. Pugin*, 1884. Brown and pink marble ALTAR with a superbly carved recumbent effigy beneath, by *R. L. Boulton*. Panelling with PAINTING on a gold ground by *Joseph Alphege Pippett*, beautiful large TILES with the Pelican in her Piety. – METALWORK by *Hardman, Powell & Co.* A War Memorial Chapel on the E side of the N transept has many tablets recording the names of the dead, and a Pietà. Also in the N transept, W side, ALTAR of Mary Queen of the Most Holy Rosary, with much accomplished painting on a gold ground. – STAINED GLASS. E window by *William Wailes*, 1856. His typical bright glass, the Virgin and saints. S choir aisle, a window – by whom? Showing St Matthew, St John with a model of the cathedral, and St George. Below, Had-field on one side holds the plan and Goldie on the other has a drawing of the reredos. Both wear pink damask robes, looking like superior dressing-gowns, over their ordinary clothes. N aisle, a good First World War memorial window with St George, by *Barraclough & Sanders* of Lancaster.

Attached, a well-grouped range of Gothic OFFICES and a former SEMINARY around a courtyard E of the cathedral, added after 1872 by *George Goldie* in matching stone. Variety in gables and chimneys, with a very pretty timber-framed lantern at the angle. The E courtyard side is of three storeys with dormers. Windows to the first two levels are divided by blind stone arcading, each pair within a giant arch, expressing the presence within of an impressive double-height space, galleried on all sides, with a coffered ceiling. This was part of the seminary, now a bookshop and information centre.

ST PHILIP, St Philip's Place. By *Robert Smirke*, 1822–4. A Commissioners' church (cost £14,670). The steeple stands s but the church is oriented. Greek Revival style, reusing the design for Smirke's St Mary, Wyndham Place, London. The tower was also used for his St Anne, Wandsworth, and is based on a design by *Stephen Riou* published in 1768, according to Dr Ivan Hall. Semicircular porch with unfluted Ionic columns, balustraded parapet, round pilastered tower in diminishing stages, with a domed cap. Clock by *Whitehurst & Co.* of Derby, 1832. The body of the church has upper high-arched windows, small square windows below. To the w is a three-bay pediment, to the E a pedimented tripartite window. The interior has its three galleries, the frieze with wreaths. The upper order absurdly slender Greek Doric. Flat ceiling. A reordering was undertaken in 1895 by *J. Medland Taylor* when a platform was inserted into the chancel and choir furnishings introduced. – STAINED GLASS. Mid- to late C19 E window by *R.B. Edmundson & Son* of Manchester. First World War memorial window in SE chapel by *Humphries, Jackson & Ambler* of Manchester.

SACRED TRINITY, Chapel Street. Founded in 1634 by Humphrey Booth, who made his fortune from the textile trade, and died soon after it was consecrated in 1635. It began as a chapel of ease, and the parish was created in 1650. The w tower was the only part to escape rebuilding in 1752–3. The w window of course belongs to the Victorian restoration (by *Holden*, 1871–4). So do the bell-openings. The rest is a strange mixture of Gothic and classical motifs, shown in an engraving of 1741 and so nothing to do with the rebuilding. Triglyph frieze below the crenellated parapet and crocketed corner pinnacles, some of them replacing urns shown in 1741. A Victorian slated spirelet replaces a taller spire. Nave with two tiers of arched windows, with blocky capitals, the doorways with alternating rustication. At the E end is a niche, originally designed for a statue of Charles I. SE chapel of 1934 in matching style. (Three galleries, and unfluted Doric columns between them and the ceiling. Victorian timber roof. Short chancel.)

INDEPENDENT CHAPEL, Chapel Street. Dated 1819, set back from the street line, symmetrical and externally a well-preserved ensemble. One storey over a tall basement. Brick with a hipped roof. Stone steps divide into two branches and lead to a stone balustraded platform serving the two main entrances, which have radial fanlights.

PUBLIC BUILDINGS

SALFORD MAGISTRATES' COURT, Bexley Square. Built as a market hall by *Richard Lane*, 1825–7, and used as the town hall from 1835. The façade and first bay are Lane's work, the rest has been rebuilt at various times to suit the subsequent uses. This was Lane's first big commission, and as with all his Greek work he used Stuart and Revett's *Antiquities of Athens* as his source. This composition seems to be based partly on a Doric portico in Athens, illustrated in the book. The wreaths in the frieze, a favourite Lane motif, were perhaps suggested by another of his favourites, the Thrasyllic Monument, but the paterae show Lane at his most decorative – later designs are all more austere. The sides of the first bay have tripartite windows, then the additions, brick with stone dressings, in matching restrained classical style with windows in stone architraves. Inside a hall has Doric columns and stairs on each side of the entrance hall lead up to the central entrance to the upper room, framed by Corinthian columns. Extensions of 1862 were by *James Evans*, the Borough Surveyor, and further enlargements of 1874–5 by the Borough Engineer, *A. Fowler*. The interior has been altered and subdivided, preserving some of the ceilings with ornate plasterwork. Alongside the building an early C20 Baroque range with ancillary accommodation was designed by *J. W. Broadbent*.

SALFORD EDUCATION OFFICES, Chapel Street. Dated 1895, by *Woodhouse & Willoughby*. Imposing, high and large, faced with yellow terracotta. The façade is in the French Renaissance style, not quite symmetrical, with a corner turret, E end. Three storeys with a central entrance.

GAS BOARD OFFICES (former), Bloom Street. Dated 1880, and closely based on Thomas Worthington's work in Manchester of the 1860s and 1870s (the Police Courts, Minshull Street, p. 287 and Nicholls Hospital, p. 361), though it seems more florid and slightly coarser in detail. No evidence has been found for Worthington's involvement. European Gothic, symmetrical, powerful central tower with pyramid roof and corner tourelles, like the Nicholls Hospital tower. The forceful beast gargoyles are typical of Worthington too.

COURT HOUSE (former), Encombe Place and Upper Cleminson Street. Of *c.* 1860–5, probably by *Charles Reeves* and his pupil *Thomas Charles Sorby*, successive Surveyors of the County Courts. A dignified seven-bay front with alternatingly pedimented first-floor windows. The ground floor is rusticated stone, with semicircular heads to the openings. The entrances on this side were for the public, s, and the judge, N. Upper two floors of brick with stone dressings, the five windows at the s end blind as they fronted the lower part of the court-room. Well finished with some individual details, e.g. the volutes in the architraves of the upper-floor windows. Sorby's involvement can be detected in the pediments on first-floor windows, the masks over the entrance and the curved walls of the courtroom, features of his other buildings. The interior was greatly altered in 1928 when open-plan offices were created on the ground floor and the courtroom subdivided. Further alterations followed in 1985. The building was closed in 1992 and later converted to offices.

LIBRARY, MUSEUM AND ART GALLERY. Salford was one of the pioneering local authorities in adopting the Museums Act of 1845 and Public Libraries Act of 1850. It bought Lark Hill mansion in 1845 for a new museum and public library, of which Queen Victoria and Prince Albert were patrons. The main promoters were the Salford M.P. Joseph Brotherton and Mayor Edward Langworthy. The library was the first free local authority library in the country, and the museum among the first of its type. The sequence of building after that was as follows. The N wing and staircase were added by *Travis & Mangnall* in 1853. The S wing, also by them, followed in 1857, and in 1878 the W wing was added by *Henry Lord*. A new E wing was built by *W.A. Walker* and *R.G. Morgan* of the Salford City Engineers' Department in 1936–8 on the site of the mansion, which was demolished.

The building presents a unified whole in appearance because later additions, including the 1930s wing, followed the 1853 building in style, fairly low-key Renaissance in red brick with stone dressings. The main front is thus symmetrical, with projecting entrance bays on each side with arcaded porticoes, to library, r. and gallery, l. Public galleries were essentially a new building type, so the architects looked for precedents from the private sphere. Travis & Mangnall, as *The Builder* records, based their design on the gallery of Lord Northwick at Thirlestaine House, Cheltenham, which was described by a critic in 1853 as being one of only two worthwhile galleries in England. The same type of sloping window above a cove was later used by Waterhouse for the Natural History Museum; though the design was probably derived from Barry's reconstruction of the Hunterian Museum at the Royal College of Surgeons, London, of the 1830s. The architects at Salford may have been introduced to Northwick's gallery by the art dealer Thomas Agnew, who became Mayor of Salford in 1851 and was a leading collector of contemporary British art. He gave generously to the collection and would have known Northwick, who shared his interests. Apart from a new stair in the l. part and a tea room, both late C20, the galleries are largely unaltered at upper level, with flat ceilings, sloping coves with plaster enrichment, and the windows above, now blocked. The MUSEUM incorporates a reconstructed street, Lark Hill Place, with shops and shop fronts, many made up from C18 and C19 buildings being torn down nearby in 1953. It opened in 1957 and was augmented through local demolitions until the mid 1960s. It was influenced by Kirkgate at the Castle Museum in York, built in 1938 for John Kirk's collections, but unlike others it has remained virtually untouched and is one of the earliest and most interesting examples of the type.*

*According to William Longshaw.

WORKING CLASS MOVEMENT LIBRARY, Acton Square, opposite the University. A former nurses' home, by *Henry Lord*, 1897–1901. An attractive eclectic composition with timbered gables, a tall channelled chimney, and bays with pretty looping parapets with crown motifs in terracotta. In 1987 it was converted to accommodate the library of Ruth and Edmund Frow, Communist bibliophiles, who had built up a large and important collection of material relating to the labour movement, with special emphasis on Britain and the North West.

CITY POLICE HEADQUARTERS, The Crescent and Albion Square. By *Bradshaw, Gass & Hope*, brick and Portland stone, in proud municipal Neo-Georgian, opened in 1957. The design could as well have been 1937. Symmetrical to the square with a portico and a pedimented tripartite window within a round-arched opening.

FIRE STATION (former), Albion Place. By *H. Kirkley*, opened in 1902. Now used as exhibition galleries. The main office range faces N over the square. Red brick and buff terracotta, central shaped gable with a clockface.

ROYAL SALFORD HOSPITAL (former), Chapel Street. The institution originated as a dispensary in 1827 and moved to this site three years later. It was extended in 1865 and additions were made thereafter. Nothing seems to be left of the earlier buildings, and the hospital suffered extensive bomb damage in the war. What survives from before then is the Pendlebury Wing, opened in 1885, by *Henry Lord*. Red brick with stone dressings, three tall storeys, modestly Queen Anne. On Chapel Street the varied roofline has pedimented dormers on either side of a central ornate Dutch gable. The bold Doric portico attached to the r. was repositioned and rebuilt, probably when mid-C20 extensions were made following war damage. Converted to flats, 2001–2, by *Provan & Makin*.

TRINITY BRIDGE, Chapel Wharf. A footbridge over the River Irwell linking Salford with Manchester. By *Santiago Calatrava*, 1993–5, his only executed work in Britain so far. It is similar to his Alamillo Bridge in Seville, i.e. with a deck supported by stainless steel cables from a sloping pylon, but much smaller in scale and correspondingly more airy and lightweight. It is white, standing out from the dark tunnel of the riverside here, with a great sense of tension and dynamism. Springing from the Salford side, the pylon is flanked by spiralling ramps and pulled at an angle towards land as it supports deck and ramps with a system of cable stays. The deck narrows and rises slightly towards the Manchester side.

For Greengate Baths, *see* Perambulation, p. 626.

UNIVERSITY OF SALFORD

The University originated as the Royal Salford Technical Institute in 1896. In 1956 one part was redesignated as a college of advanced technology, the other remaining a technical college. In 1967 the former became the University of Salford. The technical college, which had moved to premises on Frederick Road, to the w, became University College Salford in 1992. Finally the two institutions merged in 1996.

The campus is shared with the Library and Art Gallery complex (*see* above) and encroaches upon Peel Park (*see* below). w of the Library, end-on to the Crescent, is the original Technical Institute building by *Henry Lord*, opened in 1896. Long, three-storeyed, Renaissance style, all in hot red Ruabon brick and red terracotta. The main front overlooks lawns in front of the Art Gallery. Symmetrical, with a grand entrance bay and varied roofline of gables and chimneys. The building is 'lifted' and given stature by the fine terracotta panels with reliefs by *Earp, Son & Hobbs*. Over the entrance allegories of Art and Science, at the top of the entrance bay a large panel with five figures representing Arts and Sciences. Panels on either side represent scientific work, building and engineering. On the side elevation to the road, female figures representing spinning and weaving. In the grounds in front of the building a terracotta GAZEBO also by *Lord*, erected to conceal a ventilation outlet duct from the laboratories in the Institute building.

Other buildings to note are as follows. The first post-war addition was the MAXWELL BUILDING, by *C. H. Simmons* of the *Lancashire County Architects Department*, 1959–60, large and restless with a lower part linked by a bridge to a long angled block, e of the art gallery. To the NW a straightforward tower block (Chemistry) designed *c.* 1960 by *Courtauld's Architectural Department*. 1970s additions were mainly by *W. F. Johnson*, including the MYERS BUILDING, a cluster of low octagonal blocks in the far NW part of the site. The CHAPMAN CENTRE, lecture theatres, also NW, has a South Bank look about it. Low massive windowless shapes in grey concrete.

The original buildings of the TECHNICAL COLLEGE lie further w at the corner of The Crescent and Frederick Road, properly speaking in Pendleton. Straightforward high blocks fronted by a big cantilevered lecture theatre, all by *Halliday Meecham*, 1963–7. In the courtyard aggressive totemic concrete SCULPTURES by *William Mitchell*, 1967.

The only other building of note is outlying to the e on the Adelphi Campus just off Adelphi Street: the CENTENARY BUILDING by *Hodder Associates* (1994–5), recipient of the first Stirling Prize in 1996. It consist of three parts, a four-storey block facing e containing studios and seminar rooms, a three-storey strip of staff and teaching rooms, and a w-facing block with lecture theatres, studios, etc. Parts of the end walls have rendered expanses, typical of Hodder's other work. The rest is glazing interrupted by dull grey panels. The N entrance façade with strong curving forms and angled swooping forms, with grey cladding and much glass, is crowned by a brise-soleil. The clear outward expression of form is what gives it punch.

PEEL PARK was established at public expense as part of a single enterprise in Manchester and Salford, along with the formation of Queen's Park, Harpurhey (p. 395) and Philips Park, Bradford, Manchester (p. 569). All were designed by *Joshua Major & Son* who won the competition, all were opened in 1846. The land for Peel Park included the late C18 Lark Hill mansion and its grounds (*see* Library, Museum and Art Gallery, above). The park seems always to have been designated by Salford Corporation as the site for other municipal endeavours – hence the foundation of a museum, art gallery and library – while the Technical Institute was built nearby in 1896 (*see* above). Subsequently the buildings of Salford University, successor to the Institute, encroached upon the park. In consequence only the area N of the campus has the character of a public park, and relatively little of the original design survives. The STATUES in front of the art gallery were moved from the park. Both are by *Matthew Noble*: Prince Albert, 1864, and Queen Victoria, 1857, on tall pedestals.

PERAMBULATION

This is rather a long walk, but one which takes in most of the churches and public buildings listed above. We start at the River Irwell on Blackfriars Street. For Blackfriars Bridge, *see* Manchester centre, p. 304. The buildings of interest are mainly on the W side. Towering above everything, HIGHLAND HOUSE, former tax offices, is by *Leach, Rhodes & Walker*, 1966. Reclad and converted to apartments *c.* 2000. A straightforward job, with funnel-like windows giving it a bit of character. Next GUARDIAN CHAMBERS, dated 1901. Much buff terracotta work in the gable and beneath the triangular pediments of the second floor. The date 1878 presumably commemorates an earlier building. No. 24, the former CROWN TAVERN, is early C19, with a late C19 pub front following the original ground-floor openings. Next on this side Nos. 14–16, the former DE JERSEY WAREHOUSE, dated 1866. By *Clegg & Knowles*, and typical of them. Red brick and stone dressings, openings with stilted arched heads and a prominent cornice. No. 10 is the former BAERLIN'S WAREHOUSE, by *Oldham & Wilson* of Manchester, 1877–9. The most distinguished of the group, quite unlike the usual Manchester warehouse type of this date, for which a palazzo style was almost universal. Sandstone ashlar, eclectic with Flemish Renaissance and Tudor features. Five storeys and an attic. Octagonal piers divide the five narrow bays and rise above the parapet and gable to finish with heraldic finials, giving strong vertical emphasis. Transomed windows, with oriels in the first and second storeys of the end bays, where the offices were. Fourth-floor centre bay gabled, all topped by a big elaborate Dutch gable with paired traceried

Salford, Baerlin's warehouse, from *Building News*, 1884

windows and blind tracery, culminating in an ornate finial. The fine carving is by *E. Williams*.

Crossing busy Chapel Street, note on the N side the former POLICE STATION, 1888–9 by *Arthur Jacob*, Borough Engineer. Red brick with terracotta dressings, making a show on the street corner with a circular slated turret. Passing Sacred Trinity Church (*see* above), continue N along Blackfriars Street beneath railway viaducts. Here the interest is all on the W side. SOLMAR HOUSE is a commercial warehouse of *c.* 1870 in the Manchester style, four storeys over a raised basement, red brick with stone dressings, ornate stone doorways. A little further N the former MISSION HOUSE and CLERGY HOUSE of Sacred Trinity Church, dated 1898. Spare, in red brick; three bays, that to the r. with paired ground-floor windows and an oriel; narrow off-centre entrance bay; three hipped dormers. Adjoining is the former SACRED TRINITY SCHOOL with datestones of 1891 and 1892. By *J. Medland Taylor*. Good in a stripped way, three storeys over a high basement with an arcade of wide round-arched windows, gabled roofline and tall chimneys. Next BLACKFRIARS BATHS (former), built for Salford Corporation in 1879–80 by the Borough Engineers *Brockbank & Wormall*. Red brick and terracotta with Renaissance motifs, symmetrical with a central entrance flanked by arcades of small round-headed windows, central raised gable. There were pools for women as well as men, an innovation in the public baths of the Manchester and Salford neighbourhood.

89   Adjacent is THE SALFORD TENNIS AND RACQUETS CLUB by *G. T. Redmayne*, opened in 1880, using designs prepared in 1876. The courts are for real tennis and racquets, and there is only a handful of other examples in the country. Red brick, terracotta dressings, gabled and domestic in character. The interruption to the upper part of the projecting entrance bay is due to insertion of a squash court in 1925–6, the only major alteration and itself early of its type. The interior is a delight, with a grand entrance and staircase hall, club rooms, dining room, changing rooms etc. as well as extensive wine cellars. The double-height tennis court has a gallery on one side, the dedans behind the server's end and a tambour at the opposite end, forming a sort of cloister arrangement. There is an opening known as a grille behind the receiver's end. Both this and the double-height racquets court have upper viewing galleries. The court layout does not substantially differ from the earliest surviving C16 example at Hampton Court, Middlesex. A skittles alley complete with original fittings is sited in a narrow space behind the tennis court. Last on Blackfriars Road, on the corner with Trinity Way, the characterful BLACK FRIAR pub. Dated 1886; by *William Ball*. Red brick, red sandstone dressings, with Arts and Crafts touches such as the tiled gables, lettered friezes and stone carvings of friars. Gabled bays with tripartite windows flank a bay with a first-floor stone oriel.

A detour may be taken here NE along Queen Street and N along Caygill Street to Collier Street, for GREENGATE BATHS by *Thomas Worthington*, 1854–5. The Manchester and Salford Baths and Laundries Co., formed in 1854, commissioned Worthington to design three public baths. This is the only one left, and one of the earliest surviving purpose-built public baths in the country. A powerful rhythmic Italianate façade. The interior has been altered, but surviving original roofs are supported by laminated timber trusses on cast-iron brackets. Opposite the baths the EAGLE INN is a good unspoiled example of a late C19 back-street pub, with a shaped-gable centre and a terracotta plaque with an eagle over the entrance.

Returning to Blackfriars Road, we retrace our steps to CHAPEL STREET, and then follow it westward. On the S side the rear of the huge Lowry Hotel and Aldine House can be seen. Turning down Dearman's Place gives views of both from

Santiago Calatrava's TRINITY BRIDGE (*see* public buildings). The LOWRY HOTEL, by *Consarc* 2001–2, has a big concave glazed front. ALDINE HOUSE, by *Leach, Rhodes & Walker*, 1967, is one of their best buildings, a group of tall white concrete office blocks with funnel-like windows around a little two-storey pavilion clad in black polished granite. Return to Chapel Street and continue beneath the railway viaduct to look along Cook Street, N side, at the former Chester's Brewery (now called the DEVA CENTRE following conversion to offices, late 1990s). By *W. A. Deighton*, dated 1896. The most striking element is the massive five-storey tower with a hipped roof topped by a raised pavilion-like turret. Lower office ranges, boiler house, etc. Continuing w takes us past the Independent Chapel (*see* above) to Bloom Street. On the r., SALFORD HOUSE is a large former model lodging house for men, by the Borough Engineer *Joseph Corbett*, 1890–4, enjoying a very different lease of life as luxury flats since 2000. Plain, brick with some sparing decoration, e.g. bands of patterned terracotta. Two gabled four-storey wings on each side of a lower gabled entrance block with the Salford arms and the legend 'Salford Corporation Model Lodging House'. The former warden's house, of three storeys, is attached on the NW side. (For the former Gas Offices *see* Public Buildings, above.)

Return to Chapel Street. Immediately opposite Bloom Street is New Bailey Street, just s of Chapel Street, crossed by three impressive RAILWAY VIADUCTS. The N one is of 1894 by *William Hunt*, engineer, for the Lancashire & Yorkshire Railway. Cast-iron columns, parapet with fluted pilasters and swags. The middle one is also for the Lancashire & Yorkshire, 1865, by *Sturges Meek*. Doric columns carrying a deck with a plain panelled parapet. The s one is by *Sir John Hawkshaw*, engineer, for the Liverpool & Manchester Railway, 1844. An impressively long stretch supported by enormous cast-iron columns with lotus-leaf capitals. Where the bridge crosses the street itself the bridge parapet has fluted pilasters with acanthus capitals.

Continue w along Chapel Street. After the busy Trinity Way, the former SALFORD CINEMA, N side, is dated 1915, and so is a relatively early example. It is on the site of a mid-C19 Presbyterian church, and reuses the stone rear wall of that building. Baroque, with an entrance under a big open cupola. The balcony has been divided off but the stalls survive with seating of *c.* 1930. Almost opposite, is the former WILLIAMS DEACON'S BANK of *c.* 1880, ashlar-faced and Gothic much à la Manchester. Corner brackets with sunflower motifs. Continuing along the busy road takes us past the Magistrates' Court, Education Offices, Roman Catholic Cathedral and St Philip's Church (*see* above). ENCOMBE PLACE lies immediately N of the church. A row of four three-storey brick houses of the early C19 with steps up to doors with Ionic cases. An elegant adjunct to the square, which has on its w side the former Court House (*see* Public Buildings, above).

DREADFUL ACCIDENT AT MANCHESTER.

Salford, Islington Mill collapse, engraving, 1824

Back on Chapel Street, the MANCHESTER AND SALFORD
SAVINGS BANK, N side, proclaims itself in a lettered frieze.
Dated 1885. Central oriel, and entrance with a triangular
pediment offset to the r. It replaced premises established in
1877. A short detour s down William Wroe Street to James
Street is required to see ISLINGTON MILL, on the corner of
Factory Lane. A six-storey cast-iron-framed fireproof mill for
cotton-spinning, put up in 1823 by the builder *David Bellhouse*.
External engine house, warehouse, offices and stables. A
second mill on the rear (w) part of the site, erected slightly
later, has been partially rebuilt. Islington Mill is important in
the history of mill construction for the highly publicized partial
collapse in 1824, caused by the failure of cast-iron beams,
which has been credited with delaying widespread introduction of fireproof construction in the textile industry.

Beside the mill on Oldfield Road the SALVATION ARMY
SOCIAL SERVICES CENTRE (originally the Stella Maris
Seamen's Hostel and Club), is by *Desmond Williams & Associates*, 1966. Good. Dark purple brick and exposed concrete.
Long low podium, the horizontals accentuated by a recessed
window strip. Three storeys above it, of which the upper two,
housing the accommodation, are cantilevered out.

Turning N along Oldfield Road leads back to Chapel Street. On
the corner a WAR MEMORIAL commemorates Lancashire

Fusiliers who fell in South Africa, 1899–1902. An evocative bronze figure of a soldier on a tall plinth by *George Frampton*. Turning w brings us to THE CRESCENT, a continuation of Chapel Street. The late C19 BLACK HORSE pub, s side, has enjoyable carvings in the ground-floor keystones: a black-smithing trophy, heads of a horse, a satyr and Bacchus. Then Georgian Salford comes at last into its own, with an unbroken row of houses and terraces overlooking a loop of the river across the road to the N. The Crescent, the adjoining Albion Place, and other streets in the area were laid out and the first leases were issued in 1793. The land had been left to the trustees of the Booth Charity by Humphrey Booth, grand-son of the charity's founder, in 1672. By 1801 twenty-two ninety-nine-year leases had been created. Restrictive covenants on the positioning and building materials applied, and the use of stone doorcases and of sash windows was specified.* Start-ing at the E end, No. 17 is a large brick house with a project-ing entrance bay and steps up to a pilastered doorcase. On each side single-storey bays with wide arches over inserted openings. Next a terrace of three with pedimented doorcases (one removed), roughcast, now used as a pub. There follows a whole long, stepped, curved terrace of houses with enjoyable doorways, most partially or wholly rebuilt in the conversion to offices. Beyond the terrace is Albion Place, where a Lancashire Fusiliers FIRST WORLD WAR MEMOR-IAL stands outside the old Fire Station, 1922 by *J. & H. Patteson*. Portland stone pedestal with the word 'Egypt' sur-mounted by a sphinx, symbol of the regiment. We are now opposite the University (*see* above). Continue w for ACTON SQUARE, where there are a number of brick early C19 houses. Three of them facing on to The Crescent; another is JOULE HOUSE, home of the scientist James Prescott Joule, facing on to the square, with a projecting Ionic porch.

OUTER SALFORD

1. Broughton

On rising land w of the centre alongside the meandering River Irwell.

ASCENSION, Church Road. 1869 by *J. Medland Taylor*. Big, tow-erless, and a little bleak. Brick with brick tracery and some brick patterns. Chancel with chapels and apsidal end. The w end has a porch flanked by two big flying buttresses. Above, blind arcading and a large rose window. The aisles have triple lancets alternating with paired windows with plate tracery. (Very plain interior which has lost most of the original fittings.

---

* These details are based on research by Jane Foster of Chetham's Library.

Circular piers, hammerbeam roof. – REREDOS with mosaic panels.)

ST JOHN EVANGELIST, Murray Street. By *Richard Lane*, 1836–9. Chancel 1846 by *J. E. Gregan*, probably in collaboration with *A. W. N. Pugin*. Between the two lies the conversion to archaeological conformity. Lane's is a typical, if cheap, example of his early C19 churches. Ashlar. W tower with very tall slim bell-openings and graceless pinnacles, flanked by porches with pitched roofs. They, the body of the church, and the tower have battlements. The way in which the pitch of the nave roof and the pitch of the porch bay roofs coincide is unusual. The nave has long windows with minimum Perp details. The chancel is an abrupt change, rock-faced rubble with Dec windows. Vestries on each side; that to the S of 1896 replaced the original. Inside, the galleries have gone, which accentuates the height and slenderness of the octagonal stone piers of the six-bay nave arcade. A late C20 partition divides the two easternmost bays of the nave from the remainder, which is to be converted for community use. Gallery stairs with traceried balustrades and wreathed rails.

The chancel is a good set-piece despite the loss of some furnishings. It was paid for by the incumbent, Thomas Baynes, and received a very favourable notice in *The Ecclesiologist*. It is not possible to be certain of the extent of *Pugin*'s involvement, but the arrangements and detailing are typical of him. Subsequently it became the subject of a furious row between Bishop Prince Lee and the churchwardens, which was conducted partly through the letters page of the *Manchester Guardian* and was notorious enough to become the subject of an editorial.* The affair is an early instance of disagreement between a High Church parish and a bishop over religious imagery in which Pugin was involved, though the record suggests he tried to distance himself from it. *The Ecclesiologist* reported that the bishop exploded in anger on his visit, flinging down altar cloths and dashing ornaments to the floor. He later denounced the chancel furnishings as 'all copied duly from Romish artists'. The churchwardens angrily refuted suggestions of popery, but the piscina was removed in 1850, and tiles with Marian symbols were taken up. Stepped SEDILIA on the S side.

Elaborate traceried REREDOS with an Agnus Dei flanked by very unusual majolica tile PANELS with embossed lettering, Decalogue, Creed, Lord's Prayer. By *Minton* with borders designed by *Pugin*. – Beautiful *Minton* TILES, with Agnus Dei symbols and emblems of the Evangelists, derived, according to Minton, from examples found at Tintern Abbey and elsewhere, and not, as the bishop suggested, copied from Pugin's designs. – STAINED GLASS by *Hardman*, recorded in 1849 and therefore designed by *Pugin*. The bishop expressed the hope that the windows would be broken by boys, and his wish has come true. They are all damaged, some badly. E window,

---

* Meriel Boyd gave me the information on this episode.

Christ surrounded by the apostles with eucharistic symbols and Agnus Dei; s side Adoration with a crowned Virgin. This motif was also singled out for condemnation by the bishop, but Hardman refused to remove it. Other chancel windows have angels with scrolls, an Annunciation and a *Noli Me Tangere* (badly damaged). In the nave mid-C19 glass by *William Wailes* and *Charles Gibbs.* w internal window, late C19 by *Kempe.*– MONUMENT. On the N side of the sanctuary. John Clowes †1846 (*see* also below). Tomb recess with a florid crocketed and ogee-arched canopy, at first sight like an Easter sepulchre. By *MrWright* of Nottingham, but was he the carver or the designer? Any functional connection with an Easter sepulchre was hotly denied by the churchwardens.

St James, Great Cheetham Street East. 1879 by *Paley & Austin*. Of light brick, with a tall bellcote at the E end of the nave. Brick window tracery. Nave windows with pointed arches, chancel windows with flat heads and tracery with lobed quatrefoils. It is a good building, but not outstanding, as Paley & Austin's can be. Their distinctive touch is seen in the impressively sheer gables and large expressive buttresses breaking through the roof to mark the position of the chancel. The large brick VICARAGE to the E must also be by them.

CONGREGATIONAL CHURCH, Upper Park Road. 1874–5 by *S. W. Dawkes*. The style is late C13. Of stone, large and elaborate, with an exceptionally high and well-proportioned SW steeple, tricked out with ornate gablets and lucarnes. Aisles, transepts, chancel chapels, the s one with an apse. Generous windows with variety in the treatment of the tracery, and a change of mood for the chancel, which is busy with continuous arcades of lancets. Converted to flats 2002–3, when rows of dormers were inserted.

GREEK CHURCH OF THE ANNUNCIATION, Bury New Road. 1860–1 by *Clegg & Knowles*, better known for their commercial warehouses in Manchester city centre. A demonstration of the wealth of the C19 Greek community. Elegant, powerful and purposeful, making a great show. Strictly classical, with a three-bay Corinthian portico and Corinthian pilasters along the sides, and windows with pediments. The carving is uncommonly carefully done, perhaps by *Simpkin & Stewart* who worked on some of the firm's Manchester warehouses. Inside, the piers and the roof are mid-C20, installed following a fire. The original polygonal apse appears oddly behind.

St Boniface (R.C.), Gerald Road. By *Mather & Nutter*, 1960–1. Brick and concrete. Saddleback tower, vertical window strips continued as openwork bell-openings. Entrance block with zigzag roof.

UKRAINIAN CATHOLIC CHURCH, Bury Old Road, a former Nonconformist chapel dated 1881. Low entrance range flanked by single-storey octagonal pavilions, the main body behind with a flèche and windows with minimal tracery.

NORTH SALFORD SYNAGOGUE, Vine Street. Converted from a mid–late C19 villa in 1953 using fittings from a demolished

synagogue. Large, brick, and rather plain, with a windowless
E wall with canted bay for the Ark. Canted entrance bay,
arched doorway with granite columns.

SWIMMING BATHS, Great Cheetham Street West. By *Scott,
Brownrigg & Turner*, 1967. The dominating feature is the deep,
flat roof which contains the air-conditioning plant, treated as
a great dark cornice, with a group of glass pyramids on top. It
is supported by slender piers, and a bold entrance bridge
connects pavement level with the first floor.

VICTORIA THEATRE (former), Great Clowes Street. By *Bertie
Crewe*, 1899. Baroque, in red terracotta with red brick. Relatively pedestrian outside, but said to have a splendid interior
with elaborate plasterwork festoons, cherubs, musical instruments, etc. and two levels of boxes with Corinthian columns.

PENDLETON CO-OPERATIVE INDUSTRIAL SOCIETY SHOPS
(former), Wellington Street West. Dated 1907, unmistakably
by *A. H. Walsingham*. Decoration is concentrated on the
octagonal corner tower. A round top and a steep conical roof,
banding and decorative detail in red, green and yellow terracotta.

HOUSES. Broughton, especially Higher Broughton, to the N, was
an area of gentlemen's houses and villas in the early C19 and
remained popular through the C19. The area known as the
Cliff, at the top of Lower Broughton Road, offered picturesque surroundings overlooking the River Irwell, and a few
early to mid-C19 examples survive there. Large mid-Victorian
houses abounded along main routes, but there have been many
losses.

BROUGHTON PARK. A villa estate laid out by the Rev. John
Clowes, a noted gardener and botanist, *c.* 1840–5. The Clowes
family came into possession through marriage to a Chetham
in 1769. Broughton Park has winding streets, centred on
Clowes Park, the site of the demolished mansion, but hardly
any of the early houses survive. One is Broughton House on
PARK STREET, probably 1860s, very large and Italianate, the
service part with a tall tower. One or two later houses to note,
e.g. No. 19 BRANTWOOD ROAD, Art Deco with a flat roof and
bold rounded bays, including a smaller central one over the
entrance, all done in bright orange brick. On HANOVER
GARDENS attractive terraces with full-height polygonal bays,
low roofs and entrances with columns, all with an Arts and
Crafts accent, 1930s and attributed to *Joseph Sunlight*.* No. 26
OLD HALL LANE is the best of the interwar houses, a dashing
Moderne composition with an expressive curved porch canopy
and recessed curving bays, flat roofs and some original
windows.

BURY NEW ROAD. Nos. 393–407. A dignified early to mid-C19

* By Dr Sharman Kadish.

classical terrace, three storeys, stuccoed, with prominent quoins. Near the junction with Singleton Road is a former TOLL HOUSE, a little Tudor-style single-storey house, stuccoed and gabled with flat hoodmoulds.

GREAT CLOWES STREET. Some large early to mid-C19 houses, mainly on the stretch between Great Cheetham Street and Broughton Lane. Most are classical, most derelict. The severe stone Nos. 258–260 is of *c.* 1830. Stately in scribed stucco and with good proportions, with large Ionic porticoes.

LOWER BROUGHTON ROAD. The best group of houses in the area. Starting near the s end, the mid-Victorian CASTLE GREEN, E side, is given a fantastic appearance by the emphatic crenellated top and crowstepped gables. A little further along on the other side is COTSWOLD TERRACE, probably early C20 and notable for the close-studded timbered front. On the opposite side are the earliest houses of the street, Nos. 388–390, set back at an angle. A pair of gabled brick houses, looking mid C19; but No. 388 is partially timber-framed, and so probably C17. Continue N for No. 435, SCAR WHEEL HOUSE, w side, an impressive Neo-Tudor house of *c.* 1840, asymmetrical, with very steep gables. The porch has a traceried parapet, and even the tall projecting chimney has traceried panels. Single-storey rear bay with pinnacles and quatrefoil cresting. The neighbouring No. 437 is in contrast classical, probably of similar date. Stuccoed, with a pilastered bay and large Greek anthemion motifs in plaster over the lower windows. The most noticeable thing about the early to mid-C19 No. 451 is the coach house with a Gothic arcaded corbel table and niches. The main house is more restrained, and stuccoed. Further along is a little terrace (w side), Nos. 453–455, early C19 and very plain, with heavy architraves and doorcases with slender Tuscan pilasters. Beside them to the N, is CLIFF HOUSE in similar style. More early and mid-C19 houses follow as the road rises to the N, including the stone Italianate No. 464 and Gothic houses of the 1840s.

RADFORD ROAD. No. 10 is ornate Early Victorian, asymmetrical, with an entrance recessed between gabled bays, and plasterwork festoons.

2. Charlestown

NW of the centre.

ST GEORGE, Whit Lane. 1858, by *E. H. Shellard*. The tower and broach spire remain. Yellow sandstone and remarkable only as a landmark.

PENDLETON CO-OPERATIVE INDUSTRIAL SOCIETY SHOPS (former), Gerald Road. Dated 1909; originally the Society's butchery department. The largest and most elaborate of the early C20 Co-op shops in Salford and North Manchester. Resplendent in red brick with liberal yellow and green terracotta, typical work of *A. H. Walsingham*. The street elevations meet at an angled corner with an octagonal domed tower. Gables on each side with upper rows of round-headed windows, roof with lantern and cupola.

3. Kersal

NW of the centre. The hamlet of Kersal was given to Lenton Priory, a Cluniac house in Notts., in the mid C12. The cell was dedicated to St Leonard and seems to have consisted of a prior and one or two monks. Buildings described as a chapel and priory were extant in the mid C18 on low-lying land off Littleton Road, beside the Irwell, but they had been demolished by c. 1800. A number of worked stones discovered on the site during the 1980s, including fragments of rib-vaulting, were ascribed mainly to the late C12–C13 and the C15. Kersal Moor is an area of high open land N and NW of the river on the Bury boundary. It was the site of fairs, race meetings and various sports from the C17.

St Paul, Moor Lane. By *A. Trimen*, 1852. A church of great archaeological ambition, with ostentatious use of irregular masonry (one can only imagine the bemusement of the masons), and grouping of windows of E.E., Dec and Perp styles to suggest different building campaigns. Transepts. Ornate W tower with recessed spire, and a stair-turret crowned by a spirelet. The sources are Magdalen Tower, Oxford, and Carisbrooke Parish Church, Isle of Wight,* evident in the treatment of the turret and paired bell-openings. Badly damaged by fire in 1987 with loss of the clerestory. Repairs and rebuilding were done by *Downs & Variava*. The new roof swoops out oddly over the S transept. The interior has been subdivided, leaving the E end for the church, the remainder for meeting rooms etc. Arcades of octagonal piers. – Stone traceried REREDOS, flanked by MOSAIC panels by *Walter J. Pearce*. – STAINED GLASS. An extensive scheme installed in 1949 by *Whitefriars* was decimated in the fire. The only complete surviving window is in the N transept, the Crucifixion. Fragments and parts of scenes have been reset in the windows elsewhere. Good E window, early C20 probably by *Shrigley & Hunt*. – MONUMENT. Jonathan Tong †1881, tablet with marble surround, beautifully lettered.

Kersal Cell, Littleton Road. A three-bay cruck-framed house of the early C16, demonstrating of the persistence of this form of construction in Lancashire even in a fairly substantial dwelling. The exact relationship with the priory is unknown, and since dendrochronology suggests a date somewhat before the Dissolution it is possible that it was either an administrative building of the priory or the home of an individual who had leased land from it. Three of the four original crucks

* I am grateful to Nell Darlington for this information.

survive, some of them mutilated, the blades resting on stone footings. The building was remodelled, probably in the mid or late C16, when cross-wings at either end were added and the hall enlarged by rebuilding an internal wall W of the original bay division. This was probably undertaken by the Kenyon family who bought the property in 1548. Damaged remains of wall paintings on both sides of the inserted wall are probably of late C16 date. A C17 plasterwork frieze at the W end of the hall has a pattern of trails, with beasts' heads and water creatures such as dragonflies, toads, newts and fish. The upper chamber has heraldic plasterwork including arms of the Byroms and the date 1692, when that family acquired the building from the Kenyons. Converted to apartments, 1990s.

4. Ordsall

An area SW of the centre, characterized mainly by clearances for late C20 low-rise housing.

ST CLEMENT, Hulton Street. 1877–8 by *Austin & Paley*. Stock brick, with a tall slated flèche on the E end of the nave. Three-light windows in the aisles, the clerestory with much bare wall and small circular windows, alternately sexfoils and stars. The tracery is all of *c.* 1300. Austin & Paley's individuality is seen mainly in the E and W ends, where there is interplay between the forms and contrast between the bare and decorated surfaces. The W front, owing to clearances, is the most visible and striking part today. A complex composition framed by two forceful buttresses stepping up in five rhythmic stages. Gabled porch with two segmental-headed portals, and above three stepped windows under one blank arch. In the gable a grid of quatrefoils in terracotta. The E end also has stepped buttresses and a window beneath a blank arch. To the side a pretty stair-turret with a blind arcade of lancets and a conical roof. (High and spacious interior, now with a module in the nave inserted by *Hayes, Turner, Buttress & Partners*, 1980. Round piers, and brick all exposed above. The chancel is brick-vaulted with moulded ribs. – Elaborate REREDOS and PANELS. Murals executed in *Doulton* tiles. – Tripartite SEDILIA.) Attached at the E end, the VICARAGE, also by *Austin & Paley*. Large, brick, with mullioned windows with arched heads.

ST IGNATIUS OF ANTIOCH, St Ignatius Way. By *Darbyshire & Smith*, 1900. Connected with the development of the area for municipal housing (*see* below). Stock brick and red terracotta. Italian Romanesque, with a wealth of detail in friezes and arcading. Big detached SW tower with a deeply recessed and shafted entrance and a pyramid roof. Another less elaborate entrance in the nave, W end. The interior has been subdivided at the chancel arch. Five-bay round-arched red sandstone nave arcade, piers with cushion capitals on high bases. Two-bay chancel where the piers are of red granite, round apse. Attached VICARAGE in restrained style.

STOWELL MEMORIAL CHURCH, Eccles Old Road, at the junction of Regent Road and the motorway. 1869 by *J. Medland Taylor*. Only the tower and spire survive as a landmark. Sandstone, with a tall steeple.

ST JOSEPH (R. C.), Ellesmere Street. 1902. A big-boned church with a thin NW corner tower. Red brick and stone dressings, Perp. The only unusual feature is the clerestory, with a big round-headed arcade with very small paired lights.

89 SALFORD LADS' CLUB, St Ignatius Way, on the corner of Coronation Street. By *Henry Lord*, opened by Baden Powell in 1904. It fronts the New Barracks Estate (*see* below), and it was not municipal but the gift rather of J. G. and W. G. Groves, who bought the land from the Corporation in 1900. Red brick, eclectic with transomed windows, oriels and domes. The interior is almost completely unaltered. Large gymnasium with viewing gallery, fives court, concert hall with gallery, offices with Art Nouveau fireplaces, etc. A remarkable survival. Balancing it at the other end of the street is the church of St Ignatius, *see* above.

CYGNUS HOUSE, Woden Street. *c.* 1996 by *Amec*. A sleek silvery warehouse beside the Ship Canal, lying low and looking alien amidst all the desolation hereabouts. A security-conscious design. Curving profile clad in silvery metal panels, inset ends with dark cladding, and very few very small porthole-like windows.

NEW BARRACKS ESTATE. A large early C20 scheme between Regent Road, N, Gloucester Street, E, Tatton Street, S, and Huddart Close, W. By *Henry Lord*, who won the competition in 1899 for Salford's first municipal housing. The site was formerly an infantry barracks. The scheme remains largely intact, though there have been losses on the S and E sides. Red brick, with sparing Queen Anne detailing, two and three storeys. There were three classes of housing, with two or three bedrooms per house, some with a parlour as well as a living room. Thirty-two shops were provided, of which only a few along Tatton Street survive. The housing is centred on Regent Square where there was to have been a public hall; the park created instead gives a sense of spaciousness.

17 ORDSALL HALL, Taylorson Street. The most important remaining timber-framed building in Salford; the seat of the Radcliffe family who secured the manor in 1354. Sold in 1662, it passed through a number of hands before acquisition in 1758 by the Egerton family of Tatton, Cheshire. It was purchased by Salford Corporation in 1959 and has been a museum since 1972.*

---

* Excavation of a site immediately W of the building in 1978–9 found evidence for a C17 barn, thought to be the one erected in 1646 by Humphrey Chetham, who owned that part of the estate at that time.

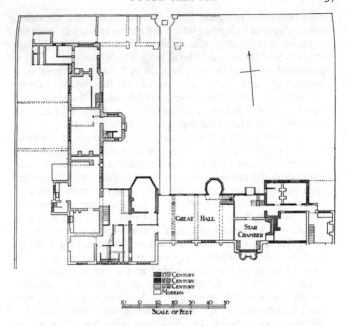

Ordsall Hall, plan.
Victoria County History of Lancashire, vol. 4, 1911

The site was originally moated, and remained partially so until the late C19. The building consists of a richly decorated timber-framed s range built in the early C16,* a brick w range of 1639, and a truncated C14 E range with a C15 or C16 extension and another of the early C17. Excavation in 1990–1 traced the demolished E wing which had been rebuilt or cased in brick, and identified a square building attached to the end of the wing which could have been a dovecote. The hall range was partially refaced or rebuilt in 1896–7 by *Alfred Darbyshire*, which is what gives the s side its present character – brick with red terracotta dressings and big Perp windows. The N side was also heavily restored, matching the original. It is decorated all over with quatrefoil panels, which have been credited with starting a fashion seen in a number of other halls in the area.[†] The Hall has a broad dais-end window on a stone base with a little vine ornament on the transom and crocketed pinnacles. Above it is a square gable containing a little room. The hall itself has a spere truss at each end, that at the low end complete with large tracery over. Three doorways from the screens passage to the service rooms are in the end wall. The posts rise

* Dendrochronology yielded a date of 1512 for the hall.
[†] For example Samlesbury, 1545, Rufford, *c.* 1540, both in North Lancashire, and Speke near Liverpool, late 1560s.

from high stone polygonal bases. They are elaborately moulded, with polygonal caps from which the timbers rise, following the complex moulding profile. This is an unusual feature, not encountered in any other local halls. The whole of the roof is patterned in quatrefoils. The dais end has one spere post remaining, and there are traces of the coved canopy formerly over the table – one curved beam on the N side and mortices in the tie-beam. Behind the dais, the wall of the C14 part survives, with some replaced timbers.

An opening on the N side leads into the truncated E WING, the oldest surviving part. Only two bays survive, housing the PARLOUR – known as the Star Chamber for the leaden stars decorating the ceiling – and an UPPER CHAMBER. Here the arch-braces of the principals can be seen, with traces of painted decoration. Above the inserted ceiling and beneath later roof structures is a crown-post roof, for which a date of c. 1360 was suggested by dendrochronology. It is tempting to relate this to the recorded acquisition of a licence for a chapel here in 1360/1. A two-storey one-room extension to the SE end of the E wing was possibly added in the C16 or earlier, and another storey was added (or the previous one completely rebuilt), probably in the early C17. The lower part was apparently timber-framed, but most of the timbers were replaced in the early C18 by brick. The first-floor room has a C15 or C16 stone fireplace and a plaster ceiling with geometrical panelling. This is probably early C17, inserted when the upper floor was added. This little top room has an early C17 stone fireplace and the Radcliffe arms in plaster.

At the other end the service rooms have been thrown together, but it is still possible to trace the kitchen passage in the mortises of the ceiling timbers. The kitchen is now in the C17 W WING. The two rooms over the services (now merged) were spacious chambers with tall kingpost roofs matching the height of the hall roof. Between the services and the W wing is a little linking range of 1512 with generous timber mullioned windows below and a little oriel above, embellished with roses set in quatrefoils above cusped arcading, with in the centre a shield with a Stanley eagle's claw badge. In the upper room the timber framing of the present end wall has been partially incorporated into the brickwork of the W wing.

The W wing is a replacement of an earlier structure, which must have included a kitchen. Dated 1639, three storeys, very plain, utilitarian even, with brick hoodmoulds and a projecting three-storey porch. At the N end is a low projection with raised basket-arch moulds over the openings, like those of similar date at Wardley Hall, Wardley (q.v.). Most of the mullioned windows were either coated in cement render or (perhaps) replaced with concrete in the 1960s, but some of those to the attic are of rendered brick. The wing was divided into apartments from the first, with rooms to the S reached from the main range, and other apartments reached from a stair in the porch. There was originally no communication

between the areas. Apart from rooms at the N end the walls of
the attics seem never to have been plastered. The KITCHEN is
one bay N of the original kitchen passage, complete with a huge
chimney. A few traces can be found of a predecessor building.
A buttress at the N end was probably originally built around a
post. Earlier brickwork at both N and S ends is also evident.*
Recent work on the building and examination of original fittings removed during the 1960s has recovered the original stair
of the 1639 W wing, which Mr Blacklay has reconstructed from
fragments. It may be returned to its original position, connecting the linking block to the first floor of the new brick
structure. Quantities of C17 and C18 oak panelling also survive.

STAINED GLASS originating in the hall oriel is kept *ex situ*
at the hall. Much of it is armorial. Figures of St Catherine
and the Virgin, of *c.* 1500, were brought from Barlow Hall (*see*
p. 413) in the C19.

5. Pendleton

Pendleton lies W of the centre of Salford. It had its own town hall
of 1865, demolished in the mid C20. It is sliced in two by Broad
Street, a busy dual carriageway, with older buildings on the N
side and 1960s development on the other. Here the area between
Liverpool Street, Cross Lane, Broad Street and Warren Street is
dominated by a forest of 1960s council tower blocks of twenty-
three, seventeen, fifteen and twelve storeys and to several different designs, interspersed with late C20 low-rise housing. The
seventeen-storey blocks around Ellor Street (Mulberry Court,
Sycamore Court, etc.) were designed by the *Architecture Research
Unit of the University of Edinburgh*, 1965. Dark infill and exposed
frame expressing single and double units. A large forbidding
SHOPPING CENTRE of slightly later date lies to the W.

St AMBROSE, Liverpool Street. By *R.B. Preston*, consecrated
    1910. Red brick and red terracotta. Dec, with one unchar-
    acteristic feature for Preston, who can be so dull: a slender tower
    to the street, slightly Arts and Crafts in character, with splayed
    corners, battlements and spiky gargoyles at the corners.
St PAUL, Ellor Street. 1855–6 by *E.H. Shellard*. Hidden amongst
    the tower blocks. When the parish was formed in 1855 it
    comprised seventy acres into which more than 7,500 people
    were packed into back-to-backs. Dec NE corner spirelet, low
    chancel, five-bay nave arcade of octagonal piers, ornate ham-
    merbeam roof. Restoration in the 1970s was accompanied by
    reordering by *Stephen Dykes Bower*, who also introduced a new
    decorative scheme. It is a great success. The chancel was
    screened off and acts as a Lady Chapel. A complex scheme of
    stencilling in a free Gothic style was executed in reds and
    greens in the nave ceiling and blues in the chancel. None of
    the original FURNISHINGS survive. – Simple LIGHT

---

* Anthony Blacklay pointed this out to me.

FITTINGS and intricate SCREENS are by *Norman Furneaux* to designs by *Dykes Bower*. The church has become a repository of items rescued from demolished or disused churches in the diocese. – BENCH SEATING and CHOIR FURNISHINGS in dark oak are from the demolished St Anne, Brindle Heath (by *F. P. Oakley*, 1914). – Very elaborate FONT with marble shafts and carved biblical scenes from St Alban, Rochdale, of 1855–6. – Early C19 ROYAL ARMS, a good carved and gilded piece. – The chief treasure is the ORGAN of 1787 by *Samuel Green*, the case surmounted by flame-like cresting and urns, from St Thomas Ardwick (*see* p. 359).

CHURCH HALL by *Dykes Bower*, 1975, using reclaimed material including doorways from demolished churches in the area. It is attached to the SE end of the church, creating a shared entrance. Matching coursed sandstone rubble and slate-clad upper storey with traceried windows. Except for the open ironwork cupola it could be early C20.

ST THOMAS, Broad Street. A Commissioners' church. An indication of the character of this area in the early C19 is perhaps given by Bishop Sumner's choice of 'How dreadful is this place' as his text on the occasion of the consecration. By *Richard Lane* and *Francis Goodwin*, 1829–31. It is clear from the correspondence and appearance that Lane did most of the work, which is typical of his early C19 churches. Ashlar, w tower with embattled parapet and pinnacles. Five-bay nave with battlemented parapets. Perp E window. INTERIOR. A good example of the type, alterations notwithstanding. Arcades of slim Perp piers, plaster vaulted ceiling, shallow apse and galleries. These have arcaded blind-traceried fronts. The w gallery, supported by quatrefoil columns, has a florid Perp canopy with the carved arms of William IV. Other galleries have been closed in below to provide meeting rooms, retaining one N bay as a chapel. Stone stairs with cast-iron balusters and wreathed rails. – STAINED GLASS. E window, upper tracery only, perhaps by *Hardman*, 1840s. N chapel also by *Hardman*, scenes from the life of St Thomas.

SEVENTH-DAY ADVENTIST CHURCH, formerly Unitarian, Cross Lane. By *Ray Cowling*, 1976. Low brick buildings including a Sunday School, offices, meeting rooms, etc., grouped together. The chapel projects towards the road. Octagonal, with a copper roof and slender concrete spire.

SALFORD UNIVERSITY, Frederick Street site. *See* inner Salford, p. 622.

HALTON BANK SCHOOL (former), Bolton Road. 1906 by *John Woodhouse*. Large, boldly done in red brick and yellow terracotta, and a satisfying Queen Anne-ish composition of blocky forms with roofs with cupolas.

BROAD STREET, near St Thomas. On the N side, a range of early C19 houses with wide doorways with radial fanlights, including No. 34, a symmetrical five-bay house with a central pedimented entrance bay. Further E a former WESLEYAN SCHOOL, dated 1887, perhaps by *W. R. Sharpe* who did the

demolished Wesleyan Church here. Gothic, with a tower surmounted by a timbered lantern, gabled to the r. with big
churchy windows.

BROUGHTON ROAD. Nos. 19–21, N of St Thomas, was one of
the principal buildings of the PENDLETON CO-OPERATIVE
INDUSTRIAL SOCIETY, with offices, warehouses, committee
rooms and assembly rooms. The part to the l. is of 1887 by
F. Smith, extended to the r. in similar style by *A.H. Walsingham* in 1903. Very ornate, red brick with terracotta and
stone dressings, tall octagonal turret and many Dutch gables
and slim octagonal piers dividing the bays. More large former
Co-op buildings of various late C19 and early C20 dates lie off
AGNEW STREET, opposite, including bakery and dairy
buildings.

BUILE HILL, off Eccles Old Road. Built for Thomas Potter, later
first mayor of Manchester, in 1825–7 by *Charles Barry*; additions of the 1860s by *Edward Walters*, who introduced a third
storey. Barry's two-storeyed villa is classical, restrained and
refined, the N entrance front rather austere, the S garden front
lighter and more decorative. Symmetrical main block with a
recessed W wing. The N side has a recessed entrance bay with
a door framed by Doric pilasters and flanked by tall narrow
lights, flanked by two bays on each side. The garden front is
similar but with tripartite windows throughout, the lights
divided by pilasters with rosettes. Projecting bay windows with
shallow balustraded balconies. The entrance has attached
columns using the order from the Tower of the Winds in
Athens. Walters added a third storey and a Greek Doric porte
cochère with two fluted columns and a triglyph frieze. He
extended the W wing southwards by one bay and furnished it
with a balustraded bay to match the others. Attached to this is
a low billiard room, matching the original building in style,
possibly by *Walters*. Walters's upper floor is almost seamlessly

Salford, Pendleton, Buile Hill, engraving, 1847

added, similarly restrained, and executed in matching stone. Deep eaves, and on top an open balustraded lantern with paterae. The original villa had a similar lantern, which seems to have been reused or copied. In this respect the design is related to Barry's original Italianate proposal (kept at the RIBA drawings collection), and to the attic over the main entrance hall of his Royal Manchester Institution, 1824–35 (*see* p. 288). The garden side overlooks a terrace with ugly concrete balustrading, probably 1930s, replacing a stone wall.

The property was purchased by Salford Corporation in 1902, when the grounds were made into a public park (*see* below) and the house converted to a natural history museum, opened in 1906. The house subsequently became a mining museum which closed in 2000. Now there are some plans to convert it to an hotel. (Interior greatly altered, with loss of some ceilings and plan form, but with an original cantilevered stair.)

Brick service buildings lie E of the house. They were greatly altered during the 1930s and again more recently. A refronted house may have provided accommodation for a gardener, other buildings around a courtyard probably originated as stables, coach houses etc.

SUMMERHILL, Eccles Old Road. An early C19 Tudor Gothic house, with some unusual details. It was the home of the most influential art dealer and patron of the arts in early C19 Manchester, Thomas Agnew, who began his career in 1816 and conducted his own business from 1824. It is possible he had the house built at about this period. Of stone, with a symmetrical centre and attached two-bay wing, l. side. The main display is reserved for the central entrance bay which is framed by octagonal piers. Elaborate porch with a Tudor-arched doorway, crenellated parapet and angle buttresses rising as spires. Above is a canted bay window, with crenellations and finials at the angles. The parapet between the octagonal piers has a strange Lombard frieze. Otherwise the whole roofline is crenellated. Elongated oblong panels with blind tracery detailing in the frieze; windows with label moulds. The interior has been altered and detail lost following late C20 fire damage.

(CHASELEY FIELD, Chaseley Road. A Gothic villa, probably 1840s or 1850s, with very good interior fixtures and fittings, including an elaborate stair.)

BUILE HILL and SEEDLEY PARK, off Eccles Old Road. The park consists of Seedley Park, SE, opened in 1876, and the grounds of Buile Hill (*see* above), opened as a park in 1903. The grounds of two more houses, both demolished, were added later. Hart Hill: NW, purchased in 1924 and Springfield, between Buile Hill and Seedley Park bought in 1927. Rolling well-wooded land, falling to the SE. Seedley Park was laid out by *Henry Moore*, head gardener at Peel Park, Salford (*see* p. 624). A tree-lined axial route runs W across the park from the main E entrance, and there is an undulating perimeter path. A steep wooded bank links the area with the grounds of Buile

Hill, which were laid out by the Salford Corporation Parks' Superintendent *A. Wilsher*. Here there are large expanses of grassland crossed by paths, and a circuit walk. The original approach to Buile Hill, which runs S and W from Eccles Old Road was improved and incorporated into the layout.

6. Salford Quays

S of the centre. The best introduction to the area is a tram ride from Manchester. Undeveloped or decayed canalside areas give way to glittering buildings as the tram crosses the Manchester Ship Canal and passes alongside the basins. Salford Quays has a special atmosphere, with its own breezy microclimate. The brashness of some of the architecture is offset by the solidity of the masonry of the basins, and there is something of a pioneer feeling, given by the contrast between the developed areas and the big open spaces awaiting new uses. The large expanses of water, now inhabited by water birds, make one long for the sight of a great ship coming up the canal, or even a little one, but that sight is rare nowadays.

The Salford side of the Manchester Ship Canal started to lose its industry in the mid C20 (for the history of the canal *see* Manchester, public buildings, p. 302). Salford Council bought the land in the early 1980s, a daring and far-sighted move. The London Docklands Development Company had become responsible for the London docks at about the same time. A development plan for the whole area was drawn up in 1985 by *Shepheard Epstein Hunter* (who had been responsible for the masterplan for the development of London's Wapping in 1976) with *Ove Arup* as consultant engineers. As in many London docks, the basins were retained and restored, and features such as bollards and some of the huge cargo cranes were retained, not always in the original positions. New canals were cut through the quays to link them, trees were planted and walkways built. The polluted water was cleaned up, and the area is now popular for water sports.

Infrastructure was completed in advance of development, which followed mainly in the form of offices and housing. It has been more of an economic than an architectural success. The housing is variously of single units and three- to four-storey blocks, the styles builders' traditional, Neo-Georgian, or with motifs borrowed from demolished warehouses. The office buildings, some of them on a huge scale, are generally in the Postmodern style of that moment, a style that this writer finds hard to like even if it is exceptionally well done, but nothing here earns that description. Architects responsible for some of the largest include *Fairhurst Design Group* (The Victoria, Harbour City, 1991–3) and the *Percy Thomas Partnership* (The Anchorage, Anchorage Quay, 1990s).

THE LOWRY, an arts centre by *Michael Wilford & Partners*, 1997– 126 2000, stands on a finger of dockland jutting into the Ship Canal. It has a nautical feel, and transparent, semi-transparent and reflective surfaces attempt, not wholly successfully, to express the presence of the solid, inward-looking core. This comprises two back-to-back theatres which are wrapped in lighter, outward-looking spaces used as galleries, cafés, etc. The cladding of angled steel shingles suggests movement, and a huge circular funnel, with openwork at the top and clad in semi-transparent gauze, anchors the building on the landward side beside the blocky entrance canopy. This takes the form of a halved cylinder, curved side down, supported by tapering props. It seems to be a sculptural statement rather than a functional element. The building is imposing, and from some angles, exciting, but ultimately – from the outside – confused. After the cool metallic hues of the exterior the intense colours of the interior shock. (In contrast the main galleries on the second floor are dead white.) From the entrance, routes lead around and into the theatres. They are both excellent and traditional in arrangement but highly flexible, so that different staging and seating can be contrived. The main galleries house Salford's collection of paintings by L. S. Lowry, their fancy gilt frames looking incongruous in the white planar setting. Other successions of spaces, some open through the full height of the building, lead to more galleries, cafés and to the waterside. All this shows how the design developed substantially after the death of Wilford's partner, James Stirling, in 1992. Apart from the strong colours there is not much here that resembles Stirling's own late style, with its Postmodern classical flavour and strongly symmetrical planning – a sign of how far Wilford has travelled in developing an architectural language of his own.

The venture was promoted by Salford City Council and funding included substantial grants from the Heritage Lottery Fund. After the abandonment of the Stirling–Wilford masterplan for the immediate area, however, the ambition of the scheme has not been extended to the setting, witnessed by the positioning of a banal multi-storey car park and shopping complexes in the path of landward views.

LOWRY FOOTBRIDGE, 1998–2000 by *W. Middleton* of *Parkman Ltd.*, linking the Lowry and Imperial War Museum sites (for the latter *see* Stretford). The deck, with horizontal flashes of blue in Perspex panels, is supported by an arch. At either end pairs of gantries house gravity lifts, allowing the deck to be raised wholesale to let shipping through.

MANCHESTER LINERS OFFICES (former), Furness Quay. Now known as Furness House. Perhaps the best of *Leach, Rhodes & Walker*'s mid-C20 buildings, opened in 1969. Nine-storey bowed block with a recessed attic and continuous window strips with greenish glass, clad in white and grey mosaic. Beside it, at an angle, a six-storey block, with, between the two, a little white pavilion, which answers the curves of the main blocks and is connected to the lower one by a bridge.

DOCK OFFICES, Trafford Road. Of *c.* 1925, by *Harry Fairhurst & Son*. Stripped classical style, concrete, E-plan. Four storeys with a central projecting pylon-like bay with a full-height arched window. Projecting cornice with an attic storey above. ENTRANCE GATEWAY, also by the *Fairhursts*. Concrete, with a flat arch and the words MANCHESTER DOCKS, supported by pylons, each with a projecting ship's keel motif.

SWING BRIDGE, Trafford Road. A mighty steel structure of 1892 crossing the Ship Canal. It no longer swings. The road is carried by two big arched trusses with diagonal braces. A small brick lookout and control booth is attached on the Salford side.

7. *Weaste and Seedley*

W of the centre between Pendleton and Eccles.

ST LUKE, Liverpool Street. By *G.G. Scott*, 1865, the chancel chapel added 1873–8, also to his design. On top of a little hill, in a bare churchyard. Slim, embraced W tower with short but powerful broach spire. Nearly all the windows are lancets. But the clerestory windows are foiled circles. Polygonal apse. The interior also has much power, despite the small size. The focus is the apse with its densely timbered scissor-braced ceiling and continuous arcade of lancets with shafts, of which alternating pairs are blind. Beautifully carved corbels. Four-bay nave with quatrefoil piers with moulded tops. The two-bay N chapel (given by the Tootal family) has an open arcade. W end with a central arch flanked by lower arches, divided by huge round piers with foliated tops which support the tower. A chapel at the E end of the S aisle has a REREDOS with rather stiff carved surround and a painting, both by members of the Home Arts and Industries classes which started in the church in 1886. – Circular FONT on short piers. – PULPIT. Stone base with Celtic-looking biting beasts on the splayed corners. – STAINED GLASS. The E window looks like *Hardman*. In the N chapel the glass is early work of *Kempe*, good but rather faded. Mid- to late C20 PAINTINGS of the Evangelists in the blind lancets of the apse.

ALL SOULS AND ST JOHN VIANNEY (R.C.), Weaste Lane. 1932–4 by *William Ellis* of Manchester in the buff brick Romanesque style favoured in the 1930s by the Catholics in that city. Channelled SW tower with very tall narrow openings and big open arches to the bell stage. Big transepts, canted apse; attached presbytery, E. Carved stone panels by *J. Lenigan*. (Romanesque high altar and baldacchino by *Dinelli & Figli* of Pietrasanta to Ellis's designs; mosaic Stations of the Cross by *Walter J. Pearce*.)

UNITED REFORMED CHURCH, Weaste Lane. By *Edward Jones* of Manchester, dated 1910. Described as 'Elizabethan Renaissance'. Red brick, red terracotta, recessed angled entrance to street corner, short NW tower with little domed finials at the corners, windows with uncusped late Perp tracery. It had double windows from the outset to block the noise from the railway. (Glass by *T.H. Lea* and *Williams Bros*.)

WEASTE CEMETERY, Cemetery Road, Weaste. The first municipal public cemetery in Salford, opened in 1857. It was
extended to the N, with a new entrance from Eccles New
Road, in 1887–8 by the Borough Engineer, *Arthur Jacob* with
planting by *Henry Moore*. The ENTRANCE LODGE, roofless and
ruinous, is probably the one designed by *Mr Collins* under
Jacob's supervision in 1886. It has a plaque recording the
opening and extension of the cemetery. The four chapels and
lodges by *Pritchett & Sons* of York, 1856, have been demolished. The older, S part is well planted and has a large collection of Victorian and later monuments with a variety of urns,
obelisks and angels, the best assemblage in Salford and one of
the best in SE Lancashire. The most prominent, and one of
the most distinguished Victorian monuments in any English
cemetery, is the BROTHERTON MEMORIAL, by *T. Holmes &
W. Walker*, who won the competition. It was carved by *T. R.
Williams*, and erected by public subscription. Gothic, tall buttressed and arcaded base, gabled and crocketed spirelet supported by open arcading with shafts in the form of angels.
Joseph Brotherton †1857 was Salford's first M.P., and the first
to be interred in the cemetery. A number of other elaborate
monuments nearby, including a pink granite obelisk with a
portrait medallion, to Mark Addy †1890, the 'Salford Hero'
who saved more than fifty people from drowning in the River
Irwell. Further S is the memorial of Charles Hallé †1895,
founder of the Hallé Orchestra, with a portrait plaque. FIRST
WORLD WAR MEMORIAL near the centre of the site. Stone
angel on a tall granite plinth.

COACH AND HORSES, No. 350 Eccles New Road. A nice
unspoiled pub, 1920s but Edwardian in style. It has a little-
altered interior with green tiles, an elaborate bar, big
Jacobean-style stair and other original fittings.

LORDS LANE. Early C19 brick house set back from the end of
the road. Central entrance bay with stone Ionic portico flanked
by slightly projecting bays with large tripartite windows.

SHAW *see* CROMPTON

SIMISTER

1½ m. NE of Prestwich, at the end of Heywood Road. The village
is almost inaccessible by road, although it sits virtually on top of
the monster roundabout connecting the M60, M62 and M66
motorways.

ST GEORGE. By *R. B. Preston*, 1914–15. Nave, chancel and S
transept, semicircular W baptistery and SW porch, in a simple
Romanesque style with Arts and Crafts influence. Beautifully
laid random rubble with a single band of ashlar. Graded slate
roofs. Uncomplicated interior, plastered white except for an

ashlar lining to the chancel. – Arcaded tub FONT. – STAINED
GLASS in the baptistery, marking the demise of the local
postman †1966, and of the post office.
LADY WILTON SCHOOL. Built by the Egertons of Heaton Park,
1850. Brick, single-storey, L-shaped.

SMALLBRIDGE *see* ROCHDALE OUTER

STAND *see* WHITEFIELD

STRETFORD
Including Old Trafford and Barton-upon-Irwell

INTRODUCTION

Stretford is part of Manchester functionally and visually and the
boundary, SW of the Manchester centre, is nowhere noticeable.
It became administratively part of Trafford Metropolitan
Borough Council in 1974. The area includes Old Trafford, E, and
Trafford Park, with the docks, N, built in connection with the
Manchester Ship Canal, 1885–94 (*see* Manchester, public build-
ings, p. 302). Barton-upon-Irwell is really the W part of Trafford
Park. The area was largely rural and villagey until the late C19.
The old municipal centre of Stretford was at the junction of
Chester Road (now a daunting dual carriageway) and Edge Lane,
where there is a dispiriting 1970s shopping centre. Trafford Park
is a flat area of industrial works and sheds, criss-crossed by fast
roads. Two things make the area special, architecturally speaking; All Saints, Barton-upon-Irwell (1863–8) is the masterwork
of *E. W. Pugin*, with some superb original furnishings and interior schemes, and *Daniel Libeskind*'s Imperial War Museum
North (1997–2002) is architecture of international quality.

Trafford Park was part of the estate of the de Trafford family
who had their mansion there (demolished 1939), built in 1762
incorporating part of the predecessor house. In the grounds in
1857 the celebrated Manchester Exhibition of Art Treasures was
held, the first British exhibition ever of works of art on such a
scale. The temporary building measured 656 by 200 ft (200 by
61 metres), of corrugated iron and glass, the architecture applied
by *Edward Salomons*, the interior decoration by *J. G. Crace*.* The

---

* *See* Ulrich Finkel, 'The Art-Treasures Exhibition', in J. H. G. Archer, (ed.), *Art
and Architecture in Victorian Manchester*, 1985.

fourth Sir Humphrey de Trafford and his wife Annette were patrons in the mid- to late C19 of local Catholic churches and schools. The fifth Sir Humphrey was a keen sportsman and his patronage, combined with good transport links with the centre of Manchester, made Old Trafford a centre of sports activity from the late C19. Stretford was the home of the cotton magnate John Rylands (*see* also John Rylands Library, Manchester, p. 290), whose house, Longford Hall, stood off Edge Lane until demolition in the late C20. The grounds have been turned into a public park.

Following the opening of the Manchester Ship Canal and development of the surrounding area, Trafford park and hall were sold in 1897. The estate was bought by E. T. Hooley, who registered Trafford Park Estates Ltd in 1896. It became the first industrial estate of its type in the world. Marshall Stevens, the general manager of the Ship Canal, was recruited as managing director in 1897 and a wide range of industries was established. One of the biggest firms was the British Westinghouse Electric Co. (later Metropolitan Vickers Electrical Co.) which erected the largest engineering works in the country. The trading importance of the Ship Canal and Port of Manchester also attracted foreign firms, including the Ford Motor Co. The Manchester architect *Charles Heathcote* was a beneficiary – he helped to design the Westinghouse works and the Ford factory, as well as numerous warehouses and stores, all of them demolished. The resulting diversification protected Manchester from the worst effects of interwar depression. Production reached its peak in the Second World War, when the Park was Britain's chief armaments centre. Decline began in earnest in the 1960s followed by modest improvements in response to various economic and development initiatives in the 1980s–90s. Heavy manufacturing has of course gone, but there is light industry of various types, mostly housed in late C20 sheds. The best places to get a flavour of the area in its heyday are along Mosley Road and on Trafford Park Way, where the former CARBORUNDUM ABRASIVES works include a range of early C20 buildings. From the 1980s development of Salford Quays (see p. 643) on the opposite side of the Canal has been an impetus for further regeneration.

Churches and public buildings are described in the usual way, then the scattering of other buildings. There is no perambulation.

CHURCHES

ALL SAINTS, Barton Road, Stretford. 1957 by *Leach, Rhodes & Walker*. Brick, with a semicircular apse and NW tower with a copper roof and cupola. Neo-Georgian windows with pediments. – STAINED GLASS. W end screen with glass by *Geoffrey Clarke*, fresh from his commission for windows at Coventry Cathedral. Large swirling designs illustrating aspects of the Trinity.

St Catherine, Redclyffe Road, Barton-upon-Irwell. The church of 1843 by *E. Welch* has been demolished. The churchyard is completely overgrown and almost impenetrable. One of the largest visible monuments is a huge stone block, to Marshall Stevens †1936, creator of Trafford Park, 'whose life work lies around this spot'. The single-storey former church school and two-storey house stand nearby, early C19 with mullioned windows, but greatly altered and overgrown with creepers.

St John Evangelist, Ayres Road, Old Trafford. 1904–8 by *R. B. Preston*. Very red brick with mechanical Perp tracery in terracotta. Big blunt sw tower.

St Matthew, Chester Road and Leslie Street, Stretford. 1841–2 by *W. Hayley*. It cost £2,700, of which the Church Commissioners gave £300. Stock brick. The usual lancets and thin buttresses. w tower with stepped lancets over the entrance and octagonal corner pinnacles in the final stage. Crenellated parapet, except on the e side (facing the road) where there is a gable with a clock. The e end was enlarged in 1861 with vestries with polychrome brick window heads and banding. Of 1906, a chancel in matching style but with plate-traceried windows. (Galleries on quatrefoil cast-iron columns. Furnishings of the 1860s. – e window by *William Wailes*.)

All Saints (R.C.), Redclyffe Road, Barton-upon-Irwell. By *E. W. Pugin*, and his masterwork. It stands beside the Ship Canal in wasteland on the w edge of Trafford Park, though it cannot be long before development spreads to this area. Begun as a family mausoleum, but intended as a parish church; now a Franciscan Friary (Friars Minor Conventual) which occupies the expanded presbytery and later buildings on the site. Sir Humphrey and Lady Annette de Trafford of nearby Trafford Hall (*see* above) paid for it. Pugin and his father A. W. N. Pugin had previously undertaken important commissions for Lady Annette's relatives, the 16th and 17th Earls of Shrewsbury.

Building started with the construction in 1863 of the de Trafford mortuary chapel, with a new church following 1867–8 alongside, so it became a n chancel chapel. The chapel looks like a precious casket or reliquary, with a debt to the Sainte Chapelle in Paris (1243–8). Steep pavilion roof and wrought-iron cross finials. There is a little rose window at the e end and the gables of the windows rise through the parapet. A carved panel showing the donors appears at the e end over the entrance to the vault. The church also displays French inspiration, with the absence of transepts, a large rose window and a flèche-like bell tower. The e end faces the road, with a high polygonal apse and tall plate-traceried windows each under separate cross-gables. Clerestory with cinquefoiled windows, aisles with plate tracery. The w end is dominated by a huge rose window with rather fussy details beneath an arch banded in red and yellow stone. Arcade of lancets beneath, and an arched entrance, all framed by buttresses topped by statues.

Above is a slightly projecting bell-turret with open arcading topped by a short stone spire.

INTERIOR. Splendid and dignified. The nave is of seven bays. The chancel arch is striped in red Mansfield and buff Painswick stone, and so are the arcades. Clustered shafts with capitals sumptuously carved with naturalistic foliage. The very high scissor- and arch-braced roof has principals rising from carved corbels. In the chancel the pitch is much higher, with stone shafts rising from angel corbels and a vaulted roof luxuriously decorated with painted roundels and gilding. There are four steps up from the nave and a further four to the altar. W organ gallery with a cantilevered stone stair, S side. At the SE end of the nave two arched entrances lead to confessionals and another arch to the presbytery. The N chapel entrance has de Trafford arms over and angels on each side. Stone rib-vaulted ceiling, encaustic *Minton* tile floor with de Trafford badges and monograms, and an inner row of slim circular pink marble piers, from which the vault springs, alongside the larger piers of the chancel. The effect is confusing and exhilarating. The configuration of arcades, which E. W. Pugin saw at St Mary, Beverley (which he and his father restored), was used earlier at his Knill Chantry in St George's Cathedral, Southwark, 1856.

FITTINGS. In the chapel, elaborate Caen stone REREDOS, beautifully carved with canopies and statues of the Virgin and attendants including minstrel angels. Altar table with four shafts of black marble and a recumbent Christ beneath. – Chancel REREDOS. Truly splendid, with highly competent figure carving. Gabled niches with statues and angels above. At the centre larger angels hold aloft a gilded crown over the niche for the monstrance. Dr O'Donnell suggests *R. L. Boulton* of Cheltenham or *Geflowski* of Liverpool as possible sculptors for both reredoses. – PULPIT. Attached to the first bay of the nave, N side. Stone with marble stair balustrade. – WALL PAINTINGS. Coronation of the Virgin, S aisle, Annunciation, N aisle, both badly damaged. Over the chancel arch, Christ in Majesty. On the chancel S wall the Adoration of the Lamb, with figures including the de Trafford family and Pugin in medieval robes, holding his plan of the church. By *J. Alphege Pippett* of *Hardman & Co.*, c. 1868 – STAINED GLASS. Mainly competent late C19 work. The E windows are by *Hardman & Powell*, but they were damaged during the Blitz. In the de Trafford chapel scenes set amid jumbled fragments brought from St John (C. of E.), Eton, in 1991. The W rose window and lancets are filled with bright, unlovely late C20 glass, the only jarring note.

PRESBYTERY, also by *E. W. Pugin.* S of the church and linked to it by a sort of cloister, now obscured and altered by a church hall added in 1950. The front faces S. Stone, with tall chimneys, asymmetrical, with a projecting gabled entrance bay with a bay window, l., beside the arched entrance, and a gabled dormer, r., above a mullioned-and-transomed window. It is all done in coursed rubble, and there are similarities with Pugin's presbytery at St Ann's Church (below).

St Ann (R.C.), Chester Road, Stretford. 1862–7 by *E. W. Pugin*. Grey stone. Tall, almost detached NW steeple. Short spire, plain pinnacles, and very tall, very thin lancets in the second stage of the tower. In its W face, low down, a medallion with the kneeling donors (Sir Humphrey and Lady Annette de Trafford, *see* All Saints, above) holding a model of the church. The W end of the nave is dominated by a large fancy rose window with a carved *crucifixus* at the centre. Low aisles, clerestory with spherical windows and a canted apse. Geometrical tracery.

INTERIOR. Smaller and less elaborate than All Saints (above), but with generosity of space and some similarities, for example in the high and elaborate scissor-braced roof. Chancel with a canted apse with ribs rising from angel corbels, and stencilled decoration by *Edward Booth*, *c.* 1998. There are five steps up from the nave, and a further three to the altar position. Nine-bay arcades of circular piers on high octagonal bases. The caps have lively fruit, flower and foliage carving, like those of All Saints. W gallery with an openwork front with diagonal braces. – Elaborate stone REREDOS. The Adoration of the Lamb with many angels, Caen stone. The altar below has been removed. – STAINED GLASS. E windows with the Coronation of the Virgin and scenes from her life, designed in 1863 by *Hardman & Co.* under the supervision of *E. W. Pugin*. W rose window with figures of the Evangelists etc., also by them of 1863. – MONUMENTS. Good brasses at the foot of the inner chancel wall on each side. Sir Thomas de Trafford †1852, N; Henry Tempest †1860, S. They appear to be by the same hand, with black and red lettering and family badges.

PRESBYTERY. W of the church and attached to it. Also by *E. W. Pugin*. Rubble with ashlar dressings, Gothic. Gabled l. bay with a bay window, entrance with two lights over, dormer, r. side. The windows have cambered heads, apart from those of the bay, which have shallow pointed heads.

St Alphonsus (R.C.), Ayres Road, Old Trafford. 1936 by *Hill, Sandy & Norris*. Brown brick with stone dressings, Geometrical window tracery. (The interior has wall-piers with low round-headed aisle passages.)

St Antony of Padua (R.C.), Eleventh Street, Trafford Park. A tin tabernacle of 1904 with a little W bellcote. A rare survival nowadays.

Martin Luther German Church, Park Road, Stretford. 1963 by *T. D. Howcroft* (of *Young & Purves*). A square block of white slabs with narrow vertical windows and a roof with a very shallow pitch. Attached HALL of brown brick with a flat roof, simply treated. The PARSONAGE is more conventional, of pale grey brick with a pitched roof. A creeper scrambling over the church has robbed it of its clean lines. It was deliberately planted there. Was there a failure of nerve?

INDEPENDENT METHODIST CHURCH (former), Barton Road, Stretford. 1879–81, reusing materials from a predecessor nearby. Symmetrical, red brick with handsome stone dressings, with Italian and Venetian Gothic motifs.

CONGREGATIONAL CHURCH, South Croston Street. A church was built in 1860 by *Poulton & Woodman*, but only a fragment survives, stone, two-storeyed, perhaps part of a vestry. The former CONGREGATIONAL CHURCH SUNDAY SCHOOL opposite, is large, of brick in header bond, gabled, and with polychrome heads to the windows. Put up in 1860, perhaps also by *Poulton & Woodman*.

UNION BAPTIST CHURCH (former), Edge Lane, Stretford. With The Claremont Chapel in Little Bolton (*see* p. 149), the grandest surviving Baptist Church in SE Lancashire. Opened by the patron, John Rylands, in 1867. The front is of stone, with an open pediment supported by a pair of huge Corinthian columns framing double doors. Arched and stepped upper windows, brick sides with tall arched windows. The architect is unknown. Converted to offices, late C20.

SHARON CHURCH, Chorlton Road, Old Trafford. Formerly a Welsh Congregational Church, late C19. Symmetrical, coursed rubble with a projecting entrance bay with paired entrances beneath pointed arches and a large plate-traceried window over. Flanking bays with upper rose windows.

FREE UNITARIAN CHURCH (former), Shrewsbury Street, Old Trafford. 1901. Large, Perp, of red brick and red terracotta with a tower with a spire with Westmorland slate. Attached hall with big Perp windows. Derelict.

STRETFORD CEMETERY, Lime Road, Stretford. Opened in 1885, with an axial layout by *John Shaw*. Beautiful CHAPEL, by *Bellamy & Hardy* of Lincolnshire. N tower with angle buttresses terminating with crocketed pinnacles and a slender stone spire. The lowest stage is steeply gabled to W, S and E, a wilful touch, with opposed tall entrances in the E and W sides forming a porte cochère. Short chancel, elaborate pinnacled S porch.

PUBLIC BUILDINGS

TOWN HALL, Talbot Road, Old Trafford. 1931–3 by *Bradshaw Gass & Hope*. An imposing pile. Large and spreading, symmetrical, of brick with vaguely Adamish detail. High central clock tower, set back at the top. Central entrance bay with a tall arched window and portico, seven-bay ranges on each side, and angled end bays with concave fronts. Gateways on each side have brick piers with urn finials. The entrance leads into a vestibule and on to the main stone stair. This goes up in one flight and divides, where on each side there are plinths with large bronze statues by the *Bromsgrove Guild*: on one side Electra holding a globe, on the other Niord with a ship and sea beasts. Circular domed council chamber with a glazed oval lantern, meeting and committee rooms with oak panelling. Furnishings by *Waring & Gillow*.

PUBLIC HALL (former), Chester Road, Stretford. By *N. Loft-house*, 1879. The gift of John Rylands, the cotton magnate whose house stood nearby on Edge Lane. It originally incorporated a free public library and lecture theatres, now used as offices. Five bays, Gothic, brick with much stone and plenty of naturalistic foliage carving. Near-symmetrical. Tall clock tower with a pyramidal slated roof, four bays on either side with overlarge corner pinnacles. On the l. side only, a large dormer. Central entrance framed by pinnacles supported by short stone shafts, paired windows divided by stone shafts with foliated caps. Large entrance and staircase hall with columns with foliated tops and a stair with cast-iron balusters. Upper lecture theatre with pretty openwork ventilators and a gallery with an ornate ironwork front.

PUBLIC HALL (former), Talbot Road, Old Trafford. By *Colin C. McLeod*, 1887–8, for the Stretford Local Board; enlarged in 1907; now an hotel. Eclectic style with a balustraded parapet, central segmental-headed gable and upper arcade of round-arched windows. Central entrance with a balconied porch.

IMPERIAL WAR MUSEUM NORTH, Trafford Wharf Road, Trafford Park. By the New York architect *Daniel Libeskind*, 1997–2002, his first building in Britain. Like the Jewish Museum in Berlin (designed from 1989) where Libeskind showed himself to be a master of complex internal forms, it is a monument in itself. The disorientating qualities of the interior can also be compared with his Felix Nussbaum Haus in Osnabruck (opened 1998). The concept, according to the architect, is a shattered sphere 'reassembled as a fundamental emblem of conflict'. The three elements are like great shards, the large down-curved part representing war on land, the high upright part the war in the air, and a smaller, up-curved element, with windows overlooking the Ship Canal, the war at sea. Clad in shiny aluminium, with few visible external openings, the first impression is given by the sculptural shape. The entrance is at the intersection of the earth and air shard, leading in to the latter, which is revealed at close quarters to be a slatted permeable structure, and open to the elements and 180 ft (55 metres) high. This part is representative, with no exhibits. There are views right up to the observation platform 124 at the top, reached by a lift from which a walkway leads to the viewing area. The platform is unnerving. The floor grid at first appears opaque, but becomes semi-transparent as it is traversed, owing to the angle of the small openings, and horrifying views down to the floor-level far below suddenly reveal themselves. The sound and feeling of wind blowing through the structure adds to a sense of vulnerability.

At the base, an opening leads to the earth shard, and here the maroon and black colour scheme asserts itself as the low space is entered. Other motifs appear, such as the slim linear zigzag ceiling lights. A shiny lift shaft veers upwards at an angle

beside stairs. The main exhibition halls are at first-floor level,
where there is an immediate change of scale: two high windowless spaces, the larger with the permanent collection, the
smaller for temporary shows. The main space has exhibits such
as aeroplanes and tanks between large, full-height white-
rendered silos which enclose more intimate areas for the
display of smaller objects. The space is arranged so that walls
and silos act as one screen for projected images, and at intervals an unsettling *son-et-lumière* on themes of war and conflict
takes place. The smaller gallery is mediated by the big angled
silvery wall of the air shard jutting through the space and dividing it. It is big and bare, with the sound of the ventilation
system calling to mind an industrial store of some sort. The
sea shard, with a restaurant, has views of the waterfront,
anchoring it to the outside world. After the big, dark spaces it
is human in scale, and a relief. This is part of the point of the
building. From the outside, the separate elements represent an
idea that is easy to grasp. Inside, the earth shard swallows the
visitor up into its own self-referential world, designed to be
unsettling and disorientating, down to details such as the
doors randomly opening towards or away from the user, and
the corrugations of the floor surfacing running at an angle to
the walls, even in the lavatories. In contrast the air shard
creates a feeling of vulnerability for its vertiginous engagement
with the elements. There is constant tension between angles
and planes throughout, in the narrow horizontal glass cases set
into the angled lift shaft, cutting across the lines of the
cladding, in the slim vertical inset lights in the angled piers of
the sea shard, and in the high opening at the head of the stairs,
revealing a seemingly inaccessible inner space, actually a
meeting room.

The building is an achievement of rare distinction, the
more so when it is realized that the project budget was
drastically cut. Funding was provided by a consortium
including Peel Holdings, owners of the Manchester Ship
Canal, and Trafford Metropolitan Borough Council, but
expected grants from other sources were not forthcoming. This
curtailed plans for landscaping the area, and other economies
were made. Despite this there is close attention to detail and
consistency of vision. It is the most original building in SE Lancashire since the Second World War; powerful, intelligent and
humane.

WAR MEMORIAL, Chester Road, Old Trafford. By *Patteson*,
1924. Lion on a tapering plinth set back before a semicircular
wall with bronze plaques recording the names of the dead.

NORTH TRAFFORD COLLEGE, Talbot Road, Old Trafford. The
college grew from the Old Trafford Institute, a technical school
founded in 1899 (*see* below). New buildings were erected SW
of the town hall in 1940 by *Stephen Wilkinson*, with additions
by the County Architect *Roger Booth* in 1963. Nothing of note,
architecturally. Brick, the older part symmetrical and vaguely
Art Deco, with a stubby tower.

OLD TRAFFORD INSTITUTE (former), Stretford Road, Old Trafford. Opened 1899 as a technical school, subsequently with a public library. Now a Buddhist centre. Long, dull, brick, with a polygonal clock turret at one end.

SEYMOUR PARK COMMUNITY SCHOOL, Northumberland Road, Old Trafford. Junior and infant schools opened in 1907 and 1910. Large, but low, appealing gabled black and white blocks with tiled roofs, grouped together. The former teacher's house at the S end of the site is similar. A very long frontage with a close rhythm of red brick piers with yellow terracotta detailing.

WAR MEMORIAL HOSPITAL, Seymour Grove, Old Trafford. Originally Basford House, lent by James Nuttall of Hale, Cheshire, as an auxiliary hospital in 1914. One of the biggest and most distinguished of the mid- and late C19 houses on Seymour Grove. Of c. 1850, Italianate, with deep bracketed eaves and narrow entrance bay with a pedimental gable and elaborate columned porch. The windows of the main elevation have stone surrounds. Semicircular bay l. side, service bay r. side. Bought in 1925 for a district hospital, it is now the Stretford Memorial Outpatients' Department. Low brick additions to the rear including an extension by J. & J. Bolchover, 1985.

ROYAL ARMY MEDICAL CORPS, now the 207 Manchester Field Hospital. At the corner of Upper Chorlton Road and Darnley Street, Old Trafford. Dated 1903. Tudor in flavour, with a gatehouse-like entrance bay to the corner with tall crenellated octagonal towers. Transomed windows. Red brick with red sandstone dressings.

OLD TRAFFORD STATION, Trafford Bar, at the corner of Talbot Road, Old Trafford. The Manchester South Junction & Altrincham Railway (MSJ&AR) was opened in 1849; the station followed, probably in the mid 1850s. Canted to the street corner, with a parapet adorned with urns and a central elaborately carved stone entrance, windows with stone consoles.

BRIDGEWATER CANAL. For the history of the canal see Castlefield, Manchester, p. 350 and Worsley, p. 686. The stretch from the Mersey through low-lying land called Stretford E'es to the N had to be traversed by means of an embankment. Stone and brick AQUEDUCTS were built c. 1776 by John Gilbert and James Brindley to carry it over the Mersey at Barfoot Bridge, where the superstructure has been partly replaced by concrete, and over Hawthorn Road, where there are two stone arches over the sunken lane. The WATCH HOUSE, on the canal side off Hawthorn Road, is a pair of small brick houses with attached stables, probably late C18 and identifiable with those shown on a plan of 1785. It was a change-over point for the horses, and a staging post for the packet boat service between Runcorn and Manchester. One of the houses is said to have been used by a foreman responsible for maintenance of canal banks. The stables have a row of (blocked) circular pitching eyes above the entrances and in the gable. Converted to a club with loss of interior fittings.

(BRINDLEY'S WEIR, off Cornbrook Road. A culvert basin and sump designed by *James Brindley* in the 1760s to allow the Corn Brook to flow beneath the Bridgewater Canal.)

93 SWING BRIDGE AND AQUEDUCT, Redclyffe Road, Barton-upon-Irwell. The aqueduct carries the Bridgewater Canal, and replaces Brindley's pioneering aqueduct of 1761. This and a swing road bridge were constructed by *Sir Leader Williams* during the construction of the Manchester Ship Canal in the early 1890s. Fabrication was by *A. Handyside & Co.* A four-storey brick control tower with a pyramidal roof stands between the two, and the bridge and aqueduct revolve on a central axis so they swing lengthways on to the canal. The road bridge has bow-string lattice girders on each side of the deck. The aqueduct is constructed so that the canal channel remains full of water when it moves. The Bridgewater Canal is still navigable and the sight of a boat crossing the aqueduct with the Ship Canal below cannot fail to thrill.

CENTENARY LIFT BRIDGE, Centenary Way, Trafford Park. Built by the Trafford Park Development Corporation as a road bridge to link the N part of the Park with routes to the M60 motorway at Eccles. By *Parkman Consulting Engineers*, opened in 1994. Paired towers on each side with a steel deck which is carried on cables and can be lifted 75 ft (23 metres).

OTHER BUILDINGS

WHITE CITY, Chester Road, Old Trafford. The site started as botanical gardens, established in the 1820s. It was subsequently used as a greyhound track. The entrance PORTAL to the gardens of 1828 now fronts a 1980s–90s retail park. It is painted white. Central arched entrance flanked by advanced bays with paired unfluted columns under a heavy parapet, with pedestrian entrances on each side and the slightly advanced façades of two-storeyed lodges with columns flanking the windows. The simplest possible Greek Ionic order is used, probably based on the Little Temple on the Ilissus but lacking any enrichment.

GORSE HILL PARK, Chester Road, Old Trafford. The entrance is formed by an elaborate relocated gateway which formed the entrance to Trafford Hall in the mid C19. Central arch flanked by pedestrian entrances with attached Corinthian columns. Heavy iron gates with vine motifs. Attached on each side, single-storey lodges.

GREAT STONE, Chester Road, at the entrance to Gorse Hill Park, Old Trafford. Possibly a medieval cross base which gave its name to the immediate locality and nearby Great Stone Road. A large gritstone boulder with two sockets in the top, moved from nearby.

ESSOLDO CINEMA (former), Chester Road, Stretford. By *Henry Elder* of *Roberts, Wood & Elder*, 1936. One of the most entertaining sights in the Manchester area, if you do not mind a building being a joke. Striking Art Deco brick entrance block designed to look like a cash register, with stepped curves falling away from a prominent central fin, and a deeply recessed entrance. The exit, on Edge Lane, has an inwardly curving wall with a curved canopy topped by a tall phallic concrete pier. Elder explained that he chose the motifs because the film industry was mainly about 'money and sex'. It seated 2,000 and is said to retain the original basic layout and murals by *F. H. Baines*.

ESSENCE FACTORY, Chester Road, opposite Northumberland Road, Old Trafford. 1896 by *Briggs & Wolstenholme*. An uncommonly stately office building fronting the works, in bright red brick and red terracotta. The end towers have octagonal corner turrets, pyramidal roofs, and two-storey oriels. They are repeated on a smaller scale on either side of the central entrance, this with a portal flanked by octagonal piers. Round-arched windows, those of the first and second floors in a giant arcade.

QUAY WEST, Trafford Wharf Road, Trafford Park. By *The Ratcliff Partnership*, 1990. Glittering Postmodern offices, with a central inset pedimented bay flanked by clustered polygonal bays. It is given a monumental feeling by the all-enveloping reflective bronze-coloured cladding, making it appear to be windowless.

THE VILLAGE, off Village Way, Trafford Park. Trafford Park Dwellings Ltd was formed in 1899 and began building housing soon after for workers at the Westinghouse factory. Streets were laid out in a grid, those running N–S named First to Fourth Avenue, the E–W streets First to Twelfth Street. Almost 550 houses had been built by 1903. Shops were built on Third Avenue, an Anglican church (St Cuthbert, demolished) on the same street in 1902, and the R.C. church of St Antony (*see* above) on Eleventh Street in 1904. Hardly any houses survived clearance in the 1970s–80s, but a block of streets between Village Way (N), Europa Way (E), Westinghouse Road (S) and Mosley Road (W) preserves something of the original character. The shops are still there, and generally a small-scale residential character has been preserved. Late C20 development, mainly offices, keeping low, clad in red brick, with pitched roofs.

TRAFFORD PARK HOTEL, Ashburton Road East, Trafford Park. 1902. Now a pub. Large and garish, in red brick and painted terracotta. Eclectic Renaissance style, with big shaped gables, one each at the front and sides carrying the name of the hotel, and a big domed clock tower.

TRAFFORD ECOLOGY PARK, Lake Road. Formed from a lake in the grounds of Trafford Hall (*see* p. 648) and its environs. The OFFICE is a small low building, designed to be energy-efficient. 1999 by *Bareham Andrews Architects*. Slatted cedar screen to the main office area, angled roofs, and walls with corrugated aluminium cladding.

LIVERPOOL WAREHOUSING CO. LTD WAREHOUSES, Trafford Wharf Road, Trafford Park. The easternmost, dated 1932, is spare and monumental with a flush façade of full-height narrow loading bays and small windows. Covering the whole of the blank E side, a MURAL by *Walter Kershaw*, 1993, depicts Park industries, replacing an earlier mural by the artist on the same theme, of 1982. The sister warehouse, dated 1925, lies slightly to the W.

Opposite the 1932 warehouse, a C20 brick warehouse on an island site, with on the E and W side late C20 SCULPTURES. Large metal loading hooks on chains set on angled brick bases.

TRAFFORD CENTRE, Barton Dock Road, Trafford Park. By *Rodney Carran* of *Chapman Taylor Partners* for Peel Holdings. 1996–8. Carran designed the Lakeside Centre in Thurrock, Essex, 1990. This is another of the giant out-of-town private shopping centres of the generation which began with the Gateshead Metro Centre in 1986. The first planning application for the shopping centre was submitted in 1986, but permission was delayed until 1995 by a public inquiry and appeals. Caesar's Palace in Las Vegas was the inspiration for this extraordinary architectural menagerie, which is as daring in scale and ambition as it is shameless for its plundered historic and cultural motifs. Modified butterfly plan with a huge central dome and smaller domes at each end. The main entrance is fronted by a giant semicircular colonnade crowned with large Neoclassical-style statues by *Guy Portelli*. Otherwise, a mixture of classical, Neoclassical, Egyptian and Tudor domestic (polychrome brick diaperwork) motifs. The main entrance leads into a huge food court, which rises through two storeys, overlooked by galleries. It is modelled on a transatlantic liner complete with a pool and lifeboats, where people dine on 'deck', beneath a screen onto which is projected a sky which changes from day to night. Beyond, a Faux Ancient Egyptian temple and an Aztec-style casino. The upper level has an exhausting profusion of architectural settings for cafés and restaurants, including a 'New Orleans French quarter' with double-height ironwork balconies and Chinatown, with 'Chinese' houses and temples.* Shopping malls on two levels stretch in an arc beyond, generously top-lit, with real palm trees, pink columns and polished marble and granite floors. It is warm, scrupulously clean, and free of smoke, exhaust fumes, dogs and beggars. People flock here to eat and shop in the safety and comfort of a fairytale world in which everything is owed to Disney and nothing to the Brothers Grimm.

LANCASHIRE COUNTY CRICKET CLUB, Warwick Road, Old Trafford. The Manchester Cricket Club moved here in 1856 and amalgamated with the Lancashire County Cricket Club in 1880. A pavilion built in 1857 was replaced in 1894–5 by *Thomas Muirhead* (who later designed the cricket pavilion at the Oval in London). Full-height towers with copper domes

---

* Terry Wyke draws attention to some noteworthy SCULPTURE: Spirit of New Orleans, by *Colin Spofforth*, 1998, and Arthur Brooke, by *Anthony Stones*, 1999.

flank the stand, which has an arcade of big arched openings at the base and open canopied seating above.

MANCHESTER UNITED FOOTBALL CLUB STADIUM, Sir Matt Busby Way, Old Trafford. The 1910 stadium was designed by *Brameld & Smith*, engineer *Archibald Leitch*, but only the old players' tunnel survives.* Otherwise it is standard late C20 stuff, though the North Stand by *Atherden Fuller* with engineers *Campbell Reith Hill* claimed to have Europe's largest cantilever roof when it was put up in 1996.

OLD TRAFFORD BOWLS CLUB, Talbot Road, Old Trafford. 1877. Unusually large and early club premises with little alteration. Traditional timber-framed style, two storeys, with a balcony overlooking the green, clubroom, billiard room, etc.

SUMMERSEAT

Immediately s of Ramsbottom, but only accessible from there on foot or by steam train. It has become a nest of upward mobility, its little roads choked with traffic and its industrial buildings and cottages mercilessly restored.

ROWLAND METHODIST CHURCH (site). The magnificent TOMB of John Robinson Kay †1872, by *J. S. Crowther*, now stands exposed on a flat grass plat. A big table-tomb of marble and granite set with fat semi-precious stones and with carved roundels personifying his virtues – Fortitudo, Humilitas etc., and raised on an octagonal platform of half-grassed-over coloured tiles. The exceptionally ambitious church, in Perpendicular Gothic, 1844–7 by *James Simpson*, and the octagonal mausoleum (also by *Crowther?*) in which the tomb stood, were demolished in 1978. Behind still stands the long Gothic SCHOOL.

BROOKSBOTTOM MILL. Established by Robert Peel in 1773. Acquired in 1830 by John Robinson Kay, who developed the surrounding village. The present building is of 1874–6 by *Russell & Whitaker* of Rochdale. Four-storey Italianate cotton-spinning mill, formerly L-shaped and with single-storey north-light weaving sheds. Integral engine house, expressed by a large arched window between pilaster-strips facing the river. The octagonal chimney has gone, but the OFFICE of 1877 remains and so does a two-storey canteen block of 1890 bridging the river. Office and mill are of polychrome stone with varied window treatments on each floor. All now converted to residential and entertainment use. VICTORIAN LANTERNS is another residential conversion – the name is the key to its sensitivity – of a goods trans-shipment shed backing onto the railway. The former MECHANICS' INSTITUTE on Hill Street, looking rather like an Italianate chapel, 'has been converted in the most insensitive manner' says Dr Leach.

*According to Simon Inglis.

MILLER STREET is a surprise among the plain stone and brick
terraces: a white Tudor-Gothic row of 1855 of some pretension,
with its back to the road. Three spaced-out gables, Gothic
doorcases, dripmoulds.

SUMMERSEAT HOUSE (Pupil Learning Centre), Summerseat
Lane. Built by Richard Hamer, mill manager, in 1836. Five-
bay, double-pile classical house, rendered except for its stone
portico, with at least some of its grounds and planting preserved. Fine interiors, particularly the square staircase hall in
the centre. The stair has swirling cast-iron balustrading, and
there are plaster acanthus and fruit baskets round the soffit of
its dome.

Close by, also on Summerseat Lane, is PEEL HALL. Multi-
period house. HEM 1706 is carved over the lintel of the purely
vernacular section.

7000   SWINTON

Between Pendlebury (NE) and Worsley (SW), and merging with
them. There is a proper centre where the church and civic buildings are, with residential areas around.

ST PETER, Chorley Road. St Peter replaces a chapel of 1791, a
quite substantial but very plain building. The new church, of
1869, and the choice of *G. E. Street* as its architect, was due
to the Rev. H. R. Heywood, son of Sir Benjamin Heywood and
brother of Sir Percival Heywood and also of Edward Stanley
Heywood, who paid for the nearby Pendlebury Church (q.v.).
The Heywoods were a Manchester banking family of Nonconformist descent. But Sir Benjamin joined the Church of
England and both Swinton and Pendlebury are the expressions
of the Tractarian convictions of his sons. The church, with
nearly all the plate, bells and organ, cost £18,000. Of this the
contract with the architect was for £12,233. The architect's fee
was £718. Of the money the incumbent gave £4,650, Sir
Benjamin £1,100 and yet another brother £1,061.

The E view of the church is of three gables, chancel and
chapels, and the higher aisle gables appearing behind. The W
side has a robust tower and the aisle W gables l. and r. of it.
The tower has a stair-turret projecting at the NW corner and
rising higher than the tower. The vestry on the N side con-
tributes two cross-gables. The roof has diamond patterns in
coloured slate. That is enough variety. The tracery is of the conventional C13 kind. The interior is robust too: four wide bays,
Dec piers, naturalistic capitals (carved by *Earp*), an ample
chancel arch, and the two-bay chapels. The chancel arcade is
simpler than that of the nave, which has slender shafts at the
angles of the quatrefoils. The chancel has a wagon roof, the
nave is of the deliberately elementary single-frame type, with
close-set timbers creating an insistent pattern. The aisles have
full kingpost roofs. The anomaly that there are five windows
to the four arcade arches is explained by an afterthought

of Street's, who felt so strongly about five windows as an improvement on four that he paid for the change himself. One looks at Swinton with respect. It has more body than Scott's Worsley (q.v.), but it lacks the elating quality of Bodley's Pendlebury. Be that as it may; we ought to be grateful for three such Victorian churches distant from each other by only a few miles. At this time England was stronger and more powerful in its Gothic churches than any other country. Pendlebury and Swinton stand out above any contemporary Gothic buildings in France or Germany.

REREDOS. Marble arcading with inlaid polychromatic marble, now with some gilding. – Beautiful open ironwork PARCLOSES. – PULPIT. Stone, with arcading inlaid with polychromatic marbles and panels with finely carved fleurons. – *Minton* TILE FLOORS, the most ornate reserved for the chancel. – FONT. Bowl carved with fleurons supported by clustered shafts. Ornate spire-like Gothic cover of painted cast-iron. – STAINED GLASS. One of the best assemblages in the region. E window by *Clayton & Bell*, who also did the W and tower windows, and two in the N aisle. N chapel E, painted glass by *Kempe*, c.1870. At the W end of the N aisle two good interwar windows by *Whall & Whall* with beautifully drawn figures on a pale ground; also in the N aisle a late C19 window by *Edward Frampton*. S aisle, three late windows by *Morris & Co.*, the westernmost Christ blessing children, dedicated in 1909; the Calling of Peter, 1902 by *J. H. Dearle* of *Morris & Co.*; the third of 1896 showing the miraculous draught of fishes. At the W end of the S aisle a window by *Powell & Sons*, 1898.

LYCHGATE. A First World War memorial. Stone, Gothic, and gabled, with statues in niches by *J. Lenigan*.

HOLY ROOD, Moorside Road. By *Henry Lord*, 1911. Large, towerless, Romanesque, red brick. There was evidently not enough money for the finely detailed terracotta dressings typical of Lord.

METHODIST CHURCH, Moorside Road. Dated 1891 and rather grand. Brick with liberal stone dressings, eclectic Renaissance style.

METHODIST CHURCH (formerly Primitive Methodist), Manchester Road, 1891. Of stone, with everything concentrated on the street elevation where a single-storey porch fronts a big gable flanked by low towers with parapets with gables, corner pinnacles and balustrading. W window with fancy tracery.

UNITED REFORMED CHURCH, Worsley Road. Typical early C20 attenuated Perp, red brick and white stone. The building of c. 1870 it replaced is now used as a hall. Gothic in the sense that it has pointed windows.

SALFORD NORTHERN CEMETERY, Cemetery Road. Buildings by *Sharp & Foster*, 1903. A LODGE and OFFICES flank the entrance. Brick, rather plain and dull. Near the centre of the site is a cruciform CHAPEL with lancets and a thin W spirelet.

MUNICIPAL BUILDINGS, Chorley Road. St Peter's Church (above) is no longer seen as it should be, owing to the large clearing made for this anaemic Neoclassical building. It is of light brick, two-storeyed, with a giant portal arch and slender middle clock tower. The entrance sequence fails to work, with the door giving to a series of poky spaces before a generous stair leads to a hall with coffered ceilings and paired columns placed axially. The council chamber also has coffered ceilings. The architects were *Percy Thomas & Ernest Prestwich* of nearby Leigh. The date is 1937. Extensions of 1973 by *Cruickshank & Seward*, 1976 by *Leach, Rhodes & Walker*, and 1989–90 by *Salford City Council Architects' Department*.

LIBRARY AND LANCASTRIAN HALL, Chorley Road. *c.* 1968, by *Leach, Rhodes & Walker*. Large, ugly, of concrete. Few of the projections and recessions represent functional necessities. The attached SHOPPING CENTRE which followed is hardly better.

ROYAL MANCHESTER CHILDREN'S HOSPITAL, Hospital Road. By *Pennington & Bridgen*, 1872–3. On the pavilion plan, and said to have been modelled on St Thomas's Hospital in London (1868–71). Pale brick with stone dressings, Italianate, the main block to the road with a truncated central octagonal tower and a projecting pedimented entrance bay with a portico. Most of the rest has been engulfed by new building and extensions, but the tall water tower at the E end of the site is still a landmark. The hospital originated as the General Dispensary for Children in 1829 and moved to this site from the centre of Manchester.

VICTORIA PARK, Manchester Road. Mid-C19 LODGE with minimal Tudor detailing, originally a toll house. Attractive cast-iron LAMPS along the main route. BANDSTAND, erected for Queen Victoria's Jubilee in 1897. Cast-iron with an octagonal canopy topped by a little cupola and with pretty cast-iron brackets.

THORNHAM *see* MIDDLETON

TOTTINGTON

7010

Pennine fringe settlement on the road NW from Bury to Turton. Across the valley ¾ m. N is Greenmount, included here. In between was a calico printworks, developed from an C18 spinning, weaving and bleaching business by Joshua Knowles. In 1841 he was employing 300, a third of them children. The figure was 450 in 1901 but the mill closed in 1928, leaving the usual series of lodges (reservoirs), an isolated chimney, and some eccentric ancillary buildings – *see* Tower Farm. Tottington's churches tell a story of robust independence, and so does its domestic architecture. This is noticeable in the details as much as in whole structures – see for instance the doorcases of the Robin Hood pub of 1708 and the Carmelo Restaurant, Market

Street, whose jambs and lintel, just three stones in the Pennine manner, are carved to look like a fully rusticated surround and flat arch.

St Anne. A preaching box of 1799 – a rare survival of what was a common type in the area, attractively placed on a green hillside. Two storeys, four bays by two, of watershot stone. Twin entrances, bellcote. Five-light Gothic window inserted in the flat E wall, probably early C20. Galleries round three sides, on iron stanchions encased in the C20 by square wooden posts. (STAINED GLASS, E by *Heaton, Butler & Bayne*, 1912.) Handsome three-bay VICARAGE, N.

   NATIONAL SCHOOL, immediately S, 1835.

St John (Free Church of England), Kirklees Street. In 1853 the vicar of Tottington appeared in the pulpit in a surplice, whereupon most of the congregation marched out, burnt him in effigy, and founded their own church. It later joined the Free Church of England, which had been founded in 1844 as a reaction against the Tractarians, with affiliations to the Countess of Huntingdon's Connexion. Plain stone building with rectangular windows and a bellcote, but with a four-column Greek portico – added in 1867, but surely reused from another building – serving as a porch. A Tractarian chancel was added in 1909–10, nullifying its *raison d'être*. The church is in a weary state today. Much of the interior, riddled with rot, has been stripped out, leaving the hammerbeam roof as just a bolted iron armature. – Simple FITTINGS, with a central block of pews, but with a full set of choir stalls and an organ (given as a war memorial in 1921) in the chancel. – STAINED GLASS. The windows have been made pointed on the inside, and some of the glass represents tracery. In the nave three windows of the 1950s signed W.W. Liverpool, presumably *Williams & Watson*. Chancel early C20 by *H. Gustav Hiller* also of Liverpool, depicting Faith, Hope, Love and Duty.

   SCHOOL, alongside. 1869, enlarged 1905; now residential.

Methodist Church, Spring Street. By *Arthur Brocklebank*, 1905. Large traceried windows over the entrance, between the characteristic shoulders for gallery stairs, and at the E end. At the sides unattractive paired round-topped lancets. (Well-preserved interior with raked seating. – Art Nouveau CHANCEL FURNISHINGS, ORGAN CASE, DOOR FURNITURE, STAINED GLASS in doors. – WAR MEMORIAL. Tablets in glass mosaic and tile, perhaps by *Walter J. Pearce*.)

   The big WESLEYAN SCHOOL of 1868, by *E. Simpkin* of Bury, faces the other way, onto Wesley Street. Seven by four bays, two storeys, classical. Restored in 2003 as fifteen apartments and now looking much brighter than the working church.

Greenmount School/Chapel (Congregational), ½ m. N. Built 1846, extended 1890. Greenmount village only came into existence with the chapel, and took its name from it. A forceful building, low and wide, in a simple Norman style, with a corbel table and widely spaced round-arched windows between flat buttresses. Bellcote at both ends. Very like the school at Elton (outer Bury, q.v.), so perhaps also by *John Harper*. The rear extension has five side gables.

CONGREGATIONAL CHURCH, Greenmount. A churchy replacement for the school/chapel (above), 1865–7, by *George Woodhouse*. Gothic, with a ritual NW spire. Galleries were intended, although they never materialized; hence the low polygonal staircase tower balancing the steeple, which alone identifies it as a Nonconformist church. Short chancel-like extension at the ritual E end, but no E window.

LIBRARY, Market Street. It was Tottington Hall, C19 home of the Nuttall family, then for a while the town hall. Its plain early C19 five-bay ashlar façade faces away from the road. Behind – i.e. towards the road – are older parts, including a nice C17 stable with gable kneelers and a mullioned corner window. Part of the garden is preserved, with extensive rockwork. WAR MEMORIAL *c.* 1920, white granite, powerfully put together and with an unusually poetic text; bronze medallions of a setting sun and a descending dove.

STORMER HILL. An interesting group, mostly of brick, on Holcombe Road. STORMER HILL HOUSE stands on the crest. Impressively large, with 1770 ES and EE/S 1762 cast on the rainwater hoppers. (Two fireplaces in the Long Room made of wooden printing blocks from Tottington Printworks.) Over the road is STORMER HILL FOLD, with a beautifully cut stone in a gable end inscribed Smalley/Edward Ellen/1759. In the valley towards the church a pair of brick cottages with a third-storey workshop on top. A long flight of external steps leads up to it.

THE DUNGEON, Harwood Road. A former lock-up, with a huge date 1835 carved over the door. Everything is exaggerated on this tiny building. The stones are gigantically rusticated, with crudely carved faces, crossed bones, and a key for variety. Great slabs for the roof. The grilled door is of massive iron with a surely unnecessary knocker in a lion's mouth. Next to it is another curiosity. No.10 is the thinnest possible house, and moreover leans perceptibly to starboard; a 10 ft (3 metre) wide slice of a terrace, but it is hard to see where the rest of the terrace could have been.

40 THE IMAGES, Nabbs House, Brandlesholme Road. A splendid Gothick folly like a castle gatehouse with two round towers. It was built by John Turner in the 1840s to get drunk in, with the same grossly pecked rustication as The Dungeon, and even more in the way of grotesquely carved faces and creatures. It had two fireplaces, with outrageous chimneys with faces, one of which remains, and was lined with carved oak panelling of which a fragment remains. It was linked to the house by a passage in the hollow boundary wall, which remains, and by two buried chambers lined with quartz, which have been removed. Close to the house is a stone bench into which *John Turner* has incorporated a stone carving of himself asleep, with his gun, powder bottles, and a brace of birds.

TOWER FARM, off Brandlesholme Road, Greenmount. It was the stableyard of Tottington Print Mill. Inscribed JK (Joshua Knowles) 1840 on the gatehouse tower, which is tall and sheer with a machicolated top ringed with pretend gunports. Arrowslits and a quatrefoil window. Joshua Knowles served his apprenticeship with the Grants at Ramsbottom, and the building was a near copy of the Grants' Nuttall Hall Farm.

BRANDLESHOLME, Brandlesholme Road, 1 m. E. Still surrounded by fields, an unkempt fold, i.e. a huddle of three or four dwellings and associated agricultural buildings. The nucleus is BRANDLESHOLME OLD HALL, originally the home of the bailiff of Tottington Forest, perhaps late C15, but possibly earlier. White and roughcast, with accretions. Only the long roof of the hall range raises expectations. The interior is all the more exciting for revealing itself bit by bit. The house place in the centre is quite a fine apartment with an enormous inglenook fireplace at the S end, with a smaller masonry fireplace inside it. Wall posts are visible, cut off by the high, heavily timbered ceiling which has evidently been inserted, perhaps in the C16 or early C17. The centre pair, with good base mouldings, stand on tall stone pads. The rest of the great hall – for that is what it is – can be seen in a little 'minstrel's gallery' to one side of the smoke hood, in the upstairs rooms, and finally by squirming into what must represent the upper part of the smoke hood. Behind the stone stack that was inserted in the smoke hood is a splendid spere truss, with cusped bracing between the massive spere posts and the wall posts. So this was the low end, and the stack was built in front of the screen. The high arched intermediate trusses can be seen, well moulded and of good quality, carrying kingposts; quatrefoil windbracing. Front and back wall plates are present, and at least the top of the W wall inside its skin of brick. At the high end (N) is another post brought forward on a dwarf wall, forming what appears to be another spere truss. This is decorated by scalloping and battlements. This could indeed be a second screens passage, resulting from dividing the property or reversing the service and family wings; but a more likely interpretation, comparing it with Little Mitton Hall, N Lancashire, or (on a larger scale) Ordsall Hall, Salford (see p. 636), is an alcove for the dais between matching spere posts, giving the hall a degree of longitudinal symmetry. In the N wing, handy from the dais, is a half-spiral stair climbing round an octagonal mast. Its midfloor is square-framed with finely moulded joists of C16 type.

The S wing is now a separate dwelling called BRANDLESHOLME HALL. It was rebuilt in Tudor style in 1849 after a fire. The division is at the spere truss, so it includes the space of the former screens passage. The insertion of the intermediate floor in the hall, and the addition of the inglenook and smoke hood may well have taken place at the same time as the division into two properties, i.e. probably in the C16 or C17. It is interesting that the inserted floor is set high, so that the house place is still taller than the other rooms.

BRANDLESHOLME HALL FARM, on the same yard, is red brick
and Late Victorian. Immediately behind it is a CRUCK BARN,
also probably C15 or C16, stone-faced with a stone roof. The
three cruck trusses have a low tie-beam and a collar set near
the apex. On either side of the W door are aisled sections.

UNSWORTH

ST GEORGE, Moss Lane. 1843, by *Mills & Butterworth*, replacing a building of 1730. Brick, lancet style, with the usual thin
buttresses, a stone bellcote, and a tiny chancel. C20 octagonal
parish room added S, in buff brick.
BRICK HOUSE FARM. ¾ m. NW, over the motorway off Castle
Lane, in a surprising but characteristic island of open country.
Of 1681. It lives up to its name, with raised diapering and
strings, mullions, and a blank oval in the gable all proudly in
brick.

URMSTON

Urmston lies W of Stretford and merges imperceptibly with
Davyhulme, NW, and Flixton, S. It was little more than a village
before the railway arrived in 1872–3. The population rose from
996 in 1871 to 4,042 in 1891.

CARR DITCH, Winchester Road, Moorside Road (line of).
Similar to Nico Ditch (*see* Denton), but not now thought to
be part of the same feature. The ditch is nowhere visible, but
it forms the ancient boundary between Flixton and Davyhulme, and it may be the ditch mentioned in a document of
1278.
ST CLEMENT, Manor Avenue. 1868 by *J. Medland Taylor*, the N
aisle by *Taylor* too, 1873–5. Lengthened to the W in 1887–8 by
Whittenbury & Mather. The tower dates from 1899–1903. The
church is in the early C14 style, with much variety of window
tracery, some of which is owed more to the imagination of the
architect than to precedent. Rock-faced stone with red sandstone banding. Friendly timbered S porch. The N aisle matches
the nave in height. Between the two at the junction with the
chancel, a little octagonal spirelet, a typical Taylor motif. The
low S aisle has windows beneath flat heads, and there is an
unexpected dormer in the nave at the E end with a spherical-
triangular window with strange tracery details. Inside there are
more odd touches, as one expects of this architect. The tall N
arcade has columns with rings, and at its E end there are
strange things happening around the pulpit, where there is a
setback between the arcade and chancel, and a niche in the
NE respond. Columns of the S arcade are alternately circular
and octagonal with plain moulded caps, except the easternmost, which is foliated. Arch- and scissor-braced nave roof,

arch-braced N aisle roof with kingposts. The chancel arch is cusped, and the N aisle E window is circular yet has mullions like a normal window with a pointed arch, reminiscent of a transept window of Taylor's St Anne, Denton (q.v.). The organ chamber at the E end of the N aisle has an unusual frontispiece of 1894; arched entrance with granite columns flanked by arched niches with organ pipes. – FONT. Large circular bowl. – STAINED GLASS. The best is the w window, the Sermon on the Mount in a lush landscape. – MONUMENT. On the s chancel wall a very good bronze portrait relief, Rev. E. Harwood Cooke, by *John Cassidy*, 1919. In the N porch, FIRST WORLD WAR MEMORIAL with alabaster arcading, by *Patteson*.

UNITARIAN CHURCH, Queen's Road. Early C20, all of hard red brick and red terracotta, with lancets. An unusual design with a central crossing with a slated spirelet and shallow transepts.

ENGLISH MARTYRS (R.C.), Roseneath Road. 1913. Attributed to *J. Spark*, but he may have just been the contractor, as he was at the Cottage Hospital (below). Pale brick with busy red brick dressings. Low towers with pyramidal roofs flank the w entrance, which has a projecting porch clad in red terracotta. Triple lancets beneath round arches. Attached former SCHOOL of similar materials.

CEMETERY, Queen's Road. Opened in 1892, when the buildings were still under construction. Large LODGE, red brick with stone dressings, Elizabethan style. Two CHAPELS on either side of a big square tower with a tall through-archway, three bell-openings, and an inset upper stage with a pyramidal roof.

JEWISH CEMETERY, Chapel Grove and Albert Street. Land at Urmston was first acquired by the Manchester Spanish & Portuguese Jews' Congregation (Sephardi community) probably in 1878, which is the date of the earliest recorded tombstone. The Ashkenazi New Synagogue (Cheetham Hill) purchased land for an extension in 1892. Simple brick OHEL (chapel) by *William Sharp Ogden* at the end of Albert Avenue, dated 1894. A second Ohel, also very low-key and of brick, was built on Chapel Grove in 1900 for the Manchester Burial Society of Polish Jews. Good varied range of late C19 and C20 monuments.

POLICE STATION, Church Road and Station Road. 1904. Elizabethan, brick and much stone, dated 1904. Tudor-arched doorways, stone bays. Unfussy and pretty.

URMSTON GRAMMAR SCHOOL, Newton Road. Opened in 1929. Brick with stone dressings and hardly any decoration except at the main entrance. Here there is a little clock turret and an elaborate Neo-Georgian porch with urns and a high pedimented gable breaking through the eaves.

COTTAGE HOSPITAL (former), Greenfield Avenue. By *Edward Hewitt* of Manchester. Dated 1897 and 1899, opened in 1900. A Jubilee project to provide nursing care for those without help at home. Three bays, with a central shaped gable and a frieze with the words Cottage Hospital (now obscured).

RAILWAY STATION, Station Road. Dated 1872. Brick with gables and bargeboards and minimal Gothic detailing.

SHOPPING CENTRE. By *Leach, Rhodes & Walker, c.* 1968. Long low blocks with projecting concrete beams and recessed walkways. Unlike so many centres of this date, it is popular and well used.

DOCTOR'S SURGERY, Station Road and Gloucester Road. An attractive large house, said to have been built for Dr Walter Mayne *c.* 1900 and still used as a doctor's surgery. Brick, asymmetrical with projecting wings with upper timbering, tall channelled chimneys.

7000

WALKDEN

NW of Swinton and merging with it.

ST PAUL, Manchester Road. 1848 by *William Young.* Made memorable by the blunt SW tower and forceful octagonal stair-turret with a pyramidal top. Nave and aisles and lower chancel. N aisle added 1881–2. Quatrefoil clerestory windows grouped in pairs, otherwise lancets. The point is that the architect of 1848 was entirely on the Pugin–Scott side, with no leftovers of the early C19 Gothic in detail or plan. Arcade of alternate circular and octagonal piers, high hammerbeam roof on corbels carved with angels in 1882 by *Mr Millson* (probably *J. J. Millson* of Manchester). Chancel with scissor-braced roof. – Chancel FURNISHINGS include an elaborate carved timber SCREEN of 1915 and a mosaic REREDOS of 1904. – STAINED GLASS. N aisle, a densely coloured late C19 window by *R. Bennett* of Manchester in the style of Burne-Jones, but badly drawn.

ST JOHN, Worsley Road North. By *J. Medland & Henry Taylor,* 1876. Polygonal crossing tower. Note the funny (typically Taylorian) way in which the stair-turret links up with the tower. Polygonal apse, no aisles.

ST PAUL, Manchester Road (N of the centre). 1874–6 by *J. Medland & Henry Taylor.* It replaced a chapel founded in 1734. Stone, W tower with broach spire added in 1897. Dec details; some of the tracery is quite individual, and though there is no immediate impression of the roguishness which characterizes the firm, the eye is soon drawn to details such as the bellcote with a perky roof, marking the chancel and underlining the fact that it is higher than the nave. Very emphatic separation of the parts. Tall paired gable chimneys to the vestry. Aisles and N transept chapel with a wheel window. (Hammerbeam roof, stone CHANCEL RAIL incorporating PULPIT and LECTERN in coloured stone, C18 baluster FONT from the previous church, STAINED GLASS by *Shrigley & Hunt.*)

MONUMENT. NW of the church, a chest tomb with husk garlands on the sides, to Margaret Hewitt of Peel Hall †1788.

ELLESMERE MEMORIAL, Manchester Road. Moved from the crossroads to the W edge of St Paul's churchyard. 1868 by *T. G.*

Walkden, Ellesmere Memorial, from *The Builder*, 1868

Jackson, then only thirty-three years old. He won a competition assessed by Street. The carving was by *Farmer & Brindley*. A tabernacle with a high pinnacle, richly decorated and topped with a cross finial. One would expect to see a statue in the tabernacle but there is only a short fat column. At the corners figures of a cotton-worker, a collier and two factory girls have been removed. Above, life-size figures of Piety, Chastity, Munificence and Prudence in elaborate canopied niches. The monument commemorates the widow of Francis Egerton, 1st Earl of Ellesmere, who was a philanthropist especially interested in the education of girls.

CIVIC AND MARKET HALL, Manchester Road. By *Shingler Risdon Associates*, 1963–5. Appallingly bleak and overscaled, in exposed concrete.

PEEL HALL, Peel Lane. The hall, of *c.* 1840–5 and attributed to *Charles Barry*, has gone. Only a fanciful little stone Tudor

GATEHOUSE on the corner of Peel Lane and Parkway and a domed brick mid-C19 ICE HOUSE in the woods just s off the entrance drive, survive. In the grounds ST ANNE'S HOSPICE, by *Rod Hackney & Associates*, 1981, a low building of warm orange brick and pantile roofs employing traditional forms, clustering around a courtyard.

8010

WALMERSLEY

Walmersley Road heads due N from Bury, long and straight. Its s end is lined with solid Victorian houses, often in short terraces with the ends turned to punctuate them. These give way to much lower terraces of stone, with an occasional open space.

CHRISTCHURCH, Walmersley Road. The SCHOOL of 1839 and SCHOOLHOUSE of 1842 remain from the previous church. Its W tower stood in front of the school, with a simple unaisled nave, 'inconvenient and out of keeping with modern ideas' towards the road. Its replacement is by *Maxwell & Tuke* and is dated 1883. Typically of the architects, it is very sparingly buttressed with precise stonework, its walls and windows looking more like a stretched envelope than a massy structure. Bar tracery of the Chartres type, very flat, or plain wide lancets. The SW tower, outside the aisle, was completed in 1913. It is much fussier in its upper reaches. The high cradle roof runs through from end to end, with no chancel arch. Circular piers, bearing, with an effort, oversized square capitals and a thick upper wall and clerestory. Transepts, or rather transeptal chapels, and a long chancel with a mosaic floor. – REREDOS and WAINSCOT are a First World War memorial. – STAINED GLASS, E, a survival from the old church, in typically glaring colours with blue predominating. The rest, all in place at the consecration, are chancel s by *Lavers, Barraud & Westlake*, s transept by *Heaton, Butler & Bayne*, and N transept by *Ward & Hughes*. Two small windows in the s aisle also by *Ward & Hughes*, 1891.

SPUR PETROLEUM next to the church, was WALMERSLEY BREWERY. Recorded in 1842, it was owned by the Chadwicks of Glorybutts Farm, along with several pubs. The buildings face a courtyard, with a tower inscribed with the name, and a square chimney. On the road a handsome early C19 house/office/pub.

BALDINGSTONE HALL, Walmersley Old Road. Long C17 stone house with a pair of round-arched windows each side of the door. Other windows have plain mullions, with extra lights for the house place.

MOUNT PLEASANT, 1 m. N on Walmersley Old Road. High up, on the shoulder of Snape Hill. It was a fold, i.e. a cluster of dwellings and farm buildings, which developed in the C18 as a collection point for hand-woven pieces, then was built up from 1819 by John Hall as a factory village. The mill was set on two sides of a square lodge (reservoir), with terraces of cottages on the other sides. John Hall Ltd expanded into the early C20 but closed in 1965. The mill complex was demolished or completely remodelled in the 1980s, when the lodge was filled in, but the cottages on their stony streets remain.

WALSHAW

A mile or so W of Bury, up the hill.

CHRISTCHURCH. Named prominently on the W wall the Jesse Haworth Memorial Church. 'Uncle Jesse', who had employed most of the village at his fustian works, died in 1887 leaving £593,000. The church was commissioned from *Lawrence Booth* of *Booth & Chadwick* by his sister and nephew in 1888, and built in 1889–92 'for the diffusion of evangelical doctrine as set forth in the book of common prayer and the thirty-nine articles of the church of England as by law established'. It is indeed a demonstration of liberality (£28,000) and of Evangelical churchmanship. Booth rose to the capabilities of the hillside site, placing the steeple at the SE where it can be admired from Bury town centre below, decking the sides with crossgables and decorating the whole with lavish carving. The style was said to be Geometric Gothic, though the windows have un-Gothic transoms. The stone is from Holcombe, 3 m. N.

The nave is as wide as the preaching houses of the Nonconformists – as wide as the tall chancel arch and its side arches together. The aisles are mere passages, behind circular piers of grey granite with shaft-rings on high octagonal bases. There are broad transepts, two bays wide. The arcade marches past them, doubled. There are chancel transepts too, the N containing the organ on a high platform, the S, under the tower, the Haworth pew under its dedication inscriptions. Broad hammerbeam roof. There is animated carving everywhere: cushion capitals with unconventional foliage, twisting and twirling angel corbels, and an arcaded REREDOS; all executed by *Richard Williams* of Accrington. – MOSAIC in the reredos by the *Venice & Murano Glass Co.* – PULPIT and READING DESK, almost matching on either side of the chancel arch, by *Pearson & Brown* of Pendleton. – Fat FONT, also carved by *Williams*, octagonal top and bottom but bulging circularly with lush foliage in the middle. – ALTAR TABLE, N transept, like a piece of polite furniture; carved relief panel in the middle. – STAINED GLASS. The complete didactic scheme, each window with its biblical reference, was in place at the consecration. All with angels above the transom. E by *Arthur Dix*, chancel N and S by *Cakebread, Robey & Co.*, the rest by *W. Pape* of Leeds.

WALSHAW CO-OP NO. 5, on the corner of Bank Street. Now J. T. R. Controls Ltd. Dated 1891. It sweeps round a corner with broad shop windows on central iron posts, inscribed on

their lintels GROCER, CLOGGER, NEWS ROOM and BUTCHER.
HIGH CROMPTON, Bentley Hall Road. Long stone C17 farmhouse with quoins and dripmoulds. The door at the NE end is
in line with the chimney, so presumably a baffle entry. Beyond
this is a short non-residential section with a taking-in door.

WARDLE

9010

A tough Pennine hamlet, grown industrial, and now residential.
Evidence for proto-industrialization the long weavers' windows,
often partly blocked, of the old houses e.g. in Wardle Fold and
Knowl Syke Street, even in the Globe Inn. Evidence for early
mills the several lodges (reservoirs), and WHITTAKER MILL of
1815, which is little different in its architecture from a row of
weavers' houses, and now indeed residential.

ST JAMES. By *George Shaw*, 1856–8, but built by Edward Taylor
of the town, not by Shaw himself as was usual. It was abandoned in 1973 and is derelict, a disturbing presence. Typical
Shaw steeple on the s side overlooking the valley with a tight
broach spire. The body of the church is austere, E.E. unusually for the architect, with lancets in ones, twos and threes. It
cost £2,700. VICARAGE, also presumably by *Shaw*, immediately w.
WESLEYAN METHODIST CHAPEL. 1874. It also accommodates
the Church of England congregation. Stone, Italianate, with
a Doric portico. (Interior subdivided horizontally at gallery
level.) Immediately N is its modest predecessor of 1809.
Immediately above the village is WATERGROVE RESERVOIR of
1930–8. In its boundary wall many datestones of drowned and
destroyed buildings, mainly C18 and C19.

WARDLEY

7000

The settlement is on the w edge of Swinton and the Salford
conurbation, merging with it but giving way to open fields to the
s and w. It was an ancient estate within the manor of Worsley
(q.v.) which passed to the Tyldesley family before being absorbed
back into the Worsley estate in the C18.

ALL SAINTS, Hamilton Street. 1912–13 by the patron *Colonel
Bertram Heywood* with the architect *T. H. Cunliffe*. An odd little
building designed as a church hall and used for worship
pending the erection of a new church, which never materialized. Bold square Neo-Georgian porch complete with urns at
the corners, an octagonal timber cupola and rustication in
raised brickwork. Otherwise a brick box with a great big red
sandstone Diocletian E window. Other windows also of stone,
with round arches.
WARDLEY HALL, Wardley Hall Lane. Built by Thurstan
Tyldesley, who inherited in 1495 and died in 1554, on the site

of a house dating from the C14. After various changes in ownership the house and lands were bought by the 3rd Duke of Bridgewater in 1760. The house later fell into decay and was restored in 1894 by *John Douglas*. It was acquired in 1930 with land for use as a cemetery (*see* below) by the Roman Catholic Church as the residence of the bishops of Salford. A campaign of repair and alteration, done in exemplary manner, was started soon after.

Wardley is a courtyard house, sitting on a large platform, with a tremendous moat. This was filled in on the N and NE sides, probably in the early C19, and landscaped to give it an irregular outline. The important thing about Wardley is that it captures that moment in the architectural development of houses where there is still a cross-passage, while the hall already had a great chamber above. A similar arrangement is seen at Wythenshawe Hall (*see* p. 499) and probably at nearby Worsley Old Hall, Worsley (q.v.). The main body of the house including E and W wings seems to be largely of one build, or done in closely spaced campaigns, as the roof trusses show. The irregular plan must have been inherited from the previous house, and the angle of the E side is said to relate to the line of the moat. Corridors and a stair-tower were added piecemeal on the inner, courtyard, sides, probably in the late C16 or C17. The outer timber-framed walls were partially rebuilt in brick, possibly in the C17, perhaps when the brick s gatehouse

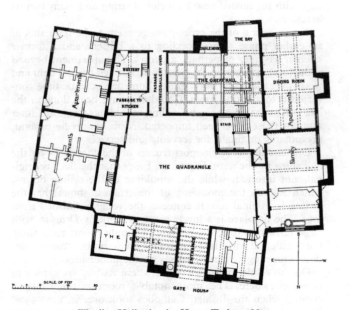

Wardley Hall, plan by Henry Taylor, 1884

range was added or rebuilt. Close-studded timber-framing survives on each side of the hall range. To *Douglas* is owed the
stone bay windows on the S and E sides, the channelled brick
chimneys, some but not all of the stacks, some brick repair
and refacing, and the stone mullions and transoms of windows
in the brick outer walls; also some fireplaces, etc.

The GATEHOUSE has very odd coved eaves to the E, and a
gabled centre with an arched entrance. It was formerly dated
1625. The outer face and mullioned windows are largely
Douglas's work, and the adjoining gabled N end of the W wing
is also late C19 or C20 work. The gatehouse inner face has
basket-arched moulds over some of the windows, like those of
the C17 brick wing at Ordsall Hall (*see* p. 636). In the cobbled
courtyard the outer corridor walls and the stair-tower all have
herringbone framing, but the roof pattern shows that there was
more than one campaign of work here.

The entrance on the S side of the yard leads into the cross-
passage with the traditional three doorways. The large
inglenook in the HALL must be *Douglas*'s work, though the
brick external stack looks as if it could be C16 or C17. The room
has been subdivided, and in the other part, to the W, is the
bay and access to the stair, while the parlour lies beyond. What
an extraordinary room this is – easily the most highly decorated of any in the house, with a forest of timbers, all deeply
moulded. Arch-braced posts on each side support heavy ceiling
beams, and there is C17 panelling. The fireplace has been
renewed, but the external stack, unlike all the others, is of
stone. Is it C17, or earlier yet? The stairs are C17, perhaps late
C17, with big turned newels, a closed string and many turned
balusters.

Two rooms E of the cross-passage seem to be remnants of
an earlier phase, corresponding to a buttery and a former
kitchen passage, or perhaps a pantry. The apartment beyond
is the loveliest room in the house, with much natural light and
views over the lawns to the moat. Someone at some time converted it to a sitting room. Could this have been done in the
late C18 as the fireplace and ceiling mouldings suggest? Either
that, or these have been imported. More rooms lie beyond,
presumably originally for servants and services.

Upstairs the large kingpost trusses of the chamber over the
hall show by the moulding at the bases that the floor is original, not inserted, while the moulding of the ceiling beams,
which follows the moulding of the trusses, shows that the
ceiling is original too. It conceals the roughly finished truss
tops. The fireplace is a lovely piece of work by *Douglas*, with
large terracotta dragons. A suite of family rooms runs along
the W side, all with the same rather crude timber trusses, this
time with roughly carved bosses on the undersides.

On the E side the roof trusses, where visible, are similar to
those elsewhere. The most notable room is the CHAPEL
created when the Roman Catholics took over in the 1930s.
It is beautifully done, with a carved oak REREDOS which

incorporates bits and pieces of C17 carved work, and attractive armorial STAINED GLASS roundels dated 1932.

STABLE. NE of the house, around a small courtyard with the COACH HOUSE on the N side. C18, brick with some multipaned windows and original stable doors. The coach house has a little cupola, and the upper part is half-timbered, perhaps as part of alterations by *Douglas*.

LODGE. NW of the house. *c.* 1894 by *John Douglas*. Two storeys, half-timbered above and stone below. Gabled with big channelled chimneys.

ST MARY'S R.C. CEMETERY, Wardley Hall Lane. The land was obtained in 1930 when the neighbouring Wardley Hall (above) was acquired by the Roman Catholic Church. The pretty little CHAPEL, looking more 1892 than its actual date, 1932, is Perp, half-timbered and with red sandstone.

WESTHOUGHTON

6000

A small town on a hill, with the inestimable benefit in this part of Lancashire of open country immediately to the W. The abbot and canons of Cockersand Abbey in N Lancashire owned a large estate in the township from the C13 or before. It is thought that their manor house was at Brinsop, in the NW corner of the township. Still only a scattered village in the 1850s, its business was mining, made infamous by the terrible Pretoria Pit disaster of 1910.

ST BARTHOLOMEW. There was a chapel of ease to Deane here, 'thatched, standing in the midst of the moors', from at least 1509. It was rebuilt in 1731. Parochial status came in 1867 and the old building was replaced in 1869–70 with a Gothic church by *Cunliffe & Freeman* of Bolton, of which we still have the NE tower and sundry bits and pieces. The rest was destroyed by fire, probably arson, in 1990. The new church, by *Dane Ashworth Cottam*, was built 1994–5. It cost about a million pounds. It is planned diamond-wise, at forty-five degrees to the old axis. But the Lady Chapel, which is aligned on the old axis, in line with the tower, has been given a street front with rescued windows, buttresses and pinnacles from the old church. Much has been made of this ambivalence, as we shall see.

Entry is into a low narthex which connects the new building with the tower (the fact they do not quite touch exempted the church from paying VAT). To the r. are the extensive offices and social spaces expected in a church of the 1990s. These are built on the old E–W axis and are clad in brick not stone.

The church itself, on its new axis, is a serene space of considerable subtlety. It is a simple enough shape, a big square or diamond, with stone niches in the cardinal faces for the altar and baptistery, and lower corner spaces to receive the structural members of the big double timber cross that forms the roof. Extending from this space on the diagonals, not the cardinal sides, are the Lady Chapel and the entrance. The church is lit by big plain windows and by a lantern whose structural timbers are an exact miniature of those on the main roof, but arranged at forty-five degrees to them. – FONT. By *John Poole*, small, of bronze on a stone pedestal and a wave-patterned mosaic base. – ORGAN. By *Nicholson* of Malvern, slung on a gallery over the entrance. A spectacular composition of silver pipes and black wood, displaying again the recurring diamond motif.

The churchyard has been extended W to form the town CEMETERY. Towards the W end of it is the PRETORIA MINE MONUMENT, of black stone lined in gold with an urn on the top. It commemorates those who lost their lives in the pit disaster in 1910.

SCHOOL, opposite the lychgate. Gothic, 1893.

ST JOHN EVANGELIST, Wingates, on the A6. 1858–9 by *George Shaw*. Built for a breakaway congregation, following a quarrel over the introduction of ritual by the incumbent of St Bartholomew in opposition to the Vicar of Deane and the Bishop. Nave, chancel and S porch only, but the porch has the conceit of a suggested upper room. There are some mighty funny traceries including a five-pointed star, W, and affronted Ss, E. There was originally a tall flèche two bays in from the W. The replacement bellcote on the W gable is too squat. Simple interior dominated by the trademark Shaw roof with four equal straight struts suggesting a wagon shape. A pair of extra descending struts terminating as pendants indicate the position of the flèche. The W gallery has been extended by a bay to create a parish centre within the nave. Shaw's furnishings must have been of the simplest to judge by the remaining FONT. – STAINED GLASS. Two supplied by *Shaw* from his Saddleworth workshop, SE and SW; Puginian, but let down by poor firing so that the faces have faded. E by *Lavers, Barraud & Westlake*.

ST JAMES, Daisy Hill. 1879–81. One of a notable group by *Paley & Austin*, which at this date means *Hubert Austin*; *see* also Atherton, Howe Bridge, and Leigh nearby in SW Lancashire. A masterly performance for relatively little cash – £6,500 – which was given by the sisters Mrs Makant and Miss Haddock. Of red brick and terracotta with stone dressings reserved for the porch and one or two other key places. Aisleless nave and chancel. Transept on the N side only, and a two-bay organ chamber and vestry. On the S side of the chancel rises the tall Spanish-Colonial-looking bell-turret that makes the building such a distinctive landmark. It has three bell-holes, one over two, and is transparent in N and S views. It is just wide enough to incorporate an octagonal winding stair and a tiny ringing chamber. Outside and in, the church has the barest minimum of motifs, but every one counts. The windows are few and large, with red terracotta tracery. A transomed two-lighter is punched through the base of the bell-turret. The interior is all bare brick too, with a simple tie-beam roof over the nave and a boarded wagon ceiling for the chancel. The chancel windows have detached inner shafts. The window in the bellcote is set very deep and has stouter shafts in consideration of what it has to carry. Two SEDILIA and an AUMBRY of terracotta. – REREDOS. By *Shrigley & Hunt*, 1924, a triptych opening out right across the E end, beautifully carved. Pre-Raphaelite figure painting by *Alfred Charles Weatherstone*. – STAINED GLASS; only two. E, a superb piece by *Morris & Co.*, 1898. It is a broad six-lighter subdivided 2 + 2 + 2. In the centre the Epiphany, flanked by saints, with angel musicians in the traceries (by *Bowman, Stokes* and *Walters*). Plenty of fat twining foliage (by *Wren*) top and bottom. The other, in the transept so not competing, is by *Edith Norris*, 1943. – MONUMENT. Only one, in memory of the first vicar †1911. Mosaic and *opus sectile* on an alabaster tablet signed *Jones & Willis*. 82

SCHOOL by the W end. 1870, of brick, with a little bellcote.

SACRED HEART (R.C.), Lord Street. 1994–5. By *Michael Taylor* of the *Pozzoni Design Group*. Of red brick with yellow brick stripes. Complex plan, which the roof ignores, sweeping over the lot and anchored outside the building by corner piers. The altar end is folded twice with a statue in a glass box under a window in the re-entrant angle. Further folds at the sides include a pair projecting transept-wise, over which the roof does break forward. The worship space is an octagon, which is not obvious from the outside. Entry is at forty-five degrees to the main axis, as at the contemporary St Bartholomew's (*see* above). – FONT, LECTERN and ALTAR designed around interlocking squares, suggesting the same motif. Extensive office and social accommodation under the same roof, and the presbytery at right angles. The cost was *c.* £450,000.

TOWN HALL. 1902–4 by *Bradshaw & Gass*. Of fierce red brick and terracotta in stripes. Mannerist in style with an open pediment, swagged pilaster capitals and large masks over the windows. Just two stone columns for the porch, monoliths with a single blocking near the bottom. A domed tower at the N end. Beyond that an extension in the same style and materials, astonishingly done in 1992. The COUNCIL CHAMBER at the S end has two oriels and early C20 wall paintings of romantic landscapes – not S Lancashire – done with thickened oils, strongly textured. Behind it and joined by a bridge is the CARNEGIE LIBRARY AND HALL of 1906, in the same style.

BRINSOP HALL, 2 m. NW, off the A6. A gaunt house of C18 or C19 brick, recently truncated at the back, on the site of a medieval grange of Cockersand Abbey in N Lancashire. It has an unexpectedly commanding situation.

HULTON PARK, *c.* 2 m. E. The mansion, a plain Grecian house with some rich interiors, was demolished in 1958. The park is intact, remarkably for an area so unaristocratic and heavily industrialized, although turned over to agriculture. It is medieval in origin and was owned by the Hultons from the C13.

8000   WHITEFIELD, STAND and BESSES O' TH' BARN

The area is generally called Whitefield these days – a pity, because Stand is such an interesting name, referring to the medieval hunting lodge in the Pilkington deer park, emparked in 1291.

41   ALL SAINTS, Church Lane, Stand. 1821–6. An early Commissioners' church, before Gothic was *de rigueur*, and when the grants were still relatively generous. Even so the first architect approached turned it down. He was John Soane. He considered that the £12,000 on offer was insufficient, but was willing to pass the job on to the young *Charles Barry*. In the end the building cost £13,729, all of which was granted by the Commission. It was Barry's first job along with the almost identical St Matthew, Campfield in Manchester (demolished).

Here we see what Barry could do in the way of Gothic without Pugin and before the Ecclesiologists. He could do accurate Grecian – *see* the Manchester City Art Gallery of 1824 – but his Gothic is highly fanciful. In later life he was apologetic about these his early efforts, but as architecture and as an ornament to the landscape Stand church could hardly be bettered.

The whole building stands tall. It is on high ground, and is moreover raised up on a platform. Barry had the unerring sense of scale and mass that comes of a classical training. The walls rise sheer, a great five-bay box with tall windows with their cusped intersecting tracery set well back, giving depth as well as mass. The galleries are clearly indicated by a band of blank arcading across each window. At the E is a full-height canted apse with the same windows. The W tower is raised up on a vertiginous open vaulted porch, its arches and especially the side lancets as thin and steep as anything in Fonthill. The tower is even slimmer and more sheer than Bell Harry at Canterbury, with its octagonal buttresses without set-offs.

The nave is exceptionally wide, with its galleries, wide as well, set well back. The slender Perp piers of the four-bay arcades (the fifth bay is for the gallery stairs) carry a plaster vault. It is the lightness and the freedom this allowed which, more than anything, make the interior so enjoyable. Barry has made his high vault of two tierceron stars, not four, each covering two bays. The half-folded fan over the apse he has repeated over the W gallery. The aisles are rib-vaulted at the same height. So this is a hall-church, symmetrical about both its axes, and strongly centralized. It is an effect of great charm, far removed from the conscientiously revived English Dec that was soon to sweep the board.

The original interior colour scheme was reinstated by *Gordon Thorne* in 1982; off-white with the ribs in stone colour. Barry's fittings have gone. A chancel was made out of the E bay in 1898, fitted with the present fine ALTAR, canopied SCREEN and PULPIT in 1921, CHOIR STALLS and side SCREENS in 1937, all by *Austin & Paley*. At ground level the reordered church reads as three bays and a chancel, strongly orientated, setting up a frisson of disagreement with the two-plus-two bays of Barry's ceiling and its E–W symmetry.

STAINED GLASS. The background is a Victorian scheme of greens and yellows replacing the original clear glass (1864). The three E windows with their strident colours and large pieces of glass are of 1841 by *D. Evans* of Shrewsbury. In the lower windows and in great contrast are two by *Lavers, Barraud & Westlake* with their usual concave faces. S under the gallery SS Thomas, Barnabas and John the Baptist, all with the same face, by *A. L. Moore*, 1912.

MONUMENTS. Under the W gallery, two sons of T. Pilkington Young and Margaret Young †1915 and 1916: a beautiful brass. Tom Ramsbottom of Old Hall, 'cut off at Naples in the 25th year of his age, 1818, while engaged in the ardent and honourable pursuit of commercial enterprise': Greek, with a portrait medallion and a maritime trophy. Chancel N, James Clegg †1836, portrait bust on a high base with relief figures of Faith, Charity and Hope; by *Dunbar*. Chancel S, James Ramsbotham †1835, portrait bust and a long eulogy, signed *Chantrey* 1858. Above is the first rector, Thomas Corser †1876. The plum is a *Sievier* monument in the SE corner, to Frances Ramsbotham †1826 aged twenty-one. She lies on a *chaise longue* with many cushions. Another young lady in Regency dress kneels by her side, holding her hand. On the floor a fallen book.

RECTORY, Church Lane. Converted by *Barry* from a farmhouse *c.* 1830. Roughcast, with hoodmoulds and decorative glazing bars.

STAND CHAPEL (Unitarian), Ringley Road, ½ m. SW of All Saints. 'Conditum 1693, Renovatum 1818, Deletum 1940, Restitutum 1952' is the laconic inscription on a foundation stone. 'Deletion' was due to an incendiary bomb. Restitution was by *J. S. A. Young* of *Young & Purves*, in pure revived Georgian, redolent of New England rather than England. Red brick and white wood, with big clear windows (renewed in plastic) and a white lantern spire. (STAINED GLASS. Chancel, 1954, by *Morris & Co.* Vestibule, 1855.)

CONGREGATIONAL CHAPEL (United Reformed), Besses o' th' Barn, Bury New Road. The chapel had its origins in the bicentenary of the Act of Uniformity, in 1862, when the Congregational Union set up a fund for new churches, and at the same time Jonathan Lees recruited a group of senior students at the Independent College in Whalley Range (*see* p. 483) to set up a Sunday School at Besses junction. The chapel, which must have loomed over the tiny hamlet, went up in 1864–5. *Alfred Waterhouse* is the unmistakable architect. It is of common red brick with patterns in yellow and blue brick, which in any other architect's work might be called jolly, filling the window spandrels and making up the arches and strings. The chapel is large and T-shaped, with plate-tracery roses in its gable ends. It has lost its painted decoration. Behind is an equally large

schoolroom, with further buildings added in 1889 stretching
back to Bury Old Road. Chapel and schoolroom have characteristic cradle roofs. It was an inexpensive job for its size –
£4,165. – STAINED GLASS by *Humphries, Jackson & Ambler*
1922, to Eliza Ragdale †1914; she is posed like Holman Hunt's
Light of the World, holding a candle lantern, not knocking but
offering medicine to a sick man.

Fashionable flats called THE ATRIUM were being built in
2003, immediately S, challenging the chapel's height. The
metal-clad top storey grows out of the brick of the lower
storeys, just like the many residential conversions in central
Manchester. To Bury New Road in front a smaller block
c. 2001 in quieter colours, called MAYFAIR HOUSE. Fat grey
roofs, glass brick stair-tower and balconies with perforated
metal guards, yellow brick, metal cladding and grey render.

CONGREGATIONAL CHURCH (United Reformed), Stand Lane
– nearly in Radcliffe. 1885, by *J.P. Pritchett* of Darlington. Of
stone, fully Gothic with tower and spire, nave and aisles, and
a short chancel. It replaces a building of 1792, hence the earlier
gravestones. (Octagonal columns and foliage capitals. Barrel
ceiling with angels. – Good STAINED GLASS by *T. Curtis* of
Ward & Hughes, 1895–8 and 1920.)

FIRST WORLD WAR MEMORIAL, W of All Saints on Higher
Lane. By *Vernon March*. An ecstatic bronze angel, stretching
skywards, stands on a concave-sided column of Portland
stone. She has strangely dishevelled wings, like a tatty drag-
onfly. At her feet a dragon coils sulkily round a globe.

STAND HOUSE, Ringley Road. Plain Georgian, of brick, with a
three-bay pediment. Ringley Road is lined with large houses
in their own grounds, from the C18 to the very recent, with
the latter predominating. Now flats are beginning to intrude,
including an extension to Stand House, and, at No. 6, a block
called THE HOLLOWS by the venerable firm of *Bradshaw Gass
& Hope*, 2003, symmetrical, with a Voysey-like mix of vernacular and C21 motifs. At the other end of the scale is THE
SQUARE, off Ringley Drive, of 1991, an unrestrained parody
of a London square of the less grand sort, by *P.J. Livesey
Group*. Three sides only. Three-storey houses with their front
doors on the middle floor, of yellow brick and rusticated
stucco. The ensemble is crammed with pediments, colonnades, balustrading, and lamps on wrought-iron arches. The
central garden is reduced to car-parking and a three-tier
Baroque fountain in a small enclosure. At the bend of Ringley
Road was STAND OLD HALL, represented today by a battered
Victorian house. The site has a long history with a succession
of houses. The great hall of the Pilkingtons, which was on a
par with Rufford and Ordsall, had long been degraded to a
barn when it fell down in the 1960s.

RAILWAY BRIDGE, Besses o' th' Barn. *c.* 1968. An enormous concrete I-beam spanning the M60 and Bury Old Road. It is balanced delicately on adjustable supports at the ends, because
the area is subject to mine subsidence. The trams, toy-like

in comparison, run along the bottom flange on either side.
Contractor *Leonard Fairclough* under the supervision of *W. F.
Beatty*, civil engineer.

BARCLAYS BANK, Bury New Road. By *Maxwell & Tuke*, 1880–3,
for the Bury Banking Co. Tall, of red brick and terracotta,
strongly urban in appearance.

WINTON

S of Worsley and W of Patricroft, with which it merges.

ST MARY MAGDALENE, Westbourne Road. By *R. T. Beckett*,
1913. A church that makes one want to see more of this architect's work. It is big in conception, even though crossing tower
and nave are unfinished. A new uncluttered W front was added
by *Donald Buttress*, 1970. The large windows have simplified
Perp tracery, the smaller just Elizabethan mullions. Three-bay
nave, with low arches beside the chancel, massive piers for the
tower, S transeptal chapel. Shallow N transept with a tall arch
to the organ chamber. Complex spaces are created, somewhat
in the manner of Austin & Paley. – REREDOS. By *Bodley &
Garner*. Panelling from the demolished St Peter, Eastbourne.
– STAINED GLASS. Late C19 figures of St John and St Peter
from St Catherine, Barton-upon-Irwell, N aisle. E chapel
window by *W. H. Cotton* of Manchester.

WORSLEY

Worsley lies to the W of the Salford conurbation, but it has the
atmosphere of a village, with open land on almost every side. The
roar of the adjacent M60 motorway is the only jarring note. The
manor was held from the C12 by the de Worsley family and passed
to various local families through marriage, culminating in the
Earls of Bridgewater. The son of the 3rd Earl was created 1st
Duke of Bridgewater in 1720. What matters in the centre is all
connected with the dukes, and their successors, the Earls of
Ellesmere. Due to the 3rd Duke, Francis Egerton, is the canal.
Lord Francis Leveson-Gower, son of the 3rd Duke's nephew,
the Duke of Sutherland, inherited and changed his name to
Egerton. He became the 1st Earl of Ellesmere in 1846. Due to
him is the church, and much else. The present character of the
place is partly owed to the work of the 3rd Earl and his agent,
Henry Hart Davis.

Coal was extracted locally from the C14, and the local quarry,
called the Delph, probably also had medieval origins. There was
a corn mill beside the Delph from the C14, and its late C18 successor had been converted to steam power by 1807. Efforts to
improve water transport date from 1737, but nothing came of the
scheme. Not until the 3rd Duke took matters in hand was a canal
finally built, following an Act of 1759. It was designed to take

coal to Manchester from the mines near the centre of the settlement. Worsley became a centre of industry, with a large lime kiln
and mortar mill, coke ovens, saw pits, carpenters' workshops,
boat building and more. Workers and craftsmen were recruited
from all over the country, including stone masons from Cumberland and boat builders from the Severn. In 1773 Josiah Wedg-
wood described it as having the appearance of 'a considerable
seaport town'.

There has been a seemingly unbroken tradition of domestic
Tudor-style timber-framed houses in the village from the 1840s
to the present day, first for the Bridgewater Estate and latterly
as private houses. The unusually early revival of the style must
be owed to the taste of the 1st Earl and the skill of his architect
James Evans, who was also the Borough Surveyor of Salford.*
Of later contributions the most notable were made by *Douglas &
Fordham* and the successor firm *Douglas & Minshull*, for the 3rd
Earl.†

51 ST MARK, Worsley Brow. 1845–6 by *Sir George Gilbert Scott* for
Francis Egerton, 1st Earl of Ellesmere. N aisle added 1851. In
a leafy position, crowning the hill with a glorious tower and
spire. This shows young Scott more playful than he later chose
to be. The spire bristles with crockets and gargoyles. The style
of the church is Geometrical to Decorated, i.e. Scott's
favourite Middle Pointed. The interior is splendid too, calm
and spacious with none of the thinness seen in so many
churches of this date. Five-bay nave, Dec piers with bossy leaf
capitals, three-bay chancel with plain caps to the piers, three-
bay family chapel on the S side balanced on the N side by an
organ chamber and vestry. Sturdy hammerbeam nave roof with
intermediate scissor-braces, simpler chancel roof, aisle roofs
with arch braces.

PULPIT. A fantastic piece made of French or Flemish C17
carved panels, including an ambitious stair-rail showing the
Presentation in the Temple with entertaining architectural
detail. – ORGAN SCREENS with panels of similar type and
origin. – LECTERN. Oak figure of St Mark beneath a canopy.
– FONT. A big octagonal bowl with richly carved sides. – ALTAR
RAIL. Brass rail and ironwork passion flowers. – REREDOS.
Alabaster with marble and mosaic, in memory of Catherine,
Countess of Ellesmere †1866. The MOSAIC PANELS with
angels above the reredos commemorate Francis Fulke Egerton
†1891. – Exquisite iron chapel SCREEN with bold three-dimen-
sional twining leaves and finials with crowns, thought to be by
J. B. Skidmore. – Original fine CHOIR STALLS, SEDILIA, and
BENCHES. – STAINED GLASS. The E window and three of the

---

* T.M. Penson built in similar style in the 1850s in Chester. Other early examples
are scattered, e.g. J. B. Papworth's Park and Lodge cottages at Basildon, Essex,
1842; a design for a villa by E. B. Lamb, 1836; and Matthew Habershon's buildings
of the 1830s.
† John Aldred is responsible for most of the attributions to James Evans and the
Douglas firms.

Tomb of the 1st Earl of Ellesmere, from *The Builder*, 1860

four chapel windows are by the same workshop. Large well-drawn figures with great blocks of jewel-coloured glass relieved by intricate patterning in the tracery over. Teresa Sladen suggests Continental origins. Chapel s side, Fortitude and Humility by *Morris & Co.*, 1905. w window, Faith, Hope and Charity, late C19; St Hilda, N aisle, probably 1930s by *C.E. Moore*, and the baptism of St Augustine, N aisle w, 1910. – MONUMENT. In the family chapel, Francis Egerton, 1st Earl of Ellesmere †1857, tomb-chest with recumbent effigy designed by *Scott* with decorative carving by *J. Birnie Philip*, but the effigy by *Matthew Noble*.

RECTORY, off Walkden Road, N of the church. A spare, asymmetrical, big-boned house dated 1850. Brick with stone dressings and prominent stone quoins. Most of the show is in the tall chimneys, clustered and set diagonally on sturdy bases. The garden front has two projecting gabled bays.

METHODIST CHURCH, Barton Road. 1878, on the site of a predecessor of 1801. Rather undistinguished, brick with Gothic windows, but with a good unspoiled interior. Continuous oval gallery on plain cast-iron columns. Pitch-pine PEWS, elaborate dominating PULPIT.

For the Public Library, *see* Perambulation, below.

WORSLEY OLD HALL, Old Hall Lane. The hall of Sir Geoffrey de Worsley recorded in 1376 is thought to have been on an unknown site to the SE. The present building is probably of C16 or C17 origin. It seems to have consisted of a hall range, s side, with wings extending N on the E and W sides. The building was remodelled during the C18 with partial refenestration and the addition of a range immediately N of the hall range, and probably other work as well. Substantial reworking followed *c.* 1855, when extensions were also made to the E wing, probably by *Blore.* More work was carried out in 1891. In 1905 the remaining space between the wings was filled in with a billiard room, and in 1906 a small wing was added on the NW side. The C19 and early C20 work was done in black-and-white style. More interior alterations followed during the C20, most recently during the 1990s when the building was converted to a restaurant. The result is that it is almost impossible to unpick the evolution of the building, or even to be certain how much of the fabric predates the C19.

The S front has on the E side a projecting timber-framed bay on a stone plinth. The remainder is rendered and has mainly multi-paned windows, probably of the C18 or early C19. Two projecting brick stacks are C19. An offset C19 porch probably reflects the position of a cross-passage. On the E side is the timber-framed gabled end of the hall, but how much of this is original? Other elevations are owed mainly to the early C20. Inside the problems continue. The beams of the hall suggest the position of a cross passage where the present entrance is, for a ceiling beam has truncated tenons on the underside, but all the timbers have been reworked so that it is not possible to be sure how many of them are original. It seems likely that the hall had a chamber over it from the beginning but retained a screens passage, as did the C16 Wythenshawe Hall, Wythenshawe (p. 499) and nearby Wardley Hall, Wardley (q.v.).

WORSLEY NEW HALL (site), Leigh Road. *Sir Edward Blore* designed a large stone Elizabethan-style hall for the 1st Earl, 1839–46. This replaced a classical brick house called the Brick Hall erected *c.* 1760 on a site to the N. The New Hall was demolished shortly after the Second World War, and parts of the cellars were incorporated into a large concrete box of a RADAR STATION erected in the early 1950s. Repositioned ENTRANCE GATES and quadrant walls stand on Leigh Road. The main gate is flanked by pedestrian entrances, Baroque style with elaborate scrollwork, designed by *Blore c.* 1850 and shown at the Great Exhibition in 1851, where they won an award. The GARDENS with fountains and huge terraces cut into the hillside overlooking the valley were designed by *W. E. Nesfield.* They are almost completely overgrown and wooded, though the bones of the design survive in the form of the terraces. An ICE HOUSE, probably of the 1840s, with a plain stone-fronted entrance, lies alongside the main drive from West Lodge. A BOATING LAKE, an enlargement of an existing lake with the creation of an island, lies S of the gardens, partly dried up, so the island has joined dry land again. The work was done at some time between 1845 and 1891. The island has on it an intriguing stone GROTTO (shown on a map of 1891) with a large chamber connected to a number of subsidiary chambers, somewhat in the manner of a prehistoric tomb. Over the entrance is a huge monolith. The main chamber has a shallow dome of brick, supported by iron beams, into which circular holes are let, which look as if they were originally glazed. When was this built and by whom?

ESTATE BUILDINGS include WEST LODGE, Leigh Road, s side. By *Douglas & Fordham*, 1894–5. Two-storeyed timber-framed house with decorative bargeboards, etc. – CHURCH LODGE, Worsley Road. Now a pub called the John Gilbert. Stone, Elizabethan style with tall chimneys and the conceit of an entrance treated as an inglenook, i.e. a projecting porch with a tall chimney rising from it. Many alterations and additions in connection with pub use. It looks mid C19. Could it be by *Blore*? – OLD HALL LODGE, Walkden Road. Similar to West Lodge, by *Douglas & Fordham*, 1895. – Another LODGE lies far to the E off Greenleach Lane, also two-storeyed and timber-framed, probably also by *Douglas & Fordham*.

THE AVIARY, off Walkden Road. By *James Evans*, 1848–9, as a hunting and fishing lodge for the 1st Earl of Ellesmere. Brick with a timber-framed upper storey. Unusual corner tower with little jettied gables on each side and a classical cupola. Gabled range with upper diagonal cusped bracing, and pretty bays with windows with margin lights. Greatly extended in matching style in 1995.

KITCHEN GARDEN, reached from a drive running s from Leigh Road. Probably mid-C19 and so probably by *Blore*. The garden has the expected brick walls and bothies. A boiler house with a large stone CHIMNEY lies on the N side, though the related glass houses have disappeared. An impressively large and elaborate Tudor-style HEAD GARDENER'S HOUSE on the W side has a full-height octagonal tower with a swept pyramidal roof. It was described in the *Gardeners' Chronicle* in 1875 as 'a very handsome, large, ornamental, stone building such as is not very often met with for a gardener's residence'.

ELLESMERE MEMORIAL, off Leigh Road. Put up to commemorate the 1st Earl of Ellesmere. By *Driver & Webber* of London, who won the competition in 1859 which was judged by Charles Barry. It still acts as a foil for the spire of St Mark's Church (above) in approaches from the w, but has been greatly diminished in height: it was originally more than 130 ft (45 metres) tall. Gothic, with two lower stages with crocketed gables and gabled angle buttresses, above which truncated octagonal column supports an octagonal spire.

DRYWOOD HALL, Worsley Road. Now a school. Dated 1855, and built for the Manchester calico printer Jonathan Wood, in a similar timber-framed style to the Court House and Nos. 3–5 Barton Road (below). Asymmetrical disposition of gables and bays, with a two-storey porch consisting of a gabled upper part supported by columns.

HAZELHURST HALL, Hazelhurst Road. Three-storey brick house with cambered window heads, an early C18 cross-wing to a demolished C17 house.

BRIDGEWATER CANAL

38   The 3rd Duke was only twenty-two years old when the first Act
for the canal was passed in 1759. His agent *John Gilbert* seems to
have been initially responsible for planning the project. The engineer *James Brindley* became involved in 1759. The route was
planned to follow a contour, avoiding the need for locks. This is
typical of early canals, and of Brindley's work. Unlike most other
navigations it did not depend on improving an existing natural
watercourse. The terminal basin is at Castlefield in Manchester
(*see* p. ••). In 1776 the canal was linked with the w coast near Liverpool, and thus with international trade routes. Amongst the
most daring and innovative developments was the construction
of an underground canal system at Worsley, where from *c.* 1760
tunnels were driven from the quarry at the Delph so that coal
could be loaded directly from the mines. The idea seems to have
grown from the need for tunnels to drain water from the mines.
The system includes an underground inclined plane built *c.* 1795
to Gilbert's design, linking the higher levels beneath Walkden
Moor, 1.9 m. N of Worsley village, with the main system. There
was a lock at the upper level, and when this was drained a loaded
boat settled on a trolley, which was lowered by ropes. As the fully
laden boat went down the slope, an empty vessel was pulled up
on the other end of the rope. In this way coal could be moved
from the upper level to the main level without having to change
boats. The canal was sold in 1887 to Manchester Ship Canal Co.
and the underground workings are now inaccessible. For structures relating to the canal *see* the perambulation, below.

PERAMBULATION

Starting on WORSLEY ROAD at the DELPH, the original CANAL
BASIN lies at the foot of the quarry walls, into which two
tunnel entrances are cut. Above the basin a stone C18 house,
much altered, was built or adapted for use by stone masons.
On the opposite side of the road No. 3, a rendered early C18
house with later stone mullioned windows, described as a
'nailers shop' in 1785. Crossing the road and taking the footpath on the r. of the bridge leads down to the towpath. The
BRIDGE was rebuilt *c.* 1760 to span the canal, and enlarged in
the C19 and C20. In the E side of the main arch are a number
of large chambers of unknown origin, though Mr Aldred suggests they may have been used to stable or rest canal horses.
The path leads over a footbridge from which the large late C18
ROCK HOUSE can be seen to the r. Brick, symmetrical, with
central entrance with columns and a fanlight. On the water
38   front is the PACKET HOUSE which originated as a group of
C18 brick houses extended with a large timber-framed wing
c. 1850, probably by *James Evans*. Altered 1900 with addition
of a shop, w side, by *Douglas & Minshull*. At the edge of the
canal, a JETTY with stone steps, probably from 1769, when

packet boat services began. The timber-framed KIOSK on the l. includes part of a lodge of 1896 by *Douglas & Fordham* moved here in 1989 from the entrance drive to Worsley Old Hall (*see* above).

Following the path s on to Barton Road and turning r. leads to the COURT HOUSE. Of 1849 by *James Evans* for the 1st Earl of Ellesmere, to accommodate the manorial court and other official functions. An interesting early example of black-and-white revival. Hall with a wing placed centrally on the N side and a small room attached on the s side. The N wing and main hall have large stone stacks, that to the hall immense, with a funny Italianate top. Elaborate w porch. Low gabled wings on either side of 1896 (could they be by *Douglas & Fordham* who did other work on the estate at this time?) Gabled oriels on each side, that to the s lighting the gallery. Close-studding with quatrefoils in the gables; bargeboards, some with Celtic-style beasts, and finials. Inside, the hall has a Tudor-style proscenium arch with an elaborate timber strapwork crest. Arch-braced roof with pendants. The stone fireplace has over it the royal arms and arms of local families. In the wing a room with *ex situ* C17 panelling and a Tudor-style chimneypiece. A late 1960s PUBLIC LIBRARY attached to the N side of the court house is low, and nicely done, by *Derek Warburton* for Worsley UDC. The palette is black and white, but it is frankly modern, a low dark brick box with a glazed screen with white panels.

Retracing our steps SE along Barton Road leads past Nos. 3–5, a pair of cottages, sw side. Dated 1851, and used at one time as a police station. Timber-framed, T-plan, with bargeboards and other details similar to the Court House (above) and so probably also by *James Evans*. Rows of cottages of *c.* 1800 on either side of the road were built for estate workers. Rendered brick with stone eaves cornices. Nos. 10–16 are relatively little altered, those opposite have been turned into shops, and are of several different builds.

Beyond is a green where the canal towpath can be rejoined. On the opposite bank an early or mid-C19 brick BOAT HOUSE with a castellated entrance arch can be seen. It was used to house the royal barge on the occasion of Queen Victoria's visit in 1851. The iron FOOTBRIDGE ahead, with a cobbled deck, was built *c.* 1907, perhaps by *Douglas & Minshull* from whom the earl's agent Henry Hart Davis requested estimates in 1906. It is a good vantage point for views down the canal to the Packet House. On the opposite side of the road, the BRIDGEWATER HOTEL, a pub by *Douglas & Minshull*, 1902, is large, asymmetrical, with a three-storey projecting central entrance bay in red sandstone. Arched entrance with a mullioned window above with strapwork carving over it. Ranges on each side have gabled timber-framed upper storeys. Back on the canal bank an C18 DRY DOCK with a C19 iron-and-timber canopy can be viewed across the canal. Reputed to be the earliest surviving canal dry dock in the country, it has a system for draining the water into the Worsley Brook which runs beneath the canal.

The other dock beside it is C19, and both are in use for their original purpose, repairing and servicing canal boats.

Now we leave the canal and rejoin Barton Road, where on the E side a building known as the GRANARY is on the site of a forge. Traces of a waterwheel on the Worsley Brook, which emerges beside the building, have been discovered. Further S are the remains of a large LIME KILN. Square, of stone, now partially damaged and overgrown. Dr Arrowsmith reports that it was probably a draw kiln, possibly of the 1760s and certainly present by 1785. It is thought to retain two internal pots for burning lime, with draw holes to feed air into it and an access tunnel. It was originally connected to the canal by an arm for loading.

Returning along Barton Road to the canal, cross the footbridge over the canal and continue NE to THE GREEN. This was the site of factories and a works yard, moved to Walkden in 1903. In that year the base of a chimney was converted to an ornamental FOUNTAIN, with a Latin inscription praising the achievements of the 3rd Duke. Groups of houses arranged in an arc on the S side were built in 1904–10. Some at least, and possibly all, were designed by *Douglas & Minshull*. Hart Davis wrote: 'I am turning the old Worsley Yard into a kind of Village Green, with cottages for his Lordship's employees'.* In 1905 Hart Davis approved plans by *Douglas & Minshull* for the block of four cottages, but asked that bathrooms be omitted for fear of misuse. This seems to have been prompted by a cutting from the *Land Agent* kept with the correspondence which reported that tenants of Lord Tredegar in Gloucestershire had moved their baths into the gardens and used them as rabbit hutches. Some houses are half-timbered, and some have Arts and Crafts motifs, including Nos. 146–149, gabled and rendered with large battered chimneys and Nos. 140–145 and 150–153, decoratively timbered with many gables and mullioned windows.

Turning E from the Green along Worsley Road takes us to more houses, this time of the 1760s, concentrated in a range called The Crescent. Modest rendered two-storey terraces, erected piecemeal, some with multipaned windows. Similar houses stand on a continuation of the Crescent, running S from the main road. They were probably used by canal workers and boat builders. Returning past the Green, turn N along MILL BROW for more groups of late C18 estate cottages, of which Nos. 113–117 are the least altered (the numbers are Worsley estate numbering, rather than street numbers). Opposite this terrace is HIGHFIELD HOUSE, a large early C19 house hidden behind high fences. Stuccoed, with a bracketed eaves cornice.

Return to Worsley Road, and turn r. MILL HOUSE, N side, is a late C18 house with windows in stone architraves, and a plaque with the Ellesmere lion, from when it acted as an estate office in the C19. Opposite, some more modest C18 houses and just beyond, the bridge and our starting point.

*We are indebted to Mr John Aldred for information on the correspondence.

GLOSSARY

Numbers and letters refer to the illustrations (by John Sambrook)
on pp. 698–705.

ABACUS: flat slab forming the top of a capital (3a).

ACANTHUS: classical formalized leaf ornament (4b).

ACCUMULATOR TOWER: *see* Hydraulic power.

ACHIEVEMENT: a complete display of armorial bearings.

ACROTERION: plinth for a statue or ornament on the apex or ends of a pediment; more usually, both the plinth and what stands on it (4a).

AEDICULE (*lit.* little building): architectural surround, consisting usually of two columns or pilasters supporting a pediment.

AGGREGATE: *see* Concrete.

AISLE: subsidiary space alongside the body of a building, separated from it by columns, piers, or posts.

ALMONRY: a building from which alms are dispensed to the poor.

AMBULATORY (*lit.* walkway): aisle around the sanctuary (q.v.).

ANGLE ROLL: roll moulding in the angle between two planes (1a).

ANSE DE PANIER: *see* Arch.

ANTAE: simplified pilasters (4a), usually applied to the ends of the enclosing walls of a portico *in antis* (q.v.).

ANTEFIXAE: ornaments projecting at regular intervals above a Greek cornice, originally to conceal the ends of roof tiles (4a).

ANTHEMION: classical ornament like a honeysuckle flower (4b).

APRON: raised panel below a window or wall monument or tablet.

APSE: semicircular or polygonal end of an apartment, especially of a chancel or chapel. In classical architecture sometimes called an *exedra*.

ARABESQUE: non-figurative surface decoration consisting of flowing lines, foliage scrolls etc., based on geometrical patterns. Cf. Grotesque.

ARCADE: series of arches supported by piers or columns. *Blind arcade* or *arcading*: the same applied to the wall surface. *Wall arcade*: in medieval churches, a blind arcade forming a dado below windows. Also a covered shopping street.

ARCH: Shapes *see* 5c. *Basket arch* or *anse de panier* (basket handle): three-centred and depressed, or with a flat centre. *Nodding*: ogee arch curving forward from the wall face. *Parabolic*: shaped like a chain suspended from two level points, but inverted. Special purposes. *Chancel*: dividing chancel from nave or crossing. *Crossing*: spanning piers at a crossing (q.v.). *Relieving or discharging*: incorporated in a wall to relieve superimposed weight (5c). *Skew*: spanning responds not diametrically opposed. *Strainer*: inserted in an opening to resist inward pressure. *Transverse*: spanning a main axis (e.g. of a vaulted space). *See also* Jack arch, Triumphal arch.

ARCHITRAVE: formalized lintel, the lowest member of the classical entablature (3a). Also the moulded frame of a door or window (often borrowing the profile of a classical architrave). For *lugged* and *shouldered* architraves *see* 4b.

ARCUATED: dependent structurally on the arch principle. Cf. Trabeated.

ARK: chest or cupboard housing the

tables of Jewish law in a synagogue.

ARRIS: sharp edge where two surfaces meet at an angle (3a).

ASHLAR: masonry of large blocks wrought to even faces and square edges (6d).

ASTRAGAL: classical moulding of semicircular section (3f).

ASTYLAR: with no columns or similar vertical features.

ATLANTES: *see* Caryatids.

ATRIUM (plural: atria): inner court of a Roman or C20 house; in a multi-storey building, a toplit covered court rising through all storeys. Also an open court in front of a church.

ATTACHED COLUMN: *see* Engaged column.

ATTIC: small top storey within a roof. Also the storey above the main entablature of a classical façade.

AUMBRY: recess or cupboard to hold sacred vessels for the Mass.

BAILEY: *see* Motte-and-bailey.

BALANCE BEAM: *see* Canals.

BALDACCHINO: free-standing canopy, originally fabric, over an altar. Cf. Ciborium.

BALLFLOWER: globular flower of three petals enclosing a ball (1a). Typical of the Decorated style.

BALUSTER: pillar or pedestal of bellied form. *Balusters*: vertical supports of this or any other form, for a handrail or coping, the whole being called a *balustrade* (6c). *Blind balustrade*: the same applied to the wall surface.

BARBICAN: outwork defending the entrance to a castle.

BARGEBOARDS (corruption of 'vergeboards'): boards, often carved or fretted, fixed beneath the eaves of a gable to cover and protect the rafters.

BAROQUE: style originating in Rome *c.*1600 and current in England *c.*1680–1720, characterized by dramatic massing and silhouette and the use of the giant order.

BARROW: burial mound.

BARTIZAN: corbelled turret, square or round, frequently at an angle.

BASCULE: hinged part of a lifting (or bascule) bridge.

BASE: moulded foot of a column or pilaster. For *Attic* base *see* 3b.

BASEMENT: lowest, subordinate storey; hence the lowest part of a classical elevation, below the *piano nobile* (q.v.).

BASILICA: a Roman public hall; hence an aisled building with a clerestory.

BASTION: one of a series of defensive semicircular or polygonal projections from the main wall of a fortress or city.

BATTER: intentional inward inclination of a wall face.

BATTLEMENT: defensive parapet, composed of *merlons* (solid) and *crenels* (embrasures) through which archers could shoot; sometimes called *crenellation*. Also used decoratively.

BAY: division of an elevation or interior space as defined by regular vertical features such as arches, columns, windows etc.

BAY LEAF: classical ornament of overlapping bay leaves (3f).

BAY WINDOW: window of one or more storeys projecting from the face of a building. *Canted*: with a straight front and angled sides. *Bow window*: curved. *Oriel*: rests on corbels or brackets and starts above ground level; also the bay window at the dais end of a medieval great hall.

BEAD-AND-REEL: *see* Enrichments.

BEAKHEAD: Norman ornament with a row of beaked bird or beast heads usually biting into a roll moulding (1a).

BELFRY: chamber or stage in a tower where bells are hung.

BELL CAPITAL: *see* 1b.

BELLCOTE: small gabled or roofed housing for the bell(s).

BERM: level area separating a ditch from a bank on a hill-fort or barrow.

BILLET: Norman ornament of small half-cylindrical or rectangular blocks (1a).

BLIND: *see* Arcade, Baluster, Portico.

BLOCK CAPITAL: *see* 1a.

BLOCKED: columns, etc. interrupted by regular projecting

blocks (*blocking*), as on a Gibbs surround (4b).

BLOCKING COURSE: course of stones, or equivalent, on top of a cornice and crowning the wall.

BOLECTION MOULDING: covering the joint between two different planes (6b).

BOND: the pattern of long sides (*stretchers*) and short ends (*headers*) produced on the face of a wall by laying bricks in a particular way (6e).

BOSS: knob or projection, e.g. at the intersection of ribs in a vault (2c).

BOWTELL: a term in use by the C15 for a form of roll moulding, usually three-quarters of a circle in section (also called *edge roll*).

BOW WINDOW: *see* Bay window.

BOX FRAME: timber-framed construction in which vertical and horizontal wall members support the roof (7). Also concrete construction where the loads are taken on cross walls; also called *cross-wall construction*.

BRACE: subsidiary member of a structural frame, curved or straight. *Bracing* is often arranged decoratively e.g. quatrefoil, herringbone (7). *See also* Roofs.

BRATTISHING: ornamental crest, usually formed of leaves, Tudor flowers or miniature battlements.

BRESSUMER (*lit.* breast-beam): big horizontal beam supporting the wall above, especially in a jettied building (7).

BRICK: *see* Bond, Cogging, Engineering, Gauged, Tumbling.

BRIDGE: *Bowstring*: with arches rising above the roadway which is suspended from them. *Clapper*: one long stone forms the roadway. *Roving*: *see* Canal. *Suspension*: roadway suspended from cables or chains slung between towers or pylons. *Stay-suspension* or *stay-cantilever*: supported by diagonal stays from towers or pylons. *See also* Bascule.

BRISES-SOLEIL: projecting fins or canopies which deflect direct sunlight from windows.

BROACH: *see* Spire and 1C.

BUCRANIUM: ox skull used decoratively in classical friezes.

BULL-NOSED SILL: sill displaying a pronounced convex upper moulding.

BULLSEYE WINDOW: small oval window, set horizontally (cf. Oculus). Also called *œil de bœuf*.

BUTTRESS: vertical member projecting from a wall to stabilize it or to resist the lateral thrust of an arch, roof, or vault (1c, 2c). A *flying buttress* transmits the thrust to a heavy abutment by means of an arch or half-arch (1c).

CABLE OR ROPE MOULDING: originally Norman, like twisted strands of a rope.

CAMES: *see* Quarries.

CAMPANILE: free-standing bell-tower.

CANALS: *Flash lock*: removable weir or similar device through which boats pass on a flush of water. Predecessor of the *pound lock*: chamber with gates at each end allowing boats to float from one level to another. *Tidal gates*: single pair of lock gates allowing vessels to pass when the tide makes a level. *Balance beam*: beam projecting horizontally for opening and closing lock gates. *Roving bridge*: carrying a towing path from one bank to the other.

CANTILEVER: horizontal projection (e.g. step, canopy) supported by a downward force behind the fulcrum.

CAPITAL: head or crowning feature of a column or pilaster; for classical types *see* 3; for medieval types *see* 1b.

CARREL: compartment designed for individual work or study.

CARTOUCHE: classical tablet with ornate frame (4b).

CARYATIDS: female figures supporting an entablature; their male counterparts are *Atlantes* (*lit.* Atlas figures).

CASEMATE: vaulted chamber, with embrasures for defence, within a castle wall or projecting from it.

CASEMENT: side-hinged window.

CASTELLATED: with battlements (q.v.).

CAST IRON: hard and brittle, cast in a mould to the required shape.

Wrought iron is ductile, strong in tension, forged into decorative patterns or forged and rolled into e.g. bars, joists, boiler plates; *mild steel* is its modern equivalent, similar but stronger.

CATSLIDE: See 8a.

CAVETTO: concave classical moulding of quarter-round section (3f).

CELURE OR CEILURE: enriched area of roof above rood or altar.

CEMENT: *see* Concrete.

CENOTAPH (*lit.* empty tomb): funerary monument which is not a burying place.

CENTRING: wooden support for the building of an arch or vault, removed after completion.

CHAMFER (*lit.* corner-break): surface formed by cutting off a square edge or corner. For types of chamfers and *chamfer stops see* 6a. *See also* Double chamfer.

CHANCEL: part of the E end of a church set apart for the use of the officiating clergy.

CHANTRY CHAPEL: often attached to or within a church, endowed for the celebration of Masses principally for the soul of the founder.

CHEVET (*lit.* head): French term for chancel with ambulatory and radiating chapels.

CHEVRON: V-shape used in series or double series (later) on a Norman moulding (1a). Also (especially when on a single plane) called *zigzag*.

CHOIR: the part of a cathedral, monastic or collegiate church where services are sung.

CIBORIUM: a fixed canopy over an altar, usually vaulted and supported on four columns; cf. Baldacchino. Also a canopied shrine for the reserved sacrament.

CINQUEFOIL: *see* Foil.

CIST: stone-lined or slab-built grave.

CLADDING: external covering or skin applied to a structure, especially a framed one.

CLERESTORY: uppermost storey of the nave of a church, pierced by windows. Also high-level windows in secular buildings.

CLOSER: a brick cut to complete a bond (6e).

CLUSTER BLOCK: *see* Multi-storey.

COADE STONE: ceramic artificial stone made in Lambeth 1769–*c.*1840 by Eleanor Coade (†1821) and her associates.

COB: walling material of clay mixed with straw. Also called *pisé*.

COFFERING: arrangement of sunken panels (coffers), square or polygonal, decorating a ceiling, vault, or arch.

COGGING: a decorative course of bricks laid diagonally (6e). Cf. Dentilation.

COLLAR: *see* Roofs and 7.

COLLEGIATE CHURCH: endowed for the support of a college of priests.

COLONNADE: range of columns supporting an entablature. Cf. Arcade.

COLONNETTE: small medieval column or shaft.

COLOSSAL ORDER: *see* Giant order.

COLUMBARIUM: shelved, niched structure to house multiple burials.

COLUMN: a classical, upright structural member of round section with a shaft, a capital, and usually a base (3a, 4a).

COLUMN FIGURE: carved figure attached to a medieval column or shaft, usually flanking a doorway.

COMMUNION TABLE: unconsecrated table used in Protestant churches for the celebration of Holy Communion.

COMPOSITE: *see* Orders.

COMPOUND PIER: grouped shafts (q.v.), or a solid core surrounded by shafts.

CONCRETE: composition of *cement* (calcined lime and clay), *aggregate* (small stones or rock chippings), sand and water. It can be poured into *formwork* or *shuttering* (temporary frame of timber or metal) on site (*in-situ* concrete), or *pre-cast* as components before construction. *Reinforced*: incorporating steel rods to take the tensile force. *Pre-stressed*: with tensioned steel rods. Finishes include the impression of boards left by formwork (*board-marked* or *shuttered*), and texturing with steel brushes (*brushed*) or hammers (*hammer-dressed*). *See also* Shell.

CONSOLE: bracket of curved outline (4b).

COPING: protective course of masonry or brickwork capping a wall (6d).

CORBEL: projecting block supporting something above. *Corbel course*: continuous course of projecting stones or bricks fulfilling the same function. *Corbel table*: series of corbels to carry a parapet or a wall-plate or wall-post (7). *Corbelling*: brick or masonry courses built out beyond one another to support a chimney-stack, window, etc.

CORINTHIAN: *see* Orders and 3d.

CORNICE: flat-topped ledge with moulded underside, projecting along the top of a building or feature, especially as the highest member of the classical entablature (3a). Also the decorative moulding in the angle between wall and ceiling.

CORPS-DE-LOGIS: the main building(s) as distinct from the wings or pavilions.

COTTAGE ORNÉ: an artfully rustic small house associated with the Picturesque movement.

COUNTERCHANGING: of joists on a ceiling divided by beams into compartments, when placed in opposite directions in alternate squares.

COUR D'HONNEUR: formal entrance court before a house in the French manner, usually with flanking wings and a screen wall or gates.

COURSE: continuous layer of stones, etc. in a wall (6e).

COVE: a broad concave moulding, e.g. to mask the eaves of a roof. *Coved ceiling*: with a pronounced cove joining the walls to a flat central panel smaller than the whole area of the ceiling.

CRADLE ROOF: *see* Wagon roof.

CREDENCE: a shelf within or beside a piscina (q.v.), or a table for the sacramental elements and vessels.

CRENELLATION: parapet with crenels (*see* Battlement).

CRINKLE-CRANKLE WALL: garden wall undulating in a series of serpentine curves.

CROCKETS: leafy hooks. *Crocketing* decorates the edges of Gothic features, such as pinnacles, canopies, etc. *Crocket capital: see* 1b.

CROSSING: central space at the junction of the nave, chancel, and transepts. *Crossing tower*: above a crossing.

CROSS-WINDOW: with one mullion and one transom (qq.v.).

CROWN-POST: *see* Roofs and 7.

CROWSTEPS: squared stones set like steps, e.g. on a gable (8a).

CRUCKS (*lit.* crooked): pairs of inclined timbers (*blades*), usually curved, set at bay-lengths; they support the roof timbers and, in timber buildings, also support the walls (8b). *Base*: blades rise from ground level to a tie- or collar-beam which supports the roof timbers. *Full*: blades rise from ground level to the apex of the roof, serving as the main members of a roof truss. *Jointed*: blades formed from more than one timber; the lower member may act as a wall-post; it is usually elbowed at wall-plate level and jointed just above. *Middle*: blades rise from half-way up the walls to a tie- or collar-beam. *Raised*: blades rise from half-way up the walls to the apex. *Upper*: blades supported on a tie-beam and rising to the apex.

CRYPT: underground or half-underground area, usually below the E end of a church. *Ring crypt*: corridor crypt surrounding the apse of an early medieval church, often associated with chambers for relics. Cf. Undercroft.

CUPOLA (*lit.* dome): especially a small dome on a circular or polygonal base crowning a larger dome, roof, or turret.

CURSUS: a long avenue defined by two parallel earthen banks with ditches outside.

CURTAIN WALL: a connecting wall between the towers of a castle. Also a non-load-bearing external wall applied to a C20 framed structure.

CUSP: *see* Tracery and 2b.

CYCLOPEAN MASONRY: large irregular polygonal stones, smooth and finely jointed.

CYMA RECTA and CYMA REVERSA: classical mouldings with double curves (3f). Cf. Ogee.

DADO: the finishing (often with panelling) of the lower part of a wall in a classical interior; in origin a formalized continuous pedestal. *Dado rail*: the moulding along the top of the dado.

DAGGER: *see* Tracery and 2b.

DALLE-DE-VERRE (*lit.* glass-slab): a late C20 stained-glass technique, setting large, thick pieces of cast glass into a frame of reinforced concrete or epoxy resin.

DEC (DECORATED): English Gothic architecture *c.* 1290 to *c.* 1350. The name is derived from the type of window tracery (q.v.) used during the period.

DEMI- or HALF-COLUMNS: engaged columns (q.v.) half of whose circumference projects from the wall.

DENTIL: small square block used in series in classical cornices (3c). *Dentilation* is produced by the projection of alternating headers along cornices or stringcourses.

DIAPER: repetitive surface decoration of lozenges or squares flat or in relief. Achieved in brickwork with bricks of two colours.

DIOCLETIAN OR THERMAL WINDOW: semicircular with two mullions, as used in the Baths of Diocletian, Rome (4b).

DISTYLE: having two columns (4a).

DOGTOOTH: E.E. ornament, consisting of a series of small pyramids formed by four stylized canine teeth meeting at a point (1a).

DORIC: *see* Orders and 3a, 3b.

DORMER: window projecting from the slope of a roof (8a).

DOUBLE CHAMFER: a chamfer applied to each of two recessed arches (1a).

DOUBLE PILE: *see* Pile.

DRAGON BEAM: *see* Jetty.

DRESSINGS: the stone or brickwork worked to a finished face about an angle, opening, or other feature.

DRIPSTONE: moulded stone projecting from a wall to protect the lower parts from water. Cf. Hoodmould, Weathering.

DRUM: circular or polygonal stage supporting a dome or cupola. Also one of the stones forming the shaft of a column (3a).

DUTCH or FLEMISH GABLE: *see* 8a.

EASTER SEPULCHRE: tomb-chest used for Easter ceremonial, within or against the N wall of a chancel.

EAVES: overhanging edge of a roof; hence *eaves cornice* in this position.

ECHINUS: ovolo moulding (q.v.) below the abacus of a Greek Doric capital (3a).

EDGE RAIL: *see* Railways.

E.E. (EARLY ENGLISH): English Gothic architecture *c.* 1190–1250.

EGG-AND-DART: *see* Enrichments and 3f.

ELEVATION: any face of a building or side of a room. In a drawing, the same or any part of it, represented in two dimensions.

EMBATTLED: with battlements.

EMBRASURE: small splayed opening in a wall or battlement (q.v.).

ENCAUSTIC TILES: earthenware tiles fired with a pattern and glaze.

EN DELIT: stone cut against the bed.

ENFILADE: reception rooms in a formal series, usually with all doorways on axis.

ENGAGED or ATTACHED COLUMN: one that partly merges into a wall or pier.

ENGINEERING BRICKS: dense bricks, originally used mostly for railway viaducts etc.

ENRICHMENTS: the carved decoration of certain classical mouldings, e.g. the ovolo (qq.v.) with *egg-and-dart*, the cyma reversa with *waterleaf*, the astragal with *bead-and-reel* (3f).

ENTABLATURE: in classical architecture, collective name for the three horizontal members (architrave, frieze, and cornice) carried by a wall or a column (3a).

ENTASIS: very slight convex deviation from a straight line, used to prevent an optical illusion of concavity.

EPITAPH: inscription on a tomb.

EXEDRA: *see* Apse.

EXTRADOS: outer curved face of an arch or vault.

EYECATCHER: decorative building terminating a vista.

FASCIA: plain horizontal band, e.g. in an architrave (3c, 3d) or on a shopfront.

FENESTRATION: the arrangement of windows in a façade.

FERETORY: site of the chief shrine of a church, behind the high altar.

FESTOON: ornamental garland, suspended from both ends. Cf. Swag.

FIBREGLASS, or glass-reinforced polyester (GRP): synthetic resin reinforced with glass fibre. GRC: glass-reinforced concrete.

FIELD: see Panelling and 6b.

FILLET: a narrow flat band running down a medieval shaft or along a roll moulding (1a). It separates larger curved mouldings in classical cornices, fluting or bases (3c).

FLAMBOYANT: the latest phase of French Gothic architecture, with flowing tracery.

FLASH LOCK: see Canals.

FLÈCHE or SPIRELET (lit. arrow): slender spire on the centre of a roof.

FLEURON: medieval carved flower or leaf, often rectilinear (1a).

FLUSHWORK: knapped flint used with dressed stone to form patterns.

FLUTING: series of concave grooves (flutes), their common edges sharp (arris) or blunt (fillet) (3).

FOIL (lit. leaf): lobe formed by the cusping of a circular or other shape in tracery (2b). Trefoil (three), quatrefoil (four), cinquefoil (five), and multifoil express the number of lobes in a shape.

FOLIATE: decorated with leaves.

FORMWORK: see Concrete.

FRAMED BUILDING: where the structure is carried by a framework – e.g. of steel, reinforced concrete, timber – instead of by load-bearing walls.

FREESTONE: stone that is cut, or can be cut, in all directions.

FRESCO: al fresco: painting on wet plaster. Fresco secco: painting on dry plaster.

FRIEZE: the middle member of the classical entablature, sometimes ornamented (3a). Pulvinated frieze (lit. cushioned): of bold convex profile (3c). Also a horizontal band of ornament.

FRONTISPIECE: in C16 and C17 buildings the central feature of doorway and windows above linked in one composition.

GABLE: For types see 8a. Gablet: small gable. Pedimental gable: treated like a pediment.

GADROONING: classical ribbed ornament like inverted fluting that flows into a lobed edge.

GALILEE: chapel or vestibule usually at the W end of a church enclosing the main portal(s).

GALLERY: a long room or passage; an upper storey above the aisle of a church, looking through arches to the nave; a balcony or mezzanine overlooking the main interior space of a building; or an external walkway.

GALLETING: small stones set in a mortar course.

GAMBREL ROOF: see 8a.

GARDEROBE: medieval privy.

GARGOYLE: projecting water spout often carved into human or animal shape.

GAUGED or RUBBED BRICKWORK: soft brick sawn roughly, then rubbed to a precise (gauged) surface. Mostly used for door or window openings (5c).

GAZEBO (jocular Latin, 'I shall gaze'): ornamental lookout tower or raised summer house.

GEOMETRIC: English Gothic architecture c. 1250–1310. See also Tracery. For another meaning, see Stairs.

GIANT or COLOSSAL ORDER: classical order (q.v.) whose height is that of two or more storeys of the building to which it is applied.

GIBBS SURROUND: C18 treatment of an opening (4b), seen particularly in the work of James Gibbs (1682–1754).

GIRDER: a large beam. Box: of hollow-box section. Bowed: with its top rising in a curve. Plate: of I-section, made from iron or steel plates. *Lattice*: with braced frame-work.

GLAZING BARS: wooden or some-times metal bars separating and supporting window panes.

GRAFFITI: *see* Sgraffito.

GRANGE: farm owned and run by a religious order.

GRC: *see* Fibreglass.

GRISAILLE: monochrome painting on walls or glass.

GROIN: sharp edge at the meeting of two cells of a cross-vault; *see* Vault and 2c.

GROTESQUE (*lit.* grotto-esque): wall decoration adopted from Roman examples in the Renaissance. Its foliage scrolls incorporate figur-ative elements. Cf. Arabesque.

GROTTO: artificial cavern.

GRP: *see* Fibreglass.

GUILLOCHE: classical ornament of interlaced bands (4b).

GUNLOOP: opening for a firearm.

GUTTAE: stylized drops (3b).

HALF-TIMBERING: archaic term for timber-framing (q.v.). Sometimes used for non-structural decorative timberwork.

HALL CHURCH: medieval church with nave and aisles of approxim-ately equal height.

HAMMERBEAM: *see* Roofs and 7.

HAMPER: in C20 architecture, a visu-ally distinct topmost storey or storeys.

HEADER: *see* Bond and 6e.

HEADSTOP: stop (q.v.) carved with a head (5b).

HELM ROOF: *see* 1c.

HENGE: ritual earthwork.

HERM (*lit.* the god Hermes): male head or bust on a pedestal.

HERRINGBONE WORK: *see* 7ii. Cf. Pitched masonry.

HEXASTYLE: *see* Portico.

HILL-FORT: Iron Age earthwork en-closed by a ditch and bank system.

HIPPED ROOF: *see* 8a.

HOODMOULD: projecting moulding above an arch or lintel to throw off water (2b, 5b). When horizontal often called a *label*. For label stop *see* Stop.

HUSK GARLAND: festoon of stylized nutshells (4b).

HYDRAULIC POWER: use of water under high pressure to work machinery. *Accumulator tower*: houses a hydraulic accumulator which accommodates fluctuations in the flow through hydraulic mains.

HYPOCAUST (*lit.* underburning): Ro-man underfloor heating system.

IMPOST: horizontal moulding at the springing of an arch (5c).

IMPOST BLOCK: block between abacus and capital (1b).

IN ANTIS: *see* Antae, Portico and 4a.

INDENT: shape chiselled out of a stone to receive a brass.

INDUSTRIALIZED or SYSTEM BUILDING: system of manufac-tured units assembled on site.

INGLENOOK (*lit.* fire-corner): recess for a hearth with provision for seating.

INTERCOLUMNATION: interval be-tween columns.

INTERLACE: decoration in relief simulating woven or entwined stems or bands.

INTRADOS: *see* Soffit.

IONIC: *see* Orders and 3c.

JACK ARCH: shallow segmental vault springing from beams, used for fireproof floors, bridge decks, etc.

JAMB (*lit.* leg): one of the vertical sides of an opening.

JETTY: in a timber-framed building, the projection of an upper storey beyond the storey below, made by the beams and joists of the lower storey oversailing the wall; on their outer ends is placed the sill of the walling for the storey above (7). Buildings can be jettied on several sides, in which case a *dragon beam* is set diagonally at the corner to carry the joists to either side.

JOGGLE: the joining of two stones to prevent them slipping by a notch in one and a projection in the other.

KEEL MOULDING: moulding used from the late C12, in section like the keel of a ship (1a).

KEEP: principal tower of a castle.

KENTISH CUSP: *see* Tracery and 2b.

KEY PATTERN: *see* 4b.

KEYSTONE: central stone in an arch or vault (4b, 5c).

KINGPOST: *see* Roofs and 7.

KNEELER: horizontal projecting stone at the base of each side of a gable to support the inclined coping stones (8a).

LABEL: *see* Hoodmould and 5b.

LABEL STOP: *see* Stop and 5b.

LACED BRICKWORK: vertical strips of brickwork, often in a contrasting colour, linking openings on different floors.

LACING COURSE: horizontal reinforcement in timber or brick to walls of flint, cobble, etc.

LADY CHAPEL: dedicated to the Virgin Mary (Our Lady).

LANCET: slender single-light, pointed-arched window (2a).

LANTERN: circular or polygonal windowed turret crowning a roof or a dome. Also the windowed stage of a crossing tower lighting the church interior.

LANTERN CROSS: churchyard cross with lantern-shaped top.

LAVATORIUM: in a religious house, a washing place adjacent to the refectory.

LEAN-TO: *see* Roofs.

LESENE (*lit.* a mean thing): pilaster without base or capital. Also called *pilaster strip*.

LIERNE: *see* Vault and 2c.

LIGHT: compartment of a window defined by the mullions.

LINENFOLD: Tudor panelling carved with simulations of folded linen. *See also* Parchemin.

LINTEL: horizontal beam or stone bridging an opening.

LOGGIA: gallery, usually arcaded or colonnaded; sometimes freestanding.

LONG-AND-SHORT WORK: quoins consisting of stones placed with the long side alternately upright and horizontal, especially in Saxon building.

LONGHOUSE: house and byre in the same range with internal access between them.

LOUVRE: roof opening, often protected by a raised timber structure, to allow the smoke from a central hearth to escape.

LOWSIDE WINDOW: set lower than the others in a chancel side wall, usually towards its W end.

LUCAM: projecting housing for hoist pulley on upper storey of warehouses, mills, etc., for raising goods to loading doors.

LUCARNE (*lit.* dormer): small gabled opening in a roof or spire.

LUGGED ARCHITRAVE: *see* 4b.

LUNETTE: semicircular window or blind panel.

LYCHGATE (*lit.* corpse-gate): roofed gateway entrance to a churchyard for the reception of a coffin.

LYNCHET: long terraced strip of soil on the downward side of prehistoric and medieval fields, accumulated because of continual ploughing along the contours.

MACHICOLATIONS (*lit.* mashing devices): series of openings between the corbels that support a projecting parapet through which missiles can be dropped. Used decoratively in post-medieval buildings.

MANOMETER or STANDPIPE TOWER: containing a column of water to regulate pressure in water mains.

MANSARD: *see* 8a.

MATHEMATICAL TILES: facing tiles with the appearance of brick, most often applied to timber-framed walls.

MAUSOLEUM: monumental building or chamber usually intended for the burial of members of one family.

MEGALITHIC TOMB: massive stone-built Neolithic burial chamber covered by an earth or stone mound.

MERLON: *see* Battlement.

METOPES: spaces between the triglyphs in a Doric frieze (3b).

MEZZANINE: low storey between two higher ones.

MILD STEEL: *see* Cast iron.

MISERICORD (*lit.* mercy): shelf on a carved bracket placed on the underside of a hinged choir stall seat to support an occupant when standing.

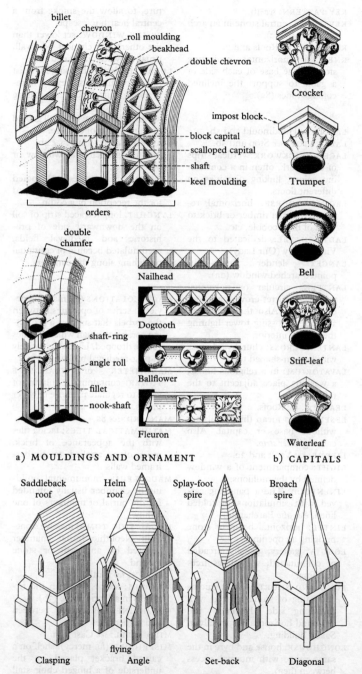

a) MOULDINGS AND ORNAMENT

billet
chevron
roll moulding
beakhead
double chevron
block capital
scalloped capital
shaft
keel moulding
orders

double chamfer

shaft-ring
angle roll
fillet
nook-shaft

Nailhead
Dogtooth
Ballflower
Fleuron

b) CAPITALS

impost block

Crocket
Trumpet
Bell
Stiff-leaf
Waterleaf

c) BUTTRESSES, ROOFS AND SPIRES

Saddleback roof
Helm roof
Splay-foot spire
Broach spire
flying
Clasping
Angle
Set-back
Diagonal

FIGURE 1: MEDIEVAL

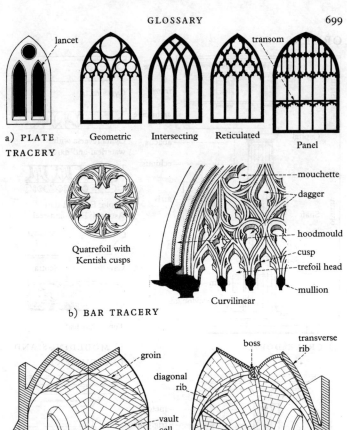

a) PLATE TRACERY

Geometric   Intersecting   Reticulated   Panel

Quatrefoil with Kentish cusps

Curvilinear

b) BAR TRACERY

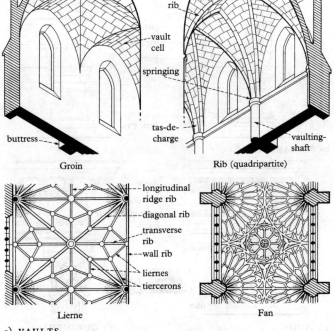

Groin

Rib (quadripartite)

Lierne

Fan

c) VAULTS

FIGURE 2: MEDIEVAL

ORDERS

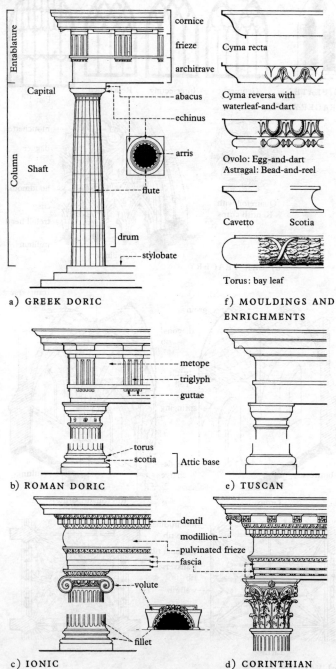

a) GREEK DORIC

- cornice
- frieze
- architrave
- abacus
- echinus
- arris
- flute
- drum
- stylobate

Entablature
Capital
Column
Shaft

f) MOULDINGS AND ENRICHMENTS

Cyma recta

Cyma reversa with waterleaf-and-dart

Ovolo: Egg-and-dart
Astragal: Bead-and-reel

Cavetto   Scotia

Torus: bay leaf

b) ROMAN DORIC

- metope
- triglyph
- guttae
- torus
- scotia   } Attic base

e) TUSCAN

c) IONIC

- dentil
- modillion
- pulvinated frieze
- fascia
- volute
- fillet

d) CORINTHIAN

FIGURE 3: CLASSICAL

a) PORTICO

Distyle in antis   Prostyle

Anthemion & Palmette   Guilloche   Key pattern

Rinceau   Husk garland   Vitruvian scroll

Console   Diocletian window   Acanthus

Broken pediment   Lugged architrave

Segmental pediment   Shouldered architrave

Venetian window

Open pediment   Swan-neck pediment   Gibbs surround

b) ORNAMENTS AND FEATURES

FIGURE 4: CLASSICAL

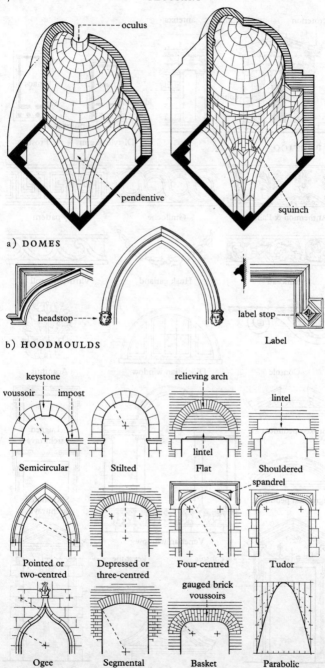

a) DOMES

b) HOODMOULDS

Label

c) ARCHES

FIGURE 5: CONSTRUCTION

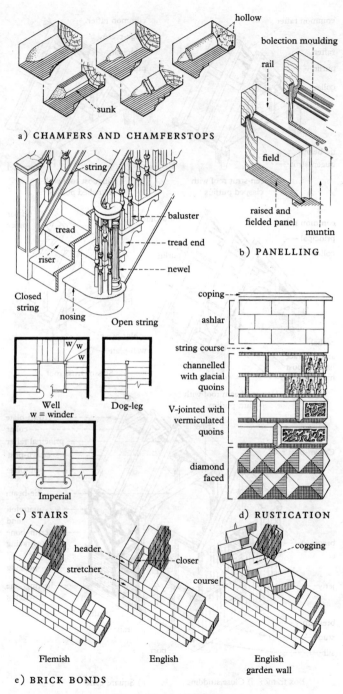

hollow

sunk

a) CHAMFERS AND CHAMFERSTOPS

bolection moulding

rail

field

raised and
fielded panel

muntin

b) PANELLING

string

baluster

tread

tread end

riser

newel

Closed
string

nosing   Open string

Well   Dog-leg
w = winder

Imperial

c) STAIRS

coping

ashlar

string course

channelled
with glacial
quoins

V-jointed with
vermiculated
quoins

diamond
faced

d) RUSTICATION

header

closer

stretcher

course

cogging

Flemish   English   English
garden wall

e) BRICK BONDS

FIGURE 6: CONSTRUCTION

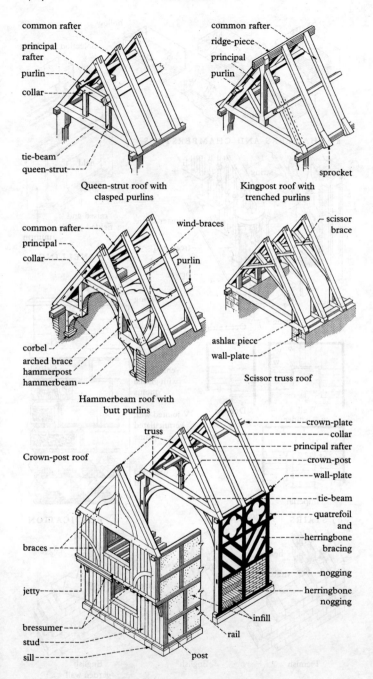

common rafter
principal rafter
purlin
collar
tie-beam
queen-strut

Queen-strut roof with
clasped purlins

common rafter
ridge-piece
principal
purlin
sprocket

Kingpost roof with
trenched purlins

common rafter
principal
collar
wind-braces
purlin
corbel
arched brace
hammerpost
hammerbeam

Hammerbeam roof with
butt purlins

scissor brace
ashlar piece
wall-plate

Scissor truss roof

Crown-post roof

truss

crown-plate
collar
principal rafter
crown-post
wall-plate
tie-beam
quatrefoil and
herringbone bracing
nogging
herringbone nogging

braces
jetty
bressumer
stud
sill
post
rail
infill

Box frame: i) Close studding   ii) Square panel

FIGURE 7: ROOFS AND TIMBER-FRAMING

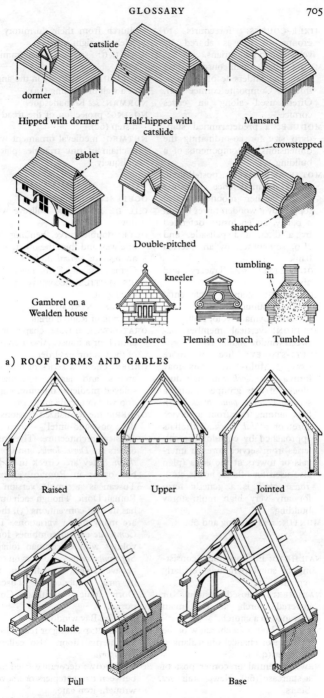

catslide

dormer

Hipped with dormer

Half-hipped with catslide

Mansard

gablet

crowstepped

shaped

Double-pitched

Gambrel on a
Wealden house

kneeler

tumbling-in

Kneelered

Flemish or Dutch

Tumbled

a) ROOF FORMS AND GABLES

Raised

Upper

Jointed

blade

Full

Base

b) CRUCK FRAMES

FIGURE 8: ROOFS AND TIMBER-FRAMING

MIXER-COURTS: forecourts to groups of houses shared by vehicles and pedestrians.

MODILLIONS: small consoles (q.v.) along the underside of a Corinthian or Composite cornice (3d). Often used along an eaves cornice.

MODULE: a predetermined standard size for co-ordinating the dimensions of components of a building.

MOTTE-AND-BAILEY: post-Roman and Norman defence consisting of an earthen mound (motte) topped by a wooden tower within a bailey, an enclosure defended by a ditch and palisade, and also, sometimes, by an internal bank.

MOUCHETTE: *see* Tracery and 2b.

MOULDING: shaped ornamental strip of continuous section; *see* e.g. Cavetto, Cyma, Ovolo, Roll.

MULLION: vertical member between window lights (2b).

MULTI-STOREY: five or more storeys. Multi-storey flats may form a *cluster block*, with individual blocks of flats grouped round a service core; a *point block*, with flats fanning out from a service core; or a *slab block*, with flats approached by corridors or galleries from service cores at intervals or towers at the ends (plan also used for offices, hotels etc.). *Tower block* is a generic term for any very high multi-storey building.

MUNTIN: *see* Panelling and 6b.

NAILHEAD: E.E. ornament consisting of small pyramids regularly repeated (1a).

NARTHEX: enclosed vestibule or covered porch at the main entrance to a church.

NAVE: the body of a church w of the crossing or chancel often flanked by aisles (q.v.).

NEWEL: central or corner post of a staircase (6c). Newel stair: *see* Stairs.

NIGHT STAIR: stair by which religious entered the transept of their church from their dormitory to celebrate night services.

NOGGING: *see* Timber-framing (7).

NOOK-SHAFT: shaft set in the angle of a wall or opening (1a).

NORMAN: *see* Romanesque.

NOSING: projection of the tread of a step (6c).

NUTMEG: medieval ornament with a chain of tiny triangles placed obliquely.

OCULUS: circular opening.

ŒIL DE BŒUF: *see* Bullseye window.

OGEE: double curve, bending first one way and then the other, as in an *ogee* or *ogival arch* (5c). Cf. Cyma recta and Cyma reversa.

OPUS SECTILE: decorative mosaic-like facing.

OPUS SIGNINUM: composition flooring of Roman origin.

ORATORY: a private chapel in a church or a house. Also a church of the Oratorian Order.

ORDER: one of a series of recessed arches and jambs forming a splayed medieval opening, e.g. a doorway or arcade arch (1a).

ORDERS: the formalized versions of the post-and-lintel system in classical architecture. The main orders are *Doric, Ionic,* and *Corinthian.* They are Greek in origin but occur in Roman versions. Tuscan is a simple version of Roman Doric. Though each order has its own conventions (3), there are many minor variations. The *Composite* capital combines Ionic volutes with Corinthian foliage. *Superimposed orders*: orders on successive levels, usually in the upward sequence of Tuscan, Doric, Ionic, Corinthian, Composite.

ORIEL: *see* Bay window.

OVERDOOR: painting or relief above an internal door. Also called a *sopraporta.*

OVERTHROW: decorative fixed arch between two gatepiers or above a wrought-iron gate.

OVOLO: wide convex moulding (3f).

PALIMPSEST: of a brass: where a metal plate has been reused by turning over the engraving on the back; of a wall painting: where one overlaps and partly obscures an earlier one.

PALLADIAN: following the examples and principles of Andrea Palladio (1508–80).

PALMETTE: classical ornament like a palm shoot (4b).

PANELLING: wooden lining to interior walls, made up of vertical members (*muntins*) and horizontals (*rails*) framing panels: also called *wainscot*. *Raised and fielded*: with the central area of the panel (*field*) raised up (6b).

PANTILE: roof tile of S section.

PARAPET: wall for protection at any sudden drop, e.g. at the wall-head of a castle where it protects the *parapet walk* or wall-walk. Also used to conceal a roof.

PARCLOSE: *see* Screen.

PARGETTING (*lit.* plastering): exterior plaster decoration, either in relief or incised.

PARLOUR: in a religious house, a room where the religious could talk to visitors; in a medieval house, the semi-private living room below the solar (q.v.).

PARTERRE: level space in a garden laid out with low, formal beds.

PATERA (*lit.* plate): round or oval ornament in shallow relief.

PAVILION: ornamental building for occasional use; or projecting subdivision of a larger building, often at an angle or terminating a wing.

PEBBLEDASHING: *see* Rendering.

PEDESTAL: a tall block carrying a classical order, statue, vase, etc.

PEDIMENT: a formalized gable derived from that of a classical temple; also used over doors, windows, etc. For variations *see* 4b.

PENDENTIVE: spandrel between adjacent arches, supporting a drum, dome or vault and consequently formed as part of a hemisphere (5a).

PENTHOUSE: subsidiary structure with a lean-to roof. Also a

separately roofed structure on top of a C20 multi-storey block.

PERIPTERAL: *see* Peristyle.

PERISTYLE: a colonnade all round the exterior of a classical building, as in a temple which is then said to be *peripteral*.

PERP (PERPENDICULAR): English Gothic architecture c. 1335–50 to c. 1530. The name is derived from the upright tracery panels then used (*see* Tracery and 2a).

PERRON: external stair to a doorway, usually of double-curved plan.

PEW: loosely, seating for the laity outside the chancel; strictly, an enclosed seat. *Box pew*: with equal high sides and a door.

PIANO NOBILE: principal floor of a classical building above a ground floor or basement and with a lesser storey overhead.

PIAZZA: formal urban open space surrounded by buildings.

PIER: large masonry or brick support, often for an arch. *See also* Compound pier.

PILASTER: flat representation of a classical column in shallow relief. *Pilaster strip*: *see* Lesene.

PILE: row of rooms. *Double pile*: two rows thick.

PILLAR: free-standing upright member of any section, not conforming to one of the orders (q.v.).

PILLAR PISCINA: *see* Piscina.

PILOTIS: C20 French term for pillars or stilts that support a building above an open ground floor.

PISCINA: basin for washing Mass vessels, provided with a drain; set in or against the wall to the S of an altar or free-standing (*pillar piscina*).

PISÉ: *see* Cob.

PITCHED MASONRY: laid on the diagonal, often alternately with opposing courses (*pitched and counterpitched* or *herringbone*).

PLATBAND: flat horizontal moulding between storeys. Cf. stringcourse.

PLATE RAIL: *see* Railways.

PLATEWAY: *see* Railways.

PLINTH: projecting courses at the

foot of a wall or column, generally chamfered or moulded at the top.

PODIUM: a continuous raised platform supporting a building; or a large block of two or three storeys beneath a multi-storey block of smaller area.

POINT BLOCK: see Multi-storey.

POINTING: exposed mortar jointing of masonry or brickwork. Types include *flush*, *recessed* and *tuck* (with a narrow channel filled with finer, whiter mortar).

POPPYHEAD: carved ornament of leaves and flowers as a finial for a bench end or stall.

PORTAL FRAME: C20 frame comprising two uprights rigidly connected to a beam or pair of rafters.

PORTCULLIS: gate constructed to rise and fall in vertical grooves at the entry to a castle.

PORTICO: a porch with the roof and frequently a pediment supported by a row of columns (4a). A portico *in antis* has columns on the same plane as the front of the building. A *prostyle* porch has columns standing free. Porticoes are described by the number of front columns, e.g. tetrastyle (four), hexastyle (six). The space within the temple is the *naos*, that within the portico the *pronaos*. *Blind portico*: the front features of a portico applied to a wall.

PORTICUS (plural: porticūs): subsidiary cell opening from the main body of a pre-Conquest church.

POST: upright support in a structure (7).

POSTERN: small gateway at the back of a building or to the side of a larger entrance door or gate.

POUND LOCK: see Canals.

PRESBYTERY: the part of a church lying E of the choir where the main altar is placed; or a priest's residence.

PRINCIPAL: see Roofs and 7.

PRONAOS: see Portico and 4a.

PROSTYLE: see Portico and 4a.

PULPIT: raised and enclosed platform for the preaching of sermons. *Three-decker*: with reading desk below and clerk's desk below that. *Two-decker*: as above, minus the clerk's desk.

PULPITUM: stone screen in a major church dividing choir from nave.

PULVINATED: see Frieze and 3c.

PURLIN: see Roofs and 7.

PUTHOLES or PUTLOG HOLES: in the wall to receive putlogs, the horizontal timbers which support scaffolding boards; sometimes not filled after construction is complete.

PUTTO (plural: putti): small naked boy.

QUARRIES: square (or diamond) panes of glass supported by lead strips (*cames*); square floor slabs or tiles.

QUATREFOIL: see Foil and 2b.

QUEEN-STRUT: see Roofs and 7.

QUIRK: sharp groove to one side of a convex medieval moulding.

QUOINS: dressed stones at the angles of a building (6d).

RADBURN SYSTEM: vehicle and pedestrian segregation in residential developments, based on that used at Radburn, New Jersey, USA, by Wright and Stein, 1928–30.

RADIATING CHAPELS: projecting radially from an ambulatory or an apse (see Chevet).

RAFTER: see Roofs and 7.

RAGGLE: groove cut in masonry, especially to receive the edge of a roof-covering.

RAGULY: ragged (in heraldry). Also applied to funerary sculpture, e.g. *cross raguly*: with a notched outline.

RAIL: see Panelling and 6b; also 7.

RAILWAYS: *Edge rail*: on which flanged wheels can run. *Plate rail*: L-section rail for plain unflanged wheels. *Plateway*: early railway using plate rails.

RAISED AND FIELDED: see Panelling and 6b.

RAKE: slope or pitch.

RAMPART: defensive outer wall of stone or earth. *Rampart walk*: path along the inner face.

REBATE: rectangular section cut out of a masonry edge to receive a shutter, door, window, etc.

REBUS: a heraldic pun, e.g. a fiery cock for Cockburn.

REEDING: series of convex mouldings, the reverse of fluting (q.v.). Cf. Gadrooning.

RENDERING: the covering of outside walls with a uniform surface or skin for protection from the weather. *Limewashing*: thin layer of lime plaster. *Pebbledashing*: where aggregate is thrown at the wet plastered wall for a textured effect. *Roughcast*: plaster mixed with a coarse aggregate such as gravel. *Stucco*: fine lime plaster worked to a smooth surface. *Cement rendering*: a cheaper substitute for stucco, usually with a grainy texture.

REPOUSSÉ: relief designs in metalwork, formed by beating it from the back.

REREDORTER (*lit.* behind the dormitory): latrines in a medieval religious house.

REREDOS: painted and/or sculptured screen behind and above an altar. Cf. Retable.

RESPOND: half-pier or half-column bonded into a wall and carrying one end of an arch. It usually terminates an arcade.

RETABLE: painted or carved panel standing on or at the back of an altar, usually attached to it.

RETROCHOIR: in a major church, the area between the high altar and E chapel.

REVEAL: the plane of a jamb, between the wall and the frame of a door or window.

RIB-VAULT: see Vault and 2c.

RINCEAU: classical ornament of leafy scrolls (4b).

RISER: vertical face of a step (6c).

ROACH: a rough-textured form of Portland stone, with small cavities and fossil shells.

ROCK-FACED: masonry cleft to produce a rugged appearance.

ROCOCO: style current *c.* 1720 and *c.* 1760, characterized by a serpentine line and playful, scrolled decoration.

ROLL MOULDING: medieval moulding of part-circular section (1a).

ROMANESQUE: style current in the C11 and C12. In England often called Norman. *See also* Saxo-Norman.

ROOD: crucifix flanked by the Virgin and St John, usually over the entry into the chancel, on a beam (*rood beam*) or painted on the wall. The *rood screen* below often had a walkway (*rood loft*) along the top, reached by a *rood stair* in the side wall.

ROOFS: Shape. For the main external shapes (hipped, mansard, etc.) *see* 8a. *Helm* and *Saddleback*: *see* 1c. *Lean-to*: single sloping roof built against a vertical wall; lean-to is also applied to the part of the building beneath.
Construction. *See* 7.
Single-framed roof: with no main trusses. The rafters may be fixed to the wall-plate or ridge, or longitudinal timber may be absent altogether.
Double-framed roof: with longitudinal members, such as purlins, and usually divided into bays by principals and principal rafters.
Other types are named after their main structural components, e.g. *hammerbeam, crown-post* (*see* Elements below and 7).
Elements. *See* 7.
Ashlar piece: a short vertical timber connecting inner wall-plate or timber pad to a rafter.
Braces: subsidiary timbers set diagonally to strengthen the frame. *Arched braces*: curved pair forming an arch, connecting wall or post below with tie- or collar-beam above. *Passing braces*: long straight braces passing across other members of the truss. *Scissor braces*: pair crossing diagonally between pairs of rafters or principals. *Wind-braces*: short, usually curved braces connecting side purlins with principals; sometimes decorated with cusping.
Collar or *collar-beam*: horizontal transverse timber connecting a pair of rafter or cruck blades (q.v.), set between apex and the wall-plate.
Crown-post: a vertical timber set centrally on a tie-beam and supporting a collar purlin braced to it longitudinally. In an open truss

lateral braces may rise to the collar-beam; in a closed truss they may descend to the tie-beam.

Hammerbeams: horizontal brackets projecting at wall-plate level like an interrupted tie-beam; the inner ends carry *hammerposts*, vertical timbers which support a purlin and are braced to a collar-beam above.

Kingpost: vertical timber set centrally on a tie- or collar-beam, rising to the apex of the roof to support a ridge-piece (cf. Strut).

Plate: longitudinal timber set square to the ground. *Wall-plate*: plate along the top of a wall which receives the ends of the rafters; cf. Purlin.

Principals: pair of inclined lateral timbers of a truss. Usually they support side purlins and mark the main bay divisions.

Purlin: horizontal longitudinal timber. *Collar purlin* or *crown plate*: central timber which carries collar-beams and is supported by crown-posts. *Side purlins*: pairs of timbers placed some way up the slope of the roof, which carry common rafters. *Butt* or *tenoned purlins* are tenoned into either side of the principals. *Through purlins* pass through or past the principal; they include *clasped purlins*, which rest on queenposts or are carried in the angle between principals and collar, and *trenched purlins* trenched into the backs of principals.

Queen-strut: paired vertical, or near-vertical, timbers placed symmetrically on a tie-beam to support side purlins.

Rafters: inclined lateral timbers supporting the roof covering. *Common rafters*: regularly spaced uniform rafters placed along the length of a roof or between principals. *Principal rafters*: rafters which also act as principals.

Ridge, ridge-piece: horizontal longitudinal timber at the apex supporting the ends of the rafters.

Sprocket: short timber placed on the back and at the foot of a rafter to form projecting eaves.

Strut: vertical or oblique timber between two members of a truss, not directly supporting longitudinal timbers.

Tie-beam: main horizontal transverse timber which carries the feet of the principals at wall level.

Truss: rigid framework of timbers at bay intervals, carrying the longitudinal roof timbers which support the common rafters. *Closed truss*: with the spaces between the timbers filled, to form an internal partition.

See also Cruck, Wagon roof.

ROPE MOULDING: *see* Cable moulding.

ROSE WINDOW: circular window with tracery radiating from the centre. Cf. Wheel window.

ROTUNDA: building or room circular in plan.

ROUGHCAST: *see* Rendering.

ROVING BRIDGE: *see* Canals.

RUBBED BRICKWORK: *see* Gauged brickwork.

RUBBLE: masonry whose stones are wholly or partly in a rough state. *Coursed*: coursed stones with rough faces. *Random*: uncoursed stones in a random pattern. *Snecked*: with courses broken by smaller stones (snecks).

RUSTICATION: *see* 6d. Exaggerated treatment of masonry to give an effect of strength. The joints are usually recessed by V-section chamfering or square-section channelling (*channelled rustication*). *Banded rustication* has only the horizontal joints emphasized. The faces may be flat, but can be *diamond-faced*, like shallow pyramids, *vermiculated*, with a stylized texture like worm-casts, and *glacial* (frost-work), like icicles or stalactites.

SACRISTY: room in a church for sacred vessels and vestments.

SADDLEBACK ROOF: *see* IC.

SALTIRE CROSS: with diagonal limbs.

SANCTUARY: area around the main altar of a church. Cf. Presbytery.

SANGHA: residence of Buddhist monks or nuns.

SARCOPHAGUS: coffin of stone or other durable material.

SAXO-NORMAN: transitional Romanesque style combining Anglo-Saxon and Norman features, current *c.* 1060–1100.

SCAGLIOLA: composition imitating marble.

SCALLOPED CAPITAL: *see* 1a.

SCOTIA: a hollow classical moulding, especially between tori (q.v.) on a column base (3b, 3f).

SCREEN: in a medieval church, usually at the entry to the chancel; *see* Rood (screen) and Pulpitum. A *parclose screen* separates a chapel from the rest of the church.

SCREENS or SCREENS PASSAGE: screened-off entrance passage between great hall and service rooms.

SECTION: two-dimensional representation of a building, moulding, etc., revealed by cutting across it.

SEDILIA (singular: sedile): seats for the priests (usually three) on the s side of the chancel.

SET-OFF: *see* Weathering.

SETTS: squared stones, usually of granite, used for paving or flooring.

SGRAFFITO: decoration scratched, often in plaster, to reveal a pattern in another colour beneath. *Graffiti*: scratched drawing or writing.

SHAFT: vertical member of round or polygonal section (1a, 3a). *Shaft-ring*: at the junction of shafts set *en delit* (q.v.) or attached to a pier or wall (1a).

SHEILA-NA-GIG: female fertility figure, usually with legs apart.

SHELL: thin, self-supporting roofing membrane of timber or concrete.

SHOULDERED ARCHITRAVE: *see* 4b.

SHUTTERING: *see* Concrete.

SILL: horizontal member at the bottom of a window or door frame; or at the base of a timber-framed wall into which posts and studs are tenoned (7).

SLAB BLOCK: *see* Multi-storey.

SLATE-HANGING: covering of overlapping slates on a wall. *Tile-hanging* is similar.

SLYPE: covered way or passage leading E from the cloisters between transept and chapter house.

SNECKED: *see* Rubble.

SOFFIT (*lit.* ceiling): underside of an arch (also called *intrados*), lintel, etc. *Soffit roll*: medieval roll moulding on a soffit.

SOLAR: private upper chamber in a medieval house, accessible from the high end of the great hall.

SOPRAPORTA: *see* Overdoor.

SOUNDING-BOARD: *see* Tester.

SPANDRELS: roughly triangular spaces between an arch and its containing rectangle, or between adjacent arches (5c). Also non-structural panels under the windows in a curtain-walled building.

SPERE: a fixed structure screening the lower end of the great hall from the screens passage. *Spere-truss*: roof truss incorporated in the spere.

SPIRE: tall pyramidal or conical feature crowning a tower or turret. *Broach*: starting from a square base, then carried into an octagonal section by means of triangular faces; and *splayed-foot*: variation of the broach form, found principally in the southeast, in which the four cardinal faces are splayed out near their base, to cover the corners, while oblique (or intermediate) faces taper away to a point (1c). *Needle spire*: thin spire rising from the centre of a tower roof, well inside the parapet: when of timber and lead often called a *spike*.

SPIRELET: *see* Flèche.

SPLAY: of an opening when it is wider on one face of a wall than the other.

SPRING or SPRINGING: level at which an arch or vault rises from its supports. *Springers*: the first stones of an arch or vaulting rib above the spring (2c).

SQUINCH: arch or series of arches thrown across an interior angle of a square or rectangular structure to support a circular or polygonal superstructure, especially a dome or spire (5a).

SQUINT: an aperture in a wall or through a pier usually to allow a view of an altar.

STAIRS: *see* 6c. *Dog-leg stair*: parallel flights rising alternately in opposite directions, without an open well. *Flying stair*: cantilevered from the walls of a stairwell, without newels; sometimes called a *Geometric* stair when the inner edge describes a curve. *Newel stair*: ascending round a central supporting newel (q.v.); called a *spiral stair* or *vice* when in a circular shaft, a *winder* when in a rectangular compartment. (Winder also applies to the steps on the turn.) *Well stair*: with flights round a square open well framed by newel posts. *See also* Perron.

STALL: fixed seat in the choir or chancel for the clergy or choir (cf. Pew). Usually with arm rests, and often framed together.

STANCHION: upright structural member, of iron, steel or reinforced concrete.

STANDPIPE TOWER: *see* Manometer.

STEAM ENGINES: *Atmospheric*: worked by the vacuum created when low-pressure steam is condensed in the cylinder, as developed by Thomas Newcomen. *Beam engine*: with a large pivoted beam moved in an oscillating fashion by the piston. It may drive a flywheel or be *non-rotative*. *Watt* and *Cornish*: single-cylinder; *compound*: two cylinders; *triple expansion*: three cylinders.

STEEPLE: tower together with a spire, lantern, or belfry.

STIFF-LEAF: type of E.E. foliage decoration. *Stiff-leaf capital see* 1b.

STOP: plain or decorated terminal to mouldings or chamfers, or at the end of hoodmoulds and labels (*label stop*), or stringcourses (5b, 6a); *see also* Headstop.

STOUP: vessel for holy water, usually near a door.

STRAINER: *see* Arch.

STRAPWORK: late C16 and C17 decoration, like interlaced leather straps.

STRETCHER: *see* Bond and 6e.

STRING: *see* 6c. Sloping member holding the ends of the treads and risers of a staircase. *Closed string*: a broad string covering the ends of the treads and risers. *Open string*: cut into the shape of the treads and risers.

STRINGCOURSE: horizontal course or moulding projecting from the surface of a wall (6d).

STUCCO: *see* Rendering.

STUDS: subsidiary vertical timbers of a timber-framed wall or partition (7).

STUPA: Buddhist shrine, circular in plan.

STYLOBATE: top of the solid platform on which a colonnade stands (3a).

SUSPENSION BRIDGE: *see* Bridge.

SWAG: like a festoon (q.v.), but representing cloth.

SYSTEM BUILDING: *see* Industrialized building.

TABERNACLE: canopied structure to contain the reserved sacrament or a relic; or architectural frame for an image or statue.

TABLE TOMB: memorial slab raised on free-standing legs.

TAS-DE-CHARGE: the lower courses of a vault or arch which are laid horizontally (2c).

TERM: pedestal or pilaster tapering downward, usually with the upper part of a human figure growing out of it.

TERRACOTTA: moulded and fired clay ornament or cladding.

TESSELLATED PAVEMENT: mosaic flooring, particularly Roman, made of *tesserae*, i.e. cubes of glass, stone, or brick.

TESTER: flat canopy over a tomb or pulpit, where it is also called a *sounding-board*.

TESTER TOMB: tomb-chest with effigies beneath a tester, either free-standing (tester with four or more columns), or attached to a wall (*half-tester*) with columns on one side only.

TETRASTYLE: *see* Portico.

THERMAL WINDOW: *see* Diocletian window.

THREE-DECKER PULPIT: *see* Pulpit.

TIDAL GATES: *see* Canals.

TIE-BEAM: *see* Roofs and 7.

TIERCERON: *see* Vault and 2c.

TILE-HANGING: *see* Slate-hanging.

TIMBER-FRAMING: *see* 7. Method of construction where the structural frame is built of interlocking timbers. The spaces are filled with non-structural material, e.g. *infill* of wattle and daub, lath and plaster, brickwork (known as *nogging*), etc. and may be covered by plaster, weatherboarding (q.v.), or tiles.

TOMB-CHEST: chest-shaped tomb, usually of stone. Cf. Table tomb, Tester tomb.

TORUS (plural: tori): large convex moulding usually used on a column base (3b, 3f).

TOUCH: soft black marble quarried near Tournai.

TOURELLE: turret corbelled out from the wall.

TOWER BLOCK: *see* Multi-storey.

TRABEATED: depends structurally on the use of the post and lintel. Cf. Arcuated.

TRACERY: openwork pattern of masonry or timber in the upper part of an opening. *Blind tracery* is tracery applied to a solid wall.
Plate tracery, introduced *c.* 1200, is the earliest form, in which shapes are cut through solid masonry (2a).
Bar tracery was introduced into England *c.* 1250. The pattern is formed by intersecting moulded ribwork continued from the mullions. It was especially elaborate during the Decorated period (q.v.). Tracery shapes can include circles, *daggers* (elongated ogee-ended lozenges), *mouchettes* (like daggers but with curved sides) and upright rectangular *panels*. They often have *cusps*, projecting points defining lobes or *foils* (q.v.) within the main shape: *Kentish* or *split-cusps* are forked (2b).
Types of bar tracery (*see* 2b) include *geometric(al)*: *c.* 1250–1310, chiefly circles, often foiled; *Y-tracery*: *c.* 1300, with mullions branching into a Y-shape; *intersecting*: *c.* 1300, formed by interlocking mullions; *reticulated*: early C14, net-like pattern of ogee-ended lozenges; *curvilinear*: C14, with uninterrupted flowing curves; *panel*: Perp, with straight-sided panels, often cusped at the top and bottom.

TRANSEPT: transverse portion of a church.

TRANSITIONAL: generally used for the phase between Romanesque and Early English (*c.* 1175–*c.* 1200).

TRANSOM: horizontal member separating window lights (2b).

TREAD: horizontal part of a step. The *tread end* may be carved on a staircase (6c).

TREFOIL: *see* Foil.

TRIFORIUM: middle storey of a church treated as an arcaded wall passage or blind arcade, its height corresponding to that of the aisle roof.

TRIGLYPHS (*lit.* three-grooved tablets): stylized beam-ends in the Doric frieze, with metopes between (3b).

TRIUMPHAL ARCH: influential type of Imperial Roman monument.

TROPHY: sculptured or painted group of arms or armour.

TRUMEAU: central stone mullion supporting the tympanum of a wide doorway. *Trumeau figure*: carved figure attached to it (cf. Column figure).

TRUMPET CAPITAL: *see* 1b.

TRUSS: braced framework, spanning between supports. *See also* Roofs and 7.

TUMBLING or TUMBLING-IN: courses of brickwork laid at right-angles to a slope, e.g. of a gable, forming triangles by tapering into horizontal courses (8a).

TUSCAN: *see* Orders and 3e.

TWO-DECKER PULPIT: *see* Pulpit.

TYMPANUM: the surface between a lintel and the arch above it or within a pediment (4a).

UNDERCROFT: usually describes the vaulted room(s), beneath the main room(s) of a medieval house. Cf. Crypt.

VAULT: arched stone roof (sometimes imitated in timber or plaster). For types see 2c.
Tunnel or *barrel vault*: continuous semicircular or pointed arch, often of rubble masonry.

Groin-vault: tunnel vaults intersecting at right angles. *Groins* are the curved lines of the intersections.

Rib-vault: masonry framework of intersecting arches (ribs) supporting *vault cells*, used in Gothic architecture. *Wall rib* or *wall arch*: between wall and vault cell. *Transverse rib*: spans between two walls to divide a vault into bays. *Quadripartite* rib-vault: each bay has two pairs of diagonal ribs dividing the vault into four triangular cells. *Sexpartite* rib-vault: most often used over paired bays, has an extra pair of ribs springing from between the bays. More elaborate vaults may include *ridge ribs* along the crown of a vault or bisecting the bays; *tiercerons*: extra decorative ribs springing from the corners of a bay; and *liernes*: short decorative ribs in the crown of a vault, not linked to any springing point. A *stellar* or *star* vault has liernes in star formation.

Fan-vault: form of barrel vault used in the Perp period, made up of halved concave masonry cones decorated with blind tracery.

VAULTING SHAFT: shaft leading up to the spring or springing (q.v.) of a vault (2c).

VENETIAN or SERLIAN WINDOW: derived from Serlio (4b). The motif is used for other openings.

VERMICULATION: *see* Rustication and 6d.

VESICA: oval with pointed ends.

VICE: *see* Stair.

VILLA: originally a Roman country house or farm. The term was revived in England in the C18 under the influence of Palladio and used especially for smaller, compact country houses. In the later C19 it was debased to describe any suburban house.

VITRIFIED: bricks or tiles fired to a darkened glassy surface.

VITRUVIAN SCROLL: classical running ornament of curly waves (4b).

VOLUTES: spiral scrolls. They occur on Ionic capitals (3c). *Angle volute*: pair of volutes, turned outwards to meet at the corner of a capital.

VOUSSOIRS: wedge-shaped stones forming an arch (5c).

WAGON ROOF: with the appearance of the inside of a wagon tilt; often ceiled. Also called *cradle roof*.

WAINSCOT: *see* Panelling.

WALL MONUMENT: attached to the wall and often standing on the floor. *Wall tablets* are smaller with the inscription as the major element.

WALL-PLATE: *see* Roofs and 7.

WALL-WALK: *see* Parapet.

WARMING ROOM: room in a religious house where a fire burned for comfort.

WATERHOLDING BASE: early Gothic base with upper and lower mouldings separated by a deep hollow.

WATERLEAF: *see* Enrichments and 3f.

WATERLEAF CAPITAL: Late Romanesque and Transitional type of capital (1b).

WATER WHEELS: described by the way water is fed on to the wheel. *Breastshot*: mid-height, falling and passing beneath. *Overshot*: over the top. *Pitchback*: on the top but falling backwards. *Undershot*: turned by the momentum of the water passing beneath. In a *water turbine*, water is fed under pressure through a vaned wheel within a casing.

WEALDEN HOUSE: type of medieval timber-framed house with a central open hall flanked by bays of two storeys, roofed in line; the end bays are jettied to the front, but the eaves are continuous (8a).

WEATHERBOARDING: wall cladding of overlapping horizontal boards.

WEATHERING or SET-OFF: inclined, projecting surface to keep water away from the wall below.

WEEPERS: figures in niches along the sides of some medieval tombs. Also called mourners.

WHEEL WINDOW: circular, with radiating shafts like spokes. Cf. Rose window.

WROUGHT IRON: *see* Cast iron.

INDEX OF ARTISTS

INDEX OF PATRONS

Indexed here are individuals or families (not bodies or commercial firms) recorded in this volume as having owned property and/or commissioned architectural work in South-East Lancashire and Manchester. The index includes monuments to members of such families and individuals, but not those to others unless they are of special interest.

INDEX OF PLACES

Principal references are in **bold** type; demolished buildings are shown in *italic*. Manchester is indexed in two separate entries: 'Manchester city centre' and 'Manchester outer districts'.